W9-CNY-906

BROADWAY

An Encyclopedic Guide to the History, People and Places of Times Square

Ken Bloom

Facts On File
New York • Oxford

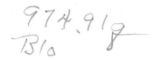

974.91p
B10

BROADWAY: An Encyclopedic Guide to the History, People and Places of Times Square

Copyright © 1991 by Ken Bloom

All rights reserved. No part of this book may be reproduced or utilized in any form or by any means, electronic or mechanical, including photocopying, recording, or by any information storage or retrieval systems, without permission in writing from the publisher. For information contact:

Facts On File, Inc.
460 Park Avenue South
New York NY 10016
USA

Facts on File Limited
Collins Street
Oxford OX4 1XJ
United Kingdom

Library of Congress Cataloging-in-Publication Data

Bloom, Ken, 1949–
   Broadway : an encyclopedic guide to the history, people, and
      places of Times Square / Ken Bloom.
    p. cm.
  ISBN 0-8160-1249-0
  1. Times Square (New York, N.Y.)—Dictionaries.   2. Broadway (New
     York, N.Y.)—Dictionaries.   3. New York (N.Y.)—Dictionaries.
     I. Title.
    F128.65.T5B56   1991
    974.7'1—dc20   90-32632

A British CIP catalogue record for this book is available from the British Library.

Facts On File books are available at special discounts when purchased in bulk quantities for businesses, associations, institutions or sales promotions. Please call our Special Sales Department in New York at 212/683-2244 (dial 800/322-8755 except in NY, AK or HI).

Jacket design by James Victore
Composition and manufacturing by The Maple-Vail Book
Manufacturing Group
Printed in the United States of America

10 9 8 7 6 5 4 3 2 1

This book is printed on acid-free paper.

Contents

To my first friend, Harry Bagdasian,
for our shared past
and in anticipation of a shared future.

Acknowledgments

The story of Times Square is replete with the history of many different factors—the theaters, the impresarios, the gangsters, the performers, etc. This broad scope required a huge amount of research. Thanks to the Billy Rose Theater Collection of the New York Public Library at Lincoln Center and especially Dorothy Swerdlove and her staff who were all patient and professional in answering my many questions. I also acknowledge the resources of the Theatre Collection and Photo Collection of the Museum of the City of New York and the collection at the New-York Historical Society. Information on theaters came in part from Save the Theaters. I also thank Michael Kerker of ASCAP for his patience and for the loan of many photos in the book. And I want to thank Tony Randall for his loan of the material on Hubert's Flea Circus.

Thanks to Nancy Andrews, Clive Barnes, Joey Bishop, Robert F. Byrnes, Dolly Dawn, Jack Goldstein, Hilary Knight, Bob Larkin, Duke Niles, Robert L. Riddell, Mel Starr, and everyone else who graciously agreed to be interviewed.

I especially thank Ellen Zeisler of Susan Bloch and Company, publicists, who was generous in her support both professionally and personally. Ellen made the daunting task of putting this book together much easier.

David Laskin, my copy editor, had perhaps the hardest job of all, deciphering my early drafts and helping me make them understandable and readable. Much of the credit for whatever success this book receives should go to David.

Barry Kleinbort, a friend with a remarkable knowledge of theater history, went over the manuscript looking for misspellings and inaccuracies. Barry made the book much better through his involvement.

Berthe Schuchat, Vicki Gold Levi and Craig Jacobs proofread the galleys with an unerring sense of history and journalism.

Thanks to David Rose, a friend who patiently tried to get me over the hurdles of dealing with a computer. He tried his hardest to explain exactly what was going on inside the machine.

Tama Starr was terrific in taking time out of her schedule to clear up many misconceptions, supply me with irreplaceable photos and give me the benefit of her unique view of Times Square and Broadway. Thanks for your patience, Tama.

Vicki Gold Levi also selflessly helped me with photo acquisitions through her extensive knowledge of both Times Square and photo research. I can hardly believe how kind she was in her help.

Debby Humphreys generously opened her private collection of Times Square and Broadway to me and loaned me many materials that I could not find elsewhere.

Louis Botto of Playbill was kind enough to supply the information on Playbill's history. Also his excellent book *At This Theater* was invaluable for the theatre history entries.

Most important, I thank my parents who sometimes didn't believe this project would ever be finished (neither did anyone else listed on this page) but supported me whole-heartedly.

I also thank my other friends who put up with my complaining, mood swings and long disappearances. They deserve a medal and my thanks for helping me through both bad times and giving me the good times. They include John Akamine, Harry Bagdasian, Bari Biern, David Bishop, Adrian Bryan-Brown, Hap Erstein, Sheila Formoy, Terry Grant, Tim Grundmann, Richard Haight, Karen Hopkins, Edward Jablonski, Ruth Levine, Robbie McEwen, Karen McLaughlin, Russell Metheny, Paul Newman, Ezio Petersen, Guy Riddick, Bill Rudman, Scott Sedar, Michael Shoop, Mike Shuster, David Simone, Bob Sixsmith, Maxine

Sullivan, Karma Urso, Carl Weaver, Joseph Weiss, Max Woodward.

My first agent and friend Lucy Stille deserves thanks as does my present agent, Heide Lange of Greenburger Associates. Heide has been remarkably supportive and a source of reason. Last but certainly not least, I want to especially thank my editors at Facts On File, John Thornton and Doug Schulkind. They did all the right things at the right times. I can't tell them how much I appreciate their guidance and support even when I was acting like a jerk. Their personal and professional support shows that they were not only excellent at their jobs but also first-rate human beings. Thanks also to Deborah Brody, a terrific editor who has become a special friend.

I am sure I have forgotten to thank many individuals who helped me compile the enormous amount of research and who gave me moral suport. If I have forgotten to thank you please accept my apologies and send your name to me care of Facts On File.

Ken Bloom
New York City

Introduction

"Broadway may only be a street to some people, but to some of the rest of us it's a religion." So claimed Eddie Foy Sr. on stage at the Palace Theater *(q.v.)*, and thousands of people have proved his statement true.

Times Square is the only spot where the hundreds of different worlds that comprise New York City meet face to face. The result has been funny, dramatic and sometimes deadly. Times Square mixes hookers, Broadway stars, gangsters *(q.v.)*, newspapermen, schnorrers and bon vivants, rubber neckers and passersby. These worlds all coexist in 10 blocks of Broadway.

Surprisingly, there has been no comprehensive history of the Times Square area. There have been short books with chatty rundowns on the nighclubs, theaters, etc., but they tended to be very vague and broad in scope. Few facts enter into the pages of those books. This book is meant to be an informal guidebook to the mercurial history of Times Square. Partly scholarly and partly anecdotal, the book, like Broadway itself, can be used by those who have an exact destination in mind or those who wish to wander aimlessly, browsing up and down the boulevard.

For those hardy souls who are purposeful in their quest, major entries are arranged alphabetically. Those subjects not covered in their own separate entries are listed in the index. My hope is that the referrals in the index will lead the interested reader to a somewhat complete idea of a person's career or a place's importance in Times Square history.

Those who would rather take a more lighthearted browse through the history can pick an entry at random and follow the cross-references to additional entries. This method might eventually take one through the entire book.

Since Broadway and Times Square have been the center of the American entertainment industry, many entries are devoted to performers, writers and theaters. But the electric atmosphere of the area also attracted many ancillary industries and individuals from other walks of life. I have tried to balance the entries accordingly.

Setting the criteria for which entries to include and which to exclude was difficult. I could have made the book more complete with shorter entries, but I felt this would result in a dry book with little room for anecdote. And it is often the stories about the individuals and locations that give Times Square its unique flavor. Also, I decided to include those individuals and institutions that might stand as symbols of their type and that are important in their own right as well. For example, Rector's is the only "lobster palace" included in this book. However it didn't differ that much in ambiance from Shanley's or the dozens of other haute cuisine restaurants that dotted Broadway in the early years of the century.

Neil Simon *(q.v.)*, Joseph Fields *(q.v.)*, Arthur Miller *(q.v.)*, Eugene O'Neill *(q.v.)* and Tennessee Williams *(q.v.)* are the only playwrights accorded their own entries. However, briefer discussion of many more authors can be discovered through the index.

Far more composers and lyricists are represented than are playwrights. This is because I feel that they had greater impact on American theatrical history than their legitimate theater brethren. After all, the musical theater is Broadway's lifeblood. Its popular songs are known throughout the world, and amateur productions have influenced many Americans beyond the boundaries of Broadway. Because the book was limited in size not every theater or playwright or restaurant could be covered.

I also tried to focus on those individuals who have had a lasting influence on the area and the art of Broadway beyond their own times. For example, John Golden

Courtesy Artkraft Strauss

was a well-known producer, director, playwright and sometimes songwriter, but today his name is practically unknown. This doesn't mean he didn't make real contributions to Broadway, but he didn't merit an individual entry. Instead, a good description of his professional life can be found through index references. On the other hand, many figures who never received much fame are included simply because they seemed to illustrate a certain ambiance in Times Square at a particular time.

Biographical entries cover actors, gangsters, critics, entrepreneurs, and many incidental but colorful characters. The biographies cover their subjects' lives and careers as they related to Broadway and Times Square.

Entries on Broadway theaters contain the opening dates of the houses, architects and opening attractions. Additional details are provided by tracing the histories of major productions and their stars.

I have tried to keep my own judgments apart from the factual entries, but Times Square is as much a subjective feeling as an actual location and the choices of who and what were included obviously reflect my personal consideration of their importance.

Times Square attracts almost 8,000,000 theatergoers a year. Each contributes over $150 to the New York City economy, and together they support over 20,000 jobs. The Theatre League estimated that $750 million is spent by people coming to Times Square to see theater.

The history of Times Square goes back to before the founding of the United States. In 1776, the English general William Howe attacked Manhattan from the East River, near what is today 37th Street. This later became the subject of Robert E. Sherwood's play *Small War on Murray Hill* and the Rodgers and Hart *(q.v.)* musical *Dearest Enemy.* When news of Howe's landing reached General George Washington, he immediately brought his troops down from Harlem, where they were headquartered. From downtown came the American general Israel Putnam (who later had a Times

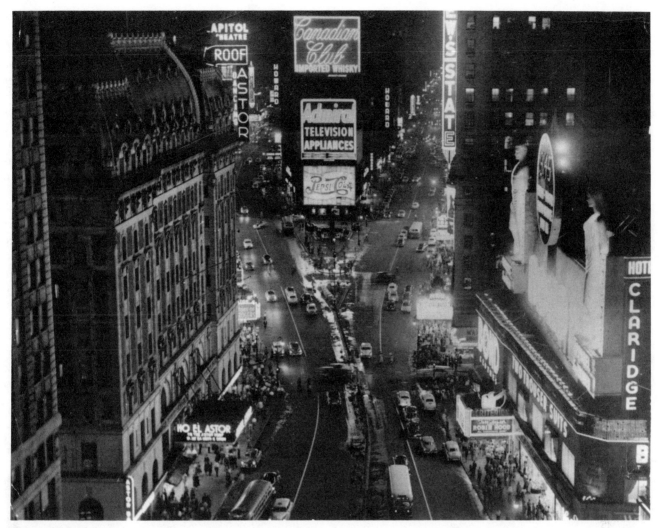

Courtesy Artkraft Strauss

Square building named after him). Putnam's guide was Aaron Burr.

Washington and Putnam occupied sites on what are now Bryant Park, behind the New York Public Library on 42nd Street between Fifth and Sixth Avenues, and the area near the present-day Broadway between 43rd and 44th Streets. Years later, Washington would enjoy taking his wife, Martha, on a carriage ride through the area.

During the early 1800s, this area was the home of squatters who settled along the creek known as Great Kill. The stream was later filled in and became 42nd Street. The area was known for its goat farms and as the site of manure dumping, a big business given the importance of the horse in the 19th century. Dutch farmers began settling the area and erecting farms.

John Jacob Astor and William Cutting purchased a 70-acre plot of land between Broadway and the Hudson River, bounded by 42nd Street to the south and 46th Street to the north, for $25,000 and built Medreef Eden farm. Astor had arrived in the country in 1784 from

Waldorf, Germany. He began a fur trade called the American Fur Company (the Astor Place subway station features a beaver in tile decoration as a tribute to Astor). Astor built a series of forts in Oregon to protect his fur business and began trading with China from the Pacific Coast. He also dealt in English pianofortes.

John J. Norton owned a large farm on the west side of 42nd Street. On September 28, 1825, he ceded a part of his farm, the Hermitage, to the city so that it could construct 42nd Street. The city paid Norton $10 for the rights of passage.

In 1829, a local paper carried an advertisment that read in part: "To let—large and commodious house and garden spot situated on Forty-second and Forty-third Streets, and 100 feet from Eighth Avenue. Well calculated for boarding school, summer retreat or private family—being pleasantly situated on high ground with view of North River. House has 25 rooms, good well and pump in cellar. Garden is laid out and at present planted for spring vegetables."

The streetcar line finally reached the summer homes

around East 42nd Street in 1839. The 42nd Street thoroughfare was used to drive cattle from the docks to slaughter houses on the East Side. The cattle arrived at 42nd Street on the Weehawken Ferry from New Jersey. Horsecar lines from the ferry also took passengers downtown.

Houses, stores, schools and churches were built in the area. Bloomingdale's Baptist Church (1841), the Forty-second Street Presbyterian Church (1868) and the Methodist-Episcopal Asylum for the Aged and Infirm (c. 1855) all opened on 42nd street. The Bloomingdale's Baptist Church became the Central Baptist Church in 1868, the Forty-second Street Presbyterian Church became St. Luke's Evangelical Lutheran Church in 1875 and the Asylum closed its doors in 1883 and was converted into the Clinton Apartment House. In 1878, St. Louis College "for Catholic boys of refined families" occupied 224 West 58th Street. The Church of St. Mary the Virgin at 228 West 45th Street was an Episcopal church with 600 members. In 1866, the Sisterhood of St. John the Baptist opened the Midnight Mission "for the reclamation of fallen women, who are here given homes, and, if found worthy, aided in obtaining permanent homes or employement." The mission was

at 208 West 46th Street. The George Bruce Memorial Circulating Library was situated at 226 West 42nd Street beginning in 1883.

The area, named after London's Long Acre, became the center of the carriage industry. Where the Winter Garden theater (q.v.) now stands was the Tattersall's American Horse Exchange. Harness shops and stables made up the majority of the businesses on Longacre Square. As the theater industry moved into the area, the carriage shops moved northward and were transformed into garages and automobile showrooms when the horse became passe.

Slowly but surely, the New York theater industry came uptown from the City Hall area to 14th Street and Union Square to 23rd Street and Madison Square to 34th Street and Herald Square. The theaters followed the diagonal swath that Broadway cut through the city.

Little by little new theaters began nearing Longacre Square. Among the first theaters built in the Longacre Square area was the Metropolitan Concert Hall at 41st and Broadway. Built in May 1880, the concert hall was never a success. It became the Metropolitan Casino, Alcazar, Cosmopolitan Theatre, a roller-skating rink and an exhibition hall. It was demolished in 1887 to

Broadway and 47th Street. 1870

make way for the Broadway Theatre, a very successful venture.

T. Henry French and two partners built the Broadway, which opened on March 3, 1888, with a production of *La Tosca* starring Fanny Davenport. French was the son of Samuel French whose name graces the still-popular play-publishing business he founded. The new Romanesque building seated 1,776 patrons with a 75-foot-wide stage. Like many theaters of the time, the Broadway was the home to acting companies, in this case led by De Wolf Hopper and Francis Wilson. Both companies specialized in comic operas. The Broadway Theatre left the legitimate field in 1908 when vaudeville and movies took over its stage. The theater was torn down in 1929 and replaced with a garment-center building.

The Casino Theatre *(q.v.),* built in 1882 at the corner of 39th Street and Broadway, was a favorite of audiences and performers. In 1900, the same year that Macy's moved from the "Ladies Mile" to Herald Square, the Casino had a roof garden built over its auditorium, the first of a popular breed of theaters around the turn of the century.

One year after the construction of the Casino, the Metropolitan Opera House opened on Broadway between 39th and 40th Streets. The arrival of the distinguished opera company gave the area a new cachet, and soon society began to look at the West Side as an attractive area. The Opera House suffered a major fire in 1892 but was rebuilt and lasted until 1966 when a new (and inferior) Metropolitan Opera House was constructed in Lincoln Center.

By 1893, New Yorkers were spending $6 million a year on entertainment. That same year (the year of the World's Columbian Exposition and Grover Cleveland's inauguration as President), land owner Robert Goelet built a theater on his plot of land on 38th Street and Broadway and called it Abbey's Theatre after producer Henry Abbey. King's Handbook of New York (1893) predicted that the Abbey would occupy "a prominent and worth place among the most notable theatres of New York and the world." But this was not to be. Abbey left the theater in 1896, and the name was changed to the Knickerbocker Theatre under the auspices of Al Hayman. The Knickerbocker was torn down in 1930.

The first theater on 42nd Street was the American Theatre built in 1893, the year of a great stock market panic. The parcel of land included property on 41st Street, 42nd Street and Eighth Avenue and was purchased for producer T. Henry French by theatrical real estate agent Hartie I. Phillips from 17 different owners. The theater was next to the Franklin Savings Bank directly on the corner and across the street from J. Wieland's Pharmacy, which stood on the northeast corner. Although the theater proper was built on land bounded by 41st Street and Eighth Avenue, the entrance, due to the plot's odd makeup, was on 42nd Street. Later theaters like the Lyric *(q.v.),* wanting a 42nd Street facade, would copy the example set by the American architect Charles C. Haight.

French promised that the 1,900-seat Spanish Renaissance-style theater would be "the largest and the handsomest combination theatre in the United States." The *New York Times* said that "the first impression one gets of it is not of great size; its lines are such that every spectator, even those in the upper gallery, is brought in close relation with the stage." The *Times* also reviewed the theater's roof garden where vaudeville acts were presented. The paper reported: "The main garden is 90 feet square, and is brilliantly lighted by arches and trefoils or powerful electric lights. It will accommodate 650 persons, who, in case of rain, can take refuge in two large roofed apartments, where free air is a feature and shelter is perfect. The stage is large, and some say it is the largest among the roof garden stages."

The main auditorium's opening production was *The Prodigal Daughter,* an import from London. The show was a spectacle with a cast of almost 200, along with 9 racehorses, which actually ran a steeplechase course, complete with water hazard and hurdles constructed on a moving treadmill. The show also had a full complement of hounds for the hunt. All did not always go well in the difficult scene. George Odell wrote in *Annals of the New York Stage:* "In the race scene, on May 26th, . . . the horse, Columbus, fell, in jumping over the hurdles, and rolled upon his rider, Guttenberg Billy. The fiery steed, Rochefort, ridden by Leonard Boyne, attempted to climb over the iron balcony. The panic was completed when Julia Arthur employed the leading lady's privilege of fainting . . . Thenceforth, so far as I know, the horses behaved according to the script of the play."

The show was a great success and the New York *Dramatic Mirror* exclaimed: "No midsummer theatrical performances in this city have ever met with the phenomenal success of those at Mr. French's American Theatre." But subsequent offerings were not successful in drawing audiences; the American suffered losses and finally became a vaudeville house, and its name was changed to the American Music Hall. It briefly presented motion pictures before turning, in 1929, to burlesque. The theater couldn't weather the Great Depression and was demolished in 1932.

In 1895, in the area known as "thieves lair" by locals, Oscar Hammerstein I *(q.v.)* built his Olympia theater *(q.v.)* complex. Electric lights had just been installed in the Long Acre area. The theaters that made up the Olympia complex on Broadway between 44th and 45th Street were not a success, although they managed to draw attention to the Square as an entertainment center.

The area along Broadway from 37th Street and 42nd

Street was dubbed "the Rialto." Soon the Longacre theater district would also be called "the Rialto." In the 1950s and 1960s, Sam Zolotow wrote a popular theater column in the *New York Times* called "News of the Rialto."

Almost 80 theaters were constructed in the Times Square area. Many were built by producers and actor/managers who headed their own stock companies. They leased the land from the original owners who were intelligent enough not to let go of their land holdings. More and more producers like David Belasco *(q.v.)* and Daniel Frohman had their own houses built. Later, just before and during the 1920s, impressarios like Florenz Ziegfeld *(q.v.)* and Earl Carroll *(q.v.)* would build theaters to house their productions.

Most of the successful theaters in the area were owned by the six members of the Theatrical Syndicate, a trust that was happy to force out its competition. The Syndicate was put out of business in 1916 and replaced by another equally powerful group—the Shubert Brothers *(q.v.)*. The Shuberts' power cannot be overestimated.

During the Depression, when breadlines snaked around Duffy Square at Broadway and 47th Street, it was the Shuberts who kept American theater alive. The Shuberts were forced to break up their near monopoly in the 1950s.

The Square's preeminence was solidified in 1904 when the *New York Times* (founded in 1851) tore down the Pabst Hotel and built its new headquarters, the Times Tower *(q.v.)*. It is telling that the entrance of the Pabst Hotel faced downtown while the new Times Tower faced uptown.

The move by the *New York Times* to the Square led to the City Council's voting to rename Longacre Square to Times Square. In April 1904, the mayor signed the designation.

The Times Tower gained prominence in the square when the Motogram *(q.v.)* electric zipper sign was wrapped around the building. The Motogram gave the latest news and thousands of New Yorkers, in the years before the widespread use of radio, would gather in the Square to see the latest reports. Even during radio's

Longacre Square south from 45th Street. Note Rector's Restaurant between 43rd and 44th Streets in front of the Cadillac Hotel. The center of the Square features Pabst's Hotel, soon to be replaced by the Times Tower. Courtesy Municipal Art Society.

and, later, television's prominence in timely news reporting, the Times Tower remained the focal point. New Yorkers gathered to see election results, news of the Japanese surrender in World War II (and the resultant V-J day *(q.v.)* celebration) and sports finals.

The Square was also used for mass rallies to sell war bonds for publicity stunts *(q.v.)*, political demonstrations and for the annual New Year's Eve celebration. Parades, including Macy's annual Thanksgiving Day parade, marched down Broadway through the Square.

On October 27, 1904, the West Side Subway was opened from Fourth Avenue to 42nd Street on the East Side then across the thoroughfare to Broadway and up to 125th Street. Within one year, the Times Square subway stop had been used by over 5,000,000 people. The laying of the new subway lines through the city; the consolidation of many train lines into Grand Central Terminal at 42nd Street and Vanderbilt Avenue in 1878; and the completion of the Third and Sixth Avenue elevated trains also in that year helped the burgeoning area of Times Square.

In 1905, gasoline-driven buses replaced the horse-drawn streetcars. The city saw its first metered taxi cabs in 1907. Unfortunately, many of the theaters were not built to screen the increased noise from the traffic. Patrons sitting in the last rows of the orchestra at the Republic Theater *(q.v.)* could not hear Mrs. Patrick Campbell in *Magda*. Press agent A. Toxen Worm had a brainstorm when George Tyler facetiously suggested that the problem could be solved if 42nd Street were covered with tan bark. Worm thought the idea was the ideal publicity stunt *(q.v.)* and ordered the street so covered.

John C. Van Dyke described Times Square in his book *The New New York*. He wrote: "At eight in the evening there is the incessant come and go of trolleys, the rattle of cabs, the shuffle and push of many feet along the street, the insistent voice of ticket speculators, and the unintelligible shout of men and boys hawking night editions of newspapers."

The construction of Madison Square Garden on 50th Street between Eighth and Ninth Avenues brought many sports enthusiasts to the area. The money to be made in area nightclubs and later speakeasies, not to mention the money laundering through Broadway investments, led to an influx of gangsters.

Madison Square Garden Courtesy Municipal Art Society.

The opening of such hotels as the Astor *(q.v.)*; the Metropole at 41st Street between Broadway and Seventh Avenue (the home of George M. Cohan and Enrico Caruso); the Vendome at Broadway and 41st Street; the Claridge *(q.v.)* and the Knickerbocker *(q.v.)* brought tourists and travelers to the area. The docks, only four avenues away, hosted the arrivals and departures of the giant luxury liners making their port in New York. The Times Square hotels were the nearest deluxe accommodations for these travelers and were halfway between the ports and the rail lines. Fancy restaurants like Rector's *(q.v.)*, Shanley's, Murray's Roman Gardens *(q.v.)* and Churchill's served upper-class patrons as Anna Held *(q.v.)* and Diamond Jim Brady *(q.v.)*. The years following World War I were boom years for Times Square. Money was plentiful and New York was the richest American city. This wealth led to changes along the Great White Way. The theatrical unions, such as Actors' Equity *(q.v.)*, gained power and demanded increases in pay. Inflation, spurred by the success of the stock market, raised production costs, and ticket prices reflected the increased costs and increased taxes needed to support the growing metropolis.

The boom era culminated both financially and artistically with the theatrical season of 1927–28, when 257 plays opened in the 71 theaters around Times Square. Shortly after this, however, the industry suffered three major blows, one financial and two artistic. The first was the stock market crash of 1929, which forced many producers and their backers into receivership. Even the powerful Shuberts lost many theaters. The second was the acceptance of sound pictures by the public. Great movie palaces were built along Broadway in the late 1920s. The construction of these massive halls culminated with the greatest of all, the Roxy Theater *(q.v.)*, under the auspices of S. L. ("Roxy") Rothafel *(q.v.)*, the man most responsible for the development of the movie palace. The third big effect on the industry was the emergence of radio as a mass-entertainment force.

During the 1930s, many theaters were darkened by the sudden drop off of theatrical ventures. Many of the houses were converted to radio (and later television) studios or burlesque houses. Still more were demolished or left empty. The Federal Theater Project *(q.v.)* managed to keep some of the theaters lit. The burlesque houses slowly led to the eventual decline of the 42nd Street area. When Mayor LaGuardia outlawed burlesque, the theaters became grind movie houses and attracted an even lower class of clientele. Soon, low entertainments like Ripley's Odditorium *(q.v.)* and Hubert's Museum and Flea Circus *(q.v.)* attracted a decidedly less-ritzy crowd to the Great White Way.

World War II brought a new prosperity to the area, but it was a middle-class and lower-class area. Still, the theater remained the center of the nation's entertainment indutry. Due to the popularity of its vigor and unique signage *(q.v.)*, especially that of Douglas Leigh *(q.v.)* and the Artkraft Strauss Sign Company *(q.v.)*, Times Square itself became a great attraction.

The 1960s and 1970s saw a worsening of the area and a drop in the number of legitimate shows produced on Broadway. Many of the 42nd Street theaters fell into further disrepair and showed kung-fu or porno films round-the-clock. The opening of the Port Authority Bus Terminal brought runaways and vagrants into the area, and Eighth Avenue became known as one of New York's most undesirable locations. Hustlers of three-card monte and other scams mixed with pickpockets. Peddlers selling fake Gucci bags and $10 imitation Rolex watches crowded the sidewalks. As drugs and prostitution flourished around 42nd Street and Eighth Avenue, numerous plans, all discarded, promised to clean up the area.

Many New York landmarks, including Lindy's Restaurant *(q.v.)*, the Astor Hotel *(q.v.)*, the Paramount Theater *(q.v.)* and the Roxy Theater were demolished for high-rise office buildings, which increased land values and destroyed the low-rise ambiance of the area. Many of the great spectacular signs were taken down and replaced by simple illuminated billboards.

During the 1980s, there was a resurgence of activity around the area. Zoning changes made it more profitable to build in the area, and more and more skyscrapers were built, pushing out still more of the ancillary businesses that served the theater industry. Preservationists waged an unsuccessful battle to save the Helen Hayes and Morosco theaters *(q.v.)*. This led to an increased determination to save the remaining theaters, and in late 1987, most of the remaining theaters enjoyed landmark status (over the objections of their owners). A major redevelopment of 42nd Street was announced by Mayor Edward Koch's administration, but condemnation of buildings in the area and new construction were stalled by a series of lawsuits. The latest stock market crash, in October 1987, made new construction less attractive. Many of the individuals involved in the redevelopment plan were indicted, and the entire plan came under increased criticism. The Koch administration, astoundingly in favor of redevelopment, insisted in pursuing the plan even after it seemed unwise and unfair to do so.

The future of Times Square as New York's entertainment center is uncertain. First-run films are not given premieres in the Square, and often open simultaneously throughout Manhattan and the suburbs. Broadway shows, with ever-increasing ticket prices and a reliance on blockbuster musicals, are pricing themselves out of existence.

Even blockbuster hits such as *Phantom of the Opera*, considered a massive Broadway show, cannot hold a candle to the spectacles of the past. Because people's

Donald Duck passes through Times Square as part of Macy's Thanksgiving Day Parade. Note the vestiges of the Pepsi Cola Spectacular on the roof of the Criterion Center. Courtesy Artkraft Strauss.

salaries are expensive and scenery can be amortized, the physical productions grow and the casts shrink. The thought of producing a show the size of Cole Porter's *(q.v.) Anything Goes* (11/21/34) with 41 principals and a chorus of 25 (and this during the Depression) is unthinkable. The recent Lincoln Center revival had a total of 33 cast members. Ziegfeld's production of the musical comedy *Show Boat* (12/27/27) had 33 principals, 31 people in the Jubilee Singers, 12 dancers, 32 ladies in the chorus and 16 gentlemen in the chorus—124 cast members in all. A more recent show, *Oklahoma!* (3/31/43), had 23 principals, 16 singers and 18 dancers. *Phantom of the Opera,* currently at the Majestic Theater *(q.v.)* has only 35 people in its cast, certainly not an extravaganza by traditional standards.

Very few productions originate on Broadway. The Shuberts and their ilk put their money behind tried-and-true productions that have been successfully mounted in London, off-Broadway or regional theaters and that will appeal to the broadest possible audience.

There is less and less room, given runaway production costs, for independent producers to put work up on Broadway. The impresario with good ideas and not much capital cannot find a foothold in the new Times Square. The early geniuses who helped make the area so unique could not possibly have succeeded in today's world. High rents and new construction are forcing out small stores and businesses and they are being replaced with chain stores and fast-food restaurants.

The increase in large skyscrapers further deprives the area of its shops, restaurants, signage locations and vital nightlife. New buildings often close at 6 P.M. and leave their surrounding blocks empty. Times Square might soon become a ghost town after dark, much as the Wall Street area becomes deserted after the business day.

When Edward Arlington Robinson, on his way to a Broadway show, wrote "The White Lights, Broadway 1906," he could not have realized just how prophetic his poem would be:

> Here, where the white lights have begun
> To seethe the way for something fair,
> No prophet knew, from what was done,
> That there was triumph in the air."

Let us hope that his words will remain true.

AARONS AND FREEDLEY Today the Shuberts *(q.v.)*, Jujamcyns and Nederlanders are the theater owners of note, but prior to the Depression, most producers owned their own theaters. This was a logical outgrowth of the 19th-century tradition of the great actor-managers. These actor-managers produced their own shows in which they starred with their stock companies. That tradition faded in the late 1920s as a new generation of producers came on the scene. Other circumstances leading to the end of the actor-managers were the creation of Actors' Equity *(q.v.)* and the increased costs of producing theater, which precluded keeping large companies on salary throughout the year.

Also, as American playwrights came into their own, their plays often replaced the European and British repertoire preferred by the old school. This change in drama led to a change in acting style, a change that was hastened by the new popularity of the movies.

As the theater district moved to Times Square, producers rushed to build theaters for their own productions. Owning their own theaters allowed producers to save costs and to avoid the control of competitors. Producers Alex Aarons and Vinton Freedley were no exception.

Alex A. Aarons was born in Philadelphia in 1891, the son of composer-producer Alfred E. Aarons. Vinton Freedley was born in the same year in the same city. Aarons produced the George Gershwin *(q.v.)* and B.G. DeSylva show *La-La-Lucille* in 1919 and *For Goodness Sake* in 1922 with a score by the Gershwins among others. Freedley acted in Aarons's production of *For Goodness Sake* in 1922 and *Elsie* in 1923.

Later that year, Aarons and Freedley teamed up and produced *Lady, Be Good!* (12/1/24; 330 performances) at the Liberty Theatre *(q.v.)*. Fred and Adele Astaire *(q.v.)* starred in the show, introducing such numbers as "Fascinating Rhythm" and "Oh, Lady Be Good!"

Aarons next produced *Tell Me More!* (4/13/25; 100 performances) again with a score by the Gershwins and B.G. DeSylva. They teamed up again with *Tip-Toes* (12/28/25; 194 performances). Queenie Smith and Jeanette MacDonald starred and the score included "Looking for a Boy," "That Certain Feeling" and "Sweet and Low Down."

Their next Gershwin show was a smash hit. *Oh, Kay!* (11/8/26; 256 performances) opened at the Imperial Theatre *(q.v.)* with Gertrude Lawrence, Oscar Shaw, Victor Moore and Betty Compton. The superior score yielded such tunes as "Maybe," "Clap Yo' Hands," "Do Do Do" and "Someone to Watch Over Me."

The success of *Oh, Kay!* led the two producers to follow in the path of others and build their own theater. The name Alvin was arrived at by combining the first letters of each producer's first names. The Alvin Theater *(q.v.)* opened with the premiere of *Funny Face* on November 22, 1927.

The production of *Funny Face* (250 performances) boasted a score by George and Ira Gershwin *(q.v.)* and starred the Astaires. The score introduced such standards as "Funny Face," " 'S Wonderful" and "My One and Only."

Next came *Here's Howe!* (5/1/28; 71 performances), remembered today, if at all, by the pop song "Crazy Rhythm." Next, Aarons and Freedley presented *Hold Everything!* (10/10/28; 413 performances) at the Broadhurst Theater *(q.v.)*. Their third premiere in 1928 was the Gershwins' *Treasure Girl* (11/8/28; 68 performances) at the Alvin Theater. The show opened with Gertrude Lawrence, Clifton Webb and Walter Catlett starring. The score featured such gems as "I've Got a Crush on You," "Oh, So Nice," "I Don't Think I'll Fall in Love Today" and "Feeling I'm Falling."

Spring Is Here (3/11/29; 104 performances) came hard on the heels of the closing of *Treasure Girl*. This time

Rodgers and Hart *(q.v.)* provided a score including the well-known "With a Song in My Heart." *Heads Up!* (11/11/29; 144 performances), another Rodgers and Hart show, opened with Ray Bolger and Victor Moore.

The stock-market crash slowed the producing team's output, and *Girl Crazy* (10/14/30; 272 performances), their next production, would not open until almost a year after *Heads Up!* It might have played longer if the country's problems hadn't caused theater business to fall off. The score was one of the Gershwins' best. It featured "Bidin' My Time," "Embraceable You," "But Not for Me" and "I Got Rhythm." The cast included Willie Howard, Ginger Rogers and, making her Broadway debut, Ethel Merman *(q.v.)*.

Girl Crazy was the last show to play the Alvin Theater under Aarons and Freedley's management. They lost their theater to the mortgage holders, as did many other theater owners during the Depression.

Aarons and Freedley continued their partnership both at the Alvin and at other Broadway houses after the loss of the Alvin. Following *Girl Crazy* came *Pardon My English* (1/20/33; 43 performances), George Gershwin's ninth and final score for Aarons and Freedley and Alex Aarons's last Broadway show. It premiered at the Majestic Theater *(q.v.)*.

After Aarons's retirement in 1933, Freedley continued on his own (Aarons died on March 14, 1943), producing *Anything Goes!* (11/21/34; 415 performances) at the Alvin. *Anything Goes!* starred Ethel Merman and featured an excellent Cole Porter *(q.v.)* score including "You're the Top," "I Get a Kick Out of You," "Anything Goes" and "All Through the Night." The show reestablished Freedley as a top Broadway producer.

Freedley's production of Cole Porter's *Red, Hot and Blue!* (10/29/36; 181 performances) at the Alvin starred Ethel Merman, Bob Hope and Jimmy Durante. The standout song was "It's Delovely."

Freedley next presented Porter's *Leave It to Me!* (11/9/38; 291 performances) at the Imperial Theatre marking the Broadway debut of Mary Martin *(q.v.)*. She became a star when, in this show, she introduced the Porter song "My Heart Belongs to Daddy." The other notable Porter songs featured in the score were "Most Gentlemen Don't Like Love" and "Get Out of Town."

Vernon Duke *(q.v.)* and John Latouche's *Cabin in the Sky* (10/25/40; 156 performances) was Freedley's next production, opening at the Martin Beck Theatre *(q.v.)*. Freedley coproduced the show with Albert Lewis. The exceptional score featured "Taking a Chance on Love," which was introduced in the show by Ethel Waters and became an instant success.

Freedley produced one more show boasting a Cole Porter score, *Let's Face It!* (10/29/41; 547 performances). The show starred Danny Kaye, Eve Arden, Benny Baker, Mary Jane Walsh and Vivian Vance.

Jackpot (1/13/44; 44 performances), a Vernon Duke

and Howard Dietz *(q.v.)* failure, returned Freedley to the Alvin. Nanette Fabray, Allan Jones and Betty Garrett starred. Jacqueline Susann, later to receive fame as an author, played a small role. Freedley's production of *Memphis Bound!* (5/24/45; 36 performances) at the Broadway Theatre *(q.v.)* was also a failure.

Freedley's last Broadway show, *Great to Be Alive!* (3/23/50; 52 performances) at the Winter Garden Theater *(q.v.)*, was another failure. Freedley died in New York on June 5, 1969.

Aarons and Freedley had their greatest successes when presenting shows by inspired talents. They were not the sort of creative producers who could save weak shows though their own talents. But their long list of hits proves that they recognized talent and could put together attractive packages that enabled the artists to work to their best advantage.

The team had seven shows by the Gershwins to their credit. Four of these shows featured libretti by Fred Thompson in collaboration with a series of talents, including Guy Bolton *(q.v.)*, who was also responsible for four scripts. Five of the shows featured the duo-pianists Phil Ohman and Vic Arden. Freedley alone produced four Cole Porter shows. Ethel Merman appeared in three of their shows.

The shows Aarons and Freedley produced were not necessarily the most artistic endeavors of the people they worked with, but they were among the most popular.

ABBOTT, GEORGE (1887–   ) George Abbott, or Mr. Abbott as he is known by his contemporaries, has enjoyed what is probably the most creative and certainly the longest career in the American Theater. He has been involved with 122 productions as playwright, producer, director, actor or play doctor. Often he held more than one role in the same show.

He was responsible for giving many people their first breaks in the theater. Among those who scored their first successes with George Abbott productions were Leonard Bernstein *(q.v.)*, Garson Kanin, John Kander and Fred Ebb, Betty Comden and Adolph Green *(q.v.)*, Jerome Robbins, Frank Loesser *(q.v.)*, Jean and Walter Kerr, Harold Prince, Richard Bissell, Jerome Weidman, Jerry Bock and Sheldon Harnick *(q.v.)*, Bob Merrill, as well as hundreds of performers, including Carol Burnett, Desi Arnaz and Nancy Walker.

George Abbott was born in Forestville, New York, on June 25, 1887. His early jobs included Western Union messenger, cowboy, steel worker, swimming instructor, basketball coach, and salesman.

His first play, *The Head of the Family*, a one-act, was presented by the Harvard Dramatic Club in 1912. He first appeared on Broadway as an actor in *The Misleading Lady* (11/25/13) at the Fulton Theater (see Helen Hayes Theater). Other early performances were in *Daddies* (9/

5/18); *The Broken Wing* (11/29/20); *Zander the Great* (4/9/23); *White Desert* (10/18/23); *Hellbent for Heaven* (1/4/24); *Lazybones* (9/22/24); and *Processional* (1/12/25).

His first writing assignment was in collaboration with James Gleason. They wrote *The Fall Guy* (3/10/25), which premiered at the Eltinge Theater (*q.v.*). He collaborated with Winchell Smith on *A Holy Terror* (9/28/25), which opened at the George M. Cohan Theatre (*q.v.*) with Abbott in a leading role. With John V.A. Weaver, he wrote and directed *Love 'Em and Leave 'Em* (2/3/26).

Abbott's first great success, *Broadway* (9/16/26; 603 performances), was written with Philip Dunning. The melodrama of gangsters and show biz opened at the Broadhurst Theater (*q.v.*) under Abbott's direction.

His next assignment was as director of *Chicago* (12/30/26; 172 performances). That show was also a success following its opening at the Music Box Theater (*q.v.*). *Coquette* (11/8/27; 366 performances) was also a hit under Mr. Abbott's direction.

With Philip Dunning coproducing, Mr. Abbott directed *Twentieth Century* (12/29/32; 154 performances). It opened at the Broadhurst Theater. With John Cecil Holm, he coauthored one of the great hits of the thirties, *Three Men on a Horse* (1/30/35; 812 performances). The fast-paced farce opened at the Playhouse Theater.

His first musical theater assignment was directing the Rodgers and Hart (*q.v.*) musical extravaganza *Jumbo* (11/16/35; 221 performances). The Billy Rose production played the old Hippodrome theater (*q.v.*) on Sixth Avenue. *Jumbo* was followed by a bona fide smash, *Boy Meets Girl* (11/27/35; 669 performances). Mr. Abbott produced and directed the farce at the Cort Theatre.

Abbott and Rodgers and Hart coauthored the script of *On Your Toes* (4/11/36; 318 performances), a musical comedy that opened at the Imperial Theatre (*q.v.*). Abbott produced and directed *Brother Rat* (12/16/36; 575 performances), followed by another great hit, *Room Service* (5/19/37; 496 performances) at the Cort Theatre (*q.v.*).

His next musical was Rodgers and Hart's *The Boys from Syracuse* (11/23/38; 235 performances). Mr. Abbott wrote the book and produced and directed the musical, which opened at the Alvin Theater (*q.v.*). He produced and directed the same team's *Too Many Girls* (10/18/39; 249 performances), which starred a young Desi Arnaz. Mr. Abbott's next musical was the controversial Rodgers and Hart show, *Pal Joey* (12/25/40; 374 performances). Gene Kelly opened in the title role at the Ethel Barrymore Theatre (*q.v.*).

The next year, he gave a break to new songwriters, Hugh Martin and Ralph Blane. Their show, *Best Foot Forward* (10/1/41; 326 performances), which Mr. Abbott directed, produced and coauthored with John Cecil Holm, opened at the Ethel Barrymore Theatre. It contained such great songs as "Buckle Down Winsocki,"

"Ev'ry Time" and "Just a Little Joint with a Juke Box." The show starred June Allyson, Danny Daniels, Stanley Donen, Rosemary Lane and Nancy Walker.

On the Town (12/28/44; 462 performances) marked the Broadway debuts of composer Leonard Bernstein (*q.v.*), lyricists Betty Comden and Adolph Green (*q.v.*) and choreographer Jerome Robbins. They were ably taught under the firm hand of director Abbott.

Abbott's next directorial hit, *High Button Shoes* (10/9/47; 727 performances), again introduced a new composer and lyricist to Broadway. Jule Styne (*q.v.*) and Sammy Cahn provided the songs for the Phil Silvers, Nanette Fabray show.

Another Broadway neophyte, Frank Loesser, was the songwriter who provided the score for Mr. Abbott's next hit, *Where's Charley?* (10/11/48; 792 performances). Abbott's musicalization of Brandon Thomas's farce opened at the St. James Theatre (*q.v.*). Abbott directed Ray Bolger and Allyn Ann McLerie in the leads. "Once in Love with Amy" was the big hit from the show.

Broadway veteran Irving Berlin's (*q.v.*) *Call Me Madam* (10/12/50; 644 performances) opened with Ethel Merman (*q.v.*) in the leading role. The show, inspired by real-life ambassador and hostess Perle Mesta, was Mr. Abbott's next hit as a director.

Composer Arthur Schwartz (*q.v.*) and lyricist Dorothy Fields (*q.v.*) collaborated with George Abbott on *A Tree Grows in Brooklyn* (4/19/51; 267 performances), the musical version of Betty Smith's beloved novel. Abbott wrote the libretto as well as provided direction for the musical. Johnny Johnson and Shirley Booth starred at the Alvin Theater.

Wonderful Town (2/25/53; 559 performances), Bernstein, Comden and Green's next collaboration, was directed by Mr. Abbott. The show, based on Ruth McKinney's stories in the *New Yorker,* opened at the Winter Garden Theater (*q.v.*) with Rosalind Russell in the lead.

The team of Richard Rodgers and Oscar Hammerstein II (*q.v.*) seemed like a sure bet for Abbott treatment. But the result, *Me and Juliet* (5/28/53; 358 performances) was one of the team's few failures. Mr. Abbott had greater success with *The Pajama Game* (5/13/54; 1,061 performances), the effort of another team of newcomers. Jerry Ross and Richard Adler wrote the score and Mr. Abbott collaborated with Richard Bissell on the libretto. Bob Fosse made his choreographic debut with the show. "Hernando's Hideaway" and "Hey There" were the two standouts in the score.

After directing a revival of *On Your Toes* (10/11/54), Mr. Abbott took on directing duties for the second and last collaboration between Adler and Ross, *Damn Yankees* (5/5/55; 1,019 performances) . It opened at the 46th Street Theatre (*q.v.*) with Gwen Verdon in her first starring role. Her song, "Whatever Lola Wants," became one of the hits of the show.

Having had a failure with Richard Rodgers, Mr. Abbott did much better with the composer's daughter, Mary. She and Marshall Barer wrote the score to the off-Broadway hit *Once Upon a Mattress* (5/11/59; 460 performances). It opened at the Phoenix Theater, and a new star was born, Carol Burnett.

He directed and collaborated on the book for the Pulitzer Prize winning musical *Fiorello!* (11/23/59; 796 performances). The show was the first hit for the team of Jerry Bock and Sheldon Harnick *(q.v.)*. Their loving portrait of Fiorello LaGuardia starred Tom Bosley in the title role. The same team, Bock and Harnick, and book writers Abbott and Jerome Weidman couldn't repeat their success with *Tenderloin* (10/17/60; 216 performances), which opened at the 46th Street Theatre. Maurice Evans was the unlikely star.

Mr. Abbott's direction of a comedy, *Take Her, She's Mine* (12/21/61; 404 performances), proved to be one of his only nonmusical successes in the latter part of his career. The show opened at the Biltmore Theater.

Stephen Sondheim's *(q.v.)* first attempt as both composer and lyricist, *A Funny Thing Happened on the Way to the Forum* (5/8/62; 965 performances), opened at the Alvin Theater with Zero Mostel. Mr. Abbott directed. Sumner Arthur Long's *Never Too Late* (11/27/62; 1,007 performances) was another comedy success for Mr. Abbott. It opened at the Playhouse Theater with Paul Ford, Maureen O'Sullivan and Orson Bean.

Mr. Abbott's career continued into the seventies and eighties, although he had progressively fewer successes. Among his later productions were *Fade Out—Fade In* (5/26/54; 271 performances), which reunited the director and Carol Burnett; *Flora, the Red Menace* (5/11/65; 87 performances), John Kander and Fred Ebb's first Broadway score and Liza Minnelli's Broadway debut; and *How Now, Dow Jones* (12/7/67; 220 performances) with a score by Elmer Bernstein and Carolyn Leigh.

A major revival of *On Your Toes,* which opened at the Virginia Theater *(q.v.)* on March 6, 1983, was Mr. Abbott's last Broadway success. A production of *Broadway* opened at the Royale Theater *(q.v.)* on June 25, 1987, Mr. Abbott's 100th Birthday. (Unfortunately, it played for only four performances.)

He still continues actively pursuing his interests by directing at small theaters and continuing to write for the theater. For exercise he enjoys his lifelong interests in golf and ballroom dancing.

ACTORS' EQUITY Actor's Equity is the labor union of all professional actors in the American theater. The organization has jurisdiction over all Broadway, off-Broadway and League of Resident Theaters performers. It represents these actors in all negotiations. Actors may join Equity by being cast in an Equity production or by amassing points in smaller regional and summer stock theaters.

The association was founded on December 22, 1912, by 112 actors as the American Federation of Actors, but it took until May 26, 1913, for the constitution and bylaws to be adopted.

Given the sorry state of the theater industry, four out of five Equity members are unemployed. In the Times Square area, Equity members can often be found as waiters and waitresses in theatrical restaurants and handing out flyers at the TKTS Booth *(q.v.)*. Less than 5% of the membership earns more than $10,000 annually in the theater.

At the turn of the century, the exploitation of actors was rife throughout the theater industry. Poor working and traveling conditions, as well as exploitative employers, made actors' professional lives difficult and precarious. This lack of basic amenities worked into the hands of unscrupulous producers who capitalized on the bad communications and great distances between them and their employees. The producers were following in the footsteps of the many captains of industry that exploited workers as a basic economic practice.

While not all producers were untrustworthy, the standard theatrical practices often left the actors stranded in cities far from their home base of New York. Actors were not paid for long rehearsal time. Often producers put shows into rehearsal without the capitalization necessary to open. Rehearsals could last months or until the producer raised the money. Performers were often expected to provide their own costumes and keep them in reasonable shape. These hardships may have made for many amusing anecdotes in future biographies, but being stranded in the middle of nowhere with hostile locals and no money wasn't something the actors looked forward to.

The Pabst Grand Circle Hotel in New York was the scene of the first meeting to create the organization. Francis Wilson was elected as the first president. The original members of the committee were Albert Bruning, Charles D. Coburn, Frank Gillmore, William Harcourt, Milton Sills and Grant Stewart.

The preamble to the constitution of Actors' Equity states that the organization will do what it can to "advance, promote, foster and benefit the profession." It spells out the conditions under which an actor may be employed, elaborates on several benefits to the membership and instructs the association to work for improved legislation on behalf of the profession.

The producers didn't take the fledgling organization seriously. Problems were exacerbated by the producers' unwillingness to discuss problems with actors' representatives. Clearly, a strong action was neccessary by the organization. Its first important action, the actors' strike of 1919 *(q.v.)*, lasted 30 days and closed 37 plays in 8 cities, prevented the opening of 16 others and was estimated to cost the industry $3 million, a huge sum at the time.

During the strike, George M. Cohan (q.v.) sided with management. He had come up through the ranks of performers and felt he had good relationships with both actors and producers. His attitude was more sentimental than logical. Marie Dressler, who remembered her days as an $8 dollar a week chorus girl, helped bring the chorus girls into the strike. She became the first president of the Chorus Equity Association, which later merged with Actors' Equity. This strike resulted in Equity being recognized as the official trade union of the acting profession.

In 1960, Broadway was again disrupted by a second strike. Contractual negotiations were undertaken between the association and the League of New York Theaters, the producers' organization. An agreement was reached under which actors received higher rehearsal salaries, higher minimum salaries, provisions for a pension plan and welfare benefits.

In 1961, the two organizations agreed that no member of Equity would be required to work in a theater "where discrimination is practiced against any actor or patron by reason of his race, creed or color."

Equity has a reputation for a wariness and distrust of producers. Its newsletter, *Equity News,* reflects the bureaucracy of the main organization and echoes the attitude of its staff and many of its more radical members. To its credit, Equity has been trying of late to represent the needs of those actors outside of the Broadway arena. But, too often, Equity seems to operate without an understanding of the legitimate problems producers and other theatrical professionals face. Critics accuse Equity of operating with too much rigidity, preferring to close shows and lose jobs rather than bend rules to allow for special exceptions.

Unfortunately, the current state of the theater industry encourages producers to cut corners and save money at the expense of others. Shows are produced by pharmaceutical heiresses, washed up television actors and purveyors of ladies lingerie. Where once there was one name above a show title, there are now often five or six. Equity can hardly be blamed for being confused as to who exactly is in charge.

It would seem time for all participants, including Actors' Equity, to make concessions in order to control ticket prices and encourage investment. Like all the other theatrical trade unions, Actors' Equity must share part of the blame for the depressed state of current theater.

ACTORS' STRIKE OF 1919   The American Federation of Actors, the precursor of Actors' Equity (q.v.), called a strike on August 6, 1919. One hundred actors closed 12 Broadway productions. The 2,700 members of Equity didn't represent all the performers on the legitimate stage. Producers wooed nonunion actors and many shows were ready to reopen with replacements. But the stagehands and musicians, already members of the AFL, joined the strike, and the shows were closed for the duration of the strike.

On September 6, 1919, the strike was resolved to Equity's advantage, and Equity was recognized as the legal bargaining agent for stage performers. The strike lasted 30 days and closed 37 plays in 8 cities, prevented the opening of 16 other shows and was estimated to cost the industry $3 million.

The only financial demand made on the producers was that performers be paid for extra matinees. It wasn't until 1933 that a minimum pay for actors was written into the Equity contract. Rehearsal minimums weren't set until 1935. But the strike did establish Equity and led the way for additional bargaining. Membership in Equity increased from 2,700 to 14,000 following the strike.

Part of the foundation of the strike was laid, oddly enough, by the producers themselves. Prior to the strike, producer John Golden met with F. Ray Comstock, J. Fred Zimmerman, Arch Selwyn, Florenz Ziegfeld (q.v.), Winchell Smith and L. Lawrence Weber. Golden's goal was to stop the constant warfare between producers, address the problems of censorship and rampant ticket speculation, set up a permanent dialogue among the different producing organizations in order to facilitate the sharing of ideas and, most important, stop rival producing organizations from stealing each other's stars. Although not much came out of this first meeting, it wasn't too painful for the parties involved, and it solidified the feelings of community among the producers.

Later, at a luncheon at the Claridge Hotel, 40 managers organized the Producing Managers Association. This organization helped convince others in the theatrical community that organization was a workable idea. It also provided a convenient entity for receiving complaints from the producers' employees, including actors.

It wasn't long before Francis Wilson, as President of Actors' Equity (q.v.), made demands of the producers.

The actors, considering themselves artists not laborers, sought to limit the amount of free rehearsal time and be paid for added matinees. They also wanted continuation of salary during layoffs in production. Prior to this, managers had stopped tours, no matter where in the country and laid off the actors without pay until new bookings came up weeks or months later.

Whether these demands had merit wasn't considered by the producers. They weren't used to having their practices questioned. When they rejected the demands, the actors went on strike.

The actors were not prepared for the strike they called but, once it was announced, they tried to solidify their stand. There were many different parties and factions.

George M. Cohan (q.v.), Louis Mann, Janet Beecher, Lenore Ulric, Francis Starr, Minnie Maddern Fiske, William Collier and others wanted no part of the strike or the American Federation of Actors. These performers split off and formed the Actors' Fidelity League.

Made bold by the apparent dissension between the two actor organizations and among factions within each group, the producers felt no need to arbitrate. They were content to socialize at their meetings and wait for the expected apology from the actors. Weeks went by, and millions of dollars were lost by the theater industry as well as the restaurant, hotel and transportation interests dependent on the theater business. Finally, the producers agreed to meet with the actors. Attending the meeting in the library of the St. Regis Hotel were Frank Gillmore, Francis Wilson, Ethel Barrymore (q.v.), Lillian Russell and others for the actors, and Al Woods, Arthur Hopkins, Sam Harris, David Belasco (q.v.), William Brady, Henry Savage and the producer responsible for the meeting—John Golden. Augustus Thomas served as the mediator.

The strike was soon settled once the producers started taking the actors seriously. The actors did not strike again until 1960.

ADELPHI THEATER   See GEORGE ABBOTT THEATER.

ALBEE, E.F., (1857–1930)   E.F. Albee was among the most disliked men in show business. With his partner B.F. Keith (1846–1914), Albee owned most of the great vaudeville theaters between Chicago and the East Coast. Keith and Albee tied up bookings for their houses with their United Booking Office. The UBO gave franchises free to agents, provided the agents didn't deal with any of Keith-Albee's competitors. This empire of over 1,500 theaters expanded to include the entire country when Martin Beck's west-coast-based Orpheum Circuit agreed to book through the United Booking Office.

Albee's power and influence were immense. To incur the wrath of Albee was to be practically blacklisted from vaudeville. Smaller chains like the Gus Sun circuit couldn't provide enough work for top names. Acts played the smaller, less prestigious houses until they improved and, step by step, worked their way up to the apex of the vaudeville performers' art, the Palace Theater (q.v.). Albee had a greater impact on the quality of the nation's entertainment than anyone at the time simply because every major vaudeville star had to please Mr. Albee first. With his partner Benjamin Keith, Albee helped make vaudeville the most successful entertainment of its time. And, due to his greed, he helped kill the golden goose.

At the end of his life, in the late 1920s, an elderly Albee was speechless when Marcus Heiman of the United Booking Office accused him of killing vaude-

ville. Heiman told Albee how his five-shows-a-day policy broke the backs of actors and audiences alike. For the actors, the five-a-day policy made the grind too much to bear. It ground vaudeville to dust.

But vaudeville was dying anyway. The newer entertainments, talking pictures and radio, had schedules far less demanding and were much more lucrative. For the odd performer who insisted on a live audience, there was always musical comedy and revue. Audiences too, grew tired of the same old acts when they could get superior talent free on radio, broadcast from the capitals of the entertainment world—New York and Hollywood. The five-a-day policy had made Albee a lot of money but, without his lifelong partner B.F. Keith to provide the showmanship, the empire crumbled.

Albee's policy of squeezing the market dry originated early in his career. He got his start while still in his teens, as an "outside ticket" or "sixty-cent" man with the circus. Albee would park a ticket wagon outside the gates to the midway. Customers would arrive at Albee's operation before they got to the main windows and would buy tickets for more than the going rate. Albee was also able to trick customers while counting change and could make a tidy profit off the hicks and rubes. His disregard for the suckers stayed with him for his whole life.

It was Albee's teaming up with showman extraordinaire B.F. Keith that got him out of the sawdust and into the spotlight. Keith was also a ruthless businessman, but he provided the partnership with elan and whatever heart it possesed. Keith and Albee began by producing tab versions of Gilbert and Sullivan. They would advertise the shows by proclaiming: "Why pay $1.50 when you can see our show for 25 cents?" Gilbert and Sullivan were in the public domain in the United States.

The profits from their production of *The Mikado* allowed them to buy the Bijou Theatre in Boston. At 10 A.M. on July 6, 1885, they offered their first vaudeville bill. The team made profits by charging a nickel or a dime for admission. Later they raised the price to 20¢. The partners expanded the empire, eventually convincing women that the theater was not for men only. They achieved this by offering clean shows in good taste. Backstage, every theater posted a notice to the performers that stated: "Don't say 'slob' or 'son-of-a-gun' or 'hully gee' on this stage unless you want to be cancelled preemptorily. Do not address any one in the audience in any manner. If you have not the ability to entertain Mr. Keith's audiences without risk of offending them, do the best you can. Lack of talent will less open you to censure than would be an insult to a patron. If you are in doubt as to the character of your act, consult the local manager before you go on the stage, for if you are guilty of uttering anything sacrilegious or even suggestive you will be immediately closed and will never again be allowed in a theater where Mr. Keith is in authority."

After Keith's death in 1914 the machine went on, but it was clear that years of bad feelings from artists and an inability to change with the times proved Albee's downfall. In 1928, the head of the Film Booking Office, Joseph P. Kennedy, convinced Albee to sell out. Kennedy, patriarch of the influential Massachusetts family and father of future President John F. Kennedy and his brothers Edward and Robert, sold a "substantial interest" in FBO to David Sarnoff's Radio Corporation of America. In October of 1928, RCA and the FBO acquired the Keith-Albee-Orpheum chain of theaters. The new company was called Radio-Keith-Orpheum. Kennedy promised to make Albee president of the new company and told him he wouldn't have to worry about the day-to-day problems of the dying vaudeville business.

When Albee sold out, the price of stock was quoted at 16. Kennedy offered Albee 21, and greed and exhaustion convinced Albee to sell. In three months, the stock was selling for 50. Kennedy dismantled the vaudeville empire and transformed the more profitable theaters to motion pictures for RKO product. Those that were unprofitable were unloaded or knocked down, and office buildings were erected on their sites.

Albee continued as titular head of the company until Kennedy lost all patience with him. The story is that Albee entered Kennedy's office one day to make a suggestion, and Kennedy informed Albee that he was through and had been for years. Albee retired to Palm Beach, Florida where he died March 11, 1930, of a heart attack.

Albee had come a long way from his birthplace in Maine. As head of the largest chain of vaudeville theaters in America and the United Booking Office, his impact on American entertainment was immense. His Keith-Orpheum circuit tied the nation together. It enabled acts to hone their art and continue working without layoffs for long periods of time. But the toll his policies took on the acts and the business proved too great.

ALGONQUIN ROUND TABLE   Legend has it that the Algonquin Round Table was the wittiest, most urbane group of people ever to eat in one place at one time. The bon mots that were ascribed to the diners would fill 20 books, yet according to its members, the Round Table wasn't anything much. Maybe, but the legend lives on through the countless autobiographies of table members.

It all started with Alexander Woollcott (q.v.), columnist, radio personality and acerbic wit. He lived close by at the City Club and enjoyed eating at the well-known hotel on West 44th Street. Robert Benchley (q.v.), the humorist and sometime actor, also had a long relationship with the Algonquin. His mother would take him into New York when he was a child, and invariably they lunched at Frank Case's Algonquin Hotel. The one time his mother took him to another restaurant, in the Astor Hotel (q.v.), the young Benchley was said to exclaim, "My, they've changed the Algonquin." So it seemed natural that when he was established in New York, Benchley would make the Algonquin his base. (For a time, Benchley lived upstairs but moved across the street to the Royalton when the distraction of the Round Table interfered with his writing.)

In the early 1920s, when the table was informally inaugurated, most of its members were just starting their careers. They were as old as the century and hellbent on changing the course of literature and the arts. Woollcott invited newspapermen Franklin P. Adams and Heywood Broun to join him for lunch, and the clubhouse was born. The informal lunch group met often enough to be assigned the same circular table and they were originally called The Board. But cartoonist Ed Duffy showed the group as knights in armor and the name was changed to the Round Table. Other names were used to describe the group, one of which was the Vicious Circle.

Adams, who was the unofficial head of the table, given the popularity of his column, The Conning Tower, was respected by playwright George S. Kaufman (q.v.). Kaufman joined and brought in his sometime collaborator, Marc Connelly. Benchley wandered downstairs and with him came Dorothy Parker. Kaufman introduced Edna Ferber to the group. Robert Sherwood, Deems Taylor and Neysa McMein rounded out the regular group.

If Adams was the major domo because of his position in the world of letters, then Woollcott was the social director simply because he said so. The remainder of the group didn't particularly care to take charge. They were content to carp and try to top each other's witticisms. The main contribution made by the Round Table was the reporting of the previous day's bright remarks. Another was the revue *No Siree!* On the night of April 30, 1922, Robert Benchley made his acting debut at the 49th Street Theatre (q.v.). He recited his Treasurer's Report, a monologue he repeated in the *Music Box Revue.*

Admission to the club was strictly by invitation. Edna Ferber, a great novelist and playwright, wrote a note, "Could I maybe lunch at the Round Table once?" Ferber was accepted as an equal, but others were scorned as too boorish, pseudo-intellectual or not witty enough.

Little by little the gang broke up; some went to Hollywood, and some were simply tired of the effort. By the early 1930s, the table was completely disbanded. Dorothy Parker, in an Associated Press interview toward the end of her life discounted the Round Table. "People romanticize it. It was no Mermaid Tavern, I promise you, these were no giants. Think of who was writing in those days—Lardner, Fitzgerald, Faulkner, and Hemingway. Those were the real giants. The Round Table was just a lot of people telling jokes and telling each other how good they were. Just a bunch of loudmouths showing off, saving their gags for days, waiting for a chance to spring them. It was not legendary. I don't mean that—but it wasn't all that good. There was no truth in anything they said. It was the terrible day of the wisecrack, so there didn't have to be any truth, you know. There's nothing memorable about them. About any of them. So many of them died. My Lord, how people die."

Maybe she was right, or maybe she was just bitter, but the truth is probably somewhere in the middle. These were witty people who did affect their era. Lardner, Fitzgerald and the others were choniclers of their time, but the Round Table members were the court jesters who entertained people with their plays, columns, books and wits.

ALLEN, KELCEY   See CRITICS.

ALVIN THEATER   See NEIL SIMON THEATER.

AMBASSADOR THEATRE 215 W. 49th Street. Architect: Herbert J. Krapp. Opening: February 11, 1921; *The Rose Girl.*   The Ambassador was the first of the Shuberts's *(q.v.)* six theaters built on 48th or 49th Street. The theater is built in brick Romanesque Revival style with the exterior ornamented through elaborate brickwork patterns. The Ambassador was built diagonally across its lot. This allowed greater seating and a closer relationship between the rear wall and the stage. In 1985, the New York City Landmarks Preservation Commission accorded landmark status to the Ambassador's interior, though it refused to so designate the exterior.

The Ambassador's opening production, *The Rose Girl,* was an undistinguished operetta by Anselm Goetzl and William Cary Duncan that played for 99 performances. The story was so bad that Jake Shubert wondered whether it would help to switch Act One with Act Three. This was an augury of times to come. Although well located in the district, the Ambassador has never had great success.

Its next production, *Blossom Time* (9/28/21; 516 performances), proved to be its longest running until almost 50 years later. The Sigmund Romberg *(q.v.),* Dorothy Donnelly operetta would again play the Ambassador on March 4, 1931, for 29 performances and again starting September 4, 1943, for only 47 performances—its last Broadway appearance. *Blossom Time* played a total of eight times on Broadway. Whenever the Shuberts were strapped for money or found themselves with a dark theater, out would come *Blos-*

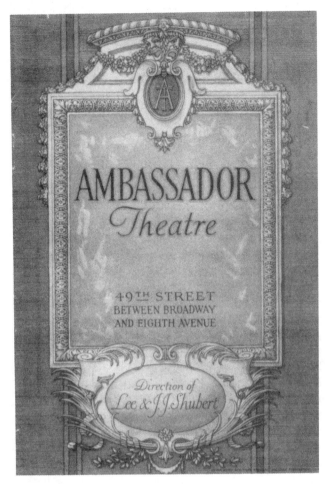

Ambassador Theatre program

som Time. This musicalization of Franz Schubert's (no relation) life would invariably bring Jake Shubert to tears. The schmaltzy story told of Franz's unrequited love, which drove him to pen what became the Unfinished Symphony.

Next came *The Lady in Ermine* (10/2/22; 238 performances). Another operetta, *The Dream Girl* (8/20/24; 118 performances), did even worse even though its score was by the great Victor Herbert *(q.v.).* This was Herbert's last operetta; in fact, he died prior to the Broadway opening. Even with additional tunes supplied by Romberg, the score couldn't redeem a shoddy book. The respectable run was more a tribute to Herbert's career and reputation than a result of the merits of the show.

The 1930s were bleak for the Ambassador. The Shuberts, like many other producers, had trouble holding on to their theaters. They sold the Ambassador in 1935. The new owners' policy of staging only dramatic works afforded the theater few opportunities for success. The only two productions of this period to achieve any notice were an eight-performance run of the Abbey Theater production of *Juno and the Paycock,* by Sean O'Casey, and a small musical revue, *The Straw Hat*

Revue (9/29/39; 75 performances). This was most notable for newcomers Imogene Coca, Alfred Drake and Danny Kaye.

Radio, movies and television occupied the Ambassador until 1956, when the Shuberts regained control of the theater. But later productions, with one exception, proved no more successful than those mounted in the past. These included Lawrence and Lee's *The Gang's All Here* (10/1/59; 132 performances), with E.G. Marshall and Melvyn Douglas, and Ira Wallach's *The Absence of a Cello* (9/21/64; 120 performances), with Ruth White, Fred Clark, Murray Hamilton, Mala Powers and Charles Grodin.

The theater's greatest success came with Robert Anderson's four one-act comedies, *You Know I Can't Hear You When the Water's Running* (3/13/67; 755 performances). Eileen Heckart, George Grizzard, Martin Balsam and Melinda Dillon were featured in the comedy.

After that success, the Ambassador resumed its revolving-door policy. *We Bombed in New Haven* (10/16/68; 85 performances) by Joseph Heller was followed by the Tom Jones-Harvey Schmidt musical, *Celebration* (1/22/69; 109 performances); a revival of Sandy Wilson's *The Boy Friend* (4/14/70; 119 performances), starring Judy Carne; *Paul Sill's Story Theater; Melvin Van Peebles's *Ain't Supposed to Die a Natural Death; The Secret Affairs of Mildred Wilde* by Paul Zindel; and *Scapino* with Jim Dale. These all had short runs at the Ambassador.

Three one-person shows next played for a time at the Ambassador—Linda Hopkins in *Me and Bessie* (10/22/75); Billy Dee Williams in *I Have a Dream* (9/20/76); and Estelle Parsons in *Miss Margarida's Way* (10/27/77).

A lame musical revue, *Eubie!* (9/20/78), ran for 439 performances due primarily to the talented cast and the fact that Eubie Blake (*q.v.*) was almost 100 years old.

The last client of note, also a musical revue, called *Leader of the Pack* (4/8/85), featured Ellie Greenwich and her songs. Her career in the late 1950s didn't last as long as Mr. Blake's but neither did her show. It ran for a disappointing 120 performances.

AMERICAN NATIONAL THEATRE AND ACADEMY The American National Theatre and Academy (ANTA) was created by an Act of Congress on July 5, 1935. President Franklin Delano Roosevelt signed the Charter, which grew out of the same idea that fostered the Federal Theater Project (*q.v.*). ANTA was meant to be a national theater that would be able to operate apart from the commercial theater atmosphere. ANTA's productions would be financed from outside contributions and would not depend on commercial success. In addition, ANTA would encourage new playwrights through readings and workshops. Actors for these productions would rise through the ranks, starting at the ANTA theater school.

As part of the WPA, the Federal Theater Project had achieved commercial success, but the politics expressed in the plays aroused opposition in Congress and eventually the plug was pulled in 1939. The founders of ANTA were determined to limit government control. To avoid any problems in censorship, ANTA was structured to receive no government funds. The founders knew that such an undertaking would be expensive and could never show a profit. So the organization was made nonprofit, enabling it to solicit funds from individuals and corporations. It was also set up to be nonsectarian and, as a reflection of the times, it would not have any honorary members.

The preamble to the Charter stated, "A national theater should bring to the people throughout the country their heritage of the great drama of the past and the best of the present, which has been too frequently unavailable to them under existing conditions."

Although it was created in 1935, ANTA had problems actually getting off the ground. The Depression was the first obstacle in its path. The United States' entry into World War II further delayed the implementation of ANTA. Finally in 1945, a reorganized Board of Directors formed from theater professionals was ready to implement the Charter. The board set up a membership structure and began to produce shows.

ANTA began its producing on a small level on February 9, 1947. The small Princess Theater was chosen, and ANTA presented five plays for five performances each. These early showcases won the Sidney Howard Award as the season's most important development in the theater. But surely no one could foresee the impact of the series on the history of the American theater, for this was among the first examples of a legitimate off-Broadway show, one that was not simply theater produced by amateur clubs for their own amusement.

Emboldened by the successes in a small arena, and dismayed by what seemed a lack of new quality works, ANTA brought a West Coast production of Bertolt Brecht's *Galileo* to the Maxine Elliott's Theatre (*q.v.*) for six performances at the end of 1947. The production starred Charles Laughton and was directed by Joseph Losey. Next came a production of *Skipper Next to God* by Jan de Hartog, featuring the Hollywood star John Garfield under Lee Strasberg's direction. It opened January 4, 1948, and was picked up for a commercial run by Blevins Davis, a member of ANTA's Board. In keeping with ANTA's charter, Laughton received the princely sum of $8 a week, and for Garfield, the salary was raised to $10 a week. Jerome Moross and John Latouche's *Ballet Ballads* was next on ANTA's schedule. This amalgam of dance, text and song was also picked up for commercial production.

On March 31, 1950, the former Guild Theater was acquired by two ANTA Board members, Robert Dowling and Roger L. Stevens, and renamed the ANTA

Playhouse. Today the theater is known as the Virginia Theater *(q.v.)*. The first season at the new space was directed by Cheryl Crawford and Robert Breen, the man who originally worked so hard to get the Charter passed by Congress.

On November 26, 1950, *Tower Beyond Tragedy* by Robinson Jeffers premiered, starring Judith Anderson. Critics were enthusiastic about the star but were mixed in their reactions to the play. Theatergoers kept the show running for 32 performances. A planned tour was dropped because of the lack of audience response. Next, Crawford and Breen presented Paul Green's reworking of *Peer Gynt* with John Garfield. This play, too, proved a failure. The next three productions, including *A Temporary Island* by Halsted Welles and starring Vera Zorina, all proved to be unsuccessful. ANTA soon found itself chronically short of funds.

During the second season in the ANTA Playhouse, Robert Whitehead, one of the theater's most respected producers, became the Managing Director. He presented more productions but, even though there were successes, the money just wasn't there to support as large and far-reaching a project as ANTA, and Whitehead departed.

During these years, ANTA presented productions of John Finch's *The Wanhope Building* (2/9/47); Arnold Sundgaard's *The Great Campaign* (3/30/47); Ben Hecht and Charles MacArthur's *Twentieth Century* (12/24/50) with Gloria Swanson and Jose Ferrer; Garcia-Lorca's *The House of Bernarda Alba* (1/7/51); Mary Chase's *Mrs. McThing* (2/20/52) with Helen Hayes *(q.v.)*; Eugene O'Neill's *(q.v.) Desire Under the Elms* (1/16/52); Clifford Odets' *Golden Boy* (3/12/52); Virgil Thomson and Gertrude Stein's *Four Saints in Three Acts* (4/16/52); as well as imported regional theater and dance companies.

The organization also concentrated on a series of benefit performances. Called the ANTA Album, the benefits featured stars performing scenes from current shows and past successes as well as new scenes performed just for the benefits. The ANTA Albums ran from 1948 through 1951 and again in 1955. Decca records released selections from the benefits on discs and helped spread the idea of an American national theater.

Lucille Lortel produced the ANTA Matinee Series at her Theater De Lys. There, she concentrated on avant garde and first-time works by such playwrights as Eugene Ionesco, Eugene O'Neill, Paul Shyre, Jean Giraudoux, Garcia-Lorca, Tennessee Williams *(q.v.)*, William Inge, Samuel Beckett, Edward Albee and others. In addition, many poets, writers and other nontheater types premiered their works. These writers included Katharine Ann Porter, W.H. Auden, e.e. cummings, Edna St. Vincent Millay, Robert Frost, Langston Hughes and Paul Vincent Carroll.

ANTA recently joined with the John F. Kennedy Center for the Performing Arts as a coproducer of the new National Theater company under the direction of Peter Sellars. The company concentrated on epic (in length and theme) productions staged with Sellars's usual disregard for the authors' intent and audience patience. The company was a dismal failure and faded without a trace, after wasting millions of dollars. The ANTA Theater, never regarded as a good house, is now owned and operated by the Jujamcyn organization, who renamed it the Virginia Theater.

AMERICAN THEATER WING   The American Theater Wing is one of the oldest service organizations benefiting the Broadway community. In recent years, it has been closely associated with the Tony Awards *(q.v.)*, which it administers. The Tony Awards are the most visible of the Wing's projects, which include grants and special entertainments. Critics have condemned the organization as existing merely to serve itself. Supporters claim it renders real service to Broadwayites. The truth is probably somewhere in the middle.

The Stage Women's War Relief was the first organization in what later became the American Theater Wing. A committee of seven women led by Rachel Crothers organized The War Relief in 1917, and they held their first meeting in the Hudson Theatre *(q.v.)*. The women, Louise Closser Hale, Josephine Hull, Minnie Dupree, Dorothy Donnelly, Bessie Tryee, Louise Drew and Rachel Crothers set up a canteen for servicemen and sent entertainers to the front to perform for the troops. The organization also sewed 1,863,645 articles of clothing for the fighting men and raised over $10 million in liberty bonds.

A men's committee was formed in 1920 to deal with problems of the returning veterans. In 1940, the American Theater Wing War Service, an affiliate of the British War Relief Society, began operations in New York. President Rachel Crothers, Vice-Presidents Helen Hayes *(q.v.)* and Gertrude Lawrence, Treasurer Josephine Hull and Secretary Antoinette Perry oversaw the women's committee. Other members of the committee included Minnie Dupree, a member of the first committee, Vera Allen, Lucile Watson, Theresa Helburn and Edith Atwater.

The men's committee was led by critic *(q.v.)* Brooks Atkinson, George S. Kaufman *(q.v.)* and Gilbert Miller. Other members of the committee were Raymond Massey, Vinton Freedley *(q.v.)*, Brock Pemberton, Billy Rose, Lee Shubert *(q.v.)* and Max Gordon. Cochairwomen were Jane Cowl and Selena Royle. Miller organized a benefit to aid British air raid-victims. The benefit earned more than $40,000.

When America entered the war, the Wing, by now an independant organization, sold war bonds, did relief work and, most important, operated the Stage Door Canteens in eight locations. The canteens were set up in many foreign cities, including London and Paris. The New York Stage Door Canteen was opened behind the Paramount Theater in a space underneath Sardi's Restaurant *(q.v.)* and the 44th Street Theatre *(q.v.)*. The Shubert Brothers donated the space. The Canteen served food and provided entertainment to soldiers returning from the front or on the way to battle.

The Canteen opened on March 1, 1942, operating from six to midnight seven days a week until the war was over. Over 1,700 Broadwayites ran the Canteen, usually committed to one three-and-a-half-hour stint per week. The actors, designers, directors and production staffers were the canteen's entire staff. They hosted the visiting soldiers and sailors, did custodial duties, served meals and kept the place operating as a restaurant, nightclub and social hall.

The canteen catered to as many as 4,000 servicemen a night, not only Americans but also visiting foreign troops. Stars entertaining at the canteen included most of the musical theater stars of the day. The dramatic stars such as Alfred Lunt and Lynn Fontanne *(q.v.)* did their part by waiting tables and dancing with the troops. "Killer Joe," an especially energetic jitterbugger, achieved notoriety. The canteen was an important feather in the cap of the Wing.

The American Theater Wing also produced USO shows for entertaining the troops overseas. The Wing donated $75,000 to the USO for entertainment. The *Barretts of Wimpole Street,* starring Katharine Cornell *(q.v.)*, was the first play sent overseas. Money for the USO was earned through proceeds from the movie, *Stage Door Canteen* and the weekly radio program of the same name. Irving Berlin's *(q.v.)* show *This Is the Army* (7/4/42) featured the song "I Left My Heart at the Stage Door Canteen." Proceeds from the show went to the Army Emergency Relief.

Over 40,000 volunteers entertained for the Wing, many in veterans's hospitals and service hospitals. The Lunchtime Follies was a touring show that entertained factory workers. The head of the production was com-

Stage Door Canteen   Courtesy Billy Rose Theater Collection.

poser Kurt Weill *(q.v.)*. Producer Kermit Bloomgarden was the general manager. Among the cast members of the various editions of the Lunchtime Follies were Jack Albertson, Milton Berle, Shirley Booth, David Burns, Howard Da Silva, Joey Faye, Arlene Francis, Sam Jaffe, Rosetta LeNoire, Fredric March, Zero Mostel, Vivienne Segal, Helen Tamaris and Benay Venuta. Songs for the revues were written by Harold Rome *(q.v.)*, Weill and others. Sketches were contributed by George S. Kaufman, Moss Hart, Maxwell Anderson, Groucho Marx, Nat Hiken, Joseph Fields *(q.v.)*, Billy Rose, S.J. Perelman, Lillian Hellman and Langston Hughes.

During the war and in the eight months following its conclusion, the Wing produced almost 1,500 auditorium shows, 350 full-length plays and over 6,700 hospital units—all in the New York area. Washington, D.C., and Boston also had their branches of the Wing.

Following the war, on September 13, 1945, members of the Wing received a letter announcing the first post-war planning meeting. A year later, on July 8, 1946, that meeting bore its first fruit when the Wing began a highly regarded Professional Training School for veterans who wanted to pursue theatrical careers. Fifty courses were offered by a prestigious faculty. Sir Cedric Hardwicke, Alfred Lunt, Jose Ferrer, Maureen Stapleton, Cyril Ritchard and Eva Le Gallienne were the acting teachers. Jose Limon was a dance instructor, along with Martha Graham, Charles Weidman, Katharine Dunham, Ray Bolger and Hanya Holm. Delbert Mann and Ezra Stone held workshops in television. Leon Barzin and Joseph Rosenstock handled budding conductors. Richard Rodgers and Oscar Hammerstein II *(q.v.)* and Harold Prince taught music for actors and directors. Oliver Smith explained the intricacies of set design, and he and Kermit Bloomgarden instructed future producers.

At each session, 1,200 students attended the unique school. Most of these students studied under the GI Bill. Illustrious alumni of the school included Marge and Gower Champion, Russell Nype, Tony Randall, William Warfield, Gordon MacRae, Pat Hingle, Charleton Heston and James Whitmore. The school remained a project of the Wing for 10 years.

In 1947, the Wing sent teams of specially trained actresses for an intensive three-and-a-half-month internship at neuropsychiatric hospitals. The actresses worked with veterans who had experienced mental problems following their discharge. Families of veterans were also in need of the Wing's services. The actresses helped veterans and their families work out problems through short plays that dramatized their plight. Discussion sessions were held after the performances.

That same year, the Wing established the Antoinette Perry (or Tony) Awards. The purpose of the awards was to honor the most distinguished members of the theatrical community.

In addition to the Tony Awards, the Wing also makes grants to off-Broadway theaters, theater schools and regional companies. The Wing hosts a Saturday Theater for Children in the public school system and sends tab (cut down) versions of Broadway shows to hospitals and nursing homes. The Wing's April and October seminars on the theater are shown on local cable television.

In 1983, the Wing received a grant from the Clarence Ross Foundation to establish a Master Class for American Actors at the Eugene O'Neill Center in Waterford, Connecticut. The class is taught by directors from England's Bristol Old Vic.

ANCO THEATER 254 West 42nd Street. Architects: J.M. McElfatrick & Co. Opening: December 5, 1904; *It Happened In Nordland.* The Lew M. Fields Theater was built by Oscar Hammerstein I *(q.v.)* as his eighth Broadway house. It was leased by producer Lew Fields *(q.v.)* who promptly named it in honor of himself. The theater was designed by Hammerstein who invented the first antifire system in any New York theater. A series of pipes led from the rooftop water tank to the stage. This early sprinkler system is still being used in concept by modern theater builders.

The opening production, Victor Herbert *(q.v.)* and Glen MacDonough's *It Happened in Nordland,* was a hit for the new theater. Fields starred in the show, which also featured Marie Cahill, Bessie Clayton, Joseph W. Herbert and May Robson and the song "Absinthe Frappe."

Hammerstein had a way of losing most of the theaters he built, and he lost this one in 1906. Producer James K. Hackett bought the theater and promptly named it in honor of himself. The theater reopened on August 27, 1906, with *The Little Stranger.* Three of the few successful shows produced at the Hackett were *The Witching Hour* (11/18/07; 212 performances), *Salvation Nell* (11/17/08) and *A Woman's Way* (2/22/09; 112 performances), the latter two starring Mrs. Fiske.

Hackett in turn lost the theater to William B. Harris, a leading producer. Harris promptly named the theater in honor of himself. He reopened a remodeled theater with *Maggie Pepper* (8/31/11). The Harris Theater was seldom successful. Productions included *Daybreak* (8/14/17), *The Lie* (12/24/14; 172 performances) and *Rolling Stones* (8/17/15; 115 performances).

Producer H.H. Frazee bought the theater and promptly named it after himself. His first production there was *The Woman of Bronze* (9/7/20). Under Frazee's leadership, the theater was the home to *Dulcy* (8/13/21; 246 performances), starring Lynn Fontanne *(q.v.)*.

A new management reopened the theater as Wallack's Theater with *Shipwrecked* (11/12/24) as the initial production. *She Got What She Wanted* (3/4/29; 118 performances) was among its most popular productions.

The Depression marked the end of the theater's legitimate policy. In 1940, it was remodeled and renamed the Anco. Under the new Times Square redevelopment plan, the Anco Theater is due to be razed.

ANDERSON, JOHN   See CRITICS.

ANDERSON, JOHN MURRAY (1886–1954)   John Murray Anderson was among Broadway's earliest jacks-of-all-trades. Anderson was the director of 33 revues and musicals, including two popular series, the *Greenwich Village Follies* and *John Murray Anderson's Almanac*. He also directed seven editions of the Ringling Brothers Circus and directed 24 shows for nightclubs, including Billy Rose's Diamond Horseshoe *(q.v.)*; wrote popular songs; staged four Aquacades, including the famous one for the 1939 New York World's Fair, 11 pageants, 61 stage presentations for movie houses; and directed one of the earliest Hollywood film musicals, *The King of Jazz,* and parts of the Esther Williams musical *Bathing Beauty*. Anderson himself compared his career with "the piecing together of a jigsaw puzzle."

Anderson had a keen eye for color and design and a intimate knowledge of the technical possibilities of modern stagecraft. He specialized in revues and directed many of the greatest. His Broadway output as a director includes *Greenwich Village Follies* (7/15/19; 232 performances) also librettist and lyricist; *What's in a Name?* (3/19/20; 87 performances) also lyricist, librettist and producer; *Greenwich Village Follies* (8/30/20; 217 performances) also lyricist; *Greenwich Village Follies* (8/31/21; 167 performances) also lyricist, librettist and producer; *Greenwich Village Follies* (9/12/22; 209 performances) also lyricist; *Jack and Jill* (3/22/23; 92 performances); *Greenwich Village Follies* (9/20/23; 131 performances) also lyricist and librettist; *Greenwich Village Follies* (9/16/24; 131 performances); *Music Box Revue* (12/1/24; 184 performances); Rodgers and Hart's early musical comedy *Dearest Enemy* (9/18/25; 286 performances); *Hello, Daddy* (12/26/28; 196 performances); *John Murray Anderson's Almanac* (8/4/29; 69 performances) also producer; *Ziegfeld Follies of 1934* (1/4/34; 182 performances); *Life Begins at 8:40,* with Ray Bolger and Bert Lahr (8/27/34; 238 performances); *Thumbs Up!* (12/27/34; 156 performances); *Jumbo* (11/16/35; 221 performances); *Ziegfeld Follies of 1936* (1/30/36; 115 performances); *One for the Money* (2/4/39; 132 performances); *Two for the Show* (2/8/40; 124 performances); *Sunny River* (12/4/41; 36 performances); *Ziegfeld Follies of 1943* (4/1/43; 553 performances); *Laffing Room Only* (12/23/44; 232 performances); *The Firebrand of Florence* (3/22/45; 43 performances); *Three to Make Ready* (3/7/46; 327 performances); *Heaven on Earth* (9/16/48; 12 performances); *New Faces of 1952,* which introduced such talents as Paul Lynde, Carol Lawrence, Eartha Kitt and Ronny Graham (5/16/52; 365 performances); *Two's*

Company (12/15/52; 91 performances); *John Murray Anderson's Almanac* (12/10/53; 227 performances).

ANNE NICHOLS LITTLE THEATER   See LITTLE THEATRE.

ANTA   See AMERICAN NATIONAL THEATRE AND ACADEMY.

ANTA THEATER   See VIRGINIA THEATER.

ANTOINETTE PERRY AWARD   See TONY AWARD.

APOLLO THEATRE   234 W. 43rd Street (originally the Bryant Theater with entrance at W. 42nd Steet). Opening: As a vaudeville and movie house in 1910; as a legitimate theater with *Jimmie* November 17, 1920.   Like other theaters, and like Times Square itself, the Apollo Theatre has seen its fortunes rise and fall. The house opened as the Bryant Theater in 1910, featuring a combination movie and vaudeville policy. As the 42nd Street corridor established itself as the leading legitimate theater block in New York, the Bryant's location made it more valuable as a venue for musical comedies, which commanded higher-priced tickets.

As a result, the Selwyn Brothers, leading producers of their day, bought the theater and renamed it the

Apollo Theatre   Courtesy Billy Rose Theater Collection.

Apollo. They christened the theater with the musical *Jimmie* (11/17/20; 69 performances). The show, starring Frances White, unfortunately did not augur well for the future of the theater.

The theater suffered a succession of failures, including Sigmund Romberg's *(q.v.) Love Birds* (3/15/21; 103 performances) and *Daffy Dill* (8/22/22; 69 performances) with a book by Guy Bolton *(q.v.)* and Oscar Hammerstein II *(q.v.)*. *Poppy* (9/3/23), starring W.C. Fields, played 346 times at the Apollo, which at that time was the theater's longest run.

The 1920s were a decade of long-running revue series. These included the *Ziegfeld Follies (q.v.)*; the Shuberts' *(q.v.) Passing Shows* at the Winter Garden Theater *(q.v.)*; Irving Berlin *(q.v.)* and Sam Harris's *Music Box Revues*; and Earl Carroll's *Vanities (q.v.)*. The Apollo was home for the *George White's Scandals* for most of its history.

The first *Scandals* (6/30/24) at the Apollo, the sixth edition, boasted a score by George and Ira Gershwin *(q.v.)* (their last for the series). The hit song "Somebody Loves Me" as sung by Winnie Lightner and the mugging of comics Tom Patricola and Lester Allen contributed to the respectable 192-performance run.

A straight play, *The Sap* (12/15/24; 15 performances) was soon followed by another edition of the *Scandals* (6/22/25; 169 performances). The team of DeSylva, Brown and Henderson *(q.v.)* replaced the Gershwins as the songwriting team and had a modest success with "What a World This Would Be."

The next edition of the annual revue opened June 14, 1926, and proved to be the most successful of the series, playing a total of 432 performances. Most of the credit for this outing's success lies with the superior DeSylva, Brown and Henderson score that seemed to mirror exactly the youthful exuberance of the Roaring Twenties. Three of its songs were among the most successful of 20th century popular songs: "Lucky Day," with its enthusiastic rendition by Harry Richman; "The Birth of the Blues"; and "The Black Bottom," perhaps the most impressive of the dance crazes to come out of musical comedy. The superior cast of Richman, Ann Pennington, Eugene and Willie Howard, Frances Williams and Tom Patricola were all *Scandals* regulars.

George White and DeSylva, Brown and Henderson were also responsible for the next hit at the Apollo, *Manhattan Mary* (9/26/27; 264 performances). White appeared in the show with comedian Ed Wynn and Ona Munson as a girl whose dream was to appear in the *Scandals*.

For the ninth edition (7/2/28; 240 performances) of the popular series, the same cast and writers of the last outing came up with another success. The big song hit was "I'm on the Crest of a Wave." The producer scored a bigger success with a new non-*Scandals* show. *Flying High* (3/3/30; 355 performances) featured a DeSylva,

Brown and Henderson score that, unfortunately, did not equal their earlier offerings. The main reason for the show's success was its star Bert Lahr and his supporting cast, including Kate Smith and Oscar Shaw.

The Apollo's bad luck with straight plays continued with its next offering, *The House Beautiful* (3/12/31; 108 performances), which is best remembered for inspiring Dorothy Parker's quip, "*The House Beautiful* is the play lousy."

The last edition of the *Scandals* to play the Apollo was the third from last in the series. It opened on September 14, 1931, and played for 204 performances. DeSylva had left the team, leaving Brown and Henderson to supply the score, which included the hits "Life Is Just a Bowl of Cherries," belted by Ethel Merman *(q.v.)*; "This Is the Mrs."; "The Thrill Is Gone"; "That's Why Darkies Were Born," explained by Everett Marshall in blackface; and "My Song" crooned by Rudy Vallee.

The last legitimate theater success at the Apollo was the musical *Take a Chance* (11/26/32; 246 performances). Buddy DeSylva returned to Broadway briefly to coproduce with Laurence Schwab. Most of the songs were by Richard Whiting and Nacio Herb Brown, although some were contributed by Vincent Youmans *(q.v.)* in his last Broadway assignment before his death. Ethel Merman repeated her previous success on the Apollo stage supported by Jack Haley, Jack Whiting, June Knight and Sid Silvers. The songs included "Eadie Was a Lady," "You're an Old Smoothie" and "Rise 'n' Shine."

The last show to play the Apollo was the unsuccessful Bill Robinson revue, *Blackbirds of 1933*. The Depression, which had shuttered so many of the Broadway theaters, finally reached the Apollo. A movie policy was initiated, and a year later, the Minsky Brothers began presenting burlesque *(q.v.)* shows on its stage. The burlesque policy remained in effect until Mayor LaGuardia's crackdown, and in 1937 the Apollo became a grind (24-hour) movie house.

Forty years later, the Broadway theater seemed to be undergoing a slight upsurge in business. There was a lack of available theaters, and the owners of the Apollo, the Brandt organization, decided to enter the legitimate theater field. Over $350,000 was spent to restore the Apollo to its former glory. Improvements both in the auditorium and backstage were completed in time for its first legitimate show under its new policy. The New Apollo reopened with *On Golden Pond* (2/28/79), starring Frances Sternhagen and Tom Aldredge. The show received mildly positive reviews. The theater's renovation received much better notices.

Although the Brandts changed the entrance to the theater from 42nd to 43rd Street, the New Apollo was still considered somewhat off the beaten track. Also, around this time, the number of independent producers operating on Broadway was severely reduced and, as a result, product grew scarce.

An unsuccessful play, *Bent,* had a short run followed by a transfer of Lanford Wilson's *The Fifth of July* from the Circle Repertory Theater. *The Fifth of July* proved to be the most successful of the house's bookings, although it hardly paid back its costs. The final offering at the New Apollo was *The Guys in the Truck,* a failure in 1983.

The theater briefly returned to its former grind policy before being shuttered. In the fall of 1987, the theater was renamed the Academy Theater with a short-lived booking of comic Redd Foxx. The theater underwent another transformation, and in September 1988 the theater's name was changed to the Alcazar de Paris. The theater was remodeled as a dinner revue theater, featuring Parisian inspired cabaret acts. It was a quick failure, and the name reverted to Academy. The last production on its stage was *Legends in Concert,* which opened and closed in May of 1989.

ARLEN, HAROLD (1905–1986) Harold Arlen, one of America's greatest composers of popular music, is just beginning to receive the respect due him. Equally at home writing for cabaret, motion picture and stage, Arlen wrote many standards for a diverse group of stars.

He was born Hyman Arluck on February 15, 1905. He first sang in the choir of the synagogue in Buffalo, New York, where his father was a cantor. He was also influenced by early jazz recordings and, when still in his teens, formed his own group, The Snappy Trio. That group soon evolved into The Southbound Shufflers. These bands played local clubs and excursion boats

Ted Koehler   Courtesy ASCAP.

around Buffalo. Then he and his friends formed The Buffalodians, for which Arlen sang and arranged the tunes. The Buffalodians were successful enough to get a small recording contract, and in 1925, Arlen was encouraged to come to New York. After his move, he became a singer, pianist and arranger with various dance bands before landing a job in Arnold Johnson's pit orchestra for the Broadway revue, *George White's Scandals of 1928 (q.v.).*

His unique singing style, influenced by liturgical singing and the techniques of black vocalists, led to jobs in vaudeville. He appeared on the Loew's Vaudeville Circuit and made it to the venerable Palace Theater *(q.v.).* Though Arlen would make his greatest mark as a composer, he continued singing, making albums throughout his career. He cut sides with the Red Nichols Orchestra and sang on his own albums for Capitol, Columbia and Walden Records.

While a rehearsal pianist for the Vincent Youmans *(q.v.)* show *Great Day,* Arlen was encouraged by songwriter Harry Warren to become a composer. A musical riff Arlen used to call the performers back from their rehearsal breaks was developed into his first hit, "Get Happy" (1930). The success of "Get Happy" led to a job writing the scores for a series of Cotton Club revues with his lyricist, Ted Koehler. In 1933, he and Koehler wrote their greatest hit, "Stormy Weather." His great success at the Cotton Club included such standards as

Harold Arlen   Courtesy ASCAP.

"Kickin' the Gong Around," "Between the Devil and the Deep Blue Sea," "I Love a Parade," "I've Got the World on a String," "Minnie the Moocher's Wedding Day," "Happy As the Day Is Long," "Ill Wind," "As Long As I Live," "Raisin' the Rent" and "You Gave Me Everything but Love." At the Cotton Club, Arlen cemented his relationships with black performers including Cab Calloway, Lena Horne and Ethel Waters. He continued providing nonstereotypical scores for black performers throughout his career.

The Cotton Club led back to Broadway and songs for musical revues, including *The Nine Fifteen Revue* (2/11/30) ("Get Happy"); *Earl Carroll's Vanities* (7/1/30) ("Hittin' the Bottle"); *Earl Carroll's Vanities of 1932* (9/27/32) ("I've Got a Right to Sing the Blues," "Rockin' in Rhythm"); *Americana* (10/5/32) ("Satan's Li'l Lamb"); *George White's Music Hall Varieties* (11/22/32); *Life Begins at 8:40* (8/27/34) ("Fun to Be Fooled," "Let's Take a Walk Around the Block," "You're a Builder Upper"); and *The Show Is On* (12/25/36).

Success in the revue format brought Arlen the opportunity to write for book shows, many of which prominently featured black performers. These shows included *You Said It* (1/19/31) ("Sweet and Hot," "You Said It"); *Hooray for What!* (12/1/37) ("Down with Love," "In the Shade of the New Apple Tree"); *Bloomer Girl* (10/5/44) ("The Eagle and Me," "Right As the Rain"); *St. Louis Woman* (3/30/46) ("Any Place I Hang My Hat Is Home," "Come Rain or Come Shine");

Johnny Mercer Corutesy ASCAP.

House of Flowers (12/30/54) ("I Never Has Seen Snow," "A Sleepin' Bee"); *Jamaica* (10/31/57) ("Ain't It the Truth," "Napoleon"); *Saratoga* (12/7/59) ("Goose Never Be a Peacock," "Love Held Lightly").

While these shows were rarely commercially successful, the scores Arlen wrote, mainly in collaboration with E.Y. Harburg *(q.v.)* or Johnny Mercer, were as rich as any on Broadway. His shows featured such greats as Lena Horne, Pearl Bailey, Diahann Carroll, Ricardo Montalban, Celeste Holm, Dooley Wilson, Ed Wynn, Bert Lahr, Ray Bolger, the Nicholas Brothers, Ray Walston, Geoffrey Holder, Josephine Premice, Ossie Davis and Howard Keel.

Arlen also had a long career in Hollywood writing for such films as *The Wizard of Oz* ("Over the Rainbow," Academy Award, 1939); *At the Circus; Blues in the Night* ("Blues in the Night," "This Time the Dream's on Me"); *Rio Rita; Star Spangled Rhythm* ("Hit the Road to Dreamland," "That Old Black Magic"); *Cabin in the Sky* ("Happiness Is a Thing Called Joe"); *The Sky's the Limit* ("My Shining Hour," "One for My Baby"); *Up in Arms* ("Now I Know"); *Here Come the Waves* ("Accent-tchu-ate the Positive"); *Out of This World* ("Out of This World"); *Casbah* ("For Every Man There's a Woman," "Hooray for Love"); *My Blue Heaven* ("Don't Rock the Boat, Dear"); *The Petty Girl; Down Among the Sheltering Palms; Mr. Imperium* ("Let Me Look at You"); *The Farmer Takes a Wife* ("Today I Love Everybody"); *A Star Is Born* ("The Man That Got Away"); *The Country Girl* ("Dissertation on the State of Bliss"); and *Gay Purr-ee* ("Paris Is a Lonely Town").

Arlen's total output doesn't match that of the greatest Broadway composers like Irving Berlin *(q.v.)*, Richard Rodgers *(q.v.)* or Jule Styne *(q.v.)* and, except for *Bloomer Girl,* he never had a major hit show. But his work was consistently brilliant. His range of compositions equals that of the most versatile theater composers: Jule Styne *(q.v.),* Frank Loesser *(q.v.)* and Cy Coleman. But Arlen's music, be it for a Tin Woodman, a runaway slave, a madam or the most innocent of naifs, always reflects Arlen's unique voice. He always wrote with a complete belief in and understanding of the character. He never let the audience know, as so many composers do, that there is a composer behind the character. His point of view was always the point of view of the character and each character's voice is both unique and unmistakably Arlen's.

Few could write as haunting a song as "Ill Wind," as stirring a song as "The Eagle and Me" or as jaunty and carefree a melody as that for "Happy As the Day Is Long." His work was inherently dramatic; even his revue songs were never simply pop songs. His work has enriched Broadway by attempting to entertain as well as subtly inform audiences about other kinds of people and different ideas and to move them with rich, true emotions.

ARTKRAFT STRAUSS

ARTKRAFT STRAUSS Of all the many companies and individuals who have influenced Times Square and our perceptions of it, none has had more impact than that of Artkraft Strauss, the company responsible for the signage *(q.v.)*, which is one of Times Square's most unique assets.

The history of Artkraft Strauss, which has designed and built virtually all of Times Square's huge outdoor displays, goes back to the turn of the century and the joining of the skills of two men, Benjamin Strauss and Jacob Starr. Times Square was just beginning to be developed; the Winter Garden Theater *(q.v.)* was still the American Horse Exchange, and Benjamin Strauss decided to follow the real estate boom uptown to 48th Street between Broadway and Seventh Avenue and begin making signs for the new theaters constructed along the Rialto.

As it happened, Jacob Starr, an immigrant metal worker and electrician, was working with a wrought iron company in the same building where Strauss had his business. Mel Starr, remembered his father relating how the two men met: "Jake used to tell the story of coming to Strauss' workshop around 1907 during the depression with a big sledgehammer and a bag full of tools and saying, 'Kannst usen ein schtarke mann?' 'Can you use a strong man?' Jake was a weakling and the sledgehammer w did. Strauss laughed but he hired l

Strauss gave him a job and they signs. It was the perfect joining technician with an instinct for tec had a burgeoning sign business. Starr, a ....., European-trained craftsman, modernized Strauss' operation by introducing specialized work into this primitive industrial area. Henry Ford would later win renown for exactly the same practice.

Theater signs at the time were gas lit. The change to electricity was inevitable, but until the electric lines were strung all the way north to Times Square at about 1915, the glow on the Great White Way was from flickering gas flames behind glass lenses set into punched out metal facades. Strauss also specialized in gold leaf and sent teams of gold leafers around the country for two or three years.

Starr left Strauss in 1919 and started a company that took burnt out light bulbs and replaced the filaments. In those days, light bulbs were very expensive and lasted for only a short time. Starr had a factory staffed with young immigrants who gently removed the glass covering and replaced the filaments. The light bulb companies frowned on Starr's business, because their continued success depended on the short life of their bulbs. They bought Starr out, and he developed an association with the Artkraft Sign Company of Lima, Ohio.

Artkraft's main business was in kitchen fixtures, and the company used the same ovens and kilns to make signs. Signs at that time were made out of porcelain covered steel which were the same materials used to make sinks and stoves. Porcelain, which has an impervious finish, is perfect for outdoor use.

Artkraft had one of the American franchises to make neon, which was invented by the Frenchman Claude in 1923. In 1927, neon was introduced to America; prior to this, all electric lights were incandescent. Now companies went public and began to merge. That same year, Starr started a company called Rainbow Lights Inc., which built electric signs. The introduction of neon marked the first time one could light signs with real colors not just white lights behind colored glass or painted bulbs.

In 1929 the Depression hit, sending the profits of both Strauss and Starr down. The two men decided to rejoin each other (Starr would say, "Sometimes zero and zero makes three."). In 1935, they merged and moved operations to the company's present location at 830 12th Avenue between 57th and 58th Street. An important client of Artkraft Strauss was Douglas Leigh *(q.v.)*, a freelance sign salesman and designer who used the Artkraft Sign Company of New York to build his creations, which were dubbed Spectaculars.

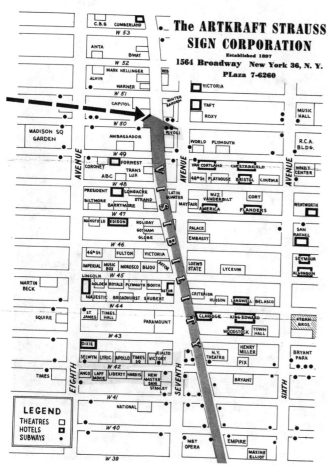

Artkraft Strauss sign locations Courtesy Artkraft Strauss.

Business began to diminish during the 1940s and 1950s. As Mel Starr remembered:

When the movie business was in its heyday, and Times Square featured first run limited showings of new movies, palaces like the Capitol, the Astor, the Victoria, the Mayfair and Loew's State would change the theatre's front every time they changed the picture by adding thousands of electric light bulbs and miles of electric tubing to the animated electrical displays.

We'd do two or three of those a week. We would do a hundred to a hundred and fifty Spectacular changes. Today, most of that is gone. The tendency is to put in plastic painted signs. There are fewer locations now. Most notably missing is the Astor/Victoria site where the Marriott Marquis Hotel now stands. Where the National Theatre is today is where the Kleenex sign was. Above the Brill Building was the Budweiser flying A and eagle. The new office buildings are replacing former sign sights. The new zoning laws mandate electric displays on the new buildings but it isn't known whether these will be permanent artistic creations or signage sights. Mel died in 1988. His daughter Tama continues the

family business. She sees the signs as an integral part of the Square: "The Square itself is the atrium of the theatre district. So these Spectacular displays, which have a surreal component, the colors and the way they're flashing, the minute you get into that environment you know you're into a theatre experience. Certainly there's a mood of glitter and fun and brightness and theatre and razzle dazzle. What makes Times Square unique is the long sight lines and the fact that the buildings are set way back so even in the middle of a crowded city, and Times Square is one of the most crowded places in a crowded city, you don't feel hemmed in like on Madison Avenue." Tama continued, "We've been doing this for eighty-eight years and we hope to be doing it for another eighty-eight."

ARTWORK Recently, due to the work of the Public Art Fund and other municipal organizations, artwork has been placed on the islands of Times Square, which separate Broadway and Seventh Avenue.

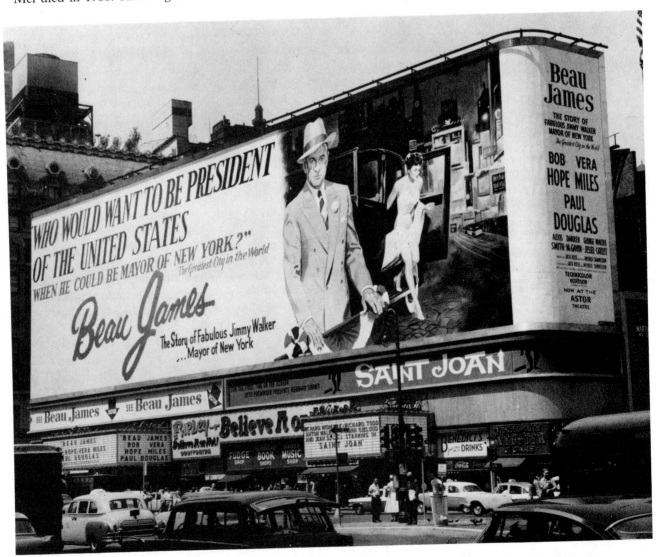

Astor/Victoria Billboard Courtesy Artkraft Strauss.

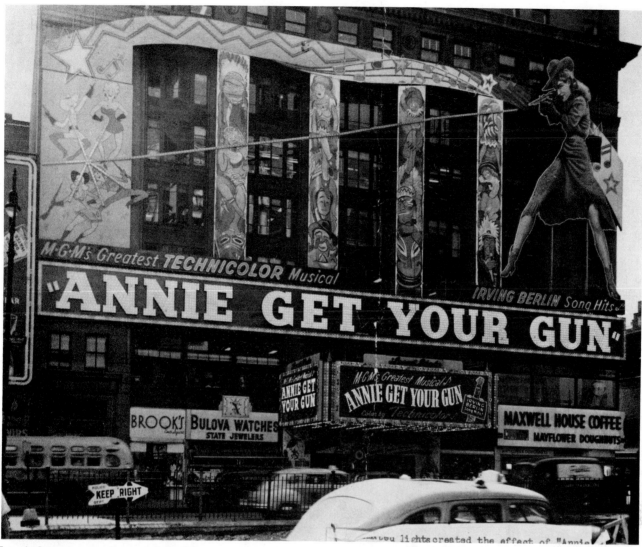

Loew's State signage Courtesy Artkraft Strauss.

There are many more traditional artworks around the square. These include the signage *(q.v.)* on buildings—commercial artworks designed to be noticed but that occasionally attract attention for their intrinsic design qualities. Sculpture also abounds in the square. The few older buildings that remain have carved cornices, gargoyles and other architectural details. Freestanding sculptures include the statues of George M. Cohan *(q.v.)* and Father Duffy and those set into the side of the I. Miller building. The statues on the I. Miller Building (northeast corner of 46th Street and Seventh Avenue) were designed by A. Stirling Calder, father of Alexander Calder. They represent Rosa Ponselle, Ethel Barrymore *(q.v.)*, Marilyn Miller and Mary Pickford. Since the I. Miller shoe store has ceased operating on the square, the statues have been neglected but have not been destroyed as have many Broadway landmarks.

The statue of George M. Cohan was designed by George Lober and erected in 1959. Cohan proudly occupies a conspicuous location across from the Palace Theater *(q.v.)* on the island between 47th and 48th Street and Broadway and Seventh Avenue.

Father Francis Duffy occupies the same island that is home to the Cohan statue. The northern end of what is usually thought of as Times Square is actually called Duffy Square after the famous "Fighting Chaplain" of New York's 69th regiment. Father Duffy was later the Pastor of the Holy Cross Church on West 42nd Street. There he became friends with many Broadway habitues. The statue was sculpted by Charles Keck and placed in the square in 1937.

A good example of the commercial artworks surrounding the square, and one that harkens back to the heyday of Times Square signage, is the neon sign over the entrance to the Howard Johnson's restaurant across from the Marriott Marquis Hotel. The sign was originally over the entrance to the Howard Johnson's restaurant at the northeast corner of 49th Street and Broadway. When that branch closed (another down the street

Marilyn Miller statue on the Miller Building   Photo Jeff Slotnick.

George M. Cohan statue   Photo Jeff Slotnick.

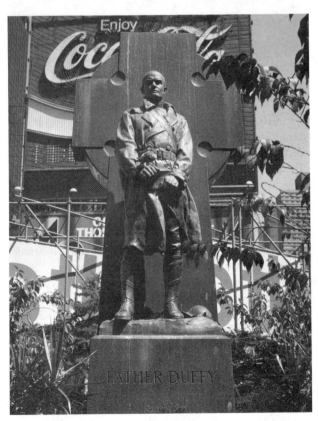

Father Duffy statue   Photo Jeff Slotnick.

also closed), the sign was renovated and moved to its present location.

The longest lasting of the newer artworks is underneath the street, unseen by passersby. But it has been heard for over a decade. Composer Max Neuhaus convinced the Metropolitan Transportation Authority to allow him the use of an abandoned subway ventilation chamber underneath the island between 45th and 46th Street.

The work, installed in 1977, contains a loudspeaker which resonates to the frequencies generated by several electronic sound generators that pick up the sounds in the ventilation chamber as the chamber resonates in response to street noise and vibration. Electricity for the piece, which cost $100,000 to install, came from a nearby light pole. Now the artwork has a direct link to the city's electricity.

In the future, new skyscrapers erected in Times Square may be required to have neon signs on their facades. Although developers have balked at the suggestion of permitting advertising on their buildings, some have agreed to allow abstract neon designs.

ASCAP The American Society for Composers, Authors and Publishers licenses the right to publicly perform the nondramatic copyrighted musical compositions of its members. ASCAP's members are the composers and lyricists who write the bulk of America's popular songs.

ASCAP collects license fees from 10,000 radio stations, 800 television stations, and over 150,000 other music users including cabarets, restaurants, nightclubs, Muzak and other background music companies, symphonies, retail stores, colleges, universities and concerts.

Though founded in 1914, ASCAP's history can be traced back to 1910. George Maxwell was the American representative for Ricordi, an Italian publishing com-

pany. Puccini was visiting America and asked Maxwell why he was not being reimbursed when he heard his melodies played in hotels and restaurants. For years Italy had a law remunerating composers for performance rights.

Puccini had good grounds for his argument. The United States copyright law of 1909 guaranteed the owners of musical copyrights the exclusive right "to perform the copyrighted work publicly for profit if it be a musical composition."

Nothing was done immediately, but in 1913, unions and other organizations were beginning to be formed. Composer Raymond Hubbell, author of "Poor Butterfly," met with Nathan Burkan, a lawyer, and George Maxwell. They believed songwriters should be paid for performances of their work.

The three men approached Victor Herbert (q.v.), the most important musical-theater composer at that time.

Eminent members of ASCAP. Victor Herbert at piano. Left to Right: Gustave Kerker, Raymond Hubbell, Harry Tierney, Louis Hirsch, Rudolf Friml, Robert Hood Bowers, Silvio Hein, A. Baldwin Sloane and Irving Berlin. Courtesy ASCAP.

Dinner given by ASCAP at Luchows, November 27, 1914 in honor of its President and Counsel, Mr. George Maxwell and Mr. Nathan Burkan. This was the first ASCAP dinner.   Courtesy ASCAP.

Herbert, a prominent fixture on Broadway and the concert stage, agreed to represent the new idea. He called a meeting at Luchow's Restaurant on 14th Street, then the center of the New York theater community.

Due to a lack of interest and inclement weather, only five people showed up to join the four men who had called the meeting. The five were composers Silvio Hein, Louis A. Hirsch and Gustav Kerker, lyricist Glen MacDonough, and music publisher Jay Witmark.

Another meeting was called on February 13, 1914, at the Hotel Claridge (q.v.). More than 100 songwriters and publishers attended the second meeting. After much discussion, ASCAP was formally created.

George Maxwell was named President. Nathan Burkan was named general counsel. Victor Herbert, who would not accept the presidency, preferred to hold the position of vice-president. He was joined by John Golden as treasurer, Raymond Hubbell as assistant treasurer and Glen MacDonough as secretary. There were 17 charter members on the first Board of Directors. Irving Berlin (q.v.) was the last surviving member of that first board.

The Fulton Theater (q.v.) on 46th Street and Broadway was the first home of the new organization. An office was rented and the staff began the difficult task of convincing others to pay for the use of the members' songs.

Despite the daunting task, the organization was quite small. The entire payroll was only $15 a week. Dues were $10 for songwriters and $50 for publishers. Today, more than 70 years later, the dues are the same.

Resistance to the organization's goals was strong. Rector's (q.v.), Broadway's premier restaurant, was the first ASCAP licensee in October of 1914. Rector's fee for that first year was $180. With the influential restaurant behind them, ASCAP found 84 more restaurants and hotels willing to sign an agreement.

Unfortunately, the fees paid by these 85 signers, which averaged only $8.23 a year, didn't cover the operating expenses of the organization. Because of the shortfall, royalties were not paid to the membership for years to come.

Widespread opposition to the concept of ASCAP continued. Since the music had been free in the past, bandleaders, hotels and restaurants didn't see a reason to pay for the use of ASCAP's members' songs.

In the summer of 1914, ASCAP fought its first court battle. John Philip Sousa and his publisher, the John Church Company, brought suit against the Hilliard Hotel Company, owners of the Vanderbilt Hotel. The orchestra in the dining room of the hotel played Sousa's march, "From Maine to Oregon," without paying for the rights. Judge Lacombe of the United States District Court for the Southern District of New York ruled in the publisher's favor. But, in the Circuit Court of Appeals, Judge Ward overturned the previous court's ruling. The decision handed down on February 9, 1915, stated in part, ". . . such persons primarily go into the saloon for refreshment and pay for what they order, and not for the music. We are not convinced . . . that the defendants played 'From Maine to Oregon' for profit within the meaning of those words in our copyright act." Since Judge Ward ruled that performances of music in hotels and restaurants were not for profit, the new organization needed to take another tack.

Victor Herbert charged that people had heard a Herbert composition, "Sweethearts," played in Shanley's Restaurant on April 1, 1915. Herbert knew because of the earlier ruling that he could not object to the use of the song as a profit-making venture. Nathan Burkan found another clause in the copyright law that gave to the copyright owner the exclusive right, regardless of profit, to the public performance of a dramatic work. Since the dramatic work was covered and since "Sweethearts" was part of the operetta of the same name, ASCAP interpreted the law as stating that any portion of the operetta must also be covered.

Shanley's made four points in its rebuttal. One, there was no cover charge, therefore the music was not a performance. Second, the platform on which the orchestra played was not a stage, therefore no theatrical performance took place. Third, the song was sung by "a young lady who was not an actress, who had never been employed in a theatrical production." The last point stated that although "Sweethearts" was a part of a theater piece, the version of the song used by the orchestra was "published as a separate musical composition by G. Schirmer, Inc., in the form ordinarily known as sheet music form, and the song as so published is a complete musical composition of itself."

Judge Learned Hand gave his decision on May 1, 1915. He stated that the previous case's ruling clearly established that performance in a restaurant was not performance for profit. He agreed with Herbert that any part of an operetta was part of a dramatic-musical production and that public performance of such a part was an infringement of Herbert's rights. However, since the song was published as a separate song and copyrighted as a unique piece, the plaintiffs had therefore abandoned their dramatic control of the song.

With the first round lost, Herbert appealed the decision. On January 11, 1916, Herbert lost the appeal. *Musical America,* a popular magazine stated, "The recent case . . . ended the campaign of the authors and composers to collect royalties from restaurants as far as the courts are concerned, with a complete defeat of the authors."

The magazine was wrong. Herbert appealed to the United States Supreme Court. The Court reversed the two lower court rulings in favor of Herbert. Justice Oliver Wendell Holmes stated that whether the work was a piece of a whole or a separate entity was irrelevant. Nor did it matter whether the patrons paid for food only or for a show. Since the restaurant paid the

orchestra and the singers a salary, then it followed that the music was an integral part of the restaurant's features. The court explained, "If music did not pay, it would be given up. If it pays, it pays out of the public's pocket. Whether it pays or not, the purpose of employing it is profit, and that is enough."

ASCAP would have more legal battles each time a new medium or new technology was introduced. Radio, television and talking pictures each had their own lawsuits, but through it all, ASCAP has persevered.

Seven years after a 1909 bill was passed by Congress, ASCAP finally collected sufficient royalties to pay its members. ASCAP's first songwriters were primarily composers and lyricists of Broadway shows. Its services eventually made it possible for many of these tunesmiths to control their work and make a living out of their art.

Through its licensing agreements, ASCAP has also had an impact on the nightclubs, dance halls, hotels and restaurants that provide so much of the glitter of the Great White Way. In later years, Raymond Hubbell wrote of the early days of the organization: "Once in a while I close my eyes and in memory I go back to that rainy October night, in 1913, at Luchow's Restaurant. I see that long table with places . . . and vision the little group of which only Jay Witmark and myself remain. Reverently I raise my glass to dear old Victor, Glen, George, Nathan, Lou, Gus and Silvio and whisper, as I think of all the blessings God has showered on ASCAP, if you fellows were here, I know we'd do it all over again!"

ASTAIRE, FRED AND ADELE The Astaires were the leading dance team of the 1920s and the best known of all Broadway dance teams. They were celebrated for their mix of sophistication and humor, combined with their grace and technical virtuosity. After Adele's retirement, Fred moved to Hollywood and continued the Broadway tradition through his teaming up with such stars as Ginger Rogers, Rita Hayworth and Cyd Charisse.

Adele was born on September 10, 1897, and Fred two years later on May 10, 1899. Both children were born in Omaha, Nebraska. In 1904, Ann Geilus Austerlitz, the children's mother, packed herself and her children off to New York City. Though Fred was four and a half and Adele was only six, Mrs. Austerlitz felt that the two children might have a career on the stage. Time, of course, proved her right. Yet one wonders what made her believe her children could become successful.

Adele had attended dance schools in Omaha and had become somewhat famous locally. Fred hadn't any lessons, although he did mimic his sister's steps. In New York, the Astaires attended the Alvienne School of the Dance. They followed their lessons with a professional debut in Keyport, New Jersey, in 1906. The engagement paid $50.

By this time, Mr. Austerlitz had legally changed his name to Astaire. He wrangled a job for the two children on the Orpheum Circuit. That 20-week tour was followed by another. At the end of the second tour, the two children found themselves unemployable. They had outgrown their act and were forced to give up the stage. Still, they practiced and took classes at the Ned Wayburn Studio of Stage Dancing. They worked on new material while studying and went to Broadway shows to observe the great dancers on the stage.

They appeared for the first time on Broadway during a benefit at the Broadway Theatre (q.v.). That led to a booking at Proctor's Fifth Avenue Theater on February 19, 1911, in an act called *A Rainy Saturday*. It was stupendously unsuccessful. The Astaires were fired after their opening performance. This failure made them persona non grata on Broadway. They were forced into touring the hinterlands. They slowly improved their technique and worked on their act. After a series of small bookings, they played their last vaudeville booking during the 1915–16 season.

They finally received their Broadway break in a Shubert Brothers (q.v.) production, *Over the Top* (11/28/17; 78 performances), at the 44th Street Theatre (q.v.). Sigmund Romberg (q.v.) and Herman Timberg contributed the music. The lyrics were by Philip Bartholomae and Harold Atteridge. Justine Johnstone and Mary Eaton were the stars of the revue.

The Astaires' contributions did not go unnoticed by the critics (q.v.). Louis Sherwin wrote in the *Globe*, "One of the prettiest features of the show is the dancing of the two Astaires. The girl, a light, spritelike little creature, has really an exquisite floating style in her capering, while the young man combines eccentric agility with humor." Despite positive reviews for the Astaires, the show did not do well. It had a brief tour under the name, *Oh, Justine!*

The Shuberts didn't ignore the Astaires' good reviews and put them into the next edition of their annual revue, the *Passing Show of 1918* (7/25/18; 124 performances). Sigmund Romberg wrote the score with Jean Schwartz. Harold Atteridge contributed the lyrics. The show also featured Lou Clayton, Frank Fay, Willie and Eugene Howard, Nita Naldi and Charles Ruggles.

The *Passing Show* received mostly favorable reviews. Heywood Broun wrote in the *New York Tribune*, "In an evening in which there was an abundance of good dancing, Fred Astaire stood out. He and his partner, Adele Astaire, made the show pause early in the evening with a beautiful, careless, loose-limbed dance, in which the right foot never seemed to know just what the left foot was going to do, or cared, either. It almost seemed as if the two young people had been poured into the dance."

Charles Darnton, writing in the *Evening World* thought that Fred and "Estelle [sic] . . . scored the hit of the show." The show undertook a long tour. When Frank Fay dropped out of the show, Fred assumed his part and played in his first sketches.

Apple Blossoms (10/7/19; 256 performances) was the team's next Broadway show. It opened under the auspices of producer Charles Dillingham. Victor Jacobi and Fritz Kreisler wrote the music to William Le Baron's book and lyrics. John Charles Thomas and Wilda Bennett were the leads. The Astaires' roles were interpolated into the proceedings, offering them the opportunity for two numbers.

The critics again gave them rave reviews. Alexander Woollcott (q.v.), writing about the "Adaires" (sic) in the *New York Times*, was especially taken with Fred's dancing. "He is one of those extraordinary persons whose senses of rhythm and humor have been all mixed up, whose very muscles, of which he seems to have an extra supply, are downright facetious."

Apple Blossoms proved to be among the most successful operettas of its time. But most of the same team, Jacobi, Dillingham, Thomas and the Astaires couldn't repeat their success when they presented *The Love Letter* (10/4/21; 31 performances).

For Goodness Sake (2/20/22; 103 performances) was the pair's next assignment. As usual, the Astaires (although they only had sixth billing) received the best of the notices. Robert Benchley (q.v.), writing in the old *Life Magazine*, said there "wasn't much to say about *For Goodness Sake* that you couldn't say about most musicals except that the Astaires (perhaps late of 'Astaire and Down') are in it." Although the Astaires constantly received good reviews, they still weren't well-known enough to carry a show by themselves. *The Bunch and Judy* (11/28/22; 65 performances) had a score by Jerome Kern (q.v.) and Anne Caldwell, but it contained no hit songs.

Alex Aarons (q.v.) had decided to produce *For Goodness Sake* in London under the title *Stop Flirting*. The Astaires were hired to reprise their performances in the West End. The show opened to rave reviews, especially for the Astaires, and it became one of the longest running shows at that time, playing a number of theaters for a total of 418 performances. Even with that long a run, the show could have gone on if the Astaires had not wished to return to the New York stage.

While they were appearing in London, Alex Aarons was busy working on their next Broadway show. Aarons had teamed up with Vinton Freedley and the new producing team hired George and Ira Gershwin (q.v.) to compose the score. Guy Bolton (q.v.) and P.G. Wodehouse contributed the libretto, which was built around the talents of the young dance team.

The title of the show was originally *Black Eyed Susan*,

but it opened on Broadway as *Lady, Be Good!* (12/1/ 24; 330 performances). The show was an immediate smash hit. Finally, doubts about whether the Astaires could handle the leads of a Broadway musical were put to rest. The Gershwins had provided them with some of their best songs—"Fascinating Rhythm," "Half of It, Dearie Blues" and "Hang on to Me."

Following a national tour and the London production, the Astaires were ready to go into rehearsals for their next Broadway show, *Funny Face* (11/22/27; 250 performances). Aarons and Freedley had again called on the Gershwins for the score, which featured such standards as "Funny Face," "He Loves and She Loves," "High Hat" and "The Babbitt and the Bromide."

Funny Face was the opening attraction of the new Alvin Theater *(q.v.)*. Woollcott enthused, "I do not know whether George Gershwin was born into this world to write rhythms for Fred Astaire's feet or whether Fred Astaire was born into this world to show how the Gershwin music should really be danced. But surely they were written in the same key, those two."

Funny Face played 263 performances in London. Its success led Paramount to give the Astaires a screen test. Apparently, the studio wasn't impressed, because they failed to pick up the team for the movies. A film version with Fred Astaire and Audrey Hepburn was released 30 years later—by Paramount.

Florenz Ziegfeld *(q.v.)* was preparing a musical called *Smiles* (11/18/30; 63 performances) to showcase the talents of Marilyn Miller. He hired the Astaires following their London engagement in *Funny Face*. Vincent Youmans *(q.v.)* composed the score which featured what became a great standard, "Time on My Hands." Despite the talents involved, *Smiles* turned out to be a great flop, "the kind of flop that even made the audience look bad," according to Fred Astaire himself.

With their next Broadway show (which would be their last appearance together), the Astaires had their greatest artistic success. *The Band Wagon* (6/3/31; 262 performances) was a smart, sophisticated revue with just the right amount of silliness. The material by Arthur Schwartz *(q.v.)* and Howard Dietz *(q.v.)* perfectly suited the Astaires' talents. Their co-stars, Helen Broderick, Frank Morgan and Tilly Losch were equally suited to what Brooks Atkinson said was "a new era in the artistry of the American revue."

The Band Wagon opened at the New Amsterdam Theatre *(q.v.)*. The critics raved about the entire production and especially about the Astaires. Richard Lockridge, writing in the *Sun,* stated, "There is something utterly audacious about the two of them; there is a lightness and flexibility and dash in whatever they do, whether it is to chase a plump and bearded Frenchman around the revolving stage or to dance in black and white before an immense encircled drum. They may be chatty and intimate, teasing themselves and the audi-

ence. They may be bizarre, tantalizing figures from a modernistic nightmare. They are in any case incomparable."

The Band Wagon went on the road for a brief tour that was marked by Adele's retirement from the stage when she married Lord Charles Cavendish. This left Fred on his own for the first time. His insecurities about performing without his sister did not stand in the way of his signing on to star in *The Gay Divorce*.

The Gay Divorce (11/29/32; 248 performances) was produced by Dwight Deere Wiman with a score by Cole Porter *(q.v.)*. The out-of-town reviews were less than favorable. The *Boston Transcript* read, "An Astaire must dance and still does very well—but not for the general good is he now sisterless."

Despite good work on the road and a score that contained at least one Porter standard, "Night and Day," the show wasn't well received when it opened in New York. One critic claimed, "Fred Astaire stops every now and then to look off-stage towards the wings as if he were hoping his titled sister, Adele, would come out and rescue him." Some reviewers, however, did enjoy Astaire's performance. Walter Winchell *(q.v.)* said, "The personable and talented brother of Lady Cavendish never before seemed so refreshing and entertaining."

In his autobiography, *Steps in Time,* Astaire wrote, "I was not upset because they missed my sister. I'd have been disappointed if they hadn't, but at any rate my job was cut out for me and the show had to be put over." Put it over he did. Still, despite the eventual long run, Fred felt the strain of supporting a show. He also realized that as long as he appeared on stage, the critics would comment on the absence of his sister. He was then receiving renewed interest from Hollywood and decided to explore this avenue.

He went on to star in 32 movie musicals with a succession of partners. But despite the brilliance and success of his film career, for many old-timers no movie could match the magic of watching Fred Astaire accompany his sister on the stages of New York. The opening night review of *Lady, Be Good!* in the *Herald Tribune* summed up the audience's enjoyment at watching the greatest dance team in Broadway history. "Fred and Adele we salute you! Last night at the Liberty Theatre this young couple appeared about 8:30 o'clock and from an audience sophisticated and over-theatered received a cordial greeting. At 8:45 they were applauded enthusiastically and when, at 9:15, they sang and danced 'Fascinating Rhythm' the callous Broadwayites cheered them as if their favorite halfback had planted the ball behind the goal posts after an 80–yard run. Seldom has it been our pleasure to witness so heartfelt, spontaneous and so deserved a tribute."

Adele Astaire died on January 25, 1981. Fred Astaire passed away on June 21, 1987.

ASTOR HOTEL Broadway between 44th and 45th Streets. The Astor Hotel was the most celebrated hotel in Times Square and perhaps the most famous in all New York. The plot of land was originally part of the Medref-Eden Farm. Around 1830, William B. Astor, Lord Astor's grandfather, purchased the property for $34,000 from the bank that foreclosed on the Medref-Eden farm. Most people felt the investment was a bad one for the site was so far uptown. Lord William Waldorf Astor willed the property to his son, Major John Jacob Astor of the British Horse Guards.

Major Astor, an important New York City real estate owner, made a lot of money off the Astor Hotel property. He received half a million dollars per year from the land lease. When the lease was renegotiated in 1928, the new lease increased the amount to $700,000 per annum, a fee the hotel could afford since the hotel's income was $2 million per year.

The 11-story hotel opened on September 9, 1904. It was an immediate success, and the opening coincided with the burgeoning importance of Longacre Square.

In 1907, a group of Japanese diplomats were entertained at the Astor. The Japanese were meeting with American dignitaries to explore improving Japanese-American relations. That same year Andrew Carnegie held a conference on his peace plan at the Astor. Forty years later, the hotel housed the United Nations personnel. General Chiang Kai-shek of China complained to the hotel's assistant manager that he would lose sleep because the "Japanese prints on the wall disturb me."

On October 10, 1910, the *New York Herald* announced that the Indian Hall grill would be reopened for the winter. The Indian Hall, decorated with museum quality artifacts, was one of the Astor's best known features.

In its more than half century of operation, the Astor

Astor Hotel

had hosted nine presidents and many celebrities. Charles Evans Hughes was staying in Suite 170 when he was running against Woodrow Wilson for the presidency. Hughes went to sleep early, sure that he was to be the next President. When he awoke, he learned that the California vote went to Wilson.

General John D. Pershing stayed at the Astor before setting out for Europe to head the American expeditionary force in World War I. General Douglas MacArthur spent his honeymoon night in Suite 386.

By 1921, rumors were already circulating concerning the fate of the hotel. A number of people were sure the "grey lady of Broadway" would be demolished. Instead, the lease was renewed and the lobby and dining rooms were enlarged. Prohibition took its toll on the Astor's profits, so 11 stores, renting for $80 a square foot, were added to the street level.

Following Prohibition, the Astor was given Hotel Liquor License Number One because of its pristine record during the dry period. In January of 1935, over 6,000 people rang in the New Year at the Astor. This was the largest turnout since Prohibition had been repealed. A local hotel newspaper described the scene at the hotel.

> A few minutes before midnight, the grand ballroom lights were dimmed, a snow scene was enacted and 'Father Time' was bombarded with colored balloons thrown by guests in the tier boxes. Simultaneously, a group of Broadway theatrical and screen stars dedicated a new enlarged bar in the Astor's cafe.
>
> Augmented orchestras under the direction of Jack Berger played until dawn. Handsome souvenirs were presented.
>
> Special parties were entertained by Fred A. Muschenheim, proprietor of the Astor, Col. Francis Gorman and William Norbert Nigey of the executive organization, in boxes overlooking the grand ballroom.
>
> Julius Brunner of 527 West 143rd Street (New York, N.Y.) surrounded by relatives and friends, celebrated his 80th birthday anniversary in the hotel's east ballroom at midnight.
>
> In the hotel's roof garden, more than 600 motion picture celebrities, attended the annual New Year's Eve charity ball and supper dance of the Motion Picture Salesmen of New York.

In 1935, the hotel was completely renovated. On January 6, 1936, Robert K. Christenberry succeeded Colonel Gorman as general manager. Gorman had been with the Astor for 25 years. Christenberry sought to upgrade the Astor facilities. By that summer, the rooms were air-conditioned. The Astor became the first fully air-conditioned hotel in the Northeast. By the late 1930s, the Astor had seven public dining rooms: the Astor Roof Garden, the Skywalk Cocktail Lounge, the Bar-Cafe, the Cocktail Terrace, L'Orangerie, the Hunting Room and the Astor Grill.

With the situation in Europe becoming more and more uncertain, the Astor introduced on September 21, 1940, chess and checkers in L'Orangerie. "Many hotel guests wish to indulge in some form of 'homey' pasttime during their leisure. The innovation will provide 'escape' to many guests whose mental burdens have increased during the current international crises."

On January 7, 1942, with its male staff drafted for service, 20 women were employed to occupy the previously exclusively male job of elevator operators. The management declared: "Employment requirements call for beauty and intelligence."

In June of 1944, Christenberry was named president, treasurer and a director of the hotel. He ordered another renovation of the hotel in 1949. By 1952, the hotel's public rooms were the Columbia Room for dining and dancing; the Astor Roof, also a dining and dancing space; the Bar Cafe; the Hunting Room; the Grand Ballroom, which was the largest in New York; the North Garden Lounge with its Japanese rock garden; the Coral Room; the Yacht Room; the Rose Room; College Hall; the East Ballroom and the outdoor, rooftop Skywalk Cafe.

In 1954, rumors of the hotel's imminent demolition were again circulating up and down Broadway. Instead, William Zeckendorf and two partners bought the hotel. Zeckendorf announced, "The principals are as one in their intention to perpetuate the Astor as a great hotel." On September 1, 1954, the deal was closed. Only 14 days later, on September 15, 1954, the Sheraton Corporation bought the hotel from the new owners.

The Sheraton Corporation changed the hotel's name to the Sheraton-Astor. They, in turn, traded the hotel back to the Zeckendorf concern in December of 1957. When the deal was completed in March of 1958, the name reverted to the Astor.

The Astor's age and the changing hotel trade in New York had dealt a blow to the venerable hotel. In late 1966, Erwin O. Schel, general manager of the hotel, stated that restoration of the hotel was impossible.

> Hotels generally are built to last 35 years. Major things need to be done to it. You simply can't expect a 65 year-old lady to be as spry as a 5 year-old. Arteries harden. Age happens. That's true of a building too.
>
> The jet plane has changed the hotel business more than any other factor. It has shortened the stay. Businessmen from Boston used to come and stay overnight. Now they fly the shuttle in three-quarters of an hour.
>
> Steamship travelers from Europe would spend two or three nights at a hotel before going home. Now they get off the boat, grab a cab, go to Kennedy Airport and wake up in Kansas City.
>
> Our guests fly over our heads. A man from Indianapolis has a 2-week vacation. He used to spend it in New York. Now he goes to Bermuda. The Rotary holds a convention in Japan. New York pales after the marvellous adventure in Tokyo.
>
> The guests used to arrive with six suitcases and stay a

week. Now they stay two days with a permanent-pressed suit and shirts they can wash out. The motels did that to the tourist habit.

There used to be a Mexican lady, a grande dame who came here twice a year with her relatives, a maid and six trunks. They expected service and they got it. I would go over their suite with white gloves.

I remember the assistant managers would greet guests while wearing morning dress or tuxedo, depending on the time of day. You would personally escort a guest to his room. Now you have push button elevators.

In 1966, the Astor was finally slated for demolition at the beginning of 1967. The property was sold for $10.5 million. Schel was especially upset over the demolition of the ballroom, which had been remodeled in 1964. "It's a shame to destroy something as beautiful as that. I don't want to be around to see it."

Big band singer Dolly Dawn remembered her time at the Astor: "I had a two room suite that I kept, even when we were on the road. Bob Christenberry was the finest gentleman that you would ever want to meet—tall and handsome and so gallant and so wonderful. He had been a colonel in the army and lost his arm halfway up to the elbow. Anyway, he had a great respect for performers. He would put us all on the sixth floor, facing Broadway. Anything that happened in Times Square, we had front row seats to it."

Jimmy Durante, who rented room 472 for over 20 years, felt that Times Square had changed—for the worst. "It just don't look and feel like New York," Durante said. "When I heard about the Astor, I thought it was a shame. My suite looked up Broadway and you could see the names going up and down on the theaters. Today that's all motion picture theaters. It ain't the same any more."

In 1967, the Astor was demolished to make way for the Minskoff Building (*q.v.*).

ASTOR THEATRE 1537 Broadway at 45th Street. Architect: George Keister. Opening: September 21, 1906; *A Midsummer Night's Dream*. Owners Wagenhals and Kemper built the Astor directly on Times Square. The theater was built with a 12-story office building above it, an unusual arrangement at the time. Annie Russell starred in the premiere attraction, *A Midsummer Night's Dream*. The classical inauguration of the theater was not an omen of all things to come.

Prominent tenants of the theater included *A Yankee Tourist* (8/12/07), which featured a young Wallace Beery in the cast; *The Man from Home* (8/17/08), which ran 496 performances, astounding for the time; and the also long running *Seven Days* (11/10/09), which ran 397 performances.

Between 1913 and 1920, the theater switched back and forth between holding live theater and motion-picture presentations. MGM leased the theater for a first-run showing of its epic *Quo Vadis* in 1913. George

M. Cohan (*q.v.*) opened two of his shows in the theater, *Hello, Broadway* (12/25/14) and *The Cohan Revue of 1916* (2/9/16). Comedian Raymond Hitchcock played the theater in *The Beauty Shop* (4/13/14). The Cohan and Harris production played for 88 performances.

The first Pulitzer Prize play, *Why Marry?* by Jesse Lynch Williams, opened on Christmas Day, 1917. It played for 120 performances. *Keep Her Smiling* (8/5/18) ran for 104 performances, followed by *Little Simplicity* (11/04/18), which held the Astor stage for 112 performances. The last performance of this decade, *East Is West* (12/25/18; 680 performances), was a huge success.

During the 1920s, legitimate theater use for the Astor ended. Productions included *Cornered* (12/8/20; 141 performances), Sigmund Romberg's (*q.v.*) *The Blushing Bride* (2/6/22; 144 performances) and *The Bronx Express* (4/26/22; 61 performances). The final legitimate offering at the Astor was *Dew Drop Inn* (5/17/23), an undistinguished musical comedy that only played 37 times.

By 1925, the theater had turned to a permanent motion-picture policy. Top pictures were frequently premiered at the Astor, beginning with the silent film *Quo Vadis*. Among the other films booked at the Astor were Billy Wilder's *One Two Three;* Vincente Minnelli's musical *Meet Me In St. Louis* with Judy Garland; *The Secret Life of Walter Mitty* with Danny Kaye; *Road to Bali* with Bing Crosby, Bob Hope and Dorothy Lamour; *Happy Go Lucky* with David Niven, Vera-Ellen and Cesar Romero; *I Wanted Wings;* Alfred Hitchcock's *Spellbound* with Ingrid Bergman and Gregory Peck; *The Vikings* with Kirk Douglas; and MGM's remake of the film that began the Astor's motion picture policy, *Quo Vadis*.

The Astor and the Victoria Theater (*q.v.*) down the block were topped by the fabulous Astor/Victoria sign. This was the largest sign in the world and is best known in recent years as the site of the Budweiser spectacular. The sign was 270 feet long and over 60 feet high. It and the Astor and Victoria theaters were torn down along with the Helen Hayes (*q.v.*) and Morosco theaters (*q.v.*) in 1982.

ATKINSON, BROOKS See CRITICS.

THE AUTOMAT Broadway between 46th and 47th Street. The Automat was one of Times Square's most enduring landmarks for more than 50 years. The coin-operated cafeteria boasted plain, sturdy food in clean, anonymous surroundings. The food was basic and cheap, and a good square meal could be bought for less than a dollar. The patron simply walked up to a wall of glass windowed doors and inserted the price of an item in its accompanying slot. The customer then opened the glass door and voila—a piece of coconut cream pie or baked beans in a crock.

The Automat was born in Germany shortly before

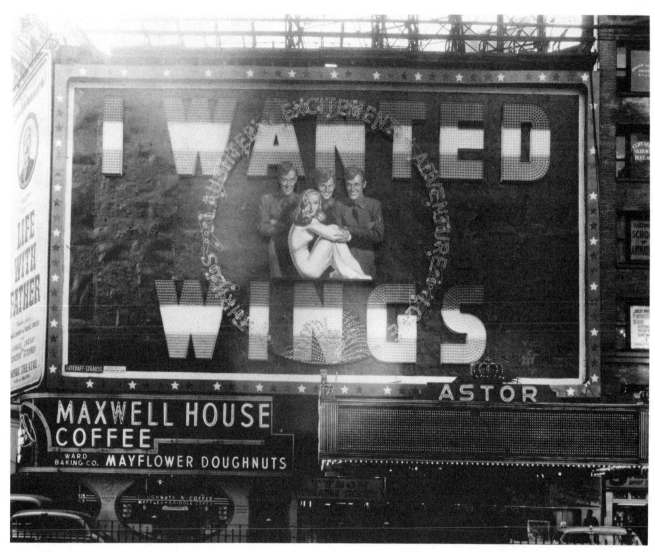

Astor Theater   Courtesy Artkraft Strauss.

the turn of the century. Joseph V. Horn and Frank Hardart brought the first Automat to 818 Chestnut Street in Philadelphia in 1902. Horn & Hardart streamlined the German equipment for Philadelphia, made it sturdier for America's greater population and gave it some modern touches. The idea—an early form of fast food for a low price—proved popular. The Automat offered a glimpse of the future in which dreams of the industrial revolution had come true. Here was machinery used to help make life easier for humans. It had the virtues of being both easy and anonymous.

The idea was so popular in Philadelphia that plans were made by Horn & Hardart to manufacture new machines and install them in New York. And what better place than the Crossroads of the World, Times Square. That other modern convenience, the subway, had reached the square, theaters were going up on every block and great, luxurious hotels like the Astor *(q.v.)* and Knickerbocker *(q.v.)* served the finest clientele. Of course there were risks. Times Square was also known

as the culinary center of New York. Nicknamed "Eatinghouse Square," by local wags, it had such restaurants as Rector's *(q.v.)*, the Cafe de l'Opera *(q.v.)*, the Knickerbocker Grill and Shanley's. How would the Automat do against these great lobster palaces?

The Automat   Courtesy Vicki Gold Levi.

To help combine the best of both culinary worlds, the opening of the Automat in July 1912 was a society bash. Director John Murray Anderson (q.v.) and Jenny Wren planned the gala opening as a benefit for charity. The top personalities in society and the theatrical world rubbed elbows, strictly by invitation. Beans in a pot, doughnuts, franks and other Automat favorites weren't in sight that first night. Sherry's, the restaurant beloved of high society, catered the affair in their grandest style. For a nickel, the hoi polloi would receive a plate of caviar from behind the glass door. From the milk spigots flowed not milk but champagne. Meyer Davis's orchestra serenaded the wealthy who ate, drank and were generally merry on both levels of the restaurant.

Few of the opening night participants would ever set foot in the Automat again, but the job was done. Word was out, and the Automat had arrived. In fact, it proved so popular that mounted police were posted to keep the crowds away from the huge leaded glass windows. On its first day, the Automat brought in 8,693 nickels.

The Times Square Automat was not only novel, but also beautiful. Its most outstanding feature was a stained-glass window 30 feet long and two stories high. The designer, Nicola D'Ascenzo also modeled windows for the Cathedral of St. John the Divine. The name "Automat" was emblazoned across the facade surrounded by garlands of fruit and flowers. Inside, the dining room featured marble topped tables on pristine white tiled floors. The central column was decorated with carvings that reached to the ceiling in a twisting pattern of leaves and vines. The Automat machinery was topped by beveled glass mirrors set into a mahogany framework.

The success of the Times Square Automat led to an expansion of the chain throughout the New York area. By the 1940s, the Automat had reached its peak of popularity, with nearly 50 outlets in the city. But the original Automat was still the flagship of the chain.

Almost all the food cost a nickel. A hamburger or bacon and eggs were two nickels. Coffee, an Automat staple, cost a nickel until the 1950s, when it was raised to a dime. Immediately, sales dropped off.

The success of the Automat reflects the changes occurring in America at the time. There was the novelty of the great machine serving humanity daily bread. Never mind that the food was all made by people in the central kitchens—first located at 47th Street and later at 50th Street and 11th Avenue—or that it was real live people who refilled the slots.

The lower classes of the city were ready for the Automat, and they could get there easily. When the great eating emporiums flourished, only the upper crust could afford transportation. A carriage ride all the way to Times Square could cost as much as a month's rent to a poor family. But the opening of the subway and the growing popularity of the automobile gave people of all classes easy access to all sections of the city.

People who couldn't afford Rector's and who didn't have the time to eat a five-course meal on their lunch hour flocked to the Automat. There was also the new immigrant class. They or the second or third generation were just getting their feet wet in the American experience. A place like the Automat was perfect for their needs. It only cost a couple of nickels, and they didn't have to face anybody. If they were unsure of dress or manners, the Automat ensured invisibility. If they didn't quite have a grasp of the language, that was fine. They didn't have to talk to anyone.

Going to the Automat wasn't like going to a restaurant simply to eat. The neat rows of windows displayed the food like merchandise. Eating at the Automat was like going shopping for lunch. You picked out the product you wanted from many choices and paid for it. This was the era when self-service was just beginning to be accepted in retailing, and the Automat followed the popular trend and translated it into restaurant terms.

The Automat was among the first hangouts for a new generation of actors, composers, lyricists and directors. While Victor Herbert (q.v.) ate at Shanley's, Irving Berlin (q.v.) was eating at the Automat. In fact Berlin set one number in his revue, Face the Music, in the Automat. Cast members Katharine Carrington and J. Harold Murray faced the Depression squarely as they dined at the Automat and sang, "Let's Have Another Cup o' Coffee."

Robert F. Byrnes, Senior Executive Vice President and Secretary of Horn & Hardart, first joined the company at the Automat in Times Square in 1925. He commented on the changes he has witnessed over his 50 years with the company: "It was the depression and people were starting to think about watching their nickels and dimes. But Broadway at that time was a seething mass of people, a class of people. They wanted to see something for nothing. They could walk down Broadway. The street was the show.

"They were getting to eat out for the first time. A different class emerged. These were the people who were offered this inexpensive means of walking in and getting a cup of coffee, nobody says anything to them, and they leave their cup on the table and walk out."

Inevitably people's tastes changed, and the Automat changed too in an attempt to keep up with the times. "At the outset there was no cafeteria. It was all Automat. There was a special window later, that if you wanted a grill item to order, you'd go to the cashier and buy a token for bacon and eggs and then walk back to a concealed cafeteria and put your token into the slot marked bacon and eggs. They didn't have to face anyone again."

As the demand for the short-order items grew, the cafeteria was opened to service. Pies, cakes, sandwiches and desserts all still came from the windows. There was no refrigeration, although there were heating units in the drums so that hot foods like baked beans in the pot could be served. By 1950, the demands of the customers forced the relationship to become 30% Automat and 70% cafeteria.

Even with the increased cafeteria service, the management that remained maintained the philosophy that everything would be made in one place. This enabled an absolute uniformity of quality in all stores. Hamburgers were premade, not cooked, and sent out to the grills. All stews and soups were centrally prepared and then warmed over at the Automat. There were four deliveries from the new commissary, which took up the square block between 49th and 50th Street and 11th and 12th Avenue.

To keep customers coming back, prices were kept low, and the places were kept immaculately clean. But social and economic conditions began to evolve after the Second World War that would kill the Automat.

Along with a saturation of the market came an increase in the price of raw materials and a rise in prices. The modes of transportation changed, the trolleys stopped and the elevated trains came down. As more and more neighborhoods were cleaned up, rents increased. The George Washington Bridge went up, the Lincoln and Holland Tunnels were opened and the population dispersed. The ethnic mix of the population changed, and many of the new immigrants didn't want to eat out. Their food was different from ours, and they weren't in as big a hurry as their predecessors to assimilate American customs. These new arrivals preferred to stay in their ghettos.

In 1939, air-conditioning was added to the restaurants. With heat in the winter and now air-conditioning in the summer, the Automats became almost too comfortable. What the company refers to as "undesirables" hung out at the Automats. Originally, there were tables that sat four people. When the Automat became crowded people shared tables. But with a change in the type of patrons, people were loathe to share their space. Robert Byrnes remarks, "There were about 200 tables and you would find 200 customers, one at each table because they didn't want to face each other."

At the same time, the counter restaurant concept came in a la Chock Full of Nuts. There, the customers could come in and not face anyone and still get out in a hurry. Even if the place was crowded, customers still weren't obliged to sit beside or across from anyone.

As its clientele changed and business slackened off, the Automat began to lose money. There was also a change in people's attitudes toward the machinery. At first, the Automat was a symbol of the future. Once the future arrived, the Automat seemed dated. With the war effort, technology changed. Transistors and computers made mechanical devices passe. When prices increased, tokens were substituted for coins. That meant the patron had to first go to a cashier for the token. The lunch counter seemed so much easier.

In the old days, the Automat was viewed as a family restaurant, but as Times Square deteriorated, fewer and fewer families frequented the neighborhood. With the great movie palaces gone and less and less product on Broadway, there was no reason for parents to take their children to the Automat. For the children brought up in the space age, the appeal of the Automat was short-lived.

The actual turning point for the company came at about 1957, when business radically changed for the worst, but the Automat hung on until 1969. By that time, things had gotten so bad that a plan was drafted for the company to go out of business. The plan was implemented through gutting their buildings and renting the space to outside concerns. In 1973, Horn & Hardart bought a mail-order company that became "a phenomenal investment." And then came the new revolution—the fast food hamburger.

The decision was made to convert the Automats to fast food restaurants. The Broadway Automat was changed over to a Burger King when the company acquired the New York Burger King franchise in 1974. They also now operate Arby's in New York and, in 1981, gained control of Bojangles Fried Chicken. The last Automat in New York is at 3rd Avenue and 42nd Street. The machines are still in use, although the cafeteria is the main draw. There is also a chocolate chip cookie shop in the space, keeping up with a current trend.

In the 1940s, the Automat system was in its heyday. There were between 45 and 50 Automats in the city and over 350,000 people were fed there every day. Robert Byrnes likes to remember this story: "One day an elderly man died in an Automat and on the same day a woman gave birth in the washroom."

AVON THEATER See KLAW THEATER.

BAER, BUGS (1886–1969) Arthur "Bugs" Baer was one of Broadway's most colorful characters and greatest humorists. Widely respected for his wit, Baer was a professional columnist who covered the Times Square scene and America at large.

Baer was born in Philadelphia. His mother had 14 children of which Baer was the seventh. Like many of his contemporaries, he was forced to leave school before graduation to find a job to help support his family. Baer left the art school he had been attending at age 14. He soon found a job designing lace that paid $12 a week.

Baer soon moved on to a job at *The Philadelphia Public Ledger* as an artist. He worked his way up the ladder until he became a sports columnist with the *Washington Times*. At the *Times*, he illustrated his column with cartoons featuring an insect with a body shaped like a baseball. The creature's name was Bugs, and this became Baer's nickname.

Baer left the *Times* to conquer New York, landing a job with *The New York World*. While at the *World* he penned one of his most quoted quips. Pete Brodie, a member of the Yankees, was thrown out while trying to steal second. Baer wrote: "His head was full of larceny but his feet were too honest."

The line captured the fancy of newspaper mogul William Randolph Hearst. The publisher hired Baer for *The New York American*. Baer later moved to the *World Journal Tribune*. His column was syndicated to over 15,000,000 people by the Hearst owned King Features.

Unbeknownst to Hearst, Baer was also moonlighting for his old paper the *World*. He wrote the 1921 column under the pseudonym of Graham Wire. The column was called "Wiregram." Damon Runyon *(q.v.)*, though a difficult man, had helped get Baer hired with Hearst, and Runyon found out about Baer's moonlighting when he came across the author working on the *World* column

at the *American*. Baer begged Runyon not to tell Hearst. "Wiregrams" was so successful that a Hearst executive sent Runyon to woo Graham Wire from the *World*. Runyon didn't known how to handle the situation until he finally told Hearst that Wire promised his mother he would never work for Hearst.

Baer was a habitue of Toots Shor's watering hole where many comics sought him out. Baer was flattered that professionals like Milton Berle would use his quips on radio and television.

Baer also appeared as a master of ceremonies and toastmaster at hundreds of dinners and charity shows. He was an active member of the newspapermen's club, The Banshees.

Some of Baer's quips have made it into popular renown. It was he who wrote the famous line, "What would you charge to haunt a house?" He called the Grand Canyon a "great place for old razor blades." He also noted, "Europe is where they name a street after you one day and chase you down it the next one." One of his best remembered lines is "Paying alimony is like buying oats for a dead horse."

Not all of Baer's remarks were totally humorous. He took his job seriously and found that he couldn't resist putting his own beliefs into his work. "I find that all humorists live in a perpetual state of indignation and are congenital reformers," he remarked.

He was against the cancellation of war debts. He stated his position in a typically humorous way. "We must make the world pay for the last war to prevent it from affording the next one." His view on prohibition was also widely quoted. "Wine, women and song are now wood alcohol, trained nurses, and 'Nearer My God to Thee.'"

He took himself seriously as a humorist and often wrote about the job. "It's a tough racket being a humorist for once having made yourself a monkey you must continue to pick up coconuts with your feet. However, I'm not complaining. If there is an easier way of making a living than doing the thing you want to, then tell me and I will picket myself for being unfair to my silhouette."

Baer died at the age of 83 on May 17, 1969.

BARNES, CLIVE See CRITICS.

BARRYMORE FAMILY The Barrymores were the greatest family in American theater history. During their notable careers (which spanned five decades on the stage) their personal lives were as well reported as their distinguished careers. Their exploits were parodied in the George S. Kaufman and Edna Ferber comedy, *The Royal Family.*

Georgiana Drew Barrymore (1856–1893) Georgiana was the daughter of Louisa Lane Drew and John Drew. Her mother first appeared on stage at the age of five in a melodrama, *Meg Murnock, or, the Hag of the Glen.* Louisa Lane specialized in playing adult roles even before she reached her teens. After two unsuccessful marriages, Louisa met John Drew, a great Irish comedian. Louisa and John Drew had three children: Louisa, who would not undertake a theatrical career; John Drew Jr., who achieved perfection in drawing room comedies; and Georgiana. Georgiana was trained by some of the greatest actors of her time, among them Edwin Booth and Lawrence Barrett, in addition to her own distinguished family. Actor Otis Skinner called Georgiana "the funniest comedian I've ever seen; she made you hold your stomach laughing, but she was never distressing." Her parents barely saw each other because John Drew was often on the road. In fact, they were only together half the time of their 12-year marriage. While her father was on the road, her mother became the first woman to run an American theater, the Arch Street Theater in Philadelphia. Georgiana was taken on the road with her father. In 1876, she married Maurice Barrymore. She died in California on July 2, 1893.

Maurice Barrymore (1839–1905) Maurice Barrymore was born Herbert Arthur Chamberlain Hunter Blyth in India. Instead of following in his family's footsteps in the Indian Civil Service, Herbert left India for England where he became the country's amateur boxing champion before launching an acting career. After two years of touring, he adopted the name Maurice Herbert Blythe and assumed the surname Barrymore. In 1875, Maurice came to America and made his debut in *Under the Gaslight.* Amy Leslie, a drama critic for the *Chicago News,* wrote of him, "He is about as near a desirable man to see across the footlights as the stage shall ever grant us." The young matinee idol made his New York debut in *Hamlet* at the Fifth Avenue Theater. Also featured in the cast were Edwin Booth making his New York bow and John Drew. After the run of the

play, Drew brought Barrymore home to Philadelphia and introduced him to Georgiana. Their marriage produced three children (Lionel, Ethel and John), each of whom achieved notable success on the stage. Maurice Barrymore died in Amityville, Long Island, on March 26, 1905.

Lionel Barrymore (1878–1954) Lionel first went on stage at the age 15 during the 1893–94 season in Philadelphia under the aegis of his grandmother, Louisa Lane Drew. He never really enjoyed performing and, following this engagement, retired from the stage for two years. He joined his uncle John Drew's acting company and made his first real success in *The Mummy and the Hummingbird* during the 1902 season, playing an Italian organ grinder. Lionel preferred character parts as if seeking to hide his real personality behind the makeup. He specialized in these parts in plays until 1906 when he again left the stage because of ill health. Whether he was actually ill or only looking for an excuse to quit the theater is uncertain.

He moved to Paris to study painting, with no intention of returning to the theater. Three years later, having achieved little success, he returned to America. In 1909, he appeared in the movies, relieved at not having to face an audience. But even the great director D.W. Griffith couldn't provide Lionel with enough work, so he was forced to return to the stage. He achieved success in *Peter Ibbetson, The Jest,* and, in 1918, *The Copperhead* in which he was first acclaimed a great star. A disasterous production of *Macbeth* followed, but he again achieved fame with *The Claw.*

In 1925, he left for Hollywood where he remained for the rest of his life. Lionel Barrymore died on November 15, 1954.

Ethel Barrymore (1879–1959) Whereas Lionel fancied himself a painter, his sister Ethel would have preferred to be a concert pianist. But the power of the family was too great, and Ethel was forced into an acting career. She made her debut as Julia in *The Rivals* in Montreal on January 25, 1894. The production was brought to New York at the Empire Theater *(q.v.).* Ethel must have made some impression on the theatrical world, for she was summoned to London by famed actor William Gillette. He starred her in his production of *Secret Service.* She followed it with parts in *The Bells* and *Peter the Great* with Henry Irving. In 1900, she returned to America under Charles Frohman's management. The play, *Captain Jinks of the Horse Marines,* was a huge success at its New York premiere on February 4, 1901.

Her early stellar vehicles included *Carrots,* a one-act play, and *A Country Mouse* (1902–03); *Cousin Kate* and *Cynthia* (1903–04); *Sunday* and *A Doll's House* (1904–05); *Alice Sit-by-the-Fire* (1905–06); *The Silver Box* and revivals of *Captain Jinks of the Horse Marines; His Excellency the Governor* and *Cousin Kate* (1906–07); *Her Sister*

(1907–08); *Lady Frederick* (1908–09). At the end of this period a critic wrote, "Ethel Barrymore now ranks with the most popular stars on the American stage, and, upon the strength of exceptional beauty, a wonderful personality and an acting talent that is constantly growing and developing, she has become one of the the most notable stage figures in this country today."

But she was not truly interested in a stage career, nor did she see herself as a great actress. She would rather have seen her brothers' careers overtake hers and was more interested in baseball and boxing than the theater. As the drama became more and more realistic with the emergence of O'Neill, Ibsen and their like, Ethel became more disenchanted. She seemed purposely to pick parts that didn't suit her. But the public still adored her, as much for her elegance and bearing offstage as her onstage performances. In 1928, the Shuberts presented her in Martinez Sierra's *The Kingdom of God* in the new Ethel Barrymore Theater *(q.v.)*. Her great success as Sister Gracia was not repeated until 1940, when she appeared in *The Corn Is Green*. Between Broadway roles, she appeared in motion pictures.

Her last stage appearance was in 1950 at a benefit for the American National Theatre and Acadamy *(q.v.)* in *The Twelve-Pound Look*. She died on June 18, 1959.

John Barrymore (1882–1942) John, too, evinced no desire for a stage career. He tried supporting himself as an artist and illustrator and, though somewhat successful, found acting to be the easiest way to make money. As the most handsome and talented of his siblings, John found acting relatively painless, although he became easily bored with long runs and as early as 1914 came on stage drunk.

He made his stage debut on October 31, 1903, at Cleveland's Theater, Chicago, playing Max in *Magda*. He made his New York debut in December of that same year, at the Savoy Theater in *Glad of It*. Later that year, he appeared as a member of William Collier's company in *The Dictator*, which also had a run in London. His sister, Ethel, arranged for him to appear with her in *Sunday* and *Alice Sit-by-the-Fire*. He then rejoined William Collier in Australia in *The Dictator*. In 1906, he again appeared with his sister in *His Excellency the Governor*.

In May 1908, he made his musical-comedy debut in the Chicago production of *A Stubborn Cinderella* and then in the Charles Dillingham production of *The Candy Shop*. Although John's musicals were successful, perhaps they proved too much effort for him. He much preferred light comedy in which he could be suave and debonair and exhibit "the great profile." He followed in his father's footsteps as a matinee idol in plays like *The Fortune Hunter* (1909) and Schnitzler's *The Affairs of Anatol* (1910). According to the press, "matinee audiences beat their breasts in admiration."

By 1916, Barrymore, bored with easy roles, found great success in John Galsworthy's *Justice*. The powerfully dramatic role of Falder enabled Barrymore to move the audience to more than breast beating. This brilliant performance was followed by one in George Du Maurier's *Peter Ibbetson* with his brother, Lionel, Constance Collier, Laura Hope Crews and Madge Evans. This triumph led to another, the part of Fadya in Tolstoy's *The Living Corpse,* retitled for Broadway, *Redemption*. Two more great performances followed, *Richard III* (1920) and *Hamlet* (1922). The reviews were astounding; Barrymore was at the peak of his talents.

Following the close of *Hamlet,* Barrymore left for Hollywood. Among his notable films were *A Bill of Divorcement, Grand Hotel, Twentieth Century* and *Counsellor at Law*. He wouldn't return until 1940, with a production of *My Dear Children* at the Belasco Theatre *(q.v.)*. By this time, Barrymore was washed up in films, and the parts that came along were mostly parodies of himself. His role in *My Dear Children* was no exception. Ill health forced the closing of the production after only four months. John Barrymore died on June 29, 1942.

BARRYMORE THEATER See ETHEL BARRYMORE THEATER.

BATTLE TO SAVE THE HELEN HAYES, MOROSCO AND BIJOU THEATERS During the latter part of 1978 and early 1979, a plan to tear down the Helen Hayes *(q.v.)*, Morosco *(q.v.)* and Bijou *(q.v.)* theaters and build a high rise hotel on the sight became public. The plan called for not only the destruction of the three theaters but also the leveling of the Piccadilly Hotel and other important structures.

Preservationists and other people became alarmed about the destruction of two of Broadway's excellent theaters and also about the impact of a massive hotel on the entire theater district. The proposed design of the hotel also received harsh attack because of the large blank walls at street level, which would effectively deaden the surrounding area. Worse, these huge, blank concrete walls faced the monumental blank walls created in 1973 by the Minskoff Building *(q.v.)* across the street.

John Portman, the builder of the proposed hotel had also built a Marriott hotel in Washington on Pennsylvania Avenue. In that case, he wanted to tear down the historic National Theatre. Portman insisted, as he did in New York, that the theater could not be saved if the hotel was to be built. Luckily for Washington, a city that has lost all but four of its historic theaters, the National was saved and Portman was proved wrong. In fact, the Marriott Hotel in Washington now boasts of its proximity to the National Theatre.

A preprinted letter addressed to government officials opposing the demolition of the theaters appeared in the

Play readings were given during the battle to save the Helen Hayes and Morosco theaters. Photo Jeff Slotnick.

New York Times on September 2, 1981. Over 2,000 people cut it out. A petition was circulated stating "I am outraged at the planned use of $55.5 million in NYC, NYS and Federal taxpayer dollars for the Portman Hotel Project, as it would destroy The Morosco, Helen Hayes, Bijou and Embassy 5 Theaters and remove no real urban blight. If the Hotel is to truly serve urban renewal and warrant subsidy, it must relocate to an alternate site or be redesigned to include the historic existing theaters." This petition was signed by over 100,000 citizens but to no avail.

New York Post drama critic Clive Barnes wrote that these theaters were, " . . . gems of theater buildings, and represent a type of theater that New York needs. They are both gorgeous to look at . . . these are two of the most handsome theaters, architecturally, in the whole city. If both of them are not protected by the Landmarks Commission to the last drop of its blood then one must question the value of the Landmarks Commission . . . Don't take away these theaters— they are part of Broadway's royal blue lifeblood and cannot ever, ever, be replaced. It would be an act that would diminish our great city, an act of the utmost folly that future generations would rue."

Brooks Atkinson, Audrey Wood, Gene Saks, Tony

Roberts, Jean Stapleton, Alec McCowen, Frances Sternhagen, Mrs. Richard Rodgers, Livingston Biddle Jr., Vivian Matalon, Oliver Hailey, Beverly Sills, Tony Randall, Elia Kazan and others wrote letters protesting the planned demolition.

Two letters written by actresses stated the case eloquently. Jane White: "There is something that an Actor puts onto his skin when you work in those theaters. A whole history of a tradition of great work that was done in a place, and those ghosts still live. And they live here."

Patricia Elliott: "[One would be] . . . throwing the baby out with the bathwater by tearing down three of the most beautiful theaters that we have on Broadway . . . if they can give me a good solid reason why we should throw out culture, heritage, art, not to mention all the vibrations of love, and feeling, and the past, and what we are as human beings . . . "

Georgio Cavaglieri, New York State Preservation Coordinator of the American Institute of Architects also wrote a letter: " . . . It will be possible to preserve the Morosco, Helen Hayes and Bijou theaters, which happen to be among the most attractive examples of theater architecture of the first quarter of our century. In my opinion, it would be possible and advisable to redesign the lower levels of the hotel building in order to incorporate in it the theaters to be preserved."

The recommendation in that letter made sense to a lot of people and Save the Theaters (*q.v.*), a nonprofit group formed to save the three theaters, hired Lee Harris Pomeroy to draw up a plan that would make the preservtion of the theaters feasible. Mr. Pomeroy was a Professor at City College and Former Director of the New York Chapter of the American Institute of Architects. Mr. Pomeroy was also an award-winning architect in his own right.

His plan offered the Portman organization many advantages. First, of course, the retention of the Helen Hayes and Morosco Theaters. The saving of these two buildings removed the need for a 1,500 seat musical theater house to be built on the third floor of the hotel. Two theaters recently built in skyscrapers, the Minskoff and Uris (*q.v.*), had proved unwieldy and unsuited to the needs of modern musical theater. These large barns never had successful shows and audiences and theater professionals alike despised their design and acoustics. The two historic theaters offered 763 more seats than the proposed 1,500 seat theater in the hotel.

Second, the hotel in Pomeroy's plan would fit in more harmoniously with the theater district. Instead of the huge blank concrete walls on the sides of the building, there would be the beautiful facades of the theaters.

Portman's design elements and the business features of his plan would be retained, although with some improvement. Shubert Alley, one of the city's most charming thoroughfares, would have been extended another block. A theater gallery lining the walkway and retail space would also replace the blank face of the hotel allowing more guest rooms to face Broadway. The shops would be lowered one level, and brought closer to Broadway and street traffic.

The revolving rooftop restaurant, one of the less appealing features of the Portman design, would be moved east, affording a better view of downtown Manhattan and Times Square.

Pomeroy probably noted that Portman didn't care about the aesthetic values of his hotel. So Pomeroy presented several financial advantages in his report: "(a) It eliminates significant cost of the proposed new 3rd level theater and over 50,000 square feet of expensive construction. (b) It allows an addition of some 15,000 square feet of space that has commercial value. (c) Portman becomes eligible for tax benefits applicable to those rehabilitating structures listed on the National Register under the Economic Recovery Tax Act of

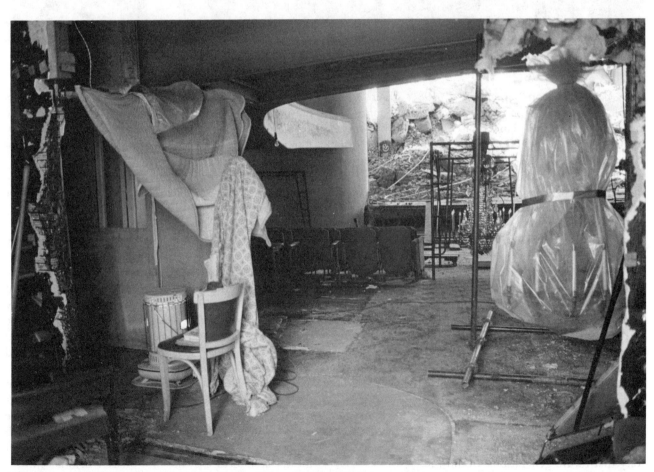

The interior of the Helen Hayes Theater during demolition   Photo Jeff Slotnick.

1981. Those benefits include 25% in investment tax credit available for rehabilitation of National Register properties. The Helen Hayes has already been designated eligible for the Register. The Morosco has received many more recommendations than necessary for designation and should be declared elibigle for the National Register.''

Perhaps Pomeroy and Save the Theaters were whistling against the wind. Even the Environmental Impact Statement (EIS) came out against the report, but the people behind the EIS hadn't bothered to consider the report fully and their objections were totally specious. For example, they objected that if the new plan was adopted the much needed new theater would not be included. But of course, the retention of the two historic playhouses obviated the need for the new theater. The EIS also stated that the proposal would preclude the atrium, but the atrium was not affected by the new plan.

With their proposal rejected, proponants of saving the theaters turned to the courts. Despite their efforts, demolition of the theaters began in March 1982, and the new hotel was built as planned. What went wrong? Jack Goldstein, Save the Theaters' Director of Preservation explains:

> There wasn't the inclination on the part of those who could have changed the project. Equity and Save the Theaters never attempted to stop the hotel. But we asked for at least a redesign of the hotel to save the theaters. All those people who said it was too late should have gone to the Department of Housing and Urban Development for an alteration of the grant and an increase in funds. It would have been less expensive than the amount of money it took to tie up that project for as long as we did. And we would have had three theaters; we would still have had an ugly hotel but we would have had the three theaters. So what went wrong was short sighted thinking on the part of the city and what we felt was a fundamental change in their perception of the historic role of this area of town.

> All of a sudden the momentum that had been gathering by development since the economic crisis in the mid-seventies based on the very important role that real estate development played in putting the city back on a firm financial standing was simply being applied to the theater district without much thought. And so we couldn't move that project. We tried to take it to the Supreme Court.

> The more unsettling thing was that immediately following the demolition of the Morosco, before the demolition of the Hayes, the City passed its new zoning ordinance for the entire midtown west area which turned what we thought was a horrible but isolated incident into something which was going to become typical. It was at that point that we decided that we would have to take on the momentum of the real estate development and we would simply have to change the mind of the city about the way it was looking at the area.

Since the building of what became the Marriott Marquis Hotel and the destruction of the theaters, the Landmarks Preservation Committee has granted landmark status to several theaters. If nothing else, this shows a change in the city's attitudes toward the area.

BEACH The Beach—the concrete island separating Broadway and Seventh Avenue across the street from the Palace Theatre (q.v.)—was the hangout for out-of-work vaudevillians in the teens and twenties. They would gather on the little island and brag about their recent bookings and hefty contracts. Usually these exploits were greatly exaggerated.

The Beach even had its poet—Philip Stack, a clerk in the Brooklyn Edison Company, who wrote poems under the pseudonym Don Wahn. Stack sent his poems to Walter Winchell (q.v.) and let Winchell print them in his column without any charge. These poems soon became an important part of the column. Wahn wrote this paean to the Beach.

> They stand nearby the Palace day on day
>   And talk in low and falsely hopeful tones,
> Their snappy clothes, pathetically gay,
>   Bespeak ability to wheedle loans;
> They swap their gags like children swapping toys,
>   And rip their lucky brothers into bits;
> Their food and drink is Broadway's blatant noise —
>   Their Bible is Variety (q.v.) or Zit's.
> So, lolling there, the weeks go swiftly by,
>   While faded clippings yellow in their hands;
> They hum the current hits and watch it die —
>   And, penniless, they quote their rash demands.
> Ah, you, who stand there seven days in seven,
> God grant you make the two-a-day in heaven.
>   —Don Wahn

BECK, MARTIN (c. 1869–1940) Martin Beck came to America from Czechoslovakia and joined a German traveling show. He then moved to Chicago and joined a North Clark Street Beer Garden as manager. Beck persuaded the owner to add dressing rooms and a stage and started his career as a vaudeville manager. Performers on the Radio-Keith-Orpheum circuit, which Beck later managed, called him "Two Beers Beck" to remind him of his humble roots.

In 1899, Beck perfected the concept of the circuit booking system. By linking together theaters on one chain, he could guarantee bookings for a whole year. This also gave him control of the actors' salaries and the content of their acts. The Orpheum Theater in San Francisco was the first theater in the chain that eventually covered the area between California and Chicago. By 1905, there were 17 theaters in the chain.

The next year, Beck came to New York and settled in the Putnam Building, which also housed the Keith-Albee (q.v.) offices and their United Booking Office. Beck built the Palace Theatre (q.v.) at Broadway and

47th Street in 1913. This enraged Keith who saw the eastern half of the country as his domain. He managed to buy out 75% of the ownership of the Palace from Beck.

Beck later built the Martin Beck Theatre *(q.v.)*, which opened in 1924. He also built the State Lake Theater in Chicago and was responsible for the first appearance in the United States of the D'Oyly Carte Opera Company in 1934.

BELASCO, DAVID (1859–1931)   David Belasco was the total theater man. Belasco was obsessed with the theater and played many different roles—playwright, producer, theater owner, actor, director and stage manager. However, although there are many anecdotes about Belasco the man, almost nothing is remembered about his work.

He began his career in San Francisco as a callboy and play adapter. He moved up to actor and made his first stage appearance in 1871 at the California Theatre in San Francisco. He later met Dion Boucicault, the greatest author of melodramas. Boucicault taught Belasco the value of theatricality and high emotion, and Belasco

began to attempt play writing. He was also influenced by the great actors with whom he performed—Edwin Booth and John McCullough performed with him in 1874.

In 1879, Belasco had his first success as a playwright with *Hearts of Oak,* which was first produced in Chicago. Emboldened by the experience, Belasco moved to New York the following year. He became stage manager of the Madison Square Theatre and by 1886 a stage manager and producer for Daniel Frohman at the Lyceum Theater *(q.v.)*.

His plays include *Lord Chumley* (1888) and *Men and Women* (1890), both written with H.C. DeMille; *The Heart of Maryland* (1895); *DuBarry* (1901); *The Darling of the Gods,* with Luther Long (1902); *The Girl of the Golden West* (1905); *Temperamental Journey* (1913); *The Return of Peter Grimm* (1921); and *Salvage* (1925). Most of these were melodramas that were popular for a time and then forgotten; as new playwrights changed the style of theater in Europe and America, melodramas like Belasco's fell by the wayside.

These new masters of the drama—Ibsen, Strindberg,

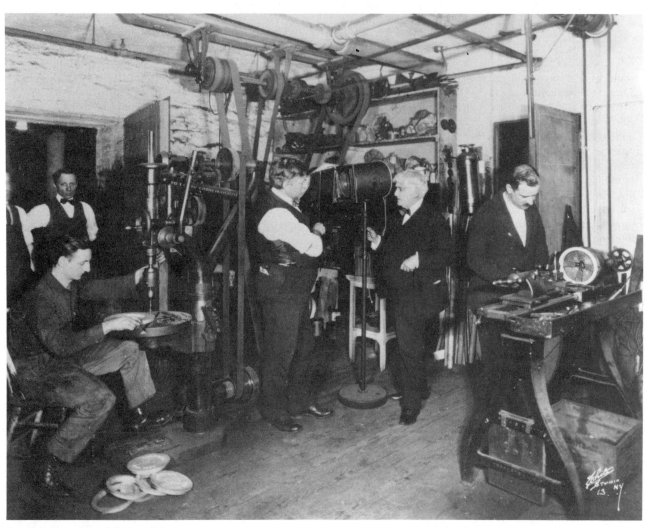

David Belasco (second from right)

Wilde, Shaw, Zola—brought realism to the stage. Belasco, realizing that tastes were changing, was entranced with the possibilities that these playwrights opened up. Belasco is thought of as the man who introduced realism into the American theater and who, as a producer, perhaps went too far. For Alice Bradley's play *The Governor's Lady* (1912), he reproduced a Child's Restaurant on the stage. And when a boarding house set was required for Eugene Walter's *The Easiest Way* (1909), Belasco actually bought one and had it reconstructed on the stage. This wasn't really art but pure showmanship. Art is in the illusion of reality, but with Belasco there was no illusion.

On his quest for realism on the stage, Belasco did make certain innovations. He pioneered stage lighting, especially at the theater he built—the Stuyvesant, which was renamed the Belasco Theatre *(q.v.)*. A favorite effect of his was re-creating a sunset. He was the first to conceal the footlights in order to make the stage even more realistic. His theater had the latest in stage equipment, which he used to produce the most astounding effects. But these were effects without emotion. The plays he produced were simply more modern versions of the melodramas with which he achieved his first fame.

Belasco wore a priest's collar and robes, although he was not particularly religious. Belasco concentrated on his facade and built his personality for its effect, just as he produced his plays. His ego enabled him to understand the importance of the director in the shaping of the drama. He might not have believed a director was necessary for others, but he could extend his control as producer by directing the actors also. But his direction relied on tricks and facade as did his producing. A favorite ruse was the temper tantrum he would throw to make the actors work harder. After lambasting the cast, he would throw his pocket watch onto the floor and crush it with his foot. This astounding action would galvanize the cast. Belasco never told them that he had a trunk full of dollar pocket watches in his office.

His legacy is in his legend. All that is left of the artist is the Belasco Theatre (the second, his first was built in 1902). Puccini adapted two of his plays into *Madame Butterfly* and *The Girl of the Golden West*. His ghost was said to show up at every opening night at his theater until that of *Oh! Calcutta!*

BELASCO THEATRE 111 W. 44th Street. Architect: George Keister. Opening: October 16, 1907; *A Grand Army Man*. The theater today known as the Belasco was called the Stuyvesant Theater when producer, director, playwright David Belasco *(q.v.)* built it in 1907. The Stuyvesant took the name Belasco in 1910 when the original Belasco Theatre reverted to its original name, the Republic *(q.v.)*. When it was built, the Belasco was the best equipped theater of its era. The

$750,000 theater boasted a huge elevator stage, areas for scene shops and the most complete lighting setup of any theater. Above the auditorium were Belasco's apartments. The technical innovations introduced by Belasco made possible all the realistic effects he doted on.

Unfortunately, for all the hits the Belasco housed, it was never considered a prime Broadway theater. Lee Shubert said it was on "the wrong side of the right street." Closer to Sixth Avenue than Times Square, the theater was somewhat off the beaten path.

Ferenc Molnar's *The Devil* was presented at the Belasco with Edwin Stevens and at the Garden Theater with George Arliss. Both productions opened on August 18, 1908, and were immediate hits. This must be the only time a play has opened in two theaters on the same day. *The Devil* was followed by *The Fighting Hope* (9/22/08; 231 performances) and *The Easiest Way* (1/19/09; 157 performances).

Belasco's love of feminine pulchritude and melodrama led to a sort of stock company of Belasco heroines, among them Blanche Bates, Lenore Ulric, Ina Claire, Jeanne Eagles and Katharine Cornell *(q.v.)*. Plays featuring these actresses included *Polly with a Past* (9/6/17), *Daddies* (9/5/18), *The Son-Daughter* (11/19/19), *Kiki* (11/29/21), *The Harem* (12/2/24), *Lulu Belle* (2/9/26) and *Mima* (12/12/28).

Vincent Youmans's *(q.v.) Hit the Deck* sailed into the

The Belasco Theatre on 42nd Street, featuring Blanche Bates in Victory

Belasco on April 25, 1927. The hit musical featured "Hallelujah" as its big number. Humphrey Bogart starred in *It's a Wise Child* (8/6/29), and Belasco's last production, *Tonight or Never* (11/18/30), starred Melvyn Douglas and Helen Gahagan.

After Belasco's death on May 14, 1931, the theater was leased to Katharine Cornell. She appeared in *Lucrece* (12/20/32) and Sidney Howard's *Alien Corn* (2/20/33). The theater was then leased to Mrs. Hazel L. Rice, wife of playwright Elmer Rice of *Street Scene* fame.

The Group Theater (q.v.) inhabited the theater in late 1934 when *Gold Eagle Guy* moved from the Morosco (q.v.). On February 19, 1935, Clifford Odets's *Awake and Sing* opened at the Belasco under the Group Theater's umbrella. These two plays, a flop and a hit, were both part of the reason for the failure of the Group. During the mounting of the first play, major rifts opened in the already strained relationship between actors and Group leader Lee Strasberg. Ruth Nelson actually tried to assault Strasberg because of his handling of Stella Adler during a rehearsal. The second play was produced over Strasberg's vigorous objections. It turned out to be a smash hit and one of the most influential plays of the thirties.

On October 28, 1935, Sidney Kingsley's *Dead End* opened to rave reviews. The production harked back to the days of Belasco's ultrarealism. The set by Norman Bel Geddes showed a dead-end street and wharf with the orchestra pit standing in for the East River.

The Group Theater presented other notable plays at the Belasco in the thirties: Frances Farmer, Luther Adler and Elia Kazan featured in Clifford Odets's *Golden Boy* (11/4/37), Odets's *Rocket to the Moon* (11/24/38) and Irwin Shaw's *The Gentle People* (1/5/39).

The forties began with an appearance by John Barrymore (q.v.) acting a parody of himself in *My Dear Children* (1/31/40). The $50,000 advance sale was one of the largest in Broadway history. It seemed that everyone wanted to catch a glimpse of the Great Profile on his way down the ladder of success. Brooks Atkinson wrote that the audience "looked as if they hoped to be present at the final degradation of Icarus. The crowds that watched the tumbrils pass in the French Revolution could not have been more pitiless or morbid."

Later that year, Helen Craig played the deaf mute in *Johnny Belinda*. The play, which opened on September 18, 1940, later became a hit movie, as did *Mr. and Mrs. North* (1/12/41). December 29, 1944, was the opening of *Trio*, a frank but tasteful treatment of lesbianism. Unfortunately, the management of the theater refused to let the play run more than two months. Judy Holliday first made her mark at the Belasco in *Kiss Them for Me* (3/20/45). Richard Widmark and Jayne Cotter (later Meadows) were the other stars in the cast.

The 1940s continued with Arthur Laurents's *Home of the Brave* (12/27/45; 69 performances), Gertrude Berg as Molly Goldberg in *Me and Molly* (2/26/48; 156 performances) and *The Madwoman of Chaillot* with Martita Hunt and Estelle Winwood (12/27/48; 368 performances).

In 1949, the Belasco became an NBC radio theater, returning to legitimate use on November 5, 1953, with the hit comedy *The Solid Gold Cadillac*. Another big hit at the theater, George Axelrod's *Will Success Spoil Rock Hunter?*, opened on October 13, 1955, with Jayne Mansfield in a leading role.

The Pulitzer Prize was awarded to the Belasco's next hit, Tad Mosel's *All the Way Home* (11/30/60), starring Arthur Hill, Lillian Gish, Aline MacMahon and Colleen Dewhurst. The British invasion of the sixties came to the Belasco in the form of *Inadmissable Evidence* (11/30/65) with Nicol Williamson. Frank Marcus's *The Killing of Sister George* (10/5/66) was the second British play presented at the theater. It played 205 performances. Al Pacino made his Broadway debut at the Belasco in *Does a Tiger Wear a Necktie?* (2/25/69), which also starred Hal Holbrook.

As Broadway's fortunes fell in the late 1960s, so did those of the Belasco. *Oh! Calcutta!* moved to the Belasco from the Eden Theater off-Broadway on February 26, 1971, and caused a sensation with critics and audiences. It also caused a sensation with the ghost of David Belasco who was often seen in his private box on opening nights. After *Oh! Calcutta!* Belasco never reappeared. Perhaps he realized that there were to be no more successes at the theater. The Shubert Organization used the theater as a final home for musicals on their last legs like *Ain't Misbehavin'*. It also leased the space to a succession of shows that had little chance for success. These included *The Rocky Horror Show* (which later became a cult movie), *An Almost Perfect Person*, *The Goodbye People* and *Hide and Seek*. These plays quickly came and went. The 1986–87 season was devoted to the works of Shakespeare presented to the city's school children by the New York Shakespeare Festival.

The New York City Landmarks Preservation Commission designated the interior and exterior of the theater a landmark. The Commission stated that it was in "An elegant neo-Georgian style reminiscent of town house architecture and specifically intended to suggest the intimate drama presented by Belasco within." The theater's interior "represents an early monument in the development of the 'little theater' movement." The theater has also been dubbed a "distressed" theater by the theater's unions which enable the theater to receive a break on minimums and fees.

BENCHLEY, ROBERT (1889–1945) Broadwayites have never felt much generosity toward their drama critics, so it's all the more amazing that nary a harsh word was

Robert Benchley

ever spoken against Robert Benchley. The Massachusetts native and Harvard graduate was dramatic editor for the old *Life Magazine* for a decade and drama critic for the *New Yorker* magazine. He was also managing editor of *Vanity Fair* magazine, which might seem like a contradiction since mismanagement was more his style.

His curious, bumbling style was best exemplified by his monologue "The Treasurer's Report," which he performed on Broadway in *No, Sirree!* and later in the *Music Box Revue of 1923*. This experience on the stage may have humbled him, for during his years reviewing plays, he seldom had a bad word to say about actors.

Benchley was a man of opposites. On the one hand, he was a chary onlooker in the game of life; when he attempted to play the game, he was often a bemused incompetent. On the other hand, he was a deft satirist who honed his skills at the Algonquin Round Table *(q.v.)*. He numbered among his closest friends Dorothy Parker, she of the rapier wit, and Robert E. Sherwood, journalist and playwright. In truth, he was a bemused optimist whose charm and poise remained unshaken until pushed beyond the breaking point.

Benchley first exhibited his off-center humor at Harvard, where his pranks included introducing a Chinese storekeeper as Professor Soong of the Imperial University of China. Benchley presented Professor Soong at a Harvard victory dinner where the learned guest lectured on Chinese football, with Benchley providing the translation.

He went to New York and to work at the *New York Tribune Sunday Magazine* in 1916 and the *New York Graphic* the following year. After his tenure at the *Tribune,* Benchley evaluated himself as the "worst reporter, even for his age, in New York."

Benchley's move to *Vanity Fair* introduced him to Parker and Sherwood. Parker and Benchley became friends with Sherwood through the kind of bizarre event that would befall Benchley throughout his life. The *Vanity Fair* offices were on 44th Street, down from the Hippodrome theater *(q.v.)*. Appearing at the time were a troop of midgets who couldn't resist hectoring the six-foot-seven Sherwood when they spied him on the street. Sherwood was afraid to go out for lunch alone and employed Benchley and Parker as bodyguards against the midget hordes.

At *Vanity Fair,* Benchley, Parker and Sherwood found themselves at odds with editor Frank Crowninshield. When Crowninshield fired Parker, Benchley and Sherwood resigned in protest. As Benchley put it, "I was getting in a rut."

Benchley was amazed to find himself on Broadway in *No, Sirree!* in which he performed the "Treasurer's Report." This show was a collaboration by members of the Round Table, and its success led to Benchley's repeating his monologue in the *Music Box Revue of 1923* and later in vaudeville. Benchley followed his Broadway appearance in many short films for MGM and some feature films that portrayed him as a somewhat bumbling drunk, which he was not. True, he was one of the great drinkers but it never seemed to affect him. It simply softened the edges of an already well rounded personality.

Benchley's wit was carefully reported by himself. He wrote his many essays with a gentle, if exasperated, wry humor. He usually attributed his more stinging barbs to Dorothy Parker.

His death on November 21, 1945, from a cerebral hemorrhage, was a shock to his family and friends, but even near death he kept up his characteristic style. The hemorrhaging was brought on by a series of nosebleeds which couldn't be stopped. Benchley had brought a book of essays to the hospital and was making notes in the margins. The last note, at the end of an essay called "Am I Thinking" by James Harvey Robinson, read: "NO. (and supposing you were?)."

Benchley's son Nathaniel became a well known author, and his grandson Peter is best known for writing *Jaws.*

BENNETT, ROBERT RUSSELL (1894–1981)   The influence of the Broadway musical extends beyond Times Square. Robert Russell Bennett, Broadway's primary orchestrator, was one of its most influential talents, one whose work reached thousands of people. In all, it was estimated that he worked on over 300 Broadway shows from *Daffydill* (1922) to *The Grass Harp* (1971). The sounds he introduced influenced the way we hear music and the way others interpreted it.

He made his first stage appearance when he was only three years old in a production starring Julia Marlow. But in spite of this early experience, acting wasn't for him. Music was more his calling, and he made his professional debut in 1910 playing the piano, violin and bass. His parents were his first teachers, and he then went on to study with composer-conductor Carl Busch. In 1919, he was commissioned by T.B. Harms Company to orchestrate several tunes including "An Old Fashioned Garden" by Cole Porter *(q.v.)*. Following that came *Daffydill* and his first Broadway orchestration, *Wildflower* (1923) with a score by Vincent Youmans *(q.v.)*, Otto Harbach *(q.v.)* and Oscar Hammerstein II *(q.v.)*. He continued to work with Hammerstein on most of the lyricist's shows—including his last, *The Sound of Music* (1959).

Bennett was awarded a Guggenheim Fellowship and studied with Nadia Boulanger in Paris in 1926. His own compositions include the "Charleston Rhapsody" (1926), "Sights and Sounds" (1929) and several symphonies. He also composed two one-act operas, *Endymion* (1927) and *The Enchanted Kiss* (1935). His full-length opera, *Marie Malibran* debuted in 1944.

He was best known for his Broadway orchestrations. He worked with most of the leading composers, including Jerome Kern *(q.v.)* (*Show Boat, The Cat and the Fiddle, Sunny*, and *Sweet Adeline);* George Gershwin *(q.v.)* (*Of Thee I Sing);* Cole Porter *(q.v.)* (*Kiss Me Kate);* Frederick Loewe *(q.v.)* (*My Fair Lady*, and *Camelot* both with Philip J. Lang); Burton Lane *(q.v.)* (*Finian's Rainbow* and *On a Clear Day*) and Arthur Schwartz *(q.v.)* (*Inside U.S.A., By the Beautiful Sea* and *A Tree Grows in Brooklyn*). His work for Richard Rodgers *(q.v.)* was best known. These shows included *Oklahoma!, Allegro, South Pacific, The King and I, Flower Drum Song* and *The Sound of Music*. He also orchestrated and arranged Rodgers' themes for the television series "Victory at Sea" (1952).

Among his many awards are an Emmy (1963) for original music composed for television and an Academy Award (1955) for *Oklahoma!*

Bennett died on August 18, 1981.

BERLIN, IRVING (1888–1989) Composer and lyricist Irving Berlin was certainly the most successful and prolific songwriter in American history. His songs span over 50 years from his first song, "Marie from Sunny Italy" (1907, lyrics only) to his last performed song, "An Old Fashioned Wedding" (1966), written for a revival of *Annie Get Your Gun*.

During the six decades of his career, he was the composer most able to chart America's taste in popular song and he influenced scores of others in his field.

Irving Berlin Courtesy ASCAP.

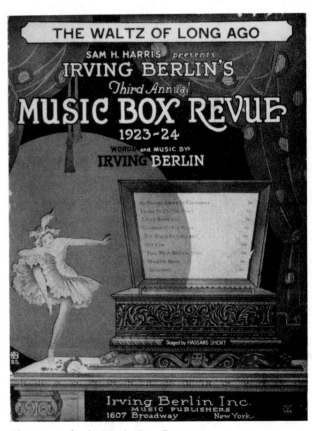

Sheet music for the Music Box Revue

He was born Israel Baline in Mohilev, Russia, on May 11, 1888. When Berlin was five, his family settled on the Lower East Side of New York. After the death of his father, when he was eight, he left school and by his teens was singing in Bowery saloons and restaurants. Songwriting was just becoming big business, and he began writing lyrics for others' tunes and plugging songs for publishers. His first song, "Marie from Sunny Italy," had music by M. Nicholson. Although he never learned to read music, Berlin was on the way to becoming a professional songwriter. In 1909, he was hired as a staff lyricist by the Ted Snyder Company, and soon Berlin matched his words to his own music. The next year, he performed in vaudeville and then musical comedy in *Up and Down Broadway*. His first big success, "Alexander's Ragtime Band," was published in 1911 and catapulted Berlin to the top of his field.

In 1914, having already had songs interpolated into revues and musicals, he saw his first full Broadway score presented. The show was *Watch Your Step* and presented the song "Play a Simple Melody." During World War I, Berlin joined the U.S. Army and was inspired to write "Oh, How I Hate To Get Up in the Morning!" The song appeared in an all-soldier revue, *Yip! Yip! Yaphank!* (8/19/18), which also featured another big hit, "Mandy." Also written for the show but unused was "God Bless America." It wasn't heard until Kate Smith introduced it in 1939.

The young composer was so successful that he was asked to contribute most of the score to the *Ziegfeld Follies of 1919 (q.v.)*. For the annual revue, he wrote the theme song of the *Follies*, "A Pretty Girl Is Like a Melody." Reacting against the extravagance of the *Follies*, Berlin joined with Sam H. Harris and built the Music Box Theater *(q.v.)*. There, the two partners presented Berlin's *Music Box Revues* (1921, 1922, 1923, 1924), a series of small scale but lush revues that introduced such songs as "Say It with Music"; "Pack Up Your Sins and Go to the Devil"; "Learn to Do the Strut"; "An Orange Grove in California"; "What'll I Do" and "All Alone." The Marx Brothers starred in Berlin's next show, *The Cocoanuts* (12/8/25).

George Gershwin and Irving Berlin Photo by George Gershwin. Courtesy ASCAP.

His next smash hit song was contributed to the musical *Betsy* (12/28/26); the song was "Blue Skies." He returned to the *Ziegfeld Follies* in 1927 with a score that included "Shaking the Blues Away," sung by Ruth Etting. Berlin's next score was for *Face the Music* (2/17/32), which featured the songs "Let's Have Another Cup of Coffee" and "Soft Lights and Sweet Music." *As Thousands Cheer* (9/30/33) followed with a cast that included Clifton Webb, Marilyn Miller and the great Ethel Waters, who introduced one of the most powerful and dramatic of all theater songs, "Supper Time." Other hits from the score were "Easter Parade"; "Harlem on My Mind"; "Heat Wave" and "How's Chances?"

Berlin spent the remainder of the 1930s in Hollywood writing, primarily for Fred Astaire and Ginger Rogers, such movie scores as *Top Hat* (RKO, 1935), *Follow the Fleet* (RKO, 1936) and *Carefree* (Fox, 1938). He also contributed scores to two Alice Faye vehicles, *On the Avenue* (Fox, 1937) and *Alexander's Ragtime Band* (Fox, 1938), as well as other films.

Berlin returned to Broadway May 28, 1940, with *Louisiana Purchase* and the songs "Fools Fall in Love," "It's a Lovely Day Tomorrow" and the title song. During World War II, Berlin wrote and appeared in another all-soldier show, *This Is the Army* (7/4/42). Berlin reprised his rendition of "Oh, How I Hate to Get Up in the Morning" and appeared in the subsequent movie version.

His greatest show, *Annie Get Your Gun,* starred Ethel Merman *(q.v.)* and Ray Middleton. The show opened on May 16, 1946, and played for 1,147 performances. The excellent score showed Berlin wasn't merely a Tin Pan Alley tunesmith, with each number supporting the plot and reflecting the character singing it. Furthermore, the songs worked equally well offstage on the hit parade. "Anything You Can Do," "Doin' What Comes Natur'lly," "The Girl That I Marry," "I Got Lost in His Arms," "I Got the Sun in the Morning" and "They Say It's Wonderful" all achieved lasting success. But the most successful of all the songs was "There's No Business Like Show Business," which has become the unofficial anthem of the entire entertainment world.

Annie Get Your Gun was followed by *Miss Liberty* (7/15/49) and *Call Me Madam* (10/12/50) with Ethel Merman starring. *Miss Liberty* featured "Let's Take an Old Fashioned Walk," and *Call Me Madam* presented "It's a Lovely Day Today" and "You're Just in Love." *Mr. President* (10/20/62) was Berlin's last score and the least successful of his shows, running only 265 performances.

Among the many awards he received are the Medal for Merit for *This Is the Army;* the Legion of Honor; a Congressional Gold Medal for "God Bless America," as well as an Academy Award for "White Christmas" (1942).

Irving Berlin contributed more hits than any of his contemporary Broadway composers. His more than 800 songs captured the spirit of the nation unlike that of any other songwriter. He died on September 22, 1989.

BERNSTEIN, LEONARD (1918–1990) Although best known for his work in the classical music field, Leonard Bernstein has had enormous success as a Broadway composer. Born in Lawrence, Massachusetts, on August 25, 1918, Bernstein began his music studies with Helen Coates and Heinrich Gebhard. He was educated at the Boston Latin School and Harvard University. At Harvard, he continued his studies with Walter Piston, Edward Burlingame Hill and Tillman Merritt. He then attended the Curtis Institute, Philadelphia, under Randall Thompson, Isabelle Vengerova and Fritz Reiner. Next, he became assistant to Serge Koussevitzky after an apprenticeship. In 1943, he assisted Artur Rodzinski as conductor of the New York Philharmonic. When guest conductor Bruno Walter became ill, Bernstein, in the best show business tradition, took over the baton and became a star.

His first show, *On the Town* (12/28/44), was based on a Jerome Robbins ballet for which Bernstein had

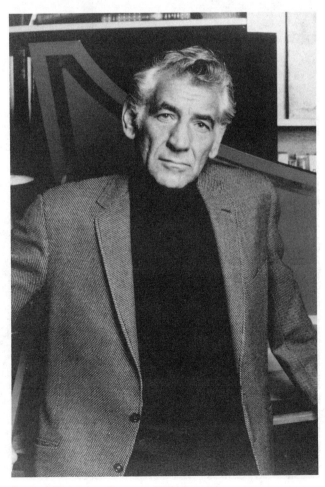

Leonard Bernstein Courtesy ASCAP.

written the music. The ballet, *Fancy Free* (1944), was adapted by Robbins, Bernstein and lyricist/librettists Betty Comden and Adolph Green *(q.v.)*. The exceptional production opened December 28, 1944, and ran for 462 performances. Comden and Green also starred in the production, which featured Chris Alexander, John Battles, Ray Harrison, Alice Pearce, Nancy Walker and ballet star Sono Osato.

The success of *On the Town* led to another collaboration with lyricists Comden and Green resulting in another great show, *Wonderful Town* (2/25/53). George Abbott *(q.v.)* directed the cast, which included Rosalind Russell and Edith Adams as two sisters from Ohio out to conquer New York. This production ran for 559 performances.

In 1950, Bernstein contributed incidental songs to a production of *Peter Pan* starring Jean Arthur. Bernstein supplied the lyrics as well as the music for the songs in *Peter Pan*, a task he repeated in 1955 for a show called *All in One*. It featured Tennessee Williams's *(q.v.)* one-act play *27 Wagons Full of Cotton* and Bernstein's one-act opera *Trouble in Tahiti*, which was written in 1952. The show was not a success and only ran for 47 performances.

His next show, *Candide* (12/1/56), was a failure, but the album, recorded by Goddard Lieberson for Columbia Records, made the show a cult favorite. It was revived in 1971—a production that closed out of town. It wasn't until 1974, when the show was revised for Broadway with Harold Prince producing and directing, that *Candide* achieved greater success, running for 740 performances. The show then entered the repertory of the New York City Opera with Harold Prince again directing.

The year after *Candide*, Bernstein's most popular musical, *West Side Story*, premiered. Arthur Laurents provided the book and Stephen Sondheim *(q.v.)* the lyrics to the retelling of Shakespeare's *Romeo and Juliet* as a love story of two New York City teenagers from different ethnic backgrounds. Larry Kert and Carol Lawrence played the lovers and introduced some of the musical theater's most enduring songs: "Somewhere," "Maria," "I Feel Pretty" and "Tonight." Jerome Robbins directed the production, which opened September 26, 1957, and ran for 732 performances.

Bernstein's heavy conducting and composing schedule prevented him from pursuing a steady career writing for Broadway. His next show, *1600 Pennsylvania Avenue*, opened on May 4, 1976, almost 20 years after *West Side Story*. Alan Jay Lerner *(q.v.)* contributed the libretto and lyrics. Unfortunately, the show only played seven performances on Broadway.

Leonard Bernstein died on October 14, 1990.

Though Bernstein did not write as much as some of the other songwriting greats like Kern, Rodgers or Berlin, the quality of his scores is unsurpassed.

BIJOU THEATRE 209 W. 45th Street. Architect: Herbert J. Krapp. Opening: April 12, 1917; *The Knife*. The Bijou was built by the Shuberts *(q.v.)*, but because of its small size, it never achieved much success. In 1918, Tallulah Bankhead made her first Broadway appearance here in *The Squab Farm*.

During the Depression, while other theaters were transformed to movies or radio use, the Bijou was shuttered. There was the occasional film booking during the forties and fifties, such as the American premiere of *The Red Shoes*.

The theater reopened as a legit house in 1957. The first production of Eugene O'Neill's *A Moon for the Misbegotten* reinstated the short-lived legitimate policy. In 1962, the theater reopened as the D.W. Griffith Theater, a movie theater. Its first presentation, *The Connection*, opened October 3, 1962.

The next year, the theater was sold again and became a Japanese cinema house called the TOHO. The film *Yojimbo* opened there January 22, 1963, as the first attraction.

In 1973, the Bijou again became a legitimate theater under its original name. However because of its small

Bijou Theatre program

Bijou Theatre featuring His Honor Abe Potash   Courtesy Billy Rose Theater Collection

size and the high operating costs of Broadway productions, the theater could be used for only small, intimate shows without stars or big production values. *Mummenschanz,* a mime theater, was the most notable tenant. It played at the Bijou for 1,326 performances. The Bijou ended its spotted history when it was demolished along with the Helen Hayes *(q.v.)* and Morosco *(q.v.)* theaters to make way for the Marriott Marquis Hotel.

THE BILLBOARD   *The Billboard* is the oldest of all amusement trade papers. It was once the most widely read until *Variety (q.v.).* W.H. Donaldson and his partner James F. Hennegan founded the paper in 1894. The first issue came out November 1, 1894, under the name *Billboard Advertising.* The monthly covered traveling shows, circuses, vaudeville, etc., only as a sideline and from the viewpoint of their use of outdoor billboard advertising. In 1897, *Billboard Advertising* became *Billboard,* and in 1900 Donaldson bought out Hennegan's

interests. Donaldson expanded the publication to include more entertainment news and in May of that year made *Billboard* a weekly. By the next year, *Billboard* was regularly covering dramatic, stock and repertory theater, music, operas, minstrel shows, vaudeville, burlesque, circuses, carnivals, street fairs and amusement parks.

Along with the news of the entertainment world, *Billboard* provided many services for performers. The paper forwarded letters to performers on the road who listed their addresses as simply, "The Billboard." *Billboard* also published complete schedules of acts and their locations.

As the years ·went by, *Billboard* marked the passing of vaudeville, variety, burlesque *(q.v.)* and other forms of entertainment. Television, movies and music became the dominant entertainment media, and *Billboard* reflected this change. In 1946, it began regularly charting the top pop artists and their record sales. By the sixties,

Variety (q.v.) had surpassed *Billboard* as the premier entertainment weekly, and *Billboard* concentrated on music news and statistics.

BILLY ROSE THEATER   See NEDERLANDER THEATER.

BILLY ROSE'S DIAMOND HORSESHOE   See CENTURY THEATER.

BILLY ROSE MUSIC HALL   See ED SULLIVAN THEATER.

BILTMORE THEATER   261 W. 47th Street. Architect: Herbert J. Krapp. Opening: December 7, 1925; *Easy Come, Easy Go* (moved from the George M. Cohan Theater). The Biltmore Theater has had a spotty history. Despite its prime location, the theater has had few long runs. It was built by the Chanin Brothers, who would eventually build, and lose, six theaters in Times Square. The Biltmore, with 1,000 seats, was an ideal size to serve plays and musicals equally well. The theater was the first built on the north side of 47th Street.

In its first years, the Biltmore's offerings were, for the most part, unexceptional. They included such moderate hits as *Kongo* (3/30/26; 135 performances); *Loose Ankles* (8/16/26; 161 performances); *The Barker* (1/18/27; 225 performances); and *Jimmie's Women* (9/26/27; 217 performances).

Later in the 1920s, the Biltmore was host to a controversial play, *The Pleasure Man* (10/1/28) by Mae West. The show was closed by the police only two days after its premiere. Among the shocking proceedings on the stage was a party of female impersonators.

A long dry spell hit the Biltmore in the midst of the Depression. It didn't have a hit until January 1, 1934 with the opening of *Big Hearted Herbert*, which played for 154 performances. But the modest success wasn't enough to keep the theater profitable. The Chanins lost the Biltmore as well as their other holdings.

To the rescue came the Federal Theater Project *(q.v.)* with its *Living Newspapers*, a series of shows that dramatized current events on the stage. *Triple-A Plowed Under* (3/14/36; 85 performances), the first *Living Newspaper*, urged farmers and consumers to join in a common goal of better incomes for the farmers and more inexpensive food for the consumer.

Injunction Granted (7/24/36) played to full houses until October 20, 1936. The play traced the history of the American labor movement and proved to be quite controversial. Like many of the *Living Newspapers*, *Injunction Granted* did not hide its point of view, which was resolutely pro labor.

Hallie Flanagan, head of the Federal Theater Project, wrote a memo to the show's creators after the opening night. In part, it stated, "The production seems to me special pleading, biased, an editorial, not a news issue.

Whatever my personal sympathies are I cannot, as custodian of federal funds, have such funds used as a party tool."

Among the only businesses showing a profit during the Depression were the movie studios. Warner Brothers bought the Biltmore and installed George Abbott *(q.v.)* as its principal producer. His first production at the Biltmore was the John Monks Jr. and Fred Finklehoffe comedy *Brother Rat* (12/16/36; 575 performances), starring Jose Ferrer, Eddie Albert, Ezra Stone and Frank Albertson. It was the theater's first big hit.

After two failures, *Brown Sugar* and *All That Glitters*, Abbott again struck gold with his production of *What a Life* (4/13/38; 538 performances). The main character of Clifford Goldsmith's comedy, Henry Aldrich, is fondly recalled by generations of radio listeners. Ezra Stone played Henry. Also in the cast were Eddie Albert, Betty Field and Butterfly McQueen.

The next big hit at the Biltmore was the terrifically successful *My Sister Eileen* (12/26/40; 866 performances) by Jerome Chodorov and Joseph Fields *(q.v.)*. They later adapted their hit play into the musical *Wonderful Town*. It starred Shirley Booth, JoAnn Sayers and Morris Carnovsky under George S. Kaufman's *(q.v.)* direction. Tragically, the real Eileen was killed in an auto accident while driving to New York to attend the opening night performance.

Abbott gave the Biltmore another hit (which would later be adapted to radio and movies) *Kiss and Tell* (3/17/43; 962 performances) by F. Hugh Herbert. It was a comedy with the unlikely subject of teenage pregnancy. The production starred Richard Widmark, Joan Caulfield and Jessie Royce Landis in the leads.

Fred Finklehoffe, one of the authors of *Brother Rat* produced the Biltmore's next hit, *The Heiress* (9/29/47 410 performances), a dramatization by Ruth and Augustus Goetz of Henry James's *Washington Square*. It was directed by the brilliant but much hated Jed Harris and starred Basil Rathbone, Patricia Collinge, Peter Cookson and Wendy Hiller.

David Merrick's *(q.v.)* first producing effort, *Clutterbuck*, opened at the Biltmore on December 3, 1949. It played 218 performances, primarily through the aggressive public relations stunts *(q.v.)* ordered by Merrick.

Beginning in 1952, the theater was leased to CBS. Another George Abbott-directed production opened at the Biltmore, reinaugurating its legitimate policy. *Take Her, She's Mine* (12/21/61; 404 performances) by Phoebe and Henry Ephron starred Art Carney, Phyllis Thaxter and Elizabeth Ashley and was produced by Harold Prince.

Elizabeth Ashley would appear also in the next attraction at the Biltmore, Neil Simon's *(q.v.)* *Barefoot in the Park* (10/23/63; 1530 performances). Mike Nichols directed the play, which also starred Robert Redford, Kurt Kasznar and Mildred Natwick.

The biggest hit in the Biltmore's history was *Hair* (4/29/68; 1,750 performances) by Galt MacDermot, James Rado and Gerome Ragni. The musical included such top-10 hits as "Aquarius," "Good Morning Starshine" and the title number. *Hair* was more than just a rock musical. It was one of the last of the truly influential Broadway musicals. The staging and loose construction of the script as well as the unconventional score influenced both theater professionals and audiences. Many audiences came to *Hair* in search of vicarious thrills while they viewed the counterculture from the safety of an orchestra seat. But *Hair* was a phenomenon of its time. A later revival presented at the Biltmore in 1977 was a failure.

Hair was the Biltmore's last big hit. On November 10, 1987, the New York City Landmarks Preservation Commission designated the interior of the theater a landmark. The Commision stated that the theater's auditorium is "a fine example" of the Adamesque style. On December 10, 1987, the Biltmore suffered a fire of mysterious origins. The stage area and front of house was damaged by the fire, but luckily no structural damage occured, although the theater's ornate plaster work was damaged. The police said that vagrants had been using the theater as a drug haven.

On February 16, 1988, the theater was auctioned off. It was sold for $5.35 million to Morris Gluck, a businessman who promised to retain the building's function as a theater. Gluck purchased the building from Sam Pfeiffer who had purchased the building two years before from David Cogan, the owner of the building since 1958.

BOCK AND HARNICK   Songwriters Bock and Harnick were the preeminent musical theater composing team of the 1960s. They showed an almost sweet regard for their characters' humanity and displayed an ability to universalize the problems and dreams of these characters in such shows as *Fiddler on the Roof* and *The Rothschilds*. But their work could also be satirical and sophisticated, especially in their shows *The Apple Tree* and *Fiorello!*

Jerry Bock (1928–   )   Composer Jerry Bock was born in New Haven, Connecticut on November 23, 1928. His early musical comedy successes included the Sammy Davis Jr. vehicle *Mr. Wonderful* (3/22/56), which ran for 383 performances.

Sheldon Harnick (1924–   )   Lyricist Sheldon Harnick was born in Chicago, Illinois, on April 30, 1924. After writing for the Northwestern University Waa-Mu shows, he achieved his first professional success as a contributor to revues including Leonard Sillman's *New Faces of 1952* (5/16/52) and Ben Bagley's *Shoestring Revue* (3/2/57).

The two songwriters collaborated for the first time on a book musical, *The Body Beautiful,* which premiered on January 23, 1958. Unfortunately, the show ran only 60 performances, but the score was well received and appreciated by Bock and Harnick's contemporaries.

Their second outing, *Fiorello!*, astounded Broadway when it won the coveted Pulitzer Prize for drama. *Fiorello!* opened on November 23, 1959, with Tom Bosley as the feisty mayor Fiorello La Guardia. Supporting him were Ellen Hanley, Pat Stanley, Patricia Wilson, Eileen Rodgers and Nathaniel Frey. *Fiorello!* played 796 performances and established Bock and Harnick as a top-grade songwriting team.

Their next effort was also a period piece. *Tenderloin* (10/17/60) starred Maurice Evans as a righteous minister who took it upon himself to clean up the notorious Tenderloin section of Manhattan. Although the show was not entirely successful, it did have a well-crafted, solid score. *Tenderloin* played 216 performances.

She Loves Me (4/23/63), a major effort for the team, was based on the Ernst Lubitsch classic film, *The Shop Around the Corner.* There were 23 songs in the superior score (a typical Broadway score only contains 12–16 songs). The title song achieved some fame. The underappreciated show was produced and directed by Harold Prince and starred Jack Cassidy, Barbara Cook, Barbara Baxley, Nathaniel Frey and Daniel Massey. *She Loves Me* managed to run 302 performances.

Their next Broadway assignment was their masterwork, *Fiddler on the Roof,* one of the greatest musicals ever written. *Fiddler on the Roof* opened on September 22, 1964. It had a superior book by Joseph Stein and brilliant direction and choreography by Jerome Robbins. Some people feel that *Fiddler on the Roof* represents the finest achievement in musical comedy. Although only "Sunrise, Sunset" achieved success outside of the show, the entire score is masterfully integrated into the script. Zero Mostel triumphed in the role of Tevye. Other cast members included Maria Karnilova, Joanna Merlin, Julia Migenes, Austin Pendleton, Beatrice Arthur and Bert Convy. *Fiddler on the Roof* played 3,242 performances, making it, for a while, Broadway's longest-running musical.

The team followed *Fiddler on the Roof* with *The Apple Tree* (10/18/66). Consisting of three one-act musicals, *The Apple Tree* featured a superb performance by Barbara Harris. She was joined by Alan Alda and Larry Blyden. The stories included Mark Twain's "The Diary of Adam and Eve"; Jules Feiffer's "Passionella" and Frank R. Stockton's "The Lady or the Tiger." The score was marvelously playful with a wide range of emotion and humor. The show played 463 performances.

Bock and Harnick's last Broadway musical as a team was *The Rothschilds.* The show opened on October 19, 1970, and, although it ran 505 performances, it was not a financial success. The show, and especially the score, were not light enough for most audiences. However, though unappreciated at the time, the show (or at least the score) is now considered an artistic success. *The Rothschilds* starred Hal Linden, Paul Hecht, Christopher Sarandon, Robby Benson, Keene Curtis and Jill Clayburgh.

After the team's breakup, Jerry Bock retired from the musical theater. Sheldon Harnick went on to provide lyrics to Richard Rodgers's *(q.v.)* music for *Rex* (4/25/76). Unfortunately, that show, Harnick's last Broadway offering, was a failure. His later attempts to mount a Broadway production included musicalizations of the movie *It's a Wonderful Life* and Dickens's *A Christmas Carol*. Neither has made it to New York.

BOLTON, GUY (1884–1979) Playwright and novelist Guy Bolton was born in Broxbourne, England, on November 23, 1884. His parents were American, and the family soon returned to the United States. He was educated at the Pratt Institute in Brooklyn and the Ecole de Beaux Arts, Paris.

Bolton was one of the most prolific playwrights and librettists of the 20th century. He wrote for productions in both New York and London in a career spanning more than 50 years. He wrote 57 musical libretti.

His first play, *The Drone*, was written in collaboration with Douglas J. Wood and premiered on December 30, 1912, at Daly's Theater, London. His last work was the musical *Anya*, which opened at the George Abbott Theater *(q.v.)* on November 29, 1965. In between, he collaborated with many authors, among them George Middleton (*Hit-the-Trail-Holiday*, 1915; *Thought*, 1916; *Polly with a Past*, 1917; *Adam and Eva*, 1919; *The Light of the World*, 1920; *The Cave Girl*, 1920; *Polly*, 1929); Philip Bartholomae (*Very Good Eddie*, 1915; *Tangerine*, 1925); Fred Thompson (*Lady, Be Good!*, 1924; *Tip-Toes*, 1925; *Rio Rita*, 1927; *The Five o'Clock Girl*, 1927; *Song of the Drum*, London, 1931; *Seeing Stars*, London, 1935; *Swing Along*, London, 1936; *This'll Make You Whistle*, London, 1936; *Going Places*, London, 1936; *Going Greek*, London, 1937; *Hide and Seek*, London, 1937; *The Fleet's Lit Up*, London, 1938; *Bobby Get Your Gun*, London, 1938; *Magyar Melody*, London, 1939; *Follow the Girls*, 1944).

His most successful collaboration was with P.G. Wodehouse. The team of Wodehouse, Bolton and Jerome Kern *(q.v.)* created the Princess Theater shows. These were considered the first successful intimate musicals, a dramatic response to the opulent revues and musicals then on Broadway. The Princess Theater shows were smart and sophisticated for their time, and they were the first attempts to link songs to characterization. Bolton's collaboration with Wodehouse included *Have a Heart*, 1917; *Oh, Boy!*, 1917; *Leave It to Jane*, 1917; *The Riviera Girl*, 1917; *Miss 1917*, 1917; *Oh, Lady! Lady!!*, 1918; *The Girl Behind the Gun*, 1918; *Oh, My*

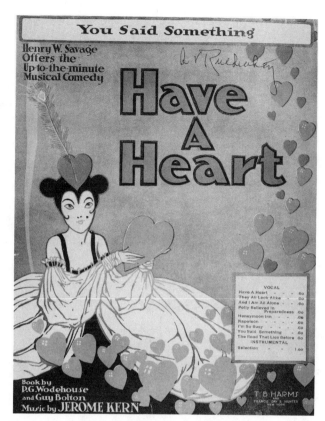

Sheet music for Have a Heart

Dear!, 1918; *The Rose of China*, 1919; *Sitting Pretty*, 1924; *Oh, Kay!*, 1926; *The Nightingale*, 1927; and *Anything Goes*, 1934.

Among the composers and lyricists who contributed scores to Bolton librettos were Cole Porter *(q.v.)*, Jerome Kern, George and Ira Gershwin *(q.v.)*, Rodgers and Hart *(q.v.)*, Wright and Forrest, Harry Tierney, Vernon Duke *(q.v.)*, Howard Dietz *(q.v.)*, Burton Lane *(q.v.)* and E.Y. Harburg *(q.v.)*.

Guy Bolton died in London, England, on September 5, 1979.

BOOTH THEATRE 222 W. 45th Street. Architect: Henry B. Herts. Opening: October 16, 1913; *The Great Adventure*. The Sam S. Shubert Theatre *(q.v.)* and the Booth Theatre were designed together as one building. The combination of the Booth and Shubert's shared facade forms Times Square's most famous pedestrian thoroughfare—Shubert Alley. The architectural firm responsible for the design of the theaters was Herts & Tallant, the firm that also designed the Helen Hayes *(q.v.)*, the Longacre *(q.v.)*, the New Amsterdam *(q.v.)*, the Liberty *(q.v.)* and the Lyceum *(q.v.)*.

The Venetian Renaissance building was built by producers Winthrop Ames and Lee Shubert *(q.v.)*. The two men had built the New Theater on Central Park West, the northernmost location for a Broadway theater. That theater failed, and the impresarios decided to

Booth Theatre Courtesy Billy Rose Theater Collection.

locate their next theater in a more traditional spot off Times Square. When their theater was finally finished in 1913, they named it after noted 19th century actor Edwin Booth.

Because building laws prohibited protruding ornamentation, the theater was decorated with polychromed stucco. The theater's intimacy is due to both its fine design and its small capacity with room for 808 people, including standees.

The first production to find success at the Booth was *Experience* (10/27/14; 255 performances), starring William Elliott. The next play, *The Bubble* (4/5/15; 176 performances), was also a hit. Another success, Clare Kummer's *A Successful Calamity* (2/5/17; 144 performances), starred William Gillette, Estelle Winwood, William Devereaux and Roland Young.

Although those shows were all hits, none had the impact of *Seventeen* (1/22/18; 225 performances), based on the story by Booth Tarkington. Ruth Gordon, Paul Kelly and Gregory Kelly starred in the comedy. *Seventeen* was followed by many now forgotten hits, including the George Arliss vehicle *The Green Goddess* (1/

18/21; 440 performances). *Seventh Heaven* (10/30/22; 683 performances), starring Helen Menken and George Gaul, was an enormous hit by Austin Strong.

Helen Hayes *(q.v.)* played a flapper in *Dancing Mothers* (8/11/24; 311 performances) with Mary Young as her mother—it was the mother who turned out to be the real hellion. James Cagney was a dancer in two editions of the *Grand Street Follies*. The first premiered in 1928 with Cagney as choreographer; the second premiered a year later.

During the 1930s, hits were scarce at the Booth. The theater's location kept it booked, but the plays did not enjoy long runs. Only when the decade was half over did the theater finally have a hit, George S. Kaufman *(q.v.)* and Moss Hart's *(q.v.)* great comedy *You Can't Take It with You* (12/14/36; 837 performances). The zany comedy won the Pulitzer Prize, as did the next great hit at the Booth—*The Time of Your Life* (10/25/39; 185 performances). William Saroyan's play starred Eddie Dowling, Gene Kelly, William Bendix, Celeste Holm, Edward Andrews and Julie Haydon.

Rose Franken's *Claudia* (2/12/41; 453 performances),

starring Dorothy McGuire and Frances Starr, was the first big hit of the forties. Elisabeth Bergner, Vera Allen, Irene Worth and Victor Jory starred in *The Two Mrs. Carrolls* (8/14/44), which eventually ran 585 performances. Another forties hit was Norman Krasna's *John Loves Mary* (2/4/47; 423 performances) starring Nina Foch in her Broadway debut.

Come Back Little Sheba (2/15/50; 190 performances), William Inge's first Broadway play, starred Shirley Booth and Sidney Blackmer. British comedienne Beatrice Lillie held forth in *An Evening with Beatrice Lillie* (10/2/52; 278 performances). Another Britisher, Cyril Ritchard, starred along with Eddie Meyeroff in Gore Vidal's sardonic comedy *Visit to a Small Planet* (2/7/57; 388 performances). Henry Fonda and Anne Bancroft starred in William Gibson's *Two for the Seesaw* (1/16/58; 754 performances). Paddy Chayefsky's spiritualistic comedy/drama *The Tenth Man* (11/5/59; 623 performances) was the last hit that the Booth enjoyed in the fifties. Tyrone Guthrie directed Broadway veterans Jack Gilford, Lou Jacobi, Jacob Ben-Ami, George Voskovec and future director Gene Saks.

In the 1960s, Julie Harris triumphed in *A Shot in the Dark* (10/18/61; 389 performances), this time appearing on the stage along with Walter Matthau, Gene Saks, Diana van der Vlis and William Shatner. Mike Nichols directed Alan Arkin, Eli Wallach and Anne Jackson in Murray Schisgal's *Luv* (11/11/64; 902 performances). The decade ended with a production of Leonard Gershe's *Butterflies Are Free* (10/21/69; 1,133 performances).

That Championship Season (9/14/72; 844 performances), was written by Jason Miller, who won a Pulitzer Prize for his efforts. The play transferred from the Public Theater to the Booth. The next hit at the Booth was also a transfer from the Public Theater—Ntozake Shange's *For Colored Girls Who Have Considered Suicide When the Rainbow Is Enuf* (8/29/76; 742 performances).

Bernard Pomerance's *The Elephant Man* continued in the growing trend of plays opening in nonprofit theaters and then transferring to Broadway. The nonprofit arena took the place of the long out of town tryout tour. *The Elephant Man* (4/19/79; 916 performances), first produced by the Theater at Saint Peter's Church, starred a series of leading men, including Philip Anglim, David Bowie and Mark Hamill.

Stephen Sondheim's *(q.v.) Sunday in the Park with George* (5/2/84), with book and direction by James Lapine, starred Bernadette Peters and Mandy Patinkin, and won the Pulitzer Prize. Herb Gardner's *I'm Not Rappaport* (11/19/85; 1,070 performances), starring Judd Hirsch and Cleavon Little was a recent long run.

On November 4, 1987, the New York City Landmarks Preservation Commission designated the interior and exterior of the theater a landmark. The Commission stated: "The Venetian-inspired design by Henry B. Herts is particularly distinguished and responsive to its prominent site" on Shubert Alley. Its interior "is expecially notable for its wood paneling, which enhances the acoustical qualities of the space."

BRADY, DIAMOND JIM (1856–1917) Diamond Jim Brady, dubbed King of the Great White Way, is the symbol of the gay nineties. A constant companion to singer and actress Lillian Russell and a great gourmand, Brady was known for his largesse and largeness.

Brady was the most flamboyant of the Broadway characters at the turn of the century. He would frequent the great lobster palaces of Broadway with a different woman on his arm nightly. It was rumored that Brady gave extravagant presents to his dates, but apparently the stories were just hype. Brady reportedly only lent the jewelry to his paramours for as long as the evening lasted. Once the lady was escorted home, her jewelry would stay with Brady.

He certainly would not have missed a brooch or two. Word on the Rialto had it that Brady owned 26,000 diamonds. He acquired his wealth from the sale of railroad equipment. At that time, before income taxes, conglomerates and foreign imports, barons of industry like Rockefeller, Carnegie and Brady could acquire vast fortunes. Brady was said to have amassed a personal fortune of $12 million.

Brady encouraged his reputation. He certainly had a sense of humor about himself, as indicated in an interview of 1909. Brady proclaimed, "The trouble with our American men is that they over dress. They do not understand that beauty unadorned is adorned the most. Now, I take it that I am considered a handsome man and one who would be called well dressed. Never by any chance do I permit more than seventeen colors to creep into the pattern of my waistcoat. Moreover, I consider that twenty-eight rings are enough for any man to wear at one time. The others may be carried in the pocket and exhibited as occasion requires. A similar rule applies to the cuff and shirt studs. My favorite stud is a petrified prune. Three of them may be worn without entirely covering the shirt bosom. Diamonds larger than door knobs should never be worn except in the evening."

No one could have made that much money and still been the bon vivant the newspapers made him out to be. In fact, Brady was a serious businessman who had excesses but never ones that affected his acumen.

Brady liked to indulge himself, and he could afford to. He arrived at restaurants sporting diamonds on his cuffs, his watch chain, and his stickpin. His diamonds were large yellow chunky stones, and it was reported in the *New York Herald* that his stickpin "lit up the road ahead of him like the headlight of a locomotive." But most of the stories and depictions of Brady were grossly exaggerated. Apparently he never wore more than a few stones at a time and then with as much reserve as a man of his size could.

Brady did live up to at least one of the legends surrounding him: He could eat vast quantities of food. The owners of Rector's *(q.v.)* reputedly called him, "the twenty-five best customers we had." According to Morris Lloyd in his book, *Incredible New York,* Brady boasted, "Whenever I sit down to a meal, I always make it a point to leave four inches between my stummick and the edge of the table. And then, when I can feel 'em rubbin' together pretty hard, I know I've had enough."

Playwright and newspaperman Channing Pollock remembers Brady eating 36 oysters as an appetizer to lunch. But for all his culinary excesses, Brady was a teetotaler. He more than made up for it with his eating habits and could sometimes down several quarts of orange juice to quench his thirst.

Once Florenz Ziegfeld *(q.v.)* accompanied Brady to dinner and ordered exactly what Brady ordered. While Brady enthusiatically cleaned his plate, Ziegfeld emptied his plate into a nearby wine bucket. At the end of the meal Ziegfeld presented the overflowing container to Brady and informed him that all that food was in his stomach. But Brady was unfazed.

Perhaps he should have listened. Brady died of an intestinal ailment at Johns Hopkins Hospital.

BRADY, WILLIAM A. (1863–1950) Producer William Brady is perhaps best remembered as a presenter of melodramas with a refined air about them. Plays like *Trilby* and Barrie's *Alice Sit-By-the-Fire* are the best known of his productions. He always mounted his productions with the utmost taste, regardless of the cost, featuring performers under his management such as Helen Hayes *(q.v.)*, Douglas Fairbanks, Grace George (his second wife), Alice Brady (his daughter), and Helen Gahagan.

Brady began his theatrical career in San Francisco in 1882. Following a move to New York, he leased the original Manhattan Theater *(q.v.)* starting in 1896 and then built the Playhouse Theater in 1911 for his own productions. The next year, he also became manager of the 48th Street Theatre *(q.v.)*.

Brady was one of the few producers—Ziegfeld *(q.v.)* was another—who saw the powers of the new art of motion pictures. Brady owned a film-distribution company, the World Film Corporation, in the late teens. He was president of the National Association of the Motion Picture Industry for five years beginning in 1915. President Woodrow Wilson appointed him chairman of a committee to organize the movie industry in 1917.

Among the plays Brady produced on Broadway were, *The Two Orphans* (3/28/04); *Way Down East* (12/14/03); *Uncle Tom's Cabin* (3/4/01); *Foxy Grandpa* (2/17/02);

The Pit (2/10/04); *Trilby* (5/8/05); *Bunty Pulls the Strings* (10/10/11); *Baby Mine* (8/23/10); *Bought and Paid For* (9/26/11); *The White Feather* (2/4/15); *The Ruined Lady* (1/19/20); *The Skin Game* (10/20/20); *Street Scene* (Pulitzer Prize) (1/10/29); and *A Church Mouse* (10/12/31).

Although Brady produced many of the most successful shows in Broadway history, he was often broke. In fact, in 1922 he admitted being broke 10 times in the preceding 20 years. *Variety* commented: "That carries no real news to Broadway, which knows that the line between solvency and stringency among Broadway producers is proverbially thin at most times. Being Broadway broke is a condition that has no equivalent in any other business save that, perhaps, of the race course. The purseless producer of today may be the prospective bonanza king of tomorrow."

Brady was broke before and would be broke again, but for all the ups and downs of his career he will be remembered as a smart entrepeneur who was able to adjust to the immense changes in popular culture as the century turned. The range of Brady's productions, from *Way Down East* to *Street Scene* was not that wide but demonstrates an ability to adapt to the changes in popular taste, an ability not shared by some of his contemporaries.

BRICE, FANNY (1891–1951) Fanny Brice was among the most beloved of all Broadway performers. Her range of characterization was incredible. She could be the broad, physical comedienne telling her Jewish-accented stories of Becky in the ballet and Mrs. Cohen at the beach as well as the lonely, soulful torch singer who introduced "My Man" to America. Later in her career, she added still another facet to her stage personality, the irrepressible hellion, Baby Snooks.

She was born in New York on October 29, 1891, and early on saw the stage as the natural outlet for her flamboyant personality. She studied under James O'Neill, and in 1910 made her stage debut in *A Royal Slave* at a Brooklyn vaudeville theater. That appearance drew the attention of Florenz Ziegfeld *(q.v.)*, who starred her in seven editions of his *Follies*—1910, 1911, 1916, 1917, 1920, 1921, 1923. She later appeared in two more *Ziegfeld Follies (q.v.)*, this time presented by the Shuberts *(q.v.)*—1934, 1936. Her other stage appearances were in *The Honeymoon Express,* 1913; *Nobody Home,* 1915; *Music Box Revue,* 1924; *Fioretta,* 1929; and two for her husband producer Billy Rose—*Sweet and Low,* 1930, and *Crazy Quilt,* 1931. Among the songs she introduced are "My Man," "Rose of Washington Square," "Second Hand Rose" and "I Found a Million Dollar Baby in a Five and Ten Cent Store."

After leaving the theater, she had a successful career on radio, mostly as Baby Snooks. She made a few movies and recordings, but they didn't reflect her importance as a star. Fanny Brice died on May 29, 1951.

Sheet music for Ziegfeld Follies of 1921

Her life provided the material for the musical *Funny Girl* (3/26/64), which was later transferred to the screen. The sequel, *Funny Lady,* also became a hit movie. Barbra Streisand portrayed Fanny Brice in all three projects.

BRILL BUILDING 1619 Broadway. Architect: Victor Bork Jr. Completed in 1930. The Brill Building has long been the home of America's music publishers. The 10-story building at the corner of 49th Street and Broadway was the embodiment of Tin Pan Alley. Until the 1960s and a wave of mergers and corporate takeovers, the Brill Building was the home to most of the large music publishers and the ancillary businesses that help to fuel the phenomena known as the American popular song.

BROADHURST THEATER 235 W. 44th Street. Architect: Herbert J. Krapp. Opening: September 27, 1917; *Misalliance.* The Broadhurst Theater was built by the Shuberts and playwright/producer George H. Broadhurst as a companion for the Plymouth Theater (*q.v.*). They were located next to another two linked theaters, the Booth (*q.v.*) and the Shubert (*q.v.*). Like the two earlier theaters, the Broadhurst and Plymouth had a pedestrian alley adjacent to their side exits. The alley, now closed off, was parallel to the more famous Shubert Alley.

The 1,155-seat theater has been among the most popular Broadway theaters, housing major hits in almost every decade since its opening. It opened with William Faversham's production of George Bernard Shaw's *Misalliance* (9/27/17; 52 performances). The New York run gave little indication of the play's later renown.

The Broadhurst was equally suitable for musicals. The first hit musical was the Nora Bayes vehicle, *Ladies First* (10/24/18; 164 performances). Rachel Crothers's *39 East* (3/31/19; 160 performances) starred Alison Skipworth. *Smilin' Through* (12/30/19; 175 performances), later a successful movie, starred Jane Cowl, who coauthored the play with Allan Langdon Martin.

During the 1920s, there were many hits at the theater, including George S. Kaufman (*q.v.*) and Marc Connelly's *Beggar on Horseback* (2/12/24; 224 performances); Michael Arlen's *The Green Hat* (9/15/25), starring Katharine Cornell (*q.v.*) as the bride whose husband commits suicide on their wedding night; and Jed Harris's production of *Broadway* (9/16/26; 603 performances) by Philip Dunning and George Abbott (*q.v.*).

Almost as successful was the DeSylva, Brown and Henderson (*q.v.*) musical, *Hold Everything* (10/10/28; 413 performances). The hit song was "You're the Cream in My Coffee." George S. Kaufman returned to the Broadhurst with *June Moon* (10/9/29; 272 performances), written in collaboration with Ring Lardner.

George Abbott and Philip Dunning produced another

The Brill Building Photo Jeff Slotnick.

hit at the Broadhurst, Ben Hecht and Charles Mac-Arthur's screwball comedy *Twentieth Century* (12/29/32; 154 performances). Another play first presented at the Broadhurst became a hit movie. The gangster drama *The Petrified Forest* (1/7/35; 194 performances) featured Leslie Howard and Humphrey Bogart in the leads. Later that year, Helen Hayes *(q.v.)* turned in an astounding performance in Gilbert Miller's production of *Victoria Regina* (12/26/35; 204 performances). The drama also starred Vincent Price.

The 1940s were marked by a series of now forgotten musicals, including *Boys and Girls Together* (10/1/40) with Bert Lahr, *High Kickers* (10/31/41) with George Jessel and Sophie Tucker and *Early to Bed* (6/17/43) with an exceptional Fats Waller score. Helen Hayes starred in Anita Loos's comedy *Happy Birthday* (10/31/46; 564 performances), one of the few nonmusicals produced by Rodgers and Hammerstein *(q.v.)*.

The 1950s were a decade of great successes at the Broadhurst. The revival of Rodgers and Hart's *(q.v.)* sardonic musical *Pal Joey* (12/25/40; 540 performances), starring Harold Lang and Vivienne Segal actually played longer than the original production. Rosalind Russell gave a tremendous performance in a role that will be forever linked with her, *Auntie Mame* (10/31/56; 639 performances). *The World of Suzie Wong* (10/14/58; 508 performances) starred William Shatner and France Nuyen. The decade closed with a huge hit, the Pulitzer Prize–winning musical *Fiorello!* (11/23/59; 796 performances). Jerry Bock and Sheldon Harnick *(q.v.)* wrote the score, and George Abbott and Jerome Weidman contributed the book with Abbott also directing. Robert E. Griffith and Harold Prince produced. Tom Bosley achieved fame as Mayor Fiorello La Guardia.

Tommy Steele starred at the Broadhurst in *Half a Sixpence* (4/25/65; 512 performances), a musicalization of H.G. Wells's novel *Kipps*. Among the outstanding elements in the production was Hilary Knight's beautiful poster *(q.v.)*. Woody Allen's comedy *Play It Again, Sam* (2/12/69; 453 performances) starred the comic along with Anthony Roberts and Diane Keaton. *Twigs* (11/14/71; 289 performances), by George Furth, featured a song by Stephen Sondheim *(q.v.)*. Sada Thompson starred.

A huge hit (for a while it was the longest running musical in Broadway history) was *Grease*. It originated off-Broadway and moved to the Broadhurst on June 7, 1972. After skipping around to other theaters, it eventually tallied 3,388 performances. Neil Simon's *(q.v.) The Sunshine Boys* (12/20/72; 538 performances) followed. *Godspell*, another long running off-Broadway musical, moved to the Broadhurst, eventually managing 2,118 performances. Bob Fosse's choreographic smash hit, *Dancin'* (3/27/73; 1,774 performances) was another hit at the popular theater. During the 1980s, the theater hosted another smash, Peter Shaffer's *Amadeus* (12/17/

80; 1,181 performances) with Ian McKellen and Tim Curry in the leads.

The Broadhurst is one of Broadway's most successful theaters. Although the shows it houses are not always hits, the theater is usually booked and always popular with producers and audiences alike.

On November 10, 1987, the New York City Landmarks Preservation Commission designated the exterior of the theater a landmark. The Commission stated that the Broadhurst was important because "the facade of the theater is a response to its Shubert Alley location and the earlier Shubert-Booth pair."

BROADWAY THEATRE 1681 Broadway. Architect: Eugene DeRosa. Opening: As the Colony motion picture theater December 25, 1924. As legitimate theater December 8, 1930; *The New Yorkers*. Vaudeville theater owner B.S. Moss opened Universal's Colony Theater as a premier motion-picture house on Christmas Day, 1924. Soon after the introduction of sound pictures, the theater adapted a legitimate policy. Its name was changed to the B.S. Moss's Broadway Theatre with the opening performance of its first show, Cole Porter's *(q.v.) The New Yorkers* (12/8/30; 158 performances). There was a previous Broadway Theatre at Broadway and 41st Street, but that theater was razed in 1929.

The 1,765 seat theater was suited only for large musicals. *The New Yorkers* filled the bill. The show, which starred Jimmy Durante, Fred Waring and His Pennsylvanians and Ann Pennington, is best remembered for the song "Love for Sale," which caused enormous controversy. In fact, the song was banned from radio broadcast.

The name of the theater was slightly altered to Earl Carroll's Broadway Theatre with the opening of his *Vanities (q.v.)* (9/27/32; 87 performances), starring Milton Berle, Helen Broderick, Robert Cummings and Patsy Kelly. Even the great Harold Arlen *(q.v.)* and Ted Koehler song "I've Got a Right to Sing the Blues" couldn't help the box office.

The failure of the first shows at the theater was a symptom of the general malaise that afflicted Broadway during the early years of the Depression. In 1932, the theater began a vaudeville policy, but it too failed. Another unsuccessful musical, *The O'Flynn* (12/27/34; 11 performances) opened at the theater and quickly closed. The theater's name reverted to B.S. Moss's Broadway Theatre on October 12, 1935, when it again showed films. The name was changed yet again to the Cine Roma on February 25, 1937, with the showing of *Lealta Di Donna*. The name was changed for the last time to simply Broadway on November 13, 1940, when Walt Disney's cartoon feature *Fantasia* opened.

Fantasia was not a success for Disney or the theater, and again the Broadway housed live theater. A number of musicals that had opened at other houses moved to

Broadway Theatre   Courtesy Billy Rose Theater Collection.

the Broadway to finish their runs. The first musical to originate at the theater under the new policy was Irving Berlin's *(q.v.) This Is the Army,* which opened, significantly on July 4, 1942 (113 performances). *This Is the Army* starred armed services members Burl Ives, Gary Merrill, Ezra Stone and Philip Truex. Composer Irving Berlin also starred, and he reprised "Oh, How I Hate to Get Up in the Morning," which he first sang in *Yip Yip Yaphank* (8/19/18).

Oscar Hammerstein II *(q.v.)* based his all-black production of *Carmen Jones* (12/2/43; 582 performances), on Bizet's *Carmen.* Another classic, *The Beggar's Opera,* was transformed by Duke Ellington and John Latouche into *Beggar's Holiday* (12/26/46; 111 performances) with

Alfred Drake, Zero Mostel, Avon Long and Herbert Ross in the cast.

During the 1950s, a series of unsuccessful productions were staged at the Broadway until Sammy Davis Jr. held forth in *Mr. Wonderful* (3/22/56; 383 performances). The show introduced a hit song, "Too Close for Comfort." A short period of Cinerama films followed before the theater hosted its finest show —David Merrick *(q.v.)* and Leland Heyward's production of *Gypsy* (5/21/59; 702 performances). Ethel Merman *(q.v.)* had the greatest role of her career singing brilliant Jule Styne *(q.v.)* and Stephen Sondheim *(q.v.)* standards.

Merman returned to the theater in its next genuine hit, the 1966 revival of *Annie Get Your Gun.* The revival moved to the Broadway from Lincoln Center. Robert Goulet and David Wayne appeared in *The Happy Time* (1/18/68; 286 performances) with a fine John Kander and Fred Ebb score.

Director Harold Prince (*q.v.*) brought his reinterpretation of the musical, *Candide* (3/10/74), by John Latouche, Leonard Bernstein (*q.v.*), Lillian Hellman, Dorothy Parker and Richard Wilbur, to the Broadway. Another revival, a black version of *Guys and Dolls,* was less successful two years later. The seventies closed with Harold Prince directing Patti LuPone in the Andrew Lloyd Webber and Tim Rice musical *Evita* 9/25/79; 1,568 performances).

The Broadway's current occupant, *Les Miserables* (3/12/87), received mixed reviews in London but it has certainly conquered American critics and audiences. As it runs, the theater is being surrounded by a new skyscraper, which incorporates the auditorium in its design. Broadwayites commended the developers for sparing the historic theater from destruction. On November 17, 1987, the New York City Landmarks Pres-

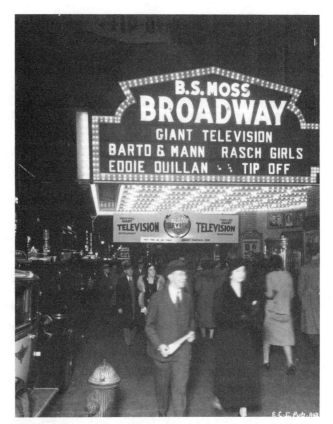

The dreaded television comes to the Broadway Theatre   Courtesy Billy Rose Theater Collection.

ervation Commission denied landmark status to the theater.

BROOKS ATKINSON THEATER

BROOKS ATKINSON THEATER 256 W. 47th Street. Architect: Herbert J. Krapp. Opening: February 15, 1926; *The Night Duel.*   The Brooks Atkinson Theater was originally owned by the Chanin Brothers, who named it after actor Richard Mansfield. The Mansfield was the third theater built by the Chanins, but they lost them all in the Depression. The 999-seat house proved perfect for intimate dramas and small revues. In its early years, when production costs were lower and musicals did not have to occupy huge barnlike theaters, some book shows held forth from the Mansfield's stage.

The Mansfield had its first hit with a now forgotten drama, *The Ladder* (10/22/26; 794 performances). Antoinette Perry, for whom the Tony Awards (*q.v.*) are named, made her second appearance at the Mansfield in this show. Despite negative reviews, millionaire Edgar B. Davis liked the show and poured over $500,000 into it to keep it running.

With *The Ladder,* the theater's only success in its first years, and unprofitable at that, the Chanin's booking policy was clearly amiss. Lew Fields (*q.v.*) took over booking the house and renamed it Lew Fields's Mansfield Theater. He opened his new theater on October 26, 1928, with Rodgers and Hart's (*q.v.*) *Present Arms*

CLIFFORD C. FISHER's

World Famous

FOLIES BERGERE

CAST OF 100
40 PRINCIPALS
60 EUROPEAN BEAUTIES

TWICE NIGHTLY

7.30 and **9.25** MATS. WED. SAT. & SUN. at 3

Prices **50¢ 75¢ $1**
(PLUS TAX)

SAT. SUN. and HOL. EVE.
75c, $1.00, $1.50 (PLUS TAX)

ALL SEATS RESERVED

World's Greatest Stage Value

SHUBERT

BROADWAY THEATRE
BROADWAY *at* 53RD ST.

Phone Circle 5-7783

Flier for Folies Bergere

(10/26/28; 147 performances) and followed it with Rodgers and Hart's *Chee-Chee* (9/25/28; 32 performances).

Fields next produced and starred in the aptly titled *Hello Daddy!* (12/26/28; 196 performances). He hired his children Herbert *(q.v.)* and Dorothy *(q.v.)* to supply the book and lyrics respectively. Jimmy McHugh wrote the music.

The theater was then renamed the Mansfield Theater, and here *Indiscretion,* a failure, opened on March 4, 1929. The theater's next show, *The Green Pastures* (2/26/30; 640 performances), was Marc Connelly's adaptation of Roark Bradford's *Ol' Man Adam an' His Chillun,* a retelling of Old Testament stories. Connelly won the Pulitzer Prize for his efforts.

When the Chanins lost the theater during the Depression, the Mansfield went dark. From March to December of 1932, there were no bookings at the theater. The Depression continued to take its toll, and the theater did not house a hit until *Behind Red Lights* (1/13/37; 176 performances), a play about prostitution on the fashionable East Side of Manhattan.

A revue, *Meet the People* (12/25/40; 160 performances), introduced Nanette Fabray to Broadway audiences. *Anna Lucasta* (8/30/44; 957 performances) arrived direct from the American Negro Theater in Harlem. Hilda Simms, Canada Lee and Earle Hyman starred. Actress Ruth Gordon's autobiographical play, *Years Ago* (12/3/46; 206 performances) starred Bethel Leslie.

After a series of failures, the Mansfield spent the 1950s as a television theater. On September 12, 1960, owner Michael Myerberg renovated the auditorium and renamed the theater after critic Brooks Atkinson. The opening show was a lively musical revue *Vintage '60.* Despite songs by such future greats as Sheldon Harnick *(q.v.)* and Fred Ebb and cast members Bert Convy and Michele Lee, the show ran only eight performances.

The first hit under the theater's new name was also Neil Simon's *(q.v.)* Broadway debut. *Come Blow Your Horn* opened on February 22, 1961, and ran for 677 performances. The success of *Come Blow Your Horn* proved to be the theater's only long-running hit in the sixties until Peter Nichols's brilliant *A Day in the Death of Joe Egg* (2/1/68; 154 performances). Bravura performances by Albert Finney and Zena Walker kept the play running until the actors strike of 1968 (June 17–19) forced it to close.

The first hit of the 1970s was Julian Barry's biographical play, *Lenny* (5/26/71; 453 performances). Cliff Gorman electrified audiences as comic Lenny Bruce. The theater's next success was the two–character comedy *Same Time, Next Year* (3/13/75; 1,453 performances) with Ellen Burstyn and Charles Grodin. Lanford Wilson's play *Talley's Folly,* moved here from off-Broadway on February 20, 1980. Judd Hirsch starred with Trish Hawkins. There would not be another hit at the

Brooks Atkinson until *Noises Off* (12/11/83), Michael Frayn's knockabout farce, starring Dorothy Loudon, Brian Murray and Victor Garber.

A surprise hit was scored by comedian Jackie Mason in his one-man show, *The World According to Me!* Borscht-belt-comic Mason opened on December 22, 1986, to rave reviews and sold out houses.

On November 4, 1987, the New York City Landmarks Preservation Commission designated the interior and exterior of the theater a landmark. The Commission stated: "Its facade is an excellent example of the romantic, eclectic 'modern Spanish' style.' Its interior, reflecting the supervision of Roman Melzer, formerly architect to Czar Nicholas II of Russia, is an unusually handsome design."

BROWN, JOHN MASON See CRITICS.

BROWN, LEW See DESYLVA, BROWN AND HENDERSON.

BRYANT THEATER See APOLLO THEATRE.

BURLESQUE The term *burlesque* conjures up images of strippers strutting down a runway before an audience of cigar-chewing dirty old men. But there were really two kinds of burlesque in America.

Of course, by the time of the strip acts, the burlesque shows of the first type were long gone. The original burlesque was broad parodies of popular plays and entertainments of the turn of the century. These burlesques were performed as afterpieces or during act breaks. The company would lampoon current hits using titles like: *Bad Breath, the Crane of Chowder; Hamlet and Egglet; Much Ado About a Merchant of Venice; Julius the Seizer; Roman Nose and Suet;* and *The Charge of the Hash Brigade.* Popular performers weren't sacred either. Jenny Lind became Jenny Leatherlungs, as portrayed by Lotta Crabtree, and Sarah Bernhardt became Sarah Heartburn. Harrigan and Hart were among the best loved presenters of burlesques. In the early 1870s, they presented *The Two Awfuls,* a satire on *The Two Orphans.*

The other burlesque was one that started with lower-class entertainments. Saloons, beer gardens and honky-tonks were poor man's vaudeville with boxing matches between the coarse acts. In 1886, Niblo's Gardens in New York presented what is generally agreed to be the precursor to modern musical comedy—*The Black Crook.* The formation of the show was entirely accidental. A French ballet troupe was due to perform at the Academy of Music in downtown New York. However, the theater burned down, and the company was stranded. At the same time, a melodrama, *The Black Crook,* was due to open at Niblo's Garden. The play was a weak reworking of the Faust legend, and William Wheatley, manager of Niblo's, brought in the ballet company to upgrade the entertainment. The show ran over five hours but the audience was transfixed at the sight of lightly clothed ballerinas.

But burlesque had an even earlier precursor. Two decades before *The Black Crook* astonished audiences in New York and around the country, Lydia Thompson arrived on our shores with her English Blondes. The show was similar to our own lady minstrel shows with double-entendre songs and artfully posed beauties clad in gauzy material. The success of these two entertainments was unique in American theater history. *The Black Crook* played for over 16 months in Manhattan and made over a million dollars. Lydia Thompson's troupe trouped across the country for over 20 years, gradually adding to their show dances and skits and comics. A Chicago newspaper critic hit the nail on the head when he observed that the girls "really had nothing to offer but their persons." These two phenomena and their common denominator, "girls, girls, girls," didn't escape the notice of showmen.

Soon small circuits or "wheels" were set up like vaudeville's Orpheum Circuit and United Booking Office. Lawrence Weber was the biggest manager, and the most extensive wheels were the Columbia and Mutual. Sam T. Jack opened the most prestigious of these theaters—the New York Theater. T.E. Miaco, Samuel Scribner and the Minsky's were other moguls of the "art." The Minsky's Winter Garden Theater on Houston Street in downtown Manhattan was their flagship, which also included the Apollo *(q.v.)* and Republic *(q.v.)* theaters in midtown.

While there were also comic sketches, illustrated songs and boxing demonstrations, it was the girls who people came to see. Burlesque was not for the faint of heart or the prudish. While vaudeville had a strict sense of morals, burlesque had none at all. The Empire Circuit gave orders to "give it as raw as it will come."

This, of course, brought trouble in the form of the local constabulary. There were often secret exits that could be used in case of a raid. Comedian Joey Bishop remembers red bulbs in the footlights that would warn a stripper not to go too far because there were police on the premises. Local jails often had a revolving-door policy. When the fine was paid, the performers went back to the theaters and then back to jail and so on.

Later, comic sketches and dances were introduced. Comedians were classified in four basic groups: the straight man, the Dutch comic, the blackface comic and the rube or pansy. They performed off-color sketches or bits that utilized essential props: the bladder, the slapstick, the blush detector, the dentist's chair and the gun. Sketches and blackouts were named by their subjects—The Butcher Bit, In the Haystack, The Schoolroom, Meet Me Round the Corner, Pick Up My Old Hat, Fireman Save My Wife, etc. The top banana or lead comedian had his own favorite sketches. Comedian

Bobby Clark originated the often-imitated courtroom sketch wherein he played the judge.

Joey Bishop recalls the attitude of the burlesque comics: "Every burlesque comic felt like burlesque was the end of the road for him. If he flopped, he had no place else to go. So he adopted an attitude that would get him through life and he did his humor that way also. There's an attitude about burlesque that you cannot teach someone . . . that's a feeling. The burlesque comic always looked like he'd rather be somewhere else besides where he was. You can't try to be funny in burlesque. You can't come out with a funny costume and then try to be funny on top of it. You must play seriously on top of it." Cuckolded husbands and disreputable doctors were forever doomed to run in and out of closets and doors, jump out windows, hide under beds and be humiliated in court.

The burlesque sketch had a rural attitude about it. It always had the farmer topping the city slicker, usually a traveling salesman. Another typical burlesque stereotype was the rube or hick. The hick was always the stupidest human imaginable. Joey Bishop recollects a sketch called "Elmer" that illustrates this. "Elmer, the hick, is lost and must go to sleep in a farmhouse. The only room available is the farmer's daughter's room. The hick and the daughter are lying in bed and she says, 'Why don't you do something to amuse me?' And he takes out a harmonica and plays it."

Joey Bishop remembers his years in burlesque as a young comic. "I worked for Izzy Herst on the Herst Circuit. We could never say 'Hell' or 'Damn' in burlesque, we could never take the lord's name in vain. So we used to say, 'Cheeeese and crackers' or 'What the hey.' I don't ever remember seeing any burlesque sketch, and I've seen them all, that was in bad taste or that was vulgar."

The dancers were direct descendants of Lydia Thompson and Little Egypt. They often had exotic names like Fatima and Mazeppa and often had specialties like Sally Rand's fan dance. These women shimmied, hootchy-cootched, belly danced and twirled their tassels across the stage in less and less clothing as time went on. In the 1890s, "leg shows" were in vogue. Then came quick-change artists who undressed and dressed in full view of the audience who could catch a glimpse of undergarment. Then around 1917 came strippers who kept their bras and panties on. These acts were usually saved as the "Extra-Added Attraction" at the end of the bill. Later, if the customer hadn't had his fill, he could often meet the teaser at the stage door. By the 1920s, the public demanded more—after all they could see legs on any flapper. So the girls showed their breasts and later disrobed down to pasties and G-strings, but they often put material under their strings to simulate pubic hair.

Soon tradition was thrown to the wind and, instead of closing the bill, striptease became the raison d'etre of burlesque. In 1923, *Variety (q.v.)* noted that burlesque was "ninety nine per cent strip with the other just to pad out the show."

Naturally the lead comics saw greener pastures in vaudeville, musical comedy, radio and the movies. If they were any good, they honed their craft and got out. Leon Errol, Rags Ragland, Danny Thomas, Phil Silvers, Jackie Gleason, Red Buttons, Abbott and Costello, Zero Mostel, Herbie Faye, Jack Pearl, W.C. Fields, Red Skelton, Joe E. Brown, Fanny Brice *(q.v.)*, Bert Lahr, Clark and McCullough and others all started in burlesque and achieved fame elsewhere.

As its talent left (even Gypsy Rose Lee, its most famous stripper, gave it up), burlesque became more and more vulgar. During Prohibition, outlawed entertainments moved into saloons, where women like Texas Guinan *(q.v.)* could be seen for free with only a small charge for bootlegged hootch. Movies, too, made inroads on the burlesque audience, and soon motion pictures came to be shown between burlesque acts. Mayor LaGuardia cracked down on New York burlesque theaters and in 1942 the city refused to renew the licenses of the burlesque houses—the end was near.

Today, burlesque is confined to seedy flop houses in a few cities, and often live sex acts are featured. Old-time burlesque is glorified in Broadway shows like *Grind* and the enormously successful *Sugar Babies,* showing that good burlesque never goes out of fashion.

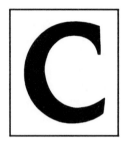

CAFE DE L'OPERA Southeast corner of 42nd Street and Seventh Avenue. The Cafe de l'Opera was the American equivalent of Paris's Cafe de Paris. This was one of the first successful cabarets in America in the years before World War I.

Louis Martin was the proprietor of the club where guests could partake of a "bottle and bird" and dance to the latest rage, the fox-trot. At midnight, a drum roll would clear the dance floor, and a show would begin featuring dance teams like Maurice and Florence Walton and Vernon and Irene Castle (*q.v.*).

The head waiter was Jules Ensaldi. He was almost as powerful as Martin himself. Ensaldi, the guard of the velvet rope, decided who was seated and who wasn't as well as more importantly where they were seated. It is thought that Ensaldi made more money than anyone at the restaurant. The more prominent patrons wanted the best tables if only to keep their social standing, and Ensaldi was the key to the best locations.

Louis Martin had the sense to keep his club intimate. Once it achieved success, Martin resisted the temptation to expand. Keeping the club small and exclusive only encouraged attempts by patrons to get reservations.

Looking down on the guests enjoying their pheasant under glass and champagne was a balcony with a mural picturing the fall of Babylon. A floor above that were the private party rooms, and on the fourth floor were the apartments for the stars of the show.

It was at the Cafe de l'Opera that many dance steps were born. After a private party for Elsie Janis on the third floor, Vernon and Irene Castle and their guests enjoyed their own band in a private ballroom upstairs. While fooling around on the dance floor, the Castles tried a new step. They went up on the beat rather than down and invented the Castle Walk. This skipping dance soon swept the country.

The Castles left the Cafe de l'Opera to open the Sans Souci with their partner Jules Ensaldi. This outing was a mixed blessing, and the place was soon closed by the fire department as it had no fire exits.

The Cafe de l'Opera lasted until World War I turned the country's thoughts to more serious matters, and the society hangouts of the early part of the century gave way to more prolitarian locales like the Automat (*q.v.*).

CANDLER BUILDING 220 W. 42nd Street. Architect: Willauer, Shape & Brady. The 24-story Candler Building, built by Coca-Cola salesman Asa Candler, was completed in 1914. The handsome terra-cotta skyscraper has remained a visual landmark since its completion.

CAPITOL THEATER 1645 Broadway, southwest corner of 51st Street. Architect: Thomas Lamb. Opening: October 24, 1919. The Capitol Theater was, at the time of its construction, the largest theater in New York. The movie palace was another step in the career of S. L. ("Roxy") Rothafel (*q.v.*), the leading manager of Broadway's motion picture theaters.

Before it became the city's entertainment hub, Times Square was an area comprised mostly of shops catering to the carriage industry. As the motor car gained popularity, the stables and carriage factories evolved into filling stations and garages. The site of the Capitol Theater was occupied by a livery stable, a blacksmith shop and a gas station. The land was owned by the Jacob Wendell estate, which was bound by somewhat Puritanical restrictions. The terms of the lease forbade the manufacture of corsets or cosmetics.

Builder Messmore Kendell recognized the importance of the underdeveloped site and leased it from the Wendell estate. He hired Thomas Lamb, a great theater architect who had already designed the Rialto (*q.v.*), and Rivoli (*q.v.*) theaters. Lamb's favorite architectural style was that of the Adam brothers. He used that and the Empire style for the auditorium, which sat 5,300 patrons.

Sherry's Restaurant, formerly on Fifth Avenue, was the source of three enormous rock-crystal chandeliers. Artist William Cotton painted beautiful murals for the auditorium walls.

Because the theater was built during World War I, construction materials, especially steel, were in short supply. Luckily, the city was constructing the IRT subway system northward from Times Square at the time. As the tunnels were completed, their trusses were sold to Kendall for use in the building of the Capitol.

When completed, the building was hailed as a masterpiece. Kendall had his own apartment at the top of the six-story building. In the apartment, Kendall could see the action on the stage by peering through a secret window. From Kendall's window above the balcony level the stage was almost a full city block away.

The stage area was the domain of Major Edward Bowes, who had an apartment suite below Kendall's. He was later known for his Amateur Hour radio show. Bowes was a part owner of the Cort Theater (q.v.) and had invested heavily in San Francisco real estate. However, Bowes had a hard time developing a viable entertainment policy for the Capitol.

The theater was beset with problems from the beginning. Right before the opening, the theater's bricklayers decided to go on strike. Left with a huge hole in the rear stage wall after the workers broke off negotiations, Kendall was forced to undertake drastic action. He called a meeting of the board and when they were assembled he passed out aprons and trowels. The board members, realizing their investment was at stake, pitched in and mended the hole.

The opening was further postponed because the lobby boasted mahogany paneling. The New York City Building Department was concerned that the theater wasn't fireproofed. They went over the entire building with blow torches, torching the mahogony to check the theater's safety.

The opening night's program consisted of a live stage show, which preceeded the feature film. The stage show was titled *Demi-Tasse*. In the cast were Paul Frawley and Mae West. Arthur Pryor's band played for the opening night revels. The evening began with an overture by the Capitol Symphony, a short color film, a travelogue, another short subject that starred a pack of talented dogs, a film of director Ned Wayburn rehearsing the evening's show and finally the revue proper.

About the only notable aspect of the revue was a song written by George Gershwin (q.v.) and Irving Caesar. The song was "Swanee," and, surprisingly, it received little attention. Gershwin's other contribution, "Come to the Moon" (written with Ned Wayburn and Lou Paley) also went unnoticed, despite its elaborate

setting. The female chorus, dressed as the Twinkle Star Girls, had electric lights in their ballet slippers that lit up on the darkened stage. By the time the opening film, *His Majesty, the American* with Douglas Fairbanks, hit the screen the battle was lost.

The show received lukewarm to negative reviews. Mae West developed a sudden case of tonsillitis after reviewers carped at her "rude way of singing." Pryor's band was also dismissed.

Although changes were made in the show, they didn't halt the theater's troubles. On October 28, 1919, four days after the grand opening, Prohibition went into effect. And at the beginning of the next week's bill, the ushers went on strike demanding the right to accept tips.

The New York Times reported on the disagreement. "Their actions attracted the attention of the audience many of whom found the strike of more interest than the screen. The boys were ordered to leave, but they refused. Several policemen were sent from the West 47th Street Station House; they arrested Herman Ingberg, one of the strikers, upon his refusal to leave, and charged him with disorderly conduct."

The negative publicity surrounding the Capitol kept audiences away in droves. The operation was losing Kendall thousands of dollars a week, money he could ill afford to lose. Kendall sold the theater to a shady character named F. J. Godsol. Godsol was owner of Goldwyn Pictures. He was also briefly jailed for selling mules to the French during World War I. Unfortunately, the French thought they had bought horses.

Godsol's first problem was what to do with Major Bowes. He decided to make the showman a vice president of Goldwyn Pictures at $25,000 a year. As managing director of the Capitol, Bowes received a similar salary. Bowes's new responsibilities at Goldwyn kept him busy, so he wasn't too upset when Godsol hired S. L. Rothafel to spruce up the theater's operation.

June 4, 1920, was the date set for the reopening of the Capitol. An advertisement boasted:

"TRIUMPHAL RE-OPENING—The Capitol—The World's Largest, Coolest, Most Beautiful Theater, Newest, Latest, Rothafel Motion Picture-and-Music Entertainment, under the Personal Supervision of S. L. Rothafel. Edward Bowes, Managing Director.

"Prices 40 cents—50 cents—75 cents—$1—No Higher (including War Tax)—Matinees, 30 cents—40 cents—No Reservations! First Come First Served!"

Roxy was busy whipping together a new gala show in the Roxy tradition. When directing the show, Roxy sat in the middle of the auditorium and shouted at the action on stage through a megaphone. The Bell Telephone Corporation's scientists were working on a new idea—the public address system. Roxy, always ready for a new invention, gladly agreed to try their experimental microphones and speaker systems.

The public address system was a huge success, saving Roxy his voice and making it unnecessary for him to run constantly from audience to stage and back. Roxy liked the idea so much that he arranged for the entire theater to be wired. Now when someone wanted to call the performers in their dressing rooms, they simply paged them over the system.

At the same time, radio station WEAF was begun in Manhattan. This early, experimental radio station even boasted sponsors like Macy's and Gimbels. WEAF wasn't content to simply broadcast from their studio. They began taking their microphones around New York and presenting live remote broadcasts. On November 11, 1922, they broadcast for the first time the Metropolitan Opera's production of *Aida* from the Kingsbridge Armory in the Bronx.

Ironically, Major Bowes was against radio for the same reason that the movies were against pay television in the fifties. He figured that people would't pay for their entertainment in theaters if it was coming into their homes for free. But Roxy saw the possibilities of the new medium and agreed to allow a broadcast from the Capitol.

On November 19, 1922, the Grand Orchestra, led by Erno Rapee, struck up "Ein Heldenleben" by Richard Strauss on the Capitol stage. It was the first time any of Strauss's music had been performed in the United States. Throughout New York and as far as WEAF's powerful signal would reach, audiences listened to the proceedings at the Capitol. Roxy was at a microphone in the wings explaining the stage action and what it meant to be in the Capitol amid all the splendor.

Of course, this made the listeners feel they were missing the action and led them to the Capitol to see for themselves the elaborate stage shows and the motion pictures. The Capitol shows became so successful that it was decided to repeat the program weekly on Sunday evenings. WEAF was also part of a small network, which meant its broadcasts were also carried in Providence, Rhode Island, and Washington, D.C.

Every Sunday, audiences heard Roxy's voice over the airwaves opening his show with the words, "Hello, everybody. This is Roxy speaking." And every show ended with Roxy signing off with the familiar words, "Good night . . . pleasant dreams . . . God bless you." Supporting Roxy, was his "gang," which included soprano Florence Mulholland, basso-profundo "Daddy" Jim Coombs and audience favorite Beatrice Belkin. The concertmaster of the Capitol Grand Orchestra was the young Eugene Ormandy.

As time went on, the radio's audience grew. The Capitol shows starring Roxy were carried by the NBC Blue Network throughout the country. Now the Capitol was the best known theater in America, and Roxy was equally famous as America's greatest showman.

The December 1925 issue of American Business Record exclaimed:

> Roxy—here is a name to conjure with! Who has not heard it—and more, who has not heard Roxy, for his is the stellar god of a new force—a "Big Timer" of the ether. When science shot lilting melodies through the air and called it radio, Roxy was born in the first pink blush of radio's morning. Before that he was S. L. Rothafel. Then came this new force. They placed a microphone before his lips, he spoke into it, and his words clutched a million hearts though the miles between were many.

Bowes wasn't happy with Roxy's success and grew increasingly miserable when people claimed they didn't even know he was associated with the Capitol. Bowes became more and more intolerant of the situation and antagonistic towards Roxy. The situation was getting worse, and clearly, something had to happen to resolve the problem. The solution came not within the Capitol Building but from without. Roxy was hired to oversee a new theater, one that would be the greatest in the world and would also, incidently, be named after him.

On July 26, 1925, Major Bowes took over the operation of the Capitol radio show and began his own career on the air. Bowes continued to present the Capitol in classy terms. He created "The Capitol Family" and continued on the NBC Blue Network.

Paul Morris in *The New York Evening World* described a typical Bowes high-class show:

> Last night I went to the Capitol Theater, where one of the most elaborate of musical entertainments garnishes the feature film. It is really extraordinary the amount of pains that are taken here to put over the music. The Capitol Orchestra is admirable. It is as large as any of the regular symphonic organizations and better than many of them. But movie fans come to be shown, not merely to be told. So there are dancers to interpret the music, and good ones, too. This week the overture was Die Fledermaus, and then they introduced Carlo Ferretti who gave us Lolita's Serenade by Buzzi-Peccia. Julia Glass, an excellent pianist, performed Rubenstein's Concerto in "Bal Masque" featuring Mlle. Desha, Miss Doris Niles and Miss Alice Wynne, and Mr. Chester Hale, the Capitol's ballet master, can be justly proud of the product of the ballet school he conducts backstage. After the feature film, a frivolous item called Soul Mates—one of those Elinor Glyn things—had been given a delightful scoring by the Capitol Orchestra, D. Melchiorre Mauro-Cottone, at the console of the Capitol's truly grand organ, rendered "Impressions of Cesar Franck" in a most admirable fashion.

Bowes realized that he needed a good assistant to help him produce Capitol revues. He found one in Chester Hale, a successful Broadway choreographer. The Chester Hale Girls, in the spirit of the later Rockettes, were terrifically popular and a great draw for the theater.

By now, the Capitol was a member of the Loew's

chain. The Loews owned a huge chain of theaters and needed shows to fill their stages. The Capitol became the flagship of the Loew's Circuit. Louis K. Sidney, who took a more egalitarian approach to the Capitol's shows, was brought in to head the work. The Capitol Grand Orchestra was headed by David Mendoza and his associate, Eugene Ormandy. It was augmented by Walter Roesner and his Capitolians.

Loew's made the Chester Hale Girls into the Chesterettes and Henry Murtaugh was hired to play the newly refurbished Capitol organ. The entire stage area was overhauled including the addition of a lift in the orchestra pit. The Capitol was now well suited to stand up to the new Roxy Theater.

Sidney changed the Capitol's shows further by introducing variety acts. One program in October 1927 featured a 55-member chorus and 40 ballet dancers in a show entitled, *The Spirit of Syncopation.* Also on the bill were performers Nora Bayes, Morton Downey, Lester Allen, Ben Bernie, Anna Case and Bobbie Arnst.

Other stars to appear on the Capitol stage were Van and Schenck, Winnie Lightner, Vincent Lopez, Georgie Tapps, James Barton, Percy Grainger, diva Mary Garden and even Sister Aimee Semple McPherson. The Capitol stage policy lasted longer than that of many of its rivals. Although in 1932 the theater claimed that 100,000 paying customers visited the theater weekly, the Depression finally took its toll and in 1935 an "all the show on the screen" policy was inaugurated.

The Capitol continued as just another movie palace, albeit a spectacular one, into the sixties. With the advent of television (a word banned on the Capitol's stage) and the flight to the suburbs, the Capitol's fortunes dwindled. The land was soon more valuable than the theater. Already, the lobby had been renovated and an escalator ran up the once glorious marble staircase.

The Capitol was razed in the mid-sixties to make way for an office block.

CARROLL, EARL (1893–1948) Earl Carroll was one of the greatest producers of extravagant musical revues in the first three decades of the century. The others were Florenz Ziegfeld *(q.v.)* and George White *(q.v.).* Carroll's revues stressed the female form and celebrated it with bawdy good humor. His shows were the closest to the burlesque *(q.v.)* tradition, and, in fact, many of his stars first achieved fame in burlesque. These included Milton Berle, Joe Cook, Sophie Tucker, Jimmy Savo, as well as Ted Healy, Jessie Matthews, W.C. Fields, Jack Benny, Helen Broderick and Patsy Kelly.

Carroll was a staff writer for a music publisher from 1912 to 1917. He wrote lyrics and music for a succession of Broadway shows, although none of his songs are played today. Among the shows he wrote for are *Pretty Mrs. Smith,* written with Alfred G. Robyn and Henry

Earl Carroll Courtesy ASCAP.

James (1914); *So Long Letty* (1916); *The Love Mill* (1916); and two editions of the *Earl Carroll Vanities (q.v.)* in 1923 and 1924.

The *Vanities* were the naughtiest of the great revues. Where Ziegfeld would make sure his girls were the best dressed showgirls, Carroll would make sure that girls he hired were the best undressed. The *Vanities* featured forgettable songs and sketches and mostly second-rate stars. The main attraction was always the girls, reflecting the producer's main interest—sex.

Carroll desired to be a producer and director, not because he felt he could contribute something to the art, but so he could capitalize on his position to meet girls. His affairs made headlines, thereby boosting ticket sales.

During Prohibition, Carroll threw a party in the Earl Carroll Theatre *(q.v.),* during which Joyce Hawley took a bath in champagne. The press exploited the party on their front pages, and the *Graphic* published a phony photo. The authorities couldn't let an event like this go unchallenged, and Carroll was hauled before a jury. He was found guilty of perjury after having stated there was no liquor at the party. Carroll served a little over half a year in jail, and again the publicity for the *Vanities* was enormous.

If anything rivaled Carroll's obsession with sex, it was his love of aviation. Carroll was a flyer during

World War I and was sent on many reconnaissance missions in France. After the war, he established a flying school in China. In 1925, Carroll became the first person to land a plane in Central Park. He received permission for the publicity stunt because he was carrying Santa Claus, who would distribute presents to children waiting in the Sheep Meadow. Joe Cook grudgingly acted as Santa Claus.

Unfortunately the weather was atrocious, with visablity next to zero and sleet beginning to fall. When Carroll attempted to land, he caught a wing of the plane on a tree. Much to the delight of the children the plane went into a ground loop before coming to rest. Carroll and Cook were unhurt but the plane was demolished.

The Depression brought bankruptcy and hard times to Broadway. Carroll was no exception, and he left New York to open the Earl Carroll Restaurant in Hollywood in December 1938. Carroll died in a plane crash on June 17, 1948. When the wreckage was located on Mt. Carmel, Pennsylvania, it was discovered that Carroll, his companion Beryl Wallace, and the crew had died before the plane hit the ground. Carbon dioxide escaped from the fire extinguishers, killing the passengers.

In an interview with *Family Circle Magazine* entitled "Your Last Day on Earth," Carroll reflected on his life. "It has been my lifework to stage and produce shows built around beautiful girls. To many people this work of mine may seem insignificant; I deal in beauty, it's true. But we are all starved and hungry for beauty; there is too little of it in the world. A hundred years from now I hope the parade of young American girls will still be walking under the sign of my theater . . . which reads: 'THROUGH THESE PORTALS PASS THE MOST BEAUTIFUL GIRLS IN THE WORLD.'"

CASA MANANA   See EARL CARROLL THEATRE.

CASINO DE PARIS   See NEW YORKER THEATER.

CASINO THEATRE (1) Broadway and 39th Street. Architects: Francis Kimball and Thomas Wisedell. Opening: October 21, 1882; *The Queen's Lace Handkerchief.*   The Casino, which stood at the southeast corner of Broadway and 39th Street, was one of the best-loved 19th century houses until it was demolished in 1930. The Moorish-style theater opened on a stormy night with a leaky roof and unfinished auditorium. But it soon recovered from its dismal premiere. Producer Rudolph Aronson presented his light opera company at the theater for its first years. In 1890, he added New York's first roof garden on top of the Casino. Productions in the 1,300-seat auditorium included early operettas and two successful shows, *Nell Gwynn* and *Erminie.*

The theater's most famous show was *Florodora,* which opened November 10, 1900, with a spectacular line of chorus girls. The original Florodora Sextette was comprised of Daisy Greene, Marjorie Relyea, Vaughn Texsmith, Margaret Walker, Agnes Wayburn and Marie L. Wilson. The Sextette elevated the chorus girl into star status. The chorus became an attraction in its own right. Florenz Ziegfeld *(q.v.)* took the concept of the Florodora Sextette and improved on it.

Florodora's publicist, Anna Marble, the wife of playwright Channing Pollock, saw that the Sextette was touted across the nation. She also pushed the show's hit song, "Tell Me Pretty Maiden," written by Leslie Stuart. The show ran for over 500 performances, one of the longest runs of the early nineteen hundreds.

Following *Florodora*'s run in 1902, the theater was involved in a lawsuit concerning its legal ownership. Lee Shubert *(q.v.)* bought the theater from the Bixby family, who owned it as an investment. The Bixbys had leased it to the Sire brothers, who in turn leased it to Charles Lederer. The affair started when Lee Shubert bought out Lederer's sublease. Lederer was happy to sell, because he was remiss in paying his rent and was about to be kicked out of the theater anyway. Shubert discovered that all the subleases were up at the same time and avoided the Sires by going to the Bixbys.

A Chinese Honeymoon (6/02/02; over 300 performances) was the Shuberts' first big hit in New York and established their reputation. Then came a succession of moderate hits, *The Runaways* (5/11/03); *Winsome Winnie* (12/01/03); *Lady Teazle* (12/24/04); and *The Earl and the Girl* (12/04/05).

The remainder of the century's first decade saw a succession of failures at the Casino. *The Social Whirl, The Blue Moon, The Gay White Way, Nearly a Hero, The Mimic World, Marcelle, Mr. Hamlet of Broadway, Havana,* and *The Girl and the Wizard* were mostly imports of English operettas with some American songs interpolated.

The Shuberts continued to keep the theater occupied with many other modest successes as well as downright flops. *The Mikado,* which had premiered at the Madison Square Roof Garden in 1902, played the Casino three times, in 1910, 1912 and 1913. None of the engagements was successful. *Up and Down Broadway* (7/18/10) contained the hit song "Chinatown, My Chinatown" by Jean Schwartz and William Jerome. *The Blue Paradise* (08/05/13; 356 performances) broke the long succession of failures with its score by Sigmund Romberg *(q.v.),* Edmund Eysler and Herbert Reynolds. The next hit at the Casino wasn't until 1922 with the production *Sally, Irene and Mary,* which ran for 318 performances.

The theater stayed dark for most of its last decade. In 1930, the Depression as well as the constant move uptown of the theater district sealed its fate, and the Casino was torn down.

CASINO THEATER (2) See EARL CARROLL THEATRE.

CASTLE, VERNON AND IRENE Vernon and Irene Castle were the premier dance team in the United States in the years preceding World War I. They were also influential in many areas outside dancing. Irene's fashions and habits were copied by thousands of young women who were just beginning to break free of the restraints of the Victorian and Edwardian eras. The couple played the major theaters in the country as well as appeared in Broadway shows and made an occasional foray into vaudeville.

Vernon Castle was born Vernon Blyth in Norwich, England, on May 2, 1887. He graduated in engineering from Birmingham University. His sister, Coralie Blyth, was married to fellow actor Lawrence Grossmith who was preparing to open his new show at the Herald Square Theater on April 8, 1907. Vernon was given a small part in the show and proved adept enough to be cast in other shows.

He appeared in *The Girl Behind the Counter* (10/1/07); *The Midnight Sons* (5/22/09); *Old Dutch* (11/22/09); and *The Summer Widowers* (6/4/10). It was during the run of the latter play that he met his future wife, Irene Foote.

Irene, born in 1893, was the daughter of the first woman to make a balloon ascension in the United States and the first man to load a Civil War cannon. She met her future husband and dance partner through social contacts and begged him to get her an audition with producer Lew Fields (q.v.). The audition was less than successful, but her friendship with Vernon eventually led to her replacing a minor character in *The Summer Widowers*. Also in the cast of that early show was a very young Helen Hayes (q.v.).

The couple were married following the closing of the show and before the opening on August 7, 1911, of their next Broadway show, *The Hen Pecks*. When *The Hen Pecks* closed, Vernon was invited to perform in a revue in Paris. His engagement was not a success; they were short of cash and decided to try their luck as a dance team in the famous Cafe de Paris. Surprisingly, they were a big hit. The French were used to rough and tumble Apache dancing, and the Castle's more romantic style took the city by storm.

On their return to the United States, they were quickly hired by Louis Martin, owner of the prestigious Cafe de l'Opera (q.v.). The restaurant was a "bottle and bird" club. Wealthy patrons dined on pheasant under glass and a bottle of champagne, while the Castles entertained. They were hired for the unheard of salary of $300 a week, which was soon raised to $600 a week.

While at the Cafe de l'Opera, they moonlighted in Broadway shows. The first was *The Sunshine Girl* (2/3/13) at the Knickerbocker Theatre. They were also playing private parties for huge sums of money. Society discovered the Castles, and soon no soiree was complete without the Castles there to entertain the guests.

One night, the team was fooling around at a birthday party for Elsie Janis. The party was in the Castles' private apartment above the nightclub. While they skipped around the dance floor, instead of coming down on the beat they went up, and a dance craze was born. The Castle Walk became the newest sensation.

The year 1913 was a year of dance crazes. There was the Turkey Trot, the Grizzly Bear, the Bunny Hug, the Lame Duck and the Camel Walk. Then came the tango and never had America seen such a suggestive and romantic a dance. The Castles excelled at them all and were at the height of their fame. A prominent critic (q.v.), Gilbert Seldes, wrote "That these two, years ago, determined the course dancing should take is incontestable. They were decisive characters, like Boileau in French poetry and Berlin (q.v.) in ragtime; for they understood, absorbed, and transformed everything known of dancing up to that time and out of it made something beautiful and new."

With everyone dancing, it seemed only natural that the Castles should open Castle House, a dignified dance hall in the Ritz-Carlton Hotel. Society was taken with the Castles and saw fit to copy not only their dance steps but their style as well. It seemed that whenever Irene changed her clothes, fashion changed also.

She wasn't really concerned with changing styles but more with wearing comfortable clothes that were easy to move in. At the beginning of her Parisian trip, she was unable to afford jewelry, so she didn't wear any and soon other women were copying her. When she received a Dutch bonnet as a present and wore it on stage, she found more and more women in the audience sporting Dutch bonnets.

By the summer of 1913, her "Castle frock" became all the rage. A newspaper article of the time described the metamorphosis. "At first, people thought she looked like a French poster and a Revolutionary heroine, and they did not think of imitating the gown. Then a young June bride had the gown copied for her trousseau. This was the beginning of several gowns a la Castle. Now the fashion has become settled as more or less artistic at smart parties."

The next year, she wore jodphurs while riding and found them more comfortable. From then on, women wore jodphurs. That same year she had her appendix removed and cut her hair into a bob in order to make it easier to handle while she was laid up. The effect was devastating. A Connecticut paper headlined the story, "Irene Castle Cuts Hair." Cecil Beaton wrote in *The Book of Beauty*, "If any one person is responsible for the appearance of the modern young lady of fashion whom we admire so much today, it is certainly Mrs. Vernon Castle."

The Castles next opened at the New Amsterdam

Theatre *(q.v.)* in the Irving Berlin show *Watch Your Step* (12/8/14). In *Watch Your Step,* Irene first wore a gown designed for her by Lady Duff-Gordon, known professionally as Lucile. The dress was an even bigger success than the show, and the Metropolitan Museum acquired it for its permanent collection.

Meanwhile, the Castles were very much in the news. They played in the roof theater of the 44th Street Theatre *(q.v.)* called Castles in the Air. They also played the basement, which was called the Castle Club. They performed there from 1:30 to 4:00 in the morning.

Vernon left to fight in World War I, and Irene continued her career. She made a few successful movies and appeared in a huge failure, Florenz Ziegfeld's *(q.v.)* revue, *Miss 1917.* On February 15, 1918, Vernon Castle died as a result of a plane crash during a training lesson in Texas. Irene tried to continue her career but without much enthusiasm. She eventually remarried and retired from the stage. She died on January 25, 1969.

Through their sense of fun and style, the Castles had influenced a generation of Americans. Arthur Murray explained why they had become such a sensation. "The Castles became all the rage by introducing elegance in modern dancing. They took long, graceful steps and danced apart, in contrast to the awkward bouncing and suggestive clinches of the animal dances. The Castles did more to make dancing acceptable in polite mixed company than any other influence."

CENTRAL THEATER See MOVIELAND.

CENTURY THEATER (1) 235 W. 46th Street, basement of the Paramount Hotel. Designer: Albert Johnson. Opening: Billy Rose's Diamond Horseshoe 1938. The Century Theater was known as Billy Rose's Diamond Horseshoe for most of its life. Impresario Billy Rose brought his show to the new theater from the Pioneer Palace of the Fort Worth Fair in 1938. The theater was designed by Albert Johnson with a patriotic color scheme—red, white and blue. The Diamond Horseshoe initially recreated an evening in the Gay Nineties as seen through the eyes of Lillian Russell and Diamond Jim Brady *(q.v.),* and Rose cast it with a number of former stars, including operatic star Fritzi Scheff, minstrel Eddie Leonard, the shimmy dancer Gilda Gray, show girl Ann Pennington and a spry 70-year-old who performed handsprings—Emma Francis. Also appearing were Joe Howard, composer of "I Wonder Who's Kissing Her Now," early talkie star Charles King and Harry Armstrong, the man who wrote "Sweet Adeline."

There was also a group of leggy chorines featuring the famous six-foot-two Stuttering Sam. She and the other beautiful chorus girls were joined by the four Rosebud girls. These women, nearly as big around as

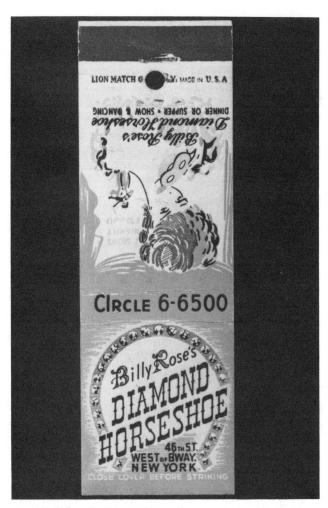

Matchbook from the Diamond Horseshoe Courtesy Vicki Gold Levi.

they were tall, taken together weighed almost 1,200 pounds.

About half way through the show's 12-year run, Rose hired Nicky Blair as manager. Blair ran other nightclubs in his career, including the Paradise, the House of (Helen) Morgan and Texas Guinan's *(q.v.)* club. Blair later opened the Carnival across the street from Madison Square Garden.

When the Diamond Horseshoe finally closed in 1951, the theater became the Mayfair. It was later renamed the Staircase and then again the Mayfair. Finally, it became the Century. Among the shows that played the Century were *On Golden Pond, Lone Star and Private Wars, Are You Now or Have You Ever Been . . .* and *Banjo Dancing.*

In the mid-1980s, the theater was devoted to the Chaiken CPA Review, a course designed to help students pass the test enabling them to become Certified Public Accountants. On November 17, 1987, the New York City Landmarks Preservation Commission denied landmark status for the theater's interior in a move that puzzled preservationists.

In January 1988, the theater was converted back to its nightclub origins. The one-time owners of Studio 54 announced that they would open the space as New York's newest club.

CENTURY THEATER (2)   See JOLSON'S 59TH STREET THEATER.

CHANIN'S 46TH STREET THEATER   See 46TH STREET THEATRE.

CHAPMAN, JOHN   See CRITICS.

CHARLES HOPKINS THEATER 153 W. 49th Street. Architects: Murphy and Dana. Opening: November 10, 1914; *The Marriage of Columbine.*   Producer Charles Hopkins built the Punch and Judy Theatre on a small parcel of land directly off Times Square in 1914. Like the Bijou *(q.v.),* which followed it three years later, the Punch and Judy was an intimate house built for small-cast, single-set plays.

The house never achieved any great success, mainly because its small size made profits difficult for even the biggest hits. Unfortunately, producers weren't interested in the limited grosses of small theaters and instead opted for medium-sized houses for their productions.

As the Punch and Judy, the theater housed few hits. In 1921, it hosted *March Hares,* a transfer from the Bijou by the Shubert Brothers *(q.v.).* The play, a romantic satire, only managed 60 performances between both houses. In 1926, in an attempt to change the theater's luck, Hopkins changed the name to the Charles Hopkins Theater. But the theater fared little better with its new name.

Productions included those on the level of *Devil In The Cheese* (12/29/26), a "fantastic comedy" that starred Fredric March and Bela Lugosi. This improbable tale concerns an archeologist who disapproves of a suitor for his daughter's hand. The hapless father eats a piece of ancient cheese discovered in the archeological dig, and the "Spirit of the Cheese" takes him inside his daughter's head where the father discovers how much

Punch and Judy Theatre   Courtesy Billy Rose Theater Collection.

she loves her boyfriend. As if this wasn't enough, the would-be husband saves everyone from bandits in the third act. Audiences were curious enough to keep the show running for 157 performances.

The next season, Hopkins presented the A.A. Milne play *The Ivory Door* (10/18/27). Henry Hull, Louise Closser Hale and Donald Meek starred in this medieval fantasy. It ran for 310 performances.

Hopkins was building a small following for what *Best Plays* editor Burns Mantle called "Charles Hopkins's funny little theater." Another A.A. Milne play was presented by Hopkins on March 4, 1931. The play was entitled *Success* when first presented in England, but the title belied its fate on Broadway. Despite the talents of Louis Calhern, Jane Wyatt, Eric Blore, Montague Shaw and Nancy Kelly, the play closed after only 72 performances. The cast would be far luckier than the play; all later achieved stardom in Hollywood.

The Depression took its toll on all Broadway theaters, and even the Charles Hopkins with its low overhead couldn't escape. Milne, one of Hopkins's favorite writers, was presented again in the theater's last legitimate season. *They Don't Mean Any Harm* opened February 23, 1932, but played for only 15 performances.

Hopkins's checkbook convinced him that the future of his theater was dim, and so, unlike many producers who couldn't accept the realities of Broadway in the Depression, Hopkins changed his theater to a movie policy.

Years later, the theater's name was changed to the World Theater and as such presented X-rated films. It was then made a member of the Embassy Theater chain, called the Embassy 49th Street Theatre. It specialized in second runs and children's fare. The theater was razed to make way for a new building in June 1987.

CIRCLE IN THE SQUARE THEATER 1633 Broadway on 50th Street. Architect: Allen Sayles. Opening: November 15, 1972; *Mourning Becomes Electra*. The Circle in the Square organization moved on November 15, 1972, to this new location in a new office building, which also houses the Gershwin Theater *(q.v.)*. As New York's premier classic theater group, Circle in the Square has brought to Times Square exactly the sort of play that is usually abhorred by legitimate producers.

Under the artistic direction of Theodore Mann and with the expertise of Managing Director Paul Libin, Circle In the Square has proved to be an important part of the Broadway theater scene. Its first full season included productions of *Medea* with Irene Papas; Siobhan McKenna in *Here Are Ladies;* a star-studded revival of Chekhov's *Uncle Vanya* with George C. Scott, Lillian Gish, Nicol Williamson, Julie Christie and Barnard Hughes; Anne Jackson and Eli Wallach in *The Waltz of the Toreadors* and Eugene O'Neill's *(q.v.) The Iceman Cometh,* starring James Earl Jones.

As a not for profit theater, the group can afford to present the kinds of shows that would be impossible to produce under normal circumstances. Other notable productions include Jim Dale's athletic performance in *Scapino* in 1974, George C. Scott's staging of O'Neill's *All God's Chillun Got Wings* in 1975 and, later that season, an exemplary revival of O'Neill's *Ah, Wilderness!,* starring Geraldine Fitzgerald, as well as an incendiary production of *The Glass Menagerie* with Maureen Stapleton and Rip Torn.

In 1976, Richard Chamberlain and Dorothy McGuire starred in Tennessee Williams's *(q.v.) The Night of the Iguana.* The next year's highlight was a revival of Moliere's *Tartuffe* with John Wood, Tammy Grimes and Mildred Dunnock.

New plays have also premiered at the theater, including *Spokesong* by Stewart Parker and *Loose Ends* by Michael Weller, both in 1979, and *Eminent Domain* by Percy Granger, starring Philip Bosco and Betty Miller. Musicals have been represented only twice and with mixed results. In 1975, Raul Julia starred in Frank Loesser's *(q.v.) Where's Charley?,* and Christopher Chadman and Joan Copeland were featured in a revival of Rodgers and Hart's *(q.v.) Pal Joey* the next year.

Other seasons have included productions of *Once in a Lifetime* with John Lithgow and Treat Williams (1978); *The Man Who Came to Dinner* with Ellis Rabb (1980); *Present Laughter,* starring George C. Scott (1982); *The Caine Mutiny Court Martial* with John Rubinstein, Michael Moriarty and William Atherton (1983); *Heartbreak House,* starring Rex Harrison and Amy Irving (1983); *Arms and the Man* (1985); *You Never Can Tell* with Philip Bosco, Uta Hagen and Amanda Plummer (1986); and Tina Howe's *Coastal Disturbances* with Timothy Daly and Annette Bening (1987).

The theater is shaped as a long oval with the audience surrounding the stage in bleacher-style seating. The tongue-shaped stage has had its detractors, but for the most part it has worked out surprisingly well. The theater seats 648 patrons, slightly smaller than the smallest commercial houses. Because of its arena setting and steeply raked seating no one in the audience is ever more than 10 rows from the stage.

CLARENCE DERWENT AWARD Actor Clarence Derwent (1884–1959) founded the award that bears his name in 1945 for the best actor and actress in a nonfeatured role. Each year, two awards are made in New York and, since 1948, two in London. The award consists of a $500 stipend to the American winners and 50 pounds to the British winners.

Past American winners of the award have included Judy Holliday, Barbara Bel Geddes, Tom Ewell, Lou Gilbert, Ray Walston, Fritz Weaver, Frances Sternhagen, George C. Scott, William Daniels, Rosemary Murphy, Gene Wilder and Gene Hackman.

CLARIDGE HOTEL Southeast corner of Broadway and 44th Street. Architect: John L. Pope. In February 1909, Charles E. Rector, owner of Rector's *(q.v.),* bought a five-story building around the corner from his famous restaurant. He hired John L. Pope to design a new hotel for the site. Unfortunately Rector was unable to purchase the corner plot that connected his restaurant and his new purchase. The land belonged to Henry Schwarzwalder, who steadfastly refused to sell. Rector was forced to lease the land from Schwarzwalder for 20 years. Looking ahead, Rector worried that in 20 years he might be unable to renew the lease with Schwarzwalder, requiring him to divide the lot back into three segments. Rector had Pope design the new building so that the placement of columns and girders required the addition of only interior walls to separate the building's three sections.

The Hotel Rector opened on New Year's Eve, 1910. It was immediately successful and became a worthy rival to the Astor Hotel *(q.v.)* across the street. Although the hotel was successful, Charles Rector went into receivership in July 1913. The hotel was sold.

The new owners changed the name to Claridge when they assumed control. Their reign was short lived. In November 1916, the hotel changed hands again. In 1922, the Claridge was sold. Owner Maximillian Zipkes renovated the building, added the Cadillac Restaurant and designed a two-story arcade containing stores. As Prohibition had gone into effect, a soda fountain and candy store replaced the hotel's bar.

The hotel was sold again in May 1923, June 1923 and February 1925. By 1928, the name was changed to the Broadway Claridge. With the Depression, the hotel's fortunes sunk even lower. It was sold once more in 1930, and in 1932 it went into foreclosure.

The hotel had one last hurrah in 1940. A sign affixed to the hotel announcing the candidacy of Earl Browder, the Communist Party nominee for President, was painted over. The Communist Party took the case to the Supreme Court. Although Justice Collins ordered the 60-foot-high by 20-foot-wide sign repainted, the order was never carried out. The Duke of Roxburghe owned the Cadillac Hotel next to the Claridge. The scaffolding needed to repaint the sign would have blocked his hotel, and his permission was needed. Since he was unavailable, the Claridge paid the Communist Party $1,187 dollars.

The Claridge building was torn down to make way for the National movie theater building.

COHAN, GEORGE M. (1878–1942)   George M. Cohan was known as "the man who owned Broadway." This actor, singer, dancer, producer, director, composer, lyricist and soft touch became the embodiment of the song and dance man, the complete performer. Through the Warner Brothers picture *Yankee Doodle Dandy* (1942),

new generations have discovered the legend of George M. Cohan.

Cohan was born on July 3, 1878. But he considered missing the anniversary of the independence of his country by only a few hours a technicality. As far as he was concerned the Fourth of July was his natal day. He took that close call with fate and made a career out of it. His shows waved the flag harder than anyone else. Cohan wrote the most successful patriotic numbers of all time with the possible exception of Irving Berlin's *(q.v.)* "God Bless America." The best known of these was "You're a Grand Old Flag." He wrote the supreme war song, "Over There," and even starred as a President of the United States in musical comedy.

Soon after his birth in Providence, Rhode Island, Cohan joined his family's vaudeville team—The Four Cohans. George, father Jerry, mother Helen and sister Josephine covered the country with their song-and-dance act. At the age of 15, George, not exactly a shrinking violet, began contributing skits and songs to the family's act. His ego, aggressive personality and unlimited energy made him continuously test himself and his fellow human beings. Nothing was ever good enough for George. He was a man of the theater, and he was determined to succeed in it as no man had ever succeeded before. As for his family, they would just have to keep up as best they could.

George made good on his first goal, Broadway, with his show *The Governor's Son* (2/25/01; 32 performances), which opened at the Savoy Theater. His next outing, *Running for Office* (4/27/03; 48 performances), also starred the Four Cohans.

George M. Cohan   Courtesy ASCAP.

Cohan took these failures and learned from them. Already he was the only Broadway author, composer and lyricist who worked in the native vernacular and whose shows weren't rehashings of the same formula operettas. Cohan was the only composer whose work was 100% American in style and tone. Not for Cohan were the staid drawing-room comedies imported from England. He translated his own brand of speed and exuberance to the stage and broke new ground by planting the seeds of American farce.

Though Cohan offstage was the gregarious, Irish upstart, his stage persona was more genteel and sophisticated. In fact, this character showed Americans that they need not be European to possess class and elan. His stage persona took the best of European sophistication and added to it the totally American qualities of enthusiasm and precociousness. As Oscar Hammerstein II *(q.v.)* wrote in the *New York Times,* "Never was a plant more indigenous to a particular part of the earth than was George M. Cohan to the United States of his day. The whole nation was confident of its superiority, its moral virtue, its happy isolation from the intrigues of the 'old country,' from which many of our fathers and grandfathers had migrated."

For his next show, *Little Johnny Jones* (11/7/04; 52 performances), Cohan again starred with his parents and wife, Ethel Levey, and he also wrote the book and composed the score. But for this outing, he added another job—director. He also began at the same time his lifelong friendship and collaboration with producer Sam H. Harris. Cohan used the show to further refine his formula, mixing a healthy dose of patriotism with a strong dash of farce and a liberal sprinkling of good old American corn. It also contained Cohan's first hit songs, "Life's a Funny Proposition After All," "The Yankee Doodle Boy," "I'm Mighty Glad I'm Living That's All" and, perhaps his most famous tune, "Give My Regards to Broadway." After a profitable hiatus on the road, *Little Johnny Jones* returned to Broadway for a run of almost four months.

Cohan's next Broadway venture, *Forty-Five Minutes from Broadway* (1/1/06; 90 performances), starred Fay Templeton, Victor Moore and Donald Brian. This score contained more Cohan standards, "Mary's a Grand Old Name," "So Long, Mary," and "Forty-Five Minutes from Broadway." One month later, Cohan, his parents, his wife and Truly Shattuck opened in *George Washington, Jr.* (2/12/06; 81 performances). This show contained his first great patriotic hit, "You're a Grand Old Flag." The original title of the song, "You're a Grand Old Rag," was changed at the urgings of patriotic groups.

Cohan's attempts at playwriting were not quite as successful. His first was titled *Popularity* (10/1/06; 24 performances). The next year, Cohan, never wanting to let a good idea go to waste, rewrote *Running for Office* as *The Honeymooners* (6/3/07; 167 performances). With his next show, *The Talk of New York* (12/3/07; 157 performances), Cohan officially became the co-producer with Sam H. Harris. This time, Victor Moore, Gertrude Vanderbilt and Emma Littlefield starred. The hit Cohan songs included "When We Are M-A- Double R-I-E-D," "When a Fellow's on the Level with a Girl That's on the Square," and "Under Any Old Flag at All."

Fifty Miles From Boston (2/3/08; 32 performances) contained the great Cohan hit, "Harrigan." Perhaps he was saving his energy for his next show, which only opened two months later. That was *The Yankee Prince* (4/20/08; 128 performances), a title that seemed to describe Cohan himself. In fact, all of Cohan's shows were semiautobiographical in spirit if not fact. *The Yankee Prince*'s run wasn't due to the score or its hits (there were none), but rather because for the first time since *Running for Office* in 1903 the Four Cohans were back together again on Broadway. Cohan premiered a third show in 1908. *The American Idea*'s (10/5/08; 64 performance) run was due more to the success of *The Yankee Prince* than its own merits.

Broadway was discovering the revue at the end of the first decade of the century. *The Cohan and Harris Minstrels* (8/16/09; 16 performances) was among the first revues seen on Broadway. Cohan and Harris next presented a straight play version of Winchell Smith's *The Fortune Hunter* (9/4/09; 345 performances), which starred John Barrymore. This first non-Cohan production presented by the team turned into a great success.

Cohan's next success was again autobiographical in title. *The Man Who Owns Broadway* (10/11/09) opened nearly a year after *The American Idea*. Cohan's next offering was a straight play, *Get-Rich-Quick Wallingford* (9/19/10; 424 performances). Hale Hamilton and Edward Ellis starred in this huge success. Cohan and Harris's next straight offering, *The Aviator* (12/6/10; 44 performances) by James Montgomery, was later adapted into the musical *Going Up* and presented to great success by Cohan and Harris.

A year later, the next Cohan musical opened, *The Little Millionaire* (9/25/11; 192 performances). Cohan, his parents and Donald Crisp, kept the show running for the longest run of his career. Exactly a month later, he coproduced the musical *The Red Widow* (11/6/11; 128 performances). In between, Cohan and Harris presented another play by Winchell Smith, *The Only Son* (10/16/11; 32 performances). The star of *The Only Son*, Wallace Eddinger, would have better luck in another Cohan and Harris production, the straight play *Officer 666* (1/29/12; 192 performances) by Augustin MacHugh.

Two months later, Cohan presented and starred in a revival of his 1906 hit *Forty-Five Minutes from Broadway*. Cohan's next Broadway outing was as author of the straight play, *Broadway Jones* (9/23/12; 176 performances), starring Cohan and his parents.

Four more straight plays followed—J.B. Fagan's *Hawthorne of the U.S.A.* (11/4/12; 72 performances) with Douglas Fairbanks in the lead; *Stop Thief* (12/25/12); Edgar Selwyn's *Nearly Married* (9/5/13; 123 performances); and finally Cohan's own *Seven Keys to Baldpate* (9/22/13; 320 performances), which starred Wallace Eddinger.

Cohan and Harris next offered the musical *The Beauty Shop* (4/13/14; 88 performances). This modest success had a score by Charles Gebest, best known as Cohan's musical director. Roi Cooper Magrue and Walter Hackett's play *It Pays to Advertise* (9/8/14; 399 performances) ran under Cohan and Harris' auspices. Cohan's next play, *The Miracle Man,* opened 13 days later and ran 97 performances.

Hello, Broadway! (12/25/14; 123 performances) was the first show to have an original Cohan score since *The Little Millionaire* more than three years earlier. Fred Ballard's comedy, *Young America* (8/28/15; 105 performances) starred Otto Kruger and Peggy Wood. Cohan collaborated with Max Marcin on *The House of Glass* (9/1/15; 245 performances). Cohan alone wrote *Hit-the-Trail Holliday* (9/13/15; 336 performances), which opened only 12 days later with Fred Niblo headlining.

Cohan again contributed a new score to Broadway, this time for *The Cohan Revue 1916* (2/9/16; 165 performances). More straight plays followed: *The Intruder* (9/26/16; 31 performances) by Cyril Harcourt; *Captain Kidd, Jr.* (11/13/16; 128 performances) by Rida Johnson Young and starring Otto Kruger; *The Willow Tree* (3/6/17; 103 performances), an English import by J.H. Benrimo and Harrison Rhodes; *A Tailor-Made Man* (8/27/17; 398 performances) by Harry James Smith; and another import, *The King* (11/20/17) by G.A. Caillavet, Robert de Flers and Emmanuel Arene.

Cohan and Harris then presented Louis Hirsch's musical *Going Up* (12/25/17; 351 performances). This was followed by the *Cohan Revue of 1918* (12/31/17; 96 performances). Its author called it "a hit-and-run play batted out by George M. Cohan." The young Irving Berlin *(q.v.)* contributed half the score to the show. Seven plays followed, the most notable being *Three Faces East* (8/13/18; 335 performances) by Anthony Paul Kelly and Cohan's *A Prince There Was* (12/24/18; 159 performances) in which he starred.

Cohan's next musical was *The Royal Vagabond* (2/17/19; 208 performances). Cohan was responsible for doctoring this European operetta while it was still on the road. He called it a "Cohanized Opera Comique."

During the run of *The Royal Vagabond* came the actors strike of 1919 *(q.v.).* Cohan was the most vocal of the managers who fought the actors. He considered the strike a personal affront and refused to join Actors' Equity *(q.v.),* the new union, for the remainder of his career. Cohan's immovable stance led to a break with his longtime friend and producing partner, Sam Harris. The strike was symbolic to Cohan of the increasingly less freewheeling atmosphere of Broadway. He grew more and more embittered and longed for the happier days when shows could be mounted with limited budgets and limitless enthusiasm. Cohan viewed the theater as a community, especially since his earliest memories were of trouping with his family. He couldn't understand why a strike was necessary at all—why "the show must go on" wasn't the most important credo to everyone in the theater. Cohan and Harris's last coproduction for 17 years was *The Acquittal* (1/5/20; 138 performances) by Rita Weiman and Cohan.

Cohan was barred from performing, since he refused to join Actors' Equity, but he continued his producing activities. His play *The Tavern* (9/27/20; 252 performances) is still produced around the country. Following a production of Augustin MacHugh's *The Meanest Man in the World* (10/12/20; 202 performances), Cohan produced and codirected the musical comedy *Mary* (10/18/20; 220 performances). His next success was a production of *The O'Brien Girl* (10/3/21; 164 performances), a musical. He then produced *So This Is London* (8/30/22; 343 performances) by Arthur Goodrich.

Cohan's next musical, for which he supplied his usual book, music and lyrics, was *Little Nellie Kelly* (11/13/22; 276 performances), which he also produced and directed. The show starred Elizabeth Hines, Georgia Caine and Charles King. Nellie was a name Cohan always liked since it was his mother's nickname. Cohan's score again contained some popular successes including, "You Remind Me of My Mother" and "Nellie Kelly, I Love You." *Little Nellie Kelly* proved to be Cohan's biggest hit.

Cohan's next musical was *The Rise of Rosie O'Reilly* (12/25/23; 87 performances). Virginia O'Brien, Georgie Hale and a young Ruby Keeler appeared in the show. His next three productions were of his own plays, *The Song and Dance Man* (12/31/23); *American Born* (10/5/25); and *The Home Towners* (8/23/26). None of these plays ran longer than 96 performances. Cohan's friends and associates banded together to force Actors' Equity to give him special dispensation to appear on Broadway; he appeared in *The Song and Dance Man* and *American Born*.

He then produced Margaret Vernon's play *Yellow* (10/21/26), which starred a young Spencer Tracy, a Cohan discovery. Tracy turned up a year later in Cohan's next production, *The Baby Cyclone* (9/12/27; 184 performances). Cohan himself appeared in his play *The Merry Malones* (9/26/27; 208 performances), and although he produced the show he did not direct it. Four more straight play productions followed, including his own *Whispering Friends* (2/20/28; 112 performances).

The last show for which he would author the book

and score was *Billie* (10/1/28; 112 performances). For his last Broadway score, Cohan contributed a big hit, the title song. Nine more straight play productions (including three revivals) followed, but they were all failures. Cohan became increasingly bitter about the Broadway scene and retired over and over again during his last years.

He produced one last show, *Fulton of Oak Falls* (2/10/37; 37 performances), with his old partner Sam Harris. Cohan wrote and starred in the show. The Theater Guild *(q.v.)* had convinced him to appear in Eugene O'Neill's *(q.v.)* only comedy, *Ah, Wilderness!* in 1933, and Cohan's last musical appearance on Broadway came in a Sam Harris production, the Rodgers and Hart *(q.v.)* musical, *I'd Rather Be Right* (11/2/37). In it, Cohan portrayed then President Franklin Roosevelt. Cohan's last appearance was in the poorly received play, *The Return of the Vagabond* (5/17/40; 7 performances), which Cohan produced, starred in and wrote.

Cohan died on November 4, 1942, at the age of 64.

At the time of his death, he was working on a new show, *The Musical Comedy Man.*

COHAN AND HARRIS THEATER   See HARRIS THEATER.

COLONY THEATER   See BROADWAY THEATER.

COMDEN AND GREEN   Betty Comden and Adolph Green are the preeminent lyricist team in the history of musical theater. They contributed to the development of the art of the musical both in the theater and on the screen. They are the longest-running writing team in Broadway history, yet because their subjects tend to be comedic rather than dramatic they have not received their due by critics and historians.

They both began their careers as members of The Revuers, a nightclub act, which also included Judy Holliday, for which they both wrote and performed. Their early collaborations for The Revuers was a success in the Greenwich Village club the Village Vanguard

Betty Comden, Jule Styne and Adolph Green   Courtesy ASCAP.

and less than a success in the more swank environs of the Rainbow Room. They went to Hollywood to star in the movie *Greenwich Village* but were mostly cut from the picture.

Leonard Bernstein *(q.v.),* a former cocamper and roommate of Adolph Green, caught their new act at the Blue Angel and convinced them to write the book and lyrics for the new musical adaptation of his ballet, *Fancy Free. On the Town* (12/28/44) was a smash hit and contained such standards as "New York, New York" and "Lucky to Be Me." The show starred Nancy Walker, Sono Osato, Cris Alexander, John Battles and Alice Pearce, as well as Comden and Green. *On the Town* played for 463 performances. This auspicious Broadway debut was under the direction of George Abbott *(q.v.),* who had led many other neophytes to Broadway success.

Unfortunately their next outing was not as successful. *Billion Dollar Baby* (12/21/45), for which they teamed up with composer Morton Gould, was a failure. And their subsequent outing with composer Saul Chaplin, *Bonanza Bound* (12/26/47), closed in Philadelphia before coming to Broadway. Discouraged by their flops, the team went to Hollywood, where they joined MGM for a series of successful film musicals. They wrote a screenplay for *Good News* (1947), penned lyrics for *Take Me Out to the Ball Game* (1949), adapted their Broadway success *On the Town* to the screen that same year and contributed a screenplay to the last pairing of Fred Astaire *(q.v.)* and Ginger Rogers—*The Barkleys of Broadway* (1949).

In 1951, the team made another attempt at Broadway and met their next collaborator, Jule Styne *(q.v.).* The initial entry in the Styne, Comden and Green canon was *Two on the Aisle* (7/19/51), a musical revue featuring Bert Lahr and Dolores Gray that ran 279 performances. Following that success, Comden and Green returned to Hollywood to write the screenplay for their best movie and perhaps the greatest movie musical of all time, *Singin' in the Rain* (1952). They followed that with another huge success for MGM, *The Band Wagon* (1953). The film was released after their next Broadway assignment, *Wonderful Town,* opened on February 25, 1953. For this tribute to New York City, Comden and Green were reunited with Leonard Bernstein. Rosalind Russell and Edith Adams starred in this modern classic, which ran for 559 performances.

They next contributed songs in collaboration with Jule Styne for the legendary Mary Martin *(q.v.)* version of *Peter Pan* (10/20/54). Their songs, "Never Never Land" and "Distant Melody," among others, perfectly captured the mood of the J.M. Barrie classic. *Peter Pan* was followed by the movie musical, *It's Always Fair Weather* (1955).

In 1956, they teamed up again with their partner from The Revuers, Judy Holliday, and had a smash hit.

The show, *Bells Are Ringing* (11/29/56), also starred Charlie Chaplin's son Sydney and the Styne, Comden and Green score yielded such gems as "Just in Time" and "The Party's Over." This resulted in their longest run to date, 924 performances. *Say, Darling* (4/3/58), a modest hit with a Jule Styne score and book by Richard Bissell, Marion Bissell and Abe Burrows, followed. It was a roman à clef about the making of a Broadway musical. Robert Morse first achieved fame in the show, which also featured Vivian Blaine, Johnny Desmond and David Wayne. "Dance Only with Me" is the best known of the largely forgotten songs.

While Jule Styne worked on *Gypsy,* Comden and Green returned to Hollywood for the screen adaptation of *Bells Are Ringing.* The threesome reunited for the Phil Silvers, Nancy Walker musical *Do Re Mi* (1/26/60). "Make Someone Happy" was the big hit from that score, which complemented Garson Kanin's tale of a small time hustler in the juke box racket. David Merrick *(q.v.),* producer of *Do Re Mi,* hired the trio for *Subways Are for Sleeping* (12/27/61), which presented Sydney Chaplin, Carol Lawrence and Phyllis Newman to good advantage. Despite a better-than-average score, which featured "Comes Once in a Lifetime," the show played only 205 performances.

Styne went on to write the smash *Funny Girl* with Bob Merrill, and Comden and Green went to Hollywood again for the all-star comedy *What a Way to Go* (1964). The three saw their next show, *Fade Out–Fade In,* premiere on May 26, 1964. The young Carol Burnett followed her success in *Once Upon a Mattress* in this show, which settled in for a long run at the Mark Hellinger Theater *(q.v.).* But Burnett claimed to have a bad back, and the show was closed while the star and creators met in court. The show reopened with Burnett, but the damage was done and it closed after only 271 performances.

The team would produce what is possibly their best score with Styne for their next show, *Hallelujah, Baby!* (4/26/67). Leslie Uggams and Robert Hooks starred in this saga of the black experience, which had a cumbersome libretto by Arthur Laurents. Styne, Comden and Green would write only one more score together, for the television musical *Getting Married* later that year.

The pair next collaborated on the Strouse and Adams *(q.v.)* musical *Applause* (3/30/70), starring Lauren Bacall. Comden and Green supplied the libretto for this musicalization of *All About Eve.* The show was a great success, but it was eight years before Comden and Green again had a show on Broadway.

In 1978, they collaborated with Cy Coleman for the remarkable, *On the Twentieth Century* (2/19/78). This wonderfully theatrical production opened with Madeline Kahn starring along with John Cullum and Imogene Coca. Kahn was soon replaced by Judy Kaye, who might have become a star overnight had the sorry state of the Broadway theater at this time not deprived her of suitable vehicles for her great talents. Kevin Kline also made his first big impression in this show. Robin Wagner's outstanding scenic design helped the glorious proceedings in what is probably the last great musical comedy.

Their last Broadway assignment was for the failure *A Doll's Life* (9/23/82) with a score by Larry Grossman. This musical sequel to *A Doll's House* was pretentious and ponderous, surely a first for Comden and Green. Between Broadway assignments, Comden and Green have starred themselves in a two person retrospective called *A Party with Betty Comden and Adolph Green.* The show was most recently on Broadway in 1977.

Green called their collaboration "an unconscious give-and-take." Betty Comden called it "mental radar." Whatever it is it has resulted in some of the most joyfully enthusiastic moments in the musical theater. Their shows, especially if they contributed librettos too, are marked by a smart, urbane innocence perfectly captured in the personality of Judy Holliday. Their characters are plain people, who express their feelings with an exuberance and joie de vivre. Comden and Green's wit, humor and slightly wry look at the world have resulted in one of the finest catalogs of productions in Broadway history. Their virtuosity is remarkable. They are the perfect collaborators both with each other and with those who have supplied the music for their shows.

COMEDY THEATER 108 W. 41st Street. Architect: D.G. Malcolm. Opening: September 6, 1909; *The Melting Pot.* The Comedy Theater, among the first Shubert *(q.v.)* theaters in New York, was not especially successful. Among its noteworthy early productions were *Affinity* (1/3/10), *A Man's World* (2/9/10), *Three Daughters of Monsieur Dupont* (4/13/10) and *The Family* (10/11/10).

The theater became William Collier's Comedy Theater with the opening of *I'll Be Hanged If I Do* (11/28/10). Shows produced during that period included *Bunty Pulls the Strings* (10/10/11) and *Fanny's First Play* (9/16/12). The name was changed back to Comedy with the opening of *Her Own Money* on September 1, 1913. *Gentlemen from Number 19* (5/1/13) and *Consequences* (10/1/14) were other productions at the Comedy.

As the theater district moved northward into Times Square, the Shuberts gave their less-promising productions to the Comedy, left behind below 42nd Street. In 1916, the Washington Square Players took over the Comedy. As a member of that company Katharine Cornell *(q.v.)* made her Broadway debut. The following year, Ruth Draper made her debut here.

The Depression hit the theater hard. The Comedy, by now well off the beaten track, was closed from 1931 to 1935. Later in the thirties, boy genius Orson Welles directed and performed at the Comedy as part of the

Federal Theater Project *(q.v.).* The theater was known as the Mercury, named after Welles' theater company. Welles presented enormously successful productions of *Doctor Faustus* and *Julius Caesar,* which opened on November 11 and 12, 1937. The Mercury Theater productions were controversial. Welles described his *Julius Caesar:* "Our Julius Caesar gives a picture of the same kind of hysteria that exists in certain dictator-ruled countries of today. We see the bitter resentment of free-born men against the imposition of a dictatorship. We see a political assassination, such as that of Huey Long. We see the hope on the part of Brutus for a more democratic government vanish with the rise of a demagogue (Antony) who succeeds the dictator. Our moral, if you will, is that not assassination, but education of the masses, permanently removes dictatorships."

Welles's productions were the great successes in the theater's history. On December 29, 1939, the theater's name and policy changed again. It became the Artef Theater, a Yiddish theater, during the run of the Yiddish drama *Uriel Acosta.* The Yiddish policy continued until the theater was razed in 1942.

CONCERT THEATER See JOHN GOLDEN THEATER.

CORNELL, KATHARINE (c.1898–1974) Katharine Cornell, Laurette Taylor, Helen Hayes *(q.v.)* and Lynn Fontanne *(q.v.)* were the great actresses of their time. Alexander Woollcott *(q.v.)* dubbed Katharine Cornell "The First Lady of the American Theater." (He disliked her husband, Guthrie McClintic, and titled a *New Yorker* Profile, "The Tyranny of the Tantrum.") At her death, critic *(q.v.)* Brooks Atkinson wrote in the *New York Times,* "If she had a great reputation it was not because she had manufactured it. It was because—in addition to that personal magnetism—she had the integrity and taste of a lady."

Katharine Cornell was born to a family with theatrical interests. Her grandfather and father were in love with the theater. There is some mystery about the year of her birth. She once claimed her birthday to be February 16, 1898. When she reached her seventies she moved the year back to 1893. She explained the discrepancy by stating, "When an actress is younger she likes to lower her age, but when she is older she likes to add to her years."

The family lived in Buffalo, New York, where her father practiced medicine. He quit the profession to become manager of a little theater. His father, in turn, had a small stage in his home where he and his friends put on amateur productions. This early background sparked her own interest in the theater. While at boarding school she produced and acted in the classics.

In 1917, Eddie Goodman, the director of the Washington Square Players, saw one of her performances at the school and invited her to come to New York. She

Katharine Cornell   Courtesy Billy Rose Theater Collection.

accepted and appeared in *Bushido*. Her only line was, "My son, my son."

She joined the Jessie Bonstelle Stock Company in Detroit and Buffalo, remaining with the company for three seasons. The company performed a new play every week for 10 performances. Jessie Bonstelle recognized the young actress's talents and brought her to London, where the company performed *Little Women*. Cornell played Jo, a leading role, and she was noticed by two women who recommended her to actor/producer Allen Pollock. He was casting Clemence Dane's drama *A Bill of Divorcement* and chose the young actress to open in the play on Broadway with himself in a leading role.

Before *A Bill of Divorcement* opened, Cornell made her Broadway debut at the Klaw Theater *(q.v.)* in Rachel Crothers' *Nice People* (3/2/21). No one took notice except casting director Guthrie McClintic. He wrote in his notebook, "Interesting. Monotonous. Watch." They were married by the following fall.

Producer Charles Dillingham opened *A Bill of Divorcement* (10/10/21) at the George M. Cohan Theatre *(q.v.)* on a particularly busy week, back in the days when Broadway might see more than one opening on a single night. Most of the leading critics attended the opening of Booth Tarkington's *The Wren* at the Gaiety Theater *(q.v.)*. However, the second-string critics were enthusiastic in their response to the drama. Their pos-

itive reviews caused the leading critics to attend the show, and they offered their opinions in Sunday editions.

Despite the acclaim, the show was floundering. The closing notice was put up, and another attraction was booked for the theater. Luckily, business began to improve, and the show was moved to the Times Square Theater *(q.v.)*, where it enjoyed a healthy run enabling audiences to discover Katharine Cornell.

Several minor roles followed, until Cornell took on the title role in George Bernard Shaw's *Candida,* which opened at the 48th Street Theatre *(q.v.)* (12/12/24). She was again acclaimed for her acting. One reviewer raved, "The tenderness, the poetry, the supreme womanliness of Katharine Cornell's impersonation of the title part puts this actress a notch ahead of anything she has yet attempted. It is an impersonation touched by the wand of genius."

Shaw was not easily amused by actresses although he was forever falling in love with those whom he admired. Shaw wrote to Cornell:

> I don't think I was ever so astonished by a picture as I was by your photograph. Your success as Candida, and something blonde and expansive about your name, had created an ideal suburban British Candida in my imagination.
>
> Fancy my feelings on seeing in your photograph a gorgeous dark lady from the cradle of the human race— wherever that was—Ceylon, Sumatra, Hilo, or the southernmost corner of the Garden of Eden!

Candida led to *The Green Hat* (9/15/25), which guaranteed her stardom. A series of undistinguished plays followed, including *The Letter* (9/26/27), *The Age of Innocence* (11/27/28) and *Dishonored Lady* (2/4/30).

She made one of her best loved appearances as Elizabeth Barrett in Rudolf Besier's *The Barretts of Wimpole Street* (2/9/31) at the Empire Theatre *(q.v.)* with Brian Aherne. Brooks Atkinson wrote in the *New York Times* that the play:

> . . . introduces us to Katharine Cornell as an actress of the first order. Here the disciplined fury she has been squandering on catch-penny plays becomes the vibrant beauty of finely wrought character.
>
> By the crescendo of her playing, by the wild sensitivity that lurks behind her ardent gestures and her piercing stares across the footlights, she charges the drama with a meaning beyond the facts it records. Her acting is quite as remarkable for the carefulness of its design as for the fire of her presence.

The play was a great triumph for the actress. After 372 performances on Broadway, she took it on a 20,853-mile tour of the country that covered 77 cities. The company also performed *Romeo and Juliet* and *Candida*.

One measure of the tour's popularity may be taken by an incident that occurred in the state of Washington. The train carrying the troupe was delayed by floods. The company finally arrived in Seattle at 11:15. The actors were surprised to find the audience had waited at the theater, determined to see the show.

Alexander Woollcott, reporting the unusual event, described the audience's enthusiasm: "The excitement, the heady compliment paid by the audience in having waited at all, acted like wine on the spirits of the troupe and they gave the kind of performance one hopes for on great occasions and never gets."

The actress explained the way the tour worked:

> We opened up the road. We made "The Barretts" and "Candida" pay for Shakespeare. "The Barretts" never played to an empty house—the receipts would be something like $33,000, then about $28,000 for "Candida" and for "Juliet" about $18,000 to $19,000, so that we came back having more than broken even. We really felt prideful.

> We continued like that for many years, alternating New York with the road, paying for ourselves with Sidney Howard's "Alien Corn," Shaw's "St. Joan" and "The Doctor's Dilemma" and some of the others—until later on, when costs got too high with "Antony and Cleopatra," we had to call in angels.

She appeared in her only Chekhov play, *The Three Sisters* (12/21/42), with Judith Anderson and Ruth Gordon at the Ethel Barrymore Theater. She seldom performed the classics, though she made a memorable Antigone. "Guthrie persuaded me to do Shakespeare, and I was very frightened of Shakespeare," Cornell once said. "If not for Guthrie, I think I would have continued just drifting. He wanted to be an actor and my career was a sublimation of his desire, because he could pour his talents through me and that was a great advantage to me."

In fact, her husband chose her roles and bolstered her confidence. He directed many of her performances and controlled her career since their marriage began. "I continued in the theater buoyed up mostly by his enthusiasm for it. He was one of those people who fascinated you always. You were never bored, sometimes upset, but never bored."

She was always an insecure, nervous performer and had to relate to her characters before she felt she could assay the role. "I was nervous from the very beginning, and it got worse as the years went on. I was conscientious and wanted to do more, always, than I was able. I don't think, when I was playing, that I was ever happy—beginning at 4 o'clock any afternoon."

She starred in S.N. Berhman's *No Time for Comedy* opposite Olivier (4/17/39) at the Ethel Barrymore Theater *(q.v.),* following the run with a six-month tour. The play was the third presentation by The Playwrights' Company *(q.v.).*

Of *No Time for Comedy* she said, "The audiences enjoyed it but I was never, not from the beginning, happy about my own performance. I have never been happy about my own performance—not in anything."

By the 1950s, her output began to slow down, and her successes grew less frequent. Her last appearance was in *Dear Liar,* which toured cross-country from October 1959 to March 1960. It opened in New York at the Billy Rose Theater *(q.v.)* on March 17, 1960. After her husband's death on October 29, 1961, she retired from the stage.

She seldom appeared on radio or television and appeared only in one movie, *Stage Door Canteen.* Her autobiographies, *I Wanted to Be an Actress* (1939) and *Curtain Going Up* (1943) were successful books.

Katharine Cornell died on June 9, 1974. S.N. Behrman called her "the most popular star in the country; an emanation of her rich and generous personality, as well as her luminous beauty, had gotten across to the American audience . . . Exhibitionism is taken for granted as the sine qua non ingredient in any acting career; Miss Cornell had less of it than any actress or actor I have ever known. Her position in the theater transcended technique; she was not, like Ina Claire and Lynn Fontanne, a great comedienne. It was something essential in herself, as a person, that the audiences sensed and reached out to."

Brooks Atkinson wrote, "she was not only a great actress but also a great lady. She was honest and considerate. She respected audiences. She worked hard because she believed that audiences of all kinds and everywhere were entitled to the best."

CORONET THEATER   See EUGENE O'NEILL THEATER.

CORT THEATRE 148 W. 48th Street. Architect: Edward B. Corey. Opening: December 29, 1912; *Peg o' My Heart.* The Cort Theatre was built by John Cort, a producer who had done most of his work on the West Coast. Cort wanted to begin production east of the Mississippi and built the Cort as his East Coast flagship theater. He built the Louis XVI-style theater on the "wrong side" of Broadway. Conventional wisdom had it that theaters east of Broadway, like the Henry Miller *(q.v.)* and Lyceum *(q.v.),* or west of Eighth Avenue, like the Martin Beck *(q.v.),* were too far off the beaten track to draw audiences. However the Cort, east of Broadway between Sixth and Seventh Avenue, was an immediate success and was thought a "lucky" theater.

The theater started its life with a huge hit, J. Hartley Manners's play *Peg o' My Heart.* The show starred Manners's wife Laurette Taylor, considered one of the greatest of all American actresses. The play had a remarkable run at the Cort Theater of 607 performances at a time when even 100 performances indicated a hit.

The Cort had another hit with its next presentation, *Under Cover* (8/26/14; 349 performances). With 999 seats the theater was suited to both plays and musicals. Its next hit, Victor Herbert's *(q.v.) The Princess Pat* (9/29/15; 158 performances) contained one hit song, the "Neapolitan Love Song."

Cort Theatre program

A revival of *The Yellow Jacket* (11/9/16) was followed by *Flo Flo* (12/20/17; 220 performances). The musical was written by Silvio Hein, a prolific composer of the time whose songs have not lasted into the present. *Abraham Lincoln* (12/15/19; 244 performances), John Drinkwater's play, starred Frank McGlyn. Produced at a time when some Americans still remembered the late president and his death, *Abraham Lincoln* struck a chord with audiences.

The 1920s were stellar years for the theater. The first hit was a somewhat unsophisticated offering. The musical *Jim Jam Jems* (10/4/20; 105 performances) featured comics Frank Fay, Harry Langdon, Joe E. Brown, Joe Miller and Ned Sparks. Producer Harry Cort even contributed some of the show's lyrics. The next hit was *Captain Applejack* (12/30/21; 366 performances).

George S. Kaufman *(q.v.)* and Marc Connelly provided one of their enduring hits with the Hollywood satire *Merton of the Movies* (11/13/22; 398 performances). Glenn Hunter starred. Eva Le Gallienne appeared in Ferenc Molnar's *The Swan* (11/23/23; 253 performances) with Basil Rathbone. Katharine Hepburn made her theatrical debut at the Cort. The play was *These*

Days which opened on November 12, 1928, and played eight performances.

The 1930s began with Jed Harris's brilliant production of Chekhov's *Uncle Vanya* (4/15/30; 80 performances). For the leads, Harris cast Lillian Gish (who almost 50 years later starred in the same play at Circle in the Square), Osgood Perkins (father of Tony Perkins), Walter Connolly and Eduardo Ciannelli.

George Abbott *(q.v.)* provided two hits at the Cort in the late thirties. The first was the hilarious *Boy Meets Girl* (11/27/35; 669 performances) by Sam and Bella Spewack, loosely based on the Hollywood adventures of Ben Hecht and Charles MacArthur. Abbott's next play was a knockabout farce of Broadway. *Room Service* (5/19/37; 496 performances), written by John P. Murray and Allen Boretz, starred Sam Levene, Philip Loeb, Teddy Hart, Betty Field and Eddie Albert.

During the next decade, the theater was equally successful. *The Male Animal* (1/9/40; 243 performances) by James Thurber and Elliott Nugent featured Nugent himself along with Gene Tierney and Don DeFore. Another often-revived play, *A Bell for Adano* (12/6/44; 296 performances) by Paul Osborn starred Fredric March.

Lady Windemere's Fan (10/14/46; 228 performances) had its most successful Broadway revival at the Cort with Cornelia Otis Skinner and Estelle Winwood featured. Cecil Beaton designed the sets, lighting and costumes as well as appeared in the play. The decade ended with Grace Kelly's Broadway debut in Strindberg's *The Father* (11/16/49). Also in the cast were Raymond Massey and Mady Christians.

Hepburn returned to the Cort in Shakespeare's *As You Like It* (1/26/50). The next Cort offering was drama critic *(q.v.)* Wolcott Gibbs's *Season in the Sun* (9/28/50; 367 performances). Jose Ferrer starred in the Pulitzer Prize drama *The Shrike* (1/15/52; 161 performances) by Joseph Kramm. Another Pulitzer Prize drama, *The Diary of Anne Frank* (10/5/55; 717 performances), starred Susan Strasberg, Jack Gilford, Lou Jacobi, Gusti Huber and Joseph Schildkraut. The 1950s were concluded with another hit, Dore Schary's drama of Franklin Delano Roosevelt, *Sunrise at Campobello* (1/30/58; 556 performances) with Ralph Bellamy as the late President.

The theater's success continued into the sixties. The first offering, Brendan Behan's *The Hostage* (9/20/60) was followed by the run of *Advise and Consent* (11/17/60; 212 performances). At the end of the decade, the theater was converted to television. Merv Griffin presented his talk show here from 1969 to 1974. The Cort reopened to live theater with the musical *The Magic Show* (5/28/74; 1,920 performances). The chief draw of the show was magician Doug Henning.

In recent years, the Cort's luck seems to have run out. As fewer and fewer shows are produced on Broadway, little quality product has been available for the Cort. Two notable tenants have been *Ma Rainey's Black*

Bottom (10/11/84; 275 performances) by August Wilson and the South African musical *Sarafina!*, which transferred from Lincoln Center on January 28, 1988.

On November 17, 1987, the New York City Landmarks Preservation Commission designated the interior and exterior of the theater as a landmark. The Commission said: "Its facade is an exceptional example of the neoclassical style" and its interior is "unusually handsome."

CRAIG THEATER   See GEORGE ABBOTT THEATER.

CRITERION THEATER   See OLYMPIA.

CRITICS   In his book *The Footlights—Fore and Aft*, publicist and playwright Channing Pollock described the critical scene around 1911.

The New York critics are about a score in number, and, during the past few years there have been many changes in the corps. Its dean, William Winter, resigned from *The Tribune*, where his post is filled by Arthur Warren. Alan Dale, of *The American*, continues to be the most widely known of our writers on theatrical topics, and we still have with us, as stand-bys, Adolph Klauber, of *The Times*; Louis De Foe, of *The World*; Rennold Wolf, of *The Telegraph*; Acton Davies, of *The Evening Sun*; Charles Darnton, of *The Evening World*; Rankin Towse, of *The Post*, and Robert Gilbert Welsh, of *The Evening Telegram*. The Press has been carrying on a lively theatrical war, and, perhaps for that reason, its reviews manifest not only ignorance but the most bumptious disregard of general and expert opinion. Arthur Brisbane having declared against "abuse," *The Evening Journal* finds good in everything; *The Sun* has had no regular critic since it lost Walter Prichard Eaton, and *The Herald* boasts that it prints only "reports" of performances. "First nights" are arranged, when that is possible, on different evenings, so that all the critics may be present at each, but, when there is a conflict, every man picks out the opening he considers most important and either lets the others go until later in the week or sends his assistant.

There are thirty or forty reviewers who represent magazines and periodicals, but, for the most part, these are de classe. They flock alone in the lobbies during intermissions, when the men from the daily newspapers congregate in groups to exchange a word or two about the play and to discuss other matters of common interest. These foyer gatherings pronounce a verdict that, as we have seen, is seldom—perhaps too seldom—overruled. Many a manager has leaned against his box office after the third act of a new piece, eavesdropping to learn what intelligence, experience, keen judgment and careful reading and rehearsing have not told him.

For there are two "anxious seats" on a "first night" in New York: One in the author's box and one in the manager's.

Some of the great critics who have shaped the history of the American theater include the following.

Kelcey Allen (1875–1951) Kelcey Allen, born in Brooklyn on November 11, 1875, changed his name from Eugene Kuttner because of his fondness for two actors, Herbert Kelcey and Viola Allen. He joined the editorial staff of the *New York Clipper* at the tender age of 18. He stayed at the *Clipper* for 20 years, also contributing articles to the *New York Recorder*. In 1914, he became drama critic for *Women's Wear Daily* and the *Daily News Record*. In his long career, Allen attended over 6,500 first nights. Allen died at the age of 75 on July 23, 1951.

John Anderson (1896–1943) John Anderson was born on October 18, 1896, in Pensacola, Florida. He was a reporter on the staff of the *New York Evening Post* in 1918. In 1924, he was appointed drama critic for the

Critics' reviews on the Winter Garden billboard   Courtesy Billy Rose Theater Collection.

Evening Post. Four years later, he moved to the *New York Journal,* which later became the *New York Journal-American.* Anderson was also the author of many books on the theater. Anderson died on July 16, 1943.

Brooks Atkinson (1894–1984) Atkinson was born in Melrose, Massachusetts, in 1894. After graduating from Harvard in 1917, he taught English at Dartmouth, worked for a short time on *The Springfield Daily News* and joined *The Boston Evening Transcript* as a police reporter and later became the assistant to the drama critic. In 1922, he found his way to New York and joined the *New York Times* as the Sunday Book Review editor. In 1925, the *Times* made him drama critic, a post he retained until 1960. Under Atkinson's tenure, the *Times'* arts reporting became the most respected in the country. He took a brief hiatus from 1942 to 1944 to serve as a wartime correspondent in China and from 1945 to 1946 in Moscow. After the war, he returned to the *Times* and his reviewing post. In 1960, he became the *Times's* critic at large. In 1965, he retired for good. Along the way, he wrote many excellent books on literature, nature and the theater, including what is probably the best history of the American theater, *Broadway* (1970). In 1947, Atkinson won a Pulitzer Prize for his Moscow reporting. He died on January 13, 1984.

Atkinson was among the most admired of New York critics. Even those who disagreed with his assessments respected his opinions because he left his personal emotions out of the reviews and made the show the focus of the piece. Atkinson wasn't overly flowery in his praise nor was he exceptionally cute or biting in his criticism. He was among the best read and most sensitive of his colleagues and reviewed shows without the wide-eyed star struck viewpoints of many of his associates. A measure of the esteem he is held in by the Broadway community is that he was until 1990 the only drama critic to have a theater named after him.

Clive Barnes (1927–   ) Barnes was born in London in 1927. In England, he held several important editorial posts on or contributed articles to such periodicals as the *Spectator,* the *London Daily Express* and the *New Statesman.* Barnes was also the dance critic for the *London Times* and for four years beginning in 1961 served as executive editor of *Dance and Dancers, Music and Musicians* and *Plays and Players.* In 1965, he came to the United States to assume the position of dance critic for the *New York Times.* In 1967, he also became drama critic. In December 1977, Clive Barnes moved (some claim he was pushed out by the *Times*) to the *New York Post* where he remains. Interestingly, when at the *Times,* Barnes held great power. When he moved to the *Post,* with New York's least respected arts coverage, he was virtually ignored by theatergoers.

Whitney Bolton (1900–1969) Bolton started his career as a drama critic in 1924 with the *New York Herald Tribune.* In 1928, he switched to the *New York Morning Telegraph* as drama critic and columnist. He left the *Telegraph* in 1938, moving to a career as publicity director for Columbia Pictures and Warner Brothers from 1941 to 1946. Bolton also served as an assistant to movie producer David O. Selznick (1943–46). He rejoined the staff of the *Morning Telegram* in 1949. He also scripted the play *Save the Pieces* (1932) as well as several screenplays.

John Mason Brown (1900–1969) Brown was born in Louisville, Kentucky, in 1900. After graduating from Harvard University, Brown joined *Theater Arts Magazine (q.v.)* as an associate editor and drama critic. He remained with *Theater Arts* from 1924 to 1928. He also lectured at the American Laboratory Theater beginning in 1924 through 1931. Brown was drama critic for the *New York Evening Post* from 1929 to 1941. He then moved to the *New York World-Telegram* for one season. During the war, Brown was on the staff of Vice Admiral Alan G. Kirk and found himself at the Sicily and Normandy landings. In 1944, he became drama critic of the *Saturday Review of Literature,* a post he held until 1955. He also had a successful academic career as a dramatic arts teacher at the University of Montana (1923, 1929, 1931), Yale (1932), Middlebury College (1935–36) and Harvard (1937–40). Brown wrote many books on the theater, including *The Modern Theater in Revolt* (1929), *Upstage: The American Theater in Performance* (1930), *The Art of Playgoing* (1936), *Two on the Aisle* (1938), *Broadway in Review* (1940), *Seeing Things* (1950), *Seeing More Things* (1948) and *Still Seeing Things* (1950). Brown also became America's best known lecturer on the American theater.

John Chapman (1900–1972) Chapman began his journalistic career as a reporter for the *Denver Times* in 1917. He moved to New York where he worked for the *Daily News* from 1920 to 1923 and from 1926 to 1929. That year, he became the drama editor for the *Daily News.* He remained in that position until 1943, when he was appointed drama critic. Chapman succeeded Burns Mantle as editor of the annual *Best Plays* in 1947 and filled the post until 1952. He then became editor of *Theater '53,* the beginning of a short lived annual on the theater. John Chapman died on January 17, 1972.

Gilbert Wolf Gabriel (1890–1952) Gabriel began his career as a reporter for the *New York Evening Sun* in 1912. From 1917 to 1924, he held the post of music critic and from 1925 to 1929 was drama critic. He assumed the same responsibilities on the *New York American* from 1929 to 1937. At the same time, he lectured on dramatic criticism for New York University. At *The New Yorker* magazine he created the "profile" feature. Like many of his contemporaries, Gabriel tried his hand at play writing. The result, *Clap Hands,* premiered in 1934, never making it to Broadway. He also wrote several books and magazine articles. Gabriel became drama critic for *Cue Magazine* from 1949 until his death in 1952. At the time of his death, he was President of the New York Drama Critics' Circle.

John Gassner (1903–1967) Gassner was a teacher at Hunter College beginning in 1928. He became a play reader for the Theater Guild (*q.v.*) in 1930. From 1935 to 1937, he served as drama critic for the *New Theater Magazine*. He then moved from magazine to magazine: *Forum* (1937–38), *Time* (1938), *Direction* (1939–43). He also taught drama at many universities, including Columbia, Bryn Mawr and Queens College. He was Sterling Professor of Playwriting at Yale. Gassner, also an editor of the annual *Best Plays* series, also wrote or edited many other theater books, including *Masters of the Drama* (1940), *Best American Plays* (1939–1963), *Treasury of the Theater* (1935–1960) and *Theater at the Crossroads* (1960).

Jack Gaver (1902–1974) Gaver spent his entire Broadway career as drama critic for United Press International. He began with the organization in 1929 and the next year was appointed theater critic and amusement columnist. He remained with UPI for over 30 years. He also wrote many books, including *Curtain Calls* (1949) and *Critics' Choice* (1954). Jack Gaver died on December 16, 1974.

Rosamond Gilder (1891–1986) Rosamond Gilder's father, Richard Watson Gilder, was editor of the *Century Magazine* and a well-respected poet. He instilled in his daughter a love for the arts and encouraged her penchant for writing. Her first important work was *Letters of Richard Watson Gilder* in 1916. She was editorial secretary for the National Theater Conference (1933–36); director of the Playwrights Bureau of the Federal Theater Project (*q.v.*) (1935–36) and drama critic and associate editor of *Theater Arts Magazine* (*q.v.*) (1925–48). Gilder sat on the editorial committee of World Theater and was associated with ANTA (*q.v.*) beginning in 1946.

Percy Hammond (1873–1936) Hammond began his career as a reporter in 1898 on the *Chicago Evening Post*. He moved to the *Chicago Tribune* the next year and wrote editorials and dramatic criticism until 1921. He then moved to the *New York Herald Tribune,* on the offer of $25,000, and he remained there as drama critic until his death in 1936. Hammond was one of the most influential and respected critics in New York. He wrote his reviews in a small closet-sized office with a companion bottle of gin. Brooks Atkinson quoted Hammond as saying: "Never praise an actress because it will bite you." He was a droll, witty man who after his death was missed greatly by both his readers and those he judged, a rare tribute to a drama critic.

Henry Hewes (1917–   ) Hewes spent his early career at the *New York Times,* beginning as a copy boy and eventually achieving the post of staff writer (1949–51). He edited the *Best Plays* series and adapted and directed many plays for regional theaters. He began his

career as drama editor of the *Saturday Review* in 1952, two years later becoming its critic. He remains at the *Saturday Review* today.

Walter Kerr (1913–   ) Kerr was born in Evanston, Illinois, in 1913. He was on the drama faculty of Catholic University during its heyday from 1938 to 1949. While at Catholic University, Kerr directed and/or wrote many plays and revues. Kerr left Catholic University and became drama critic for *Commonweal* for two years beginning in 1950. He became drama critic for the *New York Herald-Tribune* in 1951 and remained at that post until the paper folded in 1966. He then moved to the *New York Times* and briefly became drama critic. In 1967, he stopped reviewing plays on a daily basis and concentrated on writing pieces on the theater for the Sunday *Times*. Though retired, Kerr continues to contribute occasional pieces to the *Times*. In early 1990, the Ritz Theatre (*q.v.*) was renamed the Walter Kerr.

When reviewing, Kerr would take hundreds of notes during opening nights. His wife, playwright Jean Kerr, once asked jokingly if he had ever "seen" a play. Kerr is well respected for a series of books on playwriting and criticism that are considered classics. These include *How Not to Write a Play* (1955), *Pieces at Eight* (1957), *The Decline of Pleasure* (1962) and *Theater in Spite of Itself* (1963).

While at Catholic University he collaborated with Leo Brady and Nancy Hamilton in the revue *Count Me In*. It opened at the Ethel Barrymore Theater (*q.v.*) on October 8, 1942. Kerr also wrote and directed the folk-music revue *Sing Out Sweet Land* (12/27/44) and the revue *Touch and Go* (10/13/49), the latter with his wife. Kerr directed his wife's play *King of Hearts* (4/1/54), which she wrote with Eleanor Broke. Mr. and Mrs. Kerr collaborated with composer Leroy Anderson on *Goldilocks,* a musical that opened at the Lunt-Fontanne (*q.v.*) on October 11, 1958. Kerr also directed *Goldilocks*.

John McClain (1904–1967) McClain was a columnist for the *New York Sun, New York American* and *New York Journal-American* for a decade beginning in 1928. He spent his time up to World War II in Hollywood as a screenwriter. On returning to New York after the war, he joined the *Sun* and *Journal-American* and finally became drama critic of the *Journal-American* in 1951. The *Journal-American* ceased publication in 1965. McClain died on May 3, 1967.

Ward Morehouse (1899–1966) Morehouse began his journalistic career as a reporter for the *Savannah Press* in 1915. He moved to the *Atlantic Journal* in 1916 where he remained until 1919. He then moved to the *New York Tribune,* where over the next seven years he assumed the posts of reporter, rewrite man, assistant night editor and drama columnist. In 1926, he transferred to the *New York Sun* as a reporter and drama columnist. He became drama critic for the *Sun* in 1943. In 1956, Morehouse moved to the Staten Island Newhouse newspapers and he eventually became drama critic and columnist ("Broadway After Dark") for the entire Newhouse chain. He also wrote a number of plays, including *Gentlemen of the Press* (1928), *Miss Quis* (1937) and *U.S. 90* (1941).

George Jean Nathan (1882–1958)   Nathan was born in Fort Wayne, Indiana, in 1882. He became one of New York's premier drama critics over the course of a 50-year career. Nathan began his professional reviewing in 1906 at the *New York Herald*. In 1908, he left the *Herald* and became the drama critic and editor of *Bohemian Magazine*. He also wrote for *Smart Set*, becoming editor in 1914, *Harper's Weekly, Esquire, Scribner's, Saturday Review of Literature, Newsweek, Puck, Judge, Life, New Freeman* and *Vanity Fair*. He was the founder and editor (with H.L. Mencken) of the *American Mercury* from 1924 to 1930. In 1932, he wrote for the *American Spectator*.

The critic was the president of the New York Drama Critics' Circle from 1936 to 1939. He worked for the *New York Journal American* from 1943. Nathan was the author of several books on the theater, including *Mr. George Jean Nathan Presents* (1917), *The Theater, The Drama, The Girls* (1921), *The Critic on the Drama* (1922), *The Testament of a Critic* (1931), *The Morning After the First Night* (1939) and a series entitled *The Theater Book of the Year* beginning in 1942.

Through his various writings, Nathan exerted an important influence on drama in America. He trumpeted early on the talents of Strindberg, O'Neill *(q.v.)*, Saroyan and Ibsen. He did not suffer foolish plays and insisted on the highest standards for both himself and the theater. However, Nathan appreciated farce and musical comedy equally well, simply demanding good craftsmanship not necessarily seriousness. Nathan was one of the few critics who felt no compunction at leaving during intermission. Nathan died at the age of 76 on August 8, 1958.

Howard Taubman (1907–   )   Taubman was born in New York in 1907. Taubman's career was associated more with music than theater, but he was the drama critic of the *Times* for a brief period. While at Cornell University, he held a part-time job at the *New York Post* copy desk. In 1929, after his graduation, he moved to the *New York Times*. A year later, he started work in the music division. In 1935, he became music editor for the *Times* and remained in that position until 1955, with a brief sojourn during World War II writing for *Stars and Stripes* in the Mediterranean. From 1955 to 1960, Taubman served as the *Times*'s music critic. For the next five years, he held the post of drama critic. In 1966, Taubman became a critic at large at the *Times*. Taubman wrote many books on music including *The Maestro: The Life of Arturo Toscanini* and *Music on My Beat*.

Richard Watts Jr. (1898–1981)   Watts was born in Parkersburg, West Virginia, in 1898. From 1922 to 1923, he worked at the *Brooklyn Times*. He moved to the *Herald-Sun Syndicate* from 1923–24, where he was assistant night editor. In 1924, he joined the *Herald-Tribune*, where he became movie critic. He held the post until 1936 when he became drama critic, replacing the late Percy Hammond. Watts stayed at the *Herald-Tribune* until 1942 and World War II. During the war, he was posted in Dublin and Chunking. In 1946, he became the drama critic for the *New York Post*. He held that position until Clive Barnes moved to the *Post*. Watts continued to contribute to the paper until his death on January 2, 1981.

Stark Young (1881–1962)   Young was born in Como, Mississippi, in 1881. He became an English teacher at the University of Mississippi in 1904 and later moved to the University of Texas and Amherst College, where he remained until 1922. He became associate editor of *Theater Arts Magazine (q.v.)* in 1921 and in 1922 was hired by the *New Republic*. In 1924, on leaving his post at *Theater Arts,* he was named drama critic of the *New York Times*. After two years at the *Times,* he returned to the *New Republic,* where he served as drama editor. Young was a lecturer at the New School for Social Research in New York from 1925 to 1928. In addition to his newspaper work, he wrote plays and novels (including *So Red the Rose*) and dabbled in painting. Young died in 1962.

DANIEL BLUM THEATRE WORLD AWARD The Theatre World Award is given by the annual publication that records the Broadway and off-Broadway season. In 1945, Daniel Blum, editor of the publication, originated the award to recognize "promising personalities" who appear in the New York theater. There is no set number of awards given each season, but there are usually at least 10 names cited by the current *Theatre World* editor.

The Theatre World Award has cited many newcomers who went on to become stars. These include Judy Holliday, Betty Comden *(q.v.)*, Marlon Brando, Barbara Bel Geddes, Burt Lancaster, Wendell Corey, David Wayne, Patricia Neal, James Whitmore, Carol Channing, Gene Nelson, Julie Harris, Charlton Heston, Grace Kelly, Audrey Hepburn, Richard Burton, Nancy Andrews, Geraldine Page, Paul Newman, Gwen Verdon, James Dean, Eva Marie Saint, Jack Lord, Julie Andrews, Barbara Cook, Andy Griffith, Laurence Harvey, Jason Robards, Jr., Alan Alda, Carol Burnett, Jane Fonda, Robert Goulet and Larry Hagman.

DELLA AUSTRIAN MEDAL This award is given by the Drama League of New York for "the most distinguished performance of the season." It has been awarded since 1935, when Katharine Cornell *(q.v.)* won for her performance in *Romeo and Juliet.* Other recipients have been Helen Hayes *(q.v.),* Maurice Evans, Paul Muni, Alfred Lunt and Lynn Fontanne *(q.v.),* Ingrid Bergman, Judith Anderson, Julie Harris, Josephine Hull, Charles Boyer and Alec Guinness.

DE MILLE, AGNES (1905–   ) Agnes de Mille was instrumental in raising the art of Broadway choreography to new heights of sophistication and psychology. She was not content simply to have her dancers perform until the music stopped. Rather her ballet-inspired choreography revealed characterization and motivation and was often narrative in form.

She had her greatest success with the composing team of Rodgers and Hammerstein *(q.v.).* Their constant attempts to stretch the conventions of musical comedy and operetta allowed de Mille to rise to the occasion time and time again.

Her first and only appearance as a dancer in a Broadway show came with the *Grand Street Follies* (5/28/28; 144 performances). She then went to London to choreograph the Cole Porter *(q.v.)* musical *Nymph Errant* (10/6/33). The show, starring Gertrude Lawrence, was mildly successful but did not cross the Atlantic. After another London assignment *(Why Not Tonight?)* she made her Broadway choreographic debut with *Hooray for What!* The show opened on December 1, 1937, with a score by Harold Arlen *(q.v.)* and E.Y. Harburg *(q.v.).* It ran 200 performances. Robert Alton, also a distinguished Broadway choreographer, shared the credit for choreography.

A jazz version of *A Midsummer Night's Dream* called *Swingin' the Dream* opened on November 29, 1939, with an impressive cast, including Louis Armstrong, Maxine Sullivan, Benny Goodman and his sextet, Bud Freeman's Summa Cum Laude Band, Dorothy Dandridge, Jackie "Moms" Mabley, Butterfly McQueen and Muriel Rahn. De Mille shared the choreographic assignment with Herbert White.

Her first solo venture on Broadway was for the landmark musical *Oklahoma!* She received ecstatic reviews from the critics *(q.v.)*; Lewis Nichols in the *New York Times* announced that these were her "most inspired dances." Howard Barnes, writing in the *New York Herald Tribune* said that she "worked small miracles." Olin Downes of the *New York Times* wrote "the dancing . . . is so original and so expressive of genuine things that lie deep in the people and the soil."

Miss de Mille's other choreograph works for the stage, with her ballets indicated in quotes, appeared in: "Venus in Ozone Heights" and "Forty Five Minutes for Lunch" for *One Touch of Venus* (10/7/43; 567 performances); "Civil War Ballet" for *Bloomer Girl* (10/5/44; 657 performances); "Carousel Waltz" for *Carousel* (4/19/45; 890 performances); "The Chase" for *Brigadoon* (3/13/47; 581 performances); *Allegro* (10/10/47; 315 performances), for which she was also director; *Gentlemen Prefer Blondes* (12/8/49; 740 performances); *Out of This World* (12/21/50; 157 performances), for which she was director only; *Paint Your Wagon* (11/12/51; 289 performances); "Pas de Deux" for *The Girl in Pink Tights* (3/5/54; 115 performances); "Huckleberry Island Ballet" and "The Town House Maxixe" for *Goldilocks* (10/11/58; 161 performances); "Dublin Night Ballet" for *Juno* (3/9/59; 16 performances); *Kwamina* (10/23/61; 32 performances); *110 in the Shade* (10/24/63; 330 performances); *Come Summer* (2/18/69; 7 performances), for which she was also director.

DESYLVA, BROWN AND HENDERSON Lyricists B.G. DeSylva and Lew Brown and composer Ray Henderson were among the most popular of Broadway composers in the 1920s and 1930s. Their upbeat numbers seemed to exactly define the bubbly, insouciance of the twenties. Though none of their shows have lasted, they wrote some of the most endearing songs in the American popular song canon.

B.G. DeSylva was born on January 27, 1895, and died on July 11, 1950. He also collaborated with George Gershwin *(q.v.),* Victor Herbert *(q.v.),* Jerome Kern *(q.v.),* Emmerich Kalman and Lewis Gensler. DeSylva moved into producing toward the end of his involvement in Broadway. He later became a respected executive at Paramount Pictures.

Lew Brown was born on December 10, 1893, and died on February 5, 1958. He also wrote with Harry Akst, Charles Tobias and Sam Stept.

Ray Henderson was born on December 1, 1896, and died on December 31, 1970. He also collaborated with Ted Koehler, Jack Yellen and Irving Caesar.

DeSylva, Brown and Henderson were responsible for the following revues and musicals with their famous songs in quotes: *La La Lucille* (5/26/19; 104 performances), DeSylva alone; *Sally* (12/21/20; 570 perfor-

B. G. DeSylva, Lew Brown and Ray Henderson   Courtesy ASCAP.

mances), DeSylva only, "Whipporwill" and "Look for the Silver Lining"; *George White's Scandals (q.v.)* (8/28/22; 89 performances), DeSylva only, "I'll Build a Stairway to Paradise"; *Orange Blossoms* (9/19/22; 95 performances), DeSylva only, "A Kiss in the Dark"; *The Yankee Princess* (10/2/22; 80 performances), DeSylva only; *George White's Scandals* (6/18/23; 168 performances), DeSylva only, "The Life of a Rose"; *Sweet Little Devil* (1/21/24; 120 performances), DeSylva alone; *George White's Scandals* (6/30/24; 198 performances), DeSylva only, "Somebody Loves Me"; *Big Boy* (1/7/25; 48 performances), DeSylva only, "California Here I Come," "If You Knew Susie," "Keep Smiling at Trouble"; *Tell Me More!* (4/13/25; 100 performances), DeSylva alone, "Kickin' the Clouds Away"; *George White's Scandals* (6/22/25; 169 performances); *Captain Jinks* (9/8/25; 167 performances), DeSylva alone; *George White's Scandals* (6/14/26; 432 performances) "Birth of the Blues," "The Black Bottom," "This Is My Lucky Day"; *Queen High!* (9/8/26; 367 performances), DeSylva only and also as colibrettist, "You Must Have Been a Beautiful Baby"; *Piggy* (1/11/27; 79 performances), Brown only; *Good News!* (9/6/27; 551 performances), "The Best Things in Life Are Free," "Good News," "Just Imagine," "Lucky in Love"; *Manhattan Mary* (9/26/27; 264 performances); *George White's Scandals* (7/2/28; 230 performances), "I'm on the Crest of a Wave"; *Hold Everything!* (10/10/28; 413 performances), DeSylva also as colibrettist, "You're the Cream in My Coffee"; *Follow Thru* (1/9/29; 401 performances), DeSylva also as colibrettist, "Button Up Your Overcoat," "Then I'll Have Time for You"; *Flying High* (3/3/30; 355 performances), Brown and DeSylva also colibrettists; *George White's Scandals* (9/14/31; 204 performances), Henderson and Brown only, "Ladies and Gentlemen, That's Love," "Life Is Just a Bowl of Cherries," "That's Why Darkies Were Born," "This Is the Missus," "The Thrill Is Gone"; *Hot-Cha!* (3/8/32; 118 performances), Henderson and Brown only and Henderson as colibrettist; *Take a Chance* (11/26/32; 243 performances), DeSylva only, also as colibrettist, "Eadie Was a Lady" "Rise and Shine" "You're an Old Smoothie"; *Strike Me Pink* (3/4/33; 122 performances), Brown and Henderson only, and both also as colibrettists, coproducers and codirectors; *Say When* (11/8/34; 76 performances), Henderson only and also as coproducer; *Calling All Stars* (12/13/34; 35 performances), Brown only, also as colibrettist, producer and codirector; *George White's Scandals* (12/25/35; 110 performances), Henderson only; *Yokel Boy* (7/6/39; 208 performances), Brown only, also as librettist, producer and director; *Du Barry Was a Lady* (12/6/39; 408 performances), DeSylva colibrettist and producer only; *Louisiana Purchase* (5/28/40; 444 performances), DeSylva producer only; *Panama Hattie* (10/30/40; 501 performances), DeSylva colibrettist and producer only; *Zieg-*

feld Follies (q.v.) (4/1/43; 553 performances), Henderson only.

DIAMOND HORSESHOE See CENTURY THEATER (1).

DIETZ AND SCHWARTZ The songwriting team of Arthur Schwartz and Howard Dietz elevated the art of revue writing to new heights. They collaborated on what is considered the greatest of all revues, *The Band Wagon*. Their long career spanned 30 years and resulted in the creation of many great standards. Schwartz and Dietz were of the most successful writers of ballads such as "Dancing in the Dark," "I Guess I'll Have to Change My Plans," "You and the Night and the Music" and "Alone Together." Their comedy and upbeat songs were equally well constructed, such as "New Sun in the Sky," "Triplets" and "That's Entertainment."

Howard Dietz (1896–1983) Howard Dietz was born in New York on September 8, 1896. He attended Townsend Harris Hall and Columbia University. While at Columbia, he frequently contributed to Franklin P. Adams's column, "The Conning Tower." His early interest in language landed him a position as a copywriter in the Philip Goodman Company ad agency. He obtained the position by writing a contest-winning advertisement for Fatima Cigarettes.

After his discharge from the Navy, Dietz obtained a job with Samuel Goldwyn, the motion picture producer. The publicity post led to a long career with what eventually became Metro-Goldwyn-Mayer.

Dietz wrote for the stage as a sideline to his publicity work for the movies. It's ironic that he felt his retirement income would come from his MGM pension. In fact, it was his ASCAP *(q.v.)* royalties that allowed him to live in comfort.

Dietz's first Broadway lyric was for *Poppy* (9/13/23; 346 performances), a W.C. Fields vehicle and the first time Fields played a legitimate role on Broadway. Dietz also contributed the dialogue for Fields's character.

Dietz's lyrics and his contributions to "The Conning Tower" did not go unnoticed. Philip Goodman, who was involved in advertising as well as the theater, suggested to Jerome Kern *(q.v.)* that he might use Dietz as lyricist on his next show. Kern took Goodman's advice, and the result was *Dear Sir* (9/23/24; 15 performances), written with Jerome Kern. This start, though inauspicious, did bring Dietz to the attention of Arthur Schwartz, a lawyer.

Arthur Schwartz (1900–1984) Arthur Schwartz was born in Brooklyn, New York, on November 25, 1900. Like Berlin *(q.v.)* and others, Schwartz taught himself to play the piano. While at school, Schwartz played piano in neighborhood movie houses. He attended New York University and Columbia University. After graduation, he taught English for the New York public

Howard Dietz   Courtesy ASCAP.

school system. Forsaking the teaching profession, he entered a legal practice in 1924. Four years later, he wrote to Howard Dietz on the advice of publisher Bennett Cerf. Schwartz had already had one of his songs published, "Baltimore M.D., You're the Only Doctor for Me," with lyrics by Eli Dawson.

Schwartz wrote to Dietz that he was the lyricist most like Lorenz Hart *(q.v.)* in style. This was a high compliment from Schwartz, but Dietz was unimpressed. He responded by suggesting that Schwartz team up with an established lyrics writer to gain from the education, as he himself had done with Jerome Kern. Then when they both became famous they could write together.

The musical *Queen High* (11/8/26) provided Schwartz with his first job. Schwartz collaborated on two songs with fellow composer Ralph Rainger and lyricist E.Y. Harburg *(q.v.)*: "Brother Just Laugh It Off" and "I'm Afraid of You." Unfortunately, by the time the show opened on Broadway, the Schwartz songs were cut.

George and Ira Gershwin *(q.v.)* were hard at work on their score for *Oh, Kay!* (11/8/26) when Ira was forced to Mt. Sinai Hospital to have his appendix removed. George chose Dietz to work on the score during Ira's recuperation. Dietz wrote the title song's lyrics, "Heaven on Earth," and the verse to "Clap Yo' Hands."

Dietz's next assignment, *Hoopla,* was probably the first show in history to close out of town after only one act. Dietz's life as a publicist was turning out much more successful than his theater career. Metro-Goldwyn-Mayer had been formed in 1924, and Dietz was made director of advertising and publicity because of his creation of the Leo the Lion trademark and the *Ars Gratia Artis* motto for Goldwyn Pictures.

Jay Gorney and Dietz had better luck with *Merry-Go-Round* (5/31/27; 135 performances), their next collaboration, than they did with *Hoopla*. Henry Souvaine contributed some of the music, with Morrie Ryskind also writing lyrics.

Arthur Schwartz Courtesy ASCAP.

At the end of the 1920s, Tom Weatherly, a producer and Broadway bon vivant, decided to put on a revue called *The Little Show*. Dwight Deere Wiman was brought in to help produce the venture, and Dietz was called in to write the lyrics. *The Little Show* was conceived as an answer to the big revues like the *Ziegfeld Follies (q.v.),* the *Passing Shows* and the *Earl Carroll Vanities (q.v.).* *The Little Show* would be an intimate revue in the manner of *The Garrick Gaieties.*

Weatherly had already hired performers Clifton Webb, Fred Allen and Libby Holman; all that was needed was a composer. Weatherly believed that he had a line on one, however. He asked Dietz whether the name Arthur Schwartz rang any bells. Dietz showed him the correspondence between Schwartz and himself, and Weatherly promptly labeled the coincidence fate. Their first song together was a satire on the movie title songs that were being foisted on the public. The new team's answer to the fad was "Hammacher Schlemmer, I Love You," a paean to the noted New York hardware company.

The Little Show (4/20/29; 321 performances) opened to immediate acclaim. Dietz and Schwartz's score was especially well received. Their first great hit from the show and a subsequent standard was "I Guess I'll Have to Change My Plan."

While Dietz was attending to his motion-picture duties, Schwartz collaborated with other lyricists. Less than a month after the opening of *The Little Show*

Arthur Schwartz wrote music to Agnes Morgan's lyrics for some of the tunes in *The Grand Street Follies* (5/1/29; 85 performances). Schwartz's next assignment was writing the music for two London musical comedies. The first, *Here Comes the Bride* (2/20/30; 175 performances) had two Dietz lyrics. The second, *The Co-Optimist,* was written in collaboration with Greatrex Newman.

Dietz and Schwartz were reunited for *The Second Little Show* (9/2/30; 63 performances), this time on Broadway. The hit song wasn't by Dietz and Schwartz. It was "Sing Something Simple" with words and music by Herman Hupfeld.

After a failed collaboration with composer Arthur Swanstrom on *Princess Charming* (10/13/30), Schwartz reteamed with Dietz for *Three's a Crowd* (10/15/30; 272 performances), the first of the great Dietz and Schwartz Broadway revues. Fred Allen, Clifton Webb and Libby Holman, all from the first *Little Show,* starred along with Tamara Geva, Amy Revere and The California Collegians, a band that included the young Fred MacMurray in its ranks. The sketches were written by some of the top comedy writers of the time—Corey Ford, Fred Allen, Arthur Sheekman, Groucho Marx, Laurence Schwab and others. The producer was the great Max Gordon, and the director was Hassard Short in the first of his collaborations with Dietz and Schwartz. The score, written by a number of writers, contained the great Dietz and Schwartz ballad, "Something to Remember You By." Another standard, "Body and Soul," by John Green, Edward Heyman, Robert Sour, Frank Eyton and Dietz was also introduced.

The Band Wagon (6/3/31; 262 performances), which opened at the New Amsterdam Theatre *(q.v.),* was produced by Max Gordon and directed by Hassard Short. The sketches for the revue were by Dietz and George S. Kaufman *(q.v.).* The cast featured Fred and Adele Astaire *(q.v.),* Helen Broderick, Frank Morgan and Tilly Losch.

The Band Wagon was the first American revue with real sophistication. The score contained the team's greatest song, "Dancing in the Dark." The rest of the score was equally good, especially the upbeat "New Sun in the Sky" and the charming "I Love Louisa." The closing of *The Band Wagon* after 262 performances marked the end of the career of Adele Astaire, who retired following a brief tour.

The next year brought another fine Dietz and Schwartz revue, *Flying Colors* (9/15/32; 181 performances). It was produced by Max Gordon, and this time Dietz directed. Dietz, Kaufman, Charles Sherman and Corey Ford wrote the sketches. The big hit ballad was "Alone Together." Other successful numbers were "Louisiana Hayride," "Fatal Fascination" and "A Shine on Your Shoes."

Buddy and Vilma Ebsen, performers very different

in style from the Astaires, were the featured dance team. Also in the cast were harmonica virtuoso Larry Adler, dancer Tamara Geva, comedians Imogene Coca and Patsy Kelly and the sophisticated Clifton Webb.

After Schwartz contributed music to a London show, *Nice Goings On,* he and Dietz presented their first book musical, *Revenge with Music* (11/28/34; 158 performances). Dietz directed a fine cast, including Libby Holman, Ilka Chase, Joseph Macaulay, Georges Metaxa and Charles Winninger. The score contained two distinguished ballads—"You and the Night and the Music" and "If There Is Someone Lovelier than You."

The team returned to the revue format with *At Home Abroad* (9/19/35; 198 performances), although the new show had a slight plot and was billed as a musical comedy. The plot, which followed a family on an around-the-world cruise, required a large number of librettists, including Dietz, Marc Connelly, Dion Titheradge, Raymond Knight and Reginald Gardiner. Gardiner wrote his own monologues for the show. His fellow cast members included Ethel Waters, Eleanor Powell, Eddie Foy Jr., Beatrice Lillie and Herb Williams. For the first time, a Dietz and Schwartz score didn't yield a hit ballad although "Got a Bran' New Suit," "Hottentot Potentate," "Love Is a Dancing Thing," "O What a Wonderful World" and "Thief in the Night" were all terrific numbers.

Schwartz composed a couple of shows with other lyricists before teaming up with Dietz again for *Between the Devil* (12/23/37; 93 performances). The Shuberts (*q.v.*) produced the show at the Imperial Theatre (*q.v.*). It starred Jack Buchanan, Vilma Ebsen, Evelyn Laye and Eric Brotherson. The Dietz and Schwartz score contained their requisite hit ballad, "I See Your Face Before Me." It also boasted such fine tunes as "By Myself" and "Triplets."

Schwartz then collaborated with Dorothy Fields (*q.v.*) on the Ethel Merman (*q.v.*) vehicle *Stars in Your Eyes* (2/9/39; 127 performances). Despite a fine score, it was a failure. The composer then collaborated with Oscar Hammerstein II (*q.v.*) on *American Jubilee,* a show at the New York World's Fair.

Dietz, meanwhile, joined forces with Vernon Duke (*q.v.*) on *Jackpot* (1/13/44; 67 performances), produced by Vinton Freedley (*q.v.*). Duke and Dietz collaborated again on *Sadie Thompson* (11/16/44; 60 performances), starring June Havoc. Both shows had good scores but were failures.

Schwartz tried his luck with Ira Gershwin on *Park Avenue* (11/11/46; 72 performances) and, despite a good score, it too was a failure. *Park Avenue* was the last Broadway score for Ira Gershwin.

In 1945, Dietz and Schwartz joined forces again for the revue *Inside U.S.A.* (4/30/48; 399 performances). Schwartz also produced the venture, which starred Be-

atrice Lillie and Jack Haley, along with Thelma Carpenter, Herb Shriner, Louis Nye and Carl Reiner. Arnold Auerbach, Moss Hart and Arnold B. Horwitt provided the sketches.

Inside U.S.A. had Dietz and Schwartz's last great score. The ballads "Blue Grass" and "Haunted Heart" received their share of fame, but the upbeat numbers "Rhode Island Is Famous for You," "First Prize at the Fair" and "Protect Me" are the best remembered.

This show, which was produced at the Century Theater (*q.v.*) was the last of the great Broadway revues. Television, the medium in which much of the cast would achieve their fame, was the death knell of the Broadway revue.

In 1950, Dietz made an excursion, rare for a Broadway lyricist, into the world of opera. He provided the English lyrics to the Metropolitan Opera's production of *Die Fledermaus*. He repeated the job for the Metropolitan in 1952 when he wrote the English lyrics for Puccini's *La Boheme*.

For *A Tree Grows in Brooklyn* (4/19/51; 270 performances), Schwartz teamed up again with Dorothy Fields. Betty Smith, the author of the novel, and George Abbott (*q.v.*) wrote the libretto. It was produced by Abbott and Robert Fryer. Shirley Booth, Johnny Johnston and Marcia Van Dyke helped inspire the songwriters to pen some of their best numbers, including "Make the Man Love Me," "I'm Like a New Broom," "Look Who's Dancing," "Love Is the Reason," "I'll Buy You a Star" and "Growing Pains."

By the Beautiful Sea (4/8/54; 268 performances) also starred Shirley Booth, and Schwartz and Dorothy Fields again supplied the score. Herbert and Dorothy Fields wrote the book, with Robert Fryer producing with his longtime partner Lawrence Carr. The score wasn't up to the team's previous show, but it did contain many good numbers, including "Alone Too Long," "More Love than Your Love" and "The Sea Song."

The Gay Life (11/18/61; 113 performances), based on Arthur Schnitzler's play *The Affairs of Anatol,* starred Barbara Cook and Walter Chiari along with supporting players Elizabeth Allen and Jules Munshin. The score contained two beautiful ballads, "Magic Moment" and "Something You Never Had Before."

The team's last Broadway show, *Jennie* (10/17/63; 82 performances), was a vehicle for Mary Martin (*q.v.*). Their final score contained another standout ballad, "Before I Kiss the World Goodbye." Personal conflicts among the creative staff and Dietz's poor health caused impossible obstacles to the show's success.

Following that disappointment, the team attempted other projects, notably a musical version of *Mrs. Arris Goes to Paris*. But none would reach the stage. Howard Dietz died in New York on July 30, 1983, after a long bout with Parkinson's disease. Arthur Schwartz died on September 4, 1984.

DONALDSON AWARD From 1943 to 1955, *Billboard Magazine (q.v.)* gave out the Donaldson Award, named for the magazine's founder W.H. Donaldson (1864–1925). In addition to the usual awards for best actor and actress in a play or musical and supporting actor and actress, the Donaldsons were awarded to the best first play, best debut performance (male and female) and best dancer. There were also prizes awarded to the music and libretto of musicals and theater sets and costumes for both plays and musicals.

DRAMATISTS GUILD The Dramatists Guild is the official guild of Broadway's playwrights. Prior to its inception, playwrights had no security or safeguards written into their contracts. Now the Dramatists' Guild acts in a union capacity, representing professional playwrights.

Like many of its fellow guilds and unions, the Dramatists Guild had a difficult birth. The fight for playwrights' rights began in 1878 when Steele MacKay and Clay M. Greene started the American Dramatic Authors' Society "to secure protection of their work." The society didn't make much headway, however, and members of the profession regarded it in a poor light.

In 1891, another attempt was made to organize. Thirty-three authors started the Society of American Dramatists and Composers. Bronson Howard was the director of the organization. Again, the results were inconclusive.

The first enduring organization was the Authors' League of America, which was founded on December 27, 1911. Though the League was made up mainly of novelists, playwrights were included in the ranks. Following that first meeting, the League had its constitution and bylaws accepted on December 13, 1912.

When the constitution was ratified, the organization elected its first officers. The American writer Winston Churchill was president and Theodore Roosevelt was chosen as vice president. Although playwrights were allowed to join, they had little representation. There were no playwrights on the executive committee and only three on the council. This situation began to improve in 1914 when a subcommittee was appointed to develop "the standardization of a dramatic contract." The subcommittee drew up a contract the next year, but it had little effect on the theater scene.

Two years later, another contract was written, but it, too, received little notice. In 1917, the producers had complete power over the theater, and they were very much against sharing that power or compromising their position. However, the union movement in the United States was gaining momentum, and in 1919 came the first actors' strike *(q.v.)*. The strike was successful and resulted in the creation of Actors' Equity *(q.v.)*.

The success of the performers didn't go unnoticed by the playwrights. Producer and playwright Channing Pollock went to the Executive Committee of the Authors' League and asked that the dramatists be allowed to form an "autonomous committee." The Executive Committee agreed with Pollock's request and 112 playwrights formed a dramatists' committee. The League acted as an overseer or holding company for the dramatists' group.

The group was the beginnings of the present day Dramatists Guild. The first president was playwright Owen Davis. The Guild's first challenge came in an action against the practices of the Fox Film Corporation. Fox, looking to Broadway as a source for movie ideas, had an agreement with several producers whereby Fox would back the plays in return for film rights. They would, as coproducers, also receive half the receipts. The Guild opposed the agreement that Fox had with seven managements. The Guild felt that bidding on the film rights should be competitive, thereby ensuring a higher price for the playwright. A group of 30 playwrights met in secret on December 7, 1925. Exactly one month later, during a meeting at the Hotel Roosevelt, playwright George Kelly revealed the planned manifesto to 121 members of the Guild.

This mobilized and inspired the playwrights, and a group was formed to write up a producer and dramatist agreement that would cover all pertinent points. The committee included Rachel Crothers, Eugene O'Neill *(q.v.)*, John Emerson, Gene Buck, Otto Harbach *(q.v.)*, George Kelly, George S. Kaufman *(q.v.)*, Channing Pollock, J. Hartley Manners, Le Roi Clemons and George Middleton acting as Chairman.

The completed Minimum Basic Agreement was presented to the membership and approved. The members all agreed to insist on the signing of the agreement on all future works. If the producers did not sign the agreement, then the plays would not be produced. A conference between the playwrights and producers was set for March 11, 1926. Surprisingly, all of the invited managers agreed to abide by the contract. Some of them actually agreed with the authors that change was necessary.

Several of the points raised in the contract were important to the playwright-producer relationship. The film rights were to be negotiated through competitive bidding. There was a minimum basic royalty by which any playwright must be compensated. That protected first-time playwrights. Established playwrights were covered by the rule that stated that there would be no ceilings to the royalty agreements. The producers could not make changes in the script without the permission of the playwright.

The Guild assured its future with two rules. No member of the Guild would be allowed to sign with any producer who was not a signatory to the Guild contract. And no manager who agreed to the Guild's terms could sign any playwright who was not a member of the Guild.

Many producers challenged the strength of the Guild by attempting to sign playwrights to the old contracts. The playwrights stood firm and refused to sign anything but the Minimum Basic Agreement. They acted together, and in six months the Dramatists Guild was firmly established.

On April 27, 1927, the five-year Minimum Basic Agreement was signed. Another step forward was taken on July 16, 1927, when members of the British Authors' Society agreed to abide by the Agreement when their plays were presented on Broadway.

Subsequent revisions of the contract came in 1931, 1936, 1941 and 1946. On June 14, 1955, a new basic agreement was signed incorporating the previous amendments and allowing for advances in technology, which included television.

In October 1964, the Dramatists' Guild Inc. and the Authors' Guild became two separate corporations, under the umbrella of the Authors' League. The Dramatists Guild today still serves its members by fighting for acceptance of the agreement, presenting seminars and workshops for its memberships and, perhaps most important, representing its members in Washington. This political arm of the organization seeks to improve laws protecting authors' rights and freedom of speech. The Guild has successfully fought off legal battles by the producers and has worked on behalf of playwrights from many foreign countries who have no voice in their homelands.

DUKE, VERNON (1903–1969) Duke was one of Broadway's master songwriters and also a classically trained musician who composed serious works under his real name, Vladimir Dukelsky. He escaped Russia during the Revolution and went to Europe. While there, he composed ballets for Diaghilev's Ballet Russe. Although his training under such greats as Reinhold Gliere and Marian Dombrovsky seemed to promise him a great classical career, Dukelsky achieved his greatest success as a pop songwriter.

He arrived in New York in 1929 after trying his hand at several musicals in London, including *Yvonne* (1926) (dubbed *Yvonne the Terrible* by Noel Coward); *The Yellow Mask* (1928) and *Open Your Eyes* (1930). His London lyricists Percy Greenbank, Desmond Carter and Collie Knox didn't sufficiently inspire him.

In New York, Duke interpolated songs into *The Garrick Gaieties* (6/4/30), before attempting a complete score. His first American score for *Walk a Little Faster* (12/7/32), written with E.Y. Harburg *(q.v.)*, included

Duke's first great hit song, "April in Paris." He then continued his collaboration with Harburg for the *Ziegfeld Follies of 1934* (1/4/34) and another hit, "I Like the Likes of You." He next contributed both music and lyrics to the standard "Autumn in New York" written for the revue *Thumbs Up!* (12/27/34). The next edition of the *Follies* in 1936 saw Duke teamed with Ira Gershwin *(q.v.)*, and they wrote another standard, "I Can't Get Started." Duke and Ted Fetter contributed some songs to the musical revue *The Show Is On*, which opened on Christmas Day, 1936.

Duke's first American book show followed in 1940. This was the classic *Cabin in the Sky* (10/25/40) with lyrics by John Latouche and starring Ethel Waters *(q.v.)*. *Cabin in the Sky* was a superior score that contained three hits, the title song, "Honey in the Honeycomb" and, perhaps Duke's greatest song, "Taking a Chance on Love," which had lyrics by Latouche and Ted Fetter. Latouche and Harold Adamson teamed with Duke for an Eddie Cantor vehicle, *Banjo Eyes* (12/25/41). Apart from a Cantoresque song, "We're Having a Baby (My Baby and Me)," there was little in the score that would last. *It Happens on Ice* (7/15/41) contained some forgettable Duke songs. The collaboration with Latouche continued with *The Lady Comes Across* (1/9/42), which played only three performances on Broadway.

Howard Dietz *(q.v.)* supplied the lyrics to two of Duke's shows in 1944, *Jackpot* (1/13/44) and *Sadie Thompson* (11/16/44). Neither was a success. Duke's last Broadway show introduced Bette Davis to the musical theater. *Two's Company* (12/15/52) had lyrics by Sammy Cahn and poet Ogden Nash. The only song to achieve any success, "Merry Minuet," had music and lyrics by Sheldon Harnick *(q.v.)*. This show, too, closed quickly when its star became ill and had to withdraw.

Duke found his next assignment off-Broadway. Impresario and director Ben Bagley brought Duke and Ogden Nash to the Phoenix Theater to contribute a score for Bagley's *The Littlest Revue,* (5/22/56).

Duke composed a score for the United States Coast Guard, *Tars and Spars,* and also contributed incidental music to the play *Time Remembered*. His last show, *Zenda* (8/5/63), closed in Los Angeles.

Duke's songs are models of cohesive melody and great emotion. They sound very simple and easy to hum, but when studied they reveal their intricacies, and they're difficult to play. Now, through the help of Bagley and singer Bobby Short, Duke's work is reaching a wider audience and his songs are being rediscovered and appreciated by a new generation of music lovers.

EARL CARROLL THEATRE Southeast Corner of Seventh Avenue and 50th Street. Architect: George Keister. Opening: February 25, 1922, B*avu.* The Earl Carroll Theatre had two lives in two theaters on the same site. The first Earl Carroll Theatre opened with a three-act melodrama, *Bavu,* written and directed by Earl Carroll *(q.v.).* The author, director, producer, composer and lyricist was best known as the producer of the annual revue series, the *Earl Carroll Vanities (q.v.). Bavu* closed after 25 performances. The show is completely forgettable save for the fact that in the cast was the future movie star William Powell.

The second and third productions at the theater were also flops. *Just Because,* a musical comedy, opened on March 22 and ran for only 46 performances. *Raymond Hitchcock's Pinwheel* was an even bigger failure. It opened June 15 and closed after 35 performances.

Finally the theater had a hit with *The Gingham Girl* (8/28/22). The show ran 322 performances. The next hit in the theater was the first edition of the *Earl Carroll Vanities.* The show opened on July 5, 1923 with music and lyrics by Carroll. He also produced and directed the show. The revue series was planned as a rival to Florenz Ziegfeld's *(q.v.) Follies (q.v.).*

With the advent of the Depression, Carroll's fortunes floundered and he was forced to rent the theater to Radio Pictures for $12,750 a month plus half the taxes. The company was going to use the theater to premiere its film production of *Rio Rita,* originally a show produced by Ziegfeld. As if in reaction to their plans, Carroll leased Ziegfeld's old stomping ground, the New Amsterdam Theatre *(q.v.),* for his next edition of the *Vanities.*

The old Earl Carroll Theater seated only 1,000 people, making it unsuitable for the large productions to which Carroll aspired. When Ziegfeld built his own new theater in 1927, Carroll, unfazed by his financial problems, set about to build a new space of his own.

William R. Edrington, a Texas oil baron, was Carroll's chief backer. They bought the land east of the original theater for a million dollars and leveled the building on that site. The builders retained the office building atop the old theater, but tore out the theater itself.

Columnist Ed Sullivan *(q.v.)* wrote about the plans for the new theater:

If you have walked along 49th or 50th Streets just east of Seventh Avenue you have seen in skeleton form the

The first Earl Carroll Theatre Courtesy Billy Rose Theater Collection.

temple that will house the Earl Carroll "wonder works" this coming season on the same site where the former Earl Carroll Theater stood for nine years. The theater is in the "strictly modern" style in the "straight and set-back" lines of the new skyscrapers.

If you've happened to notice a man hurrying here and there in an old smock "riding the whole horse," watching the builders, experimenting with costumes and colors and listening to the boys from Tin Pan Alley as they chanted their melodies, it was the indefatigable Mr. Carroll. It is hard work but he can stand it because he "grew up in theaters."

In dwelling on the impending innovations, of this, his latest and greatest project, he said, "What I want to be remembered for are the changes I have made in the theater, even if they are quickly forgotten."

A very canny showman is Mr. Carroll, and a student of the public. So he has thought it all out. He took time out to say, "All that is wrong with show business today is the prices that are charged." The way around high prices, he intimated, is by mass production, and "The form to which mass production best adapts itself is the big revue."

So Mr. Carroll, a logician for all his persistent elegance, will concentrate on big revues, and his new edifice will seat 3,000 people with a $3 top, even for opening night.

Next Thursday evening, therefore, Earl Carroll—who knows how to make an entrance—will submit that a new $4,500,000 theater, bearing his name, will be opened and ready with the ninth Vanities to do business. It will be a milestone. One has Mr. Carroll's word for this.

The new lobby was three times as large as the old one. Remarkably, the new theater's seating capacity was also tripled. There were seats for 1,500 patrons in the orchestra alone. The boxes sat 200 people and the loge and balcony areas seated 1,300.

To utilize the space to its maximum, the 60-by-100-foot space under the balcony was given to lounge areas and balcony space. The theater was the first to be completely cooled backstage, in the auditorium and in the public areas.

The interior of the building was a classic art deco design. The walls were covered with black velvet. Brushed aluminum accented the interior. The lobby area was covered in polished black vitrolite, streaked with brown. The carpeting was in three shades of green and the seats covered in plush, coral colored fabric. The orchestra seats were equipped with little lights so patrons could refer to the program during the show.

The dressing rooms, decorated in chromium, silk and satin, were as well appointed as the audience area. The performers had their own tables with triple mirrors. There was also a complete intercom system as well as a gymnasium, showers, a safe for valuables, a refrigerator and by the stage a mirror room for last minute checks on makeup and costumes.

The stage area boasted two elevator platforms, like those in Radio City Music Hall, which enabled the orchestra to be raised from the basement to stage level while playing. Sixty stagehands were required to operate the stage machinery. Five thousand Berliner acoustical discs were put into the walls to control the acoustics. Six speakers were placed in the auditorium to boost the stage sound, and 20 more were placed in the lounges and lobby.

Because of the highly polished and reflective surfaces throughout the theater lighting became very important. In true art deco style, the lighting was concealed. The indirect lighting effects were controlled by a console in the orchestra pit. Each fixture had four colored circuits—red, blue, white and green. This idea was later copied by Radio City Music Hall.

Carroll finished off the theater, which cost a total of $4.5 million by hanging the now famous sign over the stage door, "Through These Portals Pass The Most Beautiful Girls In The World."

The theater's premiere attraction was the *Earl Carroll's Vanities of 1931* (8/27/31), which opened with the Depression in full swing. There was a staff of 84 men in the house. They were all at least six feet tall and dressed in dark uniforms with chrome highlights, to match the inside of the theater. There was no box office, but rather a long table with eight attendants in front of the ticket racks. During intermission, the ushers wheeled a huge chromium-plated tank down the aisles and dispensed free ice water to the audience.

Carroll couldn't make the theater a success. The show was especially lavish and could not recoup its cost on the low ticket prices. It also was expensive to operate the giant theater and maintain its lavish interior. Within six months, Carroll lost the theater. He was sued by the Seven Fifty-five Corporation for $366,632.90. Carroll also owed $64,952.20 for three months back rent, taxes and interest.

Ziegfeld decided to take it over. He changed its name to the Casino and reopened the space with a revival of his great hit, *Show Boat* (q.v.) (5/19/32; 181 performances). During the run of *Show Boat*, Ziegfeld died and the show closed.

George White (q.v.), the other of the big three to produce an annual revue series, used the theater for *Melody* (2/14/33; 80 performances), one of the last Broadway operettas. It was written by Sigmund Romberg (q.v.) and Irving Caesar.

A vaudeville show entitled *Casino Varieties* opened next with, in an attempt to counter the effect of the Depression on the box office, a top ticket price of $1.50. This was the theater's last legitimate show. It closed only four years after its opening.

Clifford Fischer, a former agent for the Orpheum Circuit, took up the theater's lease. He took out the seating and put tiers in the balcony and orchestra upon which he installed tables. Fischer, responding to a French wave that was sweeping over New York, called the new theater-restaurant The French Casino. It was the second such conversion, following the lead of the Casino de Paris *(q.v.),* which had been the Gallo Theater. Later, the Manhattan Casino was made out of Hammerstein's Theater *(q.v.)* on Broadway at 53rd Street. Of all the Manhattan casinos, the French Casino was the most successful.

The theater opened on Christmas Day, 1934, featuring a show modeled on the Folies Bergere—ironic, since this was Earl Carroll's inspiration also. The revues at the French Casino were very successful. The glamorous theater was perfectly suited to the spectacular shows on the stage.

The French Casino prospered until showman Billy Rose, owner of the Casino de Paris, bought the building. He redecorated the interior in a more Latin manner and extended the stage out from the proscenium. He renamed the space the Casa Manana, featuring a $2.50 price for dinner, dancing and the show. It opened on January 10, 1938, and closed by the end of the year.

In 1939, the six-story office building fronting Seventh Avenue was razed. The auditorium and stage house still stand, but the interiors were replaced with retail space. A Whelan's Drug Store and then a Woolworth's took the place of the magnificent theater. Historians have wondered whether any vestige of the art deco masterpiece remains behind the false walls of the retail space.

EARL CARROLL VANITIES   There were three great revue series that graced Broadway in the early years of the century—the *Ziegfeld Follies (q.v.),* the *George White's Scandals (q.v.)* and the *Earl Carroll Vanities.* Each of the three had its own trademark, the special stamp of its producers. Florenz Ziegfeld *(q.v.)* relied on star-filled extravaganzas featuring top talents performing material by some of America's greatest composers. George White *(q.v.)* produced jazzy, fast moving revues with flappers and sheiks and a hint of bawdiness. Earl Carroll *(q.v.),* on the other hand, employed few great stars, relied on mostly second-rate material but surpassed his competitors with vulgarity, burlesque *(q.v.)* inspired humor and ample nudity.

There were 11 editions of the *Vanities* and two *Earl Carroll Sketchbooks.* Among the stars who appeared in the series were Patsy Kelly, Peggy Hopkins Joyce, Joe Cook, W.C. Fields, Milton Berle, Ray Dooley, Jack Benny, Helen Broderick, Lillian Roth and Jimmy Savo.

Carroll was author of the famous sign that hung over his stage door, "Through These Portals Pass the Most Beautiful Girls in the World." It was a direct challenge to Ziegfeld whose aim was "Glorifying the American Girl."

The first edition of the *Vanities* (7/5/23; 204 performances) was the Earl Carroll Theatre's *(q.v.)* premiere

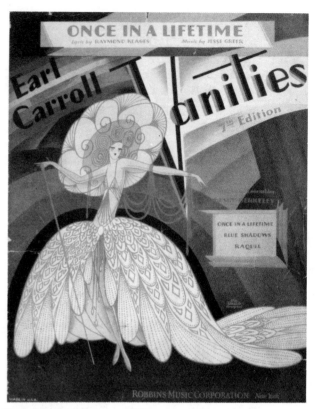

Sheet music for Earl Carroll Vanities

production. Carroll himself supplied the music and lyrics. The revue's first number was entitled, "The Birth of a New Revue." Show girls came out representing the other revue series on Broadway—the *Cohan Revue,* the Winter Garden Theater's *(q.v.) Passing Shows,* the *Scandals,* the *Music Box Revue,* the *Greenwich Village Follies* and the *Ziegfeld Follies.* Once these lovelies had paraded across the footlights, out came the loveliest of all, Alice Weaver, representing the *Vanities.*

Like Ziegfeld, Carroll himself handpicked the girls in his revue. He stated, "The Ziegfeld clotheshorse is passe. It's not enough for a girl to be beautiful and dumb. Today vivacity must be a girl's outstanding characteristic, for vivacity means youth and the speed of modernity. And the girl must be intelligent." Carroll's girls were certainly not clotheshorses. So much of them was exposed that Carroll's barber personally shaved every inch of their bodies.

The next edition of the *Vanities* (10/10/24) opened at the Music Box Theater *(q.v.).* For this edition, Carroll expanded his role, directing and supplying the libretto in addition to producing and songwriting. The show featured a scene in which, to the rhythms of Ravel's "Bolero," a bevy of show girls paraded in King Solomon's court wearing nothing but peacock headdresses. Each girl was armed with a fan and what was called "Carroll's chastity belt," a thin strip covering her privates. This came to the attention of the local authorities who assigned patrolmen to a performance. When, in the opening number, Kathryn Ray swung nude on a giant pendulum, the police made their move. The show girl was pulled from her upside-down position and covered with a blanket. She tore the blanket off and, to the amusement of the audience, was chased by a phalanx of cops. The audience thought the incident was part of the show. Then Carroll stepped before the footlights and asked the audience which it preferred, the show as presented on opening night or a bowdlerized version that would pass the censors' criticisms. The audience, of course, demanded the original version, and the show continued. The police realized an attack on the show itself might not succeed. After all, the members of the audience were well aware of what they were getting when they purchased their tickets. So the authorities cooked up another scheme.

Carroll was arrested for exhibiting lewd and indecent pictures of his show girls in the front of the theater. The police charged that minors might be badly affected if they happened to see the pictures.

The judge refused to allow testimony by artists as to the artistic merits of the pictures, which were painted by George Maillard Kesslere. Even the prestigious *New York Times* felt obliged to print an editorial in Carroll's defense. Carroll went to jail instead of posting the modest bail. He proclaimed, "I'm going to jail not for publicity but to focus attention on these self-appointed censors. If I gave the bail of $300 set by the judge, this case would be merely one of many. I want it to stand out so the real people of New York, who are against fanatical censorship, will see what is being done. It is all a very serious affair to me, for conviction could mean the end of my career."

Immediately, the box office improved and continued to do so each day the producer remained in stir. Finally, Carroll's brother Jim, his business manager, persuaded him to pay the bail. The trial commenced with Carroll pointing to the nude marble statues on the facade of the New York Public Library. The showman won his case, and the *Vanities* were allowed to continue, treading a fine line between titillation and indecency.

The 1925 edition of the *Vanities* was the most successful to date, although none of its elements were especially notable. Its long run, 440 performances, might again be explained by the strength of publicity. On February 22, 1926, Carroll held a joint birthday party for George Washington and William R. Edrington, a Texas oil man and chief backer of Carroll's productions. To add spice to the proceedings, Carroll arranged for show girl Joyce Hawley to frolic in a bathtub filled with champagne. Phil Payne, a reporter on the *New York Daily Mirror* broke the story in the next day's edition, much to the consternation of his rival dailies. *The Graphic,* one of the sleaziest of New York's dailies, printed a picture of the incident on its front page. The photo was one of the *Graphic's* infamous composite

shots, that is, faked. This came to the attention of the federal government, which charged Carroll with breaking the laws of Prohibition.

Carroll, remembering his last brush with the law and its succeeding impact at the box office, refused to settle for a plea of disorderly conduct and a small fine. He insisted that no crime had been committed because the bathtub actually contained no champagne but mostly ginger ale with a dash of sherry for color. The fact that it wasn't illegal to bathe in ginger ale was immaterial, Carroll had clearly lied and that was against the law. Carroll had testified before a grand jury that no one had gotten in the bathtub. Carroll was sentenced to a year and a day in prison, guilty of perjury. After the opening of the 1927 edition of the *Vanities,* he was sent to the penitentiary in Atlanta where he remained for 4 months and 11 days.

That edition of the *Vanities* evolved into the *Earl Carroll's Vanities Featuring The New Charlot Revue.* That show, in turn, further changed into the *Earl Carroll's Vanities of 1927.* Though the edition was not a success by any title, Carroll was not fazed. He made plans to expand his empire by building a new theater on the site of the original Earl Carroll Theater.

In the *New York Times,* Sidney Skolsky described the making of the next *Vanities,* the 1928 edition:

There were the days when Earl Carroll started to assemble the girls. Then came nights of rehearsal. Carroll standing out in the orchestra in a lemon-colored smock watching Busby Berkeley put the girls through a dance routine until two in the morning.

Then more nights of rehearsal. Warm nights. Hot nights. Everybody sweating. Chorus girls and stars. Legs dancing; gags cracked without feeling funny. Carroll giving every girl a brand new silver dollar for learning a new routine.

Then came more days and nights of rehearsal, from eleven in the morning until five the next morning. Soon no one knows, and it doesn't matter, whether it is day or night. A final dress rehearsal and everything moves laboriously and seems to be wrong. A tryout in Atlantic City. This is merely a rehearsal with an audience looking on. After the audience goes, the players work on.

A week at Atlantic City and not one member of the Vanities was on the beach. Atlantic City. It's just another theater. Days and nights and weeks of this, and then finally, the little item: Tomorrow evening at the Earl Carroll Theater the seventh edition of the Earl Carroll Vanities starring W.C. Fields.

That 1928 edition of the *Vanities* marked Carroll's return to the theater. He hadn't lost his touch. The *New York Times* stated, "Considering Mr. Carroll's past achievements in the theater and out, it is conceivably not too foolhardy a procedure to come out here with the unqualified statement that this is the best Vanities of them all." The show ran 200 performances.

Florenz Ziegfeld had just opened his luxurious Ziegfeld Theater (q.v.) on Sixth Avenue and 54th Street. Carroll was determined to outdo the legendary showman with his own art-deco palace. While it was being constructed, Carroll mounted his next edition of the *Vanities* (there was no 1929 edition) in the theater that Ziegfeld made famous, the New Amsterdam (q.v.). A young Vincente Minnelli, just coming from his success at Radio City Music Hall, designed the costumes. The score, for once, contained some hit songs, notably those of Harold Arlen (q.v.) and Ted Koehler, including "Contagious Rhythm" and "Hittin' the Bottle." Jack Benny made his Broadway debut in the production.

In the show, Carroll featured a number called "Modes—Window at Merl's." He placed five chorus girls in the window of a store. Comedian Jimmy Savo entered the window and on the pretext of changing the mannequins' outfits completely undressed them. At the first matinee, the show was raided and again Carroll was in front of a court. He won the case, foiling the censors again. The show ran 215 performances.

The new Earl Carroll Theater (q.v.) was opened on August 27, 1931, with the *Earl Carroll's Vanities of 1931*. The show and theater building together cost $4.5 million.

Ziegfeld was known for his tableaux, designed by Ben Ali Haggin, which featured women in skin colored tights arranged artfully in dramatic poses. Carroll emulated this Ziegfeld trademark with his "living curtains," only Carroll usually left out the tights. The living curtains were based on similar routines performed at the Folies Bergere. In this edition, Carroll had two living curtains: a perfume curtain with the girls posed on a drapery that sent gusts of Odor de la Noche through the audience and a dinosaur curtain staged to the music of "Dance of the Dinosaur" (composed by Hyman Grossman). This last great edition of the annual series (and the only edition to play the new theater) closed after 300 performances.

The next *Vanities* opened on September 27, 1932, at the Broadway Theatre (q.v.). It played only 87 performances, yet it contained one of the greatest songs to come out of any Broadway show, "I Got a Right to Sing the Blues" by Harold Arlen and Ted Koehler. With the country suffering from the hardships of the Depression, the face of Broadway was changing. Carroll himself had troubles with capital, and Carroll's chief backer, William R. Edrington, himself went bankrupt. Carroll was forced to give up his theater after the premiere production. It was later a home to others' productions including, ironically, a revival of Ziegfeld's greatest success, *Show Boat* (q.v.).

The final *Vanities* opened at the St. James Theatre (q.v.) eight years later on January 13, 1940. The 1932 edition had suffered from the nation's preoccupation with the Depression. This one was a victim of the coming of World War II. It proved a sad finale to the once-popular series, lasting only 25 performances. Carroll was killed with show girl Beryl Wallace in a plane accident on June 17, 1947.

EDISON THEATER 240 W. 47th Street in the Edison Hotel. Opening: March 5, 1970; *Show Me Where the Good Times Are*. Producer Norman Kean built the Edison Theater for those shows that were too small for ordinary Broadway houses. The Edison didn't achieve much success despite the quality of some of its offerings, which included *Happy Birthday, Wanda June, Don't Bother Me I Can't Cope, Sizwe Banzi Is Dead* and *The Island* and *Me and Bessie*. However, the theater finally hit pay dirt when it presented *Oh! Calcutta!*. The show had previously played at the Eden Theater off-Broadway, where it opened on January 17, 1969. Its audiences were made up of Japanese tourists. Kean committed suicide in January 1988, and *Oh! Calcutta!* finally closed in 1989, making it the second longest-running show in Broadway history.

ED SULLIVAN THEATRE 1697 Broadway between 53rd and 54th Streets. Architect: Herbert J. Krapp. Opening: November 30, 1927; *The Golden Dawn*. In 1910, Arthur Hammerstein (q.v.) was determined not to ever speak to his father, Oscar Hammerstein I (q.v.), again. By 1927, eight years after Oscar's death, Arthur was left to run the Hammerstein empire on his own. By then, Oscar II (q.v.) had made a name for himself on Broadway. Arthur decided to build the Hammerstein Theater on Broadway as a tribute to his father, using his profits from the Rudolf Friml/Herbert Stothart operetta *Rose-Marie* to finance the project.

For the first show, *Golden Dawn* (11/30/27; 200 performances), he hired Oscar II, Emmerich Kalman, Herbert Stothart and Otto Harbach to write the libretto and score. Oscar II's brother Reginald directed the proceedings. The next success at the theater was the Jerome Kern (q.v.), Oscar Hammerstein II show, *Sweet Adeline* (9/3/29; 233 performances) with Arthur producing and Reginald directing. The cast included Charles Butterworth, Irene Franklin and Gus Salzer. Torch singer Helen Morgan stopped the show with "Why Was I Born?" and "Don't Ever Leave Me."

Arthur, a heavy investor in the stock market, lost most of his fortune in the crash. Arthur needed a hit show. Unfortunately his next production, *Luana* (9/17/30; 21 performances) was not it. Rudolf Friml (q.v.) and J. Keirn Brennan wrote the operetta's score. By the thirties, the operetta was going out of favor.

With his theater dark and no prospective show in the wings and its neighboring office building almost empty, Arthur was forced to sell. Later that year, after one more producing attempt, he declared bankruptcy. The theater was bought by the young producing team of Frank Mandel and Laurence Schwab. They joined with

Oscar II to present shows in what was renamed the Manhattan Theater.

The first production in the Manhattan was *Free for All* (9/8/31; 15 performances). Richard Whiting provided the music and Oscar II the libretto. Oscar also coauthored the libretto with Laurence Schwab, who was also the director. In the cast were Jack Haley, Tamara and Benny Goodman's orchestra. Schwab, Mandel and Hammerstein's next offering at the Manhattan Theater was *East Wind* (10/27/31; 23 performances). Sigmund Romberg *(q.v.)* composed the score, and this time Frank Mandel collaborated with Oscar on the libretto.

Composer Vincent Youmans *(q.v.)* produced the next show at the Manhattan Theater, *Through the Years* (1/28/31; 20 performances). The musical, with music by Youmans and lyrics by Edward Heyman, was also a failure; however, the title song and "Drums in My Heart" were hit songs.

The theater remained dark until Billy Rose *(q.v.)* bought it and renamed it the Billy Rose Music Hall. Rose opened it on June 21, 1934, as a theater restaurant. Rose's luck was no better than that of his predecessors. He sold it, and on November 27, 1934, the theater reopened as the Manhattan Music Hall.

The Manhattan Music Hall was also a failure, and on February 14, 1936, the theater was renamed the Manhattan Theater. The Federal Theater Project *(q.v.)* presented a play by Edwin and Albert Barker—*American Holiday* (2/21/36; 20 performances).

The closing of *American Holiday* marked the end of the theater as a live venue. CBS bought the theater and made it a CBS Radio Playhouse in September 1936. When television took over the airwaves, CBS converted the space into a television studio. Its most famous tenant was the "Ed Sullivan Show." In 1967, the theater was renamed, in the emcee's honor, the Ed Sullivan Theatre. In the eighties, the theater was used by the Reeves Communications Company to tape their television production "Kate and Allie."

ELLIS, ABRAHAM (1901–1985) Abraham Ellis was known as the "Hatcheck King." He was one of the many poorly educated men who made their fortunes on Broadway by using their brains. He was born in a tenement on the Lower East Side of Manhattan. His father tried to support the family by pressing pants. Young Abraham helped support the family through a series of odd jobs. He was a delivery boy at 11, and at 14 he was a candy butcher in Oscar Hammerstein I's *(q.v.)* Manhattan Opera House. Twenty-three years later, Ellis would buy the building for $750,000.

Ellis moved from selling candy to checking hats and coats at Webster Hall in Greenwich Village. He was promoted when his boss left to fight in World War I.

He paid $500 to take over the concession and made the first of many improvements.

When the Lusitania sank, among the passengers to perish was a Yiddish actor who had willed his money to his daughter. This daughter, Yetta Samuel, married Ellis, and her inheritance went to buy the hatcheck concession at the Brooklyn Elks Club for her new husband.

Ellis wasn't content to stay at the Brooklyn Elks Club. By the 1940s, he held the concessions at the Latin Quarter *(q.v.)*, the Algonquin, the Copacabana, and the St. Regis. At these and other clubs he introduced the first hatcheck girls and numbered claim checks. In these same nightspots, he also operated concessions for photographs, washroom towels and cigars.

In 1951, the *New Yorker* profiled him as a man who "squirms, slouches, slumps and bounces up and down." He divorced his first wife and agreed to pay her $1,000 a week and give her custody of their children after she accused him of raising the children at nightclubs and prizefights. The trial was right out of Damon Runyon's *Little Miss Marker*.

ELTINGE THEATRE   See EMPIRE THEATER (2).

ELYSEE   See JOHN GOLDEN THEATER.

EMBASSY 49TH STREET THEATER   See CHARLES HOPKINS THEATER.

EMPIRE THEATER (1) 1430 Broadway at 40th Street. Architect: J.B. McElfatrick. Opening: January 25, 1893; *The Girl I Left Behind*. Producer Charles Frohman built what was to become the most beloved theater in New York history. Frohman hired J.B. McElfatrick as architect of the Empire, the first of seven theaters that the architect designed. The Empire building was five stories tall and achieved many firsts. It was the first theater to have electricity, although it also had a backup gas system in case the electricity went out. The theater was also the first to be built entirely on the first floor. Other theaters, following the example of English predecessors, were built with the balcony at ground level and the orchestra underground. The Empire was probably also the first theater to have an electric sign. It was also the first theater to follow the 1892 building code, which provided greater fire-prevention measures. Finally, the Empire hosted three companies in their initial engagements: those of John Drew, Maude Adams and owner Charles Frohman.

Frohman's initial attraction, *The Girl I Left Behind,* was an immediate success, as was the new theater. *The New York Times* exclaimed: "Every spectator is near enough the stage to be in sympathy with the actors." The critic's only reservation was that "the rows of seats are entirely too close for complete comfort, but that is

Empire Theater Courtesy Billy Rose Theater Collection.

a fault common to most theaters." According to the critic, the "decorations of the interior are handsome and tasteful. The prevailing tints are subdued red, terra cotta, cream and dull green."

Surprisingly, although reviews of the theater were favorable, Frohman decided to gut the interior and hire John M. Carrere and Thomas Hastings to redo it. The New Empire Theater opened on October 13, 1903, with John Drew starring in *Captain of Dieppe*. Again the *Times* was enthusiastic: "The elimination of all columns in the rear of the house and the introduction of broad promenades at the rear on each floor are features which add to the practical conveniences of the house. Another advantage which will be appreciated is the installation of seats modeled after a pattern designed by Mr. Frohman. These are roomy and have exactly the right shape, with pneumatic air cushions."

The first years of the Empire's history saw many classic productions. Among them were Dumas's *Lady of the Camellias* (1895) with Olga Nethersole, Oscar Wilde's *The Importance of Being Ernest* (1895) with Henry Miller, Viola Allen and William Faversham and *When*

Knighthood Was in Flower (5/2/04) with Julia Marlowe and Tyrone Power, Sr.

Among the most famous of all productions at the Empire was the J.M. Barrie classic, *Peter Pan* (11/6/05; 223 performances) starring Maude Adams. By most accounts, the greatest of all Pans, Adams, returned to the Empire as Peter Pan in special holiday attractions in 1906, 1912, and 1915. Adams had previously appeared at the Empire with leading man Robert Edeson in Barrie's *The Little Minister* (9/27/1898). Later, she also appeared at the Empire in another Barrie play, *Quality Street* (1/6/08). Another success at the Empire for Adams was *The Pretty Sister of Jose* (11/10/03). On February 6, 1905, she opened two plays in repertory— *'Op o' My Thumb* and a revival of *The Little Minister*. On January 15, 1908, she appeared at the Empire in *The Jesters*.

Other notable productions at the theater in its earliest years were *The Good Hope* (1907) with Dame Ellen Terry, Edith Craig and Beatrice Forbes-Robinson; George Bernard Shaw's *Captain Brassbound's Conversion* (1907) with Dame Ellen Terry; and Sir Arthur Wing

Pinero's *Trelawny of the Wells* (1/1/11) with Ethel Barrymore, Louise Drew, Constance Collier and Edward Arnold.

Frohman, one of the greatest producers of his time, died on May 7, 1915, when a German submarine sank the Lusitania. Frohman's brother Daniel, a legend in his own right, was an executive of Paramount Famous Lasky Corporation. The corporation took over management of the Empire, but it was both unsuccessful and insensitive to the Empire's artists. In 1920, producer Gilbert Miller took over the management.

J.M. Barrie had other productions at the theater without star Maude Adams. Among them were *Dear Brutus* (12/23/18) with Helen Hayes (*q.v.*) and William Gillette and *Mary Rose* (12/22/20) with Ruth Chatterton.

Other notable productions of the 1920s were *Blood and Sand* (9/20/21) with Otis Skinner and Cornelia Otis Skinner; *The Dove* (2/11/25) with Judith Anderson, Holbrook Blinn, Sidney Toler and William Harrigan; Noel Coward's *Easy Virtue* (12/7/25) with Jane Cowl and Joyce Cary; *The Captive* (9/29/26) with Helen Menken and Basil Rathbone; *Her Cardboard Lover* (3/21/27) with Jeanne Eagles and Leslie Howard; and P.G. Wodehouse's *Candle-Light* (9/30/29) with Gertrude Lawrence and Leslie Howard.

Maude Adams wasn't the only star associated with the Empire. Katharine Cornell (*q.v.*) opened in the *Age of Innocence* on November 27, 1928. Her subsequent appearances at the Empire included *Wingless Victory* (12/23/26; 108 performances); the classic play *The Barretts of Wimpole Street* (2/9/31; 372 performances); and *Candida* (3/10/37).

John Gielgud starred on the Empire Stage in *Hamlet*. The production opened on October 8, 1936, and played 132 performances, the longest-running *Hamlet* in New York history until the 1964 production starring Richard Burton, which played only five more performances. Assisting Gielgud were fellow cast members Lillian Gish, Judith Anderson and Malcom Keen West.

Gilbert Miller's reign at the Empire drew to a close in 1931. The theater was sold to the 1432 Broadway Corporation. Luckily, they were adept at booking the theater. Their first offering was *The Barretts of Wimpole Street* on February 9, 1931, with Katharine Cornell's acclaimed portrayal of Elizabeth Barrett Browning.

During the 1930s, there was the American premiere of Kurt Weill (*q.v.*) and Bertolt Brecht's *The Threepenny Opera*. The musical opened at the Empire on April 13, 1933. Unfortunately the show wasn't a success and only played 12 performances. Elmer Rice's *We the People* (1/20/33) fared little better, only running 50 performances. In 1934, Gertrude Stein and Virgil Thomson's brilliant *Four Saints in Three Acts* (4/2/34) was revived for 18 performances. Zoe Akin's *The Old Maid* (1/7/35) did better with Judith Anderson, Helen Menken

and Margaret Dale starring. The Edith Wharton story played for 298 performances. The great Ethel Waters played the Empire in Dorothy and DuBose Heyward's *Mamba's Daughters*. The play opened January 3, 1939, and ran 162 performances.

The Empire's most famous tenant was *Life with Father*. The classic comedy was written by Howard Lindsay and Russel Crouse. Mrs. Lindsay, Dorothy Stickney, starred in the play along with her husband. *Life with Father* opened on November 8, 1939, and ran eight years, 3,224 performances, the longest-running play in theater history. One of the many children who played in *Life with Father* was John Drew Devereaux who originated the role of Clarence. The boy's grandfather was John Drew, one of the most popular actors of his time.

The Empire changed hands again on July 31, 1946, when it was purchased by real estate operator Jacob Freidus. The new owner was, unfortunately, not interested in theater and saw the Empire for its development possibilities. Then playing at the Empire were Alfred Lunt and Lynn Fontanne (*q.v.*) in Terrance Rattigan's comedy *O Mistress Mine*. The comedy opened on January 23, 1946, and proved to be the Lunts' longest running hit, eventually playing 451 performances.

Howard Lindsay, Dorothy Stickney and John Drew Deveraux returned to the theater in the Lindsay and Crouse play *Life with Mother*. The comedy opened October 20, 1948, and ran 265 performances.

Two years after he purchased the theater, Freidus sold the property to the Astor family. On October 11, 1952, Viscount Astor II died. The family hurriedly sold their properties to raise capital. A textile firm, M. Lowenstein & Sons, purchased the theater.

Three other hits were to play the Empire. In Carson McCullers great play, *Member of the Wedding,* Ethel Waters returned to the Empire's stage. She was joined by Julie Harris and Brandon deWilde, both giving wonderful performances. *Member of the Wedding* opened on January 5, 1950, and played 501 performances. John Van Druten's drama *I Am a Camera,* based on Christopher Isherwood's Berlin stories, also starred Julie Harris. It opened on November 28, 1950, and ran 262 performances.

Shirley Booth opened in the Empire's last tenant, *The Time of the Cuckoo* by Arthur Laurents, on October 15, 1952. After 263 performances, on May 30, 1953, the play closed. On that date, Shirley Booth led the audience in singing "Auld Lang Syne," and the curtain came down for the last time.

Brooks Atkinson wrote of the Empire: "It had the finest auditorium of any theater in its time, the largest and most hospitable lobby and all the comforts of a cultivated institution. The ticket-taker wore full dress and silk hat. The Empire retained its prestige long after

Charles Frohman died. He built so well that the pride and luster of his theater outlived him."

Cornelia Otis Skinner lead a benefit for the American National Theater Academy *(q.v.)* on Sunday, May 24, 1953, at the Empire. The benefit's theme was "Highlights of the Empire." She described the theater as "That beloved gilt-prosceniumed and red-plush theater which really IS theater. It was a lovely and exciting temple."

The Empire was replaced by an office building.

EMPIRE THEATER (2)

EMPIRE THEATER (2) 236 W. 42nd Street. Architect: Thomas W. Lamb. Opening: September 11, 1912. Producer A.H. Woods hired Thomas W. Lamb, one of the preeminent motion picture theater architects in the twenties and thirties, to design the Eltinge Theatre, named after famed female impersonator Julian Eltinge. Lamb came up with a distinguished beaux-arts design for his theater.

The theater was successful, but Woods, like other producers, fell on hard times when the Depression hit. He lost the theater, and it became a burlesque *(q.v.)*

Eltinge Theatre Program

house. When Mayor Fiorello LaGuardia cracked down on burlesque in 1943, the theater was converted to a movie policy as the Laff-Movie. In 1954, it became the Empire Theater.

Because the Empire contains only 759 seats, which are spread over two balconies and an orchestra, the 42nd Street Redevelopment Project has not recommended that the Empire be saved. Only the facade would be incorporated into the plan, probably as a larger lobby for a shopping arcade or adjacent theater. If alternate usage is adopted, the Empire's interior still might be saved.

ETHEL BARRYMORE THEATRE

ETHEL BARRYMORE THEATRE 243–49 W. 47th between Seventh and Eighth Avenue. Architect: Herbert J. Krapp. Opened: December 20, 1928; *The Kingdom of God.* Ethel Barrymore *(q.v.)* was, in the 1920s, considered one of the top Broadway actresses. The Shuberts *(q.v.)* admired her artistry and wanted to put her under contract. They offered to build a theater in her name if she would join the Shubert fold. She agreed, and the Shuberts hired Herbert J. Krapp, noted theater architect, to design the building.

On December 20, 1928, the new theater opened with the eponymous star in G. Martinez Sierra's *The Kingdom of God.* The theater was hailed as ideal. It would later also prove to be a popular theater, housing successes in every decade. Of Ethel Barrymore's performance in *The Kingdom of God,* critic *(q.v.)* Heywood Broun wrote: "Miss Barrymore's performance is the most moving piece of acting I have ever seen in the theater."

The Kingdom of God and the theater's next attraction, *The Love Duel* (4/15/29), were directed by E.M. Blythe. Blythe was in reality Miss Barrymore herself. Several plays were next presented at the theater without Miss Barrymore, among them *Death Takes a Holiday* (12/26/29). The play, written by Walter Ferris, was adapted from the original Italian play written by Alberto Casella. Death decides to come to earth where he falls in love with a mortal who willingly agrees to return with him to the other side. The play was originally a comedy but when adapted by Mr. Ferris became a drama.

Ethel Barrymore returned to the theater in her next play, *Scarlet Sister Mary* (11/25/30). Its 23-performance run wasn't exactly a surprise, given that Miss Barrymore appeared in the play in blackface.

British author Ivor Novello's drawing room comedy, *The Truth Game* (12/29/30; 105 performances), marked Billie Burke's return to the stage following the death of her husband, Florenz Ziegfeld *(q.v.).*

The star for whom the theater was named returned in a revival of *The School for Scandal* (11/10/31). The production introduced her son John Drew Colt to Broadway. Her daughter, Ethel Barrymore Colt, had been introduced in her mother's production of the short-lived *Scarlet Sister Mary.*

Ethel Barrymore Theatre   Courtesy Billy Rose Theater Collection.

The Barrymore was a perfect midsize house for the production of musicals. Its first, Cole Porter's *(q.v.)* *The Gay Divorce* (11/29/32), opened with Fred Astaire *(q.v.)* (his first appearance without his sister, Adele), Claire Luce, Eric Blore, Betty Starbuck, Erik Rhodes and G.P. Huntley. The show included such Porter hits as "After You, Who?," "I've Got You on My Mind," and "Night and Day."

After *The Gay Divorce* moved to the Shubert Theater *(q.v.),* another sophisticate premiered his work at the Barrymore. Noel Coward's sparkling *Design for Living* (1/24/33) starred Alfred Lunt and Lynn Fontanne *(q.v.)* and the playwright.

The next success on the Barrymore stage did not come until Clare Boothe's comedy drama *The Women* (12/26/36; 657 performances). The play starred Ilka Chase, Margalo Gillmore, Betty Lawford, Audrey Christie, Marjorie Main and Arlene Francis.

The next musical to play the theater, *Knickerbocker Holiday* (10/19/38), starred Walter Huston. The Kurt Weill *(q.v.),* Maxwell Anderson score is best remembered for "September Song." It was followed by S.N. Behrman's *No Time for Comedy* (4/17/39), starring Katharine Cornell *(q.v.),* Laurence Olivier and Margalo Gillmore.

Ethel Barrymore appeared for the last time in the theater in *An International Incident* (4/2/40). Unfortunately it ran a scant 15 performances. Its failure was deserved, but the failure of its next tenant was not. *Pal Joey* (12/25/40), with a score by Rodgers and Hart *(q.v.),* opened with Gene Kelly, Vivienne Segal and June Havoc starring. "Bewitched, Bothered and Bewildered" and "I Could Write a Book" were the standouts in an exceptional score. An antihero was unheard of as the lead in a musical, and audiences and critics found the conceit difficult to accept. In a now famous review, Brooks Atkinson wrote in the *New York Times:* "Although it is expertly done, can you draw sweet water from a foul well?" When the show was revived in 1952 at the Broadhust Theater *(q.v.),* times had changed and Atkinson and his colleagues raved.

Best Foot Forward (10/1/41) had a sparkling score by Hugh Martin and Ralph Blane, which included "Buckle Down Winsocki" and "Ev'ry Time." Nancy Walker, Rosemary Lane, June Allyson and Maureen Cannon starred. George Abbott *(q.v.)* produced and directed.

A series of successful transfers and revivals followed. Its next great tenant was Tennessee Williams's *(q.v.)* classic *A Streetcar Named Desire* (12/3/47). The Pulitzer Prize winning drama top-lined Jessica Tandy, Kim Hunter and Karl Malden and made a star of Marlon Brando whose performance as Stanley Kowalski electrified theatergoers.

During the 1950s, husband and wife Rex Harrison and Lilli Palmer starred in John Van Druten's *Bell, Book and Candle* (11/14/50; 233 performances). Another husband and wife team, Hume Cronyn and Jessica Tandy, starred in the theater's next big hit, *The Fourposter* (10/24/51). Jan de Hartog's comedy was directed by Jose Ferrer who had previously appeared at the theater in a transfer of his classic performance in *Cyrano de Bergerac* (1946).

The theater's next hit was the drama *Tea and Sympathy* (9/30/53; 712 performances), which marked Robert Anderson's Broadway debut as a playwright. Its plot concerned charges of homosexuality leveled against a private school student. The play explored the themes of responsibility, loneliness and society's ability to define morality to judge individuals without prejudice. Deborah Kerr, John Kerr and Leif Erickson starred.

The Desperate Hours (2/10/55; 212 performances) starred Nancy Coleman, Patricia Peardon, George Grizzard, Mary Orr, James Gregory, Paul Newman and Karl Malden. Enid Bagnold's *The Chalk Garden* (10/26/55; 182 performances) was produced by Irene Mayer Selznick who had previously produced *A Streetcar Named Desire* and *Bell, Book and Candle* at the Barrymore. The show starred Fritz Weaver, Gladys Cooper, Siobhan McKenna and Betsy von Furstenberg.

Leonard Sillman produced a sequel to his series of *New Faces* (6/14/56; 220 performances) revues at the Barrymore in 1956. The series introduced new talents to Broadway. Among the new faces that year were T.C. Jones, Maggie Smith, Jane Connell, John Reardon, Virginia Martin and Inga Swenson.

The Barrymore premiered another Pulitzer Prize-winning attraction with Ketti Frings' play *Look Homeward Angel* (11/28/57; 564 performances). Anthony Perkins, Arthur Hill, Jo Van Fleet and Rosemary Murphy opened in the show. *A Raisin in the Sun* (3/11/59; 530 performances) by Lorraine Hansberry opened at the Barrymore with Sidney Poitier, Diana Sands, Ruby Dee, Louis Gossett and Claudia McNeil.

Irene Mayer Selznick produced one last show at the Barrymore, *The Complaisant Lover* (11/1/61; 101 performances). Michael Redgrave, Googie Withers and Sandy Dennis headlined the Graham Greene play. Another British playwright, Peter Shaffer, had a hit production later in the sixties, *Black Comedy* (2/12/67).

As the number and quality of shows produced on Broadway declined in the seventies and eighties, the theater suffered from a scarcity of first-rate material. The Barrymore had a hit in the Michael Stewart and Cy Coleman musical *I Love My Wife* (4/17/77; 857 performances). The musical, *Baby* (12/4/83; 231 performances), by Richard Maltby Jr. and David Shire was not a success.

The Barrymore has proven itself to be an ideal and highly versatile Broadway theater, suited to musicals, dramas, comedies, revues and even one man shows. The theater, owned by Shubert Organization, remains an integral part of the Broadway theater scene.

On November 4, 1987, the New York City Landmarks Preservation Commission designated the exterior of the theater a landmark. The Commission stated: "Its facade is an exceptionally handsome design, featuring an unusual giant terra-cotta grillework screen and fine beaux-arts style ornament." On November 10, 1987, the Commission designated the interior of the theater a landmark, noting the plasterwork ornamentation of its ceiling and the ornamental treatment of its boxes.

EUGENE O'NEILL THEATER 230 W. 49th Street. Architect: Herbert J. Krapp. Opening: November 24, 1925; *Mayflowers*. The Shuberts *(q.v.)* built this theater as the Forrest, named after the great American actor Edwin Forrest. The theater's 1,200 seats (later reduced to 1,101) meant that the stage could accommodate both musicals and straight plays. The early years of the Forrest were marked with failure. James Cagney, Mary Boland, and Osgood Perkins starred in *Women Go On Forever* (9/7/27; 118 performances), which was a hit despite critical drubbing.

Another series of failures followed until Edgar Wallace's play *On the Spot* (10/29/30; 167 performances) opened at the then-dubbed Wallace's Forrest Theater. The crime melodrama starred Anna May Wong and Glenda Farrell. Another bleak period followed, which was relieved by only the modest success of Rachel Crothers's *As Husbands Go* (1/19/33; 144 performances).

Then, after seven more flops, came one of the American theater's greatest successes, *Tobacco Road*. Jack Kirkland's play, based on the Erskine Caldwell novel, opened at the Masque Theater on December 5, 1933. It soon moved to the Forrest where it enjoyed an enormous run, playing from September 1934 to May 1941. The show finally totaled a run of 3,224 performances, making it the second longest-running play in Broadway history.

The Forrest went from feast to famine after *Tobacco Road*, and another four years of failure followed. Finally, in 1945 the theater was sold and redecorated, and on October 25, 1945, it reopened as the Coronet with *Beggars Are Coming to Town*. The Coronet had better luck than the Forrest. Its second offering was Elmer Rice's hit *Dream Girl* (12/14/45; 348 performances). Rice's wife Betty Field starred along with Wendell Corey and Evelyn Varden.

The theater's success continued with Arthur Miller's *(q.v.)* Broadway debut. *All My Sons* (1/29/47; 328 performances) starred Ed Begley, Arthur Kennedy, Lois Wheeler and Karl Malden. A lightweight musical revue, *Angel in the Wings* (12/11/47; 308 performances), followed with stars Elaine Stritch and Grace and Paul Hartman introducing such hits as "Big Brass Band from Brazil" and "Bongo, Bongo, Bongo." The success of one revue led to another. *Small Wonder* (9/15/48; 134 performances) opened with Jack Cassidy, Joan Diener, Tom Ewell, Mort Marshall, Mary McCarty, Alice Pearce and Tommy Rall.

A revival of *Diamond Lil* (2/5/49; 181 performances) starred the play's author, Mae West. Another hit revue with the Hartmans, *Tickets Please* (4/27/50; 245 performances) also featured Larry Kert, Roger Price and Dorothy Jarnac.

The theater changed names again with the opening of William Inge's *A Loss of Roses* (11/11/59). It was then dubbed the Eugene O'Neill Theater. The first hit at the O'Neill was *Show Girl* (1/12/61; 100 performances), a revue with Carol Channing. Herb Gardner's comedy *A Thousand Clowns* (4/5/62; 428 performances) starred Sandy Dennis and Jason Robards Jr.

Bock and Harnick's *(q.v.)* underappreciated musical *She Loves Me* (4/23/63; 302 performances) was directed by Harold Prince *(q.v.)*. The exceptional cast included Barbara Cook, Daniel Massey, Barbara Baxley and Nathaniel Frey.

Neil Simon *(q.v.)* bought the theater at the end of the sixties and installed a number of his own productions. The first was *Last of the Red Hot Lovers* (12/28/69; 706 performances), which starred James Coco and Linda Lavin. Peter Falk, Vincent Gardenia and Lee Grant starred in *The Prisoner of Second Avenue* (11/11/71; 780 performances). Two less successful Simon shows opened next at the O'Neill—*The Good Doctor* (11/27/73; 208 performances) and *God's Favorite* (12/11/74; 119 performances). With some unexceptional interludes, the

Simon reign continued. Simon's *California Suite* (7/2/ 77; 445 performances) starred Tammy Grimes, George Grizzard and Jack Weston. *I Ought to Be in Pictures* (4/ 3/80; 324 performances) was another hit for Simon. Simon's next offering, *Fools* (4/6/81; 40 performances) was not a success. The Neil Simon, Cy Coleman and Carolyn Leigh musical *Little Me* (1982) was revived to poor reviews and closed quickly.

The Jujamcyn Theaters organization bought the O'Neill from Simon and installed a string of failures.

Finally they struck gold with *Big River* (4/25/85; 1,005 performances), Roger Miller's tepid musicalization of *Huckleberry Finn.*

On December 8, 1987, the New York City Landmarks Preservation Commission designated the interior of the theater a landmark. The exterior was denied designation by the Commission. The Commission stated that the interior had "elaborate cameolike ornamental plasterwork including profiles, theatrical masks and panels with classical scenes."

FALLON, WILLIAM J. (1886–1927) William J. Fallon was one of Broadway's great criminal lawyers. He represented all types and saw to it that they were either acquitted or spent a long time in getting to jail. Gene Fowler's biography of Fallon was titled *The Great Mouthpiece;* Fallon was also dubbed "the Jail Robber" by author Donald Henderson Clarke.

During Fallon's 10-year tenure as a member of the New York Bar, he never saw one of his over-100 clients get the chair. Fallon depended on both legal and illegal means for his success in court. He would often pick out one member of the jury to whom he made his case. This resulted in many hung juries. He was also inclined to bribe members of the jury when the need arose.

Fallon was indicted himself on bribery charges, based on a story in the *New York American.* He denied bribing the jury and decided to represent himself, going so far as to put himself on the stand. Fallon turned the case around by accusing William Randolph Hearst, publisher of the *American,* of carrying out a personal vendetta against him. Naturally the jury acquitted Fallon.

For entertainment, Fallon followed singer Texas Guinan *(q.v.)* around town to whatever speakeasy she was currently entertaining in. Fallon, regarded as one of Broadway's most colorful playboys, enjoyed his liquor and it eventually did him in. He died in 1927 at the age of 41 of alcoholism and heart disease.

At his death, Mark Hellinger *(q.v.)* wrote, "Bill Fallon is dead. And in those four words rests the greatest sob story that Broadway ever knew. He played Broadway until Broadway finally got him. When he tried to pull out, it was too late. It always is. And so Fallon, who was still a young man, is dead. Perhaps, after all, he was satisfied to go. For his early days had been filled with love and happiness and fame. And when the future holds hope for none of these, it is then time to go."

FEDERAL THEATER PROJECT The Federal Theater Project was an arm of the Works Progress Administration during the Depression. It provided federal subsidy of the theater in order to increase employment and stimulate the nation's economy. Broadway was hard hit by the Depression. Fewer shows were produced as angels (Broadway investors) found their resources wiped out by the stock-market crash. Audiences, too, forsook the theater as an unneccessary luxury. Without product or audience, many theater owners went into receivership, and the map of Broadway was changed forever.

Theaters were demolished, turned into burlesque *(q.v.)* houses or radio studios or simply left abandoned. Actors, ill suited for other jobs, which didn't exist anyway, had nowhere to turn. Relief Administrator Harry Hopkins realized the needs of artists, including actors. He saw to the establishment of the Federal Music Project, Federal Art Project, and Federal Writers' Project. Mrs. Hallie Flanagan of Vassar College was hired by the government to oversee the fourth such program, dubbed the Federal Theater Project. Altogether, the WPA employed 40,000 artists by the end of 1936.

Hopkins explained the project to Flanagan. "This is a non-commercial theater. It's got to be run by a person who sees right from the start that the profits won't be money profits. It's got to be run by a person who isn't interested just in the commercial type of show. I know something about the plays you've been doing for ten years, plays about American life. This is an American job, not just a New York job. I want someone who knows and cares about other parts of the country. It's a job just down your alley." He also advised Flanagan that, "whatever happens you'll be wrong."

Of the thousands of performers and stage technicians who found employment were such later luminaries as John Houseman, Orson Welles, Arlene Francis, E.G. Marshall, Arthur Kennedy, Will Geer and Joseph Cotten. Composers Marc Blitzstein and Virgil Thomson and playwrights Arthur Miller *(q.v.)* and Dale Wasserman also worked on the experimental project. Future directors John Huston and Nicholas Ray received training on the project. Scenic and costume designers such as Howard Bay and Fred Stover were joined by such lighting designers as George Izenour.

The Project officially began on August 27, 1935, inaugurated by Hopkins as a "free, adult, uncensored" federal theater. Its first production, *Black Empire,* opened at Los Angeles's Mayan Theater on March 26, 1936. The first New York production was *Injunction Granted,* which opened at the Biltmore Theater *(q.v.)* on July 24, 1936. Other productions by the Broadway contingent of the Project included *Horse Eats Hat* (9/26/36) at the Maxine Elliott's Theatre *(q.v.); It Can't Happen Here,* which opened at 22 theaters around the country on October 27, 1936; *Doctor Faustus* (1/8/37) at the Maxine Elliott's Theatre; *Revolt of the Beavers* (5/20/37); *Processional* (10/13/37) at the Maxine Elliott's Theatre; *S.S. Glencairn* (10/29/37), including *Moon of the Caribbees, In the Zone, Bound East for Cardiff* and *The Long Voyage Home* at the Lafayette Theater; *One-Third of a Nation* (1/17/38) at the Adelphi Theater *(q.v.); Haiti* (3/2/38) at the Lafayette Theater; *Big Blow* (10/1/38) at the Maxine Elliott's Theatre; *Sing for Your Supper* (4/24/39) at the Adelphi Theater; and *Life and Death of an American* (5/19/39) at the Maxine Elliott's Theatre.

The project wasn't limited to only traditional plays. Flanagan, seeking to build a national theater out of the Federal Theater Project, encouraged all kinds of theater—circuses, marionette and children's shows, vaudeville *(q.v.)* and variety. Emmet Lavery, head of the National Service Bureau of the Project, stated, "If the Federal Theater could have survived for six months more, the second emergency, the actuality of war in Europe, would have perhaps extended the base of the first theater operation . . . This start on theater, which was justified by the first emergency—the necessity of feeding hungry actors—could be held together on a more limited but very professional basis as a necessary arm of entertainment with the army. And if that had happened, we would have the national theater."

But the Federal Theater, which vowed to be "uncensored," proved to be a problem for conservatives. The shows couldn't help being controversial since they reflected the state of the country and its politics. One of the more objectionable parts of the project was the series of "living newspapers." The experimental theater took subjects from the headlines and created plays around the issues. These shows personalized the facts of the news stories and brought them home to the project's surprisingly mixed audience. Audiences were reflective of the entire range of societal makeup. The stories were documentary in form and after exploring the breadth of the problems asked the government and industry to take action against the problem.

The first living-newspaper production, about the Ethiopian war, was canceled by the government. *Triple-A Plowed Under* was the second and dealt with the agriculture problems of the country. Others dealt with problems like housing, cooperatives, health care, labor unions, race relations, industry, movies, natural resources and public utilities.

The newspaper's most famous editions included *Power,* produced at the Ritz Theatre *(q.v.). Power* was an examination of a power failure and solutions to the problem. As the play progressed, the audience followed a typical consumer, Angus K. Buttonkooper, as he learned how electricity got to the consumer and the problems of monoplistic utilities.

The Project dealt with American issues, sometimes provoking controversy, sometimes not. Historical dramas received their due with five revolving around the character of Abraham Lincoln. Two of these were called *Abraham Lincoln,* one written by John Drinkwater and another by Ralph Kettering. *Mrs. Lincoln* was written by Ramon Romero and *The Lonely Man* was scripted by Howard Koch.

The most successful drama about Lincoln was *Prologue to Glory* by E.P. Conkle. After almost a year's run in New York, the production moved to the New York World's Fair in Flushing Meadows. There were also productions throughout the country for hundreds of thousands of theatergoers. In New York, Lincoln was played by Erford Gage, an actor who might have become a big star were it not for his untimely death. Lincoln's love, Ann Rutledge, was played by an actress of the same name who was actually her great-grand-niece.

Burns Mantle, editor of the *Best Plays* series stated, "If the Federal Theater had produced no other single drama, this production of *Prologue to Glory* would doubly justify its history and all its struggles." However, like most Federal Theater Project productions, *Prologue to Glory* also received its share of criticism. Republican Congressman J. Parnell Thomas labeled it "a propaganda play to prove that all politicians are crooked." He thought it was simply "Communist talk."

With the government on the lookout for Communists behind every proscenium, the Federal Theater Project was doomed to be censored and, finally, disbanded. The most famous case of censorship involved the production of the Marc Blitzstein musical, *The Cradle Will Rock,* a pro union expose of the steel industry. Orson Welles and John Houseman were the producers of the controversial piece. It was scheduled to open on June 16, 1937. Since the nation was then going through deadly strikes, the subject was especially timely and controversial—so controversial that the government sent a memo to Flanagan ordering that "no openings of new productions shall take place until after the beginning of the coming fiscal year." Actually, *The Cradle Will Rock* was the only opening scheduled.

With the opening canceled, the company was doubly intent on presenting the show. Actor's Equity *(q.v.)*, always distrustful of the WPA, had ruled that its members could not perform on stage in a Federal Theater Project play. The musicians' union also disliked the Project and forbade its members from playing in the show, despite its pro-union slant.

So on the opening night, Houseman and Welles told the audience assembled outside the theater about their problems and marched the entire group to the little Venice Theater. Marc Blitzstein was seated at his piano, alone on stage. The actors, forbidden to appear on the stage, simply took seats around the audience and stood up to say their lines. The result was tremendously exciting, and *The Cradle Will Rock* is remembered as one of the greatest triumphs of the thirties. It ended up playing 104 performances.

The House Un-American Activities Committee was quick to identify the Federal Theater as one of its targets when it began its inquiries in August 1938. Congressman J. Parnell Thomas (later jailed for defrauding the government) blasted the Project: "It is apparent from the startling evidence received thus far that the Federal Theater Project not only is serving as a branch of the Communistic organization but is also one more link in the vast and unparalleled New Deal propaganda machine."

The Federal Theater Project couldn't survive the storms of controversy. On June 30, 1939, the Project was disbanded. Hallie Flanagan described her vision of theater, a vision that the Federal Theater had fulfilled:

> We live in a changing world; man is whispering through space, soaring to the stars in ships, flinging miles of steel and glass into the air. Shall the theater continue to huddle in the confines of a painted box set? The movies, in their kaleidoscopic speed and juxtaposition of external objects and internal emotions are seeking to find visible and audible expression for the tempo and the psychology of our time. The stage too must experiment—with ideas, with psychological relationships of men and women, with speech and rhythm forms, with dance and movement, with color and light—or it must and should become a museum product.
>
> In an age of terrific implications as to wealth and poverty, as to the function of government, as to peace and war, as to the relation of the artist to all these forces, the theater must grow up. The theater must become conscious of the implications of the changing social order, or the changing social order will ignore, and rightly, the implications of the theater.

FIELDS FAMILY   The Fields family spanned almost a century of the American theater and spread their talents over a wide variety of roles. Lew Fields and his sons and daughter (Herbert, Joseph and Dorothy) concentrated their talents on the musical theater—Lew as a producer, director and performer, Herbert as a librettist, Joseph as a librettist and playwright and Dorothy as a librettist and lyricist.

Lew Fields (1867–1941)   Lew Fields, the patriarch of the Fields family, is credited with giving the young songwriting team of Rodgers and Hart *(q.v.)* their first important professional commissions to write Broadway musicals. He also enjoyed a long career as partner of Joseph Weber with whom he presented many popular burlesques *(q.v.)* on Broadway hits of the time.

Herbert Fields (1897–1958)   Herbert Fields enjoyed long collaborations as librettist to many of Broadway's preeminent songwriters. He began his career with Rodgers and Hart and then wrote a number of musical comedies with Cole Porter *(q.v.)*. He collaborated on eight shows with his sister Dorothy who was also a lyricist.

Dorothy Fields (1904–1974)   Dorothy, the baby of the family, overcame much sexism to become one of Broadway's preeminent lyricists. One strength lay in her ability to utilize current slang in her lyrics. Throughout her long career, she remained in the vanguard of the musical theater, always up-to-date and able to change along with popular taste. She was the only member of her family to make a successful transition to film, writing for such great composers as Jerome Kern *(q.v.)*.

Joseph Fields (1895 -1966)   Joseph wrote many successful comic plays, usually in collaboration with Jerome Chodorov. He also collaborated with Oscar Hammerstein II *(q.v.)* and Anita Loos on musicals and plays. He pursued his career apart from his father and siblings. His sweet and somewhat sentimental works are discussed after those of the rest of his illustrious family.

* * * * *

The saga of the Fields family started when Lew Fields began his more than 50 years in the American theater as the boyhood partner of Joseph Weber. The team were "Dutch comics" in early musical comedies. They based their characters on stereotypes of New York's Dutch population. Weber and Fields were the most popular comedy team of their time, and the partners billed themselves the Dutch Senators. By 1885, they were able to put together their own company of performers. On March 27, 1896, they took a lease on the Broadway Music Hall at Broadway and 29th Street and soon renamed it the Weber and Fields Music Hall. The team wrote and performed burlesques of other theater productions and presented well-known vaudeville performers. The theater opened with its first burlesque, *The Geezer,* on September 5, 1896. *The Geezer's* company members included Sam Bernard, John T. Kelly, Josephine Allen and Lillian Swain. Other popular burlesques were *Pousse Cafe* (1897); *Hurly Burly* (1898); *Whirl-I-Gig* (1899); *Fiddle Dee Dee* (1900); *Hoity Toity*

Jerome Kern, Dorothy Fields and George Gershwin Courtesy ASCAP.

(1901); *Twirly Whirly* (1902); and *Whoop-Dee-Doo* (1903). On May 28, 1904, the team broke up following a performance at the New Amsterdam Theatre *(q.v.)*. Weber continued his management of the theater on his own under the name Weber's Theater.

On December 5, 1904, along with two partners, Henry Hamlin and Julian Mitchell, Lew Fields opened the Lew Fields Theater on 42nd Street. Marie Cahill was the chief member of Fields's new company, which presented the Victor Herbert *(q.v.)* and Glen Mac-Donough musical *It Happened in Nordland*. Oscar Hammerstein I *(q.v.)* was the owner of the theater who leased the venue to Fields and his partners. Fields's name was taken off the theater in 1906 when it was renamed the Hackett Theater. Fields then leased the Herald Square Theater downtown, beginning operations on August 30, 1906. When Weber lost his theater in 1912, he reteamed with Fields.

They built their own theater on 44th Street and named it the Weber and Fields New Music Hall *(q.v.)*. The team didn't hold onto the theater's lease for long,

for in late 1913 the Shubert Brothers *(q.v.)* took over the theater's operation. On June 5, 1913, Fields moved his operation to the space above and called it the Lew Fields 44th Street Roof Garden *(q.v.)*. The Shuberts also owned this roof garden theater. Typically, Fields lost the space by the end of the year. The last theater named for Fields was the Lew Fields Mansfield Theater, which bore his name from April 26, 1928, to March 4, 1929. Today the theater is known as the Brooks Atkinson Theater *(q.v.)*.

As he got older, Fields turned more and more to producing. Like most producers, he had his favorite performers. These included Vernon Castle *(q.v.)*, Nora Bayes, Fay Templeton, Lillian Russell, DeWolf Hopper, Marie Dressler and Helen Hayes *(q.v.)*.

Fields hit his stride in the twenties with the production of a series of musicals by Richard Rodgers and Lorenz Hart *(q.v.)*. Fields produced the shows of which many had a libretto by his son Herbert.

Lew Fields was the librettist and producer of *A Lonely Romeo* (6/10/19; 87 performances). On August 26, 1919,

Lew Fields added a song, "Any Old Place with You," by Rodgers and Hart. This was their first Broadway song and their first professionally written song.

Lew Fields continued his support of the young team of Rodgers and Hart with *Poor Little Ritz Girl* (7/27/20; 93 performances). Unfortunately, much of the team's score was cut when the show was in its out of town tryouts and new songs by Sigmund Romberg *(q.v.)* and Alex Gerber were added. Richard Rodgers was just 18 when the show opened on Broadway.

Blue Eyes (2/21/21; 48 performances) starred Fields and Delyle Alda. They repeated their teaming with the Fields production *Snapshots of 1921* (6/2/21; 44 performances) that same year. Fields next directed two successful editions of the popular revue series, *The Greenwich Village Follies* in 1923 and 1924. His production of *The Melody Man* (5/13/24; 56 performances) was not a hit. Rodgers and Hart, the authors of the score, were still practically unknown on Broadway.

Herbert Fields made his Broadway debut choreographing the *Theater Guild (q.v.)* production *The Garrick Gaieties* (5/17/25; 231 performances), the revue which catapulted Rodgers and Hart to fame. The team's hit song from the show was "Manhattan," one of their most enduring standards. While it was running, Herbert saw his first book musical, *Dearest Enemy* (9/18/25; 286 performances), open. Rodgers and Hart provided the score, and it was one of their best. The American Revolution was the scene of *Dearest Enemy.* Herbert's book was the story of Mrs. Robert Murray, a woman who stalled the British General William Howe while the American troops got into position for a surprise attack. *Dearest Enemy,* actually written before the *Garrick Gaieties,* starred Helen Ford, Charles Purcell, Flavia Arcaro and Andrew Lawlor Jr. Writing in the *New York Evening World,* E.W. Osborn said that the book was "wise and truly witty and genuinely romantic."

Herbert Fields wrote the libretto to his father's production of Rodgers and Hart's *The Girl Friend* (3/17/26; 301 performances), a typical twenties musical. The title tune was a big hit. Abel Green, writing in *Variety (q.v.)* claimed that "The book is the best libretto Fields has contributed so far and is only parred by the songs with ultra smart lyrics and oddly rhythmed and fetching tunes."

Herbert choreographed the second edition of the *Garrick Gaieties* (5/10/26) with its Rodgers and Hart score. The big hit of this edition was "Mountain Greenery." Herbert's third Rodgers and Hart show of 1926 was *Peggy-Ann* (12/27/26; 354 performances). His father, Lew, produced in association with Lyle D. Andrews. *Peggy-Ann* was a strange musical with surrealistic overtones. The majority of the show illustrated Peggy-Ann's dreams. In one dream, a yachting trip, Peggy-Ann meets a talking fish. The *New York Times*

commended Herbert's libretto with its "frequent flights of imagination." Alexander Woollcott *(q.v.),* then writing for the *New York World,* admired the songs "but it is the libretto which arrests attention . . . It was all like a chapter out of Alice in Wonderland."

Herbert Fields was clearly becoming a major talent in the American musical theater. His next two shows, both produced by his father, were among the biggest successes of the twenties. The first was *Hit the Deck* (4/25/27; 352 performances), which opened at the Belasco Theatre *(q.v.).* Vincent Youmans *(q.v.),* Leo Robin and Clifford Grey wrote the score, which contained two huge hits, "Sometimes I'm Happy" and "Hallelujah." Lew Fields codirected with Alexander Leftwich as well as coproducing with Youmans.

The second smash hit of 1927 for Herbert and Lew was *A Connecticut Yankee* (11/3/27; 421 performances) with a score by Rodgers and Hart. Herbert's libretto received mixed notices. Alexander Woollcott wrote: "The libretto did not seem to me quite as funny as it set out to be." Alan Dale, in the *New York American,* said the show had "a poignantly amusing book . . . lovely, quaint, deliciously droll."

Lew wrote three libretti in 1928 with moderate success. *Present Arms* (4/26/28; 147 performances) had a Rodgers and Hart score and a production mounted by Lew. *Chee-Chee* (9/25/28; 32 performances) was a downright failure for Rodgers, Hart and the two Fields. Herbert's source, *The Son of the Grand Eunuch,* a novel by Charles Petit, had a subject that wasn't attractive to most Broadwayites. For *Hello Daddy!* (12/26/28; 196 performances), Herbert wrote the libretto, father Lew produced and starred (in his last appearance on Broadway) and Dorothy acted as lyricst to Jimmy McHugh's music. She had previously made a splash with her lyrics to Jimmy McHugh's music for *Blackbirds of 1928* (5/9/28; 519 performances). The team's hit song for the Lew Leslie revue was "I Can't Give You Anything But Love."

Lew Fields's last Broadway show was the *Vanderbilt Revue* (11/5/30; 13 performances). He coproduced and codirected the proceedings, which boasted a score by a variety of writers, including daughter Dorothy and Jimmy McHugh. Lew Fields decided to retire rather than buck the declining opportunities of Broadway during the Depression.

Herbert began his long collaboration with Cole Porter in 1929 with the show *Fifty Million Frenchmen* (11/27/29; 254 performances). The opening night performance almost didn't happen as planned. Singer Betty Compton complained that her dressing room at the Lyric Theater *(q.v.)* didn't suit her stature as a star. She rectified the situation by calling her boyfriend, Mayor James J. Walker. The theater was hit with six code violations, and the show's opening was threatened.

Jimmy McHugh   Courtesy ASCAP.

Luckily, Helen Broderick, also starring in the show, agreed to switch dressing rooms.

Dorothy had her final Broadway collaboration with Jimmy McHugh in *The International Revue* (2/25/30; 95 performances). They contributed one smash hit, "On the Sunny Side of the Street," to the Lew Leslie production. Dorothy and Jimmy McHugh's final collaboration, *Clowns in Clover*, closed out of town in 1933. They went out with a bang, for the score contained another standard, "Don't Blame Me."

Herbert continued his collaboration with Porter with *The New Yorkers* (12/8/30; 158 performances). The one song that might have become a hit, "Just One of Those Things," was cut prior to the opening. Herbert then collaborated for the last time with Rodgers and Hart on their show *America's Sweetheart* (2/10/31; 135 performances). The show, a gentle satire on Hollywood, starred Inez Courtney, Jack Whiting and Harriette Lake (later better known as Ann Southern). Most of the reviews were positive, except Dorothy Parker, writing in *The New Yorker* stated: "Mr. Fields has, apparently, compiled his libretto with a pair of scissors and his poor thumb must be awfully sore after all that clipping of jokes."

Herbert's next assignment was a collaboration with George and Ira Gershwin *(q.v.)* on *Pardon My English* (1/28/33; 43 performances), produced by Alex A. Aa-

rons and Vinton Freedley *(q.v.)*. *Pardon My English*, despite an excellent score, was the least successful of all the Gershwin brothers' musicals.

Both Herbert and Dorothy took a long break from Broadway in the late thirties and both returned, with different shows, in 1939. Dorothy made her return to the theater after six years with *Stars in Your Eyes* (2/9/39; 127 performances), starring Ethel Merman *(q.v.)* with music by Arthur Schwartz *(q.v.)* and book by J.P. McEvoy. The show was meant to be a somewhat leftish look at Hollywood but, under Joshua Logan's *(q.v.)* direction, turned out to be a simple satire. The songwriters wrote a very good score, although none of the songs achieved lasting fame. *Stars in Your Eyes* closed just in time for Merman to join the cast of Herbert's next show.

For Herbert, it was back to Cole Porter. The show was *Du Barry Was a Lady* (12/6/39; 408 performances), and Herbert collaborated with producer B.G. DeSylva on the hilarious book. The story was about a washroom attendant (Bert Lahr) at a popular nightclub who hits his head against a sink and dreams he is King Louis XV. In his dream, Ethel Merman, in real life a singer at the Club Petite, is Madame Du Barry. John Mason Brown called the show "a rowdy, boisterous, high-spirited extravaganza which stops at just this side of nothing and makes much of little." The show was a change from the polite comedies Herbert had written for Rodgers and Hart.

Herbert, Porter, DeSylva and Merman were reteamed for *Panama Hattie* (10/30/40; 501 performances). *Panama Hattie* was Herbert's last libretto written without his sister Dorothy. She joined Herbert at book writing while still contributing occasional lyrics to shows. Their first project as a team was Porter's *Let's Face It!* (10/29/41; 547 performances), a wartime musical with Eve Arden, Danny Kaye, Nanette Fabray, Mary Jane Walsh and Vivian Vance. The Fields supplied a sassy script to Porter's equally sassy music and lyrics.

Another Porter show, *Something for the Boys* (1/7/43; 422 performances) followed. The scene was a military base in Texas, and Ethel Merman was the star. Michael Todd produced and Herbert, in addition to coauthoring the libretto with Dorothy, codirected with Hassard Short. *Something for the Boys* wasn't top-notch Porter or Fields.

Porter, Herbert and Dorothy, Hassard Short and Mike Todd repeated their assignments (although Herbert did not direct) for *Mexican Hayride* (1/28/44; 479 performances). It, too, was a crowd pleaser but not especially notable. June Havoc, Bobby Clark and Wilbur Evans were the leads.

European style operetta, pronounced dead at the end of the twenties, made a surprisingly successful return to the Broadway stage with *Up in Central Park* (1/27/

45; 504 performances). Sigmund Romberg wrote the music, and Dorothy returned to lyric writing for the show. She also collaborated with Herbert on the book. To everyone's surprise, the Mike Todd production enjoyed a long run. The songwriters wrote a lovely, melodious score with "Close as Pages in a Book" the hit.

Herbert and Dorothy's entertaining but minor efforts for Porter didn't prepare Broadwayites for the genius of their next show, *Annie Get Your Gun* (5/16/46; 1,147 performances). The Irving Berlin (*q.v.*) score was his finest, and the book by the Fields siblings was their masterwork. Ethel Merman perfectly adapted the role of sharpshooter Annie Oakley to her talents, with Ray Middleton playing her chief rival and chief love, Frank Butler. Rodgers and Hammerstein (*q.v.*) produced and Joshua Logan directed. *Annie Get Your Gun* proved to be one of the top Broadway musicals of all time.

Surprisingly, the team's next show, *Arms and the Girl* (2/2/50; 134 performances), showed little of the talents they exhibited in *Annie Get Your Gun*. The Theater Guild (*q.v.*) along with Anthony Brady Farrell produced the show, which was based on a play by Theater Guild managers Armina Marshall and Lawrence Langner. Dorothy wrote lyrics to Morton Gould's music and collaborated with Herbert and director Rouben Mamoulian on the script.

While Herbert took a break, Dorothy collaborated again with composer Arthur Schwartz. The show, *A Tree Grows in Brooklyn* (4/19/51; 267 performances), became a vehicle for the great Shirley Booth. George Abbott (*q.v.*) produced and directed in his usual charming style and collaborated on the book with the novel's author, Betty Smith. Fields and Schwartz came up with a score that had real emotional power. "Make the Man Love Me" became a hit and a standard of pop singers. Nonetheless, the show, about a ne'er-do-well, was not upbeat enough for Broadway audiences. The songwriting team, who brought out the best in each other, collaborated on their next show, *By the Beautiful Sea* (4/8/54; 268 performances). This time, Herbert joined Dorothy on the script but the results were weak. The show was simply too much a vehicle for Shirley Booth, playing the same sort of character she undertook in *A Tree Grows in Brooklyn*.

Herbert's last show was *Redhead* (2/5/59; 452 performances). He collaborated again with his sister on the book. Additional librettists were David Shaw and Sidney Sheldon (later to be a major novelist).

Albert Hague (later to play the music teacher in the television show "Fame") collaborated with Dorothy on the score but only one song, "Merely Marvelous," was heard after the show closed. Gwen Verdon, one of the musical theater's greatest performers, costarred with Richard Kiley.

Herbert Fields died on March 24, 1958.

After a seven-year break, Dorothy resumed her career without her brother. The show was another vehicle for Gwen Verdon—*Sweet Charity* (1/29/66; 608 performances). Cy Coleman collaborated with Dorothy on the score, and Neil Simon (*q.v.*) wrote the libretto. The direction and choreography were by a truly unique talent, Bob Fosse. Dorothy's lyrics perfectly matched Coleman's jazzy rhythms, providing exactly the right tone for the alternately romantic, vulgar and sentimental score. "Hey Big Spender" was the big hit, but the rest of the score was much more sophisticated and entirely more worthy of public acclaim.

Dorothy Fields's last Broadway show, *Seesaw* (3/18/73; 296 performances), was also written in collaboration with Cy Coleman. But the result on opening night wasn't as satisfactory as *Sweet Charity*. The libretto, based on William Inge's play *Two for the Seesaw*, was attempted by a number of authors with director/choreographer Michael Bennett finally taking credit. The attempt to open up a two-character play into a full-blown Broadway musical was not successful; the show simply rang false.

Dorothy Fields died on March 28, 1974. Of all the Broadway lyricists, she was most able to keep abreast of her times. She utilized slang and idiomatic phrases without sounding forced or trendy. Her more poetic lyrics never become cloying, and her imagery remains sharp, fresh and hip. It's to her credit that she could collaborate with composers as widely divergent in style as Arthur Schwartz, Jerome Kern (in the movies) and Cy Coleman. In a field largely dominated by men, she held her own and was never forced into a "feminine" viewpoint.

* * * * *

Joseph Fields's first Broadway production was *Schoolhouse on the Lot* (3/22/38; 55 performances), written in collaboration with his longtime partner Jerome Chodorov. The two had met while working in Hollywood at Republic Pictures. The team's next collaboration, *My Sister Eileen* (12/26/40; 865 performances), was decidedly more popular. The comedy, based on a series of stories by Ruth McKenney published in *The New Yorker*, starred Shirley Booth and Jo Ann Sayers as the two girls from Ohio who try to make it in the big city. Max Gordon produced and George S. Kaufman directed. Kaufman was an expert play doctor and supervised the young playwrights' rewrites. Though he didn't mind working on the play, Kaufman thought the candy in the writers' hotel room terrible. "In the ensuing weeks they did valiant work with the script," Kaufman admitted, "the candy, however got no better." Kaufman estimated that the writers wrote no less than six scripts worth of words: "It was a rare day, in the weeks preceding rehearsals, that they did not come along with eight or ten new scenes."

Chodorov and Fields repeated the success of *My Sister*

Eileen the following season with *Junior Miss* (11/18/41; 246 performances), produced by Max Gordon. Again, the authors picked a series of stories from *The New Yorker* as their source. The stories, written by Sally Benson, were more simple and tender than those of Ruth McKenney. The director was Kaufman's sometime partner, Moss Hart. Patricia Peardon starred as the 14-year-old title character. Lenore Lonergan co-starred.

Fields went it alone with his next play, *The Doughgirls* (12/30/42; 671 performances). Pearl Harbor had been bombed three weeks after the opening of *Junior Miss*, and wartime comedies became very popular. Again, George S. Kaufman directed and instructed Fields in rewrites. Out of town, the show was in trouble, but Kaufman managed to whip Fields's script into shape for the opening at the Lyceum Theater *(q.v.)*. Virginia Field, Doris Nolan and Arleen Whelan were the stars, but Arlene Francis, playing a Russian guerilla fighter, got the notices. The critical reception was mixed, with most crediting Kaufman for keeping the play proceeding rapidly. John Anderson wrote, "If Mr. Fields's little story is as flimsy as a piece of tissue paper at least Mr. Kaufman blows it around in some gusty patterns and keeps it dancing."

Fields next directed *The Man Who Had All the Luck* (11/23/44; 4 performances) at the Forrest Theater *(q.v.)*. He teamed up with Ben Sher to write the play *I Gotta Get Out* (9/25/47; 4 performances) which opened at the Cort Theater *(q.v.)*.

Fields's two flops were followed by two of his biggest hits, the musicals *Gentlemen Prefer Blondes* and *Wonderful Town*. He wrote both libretti in collaboration with his partner Jerome Chodorov. *Gentlemen Prefer Blondes* (12/8/49; 740 performances) opened at the Ziegfeld Theater *(q.v.)* with Carol Channing and Yvonne Adair in the leads. Jule Styne *(q.v.)* and Leo Robin wrote the score. *Wonderful Town* (2/25/53; 559 performances), was based on Chodorov and Fields's play *My Sister Eileen*. The score was by Leonard Bernstein *(q.v.)* and Betty Comden and Adolph Green *(q.v.)*. Rosalind Russell and Edith Adams starred, and George Abbott *(q.v.)* directed. According to Abbott, Fields and Chodorov were shocked when they heard the sophisticated, satirical score by Comden and Green and Bernstein. In their minds, they saw the show taking shape in the same warmly humorous vein as their play. The authors lost control of their emotions and cursed the entire production and all the creative staff. Luckily the show was a smash hit at its opening. Ironically the writers won the Donaldson Award *(q.v.)* and the New York Drama Critics' Circle Award *(q.v.)* for *Wonderful Town*, their only major awards.

The team's next musical, *The Girl in Pink Tights* (3/5/54; 115 performances) opened at the Mark Hellinger Theater *(q.v.)* with a score by Sigmund Romberg, the same composer who had collaborated with Joseph's brother and sister on *Up in Central Park*. Romberg had died three years before the opening of *The Girl in Pink Tights*, and orchestrator Don Walker put together the songs from Romberg's jottings and unfinished songs. Leo Robin added lyrics.

The team's next play, *Anniversary Waltz* (4/7/54; 615 performances), opened at the Broadhurst Theater *(q.v.)*. Fields next directed the play *The Desk Set* (10/24/55; 296 performances) at the Broadhurst Theater. Chodorov and Fields were back with *The Ponder Heart* (2/16/56; 149 performances) at the Music Box Theater *(q.v.)*. Fields collaborated with humorist Peter DeVries on *The Tunnel of Love* (2/13/57; 417 performances) at the Royale Theatre *(q.v.)*.

Fields tried his hand in collaboration with Hammerstein at supplying a libretto for the Rodgers and Hammerstein musical *The Flower Drum Song* (12/1/58; 600 performances), a lightweight examination of the clash of cultures between the "younger generation" and older Chinese immigrants, at the St. James Theatre *(q.v.)*. Fields also coproduced the show with the songwriters. Fields coproduced *Blood, Sweat and Stanley Poole* (10/5/61; 84 performances) at the Morosco Theatre *(q.v.)*.

Joseph Fields died on March 3, 1966. His work was solid and skillful with a rich humanity and sentimental side. He was a witty man whose plays took everday occurrences and extracted the comedy inherent in the situations in a warm, loving manner.

58TH STREET THEATER   See JOHN GOLDEN THEATER.

51ST STREET THEATER   See MARK HELLINGER THEATER.

54TH STREET THEATER   See GEORGE ABBOTT THEATER.

FILMARTE   See JOHN GOLDEN THEATER.

FINE ARTS THEATER   See JOHN GOLDEN THEATER.

FOLIES BERGERE   See HELEN HAYES THEATER.

FORREST THEATER   See EUGENE O'NEILL THEATER.

48TH STREET THEATRE 157 W. 48th Street. Architect: William A. Swasey. Opening: August 12, 1912; *Just Like John*. The 48th Street Theatre was built by producer William A. Brady. Though it housed many successes, his theater was not to have an especially notable history. The theater's first successes were *Never Say Die* (11/12/12; 151 performances); *Today* (10/6/13; 280 performances); *The Midnight Girl* (2/23/14; 104 performances); *Just a Woman* (1/17/16; 136 performances) and *The Man Who Stayed at Home* (4/3/18; 109 performances).

The Storm (10/2/19; 282 performances) was a melodrama of the Canadian woods. Edward Arnold appeared as Burr Winton, a dashing prospector. Winton competes for the hand of Manette with cultured Englishman David Stewart. The girl just can't make up her mind. The two men are best friends, and at the end of the play, they successfully battle a forest fire. Finally, Manette decides to marry the prospector. *Opportunity* (7/30/20; 135 performances) was another hit play at the 48th Street Theatre. Owen Davis wrote the comedy, which featured subsequent Hollywood movie star Nita Naldi.

The theater was renamed the Equity 48th Street Theatre on October 2, 1922, with the opening of *Malvaloca*. A successful revival of Ibsen's *The Wild Duck* (2/24/25; 110 performances) was the theater's next success. The name was changed back to the 48th Street Theatre on June 1, 1925, with the play *Spooks*.

A series of plays with improbable but all too typical plots followed. The comedy *Puppy Love* (1/27/26; 112 performances) starred Spring Byington. It concerned a young man who, hopelessly in love with an unattainable young woman, decides to become her chauffeur to get closer to her. To nobody's surprise, the boy gets the girl in the end.

Jean Bart's drama *The Squall* (11/11/26; 262 performances) opened at the 48th Street Theatre with a cast headed by Blanche Yurka, Romney Brent and Dorothy Stickney. Also featured was Suzanne Caubet who played Nubi, a gypsy woman who blows into the play along with the title storm. Her chief is following her, and she begs the Mendez family to hide her. The family does as she asks. In the meantime, Nubi is kept busy. She seduces the Mendez's son Juan and then moves on to Juan's father, Jose, and then to Pedro, the hired hand. Finally, El Moro, the gypsy leader, arrives to bring her back alive.

Unexpected Husband (6/2/31; 120 performances) starred Josephine Hull. The comedy unfolded an incredible tale: Dorothy Atwater, a bored and restless Texan, runs away to New York in order to pursue Broadway playboy Willie Van Loan. Her adventures on the way land her in a hotel bed with a stranger and, after Dorothy's father and a tabloid reporter in pursuit of dirt discover them, there is nothing for the couple to do but get married. They do, and everyone lives happily ever after.

The Pagan Lady (12/27/30; 152 performances) was a name few audiences could resist. The drama starred Lenore Ulric as a woman who is tempted by the son of an evangelist. Although she is living with another man, she and the evangelist's son swim away to an island where they spend the night. The would-be evangelist is depressed and returns to the church. Lenore Ulric's character is happy that he will now be more tolerant of sinners since he has sinned himself.

In the 1930s, the Depression forced the sale of the theater. In 1937, the Labor Stage, an arm of the International Ladies Garment Workers Union, used the space for plays, lectures and meetings. It was called the Windsor Theater during this period, which began with the production of *Work Is for Horses* (11/20/37). The union's other theater, also called the Labor Stage, was originally the Princess Theater *(q.v.)*.

On September 1, 1943, the Windsor became the 48th Street Theatre again. Its big hit, the biggest of its entire life, was Mary Chase's classic comedy *Harvey* (11/1/44; 1,775 performances). Frank Fay starred in the fantastic play as the pixilated Elwood Dowd. Another big hit at the theater that was transferred successfully to Hollywood was *Stalag 17* (5/8/51; 472 performances).

In 1955, a water tower on the roof fell apart, and the theater was flooded. The damage was extensive, and the theater was razed.

44TH STREET THEATRE 216 West 44th Street. Architect: William A. Swasey. Opening: January 23, 1913; *The Man with Three Wives.* The theater was built as Weber and Fields Music Hall. Soon after, the Shuberts *(q.v.)*

Program for the 48th Street Theatre

44th Street Theatre   Courtesy Billy Rose Theater Collection.

purchased the property and renamed it the 44th Street Theatre. The basement of the theater was home to the Little Club, a speakeasy. Its roof was also utilized for a roof-top theater, which went through many names and managements. The best known was the Nora Bayes.

The first musical presented at the theater, *The Girl on the Film* (12/29/13; 64 performances), was a modest success. Like many of its contemporaries, it was based on a European operetta. The operetta *The Midnight Girl* (2/23/14; 104 performances) was another successful European transplant. Yet another European operetta was *The Lilac Domino* (10/28/14; 109 performances). *Katinka* (12/23/15; 220 performances) was an even bigger suc-

cess for the theater. Rudolf Friml *(q.v.)* and Otto Harbach wrote the operetta, now forgotten but at the time an enormous hit. Arthur Hammerstein *(q.v.)* produced the show.

The Shuberts made a stab at an annual series of revues with their production of the *Shubert Gaieties of 1919*. The fine cast included Gilda Gray, George Jessel and Ed Wynn. The show was a modest success with 87 performances, but the Shuberts decided not to present another edition.

The producers had one of their greatest hits in another operetta *Blossom Time*. The 44th Street hosted the first revival of *Blossom Time* (5/21/23; 16 performances) (there were eventually seven). The short run was not the failure it seemed, for the Shuberts never had any intention of running *Blossom Time*—they just wanted to be able to advertise the ensuing tour as "direct from Broadway."

Betty Lee (12/25/24; 98 performances) starred Joe E. Brown, Gloria Foy and Hal Skelly. The score was by Louis A. Hirsch, Con Conrad, Otto Harbach (*q.v.*) and Irving Caesar. An unlikely success was Arthur Hammerstein's operetta *Song of the Flame* (12/30/25; 214 performances), which had a strange grouping of songwriters. There was music written in the operetta style by Herbert Stothart and more modern melodies written by George Gershwin (*q.v.*). The lyrics were by Otto Harbach and Oscar Hammerstein II (*q.v.*). The musical was set in Russia.

An English operetta, *Katja, the Dancer* (10/18/26; 113 performances), was brought to the theater and was a success. *A Night in Spain* (5/3/27; 174 performances) was a popular revue, which bore only a passing resemblance to anything Spanish.

By the end of the 1920s, operettas were going out of favor with audiences. The 44th Street Theatre followed the trends and hosted one of the new jazz-influenced musicals, Bert Kalmar and Harry Ruby's *The 5 O'Clock Girl* (10/10/27; 278 performances), starring Mary Eaton, Pert Kelton, Oscar Shaw and Danny Dare. The hit song was "Thinking of You."

The most famous tenant of the 44th Street Theatre was another Kalmar and Ruby show, the Marx Brothers classic *Animal Crackers* (10/23/28; 213 performances). Joining Groucho, Harpo, Zeppo, and Chico was Marx regular, Margaret Dumont. The score featured what would become Groucho's theme, "Hooray for Captain Spalding!"

Unfortunately, *Animal Crackers* was just about the only successful presentation at the theater in this period. The next offering, *Broadway Nights* (7/15/29; 40 performances) was a flop. Producer Billy Rose presented *Billy Rose's Crazy Quilt* (5/19/31; 67 performances) with a terrific score by Harry Warren, Mort Dixon and himself. Despite a big hit song, "I Found a Million Dollar Baby (in a Five and Ten Cent Store)" and the efforts of cast member Fanny Brice (*q.v.*), then Mrs. Rose, the show failed.

A Little Racketeer (1/18/32; 48 performances) is notable only because composer Dimitri Tiomkin contributed several melodies. The E.Y. Harburg (*q.v.*) and Lewis E. Gensler revue *Ballyhoo of 1932* (9/6/32; 94 performances) didn't catch on, despite the talents of Grace and Paul Hartman, Bob Hope, Willie and Eugene Howard and Lulu McConnell.

The theater housed two shows in 1934, which were appreciated only after they closed. The first was Virgil Thomson and Gertrude Stein's opera *Four Saints in Three Acts* (2/20/34; 32 performances). The second was

Noel Coward's musical, *Conversation Piece* (10/23/34; 55 performances). Coward wrote the book, music and lyrics, including the now famous "I'll Follow My Secret Heart." Yvonne Printemps and George Sanders starred.

Marc Connelly's Pulitzer Prize-winning play *Green Pastures* (2/26/35; 71 performances) enjoyed a revival at the 44th Street Theatre. Kurt Weill's antiwar musical *Johnny Johnson* (11/19/36) featured Luther Adler, Morris Carnovsky, Lee J. Cobb, John Garfield, Elia Kazan, Robert Lewis, Sanford Meisner and Art Smith. The Group Theater (*q.v.*) production had a book and lyrics by Paul Green.

The revue *Crazy with the Heat* (1/30/41; 92 performances), another failure, featured music and lyrics by Dana Suesse. Another revue, *Keep 'Em Laughing* (4/24/42; 77 performances) was also a failure.

The theater hosted a few straight plays. One of these, *Winged Victory* (11/20/43; 212 performances) was produced by the U.S. Army Air Forces. The two-act drama was written by Moss Hart and starred Private Red Buttons, Sergeant Kevin McCarthy, Private Barry Nelson, Private First Class Edmond O'Brien, Private Whitney Bissell, Private Grant Richards, Staff Sergeant Daniel Scholl, Corporal Gary Merrill, Private First Class Edward McMahon, Private Philip Bourneuf, Sergeant George Reeves, Sergeant Ray Middleton, Private Karl Malden, Staff Sergeant Peter Lind Hayes, Private First Class Martin Ritt and Private Lee J. Cobb. The show was as large in scale as a musical and, in fact, had original music composed by David Rose.

The 44th Street Theatre's short life ended when the Astor estate, which owned the theater's land, sold the property to the *New York Times*. The newspaper tore down the building in 1945 and built an addition to its printing plant.

49TH STREET THEATRE 235 W. 49th Street. Architect: Herbert J. Krapp. Opening: December 26, 1921; *Face Value*. The Shuberts (*q.v.*) built the 49th Street Theatre, but it wasn't one of their more successful houses. An early hit was the revue *Chauve-Souris* (2/1/22; 544 performances). Despite the Russian theme, the show was, typically, ersatz Russian. American composers, including L. Wolfe Gilbert and Abel Baer, wrote a number of tunes in a slightly Russian manner. Hit songs from the show included "Dark Eyes" by A. Salami, "Two Guitars" and the "Volga Boat Song." The show was so popular that it eventually had four revivals and a new edition in 1943. The second revival opened at the 49th Street Theatre on January 14, 1925, and ran 69 performances.

The theater was the home for a number of hit plays with somewhat thin plots including, *Whispering Wires* (8/7/22; 356 performances), a mystery thriller. *Give and Take* (1/15/23; 188 performances), a farce by Aaron Hoffman, concerned John Bauer (played by Louis Mann)

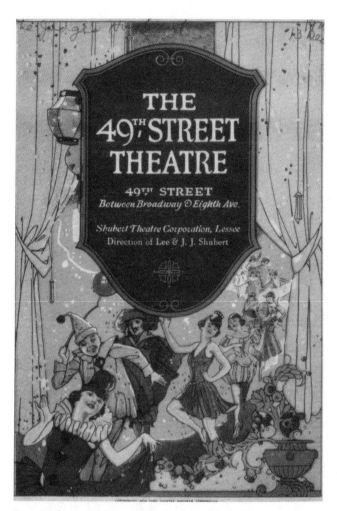

Program for the 49th Street Theatre   Courtesy Billy Rose Theater Collection.

46TH STREET THEATRE 226 W. 46th Street. Architect: Herbert J. Krapp. Opening: December 24, 1924; *Greenwich Village Follies*.   Chanin's 46th Street Theatre was one of the six Broadway theaters built by the Chanin brothers, prominent New York developers. They commissioned theater architect Herbert J. Krapp to build the theater, and he came up with a unique idea. Instead of dividing the theater into orchestra and balcony, he raked the seats bleacher style to the upper back wall.

Most of the early shows to play the 46th Street had opened at other theaters and were moved here to end their runs. The opening presentation, *The Greenwich Village Follies of 1924,* was no exception. It had run previously at the Shubert *(q.v.)* and Winter Garden theaters *(q.v.)* and closed soon after arriving.

The theater had its first big hit with the college musical, *Good News* (9/6/27; 551 performances). De-Sylva, Brown and Henderson *(q.v.)* contributed an enthusiastic score to the show. The hit songs included "The Best Things in Life Are Free," "Just Imagine," "The Varsity Drag," "Lucky in Love" and the exhilarating title song.

Zelma O'Neal starred in *Good News* as well as the

Program for the 46th Street Theatre

whose son comes back from college full of the fire of Communism. He convinces his father to turn his fruit-canning factory over to the employees. The factory failed, but a millionaire industrialist with a new selling scheme arrives on the scene and, despite the fact that he has just been released from a mental institution, his ideas save the factory.

The Judge's Husband (9/27/26; 120 performances) was another success. The plot was no less incredible than that of *Give and Take*. Joe Kirby teaches his wife the law, and his wife is later elected a judge, while Joe becomes a house husband. When Joe disappears for two days, his wife assumes that Joe had an amorous affair with one of the maids. She brings suit against Joe for divorce and tries the case herself. As it turns out, Joe was actually helping their daughter through a nasty time, and all is forgiven.

The Shuberts lost the 49th Street Theatre when the Depression hit. The Federal Theater Project *(q.v.)* leased it for a time. In 1938, it became a movie house, and in the 1940s it was torn down.

46th Street Theatre

theater's next hit, *Follow Thru* (1/9/29; 401 performances). DeSylva, Brown and Henderson again provided a superior score, including "Button Up Your Overcoat." In addition to Zelma O'Neal, the cast included Jack Haley and Eleanor Powell.

Top Speed (12/25/29; 104 performances) opened with Ginger Rogers making her Broadway debut. Billy Rose presented a revue, *Sweet and Low* (11/11/30; 184 performances). Hit songs included "Cheerful Little Earful" with music by Harry Warren and lyrics by Ira Gershwin (q.v.) and Billy Rose. An even bigger hit was "Would You Like to Take a Walk," with music by Warren and lyrics by Mort Dixon and Rose. Other song titles such as "I Wonder Who's Keeping Him Now," "Ten Minutes in Bed," and "When a Pansy Was a Flower" point up some of the naughtier aspects of the revue. Busby Berkeley and Danny Dare choreographed the proceedings, which featured Fanny Brice (q.v.), George Jessel, James Barton, Borrah Minevitch and Arthur Treacher in the cast.

Harold Arlen (q.v.) and Jack Yellen wrote the score to *You Said It* (1/19/31; 192 performances). Benny Baker, Lyda Roberti and Lou Holtz starred in the musical.

The Depression hit Broadway hard, and the Chanins lost their theaters. Though their name was dropped from the marquee, the 46th Street Theatre continued as one of Broadway's most successful.

Howard Lindsay had a hit comedy at the theater with *She Loves Me Not* (11/20/33; 367 performances). Burgess Meredith, John Beal and Polly Walters starred in the backstage/college thriller/comedy. In the show, Walters is a nightclub singer who sees a murder and has to hide out in a college. Along the way she gets to sing two songs by Arthur Schwartz (q.v.) and Edward Heyman: "After All, You're All I'm After" and "She Loves Me Not."

The Farmer Takes a Wife (10/30/34; 104 performances) was Henry Fonda's entry to Hollywood. He and Margaret Hamilton appeared in both the film version and the Broadway production.

One of the biggest hits in Broadway history, *Hellzapoppin* (9/22/38; 1,404 performances), opened at the 46th Street Theatre to mostly negative reviews. However, audiences loved it. They were convinced to attend by columnist Walter Winchell (q.v.), who used his vast power to plug the show whenever possible. Ole Olsen and Chic Johnson were responsible for the craziness on stage (and sometimes in the audience and lobby) that ranged from cheap burlesque (q.v.) jokes to cheaper vaudeville acts. *Hellzapoppin* might be compared with the latter-day television hit "Laugh In." Actually, "Laugh In" was more sophisticated. The revue moved to the larger Winter Garden Theater (q.v.).

Cole Porter (q.v.) returned to the 46th Street Theatre (*Anything Goes* moved there from the Alvin Theater (q.v.)) with a zany show, *Du Barry Was a Lady* (12/6/39; 408 performances). Du Barry, the story of a washroom attendant who falls asleep on the job and dreams he is Louis XV starred Bert Lahr and Ethel Merman (q.v.). The show also featured Betty Grable, Benny Baker, Ronald Graham, Adele Jergens and Charles Walters. Porter's inspired score included two big hits, "Friendship" and "Do I Love You."

Merman and Porter were back at the 46th Street with *Panama Hattie* (10/30/40; 501 performances). Porter's score included "Make It Another Old-Fashioned, Please," and "Let's Be Buddies." Also in the cast were Arthur Treacher, Pat Harrington Sr., Oscar ("Rags") Ragland, Joan Carroll and Betty Hutton.

After the successful run of the eerie play *Dark of the Moon* (3/14/45; 318 performances) came a revival of Victor Herbert's (q.v.) operetta *The Red Mill*. Then another classic musical, *Finian's Rainbow* (1/10/47; 725 performances), opened at the 46th Street. Burton Lane (q.v.) and E.Y. Harburg (q.v.) wrote the brilliant score and Harburg and Fred Saidy contributed the alternately fantastic and trenchant book. The superior score included "How Are Things in Glocca Morra?," "If This Isn't Love," "Old Devil Moon," "Look to the Rainbow" and "When I'm Not Near the Girl I Love." The delightful cast included David Wayne, Ella Logan and Albert Sharpe.

The next three shows at the 46th Street received

mixed reviews. The first, *Love Life* (10/7/48; 252 performances), was a underappreciated gem by Alan Jay Lerner *(q.v.)* and Kurt Weill *(q.v.)*. Elia Kazan directed the cast, which included Nanette Fabray, Ray Middleton and Lyle Bettger. Producer Cheryl Crawford presented *Love Life* and also the 46th Street's next offering, Marc Blitzstein's opera *Regina* (10/31/49; 56 performances). Based on Lillian Hellman's *The Little Foxes, Regina* starred Priscilla Gillette, Brenda Lewis, Russell Nype, Jane Pickens and William Warfield. Nanette Fabray returned in *Arms and the Girl* (2/2/50; 134 performances), with a score by Morton Gould and Dorothy Fields *(q.v.)*.

The 1950s continued the theater's good fortune with one of Broadway's greatest hits, Frank Loesser's *(q.v.)* masterpiece *Guys and Dolls* (11/24/50; 1,194 performances). The musical boasted a superior book by Jo Swerling and Abe Burrows. George S. Kaufman *(q.v.)* directed the exceptional cast, which included Vivian Blaine, Robert Alda, Isabel Bigley, Stubby Kaye and Sam Levene. The score included "Adelaide's Lament," "I'll Know," "I've Never Been in Love Before," "If I Were a Bell," "Luck Be a Lady," "Sit Down You're Rockin' the Boat" and the title song.

Audrey Hepburn starred in *Ondine* (2/18/54; 156 performances) with Mel Ferrer. Maxwell Anderson's *The Bad Seed* (12/8/54; 334 performances) was another hit at the 46th Street. Patty McCormack played the murderous child, and Nancy Kelly played her mother.

Gwen Verdon began a long run at the 46th Street in three different musicals. The first was the Jerry Ross and Richard Adler hit *Damn Yankees* (5/5/55; 1,019 performances). George Abbott *(q.v.)* directed. Hit songs included "Heart" and "Whatever Lola Wants." Bob Fosse was the brilliant choreographer.

Gwen Verdon kept her dressing room and opened in Bob Merrill's *New Girl in Town* (5/14/57; 431 performances). The show was also written and directed by George Abbott and choreographed by Bob Fosse. The musical version of Eugene O'Neill's *(q.v.) Anna Christie* contained two wonderful songs, "Look at 'Er" and "It's Good to Be Alive." Verdon's costars were Eddie Phillips (also of *Damn Yankees*), Cameron Prud'homme, George Wallace and Thelma Ritter.

Verdon stayed at the theater for *Redhead* (2/5/59; 452 performances). Albert Hague and Dorothy Fields provided the score, including two hits, "Look Who's in Love" and "Merely Marvelous." For *Redhead*, Bob Fosse not only choreographed but also directed. *Redhead* ended Gwen Verdon's long reign at the 46th Street Theatre.

Bock and Harnick *(q.v.)* wrote the score to *Tenderloin* (10/17/60; 216 performances). Jerome Weidman and George Abbott's book was about a priest's attempt to clean up Manhattan's notorious Tenderloin district. The cast included Maurice Evans, Ron Husmann, Rex Ev-

erhart, Eileen Rodgers and the ubiquitous Eddie Phillips.

Frank Loesser returned to the 46th Street Theatre with a Pulitzer Prize-winning musical, *How to Succeed in Business without Really Trying* (10/14/61; 1,417 performances). The satire made a star of Robert Morse, who costarred with Rudy Vallee, Claudette Sutherland, Charles Nelson Reilly, Virginia Martin, Bonnie Scott and Ruth Kobart. Abe Burrows provided the direction and Bob Fosse and Hugh Lambert choreographed. *How To Succeed*'s big hit song, "I Believe in You," was sung in the show by the hero—to himself.

Next came veteran Richard Rodgers *(q.v.)* and Stephen Sondheim's *(q.v.) Do I Hear a Waltz?* (3/18/65; 220 performances). Arthur Laurents based the libretto on his own play, *The Time of the Cuckoo*. The show had many assets, including performances by Elizabeth Allen, Sergio Franchi and Carol Bruce.

Mary Martin *(q.v.)* and Robert Preston were the sole cast members of the enchanting *I Do! I Do!* (12/5/66; 560 performances), a musical version of Jan de Hartog's *The Fourposter*. Tom Jones and Harvey Schmidt wrote the score, David Merrick *(q.v.)* produced and Gower Champion directed and choreographed.

The theater's next hit had an unlikely subject for a musical. *1776* (3/16/69; 1,217 performances) traced the founding of the United States. Sherman Edwards' score and Peter Stone's libretto made the proceedings dramatic. *1776* starred William Daniels, Howard Da Silva, Betty Buckley, Ken Howard and Virginia Vestoff.

In 1971, a revival of the tremendously successful *No No Nanette* opened. Ruby Keeler, Helen Gallagher, Susan Watson, Jack Gilford and Bobby Van starred. The hit even brought Busby Berkeley back to Broadway. The spirited revival ran 861 performances.

Raisin (10/18/73; 847 performances) was a musical version of Lorraine Hansberry's *A Raisin in the Sun*. The theater was again host to Gwen Verdon and Bob Fosse with the John Kander and Fred Ebb musical *Chicago* (6/1/75; 947 performances). It costarred Chita Rivera and Jerry Orbach.

The next show, *The Best Little Whorehouse in Texas* 4/17/78; 1,584 performances), broke the theater's long-run record. Carol Hall provided music and lyrics, and Larry L. King and Peter Masterson wrote the libretto. The show was a popular hit due in part to Tommy Tune and Peter Masterson's energetic direction.

Another offbeat subject, Federico Fellini's *8-1/2*, a movie about an artistically blocked film director, was the basis for a hit musical at the 46th Street. *Nine* (5/9/82; 729 performances) was another success for director Tommy Tune. *Fences* (3/26/87), by August Wilson, starred James Earl Jones and was awarded the Pulitzer Prize.

On November 17, 1987, the New York City Landmarks Preservation Commission granted landmark status to the interior and exterior of the theater. The Commission stated: "Its facade is an exceptional design based on Renaissance and neo-classical sources" and its interior was "designed in the 'stadium' plan, an innovation."

FORUM THEATER   See MOVIELAND.

FREEDLEY, VINTON   See AARONS AND FREEDLEY.

FREEMAN, DON (1908–1978)   Don Freeman was a noted illustrator who used Times Square as the backdrop for many of his highly regarded works. He was also a famed author who won many awards for his children's books and contributed poster art to plays and musicals.

Freeman was born in San Diego on August 11, 1908. He received his early schooling at the San Diego School of Fine Arts. After graduation, he moved to New York to study at the Art Students League. In his spare time and to make some money, Freeman played trumpet in a succession of jazz clubs.

Freeman had to choose between pursuing a career in music and becoming a professional artist. The decision was made by fate. While riding the subway with his sketch pad and trumpet, Freeman decided to sketch his fellow passengers. He became so immersed in the drawing he almost missed his stop. Just in time, he jumped from the car. Unfortunately, his trumpet remained on the train.

Freeman began submitting his drawings of scenes from New York life to the *Herald Tribune*. He also found a publisher for his works in the *New York Times*. His drawings pictured a Times Square that was rambunctious, turbulent and exciting. He was the artist who, more than any contemporary, captured the feeling of Broadway in the 1930s and 1940s.

Freeman also illustrated more than 50 books. Among the best known are William Saroyan's *The Human Comedy* and James Thurber's *The White Deer*. Freeman's children's books included *Norman the Doorman, Pet of the Met, The Circus in Peter's Closet* and *Mop Top*. Among his theater works are illustrations for the Ethel Merman *(q.v.)* musical, *Stars in Your Eyes*.

Freeman died on February 1, 1978.

FRENCH CASINO   See EARL CARROLL THEATRE.

Don Freeman's artwork for Stars in Your Eyes

FRIML, RUDOLF (1879–1972) In the early part of the century, the musical theater took two separate paths: (1) the homegrown American musical comedy represented by the works of George M. Cohan (q.v.), Irving Berlin (q.v.) and Jerome Kern (q.v.), and (2) the European operetta represented by Victor Herbert (q.v.), Sigmund Romberg (q.v.) and Rudolf Friml. Friml was one of the masters of this now outmoded form. From his operettas came some of the best loved melodies of the early years of American popular song.

Friml was born in Prague, Bohemia (now Czechoslovakia) on December 7, 1879. At the age of 11, one year after composing a barcarolle, he attended the Prague Conservatory where he studied under the tutelage of Dvorak and Jiranek. He completed the normal six-year course in half the allotted time and soon began touring Europe with violinist Jan Kubelik. He made his first appearance in the United States in 1901. He returned to play solo piano at Carnegie Hall in 1904 and again in 1906 to perform his own work, Piano Concerto in B-Major with Walter Damrosch conducting the New York Symphony Society.

When diva Emma Trentini broke relations with Victor Herbert, producer Arthur Hammerstein (q.v.) was forced to find a composer to write a score for his production of *The Firefly* (12/2/12; 120 performances). Trentini was a major star who had just triumphed in Herbert's *Naughty Marietta,* and finding a composer equal to her volatile temperament was not easy. Through music publisher Max Dreyfus, Hammerstein found Friml and commissioned him to write the score with librettist Otto Harbach (q.v.). The score contained three Friml standards, "Giannina Mia," "Love Is Like a Firefly" and "Sympathy."

The success of *The Firefly* led Hammerstein to sign Friml for additional projects. The first, *High Jinks* (12/10/13; 213 performances), got its title from the name of a perfume which, when sprayed on its target, produced uncontrolled mirth. Of course, this led to many humorous complications in the plot. As an added fillip,

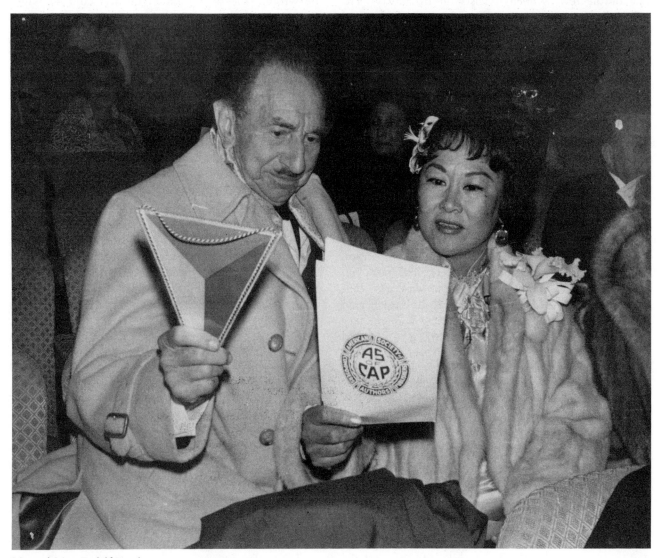

Mr. and Mrs. Rudolf Friml   Courtesy ASCAP.

the perfume was sprayed on the audience during the proceedings.

The Shuberts (q.v.) borrowed Friml's talents from Hammerstein for *The Peasant Girl* (3/2/15). Friml contributed additional numbers to the Oscar Nedbal score. Although Friml was reunited with Trentini, he wasn't sufficiently inspired to contribute any standards.

Back with Hammerstein, Friml and Harbach came up with *Katinka* (12/23/15; 220 performances), starring Adele Rowland. *You're in Love* (2/6/17; 167 performances), starred Marie Flynn as the sleepwalking heroine who made an impressive stroll on a ship's boom hanging over the audience. The play is notable today for giving Oscar Hammerstein II (q.v.) his first Broadway assignment, that of assistant stage manager.

Surprisingly, the next Harbach/Friml partnership resulted in a quick flop, *Kitty Darlin'* (11/7/17; 14 performances). Maybe Arthur Hammerstein's astute producership was the missing element. In the next Friml show, Hammerstein paired him with Rida Johnson Young, one of the few women lyricists on Broadway. The result, *Sometime* (10/4/18; 283 performances), featured popular comedian Ed Wynn and the sultry Mae West in an early Broadway appearance. She played Mayme, a vamp who used "Theda Bara tricks" to get her men.

Gloriana (10/28/18; 96 performances), the next Friml offering, opened only 22 days after *Sometime*. For *Gloriana*, Friml teamed up with another woman lyricist, Catherine Chilsholm Cushing. Harbach, Hammerstein and Friml were successful again with *Tumble Inn* (3/24/19; 128 performances), a minor musical. *The Little Whopper* (10/13/19; 224 performances), starred Vivienne Segal and was based on a silent movie, *Miss George Washington, Jr.* Friml's next score came more than two years later. Unfortunately, *June Love* (4/25/21; 50 performances) proved less endearing than its predecessor.

Friml had his songs interpolated into the 15th edition of the *Ziegfeld Follies* (q.v.) (6/21/21). The next full score under the Hammerstein banner was *The Blue Kitten* (1/13/22; 140 performances). Friml was again teamed with Harbach who was joined by William Cary Duncan as a colyricist. *The Blue Kitten* was followed by the premiere of *Cinders* (4/3/23; 31 performances). The failure of *Cinders* and Friml's sporadic output in the early twenties led many people to believe that he was washed up as a composer, but his next show proved to be his most popular.

Hammerstein, who still believed in Friml, paired him with his nephew Oscar for *Rose-Marie* (9/2/24; 581 performances). Herbert Stothart also contributed music to the operetta. Mary Ellis played the title role, and operetta favorite Dennis King played her lover. The score yielded three giant hits; "Indian Love Call" remains the best known, albeit often parodied with its oo-oo-oo lyrics. The title song shows little of the European influence of earlier Friml melodies, and the

"Song of the Mounties" (with music by Friml and Stothart) was the rousing male chorus number necessary in any good operetta. Hammerstein revealed his yearnings for a truly integrated score, one in which all songs related to the action on stage, instead of being just vaudeville turns stuck into the plot to relieve boredom. Hammerstein wrote in the program that the individual songs would not be listed because, "The musical numbers of this play are such an integral part of the action that we do not think we should list them as separate episodes. The songs which stand out, independent of their dramatic associations are Rose-Marie, Indian Love Call, Totem Tom-Tom, and Why Shouldn't We? in the first act, and Door of Her Dreams in the second act." *Rose-Marie* wasn't an entirely integrated work; Hammerstein's later *Show Boat* came much closer to this ideal, but it was another step on the road to a truly American operetta, a form that had its greatest success with *Oklahoma!*

The critics didn't fully agree with Hammerstein when he wrote, "the revolution in musical comedy which Rose-Marie has wrought was not accidental. It was a carefully directed attack at the Cinderella show in favor of operatic musical comedy." The *New York Times* called the plot "slightly less banally put forward than has been customary." Surprisingly, the song the critics most singled out for praise was "Totem Tom-Tom."

Rose-Marie also became the greatest financial success in Broadway history until Rodgers and Hammerstein's (q.v.) *Oklahoma!* in 1943. The Broadway production had a $4.40 top ticket price. Seven tours criss-crossed America beginning in February 1925 and ending in September 1928. The London production opened at the Theater Royal, Drury Lane, on March 20, 1925, and played even longer than the Broadway production for a total of 851 performances. Both of those productions were dwarfed by the Paris production, which premiered April 9, 1927, and lasted 1,250 performances. Productions in Berlin, Stockholm and Moscow were mounted, and the show returned to London for an additional 100 performances in September of 1929.

Movie versions were produced in 1928, 1936 and 1954. The first was a silent version, which starred Joan Crawford as Rose-Marie and the second was the MGM classic with Jeanette MacDonald and Nelson Eddy, which opened in 1936. The third starred Ann Blyth and Howard Keel to little effect.

Friml's next Broadway show, *The Vagabond King* (10/21/25; 511 performances), proved almost as successful as *Rose-Marie*, with Friml returning to his European roots. The production, with lyrics by Brian Hooker, starred Dennis King and Carolyn Thomson. Friml again supplied an exceptional score with the numbers "Only a Rose," "Song of the Vagabonds," "Some Day" and "Huguette Waltz" achieving the longest-lasting fame.

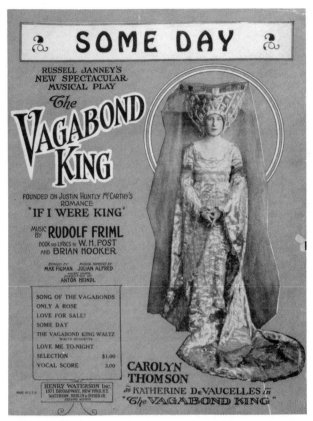

Sheet music for The Vagabond King

Florenz Ziegfeld *(q.v.)* interpolated Friml songs into his next revue, *No Foolin'*. It was also called *Ziegfeld's American Revue of 1926*. Friml's songs included "Florida, the Moon and You," which celebrated the state's current vogue on Broadway. (Irving Berlin's *Cocoanuts* also featured the new vacationland.) Friml's next show,

The White Eagle (12/26/27; 48 performances), was not a success.

In his last Broadway success, *The Three Musketeers* (3/13/28; 319 performances), Friml worked in familiar territory, musicalizing a classic European work as he had done with *The Vagabond King,* based on Justin Huntley McCarthy's novel, *If I Were King.* Dennis King repeated his prior successes in Friml shows. P.G. Wodehouse and Clifford Grey created the lyrics for the spectacular score. Among the best songs were the tremendously popular "March of the Musketeers," "Ma Belle," "My Sword and I" and "Your Eyes and One Kiss." The opening night's performance lasted well past midnight, causing Alexander Woollcott *(q.v.)* to comment, "I did greatly enjoy the first few years of Act I."

During the 1930s, Broadway audiences' tastes were changing. New American songwriters like Rodgers and Hart *(q.v.)* and DeSylva, Brown and Henderson *(q.v.)* were capturing Broadway's fancy. Operetta was seen as more and more passe. Friml's last two shows, *Luana* (9/17/30; 21 performances) and *Music Hath Charms* (12/29/34; 29 performances) were failures.

Because Friml could not change his writing style, his career languished for the remainder of his life. He wrote an occasional song for film adaptations of his stage shows. Friml also concentrated on recordings, featuring him at the piano leading orchestras through his repetoire. In 1956, he worked with lyricist Johnny Burke on new songs for the remake of *The Vagabond King.* This was his last assignment. He was saluted by ASCAP *(q.v.)* on his 90 birthday.

Rudolf Friml died on November 12, 1972.

FULTON THEATER   See HELEN HAYES THEATER.

GABRIEL, GILBERT WOLF   See CRITICS.

GAIETY THEATER 1547 Broadway between 45th and 46th Streets. Architects: Herts and Tallant. Opening: September 4, 1909; *The Fortune Hunter.* Klaw and Erlanger built the Gaiety for George M. Cohan, *(q.v.)* who shared in its management. The theater was noted for several architectural features. The audience area was built in what was known as the "mushroom" design, which reflected its configuration. The theater was also noted for the abscence of pillars holding up the balcony, which in earlier theaters had drastically hampered sightlines. With cantilevered balconies, pillars became unnecessary. Another innovation featured in the new house was the orchestra pit. Prior to this, most orchestras were on the audience level and stages were raised accordingly. This "invisible orchestra" allowed the stage height to be lowered and the sight lines of the first rows to be improved and brought forward.

The first production was Cohan's *The Yankee Prince,* which played a few performances in the theater prior to opening in Washington, D.C., on September 20, 1909. This served as a dress rehearsal for both the new theater and the touring cast of the show.

Surprisingly, although the house was known for its orchestra pit, it was never to house a musical comedy. The first full production at the theater came with the opening of *The Fortune Hunter* (9/4/09; 345 performances). Other productions in the Gaiety's first decade included *First Lady of the Land* (12/4/11; 64 performances); *Officer 666* (1/29/12; 192 performances); *Stop Thief* (12/25/12; 149 performances); *Nearly Married* (9/5/13; 123 performances); *Erstwhile Susan* (1/18/16; 167 performances); *Turn to the Right!* (8/18/16; 435 performances); and *Sick-A-Bed* (2/25/18; 80 performances).

The huge success of *Turn to the Right!* did not prepare

the theater owners for the Gaiety's greatest hit, *Lightnin'* (8/26/18; 1,291 performances). The show, written by Frank Bacon and Winchell Smith, was the story of Lightin' Bill Jones, a landlord whose hotel conveniently straddled the border of Nevada and California. When the constabulary came after him, Lightin' would simply cross the border into another jurisdiction. Frank Bacon also starred in the comedy, which ran for three years. This made Lightnin' the longest-running play in Broadway history, a position it held until *Abie's Irish Rose* overtook it in the mid-1920s. When *Lightnin'* closed, there was a spectacular parade down Broadway. Mayor John F. Hylan, Commissioner Grover Whelen, Winchell Smith, Frank Bacon and producer John Golden led the march to Pennsylvania Station where the cast embarked on a nationwide tour. The great Lightnin' Parade *(q.v.)* was one of the first events that was not totally manufactured by an overly avid press agent.

Following *Lightnin',* the Gaiety housed a string of failures: *The Wheel* (8/29/21; 49 performances); a revival of *Alias Jimmy Valentine* (12/8/21; 46 performances); and *Madeleine and the Movies* (3/6/22; 80 performances). The next hit was *Loyalties* (9/27/22; 220 performances) by John Galsworthy, chosen as a best play by Burns Mantle, editor of the *Best Plays* series.

The next play, *If Winter Comes* (4/2/23; 40 performances) was a failure, but the theater's fortunes picked up with a production of Frederick Lonsdale's comedy, *Aren't We All?* (5/21/23; 284 performances) with Leslie Howard, Jack Whiting, Cyril Maude and Marguerite St. John.

The Youngest (12/22/24; 100 performances) was followed by *Loggerheads,* which moved to the Gaiety from the Cherry Lane Theater off-Broadway. *These Charming People* (10/6/25; 97 performances) was followed by *By the Way* (12/28/25; 177 performances).

The theater's last year of operation as a legitimate

house was 1926. Its last show was the modest hit *Love in a Mist* (4/12/26; 120 performances).

Following the run of *Love in a Mist,* the theater was closed and soon reopened as a motion picture house. In 1932, the theater was converted to burlesque *(q.v.)*. In 1943, the name was changed to the Victoria. The first movie to play the Victoria was *The City That Stopped Hitler—Heroic Stalingrad,* which opened on September 4, 1943.

The Victoria and its next-door neighbor the Astor Theater *(q.v.)* had the world's longest sign positioned on their shared roofs. The signage *(q.v.)* location above the two theaters was used primarily as an advertisement for their current movie attractions. The most spectacular of these was for *The Vikings.* When the theaters ceased to show first-run features, the sign was put to more prosaic uses. The huge Budweiser billboard was perhaps the best known of these.

The Victoria was demolished along with the Astor, Morosco *(q.v.),* Bijou *(q.v.)* and Helen Hayes *(q.v.)* theaters on March 22, 1982. Its destruction and that of the other theaters led to the establishment of Save the Theaters *(q.v.)* and a renewed interest in historic preservation.

GANGSTERS Broadway and Times Square have long been the turf of gangsters and hoodlums. In the 1930s, during Prohibition, the area was known for its night-clubs and speakeasies, which afforded the bootleggers ample opportunities to sell their wares and the crime syndicates opportunities to launder money. In more recent times, with the social disintegration of the area, prostitutes and drugs have taken their hold. And throughout its history, the Broadway musical has been a perfect money-laundering device.

The Prohibition years were the most fruitful for gangsters. Since the era roughly coincided with the Depression, legitimate operators had been wiped out, and gangsters moved in to take control of New York's entertainment areas. Mob associated hoodlums had cash to spare and, in addition to backing Broadway shows and running nightclubs, they also laundered their money through real estate holdings. They bought up a lot of prime midtown property, and their families still control many choice plots of land in Times Square. The exploits of notorious hoodlums were duly recorded by journalists like Damon Runyon *(q.v.)* and Walter Winchell *(q.v.)*. Their favorite subjects were Legs Diamond, Lucky Luciano, Arnold Rothstein and Herman Rosenthal. The supporting cast included Gyp the Blood, Whitey Lewis and Lefty Louis.

Legs Diamond (1896–1931) operated the Hotsy Totsy Club, a front for criminals, on Broadway between 54th and 55th Street. The manager of the club was ostensibly Hymie Cohen. Diamond used the club as his head-quarters. Many men met their end in the back room and were then carried out "drunk" through the bar.

The murders reached their apex in July 1929. A fight erupted, supposedly over whether prizefighter Ruby Goldstein was a capable fighter. The argument turned into a full-fledged gun battle with Charlie Entratta (Green) and Legs Diamond in the middle. They both disappeared after shooting gangster Red Cassidy. A bystander, Simon Walker, was also killed as were a waiter and bartender. The hatcheck girl and cashier were never found, and three other witnesses were later found dead. Hymie Cohen was also missing. Because there were no witnesses, Diamond and Entratta got off scot-free. The club closed soon after the murders.

Diamond, much hated, was the target of many attacks on his life. However, each time he recovered and set about to control an ever larger piece of the Broadway pie. He was finally killed by two unknown assailants on December 18, 1931, in Albany, New York.

One of Diamond's chief rivals was Waxey Gordon (1888–1952), a bootlegger and nightclub owner. Gordon made almost $2 million a year in his bootlegging industry. However he claimed only $8,125 in his income tax, and that resulted in his downfall. He was probably lucky. If he had stayed out of jail, Gordon's feuds with Lucky Luciano and Meyer Lansky would have certainly resulted in his death. When Gordon got out of Leavenworth in 1940, he announced the death of Waxey Gordon and the birth of Irving Wexler, salesman. He took a suite of offices at Broadway and 42nd Street and dabbled in drug dealing. Gordon was also a backer of many Broadway shows. Those he had a stake in always featured his current flame somewhere in the chorus.

Lucky Luciano (1897–1962), Gordon's enemy, was another of the gangsters who enjoyed fame on The Great White Way. He was a leading member of the syndicate and perhaps its most important figure. Luciano operated out of several speakeasies and clubs as a board member of the Broadway Mob. The group of rumrunners was headed by Joe Adonis (1902–1972) with Frank Costello (1891–1973) also on the board. The Broadway Mob, which controlled all liquor distribution in the Times Square area, supplied Jack and Charlie's 21 Club, the Stork Club, the Silver Slipper and other smaller outlets. Meyer Lansky and Bugsy Siegel were made members of the club so their gangs could provide protection for the Mob.

Arnold Rothstein (1882–1928) was called, variously, "the banker for racketeers," the Big Bankroll, the Fixer, the Man Uptown and Mr. Big. Damon Runyon dubbed him The Brain. Rothstein was a fixer, one who could bribe almost any official no matter how high the office. He was an inveterate gambler who also bankrolled such biggies as Legs Diamond and Waxey Gordon. Rothstein had almost $3 million in real estate investments as well as his own personal wealth, made when he sold his liquor importing business in the mid-1920s.

While at Lindy's Restaurant (q.v.) on November 4, 1928, Rothstein made about $600,000 in bets on the Presidential election. Rothstein supported Hoover over Al Smith and Franklin Roosevelt as New York's next governor. He would have made a lot of money had he lived to see the election.

A few days earlier he had lost heavily to racketeer George McManus. Rothstein claimed the poker game was fixed and tore up over $300,000 in IOUs. McManus called Rothstein at Lindy's and suggested that Rothstein meet him at the Park Central Hotel. That night Rothstein was found dead at the servant's exit on 56th Street.

Though there were no indictments, it was clear to Broadwayites that Nigger Nate Raymond and Titanic Thompson, Rothstein's poker partners, authorized the hit.

Rothstein, as mentioned earlier, was the inspiration of the Damon Runyon character, The Brain. Runyon wrote that "nobody knows how much dough The Brain has, except that he must have plenty because no matter how much dough is around, The Brain sooner or later gets hold of all of it." The Brain also had some characteristics of Herman Rosenthal.

Rosenthal, a Times Square gambler and club owner, is best known as the man who stood up to Lieutenant Charles Becker (1869–1915). Becker was a New York City policeman who wanted to muscle in on Rosenthal's territory through "legitimate" police protection. When Rosenthal refused to play ball and threatened to turn Becker in to the newspapers, he was murdered in front of the Metropole Cafe at 43rd Street and Broadway on July 16, 1912. Gyp the Blood, Dago Frank, Whitey Lewis and Lefty Louie were the hit men. They were hired by Big Jack Zelig who Becker arranged to have released from jail to undertake the job. Becker was protected from prosecution by his boss, police Commissioner Rhinelander Waldo. Waldo saw to it that important leads were "lost" and a witness was locked up in jail away from the police's search. Becker, called "the crookedest cop who ever stood behind a shield," was eventually sentenced to death along with the hit men. District Attorney Whitman was instrumental in bringing Becker to the electric chair.

Becker wasn't the only public official who was in on the graft and crime surrounding Times Square. New York Supreme Court Judge Joseph Force Crater (1889–1937) disappeared off the streets of Times Square on August 6, 1930. Crater had previously bought tickets to a musical and had exited Billy Haas's restaurant at 332 West 45th Street where he had lunched with theatrical lawyer William Klein and showgirl Sally Lou Ritz. A little after 9:00 P.M., Crater got in a cab and disappeared. Despite hundreds of leads, he was never

found. Frederic Johnson, Crater's law clerk, claimed that he knew why Crater disappeared. Johnson stated, "He died because he knew too much."

Not all the law enforcers on the payroll were crooked. Among the most honest, and toughest, was police officer Johnny Broderick (1894–1966). To "broderick" someone meant to deck him or her with a powerful punch, a slang (q.v.) term that described Broderick's rough method of justice. Broderick seldom used his gun; usually, he used his fists or any useful object that was close at hand. For example, once Broderick found a criminal he was searching for in a Broadway cafeteria. He strode up to the man and knocked him out with a sugar bowl. Broderick announced to the amazed gathering, "Case closed."

Broderick's most famous exploit concerned Legs Diamond. The two were experts at their respective jobs, and neither held the other in much regard. Diamond, fed up with Broderick, announced that he was taking the cop on and was going to teach him a lesson. Diamond and his boys hit all the spots that Broderick frequented—Lindy's (q.v.), Toots Shor's, the Astor Hotel (q.v.) Bar and Leone's.

Broderick wasn't one to avoid confrontation, so he set out on his own search for Diamond. The two men met on Broadway at 46th Street. When confronted with the 5-foot-10, 170-pound Broderick, Diamond's henchmen ran away. Without his bodyguards, Diamond was less brave. He asked Broderick whether he could take a joke, to which Broderick responded by picking Diamond up and depositing him head first into a trash can.

Mayor James J. Walker later commented, "Broderick as good as killed Diamond with that garbage can stunt. It finished him as a leader."

Walker was right. Diamond was later rubbed out while hiding out in an Albany hotel room. Broderick went on to enjoy a 24-year-long career patrolling Times Square before his retirement in 1947.

Today's criminals along The Great White Way have none of the flash or panache of Diamond or Rothstein. Today's crooks deal in the distribution of crack and cocaine and in prostitution. Other petty criminals deal in three-card monte rackets set up on cardboard boxes not far from the Metropole site on 43rd Street, where three-card monte was invented.

GASSNER, JOHN   See CRITICS.

GAVER, JACK   See CRITICS.

GEORGE ABBOTT THEATER 152 W. 54th Street. Architect: R.E. Hall & Co. Opening: December 24, 1928; *Potiphar's Wife.* The Craig Theater couldn't have opened at a worse time—just as the Depression was changing the face of Broadway. Producers lost millions in the market as well as their theater holdings. The theater's location north of the theater district proper sealed its fate. From the beginning, the Craig was a disaster.

On November 27, 1934, the original owners, the Houston Properties Corporation, lost the theater, and it was renamed the Adelphi. The first show, *The Lord Blesses the Bishop*, didn't bode well for the success of the new venture when it closed after only seven performances. The theater remained a failure, and it was taken over by the Federal Theater Project *(q.v.)*.

Under the new management, the theater became successful for the first time. *It Can't Happen Here* (95 performances) was an enormous hit for the theater and the Federal Theater Project. The show was written by Sinclair Lewis and was unique in that it opened on October 27, 1936, in 18 cities. New York alone had four productions. The show was the story of a fascist politician who becomes president of the United States. Hallie Flanagan, director of the Federal Theater Project, commented: "The play says that when dictatorship comes to threaten such a democracy, it comes in an apparently harmless guise, with parades and promises; but that when such dictatorship arrives, the promises are not kept and the parade grounds become encampments."

Playwright Arthur Arent's *One-Third of a Nation* (1/17/38; 237 performances) was one of the Federal Theater Project's Living Newspapers. The show was the best known of all the Project's presentations, seen by over 2,000 people in New York alone. Ten other cities later presented the show. The theme of *One-Third of a Nation* was the problems of the nation's slums. The title of the piece was taken from Franklin Roosevelt's second inaugural address.

The last significant production at the Adelphi by the Federal Theater Project was *Sing for Your Supper* (4/24/39; 60 performances). Its best known song was "Ballad for Americans" by Earl Robinson and John Latouche.

With the end of the Federal Theater Project, the Adelphi was taken over by the Royal Fraternity of Master Metaphysicians. In December 1940, they changed the name of the theater to the Radiant Center. Three years later, on October 18, 1983, the theater became the Yiddish Art Theater. Its opening production was *The Family Carnovsky*. But the theater wasn't successful as a Yiddish theater either.

On April 20, 1944, the theater became the Adelphi Theater again. The musical *Allah Be Praised!* opened at the Adelphi but only ran 20 performances. When out-of-town producer Alfred Bloomingdale asked play doctor Cy Howard what to do, Howard suggested to Bloomingdale that he "Close the show and keep the store open nights."

Finally, the theater's luck changed with the opening of *On the Town* (12/28/44; 462 performances). The show was directed by George Abbott *(q.v.)* who gave three talents—Leonard Bernstein *(q.v.)*, Betty Comden and Adolph Green *(q.v.)*—their first Broadway break. It starred such talents as Nancy Walker, Sono Osato, Cris Alexander, John Battles, Alice Pearce and Comden and Green. The big song was "New York, New York."

Unfortunately, *On the Town* led the way to another series of flops. *Carib Song* (9/27/45; 36 performances) starred the great choreographer and dancer Katharine Dunham. *Nellie Bly* (1/21/46; 16 performances), with a score by Johnny Burke and James Van Heusen, starred William Gaxton, Marilyn Maxwell and Victor Moore. *Three to Make Ready* (3/7/46; 327 performances) was the third in a series by Morgan Lewis and Nancy Hamilton. *Three to Make Ready* moved to the St. James Theatre *(q.v.)* to make way for the next tenant, another failure about world travelers, but a spectacular one.

Around the World in Eighty Days (5/31/46; 75 performances) was the brainchild of Orson Welles, who wrote the extravaganza's book and directed the show. In addition, Welles became producer when Michael Todd decamped while the show was in tryouts. Cole Porter *(q.v.)* wrote music and lyrics to the show, but none of the songs achieved any success. Broadway wags called the show "Wellesapoppin'" after Olsen and Johnson's hit *Hellzapoppin'*. When it opened on Broadway, the 36 scene changes required 55 stagehands. (At the time, the Adelphi was not air-conditioned.) Welles also starred in the show after taking over for an actor while the show was out of town. Welles's contract with CBS Radio had him committed to a Friday night radio show. Therefore, the musical could not play Friday nights. All in all, the show lost almost half a million dollars.

Kurt Weill *(q.v.)* saw his musical version of Elmer Rice's play *Street Scene* open at the Adelphi Theater (1/9/47; 148 performances). The wonderful score, with lyrics by Langston Hughes, was ably rendered by Anne Jeffreys, Polyna Stoska, Brian Sullivan, Sheila Bond and Danny Daniels.

Music in My Heart (10/2/47; 124 performances), a musical with melodies by Tchaikovsky, was not a success. *Look Ma I'm Dancin'* (1/29/48; 188 performances) probably should have been a bigger hit than it was. Hugh Martin wrote the catchy score, and Jerome Lawrence and Robert E. Lee contributed the libretto. George Abbott produced and directed in association with Jerome Robbins. Robbins also choreographed the musical, which starred Nancy Walker, Harold Lang, Tommy Rall and Alice Pearce. *Hilarities* (9/9/48; 14 performances) was apparently a misnomer for a revue that closed quickly.

Radio and television took over the theater for much of the 1950s. It was renamed the 54th Street Theater on October 8, 1958, with the opening of *Drink to Me Only*.

Richard Adler, without his late partner Jerry Ross, tried his hand at both music and lyrics for *Kwamina*

(10/23/61; 32 performances), starring Robert Guillaume and Sally Ann Howes.

Richard Rodgers (q.v.) opened his first show without either Lorenz Hart (q.v.) or Oscar Hammerstein II (q.v.) with *No Strings* (3/15/62; 580 performances). Rodgers provided both music and lyrics. The show starred Diahann Carroll, Richard Kiley, Noelle Adam, Alvin Epstein and Don Chastain. The score contained such hits as "The Sweetest Sounds" and the title tune.

What Makes Sammy Run? (2/27/64; 541 performances) was a musicalization of the famous novel by Budd Schulberg. Ervin Drake composed the score and wrote the lyrics of the score, which included a popular song "A Room without Windows." Steve Lawrence, Robert Alda, Sally Ann Howes and Bernice Massi starred in the show.

La Grosse Valise (12/14/65; 7 performances) had music by Gerard Calvi and lyrics by Harold Rome (q.v.). This was the last show to play the theater before it was renamed the George Abbott Theater.

Darling of the Day (1/27/68; 32 performances) was a failure by the usually reliable Jule Styne (q.v.) and E.Y. Harburg (q.v.). *Buck White* (12/2/69; 7 performances) was a musical failure, most notable for the Broadway debut of Cassius Clay (Muhammad Ali). The theater's last show did even worse. *Gantry* (2/14/70) opened and closed in one day. The George Abbott theater was demolished in 1970.

GEORGE JEAN NATHAN AWARD   George Jean Nathan (1882–1958) founded the award "to encourage and assist in developing the art of drama criticism and the stimulation of intelligent theatre going." The award winner is decided by a committee of English department chairpeople from Cornell, Princeton and Yale. The award comes with a $4,000 stipend and is given to the author of "the best piece of drama criticism published during the previous year, whether an article, treatise or book."

GEORGE M. COHAN THEATRE   1482 Broadway at southeast corner of 43rd Street; main entrance on 43rd Street. Architect: George Keister. Opening: February 13, 1911; *Get-Rich-Quick Wallingford*.   The George M. Cohan Theatre was built by the team of George M. Cohan (q.v.) and Sam H. Harris, among the busiest producers of the late teens. They also managed the Harris Theater (q.v.), the Grand Opera House, the Astor Theatre (q.v.), the Gaiety Theater (q.v.), and the Bronx Opera House as well as Cohan's Grand Opera House in Chicago.

The first great hit at the Cohan Theatre was *The Little Millionaire* (9/25/11; 192 performances). It featured Cohan as composer, lyricist, librettist, director, co-producer and star. The musical also starred Cohan's parents and Donald Crisp.

The George M. Cohan Theatre   Courtesy Billy Rose Theater Collection.

In *Broadway Jones* (9/23/12; 176 performances), Cohan playing a Broadwayite who finds himself in the sticks. *Theater Magazine* said that the plot "is so simple that it is almost juvenile. But Mr. Cohan is a true observer of men and conditions, and applies the little comic and pathetic touches of life in a way which makes his completed fabric something distinctly vital and real." The show marked the end of an era, the last time the Four Cohans would appear together on Broadway. During its subsequent tour, Cohan's parents retired from the stage.

The comedy *Potash and Perlmutter* (7/16/13; 441 performances) was a huge hit. Roi Cooper Megrue and Walter Hackett's play *It Pays to Advertise* (9/8/14; 399 performances) starred Grant Mitchell. *Pom-Pom* (2/28/16; 128 performances) had music by Hugo Felix and book and lyrics by one of Broadway's few women lyricists, Anne Caldwell. Mitzi Hajos had the lead. Later that year, *Seven Chances* (8/8/16; 151 performances) opened to acclaim. Another of the theater's early successes was *Come Out of the Kitchen* (10/23/16; 224 performances).

The Kiss Burglar (5/9/18; 100 performances) was a minor musical by Raymond Hubbell and Glen Mac-Donough. *Head Over Heels* (8/29/18; 100 performances) was an early musical by Jerome Kern (q.v.). *A Prince There Was* (12/24/18; 159 performances) had as its author Robert Hilliard, who also starred. Cohan rewrote the play and made it a success.

Elsie Janis and Her Gang opened at the Cohan Theatre (12/1/19; 55 performances), featuring the talented actress Eva Le Gallienne. Charles Dillingham and Florenz Ziegfeld (q.v.) produced the show. *The Genius and the Crowd* (9/6/20; 24 performances), a comedy by John T. McIntyre and Francis Hill, was significant because it was the first show Cohan produced on his own following a split with Harris.

Cohan had a great hit with his melodrama, *The Tavern* (9/27/20; 252 performances). The story of Francois Villon was meant by Cohan to be an affectionate travesty, but opening night critics took it seriously and panned the proceedings. However, Robert Benchley (q.v.), Dorothy Parker and Robert E. Sherwood enjoyed the play in the spirit in which it was presented and gave it rave reviews. Benchley noted that, "There can no longer be any doubt that George M. Cohan is the greatest man in the world. Anyone who can write *The Tavern* and produce it as *The Tavern* is produced places himself automatically in the class with the gods who sit on Olympus and emit Jovian (or is it Shavian?) laughter at the tiny tots below on earth. In fact, George M. Cohan's laughter is much more intelligent than that of any god I ever heard of." It was revived five times on Broadway and countless times across the country.

Two Little Girls in Blue (5/3/21; 135 performances) had music was by Vincent Youmans (q.v.) and lyrics by Arthur Francis, better known as Ira Gershwin (q.v.). The musical starred Madeleine and Marion Fairbanks.

One of the theater's biggest successes was Clemence Dane's drama *A Bill of Divorcement* (10/10/21; 173 performances). Katharine Cornell (q.v.) starred. *A Bill of Divorcement* moved on to make way for the opening of Ed Wynn's musical, *The Perfect Fool* (11/7/21; 275 performances). George Gershwin (q.v.) composed two of the numbers in the show. *The Love Child* (11/14/22; 169 performances) starred Janet Beecher and Sidney Blackmer.

Adrienne (5/28/23; 235 performances), a musical with a score by popular favorites Albert Von Tilzer and A. Seymour Brown, had as its musical director Max Steiner, who would make a name for himself as one of Hollywood's greatest composers.

Owen Davis's farce *The Haunted House* (9/2/24; 103 performances) starred Wallace Edinger as an author who lives his life in the style of the book he is writing. While writing about a haunted house he scares everyone

Program for the George M. Cohan Theatre

he is in contact with. Another farce by Davis to play the Cohan was *Easy Come, Easy Go* (10/26/25; 180 performances). The show starred Edward Arnold, Otto Kruger, Victor Moore and Betty Garde.

A Frank Craven play, *The 19th Hole* (10/11/27; 119 performances), followed the downward path of a golf addict. Craven himself played the inveterate golfer whose compulsion only ends when his livelihood and marriage are threatened by the game.

Milton Ager and Jack Yellen wrote the score to *Rain or Shine* (2/9/28; 360 performances). Heywood Broun organized a show to give out-of-work actors some employment. The result, *Shoot the Works* (7/21/31; 87 performances), had as contributors to the score and sketches Peter Arno, Broun himself, Dorothy Parker, Nunnally Johnson, Sig Herzig, E.B. White, Ira Gershwin (q.v.), Irving Berlin (q.v.), Leo Robin, Dorothy Fields (q.v.), Jimmy McHugh, Jay Gorney, E.Y. Harburg (q.v.), and Vernon Duke (q.v.). Among the performers the show helped out were Imogene Coca, Jack Hazzard, George Murphy and Broun.

There You Are (5/16/32; 8 performances) was a short-lived musical that marked an end to the theater's legitimate policy. Along with many other Broadway houses, during the Depression the theater adopted a movie policy. In 1938, the theater was torn down along with the FitzGerald Building, which shared its facade.

GEORGE WHITE'S SCANDALS

George White's Scandals were a long running (1919–1939) annual series of revues produced and sometimes written by George White (*q.v.*). The *Scandals* were one of the most important of the revue series, a popular genre in the first part of the century.

Other important revue series were the *Ziegfeld Follies* (*q.v.*), *Earl Carroll's Vanities* (*q.v.*), the Shubert Brothers' (*q.v.*) *Passing Shows* and Irving Berlin's (*q.v.*) *Music Box Revues*. The *Follies* were distinguished for their elaborate production numbers and big stars. The *Vanities* were notorious for their risque numbers featuring scantily clad chorines. The *Passing Shows* were simple entertainments without much to distinguish them, and the *Music Box Revues* were intimate shows featuring Irving Berlin's songs. What made the *Scandals* noteworthy was the high quality of their material. They were the first revues to assign complete scores to songwriting teams. Until the *Scandals*, songs were submitted to producers who would pick and choose the best. White also put an emphasis on dance, since he was a former hoofer in the *Ziegfeld Follies* and other Broadway shows.

White came up with the idea for the *Scandals* while he was in the *Follies*. He realized Ziegfeld was immersed in the producing styles of the teens and earlier, and he believed he could improve on the revue format. White was sure he could move the revue into more modern fashion in his own series. His revues were much faster paced than Ziegfeld's, reflecting a new trend in jazzy entertainment.

The first *George White's Scandals* was the 1919 edition (6/2/19; 128 performances). White contributed some sketches and lyrics in addition to starring in the revue. He hired Ann Pennington, a dancer who had also appeared as his partner in the *Follies*. Pennington would become a *Scandals* regular, appearing in five editions. White hired up-and-coming composers Richard Whiting and Herbert Spencer for the tunes. Arthur Jackson and White himself handled lyric chores.

White certainly had a knack for finding other young talents. His next edition featured a score by the young George Gershwin (*q.v.*) and Arthur Jackson. Ann Pennington, Lou Holtz and White reappeared as headliners. The 1920 edition (6/7/20; 134 performances) introduced a new dance step to Broadway, the scandal walk. For this edition, White codirected with William Collier.

White again codirected, coauthored, produced and starred in his next *Scandals* (7/11/21). Gershwin and Jackson had a hit with their score, which featured "Drifting Along with the Tide." Pennington was back as was Lester Allen, who had made his first appearance

in the previous edition. Rounding out the cast were Tess Gardella (also known as Aunt Jemima), Bert Gordon and Charles King.

For the fourth edition (8/28/22), White assumed his usual roles with an assist on the libretto by Andy Rice and Ziegfeld star W.C. Fields. This time B.G. DeSylva and E. Ray Goetz provided lyrics to Gershwin's tunes. The hit song of this edition was "I'll Build a Stairway to Paradise," with lyrics by DeSylva and Arthur Francis (a pseudonym of Ira Gershwin (*q.v.*)). Lester Allen, Delores Costello, W.C. Fields, Winnie Lightner, Paul Whiteman and His Orchestra and George White were featured.

In the next *Scandals* (6/18/23; 168 performances), the DeSylva and Goetz lyrics were augmented by Ballard Macdonald's contributions to Gershwin's tunes. The score was undistinguished, resulting in no lasting hits. Allen and Lightner reappeared with an assist by Olive Vaughn and Tom Patricola. The latter would join the list of *Scandals* regulars. For the first time, White wasn't in the cast of his annual revue. He wouldn't return to the stage until the 1929 edition.

The 1924 edition (198 performances) opened on June 30 with Costello, Lightner, Patricola and the Williams Sisters starring. The Gershwin and DeSylva score presented one great standard, "Somebody Loves Me," which featured additional lyrics by Ballard Macdonald.

For the next edition (6/22/25; 169 performances), George Gershwin, who had abandoned the revue field to concentrate on book musicals, was replaced by the songwriting team of DeSylva, Brown and Henderson. This was the first uniting of the noted songwriting team, who would provide some of their greatest hits for the *Scandals*, but this show did not contain any big hits. Tom Patricola was the only *Scandals* regular to appear in the cast. He was joined by Helen Morgan, Harry Fox, Gordon Dooley and the successful black performers Flournoy Miller and Aubrey Lyles.

In the 1926 edition (6/14/26; 432 performances), the songwriting team was in top form. The trio presented White with three smash hit songs. "The Birth of the Blues" was the most highly regarded, especially as energetically presented by Harry Richman. "The Black Bottom" was the next big dance craze to come out of the *Scandals*. These were the days when many of the dance steps that swept the nation originated on Broadway. The last big song was "Lucky Day," an enthusiastically upbeat number typical of DeSylva, Brown and Henderson. Former *Scandals* contributor George Gershwin returned with an interpolation of his "Rhapsody in Blue." The show was a reunion of sorts for other former *Scandals* stars. Ann Pennington was back along with Tom Patricola and Frances Williams, who had appeared in the 1924 *Scandals* as one of the Williams Sisters. Several sibling groups also appeared: Willie and

Eugene Howard, the Fairbanks Twins and the Mc-Carthy Sisters. White charged $55 a ticket for seats in the front of the orchestra on opening night. He was right to do so, for the show was a huge success.

Because of the long run of the 1926 edition, there was no 1927 show. The next *Scandals* (7/2/28) didn't have a particularly good score; in fact, one song was titled, "Not As Good As Last Year." The Howards, Tom Patricola, Ann Pennington, Harry Richman and Frances Williams all returned, but the show wasn't as successful as the previous edition. However, it did manage a 230-performance run, mostly because of the previous edition's success.

For the next edition (9/23/29; 159 performances), George White contributed songs to one of his own shows. His lyricist was Irving Caesar. Cliff Friend wrote the rest of the unmemorable score. White seemed to enjoy performing teams, and this edition featured the Abbott Dancers, the Elm City Four, Willie and Eugene Howard, Mitchell and Durant and the Scott Sisters. White rejoined the cast of his series. Frances Williams was practically the only other cast member unrelated to another performer on the bill.

In 1930, White was producer and director of a book show, *Flying High*. He returned to his *Scandals* the next year. The 1931 edition (9/14/31; 204 performances) boasted a score by Brown and Henderson, but this time without DeSylva. The duo didn't seem to miss their former collaborator, for the score contained five huge hits—"Ladies and Gentlemen That's Love," "Life Is Just a Bowl of Cherries," "That's Why Darkies Were Born," "This Is the Missus" and "The Thrill Is Gone." The cast, too, was the greatest in *Scandals* history. Ethel Merman (*q.v.*), Rudy Vallee, Alice Faye, Ethel Barrymore Colt, Ray Bolger, Everett Marshall and Willie and Eugene Howard were the stars. However, the country was in the middle of the Depression, and theater was suffering. So despite the excellent cast and material, the show didn't run as long as it might have in better times.

There was no *Scandals* the next year, although White did present a revue, *George White's Music Hall Varieties* (11/22/32). The Depression took its toll, and the next *Scandals* was not produced until 1936. The show opened on Christmas Day of 1935 (110 performances) at the New Amsterdam Theater (*q.v.*), site of most of the *Ziegfeld Follies*. Ray Henderson was the only one of the songwriting trio left. His lyricist was Jack Yellen. The cast included Rudy Vallee, Bert Lahr, Cliff Edwards, Hal Forde and Willie and Eugene Howard.

The last *Scandals* was the 1939 edition (8/28/39; 120 performances). The score was mostly by Sammy Fain and Jack Yellen. They supplied the standard, "Are You Havin' Any Fun?," which was introduced by singer Ella Logan. The two other hits were by Yellen and

Herb Magidson, "Something I Dreamed Last Night" and "The Mexiconga." Additional cast members included the Three Stooges, Ben Blue, Ray Middleton, Ann Miller, and Willie and Eugene Howard.

The last *Scandals* was White's last Broadway show. He retired from the stage, leaving behind a wealth of great songs and the satisfaction of knowing that he helped boost the careers of many newcomers. The *Scandals* were certainly the revue series most in step with the times, and it was the vision of George White, their producer, director, writer, composer, choreographer and star, that created them.

GERSHWIN, GEORGE AND IRA

George Gershwin (1898–1937)   George Gershwin was born in Brooklyn, New York, on September 26, 1898, to a poor family of first generation immigrants. In 1912, his parents purchased a piano so that brother Ira could take lessons. But it was George who showed the natural predilection for music. He amazed his family when he sat down at the new piano and played simple tunes.

In fact, George had begun his "studies" at a neighbor's house where he taught himself the basics of piano playing. He went on to more structured schooling with Charles Hambitzer. Hambitzer in turn urged George to study theory, orchestration and harmony with Edward Kilenyi.

George had ambitions to become a concert pianist, but his teachers convinced him that such a dream was impractical. Luckily, he had an interest in the burgeoning field of American popular song. Like most of his contemporaries, he idolized Jerome Kern (*q.v.*) and Irving Berlin (*q.v.*), two composers who, with George M. Cohan (*q.v.*), were most responsible for bringing an American sensibility to what had been a predominantly European art.

"When You Want 'Em, You Can't Get 'Em (When You Got 'Em, You Don't Want 'Em)" was the title of George's first published song, copyrighted in 1916 with lyrics by Murray Roth. George's first Broadway song, "The Making of a Girl," was written for *The Passing Show of 1916* (6/22/16) in collaboration with Sigmund Romberg (*q.v.*) with lyrics by Harold Atteridge.

George created his first important song, "Swanee," which was written for the Capitol Theater's (*q.v.*) revue *Demi-Tasse* (10/24/19) and was later interpolated into the Al Jolson (*q.v.*) show *Sinbad* (2/14/18) after its opening. "Swanee," written with Irving Caesar, was an enormous hit as a result of its exposure in *Sinbad* and led to composing offers by Broadway producers.

La, La, Lucille (5/26/19; 104 performances), George's first Broadway show, opened at the Henry Miller Theatre (*q.v.*) with a libretto by Fred Jackson and lyrics by Arthur J. Jackson and B.G. DeSylva (*q.v.*). *Morris Gest's*

Ira and George Gershwin   Courtesy ASCAP.

Midnight Whirl (12/27/19) with lyrics by B.G. DeSylva followed.

George White's Scandals of 1920 (6/7/20; 134 performances) was a successful installment of the annual revue. George White *(q.v.)* had the foresight to hire George Gershwin when the composer was just beginning to make a name for himself. Arthur Jackson contributed the lyrics.

George's next Broadway attempt, *A Dangerous Maid,* closed out of town in Pittsburgh. The show is notable as the first for which Ira Gerhswin wrote all the lyrics. Ira was concerned that it would appear he was hired only because he was George's brother, so he assumed the name Arthur Francis, the first names of their brother and sister.

Ira Gershwin (1896–1983)   Ira was born on December 6, 1896, on the Lower East Side of New York City. He was always interested in language, having written light verse all through school. Ira saw his work published by Franklin P. Adams in Adams's newspaper column, The Conning Tower. Other lyricists whose work appeared in The Conning Tower were Howard Dietz *(q.v.)* and E.Y. Harburg *(q.v.).*

The first song with lyrics by Ira and music by George to appear in a Broadway show was "The Real American Folk Song Is a Rag." It was put into *Ladies First* (10/24/18; 164 performances) where it received little notice and wasn't published until years later. The first published song with music by George and lyrics by Ira was "Waiting for the Sun to Come Up," which was written for *The Sweetheart Shop* (8/31/20).

Their next Broadway show was *Two Little Girls in Blue* (5/3/21; 135 performances), which opened at the George M. Cohan Theatre *(q.v.).* Vincent Youmans *(q.v.)* and Paul Lanin also wrote some of the music for the score. The show starred Madeline and Marion Fairbanks, who were known as the Fairbanks Twins.

George White's Scandals of 1921 (7/11/21; 97 performances) had lyrics by Arthur Jackson and music by George. The only semisuccess in the score was "Drifting Along with the Tide." The following year's edition of the *Scandals* (8/28/22; 88 performances) contained the Gershwins' first standards as a team. The show opened with lyrics also supplied by B.G. DeSylva and E. Ray Goetz. The biggest hit was "I'll Build a Stairway to Paradise," with lyrics by DeSylva and Ira.

For a while, it seemed that George composed minor scores to minor musicals. These included *Our Nell* (12/4/22; 40 performances) (with interpolated songs by George); *The Rainbow* (4/3/23; 113 performances); the 1923 edition of the *Scandals* (6/18/23; 168 performances) at the Globe Theatre (*q.v.*); and *Sweet Little Devil* (1/21/24; 120 performances) at the Astor Theatre (*q.v.*).

On February 12, 1924, *Rhapsody in Blue* premiered at Aeolian Hall. The first show of the year for George was another edition of the *Scandals* (6/30/24; 192 performances) at the Apollo Theatre (*q.v.*). The show's lyrics were by B.G. DeSylva, who contributed the lyrics to the show's big hit, "Somebody Loves Me," with Ballard Macdonald. The song has remained a standard more than 60 years after the show's premiere.

Primrose (9/11/24; 255 performances) opened at the Winter Garden Theater in London with lyrics by Ira and Desmond Carter. The libretto was written by George Grossmith and Guy Bolton (*q.v.*). It was the Gershwin's biggest hit to date and it paved the way to a successful return to America.

The brothers' next show, with Ira writing under his own name, was a huge hit. *Lady, Be Good!* (12/1/24; 330 performances) opened at the Liberty Theatre (*q.v.*) on 42nd Street, produced by Alex A. Aarons and Vinton Freedley (*q.v.*) with a book by Guy Bolton (*q.v.*) and Fred Thompson. The stars were Fred and Adele Astaire (*q.v.*), Walter Catlett and Cliff Edwards.

Lady, Be Good!'s jaunty score contained at least two standards—the title song and "Fascinating Rhythm." The show was subsequently produced in London on April 14, 1926, with the Astaires. *Lady, Be Good!* established the brothers as a successful team, and for the next 20 years they wrote together.

Tell Me More! (4/13/25; 100 performances) wasn't as big a success as *Lady, Be Good!* The lyrics by Ira and B.G. DeSylva accompanied one moderately successful song, "Kickin' the Clouds Away." Another song had an interesting title—"My Fair Lady," originally the show's title song. The show was conducted by Max Steiner, who would later achieve renown as a composer of Hollywood epics like *Gone With the Wind*.

Tip-Toes 12/28/25; 194 performances) at the Liberty Theatre (*q.v.*) was twice as successful. Alex A. Aarons, who produced *Tell Me More!*, produced this show too, this time with Vinton Freedley. The Gershwin brothers' score contained several hits, including "Looking for a Boy," "That Certain Feeling" and "Sweet and Low Down."

George's Concerto in F premiered at Carnegie Hall on December 3, 1925. Seven days later, *Song of the Flame* opened, George's third Broadway show of the year. *Song of the Flame* was an old-fashioned operetta with music also by Herbert Stothart. Otto Harbach (*q.v.*) and Oscar Hammerstein II (*q.v.*) wrote the lyrics.

Reunited with his brother Ira, George wrote some of his best tunes for the Aarons and Freedley musical *Oh, Kay!* (11/8/26; 257 performances) at the Imperial Theatre (*q.v.*). The book was by Guy Bolton and P.G. Wodehouse. The cast included Gertrude Lawrence, Victor Moore, Oscar Shaw, Betty Compton and Harland Dixon.

The score was one of the brothers' best. "Maybe," "Clap Yo' Hands" and "Do, Do, Do" were all hits, but they were overshadowed by "Someone to Watch Over Me."

The Gershwins' next show, *Strike Up the Band*, closed in Philadelphia in September 1927. That temporary setback was partially compensated by their next smash hit, *Funny Face* (11/22/27; 250 performances), the show that Aarons and Freedley used to open their new Alvin Theater (*q.v.*). The theater and the show were an immediate success. Fred Thompson and Paul Gerard Smith provided the book, which was mainly an excuse for the great Gershwin songs. The conductor was Alfred Newman, who, like Max Steiner, found greater fame as one of Hollywood's top composers. The show subsequently opened a successful engagement in London on November 8, 1928.

Florenz Ziegfeld (*q.v.*) commissioned George and Sigmund Romberg to compose the score of *Rosalie* (1/10/29; 335 performances). P.G. Wodehouse and Ira Gershwin supplied the lyrics to the hit show. It opened at the New Amsterdam Theatre (*q.v.*) and starred Marilyn Miller, Frank Morgan and Jack Donahue. The most famous of the Gershwin brothers' songs was "How Long Has This Been Going On?"

The Gershwins' next show was equally successful. *That's a Good Girl* (6/5/28; 365 performances), their third show to premiere in London, opened at the London Hippodrome.

For *Treasure Girl* (11/8/28; 68 performances), the brothers were back at the Alvin Theater under the auspices of Aarons and Freedley. Gertrude Lawrence, Clifton Webb and Mary Hay introduced a fine score, including "I've Got a Crush on You," "I Don't Think I'll Fall in Love Today" and "Feeling I'm Falling."

George's *An American in Paris* premiered at Carnegie Hall on December 13, 1928. Walter Damrosch conducted the Philharmonic Symphony Society of New York.

Ziegfeld used the Gershwins' talents for his production *Show Girl* (7/2/29; 111 performances). Gus Kahn collaborated on the lyrics. Ruby Keeler, Eddie Foy Jr., Frank McHugh and Clayton, Jackson and Durante starred with Duke Ellington's Orchestra in the pit. As with many shows of the same period, *Show Girl's* run was cut short by the Depression.

Ziegfeld again commissioned a Gershwin score, this time for *Ming Toy*. The Depression hit Ziegfeld hard, and the show was never produced. In the score was a Gershwin song that became an enduring standard—"Embraceable You," later used in the hit *Girl Crazy*.

The 1930s began for the Gershwins with a revival of *Strike Up the Band* (1/14/30; 191 performances). The revised version opened at the Times Square Theater *(q.v.)*. Bobby Clark, Paul McCullough, Blanche Ring and Dudley Clements starred in the early satire. The score included "Soon," "Strike Up the Band" and "I've Got a Crush on You" (previously in *Treasure Girl*).

The Gershwins' next score accompanied another great success. Aarons and Freedley opened *Girl Crazy* (10/14/30; 272 performances) at their Alvin Theater *(q.v.)*. Guy Bolton and John McGowan devised the libretto. The cast included Ginger Rogers, Allen Kearns, William Kent, Willie Howard and, making her Broadway debut, Ethel Merman *(q.v.)*. The show's orchestra was equally luminous. Among its members were Benny Goodman, Glenn Miller, Red Nichols, Jimmy Dorsey, Jack Teagarden and Gene Krupa. The show contained five standards—"Bidin' My Time," "Embraceable You," "I Got Rhythm," "But Not for Me" and "Boy! What Love Has Done to Me."

The Gershwins took a brief sojourn in Hollywood to write the score for *Delicious*, released by Fox Film Corporation on December 3, 1931. Five days later, the Gershwins' *Of Thee I Sing* (441 performances) opened at the Music Box Theater *(q.v.)* under the leadership of producer Sam Harris. George S. Kaufman *(q.v.)*, who had written the first book of *Strike Up the Band*, collaborated with Morrie Ryskind, the author of the revised *Strike Up the Band*. William Gaxton starred as President John P. Wintergreen in the mildly satirical show. Victor Moore created one of his most successful characters in Alexander Throttlebottom, the hapless vice-president. Lois Moran, Grace Brinkley and future United States Senator George Murphy completed the leads.

The score included three standards, the title song, "Love Is Sweeping the Country" and "Who Cares." *Of Thee I Sing* proved to be an enormous success and won the Pulitzer Prize *(q.v.)*. It played 441 performances.

Following the premieres of his *Second Rhapsody* on January 29, 1932, and his *Cuban Overture* on August 16, 1932, George saw *Pardon My English* (1/20/33; 46 performances) open at the Majestic Theater *(q.v.)* with Aarons and Freedley producing. The score contained several hit songs, "My Cousin in Milwaukee," "The Lorelei" and "Isn't It a Pity."

Let 'Em Eat Cake (10/21/33; 90 performances) was a sequel to *Of Thee I Sing*. The song "Mine" was the big

hit from the score. William Gaxton, Victor Moore and Lois Moran repeated their roles from *Of Thee I Sing*.

While George was working on his monumental opera *Porgy and Bess*, Ira worked on his first collaboration with another composer. The Shuberts *(q.v.)* presented *Life Begins at 8:40* (8/27/34; 227 performances) at their Winter Garden Theater *(q.v.)*. The music was written by Harold Arlen *(q.v.)* and the lyrics by Ira and E.Y. Harburg *(q.v.)*. Bert Lahr, Ray Bolger, Luella Gear and Frances Williams starred in the show. The hit songs included "You're a Builder Upper," "Fun to Be Fooled" and "Let's Take a Walk Around the Block."

George Gershwin's last Broadway score and what most people consider his masterpiece was *Porgy and Bess* (10/10/35; 124 performances). The show was presented by the Theater Guild *(q.v.)* at the Alvin Theater. The lyrics were written by Ira and Du Bose Heyward. Todd Duncan, Anne Brown, John W. Bubbles and Ruby Elzy starred. The show contained George's richest melodies and most theatrical ballads. "Summertime," "My Man's Gone Now," "I Got Plenty o' Nuthin', " "Bess, You Is My Woman Now" and "It Ain't Necessarily So" are among the greatest songs written for the American musical theater.

The show received a surprisingly mixed reaction from critics. They couldn't understand whether the piece was opera or musical theater. This inability to

DuBose Heyward Courtesy ASCAP.

place the show in a convenient pigeon hole seemed to throw off their critical acumen. Other performers and the team's close friends knew that the work was a masterpiece, but George in particular was distraught at the critical reaction.

Ira again collaborated with another composer, this time Vernon Duke (q.v.). The show was the *Ziegfeld Follies of 1936* (1/30/36; 227 performances), which was presented by Ziegfeld's widow, Billie Burke, and the Shuberts. It opened at the Winter Garden Theater and starred Fanny Brice (q.v.), Bob Hope, Eve Arden, Gertrude Niesen and Josephine Baker. The only hit to emerge from the score was "I Can't Get Started."

George and Ira went to Hollywood to script the songs to three movies. *Shall We Dance* was released by RKO in May, 1937. *A Damsel in Distress* was released in November that same year by RKO. Goldwyn released *The Goldwyn Follies* in February 1938.

While in Hollywood, George began having frequent headaches. At first doctors were unable to find anything wrong. As the illness progressed, it was discovered that he had a brain tumor. After an unsuccessful operation, George Gershwin died in Hollywood on July 11, 1937. He was 38 years old.

The Goldwyn Follies was completed after George's death by Vernon Duke and by Kay Swift, who used George's notes to complete the songs. Ira was devastated by the loss of his brother.

Ira collaborated with Kurt Weill (q.v.) on the score to *Lady in the Dark* (1/23/41; 467 performances), which boasted a book by Moss Hart and opened at the Alvin Theater. The show starred Gertrude Lawrence, Danny Kaye, Victor Mature and Macdonald Carey. *Lady in the Dark* was one of the first shows to examine psychoanalysis. The subject lent itself to several magnificent dream sequences.

Ira wrote a score for the movie *The North Star*, released by RKO in October 1943. He was teamed with an unlikely partner, Aaron Copeland. The screenplay was written by Lillian Hellman. A more lighthearted assignment followed when Ira teamed up with Jerome Kern for the movie *Cover Girl*. It was produced by composer Arthur Schwartz (q.v.) for Columbia, which released it in April 1944.

Kurt Weill was again Ira's collaborator for *The Firebrand of Florence* (3/23/45; 43 performances) based on the life of Benvenuto Cellini. The show was a failure, opening at the Alvin Theater.

Weill and Gershwin went to Hollywood to supply the score to *Where Do We Go From Here?* The movie was released by 20th Century-Fox in May 1945.

Ira returned to New York for his last Broadway show, *Park Avenue* (11/4/46; 72 performances). Arthur Schwartz, producer of *Cover Girl,* was Ira's collaborator. The show was presented by Max Gordon at the Shubert Theatre (q.v.). The score was a bright spot in an otherwise unsuccessful show.

Ira settled permanently in Hollywood, where he supplied the lyrics to a succession of film musicals. The score for *The Shocking Miss Pilgrim* (20th Century-Fox 1947) was built around jottings George had left at his death. Ira wrote the *Barkleys of Broadway* (MGM 1949) with Harry Warren. It would prove to be the last film featuring the team of Fred Astaire and Ginger Rogers.

A minor effort, *Give a Girl a Break,* was an MGM film released in 1953. It had music by Burton Lane (q.v.). Harold Arlen was the composer of one of Ira's biggest movie hits, *A Star Is Born.* Warner Brothers released the movie starring the Judy Garland and James Mason in October 1954. Ira's last score was written for the Paramount Pictures *The Country Girl* with music by Harold Arlen. It was released in December 1954. *Kiss Me, Stupid,* a Billy Wilder film, contained three previously unpublished songs by the Gershwin brothers. It was released by United Artists in December 1964.

Ira Gershwin died in Hollywood on August 17, 1983.

GERSHWIN THEATER 1633 Broadway between 50th and 51st Street. Designer: Ralph Alswang. Opening: November 28, 1972; *Via Galactica.* This theater, originally called the Uris, was the first new Broadway theater built in New York since the Earl Carroll Theater (q.v.) went up in 1931. Designer Ralph Alswang de-

Uris Theatre

scribed his theater: "The Uris represents what I think is the total philosophy of a modern musical comedy house—seating, sight lines, acoustics—the economy and aesthetics for this kind of theater." Critics disagreed, calling the theater an ugly barn with poor acoustics and too deep an auditorium. The 1,900 seat theater was built on the site originally occupied by the Capitol Theater *(q.v.),* a huge movie palace that critics thought would have served the same purpose as the Uris with more style. However the Uris was definitely an afterthought. The first priority was to build a massive office building on the site. This was one of the first giant offices in Times Square and was criticized for ruining the low-rise area. Critics at the time prophesized correctly that the Uris was only one of the first of many skyscrapers that would forever change the special qualities of Times Square.

Included in the theater is what is referred to as the Theater Hall of Fame. This consists of names of theater greats tacked up on a huge side wall. There is no explanation of who the people are nor are there any exhibits. There are just the names on the wall. It should also be noted that some of the names are misspelled.

The Uris opened with a short-lived musical, *Via Galactica,* which had music by Galt MacDermot, composer of *Hair,* and lyrics by Christopher Gore. The show ran for only 7 performances.

Cy Coleman and Dorothy Fields *(q.v.)* wrote the score to *Seesaw* (3/18/73; 296 performances), the next offering at the Uris. *Seesaw,* under Michael Bennett's direction, was not successful. More failures followed in the Uris's early years. A revival of *Desert Song* opened in late 1973 and lasted only 15 performances, and a stage adaptation of Lerner and Loewe's *(q.v.)* film *Gigi* played 103 performances.

In 1975, the theater found no legitimate bookings. Instead the Uris presented a series of concerts by pop stars. The next year, with the short-lived exception of *Treemonisha* (10/21/75; 64 performances), a previously unproduced opera by ragtime great, Scott Joplin, the theater hosted more pop concerts and ballet companies. The Houston Grand Opera, which had been responsible

Interior of the Gershwin Theater

for the production of *Treemonisha*, revived *Porgy and Bess* in 1976. It was followed by still more concerts.

Finally, the theater had a success with a revival of Rodgers and Hammerstein's *(q.v.)* *The King and I* (5/2/77; 719 performances). The musical featured original cast member Yul Brynner and Constance Towers. Angela Lansbury assumed the role of Anna with Michael Kermoyan as the King while Brynner was on vacation.

Lansbury returned in another long running show, *Sweeney Todd* (3/1/79; 557 performances), which was the Uris's next tenant. The musical had a score by Stephen Sondheim *(q.v.)* and book by Hugh Wheeler. Len Cariou costarred as the demon barber of Fleet Street. Todd murdered his enemies and Mrs. Lovett, the Lansbury character, baked the victims' remains into meat pies. Sweeney Todd ran an impressive 557 performances but was not a financial success. Blame was put on the huge theater with its large weekly operating cost and the overblown production necessary to fill its cavernous stage.

Following some bookings of ballet companies, the Uris hosted Joseph Papp's Public Theater production of Gilbert and Sullivan's *The Pirates of Penzance* (1/1/81; 772 performances). The operetta opened with Linda Ronstadt, Kevin Kline and Rex Smith headlining the cast.

Another musical revival, *My Fair Lady* (8/18/81; 124 performances), opened with Rex Harrison repeating his starring role as Henry Higgins and Nancy Ringham playing Eliza Doolittle. Next came *Annie,* which moved from the Eugene O'Neill Theater *(q.v.)* to end its 2,377 performance run.

The Houston Grand Opera opened a production of Jerome Kern *(q.v.)* and Oscar Hammerstein II's *(q.v.)* musical *Show Boat* (4/24/83). On June 5, 1983, during *Show Boat*'s run, the name of the theater was changed to the Gershwin, after composer George Gershwin *(q.v.)*. Critics felt that the songwriter would have been embarrassed to have such a poor theater named after him. They also pointed out that the Alvin *(q.v.)* was really the theater that should have been renamed the Gershwin, since the Gershwin brothers both had such great successes there.

A lackluster revival of *Mame* (7/24/83) (Lansbury's third appearance at the theater) quickly closed. The Royal Shakespeare Company presented two fine productions, *Cyrano de Bergerac* and *Much Ado About Nothing,* in repertory at the Gershwin beginning October 14, 1984. The limited run was extremely successful.

Another classic Hollywood musical, *Singing in the Rain,* opened at the Gershwin in 1985 and was a failure. The theater finally had a moderate success with Andrew Lloyd Webber's musical *Starlight Express* (3/15/87; 761 performances).

GILDER, ROSAMOND   See CRITICS.

GLOBE THEATRE   See LUNT-FONTANNE THEATER.

GOLDEN THEATER   See JOHN GOLDEN THEATER.

GOODMAN, ALFRED (1890–1972)   Al Goodman was an important Broadway conductor who occasionally composed for Broadway shows but without much success. He is best known for the recordings of studio-cast albums of Broadway shows, which he made primarily for RCA Victor.

He was born in Nikopol, Russia, on April 12, 1890. After arriving in the United States, he attended Peabody Conservatory on scholorship. In 1907, he made his theatrical debut playing piano in a nickleodeon in Baltimore, Maryland. Following this inauspicious beginning, he joined the Aborn Opera Company as a singer. Apparently his singing wasn't as good as his conducting, and he soon became the company's musical director. The Aborn Opera Company was one of many small opera companies that produced original operas and revivals. Goodman received valuable training with the short runs and many productions that the Aborn company produced every year.

Goodman's talents were brought to the attention of the Shubert Brothers *(q.v.)* who hired him as a staff conductor for the Winter Garden Theater *(q.v.)*. He made his Broadway debut conducting *The Passing Show of 1912,* which opened July 22. This was the first in a series of *Passing Shows (q.v.)* that were the Shuberts' entry in the revue field.

The Shuberts, operating under the title Winter Garden Theater Company, had many artists and performers under exclusive contract. In addition to Goodman, these included composer Sigmund Romberg *(q.v.),* lyricist and librettist Harold Atteridge, director J.C. Huffman, choreographer Allan K. Foster and musical director Oscar Radin. These men worked on almost all the *Passing Shows.* Goodman took over the baton from Radin when Radin was called to conduct another Shubert show.

In all, Goodman conducted 14 *Passing Shows*—each year from 1912 through 1926, except for the 1919 edition. Among the stars he accompanied were Charlotte Greenwood, Willie and Eugene Howard, Marilyn Miller, John Boles, Ed Wynn, Fred and Adele Astaire *(q.v.),* George Raft, Blanche Ring, Fred Allen, George Jessel and Nat Nazzarro Jr. All these stars and more appeared in the yearly series. Unfortunately no famous songs emerged from the *Passing Shows.*

In between Goodman's annual assignments at the Winter Garden, the Shuberts called on him to conduct other shows. These included *So Long Letty* (10/23/16) and *Sinbad* (2/14/18) with Al Jolson *(q.v.)*. Goodman also convinced the Shuberts to give him a chance writing original musicals. The first was *Linger Longer Letty* (11/10/19; 69 performances), one in a series of musicals starring Charlotte Greenwood as the popular Letty. Bernard Grossman supplied the lyrics. Goodman's second composing job was with Bert Grant for *Cinderella on Broadway* (6/24/20; 126 performances). Harold Atteridge provided the lyrics.

With Lew Pollock and Gustave Kerker he wrote *The Whirl of New York* (6/13/21; 124 performances). The modest success of these outings led to more assignments by the Shuberts, including collaborations with Jean Gilbert on *The Lady in Ermine* (10/2/22; 238 performances) and with Edward Ridemus on *Caroline* (1/31/23; 151 performances). He also contributed songs to the *Passing Show of 1922* (9/20/22) and the score to *Dew Drop Inn* (5/17/23; 37 performances).

Meanwhile, he was still conducting for Shubert productions. He was musical director for one of the Shuberts' biggest successes, *Blossom Time* (9/28/21; 516 performances). Again, Goodman replaced Radin as conductor of the long running hit. He worked again with Al Jolson in *Bombo* (10/6/21; 218 performances), which played the Jolson Theater (*q.v.*). In *Sinbad* and *Bombo*, Goodman helped Jolson in presenting many of his greatest hits. Among these are "April Showers," "Avalon," "Toot, Toot, Tootsie," "My Mammy," "Swanee" and "Rock-A-Bye Your Baby to a Dixie Melody."

He contributed songs to *Artists and Models* in 1923, 1924 and 1925. This was a short lived series of annual revues presented by the Shuberts. He also had songs added to the score of *Sky High* (3/2/25) and the score of *Gay Paree* (8/18/25). Although some of these shows were successful, none of Goodman's songs were; he made his mark as conductor, rather than as composer, of some of the greatest Broadway shows.

Goodman was musical director for the smash hit *Rio Rita* (2/2/27; 494 performances) with a score by Harry Tierney and Joseph McCarthy. He also conducted *Good News* (9/6/27; 551 performances) with its up-to-date score by DeSylva, Brown and Henderson (*q.v.*). The *New Moon* (9/19/28; 519 performances) boasted a score by Sigmund Romberg and Oscar Hammerstein II (*q.v.*). He continued his lucky streak with DeSylva, Brown and Henderson's *Follow Thru* (1/9/29; 401 performances). The last show of the twenties with musical direction by Al Goodman was *Sons O' Guns* (11/26/29; 297 performances).

During the thirties, Goodman, in the pit of the New Amsterdam Theatre (*q.v.*) conducted what is probably the greatest revue of all time, *The Band Wagon* (6/3/31; 262 performances). The Dietz and Schwartz (*q.v.*) show starred Fred and Adele Astaire (*q.v.*), Tilly Losch, Helen Broderick and Frank Morgan. Goodman conducted such songs as "I Love Louisa" and "Dancing in the Dark."

Jerome Kern (*q.v.*) and Otto Harbach's (*q.v.*) *The Cat and the Fiddle* (10/15/31; 395 performances) was

next. Under Goodman's direction, Bettina Hall, Georges Metaxa and Odette Myrtil sang such Kern and Harbach standards as "Try to Forget," "She Didn't Say 'Yes' " and "The Night Was Made for Love."

By now, Goodman was considered the top Broadway conductor. Released from his Shubert contract in 1927, he was able to pick and choose his assignments. He chose to work with only the top composers on shows that looked like hits or that had interesting scores. After *The Cat and the Fiddle,* he worked with songwriters Howard Dietz and Arthur Schwartz on *Flying Colors* (9/15/32; 181 performances) which introduced such standards as "Louisiana Hayride" and "Alone Together."

He worked again with Ray Henderson and Lew Brown on *Strike Me Pink* (3/4/33; 122 performances) at the Majestic Theater (*q.v.*). A revue, *Life Begins at 8:40* (8/27/34; 238 performances), was next with its jaunty score by Harold Arlen (*q.v.*), E.Y. Harburg (*q.v.*) and Ira Gershwin (*q.v.*). The show introduced "Let's Take a Walk Around the Block."

Calling All Stars (12/13/34; 35 performances) was one of Goodman's few flops on Broadway. His next show, *Music Hath Charms,* was also a flop, opening only 16 days after *Calling All Stars*. Despite a Rudolf Friml (*q.v.*) score, the show played only 25 performances.

He was on the upswing again when conducting more Dietz and Schwartz tunes for *At Home Abroad* (9/19/35; 198 performances). The loosely constructed musical opened with Eddie Foy Jr., Beatrice Lillie, Eleanor Powell, Ethel Waters and Reginald Gardiner. The score included "Love Is a Dancing Thing," "O What a Wonderful World" and "Thief in the Night."

Arthur Schwartz also composed Goodman's next assignment, *Stars in Your Eyes* (2/9/39; 127 performances). This time, Dorothy Fields (*q.v.*) supplied the lyrics for the Ethel Merman (*q.v.*) starrer. Goodman's last Broadway show was the Rodgers and Hart (*q.v.*) musical, *Higher and Higher* (4/4/40; 84 performances), one of their less successful shows.

Goodman was a workaholic who often moonlighted on national radio shows. He began his radio work in 1932 and continued after leaving his Broadway conducting chores. Among the shows for which he conducted were "Ziegfeld Follies of the Air," "Your Hit Parade," the "Fred Allen Show," "Millions for Defense," "The Family Hour," "Star Theater," "Show Boat Hour," "Your Hollywood Hit Parade" and "Al Goodman's Musical Album."

He moved to television conducting in 1949. He also continued working on records, conducting 42 studio cast recordings and original-cast recordings. His last recording of a show score was for *Fiddler on the Roof* in 1964.

Goodman affected the history of Times Square and Broadway as few others have. Through his conducting of Broadway scores, he helped introduce and set the sound of hundreds of standards. He popularized many of these shows and others through his national radio programs. His records reached still more Americans who might never have heard a Broadway show. In this way, he helped carry the spirit of Broadway to thousands of people for almost 50 years.

GREEN, ADOLPH See COMDEN AND GREEN.

GROUP THEATER The Group Theater, described by itself as "An organization of actors and directors formed with the ultimate aim of creating a permanent acting company to maintain regular New York seasons," was an outgrowth of the Theater Guild (q.v.). The group was determined to follow the tenants of method acting espoused by Konstantin Stanislavsky and practiced at the Moscow Art Theater. During its decade-long existence during the 1930s, the Group changed the course of American theater.

The Group originated as the Theater Guild Studio, which tried to present somewhat experimental plays for the masses. Therefore its offerings, while experimental in technique, were easily accessible to mainstream audiences. The first production, *Red Rust* (12/17/29), was presented at the Martin Beck Theatre (q.v.). Other early productions were Waldo Frank's play *New Year's Eve* and Padraic Colum's *Balloon*.

The breakthrough production was Paul Green's *House of Connelly* (9/23/31), which opened at the Martin Beck Theatre. The Group organization was lead by Cheryl Crawford, Harold Clurman and Lee Strasberg. With the success of *House of Connelly,* the Group Theater was officially launched as a separate entity from the Guild.

Toward its goal of forming a permanent company, the Group gathered a strong core of actors, including Luther Adler, Ruth Nelson, Morris Carnovsky, Art Smith, Elia Kazan, Lee J. Cobb and Roman Bohnen. The core was augmented by such Hollywood stars as Francis Farmer and Sylvia Sydney. Conversely, some of the Group's actors went on to earn fame in Hollywood. These included Franchot Tone, J. Edward Bromberg and John Garfield.

The Group also had its favorite playwrights. The most frequently produced was Clifford Odets, a one-time actor who decided to pursue play writing when his one-act play *Waiting for Lefty* won an award from *New Theater Magazine* for plays of social significance. Odets's first full-length play, *Awake and Sing* (2/19/35; 104 performances), was produced at the Belasco Theatre (q.v.). Another of Odets's successes was *Till the Day I Die* (3/26/35; 135 performances), which was presented with *Waiting for Lefty* at the Longacre Theater (q.v.). Other hits of Odets and the Group were *Paradise Lost* (12/9/35; 72 performances), which opened at the Longacre Theater, *Rocket to the Moon* (11/24/38; 131 perfor-

mances) and, the most successful of all, *Golden Boy* (11/4/37; 248 performances).

The Group also had success with the work of other modern dramatists. These included Dawn Powell's *Big Night* (1/17/33); Maxwell Anderson's *Night Over Taos* (3/9/32); John Howard Lawson's *Success Story* (9/26/32); Sidney Kingsley's Pulitzer Prize (q.v.) winning drama *Men in White* (9/26/33); Irwin Shaw's *The Gentle People* (1/5/39); and William Saroyan's *My Heart's in the Highlands* (4/13/39).

The Group disbanded in 1941.

GUDE, O.J. (1862–1925) Gude was the leading pioneer of the electric sign. He was named the "Creator of the Great White Way" after his early experiments in signage (q.v.). He was born in New York on March 29, 1862, and was forced to leave school at 17 because of the death of his father. Gude entered the advertising field and spent the following years with a variety of companies.

In 1889, he began his own firm, O.J. Gude Company. The company was a steady success, growing into one of the largest advertising firms in the country. He specialized in representing various food-processing companies. He made history around 1900 when he erected the first electric advertising sign on the site of what is now the Flatiron Building. The sign was an immediate success, although it was modest in size by today's standards.

As Manhattan's population moved uptown, so did Gude's sign locations. His most famous sign was the Wrigley's Gum spectacular at Seventh Avenue and 43rd Street above the Putnam Building.

Gude retired from the business in 1918 because of ill health. He went to Europe for sightseeing and to take the cure. He died in Bad Nauheim on August 15, 1925. At the time of his death, Gude was Chairman of the Board of Directors of the O.J. Gude Company, an outdoor advertising specialist. He also was a director of the Poster Advertising Company and the Van Buren New York Bill Posting Company.

GUILD THEATER See VIRGINIA THEATER.

GUINAN, TEXAS (? –1933) Texas Guinan was the owner of or principal attraction at many speakeasies during Prohibition. She was born Mary Louise Cecilia Guinan in Waco, Texas. While still in Texas, she enjoyed a brief career as a bronco buster and received the nickname Texas. She then appeared in some two-reel movie westerns for which she was publicized as "The Female Two-Gun Bill Hart." When she arrived in New York, she found work for the Shuberts (q.v.) as a chorus girl in the *Passing Show* series at the Winter Garden Theater (q.v.).

During World War I, she entertained the troops

overseas. She once claimed that she spent the time "driving an ambulance and working as an entertainer in spare time. I met Albert, King of Belgium—was saluted and entertained by Clemenceau, did social service work with Queen Marie of Roumania. I toured the trenches along with an all-star cast which included Elsie Janis, Mme. Ernestine Schumann-Heink and Elizabeth Brice. Maybe they sang better but I sang louder."

The hostess made her fame as the originator of such lines as "Let's give the little girl a great big hand" and "Hello, sucker." Guinan also popularized calling wealthy patrons "the big butter-and-egg man." Other quips ascribed to Guinan are "Never give the sucker an even break," "Her brain is as good as new," "It's having the same man around the house all the time that ruins matrimony," "A guy who would cheat on his wife would cheat at cards" and "I'm a country girl who came to Broadway to make enough money to go back and live in the country."

Though Guinan was herself a teetotaler, she reigned over some of the most popular speakeasies in Manhattan. Her acquaintances ranged from mobsters like Al Capone to clergymen and even the Mayor of New York, James Walker.

Her oversized personality enabled Guinan to relate as easily to the business executives who were her customers as to the gangsters (q.v.) who were her bosses. The gangster with whom she mainly associated was Larry Fay, a one-time cab driver who used his wiles to gain control of an entire fleet of cabs. Fay discovered Guinan at the Beaux Arts club and promptly stole her away so she could oversee his new El Fay Club. The El Fay was in the Parisian style, although Guinan was all-American in style. Guinan's renown soon spread, and the club did a booming business as a popular hangout for the denizens of Times Square.

Guinan realized she was the principal attraction and left to form her own club, The Three Hundred Club. When Guinan left, the El Fay club faltered. Finally Fay gave away the club to a friend as a present. The Three Hundred Club was soon closed by Prohibition agents. Undaunted Guinan opened Texas Guinan's. When the same fate befell that club she opened the Club Intime. Among those discovered by Guinan as performers in her clubs were Lon Chaney, Jack Oakie, Ruby Keeler, Barbara Stanwyck and Rudolph Valentino.

Guinan died of chronic colitis just a few months before the end of Prohibition on November 5, 1933. Before her death, she left instructions that she be taken to Campbell's Funeral Home where she wanted an open casket so "the suckers can get a good look at me without a cover charge." The pallbearers at her funeral included O.O. McIntyre, Mark Hellinger (q.v.), Ed Sullivan (q.v.), Louis Sobol, Paul Yawitz and Heywood Broun. The journalists were among Guinan's greatest admirers.

The funeral cortege passed down Broadway and passed the Rivoli Theater (q.v.) where Guinan's name was in lights as star of the motion picture Broadway Through a Keyhole. At the cemetery Guinan had a grand, if unruly, send-off. As she herself put it a few days before her death, "I've broken box-office records most of my life. Don't let me flop in death." She didn't; the 2,000 onlookers rioted and ran for the vault. The flowers topping Guinan's casket were stolen, and the vault was damaged by the hysterical crowd.

The Queen of Whoopee, as Guinan was dubbed, gave Prohibition some of its livelier moments.

HAMMERSTEIN, ARTHUR (1872–1955) Arthur Hammerstein, the least flamboyant of the Hammerstein family, is the least remembered. But of all of Oscar Hammerstein I's *(q.v.)* sons, it was Arthur who would have the most influence on the American theater.

Arthur was one of the most successful Broadway producers of his time. Most of his productions were operettas, primarily by Rudolf Friml *(q.v.)* and Otto Harbach *(q.v.)*. Arthur, unlike such great producers as Florenz Ziegfeld *(q.v.),* David Belasco *(q.v.)* and George White *(q.v.),* did not put his own stamp on productions, but they were marked by an emphasis on strong production values. His settings, lighting and costumes were all exquisitely designed and executed.

He was born on December 21, 1872. His father, Oscar Hammerstein I was Broadway's most important pioneer. Arthur was the second son of the impresario, and it was always assumed that he would enter the family's profession. He began his working life as a building contractor, a job well suited to the needs of his father who was always planning to build a new legitimate theater or opera house. The Victoria Theater *(q.v.)* on Broadway was the younger Hammerstein's first important job. He supervised the construction to his father's architectural plans. Naturally, the Victoria, like many of Oscar Hammerstein's productions, was ready only at the very last minute on March 2, 1899.

In 1905, Arthur was hired by his father to build the Manhattan Opera House down the street from its rival, the Metropolitan Opera House. He inherited his father's interest in opera, and in 1908 he took his first steps towards becoming a producer. The younger Hammerstein's first major move was to sign the great opera singer, Luisa Tetrazzini. She repeated her triumphant London success with her American debut at the Manhattan Opera House.

Hammerstein's success led to his assisting his father in managing the opera house. He entered into negotiations with financier Otto Kahn, a noted member of the Metropolitan Opera board. The rivalry of the two operations was hurting both institutions. The result of the meetings was that the Hammersteins agreed not to produce opera in New York, Philadelphia, Boston or Chicago for the decade beginning in 1910. In return, the Metropolitan agreed to pay the Hammersteins over a million dollars.

Later, in 1910, Oscar, looking for new horizons, wanted to go to London. Arthur took a loan on his life insurance to finance his father's trip. When Oscar announced plans to build a new opera house in London, Arthur, fed up with Oscar's money-losing schemes, was so incensed that he vowed never to speak to his father again.

Arthur decided to become a producer himself. His first production, under his father's auspices, was Victor Herbert's *(q.v.)* newest operetta, *Naughty Marietta* (11/7/10; 136 performances). The show, presented at the New York Theater, drew heavily on the Manhattan Opera House's talents, including soprano Emma Trentini, Orville Harrold, the chorus, most of the orchestra and the conductor. The show was an immediate success and contained one of Broadway's finest scores, including " 'Neath the Southern Moon," "Ah! Sweet Mystery of Life," "I'm Falling in Love with Someone," "Tramp! Tramp! Tramp!" and the "Italian Street Song."

Arthur's first solo production and the first of 10 collaborations with composer Rudolf Friml *(q.v.)* was *The Firefly* (12/2/12; 120 performances) with book and lyrics by Otto Harbach *(q.v.)*. Emma Trentini repeated her great success in *Naughty Marietta* with the new show. The songs included "Giannina Mia," "Love Is Like a Firefly" and "Sympathy."

The next year, Arthur produced another Friml and Harbach show, *High Jinks* (12/10/13; 213 performances). Surprisingly, although the show was a huge hit, the score contained no standards.

In 1914, three of Oscar's sons died. The loss of Abe, Harry and Willie was an immense blow to their father and caused Arthur, the surviving brother, to forgo his own productions that year. He took over the Victoria, but it was already suffering from the success of the new Palace Theater (q.v.), the opening of which was facilitated by Oscar's selling his exclusive right to present vaudeville in Times Square. In 1915, Oscar sold the Victoria as well as the Lexington Opera House and was forced into retirement.

Free to produce on his own again, Arthur presented another Friml and Harbach musical, *Katinka* (12/23/15; 220 performances). He produced two shows in 1917, *You're in Love* and *Furs and Frills*. *You're in Love* (2/6/17; 167 performances) boasted a Friml score with book by Edward Clark and Harbach and lyrics by Clark. *Furs and Frills* (10/9/17; 32 performances) was Arthur's first failure. It had a score by Clark and Silvio Hein, a minor composer. The show did contain an important song, "Make Yourself at Home." It was his nephew Oscar Hammerstein II's (q.v.) first professional song.

Arthur also produced two shows in 1918. The first, *Sometime* (10/4/18; 283 performances), had music by Friml and lyrics and libretto by the author of *Naughty Marietta*, Rida Johnson Young. The cast, an unusual blend of talents, featured Francine Larrimore, Mae West and Ed Wynn. The second Arthur Hammerstein production of 1918 was *Somebody's Sweetheart* (12/23/18; 234 performances) with music by Anthony Bafunno and libretto and lyrics by Alonzo Price. In 1919, Arthur produced only one show, *Tumble Inn* (3/24/19; 128 performances). It featured a Friml and Harbach score.

Always You (1/5/20; 66 performances) was Arthur's first show of 1920. It was also the first complete score written by Oscar Hammerstein II. *Tickle Me* (8/17/20; 207 performances), the second of Arthur's 1920 shows, had music composed by Herbert Stothart and book and lyrics by Harbach and Oscar Hammerstein II. Frank Mandel also collaborated on the libretto. A gimmick in *Tickle Me* almost landed Arthur in jail. During the song, "We've Got Something," the chorus girls went into the audience and distributed bottles labeled, "Compliments of Arthur Hammerstein, a Tickle from *Tickle Me*—Carstair's Whiskey." When the Federal Prohibition Enforcement Bureau heard of the stunt (q.v.), it dispatched agents to the theater and the next day arrested Arthur in his office. Arthur informed them that the bottles contained only iced tea. *Jimmie* (10/17/20; 71 performances) was the third show presented by Arthur that year. It had the same authors as *Tickle Me*.

Another Friml and Harbach operetta, *The Blue Kitten* (1/13/22; 140 performances), started the new year for Arthur. William Cary Duncan helped on the libretto and lyrics. *Daffy Dill* (8/22/22; 69 performances), a

Stothart, Oscar Hammerstein II and Bolton musical was the second 1922 show.

For Arthur, 1923 was a banner year. The first of his three shows that year, *Wildflower* (2/7/23; 477 performances), was Arthur's first show with Vincent Youmans (q.v.). Harbach and Hammerstein supplied the libretto and lyrics. Herbert Stothart also contributed to the music. It was followed by Arthur's first and last foray into the revue field, *Hammerstein's Nine O'Clock Revue* (10/4/23; 12 performances). The third 1923 show, *Mary Jane McKane* (12/25/23; 151 performances), was written by Youmans, Stothart, Duncan and Oscar Hammerstein II.

Arthur's sole 1924 production was also his biggest success—*Rose-Marie* (9/2/24; 581 performances). The Friml, Stothart, Harbach and Oscar Hammerstein II show contained such fine songs as "Indian Love Call," "Only a Kiss," "Pretty Things," "Rose-Marie" and "Totem Tom-Tom." The show broke box-office records and earned Arthur $2,500,000.

George Gershwin's only operetta, *Song of the Flame* (12/30/25; 214 performances), had additional music by Stothart with book and lyrics by Oscar Hammerstein II and Harbach.

Next, Arthur produced *The Wild Rose* (10/20/26; 62 performances), one of the few Friml, Harbach and Oscar Hammerstein II flops. *Golden Dawn* (11/30/27; 200 performances), an Emmerich Kalman, Stothart, Harbach and Oscar Hammerstein II musical, might have been a greater success but by this time the operetta was losing its vogue. *Golden Dawn* did contain two Broadway firsts—the first topless chorus girl and the Broadway debut of Archie Leach. He would become better known in Hollywood as Cary Grant.

Arthur's production of *Good Boy* (9/5/28; 253 performances) was a collaboration between Oscar Hammerstein II and Harbach and Bert Kalmar and Harry Ruby. It featured Helen Kane, Charles Butterworth and Borrah Minevitch.

One of Arthur's rare forays into musical comedy, *Polly* (1/8/29; 15 performances), was written by Philip Charig and Irving Caesar. *Sweet Adeline* (9/3/29; 233 performances) was Arthur's only production of a Jerome Kern (q.v.) show. Oscar Hammerstein II provided the book and lyrics. Helen Morgan, Irene Franklin and Gus Salzer starred.

With operettas out of vogue and the Depression hurting Broadway's business, Arthur moved to Hollywood to produce movies. His daughter Elaine had already enjoyed a successful acting career on the screen. But his only production, *The Lottery Bride* (1930), made for United Artists, was a failure. He returned to Broadway.

Arthur's last year of producing included two productions on Broadway that were both failures. A Rudolf Friml and J. Keirn Brennan score was featured at the opening of *Luana* (9/17/30; 21 performances). Arthur's last Broadway show, *Ballyhoo* (12/22/30; 68 performances), had a score by Louis Alter, Harry Ruskin, Leighton K. Brill and Oscar Hammerstein II. The show starred W.C. Fields.

The failures of his Hollywood foray and his last two Broadway shows forced him into bankruptcy. At the courthouse he was quoted as saying, "When Mayor Walker comes back into the city I will ask him to take the statue of my father and put it in some public place—possibly around Times Square. It is a curious thing that when he was exactly my age, my father went through the same thing. In 1897 he lost under foreclosure the Olympia Theater [*q.v.*] . . . In a couple of years, when conditions improve, I'll be back again, bigger than ever." But unlike his father, Arthur didn't bounce back. His producing days over, Arthur led a quiet retirement. He dabbled in inventions and even collaborated on a number one song on the Hit Parade, "Because of You." The 1950–51 hit was certainly a surprise to the family. He died in Palm Beach, Florida, on October 12, 1955.

HAMMERSTEIN I, OSCAR (1847–1919) Of all the individuals responsible for the emergence of Times Square as the entertainment center of New York, producer and developer Oscar Hammerstein I was the most important. As the century turned, Hammerstein changed the face of opera and theater in America. "The Father of Times Square" was also the founder of the greatest theatrical family in the history of the American theater.

The five-foot-four-inch producer was a striking figure as he sauntered down Broadway. He sported a pointed goatee and always carried a cigar. His favorite dress was a Prince Albert coat, striped trousers and an ever-present hat that he designed himself.

Biographer Carl Van Vechten wrote of Hammerstein, "Surely no adventurer, however gifted or successful, gets half the fun out of his adventuring unless he is able to watch himself all the time and smile and marvel at the tricks and turns of destiny. Hammerstein had this quality."

Hammerstein was born in Germany on May 8, 1847. He entered a Berlin music conservatory when he was 12. Although he worked hard on the violin, he proved only a fair student. However, he did acquire one thing in the conservatory—his love of grand opera. After the death of his mother, his relationship with his father deteriorated. With the army in his future and an unhappy life at home, the 15-year-old Hammerstein ran away and arrived in New York City in 1863, penniless and unable to speak the language. Like many immigrants before him, he found piece work in a cigar factory at two dollars a week. Hammerstein's intelligence allowed him to prosper in the cigar works. He invented many gadgets that he gave to his bosses before he learned of the patent system.

Oscar Hammerstein I   Courtesy ASCAP.

In 1868, Hammerstein married Rose Blau, and they had their first son, Harry, the following year. Harry would, like his siblings, be brought into his father's theatrical business. Hammerstein had a distant relationship with his family. His grandson, Oscar Hammerstein II *(q.v.)* met his grandfather for the first time when he was seven. He expected his sons to become his co-workers, and they did.

Hammerstein quit his job in 1871 against his wife's wishes. He took their savings and invested it in a friend's scheme to present opera in German. The opening night proved successful, but the undertaking failed when audiences fell off during the run. The entire investment was lost (the first of many bankruptcies) but Hammerstein was unconcerned. He had a marvelous time and was bitten with the theatrical bug. Although he returned to the cigar business, he now had a new goal—to become a producer himself.

Hammerstein's second son, Arthur *(q.v.)* was born in 1872. That same year, Hammerstein became an American citizen and patented his first invention—a multiple cigar mold. He received $1,500 from the sale of the patent. The success of his patent sale gave Hammerstein courage. In 1874, he established The *United States Tobacco Journal* with $50. The highly successful journal became a leading voice in the business. Hammerstein followed the lead of other publishers of the day and indulged in a little yellow journalism in order to drum up advertising revenue. The journal is still published today.

That same year, Hammerstein acted as guarantor for the opening of his producing friend's Germania Theater. Hammerstein decided that he could write plays and had five premieres at the theater. He even had his incidental music performed at the Germania. The theater survived somewhat longer than the two men's previous theatrical outing. The Germania closed three and a half years later when it became Tony Pastor's.

Hammerstein's third son, William *(q.v.)*, was born in 1874; another son, Abraham Lincoln Hammerstein, came along two years later. Their mother Rose died, and Hammerstein's younger sister Anna was brought from Germany to help him raise his four sons.

Two years later, in 1878, Anna left to marry Harry Rosenberg. Their son Walter, Hammerstein's nephew, would also enter the theater business. (He owned the Broadway Theatre *(q.v.)* and later established a chain of movie theaters under the Walter Reade name.) After Anna's departure, Hammerstein married Malvina Jacobi. They would later have two daughters of their own, Rose and Stella.

Hammerstein still had the urge to embark on a theater career, and in 1882 he backed a play called *The Perjured Peasant*. The star was Heinrich Conried who achieved fame in the role. Hammerstein and Conried would be forever linked as enemies. Their disagreements forced the closing of *The Perjured Peasant*. Later, when Conried became general director of the Metropolitan Opera, the feud intensified.

Meanwhile, Hammerstein was still involved in the cigar business. He founded the New York Leaf Tobacco Dealers Protective Association and the New York Leaf Tobacco Board of Trade. In 1884, he invented a pneumatic cigar-making machine, a device that would make a million dollars. Unfortunately, Hammerstein sold the patent for $6,000.

In addition to opera and tobacco, Hammerstein's interests extended to real estate. In 1888, he took his $6,000 from the pneumatic cigar-making machine and a loan against his interests in the Tobacco Journal and built an apartment house, the Kaiser Wilhelm on 7th Avenue between 136th and 137th Street. He would eventually build 24 apartment buildings and 30 houses.

As Hammerstein's interest in the Harlem neighborhood increased, he figured that Harlem, then a place of middle-class residences, needed its own opera house. To finance the theater, Hammerstein sold the Tobacco Journal for $50,000. His first theater, the Harlem Opera House, was built at 125th Street between 7th and 8th Avenue. That theater, like all his others, was designed by Hammerstein himself. In what was an amazingly ironic comment on Hammerstein's career, he forgot only one thing in his design—the box office.

The new theater opened in 1889. Among the stars who appeared were Joseph Jefferson, Mme. Modjeska and Edwin Booth. They insisted on receiving higher salaries since the theater was so far uptown. Jefferson received 90% of the gross. The theater was a success, but Hammerstein, typically, lost money. Hammerstein could always rely on his inventive genius to pull him out of debt. In 1890, he sold another patent that gave him $65,000.

Hammerstein began his lifelong battle with the Metropolitan Opera when its management denied his request to present their stars in Harlem. So he instead created his own company. Soprano Lilli Lehmann was his star and his main draw. The week-long season was a tremendous success, but Hammerstein lost $50,000. Walter Damrosch, conductor on the engagement, remembered Hammerstein's attitude towards the failure: "That didn't faze the indomitable Hammerstein. He ran his hand deep into his trouser pocket, made up the deficit without a murmur, and when everything had been settled, he said to me, 'Someday I will be an impresario.' "

Despite his mixed success with the Harlem Opera House, Hammerstein decided to build another theater in the neighborhood. The Columbus Theater on 125th Street between Lexington and Fourth Avenue opened in October 1890. This time Hammerstein booked vaudeville and minstrel shows into the theater, which ended its first season with three weeks of opera. The theater was a success and drew a steady audience.

In 1891, Hammerstein mounted the American premiere of Mascagni's *Cavalleria Rusticana*. Although he held the exclusive rights to the opera, another production was mounted by a competitor taking advantage of a loophole in the copyright laws. Hammerstein's production was a tremendous success and emboldened Hammerstein to increase his empire.

The first Manhattan Opera House was constructed by Hammerstein in Herald Square. The theater opened in 1892 with the play *Lena Despard*. Although it was a tremendous bomb, Hammerstein wasn't particularly concerned. The failure merely proved to him that grand opera was the only thing that would succeed in the new house.

He was proven wrong. The opera season was an abject failure. Koster and Bial, successful vaudeville producers, teamed up with Hammerstein to present Koster and Bial's Music Hall in the Manhattan Opera House. It was an immense hit.

Hammerstein hadn't forgotten his foray into writing music for the Germania Theater. He bet $100 that he could write an opera in two days. Hammerstein set to work despite his friends' attempts to distract him. They placed organ grinders outside his window at the Gilsey House round the clock. The result, *The Kohinoor,* was deemed unproduceable, and Hammerstein was refused the $100. So naturally, he mounted the production at Koster and Bial's Music Hall. It lost $10,000 but Hammerstein did get his $100.

Hammerstein was never an easy man to get along with, and his relationship with Koster and Bial grew strained. George Kessler, a salesman for Moet and Chandon, tried to get Hammerstein to present his girlfriend Marietta del Dio at the Manhattan Opera House. Hammerstein disliked both the playboy and the singer. When Hammerstein refused, Kessler approached Koster and Bial. They were only too happy to show Hammerstein who was boss and immediately signed del Dio. On opening night, Kessler and Hammerstein were seated in the same box. During del Dio's curtain call, Hammerstein stood and booed the singer. Kessler threw a punch at the producer, and the audience was treated to the sight of the two men fighting. They carried their fight to the street after being forcibly ejected from the theater. The police were called, and both men were arrested.

Koster brought Kessler's bail money but refused to spring Hammerstein. A friend later showed up to post Hammerstein's bail. When the case came to court, the judge ruled that Hammerstein had the right to boo in his own theater. Koster and Bial tried to force him out of the theater, but he sued them and won. In fact, Hammerstein proved to be a master of the lawsuit. Once, he had 40 suits pending concurrently. Koster and Bial paid Hammerstein $370,000. He took that money and an additional $2 million and changed history.

In 1895, he made his most important move. He took an option on a piece of land between 44th and 45th Street on the east side of Broadway, and on it he built a complex of four theaters, the largest theater group at the time. Although the Olympia *(q.v.)* created a sensation, it never proved very profitable. The opening was marred by wet paint and a near riot. But the Olympia firmly established Longacre Square, the original name for Times Square, as the new theater district.

Hammerstein featured French music hall star Yvette Guilbert as his star at the Olympia. She drew a large crowd to the theater, and receipts totaled over $15,000 a week. But in 1896, with his usual penchant for argument, Hammerstein lost Guilbert. He devised an original ballet and put it on in the Olympia. The receipts fell to $4,000 a week. Hammerstein couldn't help but realize his error, and he replaced the ballet with a series of *Living Pictures.* The main attraction of the *Living Pictures* was scantily clad women.

Lillian Russell was drawing crowds into the Harlem

theaters, and George Bernard Shaw's *Arms and the Man* premiered uptown. Downtown, the less artistic fare continued. Hammerstein and his sons, now all in the business with their father, were arrested for offending public morals. They were released, and Hammerstein learned the lesson of publicity with the resultant rise in profits at the Olympia.

The success brought on by the publicity didn't last long, however. In 1898, the New York Life Insurance Company foreclosed on the Olympia and it was sold at auction. The president of the insurance company wrote Hammerstein that the company would continue to run the theater. Hammerstein answered the letter by writing, "I am in receipt of your letter which is now before me, and in a few minutes will be behind me. Respectfully yours, Oscar Hammerstein." Hammerstein was legally barred from the premises. He owed over a million dollars by this time.

At this time, Hammerstein met a friend on Broadway and gave him a cigar. "I have lost my theaters, my home and everything else. My fortune consists of two cigars. I will share it with you." The story was more than just a humorous anecdote. Hammerstein was by turns despotic and benevolent and seemed unfazed by the roller-coaster quality of his fortunes.

The following year, he recovered enough to build the Victoria Theater *(q.v.)* at Seventh Avenue and 42nd Street. He raised part of the capital by selling more patents. He announced that he chose the name Victoria because "I have been victorious over mine enemies—those dirty bloodsuckers at New York Life."

Ready at the last minute, the Victoria opened as scheduled, and Hammerstein won a suit of clothes on a bet he made that the theater would open on time. Hammerstein wore the suit on the opening night.

Theater was America's leading form of entertainment. The public followed Hammerstein's rise and fall in the same way current audiences follow the careers of movie stars. Audiences packed the Victoria at its opening, and the theater proved a constant success. Hammerstein not only opened the path to theater development in Times Square but his optimism and ability to recover from blows that would have ended the career of a lesser man proved an inspiration to succeeding generations of Hammersteins and other theater professionals. He was once quoted as saying, "I am never discouraged. I don't believe in discouragement. I was not cast down. I merely discovered my inability to do what I thought I could do. That discovery did not fill my heart with tears or regrets, neither did it destroy my self-esteem. To do anything in this world, a man must have full confidence in his own ability. If I haven't confidence in myself, others will not have confidence in me."

Hammerstein himself appeared on the Victoria stage. When Lew Dockstader, the minstrel man, complained about the difficulty in finding qualified talents, Hammerstein nominated himself. The press was duly informed and Hammerstein appeared for one performance making his "Debut Extraordinary."

As the century turned, the impresario built the Republic Theater (q.v.) on a plot next to the Victoria. On the shared roof, he opened the Paradise Garden (q.v.). The roof garden opened with another of Hammerstein's attempts to write opera, but it was a success nonetheless. The Paradise Garden featured the Swiss Farm with barnyard animals and New York's first singing waiters. In 1901, Hammerstein leased the Republic to producer David Belasco (q.v.) who promptly rechristened it the Belasco Theatre.

Leo Tolstoy's drama *Resurrection* (1902) with Blanche Walsh as the star became a big hit. It ran for almost two years at the Victoria and netted $100,000 for Hammerstein. After the run of *Resurrection,* Hammerstein changed the policy of the Victoria to vaudeville. Willie was installed as manager with his father, operating in an office and apartment off the balcony, close by.

The Victoria's success led Hammerstein to construct a theater on 42nd Street. When comic Lew Fields (q.v.) leased it, he named it, appropriately, the Lew M. Fields Theater (q.v.). The theater was the first to have a fire-fighting system in which water is carried from a tank on the roof.

When Macy's moved to 34th Street, the Manhattan Opera House was demolished. Hammerstein decided to take on his old rival the Metropolitan Opera. He built what he declared would be the largest theater in the world, choosing once again the Herald Square area, a few blocks from the Metropolitan Opera House. The New Manhattan Opera House opened on December 3, 1906, on 34th Street, west of Eighth Avenue (the theater is now known as the Manhattan Center). Again, the theater opened just in a nick of time. When asked what he was opening with, Hammerstein responded, "With debts." The 3,100 seat theater's opening was a tremendous success.

That success received worldwide notice. Nellie Melba joined the company and the box office was boosted. The productions were expensive to mount; whenever box office fell off the debts multiplied. Frank Woolworth, owner of the Woolworth chain, was convinced by Hammerstein to lend $400,000 to the Opera House. Hammerstein secured the talents of Emma Calve and the Opera House turned a profit. Artistically and financially, the theater had a successful 1906–07 season—and the Metropolitan suffered its first loss in years. The 1907–08 season began auspiciously with *Tales of Hoffman* and the American premiere of *Thais* with Mary Garden singing the lead. In the next few years, Hammerstein presented many other notable operas. His son Arthur signed Luisa Tetrazzini to appear in *La Traviata, Rigoletto* and *Lucia Di Lammermoor.* The American premiere of Debussy's *Pelleas et Melisande* with Mary Garden in the lead proved triumphant.

With the Manhattan Opera House a raging success, Hammerstein appointed Arthur to oversee the construction of a new 4,100-seat theater in Philadelphia. Though the Manhattan and Victoria theaters were bringing in profits, the Philadelphia theater's construction costs drained the family's coffers. To raise capital, Hammerstein sold the Lew M. Fields Theater for $225,000.

By the end of 1908, the Philadelphia theater opened to great acclaim. Back in New York, Mary Garden opened the Manhattan Opera House in *Le Jongleur De Notre Dame.* She played the boy's role at Hammerstein's insistence and critical huzzahs. Later that year, Richard Strauss's *Salome* was another smash at the 34th Street theater, but the Philadelphia house's fortunes declined.

Part of Hammerstein's reason for opening the Manhattan Opera House was to provide opera for the middle class. He never liked society and hated the snobbish attitude at the Metropolitan. He insulted one of his wealthier backers, and when she withdrew her support his conductor, Campanini, set sail for Italy. Hammerstein was undisturbed. In 1909, he commenced buying land in Brooklyn, Cleveland and elsewhere to build opera houses. As his son Arthur observed, "If Father could buy enough plush to make a theater curtain, there would be a theater built around it." A tour of his New York operatic successes to Boston, Pittsburgh and Chicago proved critically popular but financially draining. In 1910, he mounted the premiere of Strauss's *Elektra,* an immense success. That same season, he presented the debut of singer John McCormack.

The Metropolitan–Manhattan feud wasn't doing either theater any good. Hammerstein met with the Metropolitan's leading backer, Otto Kahn, in order to arrange some sort of understanding. The result was that the Metropolitan payed Hammerstein $1,250,000 to forgo all producing of opera in New York, Chicago, Boston, Philadelphia for a period of 10 years. Hammerstein sorely needed the money and accepted the deal. He sold the Philadelphia theater for $400,000, which paid off the mortgage.

Looking for new worlds to conquer, Hammerstein sailed to London on money given to him by his son Arthur. Arthur took a loan on his life insurance to pay for the sailing. In London, Hammerstein bought property that he announced would soon see the construction of another Hammerstein Opera House. As Hammerstein himself commented, "Opera's no business. It's a disease."

He kept his promise, and the London Opera House opened on Kingsway in November 1911. The theater appeared at first to be popular, but after seven months he had lost a million dollars.

In 1913, Hammerstein's fortunes suffered a major

blow when he sold the exclusive rights to present vaudeville in Times Square for $250,000. That ended the Victoria's monopoly on the popular art and opened the doors to competition. From that time, the Victoria, Hammerstein's sure breadwinner, began its decline. But he had other ideas for the $250,000. He used it to open the Lexington Opera House, where he intended to present operas in English. Hammerstein felt that gimmick would get him around his agreement with the Metropolitan. At the Manhattan Opera House he presented comic opera.

The year 1914 proved especially tragic for the impresario. His sons Abe, Harry and Willie all died. The Metropolitan Opera House sued Hammerstein and won. He was prevented from opening the Lexington theater as an opera house and it switched to a movie policy.

In 1915, with his fortunes diminished, Hammerstein sold the Victoria and Lexington. At the age of 68, he bought a home in New Jersey and married Emma Swift. His last years were spent in a forced retirement. On August 1, 1919, the man who, John Philip Sousa said, "has done more for music than any other man in America" died.

The *New York Times*'s editorial page contained a tribute to the showman.

> In the popular mind Hammerstein's fame rests on the minor aspects of his greatness . . . His name will always recall the eccentric silk hat of his prime, with a black cigar tilted up beneath it. It will recall his tireless energy, his fertility of resource, his amazing faculty of enlisting the support of men and money, his building of gigantic theater after theater—most of which failed through being located according to ideas of real estate values which were true in themselves but too far ahead of his time. It will recall his cheerful courage in failure and his quick turns of speech at all times. It will recall the amazing publicity expert who used his own eccentricities to their limit for public effect. One sentence reveals vividly the intense workings in his mind, "Nature's greatest mistake is her failure to equip us with a switch to turn off our thought." The restless energy of his mind and his inexhaustible fertility of invention made him, during one brief period, the regenerator of our musical life; but first and always he was a character of almost titanic force and picturesqueness.

HAMMERSTEIN II, OSCAR (1895–1960)   Oscar Hammerstein II, the son of William Hammerstein *(q.v.)*, the manager of the Victoria Theater *(q.v.)*, grandson of the great theater builder and impresario Oscar Hammerstein I *(q.v.)* and nephew of noted producer Arthur Hammerstein *(q.v.)*, was the scion of the greatest theater family of its time. Oscar's career as lyricist and librettist was equaled in length and breadth only by author, director, producer George Abbott *(q.v.)* and by Oscar's partner Richard Rodgers *(q.v.)*. Oscar was Broadway's preeminent librettist and lyricist. He was among the first authors to attempt a true integration of

Oscar Hammerstein II   Courtesy ASCAP.

songs and script in the new American form of musical comedy.

The Right Honorable Earl Attlee, past prime minister of Britain, commented on Hammerstein's career in 1962. "Oscar Hammerstein's vision was not limited by the boundless, yet confined area of the theater. He was deeply aware of the world in which he lived and deeply sensitive equally to human emotion and to human folly. Hatred was his chief abomination . . . If the world is to be made one, we have to see ourselves as Oscar did, as individual members of a great human family . . . " Mr. Attlee caught the thread that ran through all of the writer's great works. His concern for understanding among people was his great hallmark.

Hammerstein was born in New York City on July 12, 1895. The young man attended Columbia University (1912–16) and Columbia Law School (1915–17). It was at Columbia that Oscar began writing books and lyrics for his first musicals. In fact, his first collaboration with Richard Rodgers was for Columbia University shows. *Up Stage and Down* (1916) was the show and the first Rodgers and Hammerstein songs were "Weaknesses," "Can It" and "There's Always Room for One More."

A year later Hammerstein found his first song, "Make Yourself at Home," with music by Silvio Hein, interpolated into the Broadway show *Furs and Frills*. His first full score was a collaboration with Herbert Stothart, who would make his mark in Hollywood as an award-winning scorer of motion pictures. Their show, *Always You* (1/5/20; 66 performances), opened at the Central Theater *(q.v.)*. The young lyricist also contributed the libretto for the show, which starred Helen Ford, a future Rodgers and Hart star.

Reviewers were quick to note the young Mr. Hammerstein's talents. The *New York Times* said the "lyrics are more clever than those of the average musical comedy." The *New York World* commented, "Mr. Hammerstein couldn't forget the dear old college days . . . the lyrics are good as a whole, and some of them are keen." The *New York Dramatic Mirror*'s review noted: "Hammerstein appears to be a far better lyricist than librettist. His lyrics have a distinct quality, while his wheezes are rather antiquated. The plot is inconsequential but it is sturdy enough not to be lost, ever."

Hammerstein had greater success with his next show, *Tickle Me* (8/17/21; 207 performances). Herbert Stothart was the composer, and the book was written by Hammerstein in collaboration with Otto Harbach *(q.v.)* and Frank Mandel.

Hammerstein and Stothart next came up with *Jimmie* (11/17/20; 71 performances). After *Jimmie* came a play, *Pop,* written with Frank Mandel. *Pop* closed in Atlantic City before opening in New York. Another Stothart show, *Daffy Dill* (8/22/22; 71 performances) was yet another flop. Hammerstein had even less success with *Queen O'Hearts* (10/10/22; 39 performances) at the George M. Cohan Theatre *(q.v.)*. The music was by Lewis Gensler and Dudley Wilkinson, and additional lyrics were written by Sidney Mitchell.

Hammerstein would have his first big hit in collaboration with Stothart and Vincent Youmans *(q.v.)*. The show, *Wildflower* (2/7/23; 477 performances), had a book by Hammerstein and Otto Harbach. The hit song, "Bambalina," had music by Youmans.

Hammerstein's *Mary Jane McKane* (12/25/23; 151 performances) with music by Youmans and Stothart opened at the Imperial Theatre. Hammerstein again attempted play writing and again found failure with *Gypsy Jim* (1/14/24; 24 performances), written with Milton Herbert Gropper. The two playwrights' next play, *New Toys* (2/18/24; 24 performances) opened and closed quickly at the Fulton Theater *(q.v.)*.

Clearly, straight playwriting was not for Hammerstein. He would receive greater acclaim as a librettist and lyricist, and in fact his next show, *Rose-Marie* (9/2/24; 557 performances), proved one of his greatest hits. This time, Rudolf Friml *(q.v.)* was the composer along with Stothart. Arthur Hammerstein, Oscar's uncle, produced. *Rose-Marie* opened at the Imperial Theatre *(q.v.)* with Dennis King and Mary Ellis. The title song, "Pretty Things," "Totem Tom-Tom" and "Indian Love Call" were all standouts in the score.

With *Rose-Marie,* Hammerstein had embarked on his quest for the perfect integration between song and story. The program for the show contained the following note: "The musical numbers of this play are such an integral part of the action that we do not think we should list them as separate episodes." *Rose-Marie* ran 851 performances in London. The musical proved equally successful on film with MGM producing three versions, in 1928, 1936 and 1954.

Hammerstein started a long collaboration with composer Jerome Kern *(q.v.)* on the show *Sunny* (9/22/25; 517 performances). Harbach worked with Hammerstein on the book and lyrics. Charles Dillingham produced the musical at the New Amsterdam Theatre *(q.v.)*. *Sunny* starred Marilyn Miller, with Clifton Webb, Joseph Cawthorn, Cliff Edwards and Jack Donahue in the cast. The score was also a hit with no less than three big numbers, the title song, "Who" and "D'Ye Love Me?" achieving great fame. *Sunny* played 363 performances in London and was filmed in 1930 and 1941.

Stothart and George Gershwin *(q.v.)* were the composers on the next Harbach and Hammerstein show, *Song of the Flame* (12/30/25; 219 performances). Perhaps the show's Russian setting was not suited to either Gershwin or Hammerstein. Harbach, Hammerstein and Friml's next outing, *The Wild Rose* (10/20/26; 61 performances) was a failure.

Harbach, Hammerstein and Sigmund Romberg's *Desert Song* (11/30/27; 471 performances) was an enormous and immediate hit. Frank Mandel, colibrettist was also producer with Laurence Schwab. Vivienne Segal, Robert Halliday and Lyle Evans sang the exceptional songs, which included "The Riff Song," "The Desert Song," "One Flower Grows Alone in Your Garden" and "Romance." The *New York Times* called the score "excellent" and "rather imposing." Hammerstein's book received weaker reviews than his and Harbach's lyrics. The *New York American* reflected the general opinion when it commented, "the 'book' is its weakest point, and even that may 'draw,' for it appeals to those who like silly, sheikish stories, with a dashing He pursuing a shrinking She." The *Desert Song* played 432 performances at the Theatre Royal, Drury Lane, London. Film versions were released by Warner Brothers in 1929, 1943 and 1953.

Hammerstein's next show, *Golden Dawn* (11/30/27), was a failure, but he followed it up with his first classic musical comedy, the enormously successful *Show Boat* (12/27/27; 572 performances). This legendary musical, with book and lyrics by Hammerstein and music by Jerome Kern, opened at the Ziegfeld Theater *(q.v.)*. *Show Boat* starred Norma Terris, Edna May Oliver, Tess Gardella, Charles Winninger, Howard Marsh, Jules Bledsoe and Helen Morgan.

Show Boat was the first show to exhibit Hammerstein's concern with human issues. The show's plot dealt with miscegenation and problems of blacks. The score, including "Bill," "Make Believe," "Can't Help Lovin' Dat Man," "You Are Love," "Why Do I Love You?" and "Ol' Man River" is still considered by many to be the ultimate musical theater work.

Show Boat embarked on a long national tour. It returned to New York in 1932 for an additional 180 performances. *Show Boat* was presented in London for 350 performances and was revived in New York in 1946, 1954, 1961, 1966, 1976 and 1983. It was filmed in 1929, 1936 and 1951. Hammerstein's next show, *Good Boy* (9/5/28; 253 performances) with music by Herbert Stothart and Harry Ruby, also had lyrics by Bert Kalmar.

The New Moon (9/19/28; 509 performances), with book and lyrics by Hammerstein and music by Romberg, opened at the Imperial Theatre. The operetta contained at least six great hits, "The Girl on the Prow," "Softly, As In a Morning Sunrise," "Stouthearted Men," "Lover, Come Back to Me," "Wanting You" and "One Kiss." Brooks Atkinson stated in the *New York Times* that, "It is not merely a good book; it is almost too good." E.W. Osborn, reviewing the show for the *New York Evening World,* called it "A glory, take it for all in all of light opera at its best, as far from the plain musical play as the sun is from the stars."

Hammerstein had another of his flops with *Rainbow* (11/21/28; 29 performances), a collaboration with Vincent Youmans. Hammerstein and Kern's *Sweet Adeline* (9/3/29; 234 performances) was a moderate success at Hammerstein's Manhattan Theater (q.v.). It featured Helen Morgan who introduced the three hits in the score, "Here Am I," "Why Was I Born?" and "Don't Ever Leave Me."

In 1931, Hammerstein had a string of failures, including *The Gang's All Here* (2/18/31), *Free For All* (9/8/31) and *East Wind* (10/27/31). None played more than 23 performances.

Another Hammerstein collaboration with Kern, *Music in the Air* (11/8/32; 275 performances), opened at the Alvin Theater (q.v.). "I've Told Ev'ry Little Star," "And Love Was Born" and "The Song Is You" were the hit songs in the score. *Music in the Air* played 275 performances in London and was filmed in 1934.

Hammerstein had two rare London premieres in 1933 and 1934. The first, *Ball at the Savoy* (9/8/33), with Paul Abraham contributing the music, ran 148 performances at the Theater Royal, Drury Lane. The second, *Three Sisters* (4/9/34; 45 performances), was written with Jerome Kern. It also opened at the Theater Royal, Drury Lane.

When Hammerstein returned to the United States, he completed two projects with Romberg. The first was a film, *The Night Is Young*. The second, the musical *May Wine* (12/5/35; 213 performances), opened at the St. James Theatre (q.v.). After that show, Hammerstein had more Hollywood assignments. *Give Us This Night* featured music by Erich Wolfgang Korngold. *Swing High, Swing Low* had a screenplay cowritten by Hammerstein and Virginia Van Upp. Kern and Hammerstein wrote the score to the film *High, Wide and Handsome,* which was a hit in 1937.

Gentlemen Unafraid was Hammerstein and Kern's next stage production. It opened in St. Louis on June 3, 1938, and closed there on June 12. Then it was back to Hollywood for *The Lady Objects* with music by Ben Oakland and lyrics by Hammerstein and Milton Drake; *The Great Waltz,* a film with music by Johann Strauss II and *The Story of Vernon and Irene Castle.* This teaming of Fred Astaire (q.v.) and Ginger Rogers had a script by Hammerstein and Dorothy Yost.

Hammerstein's bad luck on the stage continued with his next collaboration with Jerome Kern. *Very Warm for May* (11/17/39; 59 performances) at the Alvin Theater contained a fine score, including "All the Things You Are," "That Lucky Fellow," "In the Heart of the Dark" and "All in Fun." Hammerstein had his only collaboration with Arthur Schwartz (q.v.) in *American Jubilee.* The show premiered at the New York World's Fair of 1940. The Romberg operetta *Sunny River* (12/4/41; 36 performances) continued his string of failures. Hammerstein was generally thought to be washed up. Aware of the talk along Broadway, he needed a hit to revive his career.

Desperate as he felt for renewal, Hammerstein was nonetheless unprepared for the amazing turnaround he was to enjoy as the lyricist and librettist in the team of Rodgers and Hammerstein, the most successful songwriting partnership in the history of musical theater. The Theater Guild (q.v.) approached Hammerstein to collaborate on a new show with Richard Rodgers. Rodgers's longtime partner, Lorenz Hart, was having his own personal problems and the composer was looking for a new collaborator.

The new team's first production changed the course of musical theater and broke most of the commonly held conventions. *Oklahoma!* began a second great chapter in Hammerstein's career.

As a retort to all those who said he was washed up artistically, he took out an ad in *Variety* (q.v.), which read:

> Holiday Greetings
> from
> Oscar Hammerstein 2nd
> author of
> SUNNY RIVER
> (6 weeks at the St. James)
> VERY WARM FOR MAY
> (7 weeks at the Alvin)
> THREE SISTERS
> (7 weeks at the Drury Lane)
> FREE FOR ALL
> (3 weeks at the Manhattan)
>
> "I've Done It Before And I Can
> Do It Again!"

For his next production, Hammerstein chose to adapt Georges Bizet's opera *Carmen*. The show, *Carmen Jones,* opened at the Broadway Theatre *(q.v.)* on December 2, 1943, to rave reviews. The all-black show was a success, running 502 performances.

Although the team of Rodgers and Hammerstein had their occasional failures their great successes, *Oklahoma!, Carousel, South Pacific, The King and I* and *The Sound of Music* introduced a unique voice into the American theater. Rodgers's melodies to Hammerstein's lyrics were more expansive and soaring than those written with Hart. Hammerstein's lyrics and libretti were warm and humane and touched on themes of tolerance and understanding. Critics have accused Hammerstein of resorting to too much sweetness, but his accomplishments with Rodgers should not be underestimated. Rodgers and Hammerstein opened the musical to new forms and formulas.

Oscar Hammerstein died on August 23, 1960. As a tribute, the lights were dimmed on Broadway and taps was played in Times Square. Dore Schary memorialized him in 1962. "Oscar Hammerstein was a rare man who wrote rare words and accomplished rare deeds. His legacy includes not only the hundreds of lyric words that are part of our lives but also the burning conviction that there can be a better future for us than the atomization of the world."

HAMMERSTEIN, WILLIAM (1874–1914) Willie Hammerstein, son of the great Oscar Hammerstein I *(q.v.)* and father of Oscar Hammerstein II *(q.v.)* became a legendary impresario in his own right. Willie dressed conservatively and was quiet in demeanor, but he was the most outgoing and showy of turn-of-the-century producers when it came to the theater he managed, the Victoria *(q.v.).*

Willie's father was a strict disciplinarian, and his childhood was not an especially happy one. He described it in a letter to his wife: "As a child growing up, I never really had the feeling of belonging. My mother, as you know, died when I was all of four years old, and, although I grew very dependent on my Aunt Anna, she too left to be married very shortly thereafter. When 'my shadow of a father' remarried, I, for one, retreated into myself. More and more I became a loner."

Willie raised his own son in the same detached way. His only contact with his son was a kiss good-bye in the morning and hello in the evening. Oscar knew his father loved him, though he didn't receive much affection.

Unlike his father or brother Arthur *(q.v.),* Willie wasn't concerned with furthering the theatrical arts or making himself known as an arbiter of taste. He wasn't really interested in the theater. He never attended others' attractions and preferred the quiet life. In contrast with his private home life was the flamboyance of his producing style. Willie's chief concern was filling his theaters, in almost any way he could. He booked both typical vaudeville acts and stars of his own making, usually some freak act or personality in the news.

The Victoria was host to the most bizarre performers. The most notorious of these acts was the Cherry Sisters, billed as "America's worst act." The Cherry Sisters more than lived up to their name—they had to be protected by a net from projectiles tossed from the audience.

Willie also made a vaudeville star of Evelyn Nesbitt, the mistress of Stanford White. Nesbitt was billed as "The Girl on the Red Velvet Swing." Nesbitt had no talents, so Willie had a tenor do the singing while Nesbitt did the swinging. White had been murdered by Nesbitt's jealous husband, Harry K. Thaw. When Thaw escaped from prison, Willie arranged for an armed guard to protect Nesbitt. Competitors said that Willie himself had orchestrated Thaw's escape to boost attendance at Nesbitt's performances.

Willie even arranged for his own dancers to be arrested for indecent exposure. He was the first producer to use motion pictures between acts. They were used initially to clear the house. Willie presented freaks, criminals and wrestlers, all in the name of ticket sales.

The one-time Gay Nineties dancer Carmencita made her stage comeback under the auspices of Willie. In fact, the real Carmencita had been dead for nine years. Sober Sue was another huge hit at the Victoria Theater. Willie challenged the leading comedians of his day to make her laugh. None ever succeeded. What Willie didn't explain was that Sober Sue's face was paralyzed.

A woman whose acquittal for murdering her husband landed her on the front pages and subsequently on the stage of the Victoria asked Willie whether she was being held over. "Not unless you shoot another man," he responded. This led to the theater's being dubbed "the great nut vaudeville house of New York."

Willie managed the Victoria Theater brilliantly. In summer months, he would advertise that the temperature inside the theater was 10 degrees cooler than it was outside. To prove it, he showed a thermometer mounted on a hidden block of ice.

Willie's wife, Allie, died in 1910 at the age of 35. The next year Willie married Allie's sister. Also in 1911, Willie expanded the Victoria's repertoire and presented some of the greatest performers of his time: Will Rogers, Vernon and Irene Castle *(q.v.),* Fanny Brice *(q.v.),* Weber and Fields, Buster Keaton, the Dolly Sisters, Al Jolson *(q.v.),* Houdini, Annette Kellerman (the "Million Dollar Mermaid") and Charlie Chaplin.

Lillian Ross quoted Chaplin's comments on Willie in *The New Yorker.*

"You know, it was Willie Hammerstein, Oscar's son, who invented pie-throwing. The legend is that Mack Sennett invented it. But when the Karno company worked for Willie Hammerstein, he loved the act, and he gave us a bit of business for the act with the dour drunks.'' Chaplin lowered his voice a couple of octaves and, putting on a pompous manner, sang, "Hail, morn, smiling morn.'' He went on, "We had a boy in the box with me, and I used to knock him over. One day, Hammerstein said, "Why don't you do it with a pie?'' So we did. The laughter we got lasted two minutes, which was a long time. Willie Hammerstein had such a sad face. But the *acts* he had. The big time. He had Eva Tanguay. Willie Howard. Acts like that.

When Marie Dressler appeared at the Victoria for a four-month engagement, her accompanist was an unknown musician named Jerome Kern *(q.v.)*. Willie had discovered Kern and arranged for him to get the job. Irving Berlin *(q.v.)* also appeared at the Victoria as "the composer of the recent hit, 'Alexander's Ragtime Band.' " Willie and Berlin would often shoot craps in the Hermitage Hotel across the street.

Although the Victoria was doing booming business, Willie resigned when he found out that his father planned to sell the Victoria. "I left the Victoria Theater because I hoped that by so doing I could save my father from himself,'' Willie said. Oscar hoped to use the proceeds from the sale of the Victoria to finance a series of opera houses across the country.

Oscar decided not to sell the theater after all, and three months later Willie returned. But instead of selling the Victoria, Oscar decided to sell the exclusive vaudeville booking rights that belonged to the theater. This enabled the rival Palace Theatre *(q.v.)* to thrive, and soon the Victoria's fortunes fell. Ironically, the Victoria was enjoying its most fruitful season when the booking rights were sold.

On June 10, 1914, Willie died at the age of 41. After suffering a mild case of scarlet fever, he entered a hospital and died of Bright's disease. The *New York Times* headlined its notice of Willie's death by writing, "Hammerstein, the Barnum of vaudeville, dead at forty.'' Just before he died, Willie made his brother Arthur promise not to let his son Oscar II pursue a theatrical career. Luckily, Arthur broke the promise.

HAMMERSTEIN'S MANHATTAN THEATRE   See ED SULLIVAN THEATRE.

HAMMOND, PERCY   See CRITICS.

HARBACH, OTTO (1873–1963)   In the American theater of the early 20th century, there were over 100 musicals premiering each season. Composers, lyricists and book writers working at that time often had the opportunity to work on as many as 5–10 shows a season. Otto Harbach was one such prolific librettist and lyricist. Although much of his work in early operetta and musical comedy has not lasted, several of his

Otto Harbach   Courtesy ASCAP.

songs, particularly those written to music by Jerome Kern *(q.v.)*, have become classics.

Harbach was born Otto Christiansen of Danish immigrant parents in Salt Lake City, Utah, on August 18, 1873. When Danish citizens were conscripted into the army in the late 1800s, their names were changed to make bookkeeping easier much as new arrivals to Ellis Island found their names changed. The Christiansens worked on the Hauerbach farm, and their name and their fellow farm workers' names were changed to Hauerbach. After attending Knox College, Otto moved to New York, where he held newspaper jobs from 1902 to 1903. He moved from journalism to advertising for the remainder of the century's first decade.

His first theatrical job brought his first hit song. *Three Twins,* written in 1908 with composer Karl Hoschna, introduced the favorite "Cuddle Up a Little Closer, Lovey Mine." Based on the popularity of the song and the star performance of Bessie McCoy, *Three Twins* ran 288 performances.

Bright Eyes (2/28/10; 40 performances) was the next musical by the Hauerbach and Hoschna team. Their next collaboration proved more successful. *Madame Sherry* (8/30/10; 231 performances) was a triumph at the New Amsterdam Theatre *(q.v.)*. For this show, Hauerbach contributed both lyrics and book. The show resulted in Hauerbach's second hit song, "Every Little Movement." After Broadway, the show enjoyed a long tour and many revivals as an early mainstay of the touring circuit.

In 1911, the successful team wrote the music for three shows *Dr. De Luxe* (4/17/11), *The Girl of My Dreams* (8/7/11) and *The Fascinating Widow* (9/11/11). None of these shows played more than 60 performances, and no standards were to come from their scores. Hoschna died at the age of 34, only 5 months after the opening of *The Fascinating Widow,* so Hauerbach was forced to find another partner.

He found an ideal one in Rudolf Friml *(q.v.)*. Their first show together turned Hauerbach's fortunes around. *The Firefly* (12/2/12; 120 performances) was all the more remarkable for being Friml's first Broadway score and producer Arthur Hammerstein's *(q.v.)* first producing venture. The show seemed doomed at the start when Victor Herbert, *(q.v.)* who had signed to compose the score, dropped out due to an argument with star Emma Trentini. Music publishers Max Dreyfus and Rudolf Schirmer encouraged Hammerstein to give the young Friml a chance. Three of the songs—"Giannina Mia," "Love Is Like a Firefly" and "Sympathy"—attained classic status.

The next year, the Hammerstein, Friml and Hauerbach team contributed *High Jinks* (12/10/13; 213 performances) to Broadway. The score was a superior operetta work, but perhaps because the big hit was interpolated ("All Aboard For Dixie" by Jack Yellen and George L. Cobb), it was seldom heard after its initial presentation. In 1914, Hauerbach contributed a libretto only to *The Crinoline Girl* (3/16/14; 88 performances). He then americanized *Suzi* (11/3/14; 55 performances).

Hammerstein, Friml and Hauerbach teamed up again for *Katinka* (12/13/15; 220 performances). The show had a workmanlike score from which no standards emerged. In 1917, the Hauerbach and Friml team contributed two shows, *You're in Love* (2/6/17; 167 performances) and *Kitty Darlin'* (11/7/17; 14 performances). Also in 1917, Hauerbach, responding to the mounting antagonism toward Americans with German-sounding names, changed his surname to Harbach.

Harbach, aware of the public's changing tastes in musical theater, tried his hand at the book and lyrics to a real American musical comedy rather than the American operettas as he had been writing. The result, written in collaboration with Louis Hirsch, was *Going Up* (12/25/17; 350 performances), Harbach's third score and libretto of 1917. Although no lasting songs emerged from the score, the effect of a full-sized biplane flying was enough to keep audiences enthralled.

Despite his success in a more modern vein, Harbach rejoined Friml for his next two shows, *Tumble Inn* (3/24/19; 128 performances) and *The Little Whopper* (10/13/19; 224 performances). *Tumble Inn* might have achieved a longer run if it wasn't for the actors' strike of 1919 *(q.v.)*. *The Little Whopper* was Friml's first attempt at a more modern style of composing.

Arthur Hammerstein produced *Tumble Inn* and also Harbach's next show, *Tickle Me* (8/17/20; 207 performances) with a score by Herbert Stothart. Stothart achieved more fame during his long career on the staff of MGM where he scored 75 pictures, among them *The Wizard of Oz*. *Tickle Me* was Harbach's first collaboration on a libretto with Oscar Hammerstein II *(q.v.)*, nephew of Arthur. In all, Oscar collaborated with Harbach on 10 libretti and/or lyrics. Frank Mandel also collaborated on the book. None of the Hammerstein/Harbach/Stothart songs achieved fame.

Harbach had another successful collaboration with Louis Hirsch in *Mary* (10/18/20; 220 performances). The show was under the direction of George M. Cohan *(q.v.)*. Its hit song was "The Love Nest." The song later achieved greater fame as the theme song for George Burns and Gracie Allen.

Harbach worked on a number of shows during the 1920s, including *Jimmie* (11/17/20), *June Love* (4/25/21), *The O'Brien Girl* (10/3/21), *The Blue Kitten* (1/13/22) and *Molly Darling* (9/1/22). None were hits. Harbach's next show, *Wildflower* (2/7/23; 477 performances), proved to be one of his biggest successes. Arthur Hammerstein was the producer, and his nephew Oscar collaborated on book and lyrics with Harbach. Vincent Youmans *(q.v.)*, one of the greatest composers of the 1920s, wrote

Sheet music for Mary

most of the score; Herbert Stothart composed the remainder. Several of the songs became quite popular, and a few became minor standards. The best songs were "Bambalina" and the title song. Edith Day starred in the show.

Jack and Jill (3/27/23; 92 performances) featured a young Clifton Webb. *Kid Boots* (12/13/23; 479 performances) had Harbach contributing the libretto in collaboration with William Anthony McGuire.

The team responsible for the great success of *Wildflower* was reunited for Harbach's next big hit, *Rose-Marie* (9/9/24; 581 performances), with music by Rudolf Friml and Herbert Stothart. Arthur Hammerstein again produced and Oscar Hammerstein collaborated with Harbach on book and lyrics. The score was one of the best of the twenties, with several songs achieving long-lasting fame, including "Indian Love Call," "The Mounties," the title song, "Pretty Things" and "Totem Tom-Tom."

The critics were enthusiastic about the new show, although sometimes in a backhanded way. The *New York Times* admitted that it was " . . . one of the big musical successes of the new season," but it went on to describe the book as "slightly less banally put forward than has been customary." Of the songs, the *Times* said, "several numbers . . . will probably become nuisances before long." The show enjoyed several extensive national tours and international productions in London, Paris and Berlin. London was an especially enthusiastic city. The show played the Theatre Royal, Drury Lane, for 851 performances. It was revived in London in 1929 for an additional 100 performances, again in 1942 for 149 performances, and yet again in 1960 for 135 performances.

In 1924, Harbach was in the midddle of his most productive period. His next show after *Rose-Marie*, *Betty Lee* (12/25/24; 98 performances), had music by Louis Hirsch and Con Conrad and starred Joe E. Brown.

Vincent Youmans was again tapped for a Harbach show, this time with Irving Caesar collaborating on lyrics with Harbach as he had on *Betty Lee*. The show was *No, No, Nanette* (9/16/25; 329 performances). Almost the direct opposite of *Rose-Marie* in tone, *No, No, Nanette* was the quintessential twenties musical with flappers, fast women and bobbed hair. The terrific score contained one of the greatest hits of the twenties, "Tea for Two," with lyrics by Caesar, and "I Want to Be Happy." Louise Groody played Nanette and appeared without her trademark curls. She was also the first star who received a percentage of the box office gross.

Harbach's second 1925 show, *Sunny* (9/22/25; 517 performances), was an even bigger hit than *No, No, Nanette*. It marked Harbach's first collaboration with the great Jerome Kern *(q.v.)*. Oscar Hammerstein again collaborated on book and lyrics. Marilyn Miller, one of the greatest stars of the twenties, headlined as Sunny.

Her supporting cast included Clifton Webb, Cliff Edwards, Pert Kelton and Jack Donahue. The score was one of Kern and Harbach's best and contained many standards including "D'Ye Love Me?," "Sunny" and "Who?" The show received almost unanimous raves; the sole dissenter was Gilbert Gabriel, who wrote in the *New York Sun*, "Kern's music is spread rather thin . . . The lyrics are at least workable." Most critics *(q.v.)* agreed with Robert Benchley *(q.v.)* writing in the old *Life*, " . . . it isn't so much that it is consistently good, but that it has practically no bad spots."

On his next outing, *Song of the Flame* (12/30/25; 219 performances), Harbach collaborated with Oscar Hammerstein II, Herbert Stothart and a young new composer, George Gershwin *(q.v.)*. Arthur Hammerstein produced. The show opened to excellent reviews for the sets and costumes and only fair reviews for the score and libretto. It contributed a hit song, "The Cossack Love Song."

The year 1926 started slowly but ended with a bang for Harbach. His fourth show of the year, after *Kitty's Kisses* (5/6/26), *Criss-Cross* (10/12/26) and *The Wild Rose* (10/20/26), *The Desert Song* (11/30/26; 465 performances), was another Hammerstein II and Harbach operetta. Sigmund Romberg supplied the rousing music with Frank Mandel helping on the book. The score included such standards as "The Riff Song" and "One Alone." A mark of its lasting qualities is the fact that it was filmed three times—in 1929, 1943 and 1953. Amazingly, Harbach had a fifth show open in 1926. *Oh, Please!* (12/17/26; 79 performances) had a book by Harbach and Anne Caldwell and music by Vincent Youmans.

Harbach's first show of 1927, *Lucky* (3/22/27; 71 performances), was followed by *Golden Dawn* (11/30/27; 184 performances). In *Golden Dawn*, Stothart, Harbach and the Hammersteins were teamed with composer Emmerich Kalman to little effect. The show concerned an English girl captured by an African tribe and saved by an American prisoner of war. The story didn't play much better than it reads, although the score received some nice notices. *Golden Dawn* was notable on two counts however. It was the debut production at Hammerstein's Theater *(q.v.)*, and it featured Archie Leach in a supporting role. Leach received more renown later in his career as Cary Grant.

Harbach's output began to slow as the twenties drew to a close. In 1928, Harbach had only one show, *Good Boy* (9/5/28; 253 performances). Hammerstein produced, and Stothart conducted and composed the score with Harry Ruby. Hammerstein II and Harbach collaborated with Henry Myers on the script, and Bert Kalmar contributed the lyrics.

Two years passed before Harbach's next show, *Nina Rosa* (9/20/30; 129 performances). Harbach contributed the libretto to the Romberg–Caesar score. Broadway's

Otto Harbach   Courtesy ASCAP.

HARBURG, E.Y. (1898–1981) E.Y. ("Yip") Harburg was perhaps Broadway's most complex lyricist. At once outspoken, liberal and uncompromising, Harburg was also sentimental, romantic and humorous. He was a man of strong moral and political beliefs who felt tolerance for those whose politics differed with his own. He believed in the power of lyrics and used that power to move audiences both emotionally and artistically in shows such as *Finian's Rainbow* and *Bloomer Girl*.

He began as a lyricist while still at New York City's Townsend Harris Hall High School along with schoolmate Ira Gershwin *(q.v.)*. While at City College, Harburg had his work published in Franklin P. Adams's influential column The Conning Tower. After graduating, Harburg followed in the footsteps of Gershwin and became a lyricist.

Harburg's first partner was composer Jay Gorney. After contributing songs to a succession of musical revues, the team struck gold with "Brother Can You Spare a Dime," which was practically the official anthem of the Depression. The show was *Americana* (10/5/32; 77 performances). Along the way, Harburg also collaborated with Harold Arlen *(q.v.)*, Burton Lane *(q.v.)* and Vernon Duke *(q.v.)*. Harburg's wit and social consciousness shone through in all his lyrics.

Three early revues contained hit songs by Harburg. *Walk a Little Faster* (12/7/32; 121 performances) featured Duke and Harburg's classic "April in Paris." People couldn't believe that Harburg had never actually visited

output had fallen off with the advent of the Depression, and Harbach's career suffered accordingly. Royalties assured him a comfortable life, so he wasn't about to work too hard to get projects on.

His next Broadway show was a success with critics and audiences. *The Cat and the Fiddle* (10/15/31; 395 performances) paired Harbach with Jerome Kern. The fine score boasted such standards as "Try to Forget," "She Didn't Say Yes" and "The Night Was Made for Love."

The following year saw Kern and Harbach contributing to one of their greatest successes, *Roberta* (11/18/33; 294 performances). Bob Hope, Sydney Greenstreet, George Murphy, Tamara, Lyda Roberti and Fay Templeton starred along with The California Collegians whose membership included Fred MacMurray. The score was one of Kern and Harbach's finest, featuring "Smoke Gets In Your Eyes," "Don't Ask Me Not to Sing," "I'll Be Hard to Handle (with lyrics by Bernard Dougall)," "Let's Begin," "The Touch of Your Hand," "Yesterdays" and "You're Devastating."

Harbach's last Broadway show, *Forbidden Melody* (11/2/36; 32 performances), featured a score by Sigmund Romberg and was one of the last European-style operettas. The show was a disappointing end to a remarkable career. Harbach was a craftsman whose writing certainly inspired others to do their best work. Harbach died in New York City on January 24, 1963, outliving virtually all of his collaborators.

E.Y. ("Yip") Harburg   Courtesy ASCAP.

Paris but got his inspiration from a travel brochure. Bobby Clark, Beatrice Lillie and Evelyn Hoey appeared in the revue.

The *Ziegfeld Follies of 1934* (1/4/34; 182 performances) also had a Harburg and Duke score, although it interpolated many songs by other songwriters. The show featured the Harburg/Duke success "What Is There to Say?" *Life Begins at 8:40* (8/27/34; 238 performances) had music by Harold Arlen and Harburg teamed with his old friend Ira Gershwin *(q.v.)*. The three songwriters came up with such hits as "Let's Take a Walk Around the Block," "You're a Builder Upper" and "Fun to Be Fooled."

Hooray for What! (12/1/37; 199 performances) was Harburg's first book show, written in collaboration with Arlen. The show starred June Clyde, Vivian Vance, Jack Whiting and Ed Wynn. Songs included "Down with Love," "Moanin' in the Mornin'" and "In the Shade of the New Apple Tree." The antiwar musical gave Harburg ample opportunity to express his pacifist leanings.

He explored both race relations and woman's rights with the show *Bloomer Girl* (10/5/44; 657 performances). The brilliant musical opened with Celeste Holm, David Brooks, Joan McCracken and Dooley Wilson singing such Arlen/Harburg hits as "Right As the Rain," "The Eagle and Me," "T'morra', T'morra'" and "Evalina." Harburg was professional enough to make sure that he not only got his points across but also entertained the audience. Harburg also codirected *Bloomer Girl* with William Schorr.

Harburg's greatest success was certainly *Finian's Rainbow* (1/10/47; 725 performances), written in collaboration with Burton Lane. Harburg also contributed the libretto along with Fred Saidy. *Finian's Rainbow* contained one of the theater's finest scores, including such brilliant songs as "How Are Things in Glocca Morra," "Look to the Rainbow," "Old Devil Moon," and "When I'm Not Near the Girl I Love." His associates felt that Harburg, who at times could be magical and mischievous himself, was closely reflected in the character of Og the leprechaun. *Finian's Rainbow* starred an exceptional cast, including David Wayne, Ella Logan, Donald Richards and Albert Sharpe.

Flahooley (5/14/51; 40 performances) was a rare failure for Harburg. However the score, with music by Sammy Fain, featured some excellent songs, including "He's Only Wonderful," "The World Is Your Balloon" and "Here's to Your Illusions."

Artistically, *Jamaica* (10/31/57; 555 performances) suffered because it was too often a vehicle for its star, the singer Lena Horne. The terrific score by Arlen and Harburg included such fine songs as "Ain't It the Truth," "I Don't Think I'll End It All Today" and "Napoleon."

Harburg tackled the Lysistrata legend for his Broadway show, *The Happiest Girl in the World* (4/3/61; 96 performances). The music was adapted by Harburg from the works of Jacques Offenbach to which he added lyrics, which perfectly reflected the Harburg view of the world. Though some thought Harburg's unofficial theme song was "When I'm Not Near the Girl I Love (I Love the Girl I'm Near)" from *Finian's Rainbow*, those who knew him the best felt his theme might be "Adrift on a Star" from *The Happiest Girl in the World*.

Harburg's last Broadway show, *Darling of the Day* (1/27/68; 32 performances), was written with Jule Styne. The show starred Vincent Price and Patricia Routledge.

Harburg is also known for his many movie songs, most notably the score for *The Wizard of Oz*. He died on March 5, 1981.

HARNICK, SHELDON See BOCK AND HARNICK.

HARRIS THEATRE 226 W. 42nd Street. Architect: Thomas W. Lamb. Opening as a movie theater, May 14, 1914, with *Antony and Cleopatra*; as a legitimate theater, August 19, 1914, with *On Trial*.   The Candler family, who had made their money from Coca-Cola, built the Candler Theatre on 42nd Street next to the Candler office building *(q.v.)*. They built the theater as a movie theater but had architect Thomas Lamb design the house so that it could also serve as a fully equipped legitimate theater. Its theatrical policy began with the show *On Trial* (8/19/14; 365 performances).

The producing team of George M. Cohan *(q.v.)* and Sam Harris took over the theater's operation, renamed it the Cohan and Harris Theatre and opened their first production, *Object—Matrimony* (10/25/16; 30 performances). After a brief sojourn by *The Intruder* (9/6/16; 128 performances), the theater had a hit with *Captain Kidd, Jr.*, written by operetta librettist Rida Johnson Young. The show starred Otto Kruger.

The theater hosted three offerings in 1917. The first, *The Willow Tree* (3/6/17; 103 performances) by J.H. Benrimo and Harrison Rhodes, had Fay Bainter in the lead. The musical revue, *Hitchy-Koo* (6/7/17; 220 performances), the first in a continuing series, starred comedian Raymond Hitchcock, Irene Bordoni, Leon Errol, Grace LaRue and Frances White. Bordoni was an immediate sensation. The French singer's message, that sex could be light and fun and gay, shocked Broadway's audiences. An even bigger hit was *A Tailor-Made Man* (8/27/17; 398 performances) by Harry James Smith. The play opened with Grant Mitchell achieving stardom in the leading role.

Another long run at the Cohan and Harris Theatre was Anthony Paul Kelly's play *Three Faces East* (8/13/18; 335 performances). Violet Heming and Emmett Corrigan opened in the play.

Cohan himself appeared in *The Royal Vagabond* (2/17/19; 208 performances) at the Cohan and Harris Theatre. The musical was originally written by Anselm

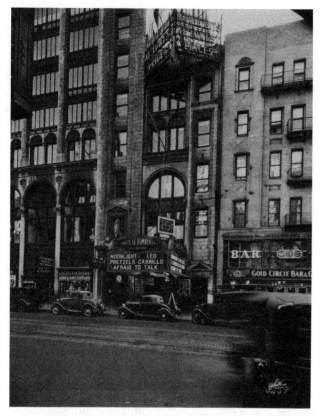

Sam H. Harris Theatre   Courtesy Billy Rose Theater Collection.

Goetzl, William Cary Duncan and Stephen Ivor Szinngey. Cohan contributed music to the show. Songs were also written by Harry Tierney and Joseph McCarthy and Irving Berlin (*q.v.*). Music publisher Isadore Witmark had approached Cohan with the original script. Cohan loved it, but for the wrong reasons. He thought it was a brilliant parody of Ruritanian operettas, or at least would be with a little rewriting. Cohan remembered that Witmark had rewritten his first song's lyrics, so Cohan found it amusing that he would now be able to turn the table on the publisher. Cohan told Witmark that he and Harris would produce it if Cohan could rewrite it. Witmark agreed, and Cohan opened the "Cohanized Opera Comique" to rave reviews.

The Acquittal (1/5/20; 138 performances), Rita Weiman's drama, was also "Cohanized." Unfortunately, the show marked the end of the Cohan and Harris producing relationship. Following *The Acquittal,* the musical *Honey Girl* (5/3/20; 142 performances) opened at the theater with a score by popular songwriter Albert Von Tilzer and Neville Fleeson.

When the partnership with Cohan dissolved, Harris took over the operation of the theater. He changed the name to the Sam H. Harris Theatre. There had previously been a Harris Theater, but its name was changed to the Frazee in 1920. *Welcome Stranger* (2/21/21; 307 performances) was the first offering under the banner of the Sam H. Harris Theatre.

Six-Cylinder Love (8/25/21; 430 performances), William Anthony McGuire's comedy, starred Donald Meek, June Walker, Ernest Truex and Hedda Hopper in the days before she became one of the most powerful columnists in Hollywood.

The theater hosted one of its most notable attractions when John Barrymore (*q.v.*) starred in *Hamlet* (11/16/22; 101 performances). Producer Arthur Hopkins presented the play at the Harris because his own Plymouth Theater (*q.v.*) was occupied with Don Marquis's comedy, *The Old Soak.* Hopkins was also producing *Rose Bernd* featuring Barrymore's sister Ethel.

Franklin Adams wrote in his column The Conning Tower on November 18, 1922: "All day at my desk and so in the evening to see Hamlet and J. Barrymore's acting of it the finest I ever saw, and all about it as close to perfection as ever I hope to see, and when my grandchildren say to me, This or that is a great Hamlet, I shall say, Ay, but not so fine as Barrymore's. And I will disinherit those babes." Other critics were equally enthusiastic. Barrymore's portrayal of Hamlet set a Broadway record for the tragedy until Richard Burton's production played for 137 performances in 1964. Barrymore might have played longer, but he was exhausted by the role and had personal problems that distracted his attention. On its closing night, over 1,000 people were turned away from the box office.

Edna May Oliver, Eva Condon and Andrew Lawlor starred in Owen Davis's Pulitzer Prize-winning drama *Icebound* (2/10/23; 170 performances). Although Owen Davis had a big success with the drama *Icebound,* he was best known as a writer of farce. His *The Nervous Wreck* (10/9/23; 271 performances) was an immediate hit with Otto Kruger, Edward Arnold, June Walker and William Holden in the cast. The play was later adapted into the musical *Whoopee.*

One Helluva Night lived up to its name. The play opened on June 4, 1924, and closed the same night. *Topsy and Eva* (12/23/24; 165 performances) was a hit musical for the theater. *Alias the Deacon* (11/24/25; 277 performances) was a comedy by John B. Hymer and Le Roy Clemens. The comedy *Love 'Em and Leave 'Em* (2/3/26; 152 performances) was written by George Abbott (*q.v.*) and John V. A. Weaver. *We Americans* (10/12/26; 120 performances) was a drama starring Muni Weisenfreund, better known later as Hollywood star Paul Muni.

The theater wasn't lucky enough to host the hit musical *No, No, Nanette* but it did host *Yes, Yes, Yvette* (10/3/27; 40 performances). The show had lyrics by *Nanette's* lyricist Irving Caesar and starred Jeanette MacDonald and Charles Winninger.

Congai (11/27/28; 135 performances), a play by Harry Hervey and Carleton Hildrith, was staged by Rouben Mamoulian and starred Helen Menken. *Mendel, Inc.* (11/25/29; 216 performances), about an eccentric inventor whose wife has to go to work to support the family, starred Alexander Carr and the sometime vaudeville team of Smith and Dale.

Rhapsody in Black (5/4/31; 80 performances), an all black revue, had an impressive cast, including Ethel Waters, Valaida and Eloise Uggams. Songs included "Till the Real Thing Comes Along" by Alberta Nichols and Mann Holiner and also George Gershwin's *(q.v.)* "Rhapsody in Blue." A play, *Sing High, Sing Low* (11/12/31; 70 performances) was a failure.

The Black Tower (1/11/32; 72 performances) was a disappointment. The plot concerns Dr. Eugene Ludlow who attempts to create the perfect statue by using his own special embalming method on real humans. When he tries to subject the heroine to his nefarious scheme, the police arrive in a nick of time.

By the mid-1930s the Shuberts *(q.v.)* had gained control of the theater. However, they, like many of their rivals, lost many of their holdings because of the Depression, and the Harris was no exception. Today, the theater is one of the city's grind movie houses. The 994-seat theater may become a twin movie theater under the Times Square Redevelopment Plan.

HART, MOSS   See KAUFMAN AND HART.

HAYES, HELEN (1900–   ) Playwright Robert Emmett Sherwood once commented that Helen Hayes "seems to regard the theater much as a champion mountain climber regards Everest: it is a challenge to her remarkable determination and courage and skill." Sherwood, writing in the theater magazine, *The Stage,* was referring to Hayes's reluctance to settle for one stage persona. Rather, she insisted on tackling a wide variety of roles. Most of her characters were genteel and seemingly civilized, but they all had an inner strength and maturity. They were marked by a sort of sly, mischievous twinkle in the eye with a promise of sexuality beneath their refined exterior.

"The First Lady of the American Theater" was born in Washington, D.C., on October 10, 1900. She evinced a talent for acting at an early age, first appearing as Prince Charles in the Columbia Players' production of *The Royal Family* in 1905 at the National Theatre *(q.v.)*. In 1908, when she was eight years old, she appeared in three more productions in her hometown: *Little Lord Fauntleroy, The Prince Chap* and the lead in *The Prince and the Pauper.*

Her New York debut was in the Victor Herbert *(q.v.)* musical *Old Dutch* (11/22/09), which premiered at the Herald Square Theater. The Gerry Society did not allow children to sing in Broadway shows, so composer Victor Herbert had Miss Hayes and another actor mime the leading couple's actions as they sang their love duet. Critics said the two children "stole the show." The *New York Herald*'s critic observed that

Helen Hayes

"Miss Helen Hayes, a wee miss, won the favor of the audience by a bit of acting that was refreshing."

Hayes made many appearances on Broadway, and she scored a great success in the role of Cora Wheeler in Booth Tarkington's comedy *Clarence* (9/20/19) at the Hudson Theatre *(q.v.)*. Also in the cast were Glenn Hunter, Mary Boland and Alfred Lunt *(q.v.)* in the title role. *Clarence* was an immense success at the time and closed after 300 performances.

Of Hayes's performances in *Quarantine* (12/16/24; 163 performances), critic Heywood Broun reported that a woman sitting behind him exclaimed "Isn't she just too cute?" no less than 21 times. The young actress desperately wanted to present a more grown-up image when she attacked the part of Cleopatra in George Bernard Shaw's *Caesar and Cleopatra* (4/13/25; 128 performances) at the Guild Theater *(q.v.)* under the auspices of the Theater Guild *(q.v.)*. Lionel Atwell played the Roman general.

The critics seemed to feel that the actress was more suited to play an ingenue than the Queen of Egypt. Broun stated: "Helen Hayes is probably the most carefully trained and expert of all the younger actresses in America, but I wish she would forget some of her tricks. Her Cleopatra is certainly a half-sister of the little girl in Clarence who would not wash her face."

Her crack at maturity would finally come with William A. Brady's *(q.v.)* revival of James Barrie's *What Every Woman Knows* (4/13/26; 268 performances). Brady had a lease on the little Bijou Theatre *(q.v.)* and still had four weeks left to use it. He approached Helen Hayes to assay the role best remembered for Maude Adams's striking interpretation. Despite her nervousness at stepping into the shoes of Maude Adams, Hayes took the job and it proved to be a turning point in her career. John Mason Brown was among the critics *(q.v.)* who noticed a change in Hayes's abilities. "In Maggie Wylie [her character in *What Every Woman Knows*] Miss Hayes has grown up, and has recaptured the grace, the charm, and, though I be excommunicated for saying it, the wistfulness of a Barrie heroine. It lights up the whole play and brings out of it the enchantments of pure magic." The play and Helen Hayes were a big hit, playing well beyond the initial four-week engagement. It later went on tour.

While *What Every Woman Knows* was playing at the Bijou, performances were constantly interrupted by the sound effects accompanying the silent picture, *The Big Parade,* playing next door at the Astor Theatre *(q.v.).* The cast was relieved when their play closed and went on tour. However, they were disappointed to find that the movie was also playing next door to their theater in Boston.

Coquette (11/8/27; 366 performances) at the Maxine Elliott Theatre was another success for Helen Hayes. The play marked her emergence as a star of the first order. Her role, written by George Abbott *(q.v.)* and Ann Preston Bridgers, proved perfect for her talents. George Cukor was the original director of the play, but he was replaced by coauthor Abbott. Producer Jed Harris, one of the most hated men in the New York theater, fired Abbott and directed the play himself. Critic Howard Taubman described the character Hayes played as full of sugared malice. Hayes's portrayal served as the basis for hundreds of similar Southern belles in movies and stage plays. Noel Coward announced that, "Helen Hayes gave an astonishingly perfect performance. She ripped our emotions to shreds." Hayes toured in the production for two years.

Ferenc Molnar's *The Good Fairy* (11/24/31; 154 performances) marked her return to Broadway after a visit to Hollywood to make several pictures that received mixed reviews. In *The Good Fairy,* Hayes played an almost too-good-to-be-true-character, but she managed to make the play enchanting rather than saccharine. Following her return to Hollywood and a starring role opposite Gary Cooper in *A Farewell to Arms,* Hayes received an Academy Award for *The Sin of Madelon Claudet.*

Her next great success on Broadway was in Maxwell Anderson's *Mary of Scotland.* Anderson had seen the actress in *Mr. Gilhooley* (9/30/30; 31 performances). Though it was a failure (audiences would not accept

their favorite little actress as a prostitute), Hayes herself received good notices and Anderson was determined to write her a play. The result was *Mary of Scotland* (11/27/33; 236 performances) in which Hayes played the title role of Mary Queen of Scots. The Theater Guild production opened at the Alvin Theater *(q.v.).* The actress and playwright imbued Mary with a bittersweet character. Especially in her scenes with her cousin Elizabeth, she was simply a vulnerable woman forced to assume her role as queen. Burns Mantle wrote: "Never in a career that began with her childhood and has included many successes has this actress approached the quality of this particular performance. And the answer is not entirely that never before has she had so fine a chance. She has in these last few years been gaining in poise and force and understanding . . . Here she stands, definitely planted near the top of her profession not, I suspect, to be again shaken from that eminence." The production enjoyed a long run, although Hayes had to return to her contract with MGM. She was replaced by Margalo Gilmore on June 1, 1934.

In her next stage appearance, she again portrayed a member of British royalty. *Victoria Regina* (12/26/35), by Laurence Housman, opened at the Broadhurst Theater *(q.v.)* with Vincent Price costarring. The original script consisted of 32 short scenes. A third of them had been used in the London production. The play spanned Victoria's life from age 17 to 60 and finally to 80. To achieve the effect of age, she had costume designer Rex Whistler make specially padded costumes. She was advised by Charles Laughton to fill her cheeks with apple slices, but when the apples proved too tasty, she replaced them with cotton wool. The final effect was not cosmetic but came from inside Hayes. She patterned her speech and carriage after her paternal grandmother. In her last scene, many audience members did not believe it was still Helen Hayes on stage. For her performances as Queen Victoria, she was hailed as the greatest American actress of her generation. After 204 performances, the play closed. It reopened at the Broadhurst on August 31, 1936, for an additional 311 performances. It then was launched on a 10-month tour of the country. While on tour, Hayes assembled the company and announced that they would perform special matinees of Shakespeare's *The Merchant of Venice.*

Shakespeare would also provide her next Broadway success as Viola in *Twelfth Night* (11/19/40; 129 performances). Maurice Evans played Malvolio in the production at the St. James Theatre *(q.v.).* Hayes had another moderate run in Maxwell Anderson's *Candle in the Wind* (10/22/41; 95 performances) at the Shubert Theater *(q.v.).* Alfred Lunt *(q.v.)* directed Hayes as an actress who attempts to win the freedom of a French journalist from a Nazi concentration camp.

In 1909, the young Helen Hayes was forbidden to sing on stage; in 1946, she was finally given the chance.

The occasion was *Happy Birthday* (10/31/46; 564 performances), a play by Anita Loos that opened at the Broadhurst Theater *(q.v.)* under the auspices of producers Richard Rodgers and Oscar Hammerstein II *(q.v.)*. The team wrote a song for the play, "I Haven't Got a Worry in the World." The Hayes character is a frustrated old woman who one day takes her first drink of liquor, and her second and third, and ends up discovering the human behind the stern facade. The play proved a pleasure to watch and perform. For her performance in *Happy Birthday*, Hayes won the Tony Award *(q.v.)* for best actress—it was the first time the award had been given.

Hayes's first appearance in London's West End came next. The opportunity arose when the great American actress Laurette Taylor died. Before her death, Taylor asked that Helen Hayes be given the opportunity to play Amanda in Tennessee Williams's *(q.v.) Glass Menagerie* if she herself could not. Helen Hayes opened at the Theater Royal, Haymarket, July 28, 1948.

Hayes had considered retirement and the death of her daughter Mary in 1949 convinced her to give up performing. But Joshua Logan *(q.v.)* enticed her back to the stage with his adaptation of *The Cherry Orchard* entitled *The Wysteria Trees* (3/29/50; 165 performances) at the Martin Beck Theatre *(q.v.)*.

Mary Chase, the author of *Harvey*, had her play *Mrs. McThing* (2/20/52; 350 performances) optioned by ANTA, the American National Theater and Academy *(q.v.)*. They convinced Helen Hayes to undertake the title role. Brandon de Wilde was her costar.

In November 1955, the Fulton Theater was renamed the Helen Hayes Theater *(q.v.)* in her honor. She told George Oppenheimer about her reaction to the news of the theater's renaming: "I got the news by phone and it seems I was overcome and cried a bit. Then I called Charlie (MacArthur) and asked him how he felt about being married to a building. He didn't seem to mind. In fact, he paid me a great tribute. He was on the way out and he had on his hat, but when I told him about it, he took it off. It's a pretty important occasion when Charlie takes off his hat."

During the run of *Mrs. McThing*, Helen Hayes's mother, Brownie, died. The actress received another blow when, on April 21, 1956, her husband, playwright Charles MacArthur, died.

After an appearance in the movie *Anastasia*, Hayes returned to Broadway in Jean Anouilh's *Time Remembered* (11/12/57; 248 performances) at the Morosco Theatre *(q.v.)*. Her costars were Susan Strasberg and Richard Burton. Although they had no scenes together, Burton and Hayes immediately took a dislike to each other. The show, however was a success, winning a second Tony Award for the actress.

Hayes played her first role in the Helen Hayes Theater in Eugene O'Neill's *(q.v.) A Touch of the Poet* (10/2/58;

284 performances). In it, she played Norah Melody, the bedraggled wife of a disheveled, drunken innkeeper. Eric Portman played the down-at-the-heels Irishman and Kim Stanley played their daughter. Whitney Brown summed up the critical opinion when he wrote, "Miss Hayes plays the pseudo gentleman's low-born Irish wife with lovely perception and a gift for using tiny and seemingly inconsequential things to build a creature of dimension and earthy grandeur."

In 1966, Hayes joined the repertory company APA—Phoenix. Not all her roles were starring ones, but she enjoyed flexing her theatrical muscles and also being away from the pressures of a normal Broadway run. While at APA—Phoenix she appeared in Sheridan's *The School for Scandal*, Pirandello's *Right You Are If You Think You Are*, *We Comrades Three* and *You Can't Take It With You*. During the next season, she was in George Kelly's *The Show Off* (12/5/67). She also appeared in her husband and Ben Hecht's classic, *The Front Page* at the Ethel Barrymore Theater *(q.v.)* in October 1969, replacing another actress for six weeks.

After her Oscar winning performance in the movie *Airplane*, Helen Hayes opened opposite James Stewart in Mary Chase's *Harvey* (2/24/70) at the ANTA Theater *(q.v.)*. Clive Barnes enthused, "She is one of those actors—Laurence Olivier is another, for she keeps the grandest company—where to watch how she is doing something is almost as pleasurable as what she is doing. Her technique is so close to the surface of her acting that it gives it a special blush." *Harvey* was her last Broadway appearance and her next-to-last stage appearance.

She retired from the stage after a 1971 production of O'Neill's *Long Day's Journey Into Night* at Catholic University in Washington, D.C. Critics raved about her performances as Mary Tyrone in the harrowing drama. Walter Kerr wrote: "By first creating the facade and by making it halfway plausible, Miss Hayes gained suspense to begin with and a heart-sinking sympathy when, inevitably, the foundation gave way . . . The standing ovation she received was in order and not simply because she had spent a lifetime being Helen Hayes. It was Eugene O'Neill she was working for, first to last."

After 65 years of professional service, Helen Hayes retired from the stage.

HELD, ANNA (1873–1918)   Anna Held was the first and most famous of the performers in what was called the Broadway Beauty Trust. The Beauty Trust referred to all the beautiful women employed on the stages of the Great White Way. Anna Held was the first great star who owed her fame as much to publicity as talent.

Debate raged as to whether she was born in Warsaw, Poland, or Paris, France. Someone even speculated she was actually reared in Illinois. Although the mists created by a great publicity machine obscured her earliest days, her later career is certainly well documented.

At eight she was singing for coins in Montmartre. When she was 12 and an orphan, she found a job at the Prince's Theatre in London in the chorus. The pay was only five shillings, but the dainty chorine rose quickly through the ranks. She soon played throughout the continent, in Amsterdam, Hungary, Germany and Scandinavia. At 15 she was already featured in Parisian revues.

Like Lillian Russell, Anna Held used her obvious assets to overcome limitations. She certainly looked the part of a Parisian chanteuse. Her 18-inch waist gave her the hour glass form so admired by both sexes.

Her first turning point came when she sang what became her theme song, "Won't You Come and Play Wiz Me." The song was adapted from "Die Kleine Schrecke" ("The Little Teaser"). Later in her career, one critic remarked "it was not an invitation; it was a demand."

Her second turning point came when she was seen by the great Florenz Ziegfeld (q.v.) at the Palace Music Hall, London. Ziegfeld brought her to the United States, where she made her debut at the Herald Square Theater on September 21, 1896. The play was A Parlor Match by Charles Hoyt. She certainly earned her salary, said to be $1,500 per week. Of her debut the New York Times observed, "As a spectacle Mlle. Held is a success, absolute and complete. Her eyes are long, narrow and heavily circled; her nose is straight; her mouth perfect; and as for her chin, people might go some ways to see it without regretting the experience." The Times realized that she was not a particularly strong singer and remarked that, "she would not be a 'sensation' at all if the idea had not been ingeniously forced on the public that she is—naughty."

For her second production, Papa's Wife (11/13/1899), Ziegfeld ingeniously forced some more ideas on her public. The most famous publicity stunt (q.v.) concerned her celebrated milk baths. Ziegfeld was given the idea from playwright Max Marcin who heard a story about a French woman's daily baths in asses milk. Ziegfeld adapted the idea for his star by arranging for a New Jersey milkman to deliver 40 gallons of milk to her apartment at the Netherland every day. Newspaper reporters were willing to print almost anything, but at this they balked. So the great impresario brought them up to Miss Held's boudoir, where they could observe her in the bath.

She exclaimed, "It is, you see, to take the beauty bath. In Paris I ate some fish and it brought out a pimple on my wrist. The milk she preserve the creamy complexion." The reporters were convinced, and milk baths became the rage across the country. Ziegfeld kept the story alive by having the milkman sue him for nonpayment.

In Papa's Wife, Held introduced the second of her great numbers, "I Just Can't Make My Eyes Behave." In this production, Ziegfeld again made headlines by decking out his star with $40,000 worth of costumes. One dress, a yellow crepe de chine with poppies embroidered on its skirt, cost $20,000.

By this time, it was announced that she and Ziegfeld had been married in Paris before she came to this country. This wasn't true, but newspapers seemed indulgent and didn't push the issue. She was recognized as his common-law wife when divorce papers were served on him in 1912.

Flo stepped up the publicity campaign as Anna brought in the money. It was reported that she saved a city judge when she overtook his runaway horse with her bicycle. Meantime, a special railroad car was outfitted in an Oriental style, and Ziegfeld took his breadwinner on the road in two plays, The Cat and the Cherub and A Gay Deceiver.

The provinces were not so liberal as the big city of New York, as witnessed in this article in the Pittsburgh Post: "Police censorship has caused the removal of portraits of Anna Held from the lobby of the Nixon Theater. The piece which Inspector McQuade especially frowned on was in a frame almost six feet square and showed a scene in an artistic studio in the second act of The Parisian Model. The police refused to countenance the exhibition of her bare shoulders and feet in the theater lobby, and there is speculation and fear as to what will happen to the production when it comes here next week." Ziegfeld's advance man, under orders from his boss, probably coerced the police to remove the offending poster.

Miss Held made a splash in other musicals: The Little Duchess (10/14/01); Higgledy Piggledy (10/20/04) and Miss Innocence (11/30/08). It was in The Little Duchess that Ziegfeld surrounded his petite beauty for the first time with tall stately showgirls. One critic exclaimed, "the nymphic Anna of the amber eyes pitted her beauty against a dozen others." Of course, she held her own magnificently and, in fact, looked all the more rare and beautiful when compared with the long-legged opposition.

Late in her career, the Shubert Brothers (q.v.) managed her while Ziegfeld was concentrating on his Follies (q.v.). Though she never had as great success without Ziegfeld as with him, Anna Held remained a top draw at the box office until her death in 1918.

By this time, Ziegfeld had already alienated her affections through his affair with showgirl Lillian Lorraine. After their divorce, Ziegfeld married another of his stars, Billie Burke (q.v.). Anna Held became ill following a road tour of Follow Me for the Shuberts. Her diagnosis was that of myeloma. The constant dieting, which kept her weight around 90 pounds, and her tightly laced corsets hastened the progress of the disease.

Her estate was settled at $257,859. Most of this was

jewels, including a $100,000 necklace. When her body left Campbell's Funeral Home, 5,000 people watched along Broadway. Ziegfeld wasn't there, although he sent a huge wreath of orchids for her coffin.

HELEN HAYES THEATER (1) 210–14 W. 46th Street. Architects: Herts and Tallant. Opening: April 27, 1911, as theater/restaurant Folies Bergere; as Fulton Theater October 20, 1911, *The Cave Man*; as Helen Hayes Theater November 21, 1955, *Tiger at the Gates.*   Producers Henry B. Harris and Jesse Lasky opened a Broadway branch of the Parisian nightclub Folies Bergere on April 27, 1911. The club, which some consider the first American nightclub, was not successful enough to continue as a cabaret. The owners renovated the space into a legitimate theater and called it the Fulton.

The theater was a success from the beginning. *Linger Longer Letty* (11/20/19; 69 performances) was written by Al Goodman *(q.v.)*, Bernard Grossman and Anne Nichols. Charlotte Greenwood starred in one of the only musical-comedy series to be based on one character. Letty Pepper, played by Greenwood, was a favorite of audiences, especially when she kicked her feet high over her head. *Linger Longer Letty's* one big hit song, "Oh by Jingo, Oh by Gee," was written by Albert Von Tilzer and Lew Brown *(q.v.)*.

Orange Blossoms (9/19/22; 95 performances) was Victor Herbert's *(q.v.)* last musical comedy produced in his lifetime. Edith Day introduced a great Herbert standard, "A Kiss in the Dark." Despite many plusses, the show received mixed reviews. Ticket prices were cut from $4.00 to $3.50 to help attract audiences, but it didn't help and the show closed.

The theater's greatest hit, and the biggest hit of the twenties, was Anne Nichols's comedy *Abie's Irish Rose* (5/23/22; 2,327 performances). The remarkably successful show was to move to other theaters before finally closing.

Nifties of 1923 (9/25/23; 47 performances) was a failure, despite a score by contributors such as Eubie Blake, Noble Sissle *(q.v.)*, George Gershwin *(q.v.)*, Irving Caesar, Harry Ruby, Bert Kalmar and Ira Gershwin *(q.v.)*. However, Ira Gershwin (writing under his pseudonym Arthur Francis) wrote lyrics to music by Raymond Hubbell, not his brother. Irving Caesar provided the lyrics to the song by George Gershwin. Gus Van and Joe Schenck headed the cast.

Sitting Pretty (4/8/24; 95 performances) was a Jerome Kern *(q.v.)*, P.G. Wodehouse and Guy Bolton *(q.v.)* musical in the vein of their Princess Theater shows—small, intimate, American-themed productions. The musical director was Max Steiner.

It might have run longer had composer Kern not banned others from performing the show's songs on radio, in clubs or on records. The composer was distraught over the treatment his tunes had received by modern orchestrators and arrangers. As he put it:

The first Helen Hayes Theater Courtesy Municipal Art Society.

None of our music now reaches the public as we wrote it, except in the theater. It is so distorted by jazz orchestras as to be almost unrecognizable.

A composer should be able to protect his score just as an author does his manuscripts. No author would permit pirated editions of his work in which his phraseology and punctuation were changed, thereby giving to his work a meaning entirely different from which he intended.

Kern went on to further lambast the new American jazz. "There is no such thing as jazz music per se, at least nothing that may honestly be called original and characteristically American. The Gypsy orchestra of Hungary knew and used similar methods years ago, but they were artists and knew how and when to apply these methods."

A drama that would, in another medium, change the history of entertainment opened at the Fulton. The play was *The Jazz Singer* (9/14/25; 315 performances), which was later made into the world's first talking picture by Warner Brothers with stage great Al Jolson *(q.v.)* in the lead. The original play was written by Samson Raphaelson and starred George Jessel as the cantor's son who wants a life in the theater rather than a life devoted to religion.

Beatrice Lillie appeared in her first American book musical, *Oh, Please!* (12/12/26; 79 performances) at the Fulton. The hit song was "Like She Loves Me." The Vincent Youmans *(q.v.)* score had lyrics by Otto Harbach *(q.v.)* and Anne Caldwell.

Hamilton Deane and John Balderston were the playwrights responsible for scaring the wits out of audiences at the Fulton Theater with their play *Dracula* (10/5/27; 265 performances), based on Bram Stoker's novel. The play starred Nedda Harrigan (daughter of Ned Harrigan and wife of Joshua Logan) and Dorothy Peterson as Lucy Harker. The Count was played by Bela Lugosi, who later replayed the character in many motion pictures. Lugosi became a star with *Dracula,* but despite his excellence as a classical actor he became typecast in the role.

The first of Leonard Sillman's *New Faces* (3/15/34; 148 performances) revues introduced actors Imogene Coca, Hildegard Halliday and James Shelton to New York audiences. But by far the greatest new face was that of Henry Fonda. The score's hit songs, written by a variety of composers, were "My Last Affair" and "The Gutter Song."

Another long-running comedy, *Arsenic and Old Lace* (1/10/41; 1,444 performances), graced the Fulton's stage. The comedy, by Joseph Kesselring with an assist by Howard Lindsay and Russel Crouse, starred Josephine Hull and Jean Adair as two maiden aunts who bury a number of lonely old men in their basement. Also featured were Allyn Joslyn, John Alexander, Edgar Stehli and Boris Karloff.

Lillian Hellman's play *The Searching Wind* (4/12/44; 326 performances) starred Montgomery Clift and Dudley Diggs in the drama, which showed how too much sentimentality can disguise true feelings and lead to ruin. Arnaud D'Usseau and James Gow's play, *Deep Are the Roots* (9/26/45; 477 performances), explored the problems of black veterans returning from World War II. The drama starred Barbara Bel Geddes, Gordon Heath and Helen Martin.

Lillian Hellman had her second Fulton Theater premiere with *Another Part of the Forest* (11/20/46; 182 performances). Patricia Neal starred in the leading role. William Wister Haines's *Command Decision* (10/1/47; 409 performances) starred James Whitmore, Paul Kelly and Paul Ford. Anita Loos adapted Collette's story *Gigi* (11/24/51; 217 performances) for the stage and cast Audrey Hepburn, Mel Ferrer and Marian Seldes in the leads.

The Seven Year Itch (11/20/52; 1,141 performances), George Axelrod's comedy about the male libido, starred Tom Ewell and Vanessa Brown. It was later made into a very successful movie with Ewell and Marilyn Monroe.

On November 21, 1955, with the opening of *Tiger at the Gates,* the theater was renamed to honor actress Helen Hayes *(q.v.).* Jose Quintero directed Fredric March, Florence Eldridge and Jason Robards Jr. in Eugene O'Neill's *(q.v.)* autobiographical drama *Long Day's Journey Into Night* (11/7/56; 390 performances). The production won the Pulitzer Prize award *(q.v.)* for

drama that year. Another O'Neill play, *A Touch of the Poet* (10/2/58; 284 performances), directed by Harold Clurman, had its Broadway premiere at the Helen Hayes. The drama starred Helen Hayes, Eric Portman, Kim Stanley and Betty Field.

Jean Kerr's comedy *Mary, Mary* (3/8/61; 1,572 performances) starred Barbara Bel Geddes and Michael Rennie. Another Jean Kerr play was the Helen Hayes Theater's next tenant. *Poor Richard* (12/2/64; 118 performances) starred Gene Hackman and Alan Bates. Brian Friel's comedy *Philadelphia Here I Come* (2/16/66; 326 performances) was a hit in the 1965–66 season.

The Prime of Miss Jean Brodie (1/16/68; 378 performances) had Zoe Caldwell in the lead. Jay Presson Allen's play was later successfully transferred to the screen. Alec McCowen also had a tour de force in his protrayal of Frederick Rolfe/Baron Corvo in Peter Luke's play *Hadrian VII* (1/8/69; 359 performances). A light comedy, Bob Randall's *6 Rms Riv Vu* (10/17/72; 247 performances), starred F. Murray Abraham, Jerry Orbach, Jane Alexander and Jennifer Warren.

The Me Nobody Knows opened at the Helen Hayes Theater after a successful run off-Broadway. It eventually played for 587 performances. The Gary William Friedman and Will Holt revue, based on children's poetry and writing, featured a cast of youngsters, including Irene Cara.

Rodgers and Hart (5/13/75; 111 performances) was a revue based on the songs of the great composing team, Richard Rodgers and Lorenz Hart *(q.v.).*

George S. Kaufman *(q.v.)* and Edna Ferber's comedy satire of the Barrymores *(q.v.), The Royal Family* (12/30/75), was mounted as an all-star revival. Among the cast members were Rosetta LeNoire, Joseph Maher, Mary Louise Wilson, Eva Le Gallienne, Sam Levene, Rosemary Harris and George Grizzard.

The classic O'Neill drama *A Touch of the Poet* (12/28/77; 141 performances) opened for a second time at the Helen Hayes Theater. This production starred Milo O'Shea, Geraldine Fitzgerald, Jason Robards Jr., Kathryn Walker and George Ede under the direction of Jose Quintero.

Perfectly Frank (11/30/80; 16 performances) was another revue that focused on the career of a major Broadway composer. Frank Loesser *(q.v.)* was the subject of the show.

The Crucifer of Blood (9/28/78; 236 performances) was a Sherlock Holmes mystery, starring Paxton Whitehead as the intrepid deducer and Timothy Landfield as his assistant John Watson, M.D. Glenn Close also starred in the mystery. *The Crucifer of Blood* was the last semisuccess to play the Helen Hayes Theater.

A long battle to save the Helen Hayes, Morosco *(q.v.)* and Bijou *(q.v.)* theaters and the Astor *(q.v.)* and Victoria *(q.v.)* movie theaters was fought in the late seventies. Despite the best efforts of preservationists, architects, theater people and audiences the prodeveloper city government and the builders won the battle, and in 1982 the theaters were torn down to make way for the Marriott Marquis Hotel.

HELEN HAYES THEATER (2) See LITTLE THEATRE.

HELLINGER, MARK (1903–1947) Mark Hellinger was the first reporter to cover the Broadway scene exclusively. His compatriots were Walter Winchell (q.v.), the first Broadway columnist, and Damon Runyon (q.v.), the author of many stories that captured the spirit of 'The Main Stem.'

In addition to his work as a reporter, Hellinger wrote thinly disguised fictional stories about the men and women who inhabited Times Square. Like Damon Runyon, Hellinger loved the eccentric characters he discovered and found their stories to be more fascinating than fiction could ever be. Hellinger was a prolific writer, and it is said that he wrote over 4,500 short stories.

Hellinger had several favorite Broadway hangouts. Billy LaHiff's tavern was the home of several journalists, including Runyon and Ed Sullivan (q.v.), and sports figures like Jack Dempsey, Bugs Baer (q.v.) and Toots Shor. Author Gene Fowler set up his typewriter next to the butcher block in the basement and wrote his first novel, *Trumpet in the Dust,* in 21 days at LaHiff's.

Another favorite hangout (for its underworld element) was Bob Murphy's Cellar. It was located a few steps downstairs at Broadway and 50th Street. A special on the menu was "eggs on a platter." However, when newcomers asked for the dish, the waiter always informed them that they had the platter but were fresh out of eggs. The Cellar was not a nice place. It wasn't frequented by a high-class clientele, which was perfect for Hellinger because his columns featured tales of shady characters. Murphy's was a mother lode of material. However, one day, the proprietor went outside for a second and was shot. After his recovery, Murphy sold the Cellar and moved to a farm in New Hampshire.

After covering Broadway for the short lived *Variety* (q.v.) competitor, *Zit's,* Hellinger was hired by the *Daily News*'s owner Captain Joseph Patterson. Hellinger was only too happy to leave *Zit's,* which was a somewhat sleazy paper. He began his coverage of Broadway for the *News* in 1923 and used the time to solidify his contacts. One year later, Winchell was given his first daily column in the *News.*

Hellinger was awarded a Sunday column beginning on July 12, 1925. He called it "About Town," soon after amended to "About Broadway." Hellinger's column often opened and closed with the phrase: "Episodes, Roscoe, Episodes."

Hellinger didn't write in the florid, sometimes sentimental, style of Runyon. Unlike Runyon, Hellinger didn't employ the language of Broadway or revel in the slang (q.v.) of the streets. He made his sentences terse and delivered them in a staccato fashion. He loved irony and sprinkled his writing with puns. He also loved sentence fragments and the modified repeat sentence. For example, he would write: "She was pretty. Very pretty. A good girl too. But sad. Very sad. She was broke. And out of a job. And despondent. Life was harsh. Then one day she met Bill. Bill wasn't good-looking. But he was honest. And noble." The Hellinger style of writing was often imitated by screenwriters, playwrights and less-talented columnists who wanted to evoke the image of a hard-boiled reporter.

On January 16, 1928, Hellinger began a daily column titled "Behind the News." He hired an assistant, Jimmy Burbridge, who handled all correspondence, answered the phone and tracked down leads. Burbridge was constantly being fired by his boss, then rehired soon thereafter. It was suggested that Burbridge was hired and fired more than any other employee in the history of journalism.

Hellinger, known as a soft touch, was often the first person visited by convicts after they served their sentences. Hellinger always had a few dollars to help them. In this way, Hellinger heard some of his favorite stories, stories that would later make their way into his columns and his books.

Perhaps his most famous and controversial short story concerned a husband sent to Sing Sing for 20 years for murdering his wife. The husband is taken away protesting his innocence, but the police have discovered a skeleton (identified as his wife through dental records) buried in the back yard. At the end of his prison term, the man is released and returns to his old neighborhood. A few months later, he discovers his wife walking down the street. The wrongly convicted husband runs over to his wife's side and strangles her. The police cannot touch him, for he has already been convicted for the crime and has paid his debt to society. Because of the laws of double jeopardy, he remains a free man.

Hellinger, Runyon and Winchell all cultivated contacts with members of the underworld. Hellinger liked and admired many of the miscreants, and they in turn trusted him. They made Hellinger the official arbiter of any arguments. Hellinger's rulings didn't hold much water, but it seemed to suit everyone's purposes to at least make the effort.

Hellinger was wooed away from the *News* by Albert J. Kobler, publisher of the *Daily Mirror.* Kobler thought Hellinger would bring 10,000 readers to the *Mirror.* Actually Hellinger brought 25,000. Obviously, Hellinger wielded much power and he demanded a $500 a week salary, 50% of his syndication profits, his picture at the top of the column, a private office, a full-blown promotion campaign and the help of Jimmy Burbridge at $45 a week.

Hellinger's move from the *News* created a merry-go-round of Broadway columnists. Sidney Skolsky took over Hellinger's job at the *News*. Louis Sobol moved to the vacated post at the *New York Journal*. Sobol's column at the *Graphic* was filled by Ed Sullivan, a former sports writer. Soon after, Sullivan replaced Skolsky on Hellinger's old column at the *News*.

Hellinger's *Daily Mirror* column was titled "All in a Day." He solidified his style and arranged his columns under several headings. One heading was People I've Met, which covered celebrities; under the heading Unsung Broadwayites, he covered those who were unknown to the general public.

Hellinger expanded his domain by collecting his columns into books, including *The Ten Million*, a title inspired by O. Henry's collection entitled *The Four Million; Broadway Bill; Moon over Broadway;* and *Six Girls and Death*.

Hellinger also wrote sketches for Broadway shows including the *Ziegfeld Follies (q.v.)* (7/1/31) and *Hot-Cha* (3/8/32). Hellinger also played the Loew's vaudeville circuit in 1930 with his wife, actress Gladys Glad. Hellinger later moved into radio and color commentary of sports events.

Clearly, the newpaper column wasn't enough for the writer. He quit the *Mirror*, publishing his last column on November 13, 1937. Hellinger then moved to Hollywood, where he became a successful screenwriter and producer. Hellinger often returned to his haunts on Broadway, confirming what one journalist wrote: "The man was born and bred a newspaperman and he only went to Hollywood to get some sucker money." Hellinger did truly love Broadway. He once wrote: "This morning being this morning we will take you on another personally conducted tour of Broadway. People in every walk of life have told us that they would give anything to pace the Broadway beat as we do. And there are others who shudder and swear that they would not adopt our life for all the money in the world. Both classes are right, depending totally on the point of view. Every hour in the night life of Broadway brings sadness, gladness, love, romance, hate, joy, laughter and sorrow. Sometimes bitterness. Sometimes happiness. And again. And again. And again . . . "

He died in Hollywood on December 21, 1947. When tycoon Anthony B. Farrell bought the Warner Brothers Theater on West 51st Street, he rechristened it the Mark Hellinger Theater *(q.v.)* in the writer's honor.

Hellinger once participated in a phony feud with his fellow *News* columnist Paul Gallico. Gallico wrote after Hellinger's death: "They wrote him up as a big tipper and a picker-up of tabs and dinner checks. It was true enough, but there were so many more things to say of Mark Hellinger . . . He was sweet. He was kind. He

was gentle. He was honest, and he was good. He worked hard. He never double-crossed his friends. He was rich in talent, and with his talent he enriched his times—when he died, he left too large a hole to fill in the hearts of many, including my own."

HENDERSON, RAY See DESYLVA, BROWN AND HENDERSON.

HENRY MILLER'S THEATRE. 124 W. 43rd Street. Architects: Harry Creighton Ingalls and Paul R. Allen. Opening: April 1, 1918; *The Fountain of Youth.* Henry Miller's Theatre, home of distinguished straight plays, especially those from London, saw its fortunes fall along with Broadway's. The theater was built by actor/manager Henry Miller to house his productions. Miller made sure that his architects included a balcony in their designs because he remembered his youth and the years when he had only enough money for the balcony seats. He wanted other young people of small means to be able to enjoy the theater too.

The first production at the theater, *The Fountain of Youth*, was a failure and closed after only 32 performances. The second offering, *A Marriage of Convenience* opened on May 1, 1918, with Billie Burke starring. It played for only 53 performances.

Coal restrictions during World War I increased theater business because people left their homes to sit in a warm theater. The first hit to play the theater was *Mis' Nelly of New Orleans* (2/4/19), which played 127 performances.

On May 26, 1919, the theater housed a musical, George Gershwin's *(q.v.) La, La, Lucille!* Alex Aarons *(q.v.)* and George B. Seitz produced the show, which was one of the few musicals produced on the Henry Miller stage. The "New Up-to-the-Minute Musical Comedy of Class and Distinction" was Gershwin's first complete score for a Broadway production. The show was well received by critics and would have run longer than 104 performances but for the actor's strike of 1919 *(q.v.)*.

The teens ended with a successful production of *The Famous Mrs. Fair* (12/22/19), which ran 343 performances, well into the twenties. Also in the early twenties were the openings for *Wake Up, Jonathan* (1/17/21; 105 performances); Booth Tarkington's *Intimate Strangers* (11/7/21; 91 performances) with Alfred Lunt *(q.v.)* and Billie Burke; *The Awful Truth* (9/18/22; 146 performances), starring Ina Claire; and *Romeo and Juliet* (1/24/23; 161 performances) with Jane Cowl and Dennis King.

Helen Hayes *(q.v.)* starred at the Henry Miller in *Quarantine* (12/16/24) along with Sidney Blackmer. The play ran 163 performances but wasn't a hit with the Broadway crowd. When Hayes's friends asked where

Program for Henry Miller's Theatre

she had been because they hadn't seen her lately, she explained, "I've been in Quarantine."

Noel Coward's *The Vortex* opened on September 16, 1925, and ran 157 performances. It was followed by Ferenc Molnar's *The Play's the Thing* (11/3/26; 313 performances) and George M. Cohan's play *The Baby Cyclone* (9/12/27). The title character Cyclone was a tiny Pekinese sold by a henpecked husband. His wife makes sure he regrets his action. *Theatre Magazine* said the play had "A not very subtle plot . . . you would not believe could possibly fill any stage from 8:45 to 11:00. But Mr. Cohan is a master of padding." *The Baby Cyclone* ran 187 performances. The house long-run record was set with *Journey's End* (3/22/29), which ran 485 performances.

During the thirties, the theater's success continued. Philip Barry's *Tomorrow and Tomorrow* opened on January 13, 1931, and ran 206 performances. Helen Hayes returned to the theater in *The Good Fairy* (11/24/31; 154 performances) by Molnar. It was followed by Sidney Howard's *The Late Christopher Bean* (10/31/32; 211 performances); Eugene O'Neill's *(q.v.) Days without End* (1/8/34; 57 performances); Lawrence Riley's *Personal*

Appearance (10/17/34; 50 performances) with Gladys George; Edward Woolf's *Libel* (12/20/35; 104 performances), which marked the emergence of director Otto Preminger as a major talent; and Terrance Rattigan's *French without Tears* (9/28/37; 111 performances).

Next, the theater presented an American classic, Thornton Wilder's *Our Town*. It opened on February 4, 1938, with little advance word. The play received mixed reviews in Boston before coming to New York. In fact, the Boston run was canceled before its scheduled closing. The show was booked into the Henry Miller, but the theater gave it only a limited guarantee, believing the show to be a sure failure. The reviews at its Broadway opening were mixed, and audiences stayed away. When the play won the Pulitzer Prize *(q.v.)*, business picked up. By this time, the play had to make room for the Henry Miller's next booking, Clair Boothe's *Kiss the Boys Goodbye* (9/28/38; 286 performances), so it was transferred to the Morosco Theatre *(q.v.)*, where it concluded its 336-performance run.

The theater's first play of the 1940s was *Ladies in Retirement* (3/26/40; 151 performances). *Harriet* (3/3/43; 377 performances) followed, starring Helen Hayes, as Harriet Beecher Stowe. Critic *(q.v.)* John Anderson wrote: "Here in beaming comedy, is proof that the hand that rules the cradle rocks the world." Julius J. and Philip G. Epstein's comedy *Chicken Every Sunday* (4/5/44; 317 performances) followed the run of *Harriet*. Norman Krasna, a popular writer of light comedies, had a major success with *Dear Ruth* (12/13/44; 683 performances). Moss Hart staged the play, which starred Virginia Gilmore and Lenore Lonergan. June Lockhart, best known as the mother in the television series "Lassie" and the daughter of Gene Lockhart, starred in *For Love or Money* (11/4/47) at Henry Miller's Theatre. F. Hugh Herbert's play ran 263 performances.

The 1950s started with a hit for the theater, T.S. Eliot's *The Cocktail Party* (1/21/50). The play starred Alec Guinness, Irene Worth and Cathleen Nesbitt. Although some critics said the play was indecipherable, it kept audiences happy for 409 performances. *The Cocktail Party* was the first big British hit to play the theater, which enjoyed a reputation as the American home of English shows.

F. Hugh Herbert had another success at the theater with *The Moon Is Blue* (3/8/51). Barbara Bel Geddes and Barry Nelson starred in the long-running (924 performances) play. Edward Chodorov's hit comedy *Oh, Men! Oh, Women!* opened on December 17, 1953, and ran for 382 performances. Another English offering, Graham Greene's *The Living Room,* opened on November 17, 1954, with Barbara Bel Geddes but lasted only 22 performances. It was quickly replaced with another import, Agatha Christie's *Witness for the Prosecution* (12/16/54), which did considerably better with its 645-performance run.

The "British invasion" continued on October 10, 1956, with *The Reluctant Debutante* by William Douglas Home. The show pleased audiences for 134 performances. A hilarious production of Feydeau's comedy *Hotel Paradiso* opened at the theater on April 11, 1957. The play starred Bert Lahr and, making her stage debut, Angela Lansbury. Harold Clurman wrote in *The Nation* that the production was "louder, faster, closer to burlesque. The changes . . . helped our audience which can more readily accept departures from realism when they are unmistakable." Audiences were thrilled for 107 performances.

Elmer Rice's last play, *Cue for Passion* opened on November 25, 1958, with Robert Lansing. Unfortunately, it was a failure and closed after 39 performances. Another failure by a great dramatist, Noel Coward's *Look After Lulu,* opened on March 3, 1959. Tammy Grimes starred in the play for 39 performances.

The next hit at the theater was Saul Levitt's courtroom drama, *The Andersonville Trial.* The play opened on December 29, 1959, with George C. Scott and Albert Dekker and ran 179 performances. Movie star Bette Davis opened on September 14, 1960, in the short-lived production, *The World of Carl Sandburg.* It closed after 29 performances. A much bigger hit was Lawrence Roman's *Under the Yum-Yum Tree* (11/16/60; 173 performances), starring Gig Young.

Joseph Stein's play *Enter Laughing* opened on March 13, 1963, with Alan Arkin and Vivian Blaine. The comedy enjoyed a long run of 419 performances. A long series of flop plays followed. Lawrence Roman's *P.S. I Love You* (10/19/64) starred Geraldine Page and Lee Patterson and closed after 12 performances. Jerome Lawrence and Robert E. Lee's *Diamond Orchid,* a drama about Eva Peron, opened on February 10, 1965, and closed after five performances. Other plays at the theater included *The Promise* with Ian McKellen; Jack Gelber's *The Cuban Thing* with Rip Torn, Jane White and Raul Julia; Terrance McNally's *Morning, Noon and Night;* and Julius J. Epstein's *But, Seriously* with Richard Dreyfuss and Tom Poston. Epstein's play opened on February 27, 1969, and closed on March 1, 1969, the last production to play the theater.

After Henry Miller's death on April 9, 1926, the theater remained in his family's hands. His son, Gilbert Miller, a noted producer in his own right, oversaw the theater's operation. In 1966, Gilbert Miller's widow sold the theater. After its last legitimate production, the theater became the Park-Miller Theatre, which showed male porno films. In 1978, the theater became the disco Xenon. Xenon continued until 1984—until the death of disco. The theater then became a dance hall, Shout!!, which features 1950s rock and roll. The theater remains open as Shout!!

On November 8, 1987, Henry Miller's Theatre's exterior was designated a New York City landmark.

The Landmarks Preservation Commission said: "Its facade is a handsome example of the neo-Georgian style [used to] express the concept of intimate productions being presented."

HERBERT, VICTOR (1859–1924)   The Irish-born composer and conductor Victor Herbert was the most important and prolific of the early composers of musical comedy and operetta. He was a major influence on an entire generation of musicians. His 30-year career included many triumphs both on stage and off. Among his best-known shows are *Babes in Toyland, The Red Mill, Naughty Marietta, Mlle. Modiste, Sweethearts, Eileen* and *Orange Blossoms.* Herbert was instrumental in the formation of ASCAP *(q.v.)*.

Herbert was born in Dublin on February 1, 1859. When his father died, his mother remarried and the family moved to Stuttgart. He attended Stuttgart Conservatory and studied with Bernhard Cossman and Max Seifriz. He spent many years as a cellist with German and Austrian symphony orchestras, including five years with the Court Orchestra of Stuttgart.

After emigrating to the United States in October 1886, Herbert became a cello soloist at the Metropolitan Opera House. He also played in the symphony orchestras of Anton Seidl and Theodore Thomas. He soon graduated to conductor, first with the 22nd National Guard Band, and from 1898 to 1904 he conducted the Pittsburgh Symphony. In 1898, he performed his own work, the Concerto No. 2 for Cello and Orchestra, Op. 30, with the New York Philharmonic.

Herbert wrote 44 complete scores for the stage. In addition, he composed two operas, *Natoma* in 1911 and *Madeleine* in 1913. They were not successful, although their music has won greater appreciation today. Herbert wrote many orchestral works, including "A Suite of Serenades" written for the Paul Whiteman Aeolian Hall concert, at which George Gershwin's *(q.v.)* "Rhapsody in Blue" also appeared.

Herbert was a portly figure known for his generosity, business sense, appreciation of fine food and drink and love for Ireland. His 1892 work "Irish Rhapsody" contains some of his most heartfelt melodies. He was also a staunch supporter of composer's rights. His suit against Shanley's Restaurant set the stage for the establishment of ASCAP.

In 1894, he was commissioned by The Bostonians to compose the score for the operetta *Prince Ananias.* This group was founded in 1879 as the Boston Ideal Opera Company to present Gilbert and Sullivan operettas.

After its success, the composer collaborated with Harry B. Smith *(q.v.)* on the great hit, *The Wizard of the Nile.* Herbert would write 13 scores with Harry B. Smith, who matched Herbert's prolificacy but not his talent. Many critics felt that Herbert never had a collaborator worthy of his talents. Although many of his

Victor Herbert Courtesy ASCAP.

of childhood to those who are facing the stern realities of life.'' Those words are just as true today as when they were written.

Herbert followed the triumph of *Babes in Toyland* with *Babette* (11/16/03; 59 performances) written with Harry B. Smith. A critic for the *Evening Post* rejoiced over Herbert's work:

Mr. Herbert is, like Johann Strauss, a high-class musician, who can adapt his style to popular taste without ever becoming vulgar; and underlying his pretty tunes there are orchestra touches which rejoice the heart of lovers of the best in music. Some of the choruses, too, are excellent; but the gem of the whole score is a quartet in the last act which got two encores and deserved a hundred. There is nothing more admirable in the whole range of operatic concerted music, and it deserves to become as famous as the quartet in "Rigoletto," to which, in fact, it is far superior.

MacDonough and Herbert's next show was *It Happened in Nordland* (12/5/04; 154 performances). During the run, Blanche Ring assumed the role usually played by Marie Cahill. Miss Cahill's temperamental replacement proved just as high strung. Blanche Ring, insulted by Lew Fields (*q.v.*), the star of the show, walked out without warning and with her costumes. A minor player who knew the role took over the part on October 16, 1905, saved the show and established herself as a top Broadway star. Her name was Pauline Frederick,

scores are famous today, their libretti and lyrics are dated or second-rate.

The Wizard of the Nile was followed by a dazzling succession of operettas that featured lush melodies, stirring ballads and delightful character songs. In 1896, Herbert premiered *The Gold Bug* with lyrics by Glen MacDonough. The next year, two shows written with Harry B. Smith premiered—*The Serenade* and *The Idol's Eye*. In 1898, Herbert and Smith presented *The Fortune Teller*. The following year, three Herbert shows made their debut: *Cyrano de Bergerac* (Smith); *The Singing Girl* (Smith) and *The Ameer* (Frederic Rankin and Kirke La Shelle).

In 1900, Herbert and Smith's *The Viceroy* opened (4/9/00; 28 performances). The first of his masterpieces opened three years later—*Babes in Toyland* (10/13/03; 192 performances), with book and lyrics by Glen MacDonough, remains a favorite more than 80 years after its opening. The songs "March of the Toys," "Toyland" and "I Can't Do That Sum" are still played in pops concerts and occasional revivals. The *Dramatic Mirror* predicted, "It will prove a perfect dream of delight to the children, and will recall the happy days

Glen MacDonough Courtesy ASCAP.

and she became one of the great Broadway actresses of her time. Ironically, after the run of *It Happened in Nordland,* she lost her singing voice and never again appeared in a musical.

Miss Dolly Dollars (9/4/05; 72 performances) with words by Smith, had a number with an enduring title, "A Woman Is Only a Woman But A Good Cigar Is A Smoke." Though Kipling originated the phrase, it entered the language through the popularity of the song.

In the same year were the premieres of *Wonderland* (10/24/5; 73 performances), written with Glen Mac-Donough, and one of the composer's greatest successes, *Mlle. Modiste* (12/25/05; 202 performances). The latter opened with Fritzi Scheff in the lead. Also in the cast in a chorus role was movie pioneer, Mack Sennett. *Mlle. Modiste* contained two of Herbert's great classics, "Kiss Me Again" and the rousing, "I Want What I Want When I Want It." Henry Blossom supplied the words to that score and to Herbert's next great hit, *The Red Mill.*

The Red Mill (9/24/06; 274 performances) contained four Herbert standards, "When You're Pretty and the World Is Fair," "Moonbeams," "Every Day Is Ladies' Day with Me" and "The Streets of New York." Largely because of its four hit songs, the show is still revived today. Three months after the opening of *The Red Mill,* Herbert and Edgar Smith saw their *Dream City and the Magic Knight* open on Broadway. The show had a plot that was ridiculous even for the time. A program note described the somewhat unusual plot:

> Elsa and her brother Godfrey have been left orphans under the guardianship of their uncle and aunt, Frederick and Ortrud, and the latter conspire to defraud them of their estates.
>
> The brother has disappeared, and Elsa is accused before the King of having made away with little Godfrey, and is about to be condemned when, as a last resource, she demands to have the herald ask for some knight errant to appear and champion her cause against her uncle.
>
> Lohengrin appears, sailing down the river in a boat drawn by a swan, and in answer to Elsa's appeal, fights and defeats Frederick, whereupon Ortrud confesses that she used her magic arts to change little Godfrey into a swan, and Lohengrin, being something of a magician himself, changes him back again and returns to Fairyland.
>
> If the audience will listen intently it is possible that the shade of Richard Wagner may be heard to turn over.

Herbert's sole 1907 offering, *The Tattooed Man* (2/18/07; 59 performances) was a minor effort by the composer and Harry B. Smith. *Algeria* (8/31/08; 48 performances), written with Glen MacDonough fared little better. *Little Nemo* (10/20/08; 111 performances), based on the comic strip *Little Nemo in Slumberland* by Windsor McKay, was an elaborate fantasy. *Little Nemo* was notable in one respect: It was among the most expensive musicals ever mounted on Broadway. The average Broadway musical in that period cost between $20,000 and $30,000. Those were the preunion days when dollars bought more. Producers Klaw and Erlanger (*q.v.*) spent an astounding $60,000 on *Little Nemo.*

The Prima Donna (11/30/08; 72 performances) was written with Henry Blossom. The program of the Fritzi Scheff vehicle carried a brief statement by producer Charles Dillingham—"Made in America." The producer meant to imply that the current spate of foreign operettas didn't come up to the standards of the home grown product.

Old Dutch (11/22/09; 88 performances) was written in collaboration with George V. Hobart. The show starred Lew Fields (*q.v.*), Vernon Castle (*q.v.*), John Bunny, Ada Lewis and Alice Dovey but is best remembered today for marking the Broadway debut of the girl who played Little Mime—Helen Hayes (*q.v.*).

In 1910, another Herbert classic premiered—*Naughty Marietta* (11/7/10; 136 performances). Herbert wrote the show with Rida Johnson Young. Together they came up with what some consider Herbert's finest score. Among the songs were the hits, "Tramp!, Tramp! Tramp!," " 'Neath the Southern Moon," "Italian Street Song," "I'm Falling in Love with Someone" and "Ah! Sweet Mystery of Life."

The show was produced by Oscar Hammerstein I (*q.v.*) under the direction of his son Arthur (*q.v.*). The popularity of *Naughty Marietta* is indicated by its financial success. The show had a $2 top ticket price. Yet it averaged $20,000 a week. The property was revived twice on Broadway and was even presented in 1964 in the Dutch Coffee House of the Astor Hotel (*q.v.*). It has also been presented thousands of times in summer theaters and stock companies throughout the world. Metro-Goldwyn-Mayer filmed it with great success in 1935; Jeanette MacDonald and Nelson Eddy starred.

Herbert followed the triumph of *Naughty Marietta* with the minor effort, *When Sweet Sixteen* (9/14/11; 12 performances), in collaboration with George V. Hobart. The composer next attempted two grand opera productions. They were nowhere near as successful as his operettas.

Herbert returned to the Broadway stage with a Shubert Brothers (*q.v.*) production, *The Duchess* (10/16/11; 24 performances). The lyrics were by Joseph W. Herbert and Harry B. Smith. Smith worked on Herbert's next show, *The Enchantress* (10/19/11; 72 performances). It was, remarkably, Herbert's third show to open in a little more than a month. The librettist, listed as Fred de Gresac, was actually Mme. Victor Maurel, the wife of a famous French baritone. *The Enchantress* starred the English actress Kitty Gordon, whose primary attribute was her beautiful back. She was talented enough, however, to carry off the title role.

During the run of *The Enchantress,* Herbert wrote of the need for an American school of light-opera composition. It may come as a surprise to modern students of the musical to note that Herbert, whose work was associated with the European tradition of operetta, knew that the musical would have to evolve and that part of that evolution would be the increasing importance of American music styles. He wrote: "We need an American School of Music in order to give our young composers a chance to develop and drive out the quacks. Our young composers are too prone to get their ideas from the old world, and their work naturally will fall into the style of foreign composition. They do not get into their music that freshness and vitality so characteristic of this country. And yet on the other hand American musical taste has developed to a point where it demands something that is native. I believe that one reason why 'The Enchantress' has had so huge a success in New York, and wherever it has played, is that I determined, when I started its composition, to disregard absolutely every foreign impulse and to write in a frank, free American style." In fact, Herbert's successor, Jerome Kern (q.v.), successfully adapted an American style to musical comedy.

The Lady of the Slipper (10/28/12; 232 performances) boasted a star-studded cast that included Vernon Castle, Elsie Janis, Montgomery and Stone and Peggy Wood. James O'Dea supplied the lyrics. According to local wags, producer Charles Dillingham was stuck on the idea for a new show. He then remembered producer Charles Frohman's byword—"When in doubt, do Cinderella."

Sweethearts (9/8/13; 136 performances) was another of Herbert's shows with a celebrated score. It had lyrics by Robert B. Smith and book by Harry B. Smith and Fred de Gresac. Two songs were standouts, "Sweethearts" and "Every Lover Must Meet His Fate." Surprisingly, a later Broadway revival that opened on January 21, 1947, surpassed the run of the original. The Bobby Clark vehicle ran 288 performances.

The Madcap Duchess (11/11/13; 71 performances) had book and lyrics by Justin Henry McCarthy and David Stevens. McCarthy was best known for his novel *If I Were King*. It later became the source of *The Vagabond King*. *The Madcap Duchess* wasn't quite as successful, but the reviews were quite positive.

The Only Girl (11/2/14; 240 performances) was "a musical farcical comedy." It had one somewhat popular song, "When You're Away." When the musical was revived in 1934, Robert Benchley, writing in *The New Yorker,* put his finger on the problem with reviving Herbert shows. "The Herbert music is, of course, perennially lovely, but those Henry Blossom librettos need a cold winter's night and an attendant air of excitement in the theatrical district to make them bearable. Even in its heyday, the book to 'The Only Girl' was not so hot, and in the not-so-very-merry month of May, 1934, you could go clamming in it."

Herbert's *The Debutante* (12/7/14; 48 performances), had Robert B. Smith lyrics. The day after its opening, *Watch Your Step* opened with Irving Berlin's (q.v.) jazzy score and pointed the way to the future of the American musical theater. As time went on, more and more shows were written in the newer musical styles, and Herbert was soon considered an old-fashioned composer. Ironically, just what Herbert proposed must happen to the American musical did happen, and the popular acceptance of the new-style American musical made his work less popular. Still, at the time, Herbert was considered America's greatest composer.

Henry Blossom penned the book and lyrics for Herbert's next venture, *The Princess Pat* (9/29/15; 158 performances), which was a success. The song that has lasted the longest is the "Neopolitan Love Song," a favorite of sopranos since its introduction.

Herbert's next show featured both the musical theater's past, represented by Herbert, and its future, represented by Berlin. Both composers created the score for the revue, *The Century Girl* (11/6/16; 200 performances). Blossom supplied Herbert's lyrics. The show was the idea of the great producers Charles Dillingham and Florenz Ziegfeld (q.v.). With Ziegfeld at the helm, it was inevitable that the show would be a lavish extravaganza. In one scene entitled "The Music Lesson," both Herbert and Berlin were portrayed on stage. Herbert's hit "Kiss Me Again" was played for the scene, and Berlin wrote a counter melody to the tune.

Blossom also wrote Herbert's next show, *Eileen* (3/19/17; 64 performances), with the great Herbert song, "Thine Alone." Ziegfeld tapped Herbert's talents for another revue, the legendary *Miss 1917* (11/5/17; 40 performances). The show opened without a chance of making back Ziegfeld's investment. Although it played to sold-out houses with a cast featuring Elizabeth Brice, Marion Davies, Lew Fields, Bessie McCoy, Vivienne Segal, Ann Pennington, Savoy and Brennan, Van and Schenck and George White (q.v.), the show lost money due to its huge weekly operating expenses. The revue had a few Herbert songs, but the majority of the score was written by Jerome Kern, whose star was rising as fast as that of Irving Berlin. As Kern and Berlin had greater and greater successes, Herbert found his shows increasingly less popular.

Her Regiment (11/12/17; 40 performances) had book and lyrics by William Le Baron. Ziegfeld hired Herbert to compose a few numbers for the *Ziegfeld Follies of 1917 (q.v.)* (6/12/17). His next operetta, *The Velvet Lady* (2/3/19; 136 performances), again featured Blossom's words. *Angel Face* (12/29/19; 57 performances), with Robert B. Smith lyrics, introduced an enduring standard, "I Might Be Your Once-in-a-While."

My Golden Girl (2/2/20; 105 performances) had book and lyrics by Frederic Arnold Kummer. It contained one interesting number, "Ragtime Terpischore," in which Herbert attempted to write in the jazz idiom. However, the show was still basically a romantic operetta. Herbert next composed a few numbers for the *Ziegfeld Follies of 1920*. His next operetta, *The Girl in the Spotlight* (7/12/20; 54 performances), teamed him with Robert B. Smith.

Herbert's fortunes fell even further with his next show *Oui Madame*. It was his last collaboration with Robert B. Smith and closed out of town in 1920. The composer's output then slowed even further. He contributed to the *Ziegfeld Follies of 1921* and *1922*.

His next to last show, *Orange Blossoms* (9/19/22; 95 performances) had lyrics by B.G. DeSylva (*q.v.*) and a book by Fred de Gresac. Herbert proved that although his output had slowed he still had much to offer and could still write a superior score. For *Orange Blossoms*, Herbert wrote a beautiful song, "A Kiss in the Dark."

He completed his usual assignment for the *Ziegfeld Follies* and followed it with a concert work, "Suite of Serenades," commissioned by Paul Whiteman for his famous Aeolian Hall concert. The Suite was a major success and reemphasized Herbert's preeminence in American music.

For the composer's final operetta, *The Dream Girl* (8/20/24; 118 performances), Rida Johnson Young supplied the lyrics and collaborated on the book with Harold Atteridge. Sigmund Romberg (*q.v.*), another top operetta composer, also composed songs for the score. The Shubert production wasn't quite up to Herbert's usual standard but was a great public success. Herbert's last Broadway assignment was for the 1924 edition of the *Ziegfeld Follies*. He composed three instrumental numbers for the revue. After Herbert's death, Ziegfeld interpolated a medley of Herbert's greatest songs.

As a newspaper gimmick, columnist S. Jay Kaufman published in the *Evening Telegram* an article presenting the winner of an informal poll on who was America's greatest composer. Herbert won handily.

Victor Herbert died on May 26, 1924. On May 28, 1924, the *New York World* published a reflection on Victor Herbert's life by noted musicologist Deems Taylor:

> Losing Victor Herbert, the musical world loses someone it will never quite replace. He was the last of the troubadours. His musical ancestor was Mozart and the family of which he was so brilliant a younger son numbered Offenbach, Delibes, Bizet, the Strausses and Arthur Sullivan among its elders.
>
> What he had was what they all had, the gift of song. His music bubbled and sparkled and charmed, and he brought the precious gift of gayety to an art that so often suffers from the pretentiousness and self-consciousness of its practitioners.
>
> The thirty years of his too short career have left us two grand operas and over forty operettas and musical comedies, all distinguished by an unending flow of melodic invention, harmonic and rhythmic individuality and brilliant instrumentation.
>
> Above all he had perfect taste. Herbert's music could be trivial at times but he never wrote a vulgar line in his life. Now that he is gone there is no one left who has quite his combination of effortless spontaneity and endearing light heartedness.
>
> He is not dead, of course. The composer of "Babes in Toyland," "The Fortune Teller," "The Red Mill," "Nordland" and "Mlle. Modiste" cannot be held as dead by a world so heavily in his debt.

HERMAN, JERRY (1932–   ) Jerry Herman is certainly the best-known musical-comedy writer currently working on the Broadway stage and may be the only contemporary Broadway tunesmith whose name is recognized by the general public, with the possible exception of Andrew Lloyd Webber. Surprisingly, this fame is due to the success of only three shows—*Hello, Dolly!, Mame* and *La Cage Aux Folles*.

Herman's works are hallmarked by smart, sophisticated women, whose characters drive them to sing a rousing, optimistic number before the curtain falls. His work defines what most people think of when asked to describe the Broadway musical. His shows are glitzy, upbeat extravaganzas, long on energy and catchy tunes that the audience is sure to hum while leaving the theater.

Herman was born on July 10, 1932, in New York City. He was educated at the University of Miami and Parsons School of Design. His first score was for *I Feel Wonderful* (10/18/54), a college revue that moved to off-Broadway. Herman followed with another revue, *Nightcap* (5/18/58), which enjoyed a 400-performance run in the Showplace night club, off-Broadway. Another off-Broadway show, *Parade*, followed in January 1960.

The modest success that Herman had thus far enjoyed certainly didn't portend the enormous successes of his Broadway book shows. The first was *Milk and Honey* (10/10/61). Molly Picon, Robert Weede and Mimi Benzell starred in the show set in Israel. *Milk and Honey* ran for 543 performances, a long run by Broadway standards, yet the young songwriter didn't receive much notice, because most critics attributed the show's success to the large Jewish audience for Broadway musicals.

His next show, *Madame Aphrodite* (12/29/61), played only 13 performances off-Broadway. Two years later, Herman would have his biggest success when David Merrick (*q.v.*) hired him to write the score to Michael Stewart's musicalization of Thornton Wilder's *The Matchmaker*. The show was *Hello, Dolly!*, and this time Herman was definitely considered a major talent.

Hello, Dolly! opened on January 16, 1964, with Carol Channing in the lead. It became one of the most successful musicals in Broadway history, achieving 2,844

Jerry Herman Courtesy ASCAP.

performances. After it passed the record number of performances held by *My Fair Lady*, *Hello, Dolly!* was for a time the longest-running show in Broadway history. It was shortly thereafter overtaken by *Fiddler on the Roof*, which opened nine months after *Hello, Dolly!*

Herman's next show proved almost as popular as *Hello, Dolly! Mame* opened on May 24, 1966, with Angela Lansbury portraying Patrick Dennis's zany character. *Mame* contained another first-rate score by Herman. Most popular were the title tune and "It's Today." Other songs that received notice were "If He Walked Into My Life" and "Open a New Window." *Mame* also gave a boost to the careers of Lansbury's costars, Beatrice Arthur and Jane Connell. It played a total of 1,508 performances on Broadway.

Lansbury, Herman and *Mame* librettists Lawrence and Lee teamed up again for *Dear World* (2/6/69), a musical version of Jean Giradoux's *The Madwoman of Chaillot*. The show did not repeat the success of *Mame* and lasted only 132 performances.

Mack and Mabel (10/6/74) followed and, despite having what some fans consider Herman's most mature score as well as the contributions of Bernadette Peters and Robert Preston, the show played only 65 performances. Although the failure of the show meant that few people were exposed to the score, two songs, "I Won't Send Roses" and "Time Heals Everything," have achieved minor success. Herman's next show per-

formed slightly worse than even *Mack and Mabel*. *The Grand Tour* (1/11/79) starred Joel Grey in an unsuccessful musicalization of S.N. Behrman's play *Jacobowsky and the Colonel*. Missing were the typical Herman ingredients for success—a strong female leading role and a rousing closing number.

With three failures in a row, critics proclaimed Jerry Herman's career finished. Skeptics pointed to the success of *Hello, Dolly!* and *Mame* as flukes and suggested that Herman's style wasn't suited to the supposedly more-sophisticated Broadway of the eighties.

But on August 21, 1983, Herman surprised Broadway with *La Cage Aux Folles*, a huge hit in the style of his previous extravaganzas. George Hearn and Gene Barry played homosexual lovers in the adaptation of the French screen hit. The most popular of the songs, "I Am What I Am," even had the rare distinction of hitting the charts in a disco version.

La Cage was a huge hit with all the Broadway pizzazz and slick professionalism associated with Herman's name.

Formerly blase Broadwayites took notice when *La Cage Aux Folles* was nominated for a Tony Award for best musical *(q.v.)*, competing against Stephen Sondheim's *(q.v.) Sunday in the Park with George*. Herman's success and the relative failure of the shows of Stephen Sondheim polarized theatergoers. Although both men were respected for their skills, they represented opposite ends of the musical-comedy spectrum. Herman's jubilant, melodic scores and cotton-candy productions contrast sharply with Sondheim's dark, intricate music featured in shows long on concept.

Certainly, Jerry Herman's fans are perfectly happy with the light, breezy tone set by his hit shows. Others, however, may hope that someday he'll match the richness of the score of *Milk and Honey* with the drama of *Mack and Mabel* for a truly great Jerry Herman musical.

HEWES, HENRY See CRITICS.

HIGH SCHOOL OF PERFORMING ARTS 120 W. 46th Street. Architect: Charles B. J. Snyder. The Romanesque-revival building was designed in 1893 as P.S. 67. Charles B. J. Snyder, the Superintendent of Buildings for the New York City Board of Education, made sure the building was the most up-to-date at the time. It had improved ventilation and fire protection, unilateral lighting and small, intimate classrooms.

The school was best known as the School of Performing Arts, or P.A., as it was nicknamed. In 1937, Dr. Franklin Keller, principal of the Metropolitan Vocational High School, found some boys skipping classes to rehearse with a band in the boiler room. Dr. Keller was quoted as saying, "I thought if we gave them music, they wouldn't have to sneak in." So New York City began the High School of Performing Arts.

Thousands of students passed extremely difficult auditions to gain entry to the school's programs. Among the most famous alumni are Liza Minnelli, Barbra Streisand, Ben Vereen, Al Pacino, Melissa Manchester and Suzanne Pleshette. The school was featured as the background for the movie and subsequent television series, *Fame*.

The school's programs were transferred to 108 Amsterdam Avenue, across from Lincoln Center, in 1985. The 46th Street building was then dubbed Liberty High School and was devoted to classes for immigrants learning English. In February 1988, the school suffered a five-alarm fire that destroyed the roof and most of the interior.

HIPPODROME Sixth Avenue between 43rd and 44th Street. Architect: J.H. Morgan. Opening: April 12, 1905; *A Yankee Circus on Mars.* For most Broadwayites, the Hippodrome is synonymous with spectacle just as the Roxy *(q.v.)* connotes lavishness. The theater, the largest in the world, certainly lived up to its reputation. It presented the biggest shows ever seen in New York or anywhere else.

The Hippodrome was the brainchild of Elmer S. Dundy and Frederic Thompson, the builders and operators of Coney Island's Luna Park. Their backer, John W. Bates, urged the team to conquer Broadway at his expense. They set to work to build the biggest and most sophisticated theater of its time.

The Hippodrome   Courtesy Vicki Gold Levi.

Thompson envisioned a stage big enough to hold 600 people. It was 110 feet deep and 200 feet wide and was divided into 12 sections. Each section could be raised or lowered by hydraulics. The Hippodrome also had a huge tank that could hold a lake big enough to float boats in or take the spill from a huge waterfall. The water pumps could handle 150,000 gallons of water. Because of the huge machinery required to run these devices, the stage weighed 460,000 pounds.

The roof and balcony of the building used 15,000 tons of steel. The roof itself was constructed from four giant steel trusses, the largest in any American building. The skeleton of the building was covered by 6,000 bricks.

A typical Hippodrome extravaganza   Courtesy Billy Rose Theater Collection.

One of the most important elements of the Hippodrome's design was the lighting system. Over 25,000 light bulbs were used to illuminate the theater and stage. Nine thousand of these were used for the stage, and another 5,000 were arranged in a stunning sunburst pattern in the auditorium.

Under the stage was a complete menagerie area where the famous Hippodrome elephants were kept. The theater also had a full complement of offices, costume shops, property houses and scenery shops. The elaborate scenery itself was changed by a unique system of cranes that would carry the equipment up to the fly area high above the stage.

The Hippodrome and its shows were a publicist's dream. On March 12, 1905, a month before it opened, the theater received its first great publicity coup when Police Commissioner William McAdoo had the building surrounded by 100 police officers. They were sent because of a complaint by the Sabbath Association that construction workers were putting in long hours on Sunday. Since construction had started in July 1904, almost a year earlier, it seems strange that action was taken only then. Nonetheless, when the next shift of workers showed up, they were stopped by the police. Thompson and Dundy took matters in hand, giving each of the workers a card that invited him into the theater as a sightseer. The police were powerless to stop the men from entering as guests of the management. After they had entered the auditorium, they were instructed to put material over the windows so that the police couldn't see what was happening inside.

The excitement rose as the building neared completion. Thompson and Dundy walked their menagerie to Manhattan all the way from Luna Park. A herd of elephants led the parade followed by camels, 175 horses and even a team of bloodhounds. They marched, on foot and in vans, over the Brooklyn Bridge, up Broadway and across 42nd Street to the theater.

By opening night, the stage was set for what was certainly the largest opening in theater history, one that had cost $4 million. On April 12, 1905, the theater was ready for opening. The ticket prices ranged from 25¢ for the cheapest seats to $2 for the boxes. The theater seated 5,200 patrons. The *New York Clipper* described the theater as "remarkable for its grandeur and magnitude, a place of magnificent distances."

The opening show was *A Yankee Circus on Mars*. The play was written by George V. Hobart. Jean Schwartz, along with Manuel Klein composed the music. They, along with Harry Williams, contributed the lyrics. The settings were designed by the brilliant Arthur Voegtlin, who created most of the great special effects that helped make the Hippodrome's fame.

The star was one of Broadway's favorite actresses, Bessie McCoy, who made her entrance in a gold chariot driven by two white horses. A 30-foot airship landed on the stage and disgorged a Martian who asked the Americans to bring a circus to his planet. At one point in the proceedings, the Barlow's Magnificent Hippodrome Elephants appeared behind the steering wheels of autos. The pachyderms drove 10 chorus girls around the Hippodrome's huge stage. The show also featured 280 chorus girls.

Apart from the Hippodrome elephants, the only other regular star of Hippodrome shows was Marceline the Spanish clown. He appeared in every Hippodrome show for a decade. Marceline became as big an attraction as the Hippodrome itself. Gretchen Finletter wrote in her autobiography, *From the Top of the Stairs*, about Marceline's pranks on stage:

> When the men appeared to set up the ring, Marceline pulled each peg out as it was hammered down and ran ahead with it to the man in front . . . The men never caught on and they would have to set up the ring three times. When the carpet was unrolled for the ponies, Marceline rolled it up again just before the ponies appeared. Marceline pulled a net out from under the highest trapeze artist as he was preparing to drop down, and folded it neatly away, thinking the act was over.
>
> The manager appeared in a red coat and high hat and protested in a loud voice. He gesticulated, he pointed up at the trapeze. Did Marceline understand! This was the Dip Of Death! He must leave the net alone! Marceline looked at the manager's gestures, pointed at the figure above, pointed at himself, shook his head, then nodded and smiled. Yes, he understood.
>
> The drums rolled again. The Dip Artist started swinging and then at the very moment he was about to plunge. Marceline jumped forward, pulled at a rope, and net and all fell on the manager in a wild tangle, knocking him over, while the trapezist by a lucky chance caught another swing.

The *Yankee Circus* was only the first part of the opening night program. Next came the *Dance of the Hours*, which featured 150 dancing girls. That piece was in turn followed by *Andersonville, or A Story of Wilson's Raiders*. This spectacular pageant traces the story of a Union officer and a Southern belle. The first scene takes place during a West Point ball. Then we are whisked to the Andersonville prison. Our hero digs a tunnel out of the prison but is spotted by the guards. They chase him to a Southern mansion. Inside, the heroine gives the soldier a horse, and he gallops away with bloodhounds in hot pursuit. The scene then changes to Rocky Ford Bridge over what appeared to the audience to be a real lake. Four hundred and eighty soldiers meet at the bridge and fight to the death. A team of horses pulling a caisson charges across the stage while the soldiers fight on the bridge and in the water. After the battle, the scene changes to the McLean House at Appomattox. The Civil War ends as the hero is united with the heroine.

The *Clipper* called the evening, "probably the most

unique and remarkable entertainment ever seen in New York." The *Evening World* exclaimed, "Even our skyscrapers will have to bow to it." The rest of the reviews all agreed that the Hippodrome show was the greatest seen on any stage. *A Yankee Circus on Mars* played for 120 performances. The run was long by the standards of the day and even more remarkable when one considers the number of patrons that the theater held.

Thompson and Dundy realized that their next offering would have to surpass the premiere attraction. They decided to mount another show with a circus theme. *A Society Circus* (12/13/05) was indeed bigger and better than the previous show. The spectacular presentation lasted four hours. Sydney Rosenfeld wrote the book and Manuel Klein wrote the lyrics. Its many elaborate set pieces included a gypsy camp complete with a gypsy wedding, a circus featuring the famous elephants, this time bowling, a ballet of lions and monkeys, a thunderstorm, the elephants performing as a marching band, *The Song of the Flowers* with 144 ballerinas and, finally, a stupendous wedding ceremony around the Hippodrome pool, which was dotted with fountains and colored lights.

The reviewers were ecstatic. The *Evening Telegram* raved "Six thousand blase New Yorkers sat from eight o'clock until nearly midnight, and then got up and cheered. Could anything more be said to show just what this new spectacle is? In every way it is the biggest and best thing of its kind ever presented in America."

Despite the rave reviews, audiences were strangely unsatisfied with the show. True, it was bigger than *A Yankee Circus on Mars,* but it was not substantially different. With business falling off, Thompson and Dundy were in trouble. They simply couldn't afford to keep the theater open without a sizable audience.

The July 1906 issue of the *Theater Magazine* reported the current state of the Hippodrome.

> The announcement that Messrs. Thompson and Dundy had retired from the management of the New York Hippodrome came as a surprise to everyone, for it was generally believed that the enterprise had proved a veritable gold mine to its founders. The truth, however, was that the receipts fell off considerably this last season, and with a concern of that magnitude, when enough money does not come in at the front door to furnish the avalanche of dollars that goes out the back door, the situation soon becomes critical. One reason given for the decreased patronage was that the prices of the seats had been advanced against the judgment of Messrs. Thompson and Dundy. A more likely reason is that the novelty of the place had worn off and that its further popularity had to depend solely on the character of the entertainment provided. The show given this last season was not nearly so good . . . We said that the splendid auditorium and vast stage of the Hippodrome presented magnificent opportunities which were not taken full advantage of. An enormous amount of money was spent

on the stage for costumes, scenery, and performers, but it was not well spent. It was all light and tinsel; there was not art in it. The ballets were poor and the gipsy camp, made a star feature of the last bill, was positively tiresome. Give a good show at moderate prices, and there will be no trouble about crowding the Hippodrome.

The only producers with enough nerve to take over the Hippodrome were the Shubert brothers *(q.v.).* They reopened a fixed-up version of *A Society Circus* on September 2, 1906, and made a popular success of the show. It ended up running 596 performances with a reduced top price of $1.50.

The next show, *Pioneer Days and Neptune's Daughter* (11/28/06), amassed an astonishing $91,000 advance at the box office. The first half of the evening's bill was a Wild West story of bad guys, good guys and Indians. Everyone was fighting each other, and stagecoaches were forever running in and out. The end of the show was a climactic battle between the Indians, the settlers and the Cavalry. Over 600 performers took part in the melee.

The second act, *Neptune's Daughter,* featured a violent storm complete with huge waves and lightning flashes. A ship capsized, and only one passenger survived—a baby. He grew up and prayed to the gods of the sea. Then, as if by magic, Neptune himself, surrounded by mermaids, appeared from the waters of the tank. The audience was thrilled. How could he have risen from the sea? The show began an hour before, surely no one could hold his breath that long. So how did he do it?

During the finale a troupe of mermaids and mermen, accompanied by sea horses, walked down a broad flight of steps that led into the pool. Down they went into the pool never to be seen again. They simply disappeared into the waters.

The audience was astonished at the trick. Word got around the city of the marvelous finale to the Hippodrome show. It swelled the box office to $60,000 a week. Considering the Shuberts needed only one-tenth that amount to break even, the show was a great success.

The water-tank trick remained a mystery for years, although reports of how it worked sometimes leaked out to the press. However, Will Page, Shubert publicist, knew he had to keep beating the drums to keep the huge theater full. He devised a series of stunts *(q.v.)* that kept the Hippodrome in the public eye.

He arranged for a carriage to be drawn through the streets by an ostrich. Alongside ran a dog with a sweater that had *Hippodrome* on it. Page took the Hippodrome's Sioux tribe, which appeared in the show, around the city in an open truck. He also arranged, in the winter, for a team of elephants to draw a sleigh through the streets. Little Hip, the baby elephant mascot of the Hippodrome, was on view daily in the theater's lobby, where he would nuzzle children and hand out flyers.

Page's gimmicks worked, and *Pioneer Days* ran 288 performances.

Next came *The Auto Race* (11/25/07; 312 performances). It also had on the bill *The Battle of Port Arthur* and *Circus Days*. The names described what occurred on stage. Drama critic and playwright George Oppenheimer remembered his experience as a child watching *The Battle of Port Arthur:* "At the first bombardment— I was ultra-gun-shy—my screams of childish fright mingled with the groans of the wounded, adding to the din but not to the realism. My parents hastily removed me from the scene of battle to the relative peace of Sixth Avenue. It was not peaceful for long. My fear of the shell and shot was as nothing compared to my rage at having been removed from them."

The next Hippodrome show, *Sporting Days* (9/5/08), was accompanied by *The Land of Birds Ballet* and *Battle of the Skies. Sporting Days* featured a depiction of a real baseball game on what was surely the only indoor stage large enough. It also featured a rowing match on the Hippodrome's pool, which stood in for the Hudson River, and a horse race. For *The Land of Birds Ballet,* 400 dancers enacted beautiful avian delights.

But it was the *Battle of the Skies* that most captured the audience's attention. It portrayed a huge battle over the streets of New York in the far away year of 1950. Above the roofs of the great metropolis slid graceful monorails. The roofs served as landing docks for giant blimps. Between the buildings, high over the streets were walkways. Across them marched small children dressed as adults. Their size helped sustain the illusion in the forced perspective of the scene. In the window of a newspaper office was a giant screen on which flashed pictures of the latest news events with commentary by a megaphone-wielding announcer. In a museum stood the last living horse in the world.

But all was not well in the future. A group of spies planned to steal America's radium gun. The spies carried flashlight-sized guns that emitted beams of light that disintegrated people in a puff of smoke. The second act was a full-scale war between hundreds of balloons and blimps. Some were equipped with the radium gun.

Cleaning the Hippodrome stage

Its deadly light beam spared neither man nor machine. A great storm broke out, full of thunder and lightning, and from the Hippodrome's tank came two submarines. One was sunk by the radium gun. On the other was the heroine. When her craft was hit also, it began to submerge. She climbed to the tower of the great ship just in time to see a balloon coming to her rescue. A line was dropped, and as her submarine slipped beneath the waves, she was hoisted into the air. Behind her, also on the rope ladder, came the villain. She climbed the swaying rope and reached the airship's perch just in time. The ladder was cut loose and the villain fell into the sea. This battle was fought twice a day for 448 performances.

A Trip to Japan (9/4/09) was next. Along with the title show was *Inside the Earth* and *The Ballet of Jewels*. The climax of the opening melodrama was a fire atop a tall building. Luckily, the hero was also a tightrope walker. To save his girlfriend, he walked across telephone wires. Another highlight of the first act was the stunt performed by Desperado. He jumped off a high platform through 40 feet of air and then hit a giant slide, which deposited him on his feet on the stage floor.

Inside the Earth actually featured an entire tribe of Maori natives who played a tribe of Incas who lived in a cave in New Zealand. The heroine was kidnapped to an island in the center of the Hippodrome's great pool. The island sank with its inhabitants, and the heroine sank beneath the waters. Despite the spectacular effects, the show was not a critical success. However audiences kept it open for 447 performances.

The International Cup (9/3/10; 333 performances) was accompanied by *The Ballet of Niagara* and *The Earthquake*. *The International Cup* had planes landing on the Hippodrome's stage. Its exciting finale featured a shipwreck at sea in a perilous storm. *The Earthquake* took place in a Central American country that contained the fabled Valley of the Moon inhabited by aliens from outer space. Naturally, there was the Earthquake of the title, abetted by the mighty hydraulics beneath the stage. Islands bearing golden moon girls rose from the Hippodrome tank. The reviews were favorable for the melodrama, ballet and special effects of the Hippodrome shows. The *New York Dramatic Mirror* stated, "To see and to enjoy everything requires an able bodied person in prime health. Others will droop before the end."

A topic ripe for the Hippodrome treatment was *Around the World* (9/2/11; 445 performances), paired with *The Ballet of the Butterflies* and *The Fairies Glen* and *The Golden Barge*. The show followed its cast from New York State to the Swiss Alps and a race on the slippery peaks and then to a battle with bedouins on the sands of Egypt. It led to a sandstorm that gave way to the slave markets of Constantinople. A circus was the entertainment at a coronation in India, and then there was a midnight gondola ride in Venice. A runaway bull highlighted the action in Spain, which led, surprisingly, to Hawaii and hula dancers. From Hawaii, the intrepid travelers somehow ended up in Ireland.

Under Many Flags (5/31/12; 445 performances) was the optimistic story of world peace brought about through the invention of a machine of destruction. A man invented a blimp that could travel 200 miles an hour and carry a payload of explosives. Another man stole the airship and traveled around the world with it to Brittany, Holland, Scotland, Arizona and Persia. As a result of the flight, the world's leaders signed the Treaty of Universal Peace.

The next Hippodrome extravaganza, *America* (8/30/13; 360 performances) was followed by a nontypical offering on April 9, 1914, Gilbert and Sullivan's *H.M.S. Pinafore*, which ran 89 performances. *Wars of the Worlds* (9/5/14; 229 performances), the next offering, was described in *Theater Magazine:* "Breathlessly, we are whisked through the centuries as man's struggle against man is depicted in a series of magnificent stage pictures." *Wars of the Worlds* was somewhat topical, since Europe was involved in the beginnings of World War I.

The Shuberts put in the *Mammoth Midwinter Circus Supreme*. It also featured a film, *The Heart of Maryland*, a cartoon, a medley of Southern songs and a dancing-waters ballet. The show wasn't successful, and the Shuberts began to get cold feet. They put in a series of films and vaudeville acts that did little to attract audiences. The Shuberts owed $100,000 in back rental, and the sum was mounting daily.

Following the Shuberts' failures came Charles B. Dillingham, an up-to-date producer of the time, who decided to clean up the Hippodrome and, instead of the customary old-fashioned extravagant melodrama, presented a fast-paced Broadway-style revue. The difference was that the Hippodrome would enable Dillingham to give the show a spectacular production.

Dillingham opened *Hip-Hip-Hooray* (9/30/15; 425 performances) in a newly scrubbed Hippodrome. For the show, he hired Broadway composer Raymond Hubbell and John Golden, a noted lyricist and producer. R.H. Burnside wrote the libretto and directed the proceedings. Bandmaster John Philip Sousa composed a new work, "The New York Hippodrome March." Sousa even appeared in the show along with comic Nat Wills and Toto, a clown who replaced Marceline.

The critics were enthusiastic about the new show. *Theater Magazine* wrote, "The name fits the show. The astonished and delighted spectator feels like cheering all the way through the really wonderful program. A spectacle of marvelous beauty and varied interest, with a host of star performers, tableaux of surpassing splendor, and no end of novel surprises—such a show has never been seen in New York!'' The show heralded a new successful era at the Hippodrome. Dillingham celebrated the theater's success with a huge parade composed of 1,274 performers.

Dillingham next presented *The Big Show* (8/31/16; 425 performances), a lavish revue that created a number of firsts in Hippodrome history. It was the first Hippodrome show to feature a genuine superstar, dancer Anna Pavlova. It was also the first to contain a smash hit song—''Poor Butterfly.''

Between editions of the Hippodrome shows and on its dark nights, Dillingham filled the theater with concerts and benefits. These featured such stars as Pavlova, Paul Whiteman's Orchestra, John McCormack, Carmella Ponselle, Al Jolson *(q.v.)*, DeWolf Hopper, W.C. Fields, Houdini, Weber and Fields, Vernon and Irene Castle *(q.v.)*, Babe Ruth, George M. Cohan *(q.v.)*, Gus Edwards, Amelita Galli-Curci, Feodor Chaliapin, Tito Ruffo, Leon Errol, and Mme. Ernestine Shumann-Heink. Vernon Castle made his last stage appearance at a Hippodrome benefit.

With the war raging in Europe, it seemed appropriate for Dillingham to call his next show *Cheer Up* (8/23/17; 456 performances). The finale of the show was a resplendent version of Coney Island in all its gaudy fame. At the end, The Disappearing Diving Girls dove into the Hippodrome tank and disappeared beneath the waters. The number was constructed around the talents of swimmer Annette Kellerman, who had become a Hippodrome regular after the run of *The Big Show*.

Dillingham's next show was aptly titled *Everything* (8/22/18; 461 performances). This revue had some music and lyrics contributed by Irving Berlin *(q.v.)*. It starred Houdini, DeWolf Hopper and Belle Story.

With America now in World War I and Prohibition about to go into effect, Dillingham had the nerve or optimism to title the next Hippodrome show *Happy Days* (8/23/19; 452 performances). The *New York Dramatic Mirror* said, ''Perhaps it is Mr. Dillingham's little joke.'' The title proved even more ironic when the actors struck the Broadway theaters in the actors' strike of 1919 *(q.v.)*. Dillingham, though sympathetic to the actors, remained a member of The Producing Managers' Association, which opposed Equity. When the Hippodrome's 412 stagehands walked out, Dillingham quit as manager of the Hippodrome. The stagehands went back on the job, and when the strike was settled Dillingham returned to the theater.

With the war over, Dillingham titled his next show *Good Times* (8/9/20; 455 performances). The show featured Abdallah's Arabs, Nanette Flack, The Poodles Hanneford Family of trick horsemen, Joe Jackson, Joseph Parsons and Belle Story.

Get Together (8/3/21) was heavy on ballet. It featured *The Thunder Bird Ballet* by Vera Fokina, directed by Russian choreographer Michel Fokine. There was also an ice ballet based on *The Red Shoes*.

Get Together was followed by *Better Times* (9/2/22). Most critics and the public felt *Better Times* was the best of all the Hippodrome spectaculars. Unfortunately it was also the last. The show ran for 405 performances, after which Charles Dillingham left the theater. Production costs were rising as the theater struggled to maintain a cast of 1,000 people as well as a massive physical plant.

Because the Hippodrome occupied a large chunk of prime property, the site was viewed with interest by a number of real estate developers. The U.S. Realty and Improvement Company owned the theater and its land and tendered offers. But the theater was saved when E.F. Albee *(q.v.)* decided to take it over and present vaudeville in the huge hall.

Albee took out all the complex stage mechanics and replaced the stage with a small wooden platform. The proscenium was brought in to a more manageable size, and the Hippodrome became just another vaudeville theater. The theater reopened on December 17, 1923, with an undistinguished vaudeville bill.

The Hippodrome presented what might be called high-class vaudeville with movies thrown in for good measure. By 1929, vaudeville was all but dead, and so was the Hippodrome. Morris Gest leased the theater to present *The Passion Play* but it closed after five weeks

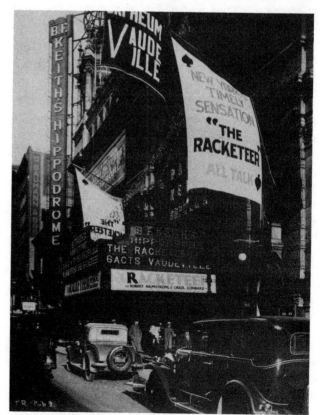

The Hippodrome in its vaudeville incarnation Courtesy Billy Rose Theater Collection.

with a $250,000 loss. In July 1930, the theater was closed tight.

RKO had inherited the theater from Albee. RKO sold it to Frederick Brown, a real estate investor. Brown then sold it to the Fred T. French Operators, Inc. for $7.5 million. The French company announced that they would tear the theater down and construct an 83-story office building on the site.

Unfortunately, the country was in the midst of the Depression, and construction was at a standstill. The Hippodrome sat empty until master showman Billy Rose decided to rent the theater to present a new musical, *Jumbo*.

Rose cleaned up the exterior of the theater and renovated the interior to resemble a huge circus arena. The seating area was altered so that it sloped in one continuous line from the far reaches of the balcony to the stage floor. Albert Johnson designed the new interior as well as the production.

Richard Rodgers *(q.v.)* and Lorenz Hart *(q.v.)* were assigned the task of writing the score for the mammoth show. Rose hired Ben Hecht and Charles MacArthur to script the proceedings. Rose employed Jimmy Durante, Gloria Grafton, Paul Whiteman and his orchestra, Poodles Hanneford, Donald Novis and Arthur Sinclair to head the cast. Then he chose 1,200 animals to appear in the circus setting. The show was so big that it needed two directors, John Murray Anderson *(q.v.)* and George Abbott *(q.v.)*. They whipped the show into shape amid countless delays. MacArthur once quipped that opening night was postponed because there were a few people who hadn't seen the show yet.

Jumbo finally opened on November 16, 1933 (221 performances). The critics were unanimous in their praise. Percy Hammond, in the *New York Herald Tribune*, called the show, "a sane and exciting compound of opera, animal show, folk drama, harlequinade, carnival, circus, extravaganza and spectacle." Gilbert W. Gabriel agreed, writing in the *New York American* that it was, "chockful of so many thrills, musical, scenic, gymnastic and humanitarian, it deserves endowment as an institution." These reviews might have applied equally well to the early Hippodrome extravaganzas. The theater itself also got good notices. Richard Lockridge, writing in the *New York Sun* stated, "It all adds up to a fairly superlative entertainment. This is largely due to what Albert Johnson has done in designing the show and, above all, the theater."

Jumbo was a huge hit but it cost so much to run that it was forced to close. The Hippodrome was closed again. In 1939, it was used briefly as a basketball court. Then in September of that year, crews came and knocked down the theater.

Ironically, development plans for the site continued to fall through. Twelve years passed before the site was finally utilized. In 1952, a garage, appropriately named the Hippodrome Garage, and an office building opened.

HOFFMAN, IRVING (1910–1968) Irving Hoffman, a caricaturist, columnist and inadvertent humorist during the forties and fifties, influenced the careers of many stars and became a confidant of many of the personalities on the Rialto.

Hoffman was born in 1910 in New York City. He dropped out of DeWitt Clinton High School a year before graduation because he found his teachers bores. In 1924, he went to the Democratic National Convention. While there, the industrious 14-year-old made caricatures of the leading lights—William Jennings Bryan, Franklin Delano Roosevelt, Alfred E. Smith and others. He sold the drawings to the *New York Evening World* and thus started his professional career.

One of his trademarks was the incorporation of the subject's initials in the drawing. For George Bernard Shaw the *G* was used to form the nose, the *B* became his mouth and Shaw's beard was defined by a flourished *S*.

The caricatures opened doors for Hoffman, and his offbeat sense of humor ingratiated him to many theatrical personages. Hoffman might not have always meant to be funny. Often the cue for his unexpected quips was his poor eyesight. Hoffman himself was aware of his unintended gaffs. As he remarked about himself in a *New York Times* quote, "I shake all the wrong hands, I offer smokers trays with olives because I think they're ash trays. I put salt on leaves of the table decorations and eat the flowers. The dinner table is lighted by candles, and I don't say a thing. People laugh and say I'm a great wit, but I feel a constricted feeling in the back of my head and wish I were at Lindy's *(q.v.)*."

Hoffman's wit got him into many elegant parties whose guests viewed him with much amusement. He turned the tables somewhat by selling gossip to such friends as columnist Walter Winchell *(q.v.)*, Ed Sullivan *(q.v.)* and Damon Runyon *(q.v.)*.

In fact, Hoffman shared a two-room apartment on West 48th Street with the three columnists. They were happy to have Hoffman as a source of material, and when he didn't come up with a tidbit they could always write about the source himself.

Hoffman was for a time a press agent for Coney Island. It was there that he got the break that propelled his career forward. Franklin D. Roosevelt had invited Queen Elizabeth and King George VI to America, and the royals took a trip to Coney Island. Hoffman arranged to have the celebrities photographed eating a Nathan's hot dog at the resort. The picture ran throughout the world, resulting in free publicity for the beach community and the hot dog company.

In 1936, Hoffman became the drama critic for the

Hollywood Reporter. He also began a column on Broadway life for the paper. Like many of his contemporaries, Hoffman used the pen to deal satirical blows at his subjects. He explained the practice by stating, "Why should I be as dull as the play."

Hoffman's column was entitled, "Tales of Hoffman." In it, he would often promote new personalities and up-and-coming talents. Among these were the young Shirley MacLaine, Lauren Bacall and Judy Garland.

Irving Berlin *(q.v.)* had a fondness for Hoffman and often used him as a sounding board for his newest tunes. Darryl F. Zanuck, head of Twentieth-Century-Fox, also sat in on these tryouts.

Hoffman acted as the go-between when the notorious gangster *(q.v.)* Louis Lepke surrendered to Walter Winchell. In his autobiography, Winchell failed to credit Hoffman's role. Perhaps it was because Hoffman was the only person who could tell Winchell to shut up when Winchell droned on bragging about the incident.

Hoffman not only helped Winchell get scoops but also aided the young columnist develop his style. Hoffman called gossip columnists "the carpet sweepers in the Hall of Fame." But as a publicist, he recognized their power. Hoffman would go so far as to actually make changes in the proofs of Winchell's column.

The clients Hoffman handled as a press agent never got a break in Hoffman's own column. He felt it would be unethical. But the fact that Hoffman had the ear of Winchell helped persuade these clients to pay him hefty retainers. His friendship with the powerful Winchell also made Hoffman wealthy through the movies. Several studios paid Hoffman a $25,000-per-year retainer to keep Winchell abreast of the latest in motion pictures.

Hoffman's close relationship with Winchell sometimes backfired on the studios. Ernest Lehman, later a noted screenwriter himself, was on Hoffman's staff. Hoffman was on retainer for Hollywood producer David O. Selznick. Lehman concocted a story about Joan Fontanne being so upset over losing the Oscar for best actress in *Rebecca* that Selznick gave her one himself. Hoffman placed the item in Winchell's column, and Selznick hit the roof. Hoffman rejoined, "We're through. I don't tell you how to make pictures; don't tell me how to write publicity."

Hoffman served as a movie reviewer, book reviewer and talent scout for Winchell. Hoffman was much better read than his friend, and many of Winchell's opinions were based solely on Hoffman's say-so.

Many felt the idea of Hoffman reviewing movies was ludicrous, since they didn't believe he could even see the screen. Once, a disgruntled producer complained about Hoffman's nearsightedness. "Yes," replied Hoffman, "but there's nothing wrong with my nose." Once, Hoffman entered a fancy party with a date on his arm and literally bumped into an acquaintance and inquired, "Tell me. Is she pretty?"

Hoffman died on December 9, 1968. Damon Runyon described Hoffman as "a great document of a tall, loose-jointed fellow, a man-about-table, a squire of dames, a bon vivant, a raconteur, and all that truck."

HOLIDAY THEATER   See MOVIELAND.

HOLLYWOOD THEATER   See MARK HELLINGER THEATER.

HUBERT'S FLEA CIRCUS   See MURRAY'S ROMAN GARDENS.

HUDSON THEATRE 139 W. 44th Street. Architect: J.B. McElfatrick & Co. Opening: October 19, 1903; *Cousin Kate*. After Oscar Hammerstein I's *(q.v.)* pioneering efforts in the new theater district growing up around Times Square at the turn of the century, the best regarded theater locations were on 42nd Street. Producer Henry B. Harris chose to build his Hudson Theater on 44th Street following the lead of Daniel Frohman's Lyceum Theater *(q.v.)* built the year before

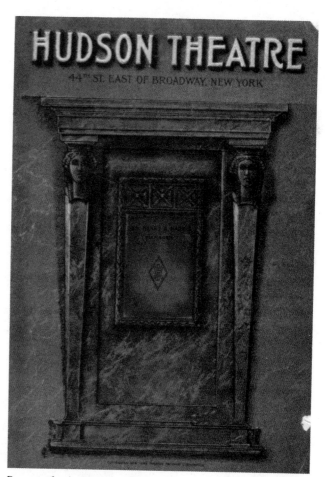

Program for the Hudson Theatre

on 45th Street. Unfortunately, the Hudson has had a spotty career.

The 1,006-seat theater, considered one of the more modern of its time, seemed to have a bright future. But Harris lost his life on the Titanic, and his widow did not have much luck in producing plays. One of the only successes at the Hudson was the black show *Hot Chocolates,* which opened June 20, 1929. It had an above-average score by Fats Waller, Harry Brooks and Andy Razaf. The songs included "Black and Blue" and the smash hit, "Ain't Misbehavin'." Cab Calloway and Edith Wilson were featured, and Duke Ellington contributed two tunes.

Like many of the other Broadway houses, the Hudson ceased legitimate use with the Depression. Mrs. Harris sold the playhouse, and the new owners leased it to CBS. It reopened as the CBS Radio Playhouse Number 1 on February 3, 1934.

Three years later the theater returned to its original use with a production of *An Enemy of the People,* which opened February 15, 1937. This return to live theater lasted just over a decade, until NBC bought it and converted it for television in 1950. In 1960, the theater again became a stage house, but except for minor productions it remained dark. Today, the theater is known as the Savoy, a disco and concert venue.

On November 17, 1987, the New York City Landmarks Preservation Commission gave the interior and exterior of the Hudson Theatre landmark status. The Commission stated that the facade is a "restrained but handsome version of Beaux-Arts classicism" and it has "unusually handsome auditorium and lobby spaces."

IATSE This union of stage workers was organized in New York City on July 17, 1893, by 11 local unions, as the National Alliance of Theatrical Stage Employees. In 1898, the word National was changed to International, although the union did not actually become international until October 1, 1902. In 1914, the American Federation of Labor added movie projectionists to the union and the name of the union became what it is today—International Alliance of Theatrical Stage Employee's and Moving Picture Machine Operators of the United States. The union currently represents press agents, stagehands, sound technicians, hair stylists, wardrobe handlers and dressers, makeup artists, set, costume and lighting designers and projectionists.

IATSE has been blamed for high production costs with the resultant high-ticket prices, loss of audience and reduction in quantity and quality of production on Broadway and the road. While the exorbitant fees and feather-bedding associated with the union has had an effect on Broadway, IATSE is not totally to blame. Like its sister unions, the American Federation of Musicians and Actor's Equity (q.v.), IATSE has its share of illogical work rules, etc., but the producers who negotiated the contracts are equally to blame. Broadway's precarious future will only be assured if the unions and producers create reasonable production contracts.

IMPERIAL THEATRE 249 W. 45th Street. Architect: Herbert J. Krapp. Opening: December 25, 1923; *Mary Jane McKane.* The 1,650-seat Imperial Theatre has proved to be among the most successful of all musical-comedy houses. Its ideal location across from the Golden (q.v.) and Royale (q.v.) theaters and down the block from the Music Box (q.v.) and now demolished Morosco (q.v.) and Bijou (q.v.) theaters gave the Shubert brothers (q.v.), its owners, a prime musical theater.

The theater opened on Christmas Day, 1923, with *Mary Jane McKane* (115 performances), a musical with music by Vincent Youmans (q.v.) and Herbert Stothart and book and lyrics by William Cary Duncan and Oscar Hammerstein II (q.v.). The producer was Oscar's uncle,

A flier for Song of Norway

Arthur Hammerstein (q.v.). Among the biggest hits were the Youmans song "Come On and Pet Me." *Mary Jane McKane* starred Mary Hay, Hal Skelly and Eva Clark.

Rose-Marie (9/2/24; 518 performances) opened with Oscar Hammerstein II again at the Imperial, this time as book and lyric writer in conjunction with Otto Harbach (q.v.). Herbert Stothart and Rudolf Friml (q.v.) composed the stirring melodies, and Arthur Hammerstein again produced. *Rose-Marie* had several hit songs, including the "Indian Love Call," "Rose-Marie," "Pretty Things" and "The Song of the Mounties."

A decidedly more modern musical, *Oh, Kay!* (11/8/26; 257 performances), boasted a superior score by George and Ira Gershwin (q.v.) and Howard Dietz (q.v.) and a serviceable book by Guy Bolton (q.v.) and P.G. Wodehouse. Among the hit songs introduced by stars Constance Carpenter, Betty Compton, Gertrude Lawrence, Victor Moore and Oscar Shaw were "Someone to Watch Over Me," "Maybe" and "Do, Do, Do." *Oh, Kay!'s* exuberant score and superior production by producers Alex A. Aarons and Vinton Freedley (q.v.) were responsible for its success.

Operetta returned to the Imperial with Sigmund Romberg's (q.v.) *The New Moon* (9/19/28; 519 performances). It had lyrics by Oscar Hammerstein II (q.v.), who also collaborated on the book with Frank Mandel and Laurence Schwab. The three librettists were also credited with the show's direction. Schwab and Mandel also handled producing chores. The songs "The Girl on the Prow," "Wanting You," "Gorgeous Alexander" and "Marianne" were minor hits from the lush score. More popular were the classic songs "Softly, As in a Morning Sunrise," "Lover, Come Back to Me" and "Stouthearted Men." *The New Moon* was among the last successful operettas mounted on Broadway.

Popular songwriters J. Fred Coots, Arthur Swanstrom and Benny Davis contributed the score to the theater's next hit, *Sons o' Guns* (11/26/29; 297 performances). Though none of the songs achieved great success (although "Why?" and "Cross Your Fingers" managed to attain a slight renown), the show was a big hit with audiences, despite the stock-market crash and the onset of the Depression.

The Depression changed the fortunes of many Broadway producers. Some, like the Chanins, lost all their holdings. The Shuberts also had some setbacks. Some of their theaters were sold to the burgeoning radio industry, and some simply went dark. But the Imperial managed to house a series of highly successful shows.

Ed Wynn was coauthor, producer and director as well as star of *The Laugh Parade* (11/2/31; 243 performances). Harry Warren, better known for his later Hollywood scores, contributed music with accompanying lyrics by Mort Dixon and Joe Young. The big hit from the score was "You're My Everything."

Broadway's preeminent revue writers, Howard Dietz and Arthur Schwartz (q.v.) had another success with their revue *Flying Colors* (9/15/32; 181 performances). Their score included such wonderful tunes as "Alone Together," "Fatal Fascination," "Louisiana Hayride" and "A Shine on Your Shoes." *Flying Colors* had skits by George S. Kaufman (q.v.), Charles Sherman, Corey Ford and Howard Dietz. Dietz also directed the show whose cast included Clifton Webb, Larry Adler, Patsy Kelly, Charles Butterworth, Imogene Coca, Vilma and Buddy Ebsen, Tamara Geva, Jean Sargent and Philip Loeb.

The Gershwins returned with *Let 'Em Eat Cake* (10/21/33; 89 performances), a sequel to their satirical musical comedy *Of Thee I Sing*. Kaufman directed the show and wrote the book with Morrie Ryskind. The show contained one of the Gershwin's most consistent scores, including the hit song "Mine." William Gaxton, Victor Moore and Lois Moran all repeated their roles from its predecessor. The show was surprisingly sophisticated by Broadway standards and is only now receiving its due. *Let 'Em Eat Cake* perhaps hit too close to home for Depression audiences.

Say When (11/8/34; 76 performances) was also not a hit, although its creators received fame later. The show had music by Ray Henderson (q.v.) and lyrics by Ted Koehler. Bob Hope, Harry Richman and Prince Michael Romanoff, later of restaurant fame, starred.

One of the greatest of all musical-comedy songs, "Begin the Beguine," graced the Imperial tenant *Jubilee* (10/12/35; 169 performances). Moss Hart (q.v.) wrote the book while sailing the seas with composer/lyricist Cole Porter (q.v.). The show was very funny and sophisticated in its telling of a royal family who is given a few days of freedom to taste the pleasures enjoyed by commoners. The show starred Mary Boland, Melville Cooper, June Knight and Charles Walters. Also included in the cast was Montgomery Clift. Another hit song, "Just One of Those Things," came from the playful Porter score.

Richard Rodgers and Lorenz Hart's (q.v.) *On Your Toes* (4/11/36; 318 performances) was the Imperial's next musical offering. The songwriters also wrote the book in collaboration with George Abbott (q.v.). Abbott also collaborated on the direction with Worthington Miner. A major contribution to the show was George Balanchine's choreography, especially for the now classic "Slaughter on Tenth Avenue." The score was brimming with great standards. These included "On Your Toes" and "There's a Small Hotel." Those songs that didn't achieve renown, such as "Quiet Night" and "The Heart Is Quicker Than the Eye" are nevertheless noteworthy.

The theater hosted a rare nonmusical production with Leslie Howard's ill-conceived version of *Hamlet*. It ran only 39 performances. The operetta form was almost totally dead, but the Shuberts opened the Franz Lehar operetta *Frederika* (2/4/37; 94 performances) at the Imperial. Despite an excellent cast and production, the public was not interested.

Dietz and Schwartz fared as badly with a book show, *Between the Devil* (12/23/37; 93 performances). Again the elements were all top-notch. Vilma Ebsen, Jack Buchanan and Evelyn Laye starred, and the score included "I See Your Face Before Me" and "By Myself."

The Imperial finally had another big hit with the return of Cole Porter. He wrote the score to *Leave It to Me!* (11/9/38; 291 performances), which accompanied the libretto by Bella and Samuel Spewack. The score contained the usual compliment of hit songs, including "Get Out of Town," "Most Gentlemen Don't Like Love" and "My Heart Belongs to Daddy." The last song was introduced by a newcomer, Mary Martin (q.v.). Also in the cast were William Gaxton, Adele Jergens, Victor Moore, Sophie Tucker and Tamara. Another newcomer included in the cast of *Leave It to Me!* was Gene Kelly, who was relegated to a part in the chorus.

Rodgers and Hart had another hit at the Imperial with their college musical *Too Many Girls* (10/18/39; 249 performances). The show had a lightweight book by George Marion Jr. As producer and director, George Abbott kept the production moving briskly. The score included the classic "I Didn't Know What Time it Was" as well as "I Like to Recognize the Tune" "Give It Back to the Indians" and "She Could Shake the Maracas." The show starred Mary Jane Walsh, Richard Kollmar, Hal Le Roy, Marcy Wescott and Eddie Bracken along with newcomer Desi Arnaz. This show also had a future star in the chorus—Van Johnson.

The 1940s were even more popular than the 1930s at the Imperial. In 1940, Irving Berlin's *(q.v.)* production of *Louisiana Purchase* (5/28/40; 444 performances) opened. Morrie Ryskind of *Let 'Em Eat Cake* fame wrote the book to *Louisiana Purchase*. Vera Zorina of *On Your Toes*, Irene Bordoni and Carol Bruce starred along with two Imperial regulars—William Gaxton and Victor Moore. Also in the show were two future songwriting stars, Hugh Martin and Ralph Blane. The Berlin score contained such enduring hits as "Fools Fall in Love" and "It's a Lovely Day Tomorrow."

Let's Face It! (10/29/41; 547 performances) was another Cole Porter vehicle to play the Imperial. The Porter score yielded no standards, but "Farming," "A Little Rhumba Numba," "I Hate You Darling," "A Lady Needs a Rest," "Everything I Love" and "Ace in the Hole" are top-drawer Porter tunes. The librettists were Herbert and Dorothy Fields *(q.v.)*. The show's wonderful cast included Eve Arden, Nanette Fabray, Benny Baker, Edith Meiser, Vivian Vance, Mary Jane Walsh, Frances and Jack Williams and newcomer Danny Kaye in his first starring role on Broadway.

Director Max Reinhardt's operetta, *Rosalinda,* moved to the Imperial to complete its 520-performance run. Mary Martin returned to the Imperial in *One Touch of Venus* (10/7/43; 567 performances), the Kurt Weill *(q.v.),* Ogden Nash musical. She perfectly personified a mortal's view of Venus. The offbeat book was by the somewhat dyspeptic humorist S.J. Perelman and poet Nash. The show was directed by Elia Kazan. Despite Nash's inexperience at lyrics, he and Weill came up with a delightful score, including the hits "Foolish Heart," "I'm a Stranger Here Myself," "That's Him" and "Speak Low." Kenny Baker, John Boles, Teddy Hart, Paula Laurence and Sono Osato completed the cast.

After a continuation of the run of *The Ziegfeld Follies (q.v.)* from the Winter Garden Theater *(q.v.)* came one of the Imperial's greatest successes. Irving Berlin's *Annie Get Your Gun* (5/16/46; 1,147 performances) toplined Ethel Merman *(q.v.)* as Annie Oakley. *Let's Face It*'s librettists Herbert and Dorothy Fields repeated the chore for *Annie Get Your Gun*. The entire show proved to be one of the classics of the American musical theater. Richard Rodgers and Oscar Hammerstein II produced with Joshua Logan *(q.v.)* directing. The Irving Berlin score was the tunesmith's finest. The hits included "They Say It's Wonderful," "Anything You Can Do," "Doin' What Comes Natur'lly," "I Got the Sun in the Morning," "You Can't Get a Man with a Gun" and the show business anthem—"There's No Business Like Show Business."

After a minor effort, *Along Fifth Avenue* (1/13/49), came another offering by Irving Berlin. *Miss Liberty* (7/7/49; 308 performances), the story of the Statue of Liberty, was not as successful as *Annie Get Your Gun*, although the score was delightful. The hit song was "Let's Take an Old-Fashioned Walk." Eddie Albert and Allyn Ann McLerie starred.

The Leonard Bernstein *(q.v.)* version of *Peter Pan* (4/4/50; 321 performances) followed, with Jean Arthur and Boris Karloff. Ethel Merman was tapped by Berlin to star in *Call Me Madam* (10/12/50; 644 performances), a slightly disguised story about Washington socialite Perle Mesta. Howard Lindsay and Russel Crouse wrote the book, and George Abbott directed. Also featured in the cast were Pat Harrington, Russell Nype, Tommy Rall, and Paul Lukas. "The Best Thing for You," "It's a Lovely Day Today" and "You're Just in Love" were the big hits.

Joshua Logan, director of *Annie Get Your Gun,* also directed the Imperial's next tenant, *Wish You Were Here* (6/25/52; 598 performances) as well as coauthored the libretto and coproduced. Harold Rome's *(q.v.)* show was not a success at first, but producers Leland Hayward and Logan worked on improving the show after it opened. The popularity of the title song also contributed to the show's long run. For the production, the Imperial had a swimming pool installed into its stage.

John Murray Anderson's Almanac (10/12/53; 227 performances) was one of the last large revues on Broadway. Hermione Gingold, Polly Bergen, Carleton Carpenter, Harry Belafonte, Orson Bean, Billy De Wolfe and Kay Medford starred.

Cole Porter's last Broadway show, *Silk Stockings* (2/24/55; 477 performances), opened at the Imperial with Don Ameche and Hildegarde Neff in the leads. "All of You" was the hit in the score.

Frank Loesser's *(q.v.)* ambitious musical version of *They Knew What They Wanted* was titled *The Most Happy Fella* (5/3/56; 676 performances). Metropolitan Opera star Robert Weede and Jo Sullivan had the leads. Also in the cast were Susan Johnson, Lee Cass and Mona Paulee. The musical epic contained some of the most sweeping melodies heard on any Broadway stage in addition to traditional musical-comedy songs, semioperatic arias and sung narrative. The show's musical comedy numbers "Big D" and "Standing on the Corner" were the big hits, but the other numbers were what made this score so unique.

Audiences loved the David Merrick *(q.v.)* production *Jamaica* (10/31/57; 555 performances) and its star Lena Horne. But the show was a far cry from what its authors contemplated. Composer Harold Arlen *(q.v.)* and lyricist E.Y. Harburg *(q.v.)* certainly didn't think they were writing the Lena Horne Show but that's how it turned out. Luckily, the score was first-rate even if it contained no major hits. Ricardo Montalban, Josephine Premice, Adelaide Hall, Ossie Davis and Erik Rhodes played second fiddle to Ms. Horne.

Harold Rome had another hit at the Imperial with *Destry Rides Again* (4/23/59; 472 performances) starring Andy Griffith and Dolores Gray. Everyone thought a western musical couldn't be a hit on sophisticated Broadway, but Rome and librettist Leonard Gershe proved them wrong with this David Merrick production.

Merrick moved *Gypsy* to the Imperial from the Broadway Theatre *(q.v.)* with Ethel Merman continuing in the starring role. He then premiered Bob Merrill's musical *Carnival!* (4/13/61; 719 performances) at the Imperial with Anna Maria Alberghetti and Jerry Orbach starring. Gower Champion directed the proceedings, and the hit song was "Love Makes the World Go Round."

Merrick retained his lease on the theater with the next attraction, a transfer of the London success, *Oliver!* (1/6/63; 774 performances). Lionel Bart's musical contained several big hit songs, including "As Long As He Needs Me," "Consider Yourself" and "Where Is Love?" Bruce Prochnik starred in the title role, ably assisted by Georgia Brown, Alice Playten, Clive Revill and Danny Sewell.

The Imperial Theatre's greatest success came next—*Fiddler on the Roof (q.v.)* (9/22/63; 3,242 performances), claimed by some to be the greatest of all musicals. Jerry Bock and Sheldon Harnick *(q.v.)* provided the score, and Jospeh Stein wrote a strong libretto. Zero Mostel had the role of his career as Tevye the milkman. Also featured were Beatrice Arthur, Bert Convy, Maria Karnilova, Julia Migenes and Austin Pendleton. The best-known song was "Sunrise, Sunset." *Fiddler on the Roof* was produced by Harold Prince and directed by Jerome Robbins to whom much of the credit for its success was given.

Cabaret moved to the Imperial from the Broadhurst Theater *(q.v.)* in 1967. It was followed by another John Kander and Fred Ebb show, *Zorba* (11/17/68; 305 performances). Joseph Stein, author of the book to *Fiddler on the Roof,* wrote the libretto to *Zorba.* Harold Prince produced and directed the show.

Minnie's Boys (3/26/70; 76 performances) was a musicalization of the early career of the Marx Brothers and starred Shelley Winters. Richard Rodgers and Martin Charnin chose as the basis for their musical *Two By Two* (11/10/70; 343 performances), the story of Noah. Danny Kaye starred in the show.

A greater success, although its material was weak, was *Pippin* (10/3/72; 1,944 performances). The show, with score by Stephen Schwartz and book by Roger O. Hirson, owed its success to the direction and choreography of Bob Fosse.

In the seventies, Broadway saw fewer and fewer musicals mounted because of the high cost of production. The Imperial hosted a revival of O'Neill's *(q.v.)* *Anna Christie* with Liv Ullmann and Victor Borge's *Comedy with Music.* Neil Simon's *(q.v.)* comedy hit *Chapter Two* (12/4/77; 857 performances) starred Judd Hirsch, Anita Gillette, Cliff Gorman and Ann Wedgeworth.

Neil Simon also provided the script to the Imperial's next tenant, the musical *They're Playing Our Song* (2/11/79; 1,082 performances), a decidedly minor effort with its Marvin Hamlisch and Carole Bayer Sager score.

Another long-running musical occupied the Imperial's stage. *Dreamgirls* (12/20/81; 1,522 performances) owed much of its success to Michael Bennett's brilliant staging. Henry Krieger provided the music and Tom Eyen the book and lyrics. The show made a star of Jennifer Holliday who scored on the pop music charts (rare for Broadway scores in the seventies and eighties) with "And I Am Telling You I'm Not Going." Other notable cast members included Obba Babatunde, Deborah Burrell, Vondie Curtis-Hall, Cleavant Derricks, Loretta Devine, Ben Harney and Sheryl Lee Ralph.

After *Dreamgirls* closed on August 11, 1985, the Imperial hosted another long-running hit, *The Mystery of Edwin Drood* (12/2/85; 680 performances) with book, music and lyrics by Rupert Holmes. George Rose, Howard McGillin, Betty Buckley, Patti Cohenour, and Cleo Laine starred in the Joseph Papp production. Shortly before closing, the show officially changed its name to *Drood*. The name change did put it further up the alphabet in the *New York Times*'s ABC theatrical listings but did little else.

INTERNATIONAL ALLIANCE OF THEATRICAL STAGE EMPLOYEES AND MOVING PICTURE MACHINE OPERATORS OF THE UNITED STATES OF AMERICA
See IATSE

JACOBS, MIKE (1880–1953)   Mike Jacobs, a ticket seller and fight promoter, was one of Broadway's most colorful characters. His domain was the world of boxing but he also had an important influence on theater and journalism.

Jacobs was born in New York City on March 10, 1880. Like most residents of the lower East Side, his family was poor and the children had to help out with part-time jobs. Jacobs left school after the sixth grade and began selling papers outside Tammany Hall. Joe Bannon, a circulation manager for the Hearst empire, tipped him a pair of tickets to the Terry McGovern–George Dixon featherweight fight; the tickets changed the young newsboy's life dramatically.

Jacobs didn't attend the fight. Instead, he took the one dollar tickets and scalped them at twice the price. Jacobs discovered the joys of ticket scalping. It was certainly easier to buy lots of tickets and scalp them than to stand outside in inclement weather to make a few cents selling newspapers.

By the time he was 16, Jacobs had built up quite a business reselling tickets to sports events. He was proud to have saved $1,000 from his speculations and later bragged, "I have never been broke since."

Jacobs's business grew under his astute leadership. His ability to gauge the popularity of an attraction was uncanny. By 1907, he had to open a storefront ticket agency to handle all his business. The office was in the lobby of the Normandie Hotel in Times Square.

The location of his business made selling theater tickets a natural, so Jacobs began augmenting the money made from sports events with theater tickets. He even found time to indulge in several other occupations, some related to his main business, some not. He backed theater projects, basketball teams and wrestling bouts. He was a concessionaire on steamboats and even owned a circus. As a personal manager, he booked great artists

of the day on concert tours. Enrico Caruso was one of his clients. Caruso was booked by Jacobs on a string of 10 one-night stands. The great tenor was guaranteed $1,000 a concert. Jacobs still made $80,000 profit.

He also backed many fighters. Walter St. Denis, sports editor of the *Globe,* introduced Jacobs to George L. ("Tex") Rickard, the greatest fight promoter of his time. Rickard was promoting the Jess Willard–Frank Moran bout for heavyweight title. Jacobs became a pupil of Rickard, and after Rickard's death in 1929 he took his place as New York's preeminent boxing promoter and speculator.

Jacobs also bought "shares" in up-and-coming fighters' careers by lending their managers money in times of need. When the fighters became successful, Jacobs often owned a substantial piece of their winnings. On the odd occasion when a fighter didn't live up to Jacobs's ambitions, the promoter would chalk up the losses to "development costs."

His proximity to the theater district and his ticket office brought Jacobs in touch with many of the leading producers of the time. It seemed that Jacobs's appraisal of a new show's chances on the Great White Way was infallible. Many would-be angels consulted Jacobs on whether the show looked like a hit or flop. In cases in which Jacobs believed a show to be a sure thing, he himself would invest heavily.

Several of the producers who Jacobs had helped became interested in boxing. William A. Brady *(q.v.)* was one such producer. He and English impresario Charles Cochran formed a partnership with Rickard to sponsor the Dempsey–Carpentier fight. Both fighters were guaranteed a purse of $200,000, regardless of the outcome of the bout. Brady and Cochran balked at the high fees and felt they could never recover their investment. They withdrew from the partnership and lived to regret it.

Rickard turned to Jacobs who proposed a plan. Jacobs agreed to invest $20,000 of his own money if Rickard would raise a $200,000 fund from other speculators. They plowed that investment and the money from advance ticket sales into building their own arena—Boyle's Thirty Acres Arena in Jersey City.

The fight was an enormous success, grossing $1,798,238, enough to return handsome profits to its investors and pay the boxers their substantial fees. Also, Rickard and Jacobs found themselves the owners of the arena. The Dempsey–Carpentier fight was the first to break the million-dollar mark.

That 1921 fight led Jacobs into other partnerships on future bouts. In 1933, his associates were journalists Damon Runyon (q.v.), Bill Farnsworth and sports editor of the *American,* Ed Frayne. But this time, the profits went to charity. Mrs. William Randolph Hearst used the proceeds for her celebrated Milk Fund.

Jacobs, flush with success, decided to challenge the biggest arena in New York, Madison Square Garden (q.v.). In 1934, he began the Twentieth Century Sporting Club with his Milk Fund partners and installed himself as president. The first bout was the Barney Ross–Billy Petrolle match held in the Bronx Coliseum.

By 1935, he had controlling interest in Joe Louis. His investment began to pay off as Louis began rising in the ranks. With Louis firmly under contract, Jacobs could really put pressure on Madison Square Garden.

The arena held a contract for a fight between the then heavyweight champion James J. Braddock and Max Schmelling. Jacobs approached Braddock's manager, Joe Gould, and convinced him that a Braddock–Louis fight would make more money. So Braddock canceled his agreement with Madison Square Garden and went on to fight Louis in Chicago for 20% of the gross. Louis won the fight and with it the championship.

Since Jacobs owned Louis's services, he could call the shots. As manager of the champion, Jacobs was at the top of his field. Louis went on to defend his title 23 times. Each fight was produced by Jacobs.

For Jacobs, money was important, but he did his share for others also. In one of the many fights that he arranged for armed-service charities, he sold $36 million in war bonds.

He broke another record with his $100 charge for ringside seats in the Louis–Conn fight. That bout grossed $1,925,564 and an additional $50,000 for the movie rights.

On December 3, 1946, Jacobs suffered a brain hemorrhage that nearly proved fatal. He retired from promotions and three years later sold the Twentieth Century Sporting Club to his old nemesis Madison Square Garden. The price was $110,000.

Jacobs achieved a further degree of fame when the block of 49th Street between Eighth Avenue and Broadway became known as Jacobs's Beach. Out-of-work pugilists would gather on the Beach in much the same way as out-of-work vaudevillians gathered on the Beach (q.v.) in front of the Palace Theater (q.v.).

Jacobs went into a part-time retirement until his death on January 21, 1953.

JOHN GOLDEN THEATER 252 W. 45th Street. Architect: Herbert J. Krapp. Opening: February 24, 1927; *Puppets of Passion.* Actually, two Broadway houses have been named the John Golden Theater in honor of the noted producer and author. The first John Golden Theater opened at 202 W. 58th Street between Broadway and Seventh Avenue on November 1, 1926, with the play *Two Girls Wanted.* Harrison G. Wiseman was the architect for this theater. The building had a stormy future. On September 17, 1935, the theater's name was changed to the 58th Street Theater with the play *Few Are Chosen.* The name was changed again to the Filmarte on September 20, 1936, with the movie *La Kermess Heroique.* On April 2, 1940, with the movie *The Life of Giuseppe Verdi,* the name was changed again to the Fine Arts Theater. On February 14, 1942, the theater briefly returned to a legitimate policy under the name the Concert Theater with the musical revue *Of V We Sing.* The show starred Betty Garrett and Phil Leeds but only lasted 76 performances. The Concert Theater became the Rock Church in 1943. It became a theater

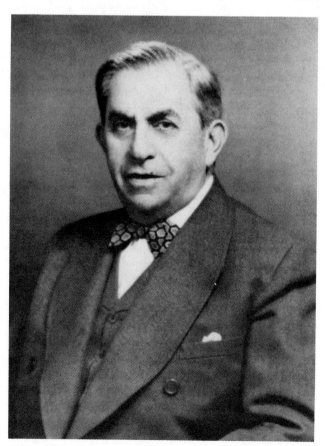

John Golden Courtesy ASCAP.

again on January 15, 1946, when it was renamed the 58th Street Theater. In April 1946, the theater became an ABC Radio Theater. On January 28, 1948, the movie *Fanny* opened at the theater, now named the Elysee.

* * * * *

The Chanin Brothers built the current John Golden Theater as their fifth theater in the Times Square area. Brooks Atkinson described the new theater, originally called the Theater Masque, in the New York Times on the occasion of its opening night: "Like all the Chanin houses the Theater Masque is pleasing and comfortable. The architecture is modern Spanish in character, and the interior of the house is decorated in pastel shades, trimmed in grayish blues and reds."

The 800-seat theater's first tenant, *Puppets of Passion,* closed after only 12 performances. In 1927 and 1928, there were other bookings but none proved successful. Finally, the first success at the Theater Masque came with Patrick Hamilton's drama *Rope's End* (9/19/29; 100 performances). The show later became the basis for the Alfred Hitchcock movie *Rope.*

As the Chanins' fortunes declined during the Depression, the theater did not fare well. Productions included the Albert Hackett and Frances Goodrich play *Up Pops the Devil* (9/1/30; 146 performances), starring Sally Bates and Brian Donlevy; the Norman Krasna comedy *Louder, Please!* (11/12/31; 68 performances) directed by George Abbott *(q.v.);* the comedy *Goodbye Again* (12/28/32; 212 performances), starring Anthony Perkins; and *Post Road* (12/4/34; 210 performances), which starred Percy Kilbride (later famous as Pa Kettle) and Lucile Watson.

A series of failures followed, and the Chanins lost the Theater Masque along with their other theaters. The first success under the new name, the John Golden Theater, was *Shadow and Substance* (1/26/38; 206 performances) by Paul Vincent Carroll, starring Julie Haydon and Sir Cedric Hardwicke.

A bona fide long running hit, the thriller *Angel Street* (12/5/41; 1,293 performances) was produced by Shepard Traube and starred Judith Evelyn, Vincent Price and Leo G. Carroll. The play had begun in London as *Gaslight.* It had been successful there, and a few summer theater productions followed. A production in Hollywood under its original title was moderately received, so when the show opened at the John Golden as *Angel Street* it was understandable that nobody expected it to be a hit. Even the lessees of the theater, the Shubert brothers *(q.v.),* had expected the play to be a quick failure. They ordered tickets printed for only the first three performances. Even Traube was not going to put his own money into the show; he had raised money by selling $15,000 shares to 15 angels. But the reviews were raves, and audiences began telling friends of the surprise hit at the John Golden Theater.

Unfortunately, *Angel Street* was not an omen for things to come. A modest comedy, *The Soldier's Wife*

(10/4/44; 255 performances) by Rose Franken, played at the John Golden and starred Martha Scott, Glenn Anders and Myron McCormick. A few more modest successes and a few failures followed, and in the middle of 1946, the theater was changed to a motion picture policy. It reverted to a legitimate policy on February 29, 1948, with the production of a one-man show featuring Maurice Chevalier. He was the first of a series of performers who presented one-person shows at the theater, including Emlyn Williams, Cornelia Otis Skinner and Victor Borge. The latter opened his show *Comedy in Music* on October 2, 1953, and played 849 performances at the theater.

An acclaimed production of Samuel Beckett's *Waiting for Godot* (4/19/56; 59 performances) was not a hit, despite raves for Bert Lahr's performance. After this, in the late 1950s and 1960s, the theater housed a series of two-person revues. First came *A Party with Betty Comden and Adolph Green.* Comden and Green *(q.v.)* were two of Broadway's most cherished lyricists, and they held their audiences in thrall for a 38-performance run commencing on December 23, 1958, and again for 44 performances commencing on April 16, 1959. The next two performers to hold forth on the John Golden stage were the English songwriters and humorists Michael Flanders and Donald Swann and their delightful show *At the Drop of a Hat* (10/8/59; 215 performances). Then came *An Evening with Mike Nichols and Elaine May* (10/8/60; 306 performances) followed by a concert by Yves Montand (10/24/61; 55 performances).

The next hit was a small revue from London called *Beyond the Fringe* (10/27/62; 673 performances) with its cast of Peter Cook, Dudley Moore, Jonathan Miller and Alan Bennett. In 1964, Victor Borge returned with his show, which had a 192-performance run. Another hit revue, twice as large as *Beyond the Fringe,* was the South African show *Wait a Minim* (3/7/66; 457 performances), which featured the traditional music of South Africa.

After a series of failures came the celebrated American comedy team of Bob Elliot and Ray Goulding with their hilarious show *Bob and Ray the Two and Only* (9/24/70; 158 performances). In 1972, David Rabe's Vietnam-era drama *Sticks and Bones* (3/1/72; 366 performances) came to the John Golden Theater via Joseph Papp's Public Theater with Elizabeth Wilson and Tom Aldredge in the leads.

Lyricist Sammy Cahn's revue *Words and Music* (4/16/74; 127 performances) was followed by a Pulitzer Prize winner, *The Gin Game* (12/31/77; 517 performances), the two-person drama that starred Hume Cronyn and Jessica Tandy. Another success was the English import *A Day in Hollywood, A Night in the Ukraine* (5/1/80; 588 performances) with Priscilla Lopez, Peggy Hewett, Frank Lazarus and David Garrison. Frank Lazarus and Dick Vosburgh supplied the score, and Tommy Tune provided the imaginative direction and choreography. Composer Jerry Herman *(q.v.)* even contributed a few songs to beef up the show.

An off-Broadway transfer, Beth Henley's Pulitzer Prize-winning *Crimes of the Heart* (11/4/81; 535 performances) gave way to David Mamet's expose of the real estate industry *Glengarry Glen Ross* (3/25/84; 378 performances). Another Pulitzer Prize winner, Marsha Norman's *'Night Mother* (4/18/84; 434 performances) starred Anne Pitoniak and Kathy Bates. Athol Fugard's powerful play *Blood Knot* (12/10/85; 96 performances) was revived at the theater with Zakes Mokae and Fugard starring.

On November 17, 1987, the New York City Landmarks Preservation Commission designated the interior and exterior of the John Golden Theater a landmark. The Commission stated: "It was designed as a small 'intimate' theater seating only 800. Its facade is a fine example of the romantic 'modern Spanish' style."

JOLSON, AL (1886–1950) Al Jolson is considered the greatest performer of all time by those who were lucky enough to see him in action. A little of his dynamic personality comes through in his movie performances, which offer an indication of his prodigous energy. Jolson was defined by his energy and humor. He introduced more hit songs than any other performer, with the possible exception of Bing Crosby. He was a unique link with America's entertainment heritage, for it was Jolson who brought the minstrel tradition into musical comedy, movies, radio and finally television. He was the one performer who embodied the complete range of the American popular arts.

Critic *(q.v.)* George Jean Nathan said of Jolson:

> The power of Jolson over an audience I have seldom seen equalled. There are actors who, backed by great dramatists, can clutch an audience in their hands and squeeze out its emotion as they choose.
>
> There are singers who, backed by great composers, can do the same. And there are performers who, aided by external means of one kind or another can do the same.
>
> But I know of none like this Jolson—or at best very few—who, with lines of prewar vintage and melodies of the cheapest tin piano variety, can lay hold of an audience the moment he comes on the stage and never let go for a second thereafter.
>
> Possessed of an immensely electric personality, a rare sense of comedy, considerable histrionic ability, a most unusual music show versatility in the way of song and dance, and, above all, a gift for delivering lines for the full of their effect, he so far outdistances his rivals that they seem like the wrong ends of so many opera glasses.

Jolson was born Asa Yoelson in St. Petersburg, Russia, on March 26, 1886. When his family came to the United States, Jolson's father found work as a cantor in a Washington, D.C., synagogue. Jolson left home

Al Jolson Courtesy ASCAP.

on several occasions to make a name for himself on the stage only to return beaten. At a Washington, D.C., vaudeville theater, Jolson was in the audience while the singer/comedian Eddie Leonard performed on stage. Jolson sang along with his big voice and Leonard, after his initial shock, was impressed. Leonard teamed with Jolson in an act which repeated their first meeting. Jolson would pretend to be a paying customer who just couldn't help joining in from the balcony.

Jolson appeared as an extra on Broadway in *The Children of the Ghetto* (10/16/1899) at the Herald Theater. Jolson joined Lew Dockstader's Minstrels in 1908 while both acts were appearing in Little Rock, Arkansas. Will Oakland, a producer and songwriter, recommended Jolson to Dockstader who hired the young performer. Jolson adopted the blackface makeup, which became a trademark for him when he was part of an early act, Jolson, Palmer and Palmer. To Jolson, the blackface was simply another gimmick for what would otherwise be simply another singing act. Somewhat shy, he also found it easier to portray a character rather than himself. Jolson was never the kind of performer who adopted blackface in order to make fun of blacks. He never assumed the stereotypes most often connected with the blackface comic. Jolson simply used the conceit as a means to make himself stand out from other singers. Later when he was inextricably linked to the character, he used the makeup to signal that a highlight of the performance was coming up. Other blackface performers, like Cantor, kept their Jewish identities and characterizations even when in blackface.

The minstrel tradition was quickly dying. Jolson realized that he would have to move on to other more sophisticated entertainments if his career was to proceed. The Shuberts (q.v.) opened their new Winter Garden Theater (q.v.) with *La Belle Paree* (3/20/11; 104 performances). The show was a typical early mishmash of styles. Its subtitle, *The Cook's Tour through Vaudeville with a Parisian Landscape,* left room for just about anything. Jolson appeared in the last scene as Erastus Sparkler and sang "Paris is a Paradise for Coons" to little effect. However the *New York Times* singled Jolson out, and the Shuberts moved him up in the show to better effect. Another of his songs, "He Had to Get Out and Get Under," was interpolated in the score, and in it Jolson introduced what became another trademark. In the second chorus, instead of singing the lyrics, Jolson whistled the tune.

Jolson's second Broadway success was *Vera Violetta* (11/20/11). This time, he was top-billed with the French star Gaby Deslys. Jolson was the smash hit of the show, and he introduced another gimmick in his performances. While singing his numbers "Rum Tum Tiddle" and "That Haunting Melody," Jolson jumped off the stage and continued performing up and down the aisles. The *New York Times* enthused, "There was Al Jolson in the role of a colored waiter who succeeded in rousing the audience into its first enthusiasm in the early part of the evening and kept them enthusiastic much of the time afterwards."

Solidly established as a Broadway star, Jolson began behaving in a way that earned him a reputation as Broadway's supreme egotist. He took out an ad in *Variety (q.v.)* stating, "Everybody likes me. Those who don't are jealous. Anyhow, here's wishing those that do and those that don't, a Merry Christmas and a Happy New Year—Al Jolson."

The Whirl of Society (3/5/12) was the third Jolson show at the Winter Garden. It opened with Stella Mayhew and Jose Collins as Jolson's costars. In it, he created the character Gus, one he would play five more times on Broadway and also in the movies.

Under New York's blue laws, performances on Sunday were illegal. But Jolson got around it by performing for show people only without sets, props or his blackface. These Jolson concerts electrified members of the Broadway community who were otherwise unable to witness Jolson in action because their own shows were running the same nights as his.

The Honeymoon Express (2/6/13; 156 performances), again at the Winter Garden, gave Jolson his first song success. "My Yellow Jacket Girl" isn't remembered today, but at the time it was a big success. Supporting Jolson was Gaby Deslys and Harry Pilcer. Fanny Brice (q.v.) was also in the cast in her third Broadway appearance. The show featured a special effect depicting the race between a locomotive and an automobile. Jolson created another sensation by stopping the show midstream and asking the audience, "Would you rather

see the rest of the show or just hear me sing?" The answer was self-evident, and for the next few hours Jolson would dismiss the cast and perform an impromptu concert. During the run, Jolson had trouble with an ingrown toenail. While singing "Down Where the Tennessee Flows," he sought to relieve the pressure on his foot by going down on one knee.

Dancing Around (10/10/14; 145 performances) was mostly undistinguished. Jolson's next Broadway appearance was in *Robinson Crusoe, Jr.* (2/17/16; 139 performances). This time, Jolson was given a Sigmund Romberg (q.v.) score, which took more and more of a backseat to Jolson's interpolations as the run continued. Jolson added several songs that he made into big successes. "Yacka Hula Hickey Dula" was another in the current wave of Hawaiian inspired songs. "Where Did Robinson Crusoe Go with Friday on Saturday Night?" was in the same spirit as "Who Paid the Rent for Mrs. Rip Van Winkle? (When Rip Van Winkle was Away)," which Jolson introduced in *The Honeymoon Express.* "Where the Black-Eyed Susans Grow" would also become a Jolson perennial, one he would sing for the rest of his career.

Jolson opened in *Sinbad* (2/14/18; 164 performances), another excuse to do his usual shtick. This time, he put in a ramp from the stage into the audience. Jolson discovered what became three of his most famous songs and interpolated them into the score of *Sinbad:* "Rock-A-Bye Your Baby with a Dixie Melody" was Jolson's

Sheet music for song from Sinbad

favorite song of all time; "Swanee," by George Gershwin *(q.v.)* and Irving Caesar, was inserted into the show while it was on the road; and perhaps the most famous of all, "My Mammy," was introduced after the show had reopened after a brief vacation for Jolson.

On November 18, 1918, the Armistice was signed, and a huge concert was scheduled for the Metropolitan Opera House for the benefit of the returning soldiers. After Enrico Caruso finished singing "Vesti la Giubba," Jolson ran on the stage before the applause was over for the great tenor. "Folks, you ain't heard nothin' yet," exclaimed Jolson, and so another piece of the Jolson legend fell into place.

Shortly after came the actors' strike of 1919 *(q.v.)*, which led to the formation of Actors' Equity *(q.v.)*. Jolson and George M. Cohan *(q.v.)* were the biggest opponents to the new union. But Jolson loved performing too much, and so to avoid being blacklisted, he gave in to the union. Cohan never joined Actors Equity and only performed on Broadway under special permission.

For Jolson's next show, *Bombo* (10/6/21; 218 performances), the Shuberts built him a new theater and named it, unsurprisingly, the Jolson Theater *(q.v.)*. Jolson had previously had a success with songs he coauthored with B.G. DeSylva and Gus Kahn—" 'N' Everything" and "I'll Say She Does," both written for *Sinbad*. Also credited on the sheet music was Al Jolson, although it was doubtful that Jolson did anything more than introduce the songs. But those songs were nowhere near as popular as the songs written for *Bombo*. Lou Silvers, *Bombo*'s conductor, and DeSylva wrote "April Showers." DeSylva also wrote "California, Here I Come," another huge hit for Jolson. Gus Kahn contributed "Toot Toot, Tootsie." *Bombo* was brought back to Broadway to the Winter Garden for an additional 32 performances on May 14, 1923.

Jolson not only took credit for songs he didn't write, but also took jokes from other shows and incorporated them into his own. Jolson would go to the popular nightclubs in the city or vaudeville houses and hear the great comics. He would then write down the jokes that got the biggest laughs and insert them into whatever show he was starring in. He would then instruct his lawyers to contact the comic and threaten to sue unless the comic removed the joke from his act.

Big Boy (1/7/25; 48 performances) had everything going for it. For one thing it costarred Eddie Cantor, who introduced one of his greatest hits, "If You Knew Susie." It also featured a horse race with real horses running on hidden treadmills on the stage floor. Jolson introduced more great songs into the score; "California, Here I Come" was reintroduced, as well as "Keep Smiling at Trouble."

Big Boy's run was prematurely halted when Jolson came down with another bout of strep throat. When Jolson left a show, that was it—there was no discussion of replacing him or having an understudy go on. Jolson knew as well as anyone else that you couldn't replace the World's Greatest Performer.

On occasion, Jolson would show up late and go onstage to apologize to the audience. He would tell them about the delicious dinner he had next door to the theater and how he just couldn't rush through it. He would then ask whether the audience minded if he put on his makeup onstage and instructed his dresser Louis Shreiber to bring on the burnt cork. He would ask the ushers to go out and buy dozens of boxes of candy, which he then passed out to the audience while he sang. After the concert, he would inform the audience that he was going back to the restaurant for dessert and if the audience would give him a half hour, they could join him there for more songs around the piano.

Jolson next appeared as a late addition to the cast of *Artists and Models,* a revue series produced by the Shuberts. He played the show for only four weeks and then took it on the road where it achieved the highest gross in history, over $60,000.

After the *Artists and Models* tour, Jolson went to Hollywood and made one of the most important pictures in the history of Hollywood, *The Jazz Singer*. Contrary to popular legend there had been other talking pictures, but before this none achieved any success. With Jolson, *The Jazz Singer* changed the future of movies forever.

Before *The Jazz Singer*'s release, Jolson was hired by the Shuberts for $10,000 a week to star in the road tour of *A Night in Spain. The Jazz Singer* opened on October 7, 1927, and for a while at least Jolson became the property of Hollywood.

By 1931, Jolson's movie career was stalled. His pictures were successes (*The Singing Fool* [1928] was the biggest money-making picture in Hollywood history until *Gone With the Wind* surpassed it), but his roles became more and more alike, and the vehicles were mostly unmemorable. Whereas Jolson on stage could stop the show and just give a concert, he was forced in the movies to stick to the script no matter how bad it was. Besides the films already mentioned, there were the disappointing *Say It with Songs* and the equally clichéd *Mammy* (1930) and *Hallelujah I'm a Bum* (1933) with a Rodgers and Hart *(q.v.)* score. Later that year, he made a movie of his stage show *Big Boy,* but it wasn't much of a success.

Jolson opened on Broadway in *The Wonder Bar* (3/17/31; 86 performances). Unfortunately, the show wasn't tailored to Jolson's talents, and none of the usual Jolson interpolations caught fire.

Jolson's last appearance on Broadway was in a book show, *Hold On to Your Hats* (9/11/40; 158 performances) with a score by Burton Lane *(q.v.)* and E.Y. Harburg *(q.v.)*. Jolson had committed to doing the show because his wife Ruby Keeler was to be given a part. But Keeler departed both the show and the marriage during the Chicago run, and Jolson was left in what to him was an increasingly alien Broadway.

Jolson could no longer control the show. He had to stick to the script. There were no more Jolson interpolations, although the script allowed him a medley of his hits. He shared billing with Martha Raye, Bert Gordon and Jack Whiting. Although Jolson and the show had received rave reviews, he lost interest. Claiming that he couldn't stand the cold of New York's winter, Jolson left the production, and it closed. It was revived briefly in July 1941 in Atlantic City. Once more, Jolson seemed unsatisfied and felt he would lose his voice if he continued.

Jolson's career went into decline, with radio appearances and touring for the USO taking up most of his time. More and more he was considered a nostalgic figure. Then the Columbia picture *The Jolson Story* (1946), starring Larry Parks as Jolson, reawakened interest in the singer. The film was followed by a new recording contract for Decca Records and a continuing radio series for Kraft. Then came *Jolson Sings Again* (1949), another big hit. Television was the new medium, and Jolson approached it warily. A final tour of Korea for the USO left Jolson exhausted and sick, and on October 23, 1950, shortly after his return home from overseas, the World's Greatest Performer died.

Robert Benchley *(q.v.)*, writing in the old *Life Magazine* of Jolson's performance in *Big Boy,* captured Jolson's unique effect on audiences:

> The word "personality" isn't quite strong enough for the thing that Jolson has. Unimpressive as the comparison may be to Mr. Jolson, we should say that John the Baptist was the last man to have such a power. There is something supernatural at the back of it, or we miss our guess.
>
> When Jolson enters, it is as if an electric current has been run along the wires under the seats where the hats are stuck. The house comes to a tumultuous attention. He speaks, rolls his eyes, compresses his lips, and it is all over. You are a member of the Al Jolson Association.
>
> He trembles his underlip, and your heart breaks with a loud snap. He sings a banal song and you totter out to send a night letter to your mother. Such a giving-off of vitality, personality, charm, and whatever all those words are, results from a Jolson performance.

JOLSON'S 59TH STREET THEATER 932 7th Avenue between 58th and 59th Street. Architect: Herbert J. Krapp. Opening: October 6, 1921; *Bombo.*   This theater had an especially difficult history. The Shuberts *(q.v.)* built the theater for one of their biggest stars, Al Jolson *(q.v.)*. He opened his successful musical *Bombo* (10/6/21; 218 performances) there. *Bombo's* score was written by Sig-

mund Romberg *(q.v.)* and Harold Atteridge. As usual, the hit songs were written by others and interpolated into the score. The most famous of these was "April Showers" by Louis Silvers and B.G. DeSylva *(q.v.)*. Other hit songs that received their first hearing in *Bombo* were "Dirty Hands, Dirty Face" by James V. Monaco, Jolson and Edgar Leslie; "My Mammy" by Walter Donaldson and B.G. DeSylva; and "Toot Toot Tootsie" by Gus Kahn, Ernie Erdman and Dan Russo. These were all enormous successes for Jolson.

Unfortunately, *Bombo* was one of the theater's few successes. After a series of failures, another huge hit opened, *The Student Prince* (12/2/24; 608 performances). This time, Romberg, along with lyricist/librettist Dorothy Donnelly, came up with a smashing score. "Deep in My Heart, Dear," "Drinking Song," "Golden Days," "Students' Life" and "Serenade" were all big hits at the time. Sixty years after its creation, *The Student Prince* is still much performed.

A couple of moderate successes followed, including a revival of the Shubert's war horse, *Blossom Time.* Romberg and Donnelly saw the curtain rise on *My Maryland* (9/12/27; 312 performances), another success.

The last three months of 1929 and the early months of 1930 were taken up by some halfhearted revivals of past operettas (*Robin Hood, Sweethearts, The Fortune Teller, The Merry Widow, Babes in Toyland, The Count of Luxembourg, The Serenade* and *Mlle. Modiste*). This series of revivals marked the end of Shubert ownership.

The Depression hit the Shuberts hard, and they were forced to sell the theater. It would never again have a success. The theater, renamed Shakespeare's Theater, reopened with *A Midsummer Night's Dream* (11/12/32). Two years later, the theater reopened as the Venice Theater with *Africana* (11/26/34; 3 performances), a new edition of the popular revue that opened originally in 1927.

The Yiddish Art Theater was the new name of the auditorium with the opening of *The Brothers Ashkenazi* (9/20/37). It was again renamed the Jolson Theater with *Comes the Revolution* (5/26/42). Yiddish theater returned, and the theater was renamed the Molly Picon Theater with the opening of *Oy Is Dus a Leben* (10/12/42).

Follow the Girls (4/8/44; 882 performances), a musical with music by Philip Charig and lyrics by Dan Shapiro and Milton Pascal, opened at what was then called the Century Theater. Surprisingly, the show was a success. *Follow the Girls* starred Jackie Gleason, Gertrude Niesen and Irina Baranova.

The success didn't transfer to other shows. On March 29, 1954, the theater was dubbed NBC Theater with the inside adapted to television. In the fall of 1959, it became the Video Tape Center. The theater was demolished around 1961.

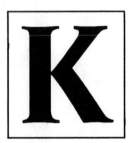

KAUFMAN AND HART

Moss Hart (1904–1961) Moss Hart, stagestruck as a youth, worked for the producer/director Augustus Pitou. Pitou produced Hart's first play. It closed out of town. Hart was introduced to Kaufman, who agreed to work on Hart's next idea, *Once in a Lifetime* (9/24/30; 305 performances).

Hart also enjoyed a successful career, mainly in musical theater, apart from his collaboration with Kaufman. Among his successes are an Irving Berlin revue, *Face the Music* (2/17/32; 166 performances); the musical *The Great Waltz* (9/22/34; 297 performances); the musical *Jubilee* (10/12/35; 169 performances); a David Freedman revue, *The Show Is On* (12/25/36; 236 performances); the musical *Lady in the Dark* (for which Hart was also codirector [1/23/41; 467 performances]); *Winged Victory,* for which Hart was also codirector (11/20/43; 212 performances); *Christopher Blake* (11/30/46; 114 performances); *Light Up the Sky* (11/18/48; 214 performances); and *The Climate of Eden* (11/13/52; 20 performances). Hart also directed the musicals *My Fair Lady* (3/15/56; 2,717 performances) and *Camelot* (12/3/60; 873 performances). He died a year after the opening of *Camelot,* on December 20, 1961.

George S. Kaufman (1899–1961) George S. Kaufman was one of the theater's most versatile participants. He was equally adept at playwriting and directing, but his greatest asset was as a play doctor. Kaufman began a journalistic career at the *Washington Times* in 1912. For nine years, he contributed a humor column. Kaufman's column was also printed in the *New York Evening Mail* from 1914 to 1915. Kaufman moved from Washington to New York where he served on the drama staffs of the *New York Tribune* and the *New York Times.*

There was no better play editor in the theater. He was often called by producers to fix ailing productions. Kaufman, a shy man, nevertheless had many followers who thrived in his presence, for Kaufman was one of the great humorists. He used his wit constructively, to teach, scold and show his affection. Kaufman's shyness was but one aspect of his insecurity. He always preferred to write with collaborators, and did so in all but two cases.

Prior to his collaboration with Moss Hart, Kaufman enjoyed many successes. Among his most notable plays, with his collaborators noted in parenthesis, were *Dulcy* (Marc Connelly; 8/13/21; 246 performances); *To the Ladies* (Marc Connelly; 2/20/22; 128 performances); *Merton of the Movies* (Marc Connelly; 11/13/22; 248 performances); the musical *Helen of Troy* (Marc Connelly; 6/19/23; 191 performances); *Beggar on Horseback* (Marc Connelly; 2/12/24; 144 performances); *The Butter and Egg Man* (9/23/25; 243 performances); the musical *The Cocoanuts* (Morrie Ryskind; 12/8/25; 218 performances); *The Royal Family* (Edna Ferber; 12/28/27; 345 performances); the musical *Animal Crackers* (Morrie Ryskind; 10/23/28; 191 performances); *June Moon* (Ring Lardner; 10/9/29; 273 performances); and the musical *Strike Up the Band* (Morrie Ryskind; 1/14/30; 191 performances).

Kaufman's collaborations with Hart include: *Once in a Lifetime* (9/24/30; 305 performances); *Merrily We Roll Along* (9/29/34; 155 performances); *You Can't Take It with You* (12/14/36; 837 performances); the musical *I'd Rather Be Right* (11/2/37; 266 performances); *The Fabulous Invalid* (10/8/38; 65 performances); *The American Way* (1/21/39; 244 performances); *The Man Who Came to Dinner* (10/16/39; 739 performances); *George Washington Slept Here* (10/18/40; 173 performances); and *Dream On, Soldier,* a special production for the American Red Cross (4/5/43; 1 performance).

During and after his collaboration with Hart, Kaufman collaborated on the following plays and musicals: the revue *The Band Wagon* (Howard Dietz *(q.v.),* 6/3/

31; 260 performances); the Pulitzer Prize-winning musical *Of Thee I Sing* (Morrie Ryskind; 12/26/31; 441 performances); *Dinner at Eight* (Edna Ferber; 10/22/32; 232 performances); the musical *Let 'Em Eat Cake* (Morrie Ryskind; 10/21/33; 90 performances); *First Lady* (Katharine Dayton; 11/26/35; 238 performances); *Stage Door* (Edna Ferber; 10/22/36; 169 performances); *The Late George Apley* (John P. Marquand; 11/21/44; 357 performances); *The Solid Gold Cadillac* (Howard Teichmann; 11/5/53; 526 performances); and the musical *Silk Stockings* (Leueen MacGrath and Abe Burrows; 2/24/55; 478 performances).

Kaufman died six months before Hart, on June 2, 1961.

KELCEY ALLEN AWARD Kelcey Allen (1875–1951) was the founder of the New York Drama Critics Circle and drama editor of *Women's Wear Daily* from 1915 until 1951. The award named for her was given each year to an individual who made a significant contribution to the American theater. The first recipient, in 1955, was Vincent Sardi Sr., owner of Sardi's *(q.v.)* restaurant.

KERN, JEROME (1885–1945) Jerome Kern and George M. Cohan *(q.v.)* were the first composers for the Broadway stage to give the musical an American feeling. Cohan brought vaudeville and music-hall influences into the musical. Kern was more in touch with the musical's European roots. He gave the European operetta a real American sound and had a greater impact than Cohan on the transition from operetta to a truly American musical theater.

Kern was born in New York City on January 27, 1885. He attended the New York College of Music, where he studied piano with Alexander Lambert and Paolo Gallico and harmony with Dr. Austin Pierce. Kern was introduced to the great operetta traditions when he went to England and Germany. When he returned to the United States in 1904, Kern found work at T.B. Harms, a leading music publisher. While at Harms, Kern became acquainted with most of the leading artists and producers of early musical comedy.

Kern began interpolating songs into American versions of foreign musicals. As an American, Kern was influenced by the harmonies and rhythms employed by America's classical and popular writers. In 1904, Kern interpolated songs into *Mr. Wix of Wickham,* an English show transplanted to America with Julian Eltinge as the star.

More important to Kern was his next interpolation, "How'd You Like to Spoon with Me?" with lyrics by Edward Laska. The song was included in the show *The Earl and the Girl* (11/04/05). The song became the first hit for Kern, and soon Broadway producers were demanding his talents.

Jerome Kern   Courtesy ASCAP.

Kern had songs interpolated into many shows that opened during the early 20th century, including *The Catch of the Season* (8/28/05); *The Little Cherub* (8/6/06); *My Lady's Maid* (9/20/06); *The Rich Mr. Hogenheimer* (10/22/06); *The Orchid* (4/8/07); *The Dairymaids* (8/26/07); *Fascinating Flora* (5/20/07); *The Great White Way* (10/7/07); *A Waltz Dream* (1/27/08); *The Girls of Gottenberg* (9/2/08); *Fluffy Ruffles* (9/7/08); *The Dollar Princess* (9/6/09); *The Gay Hussars* (7/29/09); and *The Kiss Waltz* (9/18/11).

Kern finally had his first full score commissioned for *The Red Petticoat* (11/13/12; 61 performances). Paul West supplied the lyrics to the Kern songs. The next year, Kern wrote his second full score for *Oh, I Say!* (10/30/13). Harry B. Smith *(q.v.)* wrote the lyrics for the show. In 1914 Kern and Smith wrote "You're Here and I'm Here" for *The Laughing Husband,* and Kern saw a great early hit, "They Didn't Believe Me," premiere in *The Girl from Utah* (8/24/14), with a lyric by Herbert Reynolds.

Kern had a banner year in 1915. He had five shows open that year, including one of his most enduring hits, *Very Good Eddie.* The first was *90 in the Shade* (1/25/15). Smith again provided lyrics, and the libretto was written by Guy Bolton *(q.v.),* who would become an important player in Kern's career. The second show was *Rosy Rapture,* a J.M. Barrie play produced in London. For *Nobody Home* (4/20/15), Bolton again supplied the book with most of the lyrics by Schuyler Greene.

Elsie Janis was the star and lyricist of *Miss Information* (10/5/15).

The final Kern musical of the year was *Very Good Eddie* (12/23/15). Schuyler Greene was the lyricist along with Herbert Reynolds. Guy Bolton and Philip Bartholomae contributed the libretto. Elisabeth Marbury and F. Ray Comstock produced the show, which was an immediate hit.

Nobody's Home and *Very Good Eddie* were the first two of what are now known as the Princess Theater shows. Elisabeth Marbury was a well-known literary agent of the day. She had the idea that a kind of permanent company devoted to the American musical should be established, similar to several companies that were at that time devoted to American drama. Comstock owned the Princess Theater, which, with only 299 seats, had difficulty finding tenants. Marbury's idea was a perfect long-term solution to his problem.

Kern and Bolton were the first writers hired as the core of the new company. The Princess shows are generally acknowledged as the first of the modern musical comedies. Because of the small size of the theater, they were necessarily intimate shows and broke away from the general operatic tradition. The songs were better integrated into the story than in the old-style shows, and the plots revolved around American characters in American settings. The shows were less overtly romantic than the typical musical comedy, and they were more in tune with current trends and feelings.

Kern's next show, produced in London, was more traditional. *Theodore and Co.* (9/19/16; 503 performances) had lyrics by Adrian Ross and Clifford Grey. Kern was back in the United States for his next show, *Have a Heart* (1/11/17), the first Kern show to boast lyrics by P.G. Wodehouse and first of five written by him in 1917. Bolton and Wodehouse contributed the book. "And I Am All Alone" was a mild success from the score. Harry B. Smith was the lyricist for *Love O' Mike* (1/15/17).

Oh, Boy! (2/20/17; 463 performances), another Bolton, Wodehouse and Kern production, contained several great songs: "The Land Where the Good Songs Go," cut prior to the opening; "Nesting Time in Flatbush," probably the funniest song in the show; and the enduring classic " 'Till the Clouds Roll By," one of the greatest of all American popular songs.

Leave It to Jane (8/28/17; 167 performances) was the third show by the successful trio. The score was one of the team's most consistent. "Cleopatterer," "The Crickets Are Calling," "The Siren's Song" and the title song all received a measure of success. The songs are enchanting and written with the humorous innocence that hallmarked the team's work:

Miss 1917 (11/5/17; 40 performances) was hailed by reviewers. It played to sold-out houses, and yet it closed prematurely. Produced by Charles B. Dillingham and

Florenz Ziegfeld *(q.v.)*, the show's running costs were greater than the ticket prices could cover. The Kern, Wodehouse and Bolton show starred Elizabeth Brice, Marion Davies, Lew Fields *(q.v.)*, Ann Pennington, Vivienne Segal, Van and Schenck, George White *(q.v.)* and Bessie McCoy.

In 1918, Kern was busy with another five shows on the boards. *Oh, Lady! Lady!!* (2/1/18; 219 performances) was the first of the year's Kern, Bolton and Wodehouse shows. None of the songs achieved great fame, but a song that was cut from the show, "Bill," would later become one of the great hits from *Show Boat*. The other 1918 efforts were all rather minor: *Toot-Toot!* (3/11/18; 40 performances), *Rock-a-bye Baby* (5/22/18; 80 performances) and *Head Over Heels* (8/29/18; 100 performances).

In 1919, Kern wrote only one musical, *She's a Good Fellow* (5/5/19; 120 performances). It is most noteworthy as the first Kern show for which Anne Caldwell supplied the book and lyrics. Caldwell was one of the only women working in what was then a male-dominated field. Her success led to a slight opening for women in the ranks of composers, lyricists and librettists.

Caldwell worked on a total of nine shows with Jerome Kern. Her second, *The Night Boat* (2/2/20; 313 performances) was the first of three shows written by Kern in 1920. Two of the songs, "Left All Alone Again Blues" and "Whose Baby Are You?," achieved some success. Anne Caldwell also contributed lyrics to Kern's next show, *Hitchy-Koo of 1920* (10/19/20; 71 performances). The annual revue starred popular comedian Raymond Hitchcock.

Kern's last show of 1920 was one of his greatest successes. *Sally* (12/21/20; 570 performances) had a book by Guy Bolton and lyrics by Clifford Grey, Anne Caldwell, P.G. Wodehouse and B.G. DeSylva *(q.v.)*. The show's great success was due to the excellence of the score and Florenz Ziegfeld's lavish production. The star was one of the most beloved performers on the American stage, Marilyn Miller. Leon Errol, Walter Catlett, Irving Fisher and Mary Hay also starred.

The score contained many great Kern melodies, including the title song, "Wild Rose" and "Whip-Poor-Will." The best song, however, was one of Kern's most enduring standards, "Look for the Silver Lining." The DeSylva lyric was perfectly married to Kern's simple melody.

Kern's next show, *Good Morning, Dearie* (11/21/21; 347 performances), also had a long run, in part because of the success of *Sally*. *Good Morning Dearie* boasted a book and lyrics by Anne Caldwell. "Ka-lu-a," "Blue Danube Blues" and "Good Morning, Dearie" are still remembered by Kern fans.

Fred and Adele Astaire *(q.v.)* were the stars of Kern's next show, *The Bunch and Judy* (11/28/22; 63 perfor-

Anne Caldwell   Courtesy ASCAP.

mances), which was followed by *Stepping Stones* (11/6/23; 241 performances).

Sitting Pretty (4/8/24; 95 performances), at the Fulton Theater (*q.v.*), was the last of the Bolton, Wodehouse and Kern shows. The musical starred Queenie Smith and Frank McIntyre.

Kern provided his only score in collaboration with Howard Dietz (*q.v.*) for *Dear Sir* (9/23/24; 15 performances). Dietz had contributed to Franklin Price Adams's column The Conning Tower under the pseudonym "Freckles." Like most of his contemporaries, he was in awe of Kern and was amazed that the master had called on him for his musical. *Dear Sir* wasn't a success, but it did give Dietz his start in musical comedy.

Kern's next show, *Sunny* (9/22/25; 517 performances), another great success, reunited the composer with his star of *Sally*, Marilyn Miller. Otto Harbach (*q.v.*) and Oscar Hammerstein II (*q.v.*) provided the book and lyrics. *Sunny* contained such big hits as "Who?," "D'Ye Love Me?" and the title song. Percy Hammond called the score "comparatively aristocratic." Alan Dale, however, found the music "not remarkable." He said, "It had some effective harmonies, however, and it was at least scholarly, and it wasn't treacle." Burns Mantle in the *New York Daily News* proclaimed the score "excellent."

For *The City Chap* (10/26/25; 72 performances) which opened at the Liberty Theatre (*q.v.*), Kern teamed with lyricist Anne Caldwell. For *Criss-Cross* (10/12/26; 210

performances), Caldwell and Kern were together for the last time. Otto Harbach also contributed to the lyrics. Fred Stone made his second appearance in a Kern show supported by his daughter Dorothy and Oscar ("Rags") Ragland. Stone played an aviator who made his entrance from the top of the proscenium, dangling from a parachute. As soon as he hit the stage, a spring action catapulted him back into the flies. Stone kept up his trademarked brand of physical humor throughout the show. In one scene, he rescued his daughter by hanging by his knees from a trapeze that was attached to the body of an airplane. As he swung over the stage, he grabbed two handles attached to the back of his daughter's costume and lofted her into the wings.

Lucky (3/22/27; 71 performances), Kern's next show, proved less strenuous for its cast. Bert Kalmar and Harry Ruby provided the lyrics and coauthored the libretto with Otto Harbach. At this time, Kern began the most important phase of his career. His last six shows, written with either Oscar Hammerstein II or Otto Harbach, contain some of the greatest songs of the American musical theater. Although some of these shows may not be well remembered today, their songs have endured for over half a century.

Show Boat (12/27/27; 575 performances) is generally considered Kern's masterpiece. *Show Boat* was presented by Florenz Ziegfeld at the Ziegfeld Theater (*q.v.*). The cast, Charles Winninger, Howard Marsh, Norma Terris, Helen Morgan, Edna Mae Oliver and

Sheet music for a song in Sunny

Jules Bledsoe perfectly personified Edna Ferber's fascinating characters.

The score was equally brilliant, containing such standards as "Make Believe," "Ol' Man River," "Can't Help Lovin' dat Man," "Life Upon the Wicked Stage," "You Are Love," "Why Do I Love You?" and "Bill." John Byram in the *New York Times* stated that the show had "an exceptionally tuneful score—the most lilting and satisfactory that the wily Jerome Kern has evolved in several seasons." Richard Watts Jr., in the *New York Herald Tribune,* said that Kern "came out of the proceedings with the highest credit." Abel Green in *Variety (q.v.)* stated that "the music is typically Kernian, titillating, infectious, refreshing and never tiring." *Show Boat* has been revived numerous times on Broadway and around the world.

Sweet Adeline (9/3/29; 234 performances), at Hammerstein's Theater *(q.v.),* was a vehicle written for one of the stars of *Show Boat* and one of the greatest Broadway stars—Helen Morgan. The torch singer was the lead character in the new show. Oscar Hammerstein II repeated his lyric and libretto duties. Two of Morgan's numbers, "Why Was I Born?" and "Don't Ever Leave Me" are among Kern and Hammerstein's most dramatic songs. Nearly all the reviews were favorable. Gilbert Seldes echoed the majority opinion when he commented in the *New Republic,* "the music is more of a concentration of the spirit of the 1890's than a reminiscence of its tunes. Kern is a master of many styles and handled the charm and rather awkward grace of the time perfectly."

Otto Harbach provided the book and lyrics to *The Cat and the Fiddle* (10/15/31; 395 performances) at the Globe Theater. The score was filled with beautiful Kern melodies, and Harbach's lyrics fitted the show's European ambiance perfectly. "The Night Was Made for Love," "She Didn't Say 'Yes'," "Try to Forget" and "One Moment Alone" have all become standards.

Music in the Air (11/8/32; 342 performances) retained *The Cat and the Fiddle*'s European feeling. Oscar Hammerstein II provided the book and lyrics for the show. Walter Slezak, Natalie Hall, Vivian Vance, Marjorie Main and Al Shean starred at the Alvin Theater *(q.v.).*

"I've Told Every Little Star" was the best-received song in the score, which also included "There's a Hill Beyond a Hill," "And Love Was Born" and "The Song Is You." Most of the reviews were favorable, with all the critics agreeing on the merits of the Kern and Hammerstein score. John Mason Brown, in the *New York Post,* said that *Music in the Air* "abounds in the sort of soft, insinuating melodies which rarely are heard along Broadway and of which Mr. Kern is a past master. It is subtle, captivating music." That opinion was typical of the critical raves that the score received.

Roberta (11/18/33; 295 performances) is one of Kern's most recognizable titles. The recognition is mostly due to the successful movie version with Fred Astaire and Irene Dunne. The stage version starred Lyda Roberti, Bob Hope, Tamara, Sydney Greenstreet, Fay Templeton and George Murphy. Otto Harbach supplied the libretto and lyrics. Among the songs featured in the show (and mostly cut from the movie version) were "The Touch of Your Hand," "You're Devastating," "Yesterdays," "Let's Begin," "I'll Be Hard to Handle" and the classic "Smoke Gets in Your Eyes."

Kern's last show was *Very Warm for May* (11/17/39; 59 performances) at the Alvin Theater *(q.v.).* Jack Whiting, Eve Arden, Hiram Sherman and Donald Brian were the stars. Oscar Hammerstein II provided the lyrics and libretto. He also codirected the show with Vincente Minnelli.

The wonderful score featured "In Other Words, Seventeen," "All in Fun," "In the Heart of the Dark," "Heaven in My Arms" and the evergreen "All the Things You Are." Reviews of the show, especially the book, were harsh, but Kern's score was well received. Brooks Atkinson, in the *New York Times,* said that Kern's work was "rich in variety and feeling and a testament to honest composing."

Following *Very Warm for May,* Kern composed the classic song "The Last Time I Saw Paris" with Oscar Hammerstein II. He wrote scores to films, including *One Night in the Tropics, Swing Time, You Were Never Lovelier, Can't Help Singing* and *Cover Girl.* After the successful sojourn in Hollywood, Kern returned to New York to work on a new musical with Dorothy Fields *(q.v.).* It was produced by Rodgers and Hammerstein *(q.v.)* and based on the life of Annie Oakley.

Before work commenced on the show, on November 5, Kern collapsed on Park Avenue and 57th Street. Because he had no identification, Kern was taken to the City Hospital on Welfare Island. Hospital personnel found Kern's membership card in ASCAP *(q.v.).* The organization informed Hammerstein, and he arranged for doctors to examine Kern. The composer was diagnosed as having a cerebral hemorrhage. He was moved to Doctors' Hospital on November 7. Kern intermittently regained consciousness, but his condition steadily worsened. On the last day of Kern's life, Hammerstein sat at Kern's bedside and gently sang "I've Told Every Little Star" hoping to rouse him. After finishing the song, Hammerstein looked at his friend and realized that he had died. The date was November 11, 1945.

KERR, WALTER See CRITICS.

KLAW THEATER 251–57 W. 45th Street between Broadway and 8th Avenue. Architect: Eugene De Rosa Opening: March 2, 1921; *Nice People.* The Klaw Theater led an unimpressive existence. On September 18, 1929, it reopened as the Avon Theater with Preston Sturges's comedy *Strictly Dishonorable.* In September 1934, CBS took it over as a radio playhouse. The theater was razed in 1954.

KNICKERBOCKER HOTEL 142 W. 42nd Street. Architects: Marvin & Davis, Bruce Price consultant. Construction on the beaux-arts-style Knickerbocker Hotel began in 1901, but because of the original owner's default on rent, construction stopped in 1904. The hotel was finally completed in 1906.

The Knickerbocker was planned as a rival to the Astor Hotel (*q.v.*). No expense was spared to make the 15-story hotel as luxurious as possible. Advertisements featured its $10,000 gold service for 60. The interior was designed by Trowbridge & Livingston, architects of the St. Regis Hotel. Their designs were a great success, especially the important artworks they commissioned. Maxfield Parrish's mural *Old King Cole and His Fiddlers Three* was the most prominent. Frederick Remington's painting *The United States Calvary Charge* was hung in the basement bar. A bas relief of Aphrodite by John Flanagen graced the Flower Room. Also in the Flower Room was a scene painted by James Wall Finn.

Concerning the design and decoration of the Knickerbocker, the 1906 *Architecture Record* stated, "There are few hotels in the country in the appearance of which such uniform good taste has been displayed; and there is certainly no hotel which will owe so much of its success to its aesthetic distinction. Its architecture is, unfortunately, not as successful as its decorative scheme. Certain architectural errors have been made, of which the failure to insert a partition between the restaurant and the Flower Room is one of the worst, because it seriously hurts the architectural effect of both these rooms. But even after all deductions have been made, the hotel marks a real advance in the art of making that sort of a building legitimately entertaining to its patrons."

Society took to the Knickerbocker and made its early years successful. The hotel, dubbed the "42nd Street Country Club," numbered among its tenants George M. Cohan (*q.v.*) and Enrico Caruso. It was so successful that on October 18, 1911, the Knickerbocker acquired

Knickerbocker Building. Photo Jeff Slotnick.

King Cole Room of the Knickerbocker Hotel

the Ryan Hotel next door. The two spaces were merged, and the Knickerbocker acquired 100 extra rooms.

However, with the onset of Prohibition, the Knickerbocker, like many other hotels, lost money. Liquor sales at bars and restaurants accounted for much of the hotel's profits. The Astor was able to add stores on the ground floor to offset the loss in revenue.

On June 14, 1920, Vincent Astor, Nicholas Biddle and S.B. Thorn bought the hotel and converted most of it to office space. The Knickerbocker's two lower floors were transformed into retail space, but the Grill was retained. Many of the interior appointments were saved in the transformation. The King Cole mural was transferred to the St. Regis Hotel.

In February 1921, the National Drug Stores chain was the first lessee. The company took nearly the entire first floor retail space. It leased the space for $3.5 million over a 21-year period.

The building's last major tenant was the *Newsweek* organization. In October 1956, *Newsweek* moved to new offices on the East Side. The mansard-roofed building still retains much of its turn of the century splendor. With the rampant development in the area, the Knickerbocker remains the last vestige of bygone Times Square. A relic of the past can be viewed in the front of the Times Square shuttle's track number one. A small door is still topped by a sign reading Knickerbocker, a forgotten vestige of the great hotel.

L

LABOR STAGE   See 48TH STREET THEATRE.

LAFF-MOVIE   See ELTINGE THEATRE.

LANE, BURTON (1912–   ) Composer Burton Lane has not had as many of his shows produced as his contemporaries, but his shows have all contained superior scores. When not writing for Broadway, Lane had a successful career in Hollywood. Each of Lane's Broadway scores, written with such greats as Harold Adamson, E.Y. Harburg (q.v.), Alan Jay Lerner (q.v.) and Al Dubin, were full of rich, inventive melodies.

Lane showed an early predilection for music; he took his first piano lessons at age three. He returned to the piano after his parents imposed a six year break so that he could concentrate on his school studies. Amazingly, Lane was so good that he was given an audience with J.J. Shubert, one of the Shubert brothers (q.v.), the two most powerful men on Broadway. Lane, only 14 at the time, was assigned the score for a new Shubert show. The show wasn't produced, because the star was not available, but had it been, Lane would have been the youngest songwriter in Broadway history.

The next year, Lane went to Remick Publishing Company, where he was given a job plugging songs. While at Remick's, Lane was befriended by George Gershwin (q.v.). He also met lyricist Howard Dietz (q.v.) who was working on the revue *Three's a Crowd* (10/15/30) with his partner Arthur Schwartz (q.v.). When the show opened, it contained two Dietz and Lane songs, "Out in the Open Air" and "Forget All Your Books."

He next had a song put in *The Third Little Show* (6/1/31) and nine in the 1931 edition of the *Earl Carroll Vanities* (q.v.) (8/27/31) with lyrics by Harold Adamson. The *Vanities* score led to Hollywood and his first film score, *Dancing Lady*, in 1933. The movie contained the first hit song of the 21-year-old composer "Everything I Have Is Yours," and also marked the film debut of Fred Astaire (q.v.).

In 1940, after a series of successful films, Lane wrote the score to *Hold On to Your Hats* (9/11/40; 158 performances). The show marked the return to Broadway from Hollywood of Al Jolson (q.v.). The great Jolson left the show after catching pneumonia, and the show quickly closed. Lane's score, written with lyricist E.Y. Harburg, contained the hits "The World Is in My Arms" and "There's a Great Day Comin' Manana."

Burton Lane   Courtesy ASCAP.

Laffing Room Only (12/23/44; 232 performances), a vehicle for Olsen and Johnson, was produced by the Shuberts at the Winter Garden Theater (*q.v.*). Lane tried his hand at writing his own lyrics for the show, which included one big hit, "Feudin' and Fightin'." The song had lyrics by Lane and Frank Loesser (*q.v.*). The Shuberts, used to challenging any and all comers, were fighting ASCAP (*q.v.*), the licensing agents for songwriters and publishers. The Shuberts decided to withhold the right to broadcast songs from their productions on radio. The producers started their own Performing Acts Society of the Theater to defy ASCAP. Broadcasters had formed their own challenge to ASCAP, BMI (Broadcast Music Incorporated). The Shuberts sided with BMI. Unfortunately, Lane was caught in the middle, unable to receive royalties from "Feudin' and Fightin' " because the Shuberts refused to allow it to be broadcast. In 1947, after the ASCAP ban was lifted, the song received its due.

Lane's next score was written with Harburg for one of the best Broadway musicals, *Finian's Rainbow* (1/10/47; 725 performances). The show opened at the 46th Street Theatre (*q.v.*) with Ella Logan, David Wayne, Donald Richards and the Lyn Murray Singers. Lane collaborated with E.Y. Harburg on the excellent score, which included "How Are Things in Glocca Morra," "When I'm Not Near the Girl I Love," "If This Isn't Love," "Old Devil Moon" and "Look to the Rainbow."

Almost 20 years passed before the next Broadway score by Burton Lane. *On a Clear Day You Can See Forever* (10/17/65; 280 performances) starred Barbara Harris, John Cullum and William Daniels. The show proved Lane had not lost his touch. With lyricist and librettist Alan Jay Lerner, Lane composed a winning score.

Lane and Lerner contributed more fine work to their next show, *Carmelina* (4/8/79; 17 performances). Unfortunately, the show had many troubles and never recovered in time for its opening. The show marked Lane's last Broadway assignment. Although his Broadway output was not extensive, the quality of his work is impressive. His songs have a depth rarely seen on Broadway. They are not just pop songs but true theatrical statements that help define their characters, advance the plots and express true emotions.

LATIN QUARTER Between Broadway and Seventh Avenue on 48th Street. The Palais Royal was the first of the famous nightclubs to operate out of the building that would later house the Cotton Club and the highly successful Latin Quarter. Paul Salvin, dubbed the King of Nightclubs, owned and ran the Palais Royal from its inception in the latter part of the teens. Salvin made the club a fashionable hangout for Eastsiders, insisting that his patrons wear evening dress. Soon, the Palais Royal rivaled Sherry's and Delmonico's. The club sometimes grossed $20,000 a week, a huge sum at the time.

Helping Salvin were his assistants Gil Boag and James Thompson. Salvin's maitres d'hotel were Pierre and Borgo. They both left Salvin and became successful in their own right. Pierre later built the famous Fifth Avenue hotel that bears his name.

Salvin's other operations were the Pavilion Royal, Rector's (*q.v.*) and the Montmartre, which was atop the Winter Garden Theater (*q.v.*). He was a man of simple taste who had a knack for making people feel comfortable. Salvin had a way of growing fond of certain words that he would use over and over again. For a period, his favorite word was *environment*. When performer Fritzi Scheff hit a sour note on the stage of the Palais Royal, Salvin told director John Murray Anderson (*q.v.*), "She has lost her environment. She can't do a thing like that in a respectable place like this." It was Scheff who had appeared in the Palais Royal's first production, which was staged by her husband, silent film cowboy Bronco Billy Anderson. She sang her great hit "Kiss Me Again," written for her by composer Victor Herbert (*q.v.*) for her appearance in his operetta *Mlle. Modiste.* John Murray Anderson staged later shows in the club, which were the first true nightclub shows. Anderson supplied the lyrics to music by A. Baldwin Sloane and Frank Harling.

The building housed the downtown version of Connie's Inn from 1933 to 1934. The Immerman brothers, owners of Connie's Inn, changed the name to the Harlem Club and made it a black-only club. However, blacks seldom frequented Times Square, and the club quickly closed. The Ubangi Club followed with a floor show featuring male and female impersonators. Among the performers were Gladys Bentley, who sang in a man's full evening dress. After a year, the Ubangi club moved farther downtown.

On September 24, 1936, Harlem's renowned Cotton Club moved downtown to this location. The Cotton Club opened under Herman Stark's direction, assisted by Big Frenchy DeMange. Columnist Louis Sobol remembered sitting in the Cotton Club and playing pinochle with DeMange, "one of the formidable chieftains of gangdom."

The first show at the club's new location starred Bill Bojangles Robinson and Cab Calloway. The songs for that first edition of the downtown Cotton Club were by J. Fred Coots and Benny Davis. The show was an immediate success.

By its third week, the club was grossing $45,000. In the first three months the club averaged a weekly gross of $30,000. The large earnings were due to the number of shows given, not to, high prices. A steak sandwich was $2.25. Scrambled eggs and sausage cost only $1.50, and a lobster cocktail cost $1.50. Filet mignon and french fries cost $3. The club offered Chinese selections also. Moo goo gai pan cost $2.25. The cover charge for a complete table d'hote was $1.50 to $2 for dinner. Otherwise, there was no cover charge.

The Cotton Club's success continued with its second revue, which was mounted in the spring of 1937. The songs were written by such greats as Duke Ellington and Andy Razaf. Ellington's band appeared in the show along with Ethel Waters, Ivy Anderson, George Dewey Washington and the Nicholas Brothers. The show was titled the Cotton Club Express. Columnist Ed Sullivan (q.v.) called it "easily the most elegant colored show Broadway has ever applauded" and said that it "would corner the hi-de-ho and ho-de-ho market." The show was an even bigger success than the club's first downtown revue. In one month, over 50,000 people attended.

Opening nights at the Cotton Club could easily rival Broadway's. Among the opening night patrons were actress Sylvia Sidney, comedian Lou Holtz and Dr. Leo Michel, nicknamed Dr. Broadway.

The Cotton Club continued its success through the thirties. But as the Depression dragged on, Stark began to have money problems. The government was watching the club closely because of its ties to organized crime. The cost of doing such lavish shows also rose, and the club's fortunes suddenly began to fall. Audience tastes were changing, and more luxurious, sophisticated clubs were gaining favor.

Louis Armstrong and Maxine Sullivan at the Cotton Club

Featured in the final Cotton Club show were Louis Armstrong and Maxine Sullivan, fresh from their star turns in the Hollywood movie *Going Places*. Also appearing were Stepin Fetchit, Midge Williams, Stump and Stumpy and Andy Kirk's Orchestra. Finally, on June 10, 1940, the Cotton Club closed.

The Latin Quarter, one of the greatest New York nightclubs for almost a quarter of a century, opened on the premises on April 1, 1942. Some New Yorkers preferred the more sophisticated East Side clubs like El Morocco and the Copacabana. But Times Square clubs like Billy Rose's Diamond Horseshoe (q.v.) and the Latin Quarter entertained more than their share of native New Yorkers. By 1945, the Latin Quarter was grossing $45,000 a week. In its first 10 years, the club grossed $10 million and served more than 5,000,000 patrons.

New Yorkers came here to mingle with the tourists who paid to see such stars as Ted Lewis, Sophie Tucker, Mae West, Harry Richman, Milton Berle and Willie and Eugene Howard. Columnist Earl Wilson wrote of the Latin Quarter that "the show was long, with acrobats, Apache dancers, jugglers, harmonica wizards—but you got a lot for your money and the chorus girls did their best to show you their breasts although they usually had to wear pasties over their nipples (sometimes the pasties came unpasted, however, or the girls forgot to apply them)."

The club was run by Lou Walters (q.v.), best known today as the father of television personality Barbara Walters. Walters ran the club with his partner E.M. Loew of Boston.

The Quarter, like other Broadway clubs, survived a number of calamities. In the 1930s, the rule in New York was that bare-chested women were allowed as long as they stood still. When police tried to enforce the law, the Latin Quarter girls threatened to hold a topless strike outside the club. In 1944, the government announced a 30% amusement tax. Many nightclubs went out of business when patrons stopped coming. The government later apologized and reduced the tax to 20%.

Later, during World War II, the club took another blow. War Mobilization Director Jimmy Byrnes announced that although he "regretted the inconvenience" there would be a midnight curfew for all amusements. The clubs were up in arms. However, Toots Shor, one of the greatest club owners, calmed everyone down when he stated, "Any crum-bum what can't get plastered by midnight just ain't tryin'." The curfew led to a resurgence in the speakeasy. These secret bottle clubs were thought to be permanently dead when Prohibition was repealed. Mayor LaGuardia proclaimed that "New York is still New York; I don't like the curfew law." He extended the curfew to 1 A.M. That was late enough for most people, and the speakeasies disappeared.

Walters saw the handwriting on the wall for the Latin Quarter and sold out his interest in 1958 but rejoined the enterprise as manager in 1965. He remained until he retired to Florida in 1967, two years before the club closed.

The chorus girls brought on the downfall of the club. Their union, The American Guild of Variety Artists, decided the chorus was not paid enough. The union's vice-president, Penny Singleton (Blondie in the movies), called for a strike. What neither she nor her union appreciated was that times had changed and the clubs were quickly disappearing. Loew, also the owner of several profitable drive-ins, wasn't intimidated at the threat of a strike. He offered the girls $130 a week, a raise of $8. Each week, the girls performed in 13 shows.

The previous January, Jules Podell, operator of the Copacabana, had fired his chorus line. Loew felt he could do the same. However, Loew was also having trouble renewing his lease. On February 20, 1969, the club was closed. Loew planned to reopen the club (sans chorus) elsewhere, but the death knell for New York nightclubs was already sounding and he abandoned the idea. The closing of the Latin Quarter marked the end of the nightclub era in New York.

With the Latin Quarter closed, the building remained empty. Several attempts to inaugurate a legitimate the-ater policy in the space failed. One of the building's names during this period was the 22 Steps Theater, so-called because of the 22 steps that the patrons had to walk up to reach the theater. Among the failures in the space during its various incarnations were *My Old Friends* (4/12/79; 54 performances) starring Cotton Club headliner Maxine Sullivan, and *The Madwoman of Central Park West* (6/13/79; 86 performances) starring Phyllis Newman. The name was then changed to the Princess Theater, and here *Censored Scenes from King Kong* (3/6/80; 5 performances) and *Fearless Frank* (6/15/80; 12 performances) played. One big hit at the Princess Theater was *Pump Boys and Dinettes,* which moved from a 132-performance run off-Broadway on February 4, 1982. *Pump Boys* eventually ran a total of 685 performances making it the only success in the space in 20 years. The name reverted to the Latin Quarter when the room was refurbished in November 1984. It reopened with the show *Harlem Nocturne,* which quickly closed. Since then, the space has remained empty. The entire block was demolished in 1990 to make room for another office tower.

LEAGUE OF AMERICAN THEATERS AND PRODUCERS Born as the League of New York Theaters and Producers in 1930, the League is the voice of the pro-

Latin Quarter Building Photo Jeff Slotnick.

ducers and theater owners. The organization was founded to fight ticket speculation. The League's charter stated its purpose to "protect the general public patrons of the theater, owners of theatrical entertainments, operators of theaters and reputable theater ticket brokers against the evils of speculation of theater tickets."

The League expanded its charter in 1931 and again in 1933. In 1938, it further expanded its role by becoming the official bargaining group for producers in negotiations with craft unions and Actors' Equity *(q.v.)*. The League's goals at that time were announced as "1. To effectuate and bring about amicable adjustment of labor disputes in the theatrical industry in the City of New York. 2. To make on behalf of its members all agreements with other organizations, to carry out one or more purposes of the League. 3. To procure and effect uniformity and certainty in the customs and usages of the theatrical industry; and those having an interest therein. 4. To effect economy in the conduct of the business of its members. And 5. To eliminate unfair and unjust practices."

The campaign against speculators worked. The League and Actors' Equity wrote a Theater Ticket Code of Fair Practice that limited the premiums on tickets sold through speculators. In 1940, the Code was revised and made a state law.

Since then, the organization has spearheaded campaigns for the cleanup of Times Square. The group also commissions studies on audience composition and marketing techniques. One of the League's most visible efforts has been the "I Love New York" tourism campaign. The League also administrates the Tony Awards for the American Theater Wing *(q.v.)*. The League expanded its domain when Broadway fortunes fell in the 1970s and 1980s by becoming the League of American Theaters and Producers. The League publishes what many consider a propagandist column in each month's issue of Playbill *(q.v.)*, given to each theater patron.

LEIGH, DOUGLAS (1907–) Times Square is

defined as much by its look as by its events. One man, more than any other, is responsible for the look of Times Square. He is Douglas Leigh, "the Lamplighter of Broadway," who invented the "spectacular" or giant advertising sign that revolutionized the face of Times Square. Since Times Square is its signs as much as anything else, Douglas Leigh can truly be called the designer of Times Square. Leigh has also had a successful career as a specialist in lighting some of New York's most impressive skyscrapers.

He was born on May 24, 1907, in Anniston, Alabama. After attending the University of Florida, he took a sales job with an outdoor advertising company that had offices in Alabama and New York.

At the age of 22, Leigh came to New York and, after a brief relationship with an outdoor advertising office, he decided to start his own advertising sales office. E.J. Kahn in a profile of Leigh in *The New Yorker* called him "perhaps the only person in the United States besides President Roosevelt who is now in charge of a going business that officially got under way on March 4, 1933."

His firm's first account was a sale of billboard space in the Bronx to the St. Moritz Hotel. Since this was the Depression, Leigh wasn't paid cash for the sale. He took meals and a place to stay from the St. Moritz.

Leigh's next assignment put him on the map and changed the look of Times Square forever. When he arrived on the scene, there were only four moving electric signs on the Square. The Atlantic and Pacific Tea Company asked him to design a sign for them on Times Square. Leigh wasn't content to settle for the usual illuminated billboard. Instead, he designed a 25-foot tall steaming coffee cup. Leigh dubbed the new type of sign a "spectacular." The A&P sign signaled the start of an era. There was no holding back either Leigh or the history of signage *(q.v.)* on Broadway.

Leigh went on to design some of Broadway's most incredible spectaculars, usually in collaboration with the artisans at Artkraft Strauss *(q.v.)*. His work included the Kool Cigarettes winking penguin, which stood atop a giant cake of ice and winked 100,000 times a day. For Ballantine Beer, he designed an effect of clowns pitching quoits to form the beer's three-ring trademark. He created the Bromo Seltzer sign, which bubbled over Times Square, and the Pepsi-Cola spectacular, which featured a 120-foot waterfall that generated 50,000 gallons of water per minute.

Leigh also imported and perfected EPOK from the Swiss. EPOK was a huge billboard covered in light bulbs. Images were projected onto photoelectric cells that then sent the signal to the light bulbs. The wonderful thing about EPOK was that the images could move, and New Yorkers were thrilled to see images of Charlie Chaplin, Fred Astaire *(q.v.)* and Ray Bolger scamper across the skyline. Old Gold Cigarettes, Wilson Whiskies and others sponsored the sign.

During a 46-year period, Leigh designed about 78 different spectaculars, each unique and individual. When World War II brought nightly blackouts, Leigh built a different kind of spectacular, the Camel smoke-ring sign, which endured on Broadway for 27 years.

Leigh also affected Times Square in his 13 years as President and Chairman of the Broadway Association, a group created to help solve Times Square's many problems. During his tenure, he pushed for a redeveloped Times Square and enhanced its streets by putting concrete planters along Broadway from 43rd Street to 46th Street.

Leigh was also instrumental in the war-bond drive. He created a bomb-burst effect and a waving flag of

The Pepsi-Cola spectacular Courtesy Artkraft Strauss.

lights in Grand Central Terminal. He also designed a war-bond show at Madison Square Garden *(q.v.)*, which raised $100 million in bonds. Later he entered the Navy's Special Services Division, where he developed a one-lens system for gunnery training—replacing seven projectors with one.

After the war, Leigh leased the fleet of surplus dirigibles owned by the Navy. He put lights on the blimps and sent them out over the city on behalf of Ford, Tydol, Wonder Bread and Mobil. The first went out for Metro-Goldwyn-Mayer, which used the airships to advertise its newest feature, *National Velvet*.

In Grand Central Station, he designed the giant clock (removed in February 1988) and an indoor spectacular for Salem Cigarettes. On a larger scale, he was appointed City Decorator for the Bicentennial and Democratic Convention in 1976 and for the convention again in 1980. Next, he undertook some of his most important assignments: the relighting of the Empire State Building, the Helmsley Building, the St. Moritz Hotel

Tower (his first client), the Citicorp Building, the Waldorf-Astoria Hotel, Grand Central Terminal and the arch in Washington Square.

Leigh owned the franchise for bus advertising for New York, and in less than three years, he doubled the City's take of the revenue. One of his most visible designs was the giant pole of lights above the MONY building, which predicted the next day's weather.

Douglas Leigh received five New York City Awards plus the most prestigious New York award—the Bronze Medallion. He has also received two first-prize Lumen Awards from the Illumination Society of America, the Key to the City, The Applause Award from the New York Sales Executives Club and the Broadway Association's award for 13 years as its President and Chairman. Today, Leigh continues his urban design work, constantly traveling around the world.

Paul Goldberger of the *New York Times* wrote, "When Douglas Leigh was in the business of creating Times Square (a business I wish he could continue along with his present one since those great signs are a much-missed part of the cityscape) he gave nighttime New York its visual identity for a whole period of our history.''

LERNER AND LOEWE

Alan Jay Lerner (1918–1986) Alan Jay Lerner was born in New York on August 31, 1918. He was the scion of a fortune that his family built through the Lerner Shops chain of women's clothing stores. Lerner was sent to the best schools in England and the United States. It was during this exceptional schooling that Lerner developed his love of the English language. He graduated from Harvard in 1940.

During college, Lerner had lost the sight in one eye during a boxing match. That injury kept him out of World War II and enabled him to pursue his writing career after graduation. He began in radio as a script writer. The career lasted two years, during which time Lerner wrote hundreds of scripts. But during his years at Harvard, Lerner had caught the theater bug. He contributed to a couple of the Hasty Pudding shows, *So Proudly We Hail* and *Fair Enough*. Like Loewe, Lerner was a member of the Lambs Club and had contributed some lyrics to *The Lambs Gambols,* a small revue.

In 1942, producer Henry Duffy was looking for a team of writers to write shows for his theater in Detroit. Duffy approached Loewe, asking to use the score to *Salute to Spring,* a 1937 failure. Earle Crooker had

Alan Jay Lerner Courtesy ASCAP.

written the lyrics to the score, which Loewe felt could use some improvement. Loewe told Duffy that a new lyricist would have to be found.

A few days later, Loewe came across Lerner playing cards in the club. Loewe approached Lerner, and two days later the two of them found themselves bound for Detroit. The first Lerner and Loewe collaboration, *Life of the Party* (10/8/42), premiered in Detroit with Dorothy Stone, Margaret Dumont, Charlie Ruggles and Charles Collins starring.

Frederick Loewe (1904–1988) Frederick Loewe was born in Berlin, Germany, to Austrian parents on June 10, 1904. His father Edmund, a leading vocalist, encouraged his son in music, and he became a child prodigy on the piano. The young Loewe studied with Eugene d'Albert and Ferrucio Busoni. At the age of 13, he became the youngest soloist to appear with the Berlin Symphony. When only 15, he wrote the song "Katrina," which was a huge hit in Europe.

The family emigrated to the United States in 1924, so the elder Loewe could appear in operetta. Unfortunately, Edmund Loewe died shortly after the family arrived in New York. Left virtually penniless, the young Loewe had to make his own way.

Time and popular taste in music worked against the young composer. Operetta was being replaced by a more distinctive American style on the nation's stages and in its clubs. Composers like Rudolf Friml *(q.v.)*

Frederick Loewe Courtesy ASCAP.

and Sigmund Romberg (q.v.) soon found their European style of composition out of favor, replaced by the syncopations of Irving Berlin (q.v.), George Gershwin (q.v.) and Cole Porter (q.v.).

Loewe found work in Greenwich Village as a piano player. A series of odd jobs followed, including work as a bus boy in a cafeteria and a short career as a riding instructor in New Hampshire. After returning to New York, Loewe tried his luck as a boxer in Brooklyn. The unfortunate loss of several teeth to an opponent led to another change in career. This time, Loewe tried his hand as a cowboy out West.

Loewe returned East and took a job on a ferry, plying the international waters between Miami and Havana, Cuba. Prohibition had been passed, and cruises to Havana suddenly became very popular. Loewe became a shipboard pianist until the end of Prohibition marked the end of his job. Loewe then returned to New York and a job in a beer garden in the Yorkville section of Manhattan.

Loewe finally broke into the theater as a rehearsal pianist for one of the last operettas, Champagne Sec (10/14/33). The job served to only whet his appetite for a composing career. He joined the Lambs Club in order to meet people working in the theater. The scheme worked beyond his wildest expectations.

While at the Lambs, Loewe became friends with actor Dennis King. King was set to appear with Oscar Shaw in the play Petticoat Fever (3/4/35) at the Ritz Theatre (q.v.). He was taken with a song, "Love Tiptoed Through My Heart," which Loewe wrote in collaboration with Irene Alexander. King decided to interpolate the song into the play. For the first time, a Frederick Loewe song was heard on Broadway.

Loewe had another song interpolated into a revue, The Illustrators' Show (1/22/36; 5 performances). The song was "A Waltz Was Born in Vienna," written in collaboration with Earle Crooker. The popularity of the song lasted longer than The Illustrators' Show.

Crooker, a script writer and sometime lyricist, collaborated with Loewe on a full-length score to a new musical, Salute to Spring (7/12/37) that premiered in St. Louis. The show was a great success but didn't transfer to New York.

Producer Dwight Deere Wiman enjoyed the team's work and commissioned them to compose the songs for his next Broadway show, Great Lady (12/1/38; 20 performances). The operetta was produced at the Majestic Theater (q.v.). In the cast were Norma Terris, of Show Boat fame, Irene Bordoni, a saucy French chanteuse, and Helen Ford, star of many Rodgers and Hart (q.v.) shows. In the dance chorus were such future stars as Nora Kaye, Alicia Alonso and Jerome Robbins.

After the failure of Great Lady, Loewe resumed his piano playing in restaurants and clubs and continued

going to the Lambs Club. But for a time, his Broadway activities stopped. In 1942, while at the Lambs, Loewe was introduced to the young Alan Jay Lerner.

* * * * *

Although not the best of friends, the two men got on well enough. They decided to team up for another show. The result was What's Up? (11/11/43; 63 performances). The directors were Robert H. Gordon and George Balanchine. The show starred Jimmy Savo, Larry Douglas and Lynn Gardner. Despite the talents on hand, the show wasn't a hit.

For their next project, the team chose The Day Before Spring (11/22/45; 165 performances), which opened at the National Theatre (q.v.). In spite of some favorable reviews and what is regarded as a good score, the show never caught on with audiences.

The Day Before Spring was Lerner and Loewe's last failure. From then on, each of their shows achieved great success. The first was Brigadoon (3/13/41; 581 performances), a story of the power of love and faith, which opened at the Ziegfeld Theater (q.v.). It starred David Brooks and Lee Sullivan as the two jaded Americans who stumble upon the Scottish town that appears only one day each century. Marion Bell and Pamela Britton were the two lassies who found their loves in the two strangers from the 20th century.

The score was a lyrical evocation of the Scottish Highlands. "Come to Me, Bend to Me," "The Heather on the Hill" and "Almost Like Being in Love" all became hits. The other songs, more traditional musical-comedy numbers, such as "My Mother's Wedding Day," were equally expert. Brigadoon was directed by Robert Lewis and produced by Cheryl Crawford. Agnes de Mille (q.v.) choreographed the proceedings. Brigadoon became an even bigger success in London, where it played His Majesty's Theatre for 685 performances after its April 14, 1949, opening.

Lerner next undertook a project with Kurt Weill (q.v.). Love Life (10/7/48; 252 performances) was the result. It opened at the 46th Street Theatre (q.v.) with Nanette Fabray and Ray Middleton. It was produced by Cheryl Crawford and directed by Elia Kazan.

Lerner returned to his partnership with Frederick Loewe for Paint Your Wagon (11/12/51; 289 performances). The show was a light-hearted adventure set against the backdrop of the California gold rush. Cheryl Crawford produced, Agnes de Mille choreographed and Daniel Mann directed. The show starred Olga San Juan, James Barton and Tony Bavaar.

Lerner and Loewe's score was, according to the reviewers, much more entertaining than the book. "They Call the Wind Maria" was a huge hit as was another of the show's ballads, "I Talk to the Trees."

Their next Broadway offering was their biggest success, but it took six years for it to reach the stage. The musicalization of George Bernard Shaw's *Pygmalion* was turned down by most of Broadway's veteran composers and lyricists. E.Y. Harburg *(q.v.)*, Dietz and Schwartz *(q.v.)*, Noel Coward *(q.v.)*, Cole Porter *(q.v.)* and Rodgers and Hammerstein *(q.v.)* all passed on the project. Lerner and Loewe attempted it and worked on the project for two years before giving up.

After the aborted attempt, both Lerner and Loewe split to pursue projects that never reached fruition. In 1954, the two songwriters reunited to tackle the project again. This time, the work seemed to come together more easily and *My Fair Lady* (3/15/56; 2,717 performances) opened at the Mark Hellinger Theater *(q.v.)*.

My Fair Lady starred Julie Andrews as Eliza Doolittle and Rex Harrison as her mentor, Henry Higgins. The supporting cast was equally excellent—Robert Coote, Stanley Holloway, Cathleen Nesbitt, Michael King and Christopher Hewitt. The show was produced by Herman Levin and directed by Moss Hart.

The illustrious score contained many hits. Perhaps the most successful was "I Could Have Danced All Night," but "On the Street Where You Live," "I've Grown Accustomed to Her Face," "Wouldn't It Be Loverly?" and "The Rain in Spain" all became standards. *My Fair Lady*'s run was a Broadway record until 1971, when it was overtaken by *Hello, Dolly!*

After the success of *My Fair Lady*, there was tremendous pressure put on Lerner and Loewe. The result was bound to be a disappointment, and *Camelot* (12/3/60; 873 performances) was considered so by most of the critics.

Prior to its opening at the Majestic Theater *(q.v.)*, *Camelot* had a stormy tryout period; director Moss Hart *(q.v.)* suffered a heart attack, and Lerner was hospitalized. The story of King Arthur and Guinevere was produced by the songwriters and Hart. The stars were Richard Burton in his only musical-theater appearance, Robert Goulet in his Broadway debut and Julie Andrews, following her great success in *My Fair Lady*.

Despite mostly unfavorable reviews, the show went on to become one of the most produced Broadway musicals. This is due in large part to the superior score by Lerner and Loewe. "I Wonder What the King Is Doing Tonight," "If Ever I Would Leave You" and "How to Handle a Woman" all won a fair amount of success on records and television. The Kennedy administration was called Camelot after the title and spirit of the show.

Camelot was presented in London with Laurence Harvey and Elizabeth Larner in the leads. It was subsequently revived in a long national tour with Richard Harris starring. Harris also starred in the movie version (Warner Brothers, 1967) alongside Vanessa Redgrave.

The difficulties that accompanied *Camelot*'s birth and Loewe's heart problems led to the composer's decision to retire. It was a decision he adhered to with the exception of brief collaborations with Lerner on a movie version of Antione de Saint-Exupery's *The Little Prince* (Paramount, 1975) and the stage adaptation of *Gigi* for which they won a Tony Award *(q.v.)*.

Lerner was not ready for retirement and searched for other collaborators. His first choice was Richard Rodgers *(q.v.)*, who also lost his collaborator, Oscar Hammerstein II *(q.v.)*, around the same time Lerner and Loewe broke up. The announced project was a musical dealing with E.S.P. and with a proposed title of *I Picked a Daisy*.

But the Rodgers and Lerner collaboration did not occur. The two professionals found they had divergent working styles, and the project was dropped. Lerner took the idea to Burton Lane *(q.v.)* with whom he had collaborated on the movie *Royal Wedding* (MGM, 1951).

The working relationship with Lane proved slightly more successful than that of Rodgers and Lerner. The result was *On a Clear Day You Can See Forever* (10/17/65; 280 performances). Barbara Harris, John Cullum, William Daniels and Byron Webster starred in the show, which was eventually made into an unsuccessful film (Paramount, 1970) starring Barbra Streisand and Yves Montand.

Lerner turned to composer Andre Previn for the music of *Coco* (12/18/69; 332 performances), a musicalization of the life of fashion designer Coco Chanel, with Katharine Hepburn in the leading role.

Failure was to dog Lerner's heels till the end of his career. *Lolita, My Love* by Lerner and John Barry closed out of town in 1971. *Music! Music!* (4/11/74; 37 performances), a revue that contained no original songs had Lerner's book. Lerner's collaboration with Leonard Bernstein *(q.v.)*, *1600 Pennsylvania Avenue* (5/4/76; 7 performances), was written to commemorate the American Bicentennial.

Lerner and Lane collaborated again in 1979 to worse results than their first outing, though the score is topnotch. *Carmelina* (4/8/79; 17 performances) was based on the film *Buona Sera, Mrs. Campbell* and starred Georgia Brown, Virginia Martin, Gordon Ramsey and Cesare Siepe.

Lerner's last Broadway outing was *Dance a Little Closer* (5/11/83; 1 performance), written with Charles Strouse *(q.v.)*. The show was based on Robert E. Sherwood's *(q.v.)* play *Idiot's Delight*. Like Lerner's other work, even this failure contained great lyrics.

Alan Jay Lerner died on June 14, 1986. Frederick Loewe died on February 14, 1988.

During their heyday, the team of Lerner and Loewe produced some of the most enduring of all American musicals. The Lerner and Loewe hallmark was witty, sophisticated and emotionally complex lyrics married to lively, passionate music that enthralled a generation of theatergoers. Their songs were sometimes sentimental, sometimes satirical and always professional.

LEW FIELDS'S 44TH STREET ROOF GARDEN 216–30 W. 44th Street between Broadway and Eighth Avenue. Architect: William Albert Swansey. Opening: June 5, 1913; *All Aboard.* The theater was one of many rooftop theaters built in the days before air-conditioning and stringent fire codes. The auditorium had an erratic career as a number of different ventures.

Soon after it opened, it was reopened as the Folies Marigny in January 1914. A little over a year later, it was rechristened Castles-in-the-Air. The theater was named for Vernon and Irene Castle *(q.v.)* and was used for their shows. They opened the theater on June 14, 1915, with a show called *Look Who's Here.*

On December 1, 1917, the date of the opening of the wartime revue *Over the Top,* the theater was renamed the 44th Street Roof Theatre. The revue had a score in part by Sigmund Romberg *(q.v.).* Fred and Adele Astaire *(q.v.),* the successors to the Castles as Broadway's top dance team, starred.

Popular comedienne, singer and songwriter Nora Bayes had the theater named after her on December 30, 1918, with her vehicle *Ladies First.* Though Bayes and Seymour Simon wrote most of the score along with A. Baldwin Sloane and Harry B. Smith *(q.v.),* the hit songs "The Real American Folk Song Is a Rag" and "Some Wonderful Sort of Someone" had music by George Gershwin *(q.v.)* and lyrics by Ira Gershwin and Schuyler Greene, respectively. *Ladies First* was a hit, running 164 performances.

The Nora Bayes Theater became simply the Bayes Theater on September 11, 1922, with *East Side–West Side.* Yiddish theater was presented beginning with the opening of *The Three Little Business Men* on September 3, 1923. The theater was renamed Thomashefsky's Broadway Theater, after actor Boris Thomashefsky. Nora Bayes again took over on May 12, 1924, with *Two Strangers from Nowhere.* The theater again became Bayes Theater.

The theater was renamed Giglio's Radio Theater on August 28, 1937, with *La Figlia Brutta.* The theater's name changed for the last time with *Fickle Women* on December 15, 1937. The name was again Nora Bayes Theater.

When the theater below was razed in July 1945 so too was the roof theater. Today, the *New York Times* printing plant occupies the site.

LEW FIELDS'S MANSFIELD THEATER See BROOKS ATKINSON THEATER.

LIBERTY THEATRE 234 W. 42nd Street. Architects: Herts and Tallant. Opening: October 5, 1904; *The Rogers Brothers in Paris.* Marc Klaw and Abraham Erlanger

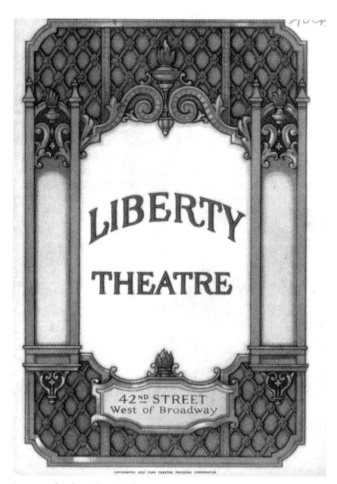

Program for the Liberty Theatre

built the Liberty for the Rogers Brothers, a couple of "Dutch" comics. The comedy team had previously opened the Victoria Theater *(q.v.)* up the block and were popular enough to assure success to the new theater's premiere, *The Rogers Brothers in Paris.* They would return to the Liberty in *The Rogers Brothers in Ireland* (9/4/05). During its heyday as one of Broadway's most successful musical houses, the Liberty presented some of the best talents on the Great White Way.

George M. Cohan *(q.v.)* had two productions play the Liberty. The first was *Little Johnny Jones* (11/7/04; 52 performances), which marked Cohan's emergence as the top musical-comedy talent of his time. Cohan wrote, directed, produced and starred in the show, which also featured his father and mother and his wife Ethel Levey. The score contained some of Cohan's most enduring hits, including "The Yankee Doodle Boy" and "Give My Regards to Broadway." Today's audiences remember James Cagney as George M. Cohan singing songs from this show in the picture *Yankee Doodle Dandy.*

Cohan's next hit at the Liberty was *Little Nellie Kelly* (11/13/22; 276 performances). The score included "You Remind Me of My Mother" and "Nellie Kelly, I Love You." By the twenties, Cohan saw his fame begin to wind down as newer talents entered the scene. One was Jerome Kern (q.v.).

Kern had several musicals premiere at the Liberty. The first, *Have a Heart* (1/11/17; 76 performances), was a minor show with a Guy Bolton (q.v.), P.G. Wodehouse libretto and Wodehouse lyrics. Though none of the songs achieved standard status, "You Said Something" had a brief vogue. Kern's next show at the Liberty, *The Night Boat* (2/2/20; 318 performances), isn't well remembered today, but the score he wrote with Anne Caldwell did contain two popular songs, "Whose Baby Are You?" and "Left All Alone Again Blues."

Charles Dillingham's production of *The City Chap* (10/26/25; 72 performances) also had a Kern/Caldwell score, but none of the songs outlasted the show's run. George Raft, Irene Dunne and Jimmy Walker's mistress Betty Compton all played secondary characters.

Two annual revues played the Liberty. The first was *Hitchy-Koo of 1919* (10/6/19; 56 performances). Raymond Hitchcock, a popular comic and monologist,

served as master of ceremonies in the annual revue's only stop at the Liberty. The score was by the young Cole Porter (q.v.) and introduced one of his earliest hits, "An Old Fashioned Garden." But the production was a flop and Porter didn't return to Broadway for five years.

George White's Scandals (q.v.) (6/2/19; 128 performances) began one of its two yearly editions at the Liberty with the 1919 version. The score by Richard Whiting and Arthur Jackson didn't have any hits, so for the next edition White enlisted George Gershwin (q.v.) to contribute tunes. The *Scandals of 1920* (6/7/20; 134 performances) introduced the "Scandal Walk," and the *Scandals of 1921* (7/11/21; 97 performances) contained "Drifting Along with the Tide." Gershwin would create better scores in two other productions which opened at the Liberty.

The first is one of Gershwin's greatest hits, *Lady, Be Good!* (12/1/24; 330 performances). The score written with his brother Ira contained many of the Gershwins' most enduring standards, "Fascinating Rhythm," "The

Liberty Theatre Photo Jeff Slotnick.

Half of It Dearie Blues'' and the title song. Fred and Adele Astaire (q.v.) starred in the show along with Cliff Edwards and Walter Catlett. The libretto was by Guy Bolton (q.v.) and Fred Thompson. The other Gershwin show to play the Liberty was *Tip-Toes* (12/28/25; 194 performances). Alex Aarons and Vinton Freedley (q.v.) repeated their roles as producers, as did the librettists and songwriters of *Lady Be Good*. Again the Gershwins provided an exceptional score, including "Sweet and Low Down," "Looking for a Boy," "These Charming People" and "That Certain Feeling."

Black shows were big successes during the late twenties and early thirties. The last big hit to play the Liberty, *Blackbirds of 1928* (5/9/28; 519 performances) was one of the most successful. It featured a stellar cast, including Adelaide Hall, Mantan Moreland, Aida Ward, Elisabeth Welch and Bill Robinson. The score by Dorothy Fields (q.v.) and Jimmy McHugh included "Doin' the New Low-Down," "I Can't Give You Anything But Love" and "Porgy." Three years later, Fields and McHugh again contributed two songs for an all-black show at the Liberty, *Singin' the Blues* (9/16/31; 46 performances), but it was not a hit.

The Liberty was one of the most successful theaters on 42nd Street. In 1932, the theater began a vaudeville policy. The Depression took a further toll, and the theater, like its neighbors, became a grind movie house.

The Liberty's orchestra and two balconies hold 1,054 patrons. The Times Square Redevelopment Plan calls for the theater to be used for nonprofit theater productions from around the country, as well as dance and small musical programs.

LIEBLING, A.J. (1904–1963) A.J. Liebling was a noted Broadway chronicler whose interests ranged from gastronomy to prize fighting. He was also a well-known watchdog of the journalism field.

Abbott Joseph Liebling was born in New York on October 18, 1904. According to Liebling, his father embodied all the traits of the Horatio Alger legend, only in reverse. It seems his father, a furrier, started wealthy and found himself penniless at his death.

Liebling enjoyed a checkered career in the halls of academe. After refusing to attend chapel, he was expelled from Dartmouth. He ended up at Columbia University's School for Journalism. He commented that Columbia had "all the intellectual status of a training school for future employees of the A&P."

Liebling received his first break shortly after graduation. He obtained a job at the *New York Times* in the sports department. He was soon fired for his somewhat cavalier disregard for facts. After the eight-month stint at the *Times,* he took a step backward to *The Providence Journal and Evening Bulletin*. His sojourn in Rhode Island was more successful. He spent almost five years at the paper, with a year off to study ancient history at the Sorbonne.

In 1930, he decided to make another attempt to crack into the New York newspaper world. Toward that end, he employed a picketer to carry a sign outside the offices of *The World*. The sign read, "Hire Joe Liebling." Liebling didn't realize that the city editor never used the front entrance, preferring, instead, to go in the back way. By the time Liebling caught the attention of the managers, *The World* had expired.

But Liebling had made an impression and was hired at the newly formed *World-Telegram*. This was the beginning of Liebling's love affair with the more unusual segments of the New York population and especially those of Broadway. His writing celebrated the misfits and colorful characters of the Big Apple. He stayed at the *World-Telegram* for five years.

In 1935, he joined the staff of the *New Yorker*. His fame increased when he served as the Magazine's Paris correspondent at the start of World War II. After the war, Liebling resumed his more freewheeling style. In 1946, he replaced Robert Benchley (q.v.) on the "Wayward Press" column devoted to criticism of the field of journalism. His more notable columns concerned the journalism community's handling of the Alger Hiss trial as well as rebuttals to various editorials and policies of the papers. Liebling was against the large newspaper chains, which he saw as a threat to free enterprise and competition.

Liebling also covered the prizefighters who inhabited the old Madison Square Garden (q.v.) on 50th Street. Liebling, who had been an amateur boxer, was always happy to point out his lack of success in the ring. He compared himself unfavorably with the young Ernest Hemingway, who Liebling allowed, was both a better pugilist and writer.

In the latter part of the 1940's, Liebling moved to Chicago. His book *Chicago: The Second City* aroused ire on both sides of the Appalachians. His boxing articles were collected in 1956 to make the book, *The Sweet Science*.

In 1953, Liebling profiled James A. Macdonald, better known as Lord Stingo, Broadway habitue and a racing columnist for the *New York Enquirer*. Liebling's profile was published as a book under the title, *The Honest Rainmaker*.

He also had a collection of essays entitled *Between Meals,* which was an autobiography of his early life. The title alluded to Liebling's long attraction to things gastronomical. He once wrote, "I used to be shy about ordering a steak after I had eaten a steak sandwich but I got used to it."

Liebling continued with the *New Yorker* up until his death on December 28, 1963.

LIGHTNIN' PARADE *Lightnin'* was a play by Frank Bacon (also its star) and Winthrop Ames that opened at the Gaiety Theater (q.v.) on August 26, 1918. John Golden was the producer of what was to become at one time the longest-running play in Broadway history. Its run of 1,291 performances was not surpassed until *Abie's Irish Rose* ran 2,327 performances in the early thirties.

When *Lightnin'* closed, the event was marked by a huge celebration at the Gaiety Theater. The idea for the ceremony and subsequent parade came from songwriter Silvio Hein. He suggested to John Golden that a small celebration might make the papers and help box office receipts in Chicago, the show's next stop.

Golden devised a plan whereby a demonstration could be arranged. He called the Actor's Equity Association *(q.v.)* to "inform" them that the Lambs Club was planning a small reception at the Gaiety. Naturally, the actors' union asked to be invited, and Golden opined that it might be all right with the Lambs. Next, the producer contacted the Lambs Club President. He was told of Equity's plans to hold a small gathering in tribute to the show and its star. The Lambs politely asked if they might attend the festivities.

Soon other groups were signing up to attend the ceremonies. Golden went to Grover Whalen, then Commissioner, and inquired whether Whalen would speak to Mayor Hylan about a parade. Hylan was more than happy to oblige, in fact he would lead the entourage. As an added bonus he would throw in the New York Police Band to augment the festivities.

The reception at the theater was attended by friends and admirers of star and coauthor Frank Bacon. Bacon and his wife were seated on stage with the cast as playwright Augustus Thomas presided over the ceremonies. They were joined on the stage by Commissioner Grover Whalen, Secretary of Labor James J. Davis and later by Mayor John F. Hylan. DeWolf Hopper, one of the greatest actors of his generation, spoke of the effect of *Lightnin'* on the morale of the theater community and specifically on the contributions of Frank Bacon to the survival of the fledgling Actors' Equity Association.

Augustus Thomas read a speech appropriately titled "Lightnin'," written by Bliss Carman. Letters in tribute to Bacon written by Will Hays, the Postmaster General, and John F. Hylan, Mayor of New York, were read aloud to the cheering audience. Secretary of Labor Davis read a letter from President Harding and presented Bacon, actor/producer Winchell Smith and Golden with gold-buckled championship belts in tribute to "the champion long-distance actor, the champion writer of American successes, and the champion producer of wholesome, American plays."

After the presentation by Secretary Davis, the audience stormed the stage. Included were stars of past and present Broadway shows. They brought Bacon, Smith, Golden and the assembled celebrities outside to Broadway and 46th Street, where thousands of well-wishers jammed Longacre Square.

The show was due to open in Chicago, and the troupe was packed and ready to go to their train. As they and their fans made their way down Broadway, additional celebrities and plain citizens joined the impromptu celebration. The Police Band struck up a march as did another band led by composer and conductor Victor Herbert *(q.v.)*. John Golden later wrote, "The sidewalks from Broadway to Eighth Avenue were impassable. Longacre Square presented the appearance of a riot."

Although the parade was unannounced, passersby became curious at the sight of police stationed on the sides of the parade route. The growing crowds were barely controlled by mounted police. Augustus Thomas observed to Bacon that although Bacon had "slipped into Broadway in gumshoes three years before, he was going out with a brass band—three or four, in fact."

Over 10,000 people joined the happy mob, stopping traffic as they made their way to Pennsylvania Station. Police estimated over 100,000 more lined the pavement, and countless thousands watched from windows along the route.

On reaching the station, the cast found the gates and cars plastered with signs wishing the company good fortune. The band began "Auld Lang Syne," and as the company entered the train, they heard the huge station echoing with thousands of voices singing the refrain.

This was certainly the greatest moment in Frank Bacon's life. It was made all the more poignant when the actor died in Chicago during the run of *Lightnin'*. He had played the part of Bill Jones over 2,000 times. Broadway would not see another such outpouring of emotion until the Valentino funeral.

LINDY'S 1626 Broadway and Northwest Corner of Broadway and 51st Street. Lindy's was the best known and greatest of the Broadway delicatessens. Leo Lindemann and his wife Clara met when Lindy was a busboy in Clara's father's restaurant, the Palace Cafe at 47th and Broadway. They opened Lindy's on August 20, 1921. "Broadway's lighting was all gold and silvery then," Leo recalled. "But mostly silvery—more like a Great White Way."

The deli was a minor success, no better than a host of other Jewish delis in the neighborhood, but Lindy's was situated in an advantageous location. Across Broadway were the Brill Building *(q.v.)*, the home of Tin Pan Alley, and the Capitol Theater *(q.v.)*. On the same side was the Winter Garden Theater *(q.v.)* home of the Shubert brothers' *(q.v.)* productions including a series of shows starring Al Jolson *(q.v.)*. Jolson, a regular patron of Lindy's, suggested that Lindy put seats in the deli and turn it into a restaurant. Lindy took Jolson's advice, and soon it was the gathering place of the stars of Broadway and vaudeville.

The deli was best known for its cheesecake, its apple pancakes and its enormous combination sandwiches. Another draw were the wisecracking waiters who sometimes treated the customers rudely and the customers loved it. Lindy was an easy mark and often had running tabs for performers who were temporarily out of luck. The restaurateur, who used to listen patiently to his clients' sad stories, was dubbed The Magnificent Ear. Lindy would give special treatment to celebrities who brought in crowds. Lyricist Irving Caesar made up a rhyme about Lindy's while strolling down Broadway with George Gershwin (q.v.).

> We take our tea at Lindy's
> We find much pleasure in this
> As we look through the windows
> To watching people pass
> With Lindy we're a trio
> Just Georgie, me and Leo
> He never takes what we owe
> He wants us for the class!

Lindy would sometimes go to extremes to keep his steady customers happy. One day, three comics, Jack Benny, Eddie Cantor and Jesse Block, and their wives discussed where to have dinner. They had dined as usual at Lindy's all week, and Benny said he wanted to go to the nearby Ruby Foo's for Chinese food. Eddie Cantor insisted on having his usual cornflakes and milk for dinner. After a coin toss, the party went to Lindy's. Benny told Lindy about the argument, and when Cantor was brought his cornflakes, the rest were served Chinese food by a battalion of waiters from Foo's.

Lindy wasn't so proud of all his patrons. Moe ("The Gimp") Snyder, a small time hood, demanded that Lindy serve only female lobsters. Snyder, married to Ruth Etting, was arrested for shooting his wife's piano player. The regulars at Lindy's sent their regards to the incarcerated Gimp who urged them to hold a rally in his defense at Madison Square Garden (q.v.). Lindy regular Chuck Green, a jewelry salesman whom Damon Runyon (q.v.) called the Doorway Tiffany, wisecracked, "The Gimp must think he's Sacco and Vanzetti."

Another infamous patron of Lindy's was gangster (q.v.) Arnold Rothstein. Clara Lindemann didn't like Rothstein and told him so. Lindy instructed his cashier to stop taking messages for Rothstein. The cashier was understandably afraid of Rothstein and took one last message—that the gangster was wanted at the Park Central Hotel. Later Rothstein was found murdered behind the hotel, and Damon Runyon helped take the heat off Lindy's. Runyon said the same might have happened to a man who left a church.

Runyon was one of Lindy's champions. He put the restaurant in his stories, thinly disguised as Mindy's. Runyon began one of his most famous stories, *Little Miss Marker,* with the line, "One evening, along toward seven o'clock, many citizens are standing out on Broadway in front of Mindy's restaurant." His story *Butch Minds the Baby* begins, "One evening along about seven o'clock, I am sitting in Mindy's restaurant putting on some gefilte fish." Lindy returned the favor by putting Runyon's latest books in the Broadway window of his restaurant. Runyon's stories were read throughout the country and were made into Hollywood movies, thereby spreading Lindy's fame.

Another reason for Lindy's early success was the Eugene O'Neill (q.v.) play *Strange Interlude* (1/30/28). The play was more than twice as long as usual plays and included a dinner break. Patrons of the John Golden Theater (q.v.) on West 58th Street found Lindy's to be a convenient restaurant. When the same show was banned in Boston and opened in the suburbs, the audience patronized a nearby restaurant owned by a struggling restaurateur named Howard Johnson.

Lindy's best patrons had their own special tables. Broadway and radio's most famous comedians had their tables as did mobsters. Songwriters sat in their own area, and political figures like Bernard Baruch, J. Edgar Hoover and Clyde Tolson sat in theirs.

Singer Dolly Dawn, who as a teenager appeared with George Hall's orchestra at the Taft Hotel, remembered some of the Lindy regulars and where they sat:

> When you came in to the left there was a bar where all the song pluggers would stand, their foot upon the rail and one elbow crooked, and they'd be watching for what celebrities would come in. They'd pounce on them and go right into their pitch. Whether it was working hours or not they were always on.
>
> To the right you had all the newspapermen—Walter Winchell (q.v.), Damon Runyon, Jack O'Brian and Ben Gross. You would see a stream of celebrities coming from one side of the room to greet the newsmen. Everybody was table hopping. It was back and forth and in and out and kissing and hugging.
>
> In another part of the restaurant would be all the comics. The big stars would be seated wherever they wanted to be seated. And in the middle of it all, Mr. and Mrs. Lindy were greeting everybody. If you ordered a piece of cheesecake—which was supposed to be the best in the world—Mr. Lindy would come over and look down over your shoulder, and he'd say, "Do you know that cheesecake killed more Jews than Hitler?" And then he would laugh, he'd say, "Go on, eat it, it won't hurtcha."
>
> The waiters would come and sit down with you. There was a waiter there named Jacobs. He'd sit down and say, "Dolly! How are you? What can I get for you?" And he'd say, "Did I have a day today! I had a bad day in the market!—I couldn't get a chicken!" He would do all the gags that he heard from the comics. The waiters were hilarious. They were so cute and so lovable and wonderful.
>
> If you wanted to avoid all the turmoil and all the commotion and all the people coming and going and have dinner quietly and get out quick you went to the "old (original) Lindy's." You know, you say you never look back, but you wish sometimes those days would come back again. They were so precious.

Lindy had a disagreement with his partner and opened a second Lindy's across the street in 1930. The new Lindy's was enlarged in 1939. By that time, the restaurant was earning $20,000 a week. Soon the "little" or "original" Lindy's patrons left to join the Lindemanns. Both restaurants prospered until July 27, 1957, when the original Lindy's closed its doors. When the second Lindy's closed in 1969, some time after Lindemann's death, fellow restaurateur Toots Shor commented, "It's a shame to see a place like this turned into a whatsiz."

The current chain of restaurants using the Lindy's name has no relation to the original restaurants.

THE LITTLE THEATRE 238 W. 44th Street. Architects: H.C. Ingalls and F.B. Hoffman Jr. Opening: March 12, 1912; *The Pigeon* Producer/director Winthrop Ames specialized in the mounting of small, intimate plays in the first decades of this century. He had trouble placing these small shows in the average Broadway house, which contained about 800 seats, so Ames built his own theater with only 299 seats. Ames wanted to give the marginally commercial plays he presented a chance, since there was no off-Broadway alternative at the time. As he himself put it, he wished to produce "the clever, the unusual drama that has a chance of becoming a library classic."

Ames had his architects design a neo-federal building with such homey amenities as a working fireplace in the lobby. The sparsely adorned auditorium contained no boxes or balcony, just a gently sloping orchestra section. Critic *(q.v.)* Brooks Atkinson called it "a gem of a theater." Above the theater proper, Ames had his offices.

The first production at the theater was John Galsworthy's comedy *The Pigeon*. The show was moderately successful with a 64-performance run. Arthur Schnitzler's *The Affairs of Anatol* (10/14/12; 72 performances) opened with John Barrymore *(q.v.)* and Doris Keane in the leads. Barrymore returned to the stage of the Little in George Bernard Shaw's *The Philanderer* (12/30/15; 103 performances).

By this time, Ames realized his plan wasn't working. Even with sell-out business, Ames could barely support a star's salary like Barrymore's. For just as he couldn't lose much money on the small productions, he also couldn't make much if the plays were hits. He announced his intention of refurbishing the house by increasing the number of seats to 1,000 by adding a balcony and enlarging the auditorium. However Ames's plan didn't reach fruition, for the cost of remodeling would have amounted to as much as he was losing in ticket sales. So instead, he opted to increase the seating to 450 seats. Ames was also involved in the construction of the Booth Theatre *(q.v.)*, which he built with the Shuberts *(q.v.)*.

The first long run at the Little was Rachel Crothers's comedy *A Little Journey* (12/26/18; 252 performances). The next offering, *Please Get Married* (2/10/19; 160 performances) starred Ernest Truex.

The First (10/20/20; 725 performances) was written by actor Frank Craven. Broadway was a more freewheeling arena in those days. When Craven told producer John Golden that acting jobs had dried up, Golden suggested that Craven write a play and stated that he would produce it sight unseen. Craven took Golden up on the offer, and eight weeks later the play was in rehearsal. Craven and Golden's attempt to repeat their success resulted in the play *Spite Corner* (9/25/22; 124 performances).

By now Ames's family fortune was being quickly depleted. By 1922, he had lost $504,372 on the operation of the Little, despite its many successes. Luckily, the Booth Theatre offset some, but not all, of the losses.

Guy Bolton *(q.v.)*, best known for his collaboration with P.G. Wodehouse and Jerome Kern *(q.v.)*, had his straight play *Polly Preferred* (1/11/23; 202 performances) produced. Bolton's straight plays were exactly like his musical libretti only without any songs.

Bolton's next offering at the Little, *Chicken Feed* (9/24/23; 146 performances), was produced by John Golden who took the lease on the theater with F. Ray Comstock and L. Lawrence Weber. Burns Mantle described *Chicken Feed* as a play that inspired "as much laughter as a farce without losing too completely its hold upon its theme,

The Little Theatre

which is fundamentally both sound and serious." The theme to which Mantle referred concerned a woman, Nell Bailey, who convinces her fellow wives and lovers to strike against their husbands and boyfriends for a share in the men's net income. The play ran to good houses when it was forced to close, because Weber wanted to move his production of *Little Jesse James* to the theater from the Longacre Theater *(q.v.).*

John Golden presented another hit play, *Pigs* (9/1/24; 347 performances), at the Little. *Pigs* was written by Anne Morrison and Patterson McNutt and directed by Frank Craven. The play was originally entitled *Johnny Jones, Jr.,* but since George M. Cohan *(q.v.)* had already written a musical *Little Johnny Jones,* Golden decided another title was in order. The authors and Golden puzzled over what would make a good title. Golden observed that since the play was about pigs, they should simply call it *Pigs.* Morrison wanted to call the show *A Pig Tale.* But Golden won, since he was set on the subtitle—*A Litter of Laughs.* Word of mouth and Golden's elaborate publicity stunts *(q.v.)* drew attention to the show.

Winchell Smith fell in love with Marc Connelly's comedy *The Wisdom Tooth* and planned to open it at the Little Theatre on February 15, 1926. However, the out-of-town tryouts in Washington, D.C., and Hartford were complete failures. The show, starring Thomas Mitchell, almost closed out of town, but Golden wired Smith. "We have had plenty of successes. Let's have a failure for a change. The Little Theatre needs a tenant. Try it out for a week or two there." Golden congratulated himself later, for *The Wisdom Tooth* proved to be a great success with a 160-performance run, and critics compared Connelly with James M. Barrie.

A bigger hit was *Two Girls Wanted* (9/9/26; 324 performances). Rachel Crothers returned to the Little Theatre as playwright and director of *Let Us Be Gay* (2/21/29; 132 performances). Another hit was Elmer Rice's *The Left Bank* (10/5/31; 241 performances).

By 1931, Ames had left the theater business. His last activity in the theater was the production of his own play *Mr. Samuel* (11/10/30; 8 performances) with Edward G. Robinson. The play marked the end of Ames's theater career. Ames died on November 3, 1937. Brooks Atkinson calls Ames "the pioneer of the modern theater" and "the greatest stage director of the time." At his death, his estate was reduced to $77,000.

In February 1935, CBS took over the theater as the CBS Radio Playhouse, but the theater returned to legitimate use on September 28, 1936, with the production of *Pre-Honeymoon,* which moved from the Lyceum Theater *(q.v.).* Anne Nichols, best known as the author of *Abie's Irish Rose,* wrote the play, and the theater was renamed Anne Nichols Little Theater.

The theater's name was changed back to the Little

Theatre with the opening of *Edna His Wife* (12/7/37; 32 performances), a one-woman show starring Cornelia Otis Skinner.

The *New York Times* took over operation of the theater in January 1942 and renamed it New York Times Hall. They used the space as a conference hall and permitted an occasional concert. The theater became an ABC television studio in 1959.

The theater returned to legitimate use with the black revue *Tambourines to Glory* (10/26/63; 24 performances). The show, by Langston Hughes and Jobe Huntley, didn't catch on. Black plays mostly disappeared from the Broadway theater after the heyday of the black musical in the teens and twenties. A substantial amount of time passed before an all-black show could succeed on Broadway.

When Frank Gilroy's Pulitzer Prize-winning play *The Subject Was Roses* moved from the Royale Theatre on September 7, 1964, the Little was renamed the Winthrop Ames Theater. Later that year, the theater resumed its original name and again became a television studio, this time for the Westinghouse network. Among the television shows that were broadcast from the stage of the theater were the "Merv Griffin Show" and the "David Frost Show." Griffin's show made the theater famous, for at the beginning of every show announcer Arthur Treacher said it was coming from "the Little Theatre off Broadway."

The theater again housed live performances with the opening of *My Sister, My Sister* (4/30/74; 119 performances) by Ray Aranha. Three years later, the theater saw the opening of its greatest hit, Albert Innaurato's comedy *Gemini* (5/21/77; 1,788 performances). The long run was abetted by a popular television advertisement. The Little was given special status by Actor's Equity *(q.v.)* and other unions to permit plays to run profitably in its small auditorium.

In 1981, the theater was redesigned by Adcadesign for its new owners, The Little Theatre Group. The next hit was Harvey Fierstein's three one-act plays, *Torch Song Trilogy* (6/10/83; 1,222 performances). Fierstein's popular play dealt with gay themes in a sometimes graphic way.

Shortly after the opening of *Torch Song Trilogy,* in July 1983, the name of the Little was changed again. It was renamed the Helen Hayes Theater as a tribute to the First Lady of the American Theater (see Helen Hayes). The previous Helen Hayes Theater *(q.v.)* had been demolished after a particularly bitter fight to save it and the Morosco Theatre *(q.v.).* Those citizens who took part in the battle to save the theaters *(q.v.)* were not appeased by the renaming of the Little Theatre.

On November 17, 1987, The New York City Landmarks Preservation Commission gave the interior and exterior of the building landmark status. The Commission stated that the theater was "An elegant neo-federal style" exterior, with an "unusual" interior "intended to suggest intimate drama."

The owners of the theater, Martin Markinson and Donald Tick bought the theater from Westinghouse for $800,000 in 1979. They decided to sell it at auction on March 24, 1988. The owners said there would be a $5 million minimum value put on the theater. Rocco Landesman, president of the Jujamcyn Theater chain said he was thinking of purchasing the theater. Apparently the owners forbade the Shuberts (q.v.) or Nederlanders from buying the house. The auction was a failure, and the theater was not sold.

LOESSER, FRANK (1910–1969)   Frank Loesser was the most versatile of all the Broadway composers. He wrote lyrics to his own tunes, and all but one of his Broadway shows were hits (another, *Pleasures and Palaces,* closed out of town.). His output on Broadway was small compared with that of his contemporaries, but each of his shows was a unique contribution to the art of the musical theater.

Loesser was born in New York on June 29, 1910. He was educated at Townsend Harris Hall, and he dropped out of City College. While holding various odd jobs, Loesser began writing song parodies to popular tunes of the day. RKO Radio Pictures hired Loesser as a staff lyricist after he published his first song, "In Love with a Memory of You," with music by William Schuman. None of Loesser's work at RKO reached the screen, and he returned to New York. He later worked at Universal Pictures. As a contract writer for Paramount Pictures, he wrote the lyrics to hundreds of songs, a high percentage of which became standards. Those that didn't become immediate hits still manage to stand the test of time.

When writing for the movies, Loesser was primarily a lyricist. He collaborated with such greats as Burton Lane (q.v.), Jule Styne (q.v.), Hoagy Carmichael, Jimmy McHugh, Arthur Schwartz (q.v.) and Victor Schertzinger. His film titles include *College Swing, Destry Rides Again, Thank Your Lucky Stars, The Perils of Pauline, Let's Dance, Happy-Go-Lucky, Seven Days Leave* and *Hans Christian Andersen.*

Among his movie songs are "The Moon of Manakoora," "Moments Like This," "Says My Heart," "Small Fry," "Heart and Soul," "Two Sleepy People," "The Lady's in Love with You," "Hey, Good Looking'," "See What the Boys in the Back Room Will Have," "Little Joe," "I've Been in Love Before," "My, My," "I Hear Music," "Delores," "I Said No," "I Don't Want to Walk Without You," "Sand in My Shoes" and "Kiss the Boys Goodbye."

Other Loesser greats are "Can't Get Out of This Mood," "What Do You Do in the Infantry," "Murder,

Frank Loesser   Courtesy ASCAP.

He Says," "Leave Us Face It We're in Love," "Spring Will Be a Little Late This Year," "Rumble, Rumble, Rumble," "Poppa, Don't Preach to Me," "I Wish I Didn't Love You So," "Tallahassee," "What Are You Doing New Year's Eve?," "That Feathery Feeling," "On a Slow Boat to China," "Baby, It's Cold Outside" (Academy Award, 1949), "No Two People," "Thumbelina," "Inchworm," "Anywhere I Wander" and "A Woman in Love."

Loesser's first Broadway assignment was with a revue, *The Illustrator's Show* (1/22/36; 5 performances). It was not an illustrious debut, but it did land him a contract with Universal Pictures as a staff writer. He then joined Paramount for a long, successful stint.

His next Broadway show was a musicalization of Brandon Thomas's farce, *Charley's Aunt,* entitled *Where's Charley?* (10/11/48; 792 performances) for which he contributed both music and lyrics. It starred Ray Bolger and Allyn Ann McLerie. Many hits emerged from the show, including "Once In Love with Amy," "The New Ashmolean Marching Society and Student Conservatory Band," "My Darling, My Darling" and "Make a Miracle." George Abbott (q.v.), known for giving many Broadway neophytes their first break, directed and wrote the libretto to Loesser's score. George Balanchine contributed the dances.

Two years later, audiences at the 46th Street Theatre (q.v.) were treated to the definitive Broadway depiction of Times Square when the curtain went up on *Guys and Dolls* (11/24/50; 1,200 performances). Abe Burrows and Jo Swerling wrote the libretto, and George S. Kaufman (*q.v.*) directed. The show starred Robert Alda, Vivian Blaine, Sam Levene, Isabel Bigley, Pat Rooney and Stubby Kaye. It was full of great Loesser tunes, including "If I Were a Bell," "Sit Down You're Rockin' the Boat," "I've Never Been in Love Before," "My Time of Day," "A Bushel and a Peck," "I'll Know" and the hilarious "Adelaide's Lament." *Guys and Dolls,* based on the stories of Damon Runyon (*q.v.*), was one of the most popular musicals in Broadway history.

With musicals based on an English farce and the New York underworld behind him, Loesser next tackled the Italian wine-making community of Napa, California, with *The Most Happy Fella* (5/3/56; 676 performances). The show was based on Sidney Howard's drama, *They Knew What They Wanted*. It tells the story of an old wine maker who uses the picture of his handsome ranch hand to send for a mail-order bride. When the woman shows up, she is so repulsed by the old man that she flees to the ranch-hand's bed. The grower, Tony, suffers injuries in a car accident, and while nursing him back to health, the bride learns to love him.

The Loesser score ably mastered the difficult material with a wealth of melody. The show was almost entirely sung, in fact some thought it closer to opera than traditional musical comedy. Loesser himself wrote the book so that the songs and story would be truly integrated. Despite the operatic overtones of the score, several of the numbers achieved success on the hit parade. The most popular were "Standing on the Corner," "Joey, Joey, Joey" and "Big D." Other hits were "Warm All Over" and "My Heart Is So Full of You." The score was considered so exceptional that Columbia records issued the entire show on a three record set, a first for a Broadway musical. *The Most Happy Fella* featured opera star Robert Weede, Susan Johnson, Jo Sullivan (later Mrs. Loesser) and Art Lund.

Loesser's next challenge was the quiet, bucolic *Greenwillow* (3/8/60; 95 performances), based on a novel by B.J. Chute. Anthony Perkins made his musical comedy debut in a cast that also included Cecil Kellaway and Pert Kelton. The one big hit from the show was "Never Will I Marry," made popular through a recording by Barbra Streisand.

Loesser's last Broadway show won him the Pulitzer Prize. *How to Succeed in Business Without Really Trying* (10/14/61; 1,417 performances) was a broad satire of the American workplace. Robert Morse attained stardom through his portrayal of the ruthless worker on his way to the top. Rudy Vallee, Bonnie Scott, Virginia Martin, Charles Nelson Reilly and Claudette Sutherland all turned in first rate performances under Abe Burrows's direction. Among the songs, "I Believe in You" achieved standard status, although people unfamiliar

with the show hardly realized the love song was sung by the hero to his own reflection.

Loesser's next attempt at Broadway, *Pleasures and Palaces* closed out of town in 1965 despite some favorable reviews.

Loesser affected Broadway in other ways besides his scores. Through his publishing company, Frank Music, he encouraged the careers of many Broadway newcomers. Loesser convinced George Abbott (*q.v.*) to hire Jerry Ross and Richard Adler to write the score of *The Pajama Game*. He also gave Meredith Willson the encouragement needed to start him on what eventually became *The Music Man*. Loesser later coproduced the show along with Kermit Bloomgarden. Loesser also encouraged composer Moose Charlap and lyricist Norman Gimbel and others.

Loesser died of cancer on July 26, 1969.

LOEW'S STATE THEATER 1540 Broadway at W. 45th Street. Architect: Thomas Lamb. The Loew's Corporation, distributors of MGM films, built their offices and flagship theater across from the Paramount Corporation's headquarters. Thomas Lamb, favorite architect of the Loew's chain, designed the theater in 1922. The 16-story building was demolished in 1987. On its site a 44-story building was erected with 850,000 square feet of office space, a shopping mall and four movie theaters.

LOEWE, FREDERICK   See LERNER AND LOEWE.

Joshua Logan   Courtesy ASCAP.

Loew's State Theater   Courtesy Artkraft Strauss.

LOGAN, JOSHUA (1908–1988)   Joshua Logan was one of Broadway's preeminent directors who also sometimes assumed the role of playwright. His main strengths lay in his vibrant staging of musical comedies, including some of the greatest in the genre. Logan was partially responsible for the success of such landmark musicals as *South Pacific* and *Annie Get Your Gun*. Logan worked with such great songwriters as Richard Rodgers *(q.v.)* (teamed with both Lorenz Hart *(q.v.)* and Oscar Hammerstein II *(q.v.))*, Irving Berlin *(q.v.)* and Harold Rome *(q.v.)*.

Logan's first musical assignment was for the Rodgers and Hart show *I Married an Angel* (5/11/38; 338 performances). He went on to direct such musicals as *Knickerbocker Holiday* (10/19/38; 168 performances); *Stars in Your Eyes* (2/9/39; 127 performances); *Two for the Show* (2/8/40; 124 performances); *Higher and Higher* (4/4/40; 84 performances) for which he was also colibrettist; *By Jupiter* (6/3/42; 427 performances); *This Is the Army* (7/4/42; 113 performances); *Annie Get Your Gun* (5/16/46; 1147 performances); *South Pacific* (4/7/49; 1925 perfor-

mances)for which he was also colibrettist, choreographer and coproducer; *Wish You Were Here* (6/25/52; 598 performances) for which he was also colibrettist and coproducer; *Fanny* (11/4/54; 888 performances) for which he was also colibrettist and coproducer; *All American* (2/19/62; 80 performances); *Mr. President* (10/20/62; 265 performances); and *Look to the Lilies* (3/29/70; 25 performances).

Logan also worked on many straight plays, although for the most part they weren't as noteworthy as his musical projects. Among the straight plays he directed are *It's You I Want* (2/5/35; 15 performances); *To See Ourselves* (4/30/35; 23 performances); *Hell Freezes Over* (12/28/35; 25 performances); *On Borrowed Time* (2/3/38; 321 performances); *Mornings at Seven* (11/30/39; 44 performances); *Charley's Aunt* (10/17/40; 233 performances); *Happy Birthday* (10/31/46; 564 performances); *John Loves Mary* (2/4/47; 423 performances); *Mister Roberts* (2/18/48; 1,157 performances) for which he was also coauthor; *The Wisteria Trees* (3/29/50; 165 performances), which he also adapted and produced; *Picnic*

(2/19/53; 477 performances), which he also produced; *Kind Sir* (11/4/53; 165 performances), which he also produced; *Middle of the Night* (2/8/56; 477 performances), which he also produced; *Blue Denim* (2/27/58; 166 performances); *The World of Suzie Wong* (10/14/58; 508 performances); *Tiger Tiger Burning Bright* (12/22/62; 33 performances); and *Ready When You Are C.B.!* (12/7/64; 80 performances).

LONGACRE THEATER 220 W. 48th Street. Architect: Henry B. Herts. Opening: May 1, 1913; *Are You a Crook?* Many Broadway producers made their fortunes in industry or business and with their profits turned to the colorful world of Broadway. One of these was H.H. Frazee, owner of the Boston Red Sox. Frazee hired architect Henry B. Herts to design his Longacre Theater. Herts had recently broken up with his partner Hugh Tallent and was anxious to prove that he could go it alone.

For the Longacre Theater, Herts chose an Italian Renaissance design and employed limestone and terracotta as the building materials. Frazee was delighted with Herts's sophisticated design and made plans to produce musicals in the 1,400-seat auditorium.

Surprisingly, his first offering was a play, *Are You a Crook?* Perhaps he should have stuck to his original notion of presenting only musical comedy, for *Are You a Crook?* closed after 12 performances. His next offering was a musical, *Adele* (8/28/13; 196 performances), by Frenchmen Jean Briquet and Adolf Philipp. The show was a hit with Georgia Caine, William Danforth, Alice Yorke and Hal Forde in the leads. The production was taken to the Gaiety Theater in London but failed to capture English audiences. It closed there after only two weeks.

John Barrymore *(q.v.)* was the next star to command the Longacre's stage in a melodrama entitled *Kick In* (10/15/14; 188 performances). It was followed by another success, *A Pair of Sixes* (3/17/14; 207 performances). *The Great Lover* (11/10/15; 245 performances), starring Leo Ditrichstein, spoofed the world of opera. *Nothing But the Truth* (9/14/16; 332 performances) was a comedy whose main character bets he can go an entire day without telling a lie. William Collier starred.

Leave It to Jane (8/28/17; 167 performances), was a musical by Jerome Kern *(q.v.)*, P.G. Wodehouse and Guy Bolton *(q.v.)*, the trio known for their small, intimate musicals with integrated libretti and scores. The show contained Jerome Kern's sprightliest score and included some of his most charming tunes, among them "Sir Galahad," "Cleopatterer," "The Crickets Are Calling," "It's a Great Big Land" and one of the most enchanting and innocent songs written for the American musical theater, "The Siren's Song."

Guy Bolton, in collaboration with George Middleton, was also responsible for the next hit at the Longacre,

Adam and Eva (9/13/19; 312 performances). The William B. Friedlander musical *Pitter Patter* (9/28/20; 111 performances) starred William Kent, Jack Squire and John Price Jones. Also in the cast was future Hollywood star James Cagney.

The Champion (1/3/21; 176 performances) starred Grant Mitchell. *Little Jessie James* (8/15/23; 385 performances) was a charming musical with a score by Harry Archer and Harlan Thompson. It introduced the hit song "I Love You." Allen Kearns, Nan Halperin and Jay Velie were featured along with the young Miriam Hopkins.

Moonlight (1/30/24; 174 performances), also a small musical, boasted a score by Con Conrad and William B. Friedlander. Conrad and Friedlander had another musical presented at the Longacre, *Mercenary Mary* (4/13/25; 136 performances).

George S. Kaufman *(q.v.)* had a big success with his play *The Butter and Egg Man* (9/23/25; 241 performances). The show starred Gregory Kelly as an out-of-towner who decides to invest $20,000 in a Broadway show. The comedy, one of Kaufman's best, is notable as the only play he wrote without the aide of a collaborator.

Miriam Hopkins had appeared at the Longacre in the musical *Little Jessie James*. She returned to its stage in a decidedly different kind of show, an adaptation of Theodore Dreiser's *An American Tragedy* (10/11/26; 216 performances). Also featured were Morgan Farley and Katherine Wilson. The play made almost as much of a splash as the novel originally had. It was among five shows that District Attorney Jacob H. Banton regarded as morally unacceptable. (The others were *The Captive*, Mae West's *Sex*, *Lulu Belle*, *The Virgin Man* and *Night Hawk*.) Philip Kearney's drama remained open, despite the government's displeasure.

Roger Pryor appeared as a Walter Winchell *(q.v.)* type of reporter in *Blessed Event* (2/12/32; 124 performances). The title referred to one of Winchell's favorite slang *(q.v.)* phrases. The Winchellian reporter was portrayed as an unscrupulous wise guy, and audiences at the first night watched the real Winchell's reaction as much as the play. A reviewer stated the next day that Winchell appeared uncomfortable. Alexander Woollcott *(q.v.)*, in his column, disagreed: "Nonsense! Winchell's emotions at *Blessed Event* if any were probably an ingenuous and gratified surprise on finding himself at thirty-five, already recognized as enough of a national institution to be made the subject of a play. If he squirmed and blanched, it was because he, and he alone, knew that the two large and unsmiling men occupying the seats behind his own were Central Office plainclothesmen, assigned by an uneasy Police Commissioner to see that Winchell should come to no bodily harm."

The Depression hurt the Broadway theater as less money because available for risky investments. The

Longacre suffered along with many other theaters. A high point of the thirties was the series of productions the Group Theater (q.v.) presented at the Longacre. The first was a double bill of Clifford Odets's two one-act plays, *Waiting for Lefty* and *Till the Day I Die* (3/26/35; 168 performances). *Waiting for Lefty* had been given a single performance at the Civic Repertory Theater on January 5, 1935, and caused an immediate sensation.

It was an incendiary play based on an actual strike of New York taxi drivers. In the play, the members of the union meet to decide whether to strike. Moderate members of the union want to wait until their leader Lefty arrives, but labor racketeers and unscrupulous union leaders urge the meeting to begin. The audience at the Longacre was treated as the union members and speeches were directed to them. As different members of the union addressed their brethren, the evening became more and more explosive. Elia Kazan, as the most vocal of the prostrike members, whipped the audience into a frenzy. At the end of the play, word comes that Lefty has been killed and the meeting explodes. The cast, on the stage and in the theater's aisles, takes up the chant, "Strike! Strike! Strike!"

The second play, *Till the Day I Die,* told of a German Communist who is tortured by police. His only recourse is to commit suicide. The cast of the two plays included Elia Kazan, Lee J. Cobb, Robert Lewis, Russell Collins, Alexander Kirkland, Roman Bohnen and Odets himself. *Lefty* continued as a classic of the American theater. After its closing at the Longacre, it toured union halls around the country.

Odets and the Group Theater returned to the Longacre with the show *Paradise Lost* (12/9/35; 73 performances), the story of a mild-mannered business man and his radical partner. *Paradise Lost* traced what Odets considered the continuing decline of the American middle class.

Another playwright, almost diametrically opposed to Odets in style and substance, also had two plays performed at the Longacre in the thirties. Paul Osborn's *On Borrowed Time* (2/3/38; 321 performances) told of a grandfather who keeps Death at bay up a tree so that he can enjoy a few more moments with his grandson. Joshua Logan (q.v.), directed the cast, which included Peter Holden, Dorothy Stickney and Dudley Digges.

Osborn's other production at the Longacre, *Mornings at Seven* (11/30/39; 44 performances) was a gentle comedy of three sisters and their families. A later revival in 1980 was a hit and ran 564 performances at the Lyceum Theater (q.v.).

Three's a Family (5/5/43; 497 performances) by Phoebe and Henry Ephron was produced by John Golden. The farce had what critic (q.v.) Burns Mantle called a "confused but possible ending." It was the last play presented at the Longacre until 1953. The theater was used for radio and television productions in the interim.

The Dorothy Parker and Arnaud d'Usseau play *The Ladies of the Corridor* (11/21/53; 45 performances) was the first play after the Longacre returned to a legitimate policy. Jean Anouilh's play *Colombe* was adapted by Louis Kronenberger as *Mademoiselle Colombe* (1/6/54; 61 performances) and starred Julie Harris as Colombe, a young innocent who discovers her own strengths in the backstage world of a Paris theater. The play was Anouilh's seventh successive failure on Broadway.

His next play, *The Lark* (11/17/55; 229 performances), changed his luck. Julie Harris starred as Joan of Arc, Boris Karloff as Cauchon, and Theodore Bikel, Sam Jaffe, Christopher Plummer and Joseph Wiseman rounded out the cast.

Samuel Taylor's *The Pleasure of His Company* (10/22/58; 474 performances) opened with Cornelia Otis Skinner, Cyril Ritchard, George Peppard, Charlie Ruggles and Walter Abel. Eugene Ionesco's anticonformist play *Rhinoceros* (1/9/61; 240 performances) opened with Zero Mostel (as the man who becomes the animal), Eli Wallach, Jean Stapleton, Anne Jackson and Morris Carnovsky. It was the only Broadway production for the Roumanian-born French playwright. *Rhinoceros* received rave reviews for Mostel's performance. The play was later revived at the Longacre on September 18, 1961, for an additional 16 performances.

A Case of Libel (10/10/63; 242 performances) by Henry Denker opened with Van Heflin, Larry Gates, M'el Dowd, Sidney Blackmer and Philip Borneuf in the cast. The play was based on Quentin Reynold's libel suit against Westbrook Pegler as reported by Louis Nizer in his book *My Life in Court.*

Lorraine Hansberry's drama *The Sign in Sidney Brustein's Window* (10/15/64; 101 performances) starred Gabriel Dell, Rita Moreno and Alice Ghostley. The play later found more appreciative audiences, and it has enjoyed many productions throughout the country. Unfortunately Miss Hansberry died on January 12, 1965, and never witnessed her play's success.

Robert Anderson's *I Never Sang for My Father* (1/25/68; 124 performances) explored the relationship of an estranged father and son, two frightened people who feel they should love each other but who bury their emotions under the protection of selfishness. *I Never Sang for My Father* starred Teresa Wright, Lillian Gish, Hal Holbrook and Alan Webb.

Terrence McNally's rollicking comedy set in a homosexual bathhouse, *The Ritz* (1/20/75; 400 performances) starred Jack Weston, Rita Moreno, F. Murray Abraham, Stephen Collins and Jerry Stiller.

The Fats Waller retrospective *Ain't Misbehavin'* moved from the Manhattan Theater Club to the Longacre on May 9, 1978. It made stars of its cast members Armelia McQueen, Ken Page, Nell Carter, Charlene Woodard and Andre De Shields. *Ain't Misbehavin'* was the best of all the revues that attempted to examine a composer's career. The credit for its success goes to director Richard Maltby Jr., who gave each of the cast members an individual character and kept the proceedings humming at a rapid clip. *Ain't Misbehavin'* ran 1,604 performances, making it one of the biggest hits of the seventies.

Deaf actress Phyllis Frelich electrified audiences in the Mark Medoff play *Children of a Lesser God* (3/30/80; 887 performances). John Rubinstein costarred in the production, which won a Tony Award *(q.v.)* and was the Longacre's last success.

On December 8, 1987, the New York City Landmarks Preservation Commission designated the interior and exterior of the theater a landmark. The Commission stated that the theater's "exceptionally handsome" neoclassical facade has five bays formed by stylized Corinthian pilasters, "adorned with elaborate ornament."

LUNT–FONTANNE THEATER 205 W. 46th Street. Architects: Carriere and Hastings. Opening: January 10, 1910; *The Old Town* In 1909, producer Charles Dillingham hired the high-class architecture firm of Carriere and Hastings to design the Globe Theatre, which later became the Lunt–Fontanne. Carriere and Hastings are best known for their designs for the New York Public Library (1898–1911), the Frick Collection (1913–1914) and the Manhattan Bridge approach (1912–1915).

Dillingham was described by Fred Stone, one of his stars, as "A swell. Dapper, meticulously dressed, his

The Globe Theatre Courtesy Artkraft Strauss.

hat always tilted a little over one eye, he was a unique figure in the theater. He knew more of the important society people than any other producer, but he preferred the company of prize fighters." Dillingham's life-style was as flamboyant as his personality, and he spared little expense in his new theater. He wanted to cater to the carriage trade, and so he made sure that the interior and exterior of the building were lavishly decorated. The theater's original entrance on 1555 Broadway was supplanted by an additional entrance on West 46th Street, which was designed for patrons who wanted to make grand entrances. Above the 46th Street doors was a balcony from which audience members could view arrivals.

Inside, the theater proper was decorated in hues of gold, blue and ivory. Above the auditorium was a dome that could be opened to the sky in good weather. Upstairs, the theater contained private apartments for Dillingham and his retinue. The six-story Renaissance-revival-style building presented an awesome facade to passersby and theatergoers.

Dillingham was primarily a producer of musicals, and so the early years of the theater were spent, almost exclusively, with musicals and revues. Dillingham's initial offering at the Globe was a Gustave Luders and George Ade musical, *The Old Town*. The main draw of the show was the popular team of Dave Montgomery and Fred Stone. Peggy Wood was also featured. Montgomery and Stone were riding high on the popularity of their last two musicals, *The Wizard of Oz* and Victor Herbert's *(q.v.) The Red Mill*. For *The Old Town*, Stone worked up a specialty act in which he twirled a lasso and danced with it. He also walked a high wire in the show. As might be evident, the plot was of little importance, and by the end of the show's Broadway run it was completely discarded. A reviewer noted that the authors had removed "the grass that was growing in the streets of *The Old Town*." *The Old Town's* 171-performance run was an auspicious success for the new theater.

Dillingham's next show, *The Slim Princess* (1/2/11; 104 performances), also included popular American humorist George Ade on the creative staff. This time, Ade's original story was the basis for the book. Leslie Stuart and Henry Blossom were responsible for the score. The cast of *The Slim Princess* included popular musical-comedy stars Queenie Vassar, Charles King, Elizabeth Brice and Joseph Cawthorn. But the biggest star in the show, and one of the biggest in the early part of this century, was Elsie Janis. *The Slim Princess* was about a country where obesity was looked on as beauty. The slim plot gave Janis plenty of opportunities for her well-known impressions.

Producer Charles Frohman's advice to fellow producers was "When in doubt, do Cinderella." Dillingham took Frohman's advice in his next offering at the Globe, *The Lady of the Slipper* (10/28/12; 232 performances). Elsie Janis returned to the Globe's stage as did Montgomery and Stone and Peggy Wood. The cast also featured dancer Vernon Castle (*q.v.*). The songs were by Victor Herbert, who had contributed uncredited music to *The Slim Princess,* and lyricist James O'Dea. *The Lady and the Slipper* also had troubles while out of town. Irene Castle had been to Paris the previous summer where she had discovered a new style in brief underwear. She took pride in her discovery and decided to introduce the style to America. As described by Elsie Janis, during the dress rehearsal in Philadelphia, Miss Castle "suddenly pulled up her skirts like a naughty little girl, showing her 'complete understanding,' Charley (Dillingham) groaned, Fred Stone looked the other way, and (my) Mother's gasp of dismay must have been heard in Trenton!" Dillingham begged the dancer to put on her Dutch bonnet and chiffon skirts but she refused and she was out of the show.

If the 232-performance run of *The Lady of the Slipper* was remarkable, then the 295 performance run of Dillingham's next production, *Chin-Chin* was almost a miracle. *Chin-Chin* (10/20/14) opened with Dillingham favorites Montgomery and Stone in the leads. The music was by Englishman Ivan Caryll, and lyrics were by Anne Caldwell and James O'Dea. Montgomery and Stone played two slaves of Aladdin's lamp. In *Chin-Chin,* Stone impersonated Paderewski. He accomplished the amazing feat of duplicating the pianist's great technique by sitting in front of a player piano on stage. Paderewski even came to one performance and complimented Stone on his playing. Stone also performed a horseback-riding trick. He was suspended by a wire while riding the horse. As he circled the stage, he slipped further and further backward until, hanging in the air, he was holding on to only the horse's tail. The trick ended when the tail appeared to come off in Stone's hand, and the actor crashed to the ground.

Dillingham was smart enough to realize that tastes in popular music were changing and the old fashioned operettas and comic operas were becoming dated. The producer hired the young Irving Berlin (*q.v.*) to write the score to the next production at the Globe, *Stop! Look! Listen!* (12/25/15; 105 performances). The show opened with a libretto by the prolific Harry B. Smith (*q.v.*). Berlin's score contained two classics—"The Girl on the Magazine Cover" and the ragtime-inspired "I Love a Piano." The fine cast included future film star Marion Davies, Gaby Deslys, Blossom Seeley and Joseph Santley.

The Globe's first straight play presentation was *The Harp of Life* (11/27/16; 136 performances). Laurette Taylor starred in the play, which was written by her husband, J. Hartley Manners. *The Harp of Life* marked Taylor's return to New York after a period in England.

In the second year of touring *Chin-Chin,* Dave Mont-

Globe Theatre Courtesy Municipal Art Society.

gomery died. Fred Stone went on to appear at the Globe in *Jack O'Lantern* (10/16/17; 265 performances). The musical had music and lyrics by Ivan Caryll and Anne Caldwell. The hit song from the show was an interpolation by Irving Berlin, "I'll Take You Back to Italy." For *Jack O'Lantern,* Fred Stone learned to ice-skate. He described another of his stunts in his autobiography: "I jumped up and down on a hay wagon which was a trampoline, pursued by the police, then ran two steps up a tree, turned a back somersault over the heads of the police, leaped on a bicycle and somersaulted with it through the window of a house." At the time, Stone was 41 years old.

Dillingham's production *The Canary* (11/4/18; 152 performances) had songs by Ivan Caryll, Irving Berlin, Anne Caldwell, P.G. Wodehouse, Harry Tierney, Harry B. Smith, Benjamin Hapgood Burt and others. Despite the large number of composers and lyricists, the show was a musical comedy, not a revue. Of course, at the time, there was sometimes little difference between the two forms.

Dillingham's production of *She's a Good Fellow* (5/5/19; 120 performances) boasted a score by Jerome Kern *(q.v.)* and Anne Caldwell. Joseph Santley (in drag), the Duncan Sisters, Olin Howland and Ivy Sawyer starred. The show's run was cut short by the actor's strike of 1919 *(q.v.),* which helped establish Actor's Equity *(q.v.).*

Along with Irving Berlin and Jerome Kern, George Gershwin *(q.v.)* was responsible for the new direction of Broadway musicals. Gershwin finally had a show of his produced at the Globe with the second edition of the *George White's Scandals (q.v.)* (6/7/20; 134 performances). Arthur Jackson was Gershwin's collaborator on the score. *Scandals* regulars Ann Pennington, Lou Holtz and Lester Allen and George White himself, starred in the show. The *Scandals* was the first show presented in the Globe that was not produced by Dillingham.

Dillingham returned to producing at the Globe with *Tip Top* (10/5/20; 241 performances). Ivan Caryll and Anne Caldwell provided the score for the show, which starred Fred Stone, the Duncan Sisters and Rags Ragland. *Tip Top* featured Fred Stone up to some new tricks. He opened the show by shooting up through a trap door in the stage with his hair covered with foam. Stone told the audience that he had added too many raisins to the bootleg hooch that he was brewing in the basement. He also learned the art of Australian whip-cracking and removed a cigarette from the mouth of an assistant with the whip. Stone's piece de resistance was when he broke resin balls with shots fired from a .22 rifle. While he shot at the airborne balls, he danced.

George White's chief rival, Florenz Ziegfeld *(q.v.),* presented the 1921 version of the *Ziegfeld Follies (q.v.)* (6/21/21; 119 performances) at the Globe. Performers included W.C. Fields, Raymond Hitchock, Ray Dooley and Vera Michelena. Fanny Brice *(q.v.)* was given the two best songs—"My Man" and "Second Hand Rose."

Jerome Kern had another show open at the Globe, *Good Morning, Dearie* (11/1/21; 347 performances). Anne Caldwell wrote the book and lyrics. Among the best songs in the score were the title tune and "Blue Danube Blues." The biggest hit in the show was "Ka-Lu-A."

George White's Scandals returned to the Globe (8/28/22; 89 performances) with music by George Gershwin and lyrics by B.G. De Sylva *(q.v.),* E. Ray Goetz and Arthur Francis. Francis was a pseudonym for George's talented brother, Ira. The cast included Lester Allen, Winnie Lightner, George White and W.C. Fields. Paul Whiteman and his Orchestra also appeared onstage. The most famous of the Gershwin songs was "I'll Build a Stairway to Paradise."

Fred Stone appeared along with his wife Allene and daughter Dorothy in the aptly titled *Stepping Stones* (1/16/23; 241 performances). Jerome Kern and Anne Caldwell wrote the score, which included the beautiful ballad "Once in a Blue Moon." On opening night, producer Charles Dillingham had a surprise for the cast. After the performance, Dillingham took Dorothy outside the theater to show her where he had put her name up in lights on the marquee.

The *Scandals* returned to the Globe (6/18/23; 168 performances) with Gershwin again supplying the score along with lyricists B.G. DeSylva, E. Ray Goetz and Ballard Macdonald. None of the songs achieved success.

Ed Wynn was composer, lyricist, librettist, producer and star of *The Grab Bag* (10/6/24; 184 performances). The show proved to be a huge hit with Wynn's hijinks. It was followed by one of the Globe's biggest hits, *No, No, Nanette* (9/16/25; 329 performances). The show's tremendous success was due mostly to the great Vincent Youmans *(q.v.)* and Irving Caesar score. The hit songs included "Tea for Two" and "I Want to Be Happy." Another factor in the great success of the show was its star Louise Groody. Groody was the first star to receive a salary plus a percentage of the box office receipts. As a result, she was the first musical-comedy star to earn over a million dollars. The actress shocked audiences when she appeared on the stage of the Globe Theatre shorn of her trademark curls. Luckily, audiences cheered her performance despite her tonsorial change.

Ziegfeld produced his revue *No Foolin'* (6/24/26; 108 performances) at the Globe. Ziegfeld planned the show as the 1926 edition of his *Follies,* but because of a breakup with his former partners and owners of the New Amsterdam Theater *(q.v.)* Marc Klaw and A.L. Erlanger he was refused the right to the *Follies* name. Out of town, the show was titled *Ziegfeld's Palm Beach Nights, Ziegfeld's Palm Beach Girl* and *Ziegfeld's American Revue of 1926.* After its Broadway opening as *No Foolin',* Ziegfeld retitled the show *Ziegfeld's American Revue.*

When the show toured following its Broadway run, Ziegfeld, having settled his argument with Klaw and Erlanger, could at last call the show the *Ziegfeld Follies of 1926*.

Jerome Kern, Otto Harbach *(q.v.)* and Anne Caldwell were responsible for the Dillingham production of *Criss Cross* (10/12/26; 210 performances). Fred Stone and his daughter Dorothy appeared in the show with Stone Sr. dropping onto the stage from the fly system above. When he reached the stage floor, a rubber contraption he was linked to jerked him back above the proscenium arch. Stone also swung 40 feet from the wings by his knees. At the bottom of his swing he picked up his daughter Dorothy and, continuing to swing from side to side, carried her to the opposite side of the stage.

Vincent Youmans's second production at the Globe, *Oh, Please!* (12/17/26; 79 performances), had a hit song, "I Know that You Know" and a talented cast, including Beatrice Lillie, Charles Winninger, Helen Broderick and Charles Purcell.

Three Cheers (10/15/28; 218 performances) was to star Fred Stone and his daughter Dorothy, but prior to the opening, Stone, who had taken up flying, crashed the plane he was piloting. His injuries prevented him from appearing in *Three Cheers*. Will Rogers, Stone's closest friend, replaced him in the show. On the opening night, Rogers told the audience, "I don't know one thing that Fred does that I can do." Rogers was smart enough not to try duplicating Stone's acrobatics, and he got laughs by admitting it. "You know, folks," Rogers would tell the audience, "if Fred Stone were here, he'd be making a standing jump up there. But I think I'll just stay where I am." Future Hollywood comedienne Patsy Kelly was also in the cast. Ray Henderson and B.G. DeSylva wrote the score, but none of the songs achieved any success. If Stone had been able to perform, the show would have been the first Globe musical featuring Stone that was not produced by Dillingham. The great producer's luck was running out.

The last show to play the Globe was the Jerome Kern and Otto Harbach musical *The Cat and the Fiddle* (10/15/31; 395 performances). The brilliantly tuneful score featured such hits as "I Watch the Love Parade," "She Didn't Say Yes," "The Night Was Made for Love" and "Try to Forget." The show starred Odette Myrtil, Georges Metaxa, Bettina Hall and George Meader.

The stock-market crash wiped out Dillingham's savings, and the great producer was forced to sell his beloved theater. Beginning in 1932, the Globe showed motion pictures. Twenty-five years later, in 1957, Roger L. Stevens and Robert W. Dowling bought the theater and had the interior completely refurbished. The second balcony was removed and a mezzanine was added. The refurbished interior was also redecorated with an 18th century motif. The theater was renamed for the greatest of all American acting teams, Alfred Lunt and Lynn Fontanne *(q.v.)*.

The renamed theater's second opening took place on May 5, 1958, with the stars who gave it their names in the leading roles of Fredrich Duerrenmatt's explosive drama *The Visit* (189 performances). Brooks Atkinson described the play as "a horrifying indictment of a cruel and greedy culture, staged with ingenuity and bravado by a gifted heretic and acted with subtlety, insight, and coolness by America's greatest actors." However, the unrelenting drama of the play kept many theatergoers away. Sadly, it marked the end of the team's career on Broadway.

The theater's greatest hit, *The Sound of Music* (11/16/59; 1,443 performances), marked the end of another great team's Broadway career. It would be the last collaboration for Richard Rodgers *(q.v.)* and Oscar Hammerstein II *(q.v.)*. The Mary Martin *(q.v.)* vehicle received decidedly mixed reviews but was an enormously popular hit with the public. Critics cited the operetta's sentimentality as its greatest fault. The score also received mixed notices, although many of the songs, chiefly "Climb Ev'ry Mountain," "Sixteen Going on Seventeen," "My Favorite Things" and the title song became standards.

One of Broadway's funniest musicals, *Little Me* (11/17/62; 257 performances), followed *The Sound of Music* at the Lunt–Fontanne. The Cy Coleman and Carolyn

Cy Coleman Courtesy ASCAP.

Leigh score was perhaps the wittiest and brashest ever to play on Broadway. It was perfectly complimented by Neil Simon's *(q.v.)* hilarious libretto. The hit songs from the score were "I've Got Your Number" and "Real Live Girl." The play was the story of Belle Poitrine, a not-so-dumb blonde, and her succession of husbands. Belle was played by two actresses. Nancy Andrews played the older Belle, and Virginia Martin the young Belle. All the husbands were played by master comic Sid Caesar. The reviews were excellent, but a newspaper strike hurt the musical's business.

Richard Burton opened in William Shakespeare's *Hamlet* on April 9, 1964. His performance was generally hailed, and the production enjoyed a 137-performance run, a record for the play on Broadway.

A series of middling musicals followed Hamlet. By now, 500 performances were usually necessary for a show to recoup its investment. Julie Harris was allowed to sing in the James Van Heusen, Sammy Cahn musical *Skyscraper* (11/13/65; 248 performances). "Everybody Has the Right to Be Wrong" was the most popular

song in the otherwise undistinguished score. The same songwriting team was responsible for the next attraction at the Lunt–Fontanne, *Walking Happy* (11/26/66; 161 performances). The title tune and Norman Wisdom's performance were the chief draw. Lyricist Carolyn Leigh teamed up with film composer Elmer Bernstein for the David Merrick *(q.v.)* production *How Now, Dow Jones* (12/7/67; 220 performances). The score contained a bona fide hit, "Step to the Rear." The show's book by Max Shulman was considered the biggest flaw in the show that starred Marlyn Mason, Anthony Roberts and Brenda Vaccaro.

Hal Linden, Jill Clayburgh, Keene Curtis and Paul Hecht starred in Jerry Bock and Sheldon Harnick's *(q.v.)* story of the Rothschild family, *The Rothschilds* (10/19/70; 505 performances).

During the seventies, there were a series of revivals at the Lunt–Fontanne. These included Stephen Sondheim's *(q.v.) A Funny Thing Happened on the Way to the Forum* with Phil Silvers and Larry Blyden; the Richard Adler and Jerry Ross hit *The Pajama Game* with Hal

The Lunt-Fontanne Theater   Courtesy Billy Rose Theater Collection.

Linden and Barbara McNair; and *Hello, Dolly!* with a return performance by Carol Channing. One nonrevival in the seventies was the Richard Rodgers and Sheldon Harnick musical *Rex* (4/25/76; 49 performances). The show, a retelling of the life of Henry VIII, starred Nicol Williamson, Penny Fuller and Barbara Andres.

A big hit for the theater was the Duke Ellington revue *Sophisticated Ladies* (3/1/81; 767 performances) with Gregory Hines, Phyllis Hyman, Judith Jamison and Hinton Battle. *Sophisticated Ladies* covered the best-known songs in the Ellington canon.

On December 14, 1987, the New York City Landmarks Preservation Commission designated the exterior of the theater a landmark. The interior was denied status. The Commission stated that the theater's facade is an "exceptional example" of beaux-arts style, with a five-bay arcade of double-height Ionic columns, a smaller version of the Century Theater that once stood on Central Park West.

LUNT AND FONTANNE The husband and wife team of Alfred Lunt and Lynn Fontanne are considered the greatest acting couple in American history. They enjoyed long careers on the Broadway stage, both together and alone from the first decade of the century until their retirement in 1960. The team was responsible for many of the great hits of the Theater Guild *(q.v.),* and they certainly accounted for the Guild's long preeminence.

Alfred Lunt (1893–1977)   Alfred Davis Lunt Jr. was born in Milwaukee, Wisconsin, to a family that had deep roots in New England. His early love for the theater launched his stage career before his 20th birthday. The year was 1912, and Lunt was in Boston ostensibly to attend the Emerson School of Oratory. He made it to only one session of one class before passing the Castle Square Theater and inquiring about employment. School was forgotten, and Lunt was hired to play small parts at $5 a week. After a month, he worked his way up to the generous salary of $20 a week. Lunt's stage debut was in the play *The Aviator,* which opened on October 7, 1912.

Lunt remained at the Castle Square Theater for three years. In 1914, he joined Margaret Anglin's touring company and remained with the company for two years. He then found work in vaudeville, supporting Lily Langtry. Later that same year, 1916, he rejoined the Anglin company.

Lunt moved to New York and made his Broadway debut at the Harris Theatre *(q.v.)* in *Romance and Arabella* (10/17/17). Two years later, he met Lynn Fontanne in a Chicago production of *A Young Man's Fancy.*

He returned to New York, and had his first great success in the title role in *Clarence.* Booth Tarkington wrote the play expressly for Lunt. *Clarence* (9/20/19) opened at the Hudson Theatre *(q.v.).* The critic *(q.v.)*

for the *Sun* wrote, "Alfred Lunt gave a most amusing performance of the entomologist, making the physical manifestations of the character broadly grotesque. He seemed at times to adopt the dramatic method of the experienced Bert Williams, even in his gait and his furtive and worried look."

After two years with *Clarence,* Lunt opened in another Tarkington play, *The Intimate Strangers* (11/27/21; 97 performances). Alan Dale, writing in the *New York American,* was relieved to find Lunt back on the stage. "A better and more satisfactory leading man could never have been secured. I had been wondering if Mr. Lunt was too good an actor to be in demand, and it was a pleasure to meet him again. Sometimes the actors who have achieved one success vanish curiously."

Lynn Fontanne (1887–1983)   London-born Lynn Fontanne made her stage debut in J.M. Barrie's *Alice-Sit-By-the-Fire* in 1905. The touring production starred Ellen Terry, the idol of Fontanne. The great actress taught the newcomer posture, interpretation and other skills. Terry gave her pupil a letter of introduction to the successful London producer Arthur Collins, manager of the Theatre Royal, Drury Lane. He cast Fontanne in one of his Christmas pantomimes, *Cinderella,* which began a long tour at the end of 1905. After other touring plays, she made her West End debut in *Billy's Bargain* in June 1910.

Fontanne's move to America was prompted by actress Laurette Taylor, who had seen Fontanne in the London production of Edward Knoblock's *My Lady's Dress* in 1914. Taylor convinced Fontanne to come to New York to act in *The Harp of Life* (12/27/16; 24 performances), a play by Taylor's husband, J. Hartley Manners. The play opened at the Globe Theatre *(q.v.).* Fontanne had already appeared on Broadway in a short lived production of *Mr. Preedy and the Countess* at the Thirty-ninth Street Theatre on November 7, 1910.

The critics noticed her performance in *The Harp of Life.* The reviewer for the *New York Times* wrote " . . . and in Lynn Fontanne, an appallingly gowned young woman who wore plum colored shoes during all the evening, the audience found a character to regard with the warmest applause. In all that she said and did was one of the few recognizable humans on the stage." A reviewer for the *Sun* exclaimed "One of the delights of the performance is the exquisite acting of a newcomer, Lynn Fontanne, who established a reputation for uncommon ability overnight. Miss Fontanne comes from England, and it is earnestly hoped that she never returns."

The uncredited reviewer's wishes were answered, for she seldom returned to England's stages. The biggest hit of her early career came in Marc Connelly and George S. Kaufman's *(q.v.) Dulcy* (8/13/21; 246 performances) which opened at the Frazee Theater. (See Lew

M. Fields' Theatre.) Dulcy was a modern Mrs. Malaprop. The actress received glowing notices in what many critics felt was her first appearance out of the shadow of Laurette Taylor.

* * * * *

Lunt and Fontanne had kept in touch following their first meeting in Chicago. They became more and more involved and finally decided to get married at New York's City Hall on May 26, 1922. The marriage took place with no fanfare. Two strangers were asked to be witnesses and were called upon to front the couple a few dollars for the license fee. This humble ceremony was the beginning of a long and successful collaboration on stage and in marriage.

After their marriage, the couple appeared separately in many productions. Notable was Lunt's first dramatic appearance in Sutton Vane's Outward Bound (1/7/24) at the Ritz Theatre (q.v.). John Corbin, writing in the New York Times, was pleased to discover the new facet to Lunt's talents. "Mr. Lunt," he wrote, "finds large scope for his acting powers as a comedian and finally does a bit of emotional acting of the first order."

The couple's first appearance together was in Sweet Nell of Old Drury, a production mounted at the 48th Street Theatre (q.v.) (5/16/23; 51 performances). There followed one of their greatest triumphs and the beginning of their long association with the Theater Guild. Ferenc Molnar's play The Guardsman was a failure when first produced on Broadway in 1913. But the Guild's offer was too good to refuse, and the acting team opened in The Guardsman (10/13/24; 274 performances) at the Garrick Theater. The play was a huge success with Dudley Digges and Helen Westley completing the cast. The team played two jealous actors. Lunt's character disguises himself as a guardsman and makes love to his unknowing wife. She claims to have known it was him all along. E.W. Osborn, writing in the New York Evening World, was among the first to recognize the couple's special powers when sharing the stage: "Alfred Lunt as the jealous actor and Lynn Fontanne as the wife who is too keen for his masquerading self are a comedy pair who need fear no compare. Their swift transition from the spats and dissension of an afternoon in their dear little home to the flirtatious byplay of the evening at the opera is wonderfully smooth and complete, and they rise most happily to the moment of confounding revelations in the third act."

A revival of George Bernard Shaw's Arms and the Man (9/14/25; 181 performances) presented by the Theater Guild at the Guild Theater (q.v.) was the Lunts' next production. They gave many other performances in Guild productions, both as a team and separately, though sometimes the productions and plays were not nearly up to the level of the team's performances.

Among the most highly acclaimed shows of their careers are Eugene O'Neill's (q.v.) nine-act marathon Strange Interlude (1/30/28; 426 performances) with Lynn

Fontanne alone; Maxwell Anderson's Elizabeth the Queen (11/3/30; 145 performances); Robert E. Sherwood's Reunion in Vienna (11/16/31; 280 performances); Noel Coward's sophisticated comedy Design for Living (1/24/33; 135 performances in a limited engagement); Idiot's Delight (3/24/36; 299 performances), the Pulitzer Prize (q.v.) winner by Robert E. Sherwood; Jean Giraudoux and S.N. Behrman's Amphitryon 38 (2/15/37; 152 performances); Robert E. Sherwood's There Shall Be No Night (9/29/40; 115 performances) at the Alvin Theater (q.v.); S.N. Behrman's comedy The Pirate (11/25/42; 176 performances); and The Great Sebastians (1/4/56; 174 performances) by Howard Lindsay and Russel Crouse.

Frederich Durrenmett's The Visit (5/5/58; 189 performances) was their last Broadway assignment and opened as the inaugural production in the newly renamed Lunt–Fontanne Theater (q.v.). Their last New York appearance was in a return of The Visit, which played City Center on March 8, 1960. Lunt served as director for the play First Love (12/25/61), which opened at the Morosco Theatre (q.v.). The team retired from the stage to Alfred's boyhood home of Genesee Depot, Wisconsin. Alfred Lunt died on August 4, 1977. Lynn Fontanne followed him on July 31, 1983.

Many authors have attempted to pinpoint the couple's unique acting style. Playwrights who had written for the Lunts were effusive in their praise. Robert Emmett Sherwood once wrote a poem about their box office appeal:

If you want a play to run many an munt
Get Lynn Fontanne and Alfred Lunt.

S.N. Behrman claimed that the Lunts were insulated and lived in their own fantasy world. One day, Lynn Fontanne rushed to the singer Alma Gluck and insisted that Gluck introduce her to Rachmaninoff. It seemed that Fontanne had run into the composer on Fifth Avenue and was so struck by his mien that she followed him around all day. When Gluck arranged for Fontanne to meet the composer (who played bridge with Gluck's husband Efrem Zimbalist Sr.), the actress was taken aback. "That's not Rachmaninoff," she exclaimed. Gluck assured her that it was indeed Rachmaninoff in the other room. It was then that Fontanne realized she had followed a stranger around Manhattan.

Brooks Atkinson, in his book Broadway, called the Lunts, "Brilliant actors with mischievious personalities and an insatiable appetite for the stage, they were the most exhilarating and enviable couple on Broadway."

Lynn Fontanne told theater historian George Freedley that people accused them of being "all tricks. What we do is exactly the opposite. We search for the truth and try to express it. We do the natural thing."

LYCEUM THEATER 149 W. 45th Street. Architects: Herts & Tallant. Opening: November 2, 1903; The Proud Prince. When producer Daniel Frohman opened his new Lyceum Theater on 45th Street, it was the first of the Times Square theaters north of 42nd Street. Other theaters had opened around Columbus Circle, and there was a healthy theater district in Harlem, but the success of the Lyceum and the other theaters surrounding it firmly established the Times Square area as the hub of legitimate theater.

The theater was considered quite modern for its time. There were no balcony supports to block the audience's view. Also, it contained shop space and dressing rooms in the rear of the theater proper. The neo-baroque interior style and beautiful facade made the Lyceum one of the most attractive Broadway houses. It was the first theater building to receive landmark status.

Frohman's private apartments contained a window from which he could view the performances below. This was a common practice in theaters whose managements liked to keep a tight rein on their companies. When Frohman's wife, Margaret Illington, acted on the Lyceum stage her husband would signal her from his window if she was overacting.

The theater has had a distinguished past, starting with its first offering, *The Proud Prince* starring E.H. Sothern, a favorite of Frohman. Soon after, William Gillette starred in J.M. Barrie's *The Admirable Crichton* (11/17/03; 144 performances). The biggest hit of the early years of the Lyceum was *The Lion and the Mouse* (11/20/05; 686 performances) by Charles Klein.

Great women graced the Lyceum stage in a number of mostly forgotten plays. Billie Burke, Ethel Barrymore, Lenore Ulric and Ina Claire all had great success at the theater.

During the twenties, Frohman, his brother Daniel and producer David Belasco *(q.v.)* all produced hits at the theater. One of the biggest successes was *Berkeley Square* (11/4/29) by John L. Balderston, starring Leslie Howard and Margalo Gillmore.

During the thirties and the Depression, Daniel Frohman's fortunes declined, but the theater still housed a number of interesting shows. Charles Laughton and Elsa Lanchester starred in *Payment Deferred* (9/30/31; 70 performances). *Sailor, Beware!* was a big hit beginning on September 28, 1933 (500 performances) and Ina Claire, who had previously starred at the Lyceum in *The Gold Diggers* (9/30/19; 720 performances) returned to the Lyceum in *Ode to Liberty* (12/21/34; 66 performances).

Having Wonderful Time (2/20/37; 310 performances), Arthur Kober's affectionate view of a summer camp for adults in the Catskills, would later be made into the musical *Wish You Were Here*. J.B. Priestley's delightful farce *When We Are Married* (12/25/39) closed the thirties.

However successful the plays staged at the Lyceum were, Frohman's career was suffering. The theater was faced with destruction. A group of investors, however, led by George S. Kaufman *(q.v.)*, Moss Hart *(q.v.)* and

Max Gordon bought the theater and allowed Frohman to live in his apartment for $1 a year.

It was natural that the first show of the forties would be Kaufman and Hart's riotous comedy *George Washington Slept Here* (10/18/40), but it didn't prove as successful as their other outings. Moss Hart then staged Jerome Chodorov and Joseph Fields's *Junior Miss* (11/18/41; 710 performances). It would later make a successful movie and a television musical. The same authors provided the theater with its next hit, *The Doughgirls* (12/30/42). Kaufman directed the Arlene Francis vehicle. Kaufman then cowrote with John P. Marquand and directed *The Late George Apley* (11/21/44; 384 performances). At the end of that play's run, the Kaufman/Hart/Gordon group sold the Lyceum. It eventually became a part of the Shubert *(q.v.)* empire.

Garson Kanin's *Born Yesterday* (2/4/46; 1,642 performances) was the Lyceum's next smash hit. It made stars of Judy Holliday and Paul Douglas.

The 1950s were also rich years for the Lyceum. Clifford Odets's *The Country Girl* (11/10/50) starred Uta Hagen, Paul Kelly and Steven Hill. Melvyn Douglas starred in *Glad Tidings* (10/11/51) and followed it with *Time Out for Ginger* (11/26/52), one of the most successful plays in the amateur market, receiving countless productions in summer stock and schools. Jean Kerr and Eleanor Brooke continued the comedy tradition at the Lyceum with *King of Hearts* (4/1/54). Drama critic *(q.v.)* Walter Kerr directed Jackie Cooper and Donald Cook in the hit comedy.

Viveca Lindfors portrayed the title role in *Anastasia* (12/29/54), written by Broadway veteran Guy Bolton *(q.v.)*. Eugenie Leontovich played the dowager empress in the production. Another drama followed, the harrowing *A Hatful of Rain* (11/9/55), starring Ben Gazzara, Shelley Winters and Harry Guardino.

During the second half of the fifties, Walter Pidgeon starred in a production of *The Happiest Millionaire* (11/20/56). The next hit was John Osborne's *Look Back in Anger* (10/1/57; 407 performances) with Kenneth Haigh, Alan Bates and Mary Ure. It reopened at the 41st Street Theatre *(q.v.)* for an additional 116 performances.

The 1960s began with Shelagh Delaney's *A Taste of Honey* (10/4/60), starring Angela Lansbury. The third hit at the Lyceum, was a British import, a production of Harold Pinter's *The Caretaker* (10/4/61) with Alan Bates, Robert Shaw and Donald Pleasence.

Ellis Rabb, artistic director of the APA Phoenix company, took over the theater for the rest of the decade. During this period of 1965–69, such plays as *War and Peace, The Cherry Orchard, The Cocktail Party* and George Kelly's *The Show Off*, starring Helen Hayes, appeared on the Lyceum stage.

The 1970s proved to be lean years for the Lyceum and Broadway in general. The best play of the decade at the Lyceum was Arthur Kopit's brilliant drama *Wings*

(1/28/79; 113 performances), starring Constance Cummings.

In 1980, an all-star revival of *Morning's At Seven* (4/10/80) opened at the Lyceum. In the cast were Nancy Marchand, Maureen O'Sullivan, Teresa Wright, Elizabeth Wilson and David Rounds. Hits since then include Athol Fugard's *'Master Harold' . . . and the boys,* Jules Feiffer's *Grown-Ups* and *As Is.*

The Shuberts restored the theater and placed their archives upstairs in Frohman's old offices. On December 8, 1987, the New York City Landmarks Preservation Commission designated the interior of the theater a landmark. The exterior had been designated in 1974. The Commission stated that the auditorium was in an "unusually handsome Beaux-Arts style design . . . with an elaborate proscenium arch and boxes adorned with elegant French-inspired ornament." The Lyceum was awarded "distressed" status among the theater's unions, enabling it to qualify for reduced minimums and fees.

LYRIC THEATER 213 W. 42nd Street. Architect: V. Hugo Koehler. Opening: October 12, 1903, *Old Heidelberg.* The Lyric is one of the most beautiful of the 42nd Street movie houses. Although the entrance to the Renaissance-style theater is on 42nd Street, the main part of the theater fronts 43rd Street. That side features a beautifully ornamented facade with cartouches inscribed "Music" and "Drama." It was cleaned in 1979 by the

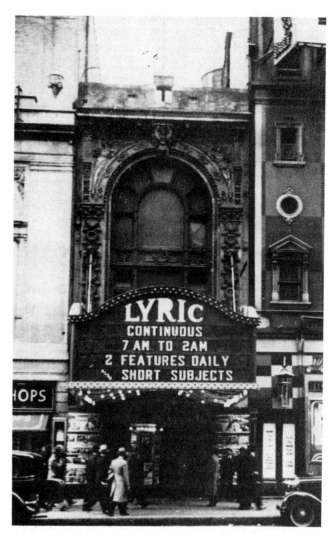

Lyric Theater (42nd Street entrance) Courtesy Billy Rose Theater Collection.

Lyric Theater (43rd Street) Photo Jeff Slotnick.

current owners, the Brandts with the expectation of reopening it as a legitimate house. But the current financial plight of the theater district has ruled out any reversal of the theater's movie policy.

The Lyric was built by the Shuberts *(q.v.)* to house Reginald DeKoven's American School of Opera. Leading man Richard Mansfield opened the house in 1903. DeKoven's troupe didn't last long, and the Shuberts subsequently booked some of the greatest actors and productions of its time—Douglas Fairbanks starred in an adaptation of Charles Norris' *The Pet;* Mrs. Fiske, George Arliss, and Dudley Diggs played in *The New York Idea* (11/19/06); Tyrone Power Sr. appeared in *Julius Caesar* (2/16/14); William Faversham also played the part at the Lyric beginning on November 4, 1912.

Musicals included Rudolf Friml's *(q.v.) The Firefly* (12/2/12) and *High Jinks* (12/10/13). *The Firefly* had lyrics by Otto Harbach and featured the Friml favorite "Giannina Mia." Fred and Adele Astaire *(q.v.)* starred in *For Goodness Sake* (2/20/22). Although the score was by Paul Lannin, William Daly and Arthur Jackson, newcomers George and Ira Gershwin *(q.v.)* contributed the hits "Someone" and "Tra-La-La." Irving Berlin *(q.v.)* supplied the score to the madcap musical comedy *The Cocoanuts* (12/8/25; 375 performances). Along with the Marx Brothers, the show featured the Brox Sisters, and the Brothers' constant foil, Margaret Dumont. The show later was made into the Brothers' first motion picture success. The great showman Florenz Ziegfeld *(q.v.)* brought his musicalization of *The Three Musketeers* into the Lyric on March 13, 1928. Rudolf Friml again delighted audiences with such songs as "Gascony," "March of the Musketeers," "My Sword," "One Kiss" and "Your Eyes." The show was a smash hit and ran 319 performances. The last legitimate show to play the Lyric was *Run, Little Chillun!* beginning on March 1, 1933.

The Lyric, like other 42nd Street theaters, became a motion-picture house because of the Depression, starting its movie policy in 1933. Luckily, as with most of the 42nd Street theaters, economics did not allow for major renovation. Thus the Lyric is almost exactly the same as when it opened more than 80 years ago. When wide screen came in, the nine original boxes were removed. Attempts to reopen the theater as a legitimate house failed in 1979 as Broadway continued its most recent decline. A huge theater with a double balcony, the Lyric seats 1,256 patrons. Because of its size, the Lyric, under the Times Square Redevelopment Plan, is supposed to be used for legitimate theater productions.

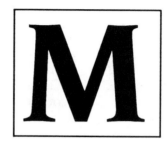

MCLAIN, JOHN See CRITICS.

MAJESTIC THEATRE 245 W. 44th Street. Architect: Herbert J. Krapp. Opening: March 28, 1927; *Rufus Le-Maire's Affairs*. With 1,800 seats, the Majestic was the largest legitimate house in Times Square. The Majestic was the last theater commissioned by the Chanin Brothers and was built as the flagship of their theater holdings. Unfortunately the Chanins lost all their theaters during the Depression.

The Majestic did not have an easy time attracting hit shows. The initial attraction, *Rufus LeMaire's Affairs*, closed after only 56 performances. Sigmund Romberg *(q.v.)*, the great operetta composer, premiered *The Love Call* (10/24/27;81 performances) with lyrics by the prolific Harry B. Smith *(q.v.)*.

Several successful transfers from other theaters held the Majestic's stage, along with a few original failures. Boxer Jack Dempsey actually starred in a Broadway play aptly titled *The Big Fight* (9/18/28; 31 performances).

The Shuberts *(q.v.)* gained control of the Majestic and filled it with their productions. *Pleasure Bound* (2/18/29; 136 performances) was a minor revue that didn't cost the producers too much, because most of its cast and creative staff were on the monthly Shubert payroll. They probably used the sets and costumes over again in another of their shows.

A Wonderful Night (10/31/29; 125 performances) was a retelling of *Le Reveillon*, the story that served as the basis for the opera *Die Fledermaus*. The music was taken from Johann Strauss. A young cast member was Archie Leach, who would later achieve fame in Hollywood as Cary Grant.

Impresario Lew Leslie, who had scored a big success with his *Blackbirds of 1928*, thought he had another hit with *The International Revue* (2/25/30; 95 performances).

He poured $200,000 into the show and hired the *Blackbirds'* songwriters Jimmy McHugh and Dorothy Fields *(q.v.)*. They came up with a couple of big hit songs, "Exactly Like You" and "On the Sunny Side of the Street." Leslie hired a wonderful cast including Americans Harry Richman and Jack Pearl, the British star Gertrude Lawrence and the Spanish dancer Argentinita. But despite their talents the show was one of the first victims of the Depression.

Romberg was back with another operetta, *Nina Rosa* (9/20/30; 129 performances). Otto Harbach *(q.v.)* wrote the book, and Irving Caesar wrote the lyrics. Stars Ethelind Terry, Guy Robertson and George Kirk couldn't overcome the audiences' antipathy toward operetta.

After a long, dark period, the Majestic presented what seemed a sure hit. Instead of a dated operetta, the Shuberts booked the modern style musical *Pardon My English* (1/20/33; 43 performances). Alex A. Aarons and Vinton Freedley *(q.v.)*, two of Broadway's most successful producers, presented George and Ira Gershwin *(q.v.)* and librettest Herbert Fields' *(q.v.)* newest creation. The score contained several standards, including "Isn't It a Pity?" and "The Lorelei." Lyda Roberti's comic song "My Cousin in Milwaukee" also achieved a bit of fame.

Ray Henderson and Lew Brown *(q.v.)* tried to buck the Depression with their production *Strike Me Pink* (3/4/33; 122 performances). Henderson and Brown contributed the score as well as coauthored the libretto, coproduced the show with silent partner Waxey Gordon, a notorious gangster *(q.v.)*, and codirected with Jack McGowan. None of their songs caught on with the public. The show starred Hal LeRoy, Jimmy Durante, Lupe Velez and Hope Williams. *Strike Me Pink's* opening-night tickets cost $25, around three times the normal ticket price.

Murder at the Vanities (9/12/33; 298 performances)

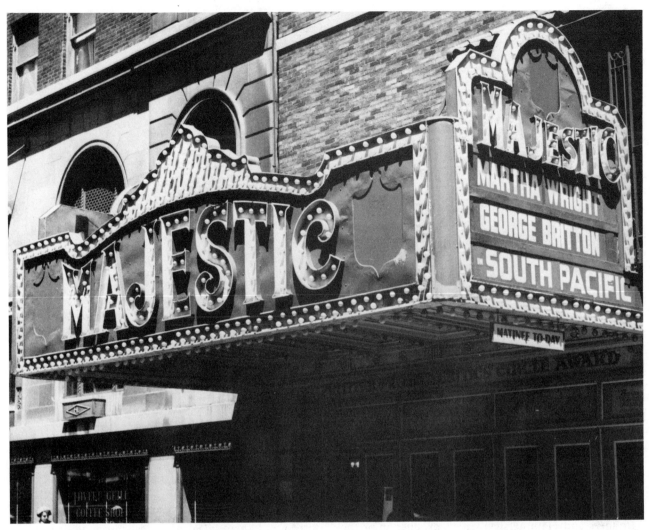

Majestic Theatre   Courtesy Billy Rose Theater Collection.

was a backstage musical mystery show produced by Earl Carroll *(q.v.)*. Carroll set the show during a performance of his *Earl Carroll Vanities (q.v.),* thus advertising his long-running revue series. The show contained a typical "Carrollian" number called "Virgins Wrapped in Cellophane." Carroll later moved his *Earl Carroll Sketch Book* to the Majestic where it concluded its 207-performance run.

A stellar cast was featured in the musical *Stars in Your Eyes* (2/9/39; 127 performances). Ethel Merman *(q.v.)* led the cast, which also featured Richard Carlson, Jimmy Durante, Mildred Natwick and Mary Wickes. Jerome Robbins, Alicia Alonzo and Nora Kaye were all in the chorus. Arthur Schwartz *(q.v.)* and Dorothy Fields provided the fine score and Josh Logan *(q.v.)* directed.

Lew Brown had another show at the Majestic, *Yokel Boy* (7/6/39; 208 performances). Brown collaborated on the lyrics with Charles Tobias, provided the libretto, and produced and directed the proceedings. Sam H. Stept wrote the music and was responsible for the one

hit song, "Comes Love." Buddy Ebsen, Judy Canova, Dixie Dunbar and Phil Silvers starred.

In 1942, Cheryl Crawford revived the Gershwin opera *Porgy and Bess.* Although it was not a success when first produced in 1935, the show scored this time around. In the cast were many of the original cast members, including Todd Duncan, Anne Brown, Ruby Elzy, J. Rosamond Johnson and Warren Coleman.

Another major revival, Franz Lehar's *The Merry Widow* (8/4/43; 321 performances) starred Jan Kiepura, Marta Eggerth, David Wayne, Melville Cooper, Gene Barry and Ruth Matteson. Audiences were ready to forget troubles in Europe and lose themselves in the Lehar music.

Richard Rodgers and Oscar Hammerstein II *(q.v.)* opened what many people consider their greatest achievement, *Carousel (q.v.)* (4/19/45; 890 performances), starring Jan Clayton, John Raitt, Mervyn Vye and Jean Darling. The Theater Guild *(q.v.)* production, under the brilliant direction of Rouben Mamoulian, proved to be the Majestic's biggest hit up to that time. *Carousel* contained such standards as "You'll Never Walk Alone," "If I Loved You" and "June Is Bustin' Out All Over."

Harold Rome's *(q.v.) Call Me Mister,* an affectionate tribute to wartime America, moved from the National Theatre *(q.v.)* with Betty Garrett, Maria Karnilova, Jules Munshin and Lawrence Winters leading the cast. Among the hit songs were "South America, Take It Away," "The Face on the Dime" and "The Red Ball Express." *Call Me Mister* struck a responsive chord and amassed a deserved 734-performance run.

Rodgers and Hammerstein struck out with their next offering, *Allegro* (10/10/47; 315 performances). The show probably wasn't as bad as critics thought, but they and the public expected more after *Carousel*. It featured John Battles, John Conte and Annamary Dickey. Lisa Kirk scored big with her rendition of "The Gentleman Is a Dope."

The songwriting team redeemed their reputation with a huge hit, *South Pacific* (4/7/49; 1,925 performances). Mary Martin *(q.v.),* Ezio Pinza, Juanita Hall, William Tabbert and the supporting company were given the opportunity to introduce such songs as "Dites-moi," "A Cockeyed Optimist," "Happy Talk," "I'm Gonna Wash That Man Right Outa My Hair," "Some Enchanted Evening," "There Is Nothin' Like a Dame," "A Wonderful Guy" and "Younger Than Springtime." Under Joshua Logan's direction, the show was an immense hit, erasing the memory of the less-than-successful *Allegro*. The musical won many awards, including the Pulitzer Prize *(q.v.)*.

Rodgers and Hammerstein's next production at the Majestic was another disappointment. *Me and Juliet* (5/28/53; 358 performances) opened with Isabel Bigley, Mark Dawson, Bill Hayes and Joan McCracken in the leads. The show made money, but critics considered it uninspired. "No Other Love" was the only hit tune in the otherwise second-rate score.

Shirley Booth was the star of *By the Beautiful Sea* (4/8/54; 268 performances), along with Wilbur Evans, Mae Barnes, Cameron Prud'homme and Libi Staiger. Though the show's score by Arthur Schwartz and Dorothy Fields didn't set off any fireworks, it was entertaining and tuneful.

An even bigger hit was David Merrick's *(q.v.)* production of *Fanny* (11/4/54; 888 performances) with wonderful songs by Harold Rome. Ezio Pinza returned to the Majestic in the show, ably supported by Walter Slezak, Florence Henderson and, also returning to the Majestic, William Tabbert. *Fanny* was not immediately a success, but with a boost from some imaginative publicity stunts *(q.v.)* by Merrick and his press agent Richard Maney *(q.v.),* the show became a hit.

Next came Meredith Willson's masterwork, *The Music Man* (12/19/57; 1,375 performances) with Robert

Meredith Willson Courtesy ASCAP.

Preston, Barbara Cook, Pert Kelton, Eddie Hodges and David Burns. The big hit tunes were "Till There Was You," "Seventy Six Trombones" and "Ya Got Trouble." Songs like "Lida Rose" and "Sincere" became standards of barbershop quartets after the Buffalo Bills introduced them. *The Music Man* accurately pictured the naive America of 1912. Later shows that attempted to cover the same territory often proved too treacly or condescending to their subjects.

In *Camelot* (12/3/60; 873 performances) Alan Jay Lerner and Frederick Loewe *(q.v.)* nearly equaled the brilliant score of *My Fair Lady*, and director Moss Hart gave the proceedings his usual polish. Julie Andrews was also a success, as was Richard Burton in his musical-comedy debut. But the libretto by Lerner seldom caught fire, and the show fell short of the brilliance of *My Fair Lady*.

A series of failures followed *Camelot*. These included Judy Holliday's return to Broadway in *Hot Spot* (4/19/63; 43 performances); Mary Martin in the Dietz and Schwartz musical *Jennie* (10/17/63; 82 performances) and Arthur Laurents and Stephen Sondheim's *(q.v.) Anyone Can Whistle* (4/4/64; 9 performances) with Angela Lansbury, Lee Remick and Harry Guardino.

Sammy Davis Jr. starred in a musical version of the Clifford Odets drama *Golden Boy* (10/20/64; 569 performances). It boasted an impressive score by Charles Strouse and Lee Adams *(q.v.)* and a mostly successful book by Odets and William Gibson.

A quick failure was a musical version of *The Teahouse of the August Moon* entitled *Lovely Ladies, Kind Gentlemen* (12/28/70; 16 performances). David Merrick's production of Jule Styne *(q.v.)* and Bob Merrill's musical version of *Some Like It Hot,* called *Sugar* (4/9/72; 505 performances), starred Tony Roberts, Cyril Ritchard and Robert Morse. Gower Champion directed.

Jerry Herman's *(q.v.)* musical set in the silent film era, *Mack and Mabel* (10/6/74; 66 performances), starred Bernadette Peters and, returning to the Majestic, Robert Preston. The all black musical version of *The Wizard of Oz* entitled *The Wiz* (1/5/75; 1,672, performances) was supposed to be a quick flop, but it caught on with audiences and was a tremendous hit.

John Kander and Fred Ebb wrote the Liza Minnelli vehicle, *The Act* (10/29/77; 233 performances). It didn't catch on with audiences or critics. *Ballroom* (12/14/78; 116 performances) was Michael Bennett's first musical following the remarkable success of *A Chorus Line,* but the material was third rate and even Bennett couldn't make *Ballroom* come alive.

It was fitting that Richard Rodgers's last show, a musical version of *I Remember Mama* (5/31/79; 108 performances), opened at the Majestic where he had enjoyed some of his greatest successes. However, *I Remember Mama,* starring Liv Ullmann, was a quick failure.

In 1981, David Merrick's *42nd Street* moved to the Majestic from the Winter Garden Theater *(q.v.),* and it remained there until 1987 when it moved across the street to the St. James Theatre *(q.v.).*

42nd Street was forced to move so that the Majestic could be made ready for what will surely be its most financially successful show, *The Phantom of the Opera* (1/26/88). The Andrew Lloyd Webber musical was an enormous hit in London and prior to opening on Broadway had almost $20 million in advance sales.

With the production of *The Phantom of the Opera,* the future of the Majestic seems rosy, at least for the next decade. On December 8, 1987, the New York City Landmarks Preservation Commission designated the interior and exterior of the theater a landmark. The Commission stated that the theater was a "fine example of the romantic 'modern Spanish' style."

MAMMA LEONE'S RISTORANTE 261 W. 44th Street at Eighth Avenue. Mamma Leone's, New York City's largest restaurant, employs over 400 people. It is primarily a tourist oriented restaurant that caters to large groups who arrive in buses or on package tours from Times Square hotels. Leone's serves huge amounts of Italian food.

The original Mamma Leone's Ristorante opened on April 27, 1906, in the Leone family's living room on West 34th Street. It seated only 20 diners, a far cry from the 1,250 patrons the restaurant seated at 239 W.

Mamma Leone's Photo Jeff Slotnick.

48th Street. The restaurant was begun at the urging of Enrico Caruso who was present at the opening night dinner. That meal, featuring seven courses, cost only 50¢. Luisa ("Mamma") Leone was the chef. Her husband Gerome was against the idea of his wife working, but Caruso convinced him to let her open the restaurant.

In 1926, the restaurant moved to the 48th Street location and slowly expanded down the block, taking over the President Theater. It occupied 35,000 square feet with 11 dining rooms. The interior was decorated in a vibrant, kitschy manner with every square inch covered by paintings, plastic plants and flowers and statuary.

The Leone's site was purchased by developers, and the restaurant's last meal on 48th Street was served on October 3, 1987. In April 1988, the restaurant relocated to the former Kippy's Restaurant in the Milford Plaza Hotel at Eighth Avenue and 44th Street, next door to the Majestic Theater *(q.v.).*

MANEY, RICHARD (1891–1968) Richard Maney was on occasion called The Boswell of Broadway or the Homer of the Great White Way but he really considered himself just a press agent *(q.v.).* True, he was probably the best in his field and he knew it, but his attitude toward his compatriots in the theater was somewhat disdainful. Maney himself described his job as "a fusion of midwife, clairvoyant, public address system and hypnotist."

He plugged away for over 300 shows in his time. Playwright Russel Crouse wrote in 1945: "The hands that feed Maney include those of practically every producer of standing on Broadway and they are practically porous with Maney's teeth marks. He has corrected Gilbert Miller's English, questioned Orson Welles's veracity, blithely deflated Jed Harris and publicly derided Billy Rose—all the while being paid by them. There must be a reason for this. Foremost, I should think, is Maney's vicious, vituperative, almost sadistic honesty. There isn't any question of Maney's talking behind your back unless you turn it."

Maney was born on June 11, 1891, in Chinook, Montana. He attended school in Seattle, graduating from the University of Washington in 1912. The next year, he began working as a press agent for the national tour of Anna Held (q.v.) and Her All-Star Jubilee. Maney didn't immediately take to the job, nor did he stay with it very long. His next position was as associate editor and then editor for *The American Angler* magazine. He put out the monthly for five years. But the theater somehow still called to him.

In 1920, he was hired as press agent for the Broadway revue, *Frivolities of 1920.* The show ran only 61 performances on Broadway, but it was enough to give Maney a foothold. He never left.

Among his biggest hits in the ensuing decades were *My Fair Lady, Camelot, Annie Get Your Gun, The Corn Is Green, The Male Animal, Arsenic and Old Lace, Private Lives, The Front Page,* and *Dial M for Murder.* He was the agent on all of Tallulah Bankhead's Broadway shows, including *The Little Foxes* and *The Skin of Our Teeth.* In fact, Bankhead had two things written into her contract: that Pete Smith be her stage manager and that Richard Maney be her publicist.

Bankhead was one of Maney's few close friends. They could drink for hours, arguing over sports, theater and politics. The saloon of choice was Bleeck's Artist and Writers Club on 40th Street near the old Herald Tribune plant. Maney was ghostwriter on Bankhead's autobiography, and she in turn wrote a tribute to Maney in the *New York Times* after his death.

Maney, like many in his profession, preferred the company of journalists to that of theatrical types. However, Maney did defend them by saying, "Despite the pettiness, the egomania and the persecution complex of stage folk, they are more amusing, more generous and more stimulating than any other professional group."

He didn't hold the same regard for producers. "Producing is the Mardi Gras of the professions," he averred. "Anyone with a mask and enthusiasm can bounce into it." Wolcott Gibbs writing in *The New Yorker* commented that Maney treated his clients (the producers) with a healthy disdain. "There are a good many press

agents in New York who operate on a sort of man-to-man basis. [Mr. Maney] is the only one who persistently treats them with the genial condescension of an Irish cop addressing a Fifth Avenue doorman." One producer asked Maney what he should wear on opening night—a black or white tie. Maney answered "a track suit."

Maney had little truck with most of the offerings presented by producers. He hated the theater and its audiences and their "notorious affair with mediocrity." He insisted that critics (q.v.) should "bat the ears off" cheap and vulgar plays. "The statutes covering indecent exposure have been teached long enough." Maney said that one of the shows he represeted "flew shut like a door."

Maney's first office was in the Empire Theater (q.v.) building. When that was razed, he moved to the 48th Street Theater (q.v.). On his retirement in 1966, he celebrated the occasion by stating:

> Richard Maney, reformed altar boy, who entered this vale of tears in Chinook, Mont. in 1891 to the obbligato of coyote yelps, after 50 years of inflating and/or deflating the theater's famous and infamous, slapped the cover over his Underwood for the last time today.
>
> "Press agentry is an exciting profession," says Mr. Maney, "for one who can tolerate the pranks and prattle of children."
>
> "What is Mr. Maney going to do? Retire to my Connecticut estate and contemplate my navel."

Richard Maney died on July 1, 1968.

MANHATTAN THEATER See ED SULLIVAN THEATRE.

MANSFIELD THEATER See BROOKS ATKINSON THEATER.

MARK HELLINGER THEATER 237 W. 51st Street. Architect: Thomas Lamb. Opening: Hollywood Theater, April 22, 1930, *Hold Everything* (movie); legitimate theater, December 13, 1934, *Calling All Stars.* The 1,600-seat Mark Hellinger is one of Broadway's most beautiful theaters and the last surviving Times Square movie palace. Thomas Lamb, designer of the theater was one of the greatest theater architects, responsible for such other former Times Square landmarks as the Strand (q.v.), Rialto (q.v.) and Rivoli (q.v.).

Originally called the Hollywood, the theater was one of the last of the great movie houses built in America. The Depression, which hurt both the movie business and Broadway, brought theater construction to a standstill. In fact, the outer lobby of the Hollywood was built to support a much taller building, but the Depression forced the abandonment of that idea. It wasn't until the mid-1980s that the building, which originally housed the outer lobby, had a building built over it. The Novotel Hotel occupies the site.

The Hollywood, which originally had its entrance on Broadway, began in 1930 as a flagship house for its

Warner's Hollywood Theater Courtesy Billy Rose Theater Collection.

owners, Warner Brothers. Four years later it housed its first legitimate production, *Calling All Stars.* Lyricist Lew Brown *(q.v.)* produced the show and contributed lyrics to Harry Akst's tunes. Brown also wrote sketches and codirected the show, which starred Judy Canova, Lou Holtz, Jack Whiting, Martha Raye, Gertrude Niesen and Phil Baker. *Calling All Stars* lasted only 35 performances, and the theater reverted to showing movies.

Two years later, on October 28, 1936, the theater was renamed the 51st Street Theater and for a time the theater's entrance was on 51st Street. The new entrance boasted an art deco design inspired by Frank Lloyd Wright. George Abbott's *(q.v.)* musical adaptation of *Uncle Tom's Cabin,* entitled *Sweet River,* opened in the renamed house but closed after only five performances.

The theater's name reverted to the Hollywood on August 11, 1937, and beginning with *The Life of Emile Zola,* movies were again presented in the ornate auditorium.

In November 1939, the last of the *George White's Scandals (q.v.)* moved from the Alvin Theater *(q.v.)* to finish its run here. The theater again became the 51st Street Theater with what everyone thought was a surefire hit—Laurence Olivier's production of Shakespeare's *Romeo and Juliet* (11/5/40; 35 performances). The audience was enthusiastic when the curtain rose, but by the end of the evening it was clear the production was not a success. The show featured Olivier's design and direction as well as a star turn as Romeo. He was supported by Vivien Leigh as Juliet, Dame May Whitty, Edmond O'Brien, Wesley Addy, Cornel Wilde and Halliwell Hobbes.

The theater again presented motion pictures under its alternate name, the Hollywood. A new musical, *Banjo Eyes* (12/25/41; 126 performances) starred Eddie Cantor as the title character with Audrey Christie, June Clyde, Lionel Stander and Bill Johnson in supporting roles. Jacqueline Susann, who later went on to become a bestselling novelist, also appeared in the cast. The show, a musical version of *Three Men on a Horse,* boasted a score by Vernon Duke *(q.v.)* and John Latouche. The hit song, "We're Having a Baby, My Baby and Me," had lyrics by Harold Adamson. The show promised to be the Hollywood's first hit and a much needed success for composer Duke. Unfortunately, Cantor became ill and the show closed prematurely.

The theater again reverted to movies. On August 15, 1947, while the film version of *Life with Father* was filling the seats, it was renamed the Warner Brothers Theater.

The theater's name was changed again when Anthony B. Farrell bought it from Warner Brothers for over $1.5 million. Farrell renamed the theater after Broadway columnist Mark Hellinger *(q.v.),* who had died on December 21, 1947. His first production at the theater was *All for Love* (1/22/49; 121 performances), a revue starring Grace and Paul Hartman and Bert Wheeler. It lost half a million dollars.

Farrell booked the theater for a while at the end of 1949 with Gilbert and Sullivan. He then mounted his second show, a musical called *Texas Li'l Darlin'* (11/25/49; 293 performances). The musical starred Kenny Delmar, Mary Hatcher, Danny Scholl and Loring Smith. The score by Robert Emmett Dolan and Johnny Mercer was a letdown. Surprisingly, the show was a hit, the first for the theater since its opening almost 20 years before.

The success of *Texas Li'l Darlin'* seemed to reverse the theater's fortunes. Despite the lukewarm reception accorded the Hartmans in *All for Love,* they had a hit with the revue *Tickets, Please!,* which moved from the

Coronet Theater (q.v.). Jack Albertson, Larry Kert, Roger Price and Dorothy Jarnac appeared with the Hartmans. Another revue, *Bless You All* (12/14/50; 84 performances), had a score by Harold Rome (q.v.) and featured Pearl Bailey, Jules Munshin, Mary McCarty and Gene Barry.

The theater's next hit, *Two on the Aisle* (7/19/51; 279 performances), headlined Bert Lahr and Dolores Gray. The revue marked the first collaboration between composer Jule Styne (q.v.) and lyricists Betty Comden and Adolph Green (q.v.). *Two on the Aisle* contained many fine revue songs, including "If You Hadn't But You Did" and "Give a Little, Get a Little Love."

Hazel Flagg (2/11/53; 190 performances), a new Jule Styne musical, had lyrics by Bob Hilliard and a libretto by Ben Hecht based on his screenplay *Nothing Sacred*. Styne produced the show himself and Helen Gallagher, John Howard, Thomas Mitchell and Sheree North starred. Jack Whiting made a comeback of sorts as the mayor of New York. He was given the show's big hit, "Every Street's a Boulevard." Another song, "How Do You Speak to an Angel," was a minor success.

The Girl in Pink Tights (3/5/54; 115 performances), Sigmund Romberg's (q.v.) last Broadway show, was posthumously produced at the Mark Hellinger. It proved a surprisingly successful cap to an amazing career. Don Walker adapted Romberg's melodies and sketches into songs that were set to lyrics by Leo Robin. As Walker noted at the time, no one simply develops a score without doing a great deal of original writing. The show starred Jeanmarie, David Atkinson and Charles Goldner. It contained Romberg's last hit song, "Lost in Loveliness."

The next original musical to play the Mark Hellinger was *Plain and Fancy* (1/27/55; 461 performances), which had an Amish setting. The show opened with Barbara Cook, Nancy Andrews, Shirl Conway, David Daniels and Richard Derr starring. The Albert Hague and Arnold B. Horwitt score contained a bona fide hit, "Young and Foolish," as well as a host of other good songs.

The next offering at the Mark Hellinger was one of the greatest Broadway shows of all time. *My Fair Lady* (3/15/56; 2,717 performances) opened with Julie Andrews, Rex Harrison, Robert Coote, Stanley Holloway, John Michael King and Cathleen Nesbitt starring. Alan Jay Lerner (q.v.) provided the witty, sophisticated lyrics and libretto, and Frederick Loewe (q.v.) provided the enchanting music. Moss Hart directed and Herman Levin produced. The score contained such standards as "On the Street Where You Live," "I've Grown Accustomed to Her Face," "Get Me to the Church on Time," "I Could Have Danced All Night," "With a Little Bit of Luck" and "Wouldn't It Be Loverly." *My Fair Lady* became the longest-running show in Broadway history, a record it held for over a decade.

After a seven month stay by Rodgers and Hammer-

stein's (q.v.) last show, *The Sound of Music,* an Italian musical, *Rugantino* (2/6/64; 28 performances), opened at the Mark Hellinger. One of producer Alexander Cohen's most misbegotten ventures, *Rugantino* played in the original Italian with subtitles. The show was one of the most expensive flops at the time.

Jule Styne, Betty Comden and Adolph Green returned to the Mark Hellinger with their gentle satire of Hollywood, *Fade Out–Fade In* (5/26/64; 271 performances). The Carol Burnett vehicle opened to mostly favorable reviews and settled in for a projected long run. Other cast members included Jack Cassidy, Lou Jacobi, Tiger Haynes and Tina Louise. Some say the star got bored with her role, so she claimed she was injured. In any case, the show closed, reopened and closed again.

On a Clear Day You Can See Forever (10/17/65; 280 performances) boasted a superior score by Burton Lane (q.v.) and Alan Jay Lerner. There were also exceptional performances by Barbara Harris and John Cullum. Lerner's libretto, however, didn't work well, and it brought down the proceedings.

Three musicals opened and closed at the Mark Hellinger without much success: *A Joyful Noise* (12/15/66; 12 performances) with John Raitt, Susan Watson and Karen Morrow and with Michael Bennett's choreography; *Illya Darling* (4/11/67; 320 performances), based on the hit film *Never on Sunday* with the film's star Melina Mercouri and director Jules Dassin; and *I'm Solomon* (4/23/68; 7 performances) with Dick Shawn and Karen Morrow in the leads.

Jerry Herman (q.v.) followed his string of hits—*Milk and Honey, Hello, Dolly!* and *Mame* with a failure, *Dear World* (2/6/69; 112 performances). Based on Jean Giraudoux's play *The Madwoman of Chaillot,* the Alexander Cohen production featured the stars of *Mame,* Angela Lansbury and Jane Connell, as well as Milo O'Shea, Kurt Peterson and Miguel Godreau.

Alan Jay Lerner had another show open at the Mark Hellinger, *Coco* (12/18/69; 332 performances), based on the life of designer Coco Chanel. Andre Previn provided the music for the underappreciated score. The show's draw was its star, Katharine Hepburn, making her musical-comedy debut.

After a horrible attempt to convert the book and movie *Exodus* to a Broadway musical entitled *Ari* (1/15/71; 19 performances) and a visit by *Man of La Mancha* came a big hit, *Jesus Christ Superstar* (10/12/71; 711 performances). The production, which was Andrew Lloyd Webber and Tim Rice's first Broadway hit, was a rock musical based on the life of Christ. The director of *Hair,* Tom O'Horgan, repeated his somewhat unconventional style of staging with this show. Jeff Fenholt starred as Jesus and future Broadway star Ben Vereen made an impression as Judas. "I Don't Know How to Love Him" was the hit song from the score.

After a potpourri of offerings, the Hellinger hosted another Alan Jay Lerner show, the much awaited *1600 Pennsylvania Avenue* (5/4/76; 7 performances), written in collaboration with Leonard Bernstein (*q.v.*). The show followed the staffs and families who inhabited the White House in its early years. The Bicentennial tribute was a tremendous flop despite an under-appreciated score.

More failures followed at the Mark Hellinger: a re-working of *Kismet* entitled *Timbuktu!* (3/1/78; 243 performances), starring Eartha Kitt; Alexis Smith in *Platinum* (11/12/78; 33 performances); the Brazilian inspired musical *Sarava* (2/23/79; 140 performances), produced by Eugene V. Wolsk with music by Mitch Leigh; and Clark Gesner's musical comedy *The Utter Glory of Morrisey Hall* (5/13/79) starring Celeste Holm, which closed on opening night.

Finally, another success opened at the theater; the raucous, exuberant salute to burlesque (*q.v.*) *Sugar Babies* (10/9/79; 1,208 performances) had former movie greats Ann Miller and Mickey Rooney in the leads. Producers Terry Allen Kramer and Harry Rigby and Ralph Allen, the show's conceiver, put together the best of burlesque and made sure that director Rudy Tronto and the entire creative staff presented the hoary old burlesque bits in a classy, imaginative setting.

Doug Henning, a superior magician, had achieved success in his first Broadway musical, *The Magic Show*. He tried to repeat his success with *Merlin* (2/13/83; 199 performances) which costarred Chita Rivera, but he couldn't transform the material into a hit.

Ben Vereen returned to the Mark Hellinger in *Grind* (4/16/85; 79 performances). The show opened with a score by Larry Grossman and Ellen Fitzhugh. Harold Prince directed the proceedings. A musical revue, *Tango Argentino* (10/9/85; 198 performances), followed *Grind*. The show featured seven pairs of tango dancers, four singers and a band.

A series of one-man shows and industrial bookings followed at the Mark Hellinger. Peter Allen's musical *Legs Diamond* was the last legitimate show to play the theater. Following that failure, the theater was leased for five years to the same church that occupied the Nederlander Theater (*q.v.*). On November 17, 1987, the New York City Landmarks Preservation Commission gave the theater's interior landmark status. The Commission called the theater "the last surviving grand movie palace in midtown Manhattan." The spaces are "an extraordinary adaptation of Baroque sources."

MARQUIS THEATER Marriott Marquis Hotel, Broadway between 45th and 46th Street. Architect: John C. Portman. Opening: July 9, 1986. The Marquis Theater was built in the new Marriott Marquis Hotel, one of the most controversial buildings in Times Square history. The hotel took the place of the Morosco (*q.v.*) Bijou (*q.v.*) and Helen Hayes (*q.v.*) theaters and The Astor (*q.v.*) and Victoria (*q.v.*) movie theaters. The Broadway community did not think the trade was worth it.

Louis Botto's excellent column in *Playbill* (*q.v.*), quotes architect/designer John Portman as claiming "Our dream was to create a new theater for the Broadway of today that could handle any type of production, any kind of light and sound equipment, provide maximum comfort for audience and actors and still convey a feeling of intimacy." Portman succeeded admirably in many of those areas, although, like all new theaters, the Marquis lacks warmth and ornamentation.

The problems with the 1600-seat theater are not in the auditorium design but in the theatergoing experience. The box office is located in an especially cramped little room. Patrons must exit the box office area and go outside again to enter the escalator to the theater proper. The theater has no real lobby of its own; instead, the hotel's common area is used as the theater lobby. This is a problem at intermission when patrons want to use the rest rooms. Since there are none reserved for theater patrons, audience members must use the hotel's rest rooms and make sure they have kept their ticket stubs in order to reenter the auditorium. The down escalator is so poorly designed that it requires the supervision of a guard. Patrons tend to bunch up at the bottom of the escalator, and so the audience is allowed access to the escalator only in small groups.

Designers and theater technicians lambaste the theater because it contains no freight elevator. All sets must be designed to be able to fit in the small elevators of the hotel. The theater has also proved terribly uncomfortable for its performers. The stage area is sometimes so cold that the cast can actually see their breath. The hotel and theater share heating and ventilation systems. The Marriott corporation is spending about $500,000 to give the theater its own heating, ventilation and plumbing systems. The systems are being overhauled because of noxious fumes that have been seeping into the backstage areas, causing nausea and dizziness. Among the causes for the fumes was an exterior vent for the sewer system, which was located only 30 feet from the theater's air intake. Ten drains in the floor of the theater were spewing sewage, which had backed up through the system.

Actors' Equity (*q.v.*) executive secretary Alan Eisenberg was quoted in the *New York Times* as saying, "We are concerned that there may be damage to the actor. They are representing to us that it will be fixed. We expect a schedule." Equity announced it would close the show if the problems were not handled.

The theater's design maddened Broadway professionals who noted no such problems in the Helen Hayes or Morosco theaters. They pointed to the problems as another result of uncaring developers who tear down

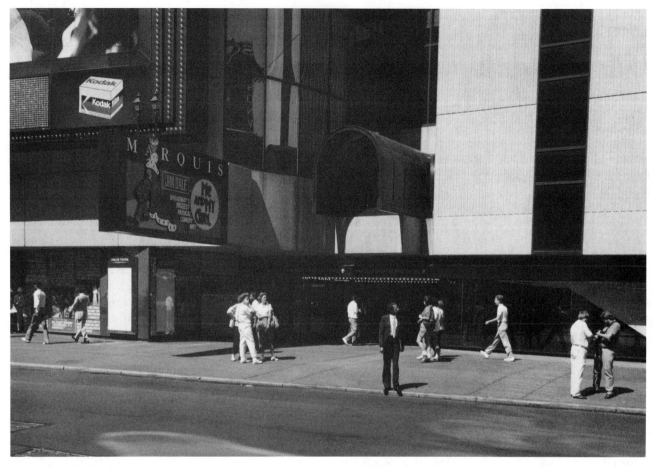

Marquis Theater facade Photo Jeff Slotnick.

excellent historic theaters and replace them with unwieldy auditoriums with poor design.

The theater, run by the Nederlander Organization, opened with a concert by Shirley Bassey and comedian George Kirby. After that dry run its first production, *Me and My Girl,* opened on August 10, 1986. The show was a smash in London and repeated its success in this country with its London star, Robert Lindsay.

The Marquis's auditorium is successful in most respects, but the inconvenient aspects of the theater's construction and the destruction of the Helen Hayes and Morosco theaters still rankle many concerned theatergoers.

MARTIN, MARY (1913–1990) Mary Martin and Ethel Merman *(q.v.)*—the two queens of the American musical theater—reflect two very different styles of singing and acting. Whereas Merman was a brassy siren, Martin portrayed a series of sly, sexy women with a tomboyish enthusiasm and spirit.

Martin was born in Weatherford, Texas on December 1, 1913. There she acquired her well-known accent. She went to Hollywood and dubbed numbers for Margaret Sullavan and Gypsy Rose Lee. Universal hired her to coach Danielle Darrieux in singing and dancing,

but the French star had her fired after Martin demonstrated a number for the film crew.

Martin arranged an audition for the Trocadero nightclub during the club's weekly Sunday–night talent show. The popular radio comedian Jack Benny was in the audience, and he was bowled over by the singer's interpretation of Arditi's "Il Bacio." Benny took Martin to his table and introduced her to Broadway producer Lawrence Schwab. Schwab invited her to appear in a musical comedy that he was planning. She signed a contract, and in the time before the show was to begin rehearsals, she appeared at the Trocadero.

Schwab meanwhile canceled plans for his musical, but he introduced Martin to playwrights Bella and Samuel Spewack, Cole Porter *(q.v.),* Sophie Tucker, Victor Moore, William Gaxton and producer Vinton Freedley *(q.v.).* They were all involved in the production of a new musical entitled *Leave It to Me!* (11/9/38; 291 performances). Martin auditioned and was hired on the spot. She replaced singer June Knight, who had introduced "Begin the Beguine" in Porter's *Jubilee.* Knight's new husband would not let her sing "My Heart Belongs to Daddy" which proved to be the hit song of *Leave It to Me!,* and forced the actress out of the show. Martin took over the role and during the

Mary Martin in South Pacific

number did a modified striptease and stopped the show.

Leave It to Me! opened at the Alvin Theater *(q.v.)*. After its run concluded, Martin was signed to a contract by Paramount Pictures. She appeared in such movies as *The Great Victor Herbert, Rhythm on the River, Love Thy Neighbor, Kiss the Boys Goodbye, New York Town* and *Happy Go Lucky*. The films, and Martin, failed to make much of a splash. Martin still owed six pictures to Paramount, when her contract was terminated.

After leaving Paramount Martin returned to the Broadway stage in the musical *Dancing in the Streets*. The show was written by Vernon Duke *(q.v.)*, John Cecil Holm, Howard Dietz *(q.v.)* and Matt Taylor. It closed in Boston prior to coming to Broadway.

After the disappointment of *Dancing in the Streets* came the joy of a starring role in the Kurt Weill *(q.v.)* and Ogden Nash musical *One Touch of Venus* (10/7/43; 567 performances). Martin appeared in the title role, a statue of the goddess that comes to life. The script was written by S.J. Perelman with Marlene Dietrich in mind. When Dietrich dropped out, Martin replaced her. Today, Martin has a pure, wholesome image typified by the characters Maria of *The Sound of Music* and *Peter Pan* but in the forties she was always considered a star with a lot of sex appeal. Her comely figure and sensuous soprano voice helped make her a convincing Venus.

One Touch of Venus opened at the Imperial Theatre *(q.v.)* with Kenny Baker, John Boles, Paula Laurence, Sono Osato and Teddy Hart also starring. She was given three exemplary songs, "That's Him," "I'm a Stranger Here Myself" and "Speak Low."

Martin's next Broadway show was the musical *Lute Song* (2/6/46; 142 performances) by Bernard Hanighen and Raymond Scott. The only song in the score to achieve much fame was "Mountain High, Valley Low." *Lute Song* opened with Clarence Derwent (who later had an award *(q.v.)* named in his honor), Mildred Dunnock and Rex O'Malley. Nancy Davis, who later became Ronald Reagan's First Lady, also appeared in the show.

After a sojourn in London at the Theatre Royal, Drury Lane in Noel Coward's *Pacific 1860,* Martin toured the United States in Irving Berlin's *(q.v.)* Annie Get Your Gun..

Oscar Hammerstein II *(q.v.)* had seen Martin in *One Touch of Venus* and swore that he would write a show for her. He made good on his promise when he, Richard Rodgers *(q.v.)* and Joshua Logan *(q.v.)* wrote *South Pacific*. The show, in which Martin gave her most mature, serious performance, is considered the high point in her career. Rodgers and Hammerstein provided her with great songs, including "A Cockeyed Optimist," "I'm Gonna Wash that Man Right Outa My Hair," "A Wonderful Guy," and "Honey Bun." *South Pacific* (4/7/49; 1,925) opened at the Majestic Theater *(q.v.)* with a record $500,000 advance sale. After two years, Mary Martin left the Broadway company to take the show to London.

Martin's next Broadway assignment was Norman Krasna's play *Kind Sir* (11/4/53; 166 performances), staged by Joshua Logan with Charles Boyer costarring. The cast also included Margalo Gillmore and Dorothy Stickney.

Kind Sir was followed by Martin's favorite role, that of *Peter Pan* (10/20/54). Producer Edwin Lester hired Martin to portray the eternally youthful character in a new musical version of the J.M. Barrie classic written by two songwriting teams. The first, Moose Charlap and Carolyn Leigh, had written an excellent score, but Lester felt more songs were needed. Jule Styne *(q.v.)* and lyricists Betty Comden and Adolph Green *(q.v.)* were brought in by Jerome Robbins *(q.v.)* after negative reviews in San Francisco. *Peter Pan* moved to Los Angeles and finally to Broadway's Winter Garden Theater *(q.v.)*. The New York engagement was planned as a dress rehearsal for a live television broadcast. Cyril Ritchard played Captain Hook and Sondra Lee played Tiger Lily. The show became a television perennial on NBC.

Martin then toured Europe in the classic comedy, *The Skin of Our Teeth* by Thornton Wilder. She brought the show to the United States and appeared in Washington, D.C., New York, Chicago and finally a television production. The New York premiere took place at the ANTA Theater (q.v.) on August 17, 1955, and played a limited run of 22 performances.

The Skin of Our Teeth was followed by national tours of *South Pacific* and *Annie Get Your Gun* and a one-woman show, *Music with Mary Martin.* She next appeared on Broadway in Rodgers and Hammerstein's last show as a team, *The Sound of Music* (11/16/59; 1,443 performances). Martin opened at the Lunt–Fontanne Theater (q.v.) along with Theodore Bikel, Brian Davies, Kurt Kasznar, Marion Marlowe, Patricia Neway and Lauri Peters.

The Sound of Music received mixed reviews, though Martin was treated kindly by the critics (q.v.). The performance and the fine score, including "Climb Every Mountain," "Sixteen Going on Seventeen," "My Favorite Things," "The Sound of Music" and "Do-Re-Mi" assured the show a long run.

Next came one of the actress's few failures, *Jennie* (10/17/63; 82 performances). The musical, based on the early career of actress Laurette Taylor, had a score by Arthur Schwartz (q.v.) and Howard Dietz, but it never jelled, and fights among the creative staff brought on a quick demise.

In 1965, the actress played Dolly Gallagher Levi in Jerry Herman's (q.v.) *Hello, Dolly!* for the troops in Vietnam following a run in Tokyo. The production was then taken to Okinawa and Korea before closing. After a break, it reopened on December 2, 1965, at the Theatre Royal, Drury Lane in London.

Mary Martin opened in the Tom Jones and Harvey Schmidt musical, *I Do! I Do!* (12/5/66; 560 performances). Gower Champion directed the proceedings, based on Jan de Hartog's play, *The Fourposter.* Martin's costar, and the only other performer in the show, was Robert Preston. *I Do! I Do!* proved to be a marvelous show as produced by David Merrick (q.v.). The show closed when the two stars left.

After *I Do! I Do!*, it was widely assumed that Mary Martin would retire. Instead, she returned to the stage twice more, although the occasions were less than felicitous. *Do You Turn Somersaults?* (1/9/78; 16 performances), costarring Anthony Quayle and *Legends* (1986) with Carol Channing, closed out of town.

MARTIN BECK THEATRE 302 W. 45th Street. Architect: G. Albert Lansburgh. Opening: November 11, 1924; *Madame Pompadour.* Vaudeville impresario Martin Beck (q.v.) built the theater bearing his name in 1924 on what many people considered the wrong side of Eighth Avenue. However, the 1,200-seat theater proved immensely popular with audiences and theater people.

The first attraction at the Byzantine-style theater was the operetta *Madame Pompadour,* with music by Leo Fall, a favorite of Viennese audiences. Broadway audiences, however, were growing tired of operetta by the end of the twenties and instead wanted musicals in a more modern vein. *Madame Pompadour* closed after 80 performances.

The famous Clyde Fitch play *Captain Jinks of the Horse Marines* was adapted into a musical called simply *Captain Jinks* (9/8/25; 167 performances). It opened at the Martin Beck Theatre with Joe E. Brown, J. Harold Murray and Marion Sunshine in the leads.

Actress Florence Reed shocked audiences as Mother Goddam in the sensational play *The Shanghai Gesture* (2/1/26; 210 performances). Reed's character kills her own daughter, a dope fiend, when it is discovered that the girl's father was a Britisher who had dumped Mother Goddam and in turn, unbeknownst to himself, slept with his daughter—a coupling her mother had arranged when she found out the man had married another woman. The play was laughed at by the critics (q.v.), but audiences couldn't wait to see the proceedings.

Actor James Gleason, who would later achieve much success as a character actor in Hollywood, wrote a play, *The Shannons of Broadway* (9/26/27; 288 performances), which opened at the Martin Beck. Following this, the Theater Guild (q.v.) took over the stage of the Martin Beck with a series of plays.

The first Guild play at the theater was *Wings Over Europe* (12/10/28; 91 performances) by Robert Nichols and Maurice Browne and directed by the great Rouben Mamoulian. The play, whose subject was the enormous destructive power of atomic energy, proved to be prophetic. The drama was chosen as one of the year's 10 best by the *Best Plays* series. Critics enjoyed the play although they admitted it was somewhat more intellectual rather than emotional.

Next, the Guild presented Dudley Digges, Claudette Colbert, Glenn Anders and Helen Westley in Eugene O'Neill's (q.v.) little-known play, *Dynamo* (2/11/29; 66 performances). O'Neill himself described the play's theme as "the passing of the old idea of a Supreme Being and the failure of Science, all-important in this day, to supplant it with something satisfying to the yearning soul of men permeated with the idea that the creations of Science are miraculous as the creations of the Supreme Being." The play was not exactly the prescription for the tired businessperson.

Miriam Hopkins, Claude Rains, Henry Travers, Helen Westley and Morris Carnovsky starred in the next Guild presentation, *The Camel Through the Needle's Eye* (4/15/29; 195 performances). The play was a natural for the Guild, which often presented middle-European light comedies. The play received good reviews from such disparate critics (q.v.) as Walter Winchell (q.v.) and Percy Hammond.

Lee Strasberg, Luther Adler, Lionel Stander, George Tobias, Gale Sondergaard and Franchot Tone starred in *Red Rust* (12/17/29; 65 performances). This was the second Soviet play to play Broadway, and it was just as unsuccessful as the first, *The First Law*. It proved to be an important event nonetheless for it was the first play presented by the Theater Guild Acting Company, which later metamorphosed into the Group Theater (*q.v.*).

Philip Barry's drama *Hotel Universe* (4/14/30; 81 performances) followed with Ruth Gordon, Morris Carnovsky, Glenn Anders and Franchot Tone in the leading roles. It opened to decidedly mixed reviews. The Guild actually printed opposing reviews next to each other in newspapers. Percy Hammond perhaps best expressed the audience's reaction to the play when he wrote: "I felt an embarrassed urge to cry out to Mr. Barry: 'Wait a minute! I didn't quite get that! Pray say it over again.' As it was, the night's pleasure was modified considerably by the feeling that I was but a yokel, astray in the court of Thespis, trying his best to join the proceedings and failing."

Roar China (10/27/30; 72 performances) featured a huge cast of mostly Asian actors. The drama concerned the Chinese rebellion and the British response. A model of a British warship filled the immense stage in a particularly stunning effect. The Lee Simonson set was among the most impressive of any in Broadway's history. Simonson wrote that director Herbert Biberman "conceived the idea of using sampan sails as a scene curtain. They floated in a tank behind the front stage ramp. The tawny, interlocking sails formed a curtain which almost hid the gunboat; only its topmast was dimly visible. At a cry of 'Sampan, sampan' they parted, gliding with incredible grace to stage right and left, where their sails in shadow gave the suggestion of a river front harbor. As they opened the warship was dramatically revealed, in towering, menacing silhouette." *Roar China* was perhaps too propagandistic for the typical audience member.

The first production of the new Group Theater, which evolved from the Theater Guild Acting Company, was *The House of Connelly* (9/28/31; 91 performances) by Paul Green. It was presented at the Martin Beck Theatre under the auspices of the Theater Guild, with Franchot Tone, Art Smith, Stella Adler, Morris Carnovsky, Clifford Odets and Robert Lewis in the cast. *The House of Connelly* was an auspicious debut for the new theater group.

After moving their successful production of *Elizabeth the Queen* to the Martin Beck, the Lunts (*q.v.*) chose the theater for the opening of their next play, Robert E. Sherwood's comedy *Reunion in Vienna* (11/16/31; 264 performances). In addition to the Lunts, the cast included Lloyd Nolan, Henry Travers, Helen Westley and Eduardo Ciannelli. Richard Lockridge reflected the majority view of critics when he wrote in the *New York Sun*: "It is as light and frisky as one always believes Viennese comedy should be, and as one so seldom finds Viennese comedy is. It needs, apparently, an American

to write it—and a couple of Americans to play it."

In 1932, another group took over the stage of the Martin Beck Theatre. The Abbey Irish Theater Players presented productions of *Playboy of the Western World*, *Shadow of a Gunman*, *The Far-off Hills* and *Juno and the Paycock* at the theater.

Next came Katharine Hepburn's return to Broadway after success in Hollywood. The play was *The Lake* (12/26/33; 55 performances), and the director was one of the most hated geniuses in the history of Broadway, Jed Harris. Soon thereafter, Dorothy Parker remarked that the actress had "run the gamut of emotions from A to B."

Yellow Jack (3/6/34; 79 performances) was Sidney Howard's dramatization of the yellow fever epidemic in Cuba and the search for its cause by Walter Reed. The distinguished cast included James Stewart, Myron McCormick, Edward Acuff and Sam Levene. *Yellow Jack* was a surprising failure.

In *Romeo and Juliet* (12/23/35; 78 performances), Katharine Cornell (*q.v.*) received raves as Juliet, as did Basil Rathbone as Romeo. The production also boasted the enormous talents of Orson Welles, Brian Aherne, John Emery and Edith Evans. It was the second-longest-running *Romeo and Juliet* in Broadway history. Cornell kept her dressing room at the Martin Beck with a revival of her classic production of *The Barretts of Wimpole Street* (2/25/35; 24 performances). The story of Robert and Elizabeth Barrett Browning also starred Brian Aherne, Brenda Forbes and Burgess Meredith. Cornell continued her stay after the run of *The Barretts of Wimpole Street* with a production of John van Druten's *Flowers of the Forest* (4/8/35; 40 performances).

Maxwell Anderson's *Winterset* (9/25/35; 178 performances) was written entirely in blank verse. Burgess Meredith, who had appeared in the last two Cornell productions, starred in the drama about Sacco and Vanzetti with Richard Bennett, Eduardo Ciannelli and Margo. A controversial play, *Winterset* was a revision of an earlier play presented by the Theater Guild—*Gods of the Lightning*. The Guild wanted Anderson's play, but Anderson was committed to a production by the Group Theater. When they decided not to produce it, producer Guthrie McClintic was given the script. Anderson's decision to bypass the Theater Guild was not unique. More and more playwrights were rejecting the Guild; preferring to have their plays presented by producers more responsive to the needs of their plays. The loss of *Winterset* was a blow to the Theater Guild. The play won the first award (*q.v.*) given by the new New York Drama Critics Circle (*q.v.*).

The Guild received another blow with Katharine Cornell's revival of George Bernard Shaw's *Saint Joan* (3/9/36; 89 performances). The Guild was the American representative of Shaw, but it was not consulted when the playwright gave permission to Guthrie McClintic, the actress's husband, to produce and direct the show. McClintic had previously produced *Winterset,* the other thorn in the Guild's side. The Guild was afraid that they would lose control of the American licensing of Shaw's work. To make matters worse for the Guild, the production, which also starred Maurice Evans, Brian Aherne, Eduardo Ciannelli, Kent Smith, Arthur Byron and George Coulouris, was an immediate hit. Tyrone Power Jr., later to achieve fame in Hollywood, was also featured in the cast.

Maxwell Anderson's next play, *High Tor* (1/8/37; 171 performances), won the second Drama Critics Circle Award. The play starred Burgess Meredith, Hume Cronyn and Peggy Ashcroft. *High Tor,* surprisingly light after Anderson's previous offering, *Winterset,* was the story of a man who owns a mountain and must deal with attempts to purchase it against his will. Ghosts of Dutch sailors waft through the play, giving the young man courage to keep his land.

Helen Hayes *(q.v.)* appeared twice at the Martin Beck in the late thirties. First she revived her acclaimed performance in *Victoria Regina* (10/3/38; 87 performances). She later appeared in the Ben Hecht and Charles MacArthur courtroom drama *Ladies and Gentlemen* (10/17/39; 105 performances).

The Martin Beck's next success was Lillian Hellman's antifascist drama *A Watch on the Rhine* (4/1/41; 378 performances) with Paul Lukas, Mady Christians, George Coulouris and Lucile Watson in the leads. The play examines the moral dilemma a man faces when forced to defend his beliefs.

In S.N. Behrman's comedy *The Pirate* (11/25/42; 176 performances), Alfred Lunt *(q.v.)* played an actor who pretends to be a notorious pirate in order to impress a young innocent played by Lynn Fontanne. Behrman's next play at the Martin Beck was even more successful. *Jacobowsky and the Colonel* (3/14/44; 415 performances), Franz Werfel's comedy, was adapted by Behrman for the talents of Louis Calhern, Annabella, J. Edward Bromberg, Oscar Karlweis and E.G. Marshall.

After a transfer of the Leonard Bernstein *(q.v.),* Betty Comden and Adolph Green *(q.v.)* musical *On the Town* from the 44th Street Theatre *(q.v.)* came an original musical, *St. Louis Woman* (3/30/46; 113 performances). The Harold Arlen *(q.v.)* and Johnny Mercer musical had a libretto by Arna Bontemps and Countee Cullen. Rouben Mamoulian directed the proceedings, which featured Pearl Bailey, Rex Ingram, June Hawkins, Ruby Hill, Juanita Hall and Harold Nicholas. The Arlen and Mercer score was among the greatest for any musical. It boasted such standards as "Any Place I Hang My Hat Is Home" and "Come Rain or Come Shine."

Eugene O'Neill's *The Iceman Cometh* (10/9/46; 136 performances) premiered at the Martin Beck with James Barton, E.G. Marshall, Nicholas Joy and Dudley Digges in the cast. Katharine Cornell again appeared in a pro-

duction of a Shakespeare play at the Martin Beck in *Antony and Cleopatra* (11/26/47; 126 performances). The impressive cast included Godfrey Tearle, Eli Wallach, Kent Smith, Maureen Stapleton, Lenore Ulric and Charleton Heston. The great actress returned to the Martin Beck stage in *That Lady* (11/22/49; 79 performances).

Another well-loved American actress, Helen Hayes *(q.v.),* appeared on the Martin Beck's stage in Joshua Logan's *The Wisteria Trees* (3/29/50; 165 performances), an Americanized version of Chekhov's *The Cherry Orchard.*

Tennessee Williams's *(q.v.)* drama *The Rose Tattoo* (2/3/51; 300 performances) was the theater's next hit. Maureen Stapleton, Eli Wallach and Don Murray opened in the passionate drama, one of Williams's many successes in the fifties. Another great American dramatist, Arthur Miller *(q.v.),* had an important play premiere at the Martin Beck, a thinly disguised indictment of the McCarthy hearings, *The Crucible* (1/22/53; 197 performances). Only five years later, the play would be revived at the Martinique Theater off-Broadway and run 633 performances. By then, the public had turned against McCarthy.

The Teahouse of the August Moon (10/15/53; 1,027 performances), a play by Kentuckian John Patrick, opened with David Wayne, Paul Ford and John Forsythe. The comedy was an immediate success and became one of the decade's biggest hits. Critics hailed the story of attempts to democratize Okinawa following World War II. John Mason Brown stated that "no plea for tolerance between peoples, no editorial against superimposing American customs on native tradition has ever been less didactic or more persuasive." Patrick's play won five Tony Awards *(q.v.),* the New York Drama Critics Award and the Pulitzer Prize *(q.v.).*

An all-star revival of George Bernard Shaw's *Major Barbara* (10/30/56; 232 performances) starred Cornelia Otis Skinner, Burgess Meredith, Eli Wallach and Glynis Johns along with director Charles Laughton. The next offering at the Martin Beck, the operetta satire *Candide* (12/1/56; 73 performances), was also an all-star production. This time the stars were the creative team including Leonard Bernstein, Dorothy Parker, Lillian Hellman, Richard Wilbur and Tyrone Guthrie.

Candide had a unusually stormy tryout run in Boston prior to New York. Luckily, Columbia Records recorded the show, and the album soon became something of a cult hit. Attempts to revive the show in 1959 (London) and 1971 also met with failure. Finally, in 1974, a much reworked version of the show opened with a brand new concept by producer/director Harold Prince *(q.v.).* This time *Candide* was a success.

Tennessee Williams had a flop at the Martin Beck when *Orpheus Descending* (3/31/57; 68 performances) opened with Maureen Stapleton. Like *The Crucible,*

Orpheus Descending fared better in a later off-Broadway run. Williams's next offering was the next success at the Martin Beck. Geraldine Page and Paul Newman starred in *Sweet Bird of Youth* (3/10/59; 375 performances). Williams summed up the play's theme (and a thread running through all his works) when he stated: "Desire is rooted in a longing for companionship, a release from the loneliness which haunts every individual."

The sixties began auspiciously for the Martin Beck with the first Broadway musical by the team of Charles Strouse *(q.v.)* and Lee Adams. They kicked off their long, successful Broadway collaboration with *Bye Bye Birdie* (4/14/60; 607 performances). Dick Van Dyke, Chita Rivera, Susan Watson, Dick Gautier and Paul Lynde starred in the affectionate lampoon of Elvis Presley's induction into the army. Strouse and Adams's light and playful score contained such hit songs as "Kids" and "Put On a Happy Face."

Next, the Martin Beck hosted the work of another Broadway newcomer who would become one of the most successful writers of the musical theater. Jerry Herman's *(q.v.)* *Milk and Honey* (10/10/61; 543 performances), the story of a group of Americans visiting Israel, starred Robert Weede, Molly Picon, Mimi Benzell and Tommy Rall.

The theater's offerings during the remainder of the sixties showed great promise, but somehow none of the shows caught on with Broadway audiences. These included Edward Albee's adaptation of Carson McCullers's *Ballad of the Sad Cafe* (10/30/63; 123 performances), which starred Colleen Dewhurst and Michael Dunn; *I Had a Ball* (12/15/64; 184 performances), a musical with a fun, bright score by Jack Lawrence and Stan Freeman and starring Richard Kiley, Buddy Hackett and Karen Morrow; the Royal Shakespeare Company's importation *The Persecution and Assassination of Marat As Performed by the Inmates of the Asylum of Charenton Under the Direction of the Marquis de Sade* (12/27/65; 145 performances) with Glenda Jackson, Ian Richardson and Patrick Magee; Edward Albee's Pulitzer Prize-winning drama *A Delicate Balance* (1/14/67; 132 performances) with Jessica Tandy, Hume Cronyn and Rosemary Murphy; and *Hallelujah, Baby!* (4/26/67; 293 performances) with a superior score by Jule Styne *(q.v.),* Betty Comden and Adolph Green and an exceptional cast, which included Leslie Uggams, Allen Case, Robert Hooks and Lilian Hayman.

At the end of the sixties, the Martin Beck at last housed a hit, *Man of La Mancha,* which moved from off-Broadway on March 19, 1968. Star Richard Kiley was given the show's big song, "The Impossible Dream (The Quest)" with music by Mitch Leigh and lyrics by Joe Darion. The show was an enormous success, playing 2,329 performances.

Edward Albee's third production at the Martin Beck,

All Over (3/28/71; 42 performances), starred Jessica Tandy, Betty Field, Colleen Dewhurst and George Voskovec. *All Over* was a disappointment in a disappointing decade. The Martin Beck Theatre finally housed a hit show in the seventies with *Dracula* (10/28/77; 925 performances). Frank Langella starred as the Transylvanian vampire count and was proclaimed one of Broadway's brightest stars. Unfortunately, this would be his only success in the theater.

The eighties have proved even more depressing for the Martin Beck than the seventies. John Kander and Fred Ebb, the songwriting team responsible for *Cabaret,* saw their musical *The Rink* (2/9/84; 204 performances) open at the Martin Beck. The show had all the ingredients for success: a libretto by Terrence McNally and two starring roles for Liza Minnelli and Chita Rivera.

Into the Woods (1/5/87; 764 performances) was the first success at the Martin Beck in almost a decade. The Stephen Sondheim *(q.v.)* and James Lapine musical garnered mostly favorable reviews. Bernadette Peters, Chip Zien, Joanna Gleason, Kim Crosby and Ben Wright starred as various fairy tale figures for whom "happily ever after" turns to tragedy.

On November 4, 1987, the New York City Landmarks Preservation Commission designated the interior and exterior of the theater a landmark. The Commission stated: "A designer primarily of movie palaces, Lansburgh created for Beck a fantastic Moorish-inspired theater, among the most lavishly decorated in the Broadway area. Its interior is an unusual Moorish design, unlike any other Broadway theater."

MAXINE ELLIOTT'S THEATRE 109 W. 39th Street between Broadway and Sixth Avenue. Architect: Ben Marshall. Opening: December 30, 1908; *The Chaperon.* Actress Maxine Elliott selected Ben Marshall, an architect from Marshall and Fox of Chicago, to design a showplace theater. Marshall designed what was the most expensive theater at that time. Elliott, a supreme beauty, was dubbed "Venus de Milo with arms." Her only drawback was her lack of great talent. However, her theater, rumored to have been built by an admiring financier, outshone its competition. The theater was among the first to have running water and carpeting. Backstage, the dressing rooms boasted full-length mirrors. Elliott's husband, Nat Goodwin, was a popular actor. He didn't seem to mind it when Lee Shubert *(q.v.)* bankrolled the theater's construction.

The theater began inauspiciously. After a string of failures, *The Passing of the Third Floor Back* (10/4/09; 216 performances) by Jerome K. Jerome opened. The next success was *The Gamblers* (10/31/10; 192 performances) by Charles Klein, known for his Hippodrome *(q.v.)* extravaganzas. Jane Cowl had the lead. Edward Sheldon's play *Romance* (2/10/13; 160 performances), starred Doris Keane. Part of its fame was due to Shel-

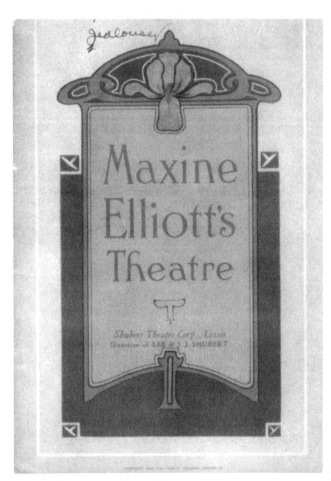

Program for Maxine Elliott's Theatre

don's plot, which concerned a preacher who was attracted to a loose woman. Audiences were relieved that the parson retained his composure throughout. Only nine years later, with the opening of *Rain,* audiences would be entranced by a minister who loses the battle for his virtue.

Musicals also occasionally occupied the Maxine Elliott's stage. Cole Porter's *(q.v.)* first attempt at Broadway, *See America First* (3/28/16; 15 performances), was unappreciated. In the cast was future movie star Clifton Webb, then a popular musical-comedy performer.

Spanish Love (8/17/20; 307 performances) by Avery Hopwood and Mary Roberts Rinehart was the first hit of the twenties. *Spanish Love* set the stage for the theater's biggest hit, Jeanne Eagels in *Rain* (11/7/22; 648 performances).

Noel Coward's *Hay Fever* (10/5/25; 49 performances), about an infuriating but fascinating family led by a grand actress, was later constantly revived throughout the world, but it was a failure at its Broadway debut. Another English playwright, Somerset Maugham, saw a near classic premiere at the theater, *The Constant Wife* (11/29/26; 295 performances).

Helen Hayes *(q.v.)* had a great success (later repeated in the movies) with *Coquette* (11/8/27; 366 perfor-

mances). The Group Theater *(q.v.)* featured Lew Ayres in *Success Story* (9/26/32; 120 performances) at the Maxine Elliott's.

The last two successes at the theater were Lillian Hellman's *The Children's Hour* (11/20/34; 691 performances) and the drama *Separate Rooms* (3/23/40; 613 performances).

In 1941, the Mutual Radio Network took over the theater for radio. In 1944, CBS brought its radio operations to the theater. CBS then transformed the theater into a television studio.

In 1959, the theater was torn down to make room for a skyscraper.

MAYFAIR THEATER See CENTURY THEATER.

MERMAN, ETHEL (1909–1984)   Ethel Merman and Mary Martin *(q.v.)* are considered the two greatest actresses in the history of the American musical theater. Merman was the more boisterous of the two women. Whereas Martin was a sexy tomboy, Merman was an up front, no nonsense dame. In an October 28, 1940, cover story on Merman, *Time Magazine* described the singer as: "A dark, bouncy, oval-faced young woman. Ethel Merman can lay no great claim to great beauty, glamor or 'legitimate' vocal quality, but she is a dynamic baggage with syncopation in every breath and gesture, and a voice with the hard, clarion, forthrightness of a jazz trumpet. Where most people hum or whistle for their personal pleasure, Ethel Merman imitates (Ta-ta-ta-ta!) the trumpet part."

Merman was the favorite of such songwriters as Cole Porter *(q.v.),* Irving Berlin *(q.v.)* and George and Ira Gershwin *(q.v.).* Her trademark voice was known for its strength and clarity. Berlin once commented: "To me, her great quality as a singer is her genius at socking the whole meaning across. She's a lyric writer's dream; nobody in show business can project the lyric of a song like Ethel. She times a lyric as carefully and brilliantly as a comedian timing a gag. She sings with feeling for the audience and will space a passage when she gets a laugh."

Ira Gershwin said she had "a no-nonsense voice that could reach not only standees but ticket-takers in the lobby." Cole Porter described watching Merman from the audience's point of view: "It was like watching a train hurtle down the tracks, undeviating, the whole performance radiating zest and spontaneity, and yet you knew that it was exactly the same yesterday, and would be the same the day after."

She appeared in many of the greatest shows in musical-comedy history, chief among them *Gypsy* and *Annie Get Your Gun.* She introduced such standards as "It's Delovely," "I Got Rhythm," "I Get a Kick Out of You," "Everything's Coming Up Roses," "There's

Jeffry Herman and Ethel Merman   Courtesy ASCAP.

No Business Like Show Business," "Life Is Just a Bowl of Cherries" and "You're the Top."

She claimed she was born in 1912. Musical theater historian Stanley Green puts her birth at January 16, 1909. Biographer Bob Thomas claims she was born a year earlier. She was born Ethel Zimmerman in Queens, New York, and was discovered by talent agent Lou Irwin when she performed in a club called Little Russia on 57th Street. Irwin arranged for her to be signed by Warner Brothers, which in 1929 was trying to conquer the new sound pictures. Warner Brothers signed her at $200 per week but couldn't quite figure out what to do with her. Her contract was not renewed after its six-month period.

Producer Vinton Freedley *(q.v.)* heard Merman sing during an engagement at the Brooklyn Paramount. He arranged for Merman to meet composer George Gershwin at the composer's apartment at 33 Riverside Drive. George was joined with his brother Ira. Merman sang "Little White Lies" and "Exactly Like You" and im-

pressed the two songwriters. They in turn performed two of the songs they had written for their new show, *Girl Crazy.*

Freedley and his partner Alex Aarons were producing *Girl Crazy* (10/14/30; 272 performances) at their Alvin Theater *(q.v.).* They offered Merman a contract at $375 per week. While she rehearsed *Girl Crazy* she was booked by Irwin into the Palace Theater *(q.v.).* The Palace engagement resulted in her first *New York Times* review, a rave: "From the night clubs to her Palace debut comes Ethel Merman, a comely ballad singer, accompanied by Al Siegel, who is not so new. Miss Merman's torch singing premiere turns out to be an auspicious event in lyric celebration of the broken Broadway heart, and promises well for her debut later this season on the musical comedy stage."

The critics's *(q.v.)* enthusiasm over her Palace engagement prepared them for Merman's musical-comedy debut. *Girl Crazy* opened with Willie Howard, Ginger Rogers and a band including Glenn Miller, Jack

Teagarden, Benny Goodman, Gene Krupa, Red Nichols and Jimmy Dorsey. Merman was introduced singing "Sam and Delilah." In her next spot she nailed her stardom with a performance of "I Got Rhythm." Critic Robert Coleman enthused, "The big surprise of the evening was Ethel Merman, a young and talented songstress with a peculiar delivery who tied the proceedings up in knots. A graduate of night clubs and motion picture theaters, this girl bids fair to become the toast of Broadway."

After *Girl Crazy* closed, Merman was booked into several clubs and a return to the Palace. George White (*q.v.*) was trying out his latest edition of his *Scandals* (*q.v.*) in Atlantic City. He wired Merman to come and join the faltering show, and she agreed. White paid Aarons and Freedley $25,000 for Merman's services, since they had an option on her next show. The amount was well spent. Merman's talents inspired songwriters Lew Brown and Ray Henderson to come up with one of their most enduring standards, "Life Is Just a Bowl of Cherries." The *Scandals* opened at the Apollo Theatre (*q.v.*) on 42nd Street on September 14, 1931. Merman also sang a duet, "My Song," with Rudy Vallee, and another effective solo, "Ladies and Gentlemen, That's Love." Brooks Atkinson caught the Merman style with an especially felicitous turn of phrase. He called her "queen of the singing announcers."

After more club appearances and another run at the Palace, Merman went into a new musical, *Humpty Dumpty*. Nacio Herb Brown, Richard Whiting and B.G. DeSylva were the composers. *Humpty Dumpty* was in trouble on the road, and the show closed in Pittsburgh. The show was reworked and opened on Broadway as *Take a Chance* (11/26/32; 243 performances). Merman was given the hit tunes "Eadie Was a Lady," "I Got Religion," Vincent Youman's (*q.v.*) "Rise and Shine" and a big hit, "You're an Old Smoothie" in a duet with Jack Haley.

Merman's performance of "I Got Religion" was described in the magazine *The Stage*: "The fluttering hands; the doubled fist extended toward you, Billy Sunday style, as though to seize your soul and raise it to heaven; the swing of the hips as she walks; the rolling of the shoulders and the accompanying wave of the head; the cocky stride ever so faintly suggestive of the ancient cake walk; the clasping of the quivering hands, imploring the audience to join in glory; the outspread palms, the raised fingers, the hands flinging at you a message of joy; and, at last, the arms stretched up to heaven, and the whole body straining to follow upward, as though one ounce more of faith would give it soaring wings."

Merman's next success also started out with a shaky out-of-town tryout. Cole Porter's *Anything Goes* originally had a book about a group of shipwrecked passengers. However, the real-life burning of the Morro Castle with 134 lives lost made the P.G. Wodehouse and Guy Bolton (*q.v.*) libretto impossible to produce. Producer Vinton Freedley approached Howard Lindsay and Russel Crouse to rewrite the libretto and keep the passengers safely on board their ship.

Anything Goes (11/21/34; 415 performances) was produced in the days before Xerox machines. Performers received only their "sides," just the scenes they were in. The script was painstakingly typed with carbon copies. With changes in the script arriving daily, Merman's experience as a secretary came in handy. She copied down the changes in shorthand and typed up the corrections for herself and her fellow actors.

The opening night at the Alvin Theater was a smash success. Porter had provided a brilliant score with many standards, including "I Get a Kick Out of You," "All Through the Night," "Blow, Gabriel, Blow," "You're the Top" and the title tune. The role of Reno Sweeney gave Merman her first opportunity to create a classic musical-comedy character.

Merman spent another unsatisfying stint in Hollywood. She returned to Broadway to appear in *Red, Hot and Blue!* (10/29/36; 181 performances), another hit show with a score by Porter. The Alvin was packed on the opening night with some patrons paying up to $50 for their tickets. They weren't disappointed when Merman, Jimmy Durante and Bob Hope sang such terrific Porter numbers as "Down in the Depths," "Ridin' High" and "It's Delovely." The title of the show refers to Merman's character "Nails" O'Reilly Duquesne, who sat on a waffle iron as a child, thereby receiving the impression that figures prominently both on her posterior and the plot.

Brooks Atkinson again summed up the Merman manner: "She is still the most commanding minstrel in the business, wearing her costumes like a drum major, swinging to the music and turning the audience into a congregation of pals for the evening."

Arthur Schwartz (*q.v.*) and Dorothy Fields (*q.v.*) gave Merman her next Broadway assignment *Stars in Your Eyes* (2/9/39; 127 performances). J.P. McEvoy's script called for Merman to play Jeanette Adair, a film star who inherits Monotonous Pictures from her late husband. Merman was joined by Jimmy Durante, Mary Wickes, Richard Carlson, Tamara Toumanova and Mildred Natwick. Toumanova wasn't the only top dancer in the cast, which also included future greats Jerome Robbins, Alicia Alonso, Dan Dailey Jr., Nora Kaye and Maria Karnilova.

Du Barry Was a Lady (12/6/39; 408 performances) was the singer's next Broadway outing. Cole Porter supplied the lively score, and La Merm, as she was dubbed, was ably supported by costars Bert Lahr and the young Betty Grable. B.G. DeSylva (*q.v.*) produced and collaborated on the libretto with Herbert Fields (*q.v.*), and the fine and funny Porter score boasted at least one standard, "Friendship." The show was a smash in its out-of-town tour but on its arrival on Broadway, the critics were not amused. They did, however, rave about Merman. John Mason Brown exclaimed in the Post: "She needs no vitamins; she has plenty to spare. Her throat houses as beguiling a calliope as Broadway knows. The Midas touch is upon her tonsils because she can turn brass into gold. She can do more than that. She can keep it brass. No one can match her in putting a song across, in trumpeting its lyrics, in personifying its rhythms. All the bright lights of Broadway seem to shine behind her face. Hard-boiled she frankly is, but she makes toughness itself an irresistible virtue. She possesses not only great energy, but a kind of shimmering dignity, too; a dignity born of her poise, her skill, her honesty and her magnificent professionalism."

DeSylva convinced Merman and Porter to reteam for *Panama Hattie* (10/30/40; 501 performances), her first solo starring role. *Panama Hattie* opened at the 46th Street Theatre *(q.v.)* with Betty Hutton, Oscar ("Rags") Ragland, Joan Carroll and Arthur Treacher in supporting roles.

Porter was also the songwriter on Merman's next show, *Something for the Boys* (1/7/43; 422 performances). Herbert and Dorothy Fields wrote the script, which at one point was titled *Jenny Get Your Gun*. The producer of *Something for the Boys* was the extraordinary showman, Michael Todd. Todd was upset by the New York critics' practice of leaving shows early so they could make deadlines. Todd had his ushers block the aisles, and he himself refused to let Burns Mantle of the *Daily News* and Howard Barnes of the *Herald-Tribune* pass. The reviews were mostly favorable, though some critics criticized the lightweight book and hitless score.

Annie Get Your Gun (5/16/46; 1,147 performances), produced by Rodgers and Hammerstein *(q.v.),* opened with an exceptional score by Irving Berlin. The Boston tryout went brilliantly, but New York had a wait-and-see attitude. It moved from Boston to New York's Imperial Theatre *(q.v.)* and was set to open when a supporting beam was broken by the heavy scenery. The show clearly could not open until the brace was repaired. The Shuberts *(q.v.)* arranged for the show to move to Philadelphia while they saw to the repairs. The theater community believed the broken-beam story was just a cover to give the authors more time to fix the show. Word on the Rialto was that *Annie Get Your Gun* was doomed.

On its opening, the show, hailed by some critics as one of the greatest in musical-comedy history, also received some less-than-favorable notices. Again, everyone praised Merman. Despite the mixed reviews, the show was an immediate smash hit. Berlin gave Merman a cornucopia of great songs. She introduced

no less than five standards in *Annie Get Your Gun:* "They Say It's Wonderful," "I Got the Sun in the Morning," "Doin' What Comes Natur'lly," "There's No Business Like Show Business" and "You Can't Get a Man with a Gun."

Berlin was also responsible for the score of her next show, *Call Me Madam* (10/12/50; 644 performances). Lindsay and Crouse wrote the script, which was based loosely on the career of hostess Perle Mesta. *Call Me Madam* presented Merman as still more of a lady, in fact ambassador to the mythical country of Lichtenburg. The show cost $225,000 to produce. The entire amount was covered by RCA, which bought the rights to the original-cast album. RCA was galled later when Decca Records, which held Merman's contract, refused to loan her to RCA for the album. RCA had to substitute Dinah Shore while Decca put out its own album of the show's songs with Merman.

Call Me Madam was in trouble while out of town, and changes were added daily until Merman announced, as she did before every show, that it was frozen. From then on, nothing could be changed. When she announced "Call me Miss Birdseye" (an allusion to the show being frozen like Birdseye foods), the authors and director knew that no amount of cajoling could change her mind. John Chapman, writing in the *Daily News,* summed up the critical opinion: "Miss Merman is her old great self, singin' like a boat whistle and leering like a female Valentino, except when that confounded Graustarkian plot slows her down."

Lindsay and Crouse also wrote the script to her next Broadway show, *Happy Hunting* (12/6/56; 412 performances). The show was not a happy experience for any of the creative staff. Merman constantly argued with her leading man Fernando Lamas. Though the score by newcomers Harold Karr and Matt Dubey did contain one hit, "Mutual Admiration Society," there was little else of interest, and Lindsay and Crouse's book was creaky. The show received more bad publicity when Lamas, after having kissed Merman on stage during a performance, wiped his hand across his mouth. When questioned by Mike Wallace, Lamas described kissing Merman as "somewhere between kissing your uncle and a Sherman tank."

Merman's last Broadway appearance in an original musical was also her greatest triumph. *Gypsy* (5/21/59; 702 performances), with a score by Stephen Sondheim *(q.v.)* and Jule Styne *(q.v.)* and libretto by Arthur Laurents, was the musical story of Gypsy Rose Lee and her sister June Havoc's adventures in vaudeville and burlesque *(q.v.)* and starred Merman as the ultimate stage mother, Rose. Styne and Sondheim provided Merman with great songs: "Everything's Comin' Up Roses," "Small World," "Together, Wherever We Go," and "You'll Never Get Away from Me." But the greatest of all and the triumphant apex of Merman's career in musical theater was "Rose's Turn." The song came at the end of the spot that is reserved for the "eleven o'clock number," the big song that kicks up the audiences' emotions before the curtain falls. "Rose's Turn" found the mother with her nerves exposed, unable to control her frustration over pushing her two daughters to be stars with no applause for herself. Producer David Merrick *(q.v.)* repeated the maneuver of Mike Todd, stationing himself at the head of the aisles to stop Walter Kerr from running out of the theater before "Rose's Turn."

In 1966, at the age of 58, Merman returned to New York to appear as Annie Oakley in a revival of *Annie Get Your Gun* for the Music Theater of Lincoln Center. Irving Berlin even wrote a new song for the occasion, "An Old-Fashioned Wedding." Merman's last Broadway appearance came in Jerry Herman's *(q.v.)* *Hello, Dolly!* The show was originally written for Merman, who vowed after *Gypsy* that she would never appear in another original musical on Broadway. She was the last in a long string of Dolly's when she assumed the part in March 1970. Russell Nype, who appeared with Merman in *Call Me Madam* on Broadway and in 1966, 1968 and 1969 in small theaters across the country, costarred in *Dolly.* On December 27, 1970, the curtain fell for the last time on *Hello, Dolly!* and on the Broadway career of Ethel Merman.

Ethel Merman died on February 15, 1984.

MERRICK, DAVID (1911–   )

Peter Ustinov called him the greatest producer of the 20th century. Others have called him the "abominable showman." But whether they love him or hate him, all agree that David Merrick is the most fabulous showman of our time, and maybe of all time. No other producer, not Florenz Ziegfeld *(q.v.)* nor the Shubert brothers *(q.v.)*, has matched his percentage of hits or his flair for publicity.

Even a partial list of his achievements includes some of the greatest shows ever presented: *Gypsy, A Taste of Honey, Irma La Douce, Hello, Dolly!, Cactus Flower, I Do! I Do!, The World of Suzie Wong, Stop the World—I Want to Get Off, Promises, Promises* and *42nd Street.*

At the height of his career during the beginning of the 1970–71 season, he was presenting seven shows on Broadway. At the same time, he also had two shows on the road, one show in rehearsal and four in the planning stages. By this stage in his career he had produced 16 shows on Broadway of which all but 3 had been hits.

Merrick's musicals have employed most of the greatest composers and lyricists of our time, including Harold Arlen *(q.v.)* and E.Y. Harburg *(q.v.)*; Jerry Herman *(q.v.)*; Tom Jones and Harvey Schmidt; Jule Styne *(q.v.)* with both Stephen Sondheim *(q.v.)* and Betty Comden and Adolph Green *(q.v.)*; John Kander and Fred Ebb and Bob Merrill.

Although best known for his big splashy musicals, he has also presented some of the most adventurous dramas, like *Look Back In Anger, The Entertainer, Epitaph for George Dillon* and *A Taste of Honey.* He introduced such unconventional playwrights as John Osborne and Tom Stoppard to Broadway and American theatergoers.

It was Merrick who single-handedly created the famous "British invasion" of Broadway in the sixties when it seemed that only shows by British authors were being produced. In addition to the above-mentioned shows, Merrick imported *Oliver!, Luther, Becket, Rattle of a Simple Man, Oh What a Lovely War, Stop the World—I Want to Get Off* and others.

American playwrights were also introduced to audiences by Merrick. Woody Allen's first plays *Don't Drink the Water* and *Play It Again Sam* were successful David Merrick productions.

Merrick introduced audiences to Barbra Streisand in *I Can Get It for You Wholesale.* He presented Thornton Wilder's *The Matchmaker* and later had it musicalized as *Hello, Dolly!* He later stunned Broadway with the all-black production of *Hello, Dolly!* and led the way to the other black musicals that flooded Broadway in the seventies and early eighties.

Most of the greatest performers of the latter half of the 20th century appeared at one time or another in Merrick shows. Mary Martin *(q.v.)*, Lena Horne, Ethel Merman *(q.v.)*, Anthony Newley, Ezio Pinza, Peter Ustinov, Woody Allen and Jackie Gleason all enjoyed success in shows produced by Merrick.

Gleason, shortly after the opening of the musical *Take Me Along,* exclaimed that "Merrick's the most terrific producer I've ever known. What a showman. What a guy!" Later, Gleason also said, after many clashes with Merrick, that "I can't stand David Merrick."

All the arguments with Gleason and others were dutifully reported in the press, but that didn't bother Merrick. He knew it only resulted in greater ticket sales. Merrick doesn't really mind what is printed about him, as long as the title of his current show is spelled correctly.

Merrick maintains an aura of mystery about his beginnings. He told a press-agent friend that he was born in 1946, the year he began his Broadway career. A decade later, he claimed he was born on November 4, 1954, the day his first big hit, Harold Rome's *(q.v.)* musical *Fanny,* opened. He has seen the press portray him as an angel or a monster or a god, but there is always a sense of wonder and awe evoked by his name.

We do know that he was born in St. Louis, the son of Celia and Samuel Margoulis. They divorced when he was 10. He graduated with a law degree from St. Louis University, whereupon he made his way to New York. His arrival in 1940 was greeted with little fanfare, and for a while Merrick was unsure of how to proceed with his theatrical plans.

He looked up producer Herman Shumlin, who was then raising money for *The Male Animal.* Merrick invested $5,000, and the success of the play returned to Merrick $20,000 and a place on Shumlin's staff.

Merrick learned about the theater by working as Shumlin's assistant and later as a stage manager of Broadway shows on the road. He waited until it was the right time to break out on his own. From his first solo producing venture, *Clutterbuck,* through his latest hit, *42nd Street,* Merrick's life has been intertwined with the life of his shows.

His love-hate relationship with the press began with *Clutterbuck* (12/3/49; 218 performances). The play received less-than-enthusiastic reviews from the critics *(q.v.),* so Merrick conceived of a series of stunts *(q.v.)* to draw public attention to the show.

Merrick's pet project was a musicalization of the Marcel Pagnol trilogy, *Marius, Fanny,* and *Cesar.* He amassed a preproduction fund from one of Herman Shumlin's assistants, and he even threw in a little money of his own. At this time, he didn't own the rights nor had he a script or score or anything but the will to make it happen. As he has demonstrated again and again, that is enough for David Merrick. He flew to France and begged Pagnol to assign him the rights. After a long battle, mainly to get Pagnol even to speak to him, the rights were attained.

Merrick wanted Joshua Logan *(q.v.),* director of *South Pacific* and other smash shows to direct *Fanny.* But Merrick didn't know Logan. He did know Edward F. Kook of the Century Lighting Company through his relationship with Shumlin. Kook introduced Merrick to the great set designer, Jo Mielziner. Mielziner arranged for Logan to attend a screening of Pagnol's film *Marius.*

Logan remembers his first impression of Merrick. "He struck me a little like he strikes everybody," Logan said. "As an undertaker. Not a very happy looking face." Logan was not impressed with the film, and a year passed while Merrick hired and fired book writers. He finally asked Logan back to see the second film of the trilogy. "It was *Fanny* and I thought it was the most marvelous thing I'd ever seen in my life," recalls Logan. "I couldn't wait to do it."

Fanny's (11/4/54; 888 performances) opening might have meant the beginning of his life to Merrick, but the critics were less than inspired. Their reviews were apathetic, and there wasn't a line at the box office window the next morning. But Merrick didn't take his defeat lying down. Just as with *Clutterbuck,* Merrick took his fight to the media.

He allowed scenes from *Fanny* to appear on "The Ed Sullivan Show." He took out the first full-page theatrical ads in *The New York Times* and the *Tribune.* He took out ads in foreign papers, hoping that tourists would see *Fanny* when they came to this country. If they came by ocean liner, they saw ads for *Fanny.* If they came via another city by train, they saw a giant billboard in Penn Station. When they alighted, they were reminded of the show again when they hailed a taxi. He put ads in over 40 American cities. When *Fanny* finally closed, the ledger books showed a handsome profit of almost a million dollars.

Merrick often had highly publicized fights with his stars. During the run of *Carnival!* (4/13/61; 719 performances), Anna Maria Alberghetti had a long running feud with Merrick. After exiting the stage at one performance, her body mike was left on while she went to the ladies' room. It was shortly after this "accident" that Alberghetti came down with a mysterious malady that prevented her from performing unless her weekly check was increased. Merrick refused to be blackmailed and instead sent Alberghetti a lovely bouquet of plastic flowers. He then fired his star and built an enormous publicity campaign around her understudy, Anita Gillette. Merrick went so far as to invite the critics to Gillette's opening night. When the show was ready to tour, Anna Maria Alberghetti's sister Carla got the part.

But all these stories pale beside the saga of *42nd Street.* Merrick's hit best illustrates his luck, charm and savvy. Based on Warner Brothers' classic 1932 musical, *42nd Street* (8/25/80), the show was planned as the most opulent musical on any stage. Merrick chose as director Gower Champion, the man who delivered Merrick's greatest hit *Hello, Dolly! Dolly's* book writer, Michael Stewart, was brought on the project with newcomer Mark Bramble. The score was the same as that used for the movie, with other Harry Warren/Al Dubin hits added.

While on the road at the John F. Kennedy Center in Washington, D.C., the show was clearly in trouble. It ran about an hour too long. The costumes were late to arrive at the opening night performance and when they did finally show up they were judged unbelievably ugly. Merrick's backers balked at putting more money into what was clearly a bomb. Merrick had been away from theater production during a five-year sojourn in Hollywood, and the talk along the Rialto was that the master had lost his touch. To top it all off, director/choreographer Champion came down with what was reported as a bad case of the flu.

Unable to raise more money through his investors, Merrick came up with an unheard of plan; he bought each investor out, saving the investors from certainly losing everything when the show finally reached New York. Merrick then proceeded to whip the show into shape. He threw out all the costumes and ordered a completely new set. By the time the show reached the Winter Garden Theater *(q.v.),* it had been totally renovated. The book was reduced to "lead ins and crossovers" according to the program. Champion had been in and out of hospitals and hadn't been seen near the theater for several days.

At the end of the opening-night performance, the audience gave the production a standing ovation. The critics had been asked to stay in their seats following the show, and the local television news teams were asked to send video crews and correspondents. Immediately after the curtain call, Merrick strode on stage amidst thunderous applause. He quieted the audience and announced the death that afternoon of Gower Champion. The resulting publicity catapulted *42nd Street* into legendary status.

The momentum that *42nd Street* gained on opening night, plus later publicity and good word-of-mouth kept the show running for over 3,000 performances. *Variety (q.v.)* carried a headline reading, "David Merrick Hits a B'way Homer. 42nd Street Owner Grosses 500G Per Week." This $500,000 was pure profit for Merrick.

Merrick was later in the news when he suffered a near-fatal stroke. While he was in the hospital, Merrick's current wife and his former wife were locked in a battle over the management of his estate. In a two-week whirlwind of legal wrangling and its resultant publicity, Merrick divorced his then current wife and remarried his previous wife. He appeared in court to prove himself competent to manage his own affairs, and to cap it all off, he escaped the hospital in a wheelchair, racing down First Avenue before being caught.

From his first productions through his triumphal return to Broadway, Merrick has infuriated, amused and astounded his public for almost 50 years. The David Merrick story is rich with fact and fiction, and it's anyone's guess as to where to draw the line. Whatever Merrick touches becomes news; each of his productions has its own story, which is also a reflection of the change in the theater since World War II.

A partial list of Merrick productions includes *The Willow and I* (12/10/42; 28 performances); *Bright Boy* (3/2/44; 16 performances); *Fanny* (11/4/54; 888 performances); *The Matchmaker* (12/5/55; 486 performances); *Look Back in Anger* (10/1/57; 407 performances); *Romanoff and Juliet* (10/10/57; 389 performances); *Jamaica* (10/31/57; 555 performances); *The Entertainer* (2/12/58; 97 performances); *The World of Suzie Wong* (10/14/58; 508 performances); *Epitaph for George Dillon* (11/4/58; 23 performances); *Maria Golovin* (11/5/58; 5 performances); *La Plume de Ma Tante* (11/11/58; 835 performances); *Destry Rides Again* (4/23/59; 472 performances); *Gypsy* (5/21/59; 702 performances); and *Take Me Along* (10/22/59; 448 performances).

In the sixties, Merrick produced *The Good Soup* (3/2/60; 21 performances); *Vintage '60* (9/12/60; 8 performances); *Irma La Douce* (9/29/60; 524 performances); *A Taste of Honey* (10/4/60; 376 performances); *Becket* (10/5/60; 193 performances); *Do Re Mi* (12/26/60; 400 performances); *Carnival!* (4/13/61; 719 performances); *Ross* (12/26/61; 159 performances); *Subways Are for Sleeping* (12/27/61; 205 performances); *I Can Get It for You Wholesale* (3/22/62; 300 performances); *Stop the World—I Want to Get Off* (10/3/62; 556 performances); *Tchin-Tchin* (10/25/62; 222 performances); *Oliver!* (1/6/63; 744 performances); *Rattle of a Simple Man* (4/17/63; 94 performances); *Luther* (9/25/63; 212 performances); *110 in the Shade* (10/24/63; 330 performances); *Arturo Ui* (11/11/63; 8 performances); *One Flew Over the Cuckoo's Nest* (11/11/63; 82 performances); *The Milk Train Doesn't Stop Here Anymore* (1/1/64; 5 performances); *Hello, Dolly!* (1/16/64; 2,844 performances); *Foxy* (2/16/64; 72 performances); *Oh, What a Lovely War* (10/30/64; 125 performances); *A Severed Head* (10/8/64; 29 performances); *I Was Dancing* (11/21/64; 16 performances); *The Roar of the Greasepaint—The Smell of the Crowd* (5/16/65; 231 performances); *Cactus Flower* (12/8/65; 1,234 performances); *We Have Always Lived in the Castle* (10/19/66; 9 performances); *Don't Drink the Water* (11/17/66; 598 performances); *I Do! I Do!* (12/5/66; 584 performances); *The Astrakhan Coat* (1/12/67; 20 performances); *Rosencrantz and Guildenstern Are Dead* (10/16/67; 420 performances); *How Now, Dow Jones* (12/7/67; 213 performances); *The Happy Time* (1/18/68; 286 performances); *Promises, Promises* (12/1/68; 1,281 performances); *Forty Carats* (12/26/68; 780 performances); and *Play It Again, Sam* (2/12/69; 453 performances).

In the seventies, Merrick's productions include *Child's Play* (2/17/70; 342 performances); *The Philanthropist* (3/15/71; 72 performances); *Vivat! Vivat! Regina!* (1/20/72; 116 performances); *Moonchildren* (2/21/72; 16 performances); *Sugar* (4/9/72; 505 performances); *Mack and Mabel* (10/6/74; 65 performances); *The Misanthrope* (3/12/75; 94 performances); and *Very Good Eddie* (12/21/75; 304 performances); *42nd Street* (8/25/80); ran for 3,486 performances.

MILLER, ARTHUR (1915–   ) Arthur Miller, the author of such American classics as *Death of a Salesman, A View from the Bridge, All My Sons* and *The Price*, is one of America's greatest playwrights. His serious and searching dramas probe the themes of human crises of identity and responsibility in relationships. Miller also explores the problems that arise when a person does not acknowledge change or current circumstances. Miller believes his plays are lessons for life.

Miller owes a debt to the realistic theater of Ibsen and has benefited from more modern techniques of scene construction. Miller's characters speak in the vernacular of the person in the street, but the language is heightened by Miller's dramatic powers and achieve a poetic quality.

Miller began his playwriting career in the early forties

Arthur Miller

as the author of radio plays. His first Broadway show, *The Man Who Had All the Luck* (11/23/44), opened at the Forrest Theater *(q.v.)* and played only four performances but certainly presaged his great talents. *All My Sons* (1/29/47), his first Broadway hit, was soon followed by what many consider his masterpiece, *Death of a Salesman* (2/10/49). The play, staged by Elia Kazan, starred Lee J. Cobb and Mildred Dunnock. It won the Pulitzer Prize.

Miller's next Broadway outing was an adaptation of Ibsen's *An Enemy of the People* (1950). It was in part a reaction to the wave of McCarthyism that was just beginning to break over the country. Next came another reaction to McCarthy's witch hunt. The subject, the Salem witch trials of 1692, seemed perfectly analogous to the American political situation in the early fifties. *The Crucible* (1/22/53) though it played only 197 performances, has received countless revivals over the years. The solid cast included E.G. Marshall, Walter Hampden, Arthur Kennedy, Jean Adair, Madeleine Sherwood, Philip Coolidge, Beatrice Straight, and Joseph Sweeney.

Miller changed his tack with his next plays, an evening of two one-acts, *A View from the Bridge* and *A Memory of Two Mondays* (9/29/55). They were sympathetic portrayals of two middle-class Americans. *After the Fall* (1/23/64) was inspired by Miller's marriage to

Marilyn Monroe. It was a much better play than initial reaction to it indicates. Critics and audiences could not separate the drama from their feelings about Monroe. That same year, his drama that was set against the horrors of Nazi Germany, *Incident at Vichy* (12/3/64; 99 performances), opened at Lincoln Center. In *Incident at Vichy*, a Jewish psychiatrist tells Prince Von Berg that he must learn to confront his collusion with the Nazis with his own humanity, a major theme in Miller's plays.

In his next Broadway production, *The Price* (2/7/68), Miller portrays two brothers who are joined by their lack of appreciation of each other's differences. Estranged for years, the brothers know only how to be capitalists, without love or heart to make them human. He followed it with other plays: *The Reason Why* and *Fame* (1970); *The Creation of the World and Other Business* (1972); *Up from Paradise* (1974); *The Archbishop's Ceiling* (1976); *The American Clock* (1984); and *Danger: Memory!* (1987).

Despite his lack of recent success on Broadway, Miller remains a major voice in the American theater. Although solidly rooted in the sensibilities of the forties and fifties, his plays have continued to speak to the common person's universal problems. Miller's humanity and compassion shine through his plays along with his profound sense of morality. Miller always believed in the importance of the theater in society. In 1951, he wrote that, "The stage is the place for ideas, for philosophies, for the most intense discussion of man's fate."

MINSKOFF BUILDING 1515 Broadway between 44th and 45th Streets. Architects: Kahn and Jacobs. The Minskoff building was erected in 1969 by Sam Minskoff and Sons on the sight of the beloved Astor Hotel *(q.v.)*. The 50-story building was the first of the skyscrapers to blight the theater district. It was also the first to take advantage of the Times Square Theater District zoning bonuses, which allowed developers to build additional stories to their buildings if they included new legitimate theaters in their designs. Unfortunately, the resulting Minskoff Theatre *(q.v.)* has more in common with a barn than a theater and is unpopular with both theatergoers and theater professionals.

The building also includes the Loew's Astor Plaza movie theater, which remains one of the only large screened movie theaters in Manhattan (the other is the Ziegfeld).

On the third floor of the Minksoff Building, overlooking Shubert Alley, are the Minskoff rehearsal rooms, used for rehearsals of Broadway shows. Many theater people consider the rehearsal rooms to be the only saving grace in a building that should never have been allowed. One architecture critic said that the building's ridiculously designed top made it look like a fifties-style spaceship that had crashed head first into Times Square.

MINSKOFF THEATRE 1515 Broadway between 44th and 45th Streets. Architects: Kahn and Jacobs. Opening: March 13, 1973; *Irene.* The Minskoff Theatre was built in the Minskoff Building *(q.v.)* on the site of the Astor Hotel *(q.v.).* Although it contains many technical innovations, the auditorium is uncomfortable, and with 1,600 seats it is far too large for optimum viewing. The theater has no ornamentation and is considered one of the coldest looking of the new theaters.

The theater's architects were quoted in *Playbill (q.v.)* as claiming that "We think we've created one of the most exciting, three-dimensional processional routes for the theatergoers—a series of forms, changes in ceiling heights, and spatial explosions. The whole processional, from the moment you enter and rise thirty-five feet to the theater level, is a theatrical event in itself." Though the walk to the auditorium is well designed, the theater is not. The balcony overhangs too far from the front of the stage and the uppermost seats are also too distant. The orchestra area has what is called continental seating—no center aisles, only two aisles on either side of the seats. Row T, for example, is 52 seats wide. Patrons who have tickets in the center of the row must cross over the feet of 25 people to get to their seats. On a matinee day, when many audience members have shopping bags, this can be extremely difficult. In its favor, however, the Minskoff was the first New York theater to be fully accessible to handicapped patrons.

The Minskoff has not attracted many successes. Its critics think that the audience's distance from the stage and the coldness of the theater's design may account for its lack of hits. Architecture, sight lines and acoustics all play their part in an audience's enjoyment of a show. While the theater can make a lot of money at capacity, most shows do not play to full houses. The Minskoff's shows might do better in a more intimate house where a full audience might equal half or three-quarters of the Minskoff's capacity.

The first show to play the theater, *Irene* (3/13/73; 604 performances), seemed to promise a bright future for the new theater. *Irene,* a revival of a successful 1919 musical that originally premiered at the Vanderbilt Theater, starred Debbie Reynolds, Patsy Kelly, Monte Markham and George S. Irving.

A series of concerts, ballets and flop musicals followed *Irene's* opening. *Rockabye Hamlet* (2/17/76; 7 performances) was directed by the usually reliable Gower Champion. But he made a mistake with *Rockabye Hamlet,* a rock version of the Shakespeare classic.

The next original shows to play the Minskoff were *Angel* (5/10/78; 5 performances), a musicalization of Ketti Frings's play, *Look Homeward Angel* that in turn

was based on Thomas Wolfe's novel; *King of Hearts* (10/22/78; 48 performances), based on the French film and *Got Tu Go Disco* (6/25/79; 8 performances).

A revival of *West Side Story* (1980) did not pay back its investors. Another revival, *Can-Can* (1981), closed after only 5 performances. For one year, the theater hosted Joseph Papp's version of Gilbert and Sullivan's *The Pirates of Penzance* which moved from the Uris Theatre *(q.v.),* another huge, modern auditorium.

The theater's failures continued unabated. Charles Strouse *(q.v.)* and Alan Jay Lerner *(q.v.)* fell under the theater's curse with their musicalization of Robert Emmett Sherwood's *Idiot's Delight,* which they titled *Dance a Little Closer* (5/11/83; 1 performance). *Marilyn: An American Fable* (12/16/83; 16 performances) was a musical version of the life of Marilyn Monroe that suffered an especially long preview period and became a legendary failure. Following a revival of *Sweet Charity* with Debby Allen, the latest failure at the Minskoff was *Teddy and Alice* (11/12/87; 77 performances), a musical starring Len Cariou. Currently, a terrific revue, *Black and Blue,* is occupying the Minskoff.

MOLLY PICON THEATER See JOLSON'S 59TH STREET THEATER.

MOREHOUSE, WARD See CRITICS.

MOROSCO THEATRE 217 W. 45th Street. Architect: Herbert J. Krapp. Opening: February 5, 1917; *Canary Cottage.* The Shubert brothers *(q.v.)* built the Morosco and named it in honor of Oliver Morosco, a West Coast producer. The Morosco enjoyed a long history of distinguished productions, including *Death of a Salesman* and *Cat on a Hot Tin Roof,* until it was destroyed to make way for the Marriott Marquis Hotel and the Marquis Theater *(q.v.)* (See BATTLE TO SAVE THE HELEN HAYES, MOROSCO AND BIJOU THEATERS.)

Oliver Morosco's first production in his new 1,009-seat theater was *Canary Cottage* (112 performances). Earl Carroll *(q.v.),* famous for his *Vanities (q.v.),* wrote the music and lyrics and coauthored the libretto with Elmer Harris. He also produced and directed the proceedings.

Following *Canary Cottage,* the theater got onto more serious affairs. The Pulitzer Prize-winning drama *Craig's Wife* (10/12/25; 360 performances) was written by George Kelly, best known as the author of *The Show-Off.* Crystal Heme played the shrewish wife who drives away her husband and neighbors and ends up an embittered, surprised, lonely woman. Also starring in the play were Anne Sutherland, Charles Trowbridge and the great Josephine Hull.

Novelist Somerset Maugham's play *The Letter* (9/26/27; 105 performances) next opened at the Morosco. The *Warrior's Husband* (3/11/32; 83 performances) is today best remembered as the first good look theatergoers had at the talents of Katharine Hepburn.

Alexander Woollcott (q.v.) tried his hand at playwriting in collaboration with George S. Kaufman. The result was *The Dark Tower* (11/25/33; 57 performances). The play was slammed by Woollcott's fellow journalists. Richard Dana Skinner, writing in the *Commonweal*, called it "a comedy of errors in taste and judgement." Woollcott took the reviews personally and was hugely depressed when the play closed.

Though *The Dark Tower* is largely forgotten, one aspect of its opening did make theatrical history and was responsible for a historic change in Broadway tradition. Producer Sam Harris was disgusted with the usual opening night audience who arrived late and noisily drunk. Harris decided to forgo the custom that offered the elite of New York society free tickets to all openings. Instead, Harris democratized his show's opening night by making up a new list of friends, critics and people he liked. Any tickets not covered by the new list were put on sale at the box office. Harris sent out a letter with the invitation that read in part: "The management of The Dark Tower has promised the distinguished players assembled for its cast the unusual luxury of giving a first-night performance before an audience not predominantly composed of Broadwayites. To this end, a list of 500 citizens of this city has been drawn up, and the first call on the opening-night seats will be reserved for them. Your name is on this list." The press attacked him, but Harris had made his point and soon all opening nights were handled in the same way.

The Dark Tower also introduced another theatrical innovation. In the play, the character of Max Sarnoff was really another character in disguise. The authors, wishing to fool the audience, felt that the plot twist might be given away if audience members noticed that there was no actor listed in the *Playbill* (q.v.) as playing Max Sarnoff. So they simply made up the name Anton Stengel. The fictitious thespian even had a fabricated biography printed with the genuine biographies of the rest of the cast.

Tallulah Bankhead and Walter Pidgeon starred in *Something Gay* (4/29/35; 72 performances). Bankhead herself reviewed the play. She said *Something Gay* was "as misleading a title as ever was hung on two hours of plot and dialogue." Critic Richard Lockridge concentrated his criticism on the author, Adelaide Heilbron—"Miss Heilbron's slight inadequacy as a writer of witty comedies apparently results only from an inability to think up any witty dialogue."

Call It a Day (1/28/36; 195 performances) starred Gladys Cooper, Frances Williams and Glenn Anders. The Theater Guild (q.v.) produced the Dodie Smith comedy. George M. Cohan (q.v.) was reunited for a brief time with his former producing partner Sam Har-

ris for *Fulton of Oak Falls* (2/10/37; 37 performances). Cohan extensively revised radio comedian Parker Fennelly's play for himself. Cohan's acting received glorious reviews, but the critics were less tolerant of his old-fashioned writing.

Noel Coward's delightfully wry comedy *Blithe Spirit* (11/5/41; 650 performances) entranced audiences with the performances of Mildred Natwick, Peggy Wood, Leonora Corbett and Clifton Webb. One of the biggest hits in the Morosco's history was *The Voice of the Turtle* (12/8/43; 1,557 performances). The John van Druten comedy starred Margaret Sullavan, Elliott Nugent and Audrey Christie. Coward wrote *Blithe Spirit* in five days. Van Druten wrote his even bigger hit in three weeks.

Arthur Miller's (q.v.) greatest success, and another Pulitzer Prize-winner for the Morosco, was *Death of a Salesman* (2/10/49; 742 performances). Lee J. Cobb created a masterful performance as washed-up salesman Willy Loman and was ably supported by Mildred Dunnock as his long-suffering wife and Arthur Kennedy as his disillusioned, alienated son.

Another great American writer, Tennessee Williams (q.v.), won a Pulitzer Prize for a play presented at the Morosco—*Cat on a Hot Tin Roof* (3/24/55; 694 performances), the theatrically vibrant drama that starred Burl Ives, Mildred Dunnock, Ben Gazzara and Barbara Bel Geddes. Elia Kazan staged the proceedings brilliantly. Ives's character of Big Daddy is one of Williams's greatest creations. Big Daddy's need for dominating his family and surroundings and fear of sickness and death clashed with the desires of his equally strong-willed family. Williams used the tortured lives of his characters to work out his own feelings of loneliness and hostility, but try as he did in this searing play and others, Williams never succeeded in exorcising his own ghosts.

Helen Hayes (q.v.), Richard Burton, Susan Strasberg Glenn Anders and Sig Arno starred in Jean Anouilh's *Time Remembered* (11/12/57; 248 performances). Vernon Duke (q.v.) composed the incidental music for the play. Patricia Moyes, the translator of the play, described it as "a joyful statement of faith in life, in common sense and in quality."

For the Morosco, the sixties was a decade of comedies, including *Generation* by William Goodhart (10/6/65; 299 performances), starring Henry Fonda, and David Merrick's (q.v.) production of Woody Allen's *Don't Drink the Water* (11/17/66; 598 performances) with Lou Jacobi, Kay Medford, Anita Gillette, Tony Roberts and Dick Libertini.

Arthur Miller's *The Price* (2/7/68; 429 performances) proved to be an exception from the comedy roster of the sixties. The drama tells of two brothers who cannot communicate because of their expectations. It starred Pat Hingle, Kate Reid, Harold Gary and Arthur Kennedy. *The Price* surprised and shocked audiences who

The Morosco Theatre after the wrecker's ball   Photo Jeff Slotnick.

were used to Broadway comedies that were more rooted in television than theater and big empty musicals with catchy title songs and little else.

Forty Carats (12/26/68; 780 performances), another David Merrick production, returned comedy to the stage of the Morosco. Jay Allen adapted a French play by Pierre Barillet and Jean-Pierre Gredy. Julie Harris starred along with Marco St. John, Polly Rowles, Murray Hamilton, Glenda Farrell and Nancy Marchand. The story concerned a 40-year-old divorcee and her romance with a young man in his twenties.

Julie Harris returned to the Morosco in Paul Zindel's drama *And Miss Reardon Drinks a Little* (2/25/71; 108 performances). The play also starred Nancy Marchand, Virginia Payne, Estelle Parsons and Rae Allen.

Alan Bates came from London with *Butley* (10/31/72; 135 performances), a play by Simon Gray. An acclaimed revival of Eugene O'Neill's *(q.v.) A Moon for the Misbegotten* (12/29/73; 314 performances) opened at the Morosco with Jason Robards, Colleen Dewhurst and Ed Flanders starring.

The Shadow Box (3/31/77; 315 performances) was a no-nonsense drama about terminally ill patients and their families. The show boasted steady performances by Laurence Luckinbill, Mandy Patinkin, Josef Som-

mer, Simon Oakland, Patricia Elliott and, particularly, Geraldine Fitzgerald. *The Shadow Box* won the Pulitzer Prize.

The Theater Guild *(q.v.)* presented William Gibson's play *Golda* (11/14/77; 108 performances) with Anne Bancroft in an acclaimed performance as Israeli political leader Golda Meir. A year later, Hugh Leonard's play *Da* (5/1/78; 697 performances) starred Barnard Hughes, Brian Murray and Mia Dillon. Leonard's sequel to *Da, A Life* (11/2/80; 64 performances), also opened at the Morosco. It was not a success. Barnard Hughes did not appear in the play; his wife, Helen Stenborg, did. Also appearing in *A Life* was Roy Dotrice and Pat Hingle.

The Morosco was locked in a battle for survival along with the Helen Hayes *(q.v.)* and Bijou *(q.v.)* theaters. Playwright Arthur Miller wrote to James Watt, the Secretary of the Interior, to condemn the plan to destroy the theater. Miller's letter stated in part: "I think it is the best theater in New York. The relationship of the auditorium to the stage is very nearly perfect; the height of the stage is optimum and the sight-lines are superb. Perhaps most vital of all, the acoustical qualities are remarkable for their trueness. All of which is probably unique in a theater that is by no means small."

The Morosco and the people of New York lost, and in 1982, the theater was demolished.

MOTOGRAM The Motogram, the world's first "moving sign" has been a prominent Times Square landmark since 1928. The Times Tower (q.v.) serves as the base for the 360 foot long sign. The sign's 14,800 bulbs have announced major events in American history as well as the daily news and weather forecast. In 1910, *New York Times* owner Adolph Ochs allowed managing editor Carl Van Anda to post round by round results of the Jim Jeffries–Jack Johnson fight from a window on the tower. Over 30,000 people jammed the square to watch the results.

In the days before radio or television, the Times Tower became the focal point of important news and, of course, the annual New Year's Eve celebration. The *Times* realized that any paper that could draw 30,000 people to its windows would soon be recognized as the most important paper in town. The management of the *Times* installed an electric sign to keep score of the Cincinnati–Chicago World Series of 1919. In 1921, 10,000 people gathered at the base of the tower to follow the course of the Jack Dempsey–George Carpentier fight.

Seven years later, in 1928, the Motogram began operation with constant news bulletins. The sign's greatest moment came on V-J Day (q.v.) when over 750,000 Americans gathered to wait for news of the Japanese surrender in World War II. At 7:03, the news came when the Motogram lit the message: OFFICIAL—TRUMAN ANNOUNCES JAPANESE SURRENDER.

In 1978, the Motogram was extinguished by the owner of the Times Tower as a protest of the decay of Times Square. However the sign was relit barely 10 years later with *New York Newsday*, a new daily paper, supplying the news.

MOVIELAND 1567 Broadway at 47th Street. Architect: Herbert J. Krapp. Opening: September 9, 1918; *Forever After*. The Shuberts (q.v.) built the Central Theater as a rival to the fabulously successful Palace Theater (q.v.) across the square. The lobby was built in a 19th century brick building that was once the Matthushek & Son piano factory. The Shuberts proved unable to compete, however, and the Central, hosting plays and musicals, led a surprisingly unsuccessful life as a legitimate theater. One of its few hits was the Lew Fields (q.v.) production of *Poor Little Ritz Girl* (7/27/20; 93 performances). Rodgers and Hart (q.v.) wrote their first Broadway score for the show. Unfortunately, much of their score was cut out of town, and new songs by Sigmund Romberg (q.v.) and Alex Gerber were added.

In 1928, the Central became a movie house. Only three years later, the Minsky brothers leased the house

from the Shuberts and made it their flagship burlesque (q.v.) house. Fiorello LaGuardia cracked down on burlesque during his administration, and the theater was returned to a film policy.

In the 1950s, the theater's name was changed to the Holiday. Once again, live shows were presented on its stage, but none were successful. Its name became the Forum 47th Street when it reverted to a movie policy. In the early eighties, the name was changed again to the Movieland. Through all the changes in policy, the Shuberts (q.v.) retained ownership. The theater closed in the late eighties.

MURRAY'S ROMAN GARDENS 228 W. 42nd Street. In the teens, 42nd Street was making a name for itself with polite society. The best-known restaurant on the street was Murray's Roman Gardens, a forerunner to the present day Mama Leone's (q.v.). Like Mama Leone's, Murray's Roman Gardens was decorated at the height of kitsch. The decor was a boldly imagined Roman Garden complete with statuary, fountains and temples. Pseudo-Roman and-Egyptian murals decorated the walls. Unlike many Roman gardens, however, the restaurant boasted a revolving floor. In the spirit of later atmospheric movie theaters, Murray's appeared to the uninitiated to actually be outdoors. A moon even traversed the starlit ceiling several times each evening.

The next incarnation of the space at 228 W. 42nd Street was Hubert's Flea Circus. Certainly lower on the entertainment scale than Murray's but ever more realistic, Hubert's actually did contain a flea circus. Hubert's opened in 1925 and was looked on skeptically by Broadwayites who still considered 42nd Street to be smart and sophisticated.

The 10¢ admission allowed the patron to enter what was essentially a carnival side show. The walls were lined with distorting mirrors such as those found in an amusement park-fun house. The pitchman at Hubert's was Karoy, "The Man with the Iron Tongue." He bade the patron to plunk down an additional 15¢ to see belly dancers, and if the patron was over 18, another 15¢ would admit the curious to an educational exhibit on human sexuality, direct from the French Academy of Medicine in Paris. Hubert's 42nd Street branch (another was on 14th Street) had such acts as Libera, a contortionist, and Ajax, the sword swallower. Later patrons gaped at Albert-Alberta, half-man and half-woman, and Chief Amok, a headhunter. Hubert's emulated the notorious Victoria Theater (q.v.) by presenting the famous as sideshow attractions. Jack Johnson and baseball great Grover Cleveland Alexander appeared on Hubert's stage.

A cleaned up, Hollywood version of Hubert's can be found in the film *The Band Wagon*. Fred Astaire (q.v.) sings the Dietz and Schwartz (q.v.) song "Shine on Your Shoes" in a Hubert's-like environment.

Patrons during the thirties might have been aghast at

Murray's Roman Gardens   Courtesy Vicki Gold Levi.

the deprivation Hubert's brought to 42nd Street. Imagine then how surprised they would have been if they could have taken a true glimpse into the future to see that Hubert's closed for good in 1975 to be replaced by a porno house named Peepland.

MUSIC BOX THEATER 239 W. 45th Street. Architect: C. Howard Crane. Opening: September 22, 1921; *Music Box Revue.* Producer Sam Harris, late of the team of George M. Cohan *(q.v.)* and Sam Harris, built the Music Box Theater with partner Irving Berlin *(q.v.)* at

the start of the 1920s. Berlin never sold his half interest. The other is owned by the Shubert Organization. (See SHUBERT BROTHERS.)

Harris and Berlin planned a series of revues for the theater. Revues were the vogue in the teens, twenties and thirties. There were the *Ziegfeld Follies (q.v.),* the *Earl Carroll Vanities (q.v.),* the *George White's Scandals (q.v.),* the *Passing Shows,* the *Artists and Models* series, the *Greenwich Village Follies* and others. The other revues stressed their opulence and girls. The big draw of the *Music Box Revues* were the scores by Irving Berlin and an almost European stylishness and refinement.

The first edition of the *Music Box Revue* (9/22/21; 440 performances) had a cast that included Sam Bernard (who said of the new theater: "It stinks of class"), the Brox Sisters, Florence Moore, Joseph Santley, Ivy Sawyer, Ethelind Terry and Berlin himself. As planned, it was the score that received the most acclaim. Chief among the songs was "Say It with Music," one of Berlin's most enduring hits. Other popular songs from the score are "Everybody Step" and "The Schoolhouse Blues."

The second edition (10/23/22; 330 performances) of the series opened with much the same creative team—Berlin writing the music and lyrics, Sam Harris producing and Hassard Short directing. This time, the cast

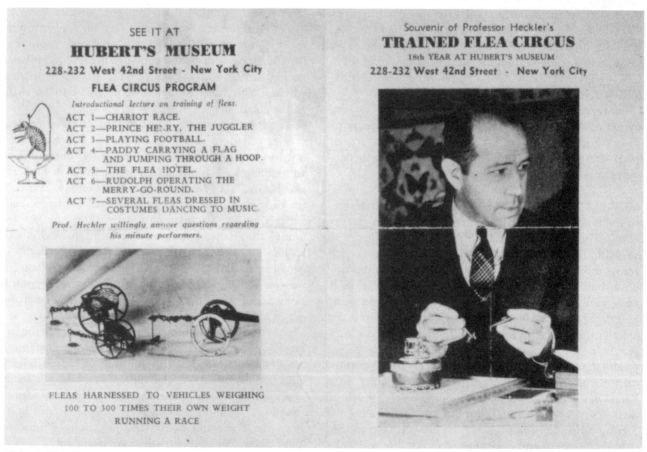

Hubert's Flea Circus program   Courtesy Tony Randall.

Sam Harris unlocking the Music Box Theater for Irving Berlin   Courtesy Billy Rose Theater Collection.

included John Steel, William Gaxton, Charlotte Greenwood, the Fairbanks Twins and Clark and McCullough. The songs included "Pack Up Your Sins and Go to the Devil," "Bring on the Pepper," "Crinoline Days," "Lady of the Evening" and "Will She Come from the East?"

The third edition (9/22/23; 277 performances) proved only a little less successful than its predecessors. The cast featured a return by the Brox Sisters, Joseph Santley, Ivy Sawyer, John Steel and Florence Moore. Newcomers included Grace Moore, Frank Tinney, Phil Baker and Robert Benchley *(q.v.).* Benchley, a popular critic, humorist and member of the Algonquin Round Table *(q.v.),* turned to acting with the popular acclaim for his droll monologue "The Treasurer's Report." Berlin provided his usual hit score, including "What'll I Do?," "Learn to Do the Strut," "The Waltz of Long Ago" and "An Orange Grove in California."

The fourth edition (12/1/24; 184 performances), the last in the series, starred Grace Moore, the Brox Sisters and the comedy team of Clark and McCullough, along-

side newcomers Claire Luce, Carl Randall, Oscar Shaw and Tamara. The biggest star, however, was Fanny Brice *(q.v.),* borrowed from her home in the *Ziegfeld Follies.* Berlin's big hit from the score was "All Alone." Each edition of the series had done slightly worse than the previous edition.

The first straight play to be presented in the theater was *Cradle Snatchers* (9/7/25; 485 performances), a comedy by Russell Medcraft and Norma Mitchell. Margaret Dale played a woman who suspects her husband of cheating when she sees him lunching with a flapper. She decides to pay her husband back by hiring a college boy to make love to her. The wife's friends, Mary Boland and Edna May Oliver, like the idea. They also don't trust their husbands. A mad party, fueled by champagne, ensues and the husbands arrive to find their wives slightly disarrayed. By curtain's end, the couples have come to an agreement, although Dale's character still decides to go to the movies with her college beau. The cast also included two future Hollywood stars, Raymond Guion (he changed his name to Gene Raymond) and Humphrey Bogart playing the character Jose Vallejo.

Another somewhat racy theme was treated in *Chicago* (12/30/26; 173 performances) in which Roxie Hart shoots her lover and with the help of a lawyer who is more theatrical director than barrister gets off without a conviction for the crime. Through the power of publicity, not only does she get out of jail, but she secures a 10-week booking in vaudeville. The Maurine Watkins satirical comedy starred Francine Larrimore, Charles Bickford, Edward Ellis, Dorothy Stickney and Juliette Crosby.

Philip Barry's comedy *Paris Bound* (12/27/27; 234 performances) was an aptly titled show for the Music Box, since the theater's next offering was Cole Porter's (*q.v.*) musical *Paris* (10/8/28; 194 performances). *Paris* was a Roaring Twenties show whose content was summed up by the title of one of its songs, "Let's Misbehave." "Let's Misbehave" was cut out of town and replaced by the hit song of the show, the equally suggestive "Let's Do It." The star of the evening was the delightful French import Irene Bordoni. Porter received some of his best early reviews with *Paris*. The *New Yorker*'s critic had high praise: "No one else writing words and music knows so exactly the delicate balance between sense, rhyme and tune. His rare and satisfactory talent makes other lyrists sound as though they'd written their words for a steam whistle."

Howard Dietz and Arthur Schwartz (*q.v.*) made history with *The Little Show* (4/30/29; 321 performances). The songwriting team was warming up for their biggest triumph, *The Band Wagon*. *The Little Show* was one of the first intimate revues that proved to audiences that all the Ziegfeldian trappings were not necessary for the enjoyment of a revue. Dietz and Schwartz contributed a big hit to the show, "I Guess I'll Have to Change My Plan." Herman Hupfeld wrote a novelty number for the show, "A Hut in Hoboken," that won some renown. Kay Swift and her husband Paul James had a hit with "Can't We Be Friends" and Ralph Rainger and Dietz wrote the classic "Moanin' Low." The latter two songs were introduced by the torchy Libby Holman. Other cast members included Fred Allen, Romney Brent, and Clifton Webb.

The thirties began with *Topaze* (2/12/30; 159 performances). The next offering was one of the great hits of the decade, George S. Kaufman and Moss Hart's (*q.v.*) *Once in a Lifetime* (9/24/30; 305 performances). The comedy marked their first collaboration. Hart had written the play and submitted it to producer Sam Harris. Harris thought it needed work and passed it on to Kaufman. The plot was a satire of Hollywood, although neither author had actually been there. The two lead characters are second-rate vaudevillians, one very shrewd and one very dumb, who decide a fortune is to be made in Hollywood now that talkies are all the rage. They become vocal coaches for movie mogul Sam Glogauer's studio. George, the dumb partner, makes a series of inept mistakes, and naturally they are hailed as genius. George is promoted again and again until he rivals Glogauer himself.

Following a particularly disastrous tryout, the play closed out of town. Further rewrites were undertaken, and the show taken out again. This time it clicked and became a smash hit when it opened at the Music Box Theater. The cast included Hugh O'Connell, Jean Dixon, Grant Mills, Spring Byington (as a Louella Parsons character), Charles Halton and George S. Kaufman himself as Lawrence Vail, a playwright whose sanity is ruined by Hollywood.

The Third Little Show (6/1/31; 136 performances), the last edition, opened at the Music Box with Edward Arnold, Constance Carpenter, Carl Randall and Ernest Truex supporting the zany comedy of Beatrice Lillie. Herman Hupfeld's "When Yuba Plays the Rhumba on His Tuba" was the only original song to achieve any success. Noel Coward's "Mad Dogs and Englishmen" was introduced to American audiences in this show.

George S. Kaufman enjoyed two more hits at the Music Box in rapid succession. The first was the George and Ira Gershwin (*q.v.*) satirical musical *Of Thee I Sing* (12/26/31; 446 performances). Kaufman wrote the book with Morrie Ryskind. The brilliant score contained a healthy dose of satire as well as great romantic numbers: "Love Is Sweeping the Country," "Who Cares" and the title song.

Of Thee I Sing starred William Gaxton, June O'Dea, Louis Moran, future politician George Murphy and Victor Moore. After seeing the show, critic (*q.v.*) John Mason Brown wrote a letter to his wife paraphrasing Lovelace: "I could not love thee, dear, so much, loved I not Victor Moore."

The authors, particularly Kaufman, were concerned that the audience would take offense at their swipes at the sacrosanct offices of president and vice president. In the thirties, when the whole country looked to the White House for relief from the Depression, the satire was quite risky. They need not have worried.

John Mason Brown wrote in the *Post* that *Of Thee I Sing* "represents not only a new and welcome departure in the world of entertainment, but also in the field of American musical comedy. Here at last is a musical comedy which dodges nearly all the cliches of its kind, which has wit and intelligence behind it, which brings Gilbert and Sullivan to mind without being derived from them."

The lone naysayer was the usually reliable *New Yorker* critic Robert Benchley who wrote, "I was definitely disappointed. *Of Thee I Sing* struck me as dull musically, and not particularly fresh satirically. The whole thing, during great stretches, was reminiscent of an old Hasty Pudding 'spoof' in which lese-majeste was considered funny enough in itself without straining for any more mature elements of comedy."

Benchley's review notwithstanding, the musical was a tremendous success, breaking the house record for the Music Box. Further proof of the show's excellence came when Kaufman, Ryskind and Ira Gershwin were awarded the Pulitzer Prize. The award was not made to George Gershwin, because the Pulitzer Prize went only to writers of words and he had written the music. Despite this obvious gaffe, the authors appreciated the Pulitzer. After all, it was the first time the Pulitzer Prize was awarded to a musical.

Ryskind was especially amused, for the person who signed his scroll was Dr. Nicholas Murray Butler of Columbia University. Years before, Dr. Butler had signed a letter to Ryskind expelling him from the university.

Before it closed, the show moved to the 46th Street Theater (q.v.) to make way for the next attraction at the Music Box—Kaufman and Edna Ferber's *Dinner at Eight* (10/22/32; 232 performances). Ferber described Kaufman's method of collaboration. As she sat at the typewriter taking down the ideas, Kaufman paced "hither, thither and yon or draped himself over and under or around such pieces of defenseless furniture as happened to be in the room." When they actually put down some dialogue, they'd "wander all over the place, deciding on positioning, and we'd experiment with the spoken lines. I might add that we didn't spare our voices in the dramatic scenes. One of my maids and the man who cared for my lawn are still, I think, a little suspicious of our sanity."

Musical theater returned to the Music Box with the Irving Berlin and Moss Hart revue *As Thousands Cheer* (9/30/33; 390 performances). Harris, who presented most of the plays in his theater, produced the proceedings, and Hassard Short directed. Berlin's score contained one of his biggest hits, "Easter Parade." Ethel Waters let loose with "Harlem on My Mind" and "Heat Wave." Her big number though was the plaintive wail of a woman who must explain to her children that their father would not be coming home because he had been lynched. The song was "Supper Time" and Berlin had his doubts as to its part in a musical comedy revue. Harris convinced Berlin to leave the song in, and Waters stopped the show with it every night. Clifton Webb sang "Not for All the Rice in China" in his impeccably clipped style. Other cast members included Marilyn Miller, the nominal star of the proceedings, and Helen Broderick.

Kaufman returned with his collaborator Moss Hart and their unconventional play *Merrily We Roll Along* (9/29/34; 155 performances). The play told its story in a reverse chronology. Audiences were not so much confused by the strange construction, but they certainly did not care for any of the cynical, disillusioned characters.

Kaufman's next assignment at the Music Box was as play doctor for the Samuel and Bella Spewack drama *Spring Song* (10/1/34; 40 performances) produced by Max Gordon. Unfortunately, Kaufman couldn't save the show.

Kaufman was one of Harris' favorite playwrights, and he returned to the Music Box with *First Lady* (11/26/35; 244 performances), written in collaboration with Katharine Dayton. Reviewers felt that the character played by veteran actress Jane Cowl was fashioned on Alice Roosevelt Longworth.

Kaufman was also responsible for the next play at the Music Box, *Stage Door* (10/22/36; 169 performances). He collaborated with Edna Ferber on the story of the performers at the Foot-Lights Club. Among the cast who played aspiring actresses were Margaret Sullavan and Jean Maitland. When Sullavan became pregnant and had to leave the show, Kaufman and Harris decided to close rather than attempt to replace her.

Kaufman directed John Steinbeck's *Of Mice and Men* (11/23/37; 207 performances), the theater's next hit. The drama opened with Wallace Ford and Broderick Crawford in the leads. Kaufman worked on the script as an editor and technician. The dialogue was all by Steinbeck, who had written the original novel with the intent of turning the property into a play or film.

Kaufman and Hart's satirical musical *I'd Rather Be Right* moved from the Alvin Theater (q.v.) to finish its run at the Music Box. The team then turned to producing with the revue *Sing Out the News* (9/24/38; 105 performances). Harold Rome (q.v.) wrote the music and lyrics and collaborated on the sketches with Charles Friedman, who directed the show. The cast included June Allyson, Mary Jane Walsh, Rex Ingram, Joey Faye and Will Geer. The show's numbers were satirical in nature as indicated by such titles as "My Heart Is Unemployed" and the "Peace and The Diplomat Ballet." Rome's hit song from the show was the exuberant "Franklin D. Roosevelt Jones."

Noel Coward's revue *Set to Music* (1/18/39; 129 performances) featured Beatrice Lillie singing such Coward songs as "I Went to a Marvelous Party" and "Mad About the Boy."

Kaufman and Hart were back at the theater with *The Man Who Came to Dinner* (10/16/39; 739 performances) starring Monty Woolley as Sheridan Whiteside, a character based on Alexander Woollcott (q.v.). The play was an immediate hit and made Woollcott an even bigger celebrity in the public's eyes. Woollcott begged to play the part, although he had originally refused it. He was finally hired to lead the Pacific Coast company.

Michael Todd's production of *Star and Garter* (6/24/42; 605 performances) opened at the Music Box with Gypsy Rose Lee, Bobby Clark, Pat Harrington and Professor Lamberti. Critics were not kind to the show, which had more in common with burlesque *(q.v.)* than musical comedy, but audiences loved being able to see burlesque in the safe environs of Broadway.

I Remember Mama (10/19/44; 714 performances) was one of the best loved comedies of the forties. The play, written and directed by John Van Druten, starred Mady Christians, Oscar Homolka, Frances Heflin and, making his Broadway debut, Marlon Brando. The first-time Broadway producers were the renowned songwriting team Richard Rodgers and Oscar Hammerstein II *(q.v.)*.

Tennessee Williams's *(q.v.)* *Summer and Smoke* (10/10/48; 102 performances) was not a success. One problem was that audiences had seen *A Streetcar Named Desire* the previous year and expected more of the same. Williams actually wrote *Summer and Smoke* before *Streetcar* and after *The Glass Menagerie,* to which it is very similar in tone.

Kurt Weill's *(q.v.)* *Lost in the Stars* (10/30/49; 281 performances) was written with Maxwell Anderson. The Playwrights' Company *(q.v.)* produced the musical which was based on Alan Paton's novel *Cry, the Beloved Country,* which dealt with race relations in South Africa. Weill and Anderson's dramatic score was well served by Inez Matthews, Julian Mayfield, Herbert Coleman and the original Porgy, Todd Duncan.

William Inge had three plays open in the Music Box in quick succession. The first, *Picnic* (2/19/53; 477 performances), starred Ralph Meeker and Janice Rule under Joshua Logan's sensitive direction. *Picnic* didn't please all the critics but they did agree that Inge had the makings of a major American playwright.

The critics were unanimous in acclaiming Inge's next play, *Bus Stop* (3/2/55; 478 performances). They praised Inge for tempering his themes of loneliness and the longing for dreams to come true. *Bus Stop* starred Kim Stanley, Albert Salmi, Elaine Stritch, Anthony Ross, Lou Polan and Phyllis Love. Harold Clurman directed brilliantly, helping Inge make the conflicts more human and sometimes even funny.

Inge's third play was *The Dark at the Top of the Stairs* (12/5/57; 468 performances). Through the story of a boy's suicide, Inge explored the unbreakable links that bind a family and the search for true freedom and tolerance. Pat Hingle and Teresa Wright starred, and Elia Kazan directed.

Claire Bloom and Rod Steiger were featured in the hit play *Rashomon* (1/27/59; 159 performances) at the Music Box, and at the end of that year Peter Shaffer's first play, *Five Finger Exercise* (12/2/59; 337 performances), opened at the theater with Jessica Tandy and Brian Bedford. Shaffer was hailed because of his excel-

lent use of language as well as his incisive understanding of class, society and sexual tensions. One of England's "angry young men" who changed the face of British drama, Shaffer impressed critics as having the artistic and technical means to convey the ideas that less-talented playwrights were raving about.

Following Henry Denker's play about Sigmund Freud, *A Far Country* (4/4/61; 271 performances), with Kim Stanley and Steven Hill, came S.J. Perleman's comedy, *The Beauty Part* (12/26/62; 85 performances). It opened to excellent reviews, but due in part to the newspaper strike of 1962-63 *(q.v.)*, it closed a failure. Marilyn Stasio described the play as "a mad show, a happy marriage of the most refined wit with the most insane low-comedy traditions. It was eighteenth-century rococo literary humor laced with pit humor. It was the world of baroque in tandem with the world of burlesque. It was a howl." Bert Lahr and the whole cast gave an inspired performance, or rather a series of inspired performances. There were 17 people in the cast playing 40-50 parts. The characters had names like Octavia Weatherwax, Vernon Equinox, April Monkhood, Chenille Schreiber and Mrs. Lafcadio Mifflin.

The comedy *Any Wednesday* (2/18/64; 983 performances) opened with Don Porter, Sandy Dennis, Gene Hackman and Rosemary Murphy. The show, Muriel Resnik's first play, suffered a particularly grueling tryout period before its opening. The playwright told the story of her play's difficult birth in one of the great theater books, *Son of Any Wednesday*. After changes in cast and directors, the show opened to rave reviews.

Harold Pinter's disturbing drama *The Homecoming* (1/5/67; 324 performances) opened direct from the Royal Shakespeare Company. The play concerns a university teacher's wife who decides to become a prostitute and move in with her in-laws. Some critics viewed the play as an indictment of the drawing-room comedy. Others felt that the play had no viewpoint. Pinter became one of the most important playwrights of his time.

Following Terrence Frisby's *There's a Girl in My Soup* (10/18/67; 321 performances) with Gig Young came Anthony Shaffer's *Sleuth* (11/12/70; 1,222 performances). The two-character mystery thriller opened with Anthony Quayle and Keith Baxter.

The British invasion continued with Alan Ayckbourn's *Absurd Person Singular* (10/8/74; 592 performances) produced by the Theater Guild *(q.v.)* and the John F. Kennedy Center. Another English import, *Comedians* (11/28/76; 145 performances) by Trevor Griffiths was followed by another show developed in England. *Side By Side By Sondheim* (4/18/77; 390 performances), a retrospective of Stephen Sondheim's *(q.v.)* works, starred the original English cast: Ned Sherrin, David Kernan, Millicent Martin and Julia McKenzie.

Playwright Ira Levin brought another thriller to the

The Music Box Theater

Music Box with *Deathtrap* (2/26/78; 1,793 performances). The play starred John Wood and actress Marian Seldes. She stayed with the show throughout its run.

The Music Box Theater's last hit was John Pielmeier's *Agnes of God* (3/30/82; 486 performances). Geraldine Page and Amanda Plummer starred in the mystery/drama.

On December 8, 1987, the New York City Landmarks Preservation Commission designated the interior and exterior of the theater a landmark. The Commission stated that the theater's neo-federal facade was "exceptionally handsome," with a double-height loggia and flanking Palladian windows. Inside are "elegant semi-circular boxes" and "classically inspired plasterwork."

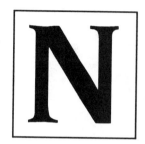

NATIONAL THEATRE See NEDERLANDER THEATER.

NEDERLANDER THEATRE 208 W. 41st Street. Architect: William N. Smith. Opening: September 1, 1921; *Swords*. The theater, built by Walter C. Jordan, a theatrical agent, opened as the National in 1921. It reputedly cost $950,000 to build and contained 1,200 seats. Its first production, *Swords*, was also the first play by Sidney Howard.

The National presented a series of fine plays with great stars. One of the biggest successes was John Willard's *The Cat and the Canary* (2/2/22; 349 performances). The thriller would be revived on Broadway in 1937 and was made into movies on several occasions. Actor/producer Walter Hampden brought a production of *Cyrano de Bergerac* (11/1/23; 250 performances) there and returned to the National in *Hamlet*, which moved from the Hampden Theater. Chester Morris and Spencer Tracy appeared in *Yellow*, (9/21/26; 132 performances); magician Harry Houdini brought his magic show, *Houdini Lives* to the theater in 1926. More great stars appeared on the National's stage in the twenties: Fredric March in *The Half-Caste* (3/29/26; 63 performances) and Ann Harding in *The Trial of Mary Dugan* (9/19/27; 437 performances).

The 1930s and the Depression, although disastrous for most theaters, proved no problem to the National. Great stars continued to grace its stage: Eugenie Leontovich, Henry Hull and Sam Jaffe in Vicki Baum's *Grand Hotel*, (11/13/30; 444 performances); Pauline Lord, Ruth Gordon and Raymond Massey in *Ethan Frome* (1/21/36; 119 performances); and *Tonight at 8:30* (11/24/36; 113 performances) by Noel Coward, starring the author and Gertrude Lawrence.

The Mercury Theater under the direction of Orson Welles presented *Julius Caesar* at the National on November 11, 1937, and followed it with Thomas Dek-

ker's *The Shoemaker's Holiday* (1/1/38; 69 performances). Tallulah Bankhead gave her greatest performance in Lillian Hellman's *The Little Foxes* (2/15/39; 410 performances). Brooks Atkinson's comment on Tallulah's performance: "She plays with superb command of the entire character—sparing of the showy

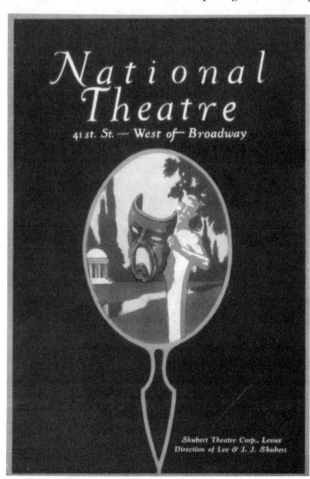

Program for the National Theatre

side, constantly aware of the poisonous spirit within." Bankhead herself described the character of Regina Giddens as "souless and sadistic, an unmitigated murderess." Much of the credit for Tallulah's performance went to her director, Herman Shumlin. He made sure she didn't rely on the tried-and-true gimmicks that served her in the past. Ethel Barrymore (q.v.) took stage in Emlyn Williams's *The Corn Is Green* (11/26/40; 477 performances).

The forties were also good years for the National. Some of the highlights of this decade were Maurice Evans and Judith Anderson in Shakespeare's *Macbeth* (11/11/41). Lerner and Loewe's (q.v.) first musical, *What's Up?* (11/11/43; 63 performances) was a quick failure. Eva Le Gallienne and Joseph Schildkraut appeared in Chekhov's *The Cherry Orchard* (1/25/44). Lerner and Loewe returned with *The Day Before Spring* (11/22/45; 165 performances), a moderate success. Harold Rome's (q.v.) musical revue *Call Me Mister* (4/18/46; 734 performances) with Betty Garrett introduced the songs "South America, Take It Away," "The Face on the Dime" and "The Red Ball Express." Judith Anderson returned, this time with John Gielgud, in *Medea* (10/20/47; 214 performances). A musical revue, *Lend An Ear* (12/16/48; 460 performances) by Charles Gaynor, followed. John Garfield appeared with Nancy Kelly in *The Big Knife* (2/24/49; 109 performances). The forties came to a close with George Bernard Shaw's *Caesar and Cleopatra* (12/21/49) with Sir Cedric Hardwicke, Arthur Treacher and Lilli Palmer.

The quality of the offerings stayed high through the 1950s. Katharine Cornell (q.v.), Grace George and Brian Aherne were featured in a revival of *The Constant Wife* (12/8/51) and Margaret Sullavan and Joseph Cotten followed in *Sabrina Fair* (11/11/53; 318 performances). The next major production at the National was *Inherit the Wind* (4/21/55; 806 performances). This huge hit, a retelling of the Scopes Monkey Trial, starred Paul Muni, Ed Begley and Tony Randall. Arlene Francis, Walter Matthau and Joseph Cotten appeared in *Once More with Feeling* (10/21/58; 263 performances). Harry Kurnitz's light comedy was the National's last success under its original name.

In 1959, showman Billy Rose bought the National and reopened it as the Billy Rose Theater on October 18, 1959, with Shaw's *Heartbreak House*. Katharine Cornell made her last Broadway appearance in Jerome Kilty's *Dear Liar* (3/17/60; 52 performances) with Brian Aherne. Edward Albee's *Who's Afraid of Virginia Woolf?* (10/13/62; 664 performances) grabbed audiences with an intensity rarely seen on Broadway. George and Martha, the play's protagonists, cannot live in peace since they cannot face their own reality. Their fantasies, supposedly their only real communication, actually keep them apart. By the end of the wrenching drama, the couple begin to take the first halting and sincere steps

at relating to each other. George Grizzard, Arthur Hill, Uta Hagen and Melinda Dillon starred in the drama.

As production on Broadway slowed, the theater had increasing spells when it was dark. Edward Albee's *Tiny Alice* was a failure of 1964 (12/29/64; 167 performances). The play examined the theme of reality through a dialogue on religion. Critics claimed to be confused about the writing, and indeed it was difficult to follow.

Tammy Grimes and Brian Bedford appeared in a notable revival of Noel Coward's *Private Lives* at the end of the sixties. The Royal Shakespeare Company came to the Billy Rose in 1971 with Peter Brook's outrageous production of *A Midsummer Night's Dream*.

Harold Pinter's *Old Times* (11/16/71; 119 performances) examined a marriage and relationships by having a husband deal simultaneously with his wife and another woman who is actually his wife at a younger age. The play proved confusing to audiences, since Pinter didn't let the audience in on his conceit. It is considered among the best of the modern plays to grace Broadway. Another English playwright, Tom Stoppard, had his play *Jumpers* presented (4/22/74; 48 performances), but it didn't translate well on the American stage and closed after 48 performances.

The English influence continued when the theater was bought by James and Joseph Nederlander and the British team of Cooney-Marsh. In 1979, the name was changed to The Trafalgar and after a refurbishment opened with Brian Clark's *Whose Life Is It Anyway?* (4/17/79; 223 performances), starring Tom Conti. Mary Tyler Moore took over the lead role—and won an honorary Tony Award (q.v.). It was followed with Harold Pinter's drama, *Betrayal* (1/5/80; 170 performances). Pinter kept up his experiments with dramatic form and constructed his play so that the first scenes took place in the most recent time frame. Each succeeding scene went further back in time. *Betrayal* was like one long flashback. The technique wasn't new; Kaufman and Hart tried it with their play *Merrily We Roll Along* in 1934. *Betrayal,* with an excellent three-person cast (Blythe Danner, Roy Scheider and Raul Julia) deserved a much longer run.

In late 1980, the theater, renamed again, became the Nederlander. Lena Horne appeared in a one-woman show in 1981. Since then a string of failures have been presented on its stage: *84 Charing Cross Road;* a musical version of James Baldwin's *Amen Corner;* Peter Ustinov's *Beethoven's Tenth;* a musical based on Kenneth Grahame's children's book *The Wind in the Willows;* a musical version of *Raggedy Ann;* and Frank Langella in *Sherlock's Last Case* have all seen short runs at the theater.

Following the run of *Sherlock's Last Case* at the end of 1987, the Nederlanders rented the theater to a church group for services. The church moved to the larger Mark Hellinger Theater in 1989. The theater has been granted "distressed" status by the theater's unions, thereby making it eligible for reduced minimums and fees.

NEIL SIMON THEATER 250 W. 52nd Street. Architect: Herbert J. Krapp. Opening: November 20, 1927; *Funny Face.* The early history of the Neil Simon Theater is also the history of the producing team of Alex A. Aarons and Vinton Freedley *(q.v.).* Like other producers, Aarons and Freedley wanted their own theater. They built it in 1927 and chose the name Alvin by combining the first letters of their first names. The Adamesque theater is best known for the many successful musicals that enjoyed long runs on its stage. This tradition began with the first production, *Funny Face.*

Funny Face (11/20/27; 250 performances) boasted a score by George and Ira Gershwin *(q.v.)* and a libretto by Paul Gerard Smith and Fred Thompson. The show starred Fred and Adele Astaire *(q.v.),* Victor Moore and Allen Kearns. The score included such standards as "Funny Face," " 'S Wonderful" and "My One and Only."

Next, a number of short-running musicals played the Alvin: *Here's Howe!* (5/1/28; 71 performances); *Treasure Girl* (11/8/28; 69 performances), a Gershwin show starring Gertrude Lawrence (with an exceptional score, including "Feeling I'm Falling," "I Don't Think I'll Fall in Love Today," "I've Got a Crush on You," "Oh, So Nice" and "Where's the Boy, Here's the Girl"); and *Spring Is Here* (3/11/29; 104 performances) by Rodgers and Hart *(q.v.).*

The Gershwins were back with a major hit, *Girl Crazy* (10/14/30; 272 performances). Ethel Merman *(q.v.),* making her Broadway debut, costarred with Willie Howard and, in her second Broadway appearance, Ginger Rogers. The score included "Bidin' My Time," "But Not for Me," "Embraceable You," "I Got Rhythm," "Sam and Delilah" and "Treat Me Rough." In the orchestra were Benny Goodman, Glenn Miller, Red Nichols, Jimmy Dorsey, Jack Teagarden and Gene Krupa.

Alvin Theater   Courtesy Billy Rose Theater Collection.

After *Girl Crazy,* the theater's ownership reverted to the firm that built it. The new owners booked the Alvin's first straight play, Maxwell Anderson's *Mary of Scotland* (11/27/33; 236 performances) with Helen Hayes (*q.v.*) as the tragic queen Mary Stuart.

Following his partner's death in 1933, Vinton Freedley returned to the Alvin to produce *Anything Goes* (11/21/34; 415 performances). Cole Porter (*q.v.*) wrote the score, and Ethel Merman, Victor Moore, William Gaxton and Vivian Vance sang such hits as "All Through the Night," "I Get a Kick Out of You," "You're the Top" and the title song.

For *Red, Hot and Blue!* (10/29/36; 181 performances), Porter, Merman and Freedley were reunited with other *Anything Goes* alumni Russel Crouse, Howard Lindsay and Vivian Vance. Merman was aided and abetted by Bob Hope and Jimmy Durante. The big hit song was "It's Delovely."

The Alvin next hosted Rodgers and Hart's *I'd Rather Be Right* (11/2/37; 289 performances). George M. Cohan (*q.v.*) made his next to last Broadway appearance as the then-current President, Franklin D. Roosevelt. The libretto by George S. Kaufman and Moss Hart (*q.v.*) allowed for some gentle ribbing of the current administration as well as room for a good score, which featured "Have You Met Miss Jones?"

Rodgers and Hart returned with *The Boys from Syracuse* (11/23/38; 235 performances) based on Shakespeare's *A Comedy of Errors.* The musical featured such great songs as "Falling in Love with Love," "This Can't Be Love" and "Sing for Your Supper." George Abbott (*q.v.*) produced, directed and supplied the book. The musical showcased choreography by George Balanchine.

Another straight play next occupied the Alvin's stage. Alfred Lunt and Lynn Fontanne (*q.v.*) starred in Robert E. Sherwood's *There Shall Be No Night* (4/29/40; 115 performances). After its New York run, the show was taken on tour and returned September 9 for an additional 66 performances before a second tour was undertaken. The play, which featured the young Montgomery Clift, won for Sherwood his third Pulitzer Prize. Altogether, the Lunts played over 1,600 performances, including a run in London, cut short when their theater was bombed during the Blitz.

The following occupant of the Alvin was among the first shows to explore psychiatry, *Lady in the Dark* (1/23/41; 162 performances). The musical starred Gertrude Lawrence, returning to the Alvin in a better vehicle than her previous offering, *Treasure Girl.* Kurt Weill (*q.v.*) and Ira Gershwin supplied the score to a libretto by Moss Hart.

Musical comedy continued at the Alvin with Cole Porter providing Ethel Merman with another starring vehicle, *Something for the Boys* (1/7/43; 422 performances). This undistinguished show enjoyed a long run, which was surprising because no hit songs came from the Michael Todd production. *Jackpot* (1/13/44; 44 performances), a Vernon Duke (*q.v.*) and Howard Dietz (*q.v.*) show, returned Freedley to the Alvin.

The Alvin was the home to distinguished performances: Ingrid Bergman in Maxwell Anderson's *Joan of Lorraine* (11/28/46; 199 performances); Maurice Evans in George Bernard Shaw's *Man and Superman* (10/8/47; 294 performances); Henry Fonda and David Wayne in Joshua Logan and Thomas Heggen's wartime comedy *Mister Roberts* (2/18/48; 1,157 performances) and Claude Rains in Sidney Kingsley's *Darkness at Noon* (1/13/51; 186 performances).

Musical comedy returned to the Alvin with *A Tree Grows in Brooklyn* (4/19/51; 267 performances), starring Shirley Booth. Novelist Betty Smith cowrote the libretto with George Abbott, who also served as director and producer. Arthur Schwartz (*q.v.*) and Dorothy Fields (*q.v.*) wrote a beautiful score.

Henry Fonda returned to the Alvin in *Point of No Return* (12/13/51; 364 performances) and Mary Martin (*q.v.*) appeared in the comedy *Kind Sir* (1/4/53; 165 performances) with Charles Boyer.

Melodies by Harold Arlen (*q.v.*) next filled the Alvin in *House of Flowers* (12/30/54; 165 performances). Truman Capote was the unlikely author of the book and coauthor of the lyrics with Arlen. Pearl Bailey and Juanita Hall starred in the show, but the best songs, "A Sleepin' Bee" and "I Never Has Seen Snow," went to newcomer Diahann Carroll.

Andy Griffith made his Broadway debut in *No Time for Sergeants* (10/20/55; 796 performances) by Ira Levin. Lucille Ball made her Broadway debut in *Wildcat* (12/16/60; 171 performances). Cy Coleman and Carolyn Leigh provided the score, and N. Richard Nash wrote the book. Stephen Sondheim's (*q.v.*) first score for which he provided both music and lyrics, *A Funny Thing Happened on the Way to the Forum* (5/8/62; 965 performances), starred Zero Mostel and Jack Gilford. *High Spirits* (5/7/64; 375 performances), top-lined Beatrice Lillie and Tammy Grimes and was based on director Noel Coward's play *Blithe Spirit.* The musical had a fine libretto and excellent score by Hugh Martin and Timothy Gray.

Liza Minnelli was the next major star to make her Broadway debut at the Alvin. The vehicle was the John Kander and Fred Ebb musical, *Flora, the Red Menace* (5/11/65; 87 performances). George Abbott (*q.v.*) coauthored the script with Robert Russell and also directed the Harold Prince production.

Rosencrantz and Guildenstern Are Dead (10/16/67; 420 performances) was hailed by the London newspaper *The Observer* as "the most brilliant debut of the sixties." Though it didn't prove as successful as expected, the David Merrick (*q.v.*) production certainly proved a remarkable introduction to the remarkable talents of English playwright Tom Stoppard.

James Earl Jones and Jane Alexander brought Howard Sackler's epic drama, *The Great White Hope* (10/3/68; 556 performances), to the Alvin. The dramatic retelling of the life of prizefighter Jack Johnson won the Pulitzer Prize. The play was originally produced by the Washington, D.C., Arena Stage and was the first important sign that America's resident theaters would play an ever-increasing role in the development of new American plays.

Company (4/26/70; 690 performances), the Stephen Sondheim musical, was next at the Alvin. Sondheim and librettist George Furth's examination of marriage was an important link between musicals of the past and the new style of musical in which the libretto moved in an often nonchronological fashion.

Shenandoah's (1/7/75; 1,050 performances) long run was based largely on the success of its television advertisement. The Gary Geld and Peter Udell score didn't have any popular songs, and the show itself received mostly lukewarm reviews.

The next musical at the Alvin became one of the most popular in the theater's history. *Annie* (4/21/77; 2,377 performances), with music by Charles Strouse *(q.v.)* and lyrics by Martin Charnin, was based on the comic strip "Little Orphan Annie." The show introduced a new standard, the song "Tomorrow." *Annie* moved from the Alvin, making room for another huge success.

The first play of a trilogy by Neil Simon *(q.v.)*, *Brighton Beach Memoirs* (3/27/83), moved to make room for the second in the trilogy, *Biloxi Blues*. Again, Matthew Broderick starred. On June 29, 1983, the Alvin was renamed the Neil Simon for its new owner.

The theater community raised a small cry over the Alvin's renaming. It seemed unfair that the Alvin, a historic name and the scene of most of the Gershwins' greatest successes, should be renamed the Neil Simon, while the Uris Theatre *(q.v.)* should be rechristened the Gershwin. But the great sign that spelled out Alvin (and had been altered to read ANNIE while that show was in residence) was changed to Simon.

The New York City Landmarks Preservation Commission designated the exterior and interior of the Neil Simon a landmark.

NEW AMSTERDAM THEATRE 214 W. 42nd Street. Architects: Herts and Tallant. Opening: November 2, 1903; A *Midsummer Night's Dream*. The New Amsterdam, called "The House Beautiful" for all its legitimate life, "is considered the most attractive of all Broadway Theaters and certainly the most deserving of preservation in the proposed 42nd Street Redevelopment Project." The theater, whose exterior and interior are designated historical landmarks by the New York City Landmarks

Program for the New Amsterdam Theatre

Commission, stands as a relic of the greatness of its productions.

Klaw and Erlanger built their new theater as the flagship of their Theatrical Syndicate. They spent $1.5 million and for their money got a legitimate theater, an office building and a 1,200-seat rooftop theater.

When the New Amsterdam opened in 1903, the *New York Times* described it for its eager readers under the headline "The House Beautiful": "In the New Amsterdam, Art Nouveau, first crystallized in the Paris Exposition of 1900, is typified on a large scale in America. The color scheme is of the most delicate reds and green and dull gold. Such painters as E.Y. Simmons and Robert Blum, sculptors, George Gray, Hugh Tallant and Enid Yandell and such designers as Wenzel and Ostertag have worked in harmony and with inspiration! The allied arts of painting, sculpture and architecture have, through their exponents, combined to produce a result that astonishes and delights, and whose effect and feeling are that of permanence, durability and extreme beauty."

The auditorium, designed in the then rare style of art nouveau, was described in the *Dramatic Mirror* as "beyond question the most gorgeous playhouse in New York." The architects used three motifs throughout the building: the history of New Amsterdam from Hendrik Hudson to 1903, the history of theater and the typical art nouveau floral and fauna motifs. Murals and friezes depict scenes from Shakespeare's *Macbeth,* Homer's *Odyssey* and the operas of Wagner. Busts of Shakespeare and Homer look down from on high above the vaulted ceilings. The theater's color scheme was basically green with mauve accents. No primary colors were used in the design.

At the time, the New Amsterdam was the largest theater in New York with seats for 1,800 patrons. It was among the first nonskyscrapers to use structural steel in its construction. The 70-ton main girder over the ceiling was the largest piece of steel in any building. The balconies did not have the common pillars blocking the audience's view. Instead, they were cantilevered into the theater's structure. The orchestra was designed to be quickly changed into a ballroom; however, the conversion never took place.

Under Klaw and Erlanger's direction, the New Amsterdam presented many of the great hits of the early 20th century. An early musical-comedy success, *Whoop-De-Doo* (9/24/03; 151 performances), had Weber and Fields (see FIELDS FAMILY), starring and producing and marking the end of their long partnership. They would change their mind years later and reteam briefly.

In 1904, the producers opened a different kind of rooftop theater. Most were summer gardens with a small platform acting like a stage. But the New Amsterdam boasted a complete miniature theater on its roof. Though it could be used year-round, it was used only during the summer months. The first shows were variety programs.

While the main auditorium presented its schedule of shows, the rooftop theater, called the Aerial Gardens, had its own schedule. It replaced variety with a series of musicals and operettas but still closed for the winter months.

New Yorkers saw their first production of Goldsmith's *She Stoops to Conquer* (4/17/05; 24 performances) at the New Amsterdam. The comedy starred Eleanor Robson. Another great American actor, Richard Mansfield, played a limited engagement at the New Amsterdam each season.

The music of George M. Cohan *(q.v.)* filled the theater when *Forty-Five Minutes from Broadway* (1/1/06; 90 performances) opened. Cohan's *The Governor's Son* was revived upstairs on June 4, 1906 with the Cohan family starring. *The Honeymooners* (6/30/07; 72 performances), which opened at the Aerial Gardens, was a revision of Cohan's musical *Running for Office.*

A smash hit for the New Amsterdam and one of the most influential shows of the early 20th century was Franz Lehar's operetta *The Merry Widow* (10/21/07; 416 performances). Its first American production opened at the New Amsterdam with Ethel Jackson portraying the widow. The play was influenced by both musical comedy and women's fashions. *The Merry Widow* hat became a quick-selling item. To celebrate the 275th performance of the show, producer Henry Savage offered each woman in attendance a free hat. What the *New York Times* referred to as a "hot skirmish" ensued when 1,300 women showed up for the June 13 matinee. Savage had bought only 1,200 hats. The producer promised the extra 100 women their own hats at a later date. *The Merry Widow* survived the stunt *(q.v.)* and moved upstairs to the Aerial Gardens for the summer of 1908. It finally closed after returning to the main auditorium.

European-style operetta continued on the New Amsterdam stage with *The Silver Star* (11/01/09; 80 performances) by Robin Hood Bowers and Harry B. Smith *(q.v.).* A new melodrama, *Madame X* (2/2/10; 125 performances), is now a sort of camp classic. It concerned a lawyer who prosecutes his mother. Of course, in the melodrama, he doesn't know who the lady is. Despite the critics' scoffing, the show enjoyed a Broadway revival and three film verisions. There was also a burlesque of the popular hit produced at the Victoria Theater's *(q.v.)* roof garden.

A European operetta, *Madame Sherry* (8/30/10; 231 performances), opened at the New Amsterdam with a popular Karl Hoschna score. Another European-influenced show that also became a smash hit at the New Amsterdam was Ivan Caryll's *The Pink Lady* (3/13/11; 312 performances). It made a star of Hazel Dawn.

A huge hit in the 1800s, Reginald DeKoven and Harry B. Smith's operetta *Robin Hood* (5/6/12; 64 performances), did not have a long run in its revival at the New Amsterdam. However, during the revival it did mark over 6,000 performances since its first presentation. Another perennial favorite, *The Count of Luxembourg* (9/16/12) featured a score by Franz Lehar, the composer of *The Merry Widow.*

Oh! Oh! Delphine (9/30/12; 248 performances) brought Ivan Caryll's tunes back to the New Amsterdam. Caryll followed this success with another, *The Little Cafe* (11/10/13; 144 performances).

The next tenant of the New Amsterdam changed its history for almost two decades, and the producer became the most successful in Broadway history. On June 16, 1913, Florenz Ziegfeld *(q.v.)* moved his *Ziegfeld Follies (q.v.)* to the New Amsterdam from the Moulin Rouge. From that year until he moved to the new Ziegfeld Theater *(q.v.)* in 1927, Ziegfeld presented an annual revue at the New Amsterdam (he missed only one year, 1926, because of a legal problem over the name Follies). Ziegfeld brought some of the greatest stars of Broadway to the New Amsterdam. Leon Errol, Bert Williams, Fanny Brice *(q.v.),* Will Rogers, Lillian

The New Amsterdam Theatre

Lorraine, W.C. Fields, Marion Davies, Carl Randall, Elizabeth Brice, Ann Pennington, Ina Claire, Mae Murray, Eddie Cantor, Joe Frisco, Marilyn Miller, John Steel, Van and Schenck, Bert and Betty Wheeler, Brooke Johns, Lupino Lane, Vivienne Segal, George Olsen, Ethel Shutta and Paul Whiteman were just some of the stars appearing in the *Follies*.

During the reign of the *Ziegfeld Follies* at the New Amsterdam, the theater housed other productions between *Follies* editions including the Victor Herbert *(q.v.)* and Robert B. Smith classic, *Sweethearts* (9/08/13), Herman Finck and C.M.S. McClelland's *Around the Map* (11/01/15), *The Girl Behind the Gun* (9/16/18) with music by Ivan Caryll and *The Velvet Lady* (2/3/19) with a score by Victor Herbert and Henry Blossom.

Ziegfeld not only produced the annual edition of the *Follies,* but he also presented many successful musical comedies and a series of revues on the New Amsterdam's roof. In 1914, he renamed the roof theater the Danse de Follies and installed a 22,000-square-foot dance floor for the summertime attraction.

Ziegfeld's musical presentations downstairs began with *Sally* (12/21/20; 570 performances). Marilyn Miller, Walter Catlett and Ziegfeld favorite Leon Errol starred in the Jerome Kern *(q.v.),* P.G. Wodehouse, Clifford Grey and Guy Bolton *(q.v.)* show. The hit songs included the title song and two with lyrics by B.G. DeSylva *(q.v.).* The first was "Whip-Poor-Will" and the other "Look for the Silver Lining," one of the greatest of all American popular songs.

Ziegfeld and his sometime-coproducer Charles Dil-

lingham refurbished the New Amsterdam's roof and opened a show called *Cinders* (4/3/23; 31 performances). The musical was presented in what was at that time called the Dresden Theater. *Cinders* had a score by Rudolf Friml *(q.v.).* On September 12, 1923, the roof garden was named the Frolic Theater with a foreign theater troupe's production of *Teatro dei Piccoli.*

Marilyn Miller and Jerome Kern were involved in another hit musical at the New Amsterdam, *Sunny* (9/22/25; 517 performances). This time, the book and lyrics were supplied by Oscar Hammerstein II *(q.v.)* and Otto Harbach *(q.v.).* The cast also included Cliff Edwards, Pert Kelton, Jack Donahue and Clifton Webb. One of the five choreographers was Fred Astaire *(q.v.).* The big songs from this score were the title song and "Who?," another smash hit for the Kern catalog.

After the short-lived run of the Rodgers and Hart *(q.v.)* musical *Betsy* (12/28/26; 35 performances) the New Amsterdam hosted an all-star production of *Trelawney of the Wells.* The stars included Helen Gahagan, John E. Kellerd, Otto Kruger, Wilton Lackaye, Henrietta Crosman, Rollo Peters, Estelle Winwood, John Drew, Pauline Lord and Effie Shannon.

For one week, the Frolic Theater hosted a play called *He Loved the Ladies* (5/10/27). The show's Thursday matinee played for no patrons. Not one audience member was present when the curtain rose. Statisticians disagree whether the play can claim to have run six performances or seven, and whether a performance counts as a performance if there is no one there to see it.

Musical comedy triumphed again at the New Amsterdam with Ziegfeld's production of *Rosalie* (1/10/28; 327 performances) boasting a score by George and Ira Gershwin *(q.v.).* Sigmund Romberg *(q.v.)* and P.G. Wodehouse contributed an equal number of songs, but they took a back seat to such future Gershwin standards as "How Long Has This Been Going On?," "The Man I Love" (cut prior to the show's opening) and "Oh Gee! Oh Joy!" The show starred the New Amsterdam favorite, Marilyn Miller, along with Jack Donahue and Frank Morgan.

Ziegfeld's next offering at the New Amsterdam was the Walter Donaldson and Gus Kahn hit, *Whoopee* (12/4/28; 255 performances). Eddie Cantor was joined by other cast members, including Ruth Etting, George Olsen's Orchestra, Tamara Geva and Ethel Shutta. The better-than-average score yielded such musical comedy gems as "Love Me or Leave Me," "Makin' Whoopee" and "I'm Bringing a Red, Red Rose." The show that followed was the fifth production of William Gillette's American classic *Sherlock Holmes* (11/25/29); it played only briefly at the New Amsterdam.

The New Amsterdam's survival at the beginning of the Depression was a testament to its good reputation with producers and audiences. The beginning of the thirties saw only a slight falling off in the number or quality of shows premiering at the theater. However, the rooftop Frolics Theater did not fare so well.

Bookings fell off throughout Times Square and only the theaters with the most advantageous location could keep lit. As 1930 turned to 1931, *Variety (q.v.)* reported that 31 theaters were dark in what was usually a busy holiday season. A theater on a roof, without a proper marquee, wasn't attractive to those producers still operating. Erlanger announced that the Frolics would undergo another transformation. The proscenium arch was filled in with a movable wall of glass. The sound-proofed wall allowed the theater to operate as a legitimate theater, a radio studio and a feature film studio. Erlanger even predicted that the theater would be used for television. In 1930, the theater became NBC Times Square Studio. Erlanger died on March 7, 1930. But his theater continued to prosper for a time.

Earl Carroll's Vanities of 1930 (q.v.) (7/1/30; 215 performances) featured Jack Benny, Patsy Kelly, Jimmy Savo and Herb Williams. Hit songs were mainly by Harold Arlen *(q.v.)* and Ted Koehler and included "Contagious Rhythm," "Hittin' the Bottle" and "The March of Time." *Vanities* was followed by probably the greatest revue in musical comedy history, *The Band Wagon* (6/3/31; 262 performances). Max Gordon produced the new revue, which boasted performances by Fred and Adele Astaire *(q.v.)*, Helen Broderick, Tilly Losch and Frank Morgan. The exceptional Arthur Schwartz *(q.v.)* and Howard Dietz *(q.v.)* score included "High and Low," "I Love Louisa," "New Sun in the Sky," "White Heat" and the classic "Dancing in the Dark."

The next New Amsterdam attraction was the Irving Berlin and Moss Hart *(q.v.)* revue *Face the Music* (2/17/32; 166 performances). This sometimes humorous, sometimes trenchant musical revue starred Mary Boland, J. Harold Murray and Andrew Tombes. The two big song hits from the score were "Let's Have Another Cup of Coffee" and "Soft Lights and Sweet Music."

Following the close of *Face the Music,* the theater had its first shaky season. The 1932-33 season found no musical presentation premiering. Producers simply didn't have enough money to launch a large number of new operettas or musical comedies. *Murder at the Vanities* (9/12/33; 298 performances) was the next hit to play the New Amsterdam. The Earl Carroll production gave audiences both a murder mystery and a full musical revue. One production number, "Virgins Wrapped in Cellophane," gives a clue to the reason for the show's long run.

Roberta (11/18/33; 294 performances), with a score by Jerome Kern *(q.v.)* and Otto Harbach *(q.v.)*, starred George Murphy, Lyda Roberti, Bob Hope, Sydney Greenstreet, Tamara and Fay Templeton, marking her 50th anniversary in the theater. A youthful Fred MacMurray appeared as one of the California Collegians. The score introduced such perennials as "Smoke

Interior of the New Amsterdam Theatre

Gets in Your Eyes," "I'll Be Hard to Handle" (with lyrics by Bernard Dougall), "The Touch of Your Hand" and "Yesterdays."

Dietz and Schwartz returned to the New Amsterdam with their new show *Revenge with Music* (11/28/34; 158 performances). The show was the only legitimate theater production on 42nd Street. The rest of the theaters had converted to sub-run motion pictures, were presenting burlesque or were closed. The musical had a superior score, including "When You Love Only One," "If There Is Someone Lovelier Than You" and "You and the Night and the Music."

Having hosted many editions of the *Ziegfeld Follies* and the 1930 *Earl Carroll's Vanities,* the New Amsterdam seemed a natural for *George White's Scandals (q.v.)* (12/25/35; 120 performances). The *Scandals* were short on material and stars but long on beautiful seminude chorines. This last edition of the *Scandals* featured hit songs including "Are You Havin' Any Fun?," "The Mexiconga" and "Something I Dreamed Last Night."

On May 7, 1936, the Dry Dock Savings Institution foreclosed on the New Amsterdam Theatre. There was $1.6 million due in interest and taxes. Max Cohen, a theater owner who also owned the Harris *(q.v.)* and Wallack's (see Lew M. Fields Theatre) theaters put up $500,000 to purchase the New Amsterdam. By then, all the owners of the theater—Erlanger, Ziegfeld and Dillingham—were dead. Cohen was forbidden to present burlesque in the theater.

The New Amsterdam reopened on July 3, 1937, with a showing of the movie *A Midsummer Night's Dream,* the film version of the first play to occupy the New Amsterdam's stage.

On September 12, 1937, the rooftop theater was renamed the WOR-Mutual Radio Theater and served as home for the show "Tim and Irene's Fun in Swingtime."

Sigmund Romberg found his popularity decreasing when *Forbidden Melody* (11/2/36; 32 performances) opened at the theater. The run reflected the change in taste along Broadway. European operettas were no longer in vogue. New composers like the Gershwins and Rodgers and Hart *(q.v.)* would inherit the mantle of popularity from such European stalwarts as Herbert, Friml and Romberg.

A production of *Othello* (1/6/37; 21 performances) was to be the last live attraction at the New Amsterdam. It featured Walter Huston in the title role. The rooftop theater returned to legitimate use as the New Amsterdam Roof with the production of *The Petrified Forest* (11/1/43; 8 performances). On September 15, 1951, the theater became the NBC Times Square Television Theater.

Downstairs a motion-picture policy took effect in 1937 and remained in effect until the New Amsterdam was shuttered in the early 1980s. At that time, the new owners, the Nederlanders, proposed to renovate the theater and open Jerry Herman's *(q.v.)* musical *La Cage Aux Folles*. Renovations took longer than expected and suddenly the Broadway theater scene was less healthy, so *La Cage* opened at the far more attractive Palace Theater *(q.v.)* in the heart of the theater district.

Other shows were announced for the theater and then withdrawn. Plans to move the lobby to 41st Street across from the Nederlander *(q.v.)* were scrapped, and subsequently major problems were discovered with the main supporting beam.

The 42nd Street Redevelopment Project states that "the combination of the New Amsterdam's facilities makes it well suited to the production of large commercial musical productions."

NEW APOLLO THEATER See APOLLO THEATRE.

NEWSPAPER GUILD OF NEW YORK (PAGE ONE) AWARD IN THEATER This award is given by a board comprised of New York journalists. There are no set categories, and past winners have included plays, musicals, critics, authors and institutions. The awards were initiated in 1945 and have been awarded annually except for 1963 because of a newspaper strike.

NEWSPAPER STRIKE OF 1962–63 The power of the newspapers over the fortunes of Broadway are amply illustrated by the newspaper strike of 1962–63. The strike forced the early closing of some shows and, incredibly enough, allowed for the run of another.

On December 8, 1962, the International Typographical Union, the newspapers' printer's union, called a strike against the New York press. New Yorkers didn't believe that the strike would last long, but it wasn't settled until 114 days later. Since the papers together printed over 5,500,000 copies each day, all those people were cut off from the Broadway theater, except for the occasional television review. The newspaper strike led to a consolidation of the television reviewers' power.

The strike deprived Broadway shows of their two major sources of promotion. The typical PR campaign consists of primary advertising and secondary publicity. Without newspapers, primary advertising was limited to billboards and fliers since television advertisement was not yet used at the time. Secondary publicity consists of the articles in newspapers that appear after the show's opening and remind the audience that the show is still running. But after the strike, there were no feature stories or gossip items to catch the public's eye. In New York, at least, it was as if the theater had simply closed up.

The fate of two shows illustrates the impact of the strike on the Broadway theaters. *The Beauty Part* was a hilarious comedy by S.J. Perleman. It received rave reviews after its opening on December 26, 1962. But the reviews on television and in the major weekly magazines had little impact, because they didn't hit all on one day the way newspaper reviews do. They just kept dribbling in.

The Beauty Part's star, Bert Lahr, commented in a *New Yorker* profile on the strike's effect on the play's box office: "It's been murder with this newspaper strike. Normally, with the kind of reviews we got, we'd be sold out for two months in advance, but as it is, we're selling out performance by performance, with a steady line of maybe six customers at the box office all day long."

Michael Ellis, *The Beauty Part*'s producer, attempted to offset the lack of publicity through a series of stunts *(q.v.)* and alternative means of advertisements. He arranged for a million bookmarks with reviews of the show to be distributed to cigar stores and book shops. People in Revolutionary War dress, complete with a bell-ringing town crier, handed out tabloid sized fliers with the reviews printed on them. Ellis put the fliers in 100,000 packages of laundry and 100,000 people found fliers slipped in with the photo prints they picked up from their local film developers. There were countless other promotions and stunts. In all Ellis spent over $50,000 in attempts to advertise the show.

None of these tricks worked. *The Beauty Part* still needed the day to day reinforcement that only a newspaper ad could bring. An additional problem for a potential audience member was figuring out what theater the show was playing at. When *The Beauty Part* moved from the Music Box *(q.v.),* to the Plymouth

Theater (q.v.) Ellis had no way to tell the public about the move. When the show had to move from the Plymouth, it was decided simply to close it after only 85 performances. Ellis commented, "Every possible kind of deal that could be made to spread the word about that show was made. But it just isn't the same thing as having that newspaper in your hand."

The Beauty Part never got off the ground without newspapers to spread the word, but Lionel Bart's musical *Oliver!* actually succeeded because of the strike. The musical opened on January 6, 1963 under the watchful eye of producer David Merrick (q.v.). Merrick, a master showman and manipulator of the press, knew *Oliver!* wasn't the greatest show. He was just as happy not to have newspaper reviewers telling the public that the show wasn't much good. Still, Merrick needed publicity.

Luckily, *Oliver!* was a musical and one with an excellent score. Merrick made sure every radio station in town had recordings of the show's hit songs—"Consider Yourself" and "As Long As He Needs Me." The airwaves were inundated with the songs, and they soon became deserved hits. When the newspapers went back to publishing and the mixed reviews were in, they had no effect. There was already solid word of mouth, and the success of the songs made the show a success in the minds of the public. *Oliver!* ran 774 performances.

Of course, the strike hurt more shows than it helped. The newspaper industry would further hurt Broadway as more and more papers folded. A few critics became all powerful, and without a wide range of opinion and outlets for advertising and stories, the entire theater community suffered.

NEW YORK DRAMA CRITICS' CIRCLE AWARD This award was begun as a protest against the awarding of the Pulitzer Prize in Drama to Zoe Akins's play *The Old Maid*. The Circle had been meeting informally since 1927 when critic (q.v.) Kelcey Allen called them together. Helen Deutsch, press agent for Maxwell Anderson's *Winterset* (one of the overlooked plays) called a meeting at the Algonquin Hotel. On October 22, 1935, the Circle adopted a constitution, and the organization stated its goal as "the fostering and rewarding of merit in the American theatre, and the awarding of a prize to be known as the Drama Critics Prize for the best new play by an American playwright produced in New York during the theatrical season." The first award went to Maxwell Anderson for his play *Winterset*. The original award was designed by sculptor Henry Varnum Poor, a plaque, featuring a depiction of the John Street Theatre. Typically, after a few years, the Circle lost the mold for the plaque, and a scroll was given to winners.

The Circle added an award for Best Foreign Play in 1938. In 1946, an award for Best Musical Production was first given. An award in each category is not mandatory, and in many years the Circle makes no award in a particular category. In 1962, the rules were altered to read: "There shall be one ballot cast for the Best Play—drama or musical, regardless of the country of its origin. If a foreign work should win the award, the Circle may if it chooses, name a Best American Play. If an American Play wins, the Circle may choose a Best Foreign Play. The choice of a musical is, as always, left to the discretion of the Circle."

NEW YORKER THEATER 254 W. 54th Street. Architect: Eugene DeRosa. Opening: as an opera house, November 7, 1927, *La Boheme*; as a legitimate theater, May 12, 1930, *The Vikings*. Opera impresario Fortune Gallo had his Gallo Theater built to house the San Carlo Opera Company. The house was not a success, and Gallo sold his building. The new owners named the theater the New Yorker Theater with their production of *The Vikings*. The Depression hurt the theater, and it was also unsuccessful.

The theater was redesigned as one of the first theater restaurants in New York, the Casino de Paree, on December 13, 1933. The club was originally called Billy Rose's Casino de Paree but the bantam producer Billy Rose (q.v.) soon sold out his interest.

The man who ran the Casino was Lew Brown, best known as a member of the songwriting team DeSylva, Brown and Henderson (q.v.). But Brown wasn't the owner; that distinction went to Tommy Lucchese. Milton Berle, recalling his first impression of Lucchese, said he "struck me as sort of naive, a nice quiet gentleman who must have been in an accident—I thought—because he only had three fingers on one hand." Berle later wised up to the fact that Lucchese was the notorious gangster "Three-Fingers Brown."

Lucchese, like most gangsters (q.v.), was paranoid. He wouldn't accept a cigar from anyone. Instead, he'd jump in a cab and go to a cigar store where he was not known. Lucchese's caution paid off. He was never arrested and lived a quiet life until he died of cancer in 1967.

Like many mob-operated clubs, the Casino de Paree was successful, but it couldn't survive the effects of the Depression. On January 16, 1936, the theater was renamed the Paladium. The Paladium was short-lived, and in 1937 the Federal Theater Project (q.v.) leased it and renamed it the Federal Music Theater.

The theater's name was changed again, to the New Yorker Theater, and returned to legitimate theater productions on March 21, 1939, with *The Swing Mikado* (86 performances). In 1943, CBS turned the theater into the CBS Radio Playhouse Number 4.

During the 1970s, the building achieved perhaps its greatest success as the disco Studio 54.

NEW YORK TIMES HALL See LITTLE THEATRE.

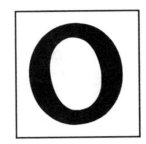

OLYMPIA Broadway between 44th and 45th Street. Architect: J.B. McElfatrick & Company. Opening for Music Hall production December 17, 1895, with Yvette Guilbert; reopened as the New York Theater, April 24, 1899, with *The Man in the Moon*. Lyric opening production November 25, 1895, with *Excelsior Jr.*; reopened as the Criterion Theater, August 29, 1899, with *The Girl from Maxim's*; reopened again as the Vitagraph Theater, February 7, 1914, as a movie theater; reopened again as the Criterion Theater, September 11, 1916, with *Paganini*. Both demolished in 1935.   The Olympia complex established Times Square as the city's theater district and served as a cornerstone for development of the whole area. Earlier in the 19th century, the theater district moved from lower Manhattan to the Herald Square area. Oscar Hammerstein I *(q.v.)* began the move northward to Times Square (then Longacre Square) in 1895 with the Olympia Theater. Hammerstein realized the potential of the area, already used as a transfer point between streetcar routes. He purchased the entire block of the east side of Broadway between 44th and 45th Streets and decided to build a huge complex called the Olympia.

In January 1895, the ground was broken. When completed, the complex contained a restaurant, a promenade or central lobby, a bowling alley, billiard rooms, a turkish bath, three theaters seating over 6,000 people, and a roof garden—an idea imported from Europe.

In an advertisement in the *New York Times*, Hammerstein bragged about "the grandest amusement temple in the world." The Music Hall, situated on the 45th Street side had prices of 75¢ to $1.50 for reserved seats. It had 11 tiers of boxes. Hammerstein boasted that it held more boxes than any other theater—124 in all.

The opening of the complex was planned for November 18, but delays pushed the opening back to November 25. Hammerstein claimed that he had lost $3,000 by postponing the opening. The *Times* accused him of overselling the house to make up the difference.

Opening night proved to be an ill omen. The crowds began to arrive in the afternoon, long before the doors were opened. The heavens then opened, and a cold rain beat down on the thousands of ticket holders who began to push and shove to get under the marquee. The *Times* reported that the crowd, "with the strength of a dozen catapults, banged at the doors of the new castle of pleasure and sent them flying open . . . puffed sleeves wilted and crimpted hair became hoydenish in the crush and the rain; toes were trampled and patent leathers and trousers were splashed, dresses were torn, and still the crowd pushed on." The staff was unable to control the throng. Hammerstein had oversold the theater by almost 4,000 seats. The police called for reinforcements to try to shut the theater doors. At 10 o'clock over 5,000 patrons, as the *Times* put it, "slid through the mud and slush of Longacre back into the ranks of

Olympia complex   Courtesy Billy Rose Theater Collection.

Program for the Olympia

Cosmopolis." A band played until 1 A.M. in the Concert Hall to try to appease the disgruntled crowd.

Hammerstein had private rooms for his guests, but unfortunately the paint was still wet and several of the elite found their clothes marked with the wall covering. The next day, Hammerstein's troubles continued. A steam pipe burst in the cellar, and two workers were killed and others badly scalded.

Yvette Guilbert was to have opened the Music Hall, but she was unavailable until mid-December, and a series of vaudeville acts filled in for her. The Lyric presented Edward E. Rice's *Excelsior Jr.,* starring Fay Templeton. "The Cornerstone of Times Square," as the Olympia was christened, never overcame the disaster of opening night.

In 1897, the president of New York Life wrote Hammerstein a note apprising him that the mortgage would be foreclosed and that a bank employee would run the theater. Hammerstein responded, "I am in receipt of your letter, which is now before me, and in a few minutes will be behind me."

The next year, Hammerstein found himself bankrupted by the Olympia. Previously, he had turned down an offer to rent the two corners of the building as a drug store and haberdashery. The proposed rental was $6,000 annually, but Hammerstein was too proud or optimistic to accept it. New York Life sold the building to producers Henry and M.L. Sire for $1 million. They in turn sold it to Klaw and Erlanger,

heads of the Theatrical Syndicate, for almost twice that amount and in 1920, a department store offered $6 million. The Music Hall became the New York Theater, specializing in vaudeville and then burlesque and the Lyric became the Criterion. The roof garden went to Klaw and Erlanger's management and was called the Jardin de Paris. The first *Ziegfeld Follies (q.v.)* was presented there in 1907.

Under Charles Frohman's direction, the Criterion offered comic opera, musical comedy, variety and straight plays. Finally, both the Criterion and the New York turned to a movie policy. The Criterion was bought by the Vitagraph company in 1914 and was renamed the Vitagraph Theater. Two years later, it was sold again and its name reverted to the Criterion. John Golden a producer, playwright and press agent wrote that the Criterion was no more successful than its predecessors. "I shall never forget the sick feeling that came over me every time I walked into the empty lobby of the Criterion Theater and saw no one at the box office except the ticket seller." One day, he and Winchell Smith stood in front of the theater and watched thousands of people passing the theater. Smith wondered why the theater was called the Criterion. Golden explained, "It's a pretty good name. A criterion is something to go by—and they're certainly going by here." The entire complex was razed in 1935.

O'NEILL, EUGENE (1888–1953) Eugene O'Neill is considered by many theater historians to be the father of 20th century American theater. O'Neill pioneered American realism, taking the theater away from the melodramatic and farcical theater that Europe bequeathed to America at the turn of the century. O'Neill was among the earliest playwrights to work in experimental techniques and nonnaturalistic styles. He delved into the psyches of his characters as few other playwrights had before him. Though some of his plays may seem overwritten and dated now, O'Neill set the groundwork for a native theater in the new century. Without his leadership, there might not have been a Group Theater *(q.v.)* or Tennessee Williams *(q.v.)* or Arthur Miller *(q.v.).* O'Neill, ever the tragedian, won four Pulitzer Prizes *(q.v.)* and the Nobel Prize for literature.

Critic *(q.v.)* George Jean Nathan hailed O'Neill in the introduction to the published version of *The Moon of the Caribees,* an early O'Neill drama. Nathan wrote of the playwright's impact on the American theater, "In O'Neill theater has found its first really important dramatist. To it he has brought a sense of splendid color, a sense of vital drama and a sense of throbbing English that no native playwright before him was able to bring . . . The essential difference between O'Neill and the majority of his contemporaries in the field of American drama lies in the circumstance that where the latter think of life (where they think of it at all) in terms of drama, O'Neill thinks of drama in terms of life."

O'Neill was born on October 16, 1888, to Irish Catholic parents, James O'Neill and Ella Quinlan, at Barrett House, on the northeast side of 43rd Street just off Broadway. Later, Barrett House was converted into part of the Cadillac Hotel around the corner from Rector's Restaurant (q.v.). O'Neill's father, a matinee idol best remembered for his performance in the play *Monte Cristo,* rivaled Edwin Booth for honors.

Eugene O'Neill's home life was especially difficult. He wrestled with his upbringing throughout his life. His parents were able to express affection only by tormenting each other, reconciling their love only by alcohol and narcotics. O'Neill worked autobiographical themes into many of his plays including, most importantly, *Long Day's Journey Into Night* (completed in 1941) and also *All God's Chillun Got Wings* (1923). In these plays he barely disguised the names of members of his family.

O'Neill spent much of the early teens on a variety of vessels sailing the world. He assisted his father on two theatrical tours and thereby learned the intricacies of the theater. Ill health forced him into a sanitarium in 1912 after a stint as a reporter in New London, Connecticut.

In 1915, O'Neill joined a group of young writers who were disenchanted with Broadway and had the youthful optimism to believe they could change the status quo. The group met on Cape Cod at a glorified shack, which they dubbed the Provincetown Playhouse, under the direction of George Cram Cook. The next year, emboldened by their efforts, they set up shop on MacDougal Street in Greenwich Village in a new Provincetown Playhouse.

The year 1917 was important for O'Neill. His talents came to the attention of the Washington Square Players, who later evolved into the Theater Guild (q.v.). The Players leased the Bandbox Theater on West 57th Street. There they presented O'Neill's one-act play *In the Zone* (10/31/17) to critical applause. The *New York Herald* reported that the play "registered so realistically that several spectators laughed awkwardly in its tense moments as a result of the nervous strain of the sustained thrill." The Provincetown Players presented O'Neill's *The Long Voyage Home* (11/17/17) to more acclaim. O'Neill was slowly getting a name for himself in the theater community and beyond.

Beyond the Horizon (2/3/20; 111 performances), the playwright's first important full-length play and first Broadway production, was produced at the Morosco Theatre (q.v.). The drama was presented during matinees only. The *New York Times* critic Alexander Woollcott (q.v.) enthused, "[*Beyond the Horizon* is] an absorbing, significant, and memorable tragedy, so full of meat that it makes most of the remaining fare seem like the merest meringue." When the Morosco's regular tenant, *For the Defense,* closed, *Beyond the Horizon* began a full Broadway schedule.

Beyond the Horizon was a naturalistic play with no melodramatic overtones. Its characters propelled the plot, not theatrical contrivance. O'Neill was criticized for over-writing and for taking a literary rather than theatrical approach to structure, but most critics agreed that *Beyond the Horizon* was a major step forward towards a new American theater. The play received the first of O'Neill's four Pulitzer Prizes for Drama.

O'Neill's career flourished as he called on his past for a seemingly infinite number of variations. He would draw on his experiences, mix them with a story in the oral tradition and experimental techniques.

Immediately following *Beyond the Horizon,* O'Neill undertook a number of tasks all at once. He had plays on and off Broadway, some with out-of-town tryouts and others commissioned or waiting to be produced. He was a prolific playwright able to juggle many projects at once, so it seems odd that he quit Broadway in the late thirties to write a cycle of plays, the production of which waited until all were finished.

The Emperor Jones (11/1/20; 192 performances) played at the Provincetown Playhouse. Set to the rhythms of tom-toms beaten at exactly the rate of the human heart beat, *The Emperor Jones* was highly experimental. The play, which was basically a long monologue, also experimented with the use of ghosts appearing on stage as manifestations of the central character's imagination.

The Pulitzer Prize-winning *Anna Christie* (11/2/21; 177 performances) was O'Neill's next success. The play was a rewrite of *Chris Christopherson,* a drama starring Katharine Cornell (q.v.) that folded in Atlantic City. *Anna Christie* was produced by Arthur Hopkins, one of the most adventurous of Broadway producers. The drama, which opened at the Vanderbilt Theater (q.v.), was an immediate success. Pauline Lord, in the title role, received glowing reviews, as did her leading man, George Marion, and the sets of Robert Edmund Jones.

Alexander Woollcott wrote in his review, "Though this Anna Christie of his has less directness and more dross and more moments of weak violence than any of its forerunners, it is, nevertheless, a play written with that abundant imagination, that fresh and venturesome mind and that sure instinct for the theater which set this young author apart." The play won for O'Neill his second Pulitzer Prize.

Expressionism, explored in *The Emperor Jones,* was again utilized for dramatic impact in *The Hairy Ape* (3/9/22; 120 performances). Louis Wolheim played the loutish Yank, juxtaposed by O'Neill with the upper-class brat Mildred. The play received decidedly mixed reviews, with the negative outweighing the positive.

All God's Chillun Got Wings ostensibly explored the travails of miscegenation. It actually had many of the overtones of O'Neill's youth. The main characters were named Jim and Ella, after O'Neill's parents. Later in a *Long Day's Journey Into Night,* O'Neill would name the mother Mary. His mother's actual name was Mary, she changed it to Ellen and later to Ella.

The opening night of *All God's Chillun Got Wings* (5/15/24; 43 performances) ran into problems before the curtain rose. The first scene, almost a prologue, featured several children. Unfortunately the Children's Society of New York refused to issue the Provincetown Playhouse a license allowing the children to perform. The objection was actually a thinly disguised attempt by racists in the government to keep the play from opening. Ku Klux Klan members had already sent threatening letters to the leads, Paul Robeson and Mary Blair as well as director James Light and O'Neill. A bomb threat was phoned in, threatening the theater with destruction if the play proceeded.

James Light addressed the defiant audience at the opening, asking them whether the play should proceed or not. After receiving a strong yes from the audience, Light proceeded to read the brief prologue since the children were legally unable to appear. The rest of the evening continued without incident. Unfortunately, the play was not a success in the critics' eyes. Heywood Broun called it "a very tiresome play." Woollcott, one of O'Neill's chief boosters, wrote, "There is a perceptible chill in the air of the theater of Eugene O'Neill at present. It is the chill of compromise—the compromise with the old realism which results in a kind of halfhearted sublimation of the material world through which his figures move." The play was revived a few months after its closing and ran an additional 62 performances.

Desire Under the Elms (11/11/24; 208 performances) was another presentation of the Provincetown Playhouse at the Greenwich Village Theater. Robert Edmund Jones designed the production and also directed the fine cast. Walter Huston, not yet established as a Broadway performer, starred along with Mary Morris. The play was not a success with the critics, who seemed to feel the dramatic construction was cliched and shopworn.

O'Neill along with Kenneth Magowan and Robert Edmund Jones presented *The Great God Brown* (1/23/26; 271 performances). O'Neill utilized masks to point up the differences between the characters' true personalities and emotions and how they are perceived by others. The lead characters let down their masks only when unafraid to bare their innermost souls. After the opening, the critics ran to their typewriters to applaud the play. Brooks Atkinson, then recently appointed as the *New York Times* drama critic, wrote that O'Neill "has not made himself clear. But he has placed within the reach of the stage finer shades of beauty, more delicate nuances of truth and more passionate qualities of emotion than we can discover in any other single

modern play." *The Great God Brown* moved from the Greenwich Village Theater to the Garrick Theater (q.v.) and finally the Klaw Theater (q.v.).

Marco Millions (1/9/28;102 performances) was the first O'Neill play to open on Broadway in four years. The previous Broadway production, *Welded* (3/17/24; 24 performances), was not a success. O'Neill's other plays had previewed at the Greenwich Village Theater and many had subsequently moved uptown. *Marco Millions* was produced by the Theater Guild (q.v.). *Marco Millions* opened at the Guild Theater (q.v.) and received mixed to positive notices.

The Guild quickly followed with the opening of *Strange Interlude* (1/30/28; 426 performances). As produced at the John Golden Theater (q.v.), *Strange Interlude* was an especially provocative play. The drama actually contained three complete three-act plays. The play was referred to by star Lynn Fontanne (q.v.) as a "six day bisexual race." O'Neill put many asides into the dialogue. Director Philip Moeller solved the problem by having the rest of the action freeze while the aside was given.

The five-hour production (excluding the dinner break) had audiences enthralled. Dudley Nichols, later a successful Hollywood screenwriter, was the critic for the *New York World.* Woollcott was the first-string critic for the paper but as he had given the play an unfavorable review in *Vanity Fair* (based on a reading of the script), Nichols was assigned opening night duties. Nichols opened his review by stating, "The Theater Guild produced Eugene O'Neill's 'Strange Interlude' last night and it needs all the restraint a reporter can muster not to stamp the occasion, without a second thought, the most important event in the present era of the American theater." Nichols went on to state that the play wasn't only "a great American play but the great American novel as well." This was what O'Neill had planned. All through his career, he strove to bring the depth and structure of a novel to the stage. *Strange Interlude* was O'Neill's greatest success to date and won for him a third Pulitzer Prize.

O'Neill based his next major work, *Mourning Becomes Electra* (10/28/31; 150 performances), on the *Oresteia* of Aeschylus. Again, New England was chosen as the background for the tragedy. Alice Brady and Nazimova starred in what was actually three plays—*Homecoming, The Hunted* and *The Haunted.* The play opened under the auspices of the Theater Guild at the Guild Theater. The show ran seven hours with the customary break for dinner. Again, O'Neill garnered great reviews. John Mason Brown, writing in the *New York Evening Post,* exclaimed "It is a play which towers above the scrubby output of our present-day theater as the Empire State Building soars above the skyline of Manhattan. Most of its fourteen acts, and particularly its earlier and middle sections, are possessed of a strength and majesty which are equal to its scale . . . It is one of the most distinguished, if not the most distinguished, achievements of Mr. O'Neill's career . . . It is an experiment in sheer, shuddering, straight-forward story-telling which widens the theater's limited horizons at the same time that it is exalting and horrifying its patrons." *Mourning Becomes Electra* was considered by many to be O'Neill's greatest achievement.

O'Neill's next success, a major departure in his usual oeuvre, was *Ah Wilderness!* (10/2/33; 285 performances), an affectionate comedy set in the New England of O'Neill's boyhood. George M. Cohan *(q.v.)* starred in the sentimental play. Critics were astounded that O'Neill would write such a light, bright comedy. Brooks Atkinson admitted, "As a writer of comedy Mr. O'Neill has a capacity for tenderness that most of us never suspected."

O'Neill had one more play premiere on Broadway, *Days Without End* (1/8/34; 57 performances), before devoting himself to writing a series of plays that he vowed would not be performed until all were finished. He took a break from the play cycle to write *The Iceman Cometh* (10/9/46; 136 performances), which premiered at the Martin Beck Theatre *(q.v.)*.

During the period that he worked on the cycle, he also completed *Long Day's Journey into Night, Hughie* and his last completed play, *A Moon for the Misbegotten.* The latter, now considered a great play, was not well received when it opened at the tiny Bijou Theatre *(q.v.)* (5/2/57; 68 performances).

O'Neill finished drafts of eight of the plays in the cycle, none of which were performed before his death on November 27, 1953. The only play of the cycle to be completed was *A Touch of the Poet.* The remainder were torn up and burned by O'Neill and his wife Carlotta. With his health declining, O'Neill feared that he would die before the plays could be finished and he was determined that no one else should work on them after his death. Only a rough, uncut draft of *More Stately Mansions* survived.

Director Jose Quintero and producers Theodore Mann and Leigh Connell presented *The Iceman Cometh* at the Circle in the Square Theater off-Broadway. Quintero later directed an acclaimed production of *Long Day's Journey* (11/7/56; 390 performances) on Broadway. The production opened at the Helen Hayes Theater *(q.v.)*. The production starred Fredric March, Florence Eldridge, Jason Robards Jr. and Bradford Dillman. O'Neill was awarded, posthumously, a fourth Pulitzer Prize.

O'Neill brought the American theater into the 20th century. He allowed it to mature until it could stand on its own against any of the European dramatists. O'Neill, Shakespeare and Shaw are the most performed playwrights throughout the world. His dramas continue to mesmerize audiences with their stark theatricality and raw emotions.

O'NEILL THEATER See EUGENE O'NEILL THEATER.

OUTER CIRCLE AWARD This award has been given since 1950 by newspaper and magazine writers who report on the New York theater from outside the New York metropolitan area. The judges of the Outer Circle Awards have always been less consistent than the judges of other major awards in adhering to fixed categories. In some years, no Best Play or Best Musical is voted. Other categories that have been selected for awards on an irregular basis are best set design, most effective and imaginative individual contribution to a stage production, best ensemble acting, achievements in staging and outstanding debut. An award was also presented to an actress for being the first American to play Eliza in *My Fair Lady*.

PAGE ONE AWARD See NEWSPAPER GUILD OF NEW YORK (PAGE ONE) AWARD IN THEATER.

PALACE THEATRE 1564 Broadway between 46th and 47th Street. Architects: Kirchoff and Rose. Opening: Vaudeville, March 24, 1913; legitimate theater, January 29, 1966, *Sweet Charity*. Perhaps the best known of all American theaters is the Palace. The Palace was to vaudevillians what Carnegie Hall was to classical musicians: a sign that the performer had reached the height of his or her art. The Palace was built by West Coast vaudeville impresario Martin Beck, who wanted to conquer the East Coast. Standing in Beck's way was the team of B.F. Keith and E.F. Albee *(q.v.)*. They controlled the East Coast vaudeville circuit and gained control of the Palace before the curtain went up on opening night.

The opening program was a matinee on March 24, 1913. The "first-class" vaudeville program was not considered a success by the trade paper *Variety (q.v.)*. The headline reporting the event was "Palace $2 Vaudeville a Joke: Double-Crossing Boomerang." The newspaper criticized the program and indulged in a prediction as to the Palace's future prospects:

The fate of $2 vaudeville at the new Palace, New York, was sealed before the house opened Monday. Since then its doom has become accepted along Broadway. Monday afternoon, following an expenditure of $4,000 for preliminary advertising of the initial variety program the Palace failed to draw capacity, even with the great quantity of 'paper' given away. In the evening the Palace held capacity on the orchestra floor but was not filled upstairs. About one-half present received free coupons.

The news of "the Palace flop" pleased the regulars around New Times Square mightily . . . Whoever arranged the opening program for the Palace presented the poorest big time vaudeville show New York has ever seen. It's also the worst exhibition of showmanship New York has known.

A betting book was made up last Friday, $100 to $75 was offered the Palace would be the first big time house in New York to close this season, and $100 even money was offered in any amount that the Palace policy will be altered by April 7.

The Palace appeared to be headed for certain failure, but appearances were deceiving. The theater that would later be referred to as "the home plate of show business"

The Palace Theatre Courtesy Billy Rose Theater Collection.

by vaudevillian Pat Rooney Sr. finally made a splash on May 5, 1913. The occasion was an appearance by the almost 70-year-old Sarah Bernhardt. The tragedian appeared on the Palace stage with her partner Lou Tellegen. Business improved and the Palace was on its way to becoming the mecca for vaudeville.

The Palace's success led to changes in Times Square. The Palace office building, surrounding the theater, quickly filled up with agents. Across the street on what is known as Duffy Square was a concrete island created by the convergence of Broadway and Seventh Avenue. Today the island holds the TKTS Booth (q.v.) and the statues of George M. Cohan (q.v.) and Father Francis Duffy. Back in the heyday of the Palace, the area was known as the Palace Beach. The Beach (q.v.) became the gathering place of performers who were between bookings.

Walter Winchell (q.v.) told his biographer Herman Klurfeld about life on the Beach when he was a young performer: "I often stood in front of the Palace for hours swapping lies. There were always jobs we turned down because the agents were either too stupid to appreciate us or unable to meet our prices. I used to wait at the Palace, hoping to meet a friend rich enough to invite me to join him across the street for a cup of coffee and a sandwich. It was all so damn frustrating and humiliating."

The theater changed its bills every Monday at a matinee performance attended by agents, producers, critics and fellow actors. The typical Palace bill consisted of nine acts. The Monday matinee performance was the most important of the week and could make or break a career. It was also considered the toughest audience of the week, and if an act failed to go over it often didn't make it to the evening show.

Most of the Monday afternoon regulars had subscriptions to the theater. In fact, 75% of the Palace's business was subscription sales. Business remained good throughout most of the 1920s until new forms of entertainment began to take hold. As radio became more and more popular, many Palace performers gave up the live stage for the microphone. The arrival of talking pictures also dealt a blow to vaudeville and the Palace. A *Variety* article summed up the Palace's declining fortunes when the paper reported on "a line in front of the Palace Monday matinee—on its way to the Roxy (q.v.)." The stock-market crash and the Depression finished off vaudeville.

There were some successful acts at the theater after the crash, but they were few and far between. Mostly, the theater resorted to gimmicks to draw patrons. The first idea was to present celebrities who were not true vaudevillians. It had worked with Sarah Bernhardt when the theater was first starting out, so show-business wisdom suggested a repeat performance. Nightclub

artists like Paul Whiteman who appeared with his band at the Palais Royal were welcomed at the Palace where they were once banned. As talkies gained hold of the public's imagination, washed-up silent-screen stars made personal appearances.

The old vaudeville spirit revived briefly when Kate Smith set a record in August 1931, with her *Swanee Revue* and an 11-week run. Musical-theater stars William Gaxton, Lyda Roberti and Lou Holtz remained at the Palace for eight weeks. But these successes were exceptional bright spots. When on March 11, 1930, E. F. Albee died, it seemed to mark the end of vaudeville forever and the end of an era at the Palace. On July 9, 1932, the last week of straight vaudeville bill was begun at the Palace.

Thereafter, the Palace added movies to its vaudeville offerings. The *New York Times* noted: "After almost twenty years of straight vaudeville, the Palace is saying good-bye to all that with its current show. On Saturday a program combining variety acts and feature motion pictures will take over the stage of what until recently was the proudest and most empurpled of all the country's former big-time music halls, the goal of vaudevillians everywhere."

Over the next few months, the vaudeville portion of the show faded and the last two-a-day vaudeville show with a movie accompaniment began on November 12, 1932. The *Times* commented: "Vaudeville is singing its swan song at the Palace this week prior to the defection of the time-honored variety house to motion pictures . . . the Honey Family are swinging the old Palace trapeze for what may be the last time. Sic transit gloria mundi."

The once great theater succumbed to the movies on November 17, 1932, with the first film to play the Palace without an accompanying vaudeville show. The movie was the Samuel Goldwyn production of *The Kid from Spain*, starring Eddie Cantor. Only 10 days later, a major competitor opened its doors for the first time—Radio City Music Hall.

A straight movie policy continued for a few months at the Palace, but it didn't draw audiences. The major studios had their own flagship theaters in Times Square, including the Warner Brothers (q.v.), the Loews State (q.v.) and the Paramount (q.v.). So the Palace was forced to scramble for product. Most of the top movies went to the major houses.

From January 7 through February 4, 1933, the Palace reinstated its vaudeville and movie schedule, but by February 11, 1933, the vaudeville was out again. The picture that opened on that day was *The Bitter Tea of General Yen*—on a second run after playing Radio City Music Hall.

On April 29, 1933, vaudeville was brought back and played in a continuous stage show/movie format, much like the Radio City Music Hall shows of later years. The continuous grind show meant the Palace could only book lesser acts who were willing to undergo the torturous regime. That policy also didn't work out, and it ended in the week beginning September 30, 1935.

For the next 14 years, the Palace stuck to a movie-only policy. The vaudeville booking office had long since moved from the sixth floor of the Palace office building to the building housing Radio City Music Hall. Yet ex-vaudevillians without much hope of ever working again still hung out on the Beach across from the Palace.

The theater itself was renovated in August 1941. *Daily News* reporter Robert Sylvester noted the occasion: "Yesterday they started to tear down and 'streamline' the old-fashioned marquee and lobby, with its twinkling little electric bulbs and displays that once were as bitterly contested for as the favors of a great beauty. The marquee still reads B.F. Keith's Palace having ignored the changes and mergers of the years. But inside the 25–year-old theater a double feature film bill was the attraction on the stage where Sarah Bernhardt once played Camille, dragging her wooden leg from stage to dressing room over a long white bearskin rug."

On May 19, 1949, vaudeville acts once more accompanied movies on stage. The idea originated with Sol Schwartz, the president and general manager of RKO Theaters. He was quoted in a *New York Times* interview with J.P. Shanley: "I think the time is ripe for a little change. Many people haven't seen 'round' actors perform on a stage for more than fifteen years. Some of the men who were in the service during the war were seeing live talent for the first time when USO shows played for them. They liked it and I think they want more." Schwartz's idea caught on with the public who oohed and aahed over the theater's $60,000 renovation.

The theater limped along into the fifties with an occasional good week, but as the decade progressed television became an increasingly greater threat to the theater's existence. On October 4, 1951, the theater closed for two weeks for sprucing up to make ready for its next incarnation.

The next turning point in the Palace fortunes came on October 16, 1951, with an appearance by Judy Garland. By this time, Garland's career in pictures was almost finished. She needed the Palace and the Palace needed her. She appeared on a two-a-day policy with such veteran vaudevillians as Smith and Dale whose act Dr. Kronkite was the inspiration for the Neil Simon *(q.v.)* play *The Sunshine Boys.* Garland was booked for a four-week run and stayed for 19 weeks. She finished on February 4, 1952, with what everyone conceded was a triumphant engagement. More straight vaudeville followed until April 12, 1952, and an appearance by

Betty Hutton, which proved almost as popular as Garland's. Ironically, it was Hutton who replaced Garland in the film version of Irving Berlin's *(q.v.)* stage hit *Annie Get Your Gun.*

Hutton ran four weeks, and then it was back to Schwartz's eight-act vaudeville policy. The next great event at the Palace took place on January 18, 1953, with an engagement by Danny Kaye. He played 14 weeks, a total of 135 performances before 243,250 patrons.

A few more imaginative bookings broke the vaudeville monotony in the fifties. Betty Hutton returned with newcomer Dick Shawn who was "discovered" and became a star. Phil Spitalny and his All Girl Orchestra held the Palace stage for a week in the summer of 1955, and in November the Grand Ole Opry took over the Palace stage.

On November 26, 1956, Judy Garland returned to a triumphant reception at the Palace. This time, comic Alan King was "discovered" at the Palace. Garland concluded another record-breaking run on January 8, 1957, after 15 weeks at a $7.50 top ticket price.

Jerry Lewis convulsed Palace audiences beginning January 8, 1957, and proved he could make it without his one-time partner Dean Martin. Lewis's four-week run had an advance sale of $90,000, and that was with a top ticket price of only $6.00. During that show television singer Edie Gorme was "discovered."

Liberace was the next superstar to appear in the Palace with an acclaimed act. However, although he had been booked for four weeks beginning on April 20, 1957, he did poor business and closed after only two weeks.

On August 13, 1957, the Palace again gave up its vaudeville policy. Blockbusters were hard to come by, and in the weeks between their appearances, the theater did not do well. If Liberace could not pack them in, then who could? The only exception to the theater's all-movie policy was a tremendously successful appearance by Harry Belafonte beginning on December 15, 1957. He was booked for eight weeks and stayed for a little over three months, playing to sold out houses.

On August 19, 1965, the theater was sold to producer James Nederlander. Nederlander restored the theater, and in August, 1965, the last movie to play the Palace—*Harlow*—premiered.

Nederlander began a new era at the Palace—legitimate theater. The first show, *Sweet Charity* (1/29/66; 608 performances), premiered with an exceptional score by Cy Coleman and Dorothy Fields *(q.v.)*. Neil Simon *(q.v.)* was responsible for the libretto, and Bob Fosse directed. Gwen Verdon perfectly captured the title character. The score contained several standout numbers including "Baby Dream Your Dream," "Where Am I Going?" and "I'm a Brass Band." But the big hit was "Big Spender."

Judy Garland made another appearance at the Palace

starting July 31, 1967, in her show *At Home at the Palace*. She appeared with her children Joey and Lorna Luft, comedian Jackie Vernon and vaudeville veteran John Bubbles. She played 24 performances. Eddie Fisher and Buddy Hackett opened at the Palace on August 28, 1967, and remained for 42 performances.

The next musical at the Palace, *Henry, Sweet Henry* (10/23/67; 80 performances), was based on the movie *The World of Henry Orient*. Despite the talents of songwriter Bob Merrill, author Nunnally Johnson and cast members Don Ameche, Carol Bruce, Alice Playten, Neva Small and Robin Wilson, the show was a failure.

Though George M. Cohan *(q.v.)* never played the Palace, the musical *George M!* (4/10/68; 435 performances), starring Joel Grey as the irrepressible Broadway star, opened there. Joe Layton staged the musical with gusto. Supporting Grey were Bernadette Peters, Danny Carroll, Jerry Dodge, Betty Ann Grove and Jill O'Hara.

The next hit to play the Palace was the Charles Strouse and Lee Adams *(q.v.)* musical *Applause* (3/30/70; 896 performances). Based on *All About Eve*, *Applause* starred Lauren Bacall, an unlikely musical comedy star. The script was written by Betty Comden and Adolph Green *(q.v.),* and choreographer Ron Field directed. Bonnie Franklin was hailed as a new Broadway star because of her rendition of the catchy title song. However, Miss Franklin subsequently left Broadway for television and never looked back.

Cyrano (5/13/73; 49 performances) was an especially dismal musicalization of Edmond Rostand's classic *Cyrano de Bergerac*. *Gentlemen Prefer Blondes,* in which Carol Channing made her first great success, was reworked into the musical *Lorelei* (1/27/74; 320 performances) featuring Carol Channing. Joel Grey returned to the Palace in one of Jerry Herman's *(q.v.)* few flop shows, *The Grand Tour* (1/11/79; 61 performances).

Lauren Bacall returned to the Palace in what seemed to be a sure success, *Woman of the Year* (3/29/81; 770 performances) with a fair score by John Kander and Fred Ebb. Despite its long run, *Woman of the Year* never paid back its investors. As a result, the Securities and Exchange Commission revised its rules for investments in Broadway shows. *Woman of the Year,* a forgetable musical, is now chiefly remembered as one of the shows that scared investors away from Broadway.

Jerry Herman recovered from the failure of *The Grand Tour* and presented the Palace his smash hit musical, *La Cage Aux Folles* (8/21/83; 1,761 performances). Harvey Fierstein wrote the libretto, based on a hugely popular French movie. George Hearn and Gene Barry starred.

La Cage might have run longer, but plans were announced to build a new 40-story office building with 364,000 square feet of office space around the theater, retaining the theater itself. It was considered too expensive to move the show.

The interior of the Palace has been given landmark status by the New York City Landmarks Preservation Commission. Gene A. Norman said: "If one theater were to be named the most famous, that privilege would fall to the Palace." This presumably means that future generations of performers can feel what Jack Haley felt when playing the Palace: "Only a performer can describe the anxieties, the joys, the anticipation, and the exultation of a week's engagement at the Palace. The walk through the iron gate on 47th Street, through the courtyard to the stage door, was the cum laude walk to a show business diploma. A feeling of ecstasy came with the knowledge that *this is the Palace.*"

PARAMOUNT BUILDING 1501 Broadway between West 43rd and West 44th Street. Architects: C.W. & George Rapp; constructed 1925–27. The Paramount Building is one of New York's most recognizable skyscrapers, yet it hasn't had nearly the acclaim of other New York landmarks. Perhaps the reason is its poor upkeep in recent years.

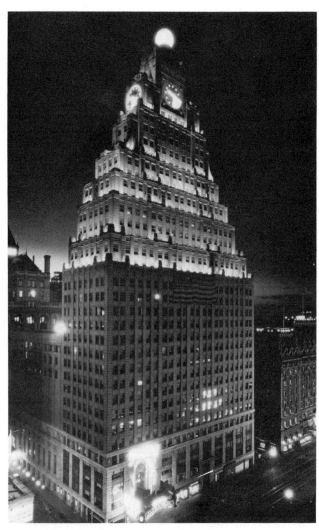

Paramount Building   Courtesy Billy Rose Theater Collection.

The 35-story building, though classically inspired, has a decided art-deco style. As it rises, the building employs a series of setbacks, culminating in a ziggurat upon which stands the magnificent clock tower. The apex of the entire structure is the 20-foot glass globe that was meant to be illuminated. The globe was perhaps inspired by the London Coliseum, which is also topped by a lighted globe, creating a beacon in London's West End.

The Paramount Building had an auspicious opening tied to the opening of the Paramount Theater *(q.v.)* over which it towered. It was built to house the New York offices of Famous Players-Lasky Corporation, the parent of Paramount Pictures. Shanley's Restaurant in the Putnam Building was demolished to make way for the 35-floor office building.

The building also contained an observation tower at its roof where sightseers could look over Manhattan for only a quarter. The 20-foot glass globe (actually hiding the building's water tower) remains atop the edifice but hasn't been lit in decades, and the giant clock faces, among the largest in the world, no longer run.

After the theater was converted to office space in 1964–65, the Paramount Building went in to a decline as did the rest of the Times Square area. Today it is one of the only original large office buildings to remain on Times Square, serving as the headquarters to many theatrical concerns.

PARAMOUNT THEATER 1501 Broadway between West 43rd and West 44th Street. Architects: C.W. & George Rapp, constructed 1925–27. Opening: November 19, 1926; *Calvacade of Motion Pictures.* The Times Square Paramount Theater was perhaps the best-loved theater on Times Square. Thousands remember lining up at the theater to hear their favorite band and vocalist. Before adopting a big-band policy, the theater mounted the usual movie-palace stage shows, similar to those that later became famous at the Roxy *(q.v.)* and other giant theaters. The Paramount is the one that remains in most people's minds as the ultimate Times Square theater.

It was built by the Famous Players–Lasky Corporation, the money behind Paramount Pictures, which

Paramount Theater   Courtesy Billy Rose Theater Collection.

constructed the Paramount Building *(q.v.)* above to house their New York headquarters.

The opening night program stated, "Thirty years ago Herald Square was the very heart of Broadway. Today it has become only a memory, and ten blocks uptown Times Square now rules as the Capital of the Amusement World. The Paramount Theater stands at the Crossroads of the world."

The opening program, staged by Broadway director, John Murray Anderson *(q.v.)*, was a typical, if overblown example of movie-palace offerings. The show was titled a *Cavalcade of Motion Pictures.* After some specialty numbers and the usual speeches, the program began. The show featured a newsreel and some vaudeville type specialties followed by the program proper. After the program came a Paramount Picture—*God Gave Me Twenty Cents,* starring Lois Moran.

Among the notables present at opening night, was a man with his white-haired wife on his arm. As the couple took their seats in a special box, the entire audience rose and gave him a standing ovation. The man was unaware of the applause for he was deaf. He was Thomas Alva Edison, the inventor of the motion picture.

Ticket prices ranged from 40¢ to 99¢. The theater opened at 10:45 A.M. and closed a little over 12 hours later. An advertisement, placed in the *New York Times* on November 23, 1926, boasted of the attendance records set by the new theater:

30,222 in Two Days! Into the Paradise of luxury, color and enchantment they came, more than 30,000 in two days. Saturday and Sunday, thrilling with new excitement at every step! The spaciousness of the place! The superb height and dignity of the Grand Hall as they entered! The decoration and equipment throughout, so beautiful that each detail made people halt to admire it alone! And then, a *show* worthy of the *setting!* These thousands are telling more thousands and they are all coming back, week after week, for there is nothing like the Paramount in all New York for sheer luxury and unprecedented entertainment values!

Patrons entered the beautiful ticket lobby and then the low ceilinged Hall of Nations, which opened into the enormous Grand Hall. The Grand Hall lobby, said to have been inspired by the lobby of the Paris Opera House, was much larger and more ornate.

The theater itself sat 3,664 people. The auditorium was criticized at the time but today is viewed in a kindlier light. The only trouble with the theater was the relatively narrow width of the proscenium arch. Later theaters featured huge stages suitable for spectacular presentations and wide-screen movies. Most shows staged at the Paramount extended a thrust stage into the auditorium over the orchestra pit. When the bigband policy went into effect, the bands played in front of the proscenium. When VistaVision wide-screen films were shown, the sides of the arch were demolished.

The August 1926 issue of *Metronome Magazine* carried an article that described other areas of the Paramount:

When the Paramount Theater opens this fall, you can meet your friends in any of 25 rooms, foyers or lobbies. Each will have a definite name and luxurious appointments. Entering at the box office lobby, one passes into the intermediate lobby, thence into the grand hall which is lined with Breche Centella marble, imported from Italy at a cost of over a half a million dollars. The main lounge will be known as the Elizabethan room, and is located in the basement where there are also a ladies' lounge, dressing room and ladies' smoking room. The men will also have a smoking room in the basement known as the University Room.

Leaving the grand hall and passing upward, one finds the intermediate mezzanine lobby, which gives access to the mezzanine loges. Here also is a men's smoking room and a ladies' rest room.

The most novel rooms ever incorporated into a theater are the period, club and fraternity rooms. Here, you can lounge in luxury and await the arrival of your friends. These rooms are named as follows: Elizabethan, Marie Antoinette, Chinoiserie, College, Jade, Club, The Galleries, Peacock Alley, Grand Hall, Hall of Nations, the Rotunda, Music Room and Fraternity Room. The College Club and Fraternity rooms will be decorated with the insignia and colors of all the clubs, colleges and fraternities, represented.

The Paramount is rapidly nearing completion. It will be one of the great art buildings of the world, with almost 50 percent of the space devoted to promenades, lounges, rest rooms and comfortable conveniences for its patrons.

The theater presented musical revues, featuring stars of the day like Fred Astaire *(q.v.)*, Beatrice Lillie and Ethel Merman *(q.v.)*, and cut-down versions of Broadway shows. There was a permanent staff, including ballet master Boris Petroff, costume designer Charles LeMaire and conductor of the Paramount Grand Symphony Nathaniel Finston. Producing directors, in addition to John Murray Anderson *(q.v.)*, were R.H. Burnside, a Shubert *(q.v.)* contract director, Jack Partington and Frank Cambria. At the Wurlitzer twin organs (called "our masterpiece" by Farny Wurlitzer, Chairman of the Board of the Wurlitzer Company) were Mr. and Mrs. Jesse Crawford.

By 1934, in the middle of the Depression, the stage shows were discontinued. Only the organ concerts remained. Then someone got the idea to present big bands and singers. The most famous appearance was that of Frank Sinatra when he sang with the Tommy Dorsey Orchestra and attained the height of his popularity.

Big-band singer Dolly Dawn also appeared there. She recalled her experiences:

The people lined up around the block, from Broadway down 43rd and around 8th Avenue. When the doors would open they would pile in. Some people would get in before 1:00 for thirty-five cents and stay in there for six shows.

The crowds at the stage door—you couldn't get out. You just stayed in and had food sent in. You slept between shows because it was just too hectic to try to get out. One hundred people would grab you.

It was exciting. I'd say to the kids coming up, if you never played that theater you hadn't really played a theater. The smell in your nose when you opened the backstage door and you'd think, "Oh my God, I'm here!" It was a certain distinct odor, I don't know how to express it.

There was an old doorman who had been an old vaudevillian, he was always called "Pop." He'd say, "If there's anything I can do for you" but you'd have to help him because he was so old.

The big thrill was when they'd ring a buzzer and say "half hour." Then "fifteen minutes." And finally "five minutes." By then whoever was supposed to be on stage had to be in the orchestra pit. When you heard that band strike up, what a thrill! What a thrill it was! You knew the orchestra lift was going to come up and there would be thousands of people applauding you.

The bobbysoxers ruled the theater. But after the big-band era came television and the beginning of the end for the Paramount. Entertainers preferred to host their own television shows for more money, bigger audiences and less work. They required inflated fees to appear at the Paramount and other theaters.

In the sixties, with the advent of rock and roll, the theater catered to a younger crowd. When school was not in session, the Paramount would draw the younger set in record numbers. But during the day and during the summer when New Yorkers were out of town, the theater died.

The Paramount finally closed on August 14, 1965. The great marquee was taken down, and the theater was gutted. Offices were put in the huge space. Dolly Dawn offered one last thought on the Paramount: "These kids have no idea what it was, and they'll never know because there will never be anything like those theaters again. And I am so grateful to the Lord that I was a part of it. And I saw it, I felt it. It's not easily forgotten and I don't want to ever forget it."

PAUL, MAURY (1890–1942) The majority of Broadwayites do not recognize the name of Maury Paul, but as Cholly Knickerbocker he exerted great influence over their lives. Knickerbocker was the name Paul signed to a society column that was widely syndicated across the country.

Paul was born in Philadelphia to a society family. He attended the University of Pennsylvania, graduating in 1914. After graduation, he joined the staff of the *Philadelphia Times* for a brief period. He soon moved to *The New York Press* as its society editor. When that paper merged with *The Morning Sun* he left journalism for Wall Street. The brokerage business didn't suit him,

and he found employment with *The New York Mail*. At the *Mail* he created a society column, using the pen name Dolly Madison.

In 1917, he moved to *The New York American* and took over the Cholly Knickerbocker column. He continued at the *American* through its merger with *The New York Evening Journal*. At the new *New York Journal-American* Paul thrived. He contributed a daily society column and contributed features to the Sunday edition.

Paul was basically a reporter and seldom expressed his own opinions in the column. He almost never reported on society's events, concentrating instead on his subjects' lives and actions. He was known to encourage feuds between himself and the doyens of society. The feuds guaranteed a lively column and a loyal readership.

Paul invented the terms "Cafe Society" and "Old Guard" and they soon entered the language. The "Old Guard," society's oldest families, were divided by Paul into two categories, A and B. The fights and controversies over placement in the two classes contributed to Paul's renown.

Paul enjoyed a remarkably long career. He remained at the *Journal-American* as Cholly Knickerbocker for 25 years until his death on July 17, 1942.

PLAYBILL *Playbill* is the most consistently recognizable aspect of theatergoing. The theater program lists all important information on the play including cast lists, technical credits, production staff, musical numbers and biographies of important contributors. Such theater programs have been a part of the audience experience since the turn of the century.

In the 18th century, playbills were introduced listing the cast members and information on the play's locale and scenes. In the 19th century, programs expanded to much the same form as today, although they had much finer design and usually gave more information on the individual productions. The early programs usually consisted of four pages: a cover, which was individualized for the show or theater; a back page, which contained a drawing of the theater layout and exits; and two interior pages with the show's credits.

In 1884, Frank Vance Strauss had the idea of combining the theater program with advertising. The Ohioan established his business the following year, and such companies as Caswell Massey, Runkel Brothers Cocoa and Schirmer pianos were among the first advertisers.

In early programs, the names of set designers and directors were listed in the back along with prop studios and costume houses. Lighting designers were almost never listed. The programs usually stated "Electrical effects by Kleigel Bros." or another lighting supply house. Individual authorship of songs in revues was usually not indicated, and typographical errors abounded.

Programs were printed for individual theaters. They

might be in any format or size. In 1891, Strauss merged operations with the only competitor left in New York. In 1905, Strauss decided to standardize the design and layout of the programs so that the makeup would be easier and the sizes of advertising space uniform.

When the programs became standardized, special features were introduced in the free handout. These included "What the Man Will Wear," one of the first men's fashion columns, "Beauty Hints," "For Book Lovers," "What the Woman Will Wear," "Doorways to Beauty," short stories, poems and sometimes biographies of the cast under the title "From Our Stageland Scrapbook." The last page, as in earlier programs, was reserved for diagrams of the orchestra and balcony levels of the theater and their exits. Each cover depicted the particular theater in which the show played. The four-color designs were especially fanciful and are much in demand today as collector's items.

In 1908 artists F. Earl Christy and John M. Burke drew "The Program Girl." The sketches appeared in the programs and were also sold in groups of three for a dime. Three years later, the program acquired a name for the first time: the *Strauss Theater Magazine Program.* Since many audience members kept their playbills and put them into scrapbooks, Strauss decided to offer for sale binders that could hold the magazine.

Strauss sold the operation in 1918 to his nephew, Richard M. Huber, who promptly renamed the handout, *The Magazine Theater Program.* In only six years, by 1924, Huber was printing over 16,000,000 playbills a year for over 60 theaters.

Huber started up operations of *Playbill*'s parent company, the New York Theater Program Corporation, in the 1934–35 season. By this time Huber's programs had completely outstripped those of competitors, and Huber's corporation had a monopoly on programs for the Broadway theater. Max Reinhardt's production of *The Eternal Road,* presented at the 34th Street Manhattan Opera House, was the only legitimate production not to use the company's program service. Even the Metropolitan Opera House passed out the magazine.

That same season a new name appeared on the program's cover, *The Playbill.* By this time, advertisements could be placed in individual programs. One advertiser who consistently took advantage of the policy was Rogers Peet Company clothing stores. They incorporated the title of the show into their advertisements. For example, the program of the revue *Rain or Shine* carried the following ad:"Rain or shine Scotch Mists are fine. Handsome, stylish overcoats that are wetproof too!" And the ad in the program for Preston Sturges's *Strictly Dishonorable,* read in part, "It's strictly dishonorable to say that a fabric is wool if there is any trace of cotton." Needless to say, some titles of productions were a challenge to Rogers Peet's advertising firm.

Since the number of advertising pages varied from show to show, the size of a *Playbill* could indicate how big a hit the show was. *Anything Goes* was 48-pages thick while *Post Road* contained only 12 pages.

During World War II, couples were requested to share one *Playbill* to help save paper for the war effort. Space was donated to war bonds just as Frank Strauss had done for liberty bonds during World War I. *Playbill* also became smaller in size to save on paper.

Covers had long featured logos or photographs from the shows rather than generic theater logos. In 1948, the cover's color was changed from sepia to ivory. In February 1951, the color was changed again from ivory to white.

The business changed hands in 1956 when Richard Huber sold *The Playbill* to producer and real estate magnate Roger L. Stevens. Stevens streamlined the design. He changed the name simply to *Playbill* and made a generic cover for all editions of *Playbill.* No longer did the name of the show appear on the cover. Of course, collectors and others railed against the change. Although the cover sketch changed each month, there was no way to tell without flipping through the magazine what show it was covering. Collectors weren't the only ones upset over the change. Stars had in their contracts that their pictures would appear on the cover of *Playbill.* By the fall of 1958, a new design was introduced; a colored band, different for each theater, was placed across the top with a show's logo or photo beneath. Then a standard yellow band was introduced.

Gilman Kraft bought the magazine from Roger Stevens in 1961. Kraft installed Arthur Birsh to head the operation. Birsh took over as publisher in October, 1965. The year before, *Playbill* had become a monthly instead of a weekly. Also, columns and staff were added to give the magazine a new, more modern look. Bernice Peck began her fashion column, "On a Personal Bias," which continues today. In 1973, the column was expanded to an entire fashion supplement. The main reason for giving her this section was to attract a wider range of advertising. Also at this time, Al Hirschfeld, noted caricaturist, started his feature, "Unlikely Casting."

By 1968, Gilman Kraft sold the magazine to Metromedia, a small chain of independent television stations that later became the basis of the Fox Television Network. The new editor-in-chief was Joan Alleman. She remains on staff to this day.

Metromedia could not have picked a worse time to buy the program. Broadway went into a dangerous slump during the late sixties and seventies. Fewer shows were being produced, audiences stayed out of the Times Square area, which was becoming increasingly sleazy and unsafe, and ticket prices were quickly rising. The result was that Arthur Birsh was able to reacquire *Playbill* from Metromedia. He remains publisher to this day.

When Birsh took over *Playbill,* the Broadway theater began a small upswing. The success of shows like *A Chorus Line, 42nd Street* and *Cats* gave the theater a base on which to build.

Unlike European theaters, Broadway theaters offer programs for free to ticket holders. *Playbill* actually pays the theaters for the rights to produce each production's programs. *Playbill* makes money through selling advertisements in the magazine. The system works much like a television network's advertising department. *Playbill* guarantees each advertiser that a certain number of audience members will receive each magazine.

Publicists on each production supply the information on the show, cast, production staff and crew to the *Playbill* editorial staff. The *Playbill* printer actually sets the type in lead instead of using more modern computer typography. The hot type is set on old Linotype machines, and the galleys are proofread by the press agents.

Production information takes up the eight and three-quarters inside pages of the distinctive yellow and white magazine. The outside pages contain articles on the theater, interviews, restaurant news, fashion sections and advertising. The production information includes the title page with all credits, scene information, musical numbers, biographies of the cast and major staff members, listings of producers and production staff and usually a column called "At This Theater."

Whereas the outside pages are printed in quantities of over a million monthly, the inside show pages are produced each week in New York. The quantity of the inner pages depends on estimates derived from past business and advance sales. The two sections are then put together and delivered weekly by *Playbill*'s yellow trucks.

In the early years of the magazine, the entire product was printed weekly. As the number of shows has fallen so has the need for weekly printings. In the old days, a *Playbill* employee named Callahan went from theater to theater and personally checked out each show's business. He then would estimate the needs of each show.

After Callahan left the post he was replaced by Herman Pepper. Pepper would also make the rounds of the theaters, checking on business and ordering the necessary number of *Playbills* to be delivered the next day. Although Pepper went into thousands of theaters during his time on the job, he sat through only one complete production, *My Fair Lady.* What he thought of the musical is not recorded. When he died, the job was assigned to the truck drivers who deliver the magazines. They check the previous night's leftovers and supply the necessary number of copies of *Playbills.*

Mistakes and typographical errors are almost non-existent today. Many theatergoers are not particularly happy with the magazine's articles, but these critics are only beginning to express their complaints. Still, despite the reservations of some, *Playbill* is a mostly excellent guide to the Broadway theater season.

PLAYERS CLUB 16 Gramercy Park. The Players Club and the Friars Club are the two performing arts clubs that cater to those in the Broadway theater. The Players was founded in 1888 by Edwin Booth, one of the greatest actors of the 19th century. The club was fashioned after the Garrick Club in England. Its charter states that the Players Club is a place where "actors and dramatists could mingle in good fellowship with craftsmen of the fine arts as well as those of the performing arts."

The club purchased the Clarkson Potter house on Gramercy Park and commissioned Standford White to redesign the brownstone as a private club. Booth lived in an apartment in the club until his death in 1893. Among the other founders of the club were Mark Twain, John Drew, General William Tecumseh Sherman, Albert M. Palmer, Augustin Daly, Lawrence Barrett and Joseph Jefferson.

The club accepts not only actors but also playwrights, artists, press agents, directors, editors, producers, publishers, cartoonists, musicians, writers and educators. There are annual pool, bridge and backgammon tournaments and dinner theater programs as well as the club's famous Pipe Nights, Ladies Day and Founder's Night celebration.

There have been nine presidents of the club: Edwin Booth, Joseph Jefferson, John Drew, Walter Hampden, Howard Lindsay, Dennis King, Alfred Drake, Roland Winters and the current president, Jose Ferrer.

An important feature of the club is the Walter Hampden Memorial Library. The research library is one of the largest in the country. It fulfills the club's manifest, which called for the creation of "a library relating especially to the history of the American stage, and the preservation of pictures, playbills, photographs and curiosities."

The library used Booth's personal library of a thousand volumes as its nucleus. The collection has since expanded greatly and now numbers over 20,000 volumes. These deal primarily with 19th century theater. Since 1957, the library has opened its doors to non-members' use for research projects.

The Players presented an annual show from 1922 through 1940. The first production was *The Rivals* at the Empire Theater, June 5–10, 1922. The cast included the leading players of the day, both male and female. These actors donated their services with 10% of the proceeds going to The Actors Fund. The total receipts for the 15 productions was $412,117.

Among the stars who graced the stage in these productions were John Drew, Pauline Lord, Mary Shaw, Otis Skinner, Tom Wise, Helen Hayes *(q.v.)*, Fay Bainter, Blanche Ring, James T. Powers, Walter Hampden,

Laurette Taylor, Elsie Ferguson, Charles Coburn, Ethel Barrymore (see BARRYMORE FAMILY), Henry E. Dixey, Philip Merivale, George M. Cohan (q.v.), Blanche Ring, Effie Shannon, Dorothy Stickney and Tyrone Power.

On April 23, 1989, The Players, an exclusively male club admitted women to its membership. Inductees included Helen Hayes, Lauren Bacall, Betty Comden (q.v.), Mary Tyler Moore, Toni Morrison, Eudora Welty, Beverly Sills, Tharon Musser, Kitty Carlisle Hart and Gwen Verdon.

THE PLAYWRIGHTS' COMPANY The Playwrights' Company was one of the more successful of the production companies established in the 1930s. Like its brethren, the American National Theatre and Academy (ANTA) (q.v.) and the Group Theater (q.v.), it proposed to establish a protective environment for the production of plays and with the goal of improving the theater. Playwright Maxwell Anderson stated the purpose of the Playwrights' Company was "to make a center for ourselves within the theater, and possibly rally the theater as a whole to new levels by setting a high standard of writing and production."

The first members of the company were playwrights Anderson, S.N. Behrman, Sidney Howard, Robert Emmett Sherwood and Elmer Rice. Later members included composer Kurt Weill (q.v.), playwright Robert Anderson, lawyer John F. Wharton and producer Roger L. Stevens.

These authors banded together for other reasons as well. They sought a more socialistic approach to the theater, whereby the occasional failure of one member could be shared by the group as a whole. They also desired more input into the production of their plays. and a freer hand in crafting important plays, regardless of the vagaries of the box office.

The first play presented by the new organization was Robert E. Sherwood's *Abe Lincoln in Illinois* (10/15/38; 472 performances). It was an immediate success at the Plymouth Theater (q.v.) due to the quality of the script and a powerful yet understated performance by Raymond Massey in the title role. Massey won the Della Austrian Medal (q.v.) for the best performance of the season. Sherwood won a Theater Club Award for the best play of the season as well as the Pulitzer Prize for Drama (q.v.). Sherwood also won in 1936 for *Idiot's Delight* and another for the Company's production of *There Shall Be No Night* in 1940.

The Company's next outing was a musical with book and lyrics by Maxwell Anderson and music by Kurt Weill. *Knickerbocker Holiday* (10/19/38; 168 performances) opened only four days after *Abe Lincoln in Illinois*. It starred Walter Huston and introduced the classic ballad "September Song." Other plays quickly followed, including Elmer Rice's *American Landscape* (12/3/38); S.N. Behrman's *No Time for Comedy* (4/17/

39); Maxwell Anderson's *Key Largo* (12/27/39); Elmer Rice's *Two on an Island* (1/22/40); Robert E. Sherwood's *There Shall Be No Night* (4/29/40); Maxwell Anderson's *Journey to Jerusalem* (10/5/40); Elmer Rice's *Flight to the West* (12/30/40); S.N. Behrman's *The Talley Method* (2/24/41); Maxwell Anderson's *Candle in the Wind* (10/22/41) and *The Eve of St. Mark* (10/7/42); and S.N. Behrman's *The Pirate* (12/25/42).

The forties continued with Sidney Kingsley's *The Patriots* (1/29/43), winner of the New York Drama Critics' Circle Award (q.v.) for Best Play; Elmer Rice's *A New Life* (9/15/43); Maxwell Anderson's *Storm Operation* (1/11/44); Robert E. Sherwood's *The Rugged Path* (11/10/45); Elmer Rice's *Dream Girl* (12/14/45); Maxwell Anderson's *Truckline Cafe* (2/27/46) and *Joan of Lorraine* (11/18/46); the musical version of *Street Scene* (1/9/47) with book by Elmer Rice, lyrics by Langston Hughes and music by Kurt Weill; Maxwell Anderson's *Anne of the Thousand Days* (12/8/48); Garson Kanin's *The Smile of the World* (1/12/49), the first nonmember-produced play; and Weill and Anderson's powerful musical adaptation of Alan Paton's *Cry the Beloved Country*, entitled *Lost in the Stars* (10/30/49).

In the fifties, the company increased its productions of plays by outside authors. The Playwright's Company began the 1950s on a sharp note with Sidney Kingsley's *Darkness at Noon* (1/31/51), which won the New York Drama Critics' Circle Award for Best Play. Other productions of the fifties included Elmer Rice's *Not for Children* (2/13/51); Jan de Hartog's *The Fourposter* (10/24/51), winner of the Tony Award (q.v.) for Best Play; Maxwell Anderson's *Barefoot in Athens* (10/31/51); Elmer Rice's *The Grand Tour* (12/10/51); Stanley Young's *Mr. Pickwick* (9/17/52); George Tabori's *The Emperor's Clothes* (2/9/53); Robert Anderson's *Tea and Sympathy* (9/30/53); Samuel Taylor's *Sabrina Fair* (11/11/53); Jane Bowles's *In the Summer House* (12/29/53); Elmer Rice's *The Winner* (2/17/54); Jean Giraudoux's *Ondine* (2/17/54) winner of the New York Drama Critics' Circle Award for Best Foreign Play; Robert Anderson's *All Summer Long* (9/23/54); Horton Foote's *The Traveling Lady* (10/27/54); and Maxwell Anderson's *The Bad Seed* (12/8/54).

The second half of the decade began with the classic production of Tennessee Williams' (q.v.) *Cat on a Hot Tin Roof* (3/24/55), which opened at the Morosco Theatre (q.v.). For his efforts, Williams received the Pulitzer Prize as well as the New York Drama Critics' Circle Award. Other plays in the Company's last decade included Baruch Lumet's *Once Upon a Tailor* (5/23/55); Jean Giraudoux's *Tiger at the Gates* (10/3/55); Joseph Fields (q.v.) and Jerome Chodorov's *The Ponder Heart* (2/16/56); Leslie Stevens's *The Lovers* (5/10/56); Robert E. Sherwood's *Small War on Murray Hill* (1/3/57); Jean Anouilh's *Time Remembered* (11/12/57), which marked Richard Burton's American debut; Noel Coward's *Nude* with *Violin* (11/14/57); Morton Wishengrad's *The Rope Dancers* (11/20/57); a revival of William Wycherly's *The Country Wife* (11/27/57); Ray Lawler's *Summer of the Seventeenth Doll* (1/22/58); Phoebe Ephron's *Howie* (9/17/58); N. Richard Nash's *A Handful of Fire* (10/1/58); Samuel Taylor and Cornelia Otis Skinner's *The Pleasure of His Company* (10/22/58); Milton Geiger's *Edwin Booth* (11/24/58); Elmer Rice's *Cue for Passion* (11/25/58); Alec Coppel's *The Gazebo* (12/12/58); Noel Coward's *Look After Lulu* (3/3/59); Joseph Stein and Marc Blitzstein's musical version of Sean O'Casey's *Juno and the Paycock, Juno* (3/3/59); Anita Loos's *Cheri* (10/12/59); Robert Bolt's *Flowering Cherry* (10/21/59); Peter Shaffer's *Five Finger Exercise* (12/2/59); Robert Anderson's *Silent Night, Lonely Night* (12/3/59); and Gore Vidal's *The Best Man* (3/31/60).

The Best Man was the last production of the Playwrights' Company. By this time, Maxwell Anderson, Kurt Weill, Sidney Howard and Robert Emmett Sherwood had died. Other members, like Roger L. Stevens, had formed new links to other producing organizations.

Although many of the plays produced by the company were failures, the Playwrights' Company had more than its share of important openings. Moreover, many plays that were ignored in their time have gone on to become part of the permanent literature of the American theater.

PLYMOUTH THEATER 236 W. 45th Street. Architect: Herbert J. Krapp. Opening: October 10, 1917; *A Successful Calamity.* The Shubert brothers *(q.v.)* backed producer Arthur Hopkins in his wish to have his own theater. The Shuberts, who already owned every other theater on the same side of the street were happy to extend their domain. The resulting Plymouth Theater, a theater worthy of the best in contemporary drama, fulfilled Hopkins's high-minded goals. Hopkins, a proponent of serious American drama, rejected the melodrama and parlor plays that typified the theater's offerings at the turn of the century. Hopkins was a staunch believer of spiritualism, and his kindly demeanor and good taste endeared him to the Broadway community. Hopkins, even after his successful years had past, had offices in the Plymouth Theater. He died in 1950.

Architect Herbert Krapp designed the Plymouth (on 45th Street) and the Broadhurst *(q.v.)* (on 44th Street) as a single unit, like their neighbors the Sam S. Shubert *(q.v.)* and Booth *(q.v.)* theaters. The shared side walls of the Shubert and Booth theaters together with the back of the old Astor Hotel *(q.v.)* formed the famous narrow walkway known as Shubert Alley. Similarly the Plymouth and Broadhurst formed an alley parallel to Shubert Alley. At the time, zoning regulations demanded a side alley exit from all theaters. The Broadhurst and Plymouth alley was almost immediately closed off to foot traffic.

The first booking, Clare Kummer's *A Successful Calamity,* had originally opened at the Booth and finished its run at the Plymouth. The first production to originate at the Plymouth was the John Barrymore *(q.v.)* vehicle *Redemption* (10/3/18; 204 performances).

After a run of Shakespeare's *Hamlet* (11/22/18) with Walter Hampden in the title role, Barrymore returned to the Plymouth's stage in *The Jest* (4/9/19; 77 performances). Barrymore was joined by his brother Lionel in the Sam Benelli drama. Hopkins produced and directed the venture, and Robert Edmond Jones, the premier set designer of his day, repeated the assignment he had carried out for *Redemption.* The three men, Hopkins, Jones and Barrymore, were fast becoming Broadway's most formidable artistic team. The Barrymore role had been played in France by Sarah Bernhardt and in Italy by Mimi Aguiglia. It was the fashion of many European stars to play men's roles. Clearly, the play was not the thing but the actors who appeared in it were, and the Barrymores took full advantage of the histrionics of the script. After a short hiatus, it reopened at the Plymouth on September 19, 1919, for an additional 179 performances. The play was to be presented at the Plymouth once more, on February 4, 1926, with Basil Sydney under Hopkins's direction. Without the Barrymores, the play failed to incite the audiences' passions, and the revival closed after 78 performances.

Rida Johnson Young, best remembered today as lyricist and librettist for a number of Victor Herbert *(q.v.)* operettas, saw her melodramatic play *Little Old New York* (9/8/20; 311 performances) open at the Plymouth. Genevieve Tobin starred as the girl who masquerades as a boy to win an inheritance rightfully the property of another lad with whom she falls in love. She wins both by the curtain's fall.

Zoe Akins's *Daddy's Gone-A-Hunting* (8/31/21; 129 performances) opened with Marjorie Rambeau in the lead. Hopkins produced and directed the comedy *The Old Soak* (8/22/22; 325 performances) by Don Marquis, with Harry Beresford in the title role and Minnie Dupree as his wife. J.P. McEvoy's play *The Potters* (12/8/23; 245 performances) was meant to be a realistic look at American family life. The comedy was really a string of episodes without the usual problem or event that is followed through to the play's conclusion.

High drama returned to the Plymouth's stage with Laurence Stallings and Maxwell Anderson's *What Price Glory?* (9/5/24; 435 performances). Hopkins produced and directed the harrowing World War I drama, which starred William Boyd (later known as Hopalong Cassidy in movies), Louis Wolheim and Brian Donlevy. The play, with its raunchy language and unromantic look at war, shocked audiences. Though the play revived several cliches, including that of comradeship in the trenches, it presented them in a more down-to-earth, no-nonsense way. The play's abundant use of swear words caused much controversy. One story tells of a prim, straitlaced woman who during intermission bent over to retrieve something from the floor and announced, "I seem to have dropped my goddam program." Controversy sells tickets as, usually, does excellence and *What Price Glory?* had both.

Philip Barry's first play at the Plymouth, *In a Garden* (11/16/25; 73 performances), starred Laurette Taylor and Louis Calhern, but it failed to catch on. Barry had better luck later. In the aptly titled *Burlesque* (9/1/27; 372 performances) Arthur Hopkins, and George Manker Watters treated audiences to what they thought was a realistic view behind the scenes in a burlesque house. The play starred Barbara Stanwyck and Hal Skelly. It let audiences into the world of cheap theatrics.

Clark Gable and Zita Johann starred in Sophie Treadwell's reworking of the story of Ruth Snyder, the first woman in America to die in the electric chair, entitled *Machinal* (9/7/28; 93 performances).

Holiday (11/26/28; 230 performances), Philip Barry's sparkling comedy, was produced and directed by Arthur Hopkins and starred Hope Williams and Ben Smith. The play is best remembered for its movie version, starring Katharine Hepburn, who was Hope Williams's Broadway understudy. The show later toured to enthusiastic response until October 28, 1929, the date of its opening in Boston. This was also the day of the Wall Street crash and the play, which was partly about getting too rich without being ready, hardly seemed appropriate any longer. Donald Ogden Stewart, who had a small role, remembered that the play was "received by the Boston mourners with an impressive two and a half hours of silence." Hopkins saw the writing on the wall, and after a commitment in Philadelphia the tour folded. This was lucky for Stewart because he had written a play.

Hopkins produced Stewart's play, *Rebound* (2/3/30; 124 performances), at the Plymouth and cast Hope Williams in the lead. Stewart also wrote a small part for himself in the comedy. The play was a hit. Alexander Woollcott *(q.v.)* stated, "The finale of that second act is one of the most exciting things I ever saw in the theater." This was high praise from a difficult critic. *Rebound* was picked by Burns Mantle as one of the year's 10 best plays.

Elmer Rice's *Counsellor-at-Law* (11/6/31; 293 performances), starring Paul Muni, reopened on September 12, 1932, for an additional 104 performances. The following year, Clare Kummer had another hit at the Plymouth with *Her Master's Voice* (10/23/33; 220 performances). It starred Laura Hope Crews and Roland Young.

Tallulah Bankhead explored the dramatic possibilities of *Dark Victory* (11/7/34; 55 performances), the story of a woman's emotional triumph over a brain tumor.

Robert Benchley *(q.v.)*, a Bankhead aficionado, wrote in the *New Yorker*, "There has always been a feeling among the admirers of Miss Bankhead that she should sometime play Camille. In *Dark Victory*, she makes a step towards this goal, without the unpleasantness of coughing." Benchley liked the George Brewer Jr. and Bertram Block play. He commented that "the sobs and sniffling which rock the Plymouth Theater at the end of the last act ought to testify to her success." Benchley wasn't alone in liking *Dark Victory*, but Bankhead had become ill and the play was withdrawn.

Samson Raphaelson wrote *Accent on Youth* (12/25/34; 229 performances), starring Constance Cummings. Robert E. Sherwood adapted *Tovarich* (10/15/36; 356 performances) for stars Marta Abba and John Halliday.

Gertrude Lawrence opened in Rachel Crothers's *Susan and God* (10/7/37; 287 performances). In 1943, the star opened City Center's drama program with the same play at affordable prices. Robert Emmet Sherwood followed *Tovarich* with his Pulitzer Prize-winning play *Abe Lincoln in Illinois* (10/15/38; 472 performances). Raymond Massey as the future president captured the hearts and minds of the audience. The play was the first production of the newly formed Playwrights' Company *(q.v.)*. Otto Preminger directed himself as a Nazi in Clare Boothe Luce's *Margin for Error* (11/3/39; 264 performances) with Sam Levene costarring.

Tallulah Bankhead returned in triumph to the Plymouth in Thornton Wilder's *The Skin of Our Teeth* (11/18/42; 355 performances). Wolcott Gibbs, the *New Yorker*'s critic, exclaimed that Bankhead gave "what may be the most brilliant and is certainly the most versatile performance of her career." Elia Kazan directed the Pulitzer Prize-winning drama, which also starred Fredric March, Florence Eldridge, Florence Reed, E.G. Marshall and Montgomery Clift.

Raymond Scott and Bernard Hanighen contributed the score to an odd bit of orientalia, *Lute Song* (2/6/46; 142 performances), the first musical to play the Plymouth. Mary Martin *(q.v.)* starred along with Clarence Derwent (namesake of the award) *(q.v.)*, Mildred Dunnock and Yul Brynner. Nancy Davis, who later became First Lady to President Ronald Reagan, also appeared in the show.

Noel Coward's *Present Laughter* (10/29/46; 158 performances) starred Clifton Webb. Bankhead made another brief appearance at the Plymouth later in the decade in a considerably lesser play, *The Eagle Has Two Heads* (3/19/47; 29 performances) (which wags dubbed The Turkey Has Two Heads). Critics were of one mind—they hated the play in spite of the fact that at each performance Bankhead fell down a flight of 10 steps. The fall received the most praise. Set designer Donald Oenslager said, "I took care to put a lot of padding under the carpet on those stairs but who except Tallulah would have taken such chances, and not once but night after night?" In his review John Lardner wrote, "Miss Bankhead spared herself nothing on opening night at the Plymouth. In a plunge that I would hesitate to make with football pads on, she toppled headfirst, majestically and in a pure line, down several stairs. She was fresh as a daisy, however, for her curtain calls, which were up to the standards of the Bankhead public."

Bankhead was back at the Plymouth in Noel Coward's *Private Lives* (10/4/48) with costar Donald Cook. The revival played 248 performances, the exact same number of performances as the original production of 1931.

Rodgers and Hammerstein (*q.v.*) produced Samuel Taylor's *The Happy Time* (1/24/50; 614 performances), with Claude Dauphin, Johnny Stewart, Eva Gabor and Kurt Kasznar. *Dial 'M' for Murder* (10/29/52; 552 performances), a thriller by Frederic Knott, starred Maurice Evans, Richard Derr, Gusti Huber and John Williams. Herman Wouk adapted his novel *The Caine Mutiny Court Martial* (1/20/54; 405 performances) for the Plymouth stage. Charles Laughton directed Henry Fonda, Lloyd Nolan and John Hodiak.

Three for Tonight (4/6/55; 85 performances) opened with Marge and Gower Champion, Hiram Sherman and Harry Belafonte. The singer later created a near riot at his one-man show at the Palace Theatre (*q.v.*).

Peter Ustinov's comedy *Romanoff and Juliet* (10/10/57; 389 performances) opened at the Plymouth with the playwright starring. Romanoff was the son of the Soviet ambassador to a small neutral country that purposely printed its stamps with mistakes to drive up their value on the collectors' market. Juliet was the daughter of the American ambassador.

The light comedy *The Marriage-Go-Round* by Leslie Stevens (10/29/58; 431 performances) starred Charles Boyer, Claudette Colbert and Julie Newmar. Elizabeth Seal created a sensation as a whore with a heart of gold, in the musical *Irma La Douce* (9/29/60; 527 performances) by Marguerite Monnot, Julian More, David Heneker and Monty Norman. The musical's big song was "Our Language of Love." Supporting Miss Seal were Keith Michell, Clive Revill, Fred Gwynne, George S. Irving, Elliott Gould, Stuart Damon and Rudy Tronto, all in producer David Merrick's (*q.v.*) production.

One of the greatest hits of the sixties was Neil Simon's (*q.v.*) *The Odd Couple* (3/10/65; 965 performances) starring Art Carney and Walter Matthau. Simon followed that success with *The Star-Spangled Girl* (12/21/66; 261 performances) which starred Anthony Perkins, Richard Benjamin and Connie Stevens. Simon returned to the Plymouth with a bigger success, *Plaza Suite* (2/14/68; 1,097 performances), an evening of three one-acts all taking place in the Plaza Hotel. Each starred George C. Scott and Maureen Stapleton. The playwright had less success with his first noncomedy dramatic attempt, *The Gingerbread Lady*. Maureen Stapleton starred as an alcoholic singer down on her luck. *The Gingerbread Lady* (12/13/70; 193 performances), though not a hit, did have its fans, and it was named one of the 10 best plays of the year by the *Best Plays* series.

For the next few years, beginning in 1973, British productions dominated the Plymouth Theater. Peter Cook and Dudley Moore opened in their two-man show *Good Evening* (11/14/73; 438 performances) in the vein of their previous success, *Beyond the Fringe*. *Good Evening* was titled *Behind the Fridge* in England.

Equus (10/24/74; 781 performances), by the English playwright Peter Shaffer, starred Anthony Hopkins as the psychiatrist of a boy who has inexplicably blinded several horses. Peter Firth starred as the youth. John Dexter's direction was hailed as were the performances. *Equus*'s theatricality sometimes overshadowed the script, but critics judged that it was for the better.

Britisher Simon Gray's play *Otherwise Engaged* (2/2/77; 309 performances) starred Tom Courteney as a man who could never get a moment's peace. After a two-year stay by the Fats Waller retrospective *Ain't Misbehavin'*, which moved from the Longacre Theater (*q.v.*), the theater hosted another English import, *Piaf* (2/5/81; 165 performances). Jane Laportaire starred as French singer Edith Piaf, and her performance won more kudos than the script.

The theater's next booking was a true theatrical event. It was the Royal Shakespeare Company's production of *The Life and Adventures of Nicholas Nickleby* (10/4/81) based on the Charles Dickens novel. Roger Rees played the title role. The play took eight hours to perform; audiences had a choice of either seeing it in one day with a dinner break or coming to the theater on two successive nights. "Nick Nick" (as it was affectionately dubbed) played to sold-out audiences for a limited engagement of 49 performances.

On January 6, 1983, David Hare's *Plenty* transferred to the Plymouth from the Public Theater where it premiered on October 21, 1982. Kate Nelligan and Edward Herrmann starred in the drama, which played 92 performances at the Plymouth in addition to the 45 performances it had enjoyed at the Public.

The Real Thing (1/5/84; 566 performances) by Tom Stoppard continued the British dominance of the Plymouth's stage. Jeremy Irons became a Broadway heart throb as a result of his performance. Then Lily Tomlin brought her one-woman show, *The Search for Signs of Intelligent Life in the Universe* (9/26/85; 398 performances), to the Plymouth for a limited engagement. Lanford Wilson's *Burn This* opened on October 14, 1987, with John Malkovich and Joan Allen in the leads.

On December 8, 1987, the New York City Landmarks Preservation Commission designated the exterior of the theater a landmark. The Commission stated that the theater's "facade is a response to its Shubert Alley location."

PORTER, COLE (1892–1964)   Of all the composers and lyricists on Broadway, Cole Porter was the most urbane and sophisticated and at times the silliest. Porter was certainly a celebrated wit and bon vivant both at home and in Europe. His wealth and social contacts made him the spokesperson and satirist of the upper classes. Whether down in the depths on the nineteenth floor or beginning the beguine, Porter was an important voice in the musical theater.

Of course he also spoke to the average person, as witnessed by the hundreds of popular songs to his credit. In his heyday, during the Depression, he fueled the dreams and fantasies of a generation. They could escape to exotic locales with the upper crust in the comfort of a balcony seat.

Porter's facility with rhythms and rhymes masked the hard work he put into the shows. This facility was all the more remarkable when juxtaposed with Porter's own personal torments.

Born in Peru, Indiana, on June 9, 1891, he showed an early talent for music and composed his first published song, "The Bobolink Waltz," at the age of ten.

Porter set out to become a lawyer. Towards that end he enrolled in Worcester Academy and then Yale at the direction of his grandfather. But Porter proved more interested in his extracurricular songwriting than in his studies. While at Yale, he wrote two of that school's

Cole Porter Courtesy ASCAP.

more enduring standards, "Bingo Eli Yale" and the "Yale Bullfrog Song." After leaving Yale for the Harvard Law School, his dean suggested that the School of Music might suit his temperament better. So Porter switched majors and began to write musical comedies.

His first break came when he met Elisabeth Marbury, the woman who produced many of Jerome Kern's (q.v.) early hits. Their show entitled *See America First* (3/28/16; 15 performances) was written in collaboration with T. Lawrason Riggs. It opened at Maxine Elliott's Theatre (q.v.) with Clifton Webb in the lead. "I've a Shooting Box in Scotland" became a minor hit.

After the failure of *See America First,* Porter abandoned the stage for three years. He didn't need to work, and so he spent the time touring the world as well as spending a brief sojourn with the French Foreign Legion. While on board a ship bound for the United States, Porter met Broadway producer and comedian Raymond Hitchcock. Hitchcock hired Porter to compose the score to the third edition of a short-lived revue series, *Hitchy-Koo.*

Hitchy-Koo (10/6/19; 56 performances), at the Liberty Theatre (q.v.), was more successful than his last outing. Porter's score yielded his first full-scale hit, "Old Fashioned Garden." Comedian Joe Cook, making his Broadway debut, introduced the song.

Even early on in his career, Porter explored themes familiar to him from his monied and leisured situation. The lyrics of "I've a Shooting Box in Scotland" were a litany of residences around the world owned by the singer. *Hitchy-Koo of 1919* contained "In My Cozy Little Corner of the Ritz" and "I Introduced," the latter a list of all the greats introduced to each other in one social outing or another.

In 1923, Porter was left over a million dollars by his grandfather, which allowed him more time to travel the world. He returned to the Broadway theater with his score for the *Greenwich Village Follies of 1924* (9/16/24; 131 performances). The show introduced "I'm In Love Again," a moderate hit at the time.

Paris (10/8/28; 195 performances) starred the French performer Irene Bordoni, known for her saucy smile and insinuating air. It was Bordoni who was largely responsible for showing Americans of the 1920s what the French knew about love. Porter provided her with what became one of his best-known songs, "Let's Do It." Through Porter's lyrics, Bordoni introduced Americans to a new concept—sex could be fun. Up to then, sex was either unmentionable or passionate in the manner of Rudolf Valentino. Bordoni and Porter were the perfect matching of talents for bringing sex into musical-comedy productions.

The reception to Porter's music was tremendous. He realized that celebrity could not only be fun but could also distinguish him from all the other bored millionaires in his circle of friends. Indeed, his popularity extended to his social strata, and he was in great demand for parties and soirees.

Porter's *Fifty Million Frenchmen* (11/27/29; 254 performances) opened at the Lyric Theater (*q.v.*). The show was the second one produced by Bordoni's husband, E. Ray Goetz. The book writer was Herbert Fields (*q.v.*) who later wrote libretti for six other Porter shows. "You Do Something to Me" was the hit of the show, which starred Helen Broderick, Genevieve Tobin and William Gaxton. The show was a big success in spite of the stock market crash, providing Porter with even more fame.

Several of Porter's songs were interpolated into an English import, *Wake Up and Dream!* (12/30/29; 127 performances). The show starred Tilly Losch, Jack Buchanan and Marjorie Robertson (Anna Neagle). The principal Porter contribution was "What Is This Thing Called Love?"

Porter's work gained new depth with each succeeding score. His melodies were uniquely his own and not based on cliched musical forms currently in vogue. His lyrics, too, showed added layers of emotion. He never relied on the moon–June–croon rhymes of his contemporaries, nor did he resort to straightforward and unimaginative contrivances.

The New Yorkers (12/8/30; 158 performances) opened at the Broadway Theatre (*q.v.*). E. Ray Goetz was Porter's producer for the third time. Herbert Fields contributed the book, and Monty Woolley directed his second Porter offering. The show starred Jimmy Durante, Hope Williams, Ann Pennington, Frances Williams, Charles King, Richard Carle, Marie Cahill, Oscar ("Rags") Ragland and Fred Waring and His Pennsylvanians. The score contained several of Porter's best work, including "Where Have You Been?," "Let's Fly Away" and "Take Me Back to Manhattan."

The song that became the biggest success and caused the biggest sensation was "Love for Sale." Percy Hammond, writing in the *New York Herald Tribune* opined, "When and if we ever get a censorship, I will give odds that it will frown upon such an honest thing." Charles Darnton of the *New York Evening World* took the opposite tack, "Love for Sale . . . was in the worst possible taste."

It proved too much even for some audiences to see the beautiful Katharyn Crawford playing a prostitute on the stage. So the character was given to Elisabeth Welch, brought on especially to sing the song. Because Welch was black, audiences seemed better able to accept her rendition of the song. The number's backdrop pictured a city street. The sign Park Avenue was simply changed to Lenox Avenue, and the show went on.

Gay Divorce (11/21/32; 248 performances), at the Ethel Barrymore Theater (*q.v.*), starred Fred Astaire (*q.v.*), in his first solo outing away from his sister Adele, as well as Claire Luce, Luella Gear and Betty Starbuck. *Gay Divorce* featured what is considered by many to be Porter's finest song, "Night and Day."

Anything Goes (12/21/34; 420 performances) featured Porter's favorite musical-comedy star, Ethel Merman (*q.v.*). Supporting her were William Gaxton, Victor Moore, Vivian Vance (later to achieve greater fame as Ethel Mertz in "I Love Lucy") and Bettina Hall. The score was among Porter's best, with no less than four gems. "All Through the Night," "I Get a Kick Out of You," "You're the Top" and the title song have all become recognized as classic examples of American popular song.

Porter's next offering, *Jubilee* (10/12/35; 169 performances) contained a score almost the equal to that of *Anything Goes*. "Begin the Beguine" and "Just One of Those Things" were the standouts. A young Montgomery Clift made his Broadway debut in the show. It might have run longer had not its star, Mary Boland, left to do a film.

Porter had hit his stride and next provided the score for a zany musical comedy, *Red, Hot and Blue!* (10/29/36; 183 performances) at the Alvin Theater. The title referred to the fact that the heroine had an identifying mark on her posterior caused by her sitting on a waffle iron. The lady in question was Ethel Merman, who was ably abetted by Jimmy Durante and Bob Hope. The score again showed Porter at the top of his class with such great songs as "It's De-lovely," "Ridin' High," and the title song.

While on vacation in the summer of 1937, Porter suffered a horrible riding accident. His horse threw him and fell on his legs, crushing them and causing extensive damage to his nervous system. Porter spent the remainder of his life in constant pain. Even after 31 operations, he never fully recovered. In 1958, his right leg was amputated. His friends doubted that he would ever write again and blamed his later failures on his great pain. But Porter bounced back creatively from this tragedy.

You Never Know (9/21/38; 78 performances), Porter's first Broadway assignment after the accident, opened at the Winter Garden Theater (*q.v.*). "At Long Last Love" was the most notable song in an otherwise inconsequential score.

Mary Martin (*q.v.*) got the Porter treatment along with William Gaxton, Victor Moore and Sophie Tucker in *Leave It to Me!* (11/9/38; 291 performances). Martin introduced "My Heart Belongs to Daddy," which made her a star.

Ethel Merman and Bert Lahr were back in *Du Barry Was a Lady* (12/6/39; 408 performances). Betty Grable, Charles Walters and Benny Baker helped round out the cast in the Porter hit. Herbert Fields and B.G. DeSylva (q.v.) wrote the book, which told the story of a lowly washroom attendant who dreams he is the King of France. "Friendship" was the archetypal Porter list song, a genre he elevated to an art form.

Merman also appeared in the next Porter musical, *Panama Hattie* (10/30/40; 501 performances), little remembered today. Arthur Treacher, Rags Ragland, James Dunn and Betty Hutton also appeared in the production.

Let's Face It! (10/29/41; 547 performances) was his second show of the forties. Danny Kaye made the biggest effect with his tongue-twisting songs "Farming" and "Let's Not Talk About Love." Eve Arden, Benny Baker, Mary Jane Walsh and Vivan Vance were also featured.

Something for the Boys (1/7/43; 422 performances), at the Alvin Theater, marked Porter's last score written for Ethel Merman. Bill Johnson, Paula Laurence and Betty Garrett were also in the wartime musical.

Mexican Hayride (1/28/44; 481 performances) was another hit show for Porter; the show had a less-than-top-notch score, though "I Love You" became a big hit. Bobby Clark and June Havoc starred. This show, like Porter's last four shows, played over 400 performances, yet none of the scores for these shows achieved the success of Porter's musicals of the thirties.

His next score was for producer Billy Rose's *(q.v.)* revue *The Seven Lively Arts* (12/7/44; 183 performances). The cast was superlative: Beatrice Lillie, Bert Lahr, Benny Goodman, Alicia Markova and Dolores Gray headlined. The revue introduced one hit, "Ev'rytime We Say Goodbye," one of Porter's greatest ballads.

Porter's next show, the monumental *Around the World in Eighty Days* (5/31/46; 75 performances) was written for the enormous talents of Orson Welles, who produced, directed and contributed the book. The young genius also starred in the show, which proved to be an expensive failure. Porter's contributions contained nothing of much interest to his fans.

Word on the Rialto was that Porter was washed up. Although he began the forties with long runs, he had few big hit tunes. Porter seemed to have lost touch with the changing scene on Broadway. After the war, high society and sophistication were decidedly out of fashion. However, at his lowest ebb, Porter came up with his greatest success.

Samuel and Bella Spewack (librettists of *Leave It to Me!*) wrote a modern adaptation of William Shakespeare's *The Taming of the Shrew,* a work totally different from the kinds of shows Porter had been writing. Porter managed to produce a masterpiece, *Kiss Me, Kate* (12/30/48; 1,077 performances). It was a show in the best tradition of what came to be known as the Rodgers and Hammerstein *(q.v.)* styled musical. The songs were not the usual star turns that Porter was so adept at writing. Instead, the songs in *Kiss Me, Kate* defined characters, advanced the plot and provided an excellent opportunity for Porter to exhibit his characteristically ingenious wordplay. The show opened with Alfred Drake, Patricia Morison, Harold Lang and Lisa Kirk heading the cast. The score is among Porter's best with "Another Openin', Another Show," "Wunderbar" and "So in Love" receiving the greatest airplay. But the rest of the score was as good as, and sometimes better than, the hit-paraded songs. Porter had proved that reports of the death of his career were premature.

Kiss Me, Kate's producers Saint Subber and Lemuel Ayers commissioned Porter's next show, *Out of this World* (12/21/50; 157 performances). Surprisingly, "From This Moment On," the song that became the best known of the score, was dropped from the show during its out-of-town tryout. The remaining songs as sung by Charlotte Greenwood, William Eythe, Priscilla Gillette and William Redfield were almost of the caliber of those for *Kiss Me, Kate.*

Porter's next to last show, *Can-Can* (5/7/53; 892 performances), was a much bigger hit. The Parisian locale was better suited to Porter's sensibilities, and the score yielded several hits: "I Love Paris," "C'est Magnifique" and "Can-Can." Lilo, Peter Cookson and Hans Conreid were the advertised stars, but by the end of the opening night at the Shubert Theater *(q.v.),* another star was born, Gwen Verdon. The production proved to be Porter's second longest run.

His last show, *Silk Stockings* (2/24/55; 478 performances) was based on the film *Ninotchka*. Hildegarde Neff had the Greta Garbo part with support from Don Ameche and Gretchen Wyler. "All of You" was the hit song of the show, which was later made into a movie musical starring Fred Astaire and Cyd Charisse. The musical proved a successful end to Porter's Broadway career.

Porter wrote two scores for the movies, *High Society* and *Les Girls,* as well as an original television musical, *Aladdin*. He died on October 15, 1964.

POSTER Of all the artifacts and mementos from long-forgotten Broadway shows, often it's the poster that gives the best idea of the spirit of a show and provides the most valuable clues to Broadway's past.

In contrast, the playbills list names (some recognizable, most not) and give facts that don't mean much unless one was lucky enough to see the show. In looking back, newspaper reviews can be used to judge the critic and the accuracy of his or her opinions, if one is familiar with the show that was reviewed. The old photographs depict actors in exaggerated poses in harsh and unflattering lighting that casts them as unmoving masses in gray costumes.

The posters, on the other hand, seem to bring the actors to life. They are dramatically posed against backgrounds that suggest the style and location of the offering. The poster may bear only a passing resemblance to the reality of the show, but the dramatic poses, the vibrant colors and the exciting typography are definitely theatrical.

Posters have always served a commercial purpose in the history of illustration. They represent a show or a show's star in a way that entices the public to the theater to buy tickets for the show.

The early poster designers of the late 19th century were staff artists working for the lithography houses that serviced the theatrical world. The artist was given snapshots of the piece and sometimes a script or a written description of what scenes were to be depicted. Louis Prang, a leading printer, explained that the job of the poster artist was "to reproduce, to imitate, not to create."

Matt Morgan of Strobridge Lithograph Company of Cincinnati is generally considered to be the first great American poster artist. At the turn of the century, the heyday of the European art-poster craze led by such fine artists as Toulouse Lautrec, Mucha and Beardsley, American posters were just beginning to show imagination and drama.

Charles Cochran, the English producer, wrote in 1898: "When I first visited America, I was struck with the horrors that looked down upon one from the hoardings. The huge theatrical posters, although beautifully printed, were entirely lacking in taste as regards design and colour. The figures were tailors' dummies without life or movement and the backgrounds were the old stereotyped German photographic reproductions of scenes from the play advertised."

Some designs were taken from photographs of the productions, and others were completely fanciful renditions of the onstage action. Taking their cue from the overstated, overblown circus poster, Broadway posters often featured incredible scenes that could obviously never be enacted on stage.

European influences soon changed the look of American posters. During the 1920s, posters reflected the growth of the field of advertising. Publicity posters received their first wide distribution when they were applied to the sides of buildings, buses and billboards. Theater posters reflected the changes brought by advertising art.

In the 1930s illustration became less important as more names were featured on the posters. Since then, the basic look of the theater poster has not changed. As fashions in art changed, so did the designs of the theater poster. Styles today are as varied as the styles of writing in the thousands of shows whose images have been "sniped" on construction walls throughout Manhattan.

Recently, the poster has tended to feature the show's logo, an image that will forever define the show in the public's mind. For the most part, the designer of the logo is also the designer of the poster, but not always. Even today, advertising agencies put together posters following contractural requirements. After fitting all the names on the poster, they find whatever place is open on the poster and jam in the logo.

Many prominent artists not primarily known for their poster work have tried their hands at theater posters. These include Thomas Nast (*The Little Corporal,* 1898), Alexander Calder (*The Glass Slipper,* 1925), Milton Glaser (*The Wiz,* 1975), Lee Simonson (*Porgy,* 1927; *Marco Millions,* 1928), John Held Jr. (*Boy Meets Girl,* 1935), Saul Steinberg (*The Waltz of the Toreadors,* 1957), Leonard Baskin (*The Ballad of the Sad Cafe,* 1963), Ben Shahn (*A View from the Bridge,* 1965), Maurice Sendak (*Stages,* 1978), and Edward Gorey (*Dracula,* 1977).

At its best, the Broadway poster excites the eye and mind and hopefully gets tickets sold at the box office. The works of great designers like Tom Morrow (*Fiddler on the Roof,* 1964; *Grind,* 1985), Eula (*High Spirits,* 1964; *Legends,* 1985), David Byrd (*Follies,* 1971), James McMullan (*Comedians,* 1976; *Anna Christie,* 1977; *I Remember Mama,* 1979), Paul Davis (N.Y. Shakespeare Festival), and Hilary Knight (*Half a Sixpence,* 1965) help define Broadway and Times Square.

PRESS AGENT The press agent's job is the most influential of all the jobs in the Broadway area. Nothing reaches the public without going through the press agent. The agent places stories and interviews in the press, invites the critics, picks the quotes for advertising and keeps the show in the public's mind.

At the turn of the century, when Times Square became Times Square, the age of ballyhoo and bumbergriff was upon us. The art of flimflammery had reached its apogee with P.T. Barnum and his cohorts. These early flacks realized the power of advertising. They would go to almost any length for valuable newspaper space. They didn't rely on polls or psychological samplings or truth in advertising. Adjectives were flung without care, landing where they may. In other fields, blatant exaggeration had led to censorship or government regulations. The Food and Drug Administration had reined in the overly effusive advertising of Lydia Pinkham and her ilk, but on Broadway, it was still anything goes.

Behind the hoopla were talented individuals who helped shape the future of the theater, press agents like Will Page, Harry Reichenbach, Walter Kingsley and Dexter Fellows. They were scorned by the newsreporters whose lives depended on the press agents' steady ouput of hype and hyperbole, which is strange when you consider most flacks had graduated from news writing themselves.

By World War I, things had calmed down. The newspapers were warier of incredible stories about the stars, and they were loath to print such features as "Marie Dressler Teaches You How to Hail a Taxicab." Puffery was out, and a new concept was introduced—journalism.

Gone were articles without bylines. Only staff writers were permitted to contribute to the papers, so press agents had to use a different kind of psychology. Instead of just fooling the public, they had to fool the editors and columnists into believing the most outrageous stories. The press agents had to change their methods of grabbing column inches. Stunts *(q.v.)* were going out of fashion; so too, were outright lies and extravagant claims.

Some press agents went so far as to change their job titles to publicity director or counselor in public relations or even propagandist. Although the names were changed, the nature of the job remained the same.

Many stars emerged from press agentry, including Herman Shumlin, producer of *Grand Hotel, Spofford, The Children's Hour* and *The Little Foxes;* Arthur Kober, author of *Having Wonderful Time;* Harry Reichenbach, author of *Phantom Fame;* Bernard Sobel, press agent for Ziegfeld *(q.v),* Erlanger, Dillingham, Earl Carroll *(q.v.)* and others; Ben Hecht, playwrighting partner to Charles MacArthur; columnist O.O. McIntyre; Jed Harris, producer of *Broadway* and *Coquette* and director of *Our Town;* and Howard Dietz *(q.v.),* author of *The Band Wagon,* lyricist of "Dancing in the Dark," "Alone Together" and other standards, and vice-president of public relations for MGM.

The most famous of all Broadway press agents was the great Richard Maney *(q.v.).* He brought back some of the flash, glitter and outrageousness of the old days. He especially excelled when teamed with a born showman like producer David Merrick *(q.v.).*

In the depressed theater atmosphere of the eighties, press agentry has lost its sting. Corporate types took over a field once dominated by free spirits who had chimpanzees drive cars down Broadway, actresses take milk baths for their complexion and who routinely described shows as "the best," "the most," "the greatest" and "positively the most amazing confluence of music and mirth seen upon any stage."

PRINCE, HAROLD (1928–) Harold Prince is currently Broadway's most successful producer and director. Recently, in the wake of a string of failures, Broadway wags announced his career dead. But with his direction of *Phantom of the Opera,* the most successful musical in decades, he has once again risen to the top of his profession.

Prince began as a stage manager for George Abbott *(q.v.).* He then became a boy wonder through his partnership with the more experienced producer Robert Griffith. Prince set out on his own when Griffith died in 1961.

Perhaps he is noted for a series of astonishing musicals he produced and sometimes directed in collaboration with songwriter Stephen Sondheim *(q.v.).* After several financially unsuccessful pairings with Sondheim, Prince moved on. The next period was rather fallow.

Some consider Prince to be an important part of the evolution of the American musical. He has an ability to control pacing and structure and a great eye toward theatricality and stage pictures. On the minus side is his penchant for overly large productions that overwhelm the humanity of the material and, sometimes an inability to work with actors on performance subtleties. Prince is often more concerned with the physical and technical elements of script and production. However, he can be brilliant at casting. Since leaving Sondheim, he has tended to work with less-than-adequate writers.

It must be said, however, that Prince's record of success is almost unequaled in the history of American theater. His shows as a producer or coproducer include *The Pajama Game* (5/13/54; 1,061 performances); *Damn Yankees* (5/5/55; 1,019 performances); *New Girl in Town* (5/14/57; 431 performances); *West Side Story* (9/26/57; 732 performances); *Fiorello!* (11/23/59; 796 performances); *Tenderloin* (10/17/60; 216 performances); *A Family Affair* (1/27/62; 65 performances) as director only; *A Funny Thing Happened on the Way to the Forum* (5/8/62; 965 performances); *She Loves Me* (4/23/63; 302 performances) also as director; *Fiddler on the Roof* (9/22/64; 3,242 performances); *Baker Street* (2/16/65; 313 performances) as director only; *Flora, the Red Menace* (5/11/65; 87 performances); *It's a Bird, It's a Plane, It's Superman* (3/29/66; 129 performances), also as director; *Cabaret* (11/20/66; 1,166 performances), also as director; *Zorba* (11/17/68; 305 performances), also as director; *Company* (4/26/70; 690 performances), also as director; *Follies* (4/4/71; 522 performances), also as codirector; *A Little Night Music* (2/25/73; 601 performances), also as director; *Candide* (12/11/73; 740 performances), also as director; *Love for Love* (play) (11/11/74; 24 performances); *Pacific Overtures* (1/11/76; 193 performances), also as director; *Rex* (4/25/76; 49 performances), as codirector only; *On the Twentieth Century* (2/19/78; 460 performances), as director only; *Sweeney Todd* (3/1/79; 557 performances), as director only; *Evita* (9/25/79; 1,568 performances), as director only; *Merrily We Roll Along* (11/16/81; 16 performances), also as director; *A Doll's Life* (9/23/82; 5 performances), as director only; *End of the World* (play) (5/6/84; 33 performances), as director only; *Grind* (4/16/85; 79 performances), as director only; and *Phantom of the Opera* (1/26/88).

PRINCESS THEATER 104 W. 39th Street. Architect: William A. Swasey. Opening: March 14, 1913; one-act plays: *The Switchboard; Fear; Fancy Free; Any Night* and *A Tragedy of the Future.* The Princess Theater, long a failure as a legitimate house, played an important role in the history of the American musical. In the teens, the Princess served as the home of the first great intimate musicals. They were written by Jerome Kern *(q.v.)*, Guy Bolton *(q.v.)* and P.G. Wodehouse. Later the theater served as the home for the long-running revue *Pins and Needles*.

The Princess, designed by William A. Swasey, was built as a small auditorium by the Shubert brothers *(q.v.)*, William A. Brady and Arch Selwyn. The site for the 299-seat theater was chosen for its proximity to the Metropolitan Opera. Unlike other theaters uptown, the Princess had a simple design. There were 14 rows of seats in the orchestra section and four boxes.

After several false starts, Holbrook Blinn was named director and F. Ray Comstock the manager of Broadway's newest venue. The theater was to feature the works of new playwrights. Four one-act plays were presented at its opening. The opening bill proved to be unpopular, and Brady and Selwyn gave Comstock their shares in the theater.

Comstock decided that a new policy was necessary and asked a leading agent, Elisabeth Marbury, for her help. She represented many of the best-known playwrights, and her business sense was legendary. She was the first agent to get her playwrights a percentage of the gross receipts of their productions instead of a flat fee. Marbury also helped the career of America's leading dance team, Vernon and Irene Castle *(q.v.)*.

Marbury suggested small, intimate musicals for the Princess's stage. Comstock agreed, but it was decided that the leading Broadway composers wouldn't be interested, given the small size of the house. Marbury approached the young Jerome Kern, who in turn suggested librettist Guy Bolton. Comstock meanwhile booked a production of a decade-old English musical, *Mr. Popple of Ippleton*. The show was entitled *Nobody Home* for its American debut.

The Dramatic Mirror contained an advertisement about the theater's new policy: "A radical change of policy is impending at the Princess Theater, on West Thirty-ninth Street, where the Barnes South African moving pictures are now being shown."

Nobody's Home (4/20/15; 135 performances) had some new Jerome Kern numbers interpolated into the original Paul Rubens score. The Shuberts were having one of their occasional fights with the *New York Times*. A statement in the program read, "This theater does not advertise in the 'New York Times.'" The producers might have considered themselves lucky that the *Times* didn't send a reviewer. Those who did attend did not like the show. Before the show closed, it was decided to move the production to the Maxine Elliott's Theater *(q.v.)* nearby. The Princess's small seating capacity simply didn't allow for a big enough profit.

Kern wrote the score for the second Princess Theater show, *Very Good Eddie* (12/23/15; 341 performances).

Philip Bartholomae and Guy Bolton contributed the book. Herbert Reynolds and Schuyler Greene wrote the lyrics to Kern's tunes. *Very Good Eddie* led the way to a succession of successful, intimate musicals at the Princess. The following Princess show, *Go To It* (12/24/16; 23 performances) was an adaptation of Charles Hoyt's 1894 hit, *A Milk White Flag*.

The Princess's next show, *Oh, Boy!* (2/20/17; 463 performances), represented another step forward in the gradual evolution of a truly American musical distinct from the European operetta tradition. The Kern, Bolton and Wodehouse musical was an immediate success. The trio continued their advancement of the musical theater form with the fifth Princess Theater show and their last collaboration, *Oh, Lady! Lady!!* (2/1/18; 219 performances) with Vivienne Segal.

For *Oh, My Dear!* (11/27/18; 189 performances), Wodehouse and Bolton collaborated with a new composer, Louis A. Hirsch. The last of the Princess Theater musicals was the Richard Whiting and Raymond B. Egan musical *Toot Sweet* (5/7/19; 45 performances).

In 1928, the name of the theater was changed for the first time. Beginning with the opening of *Sun-Up* (10/22/28; 137 performances), the theater was called the Lucille La Verne Theater.

The theater was renamed the Princess with *He Walked in Her Sleep* (4/4/29; 20 performances). The old name lasted only a few months. On October 16, 1929, with the opening of the play *Lolly* (29 performances), the Princess became the Assembly Theater.

The Depression took a toll on Broadway theaters, and the Assembly was no exception. In 1933, the theater became a movie house, the Reo. The International Ladies Garment Workers Union bought the building and used it as a union hall. They presented a show in their theater, which they called the Labor Stage.

The result was Harold Rome's *(q.v.)* surprise success, *Pins and Needles* (11/27/37; 1,108 performances). The topical revue starred members of the Union, many of whom were making their performing debuts. *Pins and Needles* became a smash hit and played several editions at the Labor Stage. Until *Hellzapoppin*, *Pins and Needles* was the longest-running Broadway musical. It played the Labor Stage for most of its run, leaving for the Windsor Theater in June 1939.

The theater changed again in 1944 when it became the Theater Workshop. On October 31, 1947, the movie *Lucia de Lammermoor* opened in the theater, which was renamed the Cinema Dante. On April 22, 1948, the movie *Not Guilty* opened. This time, the theater was called the Little Met. Its name was changed one last time on April 16, 1952, with the opening of the movie *La Forza Del Destino*. The theater's last name was Cinema Verdi.

In June 1955, the theater, which had figured so strongly

in the history of the musical, was razed to make room for an office building.

PULITZER PRIZE FOR DRAMA The controversial Pulitzer Prize for drama has been awarded since 1917–1918 when the first recipient was *Why Marry?* by Jess Lynch Williams. The prize is given to "the original American play performed in New York which shall best represent the educational value and power of the stage in raising the standard of good morals and good manners." The award choices proved unpopular with members of the critical community in the twenties and early thirties. The choice of Edith Wharton's *The Old Maid* over such later classics as Lillian Hellman's *The Children's Hour,* Clifford Odets's *Awake and Sing* and Robert E. Sherwood's *The Petrified Forest* angered the critical community and led to the founding of the New York Drama Critics' Circle Award *(q.v.).*

The first Pulitzer Prize for a musical was given to *Of Thee I Sing* in 1931–1932. However, since the judges felt this was a literary award, composer George Gershwin *(q.v.)* was not included. In some years, no Pulitzer Prize for drama has been given. On occasion, the judges' choices have been rejected by the Pulitzer board, and other plays have been awarded the prize.

PUNCH AND JUDY THEATRE See CHARLES HOPKINS THEATER.

RADIANT CENTER See GEORGE ABBOTT THEATER.

RECTOR'S RESTAURANT Broadway between 43th and 44th Street. Rector's was the most lavish and most important of the "lobster palaces" that dotted Broadway at the turn of the century. When its doors were opened on September 23, 1899, a new era of fine dining was born in what was then Longacre Square.

Charles Rector's father was a short-order cook at the Frontier House in Lewiston, New York. Charles Rector moved to Rockport, a location near the Erie Canal. At his restaurant the Sign of the Griffin, the elder Rector refined his culinary skills on traders and travelers going up the Erie Canal.

Charles Rector was an ambitious teenager. After a term in the Civil War and a subsequent tour of duty driving a Second Avenue horsecar, Rector moved to Chicago where he found a job with railroader George Pullman. He managed the first Pullman Hotel Dining Car to cross the continent.

With Pullman he got a taste of society, and he left to open his own restaurant at the corner of Clark and Monroe Streets in Chicago. Rector's Oyster House was the first to serve the upper classes live oysters. Live lobsters were brought in by train from the East Coast. And to complete the innovations, he used the only cash register with a bell west of the Appalachians.

When the Chicago World's Fair of 1893 opened, Charles Rector held the only restaurant license for the fairgrounds. At that time, Chicago was an important industrial and theatrical city. The added drawing power of the Fair ensured Rector's new Cafe Marine an important clientele. There Rector met Diamond Jim Brady *(q.v.)* and George M. Cohan *(q.v.),* both of whom implored the restaurateur to try his luck in New York. Jack Dunston and Thomas Healy had erected a building

but couldn't afford to finance their operation, so Rector was convinced to take over the building and open an exclusive restaurant.

From the outside, Rector's was a sight to behold. The two-story yellow facade was dominated by the huge griffin standing guard over the first revolving door on Broadway. Legend had it that Gentleman Jim Corbett and his wife were the first patrons to be spun into the $200,000 interior. They were ushered into a green and yellow wonderland of crystal and gold in an exaggerated Louis XIV style. Chandeliers especially commissioned for the restaurant shone over the huge main floor. Floor-to-ceiling mirrors enabled all patrons to see who was entering the revolving door.

The bottom floor held over 100 tables, and the second floor an additional 75. There were an additional four private dining rooms for large private parties and exclusive tete-a-tetes. But most patrons wanted to be noticed; that was part of the fun of dining at what was termed "The Cathedral of Froth" or "The Court of Triviality." The fun and patrons of Rector's heyday were described in a song written by Raymond Hubbell and Will D. Cobb and sung by comedian Nat Wills in the *Ziegfeld Follies of 1913.*

Rector's was expensive to maintain. The rent on the building was an astronomical $10,000 a year. Hammerstein's Olympia *(q.v.)* on the next block clearly illustrated the future of the area. The mustachioed proprietor realized that in order to pay the rent and make a profit, no expense could be spared. He furnished his new surroundings with $30,000 in linen from Belfast. Only a year later, a third would have to be replaced due to thefts and wear and tear. Each year, $20,000 worth of silver was stolen for souvenirs.

Rector managed to turn a profit, although his prices averaged only $2 for each dinner bill. Still, patrons like Diamond Jim Brady and Commodore Cornelius Van-

Rector's Restaurant

derbilt might run up tabs of up to $15 for dinner for two.

To get patrons to part with such sums, Rector knew the kitchen must be as professional as the front of house. All the silver and crystal would not keep his clientele if the food was not also exquisite. He sent his son George to France to study the great eating establishments of Paris. George returned a graduate of the Cordon Bleu after studying at Marguery's and the Cafe de Paris.

Eight captains commanded 60 waiters in full evening dress with divided coattails and white vests. The maitre d'hotel received a salary of $150 a month. In addition, he might make $30,000 in tips during the holiday season. The waiters were paid $25 from the captains and received almost $1,000 a month in tips. The coat room alone brought in $10,000 a year.

The orchestra was well versed in the latest song hits, and when Lillian Russell *(q.v.)* or Anna Held *(q.v.)* entered, they were serenaded with the theme songs from their latest Broadway successes. The stars of the Great White Way all flocked to the new restaurant.

George Rector is quoted as saying, "While others are forced to pay to see the theatrical stars of the day, the theatrical headliners paid to see Rector's."

By the end of the decade, the area around Rector's was known as "Eatinghouse Square." Charles Rector once said, "I found Broadway a quiet little lane of ham and eggs and left it a full blown avenue of lobsters and champagne." Surprisingly, it was Rector's fame that eventually led to its demise.

Paul Potter, a second-rate dramatist, opened his newest musical comedy at Weber's Theater on February 1, 1909. It was called *The Girl from Rector's* and told the story of a married woman who led a double life. In her own town, she was simply Mrs. Grimes Caperton, but she also kept house in New York as the mistress of Richard Van Arsdale, a playboy of the upper crust. By the end of the play, it was clear that Rector's and other midtown haunts catered to loose women.

The reputation of Rector's was sullied in the public's mind, and attempts to resuscitate the restaurant failed. In 1911, the dining room was remodeled, but the restaurant continued to lose $1,000 a day. George M. Cohan tried, with brief success, to lend his name to the cause. Charles Rector retired, and son George tried his hand at a new address on 48th Street and Broadway.

The final blow came with Prohibition. On New Year's Day 1919, Rector's closed forever.

REPUBLIC THEATER 207 W. 42nd Street. Architect: J.B. McElfatrick & Co. Opening: September 27, 1900; *Sag Harbor*. After building the Victoria Theater *(q.v.)* on the corner of 42nd Street and Seventh Avenue, Oscar Hammerstein I *(q.v.)* built the Republic next door on 42nd Street. The Republic thus became the first theater built on 42nd Street. The Republic and Victoria share the same roof and on it Hammerstein built the Paradise Garden *(q.v.)*.

Hammerstein wasn't interested in operating his new theater and leased it in 1902 to David Belasco *(q.v.)*, who immediately rechristened the house the Belasco. Belasco's first production was *Du Barry,* which premiered September 29, 1902, starring Mrs. Leslie Carter. When the current Belasco Theatre *(q.v.)* was built, the producer changed the name back to Republic. The name was changed September 11, 1910, during the production of *Bobby Burnit,* which opened August 22, 1910.

The Republic was host to a variety of presentations for the next decade. Attractions included the New York premiere of *Peter Ibbetson* in 1917; the transfer of *Abie's Irish Rose (q.v.)* from the Fulton Theater *(q.v.)* and *Common Clay,* 1915.

Like most of the 42nd Street theaters, the Republic ceased to stage legitimate productions during the Depression. The Republic became a burlesque house in 1931, but after LaGuardia's crackdown on burlesque it was renamed the Victory Theater. The Victory instituted a movie policy on May 9, 1942. It continues as a movie theater and is included in the Times Square Redevelopment Plan. It seats 769 people, but the fact that it has two balconies is thought to make it unsuited as a viable modern commercial theater. The plans are to turn the "architectural treasure" into a recital hall that could present chamber music and dramatic programs.

RIALTO THEATER Northwest corner of 42nd Street and Broadway. Architect: Thomas Lamb. Opening: April 21, 1916. The Rialto was built on land occupied by Oscar Hammerstein I's *(q.v.)* Victoria Theater *(q.v.)*. Like its sister theater the Rivoli *(q.v.)*, the Rialto was built by Crawford Livingston and Felix Kahn, owners of the Mutual Film Company. This "Temple of the Motion Picture—Shrine of Music and the Allied Arts" was designed by Thomas Lamb, one of the greatest architects of motion-picture theaters.

Lamb designed the interior of the theater in his favorite style, that of the Adam brothers. The Rialto,

which opened in 1916, was probably the first theater built expressly to show motion pictures. This was the dawn of feature pictures. The Rialto had no stage area. The screen was mounted directly on the back wall of the theater.

On either side of the screen were two platforms on which soloists performed between shorts and while reels were changed. The same policy was later used by S.L. ("Roxy") Rothafel *(q.v.)* in Livingston and Kuhn's Rivoli Theater *(q.v.)*. In the orchestra pit, Hugo Reisenfeld conducted the symphony orchestra that accompanied the silent films.

Lighting dimmers were just coming into use and Roxy and Lamb installed a series of lights throughout the auditorium that could be faded from one color to the next. The Rialto's "color harmonies" were widely imitated and can be seen today at Radio City Music Hall.

The Broadway facade was marked by a huge sign in a pinwheel shape with sparks that seemed to shoot out and spell the word *Rialto.* Above the sign, an American eagle beat its electric wings. Atop the eagle, also designed in lights, was the Stars and Stripes.

Livingston and Kuhn were smart enough to hire "Roxy" Rothafel to manage their new theater for $200 a week. Roxy was the genius behind the operation of

Program for the Rialto Theater

the Strand Theater, one of the first motion-picture palaces.

The theater's opening was delayed, in part because of meddling by Hammerstein. He made sure he would have an office in the new Rialto Theater. Hammerstein's impish nature took over, and he plotted his revenge on Livingston and Kahn. First, he refused to leave the Victoria, even as it was being demolished. Then he decided to move into the new Rialto on the date specified on his lease. Naturally, the space wasn't ready yet. Hammerstein insisted on occupying the office. When workmen threw him out he went to the West 47th Street Police Station.

Roxy explained the altercation by saying Hammerstein was "politely but firmly refused admission to the building because it was feared that he might make a speech to the workmen and delay the completion of the theater, now months overdue."

The *New York Times* quoted Roxy further in an article entitled "Oscar in Three Reels." "S.L. Rothapfel, director of the Rialto, stole the last scene in the episode, 'Mr. Hammerstein's little affair,' he said, 'is jeopardizing our opening which has been set for a week from Saturday. That is his loss as well as ours, for I had him on the invitation list and was arranging a little complimentary feature in his honor in consideration of his long managerial activities on that corner. If he continues to give an imitation of Mt. Vesuvius in eruption, we may have to withdraw the invitation out of consideration for our other guests on that occasion.' "

The Rialto opened on April 21, 1916. The opening night was a glorious affair with Mary Pickford, Adolph Zukor, and Marcus Loew present. Also at the opening was R.A. Rolfe, Roxy's replacement at the Strand. Everyone was curious to see how Roxy could top his achievements at the Strand.

The *New York Times* called the theater "a new palace of polite pleasure for the thousands." The ads for the Rialto's opening boasted, "The World's Largest Grand Organ—Superb Concert Orchestra—Most Wonderful System of Electrical Effects Ever Installed in Any Theater—15 cents—25 cents—50 cents—No Higher."

Roxy outfitted his ushers with his usual pomp and circumstance. Their uniforms were scarlet, the tunics featured gold piping and tassels. Every usher also carried a swagger stick whose mother-of-pearl tips lit up in the dark. To add to the splendor, the head usher carried a bugle. According to a press release, the ushers were all versed in first aid and knew how to use their swagger sticks as tourniquets.

The Rialto was so successful that its owners decided to lease the site of the Palmer-Singer Garage and built the Rivoli Theater *(q.v.)*. After taking control of both the Rivoli and the Rialto, Roxy moved on to the Capitol Theater *(q.v.)*.

The Rialto fell on hard times with Roxy gone and the Mutual Film Corporation unable to make the transition to sound. The Depression hit Broadway hard. The Rialto was sold and razed. In its place was built another Rialto Theater.

The new Rialto had an uneventful life. In 1980, the theater was refurbished, and a legitimate theater policy was attempted. Among the theater's shows (all failures) were *Musical Chairs* (5/14/80) and *A Reel American Hero* (closed in previews). After this brief period (the shows played less than a month combined time), a movie policy was renewed. The entrance reverted to 42nd Street, and kung-fu movies again became the norm. In May 1987, the theater was in the process of being twinned, having been bought by the Cineplex Odeon chain. Today, the theater is operated as a first run movie house. The Times Square Redevelopment Project *(q.v.)* calls for the theater to be replaced by an office building.

RICHARD RODGERS THEATER See 46TH STREET THEATER.

RIPLEY'S WAX MUSEUM 1539 Broadway between 43rd and 44th Street. Ripley's Wax Museum was a Times Square landmark for 23 years until it closed just before New Year's 1972, when Ripley's executive vice-president called Times Square the "Avenue of Perverts." Attendance at the house of horrors, sometimes called the Odditorium, had been falling steadily as the Times Square area declined in the late sixties. The last manager of the museum, Richard Carputo, had urged the parent organization, which also owned outlets in Niagara Falls; St. Augustine, Florida; San Francisco; Goodlettsville, Tennessee; and Chicago, to upgrade the Times Square exhibits but to no avail.

At its high point in 1961, the basement wax museum made $280,000. But by the time the decision to close the museum after the 1971 Christmas season came, revenues dropped by half while the cost of rent and upkeep had increased dramatically. There had also been two suspicious fires in February and May of 1971. After

Ripley's Odditorium.

the Times Square museum closed, the wax statues and simulated torture devices were packed up and sent to Los Angeles. Ripley's later opened an exhibit in the basement of the Empire State Building.

RITZ THEATRE 223 W. 48th Street. Architect: Herbert J. Krapp. Opening: March 21, 1921; *Mary Stuart*. The Shubert brothers *(q.v.)* built the Ritz in only 66 days as a sister theater to the Ambassador *(q.v.)*. The opening production at the Ritz was John Drinkwater's *Mary Stuart* (3/21/21; 40 performances). The first hit was *Bluebeard's Eighth Wife* (9/19/21; 155 performances) with Ina Claire and Edmund Breeze. Claire played a woman whom an American buys as his wife. She works up a prenuptial agreement with her future husband for double the alimony he is paying his other seven wives. After they are married, she refuses to live with him and arranges to be found with another man in her husband's bed. The marriage is annulled and—legally free from each other—the former husband and wife can now wed for love.

In Love with Love (8/6/23; 122 performances) starred Lynn Fontanne *(q.v.)*. Sutton Vane's imaginative play *Outward Bound* (1/7/24; 145 performances) starred Fontanne's future partner, Alfred Lunt *(q.v.)*. Vane's play took place on a boat carrying dead passengers to the other side. The drama opened with Leslie Howard and Margalo Gillmore also in the cast.

The first musical production at the theater was *Hassard Short's Ritz Revue* (9/17/24; 109 performances). Short was one of the revue format's greatest directors. He later directed such classics as *The Band Wagon* and Irving Berlin's *(q.v.)* As *Thousands Cheer*. The revue opened with Charlotte Greenwood, Raymond Hitchcock and Madeleine Fairbanks.

Ina Claire, Lynn Fontanne and Margalo Gillmore were only the first of a string of great actresses to play the Ritz Theatre. Others included Claudette Colbert in *The Kiss in a Taxi* (8/25/25; 103 performances), Helen Hayes *(q.v.)* in *Young Blood* (11/24/25; 72 performances), Grace George in *The Legend of Lenora* (3/29/27; 16 performances), Alice Brady in *The Thief* (4/22/27; 86 performances), Miriam Hopkins in *Excess Baggage* (12/26/27; 216 performances), Janet Beecher in *Courage* (10/8/28; 283 performances) and Bette Davis in *Broken Dishes* (11/5/29; 165 performances).

The thirties featured other great performers. Mildred Natwick appeared in *The Wind and the Rain* (2/1/34; 119 performances). Dennis King starred with Leo G. Carroll (television's Topper) in *Petticoat Fever* (3/4/35; 137 performances).

When the Depression changed the face of Broadway, the Ritz found bookings hard to come by. The Federal Theater Project *(q.v.)* took over the stage on February 16, 1938, with the world premiere of T.S. Eliot's *Murder in the Cathedral*. The drama of Thomas Becket proved

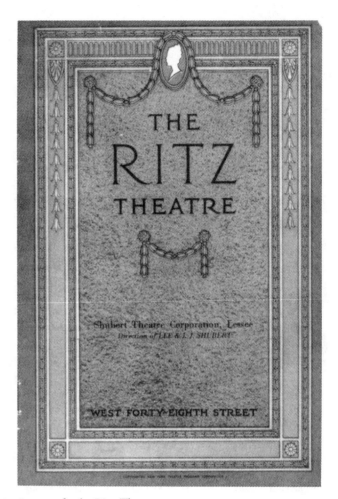

Program for the Ritz Theatre

to be a huge success, and its six-week run played to over 39,000 people.

Though the Federal Theater Project was not wealthy, its productions actually benefited from their tight budgets. The directors and designers were forced to use their imaginations to overcome their financial limitations. *Murder in the Cathedral* was designed and directed by Yale professor Halsted Welles. Welles chose to use platforms and minimal set pieces to suggest settings. He deployed his actors and props in geometric patterns that gave shape to the stage. Most of the important effects came from the imaginative use of lighting to create shadows, silhouettes and stark contrasts in mood. These abstract stage pictures brought the play out of its period and distinguished it from ordinary costume dramas.

One of the Federal Theater's director's goals was to use theater to communicate to people about the time and place in which they lived. Productions like *Murder in the Cathedral* made audiences conscious of how history was being replayed in their own lives. *Billboard (q.v.)* attested to the power of the production: "A hard-boiled audience of Broadway professionals stood up and cheered, literally stood and cheered as this reporter has seldom if ever heard an audience cheer in the theater.''

The Project's *Living Newspaper* series dramatized issues from the front pages of the nation's newspapers. *Power* (2/23/37; 142 performances) advocated public ownership and control of utilities. The play was also presented by other Project companies in Seattle, Chicago, San Francisco and Portland, Oregon.

Power presented a typical American, Angus K. Buttonkooper, as he tours his local power company. Worried that his electric bill is too high, Buttonkooper asks questions about just how and why the power system works. By the end of the first act, he is fighting mad but powerless to change the system. The second act begins with the government's establishment of the Tennessee Valley Authority, a series of dams constructed to provide inexpensive electricity. Some government officials, and the power companies, challenged the right of the government to go into the power business. At the play's end, a voice on the public address system asks: "What will the Supreme Court do?"

Power was instructive and entertaining and, as far as the government was concerned, not controversial. Harry Hopkins, one of the prime architects of the New Deal, commented: "It's fast and funny, it makes you laugh and it makes you cry and it makes you think—I don't know what more anyone can ask of a show . . . People will say it's propaganda. Well, I say what of it? It's propaganda to educate the consumer who's paying for power. It's about time someone had some propaganda for him. The big power companies have spent millions on propaganda for the utilities. It's about time that the consumer had a mouthpiece. I say more plays like Power and more power to you.''

Of course, when the Project began to explore views that were unpopular with the government, the politicians were not so amused or supportive. Until that happened, the Project was riding high and, in the government's opinion, fulfilling its mandate.

Pinocchio (12/23/38; 197 performances) was one of the most popular of all the Federal Theater offerings. The play was developed and directed by Yasha Frank, who got many of his ideas while working at the Roxy (q.v.) and Capitol (q.v.) theaters. Frank even went so far as to scent the theater with perfume during certain scenes. *Pinocchio* was part of a children's theater unit, but it had a grown-up message, which Frank explained as: "one should share his pennies with poorer folk.''

Frank also used some unusual staging techniques. As he explained: "We achieve success because we invite the children in the audience to take part in the performance. They are asked their opinion in critical situations and, afterward, they share in the distribution of goodies that have been used in the play. This creates for them an intensely personal experience and they remember the points that have been driven home.''

Surprisingly, almost three-quarters of the audience were adults who returned again and again to see the play. Robert Rice wrote in *The New York Telegraph,* "In it there are sequences which approach more closely the classic works of Walt Disney than anything I have seen the stage produce.'' In fact, Disney and his staff attended eight performances of the Los Angeles production. They then announced their next cartoon feature to be—*Pinocchio.*

The Federal Theater was disbanded on June 30, 1939. *Pinocchio* was still playing to packed houses at the Ritz Theater. At the closing night performance, *Pinocchio* finished the play inside a simple coffin. Children held signs reading, "Who killed Pinocchio?" The curtain remained up after the curtain call, and with the audience still in the theater, stage hands tore down the fanciful sets.

With the Federal Theater Project out of the picture, the Ritz went dark. At various times, all three broadcast networks used the theater. CBS used the Ritz as a radio studio. Alexander Woollcott (q.v.) broadcast his "Town Crier" radio show from its stage.

The Ritz returned to legitimate theater when Leonard Sillman presented his *New Faces of 1943* (12/22/42; 94 performances). The show starred such new faces as Alice Pearce and John Lund as well as producer and director Sillman.

Tobacco Road moved to the theater for a brief period. Then in 1943, NBC took control for their radio operations. Later, ABC used the theater for radio and television.

On January 12, 1971, the theater reopened for legitimate productions with a rock musical called *Soon.* Peter Allen, Barry Bostwick, Nell Carter, Richard Gere, Marta Heflin and Marion Ramsey starred. Although the talent was impressive, the show was not and it closed after three performances. Viveca Lindfors and Rip Torn played in a short-lived revival of Strindberg's *Dance of Death* later that season.

In 1971, the theater was closed for renovation and it reopened on March 7, 1972, with Gwen Verdon in *Children! Children!* The play opened and closed at the same performance. The theater was again dark until Maureen O'Sullivan opened in *No Sex Please, We're British* (2/20/73; 16 performances). The play, which was a huge hit in England, playing over a decade, closed quickly in New York.

The theater closed again, and for a while was called the Robert F. Kennedy Theater with plans to make it a national children's theater. But the Kennedy family sued to have the name changed, and the project folded for lack of funds. The theater was thereafter used to store posters. During that time, the roof began leaking, causing major interior damage. The Jujamcyn chain bought the theater from the city and spent $1.5 million dollars on restoration. The interior was redesigned by Karen Rosen to approximate its original splendor.

The first production at the restored Ritz was *The Flying Karamazov Brothers* (5/10/83; 47 performances), a juggling act. The Karamazovs later reopened the Vivian Beaumont Theater at Lincoln Center.

Producer Morton Gottlieb reached a unique deal with Actor's Equity *(q.v.)*, allowing the Ritz to present plays that might not otherwise have much chance for success. The theater's capacity was reduced by roping off sections of seats. One of the plays presented under this policy was David Wiltse's *Doubles* (5/8/85; 277 performances). A British revue called *Jerome Kern Goes to Hollywood* (1/23/86; 13 performances) had as its only asset a charming performance by the great Elisabeth Welch.

Magicians Penn and Teller (12/1/87) worked their magic on the Ritz's stage in the theater's last hit. The limited engagement was extended and the theater finally had a hit.

In late 1989, the Ritz was completely renovated. It reopened with August Wilson's *The Piano Lesson*. The theater was renamed the Walter Kerr Theatre.

RIVOLI THEATER 1620 Broadway, and 720 Seventh Avenue at W. 49th Street. Architect: Thomas W. Lamb. Opening: 1917. S.L. ("Roxy") Rothafel *(q.v.)* was the genius of the movie palace. His fame grew as he moved from new theater to new theater, improving and refining the concept of the movie palace. One of the theaters Roxy put his mark on was the Rivoli at Broadway and 49th Street.

When the Rivoli was built Roxy was at the Rialto Theater *(q.v.)* on 42nd Street, which was also owned by Crawford Livingston and Felix Kahn. The two builders were happy with the Rialto's performance and decided to increase their holdings. Six blocks uptown at 49th Street stood the old Palmer-Singer garage, owned by Maurice Heckscher. Livingston and Kahn bought the land and hired Thomas W. Lamb to design their new theater. Lamb was one of the three greatest motion-picture theater architects along with John Eberson and the team of Rapp & Rapp.

Lamb gave the new theater, dubbed the Rivoli, one of Broadway's most imposing facades. The glazed terracotta design was based on the Parthenon. Inside, the theater was decorated in Lamb's favored Adamesque style. The Rivoli had no stage and thus it never held large stage shows, presenting, rather, a series of movie shorts that alternated with soloists.

Livingston and Kahn hired Roxy to run the new theater, which opened on December 19, 1917, featuring the Douglas Fairbanks vehicle *A Modern Musketeer*.

Roxy was never one to stint, and the operation of the Rivoli cost Livingston and Kahn dearly. The weekly operating budget was $13,000, which the theater barely met. In fact, few of the Broadway picture palaces made

money. Rather their cachet was that they enabled the producers to advertise that their pictures had come from a triumphant run on the Great White Way.

The Rivoli shared some of its staff with the Rialto. Hugo Reisenfeld was the conductor of the Rialto orchestra and also oversaw that of the Rivoli. Erno Rapee usually conducted the Rivoli's orchestra. Hungarian born Rapee used the Rivoli as a stepping stone to greater fame when he moved with Roxy to the Roxy Theater *(q.v.)*.

Soprano Gladys Rice also began her long association with Roxy at the Rivoli. Roxy preferred to keep his "family" with him as he went from triumph to triumph.

Roxy presented a program that would become a standard feature at motion-picture palaces. It began with an overture by a symphony orchestra, then the Rialto Male Quartet, a newsreel or educational featurette, a number sung by Gladys Rice with the accompaniment of Sepp Morscher on harp, William Feder on cello and Professor Firmin Swinnen on organ. Finally, the feature picture would be presented.

Roxy's mounting extravagances eventually got him in trouble. He was making almost $700 a week and had his spacious offices moved to the Rivoli. Livingston and Kahn's theaters were associated with their Mutual Film Company, and they could ill afford the losses that began to quickly mount up. They replaced Roxy with Hugo Reisenfeld as director of operations at the Rivoli

Rivoli Theater

Rivoli Theater prior to demolition. Note how the center column was covered and the others were damaged in order to make sure the building would not be landmarked. Photo Jeff Slotnick.

and Rialto. Roxy moved on to the Capitol Theater *(q.v.)* a few blocks uptown.

With Roxy gone, the owners removed the soloist platforms and replaced them with a full stage. They instituted full-blown productions by Frank Cambria, who came fresh from staging shows for theater owners Balaban and Katz in Chicago.

The Rivoli was the site of the first presentation of Lee De Forest's Phonofilm process. It premiered at the Rivoli on April 15, 1923. Phonofilm was a sound-film process that featured De Forest's audion amplifier. De Forest took sound movies of vaudeville's top stars, including Noble Sissle *(q.v.)* and Eubie Blake, Eddie Cantor and Weber and Fields. The experiments were somewhat successful and popular with audiences. But De Forest's system never really caught on, and the Rivoli returned to a silent-film policy. Years later, the Rivoli made another attempt at presenting talkies to much greater acclaim. On May 25, 1929, the Rivoli installed the Warner Brothers' Vitaphone sound system.

The interior of the Rivoli had been completely changed through the years. The stage area, behind the screen was turned into shops, which fronted Seventh Avenue. Around 1985, scaffolding went up over the theater's facade, and some of the design was covered over with concrete. Work stopped in late 1986, and the theater, called the UA Rivoli was twinned. In July, 1987, the Rivoli was razed.

ROCK CHURCH See JOHN GOLDEN THEATER.

RODGERS, RICHARD See RODGERS AND HAMMERSTEIN, RODGERS AND HART.

RODGERS AND HAMMERSTEIN Richard Rodgers and Oscar Hammerstein II *(q.v.)* are considered to be the masters of the American musical comedy. Their formula for musical theater consisted of well-integrated songs and book, with songs that reflect the characters' personalities both in words and music. This formula or pattern for show construction and writing has been emulated since the years of their first big hit, *Oklahoma!*

The success of *Oklahoma!* came at a crucial point in both their careers and at a crucial point in the history of the Theater Guild, *(q.v.)* its producer. Rodgers had already enjoyed a successful career with his longtime partner, Lorenz Hart. The team of Rodgers and Hart *(q.v.)* were known for their sophisticated, witty contributions to a series of mostly playful, lighthearted shows. When Hart's personal problems stood in the way of further collaboration, Rodgers was forced to seek another partner. He turned to Oscar Hammerstein II, the scion of a great theatrical family.

Hammerstein at the time had his own problems. His last productions were failures, and it was whispered along Broadway that he was washed up as a creative artist. He had already enjoyed a distinguished career with such offerings as *Show Boat (q.v.)*, *Rose-Marie* and *The Desert Song* to his credit. Hammerstein was looking for a new partner, one who would challenge him to new artistic heights.

The Theater Guild was also suffering. Their recent productions had proven unsuccessful at the box office, and the producing organization was close to bankruptcy. Theresa Helburn, codirector of the Guild, had recalled an earlier Guild-produced play, *Green Grow the Lilacs,* and thought that it might work as the basis for a successful musical.

The Guild approached Rodgers, who in turn approached Hammerstein. Rodgers had previously helped the Guild when his early musical *The Garrick Gaieties,* written with Hart, proved to be a great success. The revue had put the early Guild on a firm financial footing.

In transforming *Green Grow the Lilacs* into *Oklahoma!,* Rodgers and Hammerstein took many liberties with the musical-comedy tradition. There was no opening chorus sung by a bevy of leggy chorines. Instead, the show opened with a lone figure singing "Oh, What a Beautiful Morning." Furthermore the villain, Jud, was a truly menacing figure, not just a two dimensional moustache twirler. Another change was that Jud is killed at the end, an uncommon occurrence in musical comedy.

Oklahoma! (5/31/43; 2,248 performances) was somewhat unique in that it dealt with three dimensional characters in an American locale. Most musicals at the time still featured the operetta conventions of exaggerated lovers in exotic, foreign locales. *Oklahoma!* boasted a dream ballet choreographed by the great Agnes de Mille. This was the first important musical-comedy ballet that actually advanced the plot and wasn't simply an excuse for dancing, though George Balanchine's *Slaughter on Tenth Avenue,* choreographed for Rodgers and Hart's *On Your Toes,* was an early attempt at integration between dance and plot.

The show opened at the St. James Theatre *(q.v.)*. The production starred a host of unknowns who would, as a result of the success of *Oklahoma!,* become famous. Alfred Drake, Joan Roberts, Betty Garde, Howard da Silva, Celeste Holm and Lee Dixon were the leads.

Oklahoma! played for five years and nine weeks in New York. That was enough to make it the long-run musical record holder until July 11, 1961, when *Hello, Dolly!* passed it. Questions as to whether Rodgers and Hammerstein could repeat their success were answered when *Carousel* (4/19/45; 890 performances) opened at the Majestic Theater *(q.v.)*.

The Theater Guild repeated its role as producer. Again, Rodgers and Hammerstein broke new ground. Their lead character, Billy Bigelow, a bully and crook, is killed in the second act and reappears as a spirit. The show was also unique in that it dealt with serious subjects that the average musical comedy, meant mainly to entertain, rarely attempted.

The cast was another talented group of unknowns. John Raitt and Jan Clayton were the two star-crossed lovers Billy Bigelow and Julie Jordan. They were given some of the songwriters greatest songs. "If I Loved You," "Soliloquy" and "What's the Use of Wond'rin' " are all among the finest songs in musical theater. Other hits in the score were "June Is Bustin' Out All Over" and "You'll Never Walk Alone." *Carousel* ran until May 24, 1947.

After a stint in Hollywood, where they wrote the movie musical *State Fair,* the team's next Broadway musical was *Allegro* (10/10/47; 315 performances). It was not nearly so successful as their previous works when it opened at the Majestic Theater. Many of Rodgers and Hammerstein's previous collaborators repeated their chores with *Allegro.* The Theater Guild produced, Agnes de Mille choreographed and moved into the director's seat. Robert Russell Bennett *(q.v.)*, the noted Broadway orchestrator, also repeated his role.

With *Allegro,* the team attempted to break more musical-theater conventions. One idea was to have the musical-comedy chorus act as a Greek chorus, but this and other ideas simply didn't work. *Allegro* closed on July 10, 1948. It did contain a minor hit, "The Gentleman Is a Dope."

The team redeemed themselves with *South Pacific* (4/7/49; 1,925 performances), an immensely successful show. It opened at the Majestic Theater with Mary Martin *(q.v.)*, opera great Ezio Pinza, Juanita Hall, William Tabbert and Betta St. John. Joshua Logan *(q.v.)* coauthored the book with Hammerstein and directed the production.

The score contained more songs destined to become standards. "Dites-moi," "A Cockeyed Optimist," "There Is Nothin' Like a Dame," "Bali Ha'i," "I'm Gonna Wash That Man Right Outa My Hair," "Some Enchanted Evening," "Younger Than Springtime" and

"This Nearly Was Mine" made up one of the greatest scores written for any musical.

Critic (q.v.) Howard Barnes, writing in the *New York Herald Tribune,* was wide of the mark when he commented, "The Rodgers music is not his finest, but it fits the mood and pace so felicitously that one does not miss a series of hit tunes." *South Pacific* ran until January 16, 1954.

Their next hit, *The King and I* (3/29/51; 1,246 performances), opened at the St. James Theatre. Gertrude Lawrence, Yul Brynner, Doretta Morrow, Dorothy Sarnoff and Larry Douglas starred. The score was up to Rodgers and Hammerstein's high standards. "I Whistle a Happy Tune," "Hello, Young Lovers," "Getting to Know You," "I Have Dreamed" and "Shall We Dance?" were the standouts. Hobe Morrison in *Variety (q.v.)* especially liked Hammerstein's lyric contributions. He wrote, "Hammerstein's lyrics are another of his characteristic blends of apparently effortless grace, pictorial beauty and irresistible sentiment."

The show followed in the Rodgers and Hammerstein tradition of breaking new ground. Throughout the show, the two leads, Anna and the King, have an adversarial relationship. At the end, they have a grudging respect for each other. Before they have a chance to enter into a typically cliched musical-comedy romance, the King dies.

The music and lyrics also contained the hallmarks of Rodgers and Hammerstein. The songs were perfectly suited to the demands of the script and exactly defined each character's personality and point of view. Typically, the songs propelled the plot forward instead of merely commenting on the themes. *The King and I* played 1,246 performances.

Me and Juliet (5/28/53; 358 performances), at the Majestic Theater, was a second failure for Rodgers and Hammerstein. The story was about two backstage romances. Isabel Bigley, Bill Hayes, Ray Walston, George S. Irving, Joan McCracken, Buzz Miller and Mark Dawson starred in the cast. "No Other Love," based on a theme Rodgers wrote for the television documentary "Victory at Sea," was the hit song in the show.

The critics didn't consider the show a failure, although all agreed it wasn't up to the team's usual standard. Richard Watts Jr., in the *New York Post,* seemed to sum up the critics opinions: " . . . if it is far from a peak achievement, it still has its pleasant virtues. For one thing, it isn't a bore. It is lively, vigorous and filled with the showmanlike craftsmanship of its makers. It has a number of attractive songs, its lyrics are bright and intelligent. But for the creative professionalism of the show, there is a curious and surprising air of the commonplace hanging over the evening."

Pipe Dream (11/30/55; 246 performances), a musicalization of John Steinbeck's novel *Sweet Thursday,* was the next show on the Rodgers and Hammerstein schedule. It opened at the Shubert Theater (q.v.). William Johnson, Mike Kellin, Judy Tyler and Helen Traubel were featured in the cast.

Again the critics were disappointed. Most were impressed with the professionalism, but as John Chapman of the *Daily News* put it, "for a surprising amount of time, it is dull." Richard Watts Jr. wrote in the *New York Post,* "The show is clearly the work of theater men who know their business. It merely appears oddly lacking in the sense of excitement that had been hoped for." Walter Kerr, writing in the *New York Herald Tribune* concurred: "The people are capable, the material keeps promising to turn into a party. But someone seems to have forgotten to bring along that gallon jug of good, red wine."

"The Man I Used to Be" and "All at Once You Love Her" received the most critical notice. All told, the reviews were mixed—not necessarily pans but not up to the team's usual raves. The audiences were also disappointed, and the show closed after only 246 performances

Cinderella was the team's next musical, written for television. It played on March 31, 1957, on CBS. Julie Andrews and Jon Cypher were the stars. Another version of the show was broadcast on February 22, 1965, on CBS. It starred Lesley Ann Warren and Stuart Damon.

Gene Kelly was the director of Rodgers and Hammerstein's next outing, *Flower Drum Song* (12/1/58; 600 performances). It opened at the St. James Theatre. *Flower Drum Song* was the story of the Chinese population of San Francisco. It starred Juanita Hall, Ed Kenney, Keye Luke, Larry Blyden, Jack Soo, Miyoshi Umeki and Pat Suzuki.

The score received modest praise. "I Enjoy Being a Girl" was the one hit. "Love Look Away" and "Sunday" were also singled out by some reviewers. They noted that while the score wasn't top-quality Rodgers and Hammerstein, it was still better than most Broadway offerings.

The show, although not as well regarded as Rodgers and Hamemrstein's greatest hits, was better received than *Allegro, Pipe Dream* or *Me and Juliet.* Brooks Atkinson, writing in the *New York Times,* said, "*Flower Drum Song* is not one of their master works. It is a pleasant interlude among some most agreeable people." Much praise went to the physical production. John Chapman in the *Daily News* described the show as "lavishly colored, delightfully tuneful and thoroughly sentimental."

That sentimentality along with a certain homogeneity, some critics felt, became more and more of a problem with each succeeding Rodgers and Hammerstein show. The blame was placed at Hammerstein's feet. Louis Kronenberger noted in *Time* that the team, "makes Chinatown almost indistinguishable from Broadway." Marya Mannes wrote in the *Reporter,* "the Chinese in San Francisco cannot be quite as quaint as Rodgers and Hammerstein make them."

That sentimentality reached its zenith with *The Sound of Music* (11/16/59; 1,443 performances), their last show. Based on the early career of the Trapp Family Singers, the show opened at the Lunt-Fontanne Theater *(q.v.).* The cast included Mary Martin, Theodore Bikel, Patricia Neway, Nan McFarland, Kurt Kasznar, Marion Marlowe, Lauri Peters and Brian Davies. The score was in the tradition of the great Rodgers and Hammerstein's shows and yielded the hits "My Favorite Things," "The Sound of Music," "Sixteen Going on Seventeen," "Do-Re-Mi" and "Climb Every Mountain."

This time, the critics were more apt to carp at the increasingly cloying aspects of the team's contributions. Walter Kerr, writing in the *New York Herald Tribune* was among the most critical. He commented, that " . . . before the play is halfway through its promising chores it becomes not only too sweet for words but almost too sweet for music . . . The people on stage have all melted long before our hearts do. The upshot? What might have been an impressive and moving entertainment will be most admired by people who have always found Sir James Barrie pretty rough stuff."

Louis Kronenberger in *Time* concurred: " . . . in general, the show's virtues are marred by its weaknesses . . . instead of offsetting sweetness with lightness, it turns sticky with sweetness and light . . . ends by making its warmheartedness as cloying as a lollipop, as trying as a lisp." Of course, not all the reviews were as unkind as these, but most critics even when praising the show, noting that it was bound to be a terrific hit, had reservations about the tone.

They were right about its success. The movie, released by Twentieth Century-Fox on March 2, 1965, was an even greater success. It became one of the top grossing pictures of all time.

Oscar Hammerstein II died on August 23, 1960, leaving Richard Rodgers without a partner. Rodgers went on to write a succession of musicals with various partners, to varying success.

For his first outing after Hammerstein's death, he contributed the lyrics himself. The show was *No Strings* (3/15/62; 580 performances) at the 54th Street Theater *(q.v.).* Diahann Carroll and Richard Kiley had the leads in the romantic musical. Rodgers again broke new ground with the new show. The book makes no comment on the racial differences in the leads.

The score yielded a great hit, "The Sweetest Sounds." Rodgers's surprisingly adept lyrics had more in common with Hart's work than Hammerstein's. Howard Taubman, writing in the *New York Times* commented, "Richard Rodgers is still a magician of the musical theater . . . a score full of romance and vivacity . . .

Richard Rodgers   Courtesy ASCAP.

enchanted music . . . his lines have a touch of the wholesome ease of Hammerstein and a soupcon of the peppery impertinence of Hart."

No Strings differed from other musicals in another regard. Taking a cue from the show's title, Ralph Burns's orchestrations featured no string instruments save a piano and harp.

The job of writing both music and lyrics was tough, and Rodgers decided to join up with a new partner for his next show, *Do I Hear a Waltz?* Arthur Laurents adapted his play *The Time of the Cuckoo* as the source for the libretto. For his new partner, Rodgers chose Hammerstein's protege, Stephen Sondheim *(q.v.).*

The two didn't see eye to eye, and their collaboration was stormy. It did, however, result in a good score. *Do I Hear a Waltz?* (3/18/65; 220 performances), starring Elizabeth Allen and Sergio Franchi, opened at the 46th Street Theatre *(q.v.).*

Rodgers next show fared slightly better. *Two By Two* (11/10/70; 343 performances) found him teamed with Martin Charnin. The show, a retelling of the story of Noah, opened at the Imperial Theatre *(q.v.).* It starred Danny Kaye in a return to Broadway after almost 25 years. The show was not one of Rodgers's best, and the score was largely undistinguished. Critics were especially disappointed in the libretto by Peter Stone and the lyrics by Charnin. Rodgers received some glowing notices for his music, but the rest of the production was, as Brendan Gill put it, "as nearly dead as a musical can be." Danny Kaye received enthusiastic notices, but as the run continued, he got bored and exhibited some unprofessional high jinks on stage.

Sheldon Harnick *(q.v.)* was Rodgers's next choice for a collaborator. *Rex* (4/25/76; 49 performances), at the Lunt-Fontanne Theater *(q.v.),* was based on an unlikely subject for Rodgers, the court of King Henry VIII. Clive Barnes, writing in the *New York Times,* reflected the general critical opinion when he stated that the show, "has almost everything not going for it.".

Rodgers's last show, though slightly more successful, was still a failure. *I Remember Mama* (5/31/79; 108 performances) opened at the Majestic Theater. His lyricists were Martin Charnin and Raymond Jessel. The musical was based on the straight play version of Kathryn Forbes's story, *Mama's Bank Account,* that Rodgers and Hammerstein had produced earlier.

Liv Ullmann was the unlikely choice to play Mama but received mostly good notices. Reviews for the show, however, were mostly devastating. Richard Eder in the *New York Times* opined, "the result is not a marriage but a divorce of talents."

Richard Rodgers died on December 30, 1979.

RODGERS AND HART Richard Rodgers and Lorenz Hart were the premier collaborators in the early years of the American musical theater. In fact, they were the first team in which the lyricist received equal billing with the composer. Rodgers and Hart were the perfect songwriting team. (Later Rodgers and Hammerstein *(q.v.)* would be equally famous as a team.) Their fame was enduring and well-deserved. Their music and lyrics were superbly integrated in a sophisticated whole. Although their personal relationship was somewhat stormy, their songs never reflected the problems they were having.

Lorenz Hart (1895–1943) Lorenz Hart was born in New York City on May 2, 1895. His parents, Max and Frieda Hart, were immigrants who instilled in their son a love of language and literature. He attended his first play when he was seven and was permanently hooked on the theater.

Rodgers wrote of their first meeting in *Theater Arts Monthly (q.v.):* "Neither of us mentioned it, but we evidently knew we'd work together, and I left Hart's house having acquired in one afternoon a career, a partner, a best friend and a source of permanent irritation."

Richard Rodgers (1902–1979) Richard Rodgers was born in New York City on June 28, 1902. This is where Rodgers and his parents, William and Mamie, lived and where his father practiced medicine. Rodgers showed an early gift for music. He could play the piano when only four years old.

Like most aspiring songwriters of his generation, the young Rodgers hoped for a career in musical comedy.

Richard Rodgers and Lorenz Hart   Courtesy ASCAP.

At that time, composing for the Broadway theater was considered the top of the art form. There were no movies or radio, and most popular songs were introduced first on the Broadway stage. Like many of his contemporaries, Rodgers sought to realize his aspirations by writing scores for amateur shows.

Rodgers' first song, for which he supplied the music and lyrics, was "Campfire Days" written while at Camp Wigwam in Maine. His first copyrighted song was "Auto Show Girl" with lyrics by David Dyrenforth. It was registered on June 30, 1917. His first complete score was written for the show *One Minute Please* (12/29/17). It was presented by the Akron Club of which his brother Mortimer was a member. Rodgers wrote the music and lyrics to the show as well as the next Akron Club presentation. *Up Stage and Down* (3/8/19), also a success, resulted in Rodgers's father paying for five of the songs to be published.

* * * * *

A friend, Philip Leavitt, introduced Rodgers to the young Lorenz Hart. Leavitt believed that the two would make a good songwriting team. So they met and began trying to write together.

Leavitt was pleased with the way the two boys got

along. He convinced Lew Fields *(q.v.)* to listen to their songs, and the producer decided to interpolate a Rodgers and Hart number in his Broadway show *A Lonely Romeo* (6/10/19; 87 performances). The song, "Any Old Place with You," was added after the show's opening. Fields was impressed with the team's effort.

Rodgers and Hart next contributed songs to another Akron Club show, *You'd Be Surprised* (1920). The show contained 11 Rodgers and Hart songs. Rodgers also collaborated with Herbert L. Fields *(q.v.)*, Robert A. Simon, and his future collaborator, Oscar Hammerstein II on three additional songs. In the cast was Dorothy Fields *(q.v.)* who would become a famous lyricist in her own right.

Rodgers enrolled in Columbia University in 1919. He and Hart supplied the songs for the Columbia University Players' Varsity Show of 1920, *Fly with Me*. The show was presented in the grand ballroom of the Astor Hotel *(q.v.)* on March 24 to 27, 1920. Oscar Hammerstein also collaborated on two songs for this show. Herbert Fields was the choreographer, so it was natural that his father, Lew Fields, attended the show. The elder Fields was even more impressed than before with Rodgers and Hart's work and decided to incorporate three songs from *Fly with Me* in his next Broadway show, *Poor Little Ritz Girl*. In addition Fields announced that he would allow the team to write the remainder of the score, their first Broadway musical.

Poor Little Ritz Girl (7/27/20; 93 performances) opened at the Central Theater. By that time, Fields had gotten cold feet and had cut eight of the Rodgers and Hart tunes. He hired Sigmund Romberg *(q.v.)* and Alex Gerber to supply additional tunes.

Heywood Broun wrote in the *New York Tribune,* "The more serious songs are from Sigmund Romberg, and they are pleasing, but hardly as striking as the lighter numbers." Both Charles Pike Sawyer in the *New York Post* and Kenneth Macgowan in the *New York Globe* also compared Romberg and Rodgers's styles. Sawyer wrote about "Romberg being in his best Viennese waltz style, while Rodgers has written some good numbers." Macgowan noted "Rodgers's hard, brisk tunes and Romberg's rich and syrupy melodies."

This distinction between the two composers' styles reflected the differences in the two predominent styles then on Broadway. As time passed Romberg's operatic scores would lose favor, and Rodgers's all-American style would prove to be the next step in the evolution of American musical theater.

Rodgers and Hart soon found themselves writing another score for the Akron Club. *Say Mama* played in the Plaza Hotel on February 12, 1921. It was followed by another Columbia Varsity Show, *You'll Never Know*. Oscar Hammerstein II directed the outing, which opened on April 20, 1921. Eight more amateur shows followed.

Herbert Richard Lorenz contributed the script and two songs to *The Melody Man* (5/13/24; 61 performances), a play produced by Lew Fields. Herbert Richard Lorenz was, of course, a nom de plume for Herbert Fields, Richard Rodgers and Lorenz Hart. It was noteworthy as the first Broadway play for Fredric March.

Rodgers and Hart received their big break in 1925. The show was a revue, *The Garrick Gaieties* (6/8/25; 230 performances). It was produced as a two-performance special fund-raiser. The Theater Guild *(q.v.)*, which was building a new theater on Broadway, had run short of money and needed the benefit to buy curtains and draperies for the new house. The show was also seen as a way for the Guild to showcase its lesser-known members, such as Stanley Holloway, Libby Holman, Romney Brent and Lee Strasberg.

The show, featuring a virtually unknown composer/lyricist team and an unknown cast was an immediate hit. Six performances were added, and they, too, sold out. Finally it was decided to run the show indefinitely. It not only proved a great success for the Guild and the cast, but Rodgers and Hart were finally established as a top-rate songwriting team.

For the show, they contributed one of best their tunes, "Manhattan." Still one of the most recognizable of Rodgers and Hart's hits, the song has continued as a standard in the jazz repertoire. The *New York Daily News* critic called the "music and lyrics well above the average Broadway output." Alexander Woollcott *(q.v.)* writing in the *New York Sun* opined, " . . . a distinct 'varsity show' character to the lyrics. They are the kind invariably written by those who set out to show up the banal sentiments and meager vocabulary of Irving Berlin *(q.v.)*—rich in sprightly elaborate rhymes and suffering only from the not unimportant qualification that they do not sing well."

The next Rodgers and Hart project was the first in a long line of Broadway musicals with book by Herbert Fields. *Dearest Enemy* (9/18/25; 286 performances) opened at the Knickerbocker Theater and was an immediate success. Helen Ford, Flavia Arcaro and Charles Purcell starred in the show, which was actually written before the *Garrick Gaieties*. "Here In My Arms" was the biggest hit of the show's delightful score. Most of the reviews were highly favorable with many of the critics calling the show a comic opera.

Frank Vreeland writing for the *New York Telegram* singled out Rodgers for praise: "He continues to improve markedly with every score, and he has such a fecund store of catchy tunes and has obviously mastered so well the peculiar technique of arranging them for popular consumption that he will go far as a composer." Of the new team of Rodgers, Hart and Fields, Vreeland wrote, "We have a glimmering notion that someday they will form the American counterpart of the once-great triumvirate of Bolton *(q.v.)*, Wodehouse and Kern *(q.v.)* . . . " Ed Barry, who reviewed the show for

Variety (q.v.), went so far as to recommend it as "a good buy at $3.30."

Billy Rose commissioned the team to write a revue called *The Fifth Avenue Follies.* It opened at the Fifth Avenue Club in January 1926. The trio was back on Broadway with *The Girl Friend* (3/17/26; 301 performances), which opened at the Vanderbilt Theater. Lew Fields, having passed on *Dearest Enemy*, saw the error of his ways and produced the new show. The title tune became a hit at the time as did "The Blue Room," which has enjoyed a somewhat longer life.

Next, Rodgers and Hart were asked to contribute songs to the second edition of the *Garrick Gaieties* (5/10/26; 174 performances) at the Garrick Theater. "Mountain Greenery" was the hit song.

They next went to London, contributing the score to *Lido Lady* (12/1/26; 259 performances), which opened at the Gaiety Theater. None of the songs achieved much success.

The team was reunited with librettist Herbert Fields for *Peggy-Ann* (12/27/26; 333 performances). The show was another success for the trio and Lew Fields, who produced in association with Lyle D. Andrews. The score was delightful with "A Tree in the Park" and "Where's That Rainbow?" worthy of additional attention. Helen Ford, star of *Dearest Enemy*, also starred as the title character in *Peggy-Ann*.

Somewhat surrealistic, the show was a departure from the usual Cinderella story told in most Broadway shows. There was no opening chorus, which was usually used to set the scene and allow the audience to settle down before the show actually began, and no songs until almost 20 minutes into the show. Nevertheless, the show was a hit, playing almost 10 times as long as Rodgers and Hart's next show, *Betsy* (12/28/26; 39 performances), a failure produced by Florenz Ziegfeld (q.v.).

The team escaped to London where they contributed a score to another revue, *One Dam Thing After Another* (5/19/27; 237 performances). Douglas Byng, Jessie Matthews, Sonnie Hale, Melville Cooper were featured in the London Pavilion show. The hit song was "My Heart Stood Still," which had its American debut in their next outing (with Herbert Fields), *A Connecticut Yankee*.

A Connecticut Yankee opened at the Vanderbilt Theater (11/3/27; 418 performances). William Gaxton, Constance Carpenter, June Cochrane and Paul Everton starred in the retelling of Mark Twain's novel. The top-notch score contained hits like "My Heart Stood Still," "Thou Swell" and "I Feel at Home with You." Busby Berkeley was the choreographer.

Without Herbert Fields, the songwriters seemed to have difficulty. *She's My Baby* (1/3/28; 71 performances) had a book by Guy Bolton (q.v.), Bert Kalmar and Harry Ruby. It opened at the Globe Theatre (q.v.).

Herbert Fields rejoined the team for *Present Arms* (4/26/28; 147 performances). Lew Fields produced and Busby Berkeley choreographed. It didn't have any big hits in the score, but the critics seemed almost unanimous in their praise.

Chee-Chee (9/25/28; 33 performances), their next show, was even more of a failure. In fact, it had the shortest run of any Rodgers and Hart show.

Spring Is Here (3/11/29; 104 performances) had a book by Owen Davis. It premiered at the Alvin Theater (q.v.). The script was much more traditional and inspired the songwriters to write one of their best tunes—"With a Song in My Heart." They followed it up with two middling productions, *Heads Up!* (11/11/29; 144 performances) and *Simple Simon* (2/18/30; 135 performances), which opened at the Ziegfeld Theater (q.v.) "Ten Cents a Dance" was featured in *Simple Simon*.

London called again for *Ever Green* (10/13/30; 254 performances) with a book by Benn W. Levy. The show was a much-needed hit at the Adelphi Theater. Jessie Matthews and Joyce Barbour starred. The hit song was "Dancing on the Ceiling."

Herbert Fields was brought back into the fold for *America's Sweetheart* (2/10/31; 135 performances). It opened at the Broadhurst Theater (q.v.) with Harriette Lake (better known today as Ann Southern) and Jack Whiting. They introduced the hit song from the show, "I've Got Five Dollars."

Like many of their Broadway contemporaries, Rodgers and Hart were wooed to Hollywood in the early thirties. They completed a series of films (some great, some bad) but they found New York more to their liking and soon returned. Their movies were *The Hot Heiress* (1931); *Love Me Tonight* (1932); *The Phantom President* (1932); *Hallelujah, I'm a Bum* (1933); *Hollywood Party* (1934) and *Mississippi* (1935).

They returned to New York with *Jumbo* (11/16/35; 221 performances), certainly their biggest show and one of the largest shows ever seen in New York. Producer Billy Rose (q.v.) rented Manhattan's enormous theater, the Hippodrome (q.v.), for the extravaganza that employed an entire circus. Ben Hecht and Charles MacArthur wrote what book managed to be seen amid the clowns, tumblers and animals. The show was so big that both John Murray Anderson (q.v.) and George Abbott (q.v.) shared directorial chores. It featured Gloria Grafton, Donald Novis, Jimmy Durante and Big Rosie as Jumbo the elephant. Paul Whiteman and his orchestra provided the accompaniment.

The production had been promised for three months before it actually opened. Most critics felt that the wait was worth it. Percy Hammond described *Jumbo* in the *New York Herald Tribune* as "a sane and exciting compound of opera, animal show, folk drama, harlequinade, carnival, circus, extravaganza and spectacle."

Despite rave reviews and a score that featured such

Rodgers and Hart perennials as "The Most Beautiful Girl in the World," "My Romance" and "Little Girl Blue," the show was a failure. It managed to run seven months but it cost an astounding $340,000, and the weekly operating cost precluded any profit.

After *Jumbo,* Rodgers and Hart entered their most productive and successful decade. It began with the opening of *On Your Toes* (4/11/36; 315 performances) at the Imperial Theatre *(q.v.).* The show was the story of a vaudeville family who get mixed up with gangsters and a Russian ballet company. It starred Ray Bolger, Doris Carson, Tamara Geva, Luella Gear and Monty Woolley. The score featured such great songs as "There's a Small Hotel," "Glad to Be Unhappy" and the title song. There was an added bonus in the two ballets, "La Princesse Zenobia" and the classic "Slaughter on Tenth Avenue." Both were choreographed by the legendary George Balanchine.

The production received surprisingly mixed reviews. Percy Hammond in the *New York Herald Tribune* opined that "The songs are mildly hearable . . . if you do not expect too much you will not be disappointed." Frank Norris in *Time Magazine* took the opposite view, "a definite milestone in the musical theater."

Following a largely unsuccessful return to Hollywood with the film *Dancing Pirate* (1936), Rodgers and Hart presented Broadway with one of their most exuberant hits, *Babes in Arms* (4/14/37; 289 performances) at the Shubert Theater *(q.v.).* They had collaborated on the book to *On Your Toes* with George Abbott. This time, they did it all alone. George Balanchine again choreographed. Ray Heatherton, Alfred Drake, Mitzi Green and the Nicholas Brothers starred. The songs were top-drawer Rodgers and Hart, and almost every song in the score became a standard. They included "Where or When," "I Wish I Were in Love Again," "My Funny Valentine," "Johnny One Note" and "The Lady Is a Tramp."

George S. Kaufman *(q.v.)* and Moss Hart *(q.v.)* contributed one of Rodgers and Hart's most unusual books. The show was *I'd Rather Be Right* (11/2/37; 289 performances), about Peggy and Phil who want to marry but can't afford to until Phil receives a promised raise. Unfortunately, Phil won't receive his raise until the federal budget is balanced. The hapless couple run into President Roosevelt in Central Park. This was the first time that a living President was depicted in a musical comedy.

For the role, they chose George M. Cohan *(q.v.).* He was certainly one of the most patriotic Americans and one who could give a mature, serious performance even when dancing and singing. The show, though more gently satirical than George and Ira Gershwin's *(q.v.)* *Of Thee I Sing,* caused some controversy. George Jean Nathan, writing in *Newsweek* questioned all the brouhaha: "Why the idea of calling George M. Cohan

Franklin D. Roosevelt should have engendered so intense an interest I can't figure out, unless it was because Franklin D. Roosevelt, on the other hand, has been called everything under the sun but George M. Cohan."

Peggy and Phil got the best song in the show, "Have You Met Miss Jones?" Cohan did have several good numbers including "I'd Rather Be Right" and "Off the Record." The show is best known today for a scene from it that was included in the James Cagney movie *Yankee Doodle Dandy.*

For their next show, *I Married an Angel* (5/11/38; 338 performances), Rodgers and Hart again supplied the book, and George Balanchine choreographed his third Rodgers and Hart show. Joshua Logan *(q.v.)* was chosen to direct the fantasy. The plot concerned a Count who states that only an angel will do as his wife. When she appears, the complications begin. Dennis King, Vivienne Segal, Charles Walters, Walter Slezak and Audrey Christie led the cast. Ballerina Vera Zorina was chosen to play the part of Angel. The show opened at the Shubert Theater. *I Married an Angel* had a wonderful score, most important of which was "Spring Is Here."

One of the team's greatest successes followed. *The Boys from Syracuse* (11/23/38; 235 performances), at the Alvin Theater, was based on Shakespeare's *The Comedy of Errors.* George Abbott contributed the book as well as producing and directing the show. The songwriters were obviously inspired by the material, for they wrote a terrific score. "Falling in Love with Love" and "This Can't Be Love" were the big hits, and the remainder of the songs were just as well crafted. The show starred Eddie Albert, Teddy Hart (Larry's brother), Burl Ives, Ronald Graham, Jimmy Savo, Wynn Murray, Muriel Angelus and Marcy Westcott. The reviews were mostly raves, with the score singled out as perhaps the team's best work to date. The book, however, received its share of criticism.

The Boys from Syracuse was made into a film by Universal in 1940. In 1963, the show was successfully revived off-Broadway at the Theater Four where it ran for 502 performances. That same year, it was revived on the West End of London but wasn't received well there and ran only 100 performances.

Rodgers and Hart followed *The Boys from Syracuse* with a show that ran longer but is almost forgotten today. *Too Many Girls* (10/18/39; 249 performances) opened at the Imperial Theater. It is noteworthy today as the Broadway debut of Desi Arnaz. Also cast were Eddie Bracken, Hal LeRoy, Marcy Westcott, Mary Jane Walsh, Diosa Costello and in a small role, Van Johnson. George Abbott was again responsible for the producing and directing. George Marion Jr. provided the book.

The score was sometimes inspired, though it was not as good as their best work. There was however one stand out song, "I Didn't Know What Time It Was." George Abbott received most of the credit for the show's youthful exuberance and snappy timing. A film version was made in 1940 by RKO. Desi Arnaz repeated his role, as did Eddie Bracken and Hal LeRoy. Also starring in the movie was Lucille Ball. The rest was television history.

Higher and Higher (4/4/40; 108 performances), their next Broadway show, was a disappointment at the Shubert Theater. A standard did emerge, the wistful "It Never Entered My Mind."

Pal Joey (12/25/40; 270 performances), their next Broadway outing, was not the typical musical comedy. For one thing, the lead character, the unscrupulous Joey, was a tough character for forties audiences to accept. He was a scoundrel—talented and attractive but a scoundrel. The score was among the team's most sophisticated and adult. In fact, "Bewitched Bothered and Bewildered" had to have its lyrics softened before radio stations would play it.

The show was not the sort one would expect to open on Christmas Day. The reviews were mixed. The critics (*q.v.*) wanted to like the show since it was clear superior talents were at work. However, most of them couldn't get past the unsentimental aspects of the show and its cynicism. Brooks Atkinson in the *New York Times* wrote, "If it is possible to make an entertaining musical comedy out of an odious story, Pal Joey is it . . . Although it is expertly done, can you draw sweet water from a foul well?"

Other critics liked the show better than Atkinson, but audiences seemed to agree with his assessment. *Time Magazine* called the show "a profane hymn to the gaudy goddess of metropolitan night life." The score received excellent reviews, though most critics frowned on the "smuttiness" of Hart's lyrics. Gene Kelly as Joey, Vivienne Segal and Leila Ernst received good notices, but the general public was simply not ready for an adult musical comedy.

Though too strong for the conventional audience, the show did play 374 performances, perhaps an indication that there were sophisticated theatergoers willing to spend an evening at the theater without the usual baggy-pants clowns. The run also indicates that it wasn't quite as big a failure as is generally assumed.

In 1952, the show was revived at the Broadhurst Theater (*q.v.*) to greater acclaim. This time, Brooks Atkinson wrote, "In 1940, there was a minority, including this column, that was not enchanted. But no one is likely now to be impervious to the tight organization of the production, the terseness of the writing, the liveliness and versatility of the score and the easy perfection of the lyrics. It is true that *Pal Joey* was a pioneer in the moving back of musical frontiers, for it tells an integrated story with a knowing point of view." This time, the show ran 542 performances.

They Met in Argentina (RKO 1941) was released prior to the opening of the team's last Broadway show, *By Jupiter* (6/3/42; 427 performances), for which they supplied the book, music and lyrics. The show opened at the Shubert Theater. It might have been their greatest success but for the fact that Ray Bolger, the star, quit to entertain troops overseas. It achieved the longest run of any Rodgers and Hart show until the revival of *Pal Joey*.

Unfortunately, it was the last full-scale collaboration between Rodgers and Hart. Rodgers was a finely disciplined man used to working regular hours with great determination and single-mindedness. Larry Hart was exactly the opposite. Whereas Rodgers knew exactly where he stood in the world, Hart was insecure and unstable, becoming increasingly more difficult as the partnership progressed. Often, he would disappear for days, forcing Rodgers to halt production or even write lyrics himself. Hart's insecurities led to more missed deadlines and more drinking. Rodgers reached the end of his patience during *By Jupiter* and began quietly to inquire about other partnerships.

Theresa Helburn of the Theater Guild wanted Rodgers to adapt the play *Green Grow the Lilacs* into a musical comedy. Rodgers reluctantly approached Hart, who realized he was not up to the role either mentally or physically. Rodgers then turned to his old friend and sometime collaborator from the early days at Columbia University, Oscar Hammerstein II. The result was *Oklahoma!* (3/31/43). Hart was present at the opening of the milestone musical and congratulated Rodgers on his success. But the show must have been a further blow to Hart's already damaged self-esteem.

The last project that the two friends worked on together was the 1943 revival of *A Connecticut Yankee*. Hart had collaborated with Rodgers on a new song for the show, "To Keep My Love Alive." Following the opening night performance on November 17, Hart disappeared. He remained missing for two days until he was found unconscious in a hotel room. He was taken to Doctor's Hospital, where it was determined he had pneumonia. On November 22, 1943, Lorenz Hart died.

A *New York Times* editorial on November 25, 1943 stated:

> The word most frequently used to describe Lorenz Hart was the word that fitted him best, puckish. He never quite grew up. He was the college boy of the Nineteen Twenties to the end. The peculiarly brittle quality of his humor stemmed from Morningside Heights, and two decades of deep immersion in Broadway never quite soaked it off. Especially when blended with the sure suavity of Richard Rodgers's tunes his lyrics were tinpanablation at its best: sophisticatedly simple, tenderly trite, like "With a Song in My Heart," "Isn't It Romantic," or "My Heart Stood Still"; gaily garrulous like "To Keep My Love Alive."

> From his long and memorable list of lyrics, a score or more gave a pleasure of that tingling sort which a vast

public instinctively demands. For twenty years the credit line 'Music by Richard Rodgers; Lyrics by Lorenz Hart' was a signal of almost sure success. They were a remarkable team. Not the lesser of the two was "Larry" Hart, whose facility with simple words added something felicitous to our lives. That his particular genius will be missed along the Broadway where his puckish figure was so familiar goes without saying. And since Broadway even today contributes greater than its share to the American culture, his death at the age of 48 is more than a local loss.

ROMBERG, SIGMUND (1887–1951) Sigmund Romberg was Broadway's most prolific composer, having had more than 60 musical productions produced in his 40-year career. Although Romberg was proficient in most musical theater styles, he achieved his greatest fame as a composer of operettas. His most enduring shows are still being performed. *Blossom Time, The New Moon, The Desert Song* and *The Student Prince* are all favorites of light opera companies and summer theaters.

Romberg's most famous songs are still sung today. These include "Will You Remember?," "Deep in My Heart," "Lover Come Back to Me," "Stouthearted Men," "The Desert Song," "Close as Pages in a Book," "Softly, as in a Morning Sunrise" and "Serenade." As Romberg said, "I don't care what the form is. But a melody is still a melody. Nothing succeeds like a popular tune—a romantic tune. Romantic music will never die because deep at the roots of all people is the theme of love."

He was born on July 29, 1887, in Nagy Kaniza, Hungary. As a young man, he attended school in Vienna to study engineering. But music was his real love, and he studied harmony and composition with Victor Heuberger. While in Vienna, Romberg had a job at the Theater-an-der-Wien, well known for its operettas.

Romberg came to the United States in 1909 where he held a variety of jobs, from work in a pencil factory for $7 a week to pianist in restaurants. While at Bustanoby's restaurant, he met Edward Marks, a prominent music publisher. Marks encouraged the young man to pursue composing and soon Romberg had his first published song, "Some Smoke (Leg of Mutton)."

The job at Bustanoby's also introduced Romberg to J.J. Shubert of the great Shubert brothers *(q.v.)* theater empire. The Shuberts needed shows to fill their theaters, including the huge Winter Garden Theater *(q.v.)*, home of the annual revues, the *Passing Shows*. Romberg's talents seemed to fit the bill perfectly.

Like many Shubert productions, the *Passing Shows* were low-cost, high-profit productions. Louis A. Hirsch had been the Shubert's house composer for the Winter Garden shows but he and the Shuberts had a falling out. So Romberg was hired to write the score for *The*

Sigmund Romberg Courtesy ASCAP.

Whirl of the World (1/10/14). The Shuberts had previously produced *The Whirl of Society,* and this new show was the second in what was hoped to be a series of "Whirls." Romberg's lyricist and librettist was Harold Atteridge, another Shubert contract writer.

As a staff writer Romberg was not expected to write good songs. The real stars of Shubert revues were the show girls. The cast and material were simply an excuse to parade a series of women in various stages of undress. Songs were freely interpolated into the shows. The Shuberts felt that if the scores needed any popular hits, they could easily be bought. Publishers were all too happy to provide songs to the revue series just to be able to print on their sheet music, "as sung by ——— in the Winter Garden show ———." Romberg obliged them by cranking out a series of good if not exceptional songs.

His next assignments for the Shuberts were a series of mostly forgettable revues and musicals with lyrics by Harold Atterdige. The *Passing Show of 1914* (6/10/14) and *Dancing Around* (10/10/14) were followed by *Maid in America* (2/18/15); *Hands Up* (7/22/15) with lyrics by E. Ray Goetz; *The Blue Paradise* (8/5/15) with lyrics by Herbert Reynolds; and *A World of Pleasure* (10/14/15). These shows were all relatively successful, and most made money for the Shuberts. *The Blue Paradise* contained Romberg's first hit song, "Auf Wiedersehen."

Romberg had six shows open in 1916. The first was

a vehicle for the great Al Jolson *(q.v.). Robinson Crusoe, Jr.* (2/17/16) did contain a hit song, "Yacki Hula Hicki Doola," but unfortunately it wasn't written by Romberg. Pete Wendling, E. Ray Goetz and Joe Young were the songwriters.

It was followed by the *Passing Show of 1916* (6/22/16); *The Girl from Brazil* (8/30/16) with Matthew Woodward lyrics; *The Show of Wonders* (10/26/16); *Follow Me* (11/29/16) with lyrics by Robert B. Smith; and *Her Soldier Boy* (12/6/16) with book and lyrics by Rida Johnson Young. Naturally, with so many shows to churn out, Romberg needed help. On most of these shows Romberg collaborated with other composers.

It was surprising that Romberg could produce anything of quality considering his output. Yet he did manage to create many successful hits. For *Maytime* (8/16/17; 492 performances), Romberg collaborated with Rida Johnson Young, a lyricist and librettist who also wrote hit shows with Victor Herbert *(q.v.) (Naughty Marietta)* and Rudolf Friml *(q.v.) (Sometime)*. She gave Romberg his first long-lasting hit and one of his greatest songs, "Will You Remember (Sweetheart)." Another of *Maytime*'s hit songs was "Road to Paradise."

The success of *Maytime* proved to Romberg that he could write a successful show by himself. He began increasingly to resent the Shubert assignments that came his way. But the Shuberts, and many of Romberg's Broadway contemporaries, felt that the success of *Maytime* was a fluke.

Following his work on the *Passing Show of 1919*, Romberg left the Shubert fold. He decided to go out on his own as a composer and to produce his own shows in association with producer Max Wilner. Their two efforts, *The Magic Melody* (11/11/19) with Clare Kummer's lyrics and *Love Birds* (3/15/21) with Ballard Macdonald, were both failures. Romberg also wrote the music to *Poor Little Ritz Girl* (7/27/20) with Alex Gerber. Richard Rodgers *(q.v.)* and Lorenz Hart *(q.v.)* had already written a complete score for the show while it was out of town prior to Broadway. But producer Lew Fields threw out most of their score and added songs by Romberg. Despite the interpolations, the show was a failure.

With three unsuccessful shows to his credit, Romberg found it difficult to get more writing assignments, so he returned to the Shubert fold. The Shuberts had Romberg on a salary, so no matter how successful the shows were, Romberg received the same amount of money. Also, because he was a contract employee in the years before ASCAP *(q.v.)* was established, Romberg did not own his own songs. The Shuberts received all the rights and royalties from them. Occasionally, Romberg would play the piano for rehearsals as well as conduct the orchestra during previews, all to supplement his salary.

The producers sought to placate Romberg by assign-

Clare Kummer Courtesy ASCAP.

ing him what eventually became *Blossom Time* (9/28/21; 516 performances). Romberg collaborated with Dorothy Donnelly on the adaptation of *Das Drei Maedelhaus,* a European operetta. The music was based on melodies by Franz Shubert and H. Berte.

George S. Kaufman wrote in the *New York Times* that Romberg's "songs of passionate longing . . . illuminate *Blossom Time* like pictures in a Christmas book." "Song of Love" was the only hit song to emerge from the score. The Shuberts were overjoyed with the success of *Blossom Time*. They sent out many national companies for years afterward and the piece became as good as money in the bank. For all the companies of *Blossom Time* that the Shuberts sent out on the road, they never redid the sets or costumes. J.J. ("Jake") Shubert always cried whenever "Song of Love" and "Ave Maria" were played. He would put the touring companies into the Ambassador Theatre *(q.v.)* for one night and then send them out on the road billed as "direct from Broadway." By February 1924, the show had earned the Shuberts an amazing $700,000.

After *Blossom Time,* it was back to the same old grind for Romberg. *Bombo* (10/6/21) was next, another Jolson starrer. There were many hit songs (none were by Romberg), and the show made $445,000 for the Shuberts. Following *Bombo* came *The Blushing Bride* (2/6/22) written with Cyrus Wood and then *The Rose of Stamboul* (3/7/22); *Springtime of Youth* (10/26/22) with

Harry B. Smith; and *The Dancing Girl* (1/24/23). Another edition of *The Passing Show* (6/14/23) followed.

In 1924, Romberg had a banner year. He fulfilled his usual assignments for the Shuberts and others with *Innocent Eyes* (5/20/24); *Marjorie* (8/11/24) produced by Rufus LeMaire and Richard W. Krakeur; the *Passing Show of 1924* (9/3/24), the last in the series; *Artists and Models* (10/15/24), the second edition of a new Shubert revue series with lyrics by Sam Coslow and Clifford Grey; and his first show for producer Florenz Ziegfeld *(q.v.), Annie Dear* (11/4/24), again with Grey.

Romberg's next hit was the biggest of his career. *The Student Prince* (12/2/24; 608 performances) was written in collaboration with Dorothy Donnelly. Its hit songs included "Golden Days," "Deep in My Heart," "The Drinking Song" and "To the Inn We're Marching." The show turned out to be the longest running of all the Romberg operettas.

The night before *The Student Prince* opened, Broadway saw the premiere of *Lady, Be Good!* The Gershwin brothers' musical was a sign of things to come. Romberg stated his opinion of the new musical style heralded by this show: "Casting no reflection, you will notice today that there are types of musical comedies which 'flop,' in the parlance of the theater. On the other hand, you will find one here and there that plays for a seemingly endless time to capacity houses. The latter, if you will observe, is usually the musical comedy which leans toward the operatic rather than the jazz type." This was more wishful thinking than fact. Unfortunately for Romberg, his style of musical became less and less popular and while the so-called "jazz style" musicals succeeded more and more with audiences. Romberg's oblique criticism of the Gershwins was all the more ironic, since a few years later they each contributed half a score to the show *Rosalie*.

The success of *The Student Prince* firmly established Romberg as a top composer who could handle a full score with skill. His next show, *Louis the 14th* (3/3/25; 319 performances) was a Ziegfeld production. It was written by Romberg and Arthur Wimperis. The show starred Leon Errol and Ethel Shutta. His second show of the season was *Princess Flavia* (11/2/25).

With his output slowing, his successes grew. *The Desert Song* (11/30/26; 471 performances), his next operetta, was another great hit. The lyrics were by Otto Harbach and Oscar Hammerstein II *(q.v.)*. Harbach, Hammerstein and Frank Mandel wrote the libretto. *The Desert Song* opened at the Casino Theatre *(q.v.)*. The superior score included the hits "Ho! (The Riff Song)," "French Military Marching Song," "Romance," "The Desert Song," "One Flower Grows Alone in Your Garden" and "One Alone."

Laurence Schwab and Frank Mandel produced the lavish show, which the *New York Times* called "floridly contrived and executed in the grand, unstinting manner

of the more affluent impresarios." Though they lauded the show, most of the reviewers did not see the score as anything special. The *New York American* said that the show had music "of a 'superior' quality. Although some of it sounds like 'left-overs' from *The Student Prince* there are one or two numbers that are delightful." Richard Watts Jr., writing in the *New York Herald Tribune* admitted, "I am perhaps ungrateful in regretting that, with the exception of one song called It, the lyrics gave indication that W.S. Gilbert lived and died in vain."

The public obviously disagreed with the nay sayers. *Desert Song* later had two national companies that played a total of 34 cities. It ran almost as long in London as on Broadway, amassing 432 performances at the Theater Royal, Drury Lane. There were three film versions, in 1929, 1943 and 1953.

In 1927, a good year for the musical theater, Romberg contributed music to four productions. *Cherry Blossoms* (3/28/27; 56 performances) was first with book and lyrics by Harry B. Smith. The failure led to his second production, *My Maryland* (9/12/27; 312 performances). Dorothy Donnelly was the author of book and lyrics of the hit show based on the play *Barbara Fritchie* by Clyde Fitch. The hit song of the show was "This Land Is My Land." Claude Greneker, the Shubert publicist, wrote Representative Emanuel Celler of New York suggesting that the song replace the "Star-Spangled Banner" as the national anthem. It didn't.

Donnelly also collaborated on the third Romberg production in 1927, *My Princess* (10/6/27; 20 performances). It, however, didn't repeat the success of the last show. *The Love Call* (10/24/27; 81 performances), written with Harry B. Smith, did little better.

The composer tried his hand at a show in a more contemporary vein with *Rosalie* (1/10/28; 327 performances). Romberg and P.G. Wodehouse *(q.v.)* wrote half the score. George and Ira Gershwin *(q.v.)* contributed the other half of the Ziegfeld production. Romberg's second production in 1928 was even more successful. *The New Moon* (9/19/28; 519 performances), another operetta, had book by Oscar Hammerstein II, Frank Mandel and Laurence Schwab. The latter two were also the producers. Hammerstein and Romberg came up with another fine score. The hits include "The Girl on the Prow," "Lover, Come Back to Me," "Marianne," "One Kiss," "Softly, As in a Morning Sunrise," "Stouthearted Men (Liberty Song)" and "Wanting You."

The success of *The New Moon* was exceptional, for by the end of the twenties the operetta was going out of vogue. The reviews were almost unanimous, although at least one reviewer, noting the divergence of the two competing styles of musical theater of the day, wondered whether even a superior operetta could still please the public. Gilbert Gabriel, of the *New York Sun* commented, "Theoretically, romantic musical comedies are all so many brave St. Georges against the dragonfly, Jazz. Every one of us howls for a return to librettos with big overstuffed plots, choral fireworks, grand ululations by heroes in hand-cuffs and heroines in tears, with overtures, reprises, finaletti and all the other earmarks of old-time operetta scores. Then as if in answer, along comes something like 'The New Moon'—which is certainly and superlatively as good as they come—and we aren't so sure."

The other reviewers had no reservations about enjoying the operatic form. Brooks Atkinson wrote in the *New York Times,* "Deep, rushing, stirring, it is one of the best scores written for many months." Robert Littell of the *New York Post* was of two minds, "even if it was long and many of the solo songs were pretty dull, there was something full-measured and gay and brightly colored about it, which was satisfying and a welcome relief from the usual cheap stuff . . . the music, which without giving you anything to take home, filled the air with something for which there is only one word—tuneful." While Charles Brackett, writing in the *New Yorker,* called the show "The best of the musical shows I've seen so far this year." He also commented, "The score, I must admit, is the sort which sends into vocalists, who do a great deal of gesturing, palms up and fingers brought to the clench on certain notes."

Nina Rosa (9/20/30; 129 performances) was Romberg's next show. It had lyrics by Irving Caesar and libretto by Otto Harbach. The next year found Romberg collaborating again with Hammerstein. The result was *East Wind* (10/27/31), a failure. After a year off, Romberg came up with *Melody* (2/14/33; 80 performances), another show with Irving Caesar. It was produced by George White (q.v.), best known for his annual revue series, the *Scandals* (q.v.). Hammerstein took his next turn with Romberg, and the result was *May Wine* (12/5/35; 212 performances). Laurence Schwab produced the show, which was a minor success. *Forbidden Melody* (11/2/36; 32 performances) had lyrics and book by Harbach.

The operetta form was practically dead on Broadway. During the thirties, Romberg occupied himself with assignments in Hollywood. In the forties, Romberg toured the country with an orchestra that featured his music. Five years passed between *Forbidden Melody* and his next Broadway opening, *Sunny River* (12/4/41; 36 performances). The Romberg and Hammerstein show was one of the first to deal with psychoanalysis, opening the same year as *Lady in the Dark.* It was also notable in that it dispensed with a chorus line, but it was still clearly an operetta. Wilella Waldorf in the *New York Post* stated, "Max Gordon made a noble gesture last night at the St. James. Mr. Gordon apparently feels that the time has come to bring operetta back to Broadway. A number of theatergoers, including this reviewer,

agree with him heartily. We must admit, however, that if 'Sunny River' is the best new operetta he could discover, it is not surprising that few producers these days are inclined to give much attention."

Apparently, other producers agreed with Gordon that the operetta was still a valid theatrical form. In 1945, Romberg was teamed up with a decidedly modern lyricist, Dorothy Fields, for *Up in Central Park* (1/27/45; 504 prformances). The Michael Todd production's surprise success was probably due as much to the renewed interest in American subjects in musicals aroused by the success of *Oklahoma!* as to the piece itself. What was more surprising was the success of the score. The hit, "Close As Pages in a Book," was among Romberg's best compositions.

Although *Up in Central Park* was a hit, it was assumed that its success was unique. While some other lesser operettas were produced, on the whole Broadway ignored the style. Romberg's next to last Broadway show was the last he would live to see. *My Romance* (10/29/48; 95 performances), written with Rowland Leigh, was, appropriately, produced by the Shubert brothers.

Brooks Atkinson, in the *New York Times,* effectively put the last nail in the coffin of operetta. "Lovers of the dramatic unities should study *My Romance* which was put on at the Shubert last evening. It is standard operetta with standard routines and situations that have not changed through the years. At one time the authors and composers may have believed in those ritualized gestures toward stock romance. But they are pure formula now with high society, passionate love that tears the vocal chords apart and sets the brasses and drums to roaring in the orchestra pit, a theme song of nobility, elegance and boredom."

On November 10, 1951, Sigmund Romberg died in New York City. But there would be one more Romberg show on Broadway, *The Girl in Pink Tights* (3/5/54; 115 performances). Leo Robin provided the lyrics to the songs that were worked up by orchestrator, Don Walker. The show contained Romberg's last hit song, "Lost in Loveliness."

Romberg's melodies continue to grace theaters all over the world. His shows are even occasionally revived on Broadway and at the New York City Opera. His most successful shows will be performed as long as musical theater is performed.

ROME, HAROLD (1908–   ) Harold Rome's output might not match that of his contemporaries in quantity, but the quality and success of his shows puts him near the top of the list of Broadway songwriters. He contributed both words and music to a variety of themes and characters. His shows have exhibited an unusual diversity in subject matter from the Old West of *Destry Rides Again* to the New York garment district of *I Can Get It for You Wholesale* to the Old South of

Harold Rome   Courtesy ASCAP.

Gone with the Wind. But it was in capturing the archetypal New York urban dweller, usually Jewish, that he first made his mark.

Like other successful songwriters, Rome studied to be a lawyer and graduated from Yale in 1929, the year of the stock-market crash. He worked for a law office and asked for lunch money. The firm refused him, and Rome quit. He began accompanying ballet classes and decided to become a songwriter.

His first show, *Pins and Needles,* was his most successful and somewhat of a miraculous success story. The International Ladies Garment Workers Union (ILGWU) owned a small theater called the Labor Stage *(q.v.).* In fact, it was originally the Princess Theater where Jerome Kern *(q.v.),* Guy Bolton *(q.v.)* and P.G. Wodehouse first presented their landmark Princess Theater shows.

But the ILGWU had other uses for the tiny stage, holding their elections and meetings in the theater. Then union leader Louis Schaffer conceived the notion of producing an amateur show featuring members of the union. The show was intended as both an outlet for talent within the union and an entertaining way to present his union's views. Schaffer hired the young Harold Rome to compose the score and play the piano.

The show was scheduled to be performed for a limited run. As it was, the rehearsals took over a year and a half since they could only be held on the performers' days off or after work. After a long gestation, *Pins and Needles* (11/27/37; 1,108 performances) opened.

Rome's song titles illustrate the lighthearted approach the show took to its serious themes—"Sing Me a Song of Social Significance," "It's Better with a Union Man," "One Big Union for Two," "The Red Mikado" and "Doin' the Reactionary."

Once the show settled into a long run, additional material was constantly added. Many more contributors were brought in to the production team, and the show evolved as it continued its remarkable run. *Pins and Needles* had become the longest running musical in Broadway history at the time of its closing.

Rome's next project was another satirical revue, this time on a grander scale than *Pins and Needles. Sing Out the News* (9/24/38; 105 performances) opened at the Music Box Theater *(q.v.).* The show starred Joey Faye, Mary Jane Walsh, Will Geer, Philip Loeb, Rex Ingram, June Allyson and Christina Lind.

Rome's score included one popular hit, "Franklin D. Roosevelt Jones," and another topical hit, "My Heart is Unemployed." Despite the libretto by Rome and Charles Friedman and the producing talents of Max Gordon, George S. Kaufman and Moss Hart *(q.v.),* the show was not a success.

Rome continued in a topical vein with his next show, written while he was in the Army. *Call Me Mister* (4/18/46; 734 performances) featured ex-servicemen in the cast in much the same manner as Irving Berlin's *(q.v.) This Is the Army. Call Me Mister* starred Betty Garrett, Lawrence Winters, Maria Karnilova, Jules Munshin and Danny Scholl. The score again contained a topical hit, "The Red Ball Express." and a popular hit, "South America Take It Away." Like *Sing Out the News, Call Me Mister* made Roosevelt the subject of a song. This time, the song, "The Face on the Dime," was more reverent.

Rome's high regard and affection for the middle class were again expressed in his next show, the lighthearted *Wish You Were Here* (6/25/52; 598 performances), which opened at the Imperial Theatre *(q.v.).* Arthur Kober and Joshua Logan *(q.v.)* wrote the story of a group of New Yorkers enjoying a brief vacation in an adult camp in the Catskill Mountains. It was based on the hit play by Kober, *Having Wonderful Time.*

The show featured an attractive cast, including Jack Cassidy, Sheila Bond, Florence Henderson, Patricia Marand, Larry Blyden and Sammy Smith. Harold Rome's fresh and youthful score included one major hit, the title song, "Wish You Were Here."

The reviews for the show weren't very positive, but in an unusual move, the creative staff stayed on the project after the opening, strengthening the book. One gimmick working for the show was the swimming pool constructed in the center of the stage. The swimming pool proved to be a great attraction. The show steadily built an audience through word of mouth, and several critics returned to the theater to review the new changes in the show. The hard work paid off and *Wish You Were Here* enjoyed a long run.

Joshua Logan (*q.v.*) in his capacity of colibrettist, director and coproducer of *Wish You Were Here* deserved most of the credit for the show's success. He took on the same responsibilities for Rome's next show, *Fanny* (11/4/54; 888 performances).

Fanny was the brainchild of producer David Merrick (*q.v.*). Merrick went to great lengths to obtain the rights from Marcel Pagnol. Three years passed before the show finally opened.

Ezio Pinza followed his spectacular musical-comedy debut in *South Pacific* with *Fanny*. Florence Henderson, who had a small part in *Wish You Were Here,* played the title character. Gerald Price, Walter Slezak and William Tabbert completed the cast.

Rome's score for *Fanny* was one of his most haunting. The score yielded another hit, the title song, "Fanny." Like *Wish You Were Here, Fanny* received mixed reviews, but producer Merrick was determined to make the show a success. He and his publicist Richard Maney (*q.v.*) concocted a series of outrageous stunts (*q.v.*) in order to keep the name in the public's eye. The strategy was successful, and *Fanny* became a big hit.

Merrick, overjoyed at the success of *Fanny,* commissioned Rome to tackle what appeared to be an improbable subject for a musical. Merrick bought the stage rights for the Universal picture *Destry Rides Again* (4/23/59; 472 performances) and hired Rome to write the score.

Andy Griffith and Dolores Gray headed the cast. Rosetta LeNoire, Jack Prince, Libi Staiger, Scott Brady and Marc Breaux comprised the supporting players. The new hit contained a typically well-crafted score by Rome, although none of the songs achieved a life after the show.

New York's garment district was the setting for Rome's next Broadway musical, *I Can Get It for You Wholesale* (3/22/62; 300 performances). The show was based on a trenchant novel by Jerome Weidman. It is perhaps best remembered as the Broadway debut of Barbra Streisand in a supporting part. Streisand's biography in *Playbill* read, "Barbra Streisand is nineteen, was born in Madagascar and reared in Rangoon." Elliott Gould, Marilyn Cooper, Harold Lang, Bambi Linn, Sheree North and Lillian Roth also starred.

Rome's final Broadway production was the play with music, *The Zulu and the Zayda* (11/10/65; 179 performances). Louis Gossett, and Menasha Skulnik played the lead roles, which combined two of Rome's favorite subjects. The Zayda, an old Jewish man was a natural character for Rome to write about. The Zulu was equally familiar to Rome since he had collected African art since 1939. (Eventually he brought together one of the most important collections in the world.) Rome was also intrigued with African music and wove a rich score combining the best of Jewish and African music.

Despite its rather unusual subject matter, *The Zulu and the Zayda* deserved a better fate. Its title was confusing to many theatergoers who couldn't tell exactly what the show was about.

Rome's next subject was again quite unlikely. Rome originally wrote a musical version of *Gone with the Wind* for a 1970 production in Japan. The show was reworked following its Japanese success and opened in 1972 in London. It finally made it to the United States in 1973, but never reached Broadway.

Rome has not had another show produced on Broadway. In recent years, he has concentrated on his collection of African art and his painting. Broadway is poorer for the absence of one of its most versatile and creative songwriters.

ROSELAND 239 W. 52nd Street. Roseland is the sole survivor of the many dance halls and tango palaces that have lined Broadway since the turn of the century. Roseland, with its restaurants, bars and huge dance floor, is by far the biggest of the halls.

Roseland was the idea of Louis Brecker who began his entrepreneurial career in Philadelphia, home of the original Roseland. Brecker and his fiancee Dorothy Faggen were students at the University of Pennsylvania. He was studying business administration by day and dancing with his fiancee by night. They had a hard time finding a place that wasn't overrun by ragtime. They longed for ballroom dancing, not the current fads. So Brecker, after receiving his degree in 1917, convinced Frank Yuengling, a local brewer, to invest $20,000 in a new high-class establishment at 12th and Chestnut streets in Philadelphia. The new dance hall proved successful beyond anyone's expectations. Despite the Sunday blue laws then in effect the original Roseland managed to pay back its initial investment in only six months.

Brecker took a trip to New York City and decided to check out the local concerns. He found that over 6,000 dancers patronized the Grand Central Palace dance hall on Sundays. Brecker decided to move to New York and try his luck. He returned to Yuengling who was delighted to provide the young entrepreneur with $40,000 to start the new venture.

In 1919, the Breckers opened the second Roseland on the sight of an old carriage factory at 51st Street and Broadway. The Broadway and Times Square area was just beginning to come into its own as the center of entertainment. Brecker, like Oscar Hammerstein I (*q.v.*), *New York Times* publisher Adolph Ochs and others, was a true visionary. These individuals realized the potential of the crossroads and established their businesses in what they believed would become the new center of the city. The opening night for Roseland took place on New Year's Eve, 1919. The location was an

Roseland

immediate success—a crowd circled the block four abreast.

Brecker had firm ideas about how the operation should be run. People had to behave in a respectable fashion at all times. The dance-hall hostesses were to be treated with respect, and customers were not allowed to fraternize with the girls after hours. Jackets and ties were always required, even as dress codes began to relax in other establishments. Brecker would provide ties and jackets for his patrons, if necessary. He believed that Roseland was an experience that should be fun and yet treated with respect. In case anyone got out of line, there were always bouncers (called housemen by Brecker) to see that miscreants were promptly evicted from the premises.

In the early days, all the dancing was ballroom dancing. Roseland was the place where many couples practiced, perfected and even invented variations on the latest dance crazes. These crazes included the Charleston, probably the biggest dance sensation in history. Certainly the fox trot has lasted longer, but the Charles-

ton took the country by storm in the decade called the Roaring Twenties.

It wasn't easy for the dance hall in its first years. Reformers took umbrage at the Sunday openings. It was bad enough that people were dancing on the Sabbath, but even worse, they were dancing the Charleston. Brecker didn't consider his establishment a dance hall. He preferred to call it a ballroom. His critics called it a "dance hell."

The violent reaction to the dance halls in the 1920s was just like the violent reactions to rock and roll music in the 1950s. Ironically, Brecker became one of the chief critics of that music when the twist burst on the scene in the early sixties.

On June 20, 1923, the New York Daily News carried the headline:

YELLOW GOLD LURES
GIRLS TO DANCE LAIRS
Many a White Maid, Whirled By
Oriental Arms, Sinks in Trysts of
Shame

Dance halls, or ballrooms, were blamed for all the evils of society. Dance-hall hostesses were labeled prostitutes, and drugs were supposedly sold in the dim recesses of the huge auditoriums.

Actually, the dance-hall hostess was a different sort altogether. Rodgers and Hart *(q.v.)* wrote what is probably the most accurate description of the average hostess's life in their 1930 musical *Simple Simon*. The song was "Ten Cents a Dance," introduced by Ruth Etting.

Etting's character never met her hero, but one or two of Roseland's hostesses did. Claire Patton married millionaire Archibald R. Graustein, the president of International Paper and Power Company, in 1919. Sandra Davis was swept off her feet by a big-time shoe manufacturer from Chicago.

But those were only two of the thousands of hostesses who lugged partners across the floor. When Roseland first opened, there were 150 taxi dancers ready, willing and able to trip the light fantastic. Florence Forder, the chaperon and management's watchdog didn't let things get out of hand. The women sat on chairs on a platform in a roped off area. Miss Forder would take the gentleman to the ladies and introduce them. After he made his selection Miss Forder would release the dance partner from the corral. There were several rules the woman had to observe. First, there was no trading of phone numbers or making dates for after hours. Second, they had to wear underwear for those times their nether regions might be in view. Third, there was no gum chewing allowed, and finally, there was no talking slang.

By 1948, the charge was 35¢ for three spins on the floor with a dancer. The hostesses received 70% of the price of a dance. Of course a man could also pay for dances by the hour. That rate was $2.80. The dancers received about $40 a week in commissions. They also received tips, which usually amounted to another $40. Sometimes, a hostess was given an especially large tip. Uncle Joe, a restauranteur, was known to hand out $100 bills as tips, but most often a hostess would be tipped $5 for an hour's work.

The hostess trade began to decline, and the Depression marked an end to the lavish spenders. Fewer and fewer customers could afford to spend their money on dancing, and so business faltered. By 1951, there were only four hostesses left on the line. That was the end of hostesses for Roseland.

Brecker wasn't sorry to see them go. In an early interview, he stated, "I should have got rid of the hostesses in 1933 when Prohibition was repealed, but I felt a certain loyalty to the girls. Sentimentality cost me a fortune, because I couldn't get a liquor license while I employed hostesses. The hostess is a ghostess. It was the happiest day of my life when I finally got rid of the hostesses. They gave the place an unsavory reputation. Don't misunderstand me. The girls we engaged were

perfect ladies, but the mere presence of them suggested a——a flesh market."

Roseland's clientele was a cross section of the population of the country. As the population changed, so did Roseland. During the war, there were always dozens of men in uniform on the dance floor, furiously attempting to return from leave in a totally exhausted state.

Brecker employed two bands that provided continuous music. The house band was usually a Latin band, and another orchestra would fill in their breaks with American rhythms. From time to time, famous guest bands occupied the bandstand. These included Paul Whiteman, Guy Lombardo, Benny Goodman, Count Basie, Glenn Miller, Harry James, the Dorseys, Xavier Cugat and Larry Clinton. There was also an emcee who got the people out on the dance floor and ran the contests and giveaways.

In the early years, the contests were quite physical. On March 6, 1923, across the Atlantic in Sunderland, England, history was made. That was the date of the first marathon dance. A couple managed to dance continuously for nine-and-a-half consecutive hours. The fad swept this country, and Brecker saw the craze as an opportunity to pack the house. Claims of endurance were made daily but were never officially verified. Brecker decided to remedy the situation by holding the official world championship at Roseland.

Nine couples took the floor and proceeded to wear down their heels. Their merriment was halted by the police, who cited a law that restricted continuous activity to 12 hours in length. Brecker was not one to capitulate even in the face of official actions. He pulled a truck up to the back of the auditorium and loaded the dancers and some band members into it. They drove to Sheepshead Bay, where the *Josephine,* a 60-foot sloop awaited the group. The *Josephine* set sail heading for the three-mile limit and out of harms' way. Unfortunately, this grand scheme didn't entirely succeed. After 16 hours a missive was received by loyal followers back in Times Square. The telegram read, "Heavy seas force cancellation of contest. Dancers suffering horribly from seasickness."

Brecker realized the importance of stunts *(q.v.)* in boosting attendance and getting publicity. His second most notorious escapade was the jazz wedding. An ad was placed offering $200 to any couple who would be willing to prove that they were "really in love" by getting married on the dance floor in Roseland. Robert Wagner, an accountant from Jersey City, and Katherine Bott answered the advertisement. Reverend Doctor William Klett, pastor of the Evangelical Lutheran Church of the Mediator performed the ceremony. He received $50 for his ministrations. The lucky bride and groom found 2,985 well-wishers, who had paid $1.10 each to witness the nuptials. Brecker threw in 20 bridesmaids and groomsmen, who paraded down the aisle to the jazzed-up strains of the "Wedding March" from Lohengrin. There were 20 flower girls followed by a overweight Dan Cupid dressed only in a diaper.

There were also sneezing contests and women's wrestling, but Roseland didn't have to resort to stunts to attract a clientele. Clifton Webb, then a Broadway musical-comedy star, frequented the ballroom, as did Tony DeMarco and Ray Bolger. In fact, most of the great dancers of the twenties and thirties polished their routines or stayed in shape between engagements at Roseland. George Raft worked there for $2.50 a night, demonstrating the latest steps.

Mayor Jimmy Walker punched Betty Compton at Roseland. Al Jolson (q.v.) met Ruby Keeler at Roseland, and Joan Crawford was also a celebrity regular. Other Roseland regulars included star ballroom dancers Johnny Lucchese, Lillian Kenyon, Joe Nobles and Rose Gerard, as well as producer/director George Abbott (q.v.).

Roseland survived the Depression, but after the war, its clientele began to get older and older. Brecker himself didn't dance with his wife at his own establishment: "Frankly the atmosphere offended me. It held too many memories of cheap publicity stunts. When my wife and I wanted to dance, we went to a hotel or one of the better night clubs. I hate to admit it, but I felt the place was an affront to my wife and children."

In 1956, a new Roseland opened on 52nd Street across from the Alvin Theater (q.v.) in what was the Gay Blades ice-skating rink. The new ballroom cost $2,750,000. The dance floor is 185 by 64 feet of maple wood over a cork padding.

The floor holds over 2,000 dancers who can retire to the Rose Bar for a refresher. The Terrace Restaurant seats 700, and there are additional facilities downstairs. Another attraction is the Wall of Fame, which displays the dancing shoes of Anna Held, Bill "Bojangles" Robinson, Ruby Keeler, Joel Grey, Sandy Duncan, Irene Castle (q.v.), Ann Miller, Betty Grable, June Taylor, James Cagney, Adele Astaire (q.v.), and Ray Bolger. Nearby the Wall of Fame is a plaque listing the names of those dancers who met at Roseland and later married.

Nancy Brecker took over the day-to-day operation of the room in the sixties. She said that "The only battle I ever had with my father was when I told him he had to put the twist in. Everybody in New York was doing it and he just had to do it. There was no way we could talk him into it, my brother and I both tried. He would not change and he was probably right. Because his dancers really didn't care that much."

In an attempt to bring new blood into the hall, she instituted disco nights. The room filled to capacity during the disco segments, which began at midnight after the regulars had gone: "I called it the metamorphosis of Roseland. The entire place changed over, the lights were all different, everything changed. It was fascinating to watch it. It was great. I set up the atmosphere of the place."

When her father first started, the admission was about $1.50. By the time Nancy Brecker took over the operations in what she calls "a trial by fire," the entry fee was up to $7, and $10 on special evenings. Private parties were sought, and they added luster to the once-faded ballroom. "We really tried to improve the image of Roseland, rather than letting it go downhill by having not only prestigious private parties but by making Wednesday night into a buffet night."

She completely redid the interior, including new carpeting and new mirrored walls to give the impression of a larger room. The purpose was to make the room appear bright and new as well as to add an air of romance to the surroundings. The regular patrons appreciated the renovation. "They would come in around 2:30 and they would stay until ten o'clock at night."

But it was still difficult to induce a younger clientele except on the disco nights. Brecker began advertising in the *New York Times* but the results were mixed. Part of the problem was that Roseland was an institution and taken for granted. "I have heard more people say, 'I've always been dying to go to Roseland and we just never did it.' "

When both Louis Brecker and his wife died, the family decided to sell Roseland. Al Ginsberg, a real estate developer bought the dance hall in 1981. He remodeled again and reinstated the taxi dancers. This time both men and women were available for $1 a dance.

Currently, there are rumors of Roseland's demolition in the wild real estate speculation surrounding the Times Square area. If it does go, hundreds of people, including Nancy Brecker will be sorry to see its passing: "There's no other dance floor anywhere in the world to rival it. It was always a very wonderful, unique place and it would be a shame to see it torn down but I suppose like everything else things change."

ROTHAFEL, S.L. ("ROXY") (1882–1936) S.L. Rothafel, better known as "Roxy," was the chief architect in the transformation of the movie theater from its humble beginnings as nickleodeon to its heyday as great movie palace. A pioneer impresario, Roxy rose quickly in his career until he became responsible for the creation of the largest and most elaborate movie theaters in history.

Samuel Lionel Rothapfel (he dropped the *p* when German-sounding names were viewed with unease during World War I) was born in Stillwater, Minnesota, on July 9, 1882. His father, Gustave Rothapfel, was a shoemaker. In 1895, the elder Rothapfel decided to uproot the family and bring them to New York in search of greater economic opportunity.

S.L. ("Roxy") Rothafel.   Courtesy Billy Rose Theater Collection.

Though the family became somewhat more comfortable financially, the young son still had to find a job. He became a cashier in the John B. Collins department store on 14th Street, where he earned $2 per week. While he was still in his teens, Roxy went from job to job. As he later recalled: "Through the next few years I had so many jobs it would take me hours just to name them all. I could not hold one more than two weeks. Usually I left, or was fired, even quicker than that."

Rothapfel lied about his age and enlisted in the Marine Corps at the age of 14. He was sent to Santo Domingo and China, where he fought in the Boxer Rebellion. Rothapfel became a drill sergeant and learned about discipline and training, and he later applied this knowledge in dealing with his staffs.

After seven years in the Corps, Rothapfel returned to the United States to find that he had no salable skill. He became a door-to-door salesman and eventually worked his way to Pennsylvania, where he tried out for the Northeast Pennsylvania League as a baseball player. He didn't get signed, but he did acquire something more valuable, his nickname. From then on he was known as Roxy.

In Forest City, Pennsylvania, he met the woman who became Mrs. Rothapfel. Roxy's father-in-law originally objected to the proposed marriage, because of Roxy's precarious financial status. Roxy took a job with his future father-in-law in the family-owned saloon. He tended bar for 18 months, saving his money toward his future married life.

Roxy married, and that year, 1907, he entered into the motion-pictures business. His father-in-law's tavern had a large assembly room in the back, which was occasionally used for sauerkraut dinners and gatherings. Roxy first decided to put a roller rink in the room but soon changed his mind, having noted the success of the new invention, motion pictures. As he told it: "I persuaded my father-in-law to let me turn this dance hall into a motion-picture theater. I bought a second-hand screen and projection machine, hired a pianist and charged 5 cents admission. In that little dance-hall theater I started in a crude way to do what I am doing now."

On Christmas Eve, 1908, Roxy put up a sign that announced, "Grand Opening in Vaudeville—Special matinee Xmas afternoon." The screen was a white sheet, the projector was an early hand-cranked Cineograph, and the chairs were borrowed from his father-in-law's funeral parlor.

The program consisted of an overture by pianist

Professor James Curry, vaudeville, illustrated songs, a one-reel comedy, and films of the "World's Series between the Chicago 'Cubs' and the Detroit 'Tigers', showing the famous plays and all the favorites in actual motion."

As business grew, Roxy began to demonstrate his penchant for showmanship. He covered the screen with a curtain that drew open at the start of each show. Professor Curry's piano was augmented with a violin and a baritone singer. A series of colored lights were added, which played on the screen. They cast their magical glow in alternating pink, green and blue.

Roxy's little theater became a success, and his ingenuity caught the attention of several local businessmen. The distributors in New York noticed that Roxy was ordering as many films as the owners of big nickleodeons. B.F. Keith, the owner of an increasingly important chain of vaudeville theaters (see E.F. ALBEE), noticed Roxy's imaginative success. Keith hired Roxy to improve the motion-picture portion of Keith's programs.

Keith had long considered the movies an insult to his vaudeville presentations. In the early days, he used movies primarily to clear the audience after each vaudeville bill. As the new medium grew, audience members began staying in their seats just to see the pictures.

Roxy was then introduced to Herman Fehr, the owner of an ailing vaudeville theater in Milwaukee. Roxy used his talents to upgrade Fehr's Alhambra into a mini movie palace. The transformation was impressive and unique at the time. The Fehr theater became one of the most profitable in the city.

By 1913, Roxy was ready to conquer New York. He became manager of the Regent Theater at 116th Street and Seventh Avenue. The Regent was the first high-class theater in New York built just for showing movies. It had an eight-piece orchestra and a string ensemble to accompany the picture, as well as the city's first movie pipe organ.

Roxy improved the auditorium and projection system and generally overhauled the entire operation. He had special arrangements written for the musicians. Roxy went on to success after success with a series of motion-picture houses—The Rialto (q.v.), the Rivoli (q.v.), the Capitol (q.v.) and, finally, his ultimate achievement, the Roxy Theater (q.v.).

Roxy's innovations were both artistic and technical. He was considered a genius in the new field of stage lighting. The Encyclopedia Britannica called him an authority in the field. Roxy also realized the importance of music in the program even after silent pictures were replaced by sound. He was the first to employ 100-piece orchestras and immense pipe organs in his halls.

Roxy also conquered radio and realized the great promotional possibilities of the new medium. On November 19, 1922, WEAF broadcast a program live from the Capitol Theater. The two-hour radio show was hosted and designed by Roxy. After the opening of the Roxy Theater, he began a national radio show on the NBC Blue Network.

He took his radio family, known as Roxy's Gang, out of the studio and into many hospitals and charitable functions. In February 1931, Roxy was the first person to receive an award from the New York City Federation of Woman's Charities. The New York Times stated, "Thousands of those who had heard his cheery 'Hello, everybody!' as master of ceremonies in the great theaters he directed became anxious to come to New York to see the man and his 'gang' and his super-show houses."

While beginning plans to open the new Radio City Music Hall in Rockefeller Center, he suffered a minor heart attack. On the day after the theater's opening, he collapsed again. After recuperating, he attempted to go back to work but found the interim management had taken firm control.

Virtually powerless at the Music Hall, Roxy put his efforts towards the RKO Roxy Theater. The RKO Roxy owners were sued by the owners of the Roxy on the basis of the similarity in names. The RKO Roxy was rechristened the Center Theater.

Roxy remained director of the two Rockefeller Center theaters for a year, but it was clear that he was not in control. He resigned in January 1934. Roxy went to London to examine the possibility of repeating his great success in that city, but the plans did not work out.

For the first time in many years, Roxy was without a theater. He went on a tour of the South with his "gang." Following that, he took over control of the Mastbaum Theater in Philadelphia. He changed the name of the huge white elephant to the Roxy-Mastbaum, but even the great showman couldn't help the immense auditorium. It closed on Christmas Day, 1934.

Roxy was distraught at the problems encountered in his last efforts. Even his once-loyal staff abandoned him, preferring the security of their new jobs at the Music Hall. On January 13, 1936, Roxy died in a suite in the Gotham Hotel.

ROXY THEATER Northeast corner of 50th Street at Seventh Avenue. Architect: W.W. Alschlager. Art Designer: Pietro Ciavarra. Opening: March 1927. The Roxy Theater, the largest theater in the world at the time of its opening in 1927, was dubbed "The Cathedral of the Motion Picture." It was the grandest of all movie palaces and a popular tourist attraction.

Developer Herman Lubin had the idea to tear down the old car barns at 50th Street and Seventh Avenue and erect the world's largest theater on the site. As Lubin's plans took shape, he began thinking about staffing the great hall. One man's name rose to the top of the list, that of S.L. ("Roxy") Rothafel (q.v.), the greatest motion-picture showman in the world. He

The Roxy Theater Courtesy Billy Rose Theater Collection.

virtually invented the idea of the deluxe motion picture house.

Roxy was then firmly ensconced at the Capitol Theater *(q.v.),* site of his latest triumphs, and he broadcast his popular radio show from the Capitol's stage. Roxy was happy at the Capitol, so it took some ingenious negotiation by Lubin to attract his services. Lubin offered Roxy a large salary, a percentage of the theater's profits, as well as stock options. To clinch the deal, Lubin offered to name the new theater after the showman.

With Roxy secured, plans for the theater began. Roxy explained his ideas for the new theater in the August 1926 issue of *Metronome Magazine:* "The matter of personality is the most important thing in the world dealing with the public. I am going to keep it in mind in my new theater. I have often said in discussing it that we should not call it a theater at all, but rather an institution which receives its stamp of individuality from the man who runs it. I cannot tell you of the many activities which it is going to represent, but the theater will be one part of it."

Naturally with Roxy at the helm, the plans for the theater grew more and more extravagant and, as a result, more and more expensive. Lubin realized he could not handle the immense financial commitment. Lubin sold the control of the theater to William Fox for $5 million and managed to reap a $3,000 profit.

When the theater was completed in 1927, it was indeed the largest in the world. The auditorium seated almost 6,000 patrons. There was standing room for 500 more in the rear of the audience. While the audience watched the show, there was room for twenty-five hundred more people to wait patiently in the lobby for the next show. Backstage, the numbers were also impressive. A hundred musicians played in the symphony orchestra, and a staff of 300 saw that the show ran smoothly both behind the stage and in the office. The ballet corps had 100 dancers in its ranks. On a sold-out night, there might be as many as 10,000 people in the theater.

The audience entered the theater through an outer foyer, which was part of the Taft Hotel. The foyer space was rented from the hotel, which opened as the

Manger in 1926. From the foyer, the audience entered the great Rotunda. Roxy would fire his ushers if they called the Rotunda simply "the lobby." The great space featured 12 green antique marble columns soaring five stories to the ceiling. The floor of the Rotunda was covered with an enormous circular carpet. The two-ton carpet was billed as "the largest oval rug in the world." The 70-foot-wide Rotunda led to the seating area. Patrons could either enter the orchestra area through gigantic bronze doors or rise to the balcony level by climbing the Grand Staircase.

Though it was advertised as seating 6,000 patrons, there was actually room for 5,920 seated patrons. When pressed, the ushers were instructed by Roxy to state that the theater sat over 6,000 but not all those seats were in the auditorium.

Also in the theater complex was a broadcasting studio from which Roxy could continue his radio broadcasts. The studio was large enough to contain also a two-manual Kimball pipe organ, usually played by Lew White, plus the 110 piece symphony orchestra, conducted by Erno Rapee, and the chorus and soloists who appeared on the Roxy stage. Immense as this studio was, there was still room left in the building for dressing rooms, a costume department, three floors of chorus dressing rooms, dry cleaner and laundry rooms, a hairdresser and a barbershop, a dining room, a ballet room big enough to rehearse in and a menagerie for the productions' animals. There was also a hospital, an immense engine room, the offices and the rehearsal room, almost as big as the stage itself. There were two stories of private dressing rooms, each containing a complete bath, closet, desk, bed and makeup table. There were also rehearsal rooms for the chorus, a private screening room that sat 100, a publicity shop, the usher's dressing rooms and lounge and the accounting department. For the staff's relaxation, there was a gymnasium, billiard room, cafeteria, nap room, library and showers.

The first movie to play the Roxy was Gloria Swanson's *The Love of Sunya*. It was accompanied by a "presentation show," which featured an overture, a ballet, a newsreel and a line of 16 dancers. The troupe's leader was Russell Markert, a dancer and Broadway choreographer who admired the English group, the Tiller Girls. In 1927, Markert put together the line of dancers and played the Missouri Theater in St. Louis. They became a hit in St. Louis and were brought to the Roxy in November 1927. Four months later, their number was doubled, and they were officially dubbed the Roxyettes. In 1932, Roxy now at Radio City Music Hall, brought the dancers with him and redubbed them the Rockettes.

Following the Roxyettes, came a cut-down version of a popular operetta or opera. It featured the chorus and perhaps a specially hired soloist. Following the tab

show came a finale, featuring the entire cast, and finally the feature production.

Author Nunnally Johnson described the Roxy's opening night:

Samuel L. Rothafel, described in the elaborate program as Roxy the Maestro and by the boys along the Rialto as just plain Roxy, opened his theater—"the world's largest and greatest"—at Seventh Avenue and Fiftieth Street last night, thus discommoding the lads who ordinarily foregather there of an evening to play "craps," shoot each other, stab one another and otherwise make merry.

It is only fair to mention in passing, however, that there were 6,500 men and women, ranging from James J. Walker, once of City Hall, later of Havana, and now again of City Hall, to my very favorite barber, Jo, who seemed to have quite a pleasant evening of it, the discomfiture of the crap-shooters notwithstanding. They, of course, were the people who possessed what looked something like paste-board (but which I guess was something else entirely) tickets entitling them to fight their way through a frenzied throng and pass solemnly into Mr. Rothafel's "lasting monument to the greatest force for wholesome amusement the world has ever known."

"The first impression on entering the Roxy is that of agreeable surprise," said a line in my program. It wasn't mine, however, for I found I had forgotten my ticket and had to come way home again for it.

The Roxy, owned by William Fox, was naturally the flagship of the magnificent Fox chain of theaters. As such, it premiered all the first-class Fox output. The box office record was held by an otherwise forgotten film, *The Cock-eyed World*. It had 208,785 paid admissions during one week in August 1929.

After Roxy's contract ran out on March 29, 1931, he resigned and later left to join the new Radio City Music Hall. Art Director, Clark Robinson, assumed Roxy's post until a new director could be found. The Fox Corporation decided to install the producing team of Fanchon and Marco, who had produced shows for the Fox chain. Fred Waring was chosen to replace Erno Rapee.

With Roxy gone, the theater lost some of its glamor. When the Depression descended, the Fox Film and Theater Company was hard hit. In April 1932, the company was forced to default on a $200,000 mortgage payment. The stockholders voted out the Fox corporation and closed the theater for eight weeks. During that time, the stage area was extended over the orchestra pit. This meant that the orchestra lift could not be used. The organ was also made inoperable, and the three consoles were moved to the basement.

Howard Cullman, a president of the Port Authority and owner of an apothecary firm, was put in charge. Despite his lack of theatrical experience, he did manage to reopen the theater. Wisely, Cullman decided to pare down the expensive operation. The 80-person ushering staff was cut down to a mere 18. The presentation shows were discarded and replaced with a vaudeville-style stage show.

In order to attract an audience, the admission was reduced to 35¢, which would enable a patron to sit in any seat in the house. The theater featured other incentives for attendance. A free massage service was offered in the ladies' lounge, the men's smoking room gave out free tobacco and the grand lounge dispensed free coffee. There were also advertising tie-ins and a couple of boxes of toothpaste or detergent could get one free admission.

After the Fox organization had been voted out, the quality of the films fell. The other movie companies had their own first-run theaters on Broadway, so the Roxy was reduced to playing B pictures or the products of independents like Monogram. Attendance suffered. Ironically, a Fox picture saved the theater.

Shirley Temple's *Baby Take a Bow* opened in June 1934. Instead of the usual one-week run, the picture was held over and eventually played four weeks. It actually sold out its engagement and gave the theater a much needed shot in the arm.

With *Baby Take a Bow* gone, the theater again went into a slump. In 1937, the new Twentieth Century-Fox corporation signed a 20-year lease on the theater. The new owners made changes in the decoration to "modernize" the look. Unfortunately, the new designs were much inferior to the originals. They hung giant red and white candy-striped draperies over the proscenium and along the sides of the audience. A new, neon marquee replaced the old marquee. The original wrought iron lighting fixtures were replaced with garish fluorescent lights. The marble floors were completely covered with checkered linoleum tiles.

The owners also decided to reinstate the organ. They placed it in one of the side boxes, only to discover that the pipes had been sealed behind concrete. Not to be thwarted, the management decided to pipe the organ music over the public address system.

Following the Depression, in 1942, A.J. Balaban of the Balaban and Katz chain took over the theater's operation. The new producing director hired top names to head the stage shows. Milton Berle, Jack Benny, Cab Calloway and the New York Philharmonic all played the Roxy. A better class of films were booked, and the theater's fortunes improved. The all-time box office champion movie, *Forever Amber,* was booked during this period.

That policy lasted only six years. Its next transformation was astounding. The stage area was covered with a 30-foot by 30-foot ice floor. The theater's seating capacity was reduced to a total of 5,886. The Center Theater on Sixth Avenue was also converted to ice, and both theaters did successful business.

In 1952, Congress made the movie companies divest their theater ownership. Metro-Goldwyn-Mayer spun off its Loew's Theater chain and Twentieth Century-Fox sold their chain to its exhibitor, National Theaters. Finally, the Roxy's curtains were removed from the auditorium, and the ice stage almost doubled to 60 feet. The orchestra pit was made larger, and black-light effects were installed.

Another major change was undertaken in September 1953. With the advent of television, the movie companies searched for ways to make their films a viable alternative to the free entertainment. They returned to an old idea, wide screen pictures. Fox had already experimented with and discarded their Grandeur process, which played the Roxy in 1930. A new screen was put into the theater, and the wide screen process, renamed Cinemascope, was introduced again. The first Cinemascope feature to play the Roxy was *The Robe.* Because of the size of the new screen, the stage show was eliminated along with part of the proscenium.

When the engagement of *The Robe* was over, the 70-foot wide screen was removed and the damaged proscenium was covered with turquoise curtains. In October 1955, Robert C. Rothafel, Roxy's nephew, took control of the theater and two months later reinstated the ice shows.

Rockefeller Center to the east was expanding, and the Roxy Theater stood in the way. In September 1956, the Rockefeller Center interests bought the Roxy and its land. They intended to hold onto the land until the time was right to tear down the theater and build a new headquarters for the Time and Life Building.

The Roxy underwent yet another transformation in 1958. An even larger screen, 100 feet across, was installed, and more of the proscenium was destroyed. The Cinemiracle process opened with *Windjammer*. The balcony and loge were closed off, and the theater's capacity was reduced to 2,710. Few of those seats were sold, and so children's rides were installed in the Grand Lounge. The Rotunda's snack bars featured clam chowder in tribute to the nautical attraction on the big screen, but business did not increase and the film was pulled.

With *Windjammer* out of the theater, more draperies were hung to cover the additional damage to the theater. Russell V. Downing, president of Radio City Music Hall, was put in charge of the theater's operations in November 1959, and he tried to revitalize the theater. A year later, he decided to stop the stage show once and for all.

In the end, it wasn't the Rockefellers who caused the Roxy's demolition. The Taft Hotel, from which the Roxy leased its foyer space, was owned by Bing and Bing Realtors, whose head was William Zeckendorf. The company bought the Roxy from the Rockefellers with the intent of expanding the Taft's room space. When the plans for the enlarged Taft fell through, Zeckendorf became the owner of a theater that was losing thousands of dollars a week. The theater also cost $20,000 a month in taxes. Zeckendorf decided to cut his losses by razing the Roxy.

On March 19, 1960, the Roxy closed its doors following the last showing of its last feature, *The Wind Cannot Read.* An auction of the theater's fixtures raised only $10,000. The 30 pairs of bronze exit doors were scrapped along with anything else that was unsold. The two-story French crystal Rotunda chandelier was offered to Cardinal Spellman, but he turned down the offer. The Roxy's 3,000-piece costume collection was given away as was the huge music library. Long Island University received the antiques and oil paintings. In August 1960, the Roxy was demolished.

ROYALE THEATRE 242 W. 45th Street. Architect: Herbert J. Krapp. Opening: January 11, 1927; *Piggy.* The Chanin Brothers built the Royale Theatre in 1927 on what is considered the most important of all Broadway cross streets. Because of its high concentration of theaters, 45th Street is the one street in the Times Square area where foot traffic is thought to affect box office.

The first offering at the 1,058-seat theater was *Piggy* (1/11/27; 79 performances), a musical comedy by Cliff Friend and Lew Brown. *Piggy* never caught on with the public. Producer William B. Friedlander even changed the name of the show to *I Told You So* during the run. The stunt *(q.v.)* didn't work, and *Piggy*, or rather *I Told You So*, closed quickly.

The Royale's next production, *Judy* (2/8/27; 104 performances), had a score by Charles Rosoff and Leo Robin. Queenie Smith starred with Charles Purcell and George Meeker. Judy made way for the musicalization of *The Importance of Being Ernest*, called *Oh, Ernest!* (5/9/27; 56 performances). The musical had a score by Robin Hood Bowers and Francis DeWitt. The next offering, *Rang-Tang* (7/12/27; 119 performances), starred the popular black performers Aubrey Lyles and Flournoy Miller. The show's songs, written by Ford Dabney and Jo Trent, included "Come to Africa," "Sambo's Banjo," "Sammy and Topsy," "Tramps of the Desert" and "Harlem." The titles indicate the general state of black musicals of the time. Only the songwriting team of Noble Sissle and Eubie Blake were able to begin to overcome the popular prejudices and stereotypes.

The Madcap (1/31/28; 103 performances) starred Mitzi, Harry Puck and Arthur Treacher. Though old fashioned, the show caught on and played a respectable run. Following it was the theater's first straight play, the mystery *Sh! The Octopus* (2/21/28; 47 performances).

The first smash hit for the theater was the Mae West vehicle *Diamond Lil* (4/9/28; 323 performances). West had written a script similar to another by Mark Linder. The two joined forces and *Diamond Lil* was born. Half the show was owned by Owney Madden, a gangster

The Royale Theatre   Courtesy Billy Rose Theater Collection.

(q.v.) best known as proprietor of the Cotton Club *(q.v.).*

The play caused a sensation following its opening. It was among a group of plays of the 1920s, including *Burlesque* and *Broadway*, that owed their success in part to their settings—the world of gangsters, prostitutes and drugs. These shows gave audiences who were accustomed to the more-refined drawing room comedies or cliched melodramas a chance to see what they thought was real life. Critic *(q.v.)* Percy Hammond described the audience of *Diamond Lil* as "persons anxious to encourage a conscience-smitten transgressor in her desire to be meritricious [sic]. Miss West, its star and author, recently under lock and key, is now more admired by her public than is Jane Cowl, Lynn Fontanne *(q.v.)*, Helen Hayes *(q.v.)* or Eva Le Gallienne." West had been arrested as a result of a previous Broadway offering, *Sex.*

Robert Garland, writing in the *Evening Telegram,* was the most vociferous admirer of the star. "So regal is Miss West's manner, so assured is her artistry, so devastating are her charms in the eyes of all red-blooded men, so blonde, so beautiful, so buxom is she that she makes Miss Ethel Barrymore *(q.v.)* look like the late lamented Mr. Bert Savoy." Savoy was a female impersonator.

Naturally, the script was loaded with typical Mae West lines. These included, "When a girl goes wrong, men usually go right after her" and "I'm one of the finest women who ever walked the streets." West later revived the show on Broadway in 1949 for 181 performances and in 1951 for 67 performances.

Diamond Lil was followed by a failure, the musical *Woof, Woof* (12/25/29; 45 performances). A bigger success was the *Second Little Show* (9/2/30; 63 performances). Howard Dietz and Arthur Schwartz *(q.v.)* wrote the songs. However, the show's hit tune, "Sing Something Simple," was written by Herman Hupfeld.

Mae West returned to the Royale in *The Constant Sinner* (9/14/31; 64 performances). Her previous Broadway offering, *The Pleasure Man,* was raided by the police and closed after only 2 performances. The play was set in Harlem, and West played a woman married to a prizefighter. On the side, she has two lovers, one black and one a millionaire. The millionaire kills the black lover (played by George Givot in blackface). The West character, who incidently has been selling dope on the side, allows her husband to be framed for the murder. In the end, the millionaire puts up the money for a first-class lawyer, and the husband is freed. She ends up with both men. West insisted on casting a real black as Givot's understudy to the chagrin of the producers (the Shuberts *(q.v.)*).

Howard Barnes, writing in the *Herald Tribune* described the play as "a melodrama nicely calculated to offend public taste and attract paying customers." Not everyone was a fan of the actress. Percy Hammond didn't mince words when he wrote: "She is so different from anything you have seen outside the zoo that you decide her impersonation is deliberately outlandish. When her various heroes ply her with jewels and admiration you suspect that they should be feeding her peanuts."

After the play's closing West moved to Hollywood and the movies. She continued to push back the boundaries of subject matter and to buck the critics and censors. West returned to Broadway in 1944 with her play *Catherine Was Great.*

A more subdued play, *When Ladies Meet* (10/6/32; 187 performances), opened at the Royale. Maxwell Anderson's *Both Your Houses* (3/6/33; 72 performances), was an expose of political morality. The play won the Pulitzer Prize *(q.v.)*.

After a few more inconsequential shows, the theater's name was changed. When producer John Golden lost his John Golden Theater *(q.v.)* on 54th Street, he leased the Royale, renaming it the John Golden Theater. George Abbott *(q.v.)* directed the first offering, Norman Krasna's *Small Miracle* (9/26/34; 188 performances). It featured Ilka Chase and Myron McCormick. *Rain from Heaven* (12/24/34; 99 performances) by S.N. Behrman opened with Jane Cowl and John Halliday.

During the Depression, the theater's fortunes fell along with Broadway's, and in 1937, it was taken over by CBS as a radio theater. Golden moved operations to the Masque Theater next door, and he renamed it the John Golden Theater. In 1940, CBS relinquished its lease, and the theater's name reverted to the Royale. After housing a series of plays that moved from other houses, the Royale housed popular comedienne ZaSu Pitts in *Ramshackle Inn* (1/5/44; 216 performances). *School for Brides* (8/1/44; 375 performances), its title a takeoff on Moliere's *School for Wives,* enjoyed a long run. Mae West then returned to the Royale in *Catharine Was Great,* which had originally opened at the Shubert Theater *(q.v.)*.

Louis Calhern and Dorothy Gish starred in *The Magnificent Yankee* (1/22/46; 160 performances) by Emmet Lavery. The play was much respected by critics. Ina Claire appeared at the Royale in *The Fatal Weakness* (11/19/46; 119 performances) by George Kelly.

Moss Hart's *(q.v.)* *Light Up the Sky* (11/18/48; 214 performances) was an affectionate and sometimes barbed spoof of the Broadway theater in the same style as his and George S. Kaufman's *Once in a Lifetime.* The satirical comedy opened with Sam Levene and Audrey Christie.

Christopher Fry's London hit, *The Lady's Not for Burning* (11/8/50; 151 performances), opened at the Royale with Richard Burton, John Gielgud and Pamela Brown.

Leonard Sillman opened the biggest hit in his series of *New Faces* revues at the Royale on May 16, 1952. The show introduced such future stars as Carol Lawrence, Alice Ghostley, Robert Clary, Eartha Kitt, Paul Lynde and Ronny Graham. The terrific songs, written by Arthur Siegel and June Carroll, included the standard "Love Is a Simple Thing." Other well-received songs in the show were "Penny Candy" and "Monotonous" by Siegel and Carroll, "Guess Who I Saw Today?" by Murray Grand and Elisse Boyd and "Lizzie Borden" by Michael Brown. *New Faces of 1952* with its 365 performance run was the last successful popular Broadway revue for years. In the early 1950s, audiences could see the same type of show in the comfort of their living rooms through the miracle of television; there was no need to go to Broadway.

Andre Gide's play *The Immoralist* (2/8/54; 485 performances), based on his novel, explored the theme of homosexuality. Geraldine Page, Louis Jourdan and James Dean were the stars. The chancy subject matter limited the play to a 104-performance run. More popular was Sandy Wilson's affectionate parody of twenties' musicals, *The Boy Friend.* The musical introduced a new star to Broadway, Julie Andrews.

Thornton Wilder's *The Matchmaker* (12/5/55; 486 performances) was a rewrite of his early failure, *The Merchant of Yonkers.* The German play on which *The Merchant of Yonkers* was based was later adapted into *On the Razzle* by Tom Stoppard. The stars were Ruth Gordon, Loring Smith, Eileen Herlie and Robert Morse.

Not all the critics appreciated the comedy, complaining that it lacked Wilder's personal stamp. The playwright who had contributed such classics as *Our Town* and *The Skin of Our Teeth* to the American theater was reduced, some thought, to writing a standard Broadway farce. They were right, but audiences were amused anyway. Later *The Matchmaker* was transformed into *Hello, Dolly!*, which critic Brooks Atkinson called "interminable."

Another comedy, *The Tunnel of Love* (2/13/57; 417 performances) by Joseph Fields *(q.v.)* and Peter DeVries starred Tom Ewell. *The Entertainer* (2/12/58; 96 performances) by John Osborne was hailed for its performance by Laurence Olivier. The play also starred Joan Plowright and Brenda de Banzie. Producer David Merrick *(q.v.)* ignored critics' carping about the play but couldn't keep it running.

Robert Dhery's revue *La Plume de Ma Tante* (11/11/58; 835 performances) did not have any hit songs or any stars, but audiences were entranced by the Gallic entertainment. Another revue, *From the Second City* (9/26/61; 87 performances), introduced Barbara Harris, Alan Arkin and Paul Sand to New York.

Bette Davis appeared at the Royale with Patrick O'Neal, Margaret Leighton and Alan Webb in Tennessee Williams's *(q.v.)* *The Night of the Iguana* (12/28/61; 316 performances). Williams's play opened to mixed reviews. Some felt he had become a parody of himself, and others found the bizarre play to be the apotheosis of the Williams style.

Lord Pengo (11/19/62; 175 performances) by S.N. Behrman opened with Charles Boyer, Agnes Moorehead, Brian Bedford and Henry Daniell. The next hit at the Royale, *The Subject Was Roses* (5/25/64; 832 performances) by Frank D. Gilroy, won the Pulitzer Prize. The play was Gilroy's first Broadway production. His prior play, *Who'll Save the Plowboy?* opened in 1962 at the Phoenix Theater. *The Subject Was Roses* opened with critics hailing Gilroy's tight dialogue and detailed realism, in great contrast to the work of the best-known Broadway dramatists of the day. Like his contemporary playwrights, Gilroy filled his drama with empathy for his characters, but he differed from them by his interest in the rituals of daily life. Jack Albertson, Martin Sheen and Irene Dailey made up the entire cast.

One of the biggest hits of the 1960s was the French farce *Cactus Flower* (12/8/65; 1,234 performances). Lauren Bacall made her Broadway debut in the comedy. Bacall was supported by Barry Nelson, Robert Moore and Brenda Vaccaro. Abe Burrows adapted the show for American audiences and directed the proceedings. The sixties was the last decade in which audiences were willing to be charmed on Broadway. Later audiences wanted to be wowed by Broadway, but in the sixties they were still content to sit back and watch a star go through his or her paces.

A notable booking at the Royale was the musical *Grease*, which moved to the theater from the Broadhurst *(q.v.)* in 1972 and remained for eight years. By the time *Grease* closed, the set was actually peeling and the cast was less than prime, but it had racked up 3,388 performances, a record at the time.

Who's Life Is It Anyway? (4/17/79; 223 performances) was a British import with Tom Conti. Brian Clark's play was a success on Broadway. Conti played a paralyzed man who wants to gain control of his life by getting the right to die. When Conti left the cast, the producers, faced with the problem of finding a replacement, made the unlikely choice of television star Mary Tyler Moore. Clark adapted the script for a female lead, and Moore received excellent reviews.

Alexander Cohen presented the American version of a British revue, *A Day in Hollywood/A Night in the Ukraine* (5/1/80; 558 performances) at the Royale. The revue was directed and choreographed by Tommy Tune and featured David Garrison, Peggy Hewett, Frank Lazarus and Priscilla Lopez. The show was reinforced with three songs by Jerry Herman *(q.v.)*, but they were not up to his usual standard.

Tim Rice and Andrew Lloyd Webber's third Broadway success, *Joseph and the Amazing Technicolor Dreamcoat* moved from off-Broadway on January 27, 1982. The show was a failure with the critics but a hit with audiences, playing 751 performances.

Andrew Lloyd Webber returned to the Royale with his show *Song and Dance* (9/18/85; 474 performances). The musical featured Bernadette Peters in the first act, a one-woman musical. The second act featured dancer Christopher d'Amboise and a small chorus. The two acts were linked by a tenuous story line.

George Abbott *(q.v.)* directed a revival of his play *Broadway*, written in collaboration with Philip Dunning. The show opened on Abbott's 100th Birthday, June 25, 1987. Unfortunately, the production was not a success, running only four performances.

The Royale was dark for a long period until the New York Shakespeare Festival's production of Caryl Churchill's English play *Serious Money* opened in January 1988. The play was not a success in its transfer from off-Broadway.

On May 3, 1988, theatergoers were treated to the premiere of David Mamet's *Speed-the-Plow*. The comedy, a production of the Lincoln Center Theater Company, featured brilliant performances by Joe Mantegna and Ron Silver. The third cast member, making her Broadway debut, was the rock star Madonna. Unfortunately, her talents proved insufficient to the play's needs. She did, however, sell tickets, and the show soon sold out. Madonna's appearance confused many theatergoers. Many patrons waited patiently for their idol to break into song. Japanese tourists were especially confused by the play with its heavy reliance on rapid fire dialogue and little action.

The Royale, suffering from the paucity of quality offerings on Broadway, remains one of the finest of all Broadway playhouses.

RUNYON, DAMON (1884–1946) Damon Runyon was a newspaper columnist, short-story writer, and inventor and recorder of slang *(q.v.)* who used Broadway and Times Square as the backdrop for many of his works. Runyon was a regular fixture at various Times Square haunts, particularly Lindy's *(q.v.),* which he immortalized as Mindy's. He achieved some of his greatest success posthumously through the production of the Broadway musical *Guys and Dolls,* which was based on several of his short stories.

Runyon was born in Manhattan, Kansas, on October 4, 1884. He inherited his interests in things literary from his father, Alfred Lee Runyon, a printer who also established newspapers.

Runyon also inherited his father's strong political beliefs in the rights of the common person. When he was just 18, he enlisted in the Spanish-American War. Runyon was accepted as a member of the Thirteenth Minnesota Volunteers. He was sent to the Philippines, arriving on July 31, 1898, two days before Manila surrendered. Later Runyon would embellish the truth and claim to have joined at the age of 14 and of participating in the battle of Manila. Both stories were untrue.

After he returned, he joined the *Pueblo Chieftain* as a reporter. He moved up to newspapers in Denver and, later, San Francisco. Like other great journalists of his generation such as A.J. Liebling *(q.v.),* Runyon first became acquainted with the characters inhabiting Times Square through his love of sports.

He moved to New York in 1911 and found employment as a sports reporter on the *American.* His byline originally read "Alfred Damon Runyon." Since brevity was a hallmark of many papers, editors shortened his name to Damon Runyon.

In those more freewheeling times, newspaper reporters were often hired for their journalistic talents rather than for their expertise in any one particular field. The young Runyon was assigned to cover murders, trials and politics as well as sports. Among the more celebrated trials that he covered were the Hall-Mills Case in 1926, the Snyder-Gray trial in 1927 and Bruno Richard Hauptman's trial for the kidnapping of the Lindbergh baby.

In 1916, the Hearst empire sent him to Mexico to follow General John Pershing in his quest for Pancho Villa—the Pershing Punitive Expedition. In 1916–17, Runyon went overseas with the First Army. He expanded his audience when he was appointed as a columnist and feature writer with King Features and the International News Service.

He eventually wrote three columns for the Hearst papers. The first began in 1926 and was titled "Both Barrels." The next year, he began "As I See It." "As I See It" was originally Arthur Brisbane's column, but Brisbane was a serious writer who wrote about solemn themes. Runyon didn't see the world in quite the same way as Brisbane. Two months later, Runyon began a column called, "The Brighter Side." His column made him a minimum of $20,000 a year during the twenties.

Like many of his fellow writers, Runyon answered a call from Hollywood. He joined RKO in 1941, and in that same year signed on with Twentieth-Century-Fox as a producer and writer. His first picture was *The Big Street.*

His many short stories appeared in the *Saturday Evening Post, Collier's, Liberty* and *Cosmopolitan.* The magazines payed $1,500 for his stories in the beginning. That rate soon escalated until Runyon was getting $5,000 a yarn.

His stories covered a wide range of subjects and locales but it was for his New York stories that Runyon received his greatest renown. He captured the characters and locations that made Times Square almost legendary to many of his readers.

Runyon was adept at giving the flavor of the street life through his descriptions and his characters' dialogue. For this, he invented or recorded many slang terms that later became a part of the language. This "Broadwayese" included several of his most famous terms such as "guys" for men and "dolls" for women. Free tickets to shows he dubbed "Chinee" because the tickets had holes punched in them and so resembled Chinese coins. Money was called "potatoes," and one "tore a herring" in one's favorite deli.

Runyon covered the night beat when the city really came alive. His headquarters was Lindy's Restaurant, where he would down dozens of cups of coffee. He would keep an ear peeled for the latest dialogue and would weave many local characters and incidents into his writing. Bugs Baer *(q.v.)* described Runyon as "harder to approach than a rodeo bull in a chute. There wasn't a time when he wouldn't throw a drowning man both ends of the rope."

Runyon's characters were the prizefighters, gangsters, theatrical agents, gamblers, producers, show girls, molls, bootleggers and beggars whose whole universe revolved around the intersection of Broadway and Seventh Avenue.

His characters were a unique blend of hard edges and soft hearts. Harry the Horse, Spanish John, Wilbur Willard, Big Butch, Frankie Ferocious, Big Nig, Madame La Gimp (formerly Apple Annie), Waldo Winchester, Dream Street Rose, Lily of St. Pierre, Light-Finger Moe, Sorrowful Jones, Little Isadore, Little Miss Marker, Dave the Dude and Joe the Joker all became well-known through his stories and later film adaptations.

Hollywood found in Runyon a gold mine of plot and characters. Among the 16 films based on his stories (a record for one author) were *Lady for a Day, Little Miss Marker* and *A Pocketful of Miracles* (a remake of *Lady for a Day*). During the Depression, he made as much as $30,000 in options on his stories.

Damon Runyon died in New York on December 10, 1946. He had suffered a long battle against cancer. Colonel Eddie Rickenbacker, following Runyon's will, flew over Times Square spreading Runyon's ashes over the streets of Broadway. The Damon Runyon Cancer Fund was established in the building that Owney Madden ran as the Club Napoleon.

In 1950, the Frank Loesser musical *Guys and Dolls* opened on Broadway. The show incorporated many of Runyon's characters and was based on his story *The Idyll of Miss Sarah Brown*. Runyon's character Sky Masterson was based on Broadway gambler Titanic Thompson. *Guys and Dolls* ran 1,200 performances in New York and played over 500 performances in London. It was later made into a successful motion picture starring Marlon Brando and Frank Sinatra.

ST. JAMES THEATRE 246 W. 44th Street. Architect: Warren and Westmore–F. Richard Anderson. Opening: September 26, 1927; *The Merry Malones.* In 1929, Abraham Erlanger, head of the monopolistic Theatrical Syndicate and among the most hated men in show business, built the Erlanger's Theatre as the flagship of his nationwide chain. Erlanger spent over $1.5 million on the 1,600-seat theater. His money was apparently well spent. The *New York Times* described the John Singraldi-designed auditorium: "There has been a studied attempt to create an intimate rather than a theatrical atmosphere. The interior design is Georgian, the color scheme coral and antique gold. Murals decorate the side walls and the proscenium arch."

With 1,600 seats to fill, Erlanger planned to present large-scale musicals. Erlanger, not really a producer but a booker of shows through his United Booking Office, chose George M. Cohan's *(q.v.)* musical *The Merry Malones* (216 performances). The musical starred Cohan and, he composed the score, wrote the lyrics and libretto, and produced the proceedings. Historians have not recorded why Cohan did not direct the show. Edward Royce and Sam Forrest both were credited as directors. Of course, any George M. Cohan production really had Cohan as director, and *The Merry Malones* was no different. Cohan had an odd way of directing—he would slump down in a theater seat with his feet on the back of the seat in front. And he would swing a foot back and forth to indicate how he wanted actors to move.

Cohan wasn't supposed to star in the play, but at the final dress rehearsal veteran actor Arthur Deagon dropped dead after doing a series of handsprings across the stage. The company was concerned that the opening would have to be canceled because of the 56-year-old actor's death. But Cohan, in the best "show must go on" tradition, declared that he would play the part. Cohan

had not performed in a musical in 13 years but he never lost the touch. *The Merry Malones* opened the next day out of town and was a smash. At Erlanger's, it repeated the Boston success. Richard Watts summed up the proceedings, which contained "all of the materials that have made the Cohan name eminent—the flags, the sentiment, the hokum, the persistent kidding of the plot, the Irish-American family humor, all managed with the most skilled of showmanship."

St. James Theatre   Courtesy Billy Rose Theater Collection.

The next hit at Erlanger's was the last musical that Cohan wrote—*Billie* (10/1/28; 112 performances). The show, although written only one year after *The Merry Malones,* seemed dated. Between the two shows, Broadway audiences had been introduced to *Show Boat,* the great musical that marked the direction in which musical comedy was heading. The critics enjoyed the show, but they did proclaim it as terribly old-fashioned.

Fine and Dandy (9/23/30; 246 performances) boasted a good score by one of the only female composers, Kay Swift, and her husband Paul James and included two hits, the title tune and "Can This Be Love." The cast included comedian Joe Cook, dancer Eleanor Powell and future Hollywood restauranteur Dave Chasen.

Erlanger's empire began to crumble during the Depression and he lost the theater. The Astor estate, owner of the land on which the Erlanger stood, took over the theater's operations.

On December 7, 1932, the theater's name was changed to the St. James. The first attraction under the new name was the revue *Walk a Little Faster* (121 performances). Beatrice Lillie, Penny Singleton (Blondie in the movies) and comedy team Bobby Clark and Paul McCullough appeared in the revue. The show's fine score was written by composer Vernon Duke *(q.v.)* and lyricist E.Y. Harburg *(q.v.).* The smash hit from the show was "April in Paris." Opening night at the St. James was a disaster. During the overture, the front curtain began its rise to the flies. Unfortunately, the bottom of the drape caught on something on the stage floor. Still, the batten holding the curtain kept rising, pulling the curtain taut. The amazed audience watched the curtain stretch until a ripping sound was heard and the great swag of material tore away from the batten, fell to the stage and over the orchestra pit. Still the band played on, despite the darkness of the muffled pit.

After short seasons of Gilbert and Sullivan and the Ballet Russe de Monte Carlo, Clark and McCullough returned to the St. James. The show was *Thumbs Up!* (12/27/34, 156 performances), with a score by a variety of songwriters. Again, Vernon Duke came up with a hit, along the same lines as "April in Paris." The song was "Autumn in New York," and Duke also supplied the lyrics. The show's other hit was James F. Hanley's "Zing Went the Strings of My Heart."

Operetta made a rare return to the New York stage with Sigmund Romberg *(q.v.)* and Oscar Hammerstein II's *(q.v.) May Wine* (12/5/35; 212 performances). Reviews were mixed, although all the critics *(q.v.)* found something nice to say. John Anderson, writing in the *New York Journal,* seemed to sum up the response: "I found it somewhat dry, with too much body, as the vintners say, and not enough alcoholic content—nothing, in fact, to get intoxicated over or on. Though some of Prof. Romberg's tunes are gracefully stimulating, and it is all sung, said and dressed up in Mr. (Laurence)

Schwab's accustomed lavish manner, *May Wine* crushes more than the grape."

John Gielgud's production of *Hamlet* moved to the St. James from the historic Empire Theater *(q.v.)* where it concluded its 132-performance run. Shakespeare held the St. James's stage with the Margaret Webster production of *Richard II* (2/15/37; 132 performances), starring Maurice Evans. The drama opened 37 years after the last American production. Surprisingly, the audiences during the Depression were overjoyed to spend their evenings with *Richard II,* but the summer heat forced the production to close. Evans then undertook a nationwide tour of the play, but it was not as successful. Evans quoted one candy butcher (candy salesman) saying to another, "Put-away the Baby Ruths and Love Nests—This is a class show." Evans brought the play back to New York on April 1, 1940, for an additional 32 performances.

Before then, Evans essayed *Hamlet* (10/12/38; 96 performances) in another Margaret Webster directed production. The play opened with Mady Christians, Katherine Locke and Alexander Scourby completing the leads. The production was the first complete and uncut version of *Hamlet* to play in the United States. The curtain rose for the first act at 6:30. The act ran two hours, and the audiences had an hour intermission for dinner. The curtain rose again at 9:30 for acts two and three and finally fell for good at 11:15. The actual production took 3 hours and 38 minutes to perform. Still, the show was a success. Two events surprised and even shocked Broadway regulars. In the first week, a more traditional cut-down version of the play was performed, but the uncut version was much more popular and the shorter version was no longer produced. The second surprise was the discovery that audiences would rather sit through the entire play without the dinner break. That break was taken out. The production was hailed by critics and audiences, but there was an understandably limited audience for Shakespeare, no matter how well presented. Margaret Webster suggested, with tongue in cheek, that the play be advertised as "Shakespeare's *Hamlet* in its entirety. Eight minutes shorter than *Gone with the Wind*." Evans would repeat the role on three successive occasions.

Evans continued his dominance of the St. James stage with Shakespeare's *Henry IV Part 1* (1/30/39; 74 performances). The play received excellent reviews. Margaret Webster again directed, Edmund O'Brien starred in the title role and Mady Christians appeared as Lady Percy. The production was successful for Shakespeare. Evans felt it would have run longer, but audiences didn't want to see him in bravura character roles but "in black silk tights."

While Evans and company toured, the last edition of the *Earl Carroll Vanities* *(q.v.)* (1/13/40; 25 performances) opened at the St. James. The show was a decided failure, supposedly marking the introduction of microphones to the Broadway stage.

Shakespeare returned with Maurice Evans in the Theater Guild (q.v.) and Gilbert Miller production of *Twelfth Night* (November 19, 1940; 129 performances). Margaret Webster directed a distinguished cast, including Evans, Wesley Addy, Helen Hayes (q.v.), June Walker and Sophie Stewart. Helen Hayes was by now 40 and playing a teenage girl. Critics were unconcerned, they preferred to spar over her interpretation. Past Violas (her character) had emphasized the poetry in Shakespeare's writing. Hayes decided to speak the lines in a conversational manner, and the arguments over this interpretation continued until the play closed.

Richard Wright adapted his novel *Native Son* (3/24/41; 114 performances) with the help of Paul Green. Orson Welles and John Houseman produced the venture. The production divided critics (q.v.) and theatergoers. The story was about the events following a black man's accidental murder of a white woman. William Randolph Hearst's *Journal American* labeled the play Communistic. *Time Magazine,* the bastion of Henry Luce, dubbed it "the strongest play of the season." Welles received his fair share of accolades by the press. Brooks Atkinson wrote of Welles: "When he applies the theatricalism of his personal nature to a stage problem something exciting comes into existence. The space and the sound of the theater, which are only partly used in ordinary productions, yield a fresh sensation. It is as if the theater had been shaken up and recharged with life." The "boy wonder" was at once brilliant and mischievous. Though no one could figure out why, Welles insisted that among the stage props be a boy's sled upon which was written the word "Rosebud."

The Shubert brothers (q.v.), by this time owners of the St. James, presented their first productions there, a repertory offering of the Boston Comic Opera Company and the Jooss Ballet Dance Theater. The offerings included a revival of *H.M.S. Pinafore* on January 21, 1942; *The Mikado* on February 3; *The Green Table* on February 10, followed by *The Big City* later that month; *Pirates of Penzance* and *The Prodigal Son* on February 17, *Iolanthe* on February 23, *Trial By Jury* on February 28, and finally, *The Gondoliers* on March 3.

The Theater Guild presented the premiere of Philip Barry's play *Without Love* (11/10/42; 110 performances) which featured Katharine Hepburn, Elliott Nugent and Audrey Christie. Its departure opened the way for the theater's most important production—*Oklahoma!* (q.v.) (3/31/43; 2,248 performances). The Rodgers and Hammerstein (q.v.) musical, considered the apex of the art form at its opening, saved the Theater Guild, which had little luck with recent offerings. Hammerstein, too, was considered washed up until the premiere of *Oklahoma!* The show also marked a turning point in the American musical theater. It's construction was fol-

lowed zealously by lesser talents, and for a while it seemed that every Broadway show had to have two couples, one the love interest and one the comic relief, a dream ballet, a nontraditional chorus and a homey, bucolic American setting. *Oklahoma!* became the model to which almost every musical aimed.

Frank Loesser (q.v.), the brilliant composer and lyricist, adapted Brandon Thomas's *Charley's Aunt* into the musical comedy *Where's Charley?* (10/11/48, 792 performances). George Abbott (q.v.), a champion of new talents, wrote the libretto and directed Loesser's first Broadway show. *Where's Charley?* opened with Broadway and Hollywood star Ray Bolger. Loesser gave him the evening's big hit song, "Once in Love with Amy," with which Bolger would forever be linked. Byron Palmer, Allyn Ann McLerie and Doretta Morrow costarred in the delightful show. *Where's Charley?* proved an auspicious debut for Loesser, Broadway's most ambitious songwriter.

Richard Rodgers and Oscar Hammerstein returned to the St. James with their great musical, *The King and I* (3/29/51; 1,246 performances). Gertrude Lawrence starred as Anna, and the King was played by Yul Brynner. Doretta Morrow, previously in *Where's Charley?,* Dorothy Sarnoff, Larry Douglas and Johnny Stewart starred. The superb production was directed by John Van Druten with choreography by the brilliant Jerome Robbins.

The critics were nearly unanimous in their praise, although they felt that Rodgers and Hammerstein had broken no new ground. Actually, they had taken many risks in *The King and I.* Brooks Atkinson, writing in the *New York Times* opined, "It is an original and beautiful excursion into the rich splendors of the Far East, done with impeccable taste by two artists and brought to life with a warm, romantic score, idiomatic lyrics and some exquisite dancing." Tragedy struck the production when Gertrude Lawrence died during the show's run.

George Abbott continued his introduction of new talents to Broadway with the musical comedy, *The Pajama Game* (5/13/54; 1,061 performances). Abbott coauthored the libretto with Broadway newcomer Richard Bissell. The charming, enthusiastic score was written by Richard Adler and Jerry Ross, marking their first collaboration on a book show. The show also marked the choreographic debut of Bob Fosse, one of the Broadway musical's most unique talents. The score contained two smash hits: "Hey There," which leading man John Raitt sang as a duet with himself (he accomplished this feat by singing the song into a dictaphone), and the tango "Hernando's Hideaway." Janis Paige, Reta Shaw, Eddie Foy Jr., Carol Haney, Shirley MacLaine, and Peter Gennaro were also featured in the fine cast. The show was also producer Harold Prince's (q.v.) first production, in association with Frederick

Brisson and Robert E. Griffith. *The Pajama Game* had the unique distinction of having a musical written about it, *Say, Darling*.

Johnny Mercer, one of Hollywood's best lyricists, collaborated with Gene de Paul on the score of the St. James's next show, *Li'l Abner* (11/15/56; 693 performances), based on the comic strip by Al Capp. Edith Adams and Peter Palmer starred as Daisy Mae and Abner, Stubby Kaye as Marryin' Sam and Howard St. John as General Bullmoose. The score was one of the funniest and most high-spirited in Broadway history. The lyrics successfully straddled the line between satire and sincerity. The denizens of Dogpatch were really just disguised characters out of black vaudeville. Michael Kidd's choreography was among the most athletic ever seen on Broadway.

The Shuberts were forced by the federal government to divest themselves of many of their Broadway holdings, and the St. James was included in the judgment. The Jujamcyn Organization bought the theater's lease as well as those of several other former Shubert properties.

The new owners of the building, Scarborough House, Inc., hired designer Frederick Fox to completely redo the theater. The interior was reduced to a shell, and the public areas were completely redesigned.

The theater reopened on December 1, 1958, with a hit show, Rodgers and Hammerstein's *The Flower Drum Song* (600 performances). Hollywood star Gene Kelly directed the proceedings with Hammerstein and Joseph Fields *(q.v.)* contributing the libretto. *Flower Drum Song*, starring Larry Blyden, Pat Suzuki, Miyoshi Umeki, Patrick Adiarte, Juanita Hall, Ed Kenney and Keye Luke, was not as successful as some of the team's past offerings. However, even second-rate Rodgers and Hammerstein was better than most musicals.

Carol Burnett and her star-making musical, *Once Upon a Mattress,* moved from off-Broadway to the St. James as a big hit. The score was written by lyricist Marshall Barer and Richard Rodgers's daughter, Mary Rodgers. The book was written by Jay Thompson and Dean Fuller. *Once Upon a Mattress,* an alternately sweet and zany retelling of the fairy tale *The Princess and the Pea,* eventually ran for 460 performances.

Laurence Olivier and Anthony Quinn opened in Jean Anouilh's drama *Becket* (10/5/60; 193 performances) at the St. James before being made into a hit motion picture.

Composer Jule Styne *(q.v.)* and lyricists Betty Comden and Adolph Green *(q.v.)* provided the scores for two of the next shows at the St. James. The first was a Phil Silvers and Nancy Walker vehicle, *Do Re Mi* (1/26/60; 400 performances). The show opened with David Merrick *(q.v.)* producing and Garson Kanin directing and writing the libretto. The score was excellent and wide in scope. "Make Someone Happy" was the pop-

ular hit, but the rest of the score was more adventurous and much underrated. John Reardon and Nancy Dussault provided the love interest.

Sydney Chaplin (Charlie's son), Carol Lawrence, Phyllis Newman (Adolph Green's wife) and Orson Bean starred in Styne, Comden and Green's second show at the St. James—David Merrick's production of *Subways Are for Sleeping* (12/27/61; 205 performances). The show was a typically jovial romp in the best traditions of the team's work together. The fine score had its expected hit, "Comes Once in a Lifetime." The rest of the score was equally bright and witty and, most important, theatrical.

Irving Berlin *(q.v.),* perhaps the greatest songwriter in American history, left Broadway with a lackluster show, *Mr. President* (10/20/62; 265 performances). Robert Ryan and Nanette Fabray tried to enliven the proceedings, but the show was clearly in trouble. The play owed more to television sitcoms than theater, and its sentimentality and patriotism seemed out of date. *Mr. President* opened with the largest advance in Broadway history until then.

Hello, Dolly! (1/16/64; 2,844 performances) was the next show to open at the St. James, and it proved to be an amazing phenomena. Carol Channing's miraculous performance and Jerry Herman's *(q.v.)* stirring score propelled the show forward in the best Broadway style. Professionalism and slickness was rampant on the stage if depth and emotion was not, an apt appraisal of all Gower Champion-directed shows.

After a 40-year absence, Shakespeare returned to the St. James. *Two Gentlemen of Verona* (12/1/71; 614 performances) set Shakespeare's words to music by Galt MacDermot with lyrics by playwright John Guare. The musical starred Raul Julia, Clifton Davis, Jonelle Allen, Diana Davila and John Bottoms.

A string of failures, including a 25th Anniversary revival of *My Fair Lady,* ran at the St. James in the mid-1970s. Comden and Green broke the jinx with *On the Twentieth Century* (2/19/78; 460 performances). Cy Coleman provided a complex score for this musical. The show joined Stephen Sondheim's *(q.v.)* *Follies* and *Company* as the best musicals of the seventies. All three shows were directed by Harold Prince. *On the Twentieth Century* starred Madeline Kahn (replaced soon after opening by Judy Kaye in a stunning debut), Kevin Kline, John Cullum and Imogene Coca. Another important feature of the show was the exemplary production, especially Robin Wagner's superb set.

Barnum (4/30/80; 854 performances), starring Jim Dale, enjoyed a two-year run with Cy Coleman and Michael Stewart's rousing score. More failures followed *Barnum.* Finally *My One and Only* (3/1/83; 767 performances) opened at the theater. Tommy Tune and Twiggy starred in the new musical that used songs by George and Ira

Gershwin *(q.v.)*. The whole affair was charming, stylish and fun.

SAM H. HARRIS THEATER   See HARRIS THEATER.

SAM S. SHUBERT FOUNDATION AWARD   This award has been presented since 1954 by the Shubert Foundation, "In recognition of the most outstanding individual contribution to the New York theatrical season." Past winners have included Victor Borge (the first recipient), David Merrick *(q.v.)*, George Abbott *(q.v.)* and Roger L. Stevens.

SAM S. SHUBERT THEATRE 225 W. 44th Street. Architect: Henry B. Herts. Opening: c. September 29, 1913; Forbes-Robertson Repertory.   When Sam Shubert died on May 12, 1905, as a result of injuries suffered in a train crash, his devoted brother Lee (see SHUBERT BROTHERS) vowed to build a theater in his honor in every city in the country. Each of the Sam Shubert theaters would have a picture of Sam hanging in its lobby.

Lee fulfilled at least part of his vow when the Sam S. Shubert Theatre opened in New York with the Forbes-Robertson Repertory Company. There is some disagreement about the actual date of the opening. Louis Botto's excellent book, *In This Theater,* lists the opening as October 2, 1913. George Freedley's *Biographical Encyclopedia* and *Who's Who of the American Theater* lists the opening as September 29, 1913. Jerry Stagg's *The Brothers Shubert* lists the opening as October 28, 1913. In the appendix of all Shubert productions, Stagg lists the opening as September 3, 1913. Whatever the opening date, the theater was a great success.

The Venetian Renaissance interior was designed by O.H. Bauer. Its 1,400 seats all afforded a clear view of the stage, and its paneled walls lent an air of refinement. Lee Shubert called the new theater "a temple of dramatic art" and "a place of beauty and dedication." He had offices built on the second floor overlooking 44th Street and the new Shubert Alley. At the time that the Shubert and Booth *(q.v.)* theaters were constructed, New York zoning regulations required all theaters to have alleys attached to their side exits. The shared side walls of the Shubert and Booth and the back of the Astor Hotel *(q.v.)* formed Shubert Alley.

After their production of *A Thousand Years Ago* (1/6/14; 87 performances), the Shuberts opened their first musical at the theater, *The Belle of Bond Street* (3/30/14; 48 performances), based on the English musical *The Girl from Kay's.* Interpolated into the score was the Fred Fisher and Alfred Bryan song "Who Paid the Rent for Mrs. Rip Van Winkle When Rip Van Winkle Was Away."

Franz Lehar's *Alone At Last* (10/14/15; 180 performances) was the theater's first big hit. The show starred

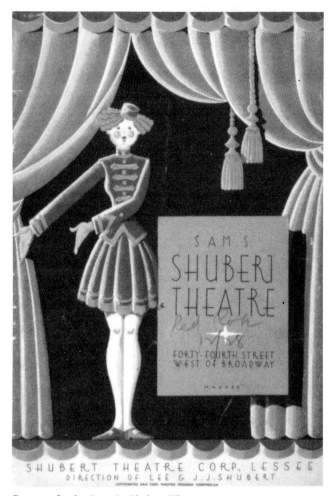

Program for the Sam S. Shubert Theatre

Jose Collins and John Charles Thomas. A bigger hit was Jerome Kern's *(q.v.)* *Love O' Mike* (1/15/17; 192 performances) with lyrics by Harry B. Smith *(q.v.)*. Clifton Webb and Peggy Wood starred.

Maytime (8/16/17; 492 performances) had music by Sigmund Romberg *(q.v.)* and book and lyrics by Rida Johnson Young. The show starred William Norris, Peggy Wood and Charles Purcell. For the first and last time in Broadway history, a second company of a hit musical was presented at the same time as the original. The second company played across the street from the Shubert at the 44th Street Theatre *(q.v.)*. *Maytime* contained one of Romberg and Young's most enduring songs, "Will You Remember," known better as "Sweetheart."

Sometime (10/4/18; 283 performances), a Rudolf Friml *(q.v.)* and Rida Johnson Young musical, was produced by Arthur Hammerstein *(q.v.)* with the somewhat unlikely team of Mae West and Ed Wynn and dramatic actress Francine Larrimore. West took the opportunity to introduce the shimmy to Broadway.

Good Morning, Judge (2/6/19; 140 performances) was a British musical by Lionel Monckton and Howard

Talbot. The show was Americanized and two songs by George Gershwin (q.v.) and Irving Caesar were added. Romberg and Frederic Arnold Kummer wrote *The Magic Melody* (11/11/19; 143 performances), which starred Charles Purcell and Flavia Arcaro. The Shubert hosted a number of revues in the 1920s.

The Greenwich Village Follies (8/31/21; 167 performances), the first edition of the show on Broadway, was staged by John Murray Anderson (q.v.). This third edition starred Ted Lewis, Irene Franklin and Peggy Hope. The next edition opened on September 12, 1922, with Savoy and Brennan, John Hazzard and Carl Randall. Two years later, after a sojourn at the Winter Garden Theater (q.v.), the *Greenwich Village Follies* returned to the Shubert, opening on September 16, 1924. This time, the score was written by Cole Porter (q.v.). None of the songs became standards. The Dolly Sisters, Georgie Hale, Moran and Mack and Vincent Lopez and his orchestra were featured. The 1924 edition ran 131 performances. The final edition to play the Shubert Theatre opened on March 15, 1926, and played 180 performances. The show was a revision of the previous year's edition, which had played the Winter Garden.

Artists and Models (8/20/23; 312 performances) was a Shubert produced revue series. The slightly risque show was the first of the American revues to emulate the *Folies Bergere*. It was also the first show on Broadway to feature topless chorines. Frank Fay starred in the show, along with Grace Hamilton and Harry Kelly. There were five more editions of the series on Broadway, though none appeared at the Shubert.

Vogues of 1924 (3/27/24; 114 performances) starred Fred Allen, May Boley, Odette Myrtil, Jimmy Savo and J. Harold Murray. The title indicates that the Shuberts hoped the show might prove popular enough to spin off into an annual series. Usually, Lee attended to the brothers' finances (his office adjoined the vault), and J.J. stuck to the artistic slate. On this occasion, J.J. was on an extended trip to Europe, so Lee decided to show his brother up and mount his own musical production.

A musical, *The Magnolia Lady* (11/25/24; 49 performances), was not a success, despite the talents of Ruth Chatterton, Skeets Gallagher and Ralph Forbes. The Shuberts presented *Gay Paree* (8/18/25; 181 performances) at the Shubert with Chic Sale, Jack Haley and Winnie Lightner. As with many Shubert shows, the hit song was interpolated into the score. *Gay Paree*'s hit was "I Can't Believe That You're in Love with Me" by Jimmy McHugh and Clarence Gaskill. The majority of the score was written by Alfred Goodman (q.v.), Clifford Grey and Harold Atteridge. The next year, a new edition opened at the Winter Garden.

The Shuberts were firm believers in the power of operettas. They insisted on producing them long after the form had gone out of favor. But when *Countess Maritza* (9/18/26; 321 performances) opened, theatergoers found they could still enjoy the old-fashioned musical entertainments. The musical starred Harry K. Morton, Carl Randall and Yvonne D'Arle. Emmerich Kallman and Harry B. Smith (q.v.) supplied the score, which featured the hit song "Play Gypsies."

Another musical, *A Night in Venice* (5/21/29; 175 performances), starred Ted Healy and not one but two troupes of dancing girls—The Allan K. Foster Girls and The Chester Hale Girls. Ranks of women dancing in unison were a staple of twenties and thirties musicals. The choreographer of *A Night in Venice* later took the idea of a corps of synchronized dancers and translated his steps to Hollywood. He was Busby Berkeley.

Everybody's Welcome (10/13/31; 127 performances) starred Ann Pennington, Oscar Shaw, Ann Sothern (then named Harriette Lake), Frances Williams and the band of Tommy and Jimmy Dorsey. Sammy Fain and Irving Kahal were responsible for most of the score, but again an interpolated song proved to be the classic. "As Time Goes By," composed by Herman Hupfeld, first appeared in the musical. Surprisingly the song did not achieve much attention until the movie *Casablanca*.

Another revue, the last of three in a series, was *Americana* (10/5/32; 77 performances). The show contained a song that became the unofficial anthem of the Depression—"Brother Can You Spare a Dime?"—composed by Jay Gorney with lyrics by E.Y. Harburg (q.v.). *Americana* is also noteworthy as the first Broadway show to offer a serious ballet. Charles Weidman was the choreographer, but the show's lack of success (and the success of "Brother Can You Spare a Dime?") overshadowed his efforts. The score contained some other songs that later achieved some renown. These included "Satan's Li'l Lamb" by Harold Arlen (q.v.), Harburg and Johnny Mercer; "Woud'ja for a Big Red Apple?" by Henry Souvaine and Mercer; and "Five Minutes of Spring" by Gorney and Harburg.

Suddenly, a spate of straight plays opened at the Shubert. First was Sidney Howard's *Dodsworth* (2/24/34; 147 performances). Walter Huston, Maria Ouspenskaya, Fay Bainter and Nan Sunderland starred. *Dodsworth* closed and then reopened on August 20, 1934, for an additional 170 performances. Next came Robert E. Sherwood's antiwar drama *Idiot's Delight* (3/24/36; 120 performances). The play won the Pulitzer Prize (q.v.) for drama. It reopened at the Shubert on August 31, 1936, and continued for an additional 179 performances. Alfred Lunt and Lynn Fontanne (q.v.) starred in the Theater Guild (q.v.) production. Dudley Digges, Margo, Henry Hull and Leo G. Carroll opened in Maxwell Anderson's *The Masque of Kings* (2/8/37; 89 performances), a failure.

Musical comedy, and a lighter air, returned to the Shubert with Richard Rodgers and Lorenz Hart's (q.v.)

smash hit musical, *Babes in Arms* (4/14/37; 289 performances). Audiences heard for the first time such classic songs as "I Wish I Were in Love Again," "Where or When," "The Lady Is a Tramp," "My Funny Valentine," and "Johnny One Note." George Balanchine contributed the choreography for a show in which dance played a role equal to the score. The young and able cast included Alfred Drake, Mitzi Green, Ray Heatherton, Wynn Murray, the Nicholas Brothers and Robert Rounseville. These were immensely talented performers.

S.N. Behrman's *Amphitryon 38* (11/1/37; 152 performances), based on French playwright Jean Giraudoux's original, starred the Lunts *(q.v.)*. The day after the Theater Guild production opened, S.N. Behrman took Giraudoux to the Shubert to see the play. The show had received raves and the theater was packed. In Paris, Giraudoux's play had played to an audience of 300. When Behrman took the playwright into the Shubert with its 697 orchestra seats, all full, Giradoux was thunderstruck. "Is there another room?," he asked. Behrman nodded and took the Frenchman upstairs to the balcony where another 762 patrons sat. Giradoux seemed upset. Behrman asked why he seemed so distressed at 1,300 seats packed with enthusiastic theatergoers. Giradoux asked the price of tickets, and Behrman figured that the weekly gross would come to $24,000. Giradoux looked even sadder and commented, "I shall have difficulty with my income tax." *Amphitryon 38* made Giradoux very wealthy.

The play opened with Jupiter and Mercury looking down from the clouds onto the mortals below. The next offering at the Shubert also had a celestial theme. The title *I Married an Angel* (5/11/38; 338 performances) was meant to be taken literally. The angel was played by Vera Zorina, ably supported by Audrey Christie, Charles Walters, Dennis King, Vivienne Segal and Walter Slezak. The score was up to Rodgers and Hart's excellent standards, although only "I'll Tell the Man in the Street" and "Spring Is Here" achieved any renown.

The Theater Guild had a huge hit with Philip Barry's *The Philadelphia Story* (3/28/39; 417 performances). Katharine Hepburn enjoyed her greatest stage success in the comedy of manners. *The Philadelphia Story* opened at the Shubert and saved the Theater Guild, which was then $60,000 in debt. Barry's almost admiring denunciation of the shallowness of the rich illustrated that even the most limited person can have a soul if you dig deep enough. *The Philadelphia Story* also starred Joseph Cotten, Shirley Booth and Van Heflin.

Rodgers and Hart returned to the Shubert with *Higher and Higher* (4/4/40; 84 performances). The elements for success all seemed to be in place—a cast including Shirley Ross (returning from Hollywood), Marta Eggerth, Jack Haley, Leif Erickson, Robert Rounseville and Sharkey the Seal; a libretto by Joshua Logan *(q.v.)* and Gladys Hurlbut and direction by Logan; and a hit tune in "It Never Entered My Mind." However, the show, an *Upstairs Downstairs* type of comedy, was a failure.

The Shuberts' next offering, *Hold On To Your Hats* (9/11/40; 158 performances), was also a failure but for different reasons. It opened with Al Jolson *(q.v.)* making a Broadway comeback, ably assisted by the hilarious Martha Raye. Jack Whiting, Gil Lamb and Jinx Falkenburg were also in the cast. The score, by Burton Lane *(q.v.)* and E.Y. Harburg, contained the hit "There's a Great Day Coming Manana." The reviewers raved about the show. Brooks Atkinson said the show was "one of the funniest musical plays that have stumbled onto Broadway for years. Hold your sides as tightly as the title directs you to hold your hat."

But Jolson was unhappy. He was constrained by the libretto and frequently threw it away completely to the delight of audiences and the chagrin of his fellow cast members. At one point during the proceedings, Jolson decided to give the audience an extra free show at the end of the curtain call, a favorite trick of his. The audience of course ate it up, and the cast stayed on stage and had a good time also. The only person in the theater not having a ball with the bonus concert was George Jessel, who had a date with one of the chorus girls. As Jolson continued running through his hits Jessel grew more and more impatient. Finally he could stand it no more. Jessel bounded on stage, took his girl friend by the hand and left the theater.

Jolson was also undergoing a messy divorce from Ruby Keeler, who had walked out of both the show and Jolson's life in Chicago to be replaced by Eunice Healy. To top it all off he caught pneumonia. Without its star, *Hold On to Your Hats* had to close.

Two notable revivals next occupied the Shubert's stage. Katharine Cornell *(q.v.)*, Raymond Massey, Bramwell Fletcher and Clarence Derwent appeared in George Bernard Shaw's *The Doctor's Dilemma* (3/11/41; 112 performances). Richard Brinsley Sheridan's 18th century comedy *The Rivals* (1/14/42; 54 performances) starred Mary Boland, Helen Ford, Bobby Clark and Walter Hampden.

Rodgers and Hart's *By Jupiter* (6/3/42; 427 performances), their last full score, opened with Ray Bolger, Ronald Graham, Benay Venuta and Vera-Ellen. The musical, sadly, contains one of the team's most neglected scores. Ray Bolger left the show to join the armed services and the show closed.

Mae West returned to Broadway in the Mike Todd and Shubert brothers coproduction of the actress's play *Catherine Was Great* (8/2/44; 191 performances). West opened to less than great reviews. Louis Kronenberger, writing in *P.M.*, reflected his colleagues' opinions when he wrote "Mae West Slips on the Steppes." However, a later headline in *Variety,* during the show's national tour, summed up the New York run best: "Critics cold but b.o. hot."

Harold Arlen and E.Y. Harburg enjoyed one of their greatest successes with *Bloomer Girl* (10/5/44; 657 performances), a delightful musical comedy with serious overtones. The show told the story of a follower of early feminist Dolly Bloomer with a subplot concerning the underground railroad. Celeste Holm starred along with David Brooks, Joan McCracken, Mabel Taliaferro and Dooley Wilson as a runaway slave. *Bloomer Girl* made powerful statements about human rights in a most entertaining way.

The Arlen and Harburg score contained one standard: "Right As the Rain." There was also a powerful song for Dooley Wilson: "The Eagle and Me." The rest of the score was equally rich and dynamic. Agnes de Mille choreographed a classic number: "The Civil War Ballet."

A revival of Victor Herbert's (q.v.) operetta *Sweethearts* (1/21/47; 288 performances) was a surprise hit with Marjorie Gateson and Bobby Clark. *Anne of the Thousand Days* (12/8/48; 288 performances) by Maxwell Anderson was a drama of Anne Bolyn and Henry VIII. It starred Joyce Redman and Rex Harrison. The Lunts returned with playwright S.N. Behrman's *I Know My Love* (11/2/49; 246 performances). The plot followed the romantic life of a couple from their youth to their eighties. The Lunts, celebrating their 25th anniversary on stage, saw the play as a parable of their own lives. The production was an adaptation of Marcel Achard's *Aupres de Ma Blonde*.

Lerner and Loewe (q.v.) wrote *Paint Your Wagon* (11/12/51; 289 performances), a story set against the California gold rush. There were two hits in the score: "I Talk to the Trees" and "They Call the Wind Maria." James Barton, Tony Bavaar and Olga San Juan starred.

Katharine Hepburn returned to Broadway and the Shubert's stage in George Bernard Shaw's *The Millionairess* (10/17/52; 84 performances) with Cyril Ritchard. Rex Harrison returned in *The Love of Four Colonels* (1/15/53; 141 performances) by Peter Ustinov. His costar was his wife Lilli Palmer.

Rodgers and Hammerstein (q.v.) slipped with *Pipe Dream* (11/30/55; 246 performances), their musicalization of John Steinbeck's novel *Sweet Thursday*. The show opened with Mike Kellin, Helen Traubel, Louise Troy, Judy Tyler and William Johnson. *Pipe Dream* had a disappointing run and many critics wondered if the team had lost its touch.

The Shubert's next show, the Theater Guild musical *Bells Are Ringing* (11/29/56; 924 performances), was a happy hit with its lead Judy Holliday. Jule Styne (q.v.), Betty Comden and Adolph Green (q.v.) concocted a delightful show with an alternately poignant and funny score. The hit songs included "Just in Time" and "The Party's Over." The strong, well-integrated score was

well served by Holliday's costars Sydney Chaplin, Eddie Lawrence and Jean Stapleton.

Bob Merrill wrote the music and lyrics to the musicalization of Eugene O'Neill's (q.v.) *Ah, Wilderness*, titled *Take Me Along* (10/22/59; 448 performances). David Merrick (q.v.) presented Jackie Gleason, Robert Morse, Eileen Herlie, Walter Pidgeon and Una Merkel. *Take Me Along* had a small hit with its title song, though "Staying Young" was the best song in the score. The show closed shortly after Gleason left and was replaced by William Bendix.

Harold Rome's (q.v.) last full-scale Broadway musical was *I Can Get It for You Wholesale* (3/22/62; 300 performances). The David Merrick production made history when on opening night a star was born. Her name was Barbra Streisand, and although she only had a small role as Miss Marmelstein, a secretary, she stopped the show. Her costars included Marilyn Cooper, Harold Lang, Sheree North and Lilian Roth. The nominal star of the show was Elliott Gould, soon to be married to Streisand.

Anthony Newley starred in David Merrick's production *Stop the World—I Want to Get Off* (10/3/62; 556 performances), which he also wrote with Leslie Bricusse. The score contained the standards "Gonna Build a Mountain," "What Kind of Fool Am I" and "Once in a Lifetime." Newley and his costar Anna Quayle handled the superior score well.

Meredith Willson, author of *The Music Man*, fared less well with his musicalization of *Miracle on 34th Street*, which he entitled *Here's Love* (10/3/63; 334 performances). The show opened with Craig Stevens and Janis Paige in the leads.

The Apple Tree (10/18/66; 443 performances) was the name of Jerry Bock and Sheldon Harnick's (q.v.) evening of three one-act musicals. Jerome Coopersmith and the songwriters wrote the libretti based on Mark Twain's *The Diary of Adam and Eve*, Frank Stockton's *The Lady or the Tiger* and Jules Feiffer's *Passionella*. The evening was wittily directed by Mike Nichols and brilliantly performed by Barbara Harris, Larry Blyden and Alan Alda.

Golden Rainbow (2/4/68; 385 performances) was ostensibly a musicalization of Arnold Schulman's play *A Hole in the Head*. But the critics announced it was more like a glorified nightclub show put on by its stars Steve Lawrence and Edie Gorme. Walter Marks wrote a good score with a smash hit song: "I've Got to Be Me."

Neil Simon's (q.v.) musical *Promises, Promises* (12/1/68; 1,281 performances) boasted a score by Broadway newcomers Burt Bacharach and Hal David brillantly orchestrated by Jonathan Tunick. David Merrick's production proved to be one of the greatest successes of the 1960s. Jerry Orbach, Jill O'Hara, Ken Howard and Marian Mercer led the cast. The musical was based on Billy Wilder's film *The Apartment*. *Promises, Promises* contained a big hit song: "I'll Never Fall in Love Again."

Tunick again supplied excellent orchestrations to a very different score that consisted only of waltzes. The show was Stephen Sondheim's (q.v.) A Little Night Music (2/25/73; 601 performances) with one of the musical theater's greatest songs, "Send in the Clowns." Hugh Wheeler based his libretto on Ingmar Bergman's film Smiles of a Summer Night. Harold Prince's adroit producing and directing and the fine performances by Glynis Johns, Len Cariou, Laurence Guittard, Patricia Elliott and Hermione Gingold equaled one of the show's greatest assets, Boris Aronson's brilliant settings.

Two plays occupied the Shubert's stage in 1975. Edward Albee's Seascape (1/26/75; 65 performances) opened with Deborah Kerr, Barry Nelson and Frank Langella. It won the Pulitzer Prize (q.v.) a year after it closed. The second play of the year was a revival of Somerset Maugham's The Constant Wife with Ingrid Bergman.

The next tenant at the Shubert Theatre made Broadway history, eventually becoming the longest-running show ever. The show was A Chorus Line, a transfer from Joseph Papp's Public Theater. A Chorus Line moved to Broadway on July 25, 1975, with a cast that included Carole Bishop, Priscilla Lopez, Robert Lu-Pone, Donna McKechnie, Thommie Walsh and Sammy Williams.

The show was an unusual success. Its score by Marvin Hamlisch and Edward Kleban contained but one hit song, "What I Did for Love." The book was by James Kirkwood and Nicholas Dante. The Pulitzer Prize-winning show's tremendous success was laid at the feet of director/choreographer Michael Bennett, a true genius. Unfortunately, A Chorus Line has outlived two of its creators, Bennett and Kleban. It closed on April 28, 1990 after 6,137 performances.

SARDI'S RESTAURANT 234 W. 44th Street. Sardi's is the preeminent theater restaurant. It hosts most Broadway opening-night parties, a tradition that began with the opening of Come Back Little Sheba on February 15, 1950.

The restaurant was opened in May 1921 down the block from its present location. It moved to the new building in 1927. Vincent Sardi Sr. and his wife, Eugenia, worked at the Bartholdi Inn prior to opening the restaurant.

Sardi's interior is dominated by the hundreds of caricatures of famous theatrical persons that line the wall. The original artist was Alex Gard who in 1929 signed a contract with Vincent Sardi Sr., exchanging his drawings for two meals a day. When Sardi's became famous for the pictures, and Gard's fame grew, the artist refused to change the agreement. He continued supplying the drawings in exchange for meals.

Upon Gard's death, he was succeeded by Don Bevan, also known as the playwright of Stalag 17. Bevan was in turn replaced by Richard Baratz, the current artist.

Vincent Sardi Jr. served as an apprentice in Sardi's kitchens following his graduation from Columbia in 1937. After an 18-month apprenticeship, he became the restaurant's host and captain. In 1946, following a stint in the Marine Corps, he took over the management of the restaurant.

In 1937, James Molinski also began work at Sardi's, as a glass washer, and worked his way up to host and dining room manager. He remained at his post just inside Sardi's front door until his retirement in 1980. Molinski was known for his good humor and paternal relationship with many of the actors whose careers he followed.

The late 1930s was Sardi's golden age. Hatcheck girl Renee Carroll worked in the restaurant from the late thirties through the forties. During slack times, she would read scripts checked by playwrights and producers. On presentation of their checks, they not only got their apparel, but also a critique of their plays by Miss Carroll. Her judgment was usually sound and was proved right by the box office once the plays were produced. Soon, she began receiving scripts even in the summer, when there was nothing to check. Once a particularly poor playwright wrote the amateur critic asking if he could send his script in, since he was too impoverished to eat at Sardi's. Miss Carroll replied that the play, a western, was probably not a good idea anyway. A far better idea would be a story about a hatcheck girl who reads scripts. She even offered to help in research—for a third of the royalties.

In 1986, Sardi's was sold to Broadway speculators, Harvey Klaris and Ivan Bloch and restauranteur Stuart Lichtenstein. The price of the sale was reputed to be $6 million. Vincent Sardi Jr. was to continue as a consultant for at least five years.

Although the food is mainly undistinguished, the prices are high and most of Broadway's new generation prefer the more intimate theater restaurants like Joe Allen's, Barrymore's and Sam's, Sardi's remains in most people's minds as the quintessential theater restaurant. It even features a special actor's menu with reduced prices for members of the profession. Richard Maney (q.v.), the great publicist, called Sardi's "the club, mess hall, lounge, post office, saloon, and market place of the people of the theater."

SAVE THE THEATERS Save the Theaters is the organization at the forefront of the movement to preserve the Broadway theater buildings, the companies that service the theater industry as well as the unique atmosphere of the theater district. It was started around 1978–79 as a committee of Actors' Equity Association (q.v.) in response to the impending demolition of the

Morosco *(q.v.)*, Helen Hayes *(q.v.)* and Bijou theaters *(q.v.)* for what is now the Marriott Marquis Hotel and Marquis Theater *(q.v.)*.

After those theaters came down in March 1982, the community realized that the rest of the Broadway theaters were also in danger of city development policies. Those concerned realized that there was a need for some organization to make sure that what happened to the Helen Hayes, Morosco and Bijou theaters didn't happen again.

Save the Theaters has a variety of other programs. The organization is concentrating on space problems off- and off-off-Broadway. It has a national program for historic theaters around the country. Furthermore, it is expanding its programs to be more responsive to the needs of the theatrical community as a whole and also the theatergoing audiences. Perhaps most important, the organization is trying to make an effort to develop new audiences and to educate the public that theater exists and is a worthwhile experience. That is clearly a long-term goal. First, the theaters must be saved.

Chris Hagedorn of Save the Theaters explains the organization's philosophy: "We're not trying to preserve theaters as empty artifacts. But I think theater is a cyclical business. Tearing them down is not an answer. There was a season maybe ten or fifteen years ago when there were only ten shows on Broadway. If we had torn all those empty theaters down where would the shows we have today go? We're not here to subsidize theaters during bad seasons. If you're in the theater business you know that plays don't always succeed and your theaters may be dark. There are certain things that we've recommended that can be done for the theaters such as tax abatements during dark periods."

The battle to protect the remaining Broadway theaters has pitted Save the Theaters against the three major Broadway theater owners—the Shubert Organization, the Nederlander Group and Jujamcyn Theaters, which together own 31 of the 35 Broadway theaters.

In December 1985, the first three theaters, the Ambassador *(q.v.)*, the Neil Simon *(q.v.)* and the Virginia *(q.v.)* were approved for landmark designation. In an unusually united front, the theater owners tried to reverse the designations of the three theaters and to postpone any further action by the Preservation Commission for a year. This last-ditch effort failed, because the theater owners never had enough votes to bring it up as a resolution.

The designation of the exterior of the Ambassador Theater *(q.v.)* was rejected unanimously. However the exteriors of the Virginia and the Neil Simon were approved unanimously, and the interiors of the Neil Simon and Ambassador were approved by a 10 to 1 vote. This dissenting vote was cast by Queens Borough President Donald Manes who later committed suicide

after being removed from office and implicated in a major New York City scandal.

This however, wasn't the only action on the theaters taken by the Commission. It also directed the Landmarks Commission to try to further define the landmark guidlines in regard to the special needs of individual productions to adapt the theaters' interiors to fit their requirements. It also directed the City Planning Commission to reconsider its policy of "buildovers" on designated theaters under the city's zoning laws.

This victory was heartening to Save the Theaters, but it was clear by the board's attitude that more work was required. Chris Hagedorn said that "Between '82 and now we've participated in the Theater Advisory Council's processes, we've completed a study of the theater district, we testified on the Landmarks Commission's hearings and got hundreds of actors and directors and producers and designers to go in and testify."

Save the Theaters remains a potent force in the planning that affects the whole of Times Square and the future of the Broadway theater.

SCHWARTZ, ARTHUR   See DIETZ AND SCHWARTZ.

SELWYN THEATRE 229 W. 42nd Street. Architect: George Keister. Opening: October 2, 1918; *Information Please.* The Selwyn, one of the grand old theaters on 42nd Street, was built by producer Arch Selwyn. The Italian Renaissance-style building has a terra-cotta facade covering both the theater and the accompanying six-story Selwyn office building.

The 1,180-seat theater was designed in a fan shape, making the farthest seat seem close to the stage. The Selwyn had separate smoking rooms for men and women and a large lounge that stood between the hustle and bustle of 42nd Street and the auditorium. The stage was lower than most, allowing for improved sight lines. The pink and blue auditorium's lighting system could be changed from white to pink to rose and to purple.

The Selwyn opened with the play *Information Please,* which ran only 46 performances. The first hit for the theater was the Rudolf Friml *(q.v.)*, Otto Harbach *(q.v.)* musical *Tumble Inn* (3/24/19; 128 performances). The show starred Charles Ruggles, Zelda Sears, Herbert Corthell, Peggy O'Neill and Johnny Ford. *Tumble Inn* was produced by Arthur Hammerstein *(q.v.)*.

The Selwyn's next booking had the delightful title, *Helen of Troy, New York* (6/19/23; 193 performances). Harry Ruby and Bert Kalmar contributed the songs with the libretto credited to George S. Kaufman and Marc Connelly. It was the first musical for the librettists. The show was produced by Rufus LeMaire and actor George Jessel. LeMaire was an important agent and an inveterate gambler. He was also constantly broke. Most of the front money for the show came from bootleggers. Though the play ended its run losing money, the reviews were good. LeMaire used the positive notices to sell his rights and move to California. There he became an executive at Universal.

The opening night program contained the following notice: "Owing to the utter unimportance of the plot, latecomers will positively be seated at all times during the play." The critics (q.v.) were generous. Percy Hammond, writing in the *Tribune,* exclaimed, "It seems improbable that I shall ever again be asked if there exists in New York any musical plays in which bare legs and barer jokes do not abound."

The Constant Nymph (12/9/26; 148 performances) by Basil Dean and Margaret Kennedy was the Selwyn's next attraction. A huge success was George S. Kaufman (q.v.) and Edna Ferber's *The Royal Family* (12/28/27; 345 performances), a slightly disguised play about the Barrymore family (q.v.). Kaufman and Ferber denied the play was about the famous theatrical family, insisting it was a composite and mainly about the Davenport family. The playwrights worked so hard and well together that their first draft turned out to be exactly what was seen on opening night. The reviews were raves, but producer Jed Harris, possibly the most hated man on Broadway, announced that any show that received those kind of reviews without selling out every performance deserved to be closed. Kaufman threatened to murder Harris, and *The Royal Family* went on to a long run.

Noel Coward's revue, *This Year of Grace!* (10/7/28; 158 performances), opened at the Selwyn with Coward, Beatrice Lillie, Florence Desmond and Queenie Leonard. The show contained two of Coward's biggest hits: "World Weary" and "A Room with a View." English impresario Charles B. Cochran served as producer. Sonnie Hale had played Coward's part in London since the author felt uncomfortable with the juvenile lead. After singing "A Room with a View," Coward announced to Cochran, "It's more than I can bear and more than one should expect of the audience!" The song was given to Billy Milton.

Cochran also produced Cole Porter's (q.v.) *Wake Up and Dream* (12/30/29; 127 performances). The score included the standard "What Is This Thing Called Love?"

Songwriters Arthur Schwartz and Howard Dietz (q.v.) had their revue *Three's a Crowd* (10/15/30; 272 performances) open at the Selwyn. It was to be the theater's last success. The revue contained two of the greatest songs of the thirties: "Something to Remember You By" and the Johnny Green, Edward Heyman, Robert Sour, Frank Eyton and Howard Dietz classic, "Body and Soul." Fred Allen and his wife Portland Hoffa starred along with Libby Holman, Clifton Webb and Tamara Geva. The show also presented a band, the California Collegians, which included a young Fred MacMurray.

Eight flops followed, the most notable being the last, *The Great Magoo* (12/2/32; 11 performances), a play by Gene Fowler and Ben Hecht. The show is notable solely because it contains the song "It's Only a Paper Moon" by Harold Arlen (q.v.) and E.Y. Harburg (q.v.).

The Depression forced the American theater into a decline, and the 42nd Street theaters suffered particularly. Most of these houses were converted to burlesque (q.v.), but the Selwyn became a movie theater. It remains a movie theater and is slated to be refurbished as part of the Times Square Redevelopment Plan. It has been suggested that the Selwyn be restored and once again become a legitimate house.

SHAKESPEARE'S THEATER   See JOLSON'S 59TH STREET THEATER.

SHUBERT BROTHERS   Lee (1873–1953), Sam S. (1876–1905) and J.J. (1878–1963) Shubert were the most prolific of all producers, concentrating on productions aimed at the widest possible audience. They were ruthless moguls who at one time owned 31 theaters in New York and 63 others across the United States, and they were at least part owners of 5 theaters in London. From their first production, *Brixton Burglary* presented at the Herald Square Theater on May 20, 1901, through the last production under the brothers' control, *The Starcross Story,* presented at the Royale Theatre (q.v.) on January 13, 1954, they presented over 520 productions on Broadway. They also were responsible for countless touring shows and even some London productions. It was estimated that fully one-fourth of the productions presented on Broadway were Shubert productions, and these shows accounted for two-thirds of the total ticket sales for Broadway. After the brothers' deaths, the Shubert Organization was formed, and it continues today as Broadway's preeminent producer.

The Shuberts' long history of play production was not marked by many high points in the American theater. They left experimental and high-minded dramas to producers with a conscience, like William A. Brady (q.v.), David Belasco (q.v.), The Theater Guild (q.v.) and others. Great musical productions were left to Florenz Ziegfeld (q.v.), Max Gordon, Sam H. Harris, Aarons and Freedley (q.v.), Rodgers and Hammerstein (q.v.) and others. Though they did present some notable productions, the Shuberts mostly catered to the broadest possible audience, concentrating on shows to please the tired businessman.

Despite the small percentage of Shubert shows that have weathered the years, the brothers did produce some near classics. Sigmund Romberg (q.v.) and Dorothy Donnelly's *Blossom Time* and the same team's *The Student Prince;* Olsen and Johnson's *Hellzapoppin!;* Vincente Minnelli's *The Show Is On;* Dietz and Schwartz's (q.v.) *At Home Abroad,* and two productions of the

Sam S. Shubert

Ziegfeld Follies (q.v.) following the great showman's death were highlights of their musical offerings. None of the Shuberts' straight plays have entered the American repertoire.

The Shubert Brothers, specifically J.J. (Jake) and Lee, were known for their lack of humor and their secretiveness. They would firmly deny rumors about productions and then turn around and make the announcement when they were ready. The two brothers were also noted for their frugality and their abhorrence of refunding ticket money no matter what the circumstances. Once, when the scenery and costumes of a Shubert production were lost in a blizzard, J.J. explained to the audience that the show would go on and made a disaster into a triumph. He managed to avoid refunds in the bargain.

Channing Pollock, a playwright and lyricist as well as a Shubert press agent *(q.v.)*, said of the brothers:

"They knew little more of literature and drama than a cow knows of the albuminous content of milk, but that was equally true of almost every manager in New York. Any of the brothers might have been mistaken for an office boy, as I mistook Sam when I applied for a position with the firm."

J.J. was in charge of the musical productions, including the negotiations with composers, musical directors and choreographers, the operation of the Winter Garden Theater *(q.v.)*, the regional theater holdings, theater upkeep and construction and personnel matters. Lee was in charge of booking the Shuberts' vast holdings, the New York theaters except for the Winter Garden, real estate transactions, straight-play productions and the company's finances. His office was conveniently located next to the vault.

The Shuberts were the first producers to hire women as ushers. They set this historical precedent in 1908 at the Casino Theatre *(q.v.)*. The Shuberts were also the first to charge for paper cups near the water fountain and the first to mix up what was called "orange drink." The liquid was made in a basement and then meted out to the various theaters. The Shuberts always had money on their minds, and that might be why they refused to supply hot water in their rest rooms. They did have hot water taps on the sinks, but no hot water came out of them. In a more serious vein, the Shuberts were first to hold tickets in racks on the wall of the box offices and also the first to provide special "count up" rooms to reconcile the books.

David Szemanski, the patriarch of the Shubert family, fled Lithuania for England and finally Syracuse, New York. He sent for his wife Catharine and their six children in 1882. Sam was the first introduced into the world of the theater. He and his brother Levi (Lee) sold papers outside the Wieting Theatre. One fateful day, Sam was invited to come in out of the cold by John Kerr, manager of the theater. Sam took a seat in the rear, and his life was forever changed. When David Belasco brought his production of *May Blossom* to the theater in 1885, he hired Sam to play a small part. Sam undertook a series of increasingly important jobs in Syracuse theaters, ending up with a post as treasurer of the Wieting Theatre.

In 1894, Sam decided to go into producing. He bought the touring rights to Charles Hoyt's *A Texas Steer*. Sam's brothers Lee and Jake joined him in the venture. The success of the abbreviated tour of the Northeast was followed by another tour of a play by Hoyt. The success of the second tour led Sam to risk another step forward in his career. He bought the Bastable Theatre and set himself up as manager. Soon thereafter, a group of speculators agreed to build the Baker Theatre for Sam to manage. Sam was contacted by Abraham Erlanger, head of the Theatrical Syndicate, which was trying to gain a monopoly on all the important American theaters. The Syndicate or Trust, operated by Hayman and Frohman, Nixon and Zimmerman and Klaw and Erlanger, controlled the plays, and if a theater owner wanted to be able to book plays he had to deal with the Syndicate or lose the show to a rival theater. Once Erlanger gained control of all the important theaters in a region, he took up to 50% of each theater's profits. But soon Erlanger lost interest in the little fiefdom the Shuberts had set up. However, the Shuberts had learned from the Erlanger method of operation.

The brothers purchased more theaters, including the Grand Opera House in Syracuse, thus giving them control of all Syracuse theaters, and then they branched out into nearby Utica. Sam was now ready for the big move. He took a lease on the Herald Square Theater in New York City from its owner Charles Evans. The brothers were warned that the Herald Square on the east side of 35th Street was a surefire failure. They ignored the warnings and contracted with the celebrated actor Richard Mansfield to present his productions at the Herald Square Theater.

The Shuberts brought Erlanger into the operation of the Herald Square to assure product and to be able to get a closer look at the despot's methods. At the same time, the Shuberts bought the rights to tour one of the biggest hits of the 1890s, *The Belle of New York*. This time, the Shuberts acquired rights for the entire country, not just the Northeast.

The first attraction at the Herald Square Theater was a western play, *Arizona* (9/10/00; 140 performances). But it was presented by Kirke La Shelle, not the Shuberts. The supposedly jinxed Herald Square Theater was now a success, but the Shuberts had to wait out two more successful productions after *Arizona* before they became Broadway producers.

Sam was gaining experience as a producer by presenting special matinee productions of new plays at the Herald Square. But the first two were abject failures, slammed by the press and scorned by the public. Sam decided that the lesson here was that he should never present a play by an unknown author (one of the plays was by George Bernard Shaw but he was unknown at the time). Sam learned his lesson well and taught his brothers. They would never again take a chance with a new playwright.

Finally, on May 20, 1901, with *The Brixton Burglary* (48 performances), Sam Shubert had his name above the title as producer at the Herald Square. The Shuberts continued their acquisition of new theaters, both in the provinces and in New York. With the Herald Square booked with other people's productions, Sam found a new outlet for his producing efforts. He bought the Casino Theatre (*q.v.*) on 39th Street.

The Shuberts opened their first bona fide smash hit, *A Chinese Honeymoon* (6/2/02; 376 performances) at the Casino Theatre. The show, presented in association with producers Nixon and Zimmerman, solidified the Shuberts' prestige in the minds of the theater community. The success gave the Shuberts enough cash to acquire their first piece of New York property—a plot of land across from the Casino on West 39th Street.

Erlanger, concerned about the burgeoning Shubert empire, tried to force the brothers out of business. The leading theatrical paper of the day, the *Morning Telegraph,* was a mouthpiece for the Syndicate. It promptly began a campaign of rumor and invective against the Shubert family. Lee retaliated in the only way he knew how, financially. He pulled all advertisements for Shubert shows and thus began a lifelong battle with the press.

Virtually every newspaper in New York felt the wrath of the Shuberts. The most famous incident concerned the Shuberts and *New York Times* critic Alexander Woollcott (*q.v.*). In 1915, the journalist had panned a Shubert production, *Taking Chances,* and was banned from future Shubert opening nights. Woollcott, a fighter at heart, simply purchased tickets for the next Shubert show, but he was met at the door to the theater by J.J. and refused entry. This charade was repeated 22 times. The *Times* brought the Shuberts to court and won an injunction against the producers. The *Times* meanwhile turned the tables on the Shuberts by not accepting their advertising. The Shuberts picked their fight with the *Times* because at the time it was a minor New York paper and posed no real threat. But the lawsuit and battle gave the *Times* and Woollcott inestimable publicity, and the *Times* became one of the most widely read New York dailies. Other producers refused to do business with the Shuberts, since a *Times* review was now important. So the Shuberts relented, and after a year, the feud was settled.

Other critics (*q.v.*) were banned from reviewing Shubert productions. These included Goodman Ace in Kansas, Philip Hale of Boston and George Holland, who got himself appointed a fire marshall and inspected the Shubert Boston theaters on every opening night. In New York, Lee barred gossip columnists Leonard Lyons and Walter Winchell (*q.v.*). The latter commented "I do not mind missing Shubert openings. I can always go the second night and see the closing." Also barred were critics Heywood Broun from the *World*, Louis Kronenberger of the newspaper *P.M.,* Gilbert Gabriel from the *Sun,* Percy Hammond of the *Post* and his successor Charles Collins, who was barred simply to keep the tradition of barring the *Post* critic going. Even Channing Pollock (formerly a Shubert employee) was forbidden entry. Pollock wore a series of disguises to Shubert productions until it almost became a game.

Pollock, in addition to acting as press agent, also screened plays for the brothers. In his role of play screener, he was given a copy of Richard Walton Tully's

Rose of the Rancho. When Tully brought the play to Pollock for his consideration, he added the caveat that the two previous producers who were asked to read the play, Kirke La Shelle and Fred Hamlin, died before they were able to pass judgment. Pollock was not a superstitious man and so gave the matter no thought. When, a few months later Tully asked for his script Pollock found it missing. It finally turned up in the bag that Sam Shubert was carrying on his fatal train ride.

This tragedy struck while the Shuberts were still battling with Erlanger over control of the American theater. A night train to Pittsburgh carrying Sam and two members of his staff collided with a parked work train. On May 11, 1905, Sam died. The blow almost made Lee give up the business, and he went so far as to meet with Erlanger with the intent of selling out the Shubert holdings to the Syndicate. The meeting collapsed, and Lee was even more resolved to keep the business. Sam's will caused an irreparable rift in the surviving brothers' relationship. Sam gave all his holdings to brother Lee. Jake was not mentioned at all in the document.

Lee effectively took control and embarked on a massive expansion. Producers Harrison Fiske and David Belasco signed agreements with the Shuberts, and Lee invited other producers to join in the fight against Erlanger. Then he announced the signing of Sarah Bernhardt, the greatest actress of her day. Other producers rallied around Lee, determined to join the "trust busters." Actually, the Shuberts were building their own monopoly, but at the time they were still the underdogs.

Erlanger ran into trouble with the beginnings of the movie industry. It was clear that the new art form was gaining favor, and vaudeville was the hardest hit popular entertainment. Erlanger was the owner of several vaudeville theaters and found his holdings threatened. He finally sold his vaudeville interests to B.F. Keith and Edward Albee *(q.v.)*, the owners of a vast vaudeville empire. Erlanger was given $500,000 to stay out of vaudeville for 10 years. Erlanger, in turn, gave half the money to the Shuberts so that they would also stay out of the vaudeville business. Lee was only too happy to concur, since they had no interest in anything but the legitimate theater.

In July 1917, the Shuberts achieved their greatest triumph. They purchased the estate of George Cox, the largest theater holder in the United States. By buying Cox's holdings for an eight-figure fee, they put the final pieces in place for a Shubert empire. Now the Shuberts could guarantee producers the pick of American cities for their tours. Forty of the greatest producers in the country booked their shows into Shubert houses, bypassing the Syndicate.

Of course, the Shuberts continued to build and buy more theaters, but their immediate problem was in supplying their chain with product. The brothers made sure that they put out a practically endless stream of shows. Those that were profitable were kept on Broadway long enough to establish a name and then were sent on the road. The brothers found that audiences never tired of some shows like *Blossom Time.* The Romberg operetta was toured almost indefinitely. The same costumes and sets were reused over and over again for each additional company. The brothers would book each tour for one performance at the Ambassador Theatre *(q.v.).* After the one performance, the show would be sent on the road advertised as "direct from Broadway." *Blossom Time* opened in 1921. Only three years later, it showed a profit of $700,000.

In 1918, the Shuberts presented 15 shows on Broadway. While the straight plays were most often flops, the musicals, especially the operettas, were hits. The Shubert factory operated in much the same way as the motion-picture industry at the height of the studio system. Among the Shubert contractees were composer Sigmund Romberg, who wrote 34 scores for the brothers, lyricist/librettist Harold Atteridge, director J.C. Huffman, set designer Watson Barratt, choreographer Allan K. Foster and jack of all trades Melville Ellis. Performers under contract to the Shuberts included Al Jolson *(q.v.),* who appeared in 11 Shubert productions, and Willie and Eugene Howard. Since the Shuberts owned the largest collection of costumes, sets and equipment in the country, they often asked their writers to compose shows around the current stock.

There seemed to be no stopping the Shuberts' dominance of the American theater scene. But in 1920, they began implementing one of their first unsuccessful policies. Lee announced that they would enter the vaudeville field. Almost immediately, the policy was a failure. The Shuberts were forced to pay too much to lure stars from their rivals Keith and Albee. Also, the Shubert theaters were too small to turn a profit even if they were sold out. Jake, whose operettas and musical revues made money, was angry. After all, the profits his shows made simply went to offset the losses of Lee's vaudeville policy.

The Shuberts even went so far as to invest in Keith's operations under the name Mr. Diamond. The fictitious Mr. Diamond was well hidden from Keith and Albee. Because Diamond was a stockholder in the Keith/Albee syndicate operation, his lawyers were able to take periodic looks at the Keith-Albee books. In this way, the Shuberts could find out exactly how their rival was doing. They learned that their vaudeville enterprise wasn't affecting the Keith-Albee dominance in the least. At least, they were making money off the Keith-Albee profits.

By 1924, the Shubert empire consisted of 86 theaters in New York, Boston, Philadelphia and Chicago. Thirty of these theaters were in New York City. They owned

Flier for The Student Prince

an additional 27 in other cities. They also controlled the booking of 750 other theaters. During some weeks, they earned $1 million at the box office.

The Shuberts kept their juggernaut rolling, despite the fact that the relationship between the brothers was constantly deteriorating. Each liked the success that the other's productions brought to the firm, but each also was jealous of the other. By 1927, their relationship had soured to the point that Lee kept his offices in the Shubert Theatre *(q.v.),* and Jake moved across the street to the new Sardi *(q.v.)* Building (which the brothers owned).

The Depression hit the entertainment industry hard, and the Shuberts lost $1 million in its first year. As the Depression deepened, Broadway suffered. Audiences would not be wooed by lower ticket prices; they were becoming more and more choosy. The days when patrons would decide to go to the theater without having a particular show in mind were over. Attendance and profits were declining at a prodigious rate. The Shuberts, never known for the artistry of their productions, were in trouble. The company lost $3 million in 1930 and 1931. At the end of 1931, the Shuberts went into receivership. The Irving Trust Company and Lee Shubert were named coreceivers.

The Shuberts were hit with a number of lawsuits, and their stockholders insisted that the books be reviewed. During the 1932–33 season only five plays were produced by the company. On January 1, 1933, a judge announced that the assets of the Shubert Theatre Corporation would be sold at auction. The auction took place on April 7, 1933. Since the theater business was failing, there were not too many interested bidders. In fact, there was only one, Lee Shubert. He bought the assets of the Shuberts for $400,000 under the name Select Theatres Incorporated. After all the bookkeeping was over with bond holders repaid, it turned out that Lee had bought his own company for $100,000. He was certainly rich enough to retire, but he knew only the theater business. He had no close friendships or relationships, and his work was his life.

The Shuberts weathered the duration of the Depression by booking their theaters for nothing in return for a piece of the box office. Thus, they "produced" shows without investing a dime. They figured rightly that every producer was undergoing bad times and would need the brothers' help. This way, the producers wouldn't have to raise the money for theater rentals, and the Shuberts would have attractions in their houses that just might turn a profit.

Jake's son John was brought into the Shubert fold and began producing shows for the brothers. He picked up where his father had left off, with operettas and musical revues. Jake was nursing wounds he suffered when Lee wouldn't let him have anything to do with the *Ziegfeld Follies (q.v.),* which the Shuberts produced. Jake prided himself on his revues, and his *Passing Show* series had rivaled Ziegfeld's. But Lee held all the aces, and in 1934, he even booked the *Follies,* the first since Ziegfeld's death, at Jake's Winter Garden Theater. The show was a hit, and that rankled Jake even more. Then, too, his own son had joined the enemy's side. He left for an extended trip to Europe.

Over 60% of the plays on Broadway during the worst of the Depression were either produced by the Shuberts or involved Shubert houses, for which the Shuberts received a part of the proceeds. By 1937, it seemed the worst was over. Lee had put over $5 million of his own money into the Shubert Organization to keep it alive, and, therefore, he was largely responsible for keeping the Broadway theater alive. Jake spent most of the Depression in Europe. He produced his first show in years, *Frederika,* in 1937. The operetta closed after only 94 performances.

In 1939, Lee began buying more theaters, many of which were theaters that the Shuberts had lost due to the bankruptcy. Although the Depression was almost over, the Shuberts did not increase their producing. They didn't have to. They managed to own pieces in 75% of the shows playing on Broadway. They either put up the additional capital needed by a rival producer or leased their 17 Broadway theaters in exchange for a piece of the box office. Even if they didn't have any money in a show, they still owned 90% of the Broadway theaters, so, in effect, they were Broadway.

In 1948, the Shuberts started the Sam S. Shubert Foundation with $500,000. It was planned that eventually all the Shubert assets would go to the foundation. The establishment of the foundation was the beginning of a plan devised by Lee and J.J. to take care of the organization when they retired.

The brothers consolidated their empire through the second largest real estate transaction in contemporary New York history (the first was Rockefeller Center). On November 10, 1948, the Shuberts purchased the Booth (q.v.), Shubert (q.v.), Broadhurst (q.v.) and Plymouth (q.v.) theaters and the Shubert Alley (q.v.) property. The deal cost almost $4 million. The transaction gave them the entire square block between Broadway and Eighth Avenue and 44th and 45th Street, except for the plots on which the Astor (q.v.) and Manhattan hotels stood.

The federal government dealt the Shuberts a serious blow when Chairman of the House Judiciary Committee, Emanuel Celler, began a probe of the Shubert operations, charging that the brothers held an unfair monopoly on American theater. Celler stated: "The Shubert interests have clamped a strangle hold on the theater. Theatrical people are afraid to testify. I have checked and I have found a malodorous picture. The Shuberts control 60 percent of New York and 90 percent of legitimate theatre elsewhere. They have allocated tickets to hit shows to 'pet' brokers, using kickbacks of all kinds."

Celler also attacked the Shuberts' house-seat policy. Every show had a certain number of the prime seats set aside for the Shuberts' use. The brothers took these tickets and sold them through speculators and ticket brokers for a huge markup. They didn't claim the profit on their taxes, only the actual price of the tickets. The press discovered, for example, that the Shuberts had held back tickets for the first 19 rows of the Philadelphia production of Annie Get Your Gun in 1946. If each of the tickets cost a top price of $6.60, they would be worth $46,200. But the Shuberts planned to sell them to illegitimate brokers who would scalp the tickets for as much as $75 each. This would bring the Shuberts $525,000. They had only to pay the amusement tax on the actual cost of the tickets—$46,200. Thus, they netted a tax-free profit of $478,800.

The Shuberts instructed their box offices to play other games with ticket sales. If the brothers had another producer's show booked into one of their theaters and they wanted the theater for one of their own productions, they could legally kick out the competition's show only if the box-office receipts fell below a certain level. The Shuberts made sure the show didn't reach its minimum by instructing their box-office personnel to simply tell all potential ticket buyers that the show was sold out. They then effectively sold no tickets.

The converse applied when the Shuberts had a show that was not doing good business but that they wanted to appear to be a success. They simply took their own money and bought out all the remaining tickets. True, there were no bodies in the seats, but the tickets were sold.

Publicity from the Annie Get Your Gun affair spurred the government's interest in Shubert practices. The attorney general of the United States held his own investigation in addition to Representative Celler's. Independent producers who were unable to get bookings in cities where the Shuberts owned a monopoly of theaters brought suit against the brothers.

The attorney general laid out his allegations against the Shuberts.

The defendants for many years have been, and are now engaged in a combination and conspiracy in restraint of interstate trade in producing, booking, and presentation of legitimate attractions.

They compel producers to book their legitimate attractions through defendants.

They exclude others from booking legitimate attractions.

They prevent competition in presentation of legitimate attractions.

They combine their power to maintain and strengthen their domination in these fields.

The government began to gather witnesses to speak against the Shuberts. Naturally the majority of the actors, producers, directors, etc., chose to remain anonymous, afraid of the all-powerful Shuberts. Lee Shubert was incensed at what he thought was cowardice and at the government's attacks. He reasoned that without the Shuberts the country's road business would collapse since there were barely enough shows produced to keep the Shubert-owned theaters open. Of course, he was right. Without the Shuberts, there would be a vacuum with no others to fill it. In regard to the anonymous complainants, Lee wanted to know where they were when the Shuberts were keeping the American theater alive almost single-handedly during the Depression.

The government was unmoved. It demanded that the Shuberts get out of either the booking business or the theater-ownership business. The brothers were also told to unload a sufficient number of theaters so that whatever competition there was could be given a chance. Lee responded by buying a half interest in Earl Carroll's (q.v.) theater in Hollywood.

Lee decided to fight the government in the courts and have the matter settled once and for all. While waiting for the government to put its case together, Lee kept up normal activities, even proposing a television series called Shubert Alley. Then on December 21, 1953, he suffered a series of strokes. He rallied for a while but died on Christmas day. The last show to be produced by the Shubert brothers was *The Starcross Story* which opened and closed on January 13, 1954.

Jake, always the Shubert in the background, would now have to assume control of the empire and fight the battles with the government. Jake had lawyer William Klein on his side. Klein had been with the brothers since 1901 and had brought about and defended thousands of suits. The government faced a temporary setback when a federal district court ruled that the Shuberts were exempt from antitrust laws. The government appealed to the Supreme Court.

Meanwhile, Jake was feuding with Lee's family over control of the empire. He systematically fired every staff member who owed any allegiance to Lee and replaced them with his own handpicked successors. His son John had come over to Jake's side before Lee's death.

As it was, Lee had always seen to the daily operation of the vast empire; Jake was a producer, not an administrator, and he knew nothing of the Shubert holdings. Not only was he in the dark as to the company's operation, but also he didn't have the necessary education to administer the vast company. Unable to grasp the big picture, Jake concentrated on the more trivial aspects of the organization.

On February 16, 1958, the government ordered the Shubert organization to sell 12 of its theaters in 6 cities in 2 years and stop entirely their booking business. Jake issued a statement in response to the government's order:

> I will live up to the decree, although I have my doubts as to whether some of its provisions will not hurt rather than benefit the legitimate theater. The decree requires us to sell a number of theaters which were assembled over half a century. Whether these theaters in other hands will continue to be operated as legitimate houses only time will tell.
>
> If we have been financially successful, the legitimate theater and the public will someday benefit from the fruits of our labor through the means of the Sam S. Shubert Foundation.

As Jake slipped into senility, his son John took over the reins of the Shubert Organization, but John was able to produce only one play, *Jules, Jake and Uncle Joe,* and that opened and closed on January 28, 1961. On November 17, 1962, John died of a heart attack.

Jake died on December 26, 1963, at the age of 86. The Shubert empire continued with Lawrence Shubert Jr. in charge, but the organization no longer produced shows. It merely managed theaters and the vast real estate holdings, and little by little the organization lost its connection to the theater and became a typical bureaucratic company.

One of the lawyers involved in defending the Shuberts against the government's antitrust suit was Gerald Schoenfeld. He brought his friend Bernard Jacobs into the business, and soon they took over operation of the Shubert Organization. Schoenfeld became the chairman, and Jacobs the president.

The two men, extremely savvy attorneys, brought the Shubert Organization back to life. They began producing and reestablished the organization's dominance of the American theater. The two men, known collectively as The Shuberts even though they are not part of the family, have used their great power to bring some of the greatest hits of the London stage to New York. These include the current blockbusters *Cats* and *Phantom of the Opera*. The two men also profess an interest in art and have at times put the Shubert resources behind chancier plays by some of the top playwrights writing in English, including Tom Stoppard, Simon Gray, Harold Pinter and David Mamet. Of course, the Shuberts did not originate any of these playwrights' productions; they were either London imports or tried out in American regional theaters. The current so-called Shuberts, like the brothers who preceded them, loathe taking chances with unproven talents.

The Shubert Organization is a subsidiary of the nonprofit Shubert Foundation, and that gives it certain tax advantages that its competition resents. The Shubert Organization, being the dominant power in American theater, receives its due share of complaints. Some are well-founded, some are just sour grapes. They control 17 theaters in New York and either own or operate others in Boston, Washington, Philadelphia, Chicago and Los Angeles. Many of the Shubert-owned theaters outside New York have been demolished and replaced with office buildings. Some view the Shuberts as real estate operators, not really producers.

Many of the smaller Shubert houses like the Belasco (q.v.) in New York sit dark for long periods. Instead of booking the theaters, or making them available to local groups, the Shuberts would rather let them sit empty. They do not like to take chances. Also, by letting the theaters sit, they prove their point that the buildings are unprofitable and local governments should allow them to be destroyed. Even the larger Shubert houses like the National in Washington, D.C., sit empty for long periods, until a big blockbuster like *Cats* or *A Chorus Line* can be booked for a six-month run. In between engagements, they remain dark in lonely downtowns.

Critics also point out that it is the Shuberts who always lead the way with higher ticket prices. True, costs have risen dramatically and the Shuberts are, some critics say, responsible for that too. After all, since their conservative producing style, booking only proven hits, guarantees they'll make money, they can afford to pay stagehands and musicians more. At the same time their competitors, who take greater chances and don't have the financial resources of the Shubert Organization behind them, can ill afford the high guarantees and inflated salaries.

To the Shuberts' credit, they have generally kept up their theater holdings admirably, although with a certain lack of taste in choice of color scheme. They also revolutionized box-office procedures through computerization and the acceptance of credit card sales. Also to their credit are the many charitable activities they support through free leases on their theaters for special events and donations to worthy causes through the Shubert Foundation. However, even now, almost 100 years since its founding, the Shubert empire is still creating controversy.

SHUBERT THEATER See SAM S. SHUBERT THEATRE.

SIGNAGE Nothing represents the popular view of Times Square so much as the giant signs that line the canyons of Broadway and Seventh Avenue. Tama Starr of Artkraft Strauss (q.v.) says the lights "create an atmosphere which is a real large part of setting the mood. And it's obvious to say but I'll say it anyway, it's unique, it's irreplaceable. What makes Times Square unique is the long sight lines and the fact that the buildings are set way back so even in the middle of the crowded city (and Times Square is one of the most crowded places in a crowded city) you still have a sense of openness and you can see the sky. You don't feel hemmed in like on Madison Avenue."

The first signs were illuminated with gas. Mel Starr of Artkraft Strauss explained their construction: "They had a gas mantle—a pipe with a string of jets, and they covered the facade with a metal sheet with the name of the attraction punched out. Each hole was covered with a little glass cap. Those were inserted into the holes. The twinkling of the lights came from the flickering of the gas flames and the color from the glass caps. Later on, bulbs emulated the twinkling of the lights."

In 1897, down Broadway at Madison Square, a sign for the "ocean breezes" of Coney Island was the first to be electrified. The first Broadway show to feature a moving electric sign was Victor Herbert's (q.v.) operetta, *The Red Mill*. Carbon bulbs outlined the mill's sails which appeared to spin around. *Florodora*, famous for its beautiful sextette, had another notable moving sign. The facade of the Casino Theatre (q.v.) at 38th and Broadway was marked by an outline of the six lovelies dancing from side to side. The first Broadway star to have her name in lights was Maxine Elliott.

Tama Starr explained the change to electricity. "It was inevitable. What you traded off by having this archaic looking twinkling you go back by having more brightness." As the years passed, the signs grew larger and larger and more and more elaborate. The introduction of neon around 1927 introduced a whole spectrum

of brilliant colors, and slowly the Great White resembled a rainbow. The neon changed the loc signs because the old light bulbs were only point light. Neon allowed designers to work with another dimension—lines.

Surprisingly the signs for Broadway shows were often just billboards, while the signs for commercial products began to dominate the Square. Among the most famous were those for Wrigley's Chewing Gum (first erected in 1917 and revised in 1935), the Pepsi-Cola waterfall, Coca-Cola, Maxwell House Coffee, Anheiser Busch, Johnny Walker, Admiral Television and Kleenex.

Some signs were simple billboards with a gimmick of one kind or another. Typical of these were Camel Cigarettes with its smoke rings and later, in the same location, Right Guard antiperspirant. Most of the more dramatic signs were designed by Douglas Leigh (q.v.).

Also dominant were the huge "spectaculars" built by Artkraft Strauss for the many movie palaces that lined the streets. The Astor and Victoria theaters (q.v.) shared facades exhibited the fanciest presentations. Each week, the massive signs would be changed to advertise the current picture. Artkraft Strauss owned an inventory of letters in different styles that could be plugged into the existing outlets to spell out the picture's title and the names of the leading players.

During World War II, the lights on Broadway were dimmed. It was discovered that the bright lights of Times Square could be seen from the ocean, and American ships were neatly outlined against the shore. Artkraft Strauss utilized reflective material on wood bases that would catch the headlights of passing cars. Color was provided by nail polish.

Artkraft Strauss leases the space for the sign from the owner of the building. Artkraft, in turn leases the rights to an advertiser. The sign company fabricates the sign, installs and supplies the space and operation and, if there is a running message, the teletypes.

Once a company decides to have a sign built, it meets with Artkraft's designers and engineers. Usually a scale model is built. After the model is approved, a single element, like one letter, is constructed in a full-size model. The letter is made to perform exactly as required on the actual sign. Sometimes, a double exposure is made, indicating how the sign will look in the context of the entire square.

Each of the large signs has carefully programmed animation. The change of lights is orchestrated much like a music score. Each element or portion of an element is noted. The elements may include the color, whether a sign "moves" in a spiral or blinks on and off and how the lights are programmed. Every two or three years, the patterns are changed. The change catches peoples' eyes in a different way, and the sign appears new.

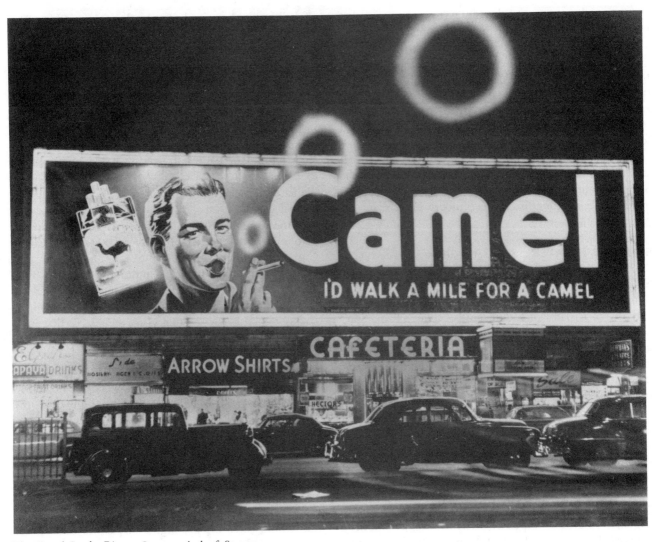

The Camel Smoke Rings   Courtesy Artkraft Strauss.

The signs' patterns can be quite intricate. The Kleenex sign at the Northeast corner of Broadway and 43rd Street featured the character Little Lulu as she skipped from one to another of the sixteen foot letters spelling *Kleenex,* lighting each letter when she passed by. When she reached the *X* she jumped down onto a sheet of pop up Kleenex and slid down onto the 50-foot-long Kleenex box. A giant neon hand then reached down, grasped a sheet of Kleenex and pulled it out to demonstrate the pop up feature of the product. There were 32 different Lulus in the operation and 8 hands, all electronically superimposed to give the illusion of a single action. In addition, the sign was wired for neon tubing, enabling the sign to repeat the entire operation in five different colors.

A final feature on the Kleenex sign was the addition of a motograph message in moving lights in letters one-story high. Operated by remote control, it permitted messages of any length, which could be changed in seconds.

Each sign is divided into individual light boxes that are individually wired. They are hoisted into place with giant cranes. The boxes usually measure six by eight feet. The neon is already placed on the light boxes. The engineer has allowed for wind resistance, the sign's weight and the supports necessary according to physics and New York City codes. The Kleenex sign boasted 1,000 transformers, 25,000 feet of neon tubing, 4,600 incandescent lamps and 500,000 feet of wire, enough to stretch from New York to Philadelphia.

Painted billboards are painted by artists using four-inch brushes directly on the billboard. The artist takes a drawing or a piece of art and squares it off, and then duplicates the grid on the billboard or wall. The artist then draws the outline of the artwork on the wall in indelible pencil. Then the artist gives the board a coat of shellac to protect the cartoon. This turns the pencil marks purple and makes them easier to see. Then the artist paints by the numbers. Skin tones and portraits of products and human beings are especially difficult. Some billboards look flat and two dimensional, but a good billboard artist can create a three-dimensional

The Joan of Arc Spectacular   Courtesy Artkraft Strauss.

look, spending a whole day on just a mouth or cheek. To get the face, often 30 or more feet tall, to not be distorted is difficult. Sometimes, the artists use a kind of pointillism for the pictures, since the drawings are seen from so far away.

The advertiser's costs include rent, maintenance, insurance, electricity and the operation and construction of the sign. Some of the large signs cost up to half a million dollars. The best-known signs, such as Coca-Cola or Fuji, would cost over $1.5 million if built today. Each sign also costs a couple of thousand dollars a month in electricity bills. The price to the companies (now mostly Japanese) is cost effective. After all, nearly 13,000,000 people pass through the square each week. As Tama explains, "The medium is unique. Elsewhere, in a magazine for example, you skip the ads or on television you go out of the room during commercials. But here people come just to see the ads."

Tama further stated that "In the old days there was an opening for every sign and sign lighting ceremonies." The Kleenex sign was turned on on Wednesday, January 30, 1957, in support of Heart Month and the

New York Heart Fund. Perry Como, dubbed "King of Hearts" of the 1957 national drive, and Ann Marie Christie, Heart Fund Poster Girl of 1957, flipped the switch illuminating the 80-foot-high and 180-foot-long sign. In addition to the lighting, the occasion included models wearing ski costumes in the five shades of Kleenex (white, blue, pink, yellow and green). The models staged a winter fashion show at the base of the sign.

Most signs aren't constructed to advertise a specific product but rather to enhance the image of a whole company. For example, Panasonic's huge sign contains only the word Panasonic without mentioning any of the company's products. The company is making its corporate image part of the landscape. Artkraft Strauss has a slogan, "Make your trademark a landmark." As Tama explains, "By having this confident, large scale appearance they are becoming more of a presence. They're looking for an architectural fantasy that makes their corporate image a permanent and bright part of civilization."

The signs are also seen around the world through

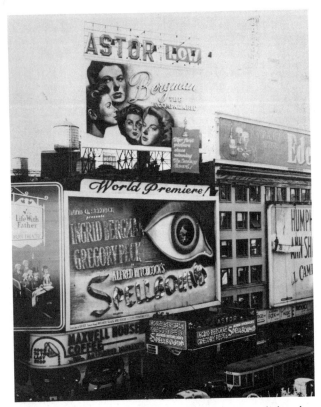

Spellbound at the Astor Theater. Note there are no lights above street level because of World War II restrictions. The sign is made from reflective materials. Courtesy Artkraft Strauss.

movies and photographs. Because the signs are in Times Square, they may have a greater impact outside New York than in the city itself.

Unfortunately, the many great sign locations are being replaced by skyscrapers. The Astor/Victoria site, once home to the largest billboard in the world, was replaced by the Marriott Marquis hotel. At one time, the location boasted the famous Budweiser sign, a billboard made up of 48 separate drawings. The National Theatre's skyscraper replaced the site of the great Kleenex sign. Up Broadway at 51st Street, the Capitol Theater *(q.v.)*, home of the Anheiser Busch eagle, is gone. The Nathan's site, originally intended to be a skyscraper, supported the TWA sign and the Budweiser bottle. Today a plain billboard occupies the rooftop. Another building intended to be a skyscraper was the Mark Hellinger Theater *(q.v.)*. That skyscraper was finally built as the Novotel Hotel, and another site was lost.

More sites may be lost if the 42nd Street Redevelopment project goes through. Tama Starr explained the problem when the designers decided to forgo signage and remove the theaters' marquees. "They were taking the position that marquees cause crime because they allow criminals to get out of the rain. Everybody knows the primary function of light is to make streets safer.

They may have taken an extreme position knowing they would have to make a compromise. The environmental impact statement, around 2,000 pages, never addressed the subject of light. They tried to brush it under the rug entirely. Now people like the Municipal Art Society say don't take away all the light. Now they're talking about putting some little bitsy neon stuff, shoe shine parlor kind of things, on the ground level of the buildings."

In February of 1987, those responsible for the project's zoning required all developers to allow for signage on their buildings. According to Robert A. Mayers, president of Mayers & Schiff Associates, a consultant on the 42nd Street project, lighting colors will be limited to white. He also would like to see the entire Times Square area surfaced with sidewalks of black granite.

Mayers also suggested that 80-foot tubular steel pylons be erected at street corners. These would hold cantilevered advertising signage. Jules Fisher, a noted Broadway lighting designer, and Paul Marantz are also consultants to the project. They envision huge interactive billboards placed on separate buildings.

Other spectacular effects are also being considered, including laser light shows, phosphorescent special effects, holographic effects in sidewalks, walls of glass and huge mirrored walls. Many of these new spectaculars are being designed by artists for strictly artistic purposes. Tama believes the insistently commercial aspects of current signage is important. "The huge signs are expensive and only a commercial advertiser can pay for it. I'd be opposed to the National Endowment for the Arts paying for this kind of thing, it's not appropriate but it is appropriate for the Canon company."

Canadian Club Spectacular A good example of the complexity and dimension of the giant signs above Times Square is the Canadian Club spectacular. The sign stood on 47th Street where the present-day Suntory spectacular recently stood. The three signs at the site are certainly the most visible in the area. The Coca-Cola spectacular, which occupied a site directly below the Canadian Club sign's old spot, is perhaps the most famous sign in the world. Both were dismantled in June 1990 to allow the razing of the building upon which they stood. It is planned to replace the signs when the new skyscraper is completed.

The Canadian Club spectacular, built by Artkraft Strauss, was 48 feet by 62 feet. The background of the sign was 3,000 square feet of yellow vitreous porcelain enameled steel. The same material is used for refrigerators and stoves, which speaks well for its ability to accommodate considerable fluctuations in temperature. Approximately 25,000 lamps (light bulbs) were used in the display. Over two miles of neon tubing covered the face of the sign. All these bulbs and tubes required over one hundred miles of wire (over 500,000 feet) to

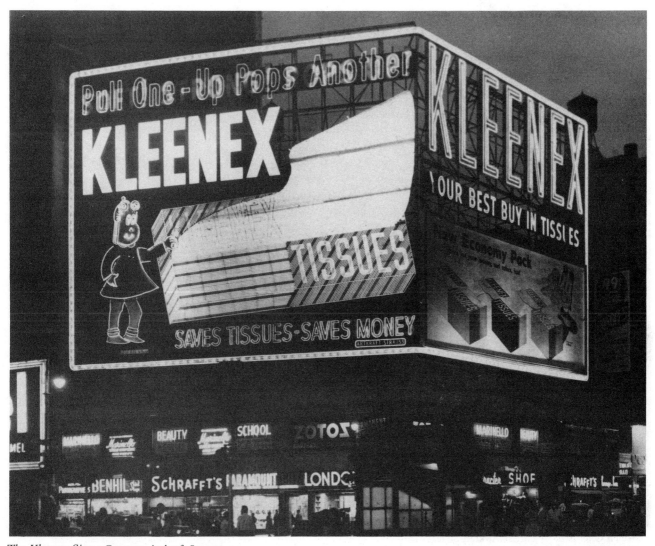

The Kleenex Sign   Courtesy Artkraft Strauss.

connect them to the 1,000 separate circuits that controlled the sign.

If all the elements of the sign were lit simultaneously, it would have consumed over 750,000 watts of electricity. It delivered over 2,500,000 candle power—two candle power for every visitor on Times Square per day.

The upper-case letters in the words *Canadian Club* were 22 feet, 6 inches high, and the lower-case letters were 12 feet high. The words *Imported Whisky* were 6 feet high. The sign was capable of 42 different animation changes. This included the colors of the sign, the pattern of the neon lights behind the letters and the order of the patterns of lights.

Vikings Spectacular   The shared roofs of the Astor *(q.v.)* and Victoria (see GAIETY THEATER) theaters was one of the greatest of the Times Square sign locations. The block-long Astor/Victoria site was the longest sign

locale in the world. Today, the Marriott Marquis Hotel and its theater take their place. Any sign erected there was bound to dominate the Square. In later years, the location was used for giant paintings without special construction or lights. The most famous of these is probably the Budweiser Sign.

When Times Square was the movie-premier capital of the world, the location was used to its best advantage. Of all the great spectaculars on the site, the sign for the film *The Vikings* was the most impressive. At the time, it was the world's largest and costliest outdoor advertising piece ever constructed for a motion picture. Because the movie opened at both the Astor and Victoria theaters, the sign and the marquee below ran for the entire block.

The sign was dedicated on June 11, 1958, by Kirk Douglas, the star and producer of the film. He was swung from the top of the sign in a bosun's chair to the boat built into the sign. He then christened the boat with sea water brought from Hardangerfjord, Norway.

Canadian Club Sign   Courtesy Artkraft Strauss.

Hardangerfjord was the home port of the real Vikings and also served as a location for the picture.

The sign was 270 feet long and 59 feet high. Across the bottom of the sign was the message "Sail the seas of passion and violence with the boldest warriors the world has ever known." The 73 letters were each 7 feet high. The title of the picture was written in letters 10 feet tall and mounted on shields. The letters on the sign were delineated in light bulbs, over 4,500 of them, each of which was expected to last only thirty hours.

The boat itself was 214 feet long, almost 3 times larger than the real Viking ships. The sail of the ship was mounted on a mast 50 feet tall. It was constructed of canvas, and the press release claimed that it was the largest single sail made for a vessel in New York. The boat was fitted with 16-foot oars, which actually moved over a sea of simulated moving waves. The oars were propelled by an elaborate series of cams and walking beams powered by a five-horsepower motor.

On both sides of the sail were 28-foot-tall portraits of the picture's stars—Kirk Douglas, Tony Curtis, Ernest Borgnine and Janet Leigh. The letters in their names were 8½ feet high and illuminated with 6,150 bulbs.

Kodak Sign 45th and 46th Street on Marriott Marquis Hotel. The Eastman Kodak sign is the largest back-lighted sign in the world. It is the first built into the facade of a building in an attempt to mollify critics of the new architecture in Times Square. The Marriott agreed to put four signs on the hotel's facade to help retain the flavor of the square. Unfortunately the signs are not integrated into the building's architecture nor can they replace the huge sign that formerly occupied what was called the Astor/Victoria site. The most prominent of these signs was the huge Vikings spectacular that extended along the entire block. Critics worry that Times Square's signage, often the definition of the Square in most tourist's minds, will be destroyed.

The Kodak sign is a 30-by-50-foot light box. The photograph that constitutes the major element of design is made of Kodak Duratrans and is essentially a huge

The Kodak Sign Photo Jeff Slotnick.

fabric slide hung on the frame. Eight hundred and eighty fluorescent lights glow behind the sign. Huge exhaust fans carry the heat from behind the sign and also serve to hold the giant picture against its frame and keep it from flapping in the air.

Artkraft Strauss built the huge box and the electronic crawl (letters defined in light bulbs) similar to the Motogram (q.v.) on the Times Tower (q.v.). The crawl advertises Kodak products for the company, which has a long-term lease on the location. The sign was officially inaugurated on November 26, 1985, with a photo advertising *Santa Claus, the Movie*. Subsequent photos have not advertised a specific product but rather show greeting card type scenes of barns, skiers, puppies, etc.

New zoning requirements insist on even more signage on the facades of new buildings in the area. Although this may not completely placate those who criticize the changes on the square, it should serve to maintain the spirit of the past.

SIMON, NEIL (1927–   ) Neil Simon is the most successful American playwright of the 20th century. He has written nearly a play a year since his first Broadway production, *Come Blow Your Horn* in 1961. Simon's output even surpasses that of Tennessee Wil-

liams (q.v.), one of the most prolific modern playwrights. Simon's dramatic language is not as poetic as Williams's, nor is he as politically motivated as Arthur Miller (q.v.) or as psychologically provoking as Eugene O'Neill (q.v.). Simon's style relies mainly on jokes and humorous situations. However, Simon does have his serious side, and more recently his plays have become increasingly emotional in content.

Simon has managed to improve his artistry while achieving popular acclaim in almost every play he has written. Some critics have ascribed Simon's success not to any special talent but to his choice of white, middle-class characters—an exact mirror of the average Broadway audience. His detractors distrust his facility in eliciting laughs, and the funnier his plays are the more he sinks in their estimation.

A chronological list of Simon's plays reveals better than anything else his maturation and continued growth. His early comedies are the closest to sitcoms, and his later works have real, honest, uncontrived emotional punch.

Simon began his career as a television writer. He contributed material for the "Phil Silvers Show" (You'll Never Get Rich) as well as the "Tallulah Bankhead Show," the "Sid Caesar Show" and the "Garry Moore Show." These programs, mostly running in the late fifties, enabled Simon to build his comic muscle. He had earlier provided sketches for shows presented at a popular summer camp, Tamiment.

Simon's first Broadway work was written in collaboration with his brother Danny, considered one of the great comic technicians in the business. The Simon brothers wrote some sketches for the musical revue, *Catch a Star!* (9/6/55; 23 performances). They also contributed material to Leonard Sillman's *New Faces of 1956* (6/14/56). Neil Simon had his first Broadway success with *Come Blow Your Horn* (2/22/61; 677 performances), the slightly autobiographical story of two brothers learning to grow up.

Simon's next project was a libretto for the Cy Coleman and Carolyn Leigh musical *Little Me* (11/17/62; 257 performances). Simon's hilarious script was based on the well-known novel by Patrick Dennis. The show, which starred Sid Caesar, Nancy Andrews, Virginia Martin and Swen Swenson, deserved a much longer run—it remains the funniest musical produced in recent times. Simon's many innovations were overlooked because the show was not "serious." Nancy Andrews played Belle Poitrine, a successful actress dictating her memoirs. Her character enjoys a series of husbands who all die in mysterious and sometimes hilarious ways. Caesar played all the husbands. Martin played the young Belle. Simon's book not only is innovative in construction, but also lampoons musical comedy techniques and keeps its tongue firmly implanted in its cheek.

Simon's next play after *Come Blow Your Horn* was *Barefoot in the Park* (10/23/63; 1,530 performances), one of the most successful productions of the sixties. *Barefoot in the Park* seemed to take up where the earlier play left off. The new piece examined a young couple's first days of marriage. Robert Redford costarred with Elizabeth Ashley.

The Odd Couple (3/10/65; 964 performances) is one of Simon's best known plays, mainly because of the popularity of the hit television series based on it. The original play opened at the Plymouth Theater (q.v.) with Art Carney and Walter Matthau as Felix Unger and Oscar Madison. With *The Odd Couple* Simon went from exploring a young marriage to a tale of two divorced and very mismatched men trying to share an apartment.

A musical, *Sweet Charity* (1/29/66; 608 performances), came next. Simon based his book on an earlier draft by director/choreographer Bob Fosse. *Sweet Charity* boasted a jazzy score by Cy Coleman and Dorothy Fields (q.v.). The show's big song, "Big Spender," was the flashiest but not the best. The book never really took shape, although many of the scenes were funny and individual pieces of stage business were excellent. The show's primary asset after the score was Gwen Verdon's touching, vibrant performance as Charity. Helen Gallagher, Thelma Oliver and John McMartin costarred. *Sweet Charity* was stylish and contained some of Fosse's best choreography.

The Star-Spangled Girl (12/21/66; 261 performances) was one of Simon's few failures. The play opened with Anthony Perkins, Richard Benjamin and Connie Stevens making up the cast. At the time of its opening, Simon was the first playwright to have four shows running simultaneously on Broadway. *Plaza Suite* (2/14/68; 1,097 performances) consisted of three one-act plays, all of which take place in the same suite in the Plaza Hotel. The show opened at the Plymouth Theater (which seemed to house only Neil Simon shows) with George C. Scott and Maureen Stapleton in the leads.

The Burt Bacharach and Hal David musical *Promises, Promises* (12/1/68; 1,281 performances) opened with Jerry Orbach and Jill O'Hara in the leads. The hip musicalization of Billy Wilder's film, *The Apartment,* gave librettist Simon ample opportunity to examine the mating habits of the white-collar worker.

In *The Last of the Red Hot Lovers* (12/28/69; 706 performances), Simon again experimented with the one-act form. The play opened at the Eugene O'Neill Theater (q.v.) with James Coco, Linda Lavin, Marcia Rodd and Doris Roberts. Coco's character, Barney Cashman, was seen in three acts trying to overcome the sexual and emotional frustration of his middle age by conquering three women.

The Gingerbread Lady (12/13/70; 193 performances) was only the second failure of Simon's decade-long career. Maureen Stapleton starred as an alcoholic singer. Audiences did not want a Neil Simon who examined loneliness. It was named one of the 10 best plays of the year by the *Best Plays* series.

In *The Prisoner of Second Avenue* (11/11/71; 780 performances), Simon was somewhat lighter in mood but still trying to expand his range. The play opened with Peter Falk and Lee Grant. Falk's character finds his life collapsing around him. The play ended on a decidedly downbeat note, but Simon sweetened the message with humor.

The Sunshine Boys (12/20/72; 538 performances) was considered a geriatric *Odd Couple.* It actually told of two vaudevillians, played by Jack Albertson and Sam Levene, who after 11 years of feuding try to reconcile their differences.

The Good Doctor (11/27/73; 125 performances) was Simon's third failure. He adapted several stories of Chekhov and added his own twists but the play (also recognized by *Best Plays*) failed to find an audience.

God's Favorite (12/11/74; 119 performances) opened at the Eugene O'Neill Theater with Vincent Gardenia and Maria Karnilova. The play was a contemporary retelling of the story of Job.

With *California Suite* (7/2/77; 445 performances), Simon began to reverse his downward spiral. The West Coast variation of *Plaza Suite* starred Jack Weston, Tammy Grimes, Barbara Barrie and George Grizzard in the four one-act plays.

Chapter Two (12/4/77; 857 performances) opened at the Imperial Theater (q.v.) with Judd Hirsch, Cliff Gorman, Anita Gillette and Ann Wedgeworth as the cast. The four-character comedy explored the attempts of a recent widower (as Simon was) to reconnect with his own emotions and those of a new woman in his life. By the end of the play, it's clear the couple will get married, and in fact Simon also remarried in real life. *Chapter Two's* run broke Simon's string of failures—for a while. Critics observed that when the author had personal problems, his plays suffered too.

They're Playing Our Song (2/11/79; 1,082 performances), a lackluster musical, didn't represent Simon or his collaborators, Marvin Hamlisch and Carole Bayer Sager, at their best.

I Ought to Be in Pictures (4/3/80; 324 performances) opened at Simon's own Eugene O'Neill Theater (q.v.) with Ron Liebman, Dinah Manoff and Joyce Van Patten. The play was the story of a Hollywood screenwriter who is visited by the estranged daughter he hasn't seen in 16 years.

Fools (4/6/81; 40 performances) starred John Rubenstein and was also a failure. It was followed by an unsuccessful revival of *Little Me,* which premiered the following year.

Simon again hit his stride with an autobiographical

trilogy beginning with *Brighton Beach Memoirs* (3/27/83; 1,530 performances). Matthew Broderick made an impressive Broadway debut as Eugene Jerome (the Simon character), winning a Tony Award *(q.v.)* in the bargain. Joyce Van Patten, Elizabeth Franz and Zeljko Ivanek costarred. By the time the play closed, its sequel, *Biloxi Blues* (2/28/85; 524 performances), had opened. Matthew Broderick was again the star. *Biloxi Blues* was the story of Eugene's induction into the Army and exposure to a different world. In the third play of the trilogy, *Broadway Bound* (12/4/86; 756 performances), Eugene is back in Brighton Beach and breaking into radio. *Broadway Bound* featured Jonathan Silverman as Eugene, Linda Lavin as his mother and Phyllis Newman as his aunt.

Simon's latest show, *Rumors* (11/17/88), received less than raves. The play was a throwback to his early farces.

SISSLE AND BLAKE Noble Sissle and Eubie Blake were the first major black songwriters to break the Broadway color barrier. Theirs were the first shows to employ blacks in the theater with a minimum of stereotyping and without resorting to weak imitations of European operettas. During the team's heyday in the twenties, their successful shows included *Shuffle Along,* which was the first all-black musical to enjoy a long run and be treated as more than an oddity.

Eubie Blake Courtesy ASCAP.

Eubie Blake (1883–1983) Eubie Blake was born in Baltimore, the youngest of 11 children, all of whom had died before he was born. His parents, former slaves, were strict disciplinarians. When their son was six, the Blakes bought an organ. During an earlier visit to a department store, Blake surprised everyone by picking out tunes on an organ.

He took lessons from his neighbor, Mrs. Margaret Marshall. Despite her warnings and those of his mother, Blake began to pick up the new ragtime syncopations. The only places to practice the new rhythms were saloons and bawdy houses. Blake got his first professional job at Aggie Sheldon's sporting house at the age of 15.

In 1901, after three years at Aggie Sheldon's, Blake joined Dr. Frazier's Medicine Show. Just two years earlier, Scott Joplin's "Maple Leaf Rag" swept the country. Blake was already composing, waiting for a big break and soaking up the new music and new techniques.

A succession of jobs followed. Minstrel shows, hotels, whore houses, and saloons were his places of employment. He finally settled in Atlantic City, playing with other classic ragtime pianists during the resort months. Blake continued writing, influenced mostly by his copioneers in the ragtime field and popular composers of the day, like the English composer, Leslie Stuart.

Noble Sissle (1889–1975) Noble Sissle was born in Indianapolis, Indiana, on July 10, 1889, the son of middle-class parents. His father was a pastor in the Methodist Episcopal Church. Sissle's parents raised him strictly, fully expecting him to follow in his father's footsteps.

In 1906, the family moved to Cleveland, where Sissle was lucky enough to attend a high school where race was not an issue. While in high school, Sissle joined the glee club and soon became chief soloist and leader. He began his professional career as a member of Edward Thomas's Male Quartet, which toured the Chatauqua circuit.

He attended De Pauw University in Greencastle, Indiana, and Butler University in Indianapolis. While at the latter school, he wrote song parodies that were sung during football games. At about this time, new dance crazes began to take the country by storm. Vernon and Irene Castle's *(q.v.)* musical director was James Reese Europe, a distinguished black musician. There was a demand for black entertainers as the syncopations of jazz replaced European rhythms.

In 1915, Sissle was asked to put together an all-black orchestra for the Severin Hotel in Indianapolis. That led to a job as vocalist for Joe Porter's Serenaders. The Serenaders were booked into River View Park in Baltimore, Maryland, for the 1915 summer season. It was then that Sissle met Eubie Blake.

Noble Sissle Courtesy ASCAP.

After Sissle and Blake met in Baltimore in 1915, Sissle went on to Palm Beach as part of Bob Young's Sextet, which entertained the elite at the Royal Poinciana Hotel. The next year they were picked to play the Palace Theatre (*q.v.*) in New York.

Later that same year Sissle and Blake worked together in the New York area. They began collaborating on songs and formed a vaudeville act, The Dixie Duo. They played throughout the country, polishing the act until it became one of the best on the circuits.

During an NAACP benefit in Philadelphia they met Aubrey Lyles and Flournoy Miller, another black vaudeville team. Miller and Lyles wanted to write and star in a Broadway musical comedy. They were tired of the treatment afforded black entertainers on the road and aspired to Broadway for both professional and political reasons.

The two teams got together to write a show based on the Miller and Lyles act, *The Mayor of Dixie*. The result was *Shuffle Along* (5/23/21; 504 performances). It was almost impossible to mount a black show on Broadway, so *Shuffle Along* endured a long, grueling tryout. The company played one-night stands in all manner of buildings in all sizes of towns.

Finally the show reached New York under the auspices of producer John Cort. It opened at the 63rd Street Theater (a rundown lecture hall). Sissle and Blake were worried about the show's reception because it was not a typical black entertainment. The cast didn't wear blackface, nor were they portraying the racist stereotypes common in that era. Whether they would be taken seriously when presenting love songs was a big concern. Because of lack of proper financing, the show was somewhat slapdash, but despite this the audiences went wild for the show.

Shuffle Along introduced a score that incorporated all the new syncopations then in vogue. The biggest hit from the show and a future standard was "I'm Just Wild About Harry." Other fine songs included, "Honeysuckle Time," "If You've Never Been Vamped by a Brownskin" and "Love Will Find a Way."

The cast included some of the greatest black performers of the time: Sissle and Blake, Lottie Gee, Roger Matthews and Miller and Lyles. The chorus and succeeding casts also featured artists who received their first important exposure through *Shuffle Along*. Florence Mills, Josephine Baker and Paul Robeson are just three of the greats who began their careers in *Shuffle Along*. The show established a new era of regard and respect for black performers. Unfortunately, it was an era that quickly passed.

The team's next Broadway attempt, *Elsie* (4/2/23; 40 performances), wasn't a success. The show had additional songs written by Alma Sanders and Monte Carlo. *The Chocolate Dandies* (9/1/24; 96 performances) was the team's next show, and this time, they contributed the complete score. The cast at the Colonial Theater included Sissle and Blake, Josephine Baker, Ivan Harold Browning, Lottie Gee, Lew Payton, Valaida Snow and Elisabeth Welch.

Shuffle Along of 1933 (12/26/32; 17 performances) was an attempt to follow the hit *Shuffle Along*. It opened at the Mansfield Theater (*q.v.*) with Sissle and Blake, Flournoy Miller, Mantan Moreland and Edith Wilson.

The team split for a while. Noble Sissle formed a band in 1933 and played long dates at the Park Central Hotel in New York City and at Billy Rose's Diamond Horseshoe (*q.v.*). Eubie Blake wrote *Swing It* (7/22/37; 60 performances) in collaboration with Joshua Milton Reddie. It was produced by the WPA Variety Theater and Frank Merlin.

In 1938 when Harry Truman ran against Thomas Dewey for the presidency, Truman chose the Sissle and Blake song "I'm Just Wild About Harry" for his campaign song. The song again became a top-10 standard, and the team of Sissle and Blake was again in demand.

In 1940, Blake teamed with Andy Razaf (lyricist of the song "Ain't Misbehavin") to write the nightclub show *Tan Manhattan*, which starred Nina Mae McKinney.

The new success of "I'm Just Wild About Harry" and the team's new fame led to their first Broadway collaboration since *Shuffle Along of 1933*. For *Shuffle Along of 1952* (5/8/52; 4 performances) Sissle and Blake were reunited with Flournoy Miller. The show was in trouble from the beginning of rehearsals and never could recover from its many problems.

The songwriters went into virtual retirement until rediscovered by musicologist Robert Kimball and musician William Bolcom. Their book, *Reminiscing with Sissle and Blake,* revived interest in the two men's careers. A Broadway revue, *Eubie* (9/20/78; 439 performances), opened to mixed reviews.

Noble Sissle died on December 17, 1975. Eubie Blake was over 100 years old when he died February 12, 1983. At one of his last birthday celebrations, he said, "If I'd known I was going to live this long, I'd have taken better care of myself."

SLANG Broadway was probably the greatest hotbed of slang in the history of the world, especially in the twenties and thirties. Slang was invented and used by the uneducated who frequented Times Square and the educated adapted slang as a way to make their lives and their speech more colorful. The slang words and sayings were picked up and trumpeted by Broadway's columnists and press agents *(q.v.).* Those most directly responsible for the invention of slang were columnist Walter Winchell *(q.v.)* and the entertainment world's "bible" *Variety (q.v.).*

Winchell was named as among the 10 most fertile contributors to American slang by lexicographer W.J. Funk. H.L. Mencken claimed that "Winchell if he did not actually invent 'Whoopee,' at least gave it the popularity it enjoyed."

Among Winchell's most ingenious contributions were slang words for marriage. The euphemisms included welded, merged, middle-aisled and Lohengrined. For divorce, Winchell used: telling it to a judge, wilted, this-and-that-way, Reno-vating, straining at the handcuffs and have phfft. In the event that the marriage was a happy one Winchell announced the birth of a baby with: blessed event, getting storked, blessed expense, bundle from heaven, preparing a bassinet, infanticipating and baby-bound. Two people in love were said to be: that way, blazing, on the verge, uh-huh, Adam-and-Eveing it, man-and-womanizing it, and cupiding.

Other Winchellisms include: sextress, intelligentleman, messer of ceremonies, debutramp (debutante), pash (passion), shafts (legs), Chicagorilla (gangster), revusical (musical revue), phewd (feud), Wildeman (homosexual), fooff (pest), dotter (daughter), giggle-water (liquor) and heheheh (mocking laugh). Times Square was dubbed the Hardened Artery, Baloney Blvd., the Bulb Belt and Hard Times Square. Winchell dubbed movies moom pictures and phlickers or flickers.

Variety was just as verbally rich and inventive as Winchell. As George Bernard Shaw commented to Bennett Cerf in 1938, "I thought I knew the English language until one day I saw *Variety* in a friend's home. Upon my soul, I didn't understand a word of it."

Many of the words coined by *Variety*'s muggs (writers) entered the English language even far away from the Main Stem (Broadway). These words include cliffhanger, soap opera, boffo, payoff, freeloader, bimbo, platter, tie-in, hoofer, smash, scram, wowed, hick, pushover, gams, disc jockey, brush-off, chiseler, corny, screwy, nix, click, whodunit, payola, baloney, palooka, nuts and emcee.

Other Varietyisms which never caught on to quite the same degree were yawner (a boring show), femme du pave (prostitute), oats opera and oater (western film), hoofologist (dancer), mitting (applauding), leerics (suggestive lyrics), ozoner and passion pit (drive-in movie), hardtop (indoor movie theater), inked (signed (especially contracts)) and authored (written).

Variety's headlines have been made famous and were loaded with slanguage. Among the best known are "WALL STREET LAYS AN EGG" and "STICKS NIX HICK PIX." Among those less well known were "BLIZ BOFFS BUFF" when a snowstorm knocked out Buffalo, New York.

Other words, not attributable to Winchell or *Variety* were recorded by Times Square journalist Damon Runyon *(q.v.).* Runyon frequently coined his own terms but mostly recorded the slang terms used by his characters, who themselves had names that were based in slang. Characters like Spider McCoy, Brandy Bottle Bates, Nathan Detroit, Madame La Gimp and Dave the Dude used slang terms that included guys for men and dolls for women. Other nicknames for men and women included John and Jane and bum and broad.

Many words revolved around the horse race betters who were regulars in Times Square. Can do, for example, meant that a horse could win a race. The morning line was the well-known newspaper, the *Racing Form.* Shooters were men who played craps with their bundle—the amount they had to bet with.

Turkey referred to a show that was produced between Thanksgiving and New Years because there were so many people attending the theater that even lousy shows succeeded at the box office. Originally, turkeys made money and were put up intentionally, although the producers knew they were bad.

With the decline of Times Square in the 1950s and especially the 1960s, the old Broadwayites left for the West Coast or Miami and stopped patronizing their old haunts. Newspapers had become more respectable and stopped accepting the overblown hype of flacks (press agents). With only three papers in New York and with the decline of radio, the gossip columnist became less important, and those who remained became serious journalists. Today's two main columnists, Liz Smith and Cindy Adams don't associate themselves exclusively with Broadway since Broadway and Times Square are no longer the center of the world's entertainment. As Broadway has been homogenized, it has lost its flash and show biz razz-ma-tazz. Even *Variety* moved its offices from the heart of Times Square to a modern office tower on Park Avenue South.

Many of the words coined along the Great White Way or the Main Stem have entered the language. Others have passed through the language and are now almost meaningless. But Broadway is certainly the poorer for the lack of slang, which gave the street so much of its unique flair.

SMITH, HARRY B. (1860–1936) Though Harry B. Smith was the most prolific of all Broadway lyricist/ librettists, his work is practically unknown today. Smith had no special style or flair for lyric writing. Although he obviously had talent, perhaps his greatest asset was his speed and satisfactory work.

He was author of 123 musicals produced in a 45-year career. Including adaptations and straight plays, Smith, by his own count, claimed authorship to more than 300 shows. Smith's greatest musical successes—*Robin Hood, The Spring Maid, Sweethearts, Watch Your Step, Countess Maritza, The Girl from Utah* and the *Rich Mr. Hoggenheimer*—were written in collaboration with such composers as Ludwig Englander, Reginald De Koven, Vic-

Harry B. Smith   Courtesy ASCAP.

tor Herbert (*q.v.*), John Philip Sousa, Robert Hood Bowers, Gus Edwards, Jerome Kern (*q.v.*), Franz Lehar, Leo Fall, Ivan Caryll, A. Baldwin Sloane, Sigmund Romberg (*q.v.*) and Emmerich Kalman.

Smith also estimated that he contributed lyrics to over 3,000 songs. His greatest success as a lyricist came with the songs "The Sheik of Araby" (from *Make It Snappy*), "Gypsy Love Song" (from *The Serenade*) and "Yours Is My Heart Alone" (from *Yours Is My Heart*). Smith's brother, Robert B. Smith, was also a successful librettist.

Harry Bache Smith was born in Buffalo, New York, on December 28, 1860. He attempted to become an operatic performer but, meeting with little interest or enthusiasm, he found a job on the *Chicago Daily News* as music critic. Smith began to write humorous verse and stories for a variety of magazines and newspapers.

His verses gained the attention of a major star, Fay Templeton. She commissioned Smith to write the libretto for her production of *Rosita, or Cupid and Cupidity*. George Schleiffarth composed the music for the operetta, which opened in Chicago in 1883. The success of that show led to another commission for *Amaryllis, or Mammon and Gammon*, with music by H.H. Thiele. That show was mounted in Milwaukee in 1884 and was also a success.

Fay Templeton next convinced Smith to abandon journalism and to move to Boston to write full time for the musical theater. She introduced the writer to Colonel John C. McCaull, a leading Bostonian producer. He, in turn, brought Smith together with composer Reginald De Koven. They collaborated on *The Bugun* (1887). Two years later came the team's next show, *Don Quixote,* produced by the Bostonians, a very successful producing organization. Henry Clay Barnabee, the star, was not strong enough for the role, and it closed after only a few months.

Smith and De Koven's greatest success, one of the biggest hits of the turn of the century, was *Robin Hood* (1891). The success of that show, written in only three weeks, convinced Smith to become a full-time writer for the theater. He moved to New York and began his career in earnest. *Robin Hood* was the first truly successful American operetta. Smith received royalties on it for over 25 years before wisely deciding to sell out his interests for a substantial sum.

In 1895, after five more collaborations with De Koven as well as two other shows, Smith teamed up with Victor Herbert. Herbert had composed a poorly received operetta produced by the Bostonians called *Prince Ananias*. The show's failure didn't deter Smith from approaching Herbert and suggesting they collaborate. Smith added new lyrics to the Herbert score as well as a new libretto. The result was *The Wizard of the Nile* (11/4/1895), which opened at the Casino Theatre (*q.v.*).

In 1899, Smith had eight shows produced, including

Papa's Wife, which starred Anna Held *(q.v.). Papa's Wife* was thought by many to be the precursor to the intimate shows that later developed into the modern musical comedy. In 1911, Smith contributed nine shows to Broadway.

His prolific career continued, although little of his work has lasted his lifetime. His later Broadway shows and their composers included *The Girl from Utah* (Jerome Kern; 8/24/14; 120 performances); *90 in the Shade* (Jerome Kern; 1/25/15; 40 performances); *Sybil* (Victor Jacobi; 1/10/16; 168 performances); *Caroline* (Edward Kunneke, Alfred Goodman *(q.v.)*; 1/31/23; 151 performances); *Princess Flavia* (Sigmund Romberg; 11/2/25; 152 performances); *Countess Maritza* (Emmerich Kalman; 9/18/26; 321 performances); *The Circus Princess* (Emmerich Kalman; 4/25/27; 192 performances); and *The Red Robe* (Jean Gilbert; 12/25/28; 167 performances).

His last Broadway musical was the 1932 *Marching By.* By then, the operetta was going out of favor and Smith's output slowed to only one or two shows a season. By the time of his death on January 2, 1936, Smith was overshadowed by such modern lyricists as Ira Gershwin *(q.v.),* Howard Dietz *(q.v.)* and E.Y. Harburg *(q.v.).* But he certainly had been hugely popular at the height of his career. Carl Van Vechten flattered Smith when he dubbed the lyricist "the Sarah Bernhardt of librettists." The *New York Times* commented in 1926 that "The name Harry B. Smith in fact became such a byword in these productions that if they were not signed by him, they just weren't comic operas."

Smith himself wrote in his 1931 autobiography, *First Nights and First Editions:* "Often my life seems all of the theater, a Chinese play lasting not through many nights but through many years. In other moods, I feel that the theater has been just a shop where I worked at a trade, and that my real life has belonged to my own people and my friends. Life is for most of us a long walk uphill against the wind, with now and then a pleasant place to rest, perhaps to laugh a little before plodding on." The quote illustrates just how much his style was mired in the florid, operatic style of the turn of the century. Smith was unable to keep pace with the changing styles of the American musical theater in which romanticism was replaced with sophistication.

SONDHEIM, STEPHEN (1930–   ) Stephen Sondheim is considered the leading composer/lyricist of the modern musical theater. Sondheim's shows, usually with Harold Prince *(q.v.)* as producer and director, have expanded the art of the musical as have those of few of his contemporaries. Sondheim's style is unmistakably his own. The hallmarks of his work are intricate rhythms and melodies composed without concern about Tin Pan Alley. These tunes exist solely for the exigen-

Stephen Sondheim   Courtesy ASCAP.

cies of the plot and characters. Sondheim's lyrics are laced with witty, intellectual rhymes and an abundance of ideas. This high level of intelligence sometimes puts off his critics who find his work coldly intellectual and somewhat emotionally uninvolving. The offbeat subjects of many of his shows and his lack of widely popular songs has sometimes kept Sondheim from achieving widespread fame among the middle-class theatergoers.

Sondheim was born on March 22, 1930. An early friend was James Hammerstein, son of Oscar Hammerstein II *(q.v.).* Oscar became the 15-year-old Sondheim's mentor. While at Williams College, Sondheim wrote musicals and prepared for a professional career on Broadway.

His first effort, *Saturday Night,* was optioned by producer Lemuel Ayers. Unfortunately, Ayers died before the production could be mounted. Among the Broadway professionals who had heard Sondheim's work was librettist Arthur Laurents. He was working on a new musical with Leonard Bernstein *(q.v.).* Laurents introduced Sondheim to Bernstein who was suitably impressed with the 25-year-old's work. Sondheim was hired to provide the lyrics for *West Side Story* (9/26/57; 734 performances).

Among the Sondheim/Bernstein songs were "Tonight," "Maria," "America," "I Feel Pretty" and "Something's Coming." The show starred Larry Kert and Carol Lawrence as Tony and Maria and Chita Rivera, Art Smith, Mickey Calin and Grover Dale in supporting roles.

Sondheim's next show was the classic *Gypsy* with music by Jule Styne *(q.v.). Gypsy* (4/21/59; 702 performances) was a musicalization of the memoirs of Gypsy Rose Lee. Arthur Laurents again contributed the libretto. The excellent Sondheim/Styne songs included the standards "Everything's Coming Up Roses," "Together," "Let Me Entertain You," and "Small World." Ethel Merman (q.v.) starred, ably assisted by Jack Klugman, Sandra Church, Paul Walker, Maria Karnilova and Jacqueline Mayro.

Although Sondheim's initial Broadway work featured only his lyrical talents, he was determined also to supply the music for his next show. The opportunity came when Burt Shevelove approached him with the idea of musicalizing the comedies of the Roman playwright Plautus. The result was *A Funny Thing Happened on the Way to the Forum* (5/8/62; 967 performances) with a libretto also by Larry Gelbart. Zero Mostel played Pseudolus, a Roman slave with aspirations for freedom. His compatriot was played by Jack Gilford. George Abbott (q.v.) and Jerome Robbins (q.v.) directed the show, and Harold Prince produced.

The success of *A Funny Thing Happened on the Way to the Forum* led to Sondheim's next show, a failure. Arthur Laurents contributed the original idea for *Anyone Can Whistle* (4/4/64; 9 performances). Angela Lansbury, Lee Remick and Harry Guardino made their Broadway musical debuts in the show. The plot concerned escapees from an asylum who find themselves in the midst of a town ruled by a crooked mayoress.

The failure of *Anyone Can Whistle* led to Sondheim's teaming with Richard Rodgers (q.v.) on *Do I Hear a Waltz* (3/18/65; 220 performances). The show was a musical version of Arthur Laurents's play *Time of the Cuckoo.* Elizabeth Allen and Sergio Franchi starred. Sondheim and Rodgers had a stormy relationship but contributed a good score.

Playwright George Furth approached Harold Prince about producing a script he had written. Prince suggested the material might be more successful as a musical, and Sondheim was brought in to complete the production team. The resulting show, *Company* (4/26/70; 706 performances), opened at the Alvin Theater (q.v.). Prince also directed the show, which starred Dean Jones, Barbara Barrie, Donna McKechnie and Elaine Stritch. The show, a ruthless examination of marriage set against an aggressively urban setting, was an immediate success.

Sondheim was by then firmly established as a superior talent. His next project was *Follies* (4/4/71; 522 performances), one of the greatest of all musicals. Harold Prince codirected and produced the show, which had a book by James Goldman. Michael Bennett codirected with Prince and supplied the choreography. *Follies* boasted an impressive physical production. The set was designed by Boris Aronson, the costumes by Florence Klotz and the lighting by Tharon Musser. The show was about a reunion of a group of former Follies performers. The action took place on two levels, the party itself and among the ghosts of the past who haunted the celebrants' present. The brilliant staging perfectly joined the two worlds. The show, however, was more than an examination of the characters' past and present lives. It succeeded in presenting a psychological examination of their feelings and thoughts. The final sequence took place in Loveland, which was actually a physical realization of the characters' problems. Their psyches were illustrated as acts in a performance of the Ziegfeld Follies.

The show starred Dorothy Collins, Alexis Smith, John McMartin, Gene Nelson and Yvonne DeCarlo. It opened at the Winter Garden Theater (q.v.). Audiences, unaccustomed to actually thinking during a musical comedy, sometimes found the show confusing and disorienting, but for many the evening was stimulating and moving.

The glamour and immensity of *Follies* led to the more intimate *A Little Night Music* (2/25/73; 601 performances), an elegant rendering of Ingmar Bergman's romantic film *Smiles of a Summer Night.* Hugh Wheeler supplied his first libretto for a Sondheim show with Prince in his usual dual role as producer and director. The show opened at the Sam S. Shubert Theatre (q.v.) with Glynis Johns, Len Cariou, Hermione Gingold and Patricia Elliott. *A Little Night Music* contained a rich and varied score all in three-quarter time. Surprisingly, one of the songs, "Send in the Clowns," attained popular status.

For his next show, Sondheim was drawn to an unlikely subject, the opening of relations between Japan and the United States in the 19th century. *Pacific Overtures* (1/11/75; 193 performances) opened at the Winter Garden Theater. A play by John Weidman was the source, which Weidman and Hugh Wheeler adapted. Prince again produced and directed the production, which featured an all-Japanese cast. The show, which used elements of the Kabuki theater to tell the story, attempted to show great events through the examination of the lives of a few common people.

The next Prince/Sondheim collaboration was the thriller, *Sweeney Todd* (3/1/79; 558 performances). The story was set against England's industrial revolution. Sweeney Todd, the lead character, was a barber who returned home from jail to seek vengeance on those who had ruined his life. His act of vengeance soon turned into full-fledged insanity, and Sweeney Todd found an accomplice in Mrs. Lovett, a baker of meat pies. As Mr. Todd dispatched friend and foe, Mrs. Lovett obligingly incorporated their corpses into her baked goods. This grand guignol production opened at the Uris Theatre (q.v.). Audiences were delighted to be scared out of their wits. Angela Lansbury and Len Cariou starred as the partners in crime.

Sondheim's next project was the last collaboration

with Harold Prince. George Furth, of *Company* fame, supplied the book for *Merrily We Roll Along* (11/16/81; 16 performances), an adaptation of the Kaufman and Hart play. The show was told in reverse order. The cast was composed entirely of teenagers and performers in their early twenties. This was a limitation that, when coupled with a misguided design and badly written book, added up to failure. Sondheim's score was typically brilliant. The show opened at the Alvin Theater.

Sondheim might have been discouraged by the failure of *Merrily We Roll Along*, but he was not about to pander to popular taste or let his work sink to the lowest common denominator. His next undertaking, *Sunday in the Park with George* (5/2/84; 604 performances) proved to be one of his most experimental outings. James Lapine contributed the book and direction to the show, which examined the painter Georges Seurat and his artistry. The first act of the musical concerned Seurat's life and took place while he is painting his masterpiece, *A Sunday Afternoon on the Island of La Grande Jatte*. The second act took place 100 years later with the story of Seurat's great-grandson, a modern artist. The show starred Bernadette Peters and Mandy Patinkin. It won the Pulitzer Prize *(q.v.)* for drama.

For his next excursion, Sondheim again chose an unlikely subject. *Into the Woods* tells the story of three fairy tales, "Little Red Riding Hood," "The Baker and His Wife" and "Jack and the Beanstalk" and what happens after "they lived happily ever after." James Lapine supplied the book as well as the direction. *Into the Woods* (11/5/87; 764 performances) opened at the Martin Beck Theatre *(q.v.)*. *Into the Woods* contained a score sung by a superior cast, including Bernadette Peters, Joanna Gleason, Chip Zien, Kim Crosby, Tom Aldredge, Ben Wright, Barbara Bryne, Daniele Ferland and Robert Westenberg. The Tony *(q.v.)* voters chose Sondheim's score over that of Andrew Lloyd Webber's *Phantom of the Opera*.

Stephen Sondheim has proven himself to be the greatest of the composer-lyricists in the Broadway tradition. The fact that he has seen fit to expand those traditions and not simply work within their confines is both his chief asset and perhaps one of his faults. His shows have mostly contained brilliant scores that have a somewhat limited appeal to the average Broadway audience. However, each of his shows has proven, sometimes in retrospect, to be an important part of the history of the American musical theater.

STAGE DOOR CANTEEN   See AMERICAN THEATER WING.

STAIRCASE THEATER   See CENTURY THEATER (1).

STARR, JACOB   See ARTKRAFT STRAUSS.

STARR, MELVIN   See ARTKRAFT STRAUSS.

STRAND THEATER 47th Street and Broadway. Architect: Thomas W. Lamb. Opening: April 11, 1914; *The Spoilers*.   The Strand was the first great movie palace in the world. It began a progression of increasingly lavish theaters, culminating in the opening of the Roxy Theater *(q.v.)*.

Since the early years of the 20th century, Times Square has had the reputation as the place to make one's mark in the world of entertainment. Thousands have come to Broadway to rise to the top of their professions. Two of these were Mitchell and Moe Mark, brothers who owned nickelodeons. They came to Times Square to erect a theater.

They chose a site at 47th Street and Broadway, the location of the Brewster Carriage Factory. They leased the land and announced their plan to build a "million dollar theater." Mitchell Mark stated, "From the first moment we conceived of erecting the Strand we made studies of all the best theaters in Europe and America."

The problem of what to put in the theater seemingly stumped the brothers. Their original plan was to build a 50¢-admission vaudeville theater. Four months before the completion of the theater, the policy still wasn't determined. At one point, almost every possible type of theatrical presentation was considered. The Marks even stated that the Metropolitan Opera would move to the new house.

Mitchell Mark made the announcement that the 2,800-seat Strand Theater would be a "national institution that would stand for all time as the model of moving picture palaces" and thus ended the speculation. Once the decision was made to use the Strand for movies, the Marks hired the greatest-motion picture impresario in the world, S.L. ("Roxy") Rothafel *(q.v.)*. He was then running the Regent Theater on 116th Street, also designed by Thomas Lamb. Roxy moved to the Strand and prepared for the grand opening.

Strand Theater   Courtesy Billy Rose Theater Collection.

Thomas W. Lamb, who became one of the greatest motion-picture palace architects, designed a magnificent theater. It was described as a theater full of "gilt and marble and deep pile rugs, crystal chandeliers hanging from the ceiling and original art works on the walls, with luxurious lounges and comfortable chairs, a thirty-piece symphony orchestra . . . and a mighty Wurlitzer."

The organ was an important part of any movie palace. Carl Edouarde, the Strand's musical director, commented that "If an exhibitor should be forced to choose between a poor orchestra and a good organist, he should consider it his duty to give the organist the preference. After all, it is quality and not quantity that really counts. Besides, it has been my experience that audiences would rather hear music played extremely well than extremely loud."

The new theater opened on April 11, 1914. The event was reported by Victor Watson in the following day's *New York Times.* "Going to the new Strand Theater last night was very much like going to a Presidential reception, a first night at the opera or the opening of the horse show. It seemed like everyone in town had simultaneously arrived at the conclusion that a visit to the magnificent new movie playhouse was necessary.

"I have always tried to keep abreast of the times and be able to look ahead a little way, but I must confess that when I saw the wonderful audience last night in all its costly togs, the one thought that came to my mind was that if anyone had told me two years ago that the time would come when the finest-looking people in town would be going to the biggest and newest theater on Broadway for the purpose of seeing motion pictures I would have sent them down to visit my friend, Dr. Minas Gregory at Bellevue Hospital. The doctor runs the city's bughouse, you know."

William Farnum, the star of the theater's first presentation, *The Spoilers,* was present as were George M. Cohan *(q.v.),* Vincent Astor and producers Daniel Frohman, Sam Harris and Abe Erlanger. The gala opening ceremony began with an artillery salute of three shots. Then came the 50-member Strand Concert Orchestra playing the "Star Spangled Banner" under the direction of Carl Edouarde.

The *Moving Picture World* reported on the stirring opening of the evening's entertainment: "We saw in lightning rapidity the scenes which inspired the deathless hymn of glory. In the roar and sweat of battle the starry flag still breezed in eloquent triumph over the brave hearts of the country's defenders. With the swiftness of thought the audience recognized the happy inspiration of sending the new theater on its career to the strains of patriotic music with the rare glimpse of American glory visualized and, as we all stood up in loving homage, no one failed to congratulate the management on its inspiration. At the same time Rothapfel

unmasked his artillery, the darkness in and about the screen was converted into a flood of light and the splendid decorations, the flowers, the hedges of green, the graceful fountains of changing color, and the pretty effects in the wings stood revealed as if by magic."

The orchestra then played the Hungarian Rhapsody No. 2. Following the concert, the screen was lit up by *The Strand Topical Review,* an up-to-the-minute newsreel featuring scenes from that afternoon's Brooklyn Federal League baseball game. A travelogue of Italy entitled *A Neapolitan Incident* came next and, since this was still the era of the silent film, a tenor hidden behind the screen sang "O Sole Mio." The Mutual Film Corporation's star, the Mutual Girl, appeared in a one-reel comedy and then made a personal appearance alongside Roxy. Another musical interlude followed with the Strand Quartet singing a selection from *Rigoletto.*

Roxy came up with another first for the new picture palace. He had four projectors put into the booth so that the nine-reel feature could be presented without interruption. This was a surprise to the audience. The *New York Times* reporter commented that the audience "absorbed the story without an effort and its interest never lagged—at 11:30 we were more interested in the fate of Glenister and all the rest than at 9:15 though we had been looking intently at the screen for more than two hours."

The opening was a tremendous success, although *Variety (q.v.)* erroneously stated that the theater would cease its motion-picture policy and present musical comedy.

The Strand changed its program every Sunday. Each consisted of "a fine picture, and an hour and a quarter's entertainment, and a first-class orchestra to boot for the same price," as described by Roxy. Those shows beginning at 2:00, 7:30 and 9:30 were called "deluxe" and contained the entire program. The other shows, at noon, 4:15, and 6:00 omitted the orchestral portion, substituting the Wurlitzer organ for the musical program.

Admissions were kept low by Roxy. During the afternoon performances, the balcony seats were 15¢, seats in the orchestra were 25¢, and loge and box seats were 50¢. On weekends, the balcony seats were a quarter, and the orchestra was split into two price ranges, 35¢ and 50¢.

Within two years, with the Strand Theater firmly established, Roxy left to open the Rialto Theater *(q.v.)* on Broadway at 42nd Street. The Strand later became the Warner Theater and after many renovations was twinned. It finally succumbed to the wrecker's ball in 1987.

STROUSE AND ADAMS Charles Strouse was one of the leading musical comedy composers throughout the 1960s and 1970s. During his most successful period, he

Lee Adams and Charles Strouse   Courtesy ASCAP.

collaborated with lyricist Lee Adams. They supplied a string of lighthearted scores to entertaining musicals. Strouse's music contains catchy themes with a dramatic flair. Adams lyrics seem simple, yet they perfectly complement the theatricality of Strouse's tunes.

Strouse was born on June 7, 1928, in New York City. His interest in music began in his early teens. Later he studied at the Eastman School of Music and under Aaron Copland and Nadia Boulanger.

Lee Adams was born in Mansfield, Ohio, on August 14, 1924. Adams had a lifelong fascination with words and worked as a staff member of *Pageant* Magazine and as editor of *This Week* Magazine.

The two met in 1949 and began writing songs at Green Mansions summer camp. Their revue songs were transferred from the camp setting to off-Broadway and a series of shows for Ben Bagley. *The Shoestring Revue* (2/28/55), *The Littlest Revue* (5/22/56) and *Shoestring '57* (11/5/56) gave the team more time to hone their skills.

They were ready to attempt a full-fledged musical comedy by the late 1950s. Their first effort, *Bye Bye Birdie* (4/14/60; 607 performances) was an immediate smash. The show, a satire on the newly emergent rock industry, starred Dick Van Dyke and Chita Rivera,

with Paul Lynde, Susan Watson and Kay Medford in supporting roles. Dick Gautier played a thinly veiled parody of Elvis Presley in the show. The score contained the team's greatest success, the jaunty "Put on a Happy Face." Their first Broadway show was also the first full musical directed by Gower Champion and the first for which Michael Stewart supplied a libretto.

For their second project, the team turned once again to a satire. Mel Brooks provided the libretto for *All American* (2/19/62; 80 performances). Despite the talents of Ray Bolger and Eileen Herlie and Joshua Logan's *(q.v.)* direction, the show was a failure. The score, which was almost as good as that of *Bye Bye Birdie*, did contain one standard, "Once Upon a Time."

The next show for which they supplied a score was a departure from their usual light satire. *Golden Boy* (10/20/64; 569 performances) was a powerful drama by Clifford Odets. It wasn't an obvious choice for musical comedy, but producer Hillard Elkins convinced the team to take it on. Certainly, the score was excellent, combining Broadway razzmatazz with the serious subject matter. Another remarkable aspect of the production was the casting of Sammy Davis Jr. as the prizefighter. Odets had died while writing the libretto and William Gibson took over the task.

For their next project, the team attempted *It's a Bird . . . It's a Plane . . . It's Superman* (3/29/66; 129 performances). The show was a pop-art depiction of the famous comic book character. The play was a tongue-in-cheek attempt to bring to the stage what Batman would later bring to television. The show enjoyed a superior score and production under the direction of Harold Prince *(q.v.)*. David Newman, coauthor of the libretto with Robert Benton, would have better luck with the same subject when he scripted *Superman*, the movie. Jack Cassidy, Linda Lavin, Patricia Marand and Bob Holiday starred.

After the failure of *It's a Bird . . . It's a Plane . . . It's Superman* came the success of *Applause* (3/30/70; 896 performances). The show was an adaptation of the movie *All About Eve*. In the lead was a newcomer to musical comedy, Lauren Bacall. Betty Comden and Adolph Green *(q.v.)* supplied the libretto. Although none of the creative contributions were particularly outstanding, the show was their longest run as a team.

Next, Charles Strouse wrote the book and lyrics to his own music for an off-Broadway show, *Six* (4/12/71; 8 performances), which opened to negative reviews, although it boasted excellent choreography by Denny Martin Flinn. The following year, the team had a failure with *I and Albert,* a musical about Queen Victoria that was staged in London.

Seven years after *Applause,* Charles Strouse opened a new Broadway musical, his second based on a comic strip character. The show was *Annie* (4/21/77; 2,377 performances) with lyrics by Martin Charnin. Andrea

McArdle played the title character, assisted by Sandy Faison, Dorothy Loudon, Reid Shelton and Raymond Thorne. The song "Tomorrow" became an anthem of prepubescent girls everywhere. The show was directed by Charnin and had a libretto by Thomas Meehan.

Strouse and Adams reunited for *A Broadway Musical* but to little result. The show opened and closed on December 21, 1978. William F. Brown supplied the book and Gower Champion the direction. That failure led to Strouse undertaking another London assignment. *Flowers for Algernon* was based on the movie *Charley* and for its American opening was retitled *Charlie and Algernon* (9/14/80; 17 performances).

Strouse and Adams's last Broadway collaboration, and Adams's last Broadway show to date, was a sequel to their first show, *Bye Bye Birdie.* Its name was *Bring Back Birdie* (3/5/81; 4 performances), and again Michael Stewart contributed the book and Chita Rivera starred. She was assisted by Donald O'Connor.

Strouse wrote a children's opera, *Nightingale* in 1982, contributing book, music and lyrics. His next Broadway outing was *Dance a Little Closer,* for which he teamed with Alan Jay Lerner *(q.v.).* Lerner also contributed the libretto and direction to *Dance a Little Closer,* an updating of Robert Sherwood's *Idiot's Delight.* The show, which opened on May 11, 1983, at the Minskoff Theatre *(q.v.),* unfortunately fared as badly as his last Broadway show, closing after only one performance. Despite the show's poor record, the score is considered a good one. The title song gained some small amount of recognition among cabaret artists.

Strouse's next Broadway score contained some of his best tunes. Unfortunately, the other elements of *Rags* (8/21/86; 4 performances) were not as well written. *Rags* had a book by Joseph Stein and lyrics by Stephen Schwartz. It starred opera diva Teresa Stratas.

At the high points of his career, Charles Strouse has shown a rare ability to time the subjects of his projects to popular taste. *Annie* and *Bye Bye Birdie* both profited by their perfect convergence with what the public was looking for in a Broadway musical. *Bye Bye Birdie* dealt with the timely, up-to-date subject of Elvis Presley's recent induction into the Army and rock and roll's popularity at a time when other teams were contributing old-fashioned scores like *The Sound of Music* and *Camelot.* Marilyn Stasio of *Cue Magazine* attributed *Annie*'s success to "an uncanny insight into what people need right now."

Of course, Strouse's timing hasn't always been so strong. *Superman* suffered by being ahead of its time. Musical comedy audiences are not always at the forefront of trends.

All of Strouse's shows, and especially those written with Lee Adams, show an exuberance and emotional fullness. The early shows, even when wedded to un-gainly books or weak productions, maintained a high level of technique and professionalism.

STUNTS Times Square, the heart of Manhattan and the center of the entertainment industry, is seldom out of the papers. Because of its proximity to the limelight, and to the offices of the *New York Times,* Times Square is the location of most of the great publicity stunts of modern times.

A publicity stunt is an unusual event designed to call attention to a performer, product or show. Most of the early stunts following the turn of the century involved the beautiful girls who graced the early musical comedies. A pretty girl with an ankle or leg showing could always be counted on to draw the papers' reporters and photographers. Stunts, called "fakes" in the old days, often became very elaborate so that editors would swallow them more easily.

Stunts have also been known to backfire. Mrs. Patrick Campbell was involved in a stunt in which it was claimed that the noted actress had won much money while playing bridge with society ladies. However, the backlash from moral readers and religious leaders made the publicity all the more damning.

As the 20th century got under way, newspapers *(q.v.)* and radio were coming into their own. There was plenty of space to fill, and press agents were there to see to it that their clients received their fair share of column inches.

The most famous and most exploited performer in her time was Anna Held *(q.v.).* Florenz Ziegfeld *(q.v.)* had met her in Paris in 1895. He immediately imported her and drummed up interest in her meager talents through a series of outrageous stunts, the most famous of which was her milk baths.

During the run of the *Ziegfeld Follies (q.v.)* Mae Daw, an unknown at the time, decided to challenge dancing star Ann Pennington to a cow-milking contest. There was no reason for her to do so except to get her name in the papers. It worked; papers the next day pictured the two women at the Long Island home of James J. Corbett.

Follies girls were forever being trotted out for one grand scheme or another. Mae Daw also spent months practicing the saxophone for a "surf jazz" party of the Follies girls. Jean Stewart traveled with a baby lamb to combat her loneliness wherever she went. Pearl Eaton almost drowned the entire line when she crashed her team's boat into another during a Central Park boat race. Luckily the stage-door Johnnies who lined the shore could swim and pulled the soaking girls from the lake.

Gilda Gray, best known for her shimmy, became a star when an enterprising press agent arranged for a suitably handsome man to wrap a $100,000 diamond

A stunt for McFadden's Flats   Courtesy Billy Rose Theater Collection.

necklace around a bouquet and toss it on stage during her number.

The same exact stunt was used for actress Julia Sanderson. This time the bouquet, thrown by a "German baron," contained an $18,000 necklace. The press bought the story again.

Press agent *(q.v.)* Will A. Page was the mastermind behind many of the above-mentioned stunts, but his personal favorite was the "Strip Golf Game." The idea grew out of an argument between chorus girls Shirley Vernon and Nellie Savage. At a party after the argument, the girls' dates insisted on their naming a date for the unusual match. The men were so insistent that plans were made to motor to Long Island and play that very next day. Before leaving, Miss Vernon had the foresight to phone Will Page and ask him to serve as referee. He agreed and made some phone calls himself, assuring press coverage.

The rules of the game were simple. If the hole was halved or tied, the girls would remain as they were.

However if the hole was lost, the loser would remove one piece of clothing. All 18 holes were to be played. Midway through the match, quite a crowd gathered and the women were reduced to their underthings. Luckily, someone came to the aid of Miss Vernon at the last minute and supplied her with a barrel. It did nothing for her game but it did make her a star. The photo of her strange garb was printed all over the world and offers for Miss Vernon's services came from Hollywood and Broadway. Ziegfeld was forced to raise her salary again and again until she replaced Marilyn Miller in *Sally*.

The teens and twenties were filled with stunts, usually built around famous actresses: Valeska Suratt's Fourth of July Christmas tree; Olga Nethersole's "Sappho" kiss; and Ruth Urban's banquet for 30, which featured a pig as the guest of honor. Harry Reichenbach put a live lion in a midtown hotel room in order to publicize the 1921 production of *Tarzan of the Apes*. However, the play managed only 13 performances.

Page, an early master of the stunt, managed to make Alice Delysia a huge star on this side of the Atlantic through a series of stunts. Luckily for Page, the performer had a well-developed sense of humor and the desire to see her name exploited.

When Page and producer Morris Gest decided to bring Delysia from the Continent during Prohibition, they wrote an unusual clause in her contract. It stated that she was to have available one bottle of wine at every meal. The reason given for this request was that the actress needed the liquor to keep up her joie de vivre and "without which Mlle. Delysia will pine away and her audience-value diminish."

When Delysia arrived in the United States, she was outfitted in a flaming-red leather dress and an ankle watch encrusted with huge diamonds. Following that, Page kept the heat on her career by a variety of ploys. A dog was trained to attack her during a luncheon. It was planned that she would then divest herself of the canine and exclaim, "More muzzles or foreign artistes will never visit these shores again." Unfortunately, the dog didn't quite understand his part, and the actress was nearly mauled, resulting in the closing of her show for three nights.

Page also cooked up a scheme for Delysia that took its leading participant by surprise. Delysia had been receiving love notes from a millionaire suitor. She wasn't interested in the man and wanted him to go away. Consulting Page, she happened to show him one of the missives in which the young man stated, "You doubt my love but you are wrong. Merely to kiss your hand, I would crawl over broken glass on my hands and knees."

Page arranged the press to be present in the actress's dressing room when the young man arrived. Little did the suitor expect to find the floor strewn with broken glass. At the other end of the trail of glass was his adored one, Delysia. She challenged him, "You said you would crawl over broken glass on your hands and knees to get me. Let me see you crawl."

This was meant to be the end of the stunt but the young man quickly dropped to his knees and actually crept across the room to the velveted Delysia. The actress and the other guests stared in horror as the man slowly crossed the room. When at her feet he rose and stated, "I've made good, now what about yourself?"

Delysia changed her mind about the man, and they enjoyed a long relationship.

Earl Carroll (q.v.), producer of the Vanities (q.v.), produced the unsuccessful The Lady of the Lamp in 1920. Carroll was desperate for the show to succeed, since it was his first producing venture. "I Am Gambling My Last Thousand Dollars," claimed headlines over the articles in which Carroll begged the public to support his show, which he had written. Carroll asserted that if audience members were unsatisfied, he personally would meet them in the lobby after the show and refund their money. True to his word, Carroll was in the lobby at the end of every performance. Luckily, most people admired the producer's pluck and left after shaking his hand. The show closed after a respectable, though not profitable, 111 performances. Carroll managed to make the event a success anyway, since, following one of the performances, a distinguished gentleman named William R. Edrington handed Carroll his card and asked to see him. Carroll made an appointment with the banker, and the result was that Carroll became owner of the Earl Carroll Theatre (q.v.).

Howard Dietz (q.v.), Broadway lyricist and head of publicity for MGM, got lots of space when he put live women in flesh colored tights on the huge sign advertising the Hollywood Revue of 1929, which was then playing at the Astor Theatre (q.v.).

Another famed fake was the bet by Margaret Mayo that she could write a play in one day. The actress was appearing in Pretty Peggy and press agent Channing Pollock needed an idea to drum up business. The scheme worked in this way. Miss Mayo made a bet with playwright Theodore Burt Sayre that she could write a play in 24 hours. To prove that the wager was on the up-and-up, it was decided that Mr. Sayre would himself provide the synopsis, which would be delivered in a sealed envelope at the start of the day.

Pollock arranged for his stenographer to aide the actress in finishing the four-act work. The night before, a finished play of Miss Mayo's was hidden around the room where the writing was to take place. All through the day Pollock and Mayo pretended to be in the throes of creativity. Between visits by reporters they enjoyed leisurely meals. Sayre, who happened to be a close friend of Pollock, assured the press that he himself wrote the synopsis. That he did, while Pollock dictated it to him over the telephone.

The newspapermen were suitably impressed when at six o'clock the next morning an exhausted Miss Mayo delivered the manuscript entitled, The Mart. Miss Mayo became an authoress in her own right with successes such as Baby Mine and Polly of the Circus.

Many stunts are instigated in order to disguise the shoddiness of a production. Edward L. Bernays was a fledgling producer in 1913 with his production, Damaged Goods. The play's title seemed entirely too apt, and so a plan was hatched. Mr. Bernays happened also to be the coeditor of the Medical Review of Reviews. The play was somewhat racy for its time and the producer decided to open it only to members of the newly formed Medical Review of Reviews Sociological Fund. Membership cost exactly the same as a theater ticket. Newly enrolled members of the Fund kept the play running for 66 performances.

Stunts often take the form of legal action. Performers are continually suing management and vice-versa. Marion Alexander might have started the idea when she sued Sam S. Shubert *(q.v.)* for $10,000 because he stated she was not beautiful.

During the run of *Fantana* in 1905, Channing Pollock hatched a stunt in which a chorus girl's dog wore expensive diamond earrings. Neither the dog nor the chorus girl owned a pair of earrings, so Pollock was happy to supply a pair of cheap fakes and the bubble gum needed to make them adhere. The press looked askance at such an obvious fraud, and the reporter from the *World* had the nerve to refuse to use the photo. So Pollock was forced to defend his honor and have the dog's ears pierced. Then Tiffanys was asked to supply a pair suitable for canine use. This time, all the papers used the photo.

Pollock drummed up business for the 1906 production *Happyland* at the Casino Theatre *(q.v.)* by announcing a matinee "for women only." To ensure coverage of the nonevent, Pollock arranged for a man to crash the theater dressed in ladies' garments. There was also a husband who insisted that his wife exit the theater immediately if he were not allowed to attend. Pollock's window dressing was unnecessary, since the event turned out to be tremendously popular and the performance was sold out.

In the days before photocopy machines, scripts had to be hand typed with crude carbon-paper copies. In order to cut down on secretarial work, actors received "sides," which contained only their lines and a few cues. Thus in the latter part of 1905, when producer Henry Miller claimed that his play *Grierson's Way* had to be postponed because the only complete script had been lost, the press bought into the lie. A $500 reward was announced to sweeten the story while the rehearsals continued. The press agent on the show was surprised to learn that Miller subsequently did lose the script and was panicked at the thought of having to pay the $500. Luckily, a stage hand found the script and accepted a small reward.

Pollock thought up many other stunts to please his producers. Nena Blake, a chorus girl with *The Royal Chef* (9/1/04) was kidnapped in costume and sent halfway across the country. Her sister, Bertha, kissed a man who had never been kissed before. Actress Adele Ritchie's niece had her name legally changed to Adele Ritchie Jr., and the namesake was wooed by a "Siamese millionaire."

Times Square has also had its share of flagpole sitters and marathon dances (see ROSELAND) and other physical feats. One of the most famous was Shipwreck Kelly who lasted 13 days atop the Paramount Hotel in 1930. He was also found on Friday the 13th atop the Chanin Building on 42nd Street. For this stunt in October of 1939, Kelly ate 13 donuts while standing on his head.

More recently, fakes have passed into disfavor. Show business is more a business than a show, and newspapers pride themselves on reporting the truth. On the other hand, publicist Richard Maney *(q.v.)* doted on fakes that were obviously fake, and in fact, too ridiculous to pass up. Maney created most of his stunts while under the employ of that master showman, David Merrick *(q.v.)*.

Facing an embarrassing failure with his first outing, *Clutterbuck* (12/3/49), Merrick arranged to have a Mr. Clutterbuck paged throughout Manhattan. Every hotel and restaurant resounded with the name Mr. Clutterbuck. Although the show was not a success, Merrick saw the value of a good stunt.

When Princess Grace was wed in Monaco, a plane circled overhead trailing a banner exhorting the wedding party to come and see the Merrick production *Fanny* (11/4/54). Closer to home, Merrick was seen in Manhattan walking an ostrich named Fanny. *Fanny* featured a belly dancer so Merrick placed a statue of her in the Poet's Corner in Central Park. The statue was nude. This enraged the sculptor who saw his art on perhaps a higher plane and again the newspapers reveled in Merrick's mischievousness.

Even this wasn't enough to satisfy the indefatigable Merrick. He found names of suburbanites listed in the phone book and called them to invite them to see *Fanny* for free, provided they brought one paying customer. When *Fanny* finally closed after 888 performances, the ledger books showed a handsome profit of almost $1 million.

Other Merrick/Maney stunts were just as colorful as those for *Fanny*. When *The Good Soup* (3/2/60) opened, someone circulated the rumor that the playwright, Felicien Marceau, was a Nazi collaborator. Much newspaper coverage ensued. When Merrick's production of *The World Of Suzi Wong* and the Rodgers and Hammerstein *(q.v.)* musical *Flower Drum Song* were both about to open in 1958, Merrick sent Asian-Americans to picket the *Flower Drum Song* box office with signs proclaiming Wong as "the only authentic Chinese show." Richard Rodgers was not amused.

History was made during a performance of the explosive drama *Look Back In Anger* (10/1/57) when a woman burst from her seat, jumped on stage and slapped actor Kenneth Haigh. This was reported in all the papers. It received attention again when Merrick admitted that the $250 he had paid the woman just might have had something to do with her outburst.

The Matchmaker (12/5/55) was given the Merrick treatment when he arranged to have a chimpanzee drive a taxi around town carrying the sign "I am driving my master to see *The Matchmaker*." Merrick's fondness for animals again became evident when, for no apparent reason, a platypus showed up at the first press conference announcing *Romanoff and Juliet*.

And as a remedy for a bad critical reception, Merrick has been known to prescribe some strong medicine. At

The giant boot on the Martin Beck Theatre for Into the Woods   Photo Jeff Slotnick.

the beginning of a live broadcast from outside the theater of one of his flops Merrick gleefully, assigned a press agent to take an ax to the television cable, thereby literally cutting off the bad review.

When faced with less than positive reviews of his musical *Subways Are For Sleeping* (12/27/61) Merrick simply went to the phone book and called people whose names matched those of New York's leading dramatic critics *(q.v.)*. The critics were Howard Taubman *(New York Times)*, Walter Kerr *(Herald Tribune)*, John Chapman *(Daily News)*, Robert Coleman *(Daily Mirror)*, Norman Nadel *(World-Telegram)*, John McLain *(Journal-American)* and Richard Watts *(Post)*.

He then brought these people to the city, wined and dined them at the Plaza Hotel's Oak Room and transported them to the theater. After, he asked them what they thought of the show and suggested they lend their names to quotes which he composed. Advertising manager Fred Golden, a Merrick favorite, made up a full page ad to be run in all the New York papers, which reprinted the erstwhile quotes, their names and pictures.

The *New York Times* discovered the stunt after its first edition and pulled it. However, the attendant publicity became so enormous that the *Times* was forced to run the ad when reporting the hoax. The other dailies did not catch the fraud.

More recently, stunts have been used sparingly and with little of the panache that earlier practitioners brought to the art. When *Grease* celebrated its fourth birthday on St. Valentine's Day, 1976, a couple was married on stage. For *Knockout* (5/6/79), a staged bout between star Danny Aiello and heavyweight Larry Holmes was held. Wilbur the pig, a cast member of *King of Hearts* (10/22/78) was treated to a limousine ride and lunch at Sardi's *(q.v.)*. For the first anniversary of *Deathtrap* on February 26, 1979, press agent Jeffrey Richards gave a party for psychics who predicted the future of the show and its cast.

Larry Blyden, who coproduced and starred in the 1972 revival of *A Funny Thing Happened on the Way to the Forum* with Phil Silvers, decided to give a free Fourth of July performance. By 11 A.M. all the tickets were gone. Josh Ellis of Solters/Roskin and Freedman had a unit of the New York Blood Program in the lobby of *Dracula* (10/20/77). For every year of its long run, *Big River* hosted a jumping-frog contest outside its theater under the auspices of publicist Adrian Bryan-Brown.

But for the most part, stunts and fakes have lost their appeal. Richard Maney once bemoaned the fact that today the authors of stunts would be "drummed out of the regiment. Hyperbole and deception no longer are effective weapons."

John Golden produced a show called *Pigs* which played in the halcyon year of 1924. In those days, a person could pull a stunt and be proud of it. For this show, a dozen of the title characters were shuttled between a stable and the theater. Harry Kline was the enterprising press agent on the show and saw to it that every day the pigs were transported in a straw-covered wagon. The driver took his squealing load up and down the streets of Times Square. On the wagon was a sign with the message: These Pigs Perform Nightly at the Little Theater.

STUYVESANT THEATER   See BELASCO THEATRE.

STYNE, JULE (1905–   )   Jule Styne is by any accounting among the most successful of all Broadway composers. His prodigious output is unequaled by his Broadway contemporaries. Many consider Styne the ultimate composer when it comes to writing to suit the talents of stars. He tailored *Gentlemen Prefer Blondes* for Carol Channing; *Gypsy* for Ethel Merman (*q.v.*); *Funny Girl* for Barbra Streisand; *Bells Are Ringing* for Judy Holliday. Although these shows remain indelibly associated with their stars, they also exist as perfect examples of cohesive, well-integrated scores that serve their theatrical needs as fully as they serve the needs of their performers. It is this versatility and superb artistry that lead many to consider Styne our greatest living composer.

He was born Julius Kerwin Stein in London, December 31, 1905. Styne's family emigrated to the United States in 1913 and settled in Chicago. By the time the youngster was a teenager, Chicago was becoming more and more of an influence in the development of jazz and popular song. The early jazz groups known as the Chicagoans did not escape the notice of the young prodigy. Despite a solid classical background (he made his debut at the age of nine as a solo pianist with the Chicago Symphony), Styne felt more and more drawn to the music of the backroom bars and nightclubs.

A scholarship to the Chicago College of Music enabled Styne to perfect his technique and to study composition, theory and harmony. He formed his own dance band for which he played the piano and contributed arrangements. He joined some of the smaller

Jule Styne   Courtesy ASCAP.

bands then touring the country, most notably that of Art Jarrett.

Styne's early days in Chicago were an important influence in his career. He was aware of all the great musicians playing at the time and called Chicago at the time "a feast."

Styne moved to New York where he earned his living as a vocal coach and then accompanist for Harry Richman, a top Broadway and nightclub performer. Styne received an offer from 20th Century-Fox asking him to come to Hollywood to coach Alice Faye, Tony Martin, Shirley Temple and other Fox stars.

Styne previously had a big hit with his first song, "Sunday," written in 1927, and it didn't take the studio long to move Styne into the composers stable. Styne moved from Fox to Republic and then to Paramount and Columbia. Among the movies for which he contributed music were: *Anchors Aweigh; Tonight and Every Night; Tars and Spars; The Kid from Brooklyn; It Happened in Brooklyn; Romance on the High Seas; Two Guys from Texas; It's a Great Feeling; The West Point Story; Two Tickets to Broadway; My Sister Eileen;* and *Meet Me After the Show.*

Styne's principal collaborators during his Hollywood years were Frank Loesser (*q.v.*) and Sammy Cahn. They collaborated with Styne on such songs as "I Don't Want to Walk Without You, Baby," "I've Heard that Song Before," "I Said No," "Victory Polka," "I'll Walk Alone," "Anywhere," "It's a Great Feeling,"

"Saturday Night Is the Loneliest Night in the Week," "Poor Little Rhode Island," "The Charm of You," "I Fall in Love Too Easily," "What Makes the Sunset," "It's Been a Long, Long, Time," "Let It Snow, Let It Snow, Let It Snow," "I'm Glad I Waited for You," "The Things We Did Last Summer," "Five Minutes More," "Time After Time," "Three Coins in the Fountain" (Academy Award, 1954) and "It's Magic."

After success in Hollywood, Cahn and Styne attempted to write a Broadway musical. The result, *Glad to See You* (1944), was planned as a vehicle for Phil Silvers. His unavailability and other problems forced the show to close out of town. However, a standard did emerge from the score, "Guess I'll Hang My Tears Out to Dry."

The team had much better luck with their next attempt, *High Button Shoes* (10/9/47; 727 performances). This time, they got their man, Phil Silvers, and he and Nanette Fabray opened the show at the Century Theater *(q.v.)*. The Styne/Cahn score contributed at least one song to the hit parade, the polka "Poppa Won't You Dance with Me." Other standouts were "Can't You Just See Yourself?" and "I Still Get Jealous."

Two years later, Styne again opened a show on Broadway, this time with Leo Robin as lyricist. It was just as big a success as *High Button Shoes*. The show was *Gentlemen Prefer Blondes* (12/8/49; 740 performances), an adaptation of Anita Loos's popular novel. It was noteworthy for several reasons, the most important being the debut of Carol Channing as Lorelei Lee. Styne and Robin provided Channing with the first song that would become her trademark, "Diamonds Are a Girl's Best Friend." The show also featured hits like "Bye Bye Baby," "A Little Girl from Little Rock" and "You Say You Care."

Styne's next show wasn't as successful, but it was important as the first meeting between Styne and his longtime collaborators, Betty Comden and Adolph Green *(q.v.)*. *Two on the Aisle* (7/19/51; 281 performances) was Styne's only Broadway revue and was written to fit the talents of Bert Lahr and Dolores Gray.

Styne's third collaborator in as many shows was Bob Hilliard with whom he worked on *Hazel Flagg* (2/11/53; 190 performances), a musicalization of Ben Hecht's movie *Nothing Sacred*. The show was a disappointment despite a fine performance by Helen Gallagher. "Every Street's a Boulevard (in Old New York)" achieved some fame.

Director/choreographer Jerome Robbins was out of town working on a musical version of *Peter Pan,* starring Mary Martin *(q.v.)*. The show was having trouble, and the writing team of Jule Styne and Comden and Green was called in to bolster the Moose Charlap, Carolyn Leigh score. The principal Styne/Comden and Green songs were "Never Never Land," "Distant Melody" and "Captain Hook's Waltz." *Peter Pan* (10/20/

54; 152 performances) played at the Winter Garden Theater *(q.v.)* before a commitment to televise the show forced the Broadway production to close. It became a perennial favorite on NBC with Martin and Cyril Ritchard having the time of their lives in the J.M. Barrie fantasy.

Next, Styne, Comden and Green collaborated on *Bells Are Ringing* (11/29/56; 924 performances), written as a vehicle for Judy Holliday. Comden and Green had cut their teeth performing with Holliday as members of *The Revuers,* an early musical-comedy act that played Greenwich Village clubs. For the new show, the songwriters gave their star two great hits, "The Party's Over" and "Just In Time."

Say, Darling (4/3/58; 332 performances), the trio's next Broadway offering was a play about a musical. The source was a thinly disguised novel by Richard Bissel that told of his experiences working as colibrettist on *The Pajama Game*. The show starred Vivian Blaine, David Wayne, Johnny Desmond and brash Robert Morse as a spoof on Harold Prince *(q.v.)*. The show unfortunately never achieved its due. The problem was that the show was more of a play with songs than a full-fledged musical. Audiences were disappointed not to find the typical musical-comedy trappings. The one hit from the score was "Dance Only with Me."

Styne then collaborated with Stephen Sondheim *(q.v.)* on what some consider the greatest musical of all time, *Gypsy* (5/21/59; 702 performances). Arthur Laurents wrote the libretto. Rose was the ultimate stage mother, and to play her the producers, David Merrick *(q.v.)* and Leland Hayward, chose the ultimate musical-comedy star, Ethel Merman *(q.v.)*. Jerome Robbins was the director and choreographer. Styne and Sondheim perfectly tailored their bravura score to the talents of Merman and also served the dramatic needs of the script. The brassy, challenging score contained several hit songs, "Let Me Entertain You," "Some People," "Together" and "Everything's Coming Up Roses." All the elements of the production fused in Ethel Merman's last number, the thrilling "Rose's Turn," a high point in the actress's career and in the history of musical theater.

Styne moved on to another collaboration with Comden and Green, *Do Re Mi* (12/26/60; 400 performances). Styne again fashioned a score for Phil Silvers. His costar in this was Nancy Walker with John Reardon, David Burns and Nancy Dussault rounding out the leads. *Do Re Mi* was the story of the mob's control of the jukebox industry and Phil Silvers's quest for a quick buck. The show's run was based mainly on the comic inventiveness of the stars and the hit song, "Make Someone Happy."

Subways Are For Sleeping (12/27/61; 205 performances) was the threesome's next offering. Sydney Chaplin, Carol Lawrence, Orson Bean and Phyllis

Bob Merrill Courtesy ASCAP.

Newman starred. The score was well received with "Comes Once in a Lifetime" achieving the most notice. The show is best remembered for a series of publicity stunts *(q.v.)* engineered by producer David Merrick.

Styne's next production was his biggest hit. *Funny Girl* (3/26/64; 1,348 performances), starring Barbra Streisand opened at the Winter Garden Theater *(q.v.).* Bob Merrill provided the lyrics to Styne's music. Garson Kanin and Jerome Robbins whipped the show into shape after a particularly stormy tryout. By opening night, it was clear that Broadway had a major hit and a major star on its hands. Regrettably, *Funny Girl* was Streisand's last Broadway appearance. The story of Fanny Brice *(q.v.)* had the same show business ambiance that had inspired *Gypsy.* The score provided another star with a Styne signature tune. Streisand introduced "People," and the song became hers alone. Other numbers in the score also received airplay. Among them are "Don't Rain on My Parade" and "Who Are You Now?."

Styne's next show also featured another young star, Carol Burnett. *Fade Out—Fade In* (5/26/64; 271 performances) didn't achieve the fame of *Funny Girl.* None of the Styne/Comden and Green songs clicked with the hit parade, and Burnett's problems with the show forced it to close, reopen, then close for good.

Hallelujah, Baby! (4/26/67; 293 performances) reteamed Styne with his *Gypsy* librettist, Arthur Laurents. The score, with lyrics by Comden and Green, was exceptional, but the book, purporting to follow the progress made by blacks in this century, proved unwieldy. The show won the Tony Award *(q.v.)* as Best Musical after it had closed. Leslie Uggams, Robert Hooks and Allen Case starred.

Darling of the Day (1/27/68; 32 performances) was another show with a fine Styne score that achieved little success. This time, the lyrics were by master lyricist E.Y. Harburg *(q.v.).*

Styne teamed up with his old partner Sammy Cahn for *Look to the Lilies* (3/29/70; 25 performances). The adaptation of *Lilies of the Field,* wasn't very strong despite the best efforts of the star, Shirley Booth. That failure was followed by *Prettybelle,* which closed out of town.

Bob Merrill, who provided Styne with such strong lyrics for *Funny Girl* and not so strong ones for *Prettybelle,* was unable to repeat his popular success with the musical adaptation of the Billy Wilder movie *Some Like It Hot, Sugar* (4/9/72; 505 performances). Cyril Ritchard and Robert Morse made their second appearances in Styne musicals along with costars Tony Roberts and Elaine Joyce.

Styne's last Broadway show, *One Night Stand,* proved not even equal to its title, closing on October 25, 1980, after eight previews. Herb Gardner provided the lyrics.

With Broadway's fitful success with musical productions in recent years, Styne has been relegated to the wings. His attempt at musicalizing *Treasure Island* got no farther than Edmonton, Canada. However, Styne still writes almost every day and is always looking forward to his next opening night.

SULLIVAN, ED (1902–1974) In the 1930s and 1940s, Walter Winchell *(q.v.),* Louis Sobol, Earl Wilson, Ed Sullivan, Mark Hellinger *(q.v.)* and Damon Runyon *(q.v.)* were the men who ruled Broadway with their newspaper columns. Each of them could make or break careers and shows with a stroke of their pens. They were night people who scoured the speakeasies and clubs for tales of those who gave Broadway and Times Square its energy.

Sullivan wasn't the most famous of the group, but he turned out to be the most influential when he began his weekly variety show on CBS in the late forties. Sullivan, like the others, believed in Broadway as a phenomenon that mattered more than any other acreage in the world. He treated it with the respect and scorn he felt it deserved. The capitals of Europe and Hollywood were viewed as distant kingdoms whose inhabitants really mattered only when on the streets of Times Square. In those days, all the great gossip columns came from New York. Hedda Hopper and Louella Parsons were important only to the movie industry. Hollywood was simply a remote outpost that existed to serve Broadway's needs. Surprisingly, residents of

Hollywood agreed with the Great White Way's ethnocentrism. The goal of many of the great movie actors was to star in a Broadway play. Columnists like Sullivan and Winchell fed that feeling with their somewhat myopic view of the world.

Ed Sullivan was born on September 28, 1902, in Manhattan. His first New York newspaper job was at the *Evening Mail* as a sports writer. He thereafter held a succession of short-term jobs—first at the *Philadelphia Ledger,* then the *Morning World,* the *Bulletin,* the *Leader* and the *Morning Telegraph.* He finally settled at the *Graphic* in 1927. He soon found himself elevated to the post of sports editor.

The *Graphic* was considered a yellow journalism rag by its contemporaries. Publisher Bernarr Macfadden's daily was even described by Sullivan as, "a step removed from pornography." Winchell, the gossip columnist, wrote a column headed "Broadway Hearsay." Winchell often fought with his editors and was soon lured to the *Daily Mirror.* Louis Sobol took Winchell's place and shortly thereafter moved to the *Journal-American.* In looking around for a replacement, the editors chose Sullivan.

The reluctant reporter accepted the job since the only alternative was looking for work on another paper. On June 1, 1931, "Ed Sullivan Sees Broadway" was printed for the first time. Sullivan was resolved not to emulate his predecessors. He believed he had a higher mission. In his first column, he attacked his forerunner's style.

"I charge the Broadway columnists with defaming the street. I have entered a field of writing that ranks so low that it is difficult to distinguish any one columnist from his road companions. I have entered a field which offers scant competition. The Broadway columnists have lifted themselves to distinction by borrowed gags, gossip that is not always kindly and keyholes that too often reveal what might better be hidden. Phonies will receive no comfort in this space. To get into this particular column will be a badge of merit and a citation—divorces will not be propagated in this column . . . In my capacity as drama critic I pledge you of the theater that if I like the show I will say so without any ambiguities of phrasing that might protect my *Variety (q.v.)* box score . . . With the theater in the doldrums, it means a decisive voice and I promise to supply it."

Naturally, Sobol and Winchell took exception to his inferences. Sobol, in his column labeled Sullivan's diatribe, "The Ennui of His Contempt-oraries." Sobol claimed that, "empty vessels make the most sound."

Sullivan didn't always keep his word, but he tried as best he could to keep his high ideals. When the *Graphic* folded on July 7, 1932, Sullivan moved to Joseph Patterson's *Daily News* for $200 a week. By this time, Sullivan had already gone into radio, starting with a sports show sponsored by Adam Hats. CBS picked him up two years later in 1932 with a program entitled "Broadway's Greatest Thrills." The sponsor was American Safety Razor, and the salary was a $1,000 a week. Since he was forced to take a $175-a-week pay cut to join the *News,* the radio salary became his major means of support. It was later called "Ed Sullivan Entertains" and was broadcast live from the 21 Club. Sullivan opened his show with the sound of a typewriter.

A reviewer wrote: "The clackety-clack of the Remington, with the carriage moved back intermittently, is a switch on the Winchellian telegraphic staccato . . . Although Sullivan's voice does not have the weight and authority for this type of work, it's no drawback. Different type pipes are welcome."

Boris Morros persuaded Sullivan to follow in Winchell's footsteps once again and he moved into live entertainment as a producer of variety shows at the Paramount Theater *(q.v.).* The shows were entitled, *Gems of the Town.* Sullivan demurred until the $3,750 per show salary was mentioned. The first *Gems of the Town* premiered with the film *Take a Chance.*

With the success at the Paramount behind him, Sullivan moved to Loew's State *(q.v.)* for a series of revues featuring Harry Rose, "the Broadway Jester" as emcee. Sullivan soon took over the hosting chores of his *Dawn Patrol* shows. At this time, Sullivan began introducing celebrities sitting in the audience, a practice he continued on television.

Sullivan's tenure at the State brought other revues to the stage. The revue of July 6, 1934, was typical. *The All-Star All-American Nightclub Revue of 1934* featured Georgie Tapps, Ken Harvey, Joan Abbott and ballroom dancers, Mr. and Mrs. Paul Mears.

It seemed natural for Sullivan to tackle Broadway next, but his offering, a revue entitled *Crazy with the Heat* (1/14/41) lasted only 99 performances. Not willing to lose everything, he moved the second act of the show into Loew's State for a two week run.

Sullivan's next stab at Broadway was an all-black revue, *Harlem Cavalcade,* which opened on May 1, 1942. It fared no better than his first try and folded after only 49 performances.

Sullivan also hosted the annual *Daily News* amateur ballroom dance competition, The Harvest Moon Ball. He began his duties in 1936 and continued for 12 years thereafter. At the 12th edition of the contest, CBS had set up a live remote from Madison Square Garden. Sullivan was unaware of the cameras until the next day when Jack Benny called to congratulate him on his work.

Thus did Ed Sullivan make his television debut on September 3, 1947. Worthington Miner was CBS's director of programming. He was impressed with Sullivan and offered him the chance to do a weekly variety series to be titled "You're the Top."

The series, retitled "The Toast of the Town," premiered at nine o'clock on Sunday, June 20, 1948. Maxine Elliott's Theater *(q.v.)* was used as the studio. Among the guests on that first show were the phenomenally successful songwriting team, Rodgers and Hammerstein *(q.v.)*. In their portion of the show, they talked about *Oklahoma!* and *South Pacific. Oklahoma!* had just closed on May 29, 1948. *South Pacific* was to open on April 7, 1949. Their third Broadway musical *Allegro* was then currently at the end of its run and received a boost from the team's appearance.

Sullivan continued plugging Broadway shows on his program, giving them the national recognition that only television could bring. He continued his newspaper column for the entire time his show was on the air. The Sullivan show moved operations to the Hammerstein Theater on Broadway between 53rd and 54th Street. As a tribute to the showman, CBS renamed the theater the Ed Sullivan Theatre *(q.v.)* in 1967. CBS finally canceled the show in 1971. Sullivan died in 1974.

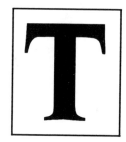

TAUBMAN, HOWARD See CRITICS.

THANATOPSIS In the 1920s and early 1930s, Thanatopsis, or more properly, The Young Men's Upper West Side Thanatopsis Literary and Inside Straight Club was the late night adjunct of the Algonquin Round Table *(q.v.).*

The organization was, to put it bluntly, a nightly poker session. Frank Case, the owner of the Algonquin Hotel *(q.v.),* was the host of the club. Case, realizing that the Round Table as well as Thanatopsis was an important publicity tool, provided a second-floor suite as well as refreshments. People would often go to the hotel merely to gape at the celebrities. They still go to see where all the history was made.

John Peter Toohey came up with the prolix title of the group, which included at one time or another most of the famous names in theater and particularly vaudeville, including Howard Dietz *(q.v.),* Brock Pemberton, Margalo Gillmore, Harpo Marx, Ina Claire, Peggy Wood, George S. Kaufman and Marc Connelly. In addition to the stage notables attending the party, there were men from the world of letters. Alexander Woollcott *(q.v.)* and his boss Herbert Bayard Swope, both of the *World,* Harold Ross, the editor of the *New Yorker* and E. Haldeman-Julius who invented the first paperbacks—Little Blue Books. Dorothy Parker, Robert Benchley *(q.v.),* John V.A. Weaver, Peggy Leech, Jane Grant, David Wallace, Herman J. Mankiewicz, Neysa McMein, Murdock Pemberton, Deems Taylor, Donald Ogden Stewart and Corey Ford all sat in on the party. Other members at one time or another were Douglas Fairbanks and Jascha Heifetz.

Swope once brought in an outside caterer from the Colony Restaurant uptown. Case put a sign on the door of the suite stating, "Basket Parties Not Welcome. Frank Case, Proprietor." The members of the club, wishing to teach Case a lesson, moved the game to the Colony for two weeks.

Swope sometimes bet as high as $10,000 dollars. Harpo Marx entered the game in 1924, invited by Alexander Woollcott. Marx's delight in gambling forced the stakes higher and higher, and many players became disillusioned as the stakes grew.

Woollcott, Marc Connelly and Heywood Broun decided they couldn't afford the higher stakes. They were in the club for entertainment, not to win money. Woollcott wrote to the other club members on behalf of his associates: "The persistent rumors that we resigned from pique at our losses are unworthy of those who circulate them. It just happens to be true that Mr. Connelly (as always) and Mr. Broun and myself, for a change, did suffer some rather severe misfortunes; but as we always say, it all evens up in the course of a year."

When Woollcott, Connelly and Broun left the group, much of its soul did too. Thanatopsis lasted, with gradual changes in membership, until the mid-thirties.

THEATER ARTS MAGAZINE (1916–1964) There have been many attempts to publish a theater-oriented magazine for the theatergoer. *Variety (q.v.), Billboard (q.v.)* and others were written for the professional. Fans of the theater needed their own organ.

In November 1916, *Theater Arts Magazine,* an illustrated quarterly published out of Detroit, Michigan, began with Sheldon Chaney as editor. The magazine sought to cover the gamut of theater interests in the country. It contained articles on Broadway, regional companies, the road and the burgeoning little-theater movement. Early contributors included such luminaries as Ruth St. Denis, Winthrop Ames, Percy Mackaye and Thomas Wood Stevens. The tone of the magazine was serious and it considered itself a progressive voice in the theater community.

A short time later, the motion picture took hold of the nation, and fan magazines like *Photoplay* became huge sellers. *Theater Arts* hung on with a small but loyal readership as the nation's theater scene became smaller and smaller. Soon the focus of the magazine was almost totally the Broadway theater with occasional forays into London's West End.

Edith J.R. Isaacs and Rosamond Gilder were later editors of what was then a monthly magazine. Their coeditors were Stark Young, Ashley Dukes, Norris Houghton, Hermine Rich Asaacs and Kenneth Mac-Gowan. Many theater luminaries contributed articles to the magazine. Among them were Norman Bel Geddes, Helen Hayes *(q.v.)*, Vincente Minnelli, John Mason Brown, Jean-Paul Sartre, Jo Mielziner and Margaret Webster. Illustrations were also important, and most issues featured photographs of stage and costume designs as well as serious studies of actors and actresses in their current roles.

Although an excellent magazine, *Theater Arts* could not compete with the movies, and as Broadway shrank so did its readership. In February 1948, the magazine folded. But in the spring of that same year, a new *Theater Arts Magazine* was born, now merged with its rival, *Stage Magazine*. Charles MacArthur was the editor, and although the tone was still serious, there was more of a lighthearted air to the proceedings.

The new magazine featured a more theatrical spirit and boasted new departments dedicated to reviews, and theater news, calendar and recordings and a dining column. The focal point of the magazine was the complete playscript included in each issue.

The new magazine was certainly more in the spirit of the new Broadway. But as Broadway continued its decline, so did *Theater Arts*. Several new editors tried to keep the magazine alive but the spring 1964 issue was its last.

THEATER CLUB AWARD This award has been given since 1926 for "the best play by an American author produced during the year." Past recipients have included George Kelly (the first winner) for *Craig's Wife,* Elmer Rice for *Street Scene,* Maxwell Anderson for *Joan of Lorraine,* Arthur Miller *(q.v.)* for *Death of a Salesman,* Richard Rodgers *(q.v.)* and Oscar Hammerstein II *(q.v.)* for *The King and I,* William Inge for *Picnic* and Frank Loesser *(q.v.)*, Abe Burrows, Jack Weinstock and Willie Gilbert for *How to Succeed in Business without Really Trying.*

THEATER DEVELOPMENT FUND No other single organization has had as great an impact on the Broadway theater as the nonprofit Theater Development Fund (TDF). Since its inception in 1968, the TDF has served both the Broadway theater community and its audiences through projects designed to increase theater attendance and to introduce new audiences to theatergoing. TDF also subsidizes important productions that might not otherwise be presented due to the brutally commercial climate of Broadway today.

The best-known of the TDF's activities is the TKTS Booth *(q.v.)* in Duffy Square. In the 1985–86 season, the TKTS Booth at Times Square sold over 1,000,000 tickets at half price. This translated into over $25 million in receipts paid to theaters. For a show close to closing, the added revenues from the TKTS Booth could mean the difference between a profitable run and a failure. Shows such as *A Chorus Line* and *42nd Street* received over $2 million of TKTS Booth sales in only one year.

Through its theater subsidy program, the TDF attempts to provide financial support to commercially produced plays on and off Broadway of artistic merit. TDF makes a commitment to a producer to buy a specified number of tickets (the average is 1,000) to a show for resale at a lower, or subsidized price to patrons on the TDF mailing list. In the 1985–86 season, TDF subsidized 12 Broadway shows, including *The Blood Knot* (6,034 tickets), *The House of Blue Leaves* (5,033 tickets), and *Loot* (4,008 tickets). In total, 53,462 tickets were sold, resulting in $562,374 dollars spent on subsidized tickets. The sale of these tickets is designed to foster an expansion of the Broadway audience.

TDF also posts an Actors' Equity Association *(q.v.)* bond for certain productions. This bond is held in escrow against the production's salaries for the cast. Some productions have difficulty raising the funds to meet their budgets, and so TDF's posting helps them put the money they have raised into actual expenses incurred by the mounting of the show.

Long-running shows may also use TDF to fill up houses without using subsidies to cover ticket costs. The producers offer the tickets to TDF's 100,000 name mailing list at a discount price. This is simply an alternative to the TKTS Booth in making discount tickets available. A producer using this service knows how many tickets are sold well in advance of the actual performance date and thus can better gauge his or her budgetary needs.

In 1985–86, 41 Broadway shows used the Nonsubsidy Ticket Program. Almost $2 million in ticket sales were generated. Some shows, like *Brighton Beach Memoirs* by Neil Simon *(q.v.)*, received over $200,000 from such ticket sales.

TDF's Group Sales Program has been in existence since 1971. Not-for-profit adult community, high school, university student, teacher, senior citizen and union groups can all avail themselves of this service. The tickets are allotted by producers and are used to encourage attendance by people who could not otherwise afford to enjoy theater or those for whom the performing arts are a new experience. This program accounts for 34% of TDF's ticket sales. Over 192,000 tickets were sold in the 1985–86 season.

The Theater Access Project was inaugurated in 1979 to "encourage and facilitate the theatergoing of persons who are deaf or hearing impaired, blind or partially sighted, physically impaired or confined to a wheel-chair." The tickets are made available to those whose handicaps would prevent them from attending theater under normal circumstances.

In the 1985–86 season, nearly 10,000 tickets were sold to disabled persons, their families, friends or teachers through TDF's Theater Access Project. Deaf persons were offered special sign interpreted performances of shows like *La Cage Aux Folles, As Is, Benefactors* and *Song and Dance* through this program.

TDF has other programs not directly connected with the Broadway theater. Through its Musical Instrument Revolving Fund, it enables small orchestras in New York State to purchase instruments. The Commercial Theater Institute holds two seminars each year to encourage fledgling producers. During the three-day conference, they are taught legal, financial and management aspects of production and a 14-week seminar on producing also is offered.

The organization also administers the Costume Collection. A warehouse contains over 100,000 donated costumes that are rented for a nominal fee to arts groups across the country. Tickets are also offered to qualified theatergoers through a voucher program aimed mainly at increasing attendance of off-Broadway and off-off-Broadway events.

Altogether, TDF handled over 2,270,000 tickets to theater, dance and music events in the 1985–86 season. The revenue received came to over $35,500,000. Because of TDF support, many shows were able to weather slow periods or to run longer than would have been otherwise possible.

Although TDF cannot actually save a failure from closing, it has been instrumental in keeping more shows alive on Broadway and giving others a larger return on their investments. It has also introduced new audiences to the live theater and has enabled other not-so-wealthy theater lovers to attend Broadway productions, despite the constantly rising price of tickets.

THEATER GUILD The Theater Guild, the oldest producing organization in America, has been producing Broadway shows since its inception in 1919. Although it has been fairly inactive in recent years, its amazingly long history has been marked by incredible highs and incredible lows. All producing organizations of note have presented great plays and all have produced flops, but the Theater Guild has had many close calls when its existence depended on the success or failure of a single production.

The Guild's often shaky finances were the result of an ambitious producing schedule and its choice of plays that did not conform to the public's expectations. Many of the playwrights whom the Guild championed are ranked with the greatest dramatists of our time, including such luminaries as Maxwell Anderson, Robert Emmett Sherwood, S.N. Behrman, Philip Barry, William Saroyan and Sidney Howard. These American dramatists were joined by many great English and European talents, chief among them George Bernard Shaw. The Guild produced 18 of Shaw's plays. The other playwright represented by the Guild through most of his career was Eugene O'Neill *(q.v.)*, considered by many to be the greatest American playwright.

The Guild branched into operating subscription programs for many theaters and also produced movies. The organization also operated the Theater Guild Abroad program, which sent Americans to European theaters. The Guild's activity slowed in the sixties and by the eighties it was practically moribund. However, the Guild has been pronounced dead before only to emerge triumphant time and time again.

The Guild was born at a time when a wave of experimentation was surging through all the arts. The Armory Show of 1913 introduced America to the new masters of European postimpressionism. Poets, musicians and playwrights were also experimenting. Many "little theaters" sprang up across the country, and these often produced the works of experimental dramatists who were breaking away from more traditional plays.

One of these organizations was the Washington Square Players, a group that produced such progressive playwrights as Arthur Schnitzler, Oscar Wilde, John Reed, Eugene O'Neill, Maeterlinck, Elmer Rice, Ibsen, Shaw, Chekhov and Basil Lawrence. Lawrence was a pseudonym for Lawrence Langner who with Theresa Helburn administrated the Guild. Among the actors who began their careers with the Players were Frank Conroy, Katharine Cornell *(q.v.)*, Glenn Hunter and Jose Ruben. Theresa Helburn was cast in a Washington Square Players' production, but her parents made her withdraw.

On May 13, 1918, with the advent of World War I and an increasing debt, the group disbanded. The closing of The Washington Square Players led the way to the Theater Guild. Helen Westley, Lawrence Langner and Philip Moeller formed a new organization described as "a little theater grown up, and should be governed entirely by a Board of Managers, to which its director should be responsible. It should be a professional theater, employ professional actors and produce only long plays, 'which should be great plays.'"

The first board members of the new Theater Guild included Westley, Langner and Moeller as well as Josephine A. Meyer, Lee Simonson, Edna Kenton, Helen Freeman and Rollo Peters. Theresa Helburn, though not a member of the board, was named Play Representative. Peters and Freeman left within the first year.

The Guild's roller-coaster financial status began with its first productions. Financier Otto Kahn helped the Guild mount its first production. Kahn, the owner of the Garrick, liked the Guild and allowed them to lease the theater rent free. Langner himself put $1,610 into the new organization. An additional $474 dollars had been raised by selling subscriptions. With $1,000 more from various sources, the Guild was ready to begin production. When the first play opened, the Guild had exactly $19.50 to its credit.

The Guild's first offering was a commedia dell' arte drama by Jacinto Benavente, which John Garrett Underhill translated and titled *The Bonds of Interest* (4/14/19; 32 performances). The show opened at the Garrick Theater on West 35th Street. It was a quick failure with a loss of $500 per week. One reason for the play's run past opening night was the Guild's 150 subscribers. These optimistic theatergoers had paid for a two-play series and so the Guild looked for another play to present.

The second Guild presentation at the Garrick was St. John Ervine's play *John Ferguson* (5/13/19; 177 performances). This time the Guild hit pay dirt. Augustin Duncan, the brother of dancer Isadora Duncan, starred in the melodrama and also directed. The success of *John Ferguson* was due to circumstances other than its questionable dramatic merits. When the actors strike of 1919 (q.v.) hit Broadway, the newly formed Actors' Equity (q.v.) closed down all Broadway productions. The Guild was spared because of its unique democratic structuring. Therefore, theatergoers who longed to see theater were faced with only two alternatives—*John Ferguson* or nothing.

Its success and popularity was almost embarrassing to the Guild since it was not a "great play." The Guild was certainly not prepared for its success. A business manager was hastily hired. He was future Hollywood director Walter Wanger. The Guild decided to move the play to the larger Fulton Theater, later named the Helen Hayes Theater (q.v.).

The play's success led to a dramatic increase in the Guild's subscribers—500 avid theatergoers signed up for the second season, which began with a series of failures. St. John Ervine was called on to save the Guild. His play *Jane Clegg* (2/23/20; 112 performances), starring Margaret Wycherly, was well received by audiences and critics.

The next season found the Guild's subscription base increased to 1,300 patrons. For its first production of its third season, it presented the American premiere of George Bernard Shaw's *Heartbreak House* (11/10/20; 128 performances). Albert Perry had the leading role at the Garrick Theater where lines formed to see the three-

and-a-half hour play. The production was important as the first directed for the Guild by Dudley Digges, a mainstay of the Guild from then on.

The third season proved very popular. A.A. Milne's *Mr. Pim Passes By* (2/28/21; 210 performances) starred Laura Hope Crews. Ferenc Molnar's *Liliom* (4/20/21; 311 performances) proved to be an even bigger success. *Liliom* starred Eva Le Gallienne, Dudley Digges, Helen Westley and Edgar Stehli. *Liliom* later served the Guild well as the basis for Rodgers and Hammerstein's (q.v.) *Carousel*.

Highlights of the next season included Leonid Andreyev's *He Who Gets Slapped* (1/9/22; 308 performances) and George Bernard Shaw's *Back to Methuselah* (2/27/22; 25 performance cycles). The Shaw play was subtitled a *Gospel of Creative Evolution*. It almost took as long as evolution itself. The Guild broke the play into sections and presented it over three separate evenings in repertory over three weeks. Four directors were called on to stage the massive undertaking. Dennis King, Margaret Wycherly, Walter Abel and A.P. Kaye starred, each playing a variety of roles. The Guild endeared itself to Shaw by this bold production. When contract negotiations were announced Shaw responded, "A contract is unnecessary. It isn't likely that any other lunatics will want to produce it." Shaw was correct, and even fewer people wanted to see it.

The Guild was broke at the beginning of its fifth season, but it did have 6,000 subscribers. Karel Capek's *R.U.R.* (10/9/22; 182 performances) opened the season at the Garrick, was hailed as one of the decade's best plays on October 9, 1922, and introduced the world to the word "robot." Elmer Rice's expressionistic drama *The Adding Machine* (3/19/23; 72 performances) was another highlight of the season.

During the next season, the Guild produced Shaw's *Saint Joan* (12/23/23; 214 performances). The play, like many of Shaw's, was long, and the Guild implored the playwright to let them make cuts because suburbanites could not get to their trains by the time the play was over. Shaw responded, "The old, old story. Begin at eight, or run later trains."

History was made again with the opening of the seventh season. Molnar's play *Where Ignorance Is Bliss* was retitled *The Guardsman* (10/13/24; 274 performances), and the comedy marked the beginning of Alfred Lunt and Lynn Fontanne's (q.v.) long and prosperous association with the Guild. The production also marked the first success of designer Jo Mielziner.

With *The Guardsman,* the Guild hit its stride and entered into its most productive period. It next presented Sidney Howard's *They Knew What They Wanted* (11/24/24; 192 performances) with Pauline Lord, Richard Bennett and Glenn Anders. *They Knew What They Wanted* won the Pulitzer Prize (q.v.).

The success of the Guild's productions was hampered

by the Garrick's small capacity and off-the-beaten-track location. The theater district had moved from Herald Square to Times Square, and the Guild was determined to move with it. They commissioned C. Howard Crane to design a new theater that would be named the Guild (q.v.). On April 13, 1925, President Coolidge pressed a button from the White House, which inaugurated the new theater.

The theater's first production was Shaw's *Caesar and Cleopatra* with Helen Hayes (q.v.) and Lionel Atwill. The production received mixed notices. A special fund-raising event was planned for a Sunday night at the Garrick Theater. The show, a musical revue, was titled *The Garrick Gaieties*. The evening of May 17, 1925, was the date set for the opening. The show was so successful that it was presented on several occasions until a full run was inaugurated on June 8, 1925. Songs for the *Garrick Gaieties* were provided by a virtually unknown Richard Rodgers and Lorenz Hart (q.v.). They wrote a delightfully witty score, which included one standard, "Manhattan." The evening also featured satires on Guild plays. For example, *They Knew What They Wanted* was satirized as *They Didn't Know What They Were Getting*.

The Guild was now firmly ensconced on Broadway, although its finances were, as usual, in a precarious state due to the expense of running its own theater. Another drain on the Guild's coffers was the permanent repertory theater it launched in New York in 1926. The public did not jump on the repertory bandwagon, and two years later the repertory idea was dropped.

Among the Guild's most successful productions of its middle years were Du Bose and Dorothy Heyward's *Porgy* (10/11/27; 367 performances); Eugene O'Neill's *Marco Millions* (1/9/28; 102 performances) and *Strange Interlude* (1/23/28; 426 performances); Shaw's *Major Barbara* (11/20/28; 73 performances) with Helen Westley, Gale Sondergaard, Dudley Digges and Winifred Lenihan; and Philip Moeller's adaptation of Sil-Vara's *Caprice* (12/31/28; 178 performances) with Lunt and Fontanne.

By the end of the 1920s, discord began to arise in the Guild's ranks. It seemed, throughout its history, that success bred failure. Perhaps the Guild needed to be lean and hungry to work well. The Guild's artistic success from 1926 to 1928 led to infighting among the Board. There were other upheavals as well. Some of the Guild's most prominent playwrights left and formed The Playwrights' Company (q.v.). Some of the Guild's best actors left and created the Group Theater (q.v.). Even the Lunts eventually left the Guild, though they later returned to act in several productions.

Despite the fighting and upheavals, there were still many successes for the Guild in the late twenties and early thirties, including S.N. Behrman's *Meteor* (12/23/29; 92 performances); Shaw's *The Apple Cart* (2/24/30; 88 performances) with Tom Powers, Claude Rains,

Morris Carnovsky, Helen Westley and Violet Kemble-Cooper; Glenn Anders, Ruth Gordon, Morris Carnovsky and Franchot Tone in Philip Barry's *Hotel Universe* (4/14/30; 81 performances); and Maxwell Anderson's *Elizabeth the Queen* (11/3/30; 135 performances) with Lunt and Fontanne.

The Group Theater presented Paul Green's *The House of Connelly* (9/28/31; 72 performances) under the Guild's auspices at the Martin Beck Theatre (q.v.). O'Neill's *Mourning Becomes Electra* (10/26/31; 150 performances) starred Alla Nazimova and Alice Brady. Hits of the thirties also included Robert Emmett Sherwood's *Reunion in Vienna* (11/16/31; 280 performances) with the Lunts; Ina Claire in S.N. Behrman's *Biography* (12/12/32; 210 performances); Eugene O'Neill's comedy *Ah, Wilderness!* (10/2/33; 285 performances) with veteran Broadway player George M. Cohan (q.v.), Elisha Cook Jr., Gene Lockhart and Marjorie Marquis; and Helen Hayes (q.v.), Philip Merivale and Helen Menken in Maxwell Anderson's *Mary of Scotland* (11/27/33; 236 performances).

After an acclaimed production of Shakespeare's *The Taming of the Shrew* (9/30/35; 128 performances) with Alfred Lunt and Lynn Fontanne came one of the Guild's most ambitious offerings, *Porgy and Bess* (10/10/35; 124 performances). George Gershwin (q.v.) composed the music for the black folk opera. His brother Ira (q.v.) and Du Bose Heyward wrote the lyrics. Heyward's libretto was directed by Rouben Mamoulian. The opening at the Alvin Theater (q.v.) met with mixed reviews. Critics differed on whether the show was an opera or a musical. Instead of concentrating on the play, the critics engaged in a war of semantics, trying to neatly pigeonhole the proceedings. The failure was a major disappointment to the Guild, which had been having its usual financial difficulties.

Tyrone Guthrie's production of Dody Smith's comedy *Call It a Day* (1/28/36; 194 performances) starred Gladys Cooper and Philip Merivale. S.N. Behrman's *End of Summer* (2/17/36; 153 performances), starring Ina Claire and Osgood Perkins, was also a success. *Idiot's Delight* (3/24/36; 300 performances), one of the Guild's greatest successes, opened at the Sam S. Shubert Theatre (q.v.). Robert Emmett Sherwood's play starred the Lunts, Sydney Greenstreet, director Bretaigne Windust, George Meader and Richard Whorf. *Idiot's Delight*'s success made three hits in a row for the Guild, but the luck was not to continue.

Behrman's *Amphitryon 38* (11/1/37; 153 performances) opened with the Lunts, Richard Whorf and Sydney Greenstreet. The play's run was an oasis in a desert of failures. One such failure was the American premiere of Anton Chekhov's *The Sea Gull* (3/28/38; 40 performances), translated by Stark Young. The limited engagement featured excellent sets by Robert Edmond Jones.

Between the success of *Amphitryon 38* and its next hit, Philip Barry's *The Philadelphia Story,* the Guild mounted nine productions, all failures. In 1936, the Guild's debits totaled $60,000. However, *The Philadelphia Story* (3/28/39; 417 performances) revived the Guild. The play opened at the Shubert with Shirley Booth, Vera Allen, Lenore Lonergan, Katharine Hepburn, Van Heflin and Joseph Cotten. The play saved the Guild from bankruptcy. As Theresa Helburn remarked, "There's no money in producing any more. The money's in authorship."

Gene Kelly, William Bendix, Celeste Holm, Will Lee, Julie Haydon, and Edward Andrews were featured in William Saroyan's *The Time of Your Life* (10/25/39; 185 performances). Also, Eddie Dowling appeared in the play and coproduced with the Guild and codirected with Saroyan. The small role of the newsboy was played by Ross Bagdasarian, better known as the creator of The Chipmunks. *The Time of Your Life* returned for an additional 32 performances.

The Lunts appeared with Alan Reed, Estelle Winwood, Juanita Hall, James O'Neill and Muriel Rahn in Behrman's *The Pirate* (11/27/42; 177 performances), which was presented in association with The Playwrights' Company.

The Guild was at another low when Richard Rodgers again stepped in to replenish the Guild's coffers. The event was one of the milestones of the American theater—Rodgers and Hammerstein's *(q.v.) Oklahoma!* (3/31/43; 2,248 performances). The musical ran for five years in addition to touring companies and foreign productions. The Guild then had a plentiful cash flow, but surprisingly its output fell. It did not even have the *succes d'estime,* which it had enjoyed in the twenties and thirties. There were other hits, but the huge success of *Oklahoma!* seemed to take the starch out of Theresa Helburn and Lawrence Langner's artistic manifesto.

A production of *Othello* (10/19/43; 295 performances) with Paul Robeson, Jose Ferrer and Uta Hagen opened to generally favorable reviews. Its run seemed to indicate that for the Guild nothing had changed. But success seemed mostly out of the producers' reach. The failures were forgettable, without the raw energy and political fervor of past flops. Blame was laid at the feet of Langner and Helburn, who were described by one dirctor as "gifted amateurs." They were accused of paying too much attention to the small concerns of the organization without being able to grasp the big picture or make educated decisions. A former staff member said they were incapable of delegating responsibility.

The Guild Theater was becoming a burden since the Guild did not have enough productions to keep it occupied, and the theater didn't have enough seats to attract other producers. In 1944, the Guild sold the theater.

The Guild's next success came with Rodgers and Hammerstein's *Carousel* (4/19/45; 890 performances) at the Majestic Theater *(q.v.)*. *Oklahoma!* was based on a previous Guild presentation, Lynn Riggs's *Green Grow the Lilacs* (1/26/31; 64 performances). *Carousel* was also based on a play that the Guild had originally presented, *Liliom.* The success of *Carousel* and the failure of most other Guild offerings led the Guild's supporters to ask, Where was the commitment to drama? Why weren't more chances being taken?

The Guild branched out into radio and began broadcasting its show "The Theater Guild of the Air" in 1945. Though the producing organization presented more successful dramas on the stage, these became less and less frequent. Eugene O'Neill's *The Iceman Cometh* (10/9/46; 136 performances) premiered at the Martin Beck Theatre *(q.v.)*. By this time Armina Marshall (Mrs. Lawrence Langner) had joined Langner and Helburn in running the Guild. The other board members had long since left in disgust.

Later hits for the Guild included William Inge's *Come Back Little Sheba* (2/15/50; 190 performances) with Shirley Booth at the Booth Theatre *(q.v.)*; *The Lady's Not for Burning* (11/8/50; 151 performances) by Christopher Fry at the Royale Theatre *(q.v.)*; and *Picnic* (2/19/53; 477 performances) at the Music Box Theater *(q.v.)*.

During the 1950s the Guild, without much theater activity to keep itself busy, turned to television. In 1953, the "Theater Guild of the Air" transferred to television. Its name was changed to honor its sponsor, United States Steel. The "United States Steel Hour" ran until 1963. The show was among the best of the anthology series to introduce new American writers. The fifties also saw the Guild branch out into motion pictures. Among the notable movies produced by the Guild were *The Pawnbroker, Judgement at Nuremberg* and *A Child Is Waiting.*

Though the 1950s and 1960s were slow decades for the Guild, the organization did mount a few notable productions. Jule Styne *(q.v.)*, Betty Comden and Adolph Green *(q.v.)* wrote the Judy Holliday musical *Bells Are Ringing* (11/29/56; 924 performances). The show introduced such standards as "The Party's Over" and "Just in Time." Dore Schary's *Sunrise at Campobello* (1/30/58; 556 performances) with Ralph Bellamy opened at the Cort Theatre *(q.v.)*. Peter Shaffer's *The Royal Hunt of the Sun* (10/26/65; 261 performances) opened at the ANTA Theater (the former Guild Theater) with George Rose, Christopher Plummer, John Vernon and David Carradine. Harold Pinter's *The Homecoming* (1/5/67; 324 performances) opened at the Music Box Theater and Allan Ayckbourn's *Absurd Person Singular* was also a success.

Since then the Guild has concentrated on managing a subscription series in other cities. Its producing days are over.

THEATER MASQUE See JOHN GOLDEN THEATER.

THEATER WORLD AWARD See DANIEL BLUM THEATER WORLD AWARD.

TIMES SQUARE THEATER 219 W. 42nd Street. Architect: Eugene DeRosa and Pereira. Opening: September 30, 1920; *The Mirage*.   The Times Square Theater had a short but noteworthy life as a legitimate theater. Built by Arch and Edgar Selwyn, the Times Square boasted a 1,200-seat auditorium designed in the Adam style. The auditorium was decorated in silver, black and a green that almost became gray. The black velvet stage curtain separated the audience from the large, 40-foot-wide stage.

The theater's facade was shared with the Apollo Theatre *(q.v.)* next door. The two theaters each had separate marquees. The theater, similar in layout to the Music Box Theater *(q.v.)*, opened with a hit, *The Mirage* (192 performances). Edgar Selwyn was the author and Florence Wood starred.

The theater's next offering was the musical comedy *The Right Girl* (3/15/21; 98 performances) written by Percy Wenrich and Raymond W. Peck and starring Tom Lewis and Robert Woolsey. The revue, *The Broadway Whirl* (6/8/21; 85 performances) soon followed. Blanche Ring, Richard Carle and Charles Winninger starred.

Three plays followed in quick succession: *The Demi-Virgin* (10/18/21; 268 performances); *Honors Are Even* (8/10/21; 70 performances) and *Love Dreams,* a "melody drama" by Anne Nichols, the author of *Abie's Irish Rose.*

The great American actress Katharine Cornell *(q.v.)* opened in *A Bill of Divorcement* (10/10/21; 173 performance) at the Times Square. The play was one of the actress's earliest successes. *The Charlatan* (4/24/22; 64 performances) followed. Tallulah Bankhead appeared at the Times Square Theater in *The Exciters* (9/22/22; 35 performances). Writing in the *Tribune,* critic *(q.v.)* Percy Hammond commented, "Few actresses can portray more convincingly than Miss Bankhead the difficult part of a pretty girl."

The next play at the Times Square was Channing Pollock's *The Fool* (10/23/22; 373 performances). The show was lambasted by the critics. Business was terrible with less than $300 in advance sales. Pollock received many letters from prominent citizens praising the play and congratulating him on writing it. The author took a quarter page ad in papers the next day with the headline, "Are All These Wise Men Fools?" Under that banner Pollock reprinted excerpts of the letters he had received. In two weeks, the box office take increased to $1,000. Apparently, clergymen had preached sermons about the play. The box office receipts for the third week totaled $14,000, enough to break even. By the fourth week the theater was sold out, and matinees were added. By Christmas, the theater had added matinees to handle the crowd, bringing the total performances for the week to 12. There were seven road companies touring the country to 85,000 people each week. The companies employed almost 300 actors with a weekly payroll of almost $40,000. In all, *The Fool* showed a $1 million profit.

The next hit to play the Times Square was *Andre Charlot's Revue of 1924* (1/9/24; 298 performances). On opening night, audiences were introduced to three great British talents: Gertrude Lawrence, Jack Buchanan and Beatrice Lillie. *Charlot's Revue* also featured a hit song, "Limehouse Blues," by Philip Braham and Douglas Furber. Theatergoers used to a four-hour Ziegfeld *(q.v.)* extravaganza were surprised at the revue's fast clip and modern theatricality.

Jerome Kern *(q.v.)* and Howard Dietz *(q.v.)* provided the score for *Dear Sir* (9/23/24; 15 performances), the next show to originate at the Times Square. Florenz Ziegfeld mounted *Annie Dear* (11/4/24; 103 performances) at the Times Square as a vehicle for his wife Billie Burke. Sigmund Romberg *(q.v.)*, Clare Kummer and Clifford Grey contributed the score. A third musical, *Kosher Kitty Kelly* (6/15/25) was an ill-disguised rip-off of *Abie's Irish Rose.*

Channing Pollock's anti-war play, *The Enemy* (10/20/25; 202 performances), like *The Fool,* garnered mostly negative reviews but was enjoyed by the public. At the end of its run, Pollock was told by the theater's ladies room attendant that she was never sorrier to see a play close. Pollock was moved, until the woman explained that she had never before enjoyed such a booming business of powder-rags. Apparently, the pacifist play was so moving that ladies retired to the lounge to cry their eyes out.

Following the closing of *The Enemy,* there was an ominous portent. The Times Square was used to show motion pictures. The policy didn't last long; on May 31, 1926, the play *Love 'Em and Leave 'Em* moved from the Apollo Theater to the Times Square.

The next hit to play the Times Square was Anita Loos's *Gentlemen Prefer Blondes* (9/28/26; 201 performances), the story of gold-digger Lorelei Lee and her friend Dorothy.

While Warner Brothers was premiering its talking picture *The Jazz Singer* to the world, the Times Square was hosting the silent film *Sunrise* by F.W. Murnau. The classic played practically the entire 1927–28 season.

The next season was taken up with Ben Hecht and Charles MacArthur's smash hit play, *The Front Page* (8/14/28; 281 performances). The comedy of the rough-and-tumble world of Chicago newspapers became one of the most enduring plays of the decade.

The Depression heralded a slowdown in the number of productions presented on Broadway. The Times

Square was home to the pacifist musical *Strike Up the Band* (1/14/30; 191 performances) with a score by George and Ira Gershwin *(q.v.)* and a satirical libretto by Morrie Ryskind and George S. Kaufman *(q.v.)*.

The Times Square hosted six productions during the 1930–31 season. The last of these, Noel Coward's *Private Lives* (1/27/31; 248 performances), was the only success. Coward, Gertrude Lawrence, Laurence Olivier, Jill Esmond and Therese Quadri comprised the cast. Coward wrote one song for the play, "Some Day I'll Find You." When the show opened, the Apollo Theatre next door was empty. So the producers featured Noel Coward's name above the title on one marquee and Gertrude Lawrence's on the other.

The 1931–32 season was a complete washout for the Times Square. None of the four plays that managed to open lasted longer than a month. The next season, the last for legitimate production at the theater, was barely better. It started with the Bella and Samuel Spewack comedy *Clear All Wires* (9/14/32; 91 performances), starring Thomas Mitchell. It was followed by *Foolscap* (1/11/33; 13 performances).

The last play to open at the Times Square was *Forsaking All Others* (3/1/33; 101 performances), a Tallulah Bankhead starrer with Thomas Mitchell directing. The drawing room comedy had the misfortune to open on the day that the federal government closed all the banks. As usual, the actress received glowing notices, although the play did not.

The Times Square Theater was then leased to the Brandts, owners or leasees of most of the 42nd Street theaters to this day. The Brandts began a movie policy for the theater and so it has remained.

TIMES TOWER West 42nd Street and Seventh Avenue. Architects: Cyrus L.W. Eidlitz and Andrew C. McKenzie, 1904; remodeled by Smith, Smith, Haines, Lundbert & Wheeler, 1966. The Times Tower is the most significant building on Times Square and the focal point of the southern end of the square. It is the scene of the annual New Year's Eve celebration *(q.v.)*. The building is a symbol of the changes the square has undergone and perhaps a guide to its future.

In what was then called Longacre Square, a quiet crossroads mainly housing carriage factories, the *New York Times* chose to build its new headquarters. The *Herald* had previously chosen a similar site on what became Herald Square, then the center of New York. Adolph Ochs, owner of the *New York Times,* wished for the same visibility. After considering a downtown site at Broadway and Barclay Street, where the Woolworth Building now stands, he realized the uptown flow of the city would make Longacre Square preeminent.

The building, completed in 1904, was the second tallest structure in the city. The triangular site, formed

The Times Tower

by the convergence of Broadway and Seventh Avenue, led to comparisons with The Flatiron Building on Broadway, Fifth Avenue and 23rd Street. However the Flatiron Building, considered New York's first skyscraper, addressed its location with more success. The Times Tower, though called "The second Flatiron Building," was a rectangular building on a triangular piece of land.

The new skyscraper, inspired by Giotto's campanile, was built on the site of the Pabst Hotel. The hotel and previous buildings occupying the site had faced south towards the city proper. But Ochs and his architects realized that the growing city would surround the tower, and so they pointed its front uptown.

The completion of the Italian-Rennaisance style tower on December 31, 1904 was celebrated with a fireworks display, the forerunner to the annual New Year's Eve celebrations.

The 375-foot-tall tower dwarfed its neighbors, none of which rose more than six stories in height. It also extended down 55 feet below the street under the new IRT Subway for which Ochs had lobbied. At one time, the building could be entered directly from the subway, a novel idea at the time.

As the area around the tower grew, so did the newspaper. By 1913, it had grown too large for its building and constructed a new headquarters down the block on 43rd Street. However, the *Times* retained an office for classified-ad placement in the tower.

As news of elections and sports results came into the paper, makeshift banners were hung outside the building. This increased the public's perception of the paper as an important news source. The impromptu celebrations following such announcements made the square a gathering place for important events. In 1928, on the eve of the presidential elections, the Motogram *(q.v.)* moving sign was inaugurated. The Motogram's lights

Times Square as Eisenhower's election is announced   Courtesy Artkraft Strauss.

wrapped around the building, spelling out the news. Perhaps the most important news flashed by the sign was the announcement of the Japanese surrender marking the end to World War II. The V-J day celebration was the most impressive demonstration surrounding the tower.

The Times retained ownership of the building until 1961. The newspaper sold the building to Douglas Leigh *(q.v.),* the designer of many of Times Sqaures most fabulous "spectaculars." Leigh sold the building to the Allied Chemical company, and the outside was stripped of its terra-cotta facade. It reopened in 1966, featuring a continuous marble skin. The stark exterior on street level encouraged gatherings by undesirable characters. As the area declined, the Times Tower, now dubbed the Allied Chemical Tower, turned a blind eye on its surroundings.

In 1974, Allied Chemical sold the building to real estate magnate Alex Parker. He already had leased 23 floors from Allied Chemical before buying the building

for a little over $6 million. Parker decided to call the building Expo America but soon simply called the building One Times Square.

Parker sold the building to Lawrence Linksman and his TSNY Realty Company for over $12 million in 1981. The new ownership is marked by the appearance in 1982 of the Spectacolor Sign. In July 1984, the building was again sold. A partnership bought the building for $16.5 million million dollars and then, one year later, sold it for $20 million.

New York Newsday currently operates the Motogram, the famous moving news "zipper" which runs around the building. Plans for the tower are on hold as the whole 42nd Street Redevelopment Plan comes under reevaluation. Park Tower Realty was the designated developer for the four ponderous office towers on parcels of land including that of the tower. The Johnson-Burgee design called for an Italianate bell tower for the site. The latest plan seems to call for the building to remain as is. Whatever building occupies the site must

The proposed Times Tower

take into account the importance of the location, both historically, geographically and symbolically.

TKTS BOOTH W. 47th Street between Seventh Avenue and Broadway. Architects: Meyers & Schiff, 1973. The TKTS Booth is the Times Square location most sought out by the thousands of tourists who flock to the Square each year. In 1982, over 1.5 million people passed through the TKTS Booth and bought half-price, same-day tickets to Broadway and off-Broadway shows. There are two additional booths, one in the World Trade Center and the other in Brooklyn.

One precedent of the half-price ticket policy was Joe Leblang's discount ticket counter in the basement of Gray's Drugstore during the 1940s. The Theater Development Fund *(q.v.)* used the idea to create the TKTS Booth.

The producers of Broadway's shows were initially wary of the booth. The idea for a half-price ticket grew out of the nature of the theater business. An owner of a clothing store can the next day sell any inventory not sold by closing time. But the theater owner has a perishable inventory—the theater seat. Each performance brings a new inventory that must be sold or lost.

This concept was difficult to explain to many of the producers who knew that a show running at 70% capacity could break even. Proponents of the booth explained to them that the 30% of tickets remaining unsold might mean thousands of dollars of profit for the show. They also pointed out that shows needing 50% of capacity to break even but only running at 40% might make up the needed revenues by selling an additional 20% of its seats through half-price ticket sales.

The public, complaining about rising prices, was quick to discover the booth and flocked to buy the cut-rate tickets. Top shows like *Cats* and *Me and My Girl* seldom used the ticket booth more than once or twice a year. But other, less-popular shows relied on daily ticket booth sales to stay open.

As time went by, more and more producers saw the usefulness of the booth, and it became firmly entrenched in the financing and planning of shows. Ticket prices continue to rise to the point where the half-price ticket of today cost as much as the full-price ticket of yesterday.

This constant inflation of prices has led some producers to question the usefulness of the booth. Some claim that big-ticket shows like *Cats* become expense-account shows, primarily attended by businesspeople and their spouses. Others attend such high priced entertainments as a special event for which they save up over the course of a year. This change in attitude has drastically affected the theater. The public no longer attends the theater as it would a movie but as a special, expensive night out.

Critics of the booth claim that it actually serves to raise the average price of Broadway shows. They argue that the producer, when making up a budget, must compare the cost of mounting and operating the show against the number of seats in the theater and the ticket price of each seat. The half-price booth is accounted for, and the producer depends on a certain number of half-price tickets to be sold for the show to stay on. Since no show can run only on a half-price policy, the

TKTS booth at Duffy Square   Photo Jeff Slotnick.

producer raises regular prices to force up the half-price numbers. Therefore, if the producer needs to sell each ticket at $20 to break even, the producer sets the ticket price at $40, knowing that all the seats won't sell at half-price and that those ticket buyers who can afford the full price will make up the difference—a classic example of the tail wagging the dog.

Furthermore, critics complain that if ticket prices were kept low, more people would attend the theater more regularly and more shows would do better and run longer. They claim that the public perceives those shows that sell half-price tickets at the booth as second-rate.

Whether the booth is a solution to a problem or a cause of the problem may be debatable, but the success of the operation is not. The architectural design of the booth is successful as well. It features canvas banners stretched on metal scaffolding surrounding and disguising the ordinary trailer that serves as a box office. Partly as a result of this design, the architects have received a commission to design the building across the way where the Coca-Cola spectacular stood.

TONY AWARDS   The Tony Awards, or more properly, the Antoinette Perry Awards, are Broadway's equivalent to the Oscars, Emmys and Grammys. Like any such awards, the Tonys have their share of detractors, and these naysayers have a point—the system and its choices aren't perfect. Despite the carping and the competition from many other annual theater awards, the Tonys are the most important of Broadway's awards and have been since their inception in 1947. Dore Schary once wrote:

There are two types of people. One type asserts that awards mean nothing to them. The second type breaks out into tears upon receiving an award, and thanks their mother, father, children, the producer, the director—and, if they can crowd it in—the American Baseball League.

However, I believe that people in the theater who receive this award have a special feeling that makes them cherish the winning of a Tony. It prevents them from going on effusively. The Tony has a special value. It was created to award distinguished achievement in the theater.

Antoinette Perry was a producer, director, actress and active member of the American Theater Wing (*q.v.*). The Wing is the sponsor of the awards named for the lady who gave herself selflessly to its activities. She was Chairperson and Secretary of the Wing during its most active period, that of World War II.

Perry began her theatrical career at the age of 18 in 1906. Her first appearance was in the David Warfield vehicle, *Music Master*. The next year, she starred in David Belasco's (*q.v.*) production of *A Grand Army Man*. In 1909, she retired from acting to raise her family.

In 1922, Antoinette Perry returned to the theater following her husband's death. She acted and later directed many plays. Among her best-known directorial efforts were Preston Sturges' *Strictly Dishonorable* (9/18/29) and Mary Chase's Pulitzer Prize *(q.v.)* winning comedy, *Harvey* (11/1/44).

After her death on June 28, 1946, Jacob Wilk talked to producer John Golden about establishing a memorial in her name. Golden approached the American Theater Wing, which took up the motion. Brock Pemberton was made chairperson of a committee formed to explore the possibilities of the memorial. They decided to honor her with an annual series of awards. A panel of theater professionals was entrusted with selecting the first recipients of the newly erected honor. The first members of that committee were Vera Allen, Brooks Atkinson (see CRITICS), Louise Beck, Kermit Bloomgarden, Clayton Collyer, Jane Cowl, Helen Hayes *(q.v.)*, George Heller, Rudy Karnolt, Burns Mantle, Gilbert Miller, Warren P. Munsell, Solly Pernick, James E. Sauter and Oliver Sayler.

On Easter Sunday, April 6, 1947, the first Tony Awards were handed out. Mickey Rooney, Herb Shriner, Ethel Waters and David Wayne entertained in the Grand Ballroom of the Waldorf Astoria. During the initial years of the Tony Awards, the winners were announced without any mention of the competition. In the first years, the award went to "distinguished" performers, designers, directors, etc. Later they went to the "best" in each category.

The earliest recipients of the Tony Award were Jose Ferrer and Fredric March for dramatic actor; Ingrid Bergman and Helen Hayes for dramatic actress; Patricia Neal for supporting actress (Dramatic) and David Wayne for supporting actor (Musical). Technical awards went to David Ffolkes for his costumes for *Henry VIII* and Lucinda Ballard won in the same category for her work on *Happy Birthday, Another Part of the Forest, Street Scene, John Loves Mary* and *The Chocolate Soldier*. Elia Kazan won for his work as director of *All My Sons,* and the talents of choreographers Michael Kidd and Agnes de Mille were also noted. Special awards went to Dora Chamberlain, Mr. and Mrs. Ira Katzenberg, Jules Leventhal, Burns Mantle, P.A. MacDonald, Arthur Miller *(q.v.)*, Vincent Sardi Sr. (see SARDI's) and Kurt Weill *(q.v.)*. That was the extent of the first year's honorees.

In later years, other award categories came and went. Stage technicians was a category in 1948 and from 1950 through 1964. At one time, there was an award for conductors. Producers had their own category once, now they share the award for best play or musical. Music and lyrics received separate awards for a few years in the late sixties and early seventies.

The first winners of the Tony Awards received a scroll documenting their honor. In addition, the men were presented with a cigarette case and the women a compact. The United Scenic Artists held a contest for a new design. The winner was Herman Rosse. His design was a medallion featuring the masks of comedy and tragedy on one side and a portrait of Antoinette Perry on the other. The new award was first issued in 1949. The Tony nominations, four in each category, were announced for the first time in 1956, and usually only one winner was announced in each category.

The Tony Awards have always had media exposure. The first ceremonies, held in hotel ballrooms, were broadcast locally on WOR radio and carried on the Mutual Radio Network. In 1956, the awards were televised locally for the first time. Channel 5, a member of the old Du Mont network, broadcast the awards. In 1967, the Tony Awards were broadcast nationally for the first time. Alexander Cohen, a Broadway producer, was in charge of the television broadcast.

The Tony television broadcast has always been considered the most entertaining and sophisticated of the many show-business award shows. However, in recent years, the ceremony has received a fair share of criticism. Critics charged the show with poor writing, inclusion of television stars as hosts rather than Broadway personalities and a second-rate variety show feel to the proceedings. In 1987, the television ceremony was broadcast for the first time without producer Alexander Cohen at the helm. The 1988 Tony Award broadcast received the lowest ratings in its history. Many have claimed that the Tonys have sold out to the needs of television and just become a poorly produced advertisement for current Broadway hits. Numbers on the awards are not even presented live. Rather they are pretaped. In the 1988 awards, not only was the *Phantom of the Opera* segment pretaped, but the actors were lipsyncing to a soundtrack. (In the theater, many of Sarah Brightman's high notes were taped while she pretended to sing.)

The Tony procedures have also come under attack on occasion. An Eligibility Committee decides on possible nominees. In recent years, some leading performers have been nominated in the supporting category. This was arranged sometimes so that they would have less fierce competition.

The Eligibility Committee sends its list to the Nominating Committee, which decides on the actual nominations. Unfortunately, this committee is made up of members who are removed from the Broadway scene. Because the Theater Wing doesn't want the committee to be accused of favoritism, the Nominating Committee is composed of members who are academicians, excritics, theater curators and ex-theater professionals. Because many of these committee members live outside the New York area, and because some shows play only a limited number of performances, the rules read, "each eligible production and performer shall have been seen by as many members as possible." Since some shows are never seen by any members of the committee or by few, the nominations are skewed towards the long-run hits.

Because of the current scarcity of quality musicals and the general decline in the number of productions, some categories have less than qualified nominees simply to make up the required four nominations in each category. On occasion, the committee has decided to limit the nominations to three or even two in each category.

The voters are made up of selected members of Actors' Equity Association (q.v.), The Dramatists Guild (q.v.), the Society of Stage Directors and Choreographers and the United Scene Artists. Members of the press on the first or second night press lists and producers who are members of the New York Theater and Producers, Inc. (q.v.) and the Board of Directors of the American Theater Wing are also allowed to vote. Press agents are not allowed to vote. The Wing feels they would not be able to overcome their urge to vote only for shows on which they have worked.

The voters must certify that they have seen all performances in each category. This is, of course, impossible. Obviously all 560 or so voters can't have seen all the nominated shows, especially those that closed after only one performance.

There have been a few major gaffs. One such "mistake" occurred in 1972 when Stephen Sondheim (q.v.) and James Goldman's musical *Follies* won seven Tony Awards, including those for Actress, Director, Score, Scenic Designer, Costume Designer, Choreographer and Lighting Designer. Nonetheless, *Two Gentlemen of Verona*, winner of the book award, carried off the award for Best Musical. Mistakes have been made in at least two instances when the wrong performer was nominated because the committee mistook the actor for another who should have been the actual nominee.

The Tony Award can mean life or death to a marginally successful play. Winning a Tony Award is a powerful publicity tool and can result in thousands of dollars in additional revenues. The Tonys have also had an impact on the theater season proper. It's no surprise that a majority of productions open in the spring at the end of the season so they'll be fresh in Tony voters' minds. In fact, the week before the nomination cutoff date sees a flurry of activity. Some shows have postponed their opening nights until after the Tony cutoff date so they would not look bad by receiving no nominations.

The Tony Award may not be perfect, but it is recognized as the leading theatrical award, and its impact on the theater is enormous.

As Jule Styne (q.v.) once commented, "The curious thing about awards is that one receives them for work one does not expect to receive them for, and does not receive them for work one does. For instance, I received the Tony for *Hallelujah, Baby!*—and not for *Gypsy!* But, the Tony, which stands for excellence in the theater is an honor whenever it comes!"

TOWN HALL 123 W. 43rd Street. Architect: McKim, Mead & White. Town Hall, a 1,498-seat concert/lecture hall has enjoyed a long history of distinguished offerings, including political meetings, readings, film showings, concerts and radio broadcasts. Although it was eclipsed by the newer Lincoln Center, Town Hall is currently battling for a rebirth.

Town Hall opened in 1921 as a lecture hall operated by the League for Political Education. The League rented out the hall to other political organizations that hosted speakers and conventions. According to the *New York Times,* the hall was conceived as "a kind of uptown Cooper Union, on the theory that efficient democratic government and healthy democratic life require a suitable meeting place for the public discussion of subjects related to the common welfare."

Speakers in the hall's early history included Booker T. Washington, William Jennings Bryan, Theodore Roosevelt and Buckminster Fuller. Margaret Sanger, lecturing on birth control, was arrested on the stage of Town Hall and taken to the 47th Street police station. The hall, which also presented silent films, hosted readings by such authors as Thomas Mann, Henry James, John Galsworthy, W.H. Auden and William Butler Yeats.

Almost from the start, the hall was regarded as a top flight concert hall. Jascha Heifetz, Fritz Kreisler, Wanda Landowska, Bela Bartok, Sergei Rachmaninoff, Mischa

Town Hall

Elman and Kirsten Flagstad all performed on its stage. Such notable classical singers and musicians as Lotte Lehman, Gina Bachauer, Joan Sutherland, Marian Anderson, Andres Segovia and Elisabeth Schwarzkopf made their debuts at Town Hall. A number of jazz musicians, including Eddie Condon, made Town Hall their home when playing for large audiences.

From 1935 to 1956, the theater hosted "America's Town Meetings of the Air," a series of public forums, lectures, speeches and debates. Among the notables who spoke on national radio via the "Town Meetings" were Eleanor Roosevelt, Winston Churchill and Richard Nixon.

When Lincoln Center was built, Town Hall lost much of its cachet. Today, after a total renovation that was completed in 1984, the hall books a variety of ethnic theater and dance companies that could not otherwise afford to perform in New York. An especially successful series at the theater are the semiannual productions of New York's only Yiddish theater company. Other companies that account for Town Hall's 90% capacity record include the Philharmonia Virtuosi, the annual jazz festival, the People's Symphony and a children's theater series that entertains 100,000 youngsters annually.

TRAFALGAR THEATER See NEDERLANDER THEATER.

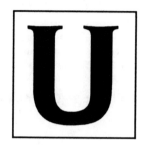

URIS THEATRE See GERSHWIN THEATER.

VARIETY "The Show Business Bible," *Variety*, has served the entertainment community with honesty and impartiality since its founding over 80 years ago. The success of the newspaper is all the more remarkable in view of the remarkable changes in the entertainment field since its inception. The paper has recognized these changes and has modified its viewpoint and content in order to remain the top show-business publication.

Variety was founded on December 16, 1905, by a young editor, Sime Silverman. Silverman, an avid baseball fan, was in love with vaudeville in all its many forms. He was equally enthralled with seal acts, plate spinners and the top comics. He had the rare fortune to be stage struck without the conceit that he might one day succeed as a performer. Silverman realized that his talent was writing, and so he wrote about his first love, vaudeville.

His first break came when George Graham Rice published the first edition of the *Daily American* in 1899. Rice's paper was designed as a competitor to the *Morning Telegraph*. To achieve success, Rice followed the example of many of his contemporaries by simply hiring the best staff members off his rival's paper.

One of these, Joshua Lowitke, secretary to editor Leander Richardson, urged Silverman to begin writing for the new paper. Silverman accepted the job over his father's objections and under the name "The Man in the Third Row" began publishing reviews.

The *American* was a success for a brief while until the Post Office closed it down. It seems that the owner only wanted the paper as a means to advertise his bookie joints. This didn't sit well with the government, and soon the staff was unemployed.

Richardson and Lowitke returned to the *Telegraph* and found an opening for Silverman when the vaudeville critic Epes W. Sargent quit. This job proved only slightly more profitable than his last. After two weeks,

Silverman, writing under the pseudonym "Robert Spear," was fired for writing unduly harsh criticism. What the paper was actually worried about was losing the advertising of the acts Silverman panned. This happened when the comedy team Redford and Winchester canceled a Christmas ad because of a Silverman pan.

So Silverman was unemployed again. While at Pabst's Columbus Circle Restaurant, Silverman drew the logo of *Variety* on a tablecloth. His idea was to form his own paper that would report honestly without regard for advertising dollar or the power of the great vaudeville empires of Keith/Albee (see E.F. ALBEE), Pantages or Loew.

Silverman picked the name *Variety* after the English word for music hall entertainments. To Silverman, it reflected the whole scope of entertainment better than the term vaudeville. Even at this time, he envisioned coverage of a wider spectrum of entertainment than simply the stage, although cinema was in its infancy and radio and television were not yet on the horizon.

Silverman borrowed $1,500 from his father-in-law and proceeded to gather a staff. The first two employees were John J. O'Connor, a one-time usher at the Alhambra Theater, and Al Greason. Silverman set up a one-room office with $40 worth of used furniture at the Knickerbocker Building on Broadway and 38th Street.

Variety began slowly to make a name for itself, and in 1906 Silverman increased the staff. Joe Raymond was appointed associate to O'Connor, who had been appointed advertising solicitor. Sam Mitnick was hired as circulation manager.

The new staff went after their tasks enthusiastically. After all, the ad reps received a 25% commission on sales. O'Connor went to the scene of his most recent job, the Alhambra, but neither Matt Keefe, a singer, nor Tony Pearl, a harpist, opted for ads. O'Connor was luckier at Proctor's Fifth Avenue. Grace Cameron, a leading entertainer, bought the first full-page ad for $50. Miss Cameron received a bonus for her support: Silverman threw in the front cover as thanks.

Joe Cook, the monologist and comedian, bought the cover for $25 in one of those early issues. *Variety*'s success, as well as Cook's, can be gauged by the fact that only a few years later, Cook bought the cover for $25,000.

By 1907, Silverman was ready to expand *Variety*'s field. O'Connor was dispatched on a 14-month voyage from vaudeville house to vaudeville house, drumming up business. He would talk up the newspaper to dealers who previously had carried only the *Clipper*. He then went to the theaters and informed the actors of *Variety*'s success and tried to drum up advertising and subscriptions. In order to expand the paper's coverage, O'Connor put a number of correspondents on retainer. In return for submitting news and reviews to the home office, the lucky reporters received free passes to their local theaters. Because *Variety* couldn't afford to pay, these early contributors were vaudeville buffs and other neophytes. As the paper's fortunes rose, Silverman replaced his early stringers with real reporters. He still didn't pay them, but at least they were professionals in the field.

Branch offices were opened by O'Connor in San Francisco and Chicago before he returned to New York to gather the fruits of his labors. Little by little, *Variety* grew and advertising rates increased with the circulation.

Ed Reynard, a well-known ventriloquist, was the first to buy a long-term advertisement. He paid $145 for a 2-inch ad that was included in the paper for a full year. Reynard proved lucky when Silverman flipped him double or nothing and lost. Silverman didn't stop there. He proposed to Reynard another flip of a coin. If Silverman won, Reynard would pay $500. If Reynard won, he would receive free advertising for the life of the paper. The coin was tossed and Silverman lost. So Reynard received a free ad for life and Silverman received nothing for his first long-term advertisement. Reynard's ad continued to run until he begged Silverman to discontinue it when *Variety* was blacklisted by vaudeville kingpin Edward Albee *(q.v.)* of the Keith-Albee chain in 1913.

Albee, who expected only good reviews befitting his position as the major vaudeville mogul in the country, resented *Variety*'s impartial attitude; He vowed to blacklist any performers advertising in the paper. Reynard was caught in the middle. On the one hand, he was receiving hundreds of dollars in free publicity. On the other hand, the ad wasn't doing him much good since he couldn't work in the majority of vaudeville houses.

Albee turned up the heat on *Variety* by convincing music publishers that if they retained their advertising

in *Variety* they would never hear their numbers performed in an Albee theater. This was a major setback to Silverman, who depended on the publishers to take out half- and full-page ads.

Silverman refused to give up the battle. Albee's competitors advanced Silverman credit, and he barely managed to keep the paper afloat. By 1914, both sides were exhausted, and the feud was clearly doing neither side any good. Albee had his assistant J.J. Murdock sign an agreement allowing advertising in *Variety* by Albee artists and allowing the *Variety* reporters into Albee's theaters.

Silverman again expanded the staff, known as "muggs." Joshua Lowitke, who got Silverman started in the first place, joined the paper. The staff called him Joe Lowe because he signed his articles "Jolo." Silverman had insisted that his employees adopt abbreviations for their bylines. Since Silverman signed his work "Sime," all others opted for four-letter pseudonyms out of respect for the boss.

Abel Green, who eventually took over for Sime became Abel; Arthur Unger, West Coast bureau chief became Ung; Jack Pulaski, the legitimate-theater editor became Ibee, although the office staff dubbed him, "The Man in the Iron Mask" because of his disfigured face.

Variety was also noted for its contributions to the English language. Its slang *(q.v.)* gave the paper its special flavor. *Variety*'s two best-known headlines have won almost legendary status. Silverman wrote the first when the stock market crashed in October of 1929. The *Variety* headline blared "WALL ST. LAYS AN EGG." When the stock market fell again in 1962, *Variety*'s headline was "WALL STREET, SON OF EGG." In 1987, when Wall Street made its biggest fall, *Variety* headlined, "WALL STREET LAYS AN EGG: THE SEQUEL." After Silverman's death, *Variety* kept up the tradition with a headline describing how farmers rejected Hollywood's attempts to woo them with rural movies. The classic banner read "STICKS NIX HICK PIX."

Surprisingly, the year that the stock market crashed and America was sent into the Depression was the first year *Variety* showed a profit.

Silverman was a strong personality and a strong editor, and for a man so loquacious he was sometimes amazingly quiet. Shortly before his death, he asked Abel Green into his office. Silverman stood up and motioned for Green to sit in his chair. Silverman said, "You sit here, Abel," and left the room. And that is how Green became the second editor of *Variety*, shortly before Silverman's death in 1933.

Abel Green brought to the editor's desk a style different from Silverman's but just as unique. Green wasn't a particularly good reporter nor was he especially good on facts. Once, the gossip column, dubbed "Chatter," was forced to admit "The attorneys for Mrs. Johnathan Bell Small announce that she did not give birth to a baby last week in Doctor's Hospital." Mr. Small was the father so Green assumed his wife was the happy mother. It was his mistress who gave birth to Mr. Small's progeny.

When the *Mona Lisa* was lent by the Vatican to the United States, the "Europe to US" column listed Mona Lisa among the celebrities making the trans-Atlantic crossing. Green didn't recognize the name and wondered if she was "some stripper."

But Green was a crackerjack editor, and his writing had all the flavor of his predecessor. Someone once remarked, "He writes faster than I can read." The paper flourished under Green's leadership with Harold Erichs acting as business manager.

Green was described by Les Brown, the television critic, as "not exactly forward looking. He was wedded to a show biz that was—and when that changed, he was wedded to nostalgia."

Silverman's grandson Syd inherited the paper when Hattie Silverman, Sime's wife, died at age 100. Though only 19 and a sophomore at Princeton, he assumed ownership with a watchful eye.

Green continued as editor until his death in 1973. Les Brown believed himself to be heir to the throne, but Syd Silverman took over operations. Syd is a quiet, introspective man whose personality couldn't be further removed from his grandfather's or Abel Green's.

Variety had over 50 people employed in its New York office at 154 West 46th Street, its headquarters since 1922. There are also 35 staffers in Hollywood who put out *Daily Variety,* the West Coast edition of the national weekly. There are also offices ranging from one- to six-person operations in London, Paris, Toronto, Washington, Madrid, Sydney and Rome. Almost 200 additional stringers report from around the world.

Circulation of the weekly *Variety* tops 50,000 issues, with the daily printing almost 20,000 copies each day. The news from the daily is often included in the weekly edition.

Variety covers movies, radio, personal appearances, television, legitimate theater, music and publishing. Special issues are devoted to spotlighting the Cannes Film Festival, the American film market, the National Association of Recording Merchandisers and other special industry events.

History was made when *Variety* was sold to a European conglomerate, Cahners Publishing Company, in July 1987. The organization moved to the Cahners offices at 32nd Street and Park Avenue South on November 10, 1987. The staff thought up the headline "VARIETY ANKLES GREAT WHITE WAY." *Variety* has lost some of its snap and spit, but it has prospered as never before. Like show business itself,

Variety has become blander and more fiscally oriented, and that is both good and bad for the industry and *Variety.*

VARIETY NEW YORK DRAMA CRITICS POLL Beginning in 1939, the theater trade newspaper *Variety* (q.v.) has published the results of a poll of New York-based newspaper and magazine critics. The categories include best performance by a male in a straight play, best performance by a female lead in a straight play, best performance by a male lead in a musical, best performance by a female lead in a musical, best performance by an actor in a supporting part and best performance by an actress in a supporting part. Awards were also given to the most promising new actor and most promising new actress. Additional awards include those for best director, best scenic designer, best costume designer, best composer, best lyricist, best librettist and most promising playwright.

VENICE THEATER See JOLSON'S 59TH STREET THEATER.

VICTORIA THEATER (1) Northwest corner of 42nd Street and 7th Avenue. Architect: J.B. McElfatrick & Co. Opening: March 2, 1899; *The Reign of Error.* Oscar Hammerstein I (q.v.) was the true pioneer of Times Square. His Olympia (q.v.) theater complex was the first entertainment attraction in what was then Longacre Square. Hammerstein's decision to build the Victoria was just another example of the amazing recuperative powers and self-confidence that allowed him to rise from the ashes of his fortunes again and again.

Just the year before, Hammerstein had lost the Olympia to the New York Life Insurance Company. After this setback, Hammerstein, then over $1 million in debt, passed an acquaintance on Broadway and offered him a cigar. Hammerstein commented, "I have lost my theaters, my home and everything else. My fortune consists of two cigars. I will share it with you."

Undaunted by his losses, Hammerstein summoned his energy and convinced the owner of the Market Livery Company on the corner of Seventh Avenue and 42nd Street to lease it to him for 20 years with no money down. Terms of the lease were reported to be $10,000 for the first year and $7,000 each succeeding year.

However, having the lease on the property didn't mean he had a theater. Hammerstein sold patents on his inventions to raise capital for the theater building. His brother Arthur (q.v.), a successful building contractor, oversaw the construction of the theater, which was scheduled to open in early 1899. Friends and associates were skeptical. One bet Hammerstein a suit of clothes that the building would be a year late in opening.

As construction continued, the question of what to put in the theater became more and more important. Hammerstein had already demonstrated his penchant for opera with the opening of his Harlem Opera House in 1889 and the Manhattan Opera House where Macy's now stands. But his forays into lighter fare had always been more successful than his operatic endeavors, notwithstanding the spectacular failure of the Olympia.

Hammerstein sent a letter to the Superintendent of Buildings stating that "the premises to be erected are not intended for theatrical or operatic performances, that there will be no excavation, room or cellar underneath a stage platform, that there will be no fly galleries, scene rooms, carpenter shop, or paintframe, . . . that we shall not provide or keep what is known as theatrical scenery on the premises, nor erect or provide stationary appurtenances necessary for performances or theatrical or operatic character; also, that no application for theatrical license will be made and that the premises when completed are to be devoted to attractions only, permitted under the existing concert licenses." Hammerstein wanted a license for a concert hall, since a theater license was much more demanding and would require a greater outlay of cash.

It was decided to open the 1,250-seat house with a variety policy. Despite what he told the Building Department, he planned on presenting vaudeville and musical comedy, both just coming into their own. The first show, *The Reign of Error,* featured a pair of "Dutch" comics, the Rogers Brothers. A poor man's Weber and Fields, the Rogers Brothers were nevertheless successful and their offering proved popular with audiences.

Though the paint was still wet on the walls, the theater opened on schedule and Hammerstein arrived for opening night wearing the new suit won on his bet. Arthur Hammerstein described the Hammerstein's unique way of theater design—"The reason the coloring was white and gold was that we had no money for paint—the 'white' was only the unpainted plaster. We covered the supporting beams with cast cornices, which I made in my shop, and highlighted the ornament with gilt. We modeled the cornices with a leaf encircling a hole for electric light bulbs to be inserted, thereby eliminating the expense of electrical fixtures."

Reportedly Arthur had his workers save every brick and board from the demolished building for use in constructing the Victoria. The carpeting was purchased for 25¢ a yard from a liner that was being refitted with new carpeting.

The *Dramatic Mirror* reported: "The decorations are in white and canary, with a little gold here and there. The effect is pretty and the house has a very bright, cheery look, which is emphasized by the warm, red colors in the chairs, carpets and hangings."

Above the Victoria, Hammerstein built a roof garden, which he named the Venetian Terrace Garden.

The space, decorated with greenery and over 2,000 electric lights, contained a small stage surrounded on all sides by the audience. The Venetian Terrace Garden opened on June 26, 1899. The theater in the round concept made hearing the acts difficult, so the theater usually booked silent acts like acrobats and jugglers. The next year, Hammerstein built the Republic Theater *(q.v.)* next to the Victoria and in 1901 built The Paradise Gardens on their shared roofs. Usually, the Victoria would be closed in the summer and the Paradise Gardens would open. Seldom were both theaters open at the same time. The Paradise Gardens' theater proper was on the Victoria's roof with a glass-enclosed auditorium allowing for an open-air feeling to the hall. On nice nights, the windows were opened to allow breezes to ventilate the hall. The Gardens offered a "Swiss Farm" with live barnyard animals on the Republic's roof and the first singing waiters in New York.

The *New York Dramatic Mirror* described the Paradise Gardens as having "a spacious platform that has tables and chairs set about, and a little pond of real water wherin disport sundry truly live ducks, not to mention a couple of property boats, one labeled 'Shamrock III.' Also there is a real water wheel that works, and a beautiful more or less arabesque arch with illuminated panels of stained glass that artistically disguises the customarily uninspiring institution known as a fire escape. Over the duck pond there is a pretty rustic bridge that takes one up to a still higher platform that boasts a Hollandish village with a little cottage, a practicable windmill, a cow-shed with property cow peering out at window, and a vegetable garden containing sprouting cabbages, potatoes, and all that sort of thing."

The following year Hammerstein leased the Republic to David Belasco *(q.v.),* who promptly renamed it the Belasco Theatre. The Victoria offered a musical *Sweet Marie,* which premiered on October 10, 1901. The show was ascribed to R. Jackson and W. Brown, but Broadway wags felt that it had actually been written by Hammerstein. The *Dramatic Mirror* stated that "there was scarcely a chance for a doubt that the managerial genius had himself written and composed the new offering just as the programme confessed that he had staged it." In any event, he had contributed a song to the proceedings. *Sweet Marie* closed after only 28 performances.

The theater presented the great actress Eleonora Duse for two weeks in November 1902. Hammerstein next presented Blanch Walsh in Tolstoy's *Resurrection* (2/17/03). The production was a huge success, despite a review in the *New York Times* that called it "a tinned-soupy Siberio-religious melodrama, with only a squint of Tolstoi." *Resurrection* ran for 88 performances at the Victoria and over a year and a half on the road. Hammerstein made more than $100,000 in profit.

The Paradise Gardens was still doing great business.

Paradise Roof Garden

The *New York Dramatic Mirror* reviewed the proceedings in the Swiss Farm. "The simple minded citizens of the great metropolis are more than eager to expend their good money for the glimpse of pastoral life that the Paradise Gardens afford and to contemplate in almost childish glee the crops that are propagated on the roof. Mr. Hammerstein's agricultural exhibition is now bigger, brighter, and better than ever, the corn belt is particularly prolific, and the prospects are excellent for the potatoes and cabbages. The ducks are even more blase than last year, but the chickens are most condescending and communicative. The cow's demeanor continues to be very 'up-stage,' and the windmill and the water wheel squeak on joyously. The attendance is enormous all the time."

In 1904, after a series of short runs by unimportant musical comedies, Hammerstein decided to change gears yet again to a strict vaudeville policy. He had always been successful with vaudeville, and he preferred to direct his attention to his opera productions. He engaged his son Willie (*q.v.*) to put the bills together. Willie, taught by vaudeville booker William Morris, proved a genius at this, and the theater continued to be financially successful. The Hammersteins assured their success and ability to weather dry periods at the box office through a slightly shady policy—they never printed the price of admission on tickets. Thus, for an act that was a big draw, the box office could command high prices. When the weather was good and patrons tended to stay outdoors in the fresh air, the ticket prices could be reduced as a draw.

Initially, the Victoria only presented high class vaudeville. The *Dramatic Mirror* opined that "Mr. Hammerstein is providing bills of extraordinary merit, using more big headliners, than any other house in the country." Each show at the Victoria was concluded with the showing of a newsreel.

As time passed, Willie turned the Victoria into a unique vaudeville house. Instead of offering top acts of the day, he created his own attractions with a combination of brilliant showmanship and sheer gall. In 1904, the Victoria began to present sensational acts right off the pages of the yellow press. The father-son team continually filled all 1,200 seats and all 30 boxes with acts like Conrad and Graham, two women who were convicted of shooting W.E.D. Stokes in the Ansonia Hotel. The two women had never appeared before the public and had to be coached on how to walk, talk and stand in front of an audience. The duo was billed as "The Shooting Stars." Unfortunately, the pair proved to have no stage ability whatsoever. But this didn't daunt the resourceful Hammersteins. They simply had Loney Haskell lecture about them while the two murderers stood by uncomfortably. The $300 they each received no doubt helped ease some of the embarrassment the two killers may have felt.

After Willie presented one murderess, Hammerstein was asked by a newspaperman whether she was to be held over for another week. Hammerstein responded, "Not unless she shoots somebody else." In 1905, Hammerstein presented The Cherry Sisters, proudly billed as "America's Worst Act." The audience was urged to throw fruit and vegetables at the two Midwesterners. To protect them, Willie had a net lowered between the audience and the hapless stars. Though it slightly dampened the fun it saved the two from concussion by legumes.

That same year, Willie presented "Captain Bloom's Demonstration of Marconi's Wireless Telegraphy" on the Paradise Gardens stage. This was the first demonstration of radio in vaudeville. He also presented "Abdul Kadar and His Three Wives in an Exhibition of Rapid Painting." Kadar was actually a Swiss artist and his three wives were his wife, daughter and sister-in-law. They arrived in the United States but were briefly not allowed entry when Willie anonymously tipped off authorities that they were not who they seemed. Willie also alerted the newspapers.

Once in the country, the trio made the rounds of the New York hotels but were refused entry, another part of the elaborate stunt (*q.v.*). Finally they ended up at the apartment Willie had booked for them.

Willie, in a constant search for the unusual person or circumstance to book for the Victoria's stage, found "Sober Sue." The billing this time was, "Sober Sue— You Can't Make Her Laugh." Top comedians of the day, Willie Collier, Sam Bernard, Eddie Leonard and Louis Mann all took the stage of the Victoria and tried to convulse the dead-panned woman. But none of them could win the $1,000 reward Willie had posted. Willie only paid Sue $25 a week but he did throw in a few $30 dresses for her costumes. At the end of her engagement, Willie confessed that Sue would never smile for her facial muscles were paralyzed.

Another typical act at the Victoria was Dorando, the Italian runner. The winner of the 1908 Olympics Marathon stood on stage like a recent immigrant while Loney Haskell lectured. A song, "Run, Run, Run, You Son of a Gun, Dorando," was written in his honor.

By 1906, Willie had decided to pepper the attractions with stars of real talent. Will Rogers, the Four Keatons, including the youngster Buster, Al Jolson *(q.v.)*, Weber and Fields, Fanny Brice *(q.v.)*, Houdini and Fred Karno's comedy troupe featuring Stan Laurel and Charlie Chaplin, all appeared on the Victoria's stage.

Willie also instituted the policy of presenting top New York cartoonists at the Victoria. Winsor McCay, Bud Fisher, Rube Goldberg and Tad Dorgan presented "chalk talks" that were great flops but did result in great publicity. Willie also presented for the first time in New York the new motion picture, *The Great Train Robbery*. The film, shot in nearby Fort Lee, New Jersey, ran for three weeks. Another film shown on the Victoria stage was the beginning of the 1908 New York to Paris auto race. Naturally, the start of the race took place directly in front of the Victoria Theater.

Of course, not all the acts were made up of talented performers. Upstairs at the Paradise Gardens, Willie had La Belle Baigneuse, Lalla Selbini, juggle while riding a bicycle. The gimmick was that she performed the act in a bathing suit. *Variety (q.v.)* reported the act was "frankly indecent." Willie later presented A. Z. Marino the "Auto Defier" who laid down upon the Victoria stage while an automobile containing four men ran over him.

When temperatures rose outside, Willie convinced patrons that the Victoria's auditorium was 10 degrees cooler by exhibiting a thermometer resting on an artfully concealed block of ice.

In 1908, the Paradise Gardens was renamed Hammerstein's Roof Garden. The most successful act to play the Victoria was Gertrude Hoffman, a popular dancer and choreographer who performed Salome's dance. The risque attraction earned $20,000 in ticket sales in its first week. Hoffman, whose specialty was dancing with the head of John the Baptist, remained at the Victoria for 22 weeks. This marked the beginning of a long fascination with Salome, which resulted in the writing of several popular songs ("Sadie Salome Go Home" by Irving Berlin *(q.v.)* among them).

Willie quit the Victoria in 1912 (the year Houdini appeared on the roof along with a real skating rink) when he discovered that behind his back his father was negotiating the future of the Victoria. By 1913, Hammerstein had sold their exclusive vaudeville booking rights to the Times Square area. This mistake would signal the beginning of the end for the Victoria.

At Arthur's insistence, Willie rejoined the Victoria and before its final fall presented one of its most infamous attractions. The act featured Evelyn Nesbitt, the wife of Harry K. Thaw who killed architect Stanford White in a jealous rage. Willie billed her as "The Girl on the Red Velvet Swing." Nesbitt also danced with her partner Jack Clifford, but it wasn't her terpsichorean talents that brought in the crowds. During their theatrical engagement in 1913, a miracle occurred. Harry K. Thaw escaped from jail. The resultant publicity was stupendous. Willie even got credit for masterminding the escape to coincide with Nesbitt's opening. Nesbitt earned the theater $175,000.

A series of events brought an end to the Hammerstein dynasty. The Palace Theatre *(q.v.)* was quickly taking the leading role in vaudeville presentation in Times Square. On June 10, 1914, Willie Hammerstein died. That same year, two of Hammerstein's other sons, Abe and Harry, also passed away. Arthur took over the management of the Victoria but did not have the showmanship of Willie. Meanwhile, Hammerstein went into an agreement with the Metropolitan Opera, which refused him the right to produce opera in New York. He was forced to convert his Lexington Opera House to a movie theater. The next year, 1915, Hammerstein was through; at the age of 68, he sold the Lexington and Victoria Theaters. Morose over his forced retirement, he died only four years later.

Hammerstein leased the Victoria to the man who would take over his mantle as the premier showman in New York—S.L. ("Roxy") Rothafel *(q.v.)*. On Sunday May 2, 1915, the Victoria Theater closed following a week of vaudeville dedicated to Willie Hammerstein. In its 17 years as the premier vaudeville house in New York, the Victoria grossed $20 million and netted $5 million.

Buster Keaton once wrote that the Victoria was "America's greatest vaudeville theater. That grand old showcase was in its day everything—and perhaps a little more—than the Palace became later. Any oldtimer will tell you, Hammerstein's Victoria was vaudeville at its all-time best." George Jessel and Will Rogers concurred with Keaton's opinion.

Roxy gutted the theater and created the Rialto *(q.v.)* movie theater. In 1935, the theater was again redesigned and became what is now known as the New Rialto. This Brandt Theater specialized in the usual kung-fu and second-run attraction found on 42nd Street. The Brandts remodeled it again in 1980, opened a Broadway entrance and attempted to present legitimate attractions at the theater. But none caught on, and the theater returned to showing kung-fu movies. In 1987, the Cineplex Odeon chain took over the theater's operations and remodeled the interior. The theater reopened as the Cineplex Odeon Warner.

VICTORIA THEATER (2)   See GAIETY THEATER.

VICTORY THEATRE   See REPUBLIC THEATRE.

VIRGINIA THEATER 245 W. 52nd Street. Architect: C. Howard Crane. Opening: As Guild Theater, April 13, 1925; *Caesar and Cleopatra*. The Theater Guild (*q.v.*), the most important producing entity of the 1920s and 1930s, was using the Garrick Theater to present its shows. The Guild decided it needed its own building to house its productions and provide space for its school, so it commissioned C. Howard Crane, Kenneth Franzheim, and Charles Bettis to design the theater. Set designers Norman Bel Geddes and Lee Simonson consulted on the project, which resulted in the Guild Theater.

At its opening, the theater was called "Home for All the Arts of the Theater." It existed "for drama, for beauty, for ideas." Strangely, the architects decided to build the theater on the second floor of the "Italian-style" building with a Spanish-tile roof. Despite the design talents involved, the Guild was judged as less than a success by artists and audiences. Lawrence Langner, the founder of the Theater Guild wrote, "We made the ghastly mistake of providing a theater with all the stage space necessary for a repertory of plays without enough seating capacity to provide the income necessary to support the repertory." The design of the auditorium was also deemed boring by audiences who were used to the European-style interior decorations of most Broadway theaters.

The Theater Guild opened the new house with a production of George Bernard Shaw's *Caesar and Cleopatra*, starring Helen Hayes (*q.v.*). President Calvin Coolidge, in Washington, threw a switch that illuminated the theater on opening night. The theater housed some of the finest work on Broadway. The Guild's eighth season began with Alfred Lunt and Lynn Fontanne (*q.v.*) in George Bernard Shaw's *Arms and the Man* (9/14/25; 181 performances). Ferenc Molnar's *The Glass Slipper* (10/19/65; 65 performances) was the next attraction, but after playing to the Theater Guild's 15,000 subscribers, it closed. During this time, the Theater Guild continued to present works at other theaters, while hits played the Guild.

The Lunts were the Theater Guild's chief acting asset. They appeared together and seperately in several productions at the Guild Theater, including *Goat Song* (1/25/26; 58 performances); *At Mrs. Beam's* (4/26/26; 222 performances); *Juarez and Maximilian* (10/11/26; 42 performances); *The Brothers Karamazov* (1/3/27; 56 performances); S.N. Behrman's *The Second Man* (4/11/27; 178 performances); Shaw's *The Doctor's Dilemma* (11/21/27; 115 performances); *Caprice* (12/31/28; 178 performances) and Behrman's *Meteor* (12/23/29; 92 performances). Lunt was featured in Eugene O'Neill's *Marco Millions* (1/9/28; 102 performances) and Lynn Fontanne starred in *Pygmalion* (11/1526; 143 performances).

While the Lunts were in rehearsal, other actors were featured on the Guild's stage. Edward G. Robinson was featured in Pirandello's *Right You Are If You Think You Are* (2/23/27; 58 performances). Dudley Digges played Mephistopheles in Goethe's *Faust* (10/8/28; 48 performances). In November 1928, Winifred Lenihan, Helen Westley, Gale Sondergaard and Dudley Digges were in Shaw's *Major Barbara* (11/19/28; 73 performances) directed by Philip Moeller. Otto Kruger, Claude Rains, Alice Brady and Gale Sondergaard opened the 12th season with *Karl and Anna* (10/7/29; 49 performances). Rouben Mamoulian directed the next production, *The Game of Love and Death* (11/25/29; 48 performances) with Alice Brady, Otto Kruger and Claude Rains.

Turgenev's *A Month in the Country* (7/17/30; 72 performances) starred Alla Nazimova, Dudley Digges and Douglas Dumbrille. Katia the maid was played by Hortense Alden, better known as Katharine Hepburn. The 12th season of the Theater Guild was brought to a close with the third edition of *The Garrick Gaieties* (10/16/30; 12 performances), a musical revue. It featured Sterling Holloway, Hildegarde Halliday, Imogene Coca and, later in the run, Rosalind Russell.

Lunt and Fontanne returned to the Guild stage in Maxwell Anderson's *Elizabeth the Queen* (11/3/30; 145 performances). The next production, *Midnight* (12/29/30; 48 performances), was undistinguished except for the inclusion in the cast of Clifford Odets. Franchot Tone, Helen Westley, June Walker, Lee Strasberg and Woodward (Tex) Ritter were among the cast in *Green Grow the Lilacs* (1/26/31; 64 performances). The play gained notice again when it was adapted for the musical *Oklahoma!* (1943).

Most of the Theater Guild's larger and more ambitious productions were staged at the Martin Beck Theatre (*q.v.*). One of its finest productions, however, opened at the Guild Theater on October 26, 1931. This was Eugene O'Neill's *Mourning Becomes Electra* (158 performances). The five-hour long production starred Alla Nazimova and Alice Brady. Shaw's *Too True to Be Good* (4/4/32; 56 performances) was not a hit, despite a cast including Beatrice Lillie, Hope Williams, Leo G. Carroll and Claude Rains. The next play was a dramatization of Pearl Buck's *The Good Earth* (10/17/32; 56 performances) with Alla Nazimova, Sydney Greenstreet, Jessie Ralph, Claude Rains and Henry Travers. Ina Claire followed next in S.N. Behrman's comedy, *Biography* (12/12/32; 210 performances). Shirley Booth, Leo G. Carroll, Judith Anderson and Humphrey Bogart appeared in Somerset Maugham's translation of *The Mask and the Face* (5/8/33; 40 performances), which closed the 15th season.

The opening of the 1933 season on October 2 marked George M. Cohan's (*q.v.*) next to last Broadway appearance and Eugene O'Neill's only comedy. *Ah, Wilderness!* (285 performances) also featured Elisha Cook, Jr. and Gene Lockhart. Its success meant that the Theater Guild had to mount the rest of the season's productions at other theaters. The 17th season opened with Ruth Gordon and Glenn Anders in *A Sleeping Clergyman* (10/8/34; 40 performances), which was followed by an epic, *Valley Forge* (12/10/34; 58 performances) by Maxwell Anderson. This production starred Philip Merivale and Margalo Gillmore. The next production of note was a revue *Parade* (5/20/35; 40 performances) starring Ralph Riggs, Eve Arden, Jimmy Savo, Charles Walters and Ezra Stone. Lunt and Fontanne opened with *The Taming of the Shrew* (9/30/35; 128 performances) costarring Bretaigne Windust, Richard Whorf, Le Roi Operti and Sydney Greenstreet. The thirties ended with highlights including Behrman's *End of Summer* (12/17/36; 152 performances) starring Ina Claire, Osgood Perkins, Shepperd Strudwick, Mildred Natwick and Van Heflin and Ben Hecht's *To Quito and Back* (10/6/37; 46 performances) with Sylvia Sidney, Leslie Banks and Joseph Buloff.

As fine as these productions were, the Theater Guild was losing money because of the relatively small seating capacity of the theater and the scale of the Guild's productions. The Guild also was at the forefront of those producers willing to take chances, so many of the typical Broadway audiences weren't ready for Guild productions. As a result, the Theater Guild found it neccessary to lease the theater to other producers. The best of these outside productions was William Saroyan's *The Time of Your Life,* which moved to the Guild in 1940. Since other producers were no more successful than the Theater Guild in paying the bills, the Theater Guild leased the theater as a radio theater in 1943.

It was renamed the WOR Mutual Theater on March 19, 1943. In 1950, the American National Theater and Academy (ANTA) *(q.v.)* bought the theater and renamed it the ANTA Playhouse. ANTA renovated the theater and opened its first production on November 26, 1950. It was Robinson Jeffers's *The Tower Beyond Tragedy* (32 performances) with Judith Anderson. Next came a hit, Gloria Swanson and Jose Ferrer in a revival of Ben Hecht and Charles MacArthur's *Twentieth Cen-*

The ANTA Playhouse　Courtesy Billy Rose Theater Collection

tury (12/24/50; 218 performances). Because it was a hit, it moved to the Fulton Theater *(q.v.)*.

Revivals at the playhouse included *Desire Under the Elms* (1/16/52; 48 performances) with Karl Malden and *Golden Boy* (3/12/52; 55 performances) with John Garfield and Lee J. Cobb. The next big hit was *Mrs. McThing* (2/20/52; 350 performances) featuring Helen Hayes, Ernest Borgnine, Jules Munshin and Brandon de Wilde. It was such a big hit that it moved to the Morosco Theatre *(q.v.)*. Helen Hayes was also in the theater's next hit, a revival of *The Skin of Our Teeth* (8/17/55; 22 performances). It also starred Mary Martin, George Abbott *(q.v.)* and Don Murray. The Lunts returned in *The Great Sebastians* (1/4/56; 174 performances) by Lindsay and Crouse.

The theater was renamed the American Academy of Dramatic Arts in 1953 and renamed again the ANTA Theater on December 21, 1954, with the opening of *Portrait of a Lady* (7 performances). A hit that actually stayed in the theater was Paddy Chayefsky's *Middle of the Night* (2/8/56; 477 performances) starring Edward G. Robinson. *Say, Darling* (4/3/58; 332 performances) starred Vivian Blaine, Johnny Desmond and Robert Morse. It was a surprise hit with a score by Jule Styne *(q.v.)* and Comden and Green *(q.v.)*. Next came the Pulitzer Prize-winning play, *J.B.* (12/11/58; 364 performances). The Archibald MacLeish drama starred Raymond Massey, Pat Hingle and Christopher Plummer.

The sixties were good years for the theater. A musical revue based on the writings of James Thurber was aptly named *A Thurber Carnival* (2/26/60; 127 performances). Hugh Wheeler's *Big Fish, Little Fish* (3/15/61; 101 performances) was directed by Sir John Gielgud. Later that year, *A Man for All Seasons* (11/22/61; 640 performances) by Robert Bolt starred Paul Scofield and became the longest run at the theater. James Baldwin's *Blues for Mister Charlie* (4/23/64; 148 performances) with Rip Torn, Diana Sands, Pat Hingle and Rosetta Le Noire was followed by *The Owl and the Pussycat* (11/18/64; 421 performances), a light comedy with Diana Sands and Alan Alda. The last big hit of the sixties was *The Royal Hunt of the Sun* (10/26/65; 261 performances) starring Christopher Plummer and George Rose.

The seventies reflected the decline in Broadway's offerings. Helen Hayes, James Stewart and Jesse White started the decade off right in a revival of *Harvey* (1970). A revival of *Cat on a Hot Tin Roof* was a hit in 1974 with Elizabeth Ashley, Keir Dullea, Kate Reid and Fred Gwynne. *Bubbling Brown Sugar* (3/2/76; 766 performances) was a surprise hit. Another was the Goodspeed Opera Company's revival of *Whoopee!* (1979). It starred Charles Repole and ran until Tom Stoppard's *Night and Day* (11/27/79; 95 performances) with Maggie Smith replaced it later that year.

The 1980s have seen even less of merit at the theater.

Oh, Brother! (11/10/81; 16 performances) with a score by Michael Valenti was an undeserved failure. In August of that year, the theater was bought by the Jujamcyn chain. The name was changed to the Virginia Theater, after Virginia M. Binger, owner with her husband James. The theater was renovated again, but still it was not considered a top Broadway house. The most notable recent production was an excellent revival of Rodgers and Hart's *(q.v.)* *On Your Toes*. *City of Angels* (12/11/89) a musical by Cy Coleman, Larry Gelbart and David Zippel is the theater's current success.

The exterior of the Virginia has been designated a historic landmark by the New York City Landmarks Preservation Commission.

VITAGRAPH THEATER   See OLYMPIA THEATER.

V-J DAY   Times Square has through most of its history served as a gathering place where New Yorkers have celebrated events ranging from prizefight outcomes to election results to the annual New Year's Eve celebration *(q.v.)*. Although the V-E day celebration on May 9, 1945, was enormous, by far the largest and most flamboyant outpouring of shared emotion was the V-J day celebration marking the end of the Second World War.

For most of these mass gatherings the focal point has been the Times Tower *(q.v.)* and the moving sign, the Motogram *(q.v.)*, that runs around the tower. Before the advent of television and the invention of the portable transistor radio, the Motogram was the fastest way for people not at home or in an office to get news. When important events were imminent, great crowds gathered at the base of the Times Tower.

Rumors had circulated all day on August 14, 1945, that Japan was about to surrender. The population of New York knew that both the first announcement and the festivities to follow would take place in Times Square. As people left work, they headed for Times Square. By 5:00, more than 200,000 people had gathered facing the Motogram. Streets were blocked off from 40th to 49th Street to accommodate the growing crowds that spilled beyond Times Square south to Herald Square and north to Columbus Circle.

At 7:03 P.M. the light bulbs on the sign spelled out the message, "Official—Truman announces Japanese surrender." The crowd, which had grown to 750,000, gasped in disbelief and then a roar went up, echoing up and down the streets of the city.

As the evening progressed, jubilant New Yorkers continued to gather in the square. By 10:00 over 2,000,000 people were jammed together in a sea of laughing, shrieking humanity. From the Paramount Building *(q.v.)* and the other surrounding structures, a spontaneous ticker-tape celebration took place. People threw paper,

Times Square on V-J Day   Courtesy Municipal Art Society.

boxes, confetti, hats and newspapers into the square. Flags were prominently displayed in windows and on flagpoles, and people brought small hand-held flags from their homes and waved them furiously. Sailors, soldiers, secretaries and survivors kissed strangers and danced together under the artificial moonlight of the advertising spectaculars (see SIGNAGE) ringing the square.

The *New York Times* reported, "The victory roar beat upon the eardrums until it numbed the senses." The huge crowd could be heard inside the many theaters up and down the avenues and side streets. Broadway shows were halted and movies interrupted as audiences left to join the celebration. After, Times Square was filled with a record amount of trash. Altogether, 5,438 tons of paper were picked up from Manhattan streets.

Although President Truman officially claimed September 2 as V-J day, since that was the actual date of the signing of the surrender papers, most Americans think of the Times Square celebration on August 14 as marking the real V-J day.

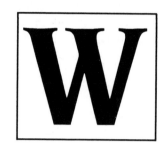

WALTER KERR THEATRE   See RITZ THEATRE.

WALTERS, LOU (1896–1977). Lou Walters, a master of the nightclub, was one of Broadway's most successful entrepreneurs. He owned and operated the popular nightclub The Latin Quarter along with many other successes.

Walters was born in London and came with his family to New York when he was 15. One of his first jobs was as an office boy in a vaudeville office. Within a few months he was earning $4 a week for scouting acts. At the tender age of 17, he entered the world of the nightclub. He began booking acts for one club, and within three years he was responsible for hiring 200 acts per week.

This early success led him to set up a business for himself in Boston. He started the concern with only $75, the cost of rent and phone hookup.

Nightclubs continued thriving even as other forms of variety were drying up. Vaudeville was all but dead, replaced by radio and sound pictures. Walters concentrated on booking clubs. In 1932, he was receiving a piece of the profits of a nightclub in Boston's Bradford Hotel.

This taste of ownership gave him the idea of starting his own club. He saved his money and in 1937 spent all but 63¢ to open his first Latin Quarter. The club was located in Boston and was an immediate success. Only three years later, in 1940, the club was earning $500,000 a year.

Walters plowed those profits into more ventures. He bought Earl Carroll's *(q.v.)* Palm Island Club in 1940. That Miami Beach supper club was also successful and gave Walters the capital to open his greatest nightclub.

In 1942, he opened The Latin Quarter in Times Square on 48th Street between Broadway and Seventh Avenue. By then, he operated clubs in Boston, Miami and New York. The new club was an immediate hit, grossing over $1.5 million in its first year. The newest Walters club capitalized on Times Square's central location and attracted a wide range of clientele. Tourists, Eastsiders, society members and celebrities from movies and theater all flocked there.

Walters explained his success through his theory of nightclub management: "I throw the book at them. I try to give them the nightclub of their dreams. Cut pile carpets, velvet on the walls, satin draperies, fountains with colored water, mirrors on the balustrade. Fill them full of food and take their breath away. Let them feel all the time they are shooting the works."

Walters's early experiences as a talent agent served him well. He drew on established stars like Sophie Tucker, Milton Berle and Ted Lewis, as well as up-and-coming faces like Patti Page and Johnny Ray. Mae West, Frank Sinatra, Mickey Rooney and Dorothy Lamour were other notables presented by Walters at the club.

Unlike many club owners, Walters insisted on a first-rate kitchen. The others felt that as long as the drinks were strong and the lights low the food didn't matter, but Walters disagreed with that philosophy. "It's a popular fallacy in this business to say that your money is made or lost in the kitchen. The man who goes to a nightclub goes in a spirit of splurging, and you've got to splurge right along with him. My motto used to be when the customer does not leave something on his plate, it's bad. I am always urging my stewards and chefs to give the customers more food than they expect."

In the first 10 years of its existence, The Latin Quarter earned over $10 million and served more than 5,000,000 people. Its success led Walters to further ventures. The theater beckoned, and his first attempt at producing was the *Ziegfeld Follies of 1943* (4/14/43; 553 performances). The show was coproduced by the Shuberts *(q.v.)*. The score was by Ray Henderson and Jack Yellen. The lavish revue starred Milton Berle, Eric Blore, Arthur Treacher and the Bil Baird Marionettes. It was an immediate success.

Unfortunately, his later theatrical ventures, *Artists and Models* (11/5/43) and *Star Time* (9/12/44) were failures. In 1953, he began Lou Walters Enterprises, a management firm, at 1576 Broadway. He sold the Latin Quarter in 1953 and began producing shows in Las Vegas. There he introduced the *Folies Bergere*.

Walters returned to The Latin Quarter in 1965, but times had changed. Costs were escalating, and the chorus line demanded union representation. Walters retired after closing the club in 1967. Another notable achievement was his daughter Barbara, today a successful ABC television personality. Lou Walters died in Miami on August 15, 1977.

WARNER BROTHERS THEATER See MARK HELLINGER THEATER.

WATTS, RICHARD, JR. See CRITICS.

WEBER AND FIELDS MUSIC HALL See 44TH STREET THEATRE.

WEILL, KURT (1900–1950) Composer Kurt Weill was born in Dessau, Germany, on March 2, 1900. His early career was primarily associated with Bertolt Brecht. Their most famous collaboration was *Die Dreigroschenoper (The Threepenny Opera)*. Another of their works, *Mahagonny*, has also endured through many productions throughout the world.

When Hitler began to come into power, Weill emigrated to the United States. He brought with him his belief in the power of the musical theater, a power never fully realized in the United States. Weill felt, correctly, that he could entertain audiences and still tackle major themes and ideas.

Because of his work with Brecht, Weill had a high regard for authors, especially poets. A hallmark of his career is the collaborations he enjoyed with many great authors whose work in the musical theater was otherwise negligible.

Weill's first Broadway production was an unsuccessful mounting of *The Threepenny Opera* (4/13/33; 12 performances). The translation was by Gifford Cochran and Jerrold Krimsky. Broadway audiences weren't ready for the serious musical theater that *The Threepenny Opera* typified.

In 1935, Weill had a production of *A Kingdom for a Cow* in London with Desmond Carter's lyrics. The play was originally written as *Der Kubbandel* by Robert Vambery, but a production in Germany was out of the

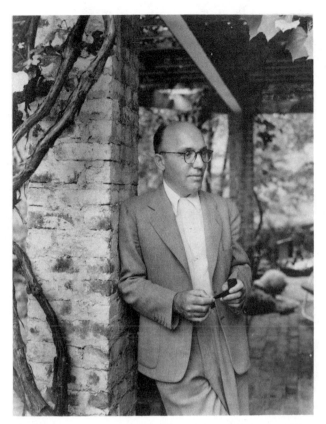

Kurt Weill Courtesy ASCAP.

question. The show opened on June 28, 1935, at the Savoy Theater. It was Weill's second failure.

He returned to the United States and wrote the music for the antiwar musical, *Johnny Johnson* (11/19/36; 68 performances). Playwright Paul Green contributed the book and lyrics to the show. The Group Theater *(q.v.)* produced the piece.

Besides the score, the most impressive of *Johnny Johnson*'s elements was its cast. It included such greats as Luther Adler, Morris Carnovsky, Lee J. Cobb, John Garfield, Elia Kazan, Will Lee, Robert Lewis, Sanford Meisner, Art Smith and Albert Dekker. But the United States wasn't ready for *Johnny Johnson*'s cautionary messages.

Weill achieved somewhat more fame with a more successful production, *Knickerbocker Holiday* (10/19/38; 168 performances) at the Ethel Barrymore Theater *(q.v.)*. The show, the story of Peter Stuyvesant in early Manhattan, also had political overtones, but they were put across in a more palatable manner.

Walter Huston, Richard Kollmar, Ray Middleton, Robert Rounseville and Jeanne Madden headed the cast. Huston made an especially strong impression in the leading role. He was lucky enough to have Weill's first popular standard to sing, "September Song."

On this show, Weill again chose a prominent playwright as his collaborator. Maxwell Anderson wrote the book and lyrics. The Playwrights' Company *(q.v.)* produced the show and Joshua Logan *(q.v.)* directed.

Maxwell Anderson   Courtesy ASCAP.

Lady in the Dark (1/23/41; 467 performances), at the Alvin Theater *(q.v.),* was Weill's first Broadway success. Weill's collaborator was Broadway veteran Ira Gershwin *(q.v.).* The show fit Weill's requirement of an adult theme. This time it was psychoanalysis. Gertrude Lawrence played the lead, a magazine editor who simply couldn't make up her mind. Through a series of spectacular dreams, Lawrence discovered the root of her problems.

The Weill and Gershwin score was among the best written for any musical. "My Ship" and "The Saga of Jenny" received the most notice. Also in the cast was Danny Kaye making his second Broadway appearance. For the occasion, Gershwin concocted an especially difficult tongue twister, "Tchaikowsky." The song was a long list of actual names of Russian composers. Macdonald Carey, Natalie Schafer and Victor Mature also had featured roles.

Weill's next big production was *One Touch of Venus* (10/7/43; 567 performances). Poet Ogden Nash supplied the lyrics to Weill's music. Nash and satirist S.J. Perelman wrote the book. Elia Kazan directed with Cheryl Crawford and John Wildberg producing. The story of a statue that comes to life was written for Marlene Dietrich and played by Mary Martin *(q.v.).* Kenny Baker was her bedeviled suitor, with John Boles, Teddy Hart and Paula Laurence rounding out the cast.

The Weill and Nash score yielded many gems. "Foolish Heart" and "Speak Low" were the popular hits.

Other songs in the score were equally good. "That's Him," "West Wind" and "The Trouble with Women" all had their partisans.

Weill and Gershwin reteamed for the unsuccessful *The Firebrand of Florence* (3/22/45; 43 performances). The show starred Melville Cooper, Earl Wrightson and Weill's wife, Lotte Lenya.

Weill again enlisted an unusual collaborator for his next production, *Street Scene* (1/9/47; 148 performances). Elmer Rice adapted his classic play for the musical. Anne Jeffreys, Polyna Stoska, Brian Sullivan, Hope Emerson, Sheila Bond and Danny Daniels starred. "Moon-Faced, Starry-Eyed" achieved some success, but for the most part this exceptional score remains largely unknown. It certainly wasn't well appreciated at the time.

Weill tried another experiment, this time with Alan Jay Lerner *(q.v.).* *Love Life* (10/7/48; 252 performances) followed a marriage against the background of changing history. The couple never aged, although time marched on. The show began in colonial times and ended at the time of the show. Nanette Fabray and Ray Middleton starred as the hapless couple. They and the rest of the cast were afforded some fine songs, including "Here I'll Stay."

Weill's last Broadway show was one of his most impassioned. *Lost in the Stars* (10/30/49; 281 performances) featured lyrics by Weill's past collaborator, Maxwell Anderson. It was based on Alan Paton's novel of black citizens in South Africa. The tragic story was well captured through Weill and Anderson's powerful and dramatic score. Todd Duncan, the original Porgy in Gershwin's *Porgy and Bess,* Herbert Coleman, Inez Matthews and Julian Mayfield headed the excellent cast. *Lost in the Stars* has won high regard as the years have passed.

Kurt Weill's final project was a musicalization of *Huckleberry Finn* written with Maxwell Anderson. Unfortunately, Weill died before the project could be finished.

Weill's most successful production occurred four years after his death. It was an off-Broadway revival of *The Threepenny Opera.* Lotte Lenya starred in the remounting of one of Weill's earliest successes. The opening at the Theater De Lys took place on September 10, 1954. It played for 94 performances. The Marc Blitzstein translation reopened on September 30, 1955. This time, it ran for 2,611 performances. Other cast members were Charlotte Rae, Scott Merrill, Martin Wolfson, Jo Sullivan, Gerald Price, Beatrice Arthur and Jerry Orbach. The hit parade success of "Mack the Knife" accounted for much of the success of the show.

Weill's early death at age 50 on April 3, 1950, was a blow to the Broadway community. His scores stand equal to those of Broadway's finest composers. Weill's themes pointed up the possiblities for the American musical theater—possibilities that still have not been fully realized.

WHITE, GEORGE (1890–1968)

George White was an actor, dancer, producer, director, choreographer, composer, lyricist and librettist. He was the force behind the *Ziegfeld Follies'* (q.v.) biggest rival, *George White's Scandals (q.v.).* As producer of the *Scandals,* White nurtured many young talents. These included George Gershwin *(q.v.),* DeSylva, Brown and Henderson *(q.v.)* and Alice Faye.

White was born in Toronto, Canada, in 1890. He learned to dance while standing on Third Avenue in New York after hawking newspapers. His first stage appearance was at the age of 12. When he was about 16, he teamed up with Ben Ryan, and together they toured vaudeville in a dancing act. A scout for producer Charles Dillingham spotted White and introduced him to Dillingham, who promptly hired White for his next show.

He made his New York debut at the Globe Theatre *(q.v.)* in *The Echo* on August 17, 1910. He next appeared at the Winter Garden Theater *(q.v.)* in *The Pleasure Seekers* (11/3/13). This led to his joining the cast of *The Midnight Girl* at the 44th Street Theatre *(q.v.)* in the middle of its run. By then, he was starting to make his reputation and was hired by Florenz Ziegfeld *(q.v.)* for the 1915 edition of his *Follies.*

After the *Follies,* White was hired by Ziegfeld for the Jerome Kern *(q.v.)* and P.G. Wodehouse revue *Miss 1917* (11/5/17; 40 performances). The show was a financial failure, although it played to standing room only houses.

White became convinced that he could outdo Ziegfeld by producing his own revues. He raised the money and opened the first *George White's Scandals* on June 2, 1919. The show featured a score by Richard Whiting and Herbert Spencer, composers, and Arthur Jackson and White himself as lyricists. This was the first instance of a team creating the entire score for a revue. Up till then, revue producers would receive entries from a variety of songwriters and pick the songs that they liked from the samples submitted. White also performed in the show as well as choreographed it.

Also appearing in the first *Scandals* was White's former dance partner from the *Follies,* Ann Pennington. She became the first in a series of regulars who starred in succeeding *Scandals*—eventually appearing in five of the annual revues. Other performers who were part of the informal company were Willie and Eugene Howard (six editions), Florence Williams (four occasions), and Lou Holtz and Winnie Lightner (each appeared three times).

Apart from the regulars, White brought in many top stars from the stage and radio. These performers included Ethel Merman *(q.v.),* Rudy Vallee (twice), Alice Faye, Everett Marshall, Charles King, Paul Whiteman and his orchestra, Dolores Costello (twice), Ray Bolger, Ethel Barrymore Colt, Cliff Edwards, Bert Lahr, Ben Blue, Harry Richman (twice), Ella Logan and Ann Miller.

White's shows were fast and snappy with a youthful exuberance. This was due in large part to the songs that were written for the series. George Gershwin *(q.v.)* contributed five scores for the series. Among the best known of the Gershwin songs are "The Scandal Walk," "Drifting Along with the Tide," "I'll Build a Stairway to Paradise," and "Somebody Loves Me." The lyrics for the Gershwin tunes were written by Arthur Jackson, Ira Gershwin *(q.v.),* Ballard Macdonald and B.G. DeSylva.

DeSylva also contributed to three other *Scandals* with his partners Lew Brown and Ray Henderson. They contributed some of the greatest songs to come out of the Broadway theater. Together they wrote "Birth of the Blues," "This Is My Lucky Day" and "Black Bottom." Henderson and Brown contributed one more score to the series but without DeSylva. The score was probably the *Scandals'* best, and it included "Ladies and Gentlemen, That's Love," "That's Why Darkies Were Born," "This Is the Missus," "My Song," "The Thrill Is Gone" and "Life Is Just a Bowl of Cherries."

Although best known for the *Scandals,* White also produced book musicals. The first was *Runnin' Wild* (10/29/23; 167 performances). This was an all-black musical, featuring Elisabeth Welch, Adelaide Hall, Flournoy Miller and Aubrey Lyles. The show was typical of the works produced by White. It was fast paced and up-to-the-minute. In fact, it was in *Runnin' Wild* that audiences first heard and saw the Charleston. Elisabeth Welch sang the James P. Johnson and Cecil Mack song as a bevy of brown beauties illustrated the dance steps. The Charleston swept through the nation and became the hottest dance craze of the twenties.

White's next non-*Scandals* show was *Manhattan Mary* (9/26/27; 264 performances). The score was composed by *Scandals* regulars, DeSylva, Brown and Henderson. White coauthored the book with William K. Wells, in addition to producing, directing and starring in the show. Ed Wynn, Harland Dixon and Ona Munson were also in the cast as were *Scandals* regulars Lou Holtz and Paul Frawley. Although the show wasn't one of the *Scandals,* it was a close relation. At the end, the heroine attains her fondest dream—joining the *Scandals.* White played himself.

Flying High (3/3/30; 355 performances), also by DeSylva, Brown and Henderson, featured Kate Smith, Bert Lahr and Oscar Shaw. By 1932, the country was deep into the Depression, and money was hard to come by both for the populace and producers. Instead of mounting an expensive *Scandals,* White presented *George White's Music Hall Varieties* (11/22/32; 71 performances), a simpler version of the same formula. Eleanor Powell, Harry Richman and Bert Lahr headlined, but the show wasn't a success. Perhaps when the curtain rose on its opening night, audiences were expecting a more lavish evening's entertainment. The songs were written by a variety of songwriting teams, including Harold Arlen (q.v.) and Irving Caesar, Cliff Friend and Herb Magidson and Carmen Lombardo. But the hit of the show, and a future standard, was Herman Hupfeld's "Let's Turn Out the Lights and Go to Bed."

The next year, White presented his last non-*Scandals* Broadway show, *Melody* (2/14/33; 80 performances). He produced and directed the show, which was a distinct change from his usual offerings. It was written by Sigmund Romberg (q.v.), mostly noted for his operettas, and Irving Caesar. The show proved to be a failure, despite the talents of Gypsy Rose Lee, Everett Marshall and Ina Ray Hutton.

Following his last *Scandals* in 1939, White toured with a tab edition called *George White's Scandals Cavalcade.* White brought the show in to Loew's State (q.v.) movie theater in June 1941. In addition to his stage chores, White ran several nightclubs. The first was the Gay White Way where he presented and directed a revue, *Midnight Scandals* in 1941. He also produced and directed an original nightclub revue, *Nice to See You* at the Versailles in April 1953. White's final nightclub show was presented in Jack Silverman's International Theater-Restaurant. The show *George White's Scandals* opened on October 9, 1963.

The *Scandals* were also filmed by Hollywood several times. Fox presented *George White's Scandals* in 1934 and *George White's 1935 Scandals* the following year. White wrote, produced, directed and appeared in the two films. *George White's Scandals* was an RKO picture that debuted in 1945. He also appeared as himself in the Warner Brothers picture *Rhapsody in Blue,* also in 1945.

White died in Hollywood on October 11, 1968. He certainly helped define the twenties through his shows, which featured such revolutionary dance crazes as the Charleston and the Black Bottom. In addition to helping the careers of many artists, he also brought Broadway's glamour to millions of people through movies and nightclub entertainments.

Close friends remember him as a shy, introverted man whose greatest pleasure was sneaking into his box offices and selling tickets. When friends would come to the box office expecting free seats, White would insist on selling them tickets at full price. It was said that his greatest ambition was to sell a ticket to one of his shows to rival producer Florenz Ziegfeld. But Ziegfeld was shrewd and bought his *Scandals* tickets through a speculator.

WIENNIG AND SBERBER'S At the turn of the century, many new restaurants were established. Rector's

(q.v.) and Shanley's attracted the upper classes, who would dine after attending an operetta or melodrama. Times Square also had its share of restaurants that catered to the actors who appeared on the stages of Broadway and vaudeville. Chief among these was Lindy's (q.v.). Another earlier example of the genre was Wiennig and Sberber's on 45th Street. The two restaurants were alike in many ways. Foremost was the presence of a real character as owner, one who was patient with the rambunctious performers and who was also sympathetic and extended credit in lean times. Whereas Lindy's had only one such person at the helm (not to ignore the contribution of Clara Lindemann), Wiennig and Sberber's had two.

Sberber was described by George Burns as the kind of man who "smelt everything before he bought it." Sberber began the habit when offered cigars. Soon the habit extended to anything offered. Napkin salesmen would find their goods held up to Sberber's nose and given a good strong sniff. If it passed muster, an order was made. Sberber was also the world's expert authority on every subject, whether he knew what he was talking about or not. No conversation could be held without Sberber butting in and making an ironclad proclamation.

Wiennig had more to do with the clientele than Sberber. This motley group mainly consisted of vaudeville performers. Wiennig couldn't seem to remember anyone's name; he preferred to associate the performers with one of their hit songs. When Al Jolson (q.v.) arrived, Sberber would greet him with a hearty "Hello, April Showers." A waiter serving Fanny Brice (q.v.) would be instructed to "Give the roast beef special to My Man." Wiennig also had the strange habit of answering any question with the answer to a previous query. For example if George Burns asked "Hello, Mr. Wiennig. Have you seen Manny Mannishaw?" Wiennig would reply "Look on the floor, maybe it fell down there."

The waiters were also eccentrics. Burns remembered them as being extremely harried. Once when a customer asked where the rest room was, the waiter impatiently replied "Please—I've only got two hands!" The waiters also distrusted each other. They always thought their coworkers were stealing their tips when their backs were turned. So they walked backward to the kitchen and yelled their orders over their shoulders.

Wiennig and Sberber's also had traditions. Whenever Wiennig and Sberber went to answer the wall-mounted phone and turned their backs to speak into the mouthpiece they would be pelted with sugar cubes. The owners learned to talk quickly and briefly to their callers, trying to keep their backs turned as little as possible. When they grew tired of ducking sugar cubes they switched to granulated sugar (after Sberber smelled it first). But business fell off—the customers were apparently let down by the elimination of ammunition.

To bring back their customers, Wiennig and Sberber brought back the sugar cubes.

WILLIAMS, TENNESSEE (1911–1983) Williams was born in Columbus, Mississippi, on March 26, 1911. His mother, much like Blanche in his masterwork *A Streetcar Named Desire,* adhered to largely irrelevant mores and a somewhat unreal idea of then current social convention. Williams's father called his son "Miss Nancy" and relentlessly expressed his disgust for the youngster. The family moved to St. Louis when Williams was eight. After college, Williams finally found the strength to escape his family, but no matter how far he fled, the memories and scars of those years stayed with him.

The Glass Menagerie (3/31/45; 561 performances), at the Playhouse Theater, was his first Broadway success. A previous play, *Battle of Angels,* was closed by its producers, the Theater Guild *(q.v.),* in Boston. The Guild actually apologized to audiences for presenting an obscene play. *The Glass Menagerie* introduced one of his career's major themes. The "memory play" juxtaposed the rebellious son, played by Eddie Dowling, with the crippled daughter, played by Julie Haydon. Both long to escape from Laurette Taylor's character, the domineering mother, but the girl does so only through her withdrawal into fantasy. Anthony Ross played the gentleman caller who reveals the possibility of escape to the brother and sister.

Williams's next work was perhaps his greatest achievement. *A Streetcar Named Desire* (12/3/47; 855 performances) opened at the Barrymore Theater *(q.v.).* The drama was a milestone in the American theater, firmly demonstrating that Williams was a major playwright. It starred Jessica Tandy as Blanche DuBois, Karl Malden as Mitch and Kim Hunter as Stella. It also introduced a new star to Broadway, Marlon Brando as Stanley Kowalski.

The character Blanche DuBois finds herself in an unstable world of violence and brutality. She can never achieve her dreams, nor can Stanley Kowalski, who wants respect as well as the good, secure life that seems always out of reach. Both characters, denied what they most want, fall prey to desire. Their impulses rule their actions as they lash out at each other in their own

Tennessee Williams and Walter Kerr

diverse ways. Williams explores the dichotomy between Stanley's intense physicality and Blanche's soulfulness. Each character's yearnings for the qualities they admire in each other take hold and destroy them. The puritanical Williams examines the pain of the two lost souls, who can only achieve catharsis through violence or madness. *A Streetcar Named Desire* won the New York Drama Critics' Circle Award *(q.v.)* as well as the Pulitzer Prize *(q.v.)*.

Williams's next play, *Summer and Smoke* (10/6/48; 102 performances) was unsuccessful at the time, perhaps because it paled in comparison with *Streetcar*. The play opened at the Music Box Theater *(q.v.)*. It has since been reevaluated and enjoys many revivals. *Cat on a Hot Tin Roof* (3/24/55; 694 performances) opened at the Morosco Theatre *(q.v.)*. The play examines the breakdown in relationships among members of a Southern plantation family who find that the only way they can communicate is through lies.

Sweet Bird of Youth (3/10/59; 375 performances), at the Martin Beck Theatre *(q.v.)*, featured powerful performances by Geraldine Page and Paul Newman. *Period of Adjustment* (11/10/60; 132 performances), Williams's attempt to write a somewhat traditional sex comedy, opened at the Helen Hayes Theater *(q.v.)*.

Night of the Iguana (12/28/61; 316 performances), produced at the Royale Theatre *(q.v.)*, was perhaps Williams's most eccentric play. It was widely parodied at the time. In *Night of the Iguana*, Williams again explored the theme of the human desire to attain peace. The sexuality and violence of Williams's earlier works are still present but tempered and relegated to the sidelines. In a way, it is Williams's most optimistic work; *Night of the Iguana* shows that peace, however impermanent, can be achieved. Although critics were divided on the play's merits, all agreed that the cast, led by Margaret Leighton, Bette Davis and Alan Webb, was superb.

Williams did not have another success on Broadway. His later plays all showed a marked change in his abilities. Although his dialogue sometimes remained as trenchant and poetic, his plays became muddled in style and insubstantial at their core. Still, Williams continued writing until his death and in the end almost seemed like a character in one of his own plays.

WINCHELL, WALTER (1897–1972) The most powerful and most controversial of all Broadway columnists was Walter Winchell. His fame grew when he conquered radio, beginning each program with the classic opening, "Good evening Mr. and Mrs. North America and all the ships at sea. Let's go to press." Winchell's colorful vocabulary was as well known as his opinions. Lexicographer W.J. Funk included Winchell among a list of the 10 major contributors of American slang *(q.v.)*. Fellow columnist Alexander Woollcott once noted

that "With a punch line at the end of a column, his own or judiciously quoted, he is capable of ending a career, or beginning a new chapter of history."

Winchell had his defenders and enemies. St. Claire McKelway, an ardent detractor of gossip, stated in a *New Yorker* magazine article that gossip's "presence in American journalism is almost entirely due to the peculiar personality of one man. This man is Walter Winchell."

Time covered Winchell in 1931 and reported that he was "no ordinary scandal-snooper. Famed is he in theater lobbies, speakeasies, nightclubs. From one gossip center to another he travels to get column material. Alert, the Winchell ear hears all. Amiable, the Winchell disposition makes friendly, easily, elicits scandal scraps. Then, at three or four in the morning, he goes back to his typewriter and two-fingers what he has learned, adding here and there the result of an imaginative mind."

Winchell's city editor at the *New York Herald Tribune*, Stanley Walker, explained Winchell's great success: "Winchell did much for journalism, for which journalism has been slow to thank him. He helped change the dreary, ponderous impersonality which was pervading the whole press. Do newspapers today print twice, or ten times, as many items about people—what they are like, what their crotchets are, what they eat and drink and wear—as they did ten years ago? Some of that credit belongs to Winchell . . . Winchell brought to his job the perfect equipment—great energy, an eager desire to know what was going on, a lack of learning and an unquenchable desire to be a newspaperman. If his background had been different, he would have been so befuddled by canons of what some people call good taste that he would have been revolted at some of his best stuff. If he had been better educated he might have been dull. As it was, everything he saw was news to him . . . "

Janet and Jacob Winchel (the added *l* was accidently added on a theater marquee and was soon adopted by young Walter) were Russian immigrants who came to New York's Harlem in 1893. Walter escaped the harsh conditions of the Harlem streets by skipping school and attending vaudeville performances. While fooling around for his school chums, Winchell discovered a talent for dancing. Since he himself admitted that, "I was the school's prize dunce," he decided, at the tender age of 13, to try his luck on the vaudeville stage.

Walter had worked as a ticket taker and usher in Harlem's Imperial Theatre along with boyhood friend George Jessel. They soon earned $4 a week leading audiences in sing-alongs during intermission. The duo added another member, Jack Weiner, and billed themselves as Lawrence, Stanley and McKinley: The Little Men with the Big Voices. The act wasn't very successful, but it brought them to the attention of Gus Edwards, a vaudevillian who toured with a kiddie act then titled the "Newsboy Sextette."

In December 1914, Winchell quit Gus Edwards's troupe and mainly hung around in front of the Palace Theatre (q.v.) along with other out of work vaudevillians. When the United States entered World War I, Winchell brought his vaudeville career to a close and enlisted into the Navy. After his release, Winchell rejoined his vaudeville partner Rita Greene and married her. The duo played around the country during 1919, and Walter began a hobby. He typed a one-page vaudeville news sheet entitled "Newsense" and distributed it to his fellow vaudevillians. The gossip sheet soon expanded to two pages and, much to Winchell's amazement, achieved some popularity. Soon Winchell began reporting newsier features in addition to the usual births, deaths, marriages and bookings, and he even began putting some of his own opinions in the paper.

Winchell began using his trademark style while writing "Newsense." He would separate items with three dots. Winchell later told his assistant Herman Klurfeld that the style was created when the dash key on his typewriter was stuck. Others attribute it to playwright and speaker Rennold Wolf in his Morning Telegraph column. It is clear that Winchell began his unique use of the English language from the beginning.

Emile Gavreau, later Winchell's editor on the Evening Graphic and the Mirror, explained how Winchell's style emerged: "His lack of newspaper experience . . . his refreshing insouciance about the difference between a subject and a predicate, became an ironical asset which preserved his personality and may have had the virtue of saving him years of learning to be like everyone else. In his pate rattled more than a grain of genius which was to produce a 'slanguage' often too puzzling for the venerable gentlemen of the courts who were not permitted to go beyond old man Webster."

While Winchell was in Chicago, the Herald and Examiner asked him to cover comings and goings at the train station. Late in 1919, he began to submit items to Billboard (q.v.). After returning to New York, his career was stalled until he landed a job with the New York Vaudeville News, a house organ of the Edward F. Albee (q.v.) vaudeville empire. Albee began the paper in order to crush Variety (q.v.), a paper that supported Albee's enemy, the White Rats actors union. Winchell began in November of 1920 and promptly drew a close to his vaudeville career and his recent marriage.

Winchell's column in the New York Vaudeville News was titled "Merciless Truth" and later "Broadway Hearsay" for which he was paid $25 a week. Winchell supplemented his salary by selling advertising space in the paper. He made sure that the advertisers also featured prominently in his column.

While at the Vaudeville News, Winchell met his second wife, June, a woman who had little interest in show business or show people. In 1924, he moved to a $100-a-week job on the New York Evening Graphic under the auspices of its owners, Bernarr Macfadden and Fulton Oursler. Winchell's column, entitled "Broadway Hearsay" and "Your Broadway and Mine," was featured each Monday. It developed into a true gossip column, with the writer putting in more and more items about personalities. Winchell's gossip was at first frowned on by Emile Gavreau, but when the column's quotient rose, so did circulation.

While at the Graphic, Winchell enjoyed his first major feud. The antagonists were the Shuberts (q.v.), the most powerful producers in the history of Broadway. Winchell had given several of the Shubert shows bad reviews, so the Shuberts banned him from their theaters. The battle drew to a close when Shubert star Al Jolson (q.v.) refused to open his latest show unless Winchell was allowed to attend.

Winning the battle with the Shuberts signified to Broadwayites and especially Graphic readers that Winchell was a powerful force along the Great White Way. He was lured away from the Graphic by publisher William Randolph Hearst, not personally a Winchell fan. On June 10, 1929, Winchell's column first appeared in the Mirror. He soon became the Mirror's leading feature, responsible for one-third of the paper's circulation. The Graphic's demise in three years was certainly hastened by Winchell's departure. Winchell remained at the Mirror until the paper folded in 1963.

The Mirror wasn't much better than the scandal sheet that was the Graphic. In fact, two months after Winchell joined the Mirror Emile Gavreau left the Graphic and became Winchell's managing editor at the Mirror. Gavreau and Winchell by this time were barely speaking and carried their feud throughout their careers.

Winchell made his radio debut on January 18, 1929, over a 42-station network. The show was called "New York by a Representative New Yorker." The success of that series led Winchell to CBS in 1932. Winchell had also made a triumphant return to vaudeville with a booking at the Palace along with fellow columnist Mark Hellinger (q.v.). Winchell also made a brief stab at the movies in a Vitaphone short titled The Bard of Broadway. Winchell himself was the thinly disguised subject of a play entitled Blessed Event that opened on February 12, 1932, at Broadway's Longacre Theater (q.v.).

Like many of his contemporaries, especially Damon Runyon (q.v.), Winchell was fascinated with gangsters (q.v.) and organized crime. He called the crimelords the "UN," for "underworld nobility." Winchell seemed to glorify their lives and deaths. He became a tool of some of the hoods themselves. But he was also a patriot who numbered J. Edgar Hoover among his friends. During the Lindburgh trial, Hoover used Winchell's column to leak information that proved damaging to

Bruno Hauptman's case. Louis "Lepke" Buchalter, the godfather of Murder, Inc., surrendered to Winchell who then handed the gangster to the police. Winchell was staunchly opposed to Hitler and Nazi activities in the United States and urged America's entry into the World War II. Winchell's power extended to the White House. Franklin Roosevelt was elected to a third term with Winchell's help.

Winchell attempted television several times but to no great success. His best-remembered television assignment was as narrator for "The Untouchables." Winchell's lack of success on television was in part due to his dwindling influence through his column. By 1960, his national domain had been reduced to 150 papers. Winchell's haunts, primarily the Stork Club, went out of favor. Time seemed to pass Winchell by, and old age was slowing down his spirit.

On October 15, 1963, the *Mirror* folded. A 115-day printers' strike forced the paper to close. It never recovered. Hearst's other New York paper, the afternoon *Journal-American* picked up the *Mirror*'s features. The *Journal-American*'s editorial staff wasn't keen on Winchell's column. An executive was later quoted in the *New York Times* as saying, "Frankly our general feeling is that Winchell was passe. In his genre I think he was the best but I don't think he has substantial reader appeal any more." But the *Journal-American* was having its own problems. The New York newspaper scene was shrinking drastically. Another strike, this one for 140 days in 1965, led to the merging of the *Herald Tribune,* the *Sun* and the *World-Telegram* into the *World Journal Tribune.* A few months later, the paper folded for good. Winchell continued to write for the Hearst Syndicate but was denied a New York outlet.

The closing of the Stork Club in October 1965 seemed to symbolize the end of an era. Winchell sank into self-pity. He simply could not handle the changes in the Broadway scene and his slide into near obscurity. *Variety* offered Winchell a weekly column, but it was unsatisfying to the newsman. He debased himself by taking out a full-page ad in *Variety* begging for a New York paper to carry his column. In 1968, Winchell found a job with the *Daily Column,* a small paper that picked up the flotsam and jetsam from New York's many newspaper closings. The new post didn't last long. Winchell retired on February 5, 1968. Despite failing health, he fought the need to slow down. When a new *Daily Mirror* began publication in 1971, Winchell was there with three columns a week.

Winchell's worsening health forced him to leave the paper, and on February 20, 1972, Walter Winchell died.

WINDSOR THEATER   See 48TH STREET THEATRE.

WINTER GARDEN THEATER 1634 Broadway between 50th and 51st Street. Architect: William A. Swasey.

Program for the Winter Garden Theater

Opening: March 20, 1911; *Bow Sing* and *La Belle Paree.* The Winter Garden Theater was built by the Shuberts (*q.v.*) on the site of W. K. Vanderbilt's American Horse Exchange. In fact, when flop shows were presented on its stage, the critics would say they could still smell the stables. The Winter Garden was named after an English theater, and the new theater "devoted to novel, international, spectacular and musical entertainments" was designed to resemble an English garden. An earlier Winter Garden Theater stood on lower Broadway near Bond Street during the mid-19th century.

The opening evening was a gala one, and scalpers were getting as much as $19 for a $2.50 ticket. A newspaper described the evening:

Crowds began to arrive at the Winter Garden long before eight o'clock until the sidewalk was almost blocked and the lobby filled to overflowing. The line of carriages and automobiles extended for two blocks when the first nighters were coming more plentifully . . .

Once inside the theater, the people seemed disinclined to go at once to their seats, but filled all of the wide promenade space back of the orchestra seats until the overture began.

Not the least attractive part of the Winter Garden is the simplicity and harmony of the decorations of the auditorium. The walls and balcony front are in old ivory and gold and the ceiling marked off in latticed squares in old ivory behind which is an artificial sky of blue . . .

The audience last night found the seats wide and comfortably spaced, with a receptacle for cigar ashes attached to the back of each chair.

The Winter Garden, built for musical presentations, opened with *La Belle Paree,* a show that included a "one-act Chinese fantasy opera" called *Bow Sing.* The Shuberts tried to pack too much into the evening. By the time Al Jolson *(q.v.),* making his Broadway debut, took the stage, the show had already run for three-and-a-half hours. Jolson was not yet well-known and when he sang "Paris Is a Paradise for Coons" in blackface, the audience was unimpressed.

Jolson's Broadway debut did not go unnoticed by the critics. Adolph Klauber wrote in the *New York Times,* "Among the very best features were those provided by the two unctuous ragtime comedians, Miss Stella Mayhew and Mr. Al Jolson, both of whom had good songs and the dialects and the acting ability to deliver every bit of good that was in them."

Despite its problems, the show was not a failure. The Shuberts cut portions and rearranged the lineup to bring Jolson into the show earlier. The critics returned to *La Belle Paree* to see what Jolson wrought and were pleased. *La Belle Paree* played 104 performances passing what *Variety (q.v.)* called the century mark—100 performances. At that time, shows were judged to be successful after only 100 performances. *Variety* had previously dubbed the show a "double sockeroo," another example of the paper's marvelous slang *(q.v.).*

Jolson certainly earned the $250 a week he was paid by the Shuberts. After the show closed, he convinced them to tour the show complete with Broadway cast and production. The Shuberts agreed, and *La Belle Paree* became the first show to tour the country following its Broadway run.

The Revue of Revues (9/27/11; 55 performances) with Gaby Deslys, Harry Jolson (Al's brother) and Ernest Hare opened next. *Vera Violetta* (11/20/11; 112 performances) again featured Al Jolson who starred along with Gaby Deslys, Ernest Hare, Stella Mayhew and Annette Kellerman. Mae West had a small part in the production but almost stole the show from Deslys.

During the show's run in New Haven, Yale students rioted because parts of the show had been cleaned up by order of the police. One account claimed that West was "in the middle of the fray, if, indeed, she did not start it." The opening at the Winter Garden went much more smoothly, probably because West was not on stage. Management claimed she was stricken with pneumonia. The show, even without West, was greeted with general acclaim by the critics. *Vera Violetta* was billed as the "largest, most elaborate production in North America."

The Shuberts then inaugurated a series of Sunday-evening concerts in the theater, taking advantage of its dark night. The concert series was a great success, since there was little other entertainment in New York on Sundays. The biggest star of the series was Jolson, who preferred to perform rather than have a day off. *Variety* proclaimed that "The Shuberts may run the Winter Garden, but Al Jolson owns it. That dandy performer does as he will with the audience, whether Sunday or on weekdays."

Jolson, Stella Mayhew and Gaby Deslys returned to the Winter Garden in *The Whirl of Society* (3/5/12; 136 performances). The show also featured another future rival of the Shuberts—George White *(q.v.),* who later mounted the *Scandals,* one of the top yearly revue series. *The Whirl of Society* is best remembered today as the first show that featured a runway down the center of the auditorium. It was a great device for Jolson, who was used to jumping off the stage and performing in the aisles. Max Reinhardt, the brilliant German director, had developed a thrust stage that broke the proscenium's "fourth wall." The Shuberts and Jolson went him one better. The runway was later dubbed "the bridge of thighs" because of the show girls who paraded up and down its length.

When Jolson was on the road, the Shuberts had to come up with an attraction for the Winter Garden. The theater was the personal responsibility of J.J., or Jake. Shubert. He controlled all the Shuberts' musical productions. His brother Lee controlled the plays and the empire's finances. Jake was mad at Florenz Ziegfeld *(q.v.),* whom he considered an arch rival. So Jake decided to outdo Ziegfeld, whose *Follies (q.v.)* were such a success. J.J. settled on an annual revue series, *The Passing Show,* so titled because the Shuberts planned them to run on Broadway for a short time and then tour the country. The shows often parodied current Broadway offerings, but their main feature was seminude chorines. The material was usually second-rate. The Shuberts even insisted that their contract writers supply songs to fit already existing scenery.

The first *Passing Show* (7/22/12; 136 performances) included songs by Louis A. Hirsch and Harold Atteridge, both Shubert contract employees. Songs were also contributed by Irving Berlin *(q.v.)* and by Earl Carroll *(q.v.),* whose *Vanities (q.v.)* later rivaled the Shuberts' revues and Ziegfeld's famous *Follies.* The *Passing Show* starred Adelaide and Hughes, Trixie Friganza, Charlotte Greenwood, Eugene and Willie Howard and Anna Wheaton.

Paris and all things French were big draws on Broadway in the early years of the century. After all, the French had the raciest of cultures, and nude show girls were guaranteed to increase ticket sales. So naturally the Shuberts' next offering at the Winter Garden was titled *Broadway to Paris* (11/20/12; 77 performances).

Interior of the Winter Garden Theater   Courtesy Municipal Art Society.

The show had little to do with anything French but composers Max Hoffman and Anatole Friedland came up with some suitably French sounding numbers.

The Honeymoon Express (2/6/13; 156 performances) featured Fanny Brice *(q.v.),* Gaby Deslys, Yancsi Dolly (of the Dolly Sisters) as well as Al Jolson. As usual, the show was overly long on opening night. So Jolson simply broke character, came down to the front of the stage, and asked the audience whether they would prefer to see the remainder of the show or sit back and hear an impromptu concert by Jolson. The question was hypothetical, for Jolson had already stopped the show cold and nothing could keep him from taking over the stage.

The Passing Show of 1913 (7/24/13; 116 performances) was typically undistinguished, but it did contain one hit song, "You Made Me Love You" by James V. Monaco and Joseph McCarthy. Usually, the only hits in early Shubert shows were interpolations of popular songs of the day. The second edition of the *Passing Show* series starred Charlotte Greenwood, May Boley, Bessie Clayton, John Charles Thomas and Carter De Haven.

The Pleasure Seekers (11/3/13; 72 performances) was

followed by *The Whirl of the World* (1/10/14; 161 performances), which introduced Broadway to one of its greatest composers, Sigmund Romberg *(q.v.).* Romberg became a Shubert contract employee and was forced to churn out shows on demand. Writing under such circumstances did not inspire Romberg, and few of his contract shows for the Shuberts contained successful songs.

The Passing Show of 1914 (6/10/14; 133 performances) also had a score by Romberg and lyricist Harold Atteridge. The show was no better than any of the Shubert offerings. However, the show did mark the Broadway debut of Marilyn Miller, a delightful dancer, who became a particular favorite with Broadway audiences. Lee Shubert discovered Miller, but he wasn't told that she was only 15 years old. Although the nominal stars of the show were Jose Collins and George Monroe, it was Miller who got the lion's share of the notices. The *Herald* proclaimed, "A hitherto unknown young woman named Marilyn Miller—an exceedingly clever person who will be much better known before long—made one of the hits of the piece. She looked well, danced well and did some capital imitations."

The finale was a fanciful recreation of the San Francisco earthquake of 1906. After the magnificent earthquake, a new, sparkling, modern city rose from the ruins. Modernity was typified by a landing strip for zeppelins. The huge blimps picked up the chorus and took them across the ocean to Paris, where the girls danced the eagle rock.

Dancing Around (10/10/24; 145 performances) starred Al Jolson, Georgia O'Ramey and Harland Dixon. Jolson again conquered Broadway despite lackluster material. The Sigmund Romberg, Harry Carroll and Harold Atteridge score failed to yield a single hit.

The *Passing Show* series continued with the 1915 edition (5/29/15; 145 performances). It opened with Marilyn Miller, starring along with Willie and Eugene Howard, John Charles Thomas and John Boles. This edition also introduced dances new to Broadway—the hula and pan Pacific drag.

The next year's edition opened on June 22, 1916, with Florence Moore and Ed Wynn. It ran 140 performances. The *Passing Show of 1917* (4/26/17; 196 performances) was the most successful edition yet. It starred Irene Franklin, DeWolf Hopper and Zeke Colvin.

Jolson returned in *Sinbad* (2/14/18; 164 performances). The musical opened with a score by Sigmund Romberg and Harold Atteridge. As usual the best songs were interpolated. These included some of Jolson's greatest hits, "My Mammy" by Walter Donaldson, Sam Lewis and Joe Young, "Rock-A-Bye Your Baby with a Dixie Melody" by Jean Schwartz, Joe Young and Sam Lewis and "Swanee" by George Gershwin (q.v.) and Irving Caesar. In *Sinbad*, Jolson introduced one of his best-loved characters, Gus. The musical director of this edition, Al Goodman (q.v.), was responsible for at least some of the success of the show. "Swanee" had been premiered at the Capitol Theatre (q.v.) to little notice, but with Goodman's arrangement and Jolson's delivery, the song became a standard.

The Passing Show of 1918 (7/25/18; 124 performances) featured the dance team of Fred and Adele Astaire (q.v.). This was the Astaires' second Broadway appearance. Also on the bill with them were Lou Clayton, Willie and Eugene Howard, Nita Naldi, Charles Ruggles and Frank Fay. Critic (q.v.) Heywood Broun singled out the Astaires for special praise: "In an evening in which there was an abundance of good dancing, Fred Astaire stood out. He and his partner Adele Astaire made the show pause early in the evening with a beautiful loose-limbed dance. It almost seemed as if the two young persons had been poured into the dance." In 1918, there was a surfeit of talent on Broadway, and the excellence of the Astaires wasn't anything out of the ordinary.

The next attraction at the Winter Garden was *Monte Cristo, Jr.* (2/12/19; 254 performances), a big hit. The show starred Jack Squire, Adelaide and Hughes and Tom Lewis.

The Passing Show of 1919 (10/23/19; 280 performances) topped all the previous editions. The show featured James Barton, Dick and George Raft, Blanche Ring, Charles Winninger, Reginald Denny and Walter Woolf. It was followed by *Cinderella on Broadway* (6/24/20; 126 performances) with George Price, Al Sexton, Shirley Royce and Flo Burt starring.

The title *Broadway Brevities of 1920* (9/29/20; 105 performances) indicated its creators were hoping the show would develop into an annual revue, but that didn't happen. Eddie Cantor, Bert Williams and George LeMaire starred.

There was no *Passing Show of 1920;* the 1921 edition (12/29/20; 191 performances) starred Marie Dressler and J. Harold Murray. One of the songs was titled "Beautiful Girls Are Like Opium."

The Whirl of New York (6/13/21; 124 performances) opened with J. Harold Murray, Mlle. Adelaide and Smith and Dale. *Make It Snappy* (4/13/22; 96 performances) opened with Eddie Cantor, Georgie Hale, J. Harold Murray and Tot Qualters in the leads. "The Sheik of Araby" by Ted Snyder, Harry B. Smith (q.v.) and Francis Wheeler was the big hit. Cantor satirized Jolson with the tune "My Yiddish Mammy."

The *Passing Show of 1922* (9/20/22; 95 performances) starred Fred Allen, George Hassell, Ethel Shutta and Willie and Eugene Howard. This edition of the *Passing Show* cost the Shuberts $36,000, a lot for a show at the

Winter Garden Roof Courtesy Municipal Art Society.

time but not near what Ziegfeld spent on his *Follies*. The sets and costumes were mainly from other Shubert productions. Fred Allen introduced one of his most inspired ideas in this show. This was the Old Joke Cemetery—a backdrop painted with tombstones upon which were written such hoary old jokes as "The church is on fire; holy smoke" or "A husband is something no respectable family should be without." The worse the jokes, the bigger the laughs. The backdrop was featured for a full five minutes with no one on stage.

The Dancing Girl (1/24/23; 142 performances) was noteworthy in that the Romberg, Atteridge and Irving Caesar score was supplemented by songs by George Gershwin and Cole Porter (q.v.). However their contribution was no better than Romberg's uninspired melodies. *The Dancing Girl* was followed by the *Passing Show of 1923* (6/14/23; 118 performances), which opened with George Jessel leading the cast.

The *Greenwich Village Follies* (9/20/23; 131 performances) (another revue series) was followed by *Innocent Eyes* (5/20/24; 119 performances). It starred Cecil Lean and Cleo Mayfield along with Mistinguett and Frances Williams. The last of the long-running series was *The Passing Show of 1924* (9/3/24; 106 performances). Romberg, Jean Schwartz and Atteridge supplied the score. Direction was by J.C. Huffman, and sets were by Watson Barrett—all Shubert contractees. The song "Nothing Naughty in a Nightie" pretty much summed up the show. In 1932, the Shuberts tried to revive the series, but the show closed out of town. A 1945 edition also closed before coming to New York.

The *Passing Shows* were over and the Winter Garden's next show, *Big Boy* (1/7/25; 48 performances) marked the last time Jolson appeared at the theater. He interpolated such hits as "California, Here I Come," "If You Knew Susie" and "Keep Smiling at Trouble." But Jolson developed an acute case of laryngitis during the run and had to leave the show.

In addition to the *Passing Shows*, the Shuberts ran a revue series called *Artists and Models*. The 1925 edition (6/24/25; 416 performances) boasted the number "The Rotisserie." It featured the chorus girls spinning on a giant spit. The scene was a big hit.

The Clifford Grey and Maurie Rubens musical *The Great Temptations* (5/18/26; 197 performances) was notable only in its casting of Jack Benny, fresh from vaudeville. In 1925, the Shuberts presented a show called *Gay Paree*. They used the title again the following year. The second *Gay Paree* (11/9/26; 175 performances) was followed by the operetta, *The Circus Princess* (4/25/27; 192 performances).

Artist and Models of 1927 (11/15/27; 151 performances) opened with Ted Lewis, Jack Pearl, Jack Squire and Gladys Wheaton. One hit song from the score, "Here Am I–Broken Hearted," was by B.G. DeSylva, Ray Henderson and Lew Brown (q.v.). Ted Lewis wove his

signature phrase—"Is Everybody Happy?"—into a song with Maurie Rubens and Jack Osterman.

The revue series *Greenwich Village Follies* returned to the theater on April 19, 1926, for its last edition. When it closed after 158 performances, it also marked the end of an era at the Winter Garden, for after this legitimate booking Warner Brothers leased the theater and converted it into a talkie movie theater. The first movie to play the Winter Garden was *The Singing Fool,* starring, who else but Al Jolson. It remained a motion-picture house until 1933.

The Winter Garden resumed a legitimate policy with the opening of *Hold Your Horses* (9/25/33; 88 performances). Orchestrator Robert Russell Bennett, best known for his work on Rodgers and Hammerstein (q.v.) musicals, tried his hand as a Broadway composer. Owen Murphy and Robert A. Simon provided the lyrics. Comedian Joe Cook, future Hollywood restauranteur Dave Chasen, Ona Munson, Tom Patricola and Harriet Hoctor starred.

Jake Shubert believed he would have the last laugh, albeit posthumously, with his archrival Florenz Ziegfeld. Shubert bought the *Ziegfeld Follies* title from Ziegfeld's widow Billie Burke. The Shubert-produced *Ziegfeld Follies of 1934* (1/4/34; 182 performances) had a score by Vernon Duke and E.Y. Harburg (q.v.). They contributed at least two standards—"I Like the Likes of You" and "What Is There to Say?" The fine cast included Eve Arden, Everett Marshall, Ziegfeld alumnus Fanny Brice (q.v.), Buddy and Vilma Ebsen, *Passing Show* favorites Willie and Eugene Howard, Robert Cummings and Jane Froman.

Life Begins at 8:40 (8/27/34; 238 performances) was the clever title of the next Winter Garden tenant. Harold Arlen (q.v.), E.Y. Harburg and Ira Gershwin (q.v.) contributed a fine score that included such hits as "Fun to Be Fooled," "Let's Take a Walk Around the Block" and "You're a Builder Upper."

In *Life Begins at 8:40*, Arlen and Harburg discovered a new, more sophisticated facet of the talents of Bert Lahr, the comic previously known for his burlesque style grotesqueries. Lahr, in turn, gave Harold Arlen his first opportunities to compose out and out comedy songs. Previously Arlen had composed his well known ballads, upbeat production numbers for the Cotton Club and racy, risque numbers for that same venue. But with Lahr, Arlen was able to break new ground in his career. Arlen and Harburg went on to create Lahr's most beloved character, the Cowardly Lion in the film *The Wizard of Oz*. The successful 238 performance run of *Life Begins at 8:40* was also due to the talents of Ray Bolger and Frances Williams.

Earl Carroll rented the Winter Garden to present *Earl Carroll's Sketch Book*. The show opened on June 4, 1935 with Ken Murray and Sunnie O'Dea starring. The score, written mostly by Murray Mencher, Charles Newman and Charles Tobias, was passable. It was

Carroll's way with beautiful women which accounted for the 207 performance run.

Another revue, *At Home Abroad,* more sophisticated than *Earl Carroll's Sketch Book,* opened at the Winter Garden on September 19, 1935 with a fine score by Arthur Schwartz and Howard Dietz. Their songs, "O What a Wonderful World," "Love Is a Dancing Thing" and "Get Yourself a Geisha" were well handled by the talented cast including Beatrice Lillie, Reginald Gardner, Ethel Waters, Eleanor Powell and Eddie Foy, Jr.

During rehearsals for *At Home Abroad,* Howard Dietz had a disagreement with director Vincente Minnelli. Their argument was not getting resolved through reasonable means, so Dietz went to his contract with the Shuberts and pointed out the clause that gave him complete control over all aspects of the production. Minnelli pulled out the contract he negotiated with Lee Shubert and found the same exact clause. With a common enemy to hate, Dietz and Minnelli decided to resolve their problems to their mutual satisfaction.

Minnelli returned to the Winter Garden to design the sets for its next offering, the *Ziegfeld Follies of 1936* (1/30/36; 115 performances). John Murray Anderson *(q.v.),* responsible for the previous *Follies* and the *Greenwich Village Follies,* directed. Vernon Duke repeated his past *Follies* assignment, but this time the lyricist was Ira Gershwin. They came up with a great song, "I Can't Get Started." It was sung by Bob Hope and Eve Arden in the production. The show also starred Bobby Clark, Josephine Baker, Fanny Brice as Baby Snooks, Gypsy Rose Lee, the Nicholas Brothers, Jane Pickens and Gertrude Neisen—a stupendous cast.

Vincente Minnelli returned to his directorial chores with *The Show Is On* (12/25/36; 236 performances). He also designed the sets and costumes for the all-star revue. *The Show Is On* brought Bert Lahr, Beatrice Lillie and Reginald Gardiner back to the stage of the Winter Garden. Lahr arranged for Arlen and Harburg to write him a song—"The Song of the Woodman"—that again perfectly captured his brilliant talents. Beatrice Lillie scattered garters, while floating out over the audience on a moon. She also made "Rhythm" by Richard Rodgers and Lorenz Hart *(q.v.)* totally her own. George and Ira Gershwin *(q.v.)* provided a sprightly waltz, "By Strauss," and Vernon Duke and Ted Fetter contributed the haunting tune "Now." Hoagy Carmichael and Stanley Adams had a hit with "Little Old Lady." Schwartz and Dietz and Herman Hupfeld also had songs in the score.

E.Y. Harburg, never one to shrink from airing his political and moral beliefs on stage, wrote lyrics with Harold Arlen for the antiwar musical *Hooray for What!* (12/1/37; 199 performances) Harburg chose Howard Lindsay and Russel Crouse to script his story with Lindsay also directing.

Hooray for What! tells the story of a meek horticulturist who invents a gas that kills insects. One of its side effects is that it also kills humans. Naturally, it then becomes a valuable commodity with the nations of the world vying for the formula.

Ed Wynn, Vivian Vance (before "I Love Lucy"), Jack Whiting and June Clyde starred. The cast included Kay Thompson as well, who also handled the vocal arranging along with Hugh Martin. Among the hopefuls trying out for the chorus was Ralph Blane. After being rejected, Blane, who would have given anything to be in an Arlen musical, simply got on line to audition for choreographer Agnes de Mille. Blane had no training as a dancer and was quickly dismissed, but he did not give up. He arranged for an agent to pester Thompson until she agreed to give Blane an audition. Exasperated, she told Blane to come to her apartment, where she was rehearsing the already assembled Kay Thompson Singers. Thompson ignored Blane while she rehearsed the group, and finally it was time to go to the theater to show the number to Shubert henchman Harry Kaufman. Kaufman was much hated by the entire company as he continually tried to quash any attempts at art in favor of cheesecake.

At the theater Blane, who had learned the song's vocal arrangement while sitting in Thompson's apartment, simply joined in with the assembled group. He tried to make himself invisible in the last row, but Harry Kaufman spotted him. "Didn't I throw you out of here twice already?" asked Kaufman. Blane, thinking fast, told Kaufman he had been hired by Thompson. This was news to her, but her annoyance with Blane was nowhere near her hatred of Kaufman. She stuck up for Blane, and Arlen, Minnelli and Harburg concurred that Blane was indeed a member of the cast.

Because of Blane's persistence, and the company's antipathy for Harry Kaufman, Blane met Hugh Martin and the two went on to write the score for *Best Foot Forward,* the MGM musical *Meet Me in St. Louis* and other musicals on stage and screen.

Hooray for What! traveled a rocky road to its Broadway opening. While out of town in Boston, Thompson was fired. De Mille's choreography was "helped" by a choreographer hired by Kaufman to juice up her classically inspired steps. Two leads were fired, and Harburg's trenchant story became more and more emasculated by Kaufman's orders.

Before she was canned by Kaufman, Thompson telephoned de Mille. The choreographer was shocked to be awakened at 2:30 in the morning and asked what could be so important. Thompson enthusiastically reported that Kaufman had fallen into the orchestra pit and had broken his back. De Mille replied, "You're just telling me this to make me feel good."

Surprisingly, despite its hazardous preopening experiences, *Hooray for What!* was a success. Critics were especially enthusiastic about the return to the legitimate stage of Ed Wynn who had enjoyed a protracted run on radio. Richard Watts exclaimed that "gone and happily forgotten are those unfortunate nights when the furious but feeble antics of the Fire Chief were demonstrating what terrible things the wanton wireless can do to a great comedian."

You Never Know (9/31/38; 78 performances) was a Cole Porter failure that contained one hit song, "At Long Last Love." Porter had a good excuse for the show's uninspired score. While working on the show, he was critically injured in a horseback-riding accident. Porter's legs were crushed by the horse, and he never fully recovered from the accident. The story, perhaps apocryphal, was that Porter worked on the lyrics to "At Long Last Love" while waiting for help.

Olsen and Johnson's phenomenally successful revue *Hellzapoppin'* had moved to the Winter Garden from the 46th Street Theatre, where it eventually completed its 1,404-performance run. The Shuberts quickly capitalized on Ole Olsen and Chic Johnson's great popularity by creating the show *Sons O' Fun* (12/1/41; 742 performances) for them. The musical comedy opened

with Joe Besser, Ella Logan and Carmen Miranda completing the cast. Sammy Fain and Jack Yellen wrote a forgettable score.

A last Shubert-produced *Ziegfeld Follies* (4/14/43; 553 performances) opened at the Winter Garden the day after the opening of *Oklahoma!* (q.v.). It ran longer than any other edition of the show. Contributing were the talents of songwriters Ray Henderson and Jack Yellen and cast members Milton Berle, Eric Blore, Ilona Massey, Arthur Treacher and the puppetry of Bil and Cora Baird. Berle was the first performer in *Follies* history to be advertised above the title.

Cole Porter returned to the Winter Garden with *Mexican Hayride* (1/28/44; 479 performances). The Mike Todd production opened with a book by Herbert and Dorothy Fields (q.v.). Bobby Clark, Wilbur Evans, June Havoc and George Givot starred. Porter's score wasn't one of his best, but it did have one hit song, "I Love You."

Olsen and Johnson returned to the Winter Garden in

Winter Garden Theater

Laffing Room Only (12/13/44; 232 performances). The revue had music and lyrics by Burton Lane (*q.v.*). Olsen and Johnson were joined on the stage by Betty Garrett and Fred Waring's Glee Club.

Marinka (7/18/45; 165 performances) was an attempt to bring operetta back to Broadway. The Emmerich Kalman music failed to catch on with audiences. Following *Marinka,* the Winter Garden abandoned legitimate production and returned to showing movies.

Three years later, a new musical comedy, *As the Girls Go* (11/13/48; 414 performances), opened at the theater. Michael Todd was the producer, Bobby Clark was the star and Jimmy McHugh and Harold Adamson wrote the score.

Todd presented his *Michael Todd's Peep Show* (6/28/50; 278 performances) at the Winter Garden. This time Bobby Clark did not appear on stage but wrote some of the sketches. Harold Rome (*q.v.*), Jule Styne (*q.v.*) and Bob Hilliard and Sammy Stept all wrote songs for the show. Several songs were written by Bhumibol, the then King of Thailand. This was certainly the only time that royalty contributed songs to a girlie show.

By the time *Top Banana* (11/1/51; 350 performances) opened at the Winter Garden, television had taken hold of the nation's imagination. Broadway was afraid of the impact of the "boob tube," as its detractors dubbed it. *Top Banana,* a satire on television with a jaunty score by Johnny Mercer, was reputedly a takeoff on Milton Berle's early adventures in the new medium. Phil Silvers, Jack Albertson, Rose Marie and Judy Lynn starred. The show was dotted with vaudeville and burlesque turns along with a stock musical-comedy plot line. It had the distinction of being filmed during an actual performance. The film was released in movie theaters to little notice.

The theater's next hit was a major one. *Wonderful Town* (2/25/53; 559 performances) reunited Leonard Bernstein (*q.v.*) with Betty Comden and Adolph Green (*q.v.*), and they came up with what can only be described as a brilliant score. Joseph Fields and Jerome Chodorov based their libretto on their play *My Sister Eileen.* Rosalind Russell made her musical-comedy debut with Edith Adams as her sister Eileen. Cris Alexander, Jordan Bentley and George Gaynes were also featured. Director George Abbott (*q.v.*) kept the show moving, and the entire proceedings were hailed by critics.

On March 1, 1957, the final edition of the *Ziegfeld Follies* (123 performances) opened at the Winter Garden Theater. Beatrice Lillie, Billy DeWolfe, Carol Lawrence, Harold Lang and Jane Morgan starred.

Leonard Bernstein collaborated with Stephen Sondheim (*q.v.*) (in his first Broadway assignment) on the score for *West Side Story* (9/26/57; 732 performances). Robert E. Griffith and Harold Prince produced, Arthur Laurents wrote the libretto, which was loosely based

on Shakespeare's Romeo and Juliet updated to contemporary New York. Jerome Robbins directed and choreographed with his usual genius. The show starred Larry Kert and Carol Lawrence (late of the *Ziegfeld Follies of 1957*) as the star-crossed lovers Tony and Maria. The cast also featured Chita Rivera (who became a star due to her fiery performance as Anita), future Broadway lyricist Martin Charnin and Marilyn Cooper.

"Tonight," "Something's Coming," "Somewhere," "Maria" and "I Feel Pretty" all became standards. *West Side Story* returned to Broadway on April 27, 1960, for an additional 249 performances.

Meredith Willson tried to repeat his success of *The Music Man* with his next musical, *The Unsinkable Molly Brown* (11/3/60; 532 performances). Tammy Grimes and Harve Presnell starred in the big hit. Willson ably captured the optimistic exuberance of the turn of the century. Tammy Grimes's energetic performance helped the show along. "I Ain't Down Yet" was the show's hit and became a popular standard. *The Unsinkable Molly Brown* was one of the last successes for the Theater Guild (*q.v.*), which coproduced the evening with playwright Dore Schary.

Robbins also had a hand in the Winter Garden's next smash hit, *Funny Girl* (3/26/64; 1,348 performances). Barbra Streisand played Winter Garden star Fanny Brice with Danny Meehan, Kay Medford, Sydney Chaplin and Jean Stapleton in supporting roles. Jule Styne and Bob Merrill wrote a great score, full of theatrically exciting melodies and rhythms. "People" became the hit of the show as well as Streisand's signature tune. "Don't Rain on My Parade" was also much performed outside the show.

A strong central performance and catchy score was also responsible for the success of the Winter Garden's next hit, *Mame* (5/24/66; 1,508 performances). The Jerry Herman (*q.v.*) show had an enjoyable libretto by playwrights Jerome Lawrence and Robert E. Lee, as well as an excellent performance by Angela Lansbury as the title character. Beatrice Arthur, Sab Shimono, Jane Connell, Jerry Lanning and Frankie Michaels made up the supporting cast. *Mame* was a smash hit at a time when the general consensus was that Broadway was dead.

A brilliant musical, the greatest production to play the Great White Way in decades, was Stephen Sondheim and James Goldman's *Follies* (4/4/71; 522 performances). Sondheim's score was in part a pastiche of the accomplishments of his predecessors in the musical theater, and it also contained sharp, scathing original numbers. Goldman's libretto broke open the traditional confines of the musical comedy. Through codirectors Harold Prince and Michael Bennett's genius, the show kept the past and present in constant juxtaposition. Boris Aronson's set design, Florence Klotz's costumes and Tharon Musser's lighting added up to make the most spectacular physical production Broadway had seen since the days of the original *Ziegfeld Follies*.

The show has a complex concept in which ghosts from past *Follies* haunt the memories of the present day performers, gathered together to remember their youthful days on Broadway. The occasion is the impending demolition of the theater that hosted the revues. By the end of the show, the audience has entered the psyches of the leading characters through a series of *Follies*-styled numbers.

Audiences either left the Winter Garden literally speechless, stunned by the force of this powerful show, or they emerged onto Broadway bewildered. For the sophisticated theatergoer, *Follies* was an unforgettable experience. There was enough theatricality and ideas in *Follies* to fuel 20 ordinary Broadway musicals.

The *Follies* cast, Dorothy Collins, Alexis Smith, Gene Nelson, John McMartin, Ethel Shutta, Yvonne De Carlo, Kurt Peterson, Marti Rolph, Virginia Sandifur, Harvey Evans and Mary McCarty brought a resonance to the show that no other musical has come close to capturing. The show won seven Tony Awards *(q.v.)* but failed to win best musical, which went to Galt McDermot's rock musicalization of *Two Gentlemen of Verona*. *Follies* failure to win for best musical stands as an indictment of the entire awards process and the Tony Awards in particular. *Follies* became a legendary production itself.

The New York Shakespeare Festival, responsible for the production of *Two Gentlemen of Verona*, which won the Tony Award over *Follies*, produced the next hit at the Winter Garden, William Shakespeare's *Much Ado About Nothing* (11/11/72; 116 performances). Critics hailed Kathleen Widdoes's and Sam Waterston's performances as well as A. J. Antoon's direction.

Angela Lansbury returned to the Winter Garden in *Gypsy* (9/23/74; 120 performances) with its masterful score by Jule Styne *(q.v.)* and Stephen Sondheim. The revival was originally mounted in London. Lansbury received a Tony Award as best actress for her portrayal of Rose, the ultimate stage mother.

The theater again resounded with the music of Stephen Sondheim when his *Pacific Overtures* (1/11/76; 193 performances) opened. The rather unconventional basis of *Pacific Overtures* was Commodore Perry's forays into feudal Japan. The show explored the different perceptions of life by the two cultures and the unavoidable changes in Japanese traditions. *Pacific Overtures* was a tragedy with a scope seldom attempted on Broadway. However, the score, which included songs like the masterpiece "Someone in a Tree" was not easily appreciated by the average theatergoer.

A revival of *Fiddler on the Roof (q.v.)* with its original star Zero Mostel played the Winter Garden for 167 performances in 1976. Unfortunately, Mostel, a mercurial actor with an amazing range, could not contain himself and constantly mugged his way through the show.

A concert performance by Beatles look-alikes, *Beatlemania* (920 performances), began previews at the Winter Garden on May 26, 1977. The producers, knowing that the Broadway critics *(q.v.)* would slaughter the show, refused to hold an official opening night. The expected bad reviews appeared anyway. But *Beatlemania*'s audiences didn't care what the *New York Times* thought. The younger set from New Jersey and Long Island jammed the theater and kept *Beatlemania* running.

A historic opening night occurred at David Merrick's *(q.v.)* production *42nd Street* (8/24/80; 3486 performances). After the curtain rang down on what most critics called a stunning success, Merrick took center stage. He announced to the assemblage that the show's director and choreographer, Gower Champion, had died that afternoon. The Broadway community was stunned; Champion was considered a fine talent and the fact that he died on the eve of what would be his greatest triumph was especially painful.

After *42nd Street* moved to the Majestic Theater *(q.v.)* (and then moved to the St. James *(q.v.)* to make way for *The Phantom of the Opera*) the Shuberts closed the Winter Garden for renovation. It reopened with the blockbuster musical *Cats* (10/7/82). *Cats*, the brainchild of Andrew Lloyd Webber and director Trevor Nunn, received mixed reviews. But the musicalization of T.S. Eliot's children's poetry was presold because of its great success in London. One wag accounted for the play's great success by claiming that everyone was interested in watching physically fit performers jumping up and down in skintight leotards. There was a hit song,

Andrew Lloyd Webber. Courtesy ASCAP.

"Memory," which many people felt owed much to Puccini. Broadwayites were astonished when Eliot, who had been dead for years and who would never have dreamed that his simple poems would become the basis for an overblown spectacle, won the Tony Award for best lyrics. *Cats* is still playing at the Winter Garden.

WINTHROP AMES THEATER   See LITTLE THEATER.

WOOLLCOTT, ALEXANDER (1887–1946) Today Alexander Woollcott is perhaps best remembered as the model for the character Sheridan Whiteside in Kaufman and Hart's *(q.v.)* comedy *The Man Who Came to Dinner.* In the play, he was depicted as a vain, vituperative sentimentalist. In real life, he was all those things and more. Woollcott was among the most important voices in the publishing world as both critic and essayist.

At the turn of the century, the theater was the primary source of entertainment, and the newspapers were the primary source of news. Stagestruck since his teens, Woollcott managed to influence both worlds with his acerbic, witty writing and boosterism. He castigated those he considered hacks and championed those he considered geniuses. His influence extended beyond the printed page to radio and to society. He was the major domo of the Algonquin Round Table *(q.v.)* and from his vantage point passed judgment on the men and women of the theater and letters.

Woollcott was born on January 19, 1887, in Phlanx, New Jersey. Most of his early years were spent in Kansas City. There he met Roswell M. Field, a newspaperman on the *Kansas City Star.* Woollcott took an immediate liking to the newspaperman who informed him that newspapermen often received free tickets to the local theatrical attractions. In fact, Field's niece took Woollcott to his first live performance.

Woollcott was hooked on the theater and journalism at the age of eight and vowed to become a newspaperman. After moving back to New Jersey and a succession of private schools, Woollcott received his first professional assignments, writing book reviews for the *Philadelphia Telegraph.* His pay was ownership of the books he reviewed and his name on the reviews. He contributed to the *Telegraph* throughout his senior year of high school.

Toward the end of his days at Hamilton College, Woollcott ran across Samuel Hopkins Adams. Adams later described Woollcott as "an odd figure . . . The youth was clad in excessively wrinkled and baggy trousers, a misshapen corduroy coat, grimy sneakers, and a red fez with a gilt tassel . . . I was struck with the owlish gravity of the eyes behind the large lenses, and an air not so much cocky as confident, suggesting the trustfulness of a tenderly reared baby."

Adams introduced Woollcott to Carr Van Anda, managing editor of the *New York Times.* Van Anda hired Woollcott, assigning him to the city room where he eventually worked his way up from cub reporter and gofer to full-fledged reporter and feature writer. When *Times* drama critic Adolph Klauber retired, Van Anda hired Woollcott as critic. Although only 27, Woollcott had firm opinions, and he set about his job with a sense of mission. Woollcott wouldn't knuckle under the influence of any producer or associate.

Most reviewers at the time were simply paid pawns of the producers. Neither they nor their editors regarded the theater as an art and most of the reviews were not really criticism but rather extended press releases. Woollcott, however, saw himself as an independent. He did not consider himself an outsider looking at the theater from afar but believed the critic was an important part of the creative force of the theater. He had been a prop boy and actor in amateur theatricals and so regarded himself better qualified than most in voicing his opinion.

He soon convinced Van Anda to give him space in the Sunday edition of the *Times.* He used this space for reflective essays under the banner "Second Thoughts on First Nights." This was the first instance of reflective journalism in the drama pages and set a precedent for essays that continue to be published even today in the *Times* and other newspapers.

Woollcott's attempts at performing left a soft spot in his heart for actors, and he tended to be kind to them. But he was not afraid of his opinions and felt that his writing should reflect the atmosphere of Times Square and the theater community. Woollcott's attitude took hold, and soon the drama pages became among the most important of the paper's sections. Critic Burns Mantle wrote in 1915 that Woollcott had "become the most talked-of and the widest-read dramatic critic in town."

Woollcott, the talk of the theater community, won the appreciation of most actors because he took their work seriously. But the producers found Woollcott and his thoughtful criticism an increasingly powerful nuisance.

The Shuberts *(q.v.),* in particular, took offense at the young reporter's refusal to write puff pieces. When they opened an insignificant play, *Taking Chances* at the 39th Street Theater on March 17, 1915, Woollcott disliked the play and said so in print, writing that there were "moments when a puzzled audience wonders what it is all about." The Shuberts expecting the negative notice, took an ad out in the same issue as Woollcott's review in which they admonished: "Do not believe everything you see in the notices today." Next they banned Woollcott from their theaters.

Times owner Adolph Ochs stood by Woollcott, and on April 1, he banned all Shubert advertising from his paper until his critic was allowed to attend Shubert openings. Thus, the battle lines were drawn with both parties backed into a corner. The *Times* took the Shuberts to court in order to obtain an injunction against the Shuberts. When the newspaper succeeded, the Shuberts dragged the matter back to court.

The Shuberts lost this appeal and immediately went to a higher court. The higher court sided with the Shuberts and held that they were allowed to admit anyone they desired, since after all, they owned the theaters. This victory by the Shuberts only served to alienate the Broadway community who considered Woollcott their champion and were inclined to root for the underdog.

As the battle raged, more and more readers were introduced to Woollcott and circulation increased; and so did advertising revenue based on increased readership. Woollcott was given more space on Sundays and a raise from $60 a week to $100 a week.

The battle was resolved late in the year through pressure put on the Shuberts by producer Oliver Morosco. Morosco was the leading West Coast producer and allowed the Shuberts rights to present his plays in New York. Morosco was an intelligent man and realized his productions were being harmed through the Shubert/Times feud. It didn't matter to Morosco whether he went with the Shuberts or another management, and he told the Shuberts that he needed the Times advertising and so would sever ties with their organization. The Shuberts saw the wisdom in his position and approached the Times to settle the feud. The Times agreed, and Woollcott once more was allowed access to Shubert theaters.

With this success, the job of theatrical reviewer was regarded in new light. The reviewer was considered a real journalist, and the arts section of the newspaper was deemed as important as the sports or front pages. It was at this time that the Times became the leading newspaper in coverage of the arts. People felt the Times critic, right or wrong, had integrity, and they read Woollcott and listened to his opinions in increasing numbers.

Woollcott, by this time a great force in society and journalism, was unhappy with his pay at the Times and so was lured to the New York Herald by its publisher Frank Munsey. His Sunday column was titled "In the Wake of the Plays."

The Herald was thereafter merged with the Tribune in the Spring of 1924. Woollcott was transferred to the other Munsey-owned paper, the New York Sun. The Sun was an afternoon paper of little importance, and Woollcott could hardly wait until August of 1925 when his contract expired and he could join the World. He replaced journalist and critic Heywood Broun, who became a news columnist.

Although Woollcott was prone to overenthusiasm in his reviews, he was also noted for his caustic comments. Producers were especially upset at Woollcott's using their hard work as an opportunity for a witty phrase or bon mot. But Woollcott couldn't resist. His best friends were the members of the Algonquin Round Table (q.v.), a group of writers and performers known for their rapier wit. This influence rubbed off on Woollcott, who could not help showing off in his reviews.

One example is in Woollcott's review of a play that concerned a pilot whose plane crashes near an Indian reservation. The pilot, badly hurt, is adopted by an Indian family. There he is nursed back to health by the warrior's daughter, who develops a crush on the airman. The mother discovers the pilot and girl in a passionate embrace and tells the father, who threatens to kill the white man.

The second act opens with the pilot proclaiming his innocence. The parents accuse him of having sex with their daughter and declare he must die. The pilot denies the accusation. At the end of the play, the pilot reveals that it was impossible for him to have made love to the girl since he was castrated in the plane crash. Woollcott commented: "In the first act she becomes a lady. In the second act, he becomes a lady."

Those who feared Woollcott's barbed reviews didn't have to worry long. Woollcott was tired of the World and resented the interference of his editor Herbert Bayard Swope and his publisher Joseph Pulitzer. When his contract ran out in May of 1928, Woollcott quit the newspaper business.

A collection of his writing, Going to Pieces, contained his thoughts on reviewing:

I find myself engaged in the business—the business, mind you—of going to the theater. I do not write plays. I do not act plays. I do not even produce plays. I merely go to see them. By contracts between the party of the first part, the party of the second part and all that sort of thing my life is actually so arranged that in the past dozen years I have not only attended two thousand first nights in New York, London, Paris and Berlin, but far from paying for the privilege, am myself paid for the inconvenience.

Professional playgoing seems to me hardly a career which a decent man would deliberately map out for himself any more than one would plan an exclusive diet of macaroons or lemon meringue pie.

Woollcott went on to write many pieces for magazines such as The New Yorker, Collier's and The Saturday Evening Post. He published many anthologies of his magazine works, many of which were on the theater. He attempted playwriting by collaborating with George S. Kaufman on The Channel Road, which premiered on November 17, 1929. The play received decidedly mixed reviews, with most of the critics making comments about drama critics attempting to write drama. The play lasted 60 performances at the Plymouth Theater (q.v.). It might have run longer but for an unfortunate bit of timing; in November of 1929, right after the stock market crash, most people's minds weren't on the theater.

Despite heavy losses in the stock market, Woollcott was able to weather the storm with his talents. He continued contributing magazine pieces, and in the fall of 1929, he found himself on the radio for the Mutual Broadcasting Network. After his 13-week run on WOR, he moved to CBS while continuing his weekly contributions to *The New Yorker* and articles for *Colliers,* and other magazines.

Despite his abdication as the theater's finest critic, Woollcott continued to influence the drama through his writing and radio broadcasts, which often revolved around luminaries of the drama and their works. But no one was ready for Woollcott's next foray into the theaters of Times Square. After trying his hand at playwriting, he decided to try acting.

Woollcott opened at the Belasco Theatre *(q.v.)* on November 9, 1931, in S.N. Behrman's *Brief Moment.* The played was presented by Katharine Cornell *(q.v.)* and Guthrie McClintic and starred Frances Larrimore. Woollcott played Harold Sigrift—a character described in the script as "very fat, about thirty years old, and lies down whenever possible. He somewhat resembles Alexander Woollcott, who conceivably might play him."

The play was a flop, but Woollcott received glowing notices. After all he had been playing the character all his adult life. Brooks Atkinson commented in the *New York Times,* "Mr. Woollcott tosses it across the footlights with a relish that the audience shares. If he enjoyed himself as much as the audience last night enjoyed him, he must have been having a very good time."

The play lasted 129 performances, mostly on the basis of Woollcott's performance. The play was selected by Burns Mantle as one of the year's 10 best. Though Woollcott played a character based on himself, he did differ from Harold Sigrift in some ways. In the first act, the character states, "Let me tell you something about vitality, my chuck. It's fatiguing to live with. I lived with a girl once who had vitality. She wore me out. Nowadays I go in for languor." Woollcott certainly never lived with a girl, considering himself a confirmed bachelor. And he definitely did not go in for languor. At this point, he was as busy as could be.

Two years later, he increased his schedule, beginning another stint on CBS Radio. This was even more successful than his first forays on the airwaves, and Woollcott again extended his influence. Later in 1933, he premiered his second dramatic collaboration with George S. Kaufman. *The Dark Tower* opened on November 25 at the Morosco Theatre *(q.v.).* The play was a failure, running only 57 performances.

S.N. Behrman used Woollcott in another of his plays, *Wine of Choice.* This opened at the Guild Theater *(q.v.)* on February 21, 1938. It fared no better than *Brief Moment* and closed after only 43 performances.

Woollcott continued his advocacy of writers who he believed did not get their due. Among these were Ernest Hemingway, Clarence Day and James Hilton. All owed much of their early success to Woollcott's efforts. He convinced Little Brown to publish Hilton's *Goodbye Mr. Chips,* and it became a huge success. He also trumpeted the talents of John Steinbeck and his sometime-collaborator George S. Kaufman.

Kaufman repaid the compliment by making Woollcott the main character in his and Moss Hart's comedy, *The Man Who Came to Dinner.* In 1934, Woollcott had become the Town Crier in a series of broadcasts for Cream of Wheat. When the sponsor objected to Woollcott's damnation of Hitler and Mussolini, he chose to drop the show. In 1937, he returned to the airwaves for the Granger Pipe Tobacco Company. In *The Man Who Came to Dinner,* Kaufman and Hart made Sheridan Whiteside (the character based on Woollcott) a radio personality who was sponsored by Cream of Mush. The play opened on October 16, 1939. Though there was some talk of Woollcott himself playing the lead, it was given to Monty Woolley with Woollcott's blessing.

The critics were unanimous in their raves. Naturally, much was made of Woollcott's reactions to being made the "irascible, not to say insulting hero of the play" as Burns Mantle put it. Woollcott, with tongue in cheek, denied everything, "Of course this is a libelous caricature. It is not true that the role of the obnoxious Sheridan Whiteside . . . was patterned after me. Whiteside is merely a composite of the better qualities of the play's two authors."

Woollcott would finally play the role in stock at the Pasadena Civic Auditorium on March 6, 1940. The next month, when Woollcott was playing the part in San Francisco, he was stricken with a heart attack. Woollcott recovered relatively quickly, and he resumed his hectic schedule. In March of 1942, after a trip to England, he returned home and was stricken again. His recuperation was only partially successful, and a long period of rest followed. During a broadcast at CBS on January 23, 1943, he collapsed and died soon thereafter.

Woollcott was both the obnoxious, literary snob and the florid sentimentalist. He was a crusader for causes and a supporter of worthy charities. He had the nerve to stake his job and reputation against the powerful Shuberts and a penchant for indulging himself in witticisms at others' expense. He adored *Goodbye Mr. Chips* and was a lifelong collector of true murder stories. In all, he was a complex man who, at his most powerful, lived an uncompromising life with himself as the star.

Edna Ferber said that Woollcott was a New Jersey Nero who mistook his pinafore for a toga. Howard Dietz *(q.v.)* dubbed him Louisa M. Woollcott. George S. Kaufman, one of Woollcott's closest friends, told Moss Hart, "Life without Aleck is like a play with a crucial scene dropped. It still plays, but something good has gone out of it."

WORLD THEATER   See CHARLES HOPKINS THEATER.

YIDDISH ART THEATER See GEORGE ABBOTT THEATER. See JOLSON'S 59TH STREET THEATER.

YOUMANS, VINCENT (1898–1946) Vincent Youmans was the quintessential twenties composer. His shows dominated the decade. The closest competitor was George Gershwin *(q.v.),* who was born one day before Youmans. Jerome Kern *(q.v.)* also provided scores to many fine shows in the twenties, including the greatest of his career, *Show Boat.* But Youmans imbued his music with a drive and rhythm that seems to define the decade, its spirit, its speed, and its humor. Zelda Fitzgerald even gave a nod to Youmans in her novel *Save Me the Waltz.*

Youmans's hits, all of which occurred in the twenties, included *No, No, Nanette, Hit the Deck* and *Wildflower.* Though these shows were wonderfully popular, Youmans's career as a whole was not as impressive as some of his contemporaries for two reasons. First, with only 93 published songs to his credit, he wasn't that prolific. Gershwin sometimes was represented by four shows in a single season. Youmans only had two shows in a single year on two occasions. Second, he was hampered by a constant battle with tuberculosis and alcoholism.

The composer was born on September 27, 1898, in New York City. He began writing songs while at the Great Lakes Training Station. The camp shows gave Youmans enough of a taste for show business, so that after his discharge, he was committed to a composing career.

Like many of his contemporaries, Youmans broke into the business as a song plugger for Remick's music publishers, his second choice having been turned down by Max Dreyfus of T.B. Harms publishing. Remick's published Youman's first popular song, "The Country Cousin," written with lyricist Al Bryan. Youmans landed his first theater job as a rehearsal pianist for producer Alex Aarons's *(q.v.)* show, *Oui Madame.* Victor Herbert *(q.v.)* was the composer. Later, composer Harold Arlen *(q.v.)* got his start in the theater as a rehearsal pianist for Youmans's *Great Day!* Youmans had his first song written for the stage interpolated into a Charlotte Greenwood vehicle, *Linger Longer Letty.* The song was "Maid-To-Order Maid" but it was only in for one performance while the show played Stamford, Connecticut. Youmans next had two songs interpolated into the show *Piccadilly to Broadway* in Atlantic City. The show closed out of town.

Youmans decided to see Dreyfus again and ask for a job. The music publisher was a sort of father figure for his employees and he took pains to give them every opportunity to develop their talents. Dreyfus hired

Vincent Youmans Courtesy ASCAP.

Youmans as a song plugger. Alex Aarons paired Youmans with composer Paul Lannin (fated to be Youmans's lifelong friend and drinking buddy) and brought in George Gershwin's brother Ira *(q.v.)* to supply the lyrics. At that time, Ira was writing under the name Arthur Francis. The resulting show was *Two Little Girls in Blue* (5/3/21; 135 performances), starring the Fairbanks sisters, Madeline and Marion. The show marked the Broadway debuts of both Youmans and Ira Gershwin. Aarons had sold his interests in the show to producer Abraham Erlanger, head of the despised Theatrical Trust. Erlanger was among the most powerful men in the theater and held the first near monopoly in the American theater. The show was a hit, which made Max Dreyfus happy, for the songs "Who's Who with You," "Dolly" and "Oh, Me! Oh, My" were all successful.

Though Youmans had passed his first test, he was not happy. He was unable to get another Broadway assignment and found himself again behind the piano working rehearsals of Victor Herbert's *Orange Blossoms.* Youmans's drinking increased, despite the fact that his second show, *Wildflower* (2/7/23; 477 performances), proved to be a great success and solidified his place in the musical theater. Arthur Hammerstein *(q.v.)* produced *Wildflower,* which had book and lyrics by Oscar Hammerstein II *(q.v.)* and Otto Harbach *(q.v.)*. Herbert Stothart also composed music for some of the songs. The show opened with Edith Day, Olin Howland and Charles Judels leading the cast.

The show received mostly excellent reviews, although Youmans and Stothart must have been taken aback when they read in the *New York Times* that the show "contains the most tuneful score that Rudolf Friml *(q.v.)* has written in a number of seasons." Charles Darnton, writing in the *New York Evening World,* stated, "at first the music seemed too good to last, but this fear proved groundless as the score offered one gay, youthful, charming melody after another." Alexander Woollcott *(q.v.)* writing in the *New York Herald,* was one of the dissenters. He was concerned that the show contained "an entirely unobjectionable mixture of songs and dances which we are going to have a mighty hard time remembering when someone asks us next September what show followed Sally, Irene and Mary at the Casino." Several of the critics predicted that the hit song would be "Bambalina."

Mary Jane McKane (12/25/23; 151 performances) opened at the Imperial Theatre *(q.v.)*. Mary Hay starred in the show along with Stanley Ridges and Eva Clark. Youmans collaborated with lyricists William Cary Duncan and Oscar Hammerstein II. Herbert Stothart also composed some songs for this show. The show received good reviews, though none of the songs achieved much success. Laurence Stallings of the *New York World* was pleased that "someone at last has staged a production number that doesn't present girls as soft drinks or popular race horses."

Youmans composed his first score without a cocomposer for *Lollipop* (1/21/24; 145 performances). He was teamed with Zelda Sears, one of the few women lyricists writing for Broadway. Youmans now had three shows running on Broadway simultaneously, for *Wildflower* and *Mary Jane McKane* were still running. *Lollipop* was another hit for Youmans. However, the show didn't contain any hit songs and didn't break any new ground. It certainly didn't prepare Broadway for his next triumph.

Youmans's next assignment, *No, No, Nanette* (9/16/25; 239 performances), proved to be an even bigger hit, although it did not run as long as *Wildflower. No, No, Nanette* was produced and directed by H.H. Frazee, past owner of the Boston Red Sox. Frazee worked out a precedent-setting deal with his star, Louise Groody, who played the title character. She was the first star in Broadway history to receive a percentage of the box office in addition to a salary.

No, No, Nanette provided Youmans with a modern setting and his talents exploded. He seemed made to compose up-to-the-minute tunes that perfectly captured the syncopation and drive of the era. Irving Caesar's fine lyrics perfectly complemented Youmans's music. The show contained one of the greatest hit songs of the twenties—"Tea for Two." Caesar claimed the lyric was a dummy lyric, used to set rhythms in his mind before writing the actual words. But the dummy lyric proved so popular that he kept it. The other smash hit from the score was "I Want to Be Happy," a title that seemed to express the mood of the entire country in the giddy years before the Depression.

Irving Caesar Courtesy ASCAP.

No, No, Nanette toured successfully and enjoyed a long life in both professional and amateur theaters for years to come. *Nanette* might have run longer on Broadway, but prior to its New York engagement, Frazee ran the show for a year in Chicago, set up three national companies and even sent a company to Europe.

A Night Out was the name of Youmans's next show, written at the behest of producer Alex Aarons. Irving Caesar and Clifford Grey collaborated on the lyrics. The show opened in Philadelphia and closed before coming to New York. *No, No, Nanette* actually opened after *A Night Out* because its pre-Broadway tour went on for so long.

Youmans paired up with lyricist Anne Caldwell for *Oh, Please!* (12/17/26; 79 performances). Caldwell wrote the libretto with Otto Harbach. The show was produced by Charles Dillingham, a gentleman producer. The cast was excellent, featuring Beatrice Lillie, Helen Broderick, Charles Purcell and Charles Winninger.

Youmans was unhappy with the way his shows were produced, so he produced *Hit the Deck* (4/25/27; 352 performances) himself in collaboration with veteran producer Lew Fields (*q.v.*). He stated: "For the first time in my life I am able to select my own singers and my own cast to interpret my music and to play the parts as I would like to have them played. For the past six or seven years, I have been completely at the mercy of the managers and of the actors." Leo Robin and Clifford Grey provided the lyrics and Herbert Fields (*q.v.*) wrote the libretto. *Hit the Deck* contained two smash hit songs, "Hallelujah" and "Sometimes I'm Happy." Louise Groody, the star of *Nanette*, was also the star here, along with Stella Mayhew and Charles King.

Though Youmans continued his producing career after the success of *Hit the Deck*, he only provided the score for his next show, *Rainbow* (11/21/28; 29 performances). It reunited Youmans with Oscar Hammerstein II, who directed and collaborated on the libretto with Laurence Stallings (the one-time critic who once reviewed Youmans). Hammerstein had just enjoyed a success with his last show, *The New Moon*, but his luck did not hold with *Rainbow*. Youmans also went from a great hit to a great failure, repeating the pattern he established with *Nanette* and *Oh, Please! Rainbow* had a particularly disastrous opening night. Gilbert Gabriel commented that, "One intermission was so long and lapsy that the orchestra played everything but Dixie to fill it up." Critics weren't totally unkind, and several found things to admire. Howard Barnes commented in the *New York Herald Tribune*, "Youmans maintains his place as one of our first jazz composers in the piece, which boasts not so much a nosegay of song hits as a coordinated score."

Youmans bounced back to form but a poor libretto, and history, would doom his next show, *Great Day!*

(10/17/29; 37 performances). He was so sure of his producing talents that he bought the Cosmopolitan Theatre, long considered a jinxed house. Billy Rose and Edward Eliscu wrote the lyrics for what was one of Youmans's best scores. It contained four big hits, "Happy Because I'm in Love," "More Than You Know," "Without a Song" and the title tune. But despite the great score, the show was a mess. It suffered a particularly painful out-of-town tryout, leading Broadway wags to dub it *Great Delay*. A week after the show opened, the stock market crashed, and Youmans, producer as well as composer, was forced to close the show.

With *Great Day* a failure, Youmans was left with an empty theater. The Depression hurt Broadway terribly, and there were no producers looking for theaters. So Youmans put a play, *Damn Your Honor* (12/30/29; 8 performers), into the house. The play opened to dreadful reviews. Youmans was unable to raise money for any further productions at the theater.

Youmans then fled New York for the more hospitable clime of Hollywood. He saw several of his stage musicals adapted for the screen and wrote an original movie musical, *What a Widow!* It was a flop, and Youmans returned to New York.

Smiles (11/18/30; 63 performances) was a Florenz Ziegfeld (*q.v.*) production at the Ziegfeld Theater (*q.v.*). Youmans had borrowed money from Ziegfeld to bring *Great Day* into New York, and in return he promised to supply a score for Ziegfeld. The result, *Smiles*, had lyrics by Clifford Grey and Harold Adamson. The cast was fine with Fred and Adele Astaire (*q.v.*), Larry Adler, Virginia Bruce, Marilyn Miller, Bob Hope and Eddie Foy Jr., but the show was a failure. Youmans and Ziegfeld fought incessantly, and Ziegfeld went so far as to get a court injunction barring Youmans from the out of town theater. The hit from *Smiles* was the standard "Time on My Hands" with lyrics by Adamson and Mack Gordon.

Youmans's career was clearly on the skids. His work wasn't bad, but personal problems prevented him from realizing his potential. Youmans had determined that his failures were due to bad management. He produced *Through the Years* (1/28/31; 20 performances), his next Broadway offering. The show was another huge failure. Again, Youmans handed in a fine score, with lyrics by Edward Heyman. "Drums in My Heart" and the title song received the most notice, but the show didn't work.

Youmans's last Broadway show was "Take a Chance" (11/26/32; 243 performances). Youmans was asked to come in to bolster the score by Richard Whiting, Nacio Herb Brown and B.G. DeSylva. They were the authors of the hit songs, "You're an Old Smoothie" and "Eadie Was a Lady." The show had a good cast, including Ethel Merman (*q.v.*), Jack Haley, June Knight, Mitzi

Mayfair and Sid Silvers. *Take a Chance* closed Youmans's Broadway career with a hit.

The composer's last assignment was for the movie *Flying Down to Rio*. Youmans tried to come to an agreement with RKO for more movies. While negotiations slowly proceeded, Youmans discovered he had tuberculosis. Though his health improved, his relationship with RKO did not. He gave up on movies and decided to tackle classical composing as Gershwin had done. Youmans's health wavered as he moved from location to location trying vainly to settle down. He was nearly broke, all the harder on him because he was used to living well. He was unemployable on Broadway, and Hollywood rejected his demands.

Youmans continued his classical lessons and occupied his last years readying a revue that would feature Latin rhythms. The show was titled *Vincent Youmans's Revue,* although there were no songs by Youmans. There was a little ballet and a few Cuban numbers by Ernesto Lecuona. Leonide Massine choreographed the ballet, and Eugene van Grona staged the Cuban numbers. The show was terribly disjointed and closed in Baltimore shortly after its January 27, 1944, opening.

The composer suffered personal disappointments, and another stab at Hollywood proved fruitless. Doctors thought Youmans could still be cured of the tuberculosis, but the patient seemed unwilling to fight. Vincent Youmans died on April 5, 1946.

YOUNG, STARK   See CRITICS.

ZIEGFELD, FLORENZ (1867–1932) Just as S.L. ("Roxy") Rothafel's *(q.v.)* name signifies, the apex of motion picture showmanship, Florenz Ziegfeld's name forever stands as a symbol of lavish showmanship in the musical theater. He was a man of superlatives for whom the show was everything. The most renowned producer of his time, he was not a good businessman, for he was often broke and preferred to plow the fortunes he made into the highly speculative world of theatrical producing. Ziegfeld's organization and methods (though not his financial practices) were the precursors to the famous Hollywood studio star system of the thirties and forties.

His monument, the *Ziegfeld Follies (q.v.)* revue series, has become a legend while his competitors' shows—the Shubert's *(q.v.) Passing Shows, Earl Carroll's Vanities (q.v.)* and *George White's Scandals (q.v.)*—are practically forgotten.

Ziegfeld also produced many book musicals. These included some of the greatest hits of the twenties: *Sally, Kid Boots, Rio Rita, The Three Musketeers, Whoopee* and his masterwork, *Show Boat.* Ziegfeld gave these musicals and others the sumptuous physical production that was his hallmark.

Ziegfeld's accomplishments go beyond his astuteness as a manager. Ziegfeld admitted to Eddie Cantor: "You know I don't have a very quick sense of humor. Half the great comedians I've had in my shows and that I paid a lot of money to and who made my customers shriek were not only not funny to me, but I couldn't understand why they were funny to anybody." Despite this, he made many of the biggest stars of Broadway, paid them stars' salaries and surrounded them with a publicity machine that kept their careers in the ascendancy. He was instrumental in introducing the American public to such stars as Anna Held *(q.v.),* Fanny Brice *(q.v.),* Eddie Cantor, W.C. Fields, Will Rogers and Bert Williams.

He was equally influential in his championing of such songwriters as Irving Berlin *(q.v.),* George Gershwin *(q.v.),* Victor Herbert *(q.v.)* (late in his career), Rodgers and Hart *(q.v.),* Sigmund Romberg *(q.v.)* and Rudolf Friml *(q.v.).* Ziegfeld's unerring sense of design led to a long collaboration with architect/scenic designer Joseph Urban.

Ziegfeld himself became his greatest creation. He had the reputation of being a flamboyant showman, Casanova, artist, magician, dictator and arbiter of popular taste. Ziegfeld represented the Broadway mogul to hundreds who sought to emulate him without success. One sign of his genius and celebrity is the fact that his personal traits and practices have become stereotypes themselves.

Ziegfeld was born on March 21, 1867, the son of Florenz Ziegfeld Sr., President of the Chicago Musical College. The Chicago World's Fair of 1893 gave the young Ziegfeld his first taste of show business. The youngster's father was in charge of supplying classical bands for the fair. His son worked with him, although the two seldom saw eye to eye. Ziegfeld junior was more drawn to the flamboyant.

Ziegfeld brought a strongman, Sandow the Great, to Chicago and the fair. Sandow became a huge hit when Ziegfeld, with an unerring sense of publicity, invited two of the doyennes of Chicago society, Mrs. Potter Palmer and Mrs. George Pullman, to step up and examine Sandow's muscles. The ladies were overwhelmed by the strongman, and soon all society lined up to feel the mighty Sandow's muscles. It was quite daring and more than a little naughty.

Ziegfeld took the muscle man to New York and another conquest of society. In 1895, after visiting Paris,

Berlin and Monte Carlo with Sandow, Ziegfeld ran out of money and became stranded in London. It was the first time he was broke, but it wasn't the last.

Ziegfeld simply couldn't save money. Nothing was too good for Ziegfeld or his productions. The reason he spent thousands of dollars on his shows was not that he felt that the added expense would pay off at the box office, but rather that he felt that anything with his name attached must mean the best. Luckily, most of the time he was successful enough to keep himself and his shows well appointed.

Charles Evans, late of the comedy team Evans and Hoey, brought the broke Ziegfeld to a music hall. There Ziegfeld discovered Anna Held (q.v.), a French chanteuse with an hourglass figure and sparkling eyes. Ziegfeld was struck by the woman's presence and immediately begged Evans for an introduction. Evans knew that the 27-year old showman would get nowhere with Held, since many American producers with greater credits and more capital had offered her their services. But Ziegfeld was adamant and even got Evans to agree to reteam with Hoey if he could convince Held to come to America with him. Ziegfeld wooed Held and came away with a contract. That he was broke was secondary, for he now had Held and Evans and Hoey for a Broadway show. Ziegfeld cabled Diamond Jim Brady (q.v.) for sufficient funds for the entourage to sail to New York.

Ziegfeld was an astute enough publicist to realize that it would be a mistake for Anna Held to burst on the Broadway scene. Instead, he opened his production, *A Parlor Match* (10/21/1896), with Evans and Hoey featured and Held relegated to a small singing part during the entr'acte. Audiences were captivated by the beauty and felt they had discovered a star.

Ziegfeld stoked the publicity machine with the famous milk-bath stunt, perhaps the greatest of all publicity stunts (q.v.). A Brooklyn milkman (paid by Ziegfeld) sued Ziegfeld for the money for milk that he had supposedly delivered to the Hotel Marlborough each day for a month. Reporters became curious, and one traced the young actress to the hotel and discovered the "secret" that Miss Held bathed in milk every day.

The stunt was the idea of playwright Max Marcin who was inspired while reading Gibbons's *Decline and Fall of the Roman Empire*. The *Sun* exposed the stunt (bringing even more publicity), but the other papers preferred to ignore the truth.

A year after *The Parlor Match* opened, Held and Ziegfeld were married. For the next few years Ziegfeld concentrated on Held's career. By the end of 1906, he was simultaneously broke and on the eve of his greatest triumph.

Held is credited with coming up with the idea for the *Follies*. She suggested that Ziegfeld could outdo the famed Paris *Folies Bergere* if he gathered together his own bevy of beauties. Ziegfeld, along with Held, producer/director Frank McKee, producer and theater owner A.L Erlanger and Ziegfeld's assistant Jerry Siegel auditioned the performers who would become The Anna Held Girls. McKee and Erlanger each owned a third interest in the *Follies*. Siegel, a man-about-Broadway, held down the fort when Ziegfeld went overseas.

A popular newspaper column, "Follies of the Day," supplied the title for the revue series. Held suggested that Ziegfeld call the show "Follies of the Year" but the superstitious Ziegfeld wanted a title with 13 letters—hence *Follies of 1907*.

The *Follies* was announced at the bottom of an advertisement for the Jardin de Paris atop the New York Theater (q.v.) on Broadway and 44th Street. The ad stated "Very soon—the Ziegfeld Revue—Follies of 1907." It was the first time that the French spelling of revue was used in this country.

The Jardin de Paris was a highly uncomfortable theater. It was topped by a glass dome, which acted as a huge magnifying lens for the sun's rays. In the days before air conditioning, it was hot, and when it rained, the audience held umbrellas over their heads because the dome leaked.

Klaw and Erlanger footed the entire bill for the *Follies*—$16,800. The show opened on July 9, 1907, and received mostly rave reviews, though critics could still be shocked at the 50 Anna Held Girls who actually showed their bloomers. One critic (q.v.) opined: "In seeking to reproduce some of the audacities of the French capital, Mr. Ziegfeld has come occasionally into collusion with a sense of propriety which still distinguishes a large portion of the public over here."

Another paper's critic observed, "Mr. Florenz Ziegfeld, Jr., has given New York quite the best melange of mirth, music and pretty young women that has been seen here in many summers. There is not a dull moment in the entire show. The many ensembles, songs and dances and the costuming of the principals and chorus carried the new review to success and assured it a long residence on Broadway."

Despite the heat in the Jardin de Paris, Ziegfeld kept the show running through the summer. Most shows closed May 31st and reopened on Labor Day.

After the *Follies of 1907*, the series became a tradition for the next 25 years. Ziegfeld advertised his *Follies* as "An American Institution" and stated their goal as "Glorifying the American Girl." The 20th and last *Follies* under Ziegfeld's auspices opened on July 1, 1931. The Shuberts (q.v.) and Ziegfeld's widow Billie Burke presented two more *Follies* in 1934 and 1936. The Shuberts alone presented a *Follies* in 1956. It was ironic that the Shuberts ended up presenting the *Follies* since the Shuberts and Ziegfeld were mortal enemies.

During their quarter of a decade under Ziegfeld's stewardship, the *Follies* featured such performers as

Nora Bayes, Mae Murray, Fanny Brice (q.v.), the Dolly Sisters, Leon Errol, Bessie McCoy, Bert Williams, Ed Wynn, W.C. Fields, Ina Claire, Marion Davies, Eddie Cantor, Joe Frisco, Marilyn Miller, Gus Van and Joe Schenck, John Steel, Gallagher and Shean, Olsen and Johnson, Paul Whiteman, Will Rogers, Ruth Etting, and Harry Richman.

The *Follies* introduced such great songs to the canon of American standards as "Shine On Harvest Moon," "The Dance of the Grizzly Bear," "Be My Little Baby Bumble Bee," "Row, Row, Row," "Hello, Frisco, Hello," "A Pretty Girl Is Like a Melody," "My Man," "Second-Hand Rose," "Strut Miss Lizzy," "Mr. Gallagher and Mr. Shean," "Half Caste Woman" and "You Made Me Love You."

Ziegfeld presented other revues tied into the *Follies*. On the roof of the New Amsterdam Theatre (q.v.), he presented a series of *Ziegfeld Midnight Frolics*. Material would be tried out in the *Midnight Frolics* before being introduced on the large stage below. The *Midnight Frolics* featured some of the stars appearing in the *Follies* downstairs. The Roof Garden above the New Amsterdam was part cabaret and part supper club. There was a $5 cover charge which usually narrowed the audience down to members of the Four Hundred.

The *Frolics* were usually directed by Ned Wayburn and had music and lyrics by Dave Stamper and Gene Buck. Buck is also credited with much of the success of the *Follies*. It was he who usually whipped Ziegfeld's ideas into shape and discovered such stars as W.C. Fields and Eddie Cantor.

Ziegfeld contributed more to the theater than just the *Follies*. In 1908, in addition to the annual *Follies* edition, Ziegfeld presented two shows: *The Soul Kiss* and *Miss Innocence*. *The Soul Kiss* (1/28/08; 122 performances) starred Adeline Genee, Cecil Lean and Florence Holbrook and was followed by *Miss Innocence* (11/30/08; 176 performances). At the time, anything over 100 performances was considered a hit.

In 1912, Ziegfeld produced two forgettable shows. The first was *Over the River* (1/8/12; 120 performances), a musical with music and lyrics by John Golden in which coproducer Charles Dillingham introduced ballroom dancing to the legitimate stage for the first time. Peggy Wood, Eddie Foy Sr. and Lillian Lorraine starred. Foy starred as Madison Parke, a gay rogue who is sentenced to 30 days on Blackwell's Island for cutting too much of a rug on Broadway. After his release, he tries to convince his wife he was in Mexico. The musical marked Foy's retirement from the legitimate theater. Thereafter, he played only in vaudeville.

A Winsome Widow (4/11/12; 172 performances), based on Charles Hoyt's *A Trip to Chinatown*, opened at the Moulin Rouge (formerly the Jardin de Paris) and contained one smash hit song, "Be My Little Baby Bumble Bee," which was originally in the *Follies of 1911*.

Raymond Hubbell wrote the majority of the show's songs with an interpolation by Jerome Kern (q.v.). The show starred the Dolly Sisters, Elizabeth Brice, Leon Errol, Charles King, Frank Tinney and Mae West.

In 1913, Ziegfeld and Held were divorced. She continued to appear under Ziegfeld's auspices in vaudeville. On New Year's Eve, 1914, Ziegfeld, attending a ball at the Hotel Astor (q.v.), ran into actress Billie Burke. Burke was later quoted by a newspaperman as saying, "I have no intention of marrying Mr. Ziegfeld or anyone else although Mr. Ziegfeld is a very charming man." The couple were married on April 11, 1914, after a matinee of Burke's show, *Jerry*. Anna Held died on August 12, 1918.

The next non-*Follies* show presented by Ziegfeld was *The Century Girl* (11/6/16; 200 performances). Irving Berlin composed the music and lyrics with some instrumental pieces composed by Victor Herbert. *The Century Girl* opened with Sam Bernard, Hazel Dawn, Marie Dressler, Leon Errol, Elsie Janis, Van and Schenck, Frank Tinney and Lillian Tashman.

The following year, *Miss 1917* (11/5/17; 40 performances), one of the most expensive productions of its time, opened with a score by Jerome Kern and P.G. Wodehouse. George Gershwin was the rehearsal pianist for the show. Even with sold-out houses, the show could not recoup its cost. Ziegfeld and Dillingham were forced to close it despite its smash hit status.

Ziegfeld's next musical comedy production, *Sally* (12/21/20; 570 performances), was a happier experience. Kern and Wodehouse collaborated on the score along with colyricist Clifford Grey. The score contained several hits, including "Whip-Poor-Will" and "Look for the Silver Lining." Both songs featured lyrics by B.G. DeSylva. Marilyn Miller starred in the production along with Walter Catlett and Leon Errol.

Eddie Cantor, who got his start with Ziegfeld, was given his first book show, *Kid Boots* (12/13/23; 479 performances). Cantor, band leader George Olsen, Harland Dixon and Mary Eaton introduced a score by Harry Tierney and Joseph McCarthy. *Kid Boots* had a $16 top ticket price at its opening. Although it was a smash hit, Ziegfeld couldn't stop trying to improve the show. He spent $20,000 on new costumes for the first-act finale. It was no surprise to Eddie Cantor when he received the following telegram from Ziegfeld on Christmas Day: "Merry Christmas to you and yours. May we remain together as long as both of us remain in show business, although profits on *Kid Boots* have been far less than *Sally*."

The Sigmund Romberg, Clare Kummer, Clifford Grey show, *Annie Dear* (11/4/24; 103 performances), opened as a vehicle for Billie Burke. Romberg wrote his second book show for Ziegfeld, *Louie the 14th* (3/3/25; 319 performances), with Englishman Arthur Wimperis. Ziegfeld favorite Leon Errol costarred with Ethel Shutta in the show.

In 1926, Ziegfeld was quarreling with Erlanger over

the name *Follies.* He was forced to title his 1926 edition of the *Follies, No Foolin'*. Later that year, the producer opened *Betsy* (12/28/26; 39 performances) by Richard Rodgers and Lorenz Hart.

In 1927, Ziegfeld produced two of his biggest successes. *Rio Rita* (2/2/27; 494 performances) opened with a score by Harry Tierney and Joseph McCarthy. The songwriters composed their finest score and one that contained many hits. The title tune, "The Rangers' Song" and "If You're in Love You'll Waltz" were recorded countless times and sold thousands of copies of sheet music. Ada May, Ethelind Terry, Bert Wheeler, J. Harold Murray and Walter Catlett starred in what was one of the last great operettas. *Rio Rita* had a top ticket price of $5.50, which was high for the time.

Ziegfeld's greatest contribution to musical-theater history came on December 27, 1927, the opening night of *Show Boat* (575 performances). The Jerome Kern, Oscar Hammerstein II *(q.v.)* musical contained what some consider to be the best musical-theater score ever written. Ziegfeld mounted a brilliant production. He did not just produce a spectacle of the eye and ear but used his unerring taste to make *Show Boat* a spectacle of the heart and mind. The musical starred Norma Terris, Helen Morgan, Jules Bledsoe, Edna May Oliver, Charles Winninger, Howard Marsh and Eva Puck. The musical, considered quite daring for its time, is still performed in major productions on Broadway and around the world.

Rosalie (1/10/28; 327 performances) continued Ziegfeld's amazing output. Where others might produce a single show each year, Ziegfeld produced two or three. *Rosalie* had a score by George and Ira Gershwin and Sigmund Romberg and P.G. Wodehouse. The Gershwins accounted for the show's hit "How Long Has This Been Going On." The classic "The Man I Love" was cut from the score prior to the show's opening (already having been deleted from the score of *Lady Be Good*). Marilyn Miller was the star, ably supported by Frank Morgan, Jack Donahue and Gladys Glad.

The Three Musketeers (3/13/28; 319 performances) was Ziegfeld's second production in 1928. Rudolf Friml, P.G. Wodehouse and Clifford Grey supplied the hit score which contained such great songs as "Ma Belle," "March of the Musketeers," "One Kiss," and "Gascony." The show was Friml's last great achievement. Operettas were on the decline as popular taste shifted to the more modern rhythms of Gershwin, Rodgers and Berlin. Dennis King, Douglas Dumbrille, Harriet Hoctor and Vivienne Segal starred. Critic *(q.v.)* Percy Hammond's review of *The Three Musketeers* in the *New York Herald-Tribune* included a summation of Ziegfeld's recent hit productions: "His enterprises were swamp lilies of the theatre, beauty arising from stagnant pools. But all of a sudden he has changed, ventured into fields more healthful, with the result that he is now the happy maestro of four pure and undefiled successes, *Rio Rita, Rosalie, Show Boat* and *The Three Musketeers.*"

Whoopee (12/4/28; 255 performances), another big hit for Ziegfeld, was written as a vehicle for former *Follies* headliner Eddie Cantor. The show has a surprisingly strong book and score, although it was written to suit Cantor's varied talents. The hit songs by Walter Donaldson and Gus Kahn included the title tune, "My Baby Just Cares for Me," "I'm Bringing a Red, Red Rose" and the classic torch song, "Love Me or Leave Me." Ruth Etting, Ethel Shutta, Frances Upton and Jack Shaw starred.

Another telegram to Cantor, on the day after *Whoopee*'s opening, illustrates Ziegfeld's taste in theater as well as his reputation (or at least his self-image) as a roue. Ziegfeld wrote: "My dear Eddie: I want to extend to you my heartiest congratulations. I knew you could do it and you did do it. You gave them an artistic, clean and enjoyable performance from start to finish. I was with sixty of the representative women of New York and they were simply enchanted."

The Gershwins and Gus Kahn contributed the score to *Show Girl* (7/2/29; 111 performances), which included the song "Liza (All the Clouds'll Roll Away)." Jimmy Durante, featured in the show with his partners Eddie Jackson and Lou Clayton, wrote his own numbers. *Show Girl* also featured Ruby Keeler, Duke Ellington and his orchestra, Eddie Foy Jr., Harriet Hoctor and Nick Lucas.

A definite departure for Ziegfeld was his coproduction with Arch Selwyn of Noel Coward's *Bittersweet* (11/5/29; 159 performances). The English operetta boasted such hits as "I'll See You Again" and "If Love Were All." The stock market crash on October 29 of that year wiped Ziegfeld out. Though he produced more shows, he never regained his fortune.

Rodgers and Hart provided a fantasy for Ed Wynn in *Simple Simon* (2/18/30; 135 performances). The show's showstopper was Ruth Etting's performance of the Rodgers and Hart classic, "Ten Cents a Dance."

Smiles (11/18/30; 63 performances) also contained a smash hit tune—"Time on My Hands" by Vincent Youmans *(q.v.),* Harold Adamson and Mack Gordon. Walter Donaldson's "You're Driving Me Crazy" was added after the Marilyn Miller starrer opened. Fred and Adele Astaire *(q.v.)* costarred along with Larry Adler, Bob Hope, Eddie Foy Jr. and Virginia Bruce.

In 1932, Ziegfeld presented a revival of his greatest hit, *Show Boat.* His last Broadway musical, *Hot-Cha!* (3/8/32; 118 performances), opened with a score by Ray Henderson and Lew Brown (see DE SYLVA, BROWN AND HENDERSON). They also contributed the libretto along with columnist Mark Hellinger *(q.v.).* Eleanor Powell, Buddy Rogers, Bert Lahr, June Knight and Gypsy Rose Lee starred. Ziegfeld financed the production with the assistance of gangsters *(q.v.)* like Dutch Schultz.

Ziegfeld had other accomplishments to his credit

besides shows. He hosted a weekly radio series and produced a color movie of *Whoopee* with Samuel Goldwyn. He was also responsible for erecting the fabulous Ziegfeld Theater *(q.v.)* with a stunning design by Joseph Urban.

Ziegfeld's health, hurt by the pressures of business and avoiding creditors, quickly deteriorated in the thirties. Bill collectors took Ziegfeld's office furniture in lieu of payment. Broadway sign makers Artkraft-Strauss *(q.v.)* owned his desk for years. Ziegfeld was stricken with pleurisy, and although he rallied for a time (he sent $6,000 worth of telegrams from the hospital), he died on July 22, 1932.

Will Rogers delivered Ziegfeld's eulogy. He commented, "He picked us from all walks of life and led us into what little fame we achieved . . . He brought beauty into the entertainment world. To have been the master amusement provider of your generation, surely a life's work has been accomplished . . . He left something that hundreds of us will treasure till our final curtains fall, and that is a 'badge,' a badge of which we are proud and want to read the lettering: 'I worked for Ziegfeld.' "

ZIEGFELD FOLLIES The *Ziegfeld Follies* was the first great revue series in the American theater and the series that defined class and entertainment when it ran during the first decades of the 20th century and for decades afterwards. Florenz Ziegfeld *(q.v.)*, the genius behind the *Follies,* saw to it that the series exhibited the best talents available in the American musical theater. Ziegfeld hired the top stars, created even more, hired great designers to create sumptuous costumes and lavish settings, commissioned the top songwriting talents from Tin Pan Alley and wove the whole proceedings together with girls, hundreds of beautiful girls.

According to Ziegfeld's publicist, Will Page, in the beginning the name Ziegfeld, The Great Glorifier, "meant a musical entertainment for tired business men which should represent almost the possible limit of what could decently be done upon the stage." Later, said Page, "the atmosphere of the *Follies* . . . changed so that naughtiness is not tolerated and more attention is paid to beauty of scenes and to gorgeousness of gowns with, of course, the finest flowers that could be collected in the garden of girls."

The *Follies* show girls were quite celebrated. It was the great couturier Lady Duff-Gordon who introduced Ziegfeld to the concept of the show girl. They were not the chorus. They did not sing, did not dance. They existed simply to be beautiful. Among the famous show girls were Olive Thomas, Dolores, Drucilla Strain, Imogene Wilson, Katherine Burke, Jessie Reed, Merle Finlay and Hazel Forbes. Some, like Irene Dunne, Peggy Hopkins Joyce, Mae Murray, Marion Davies, Billie Dove, Justine Johnstone, Paulette Goddard, Lilyan

Tashman, Barbara Stanwyck and Vera Maxwell, went on to become stars in their own right. For other show girls, their beauty was their primary talent. It was enough for Ziegfeld. The showman's favorite words were glorification, femininity and pulchritude. All three applied to his show girls. Where other producers paid their girls $30 a week, Ziegfeld paid his girls $125. The women were never presented in the nude, and Ziegfeld insisted that they be treated with respect. Sex was the byword of Ziegfeld's rivals Earl Carroll *(q.v.)*, George White *(q.v.)* and the Shuberts *(q.v.)*, but Ziegfeld admired women simply for their statuesque beauty.

Ziegfeld had his favorite performers, most of whom he discovered. Fanny Brice *(q.v.)*, comedian Bert Williams, Ann Pennington, W.C. Fields, Will Rogers, Leon Errol, Ray Dooley, Lillian Lorraine, Nora Bayes, Eddie Cantor and Van and Schenck all appeared in multiple editions of the *Follies.*

The *Follies* also boasted a long relationship with its production staff. Many of the *Follies* cost as much as $200,000 to produce. A huge part of the budget was taken up with sets and costumes. Though Ziegfeld was extravagant with money, he had the good taste and design sense to make sure every dime was visible on the stage. Ziegfeld would get his inspiration for *Follies* numbers from the day's headlines, pictures in magazines, postcards and idle comments. He would jot down his ideas and then tell his staff to put together a scene around a specific design element.

Joseph Urban, a noted architect, designed many of the great drops and set pieces for the *Follies.* Ben Ali Haggin designed the scenes called tableaux vivants or living pictures for the *Follies* from 1917 to 1925. The tableaux were artfully posed groupings of seminude show girls draped in fine fabrics. Ziegfeld's costumers included such noted couturiers as Lady Duff-Gordon (Lucile), Cora McGeachy and Alice O'Neil. Gene Buck wrote lyrics for many of the shows and is generally credited with fulfilling Ziegfeld's visions on stage. Ned Wayburn, a noted choreographer, staged the dances as well as directing most of the proceedings. The contribution of Albert Cheney Johnston should not be overlooked. The great photographer was the official portraitist for all the *Follies* girls. Since only a limited number of people could see the *Follies* in any one year, Johnston's photos were the only glimpse many people had of the magical Ziegfeld touch.

Ziegfeld didn't put as much stock in the songs. He was happy as long as the shows were sumptuous and the girls beautiful. However, many great songs were introduced in the *Follies,* either written specifically for Ziegfeld or as popular songs interpolated into the shows. These included "My Man," "By the Light of the Silvery Moon," "Be My Little Baby Bumble Bee," "Row, Row, Row," "Hello, Frisco, Hello," "A Pretty Girl Is Like a Melody," "Second Hand Rose" and "Shaking the Blues Away." Favorite songwriters of Ziegfeld were Irving Berlin (q.v.) (the first to write an entire *Follies* score by himself), Victor Herbert (q.v.), Dave Stamper and Gene Buck, Louis A. Hirsch, and Raymond Hubbell. Sketches were contributed by Harry B. Smith (q.v.), George V. Hobart, Rennold Wolf and Channing Pollock.

Eddie Cantor and Dave Freedman in their Ziegfeld biography entitled *The Great Glorifyer* described the *Follies* atmosphere: "Girls from every part of the country stood backstage on the threshold of glorification. The dressing-rooms were filled with so many stars that the skies looked deserted. Forty-second Street was a bobbing black sea of high-powered imported cars. The lobby of the New Amsterdam Theatre (q.v.) glittered with aristocracy."

The *Follies* did not begin on quite such a prestigious note. Credit for originating the idea for the *Follies* goes to Ziegfeld's wife, Anna Held (q.v.), who suggested Ziegfeld model a revue on the French *Folies Bergere*. Librettist/lyricist Harry B. Smith (q.v.) suggested the showman name his show after an old newspaper column of Smith's, "Follies of the Day." But Ziegfeld, who was superstitious, wanted the name of the show to contain 13 letters. He settled on *Follies of 1907*. The first *Follies* took place at a rooftop theater, the Jardin de Paris, on July 9, 1907. The revue (Ziegfeld was the first to use the French spelling of review), starred Emma Carus, Grace La Rue and Lillian Lee. The first *Follies* was an immediate hit, following a move to the Liberty Theatre (q.v.), and became the first Broadway show to run through the hot summer months.

The show's success led Ziegfeld to announce a new edition of the *Follies*, and thereafter the revue became an annual event on Broadway. Ziegfeld's partner in the *Follies* was Abraham Erlanger, one of the most hated producers in theater history. Erlanger owned and operated a string of theaters across the country that was practically a monopoly. If the producer of a show or act wanted to play an Erlanger house, the producer would be forced to join Erlanger's Syndicate. Erlanger tried to dictate to Ziegfeld the content of the *Follies*, but Ziegfeld would have none of it.

In 1911, Ziegfeld joined his name to the *Follies* for the first time. In 1913, after six editions, Ziegfeld finally had enough faith in the series to move it to a large legitimate theater, the New Amsterdam (q.v.). The *Follies* remained at the New Amsterdam (with one exception) until the last edition under Ziegfeld in 1931. That last Ziegfeld show opened at the new Ziegfeld Theater (q.v.).

In all, there were 21 *Follies* presented by Ziegfeld and some of them had more than one edition. By the time Ziegfeld died in 1932, the *Follies* truly lived up to their reputation as "A National Institution Glorifying the American Girl."

After the showman's death, Ziegfeld's rivals, the Shuberts, bought the right to produce their own edition of the *Follies* from Ziegfeld's widow, Billie Burke, for $1,000. Ziegfeld's estate received 3% of the gross. The Shuberts presented three *Follies*, in 1934, 1936 and 1943. There was one revue using the *Follies* name in 1957.

But no *Follies* following the master's death could truly lay claim to the title *Follies*. For one thing, no post-Ziegfeld follies were as lavish because other producers, particularly the Shuberts, were fiscally more responsible and placed a higher priority on making money than on sumptuous productions. Ziegfeld himself, though notoriously heedless of the bottom line, never lost money on a *Follies*, and they often realized a profit after Broadway while touring. Ziegfeld made sure that the annual series that bore his name reflected the pride he had in himself. Hollywood, television and the literary world all used the example of the *Follies* to portray the glamour, romance and extravagance of Broadway when in fact few other shows exhibited these qualities in such quantity. Today the *Follies* and Ziegfeld are still considered the epitome of Broadway's art.

ZIEGFELD THEATER Northwest corner of Sixth Avenue and 54th Street. Architects: Joseph Urban and Thomas A. Lamb. Opening: February 2, 1927; *Rio Rita*. The Ziegfeld was the most modern theater of its time. Not quite art deco, the beautiful auditorium was designed with few right angles, and a smooth proscenium arch blended into the auditorium walls, which were embellished with a fanciful mural. Urban described his theater as, "A modern playhouse for musical shows animated by gay detail to unite actor and audience."

Until the mid-1920s, Sixth Avenue was a street of three-story brownstones under a permanent shadow of the elevated train. When the Sixth Avenue el was torn down in 1927, the real estate market, driven by a bearish Wall Street, boomed. Speculators abounded and parcels of the thoroughfare were acquired quickly in the new land rush.

Producer Florenz Ziegfeld (q.v.) had long considered the New Amsterdam Theatre (q.v.) his home base. But this magnificent 42nd Street theater was owned by Abe Erlanger, a man of quick temper with as ruthless a business sense as Ziegfeld himself. So Ziegfeld was not averse to a move.

The owner of the property at Sixth Avenue and 54th Street was none other than media mogul William Randolph Hearst. The newspaper giant owned several large plots of land surrounding the future site of the Ziegfeld Theater and in fact had just constructed the Warwick Hotel on an adjacent block. Hearst recognized that a theater across the street from the Warwick would drive up the value of his as yet undeveloped plots. When plans to dismantle the el were announced, Hearst and

Ziegfeld Theater

his partner Arthur Brisbane approached Ziegfeld. The producer immediately hired Joseph Urban in 1926.

Ziegfeld's daughter Patricia cemented the cornerstone that contained a program from Ziegfeld's musical *Sally,* photos of the Ziegfeld family, a program from the original *Follies of 1907,* and a brick from an ancient Greek theater.

The cornerstone was laid with appropriate Ziegfeldian fanfare on December 9, 1926, at 2:47 P.M. Over 800 people, including stars of past and future Ziegfeld productions, watched while a huge audience followed the proceedings on the radio.

The theater's facade featured a tan stone, and it curved to reflect the oval auditorium inside. The oval interior eschewed right angles and the typically baroque decoration of most New York theaters. The walls were covered with a modernistic mural by Lillian Gaertner, one of Urban's pupils. This painting, entitled *The Joy of Living,* was said to be the largest oil painting in the world.

The new theater was opened on February 2, 1927, with *Rio Rita* (504 performances), an operetta boasting a score by Harry Tierney and Joseph McCarthy. The top ticket price for the new show was $5.50.

Ziegfeld's greatest production, *Show Boat* (12/27/27; 575 performances) opened next at the theater. The Jerome Kern *(q.v.)* and Oscar Hammerstein II *(q.v.)* adaptation of Edna Ferber's novel became one of the

seminal works of the American musical theater. Hammerstein's treatment of serious social issues and the superior score made *Show Boat* an almost legendary musical. The cast included Norma Terris, Tess Gardella, Edna May Oliver, Charles Winninger, Eva Puck, Sammy White, Helen Morgan, Howard Marsh and Jules Bledsoe.

George and Ira Gershwin's *(q.v.)* musical *Show Girl* (7/2/29; 111 performances) followed. The production might have run longer but for the stock market crash on October 29, 1929. Ziegfeld was practically wiped out by the crash and his landlord William Randolph Hearst was badly shaken too.

Meanwhile, the theater was leased to other managements who presented a string of successes on its stage. The first was Noel Coward's London import, *Bittersweet* (11/5/29; 159 performances). It was followed by a Ziegfeld production, *Simple Simon* (2/24/30; 135 performances) starring Ed Wynn and Ruth Etting. The Rodgers and Hart *(q.v.)* score contained the hit "Ten Cents a Dance."

Ziegfeld's last *Follies* opened at his theater on July 21, 1931. The score was by Mack Gordon and Harry Revel. The show played for 165 performances before closing. The next Ziegfeld production at his theater, *Hot-Cha!* (3/14/32; 118 performances), boasted a score by Ray Henderson and Lew Brown (see DE SYLVA, BROWN AND HENDERSON). Ziegfeld was forced to raise the capital for the production from mobster, Dutch Schultz. Despite the talents of Bert Lahr, Gypsy Rose Lee, Lupe Velez and Eleanor Powell, the show was a failure.

Ziegfeld died on July 22, 1932, and management of the theater reverted to the Hearst Company. After the dismal run of *Hot-Cha!,* the theater was converted to motion-picture presentations. Loew's Theatrical Enterprises took over the management for Hearst.

Movies were doing slightly better than theater during the Depression, and the Loew's chain eyed the site. Hearst was having his own financial problems and was forced to sell off vast sections of his financial empire. Obviously, the theater was high on the list of expendable properties. Just before Hearst signed over the deed to the movie chain, in stepped showman extraordinaire Billy Rose.

Rose had long admired the beautiful theater and especially coveted the huge private apartment that Urban had included. Rose saw himself as equal or more than equal to Ziegfeld, so it seemed logical that as Ziegfeld's natural successor he should also possess the late showman's prize asset.

Rose acquired the theater for only $630,000 in 1944. Ziegfeld's spectaculars were marked by his own great taste. Rose may have equaled Ziegfeld in his vision, but his taste was more vulgar and more populist than his predecessor's. Rose did, however, appreciate the beauty of the theater and hired Gretl Urban, daughter of the late architect, to restore the Ziegfeld to its former glory. To Rose's credit, he always kept the theater in top condition.

Rose reestablished the legitimate policy and presented his production of *The Seven Lively Arts* (12/7/44; 182 performances). Cole Porter contributed the score which featured "Ev'rytime We Say Goodbye" as its hit. The show starred Beatrice Lillie, Bert Lahr, Benny Goodman, Helen Gallagher and Dolores Gray.

Following a short-lived show, *Concert Varieties* (6/1/45) came one of the theater's biggest successes, a revival of *The Red Mill* (11/4/45; 531 performances), which ran almost twice as long as the original 1906 production. This unexpected success was followed with a revival of *Show Boat* (1/5/46; 418 performances).

These two smash-hit revivals led to another classic musical attraction, *Brigadoon* (3/13/47; 581 performances). The Lerner and Loewe *(q.v.)* score contained an overabundance of marvelous songs, including "Come to Me, Bend to Me," "Almost Like Being in Love" and "The Heather on the Hill."

The theater's next big success came with the hit show *Gentlemen Prefer Blondes* (12/8/49; 740 performances). Carol Channing and Yvonne Adair starred as Anita Loos's classic golddiggers. The Jule Styne *(q.v.)* and Leo Robin musical comedy included Carol Channing's signature song "Diamonds Are a Girl's Best Friend."

Laurence Olivier and Vivian Leigh played the Ziegfeld in a revival of *Caesar and Cleopatra* (12/20/51; 67 performances) by George Bernard Shaw. The drama was followed by a revival of the Gershwin's *(q.v.) Of Thee I Sing* on May 5, 1952. It played a few months.

The next hit for the theater was another revival by the Gershwins. *Porgy and Bess* enjoyed a 305 performance run commencing March 10, 1953. This made

way for another huge success, *Kismet* (12/3/53; 583 performances) with songs based on melodies by Borodin. The Wright and Forrest score included such standards as "Baubles, Bangles and Beads" and "Stranger in Paradise." Alfred Drake and Joan Diener starred in the Arabian fantasy.

Following *Kismet,* the theater was rented by NBC beginning in 1955. Television occupied its stage until 1963, when live entertainment was again featured. Jack Benny and Danny Kaye presented solo appearances in that year.

A flop musical, *Foxy* (2/16/64; 72 performances) with Bert Lahr, briefly played the theater and was replaced by another Wright and Forrest show, *Anya* (11/29/65; 16 performances). But Anya was not to follow the success of *Kismet,* the team's previous offering.

With *Anya*'s closing also came the closing of the Ziegfeld Theater. Billy Rose had passed away and his estate sold the theater for $17 million. The *World Journal Tribune* of Sunday March 19, 1967, carried the following story:

A STONE FOR THE ZIEGFELD

The Ziegfeld Theater, or what is left of it, is due for one last show next month. There will be ceremonies when the demolition crew gets down to the corner stone. Patricia Ziegfeld, daughter of the late illustrious impresario, will fly in from Los Angeles. She is now Mrs. William Stephenson, married to a California architect. The memorabilia in the corner stone will be presented to the Smithsonian Institute.

Incidently, the two enormous reclining figures above the Ziegfeld entrance have already been claimed by souvenir hunters. One entire figure, weighing a ton, will go to the East Hampton estate of theater angel, Evan Frankel. The head of the second statue is earmarked for the Sutton Place Terrace of Zachary Fisher who is building a new skyscraper on the site.